THE YEARBOOK OF EUROPEAN ENVIRONMENTAL LAW

Volume 4

THE YEARBOOK OF European Environmental Law

Volume 4

T.F.M. ETTY
Researcher at the University of Amsterdam

H. SOMSEN
Professor at the University of Amsterdam

(EDITORS-IN-CHIEF)

T.F.M. ETTY
Researcher at the University of Amsterdam
CURRENT SURVEY EDITOR

J. SCOTT
Lecturer at the University of Cambridge

M. LEE
Lecturer at the King's College London

BOOK REVIEW EDITORS

L. KRÄMER
DG Environment, Commission of the European Communities
DOCUMENTS EDITOR

OXFORD
UNIVERSITY PRESS

OXFORD
UNIVERSITY PRESS

Great Clarendon Street, Oxford OX2 6DP

Oxford University Press is a department of the University of Oxford.
It furthers the University's objective of excellence in research, scholarship,
and education by publishing worldwide in

Oxford New York

Auckland Cape Town Dar es Salaam Hong Kong Karachi Kuala Lumpur
Madrid Melbourne Mexico City Nairobi New Delhi Shanghai Taipei Toronto

With offices in

Argentina Austria Brazil Chile Czech Republic France Greece
Guatemala Hungary Italy Japan Poland Portugal
Singapore South Korea Switzerland Thailand Turkey Ukraine Vietnam

Oxford is a registered trade mark of Oxford University Press
in the UK and in certain other countries

Published in the United States
by Oxford University Press Inc., New York

First published 2005

British Library Cataloguing in Publication Data
Data available

Library of Congress Cataloging in Publication Data
Data available

ISBN 0-19-926786-3

1 3 5 7 9 10 8 6 4 2

Typeset by Kolam Information Services Pvt. Ltd, Pondicherry, India
Printed in Great Britain by
Antony Rowe Ltd, Chippenham, Wiltshire

Editors' Preface

The articles published in this volume of the *Yearbook of European Environmental Law* cover three important themes that are profoundly altering the European environmental landscape.

The most important event that has occurred, undoubtedly, is the enlargement of the European Union (EU) with ten Member States, which took effect from 1 May 2004. Not only the increased geographical scope of European Community (EC) environmental law, but in particular the limited experience of these new Member States with environmental policy and law forms a formidable challenge for the EU.

In this light, the significance of the United Nations Economic Commission for Europe (UN/ECE) Convention on Access to Information, Public Participation in Decision-Making and Access to Justice in Environmental Matters (Aarhus Convention)[1] can hardly be overstated. The Convention was signed by the European Union and its Member States in 1998, and necessitated elaboration of legislative measures to ensure compliance both of Member States and EU Institutions with its provisions. These measures have now mostly been adopted, and Member States and the Institutions of the EU will in future have to conduct their environmental affairs in ways consistent with the spirit and wording of the Aarhus Convention. In brief, this means that access to environmental information, public participation in environmental decision-making, and access to justice in environmental cases will have to be greatly facilitated.

That *Krämer*, with his many years of experience in DG Environment, should approach the subject of access to environmental information as enshrined in Directive 2003/4/EC on Public Access to Environmental Information and Repealing Directive 90/313/EEC (Access to Information Directive)[2] so much as a power struggle between public administrations and citizens, certainly provides food for thought. In this perspective, the Aarhus Convention and the Community instruments to which it has given rise endow citizens with powers to force reluctant administrations with hitherto almost unfettered environmental prerogatives to account for their decisions, both *ex ante* and *ex post.*

This paradigm, which hence is informed by power relations between public authorities and citizens, finds support in modern literature. Thus, Kohr has observed:

[1] Aarhus (Denmark), 25 June 1998 (entered into force 30 Oct. 2001) (1999) 38 *International Legal Materials* 3, 517.

[2] [2003] OJ L41/26.

> the chief danger to the spirit of democracy in a large power stems from [the] technical impossibility of asserting itself informally. In mass states, personal influences can make themselves felt only if channelled through forms, formulas and organizations. It is these latter rather than the individual who become increasingly the true agents or assertors of political sovereignty, so that we should speak of a group or party democracy rather than of an individualistic democracy.[3]

Negotiations leading up to the adoption of the directives and regulations that implement the Aarhus Convention, indeed, would seem to reveal a policy to limit any erosion of powers held by national and EU administrations as much as possible. Thus, the provisions of the Aarhus Convention often have been transposed literally, occasionally even falling short of its requirements, and use has rarely been made of the explicitly provided possibility to grant citizens more extensive rights.

At the same time, *Verschuuren* places emphasis on advantages associated with participation in decision-making, the subject matter regulated in the second pillar of the Aarhus Convention. This introduces a deliberative element in democratic decision-making processes, has been shown to increase the quality of decisions, increases legitimacy of public environmental decision-making, and at the same time reduces risks of capture. For Community Institutions in particular, which are equally bound by the provisions of the Convention, the public will become an important source of information additional to national public authorities, on which, at present, they are overly dependent. The Aarhus Convention initiates a process of emancipation of the Community from the Member States, in that it will have access to a novel and autonomous source of information.

In respect of access to justice (third pillar of the Aarhus Convention), *Betlem* argues that the fact that access to civil courts has been left unregulated in the Proposal for a Directive on Access to Justice in Environmental Matters[4] goes against the spirit of the Aarhus Convention. Thus, the proposed Directive defines the notion of 'environmental proceedings' as 'administrative or judicial review proceedings in environmental matters, other than . . . criminal matters', hence excluding civil proceedings.

Of crucial importance in assessing the Aarhus Convention's effectiveness in delivering on its promise to increase participation of the public in the management of the environment, are two more general questions that transcend the way in which its provisions have been drafted and are now being transposed by the EU. Its underlying premise is that non-governmental organizations (NGOs) can be equated with 'the public'. *Morrow* subjects this premise to a critical analysis. Secondly, the Aarhus Convention presumes that it will be possible to transplant

[3] L. Kohr, 'Small is Democratic' in N. Albury and M. Kingsley, (eds.) *How to Save the World—A Fourth World Guide to the Politics of Scale* (Wellingborough: Turnstone Press, 1984), 59.

[4] COM(2003)624.

what have traditionally been domestic policies regarding public participation to the international or EU level, which is a presumption that *Morrow*, again, critically reviews.

Closely related to the Aarhus Convention are issues related to the enforcement of EC environmental law. After all, the Convention provides access to information and access to justice in environmental cases, both prerequisites for effective private enforcement of Community environmental legislation. In this respect, the Protocol on Pollutant Release and Transfer Registers (Kiev Protocol),[5] which was signed in the context of the Aarhus Convention in May 2003, could be particularly significant for the enforcement of Directive 96/61/EC on Integrated Pollution Prevention and Control (IPPC Directive).[6]

An increasingly clear picture is thus emerging of the character of environmental governance in the twenty-first century. Environmental standards and decisions are elaborated by public authorities, with public involvement of the public. These standards are subsequently articulated in an ever wider range of instruments, including command-and-control regulation, financial instruments, private instruments, and various forms of self-regulation. One example of this type of environmental governance may be found in the field of the regulation of chemicals. *McEldowney*'s analysis of the EU's proposed regime for chemicals provides fascinating insights into how responsibilities are shifting from public authorities to private firms, and how the precautionary principle is operationalized.

When it comes to enforcement of these standards, the public is increasingly mobilized to complement the enforcement activities of public enforcement authorities. This is made possible by the Aarhus Convention, but also by novel instruments that empower NGOs and individuals to take action.

In this latter respect, *Betlem* and *Wennerås* deal with Directive 2004/35/EC on Environmental Liability with Regard to the Prevention and Remedying of Environmental Damage (Environmental Liability Directive).[7] Originally conceived as a private law instrument, the Environmental Liability Directive effectively has come to embrace a regime of public liability. Nonetheless, in Article 12, the Directive grants natural or legal persons with a sufficient interest a right to submit to competent authorities a request to take action, where the interest of NGOs is deemed to be sufficient.

Both authors are critical about the effectiveness of the Environmental Liability Directive. *Betlem* finds inspiration in national liability regimes pertaining to mining activities to suggest various improvements, including the scope of the Directive (in particular the inclusion of genetically modified organisms (GMOs)),

[5] Kiev (Ukraine), 21 May 2003 (not yet in force).

[6] [1996] OJ L275/26.

[7] Adopted after completion of this chapter, [2004] OJ L143/56. See G. Betlem and E. Brans, 'The Future Role of Civil Liability for Environmental Damage in the EU' (2002) 2 *Yearbook of European Environmental Law*, 183–222.

the burden of proof, and access to justice. *Wennerås* makes a compelling case to show that systems of permit defence, as included in Article 8 of the Environmental Liability Directive, are incompatible with both the overall aim of the Directive in particular, as well as regimes of 'strict liability' more generally.

The Environmental Liability Directive would also seem to curtail national discretion in deciding the kind of enforcement action that needs to be taken in response to breaches of EC environmental law. This is an important observation in light of the chapter by *Blomberg* and *Michiels*, who take up the difficult challenge to explain and in part defend Dutch policy in certain cases to tolerate breaches of environmental law. The extent to which such policies, irrespective of their environmental merits, are compatible with European Court of Justice (ECJ) case law remains a controversial issue.

This question has only gained in importance in the light of recent EU and EC initiatives to introduce a compulsory regime of *criminal* environmental law enforcement. *Comte* provides unique insights in the institutional wrangle caused by simultaneous initiatives in the first and third pillars to adopt such a mandatory regime at EU level, and passionately argues that the ECJ should acknowledge and give precedence to first pillar powers.

The third and final strand which, together with issues surrounding adoption of the Aarhus Convention and questions pertaining to the enforcement of EC environmental law, forms the backbone of this volume, relates to the integration of environmental concerns into other policy fields. Both *Dhondt* and *Williams* examine in detail the integration of environmental concerns into the Community's energy and development policies, respectively. *Dhondt* concludes that, where external objectives and environmental imperatives coincide, integration, unsurprisingly, causes few problems. In cases where objectives clash, however, very little progress seems to have been made in terms of integration. For the Community's development policy, the picture painted by *Williams* looks even bleaker: the EU is not prioritizing aid to the poorest, although poverty remains one of the main causes of environmental degradation. Nor does its development policy appear to be influenced in any significant way by environmental prerogatives.

In sum, this volume catalogues real progress in the sphere of public participation in environmental affairs, as well as less convincing attempts to close the enforcement gap which from its inception has threatened the success of the EC environmental law. Finally, as for integration—the acid test for the Union' quest to achieve sustainable growth—further progress is badly needed.

THIJS ETTY
HAN SOMSEN
(*Editors-in-Chief*)

Acknowledgements

We should like to thank a number of individuals and institutions who have contributed to the realization of this volume.

Some of the papers published in this volume were first presented at an international conference convened in Leuven on 29 and 30 August 2003, which was organized jointly by the Institute for Environmental Energy and Law of Leuven and the Centre of Environmental Law of Amsterdam (CELA). Kurt Deketelaere spent many weeks preparing this stimulating event, and proved an excellent host during the two days of the conference.

As in previous years, CELA has generously financed part of the editorial assistance that has been necessary to produce this volume. Marjan Oomens, Yvonne ter Horst, and Stefan Dimitrov spent many hours incorporating our unintelligible editorial notes into the final copy. Yvonne also secured smooth communication between the authors and the editorial team.

Rissa Philip and Frederik Somsen also deserve praise for their irreplaceable assistance and patience with the editors.

We are particularly grateful for the continued support of our anonymous referees who provide invaluable help in assisting authors and the editors in their ambition to produce articles of the highest possible academic quality. Finally and most importantly, we are indebted to all authors of articles, current survey entries, book reviews, and documents for continuing to entrust their work to the *Yearbook of European Environmental Law.*

THIJS ETTY
HAN SOMSEN
(*Editors-in-Chief*)

Contents

REVIEWS OF BOOKS

DOCUMENTS

List of Contributors

Gerrit Betlem graduated with a law degree from the University of Groningen and in 1993 obtained his PhD from Utrecht University (The Netherlands) for his prize-winning book *Civil Liability for Transfrontier Pollution* (London: Graham & Trotman, 1993). Presently, he is a Reader in European private law at School of Law of the University of Exeter (UK), where he teaches EU and international business law courses. His research interests focus on European private (international) law, including the private enforcement of Community law and Francovich liability, as well as on comparative tort law, in particular environmental liability. His most recent publications include contributions to *Towards a European Civil Code* (A. Hartkamp (ed.), Nijmegen: Ars Aequi Libris, 1998), *European Journal of International Law, Environmental Liability* and the *Oxford Journal of Legal Studies.*

Aletta Blomberg is Senior Lecturer at the Institute of Constitutional and Administrative Law of Utrecht University. She has published extensively on the issue of the enforcement of environmental law, including her PhD thesis (*cum laude*) on integral enforcement of environmental law (*Integrale handhaving van milieurecht*; Den Haag: Boom Juridische Uitgevers, 2000). She is currently involved in a research project concerning the relationship between administrative and criminal enforcement of environmental law in a European context.

Françoise Comte has worked at the European Commission since 1990. After working for DG Competition, she joined DG Environment. She graduated in law from the University of Paris-Sorbonne and from the College of Europe of Bruges. She has published numerous articles on issues related to European environmental law.

Nele M.L. Dhondt studied in Ghent (Belgium) and London (UK). While carrying out research for her PhD thesis, she worked for the Centre for Environmental Law at the University of Amsterdam. She has lectured and published in the area of EC environmental law. After having been awarded a *cum laude* for her PhD thesis, *Integration of Environmental Protection into other EC Policies* (Groningen: Europa Law Publishing, 2003), she started practising as a lawyer in Amsterdam.

Ludwig Krämer has long held a wide range of responsibilities in the European Commission. Currently he is serving the DG Environment's Legal Affairs and Governance Unit. He is also Professor at the Faculty of Law at the University of Bremen. His numerous publications in the field of European Community environmental law include *European Environmental Law* (London: Sweet &

Maxwell, 1993), *Focus on European Environmental Law* (2nd edn., London: Sweet & Maxwell, 1997), and *EC Treaty and Environmental Law* (4th edn., London: Sweet & Maxwell, 2000). His most recent co-authored book (with Keith Clement) is *Economic Development and Environmental Gain: European Integration and Regional Competitiveness* (London: Earthscan, 2001).

Sharron McEldowney, BSc (Aberystwyth) and PhD (University of Warwick), is Principal Lecturer in Bioscience at the University of Westminster. Her publications include: (with J.F. McEldowney) *Environmental Law and Regulation* (London: Blackstone, 1998); *Environment and the Law* (London: Longman, 1996); (with D. Hardman and S. Waite) *Pollution—Ecology and Biotreatment* (London: Longman, 1993) and 'A Case Study in Environmental Risk and its Assessment in the BSE Epidemic—Lessons for the Future', in *Anglo-Japanese Academy Proceedings of the Conference on National, Regional and Global Transition—A Common Agenda for Anglo-Japanese relations in the Twenty-First Century* (Tokyo: University of Tokyo, 2001), and numerous other articles.

Lex Michiels is Professor of Environmental Law at the Institute of Constitutional and Administrative Law of Utrecht University, and Director of the Center for Environmental Law and Policy. His numerous publications concern enforcement and various other aspects of environmental law, as well as administrative law more generally. He is Chairman of the Dutch Association of Administrative Law and member of the Steering Committee Elevating Enforcement ('Handhaven op Niveau'). In addition, he was Chairman of the Evaluation Commission of the Environmental Management Act for the Dutch Ministry of Housing, Spatial Planning, and the Environment (2000–3).

Karen Morrow is Senior Lecturer in Law at the University of Leeds and assistant coordinator of the Society of Legal Scholars' environment panel. Her research interests include environmental law, planning law, public law, and the law of torts. She is co-author of the following books: (with Sharon Turner) *Northern Ireland Environmental Law* (Dublin: Gill & Macmillan, 1997) and (with Sean Coyle) *A Philosophical Foundation for Environmental Law* (Oxford: Hart Publishing, 2003). She has also published a range of articles in the above areas of research expertise.

Jonathan Verschuuren is professor of European and international environmental law at the Centre for Legislative Studies of the Schoordijk Institute for Jurisprudence and Comparative Law at Tilburg University. He is member of the Commission on Environmental Law of the World Conservation Union (IUCN), member of the board of the Netherlands Committee of the IUCN, and was secretary and reporter for the Evaluation Commission Environmental Management Act for the Dutch Minister of Housing, Spatial Planning, and the Environment (until 2003). He has widely published in various academic journals. His latest book is *Principles of Environmental Law, The Ideal of Sustainable*

Development and the Role of Principles of International, European, and National Environmental Law (Baden-Baden: Nomos Verlag, 2003).

Pål Wennerås is researcher at the Centre for Environmental Law, University of Amsterdam. He has published on EC environmental law in several European law journals and is a regular contributor to the *Yearbook of International Environmental Law.* Mr Wennerås is currently working on his PhD thesis concerning the private enforcement of EC environmental law in national and Community courts.

Rhiannon Williams is a Doctoral Research Fellow at the Institute for European Studies, Vrije Universiteit Brussel, and a member of Ecosphere, the European Centre on Sustainable Policies for Human and Environmental Rights. Her research concerns the impact of globalization on European Community environment and development law. She has previously worked in the Legal Affairs Unit of DG Environment of the European Commission, as a Lecturer at the University of Liège, and as a solicitor specializing in environmental law with Renouf & Co. (now CrosbyRenouf). She has published on the enforcement of Community environmental law, access to information concerning Community environmental law, Community development cooperation law and policy, and various issues of substantive Community environmental law.

Table of Cases

European Union

Alphabetical

Chronological

Finland

United Kingdom

Table of Legislation

Austria

European Union

Treaties

Decisions

Directives

Regulations

Finland

France

Greece

Italy

Norway

Poland

Portugal

Statutory Instruments

United States of America

Access to Environmental Information in an Open European Society—Directive 2003/4/EC

*Ludwig Krämer**

I. Introduction: Access to Environmental Information in the European Union

Information generates knowledge and knowledge generates power. Although in all Member States of the European Community (EC) the duty to protect the environment rests with the administration, it is obvious that the administration does not own the environment, which belongs to everybody. It is for this reason that administrative decisions which affect the environment must be transparent, and strike a balance between the general interest to preserve, protect, and improve the quality of the environment on the one hand, and specific private or public interests on the other hand. In order to allow at least a degree of control as to whether the administration strikes the right balance between the need to protect the environment and other legitimate or less legitimate needs, it appears self-evident that information on the environment in the hands of public authorities must be made available to the public.

The European Union (EU) is conceived as an open society 'in which decisions are taken as openly as possible and as closely as possible to the citizens'.[1] The concept of open decision-making presupposes that public authorities openly provide the facts, data, studies, and monitoring results on which they intend to base their decisions, including decisions not to act. Such openness enables citizens and organizations to participate in environmental decision-making, which implies discussing the facts, and the necessity and viability to take action, thereby giving a voice to the environment and to future generations.[2]

In order to improve access to information on the environment, in 1990 the EC adopted Directive 90/313/EEC on the Freedom of Access to Information on the

* Commission of the European Communities, DG Environment, Legal Affairs and Governance Unit, Brussels (Belgium). The author expresses his personal opinion.

[1] Treaty on European Union [2002] OJ C325/5, Art. 1.

[2] See also L. Krämer, 'The Open Society, its Lawyers and its Environment' (1989) 1 *Journal of Environmental Law*, 1.

Environment (Access to Information Directive) with the objective to 'ensure freedom of access to, and information of, information on the environment held by public authorities'.[3] It established EC-wide basic terms and conditions under which such information was to be made available, defined in particular the terms 'information on the environment' and 'public authorities', laid down an exhaustive list of grounds on which the authorities could exceptionally refuse access to information, stated that against a refusal a judicial decision could be sought, and provided for some rules for active information on the environment to be made available to the public by Member States.

According to Article 9 of the Directive, Member States had to transpose the Access to Information Directive into national law by the end of 1992. They all did so, although sometimes with delay and not always completely or correctly. In its report on the application of the Access to Information Directive, the Commission listed 131 legislative and regulatory instruments which Member States had notified as national and regional transposition measures.[4] Furthermore, Member States had to report on the Directive's application by the end of 1996. With the exception of Luxembourg, they all did so with delay.[5]

II. The Elaboration of Directive 2003/4/EC on Public Access to Environmental Information and Repealing Council Directive 90/313/EEC

A. The Aarhus Convention

In June 1998, the Convention on Access to Information, Public Participation in Decision-making and Access to Justice in Environmental Matters, the so-called Aarhus Convention, was opened for signature in Aarhus, Denmark, and signed by all EC Member States and the EC itself. Germany signed the Convention at the end of 1998. Its provisions regarding access to information sometimes deviated from the wording of the Access to Information Directive, on which to a large extent it had been modelled. This meant that the Access to Information Directive had to be amended in order to be in full compliance with the requirements of the Aarhus Convention. As observed, in 2000 the Commission reported on the experience gained in the application of the Access to Information Directive. This report was based on (a) the fifteen national reports submitted by the Member States mentioned above; (b) an examination of 156 complaints which had been

[3] [1990] OJ L158/56; see also L. Krämer, *Focus on European Environmental Law* (London: Sweet and Maxwell, 1992), 290–309.

[4] Commission, Report on the Experience Gained in the Application of Council Directive 90/313 of 7 June 1990, on Freedom of Access to Information on the Environment COM(2000)400.

[5] Commission, COM(2000)400, ibid., Annex B. Luxembourg sent its report in Sept. 1996, Portugal in Apr. 1999; the other Member States sent their reports between Feb. and July 1997.

submitted to the Commission concerning alleged non-compliance with the requirements of the Access to Information Directive; (c) two judgments of the European Court of Justice (ECJ);[6] and (d) two reports which represented the view of non-governmental organizations (NGOs) and other experts.[7]

B. The Commission's Proposal for a Directive

On the basis of this documentation, the Commission submitted a proposal for a new directive on access to information on the environment.[8] The proposal had three objectives: (1) to correct the shortcomings identified in the practical application of the Access to Information Directive; the Commission underlined that the wording of the Aarhus Convention had already addressed these shortcomings; (2) to pave the way to the ratification of the Aarhus Convention; and (3) to adapt the Access to Information Directive to developments in information technologies. The Commission underlined that it preferred, in the interest of increased transparency and legal certainty, to replace the Access to Information Directive by a new Directive rather than to amend it, but stressed that 'the existing *acquis* is not open for discussion'. As the proposal thus built on the provisions of the Aarhus Convention, which in turn had been based on the Access to Information Directive, it came as no surprise that the proposal very largely maintained the structure and even the wording of the Access to Information Directive, and only fine-tuned the different provisions, adapting them to the wording of the Aarhus Convention and eliminating ambiguities which had caused concern.

The proposal took up a very limited number of innovations. The most important one concerned the privatized industry. The Commission suggested extending access to information also to 'any legal person entrusted... with the operation of services of general economic interest which affect or are likely to affect the state of elements of the environment', and expressly mentioned gas, electricity, water, and transport. It explained that a different treatment of services by public administrations or utilities and privatized companies was not justified where services of general economic interest were at stake. Other changes in the proposal concerned the shortening of the time-period for answering applications from two months to one month, and a considerable extension of the obligation actively to deliver information on the environment. In both these aspects, the proposal followed the Aarhus Convention.

6 Case C-321/96, *Mecklenburg* v. *Kreis Pinneberg—Der Landrat* [1998] ECR I-3809; Case C-217/97, *Commission* v. *Germany* [1999] ECR I-5087.

7 Stichting Natuur en Milieu, Utrecht: Access to Environmental Information: The Review and further Development of Directive 90/313, Workshop Report (1998); Stichting Natuur en Milieu, Utrecht: Recommendations for the Review and Revision of Directive 90/313 on the Freedom of Access to Information on the Environment (1998). Both Reports are mentioned as sources in COM(2000)400, n. 4 above.

8 Proposal for a Directive on Public Access to Environmental Information [2000] OJ C337E/156; Explanatory Memorandum in COM(2000)402.

Other innovations which Member States had introduced into their national legislation were not taken up by the Commission, such as the provision that access to information on the environment should, in principle, be free of charge, or provisions in Austrian legislation that private companies with a duty to measure and record emission data had regularly to publish these data.[9]

C. Economic and Social Committee; Committee of the Regions

The Economic and Social Committee welcomed the Commission's proposal, including the provision on privatized industries.[10] It suggested a number of minor amendments which were, in the final version of the Directive, almost all ignored. More successful with its Opinion was the Committee of the Regions;[11] about two-thirds of its suggestions for amendments were reflected in the final text of the Directive, although it is true that most of them concerned issues of drafting or were otherwise of a less important nature. The Opinion reflected experience which local or regional authorities had gained with questions concerning access to information, for instance with criteria for the transfer or the refusal of requests, charges, or the dissemination of environmental information.

D. The European Parliament

The European Parliament (EP) adopted, in its first reading, 30 amendments.[12] However, this figure obscures the fact that amendments typically concerned a single specific provision. For example, the EP suggested no less than eleven amendments to the wording of Article 2 concerning definitions, thirteen amendments to Article 3, and fifteen to Article 4.

The political parties in the EP very largely agreed among themselves: only five of the amending proposals suggested by the rapporteur, Mrs. E. Korhola (European People's Party (EPP)/Finland) were voted upon separately, four of them being put to a vote by the rapporteur's own political party.[13] These amendments concerned, in particular, the reduction of the answering time to two weeks instead of one month as suggested by the Commission; a minimum content for practical arrangements; free access to information for educational purposes;

[9] Austria, Bundesgesetz über den Zugang zu Informationen über die Umwelt, Article 13: 'Wer... verpflichtet ist, Emissionen aus seiner Betriebsanlage zu messen und darüber Aufzeichnungen zu führen, hat... (diese) Aufzeichnungen in allgemein verständlicher Form an einer allgemein leicht zugänglichen Stelle (monatlich und jährlich) bekanntzumachen'. (A person who is... obliged to measure emissions from his or her installation and to record them, shall be obliged to publish these records in an easily comprehensible form in an easily accessible way (once per month or per year)).

[10] Economic and Social Committee, Opinion of 15 Nov. 2000 [2001] OJ C116/43.

[11] Committee of the Regions, Opinion of 14 Feb. 2001 [2001] OJ C148/9.

[12] EP Res. of 14 Mar. 2001 [2001] OJ C343/165.

[13] [2001] OJ C343/104.

the ban of advance payment; and the possibility to introduce sanctions against officials for clearly wrongful refusal of a request for environmental information. All votes were lost by the EPP, but ultimately none of the amendments were retained in the final text of the Directive.

The EP's consensus was demonstrated in the final vote, where the Korhola report was adopted with 505 votes in favour, two abstentions and no vote against it.[14] The Commission then amended its proposal;[15] it accepted one EP amendment in full, twelve in part, and declared seventeen amendments unacceptable. The main reasons given were that the Directive was a framework directive, that the EP tried to impose excessive details, and that, for reasons of subsidiarity, Member States should have greater flexibility in fixing details.[16]

E. The Council of Ministers

Discussions in the Council of Ministers were marked by the determination of practically all Member States to adapt Community legislation to implement the Aarhus Convention, but not to go beyond the requirements of that Convention. This last aspect was mentioned twice in the statement of reasons in the Council Common Position which was reached in early 2002.[17] The Common Position accepted one EP amendment in full, two amendments in a different form, and eight amendments in part. It rejected the remaining eighteen amendments.

Induced by the almost unanimous vote during the first reading, the EP reintroduced, for the second reading, practically all the amendments which it had suggested at the first reading, this time split up in 47 amendments.[18] As the Council of Ministers did not wish to deviate in any significant way from its Common Position, a conciliation procedure was started. In December 2002, an agreement was reached which remained rather close to the Common Position. This allowed the Directive to be finally adopted on 28 January 2003 and published as Directive 2003/4 of the EP and of the Council on Public Access to Environmental Information and Repealing Council Directive 90/313/EEC (The New Access to Information Directive).[19] Member States will have to transpose the Directive into national law by 14 February 2005. The Access to Information Directive will be repealed on that same day.

An analysis of the approximately 30 months of discussion leading up to the adoption of the Directive reveals a very large degree of consensus among the

[14] [2001] OJ C343/134.

[15] Amended proposal [2001] OJ C240E/289.

[16] Each of the four key words 'framework directive', 'excessive details', 'subsidiarity', and 'flexibility' was used four times in the Commission's text.

[17] Common Position of 28 Jan. 2002 [2002] OJ C113E/1.

[18] EP Position of 30 May 2002 [2003] OJ C187E/118.

[19] OJ [2003] L41/26.

institutions on the principle of free access to information on the environment. Differences of opinion appeared as soon as details were discussed. In general, the provisions of the Aarhus Convention guided the drafting process of the new legislation. Only exceptionally were the Council and the Commission prepared to go beyond the requirements of that Convention. The EP tried, on a considerable number of points, to provide for more elaborate rights for citizens than guaranteed by the Aarhus Convention, and to curtail administrative discretion, but remained largely unsuccessful. During the conciliation procedure, the greater experience, efficiency, and professionalism of the Council secretariat, backed in particular by the Danish Council Presidency's staff, and also by Member States' administrations in the fifteen capitals, prevailed over the EP, which had fewer human resources, less profound knowledge of the topic, and less drafting capacity than the Council of Ministers.

III. The Main Provisions of the New Access to Information Directive

A. Access to Information or to Environmental Information?

At no point was there any discussion in the EP or in the Council that there should be EC legislation on the right of access to information. If one considers the principles of open society, briefly alluded to above, there is no reason to limit the right of access to information concerning the environment. In addition, Article 1 of the Treaty on European Union (TEU) does not exclude environmental issues. Finally, Article 255 EC states that 'every citizen of the Union . . . shall have the right of access to EP, Council and Commission documents', a provision which is repeated almost word for word by Article 42 of the Charter of Fundamental Rights.[20] This right of access to documents[21] is general, but is limited to the European level. There is no EC legislation establishing such a duty to provide access to documents or information for Member States.

The reason for the absence of such general legislation seems clear. Article 42 of the Charter of Fundamental Rights is placed in the Chapter of 'Citizens Rights', and Article 255 EC belongs to the chapter 'Provisions common to several institutions'. EC institutions do not systematically seek to develop the rights of citizens in the EU, and the European Commission does not specially look into the question of citizens' rights. There thus exists no administrative unit that could take such an initiative, and propose a general directive on access to information.

[20] The Charter of Fundamental Rights of the European Union [2000] OJ C364/1, repeats this provision in Art. 42, but also limits itself to the European level.

[21] See also Reg. (EC) No. 1049/2001 regarding Public Access to EP, Council and Commission Documents [2001] OJ L145/43.

This remains regrettable and to some extent arbitrary. Why should there not be a right for citizens to obtain access to the information which the administration holds on genetically modified food, on the results of food contamination controls, on the quality of drinking water, or even on data concerning trucks which have exceeded relevant speed limits? No other justification for this exists, other than the fact that such knowledge would give more power to citizens. Administrations do not wish this to occur. In a democratic society, where administrations exist to serve citizens, this policy is extremely conservative, and even reactionary. There remain sufficient exceptions to the rule of free access to information to preserve the legitimate interests of policy-makers, private persons, or economic operators where these interests are truly legitimate.

Also, the interpretation difficulties as to whether specific information must be considered 'environmental information', and thus falls within the scope of the New Access to Information Directive, demonstrate how arbitrary the borderline between 'information' and 'environmental information' is.

B. A Right of Access to Environmental Information

The Commission stated in its proposal for the New Access to Information Directive that the Access to Information Directive 'only ensured freedom of access to environmental information',[22] and suggested establishing, in the new Directive, a right of access to environmental information. This proposal, which aligned Community legislation with the Aarhus Convention, did not meet objections and was adopted.

However, the Commission's argument that the Access to Information Directive did not establish a right of access to environmental information, is incorrect. Indeed, Recital 6 of the Access to Information Directive declared that 'it is necessary to *guarantee* to any natural or legal person . . . free access to available information on the environment' (emphasis added). Recital 7 allowed the refusal of a request for information 'in certain specific and clearly defined cases'. However, such a refusal 'must be justified' (Recital 8). The applicant had the possibility to appeal against such a refusal (Recital 9 and Article 4). All these provisions reflected the existence of a right, not merely an obligation for administrations. The only part which was lacking in this system was the mention of the word 'right'. This interpretation was also followed by the ECJ which stated that 'the purpose of the Directive is to confer a right on individuals which assures the freedom of access to information on the environment'.[23]

However, this legal construction should not obscure reality. Where a citizen is confronted with a local, regional, or national administration with responsibilities not only for the environment but also, for example, for transport, the economy,

[22] COM(2000)402, n. 8 above.

[23] Case C-217/97, *Commission* v. *Germany*, n. 6 above, para. 47; see also Case C-321/96, n. 6 above, para. 28; Case C-233/00, *Commission* v. *France* [2003] ECR I-6625.

or energy, it will be helpful for the applicant to be able to point out that he has a 'right' of access to information. It is for this reason that it is important to find the word 'right to access to environmental information' back in national implementing legislation, although this aspect should not be exaggerated: the devil is in the detail of granting or refusing access to information on the environment.

C. Environmental Information

The Access to Information Directive contained a rather extensive definition of 'information relating to the environment'.[24] Practical application of this provision showed, however, that the enumeration in the Directive put administrations in a position to question whether information that was not explicitly mentioned really belonged to the information that was covered by the Access to Information Directive.

The Commission's proposal for the New Access to Information Directive tried to reduce restrictive interpretations, and to be more unambiguous.[25] Therefore, it specifically included information on emissions and other releases into the environment, genetically modified organisms, as well as cost-benefit and other economic analyses. All these elements had already been placed in the corresponding definition of the Aarhus Convention, except for the reference to releases into the environment.

The EP also wanted wetlands and coastal and marine areas to be included in the definition, an amendment which the Council accepted. In contrast, the Council did not accept that 'energy' be specified by including 'nuclear fuel and energy', because these elements 'do not appear in Aarhus and . . . are covered by "energy radiation and radioactive waste"'.[26] There was thus consensus that such information was part of 'information on the environment'.

The EP also wanted to see 'reports on the implementation of environmental legislation' to be specified, which the Council accepted during the conciliation procedure, even though such reports were not mentioned in the Aarhus Convention's definition.

More contentious was the EP's request for 'food safety' to accompany 'the state of health and safety', which is not mentioned in the Aarhus Convention. The Commission opposed this amendment, on the basis that it was not laid down in the Aarhus Convention.[27] The Council also argued that such an amendment

[24] Dir. 90/313/EEC, n. 4 above, Art. 2(a): '"information relating to the environment" shall mean: any available information in written, visual, aural or data-base form on the state of water, air, soil fauna, flora, land and natural sites, and on activities (including those which give rise to nuisances such as noise) or measures adversely affecting or likely so to affect these, and on activities or measures designed to protect these, including administrative measures and environmental management programmes'.

[25] n. 8 above.

[26] Common Position, n. 17 above, para. VI.3.

[27] Amended proposal, n. 15 above, para. 3.4.

'would too much widen the scope of the Directive'.[28] During the conciliation procedure, the formula 'the contamination of the food chain, where relevant' was agreed. This means that information on food contamination caused by pesticides, heavy metals or other contaminants is covered by the Directive. Again, it is not clear why the public should not have access to information available on other sources of contamination of the food chain.

D. Public Authorities

The Access to Information Directive defined as 'public authorities' any public administration at national, regional, or local level, with responsibilities, and possessing information, relating to the environment. This included, according to Article 6 'bodies with public responsibilities for the environment and under control of public authorities'.

The Commission proposed the following amendments: (a) a reference to 'government'; (b) a reference to persons having public responsibilities or functions, or providing public services, relating to the environment under a public administration; (c) a reference to any person entrusted with the operation of services of general economic interest which affect the environment. The exception for courts and parliaments was also discussed (d).

i. Government

The inclusion of the concept 'government' within the notion of 'public authorities' was never in dispute. Under the Access to Information Directive, the question had arisen in the United Kingdom (UK), whether central government would also be covered by 'public authorities'.[29] The EP wanted 'advisory bodies' to be included in the definition of public authorities.[30] The Commission opposed this amendment, as the Aarhus Convention did not mention it. In its Common Position, the Council also opposed the amendment, 'as this would expand too much the scope of the Directive and would give rise to the serious problem of designating those bodies'.[31] In the second reading, the EP repeated its proposal which the Council finally accepted in the form of 'public advisory bodies'.

Reading the notion of 'public authorities', it seems a strange interpretation to consider that advisory bodies should not come under 'any administration' (Access to Information Directive). The purpose of the Access to Information Directive—as well as of the New Access to Information Directive—is to give broad access to

[28] Common Position, n. 17 above, para. VI.3.

[29] See P. Roderick, 'United Kingdom' in R. Hallo (ed.), *Access to Environmental Information in Europe. The Implementation and Implications of Directive 90/313/EEC* (London/The Hague/Boston: Kluwer Law International, 1996), 249–76.

[30] Res., n. 12 above, Amendment 15.

[31] Common Position, n. 17 above, para. VI.3.

available information held by public authorities. And where public advisory bodies hold information on the state of the environment—for instance a study, an assessment of the impact of any envisaged measure, the results of monitoring data, and so on—it appears normal that such information is made available to citizens. It cannot be repeated often enough that administrations do not own the environment, and that it is therefore reasonable that such information is shared.

ii. Persons Having Public Responsibilities or Functions

The Commission explained its proposal with the argument that some bodies, for instance in the transport or energy areas, had been excluded from the scope of application of the Access to Information Directive with the argument that they had responsibilities not for the environment, but for transport or energy. Reflecting the integration principle, the new proposal therefore should also include entities whose responsibilities lie outside the realm of environmental policy, such as transport or energy bodies.

The EP accepted this explanation and the new wording. The Council slightly changed the proposed wording, so that Article 2(2)(b) of the final version of the New Access to Information Directive referred to 'any natural or legal person performing public administrative functions under national law, including specific duties, activities or services in relation to the environment'.

iii. Private Bodies and Privatized Industries

The Commission suggested including in the notion of 'public authorities' any person that was entrusted by law, or under arrangements with a public authority, 'services of general economic interest which affect or are likely to affect the state of elements of the environment'. It explained that some services, such as gas, electricity, water, or transport, were in some Member States performed by public authorities or utilities, while in other Member States, they were performed by private bodies. Unequal treatment of access to information was, however, not justified as these services were essentially the same, and differentiation between private and public services could occur within a single Member State. The Commission therefore considered it necessary to go beyond the wording of the Aarhus Convention, and to include all bodies which provided general interest services in the definition of 'public authorities'.

The Economic and Social Committee[32] and the Committee of the Regions[33] agreed to the Commission's proposal, but the EP rejected it. The Greens in the EP tried, during the First Reading, to maintain the Commission's proposal, but remained unsuccessful.[34] The Council declared that it did not wish to follow the Commission's proposal, 'sharing the EP's reluctance to assimilate to a public authority services of general economic interest such as transport, waterworks or

[32] Opinion, n. 10 above, para. 2.4.1.

[33] Opinion, n. 11 above, para. 4.

[34] [2001] OJ C343/105.

telephone'.[35] The Commission did not fight for its proposal which was thus incorporated into the final version of the New Access to Information Directive.

In general, I agree with the basic decision that there should be a differentiation between public administration and private bodies. The notion of 'services of general economic interest' is used in Article 16 and Article 86(2) EC without this notion having a well-defined meaning.[36] In the environmental sector, public transport, urban waste management, nuclear and other energy services, drinking water, and waste-water management are examples of services which may be considered as of general economic interest. Where a Member State allows a specific sector to organize itself privately, there is not much reason to ask for access to environmental information held by such private companies: the profit-making aim normally distinguishes the private from the public service, although it is readily recognized that the difference between a public and a private body depends on more criteria than the profit-making aspect. Certainly, the fact that some services in the past were organized as public services and subsequently were privatized, cannot be a decisive factor. At least in continental Europe, some two hundred years ago all economic activities were public, and were only progressively privatized.

Why non-public bodies should be obliged to grant access to available information on the environment is not evident. Public bodies have general interests to take care of, while private bodies in principle have their own interests to consider. Requiring private bodies to grant access to information on the environment would just create new difficulties between private bodies which act in the general economic interest, and private bodies which do not. Such a differentiation is even more difficult to maintain.

Austria has a rather interesting provision in its national Environmental Information Act, obliging private companies that are legally obliged to measure releases into the environment from their installations, and to keep records on them, to publish them regularly in a manner that is easily accessible and understandable.[37] Although the Commission mentioned this provision, it did not consider making a corresponding proposal for the whole of the EC,[38] and neither the Council nor the EP took any initiative in the direction of granting access to environmental information held by private companies.

iv. Judicial and Legislative Bodies

The Access to Information Directive had excluded access to information held by bodies 'acting in a judicial and legislative capacity'. When the Commission took

35 Common Position, n. 17 above, para. VI.3.

36 See also Commission, Report on Services of General Interest COM(2001)598; Commission Communication: A Methodological Note for the Horizontal Evaluation of Services of General Economic Interest COM(2002)331, 18 June 2002.

37 Bundesgesetz über den Zugang zu Informationen über die Umwelt, Art. 13.

38 See also the discussion on emissions into the environment, para. III.E.iii, below.

legal action against Germany because it had in a general fashion exempted courts, criminal prosecution authorities, and disciplinary courts, the ECJ judged that the Commission had not shown that these bodies had information on the environment obtained outside their judicial activities.[39] This judgment caused the Commission to suggest the wording that judicial and legislative bodies should be excluded from the definition of public authorities 'when and to the extent that they act in a judicial or legislative capacity'. The Council originally returned to the wording of the Aarhus Convention ('bodies or institutions acting in a judicial or legislative capacity'): because in the second reading, the EP insisted on the wording originally proposed by the Commission, agreement was finally found on the wording 'when acting in a judicial or legislative capacity'.

This controversy seems to have been caused by the ECJ's judgment, which does not convince me. Indeed, it is quite interesting for the public to know, for instance, how many environmental crimes or other offences were brought to the knowledge of a public prosecutor, how many of these cases were actually pursued, how many judgments were delivered or other sanctions imposed, how many acquittals occurred, and how often a polluter has actually gone to jail. All this information is not obtained 'in a judicial capacity', but is statistical information, and should therefore be generally accessible. The Commission had expressly mentioned statistical data,[40] but was not able to persuade the ECJ. In view of this judgment, it may be doubted whether the new wording of the New Access to Information Directive will really constitute a change.

E. Grounds for Refusal

In Article 3(2), the Access to Information Directive enumerated twelve grounds on which public authorities were entitled to oppose the right of access to information, and in Article 3(3) four more grounds were specified. The Aarhus Convention contained the same number of exceptions. The Directive maintains once more the same number and even the substance of the grounds for refusal, but fine-tunes their wording and, furthermore, adds statistical confidentiality and tax secrecy. Following the Aarhus Convention, the New Access to Information Directive also indicates that the grounds for refusal have to be interpreted in a restrictive way, a rather exceptional provision for an EC Directive. Furthermore, Article 4(2) mentions that, in each particular case, the public interest served by disclosure 'shall be weighed against the interest served by the refusal'. It will thus be not so much the Directive or the future transposing legislation which will decide whether access to information will be granted in a specific case or not. The discretion of the public authority will be decisive. For that reason, much of the practical application of the New Access to Information Directive will depend on the basic decision whether an administration is prepared to share its knowledge

[39] Case C-217/97, n. 6 above, para. 24.

[40] ibid., para. 20.

on the environment with applicants or not. In any case, the two provisions of Article 4 about a restrictive interpretation of the exceptions and of the weighing of the respective interests, together with the general establishment of a 'right' of access to environmental information in Article 1, clearly indicate the Directive's bias in favour of openness and transparency. Whenever public authorities weigh diverging interests under the New Access to Information Directive or its implementing national provisions, they will have to take into account this basic tenet of the EC legislation in favour of free access to environmental information.

Among the numerous exceptions to the right of access to information, the following deserve more detailed examination.

i. Material in the Course of Completion or Unfinished Documents

Article 3(3) of the Access to Information Directive allowed Member States to refuse a request for information where it would involve the supply of unfinished documents or data. The Aarhus Convention provided that access could be refused for material in the course of completion; the same wording was taken over by the Commission's proposal for the New Access to Information Directive. The EP did not ask for an amendment, but the Council thought it wise to combine these formulas, and provided for an exception for unfinished documents as well as for documents or data in the course of completion. In the second reading, the EP tried to mitigate the scope of this provision, requesting that in the statement of refusal the name of the person or authority preparing the material and the estimated time of completion be indicated.[41] The Council accepted this only for material in the course of completion, and only with regard to the name of the authority that prepared the material.[42] The result is that refusal may be based on the argument that documents or data are unfinished, without any information being released when the documents or data would be finished.

It might be worthwhile mentioning that the Commission itself reported that environmental organizations and experts had asked for 'unfinished documents' to be deleted altogether from the grounds for refusal, as the notion that data can be withheld pending processing was difficult to defend. Furthermore, such documents should not be capable of being withheld if they have been considered by a public authority in arriving at a decision.[43]

ii. Internal Documents

Article 3(3) of the Access to Information Directive allowed Member States to refuse access to 'internal communications'; the same wording was used in Article 4(3)(c) of the Aarhus Convention and in the Commission's proposal for the New Access to Information Directive. The EP wanted this exception to be deleted,[44]

[41] EP Position, n. 18 above, Amendment 27.

[42] Dir. 2003/4, n. 19 above, Art. 4(1), last subparagraph.

[43] n. 4 above, Annex C.

[44] n. 12 above, Amendment 20.

which the Commission considered unacceptable,[45] and the Council also rejected.[46] The EP repeated its suggestion in the second reading. In the conciliation procedure, the exception was formulated in Article 4(1)(e) as allowing refusal of access to environmental information, where 'the request concerns internal communications, taking into account the public interest served by disclosure'.

Whether this formula will change the administrative reality that internal communications are not released remains to be seen. What is interesting is the parallel development of access to information held by the EC institutions Council, Commission, and the EP. The Commission's proposal for a regulation to implement Article 255 EC provided that internal documents did not come under those documents which had to be released.[47] However, the EP and the Council did not agree. The final wording of Regulation (EC) No. 1049/2001 regarding Public Access to EP, Council and Commission Documents (Access to Community Documents Regulation)[48] included internal documents into the field of application of the Regulation, and stated:

> Access to a document, drawn up by an institution for internal use or received by an institution, which relates to a matter where the decision has not been taken by the institution, shall be refused if disclosure of the document would seriously undermine the institution's decision-making process, unless there is an overriding public interest in disclosure.
>
> Access to a document containing opinions for internal use as part of deliberations and preliminary consultations within the institution concerned shall be refused even after the decision has been taken if disclosure of the document would seriously undermine the institution's decision-making process, unless there is an overriding public interest in disclosure.

Member States thus enjoy a considerably wider discretion to refuse access to internal communications than the EC institutions. And one might wonder whether similar provisions under national law would not be more appropriate in order to address the concern of some Member States.

iii. Emissions into the Environment

Article 3(2) of the Access to Information Directive allowed Member States to refuse access to information where such access could affect 'commercial and industrial confidentiality, including intellectual property, the confidentiality of personal data and/or files'. Article 4(4) of the Aarhus Convention stated: 'A request for environmental information may be refused, if the disclosure would adversely affect: ... (d) The confidentiality of commercial and industrial information, where such confidentiality is protected by law in order to protect a

[45] Amended proposal, n. 15 above, para. 3.4. [46] Common Position, n. 17 above, para. VI.5.
[47] [2000] OJ C177E/70. [48] [2001] OJ L145/43.

legitimate economic interest. Within this framework, information on emissions which is relevant for the protection of the environment shall be disclosed'.

The Commission's proposal for the New Access to Information Directive, without giving any justification, reformulated the last phrase of the Aarhus Convention formula as follows: 'Member States may not, by virtue of this paragraph, provide for a request to be refused where the request relates to information on emissions, discharges or other releases into the environment which are subject to provisions of Community legislation'.[49]

The EP made of this phrase on emissions a separate subparagraph, so that it related to all grounds of refusal mentioned in Article 4(2) and read: 'Member States may not, by virtue of this paragraph, provide for a request to be refused where the request relates to information on emissions, discharges or other releases into the environment'.[50] The Commission was of the opinion that this derogation went too far and that, in certain cases, public authorities should be allowed to refuse access to such information.[51] The Council, then, tried another compromise: it replaced the last phrase of Article 4(4)(d) of the Commission's proposal in the section on commercial or industrial information of Article 4(2)(d), but added at the end of Article 4(2) that all the grounds for refusal should be interpreted in a restrictive way, 'taking into account... whether the information requested related to emissions into the environment',[52] and justified this by the wording of the Aarhus Convention.

The EP did not accept this compromise, and repeated its proposal from the first reading. The final compromise which went into the text of the New Access to Information Directive consisted of prohibiting refusals of information on emissions in the cases of proceedings of public authorities, commercial or industrial information, personal data and/or files, information supplied on a voluntary basis, and information pertaining to the protection of the environment.

The provision that access to information on emissions, discharges, and other releases into the environment may not be refused because of the confidentiality of commercial and industrial information is very important. All too often, economic operators argue that competitors could, through the chemical composition of emissions or releases, obtain information on the production methods and that therefore the emissions should be kept confidential. This argument was never convincing. Indeed, in the same way as a producer who puts a product into circulation or on the market may not invoke commercial or industrial confidentiality, he has to accept that emissions into the environment may no longer be kept confidential. The environment is not the producer's property. If he wants to keep the composition of his emissions confidential, then he should capture them within his installation and prevent them from going public. But he should not be entitled to both emissions into the public domain *and* the maintenance of

[49] Commission, n. 8 above, Art. 4(2.d).
[50] Res., n. 12 above, Amendment 21.
[51] Amended proposal, n. 15 above, para. 3.4.
[52] Common Position, n. 17 above.

commercial secrecy. As regards the placing of products on the market, this principle has long since been recognized, and patent law offers sufficient protection to protect the interests of producers. It was high time that this principle also came to be recognized for emissions into the environment. The wording of the Aarhus Convention which paved the way for the New Access to Information Directive is therefore more than welcome.

In my opinion, releases, discharges, and emissions into the environment should, in principle, always be made public. I therefore sympathize with the Norwegian Act on Environmental Information of February 2003, which states in Article 12 that access to information shall always be provided on (a) pollution damaging to health or pollution which may cause serious damage to the environment, (b) measures to prevent or reduce damage, and (c) illegal intervention or illegal damage to the environment. Into this line of thinking also fits Article 16, which states that 'everybody is entitled to information from enterprises and activities... concerning factors related to the enterprise and activity, including production factors and products, which may have noticeable effect on the environment. The right to environmental information... also applies to information about effects on the environment from production or distribution of a product taking place outside Norwegian borders, to the extent that such information is available'.

It is likely that greater environmental transparency will, in future, be considerably influenced by this new provision and its underlying concept. A first and very important step was taken when, in 2000, the EC set up, after many years of discussion, a European Pollution Emission Register (EPER),[53] which requires Member States to report, for approximately 20,000 individual industrial installations,[54] emissions into the air and water of some 50 pollutants, and which will allow for better knowledge about pollution hot spots within the EC. First data in the context of EPER should be available in 2003.

F. Modalities of Access to Information

Article 3 of the New Access to Information Directive organizes the modalities of granting access to environmental information. It does not really contain new provisions compared to the Access to Information Directive, but specifies the issues in more detail. The most relevant innovations are discussed briefly below.

i. Time Limits

The Access to Information Directive granted Member States two months, but the Aarhus Convention had already provided for a period of one month to respond

[53] Dec. 2000/479/EC on the Implementation of a European Pollutant Emission Register (EPER) [2000] OJ L192/36.

[54] This is the estimated number of installations which come under Dir. 96/61/EEC Concerning Integrated Pollution Prevention and Control [1996] OJ L257/26, under which EPER was set up.

to requests for access to environmental information. Decisions on requests for access to documents held by the EC institutions must normally be taken within fifteen working days,[55] and the EP had in vain requested a regular period of two weeks for the application of the New Access to Information Directive. The Commission considered two weeks too short, and this opinion was shared by the Council which declared that it is often 'impossible—in particular in smaller services' to reduce the answering time to two months. This became the final text; in voluminous or complex cases, the period may be prolonged to two months.

ii. Proving an Interest

The Access to Information Directive stated that the applicant making a request for information did not have to 'prove' an interest. The Commission suggested changing this, and not requiring applicants to 'state' an interest, as the applicant did not have to explain why he was interested in the information requested and the word 'prove' had given rise to some difficulties. This amendment was not questioned and thus was introduced in the final version of the Directive.

iii. Delay for Responding

Article 3(4) of the Access to Information Directive obliged public authorities to 'respond' to a request for access to information within two months. Some Member States had understood this provision as allowing authorities to give, for instance, a provisional reaction within two months after receiving the request; the substantive answer to the request could be given much later.[56] The new wording proposed by the Commission indicated that the answer 'shall be made available' within one month. This wording was accepted without problems and became, with a slight change, the wording of the New Access to Information Directive.

iv. Forms and Formats

The Access to Information Directive left it to Member States to decide in which form the information had to be made available to the applicant. Article 4(1) of the Aarhus Convention is more specific, stipulating that the information be made available in the form requested, including copies of the actual documentation which contained or comprised the information, unless the information is already publicly available in another form, or it is reasonable to make it available in another form. The Commission's proposal for the New Access to Information Directive followed the Aarhus Convention, but added that the information had to be easily accessible to the applicant; this addition was intended to cope with situations where, for instance, an applicant did not have access to the Internet.

[55] Reg. (EC) No. 1049/2001, n. 48 above, Art. 7.

[56] See T. Schomerus, C. Schrader, and B. Wegener, *Umweltinformationsgesetz—Handkommentar* (Baden-Baden: Nomos Verlag, 2002). Germany amended its legislation in 2001.

The EP was of the opinion that the applicant should always obtain the information in the requested form, provided it was readily reproducible to that form or format.[57] The Commission rejected this amendment, as it was not sufficiently flexible, and could be too burdensome for public authorities.[58] In its Common Position, the Council followed the Commission. At the insistence of the EP, the final version of Article 3(4) of the New Access to Information Directive allows public authorities to refer an applicant to other forms of publicly available forms, only if these were easily accessible by the applicant. Furthermore, some non-binding wording is added in order to promote electronic communication.

v. Refusal to Make Information Available

There could have been little doubt under Article 3(4) of the Access to Information Directive[59] that an applicant was entitled to receive a—positive or negative—answer within two months of the application. Nevertheless, the ECJ had to condemn France for having included a provision in French law according to which the applicant had expressly to request to learn the grounds of a refusal, where the administration had remained silent.[60] The ECJ ruled that applicants are entitled to learn the grounds for the administration's refusal without having to ask for it, although that information did not necessarily have to be delivered within the two months. In substance, the ECJ recognized that an administration, by remaining silent for two months, could tacitly refuse an application.

The wording of the New Access to Information Directive avoids this ambiguity, as Article 3(4) now provides that the reasons for a refusal to make information available shall be provided to the applicant within the time of one month, exceptionally within two months.

G. Charges

The question of administrative charges was particularly contested. Article 5 of the Access to Information Directive was relatively succinct in this regard, stating that 'Member States may make a charge for supplying the information, but such charge may not exceed a reasonable cost'. Article 4(8) of the Aarhus Convention follows this line, but also asks for a schedule of charges to be made available to applicants containing the details of the charges.

The Commission's proposal for the New Access to Information Directive specified the question of charges in more detail. The principle remained that

[57] Res., n. 12 above, Amendment 18.

[58] Amended proposal, n. 15 above, para. 3.4.

[59] Dir. 90/313/EEC, n. 4 above, Art. 3(4): 'A public authority shall respond to a person requesting information as soon as possible and at the latest within two months. The reasons for a refusal to provide the information requested must be given.'

[60] Case C-233/00, n. 23 above, paras. 88–119.

reasonable charges should be allowed, although no advance payment would be permitted. Examinations *in situ* of the information requested and access to public registers or lists should be free of charge. Finally, public authorities were to publish and make available to applicants a schedule of charges.[61]

The EP agreed to the principle of reasonable charges. However, the EP also suggested that requests for information for educational purposes should be free of charge. The actual cost of reproducing material could be charged for, but not the staff time spent on searches or compiling the information.[62] The Commission rejected the amendment on educational material, but accepted the other amendments.[63] In its Common Position, the Council only accepted that the consultation *in situ* should not lead to raising *additional* charges, but rejected all other amendments. It explained that 'searches may be very time-consuming and costly, freedom of charge may give rise to frivolous requests for information, and the notion of "education" is very vague'.[64]

In the second reading, the EP did not ask for the staff time to be explicitly mentioned, but suggested that 'a charge shall be reasonable and shall not exceed the actual cost of reproducing the material requested'.[65] However, except for the statement that examination *in situ* of the information requested should be free of charge, all the EP's amendments were rejected. Recital 16 of the New Access to Information Directive even laid down that advance payment may be required, although instances of advance payment should be limited; that, as a general rule, charges 'may not exceed actual costs of reproducing'; and that 'where public authorities make available environmental information on a commercial basis and where this is necessary in order to guarantee the continuation of collecting and publishing such information, a market-based charge is considered to be reasonable'.

Whether these provisions will help to stop past uses and abuses of the provision on charges by deterring persons from requesting access to environmental information is doubtful. Environmental organizations and private persons have often complained about high charges and asked, *inter alia*, that there should be no charge for a fixed initial amount of search time, and that there should at least be a possibility for not charging costs if the information was requested for non-commercial purposes. Charges of €1 per photocopy are apparently rather common. Germany (Hessen) charges between €11 and €16 per 15 minutes of an official's time.[66] Representative figures on charges that are actually imposed are difficult to obtain;[67] no research seems ever to have been undertaken in this regard.

[61] n. 8 above, Art. 5. [62] n. 12 above, Amendment 24.

[63] n. 15 above, paras. 3.2 and 3.3. [64] n. 17 above, para. VII.15.

[65] n. 18 above, Art. 5.

[66] M. Schmillen, *Das Umweltinformationsrecht zwischen Anspruch und Wirklichkeit* (Berlin: Erich Schmidt Verlag, 2003), 47. The cost regulations of the German Länder were not notified to the Commission, see n. 4 above, Annex A.

[67] n. 4 above, para. 3: 'In some cases, unreasonable charges have been demanded'.

H. Access to Justice

As mentioned above, the Access to Information Directive provided in its Article 4 that a person who considered that his request for information had been unreasonably refused or ignored, or had been inadequately answered, had the right to seek judicial or administrative review of the decision. This provision left the details of the judicial procedure to national legal systems. The Aarhus Convention provides in Article 9(1) for a review procedure before a court or 'another independent and impartial body established by law'. Where a court procedure is foreseen, the Aarhus Convention requires in addition a review procedure by a public authority or an independent and impartial body 'other than a court of law'.

In its proposal for the New Access to Information Directive, the Commission very closely followed the provisions of the Aarhus Convention. This decision may also have been influenced by the fact that the Commission, when making its proposal, had not planned to present a separate proposal for a directive on access to justice, but had thought that it could satisfy the requirements of the Aarhus Convention by inserting provisions on access to justice into the New Access to Information Directive and the parallel Directive 2003/35/EC Providing for Public Participation in Respect of the Drawing up of Certain Plans and Programmes Relating to the Environment and Amending Directives 85/337 and 96/61 on Participation in Environmental Decision-Making.[68] The Commission's proposal first repeated the provisions of the Access to Information Directive, and added a provision, according to which, in addition, an applicant could have the administrative decision reviewed 'by that public authority or reviewed administratively by another body established by law'.[69] Such a procedure had to be expeditious and either inexpensive or free of charge. The Commission explained that this procedure was proposed, because 'judicial appeal procedures often involve high costs or long delays'.[70]

The Economic and Social Committee approved of the proposal, but suggested an additional cooling-off period of 30 days before an applicant could ask for an administrative review.[71] The Committee of the Regions was lukewarm about the proposal.[72] The EP wanted to add to the Commission's proposal that different administrative bodies had to be independent and impartial, that the Directive's ground for refusal would not be applicable to requests from a court, and that Member States should be obliged to consider the introduction of provisions on

[68] [2003] OJ L156/17.

[69] n. 18 above, Art. 6(2).

[70] n. 8 above.

[71] n. 10 above, para. 2.12.1.

[72] n. 11 above, para. 6: 'The Committee of the Regions stresses the importance of an effective access to justice (timely, transparent, affordable and comprehensive); the practical arrangements for this should be based on national law: The process should not entail such high costs that the right of appeal cannot be effectively used'.

the recovery of legal costs, as well as sanctions against authorities or officials for manifestly wrongful refusals.[73]

The Commission accepted that the different administrative bodies had to be independent and impartial, but considered the other amendments to be excessively detailed and not compatible with the subsidiarity principle. This position was repeated by the Council in its Common Position which, for the remainder, changed the order of the provisions. An applicant could have a negative administrative answer reviewed by either the authority responsible, or reviewed administratively by an independent and impartial body established by law. In addition, the applicant had access to a review procedure before a court of law or another independent and impartial body established by law. Member States were also given the possibility to allow third parties incriminated by the disclosure of information to have access to legal recourse—a possibility which, of course, Member States already had before. This text then became the final version of Article 6.

In line with the Aarhus Convention, the new element in the procedure is thus that there is first an administrative review procedure, and then a procedure before a court of law or another administrative body. Whether this will help reduce costs for the applicant, the declared objective of the innovation, remains doubtful.

I. Active Provision of Information

Article 7 of the Access to Information Directive asked Member States to provide general information to the public on the state of the environment. The Aarhus Convention suggested very extensive active provision of information, *inter alia*, by reports on the state of the environment, publication of legislative texts, plans, and programmes, and so on. The Commission followed that line, and suggested that Member States disseminate detailed information on the environment, including legislative texts, policies, plans and programmes, implementation reports, reports on the state of the environment, and monitoring data.[74]

The EP sharpened these proposals to a certain degree, and added an amendment on the quality of the information on the environment actively disseminated, which had to be, if possible, up to date, clear and comprehensible, and scientifically sound in terms of accuracy and comparability. It also asked the Commission to submit a draft for harmonization of emission measurement procedures.[75] The Commission considered this request 'unduly burdensome on public authorities' and rejected it.[76] The Council opposed, in its Common Position, the amendment to add an article on the quality of active environmental information, and considered the EP's amendments to be unduly burdensome. Furthermore, harmonization of emission measurement procedures would fall

[73] n. 12 above, Amendment 25. [74] n. 8 above, Art. 7.
[75] n. 12 above, Amendments 26 and 27. [76] n. 15 above, para. 3.4.

outside the scope of the Directive.[77] As the EP repeated practically all of its amendments in the second reading, the matter went into the conciliation procedure. Here the Council accepted an Article 8 on the quality of information, which asked Member States to ensure 'so far as is within their power' that information be up to date, accurate and comparable. Furthermore, on request, Member States should inform applicants 'on the place' where information on measurement procedures could be found.

The different additions 'if possible', 'if available', 'as appropriate', etc. will make sure that public authorities are not unduly burdened by the obligation to disseminate information. The provisions on active information and its quality are hardly enforceable, and it will be seen to what extent they will change the reality of environmental transparency within the EU, in particular at local or regional level, where citizens are most affected and involved.

Two practical examples may illustrate these difficulties. Article 7(2)(g) of the New Access to Information Directive requires Member States to make available and disseminate environmental impact studies. However, in Directive 85/337/EEC on the Assessment of the Effects of certain Public and Private Projects on the Environment (EIA Directive),[78] the word 'studies' does not appear. Normally, one considers 'studies' to be the factual information which an operator is obliged to submit under Article 5 of the EIA Directive, together with his application for planning permission. Much more relevant is the administrative environmental impact assessment of a project. In this regard, Article 3 of the EIA Directive requires Member States to 'identify, describe and assess' the effects of a project on the environment. However, the EIA Directive does not stipulate that such an assessment has to be made in writing—although it is not clear how one can 'describe' effects other than in writing. And Article 7 of the New Access to Information Directive does not require that the assessment of the environmental impact of a project be made available or disseminated—or even that such an assessment be laid down in writing.

The second example concerns information on the quality of drinking water. There has been EC legislation on this subject since 1980,[79] although no obligation existed to publish data on the quality of drinking water which would have allowed individual persons to decide whether to use tap water or resort to bottled water. The European Commission has not published any report on drinking water either, an approach that is different, for example, to the approach regarding the quality of bathing water, where an annual report is published which indicates the quality of almost 20,000 bathing-water locations in the EC.

[77] n. 17, para. VII.16 and 17.

[78] [1985] OJ L175/40, amended by Dir. 97/11/EC [1997] OJ L73/5.

[79] Dir. 80/778/EEC Relating to the Quality of Water Intended for Human Consumption [1980] OJ L229/11. In 2003, this Directive will be replaced by Dir. 98/83/EC [1998] OJ L330/32.

A directive of 1991 on the improvement of environmental reporting[80] led to publication of a report on water issues which included information on the drinking-water directive.[81] However, the report contained no data on the quality of drinking water within the EC.

Article 7(2)(c) of the New Access to Information Directive requires Member States to make available and publish progress reports on the implementation of, *inter alia*, Community legislation, 'when prepared or held in electronic form by public authorities'. This provision thus does not require the dissemination of information on the quality of drinking water. Rather, it depends on the determination and will of the public authorities whether they will disseminate such data. It is comforting, however, that Article 13 of Directive 98/83/EC on the Quality of Water Intended for Human Consumption (Drinking Water Directive)[82] requires Member States to publish, as of 2005, reports on the quality of drinking water. But it is significant that this added value in transparency does not come from the New Access to Information Directive, which could have provided for precise horizontal provisions regarding publication of data. As (drinking) water is not the only sector where data is relevant and interesting for citizens, one would have wished to see clearer provisions in this regard in the New Access to Information Directive. Instead, these provisions allow or make possible the active dissemination of information on environmental data if there is the corresponding political will and determination to do so, but at the same time allow existing publication practice to remain unchanged.

IV. Concluding Remarks

A. Transparency in EC Law-Making

If one considers the legislative process, it is striking how much the European legislative process itself has become transparent since 1990, when the Access to Information Directive was adopted. The two readings of the EP are now published, as well as the Council Common Position, with the statement of reasons on each of the EP's amendments and the content of the Commission's amending proposal which follows the EP's first reading, and which also explains why the Commission accepts or rejects the EP's amendments. What is not published is the Council's decision to follow or reject the EP's amendments of the second reading, which constitutes the point of departure for the conciliation

[80] Dir. 91/692/EEC on the Standardization and Rationalization of Environmental Reports [1991] OJ L377/48.

[81] Commission, *The Reporting Directive: First Report on the Application of Reports from Member States (1993–1995)*; (2000) Luxembourg.

[82] n. 79 above.

procedure. Taken together, the published documents allow a rather detailed understanding of the legislative process, although this becomes possible only several weeks or months after the event. This *ex-post* transparency of the legislative process cannot, therefore, substitute for public debate and voting as exists in national, regional, or local legislative decision-making bodies.

B. Compliance with the Aarhus Convention

The next question is whether the New Access to Information Directive fully transposes the provisions of the Aarhus Convention into EC law. As regards EC institutions—including the Economic and Social Committee, the Committee of the Regions, the European Environmental Agency, and the European Investment Bank, which are all public authorities in the sense of the Aarhus Convention—this is not the case. This is because there are currently no applying provisions on access to information which apply to them. The Access to Community Documents Regulation is limited to the EP, Council, and Commission, and contains a number of elements which are not in line with the Aarhus Convention.

In contrast, the New Access to Information Directive constitutes a rather true reflection of the provisions of the Aarhus Convention. I did not discover any significant discrepancy between the information provisions of the Aarhus Convention and the New Access to Information Directive.

However, this is only part of the problem, as under Article 10 of the New Access to Information Directive, Member States will have to adapt their legislation to the requirements of the Directive by 1 February 2005. Only when the transposing national and regional legislation is available, can any final statement be made. It should be remembered that implementing legislation under Article 10 also covers regional legislation. This is of particular importance to Member States with a regional or federal structure, in particular the UK (Scotland, Wales, Northern Ireland, Gibraltar), Belgium, Spain, Italy, Austria, and Germany.

C. A High Level of Protection

Article 174 EC requires Community policy and law to aim at a high level of environmental protection, and one may wonder whether the New Access to Information Directive fulfils this objective. The details of the legislative procedure, described above, demonstrate that numerous formulations of the EP which aimed at reducing administrative discretion were not included in the final text. As the case is, this can only be due to the Council's attitude. Other options of drafting were available, had there been the political will to attain such a reduction of administrative discretion.

In other aspects, the aim of an open society was only half-heartedly realized. This is due to, for instance, the limitation of access to information on the environment, rather than encompassing all information on factual circumstances which are in the hands of the administration; the principle that citizens have a right to know what emissions and other releases are released into the environment, not only vis-à-vis public authorities, but also vis-à-vis private enterprises; the fact that access to environmental information should, as a principle, be free of charges which go beyond reproduction costs; and the fact that there should be no advance payment requirement and other means to deter citizens from exercising their right of access to information.

The argument, so often invoked during the legislative procedure, that subsidiarity prevented more precise provisions, is not a convincing argument. Indeed, if the subsidiarity principle does not oppose, for example, the explicit stipulation that advance payment is allowed, it would also have been possible to mention that advance payment is not allowed. If the subsidiarity principle does not oppose the provision that some forms of access to information are free of charge (Article 7(1)), it would also have been possible to make a general statement that, in principle, no charges should be levied.

In defence of the actual text, it should be realized that in most EC Member States the concept of an open society is still far from being fully accepted. Knowledge gives power and public authorities, the ruling political parties, or economic operators and other vested interests normally have no great interest in transparency of public administration. Seen from this angle, and comparing the environmental sector with other sectors such as food, health, transport, state aid, or energy, it remains remarkable that the New Access to Information Directive achieves, in the follow-up to the Aarhus Convention, this amount of openness of public administrations. I therefore consider that this legislation complies with the objective of a high level of environmental protection as laid down in Article 174 EC.

D. Practical Application

It became clear from the different provisions of the New Access to Information Directive which were analysed above that the Directive, as much as its predecessor, the Access to Information Directive, to a large degree lays down framework provisions, but leaves considerable discretion to local and regional administrations in putting the provisions into practice. This leads once more to the conclusion that the practical application of the Directive will be the decisive criterion for assessing its efficiency. Where public authorities have the will to approach the model of an open society in environmental matters, the Directive will constitute a useful tool; where this will does not exist, there will continue to exist numerous possibilities not to grant access to information on the environment.

Looking at the issue of access to environmental information from the point of view of the citizen, it becomes clear that improved access presupposes a more active citizen. It is known from the peoples' democracies of the former Eastern

Europe that the external structures of a society are not the decisive criterion for assessing a society's character. In the same way, the legislation on access to information will only fulfil a useful function where citizens use it and use it progressively to realize transparency in environmental issues. This concerns planning permissions for infrastructure or urbanization projects and hundreds of other administrative decisions which impact on the environment without this impact being made visible. Of course, citizens are mainly interested in issues which concern their direct neighbourhood, food, shelter, energy and transport, water, waste, and air pollution aspects. Citizens and citizen initiatives, environmental groups and associations, and other societal groups should systematically use the possibilities offered by the New Access to Information Directive and the legislation which transposes it into national law. Why can daily information on air pollution be made public in Austrian, but not in Spanish or Greek cities? Why do public authorities not inform their citizens as soon as parameters of the Drinking Water Directive—for instance for lead, pesticides or nitrates—are exceeded, so that citizens may decide themselves whether to use tap water or buy bottled water? These examples could be multiplied.

Journalists and the academic profession have a particular role to play. For example, a local discussion about the existing air pollution and its potential effects on the respiratory systems of persons, in particular of small children, may lead to the fixing of new local priorities such as roads reserved for passengers, bypasses for cars, or changes in the public transport system. Scientific research may well reveal what the causes and sources of a specific environmental impairment are, and how similar problems were tackled in other parts of the world. The activity of researchers may go much further. In 2003, a German dissertation examined the number and content of requests for access to environmental information in a region of some eleven million persons and found that, in three years, only 214 such requests had been submitted.[83] While the results of the survey might in parts be questionable, it would be interesting to see whether the number of requests in other EC Member States is more or less similar, as nine of the present and nine of the ten new EC Member States have a population of less than eleven million persons.[84] Other research initiatives might examine the impact of paying charges, pre-payments, delays, the accuracy of information given, differences between environmental and, for example, transport administrations, between small communities and large agglomerations, and so on.

These observations suggest some professionalization of environmental organizations, academic researchers, and journalists. An open society needs open, active citizens. Environmental organizations should try systematically to make more transparent sources of environmental impairment, omissions in monitor-

[83] Schmillen, n. 66 above.

[84] Denmark, Sweden, Finland, Ireland, Belgium, Luxembourg, Austria, Greece, and Portugal; all new EC Member States, Poland being the exception.

ing, impairment of nature, and to clarify in this way the price which the environment has to pay for the lifestyle which we practise at present. Present communication technologies allow networking across national boundaries, and thus increase transparency within the EU. Such research, instead of yet another study of what might have been meant by a notion such as sustainable development, or of whether the polluter shall, should, or does not pay, is more down to earth, closer to the citizen, and more relevant to him. The slogan of thinking globally, but acting locally, which was used in the past by environmental organizations, also deserves to be taken seriously by researchers.

In general, it may well be that the New Access to Information Directive represents the present state of the art on access to environmental information in Europe. Significant legislative progress towards more openness, more transparency, and less discretionary power for administrations, if ever this is aspired to, is likely to be achieved only if evidence can be produced that the present rules are applied in a way which is contrary to the concept of an open, democratic, and transparent society. Such evidence will only arise by factual research and examination of administrative practice. However, there should be no doubt that full application of the New Access to Information Directive according to its words and to its spirit, in all parts of the enlarged EU, would already constitute an important achievement on the long and difficult way towards an open European society.

Public Participation regarding the Elaboration and Approval of Projects in the EU after the Aarhus Convention

*Jonathan Verschuuren**

I. Why Participation is Useful

According to one of the preambular paragraphs of the United Nations Economic Commission for Europe (UN/ECE) Convention on Access to Information, Public Participation in Decision-Making and Access to Justice in Environmental Matters (Aarhus Convention),[1] participation in decision-making is considered necessary in order to be able to assert the *right* to live in an environment adequate to a person's health and well-being, and in order to observe the duty to protect and improve the environment for the benefit of present and future generations. In literature, it is also generally accepted that the right to participate in decision-making processes regarding the environment is a procedural right that can be seen as a part of the fundamental right to environmental protection.[2] This is despite the fact that the right to live in a healthy environment still has not been acknowledged in a binding human rights document, nor laid down in all national constitutions or national bills of rights. International[3] and national[4] human rights documents usually refer to the right to live in a healthy environment as a (discretionary) duty of the state, not as an individual right that can be enforced in a court of law in a case vis-à-vis others or the state. In the slow process of the gradual acceptation of the (constitutional) right to environmental protection, the Aarhus Convention is an important step forward. For the first time, an international convention acknowledges, in Article 1, 'the right of every person of

* Professor, Centre for Legislative Studies, Tilburg University, Netherlands.

[1] Aarhus (Denmark), 25 June 1998 (entered into force 30 Oct. 2001) (1999) 38 *International Legal Materials* 3, 517.

[2] P. Birnie and A. Boyle, *International Law & The Environment* (Oxford: Oxford University Press, 2002), 261–5 and extensively (in Dutch) J. Verschuuren, *Het grondrecht op bescherming van het leefmilieu* (Zwolle: W.E.J. Tjeenk Willink, 1993), 279–89 and 393.

[3] Birnie and Boyle, n. 2 above, 252.

[4] R.J.G.H. Seerden, M.A. Heldeweg, and K.R. Deketelaere (eds.), *Public Environmental Law in the European Union and the United States* (The Hague/London/New York: Kluwer Law International, 2002), 566.

present and future generations to live in an environment adequate to his or her health or well-being'.

In several international legal documents and conventions, such as the Rio Declaration on Environment and Development,[5] public participation has been considered a *principle* of environmental law.[6] In my view, the human-rights approach towards participation in the Aarhus Convention is to be preferred. Rights and principles both are legal norms, but they are fundamentally different.[7] Constitutional or human rights can be considered (fundamental) legal *rules*: they are very much associated with individual persons, and can be enforced by individuals against (mostly public) authorities; they form the basis of the constitutional democratic state. Environmental legal principles provide general direction to decisions by public authorities, judges, and organizations in the field of environmental policy and law, including decisions that may or may not infringe citizens' rights. Like other rules, rights can be influenced by principles, but the main difference is that rights can be directly invoked in courts, whereas principles can only play a role in combination with a legal rule.[8]

Whether public participation is expressed as a principle or a human right, in either case it is clear that it indicates an important legal instruction to provide for public participation. Birnie and Boyle argue that states which operate with openness, accountability, and civic participation are more likely to promote environmental justice, to balance the needs of present and future generations in public decisions, to integrate environmental considerations in decisions, and to implement and enforce exisiting environmental standards.[9] According to Ebbesson, public participation in environmental matters reflects an expansive notion of democracy: the involvement of citizens and Non-Governmental Organizations (NGOs) in governance not only furthers the selfish interests of each participating actor, but may also contribute to promoting public interests and concerns.[10] Two additional, more practical, arguments indicate why participation is useful. These arguments have recently been elaborated by Lee and Abbot,[11] but also follow from various evaluations of national procedural law relating to the environment.

First of all, research shows that a state decision receives wider acceptance when all persons involved are able to participate in the decision-making process. Transparency and regular contacts between competent authorities and citizens

[5] Rio de Janeiro (Brazil), 14 June 1992 (1992) 31 *International Legal Materials* 4, 876–80.

[6] J. Verschuuren, *Principles of Environmental Law* (Baden-Baden: Nomos Verlagsgesellschaft, 2003), 69–71.

[7] Ibid. 16.

[8] See Verschuuren, n. 6 above, especially at 19–50.

[9] Birnie and Boyle, n. 2 above, 261.

[10] J. Ebbesson, 'The Notion of Public Participation in International Environmental Law' (1997) 8 *Yearbook of International Environmental Law*, 56.

[11] M. Lee and C. Abbot, 'The Usual Suspects? Public Participation under the Aarhus Convention' (2003) 66 *Modern Law Review*, 83.

(either individually or organized within an NGO), and especially between companies applying for permits and citizens, significantly contributes to wider acceptance of the final decision.[12] Lee and Abbot indicate that this is due to the highly technical nature of environmental decision-making.[13] The belief that complex technical environmental issues can only be decided by technical experts leads to a strong, authoritarian, non-democratic approach that must be balanced through public participation. Although it is often thought that only experts are able to decide on complex environmental matters, participation of the public is actually important, because usually value judgements must be made as well. This is especially true when there exist knowledge gaps, doubt as to the appropriate level of safety or distribution of costs and benefits of an activity, or when fundamentally divided interests are at stake.[14]

Traditional representative democracy has often been criticized in the context of environmental decision-making for its inability to reach decisions that respect (environmental) rights of certain individuals or groups,[15] or ecological (non-anthropocentric) interests.[16] Public participation is one of the means to introduce deliberative elements in democratic decision-making processes.[17] Communicative forms of discourse between the people involved, from their respective subjective views, are needed to foster validity and legitimacy.[18] According to Habermas, *regulated* public participation and transparency are essential for the legitimacy of law: the procedure must not only provide for public participation, but also give equal opportunities to the parties involved to influence one another, and limit the authorities' discretion when making the final decision.[19]

Secondly, participation leads to better decisions. Evaluation shows that decision-making processes in which citizens have actively participated and could raise objections against draft decisions or projects result in higher quality decisions. In particular, the grounds of a decision are better motivated.[20] Better decisions are observed both in cases of participation by individual citizens, such as local residents, as well as in cases of participation by NGOs, although the quality of decisions is higher in the latter case.[21] A public hearing during which applicants, competent authorities, and members of the public are present further

[12] R.H.J. Mooren, B. van de Putte, J. Verschuuren, and K. Jesse, *Positioneringsonderzoek milieueffectrapportage* (Den Haag: Evaluatiecommissie Wet milieubeheer, 1996), 41.

[13] Lee and Abbot, n. 11 above, 84.

[14] ibid.

[15] Ebbesson, n. 10 above, 56.

[16] See extensively J.S. Dryzek, *Deliberate Democracy and Beyond—Liberals, Critics, Contestations* (Oxford: Oxford University Press, 2000), esp. ch. 6. It should be noted that public participation is only one element of a discursive democracy as advocated by Dryzek.

[17] Lee and Abbot, n. 11 above, 85.

[18] J. Habermas, *Between Facts and Norms—Contributions to a Discourse Theory of Law and Democracy* (Cambridge, Mass.: MIT Press, 1996), 228–9.

[19] Shown by Ebbesson, n. 10 above, 79.

[20] Mooren *et al.*, n. 12 above, 45.

[21] ibid. 45.

enhances the quality of the decision.[22] Involvement of the public might also contribute to keeping the competent authorities on the road paved by the legislature, diminishing the danger of capture or even corruption.[23]

The same advantages are acknowledged, in somewhat different words, in the Aarhus Convention Implementation Guide. According to this guide, issued by the UN in 2000, the public has the desire to take part in the process of gathering information, and discussing options for decision-making, actuated both by self-interest and by their responsibility to protect the environment.[24] Also, the public is a major source of information at a time when decisions become increasingly complex, and when it is therefore vital for competent authorities to be in possession of accurate, comprehensive, and up-to-date information.[25]

Three disadvantages have been observed as well. First and foremost, wider acceptance of decisions does not necessarily lead to a reduction of court cases. In fact, in 1998 the Dutch Evaluation Committee on the Environmental Management Act (the Evaluation Committee) expressed concern that procedures during which objections were raised in the participation phase increasingly ended up in court.[26] This can probably be explained by the fact that decision-making processes in which people actively participate are more likely to involve disputed projects than processes in which the public is not very interested. When many people are involved, there is bound to be someone who does not agree with the final outcome of the process.

The Evalution Committee also noted that better decisions take more time. Arguments brought forward by interested parties lead to the need to re-evaluate the draft decision or even to do further assessments before a final decision can be concluded. As a consequence, legal time limits are sometimes not met.[27]

Thirdly, some do not regard public participation as an opportunity to improve traditional representative democracy (as shown above), but rather as a threat to representative democracy. Elected representatives have to consider all relevant interests at stake, whereas in public participation only the interests of those actively involved are brought forward. Social interests, for instance, can be disregarded in a debate between an environmental NGO and the company involved.[28] It could be argued that this is not a problem because, in the end, the competent administrative body has to take a decision based upon the participation process, but also based upon its own legal power and discretion. However, the authorities face the risk of being accused of non-democratic

[22] ibid. 55.

[23] Lee and Abbot, n. 11 above, 83.

[24] S. Stec, S. Casey-Lefkowitz, and J. Jendroska, *The Aarhus Convention—An Implementation Guide* (New York/Geneva: United Nations, 2000), 85.

[25] ibid.

[26] Evaluatiecommissie Wet milieubeheer, *Om de kwaliteit van de vergunning* (Den Haag: Evaluatiecommissie Wet milieubeheer, 1998), 55.

[27] ibid. 55.

[28] Lee and Abbot, n. 11 above, 87.

behaviour when ignoring the outcome of public participation or when people feel that the authorities only offered public participation as a means to neutralize conflict.

Reconciling genuine public participation (i.e., participation that really matters as far as the content of the decision is concerned) with current forms of representative democracy in Europe is perhaps the most important challenge of the Aarhus Convention, a challenge that has not yet been broadly recognized.[29]

II. Participation in Decision-Making regarding Projects according to the Aarhus Convention

What was actually laid down in the Aarhus Convention with regard to participation concerning decision-making processes on projects? Article 6 of the Convention deals with public participation in decisions on specific activities. This provision applies to three categories of decisions (Article 6(1)):

— decisions concerning activities listed in Annex I. This Annex contains a long list of activities, which is almost (but not entirely!) identical to the list of installations in Annex I of the Directive 96/61/EC on Integrated Pollution Prevention and Control (IPPC Directive),[30] as well as a reference to: 'any activity not covered by the above where public participation is provided for under an environmental impact assessment procedure in accordance with national law';

— other decisions on proposed activities which may have a significant effect on the environment, insofar as parties have determined that such a proposed activity is subject to Article 6;

— decisions permitting the deliberate release of genetically modified organisms, but the latter only 'to the extent feasible and appropriate' (Article 6(11)).[31]

According to Annex I, a decision allowing a change or extension of one of the activities listed in Annex I is also subject to Article 6, but only where such a change or extension itself meets the criteria or thresholds set out in the Annex. However, Article 6(10) simply states that the provisions of Article 6 apply to any decision reconsidering or updating the operating conditions 'where appropriate'.

[29] ibid. 107.

[30] [1996] OJ L275/26.

[31] In this contribution, I will not go further into the issue of genetically modified organisms (GMOs), except for referring to the Guidelines on Access to Information, Public Participation and Access to Justice with Respect to Genetically Modified Organisms adopted as a voluntary instrument by the parties of the Aarhus Convention in October 2002. These guidelines are available on the UN/ECE Aarhus Convention website published on the Internet at: http://www.unece.org/env/pp/mop1.htm.

As a consequence, in my view, when part of an installation is changed, for instance, because an operator introduces a new technology (usually comprising an increase in production capacity), and a permit, therefore, has to be adapted to the new situation, public participation must be initiated, in spite of the fact that the change itself does not meet the criteria set out in Annex I.

National law may provide for not disapplying Article 6 if it is determined on a case-by-case basis that application of Article 6 would have an adverse effect on national defence purposes.

A right to participate under the Aarhus Convention has been granted to the *public*, defined in Article 2(4) as 'one or more natural or legal persons and, in accordance with national legislation or practice, their associations, organizations or groups'. According to the Implementation Guide, this definition covers 'any person'.[32] However, some provisions are only aimed at the *public concerned*, that is, people affected by, likely to be affected by, or having an interest in the decision. Environmental NGOs are deemed to have an interest under Article 2(5). Under national law, requirements can be set to limit the number of NGOs that are actually entitled to participate in the decision-making process. Basically, duties for the authorities actively to inform or contact its citizens apply to the public concerned, whereas rights of citizens to address the authorities are granted to the public, in which case authorities remain more passive.

Pursuant to Article 6(2), the participation phase of the decision-making process starts with the publication of the proposed activity. The draft decision or the nature of possible decisions has to be published, including the public authority responsible for making the decision, details of the envisaged procedure (such as opportunities to participate, time and venue of public hearing—if any—and so on), as well as the fact that the activity is subject to a national or transboundary Environmental Impact Assessment (EIA) procedure.

In accordance with Article 6(3) and (4), participation must be initiated early, when all options are still open, and within reasonable time-frames, allowing sufficient time for the public to prepare. The public concerned must be given access to all kinds of information, free of charge and as soon as it becomes available, specified in Article 6(6). This includes a description of the site, the characteristics of the proposed activity, an estimate of expected residues and emissions, a description of the significant effects on the environment and of the measures envisaged to prevent or reduce these effects, a non-technical summary, an outline of the main alternatives studied by the applicant (note that the applicant is not under the obligation to study alternatives), and the main reports and advice issued to the authorities on the project.

As Article 6(7) makes clear, participation takes place through the submission of written documents (comments, opinions, etc.), or by expressing one's opinions at a public hearing. Organizing a public hearing is only necessary 'where

[32] Stec *et al.*, n. 24 above, 39.

appropriate'. If not appropriate, the public at least has to be able to bring forward written opinions.

Article 6(8) obliges competent authorities to take due account of the outcome of the public participation in its decision. Article 6(9) adds that the public must be promptly informed of the decision and the considerations on which the decision is based.

III. Participation in Decision-Making according to Directive 2003/35/EC

In June 2003, Directive 2003/35/EC Providing for Public Participation in Respect of the Drawing up of Certain Plans and Programmes Relating to the Environment and Amending with regard to Public Participation and Access to Justice Council Directives 85/337/EEC and 96/61/EC (Public Participation in Plans and Programmes Directive) was adopted.[33] As far as participation in decision-making on projects is concerned, the relevant provisions of the Aarhus Convention have been implemented through changes in Directive 85/337/EEC on the Assessment of the Effects of Certain Public and Private Projects on the Environment (EIA Directive)[34] and the IPPC Directive.[35] These changes will be briefly dealt with below.

A. Participation in EIA

Although the projects subject to public participation listed in Annex I of the Aarhus Convention are mainly 'IPPC installations', the Public Participation in Plans and Programmes Directive introduces the additional duty to initiate a public participation procedure for all projects that are subject to an EIA according to the EIA Directive. This is a consequence of the provision in Annex I of the Aarhus Convention that its provisions on participation also apply to activities where public participation is provided for under an EIA procedure in accordance with national legislation. Pursuant to Article 6 of the original version of the EIA Directive, all Member States should have participation clauses in their national EIA legislation.

For the most part, the provisions of the Aarhus Convention were carefully, mostly literally, transposed in the amended EIA Directive. The definitions of 'the public' and 'the public concerned' were literally transposed into Article 1(2) of the EIA Directive, as was the exemption for national defence projects in Article 1(4). However, for some reason, the difference between the concepts of 'public' and 'public concerned' in the Directive has been mixed up. For instance, according to Article 6(2) of the Aarhus Convention, the public concerned shall

33 [2003] OJ L156/17. 34 [1985] OJ L175/40. 35 [1996] OJ L257/26.

be informed of the proposed activity, nature of the possible decisions, etc. After the revisions brought about by the Public Participation in Plans and Programmes Directive, Article 6(2) of the EIA Directive provides that the public shall be informed of all these aspects. Article 6(7) of the Aarhus Convention allows the public to submit any comments, opinions, etc. Article 6(4) of the amended EIA Directive, however, restricts this opportunity to the public concerned. This, of course, is quite an important deviation from the Aarhus Convention. The right to send in written objections, or the right to participate in a hearing, has been limited to persons who are able to show a specific interest in the case, whereas this right is granted to any person in the Aarhus Convention.

This was probably not an accidental mistake. Most Aarhus provisions were meticulously copied, and it seems odd that one of the most important concepts of the Convention was changed in the process by accident. There may have been opposition from Member States against general participation. Opposition may have been fuelled by the fact that, once a member of the public has entered the participation process, he or she becomes a member of the 'public concerned' and acquires 'sufficient interest' in the sense of Article 9(2), thus allowing that person to go to court. This line of reasoning is found not only in the literature,[36] but in the UN/ECE 'Aarhus Implementation Guide' as well.[37] This logic brings about an indirect *actio popularis*, something that many Member States are totally opposed to.[38]

The Aarhus provisions specifying what information, and at what time, should be presented in order for the public to prepare for participation in the decision-making process were implemented in the revised Article 6 of the EIA Directive as well. Apart from confusing the terms 'public' and 'public concerned', this was done almost literally, so I shall not go into great detail here. In addition to the Aarhus Convention, the Public Participation in Plans and Programmes Directive in Article 6(3)(c) also requires the authorities to make available to the public any information that becomes available after the time the public concerned was informed. This seems to be an important addition that is especially necessary for participation in decision-making on large projects for which an EIA has to be undertaken. Because they are so complex, it can take considerable time before a final decision on such projects is reached. Participation on the basis of outdated information is not very useful, and the additional requirement therefore is a sensible one. Like the Aarhus Convention, Article 6(4) of the amended EIA Directive now states that early and effective opportunities must be granted to the public concerned to participate in environmental decision-making procedures. Article 6(5) of the Directive allows Member States to determine more detailed arrangements for informing and consulting the public concerned 'for example by written submissions or by way of public inquiry'.

[36] F. de Lange, 'Beyond *Greenpeace*, Courtesy of the Aarhus Convention' (2003) 3 *Yearbook of European Environmental Law*, 239.

[37] Stec *et al.*, n. 24 above, 108.

[38] See further sect. V. below.

In the amended EIA Directive, substantially more attention is paid to participation in decision-making on projects with transboundary environmental effects than in the Aarhus Convention. Whereas the Aarhus Convention does not provide anything specific for projects with a transboundary environmental impact, the amended Article 7 of the EIA Directive provides that the information that is made available to the public on the proposed project and the decision that may be taken also must be sent to another Member State if significant environmental effects take place in that Member State. The other Member State can then decide, according to Article 7(2), whether it wishes to participate in the decision-making process, and whether it will enable the public concerned in this (other) Member State to participate in the decision-making process as well. When the other Member State indicates that it will participate, then all other relevant information that is made available to the public also has to be sent to the other Member State according to Article 6 of the Directive. The public affected in the other Member State then has the opportunity to actively participate in the decision-making process in the neighbouring state.

Although it could very well be argued that the 'public involved' is not limited to the public within national borders, the Aarhus Convention does not necessarily impose a duty to involve citizens from neighbouring states. However, it is in line with the obligations of the United Nations (UN) Convention on Environmental Impact Assessment in a Transboundary Context (Espoo Convention)[39] to grant citizens from neighbouring states participation rights. Article 3(8) of the Espoo Convention obliges the authorities to:

> ensure that the public of the affected Party in the areas likely to be affected be informed of, and be provided with possibilities for making comments or objections on, the proposed activity, and for the transmittal of these comments or objections to the competent authority of the Party of origin, either directly to this authority or, where appropriate, through the Party of origin.

In the past, this provision of the Espoo Convention sometimes led to the situation that citizens or NGOs from the neighbouring country were offered a wider opportunity to participate in the decision-making process than they would normally have had in their own country.[40] Directive 97/11/EC amending Directive 85/337/EEC on the Assessment of the Effects of certain Public and Private Projects on the Environment (EIA Directive)[41] did not really change this, since it simply stated that the (foreign) public concerned had to be given the opportunity to 'forward their opinion'. The newly amended EIA Directive offers better safeguards for actual and effective involvement of citizens of the neighbouring state and harmonizes participation rights within the European Union (EU).

[39] Espoo (Finland), 25 Feb. 1991 (entered into force 10 Sept. 1997) (1991) 30 *International Legal Materials* 3, 802.

[40] M. Hildén and E.R. Furmann, 'Assessment Across Borders—Stumbling Blocks and Options in the Practical Implementation of the Espoo Convention' (2001) 21 *Environmental Impact Assessment Review*, 545.

[41] [1997] OJ L073/5.

Finally, Article 9 of the EIA Directive was slightly amended to ensure that no decision is taken without explicitly examining the concerns and opinions expressed by the public concerned in the participation process. The competent authority, in considering the decision, has to show explicitly what has been the influence of the opinions brought forward in the participation process.

B. Participation in IPPC

Article 15 of the IPPC Directive only provided that Member States must take the necessary measures to ensure that applications for permits for new installations or for substantial changes are made available to the public for an appropriate period of time, to enable it to comment on them before the competent authority reaches its decision. This meagre provision on participation has now been replaced, not only by a more elaborate provision, but also by the new detailed Annex V on public participation. The new Article 15 as well as the text of Annex V is almost literally the same as the amendments made to the EIA Directive, including the mixing up of the terms 'public' and 'public concerned'. So again, only the public concerned is given the right to engage in the participation process, whereas the Aarhus Convention enables 'the public' (any person) to participate. Standing out as the main difference between the adaptations in both EC Directives is the fact that the rules on participation in the IPPC Directive were mainly laid down in an Annex to the Directive, whereas in the EIA Directive, they were included in the relevant articles of the Directive.

IV. Comparing the Participation in Plans and Programmes Directive with the Aarhus Convention

When comparing the provisions on participation regarding projects of the Participation in Plans and Programmes Directive with the provisions on participation of the Aarhus Convention, we can conclude that there is one important aspect in which the Directive differs from the Aarhus Convention. The Directive grants the right to participate in the decision-making process to a more restricted group of people (only people who are affected by or have an interest in the decision) than the Aarhus Convention. Who is going to bring the European Community or any EU Member State that implements the provisions of the Directive, rather than the stricter provisions of the Convention, before the Aarhus Convention Compliance Committee? Members of the public are allowed to bring cases of non-compliance to the attention of the Compliance Committee.[42] NGOs have already objected against attempts made by states to limit

[42] Decision I/7 on review of compliance, adopted October 2002, see the UN/ECE Aarhus website published on the Internet at: http://www.unece.org/env/pp/compliance.htm.

participation to the public concerned during the First Meeting of the Parties of the Aarhus Convention in October 2002.[43]

For the remainder, the Directive is in line with the obligations as laid down in the Aarhus Convention. The activities for which decisions have to be open for public participation are either covered by the EIA or the IPPC Directive. This means that there are no activities that should be open for participation according to the Convention but not according to EC law. On the contrary, when comparing thresholds for the two Directives and the Aarhus Convention, it becomes clear that the drafters of the Aarhus Convention used the lists of activities of the IPPC Directive as a model. For instance, decisions to allow the operation of an installation for the intensive rearing of poultry or pigs with more than 85,000 places for broilers, 60,000 places for hens, 3,000 places for production pigs (over 30 kg), or 900 places for sows, are subject to an EIA according to Directive 85/337. The same installations have to be granted a permit under the IPPC Directive when they consist of 40,000 places for poultry, 2,000 places for production pigs (over 30 kg), or 750 places for sows. The latter is exactly the threshold level for the Aarhus Convention.

The provisions on the formal aspects of the participation phase of the decision-making process were carefully transposed as well, mostly literally, sometimes going beyond what is in the Convention. In the latter cases, this is usually a logical consequence of existing EC law (see the above example of the Espoo Convention and the provisions already in the EIA Directive). The only provision that was not explicitly transposed in the Participation in Plans and Programmes Directive is Article 6(5) of the Aarhus Convention, which requires the parties to encourage prospective applicants to identify the public concerned, enter into discussions, and to provide information regarding the objectives of their application before applying for a permit. This provision, which will probably become increasingly important in the near future, will be further dealt with in section V. below.

V. Some Observations with regard to the Implementation of the Participation in Plans and Programmes Directive in the Member States

Since the transposition of the Aarhus Convention into the Participation in Plans and Programmes Directive in 2003, as far as participation regarding the elaboration and approval of projects is concerned, has not added a great many new features to the public participation provisions of the Aarhus Convention, and since both the Convention and the Directive still leave much discretion to the

[43] The European ECO Forum Carignano-Lucca Declaration, para. 3.3. This declaration is available at the UN/ECE Aarhus website, published on the Internet at: http://www.unece.org/env/pp/mop1.htm.

Parties, I will now turn to the implementation of the two documents into the national legal systems of the Member States.

It is not useful to discuss in great detail all the possible practical implications of the provisions on public participation, since this has already been done. The above-mentioned UN Implementation Guide[44] and the Good Practices Handbook on Public Participation in Making Local Environmental Decisions[45] go into almost every possible question, and show a range of possible solutions to all kinds of very specific problems.[46]

Instead, two seemingly contrary developments that can be observed in several Member States, and that will influence national discussions in the implementation process of Participation in Plans and Programmes Directive, will be dealt with: the negative consequences of (overly) liberal participation rights, and criticism of the traditional notion of participation.

A. Discussions on the Negative Consequences of Public Participation

Arguments made against public participation are as old as the notion of public participation itself. In discussions, the disadvantages mentioned above[47] are often simplified or exaggerated. Participation is costly, time-consuming, and obstructive.[48] Participation could even be argued to repress differences that exist, and always will exist in a complex and diverse society, since it is aimed at marrying all opinions into one decision.[49] Participation is a threat for representative democracy. It leads to a delay of important projects that have already been approved by democratically elected and controlled authorities. The authorities that are responsible for taking decisions to benefit the general social and economic interest can no longer adequately do so, because they are hampered by participation procedures, especially when these are followed by court procedures. The latter is often the case since in many countries the right to access to justice is granted to members of the public who have participated in the decision-making process,[50] although it is not entirely clear whether the Aarhus Convention necessitates a linkage between participation and access to justice. As mentioned above,[51] it can

[44] Stec *et al.*, n. 24 above.

[45] Department of the Environment, Transport and the Regions, *Public Participation in Making Local Environmental Decisions—Good Practices Handbook* (London: Department of the Environment, Transport and the Regions, 2000).

[46] Stec *et al.*, n. 24 above, 96.

[47] Para. I.

[48] Ebbesson, n. 10 above, 62.

[49] Dryzek, n. 16 above, 62.

[50] For instance, in Germany and the Netherlands, see M. Dross, 'Country Report Germany' in N. de Sadeleer, G. Roller, and M. Dross, *Access to Justice in Environmental Cases, Annex 4a* (Brussels: CEDRE, 2003), 5, and J.M. Verschuuren, 'Country Report The Netherlands' in N. de Sadeleer, G. Roller, and M. Dross, *Access to Justice in Environmental Cases, Annex 6a* (Brussels: CEDRE, 2003), 4, respectively.

[51] Sect. III.

be argued that a person who participates in the decision-making process, as a consequence, gains interest in the case. When looking solely at Participation in Plans and Programmes Directive, there can be no misunderstanding: only people affected by or interested in a decision are able to participate in the first place.

No doubt these arguments will be brought forward (again) in countries where Participation in Plans and Programmes Directive leads to an extension of participation rights. Discussions on limiting participation and standing rights are especially vivid in countries that have liberal legislation on these two aspects. For instance, in the Netherlands, which probably had the most liberal participation and standing requirements in its administrative legal system, procedural rights are now being restricted. Until now, *anyone* (including any NGOs) has had a right to participate in decision-making processes concerning environmental permits (including those governed by the IPPC Directive) or planning decisions. Consequently, anyone who has participated in the decision-making process has a right to go to court on each issue that he or she complained about during the participation process, even if this concerns an issue that does not affect him or her personally. This is called an indirect *actio popularis*.

Recent Dutch legislation, part of which has already been adopted, is changing this. Under new legislation, only interested parties are allowed to participate.[52] This means that citizens have to show that they have a specific interest in the case. Environmental NGOs are deemed to have an interest in environmental matters. As already stated above, this is in line with the Participation in Plans and Programmes Directive, but contrary to the Aarhus Convention. As a consequence of the new legislation, the indirect *actio popularis* will be abandoned.[53]

In 2003, the newly formed government announced further restrictions upon procedural rights in its fight against 'administrative burdens' and bureaucracy.[54] The government is currently studying the possibility of introducing a *Schutznorm* test: interested citizens can only invoke arguments based on legislation that is specifically intended to protect their own interests. Sometimes it is even proposed to drop the presumption that environmental NGOs have an interest when the environment is at stake.[55]

The latter suggestion would clearly violate both the Aarhus Convention and Participation in Plans and Programmes Directive. The Dutch Minister for the Environment has therefore pointed out in parliament that he cannot support proposals to that effect.[56] It could even be argued that any limitation of existing

[52] *Staatsblad* [Bulletin of Acts and Decrees] *2002*, No. 54.

[53] *Kamerstukken* [Parliamentary Documents] II, 2002–3, 28 916, No. 3, 33.

[54] See the May 2003 Coalition Agreement 'Participation, Employment, Deregulation', published on the Internet at: http://www.government.nl.

[55] J.M.H.F. Teunissen, 'De algemeen belangorganisatie als bestuursrechtelijk (pseudo-) Openbaar Ministerie?' (2003) 153 *Gemeentestem*, 7179.

[56] *Kamerstukken* [Parliamentary Documents] II, 2002–3, 28 600 XI, No. 95, 6.

rights is contrary to the Aarhus Convention because Article 3(6) states that the Convention 'shall not require any derogation from existing rights of... public participation in decision-making'. Still, it is interesting to find out why a country with far-reaching procedural rights is now going in the opposite direction.

Originally, one of the basic arguments to limit participation and, especially, standing rights, was the overload of cases that were pending before the courts. As already mentioned above, evaluations in the late 1990s indeed show some delay and some additional court procedures as a consequence of public participation. However, this has changed quite drastically since the vast majority of installations that needed an environmental permit now only have to meet standard requirements that are laid down in Orders in Council, rather than in individual permits. As a consequence, no individual decisions need to be taken for 75 per cent of the installations that are governed by environmental legislation, so no participation and no court procedures will be brought for any of these. The number of environmental and planning cases before the Administrative Law Division of the Dutch Council of State has declined from 3,867 in 1997 to 2,276 in 2001.[57]

In 2002 and 2003, a dramatic further decline in court cases took place. By 31 December 2002, the number of cases had been reduced to only 1238.[58] This is thought to be one of the consequences of a political assassination. On 6 May 2002, the leader of a new right-wing political party, Pim Fortuyn, who was in favour of abolishing animal welfare legislation, was killed by a person who was working for an animal rights NGO, Vereniging Milieuoffensief. This particular NGO mainly operated through court procedures against environmental permits that were issued for cattle-raising installations. Vereniging Milieuoffensief accounted for about 50 per cent of all cases in this field of environmental law that were brought before the Administrative Law Division of the Council of State. The legal activities of this NGO practically came to a halt after the assassination. Other NGOs have kept quiet since the assassination as well.

At the same time, the political climate in the Netherlands turned against environmental policy. This was mirrored in a decline in the number of cases brought before the Council of State. People seem to be reluctant to start court procedures on environmental issues. The same may be true of the participation phase of the decision-making process.

A third reason for the decline in 2002 and 2003 is a discussion on the effect of court procedures. NGOs feel that they may often win cases on legal issues, but that the effect of a succesful court case is very limited. Usually, the competent authority takes a new decision, this time without making procedural mistakes, and then the plan or project goes ahead anyway. This is usually a consequence of the rather formal approach of the Administrative Law Division. The Adminis-

[57] Verschuuren, n. 50 above, 35.

[58] See the 2002 Annual Report, available at the Council of State website published on the Internet at: http://www.raadvanstate.nl.

trative Law Division tends to annul decisions on the procedural ground that they have not been carefully prepared (e.g., without a thorough study of the environmental effects), or because they are ill-motivated. When a decision has been well prepared and properly motivated, administrative courts usually review only very minimally. This matter will be further elaborated below.

Since 2002, the main argument has been of a socio-economic nature (as opposed to the original arguments against public participation). Decision-making procedures with a strong emphasis on public participation, followed by court procedures, are considered to be 'administrative burdens', hampering much needed socio-economic development. More generally, elected politicians feel the need to regain control of decision-making processes. The public expects them to show leadership. But how can they do so when NGOs, companies, groups of citizens, or individual citizens play a substantive role in the decision-making process? The clash between public participation and representative democracy comes to the fore here.

The problem with the latter argument is that it is not based on empirical data. There is a general impression, based on a small number of much-publicized cases that were won by environmental NGOs and on a lot of bad publicity following the Fortuyn assassination, that NGOs are too powerful. The advantages of participation mentioned above, and the risks involved with reducing procedural rights, are underexposed. These risks include lengthy discussions in each and every case whether a certain member of the public meets the new requirements (thus increasing the administrative burden), a reduction in the quality of decisions, reduced public acceptance of public decisions, and less democratic governance altogether.

As stated above, it is essential to reconcile public participation with representative democracy, rather than to simply limit public participation. Public participation need not thwart political leadership and vice versa. The outcome of the decision-making process remains a state decision; political power will always be able to override the outcome of public participation. However, it is up to politicians to combine the problem-solving effectiveness of public participation with democratic authenticity.[59] It is hoped that the Member States, when implementing the provisions of the Participation in Plans and Programmes Directive, will realize the important advantages of an effective and easily accessible system of public participation in the long run.

B. Criticism of the Traditional Notion of Participation

Simultaneously, an entirely different development is taking place that is partly connected with the discussions mentioned. There is also a great deal of criticism of the way public participation usually functions. Public participation is often

[59] Dryzek, n. 16 above, 173.

limited to 'listening' to interested citizens as part of a carefully regulated formal procedure, followed by autonomous decision-making by the competent authorities. This was suggested in section I to be one of the disadvantages of public participation. In the view of many of the participating citizens, the authorities listen, but then go ahead as planned, resulting in the feeling that 'it is no use' to participate. As a reaction, but also because of the idea that, in our complex society, it is becoming increasingly difficult for the state to balance all interests involved, experiments with forms of negotiated (or collaborative) decision-making (*Kooperative Verwaltung*) have been undertaken since the 1990s in various European countries, such as Belgium, Denmark, Germany, and the Netherlands.[60] In negotiated decision-making, the authorities, in theory, bring together the parties involved, for instance, the operator of an installation, the local residents, and an interested NGO. These directly involved parties negotiate, usually within existing legal frameworks,[61] on the decision to be taken. When they have reached an agreement, the authorities more or less affirm the result of the negotiations in a formal decision. In practice, the state's role is usually not just procedural. Instead, we observe that the authorities themselves are actively involved in the negotiations as well. The main goal of these kinds of decision-making processes is to get people involved and committed, and thus create the opportunity of achieving results that might otherwise have seemed impossible to obtain, utilizing the knowledge and creativity in society, and reducing the risk that decisions are challenged in court.

Although aimed more at setting standards than at decision-making with regard to projects, similar ideas have been presented at the EU level by the European Commission, not only in the White Paper on Governance,[62] but also in the sixth Environmental Action Programme. The latter states that flexible means of addressing environmental problems should be introduced, for instance, by 'setting a regulatory framework establishing policy objectives and leaving the practical implementation measures to be defined by industry in a consensual manner, in support of the legal framework ("co-regulation")'.[63] It may be assumed that the words 'consensual manner' indicate that local residents and NGOs should be involved in the process as well. As far as European policy-making is concerned, 'real efforts are to be made to ensure that the full range of interested groups are given the opportunity to influence decision making'.[64]

[60] See extensively B. de Waard (ed.), *Negotiated Decision-Making* (The Hague: Boom Juridische Uitgevers, 2000).

[61] In the Netherlands, the City and Environment Experiments Act (*Experimentenwet stad en milieu*) allows local authorities to derogate in certain cases from existing environmental standards if necessary to facilitate the negotiations, see R. Weigel, 'The Compact City in the Spotlight of the Law' in de Waard, n. 60 above, 47–66.

[62] COM(2001)428.

[63] COM(2001)31, 61.

[64] ibid. 62.

At all levels, from local to international, partnerships between NGOs and corporations can be considered an even further step towards decision-making by the actors themselves with limited or even without government interference. NGOs and business corporations together are active in various fields of law, that is norm setting, implementation, monitoring and enforcement, and even dispute resolution. From the perspective of businesses, such cooperative action can be used to legitimize their actions at a time where government approval alone is no longer considered to be sufficient to demonstrate adequate environmental performance.[65] Moreover, NGOs can provide corporations with ecological, scientific, and legal expertise, and they can help corporations build social networks with other stakeholders.[66] Perhaps the best-known example is the Forest Stewardship Council (FSC).

The FSC, founded in 1993 by environmental groups and the timber industry, was a reaction to the failure of governments to reach agreements on sustainable forestry within the International Tropical Timber Organization.[67] The FSC rapidly grew into an organization with more than 500 members, including representatives of environmental and social groups, the timber trade and the forestry profession, indigenous people's organizations, community forestry groups, and forest product certification organizations from around the world. Government organizations are excluded from membership.

Such developments indicate that 'public participation' can be, and should be, more than just expressing a view in a hearing or in a letter to the competent authority. In the Aarhus Convention, there is one indication that the drafters of the Convention realized this. Article 6(5) of the Aarhus Convention requires parties to encourage prospective applicants to identify the public concerned, to enter into discussions, and to provide information regarding the objectives of their application before applying for a permit. Unfortunately, a similar provision was not included in the Participation in Plans and Programmes Directive. This is a missed opportunity. The authorities will have to accept that their role has changed. Adopting a more open policy style implies a greater role for the public involved. This does not mean that the authorities lose control. Again, they should balance their own democratic responsibilities with public participation outcomes. Many businesses are well aware of the need actively to involve local residents and the relevant NGOs. An intriguing question is: does 'private' participation reduce the number of court procedures, where public participation does not (or not necessarily, see section 1 above)? There is no evidence yet to

[65] J. Grolin, 'Corporate Legitimacy in Risk Society—The Case of Brent Spar' (1998) 7 *Business Strategy and the Environment*, 220.

[66] E.R. Stafford, M.J. Polonsky, and C.L. Hartman, 'Environmental NGO-Business Collaboration and Strategic Bridging—A Case Analysis of the Greenpeace-Foron Alliance' (2000) 9 *Business Strategy and the Environment*, 123.

[67] E.E. Meidinger, '"Private" Environmental Regulation, Human Rights, and Community' (1999–2000) 7 *Buffalo Environmental Law Journal*, 131.

answer this question unconditionally in the affirmative. Whatever the answer is, businesses feel it is better to negotiate beforehand than risk lengthy court procedures or bad publicity. The evaluation projects referred to above showed that public decisions involving business corporations that had actively informed and involved local residents and NGOs in their 'internal' decision-making processes at their own initiative were very well accepted by these actors.[68] This finding underlines the importance of the provision of Article 6(5) of the Aarhus Convention. It is hoped EU Member States will not overlook this provision.

VI. Conclusion: A Glance at the Near Future

Administrative environmental decision-making is becoming increasingly difficult for elected administrative bodies. Their power is diminished by experts, on the one hand, and by members of the general public involved in public participation, on the other. This shows that representative democracy is not fully suited to legitimizing environmental decisions. In this article, I have endeavoured to show that public participation should not be regarded as a threat to democracy, but as one of the means to strengthen the legitimacy of administrative decisions. Public participation does not only lead to better decisions, it balances the power of technical experts in cases where a value judgement must be made. Public participation is also one of the means to introduce more deliberative elements in democratic decision-making processes, thus enhancing legitimacy. The biggest challenge for elected government officials is to combine the problem-solving effectiveness of public participation with leadership and democratic authenticity. This is not an easy task.

Although there are some practical disadvantages attached to extensive public participation such as a delay in the decision-making process and possibly a slightly higher number of court cases, the advantages definitely outweigh the disadvantages. Therefore, it must be hoped that the reserved stance of many Member States towards extending participation rights will not be reflected in the national implementation process of the Aarhus Convention and Participation in Plans and Programmes Directive. Unfortunately, the Directive has already weakened the provisions on public participation regarding projects by allowing participation only for persons affected by a decision and for NGOs. In the Lucca Declaration,[69] Parties to the Convention were called upon to consider going further in providing access to public participation than is required by the Convention, but it would not come as a great surprise if only a few are actually prepared to consider this.

[68] Mooren *et al.*, n. 12 above, 41.

[69] Para. 13. UN/ECE Distr. GEN MP.PP/2002/CRP.1, available at the UN/ECE's Aarhus Convention website published on the Internet at: http://www.unece.org/env/pp/mop1.htm.

Although most of the provisions on public participation concerning the elaboration and approval of projects laid down in the Participation in Plans and Programmes Directive are in line with the Aarhus Convention, this Directive is only a first step towards a more active involvement of the public in environmental decision-making. In my view, there are at least three issues that need further attention in the coming years.

First of all, participation should not be limited to IPPC installations or EIA projects. As a matter of fact, it is surprising that the EC has not decided—under Article 6(1)(b) of the Aarhus Convention—to bring a proposed activity that is regulated under either Directive 79/409/EEC on the Conservation of Wild Birds (Birds Directive)[70] or Directive 92/43/EEC on the Conservation of Natural Habitats and of Wild Fauna and Flora (Habitats Directive)[71] under the Participation in Plans and Programmes Directive, given the great importance the Proposal for a Directive on Environmental Liability with Regard to the Prevention and Remedying of Environmental Damage gives to species and habitats protected under the two directives.[72] This would have been all the more obvious now the Habitats Directive, in Article 6(4), provides that 'the competent national authorities shall agree to the plan or project only after having ascertained that it will not adversely affect the integrity of the site concerned *and, if appropriate, after having obtained the opinion of the general public*' (emphasis added). Many projects that are subject to Article 6 of the Habitats Directive may already be within the scope of the Participation in Plans and Programmes Directive because they either concern IPPC installations or EIA projects. But there are many smaller projects that can have significant consequences for a Special Area of Conservation (SAC) or for a protected species. And what about smaller installations? They too may cause considerable nuisance or environmental damage. Smaller installations are more likely to be located within or close to populated areas than the very large installations that fall under the scope of the EIA and IPPC Directives. The latter are usually located in industrial zones. It is not easy to explain to a local resident that he has no right to participate because the installation remains slightly below the IPPC threshold.

Secondly, there is already an ongoing debate on participation at an international level,[73] and at the level of the EU. The Commission should consider following a public participation procedure in accordance with the Aarhus Convention on its decisions, for example, decisions to finance projects that may have a significant effect on the environment.

70 [1979] OJ L103/1.

71 [1992] OJ L206/7.

72 COM(2002)17.

73 'Access to Information, Public Participation and Access to Justice in International Forums', paper for the UN/ECE Committee on Environmental Policy, UN/ECE Distr. GEN MP.PP/2002/18 CEP/2002/13, available at the UN/ECE Aarhus Convention website published on the Internet at: http://www.unece.org/env/pp/pre.mop1.htm.

Thirdly, and finally, we can expect a growing call for more open decision-making processes, such as negotiated decision-making. Adapting existing procedural and substantive environmental law to these new types of decision-making without losing the benefits of representative democracy and, more generally, reducing tensions between representative democracy and increased involvement of society in decision-making will be a major task that is still ahead of us.

Public Participation in the Assessment of the Effects of Certain Plans and Programmes on the Environment—Directive 2001/42/EC, the UN/ECE Espoo Convention, and the Kiev Protocol

*Karen Morrow**

I. Introduction

Early indications are that, as the twenty-first century gets under way, we are set to see the emergence of a new era in international environmental law. Developments in this area are premised by the perceived need to create a role for public participation in environmental decision-making in order to increase transparency, legitimacy, and accountability. These developments are motivated by the increasingly prevalent idea that, in order for environmental decisions and the arrangements for making them to be effective, they must be owned by the public, and not simply imposed by states. This bottom-up perspective is given a key role in the sustainable development rhetoric that flavours current environmental discourse, and can arguably be viewed as representing an emerging paradigm in environmental decision-making in a more concrete form as well. Substantive developments in the well-established area of environmental assessment (EA) and emerging law and policy on strategic environmental assessment (SEA) arguably exhibit one of the most refined manifestations of applied sustainability-related decision-making to have emerged to date. The concept of public participation in this area first came to the fore in domestic law and is currently coming to play a role in international law as EA and SEA are applied in a transboundary context. Given the rationale underpinning the EA concept, it has great potential to adapt well to the sustainability agenda, and the two areas are arguably developing symbiotically.

The chapter will first examine the rationale, role, and development of public participation in international environmental law and policy. In particular, discussion will focus on the potentially problematic tendency to equate the role of

* Senior Lecturer in Law, University of Leeds, Department of Law, Leeds (UK).

Non-Governmental Organizations (NGOs) with that of the public in attempting to address the desire for broader participation in environmental decision-making in an international law context. The chapter will then proceed to examine concrete examples of provision for public participation in the environmental assessment of plans, programmes, and policies in the mutually reinforcing regimes under European Community law (in particular Directive 2001/42/EC on the Assessment of the Effects of Certain Plans and Programmes on the Environment (SEA Directive)) and the United Nations (UN) Convention on Environmental Impact Assessment in a Transboundary Context (Espoo Convention) and its Protocol on Strategic Environmental Assessment Protocol (Kiev Protocol).[1] The nature of the entitlements to public participation in these instruments will be examined and special attention will be paid to the way that they function in the acutely problematic transboundary context at a strategic level.

It will become clear that the integration of public participation into this area of environmental activity should be represented not so much as a linear progression, but rather as the development of a web of interlinked and mutually reinforcing arrangements resulting from a variety of international initiatives. On the surface it would appear that the very nature of international environmental law is being changed by the inclusion of public participation as a key element in the decision-making process. On closer examination, though, it will be argued that, while public participation has gained broad exposure in international environmental law and policy, it has not at the same time achieved deep infiltration. It appears that the international legal system (and even the relatively progressive environmental law sphere within it) remains, in substance, a state-driven, top-down system, loosely modelled on representative democracy. This is the case despite the fact that more participative democracy-styled elements are beginning to be introduced into the regime, as to date they place only a gloss on the existing order. As law and policy move on to even more demanding sustainable development assessments (SDAs), it will be necessary to their success to ensure that public participation is a central substantive element in the decision-making process, rather than a largely formal requirement. Thus far, however, it would appear that the ideology of sustainability is outstripping the political will to make this a reality.

The current near-mania for promoting public participation in international environmental law is rooted in the need to address the central problem posed by the lack of legitimacy in international law more generally. This universal problem arguably manifests itself in one of its most acute forms in the context of international environmental law which, given its increasing range of influence

[1] Dir. 2001/42/EC on the Assessment of the Effects of Certain Plans and Programmes on the Environment OJ L197/30 (the SEA Directive); Espoo (Finland), 25 Feb. 1991 (entered into force 10 Sept. 1997) (1991) 30 *International Legal Materials*, 3.

and its novel and often contentious nature,[2] pushes at the boundaries of traditional international law mechanisms. The unprecedented quantity of international environmental law and policy, and the accompanying evolution of new institutional awareness and activism, only serve to render the problem of legitimacy more visible.

Environmental issues demonstrate all too often that the state is at the same time too large and too small to deal with problems that are local in origin and global in scale. The need for international solutions to some problems and local ones to others places traditional legal systems under a great deal of pressure. In this context, the limitations of a traditional view of international law based largely on the notion of state sovereignty are very apparent. These observations explain, at least in part, the emergence of modern views of the global legal order which, although they continue to regard states as the prime actors in the system, also regard other players as enjoying significant roles in the complex processes of law and policy-making. The group of new key actors includes international governmental organizations (IGOs), transnational corporations (TNCs), and non-governmental organizations (NGOs).[3] Such pluralistic views of the international law-making community advocate the influence of a broader range of actors on the development of law and policy as a positive virtue and additional source of legitimacy. The extension of the range of input that is considered desirable or even necessary to decision-making processes is often presented in terms of promoting public participation. Public participation, in its manifold forms, exhibits a number of legitimizing characteristics, both intrinsic and instrumental, including: 'direct, non-representational, popular participation in decision-making', improved quality decision-making through broader input and discussion, consciousness raising and improved norm realization.[4] The emergence of a commitment to broadening participation, in addition to having demonstrable benefits in its own right, is also in harmony with the notion of a more participative approach to decision-making that is actively promoted by the philosophy of sustainable development.

In any event, the international legal and policy community is now more complex than ever before, and is in a state of swift development and pronounced, if not profound, change. As problems are increasingly recognized as global in nature and international legal and institutional responses are put in place, society evolves to respond to the challenges and opportunities that result. In turn, international institutions engage with new societal developments, and thus the

[2] See D. Bodansky, 'The Legitimacy of International Governance—A Coming Challenge for Environmental Law?' (1999) 93 *American Journal of International Law*, 596–624.

[3] J. Boli and G. Thomas, 'INGOs and the Organization of World Culture' in J. Boli and G. Thomas (eds.), *Constructing World Culture—INGOs since 1875* (Stanford, Calif.: Stanford University Press, 1999).

[4] R. McCracken and G. Jones, 'The Aarhus Convention' (2003) *Journal of Planning and Environmental Law*, 802.

opening up of environmental law and policy becomes self-perpetuating, if not convincingly self-justifying.[5]

In the search for firmer foundations for international environmental law, experiments with new methods of reinforcing authority and exploiting new sources of legitimacy can be identified. Encouraging public participation is one strategy[6] that is currently being put to the test in a range of areas from sustainable development through biodiversity to environmental assessment. This is a manifestation of the trend of importing democratic values into the international legal system, in particular those values associated with open government and transparency. The current preoccupation with public participation is hardly surprising, given the dominance of the ideology of liberal democracy following the end of the Cold War. Modern liberal democracy is, however, highly individualistic in its orientation, which in part explains the rising prominence of human rights questions in this area. Arguably, this represents at least a partial remodelling of liberal democratic systems in order to put them to use, if not for a new purpose, then at least in a new context. One commentator has argued that democratic strategies are being pressed into service to secure a form of accountability that is otherwise lacking in international law.[7] While this view certainly accounts for some recent developments in the law, it only tells part of the story, particularly in the absence of rights[8] for the public to pursue complaints under most international environmental law regimes. The emergence and mainstreaming of broader participation rights for the public in some areas of international environmental law arguably points to a more fundamental search for legitimacy by widening the sense of ownership over environmental law. There do, however, remain questions as to how effectively the public can actually engage with monolithic international law and policy-making processes. Certainly individual participation does not mesh well at this level in many ways, not least in terms of scale.

Increasingly, the limits of classical or representative democracy to deliver solutions to modern complex societal problems are being recognized.[9] These

[5] Meyer (1994), quoted in Boli and Thomas (eds.), n. 3 above, 30.

[6] Bodansky, n. 2 above, identifies three commonly employed conceptions of democracy in international law, the third of which, encapsulating democratic values, is most relevant to the purposes of the topic of this chapter, 613.

[7] M. Mason, 'Transnational Environmental Obligations—Locating New Spaces of Accountability in a Post-Westphalian Global Order', published on the Internet at: http://www.ethos.freeuk.com/polis/symposium1b.doc.

[8] The law is arguably beginning to develop in this way, as for example in the establishment of a new compliance mechanism under the United Nations Economic Commission for Europe (UN/ECE) Convention on Access to Information, Public Participation in Decision-Making and Access to Justice in Environmental Matters (Aarhus Convention); Aarhus (Denmark), 25 June 1998 (entered into force 30 Oct. 2001) (1999) 38 *International Legal Materials*, 3, 517. As of 23 Oct. the public will be able to bring alleged instances of non-compliance before the Convention's Compliance Committee. UN/ECE's Press Release ECE/ENV/03/P04, published on the Internet at: http://www.unece.org/press/pr2003/03env_p04e.htm.

[9] T. Fischer, 'Strategic Environmental Assessment in Post-Modern Times' (2003) 23 *Environmental Impact Assessment Review*, 155–70.

manifest themselves in a number of ways, not least in the recognition of the need to introduce bottom-up or participatory models of behaviour (though not necessarily based on individual participation) in order to progress the sustainable development agenda. The rationale underpinning this type of development is summarized by Kohr:

> The chief danger to the spirit of democracy in a large power stems from [the] technical impossibility of asserting itself informally. In mass states, personal influences can make themselves felt only if channelled through forms, formulas and organizations. It is these latter rather than the individual who become increasingly the true agents or assertors of political sovereignty, so that we should speak of a group or party democracy rather than of an individualistic democracy.[10]

These observations are, if anything, even more cogent in the international sphere.

At the same time as the loss of faith in representative democracy to adequately represent the public interest, there has been loss of confidence in technocratic and professional decision-making processes,[11] or at least the emerging belief that such elements may be necessary but are not sufficient for informing environmental decisions. This development too creates a space for public participation to provide an alternative view of the public interest and an additional source of legitimization.

In any event, the whole concept of modelling international law making on domestic democratic values, signalled by the inclusion of public participation elements in international legal instruments, begs a number of important questions. While democracy is certainly a viable source of legitimacy for state law and governance, it does not necessarily hold true that it can be effectively extrapolated to the international level in all respects.

II. NGOs as Agents of Public Participation—Questions of Principle

Despite its almost totemic significance in international environmental law and policy, there is no real consensus on what the term 'public participation' actually means in this context. It is potentially capable of bearing a vast range of possible interpretations from mere consultation at the low end of the scale to full involvement with and influence over the outcomes of decision-making processes.[12] At its most fundamental, it can be viewed as an essential hallmark of a democratic regime which 'involves not simply public participation, but the ability of the

[10] L. Kohr, 'Small is Democratic' in N. Albury and M. Kingsley (eds.), *How to Save the World—A Fourth World Guide to the Politics of Scale* (Wellingborough: Turnstone Press, 1984), 59.

[11] M. Lee and C. Abbot, 'The Usual Suspects? Public Participation Under the Aarhus Convention' (2003) 66 *Modern Law Review*, 80–108.

[12] See A.K. Wolfe, N. Kerchner, and T. Wilbanks, 'Public Involvement on a Regional Scale' (2001) 21 *Environmental Impact Assessment Review*, 431–48.

public to make decisions, either directly or through the election of representatives'.[13]

If public participation is to be thrust into such a prominent role, then it becomes crucial to identify the public for any given purpose. This process can itself be problematic, and it is advisable to adopt a generous approach in order to prevent certain sections of the public from becoming aggrieved. It is prudent then to allow to engage with the process, not only those directly affected by it, but also those indirectly affected by it and: 'those who have an interest in the particular potential impacts that may be able to support and assist those directly and indirectly affected'.[14]

In an international environmental law context, public participation in this sense presents considerable practical problems. Theoretical approaches to public participation tend to err in characterizing it as an unalloyed advantage to the public, omitting to recognize that the practicalities of engagement can prove to be extremely onerous. There are considerable practical problems in rendering public participation a substantive reality, rather than a formal illusion. These include barriers to effective engagement with decision-making processes and fall into three broad categories: timing, process unfamiliarity, and information overload, each of which can have a chilling effect on public participation. As a result, in real terms, 'public participation' in this area tends normally to be equated with NGO participation.[15] In this context, NGOs act as substitutes for affected publics in any or all of the categories represented by those directly or indirectly affected and those playing an enabling role. There are numerous definitions of NGOs, a workable one for the purposes of this chapter being: 'private organizations not established by a government or by international agreement which are capable of playing a role in international affairs by virtue of their activities'.[16]

The rapid mainstreaming of the tendency to regard NGOs as agents of public participation is partially indicated by their increasingly frequent inclusion in international environmental law instruments. It is highly significant that not only states and IGOs, but also NGOs themselves, see a significant role for them to play in this regard. Favourable views of NGO participation are usually based on the notion that such groups are 'acting as the identifiable voices of broad segments of civil society',[17] importing the notion of the desirability of their

[13] Bodansky, n. 2 above, 614.

[14] P. Stookes and J Razzaque, 'Community Participation—UK Planning Reforms and International Obligations' (2002) *Journal of Planning and Environment Law*, 786–95. See also W.M. Tabb, 'Environmental Impact Assessment in the European Community—Shaping International Norms' (1999) 73 *Tulane Law Review*, 923–60.

[15] Bodansky, n. 2 above, 619.

[16] *Encyclopaedia of Public International Law* quoted in S. Charnovitz, 'Two Centuries of Participation—NGOs and International Governance' (1997) 18 *Michigan Journal of International Law*, 186.

[17] F. Yamin, 'NGOs and International Environmental Law—A Critical Evaluation of their Roles and Responsibilities' (2001) 10 *Review of European and International Environmental Law*, 150.

playing a representative or at least quasi-representative role. This is potentially problematic, as NGOs tend to operate internally (at a certain level) as a form of grassroots participative democracy but are being pressed into service in an external role in a very different fashion.

The employment of NGOs as a form of proxy for the general public leads to a view of public participation that, while workable and certainly convenient, is, at the same time, inevitably reductionist and potentially problematic. It is arguable that the incorporation of NGOs as players in international environmental law and policy allows IGOs and states to take a useful shortcut to some sort of democratic credibility at comparatively little financial cost and less effort.[18] It allows them to pay lip service to the ideals of public participation without having to tackle the difficulty of getting the public in its broader guise to engage with the decision-making processes in question. By bringing NGOs into the fold, states and international governmental organizations (IGOs) can access both useful resources and more importantly credibility for their efforts.[19]

The proxy role accorded to NGOs in international environmental law does, however, give significant cause for concern as, by employing this subtly bastardized version of public participation, its whole character is in fact altered from a notional mechanism of participative democracy to a practical alternative form of representative democracy. This proves problematic in its own right as, once NGOs reach a certain critical mass, they cease to be organs of participative democracy and become *de facto* representative in their function—but without an electoral mandate. This means that they must seek their legitimacy by other means, for example though their expertise. These arguments may also serve to justify the quasi-representative role of NGOs in international environmental law. An alternative lens through which to view the 'representative' function of NGOs can be found in regarding them not as representatives of individual members of the public in the same way as an elected politician, but instead as representatives of otherwise inadequately covered interests.[20] In this way the quasi-representative role of NGOs could be viewed as complementary to that of mainstream representative democracy rather than inimical to it. In any event, the need to legitimize the role of NGOs as agents of public participation before this can in turn legitimize international environmental decision-making must be addressed.

In practical terms the development of a recognized role for NGOs in decision-making acknowledges the tendency of the public to self-organize its engagement with decision-making processes as ad hoc groupings crystallize into more organized community and interest groups in order to rationalize the burden of

[18] See generally Boli and Thomas, n. 3 above.

[19] D.J. Frank, A. Hironalia, J.W. Meyer, and E. Schofer, 'The Rationalization and Organization of Nature in World Culture' in J. Boli and G. Thomas (eds.), *Constructing World Culture—INGOs since 1875* (Stanford, Calif.: Stanford University Press, 1999), 99.

[20] C. Stone, *Should Trees Have Standing: Toward Legal Rights for Natural Objects* (New York: Avon Books, 1975).

participation. As Durkheim states, arguably making a virtue of necessity: 'A nation can be maintained only if, between the State and the individual, there is intercalated a whole series of secondary groups near enough to individuals to attract them strongly in their sphere of action and drag them, in this way, into the general torrent of social life'.[21]

These comments are even more apposite when applied to the international sphere, where matters of scale alone make it necessary for citizens to band together in order to have an audible voice in the matters that affect them. While this approach necessarily dilutes the participatory democracy element of public participation,[22] it arguably serves to create a grassroots form of representative democracy in its place that can do much to cure the problems encountered with participatory approaches to environmental decision-making. This is particularly the case where public input is required with great frequency or in respect of very complex issues.

Given the general reluctance of the public at large to engage with public decision-making processes, due to a combination of factors ranging from practical difficulties to simple apathy, NGOs may in fact optimize public participation in decision-making processes. NGOs certainly have a great deal to contribute to decision-making processes, bringing new or additional voices[23] to the fore, providing alternatives to the dominant official version of the public interest. Even more significantly, NGOs can bring considerable and varied[24] expertise to the decision-making process[25] and this is augmented by their ability to exploit established networks to add breadth and depth to their input.[26] The ability of NGOs to make linkages across geographical, political, and hierarchical barriers and their (albeit flawed) ability to give voice to otherwise poorly or even unrepresented interests, such as those of the planet or future generations, places them in a good position to augment traditional state and IGO inputs into law and policy-making processes. Additionally, NGOs may potentially act as conduits between IGOs and the general public,[27] facilitating dialogue between them. NGOs also potentially have a role to play in holding IGOs to account.[28] In practical terms, NGOs stand to gain at least some of the advantages that experience brings to repeat players in law and policy-making processes. At the very least, NGOs can serve as a catalyst for bringing the critical assessment of international environmental law and governance into the public sphere.

[21] Durkheim (1964), quoted in M. Stallworthy, *Sustainability, Land Use and Environment—A Legal Analysis* (London: Cavendish, 2002), 310.

[22] Fischer, n. 9 above, 158.

[23] H. Cullen and K. Morrow, 'International Civil Society in International Law— The Growth of NGO Participation' (2001) 1 *Non-State Actors and International Law*, 31.

[24] This ranges from scientific through technical to policy expertise.

[25] Cullen and Morrow, n. 23 above, 32 and Bodansky, n. 2 above, 620.

[26] Cullen and Morrow, n. 23 above, 34 and Yamin, n. 17 above, 151.

[27] P. Bombay, 'The Role of NGOs in Shaping Community Positions in International Environmental Fora' (2001) 10 *Review of European Community and International Environmental Law*, 166.

[28] Cullen and Morrow, n. 23 above, 36 and Yamin, n. 17 above, 152.

In light of their own problems of legitimacy, there is also a real appeal for NGOs in augmenting their position by embedding themselves in the work of IGOs and in the development of international environmental law and policy. There are however dangers for NGOs in being drawn into the IGO arena. A very real inequality of power (though their position is more favourable than that of the public at large) exists in the context of NGO relationships with such bodies, which means that they are in danger of being subsumed by official systems and structures. The process of co-option potentially comes at a significant cost to NGOs, attacking important elements of their distinctive identity. Even if such a result does not occur, NGOs that overenthusiastically embrace co-option are at best perceived (whether accurately or not) as 'going native'. This is particularly the case where official sources foster NGO participation by providing necessary funds. Such problems are difficult, if not impossible, to resolve. Increased influence can come at the cost of independence, and fuller involvement almost inevitably decreases objectivity.

There is an additional caveat that should be kept in mind when considering NGOs as the prime harbingers of public participation in international environmental law and policy, in the form of the danger of NGOs becoming the new technocracy, squeezing out less officially sanctioned forms of public participation. Favoured status for certain NGOs may even push less favoured NGOs out of the arena. The net result is the creation of a new type of decision-making 'closed shop', as cut off from outside influence as that which it replaced. This is a very real danger given the convenience and benefits that accrue to IGOs and NGOs in their interactions with one another.

Although it is clear that NGOs have a great deal to offer in terms of channelling public participation, there remain fundamental limitations on the legitimizing role that NGO involvement can play in international environmental law. While undoubtedly significant, NGO power is also special and 'cannot be equated with, or reduced to, the kind of power exercized by States'.[29] Further: 'For reasons of democratic public accountability... the fact that both (NGOs and governments) do have respective and essentially different roles should not be lost'.[30]

While keeping this essential caveat in mind, it can be argued that, on balance, there is a sufficient community of interest in place to justify the role of NGOs as proxies in this regard. The view that, on the whole, the advantages of NGO participation outweigh the disadvantages would seem to be borne out by established practice. Such is the perceived importance of the role of NGOs that their participation in international environmental law and policy has become part of accepted orthodoxy as expressed by then UN Secretary-General Boutros Boutros-Ghali: 'non-governmental organizations are a basic form of popular representation in the present day world. Their participation in international organizations is, in a way, a guarantee of the political legitimacy of those international organizations'.[31]

[29] Yamin, n. 17 above, 154. [30] Bombay, n. 27 above, 167.

[31] Quoted in P. Mucke, 'Non-Governmental Organizations' in F. Dodds (ed.), *The Way Forward—Beyond Agenda 21* (London: Earthscan, 1997), 94.

III. NGOs as Agents of Public Participation—Current Practice

In international environmental law the potential for NGOs to make a substantive contribution to environmental decision-making processes truly came to the fore at the United Nations Conference on Environment and Development (UNCED) at Rio in 1992. The UNCED accorded a prominent role to NGOs, not only in special parallel proceedings, but also by granting them observer status in the main proceedings.[32]

Public participation ultimately featured prominently in the hard and soft law produced at Rio, playing a thematic role in the Rio Declaration on Environment and Development,[33] in particular in Principle 10:

> Environmental issues are best handled with the participation of all concerned citizens, at the relevant level. At the national level, each individual shall have appropriate access to information concerning the environment that is held by public authorities, including information on hazardous materials and activities in their communities, and the opportunity to participate in decision-making processes. States shall facilitate and encourage public awareness and participation by making information widely available. Effective access to judicial and administrative proceedings, including redress and remedy, shall be provided.

and in Agenda 21,[34] the UNCED 'blue-print for sustainable development'. The latter document arguably narrows the focus of public participation by identifying NGOs, whether formal, informal, or grassroots-based as playing: 'a vital role in the shaping and implementation of participatory democracy'.[35]

Most NGOs are assumed to be internally democratic and therefore offer opportunities for individuals to achieve what Agenda 21 terms 'real participation'.[36] To this end the independence of NGOs is prized by the UN as both a major attribute and a precondition of public participation. The notion of this type of participatory approach to democracy may, at first glance, appear to be quaint at best and archaic at worst, in a world dominated by the norms of representative democracy espoused by western liberal thought, but it fits surprisingly easily with the imperatives of the sustainable development agenda. Sustainable development, and Agenda 21 as the means to achieve it, are groundbreaking

[32] For accounts of the role of NGOs in this context, see A. Grubb *et al.*, *The Earth Summit Agreements—A Guide and Assessment* (London: RIIA/Earthscan, 1998) and P. Willetts, 'Consultative Status for NGOs at the United Nations' in P. Willetts (ed.), *The Conscience of the World—The Influence of Non-Governmental Organizations in the UN System* (London: Hurst & Company, 1996), 54 ff.

[33] United Nations Conference on Environment and Development, Rio Declaration on Environment and Development (New York: UN, 1994).

[34] *Earth Summit Agenda 21—The United Nations Programme of Action from Rio* (New York: UN, 1994).

[35] ibid. 27.1.

[36] ibid.

in international environmental law terms, since they target not only the activities of international institutions and states but at their heart focus on the role to be played by communities and individuals, taking the view that: 'people's rights and responsibilities form the crux of any discussion of sustainability'.[37] Sustainable development has, since its inception in a populist guise in the Brundtland Report in 1987,[38] stressed the need for a 'bottom-up' approach to changing human attitudes and practices and NGOs have a great deal to offer in the 'vast campaign of education, debate and public participation'[39] necessitated by such an ambitious goal. NGOs are identified by the Brundtland Report as having a legitimate, significant, and increasing role to play in this regard at local, regional, national, and international levels.[40] They are in many ways well placed to facilitate the growth of sustainable development. The relative independence of NGOs and their range of expertise[41] are officially recognized as enriching dialogue and partnerships with government.[42] NGOs also offer an established and active global network of mutual contact and information exchange that has much to offer in the context of sustainable development.[43] The infrastructure of this aspect of civil society was recognized at the UNCED as a resource worthy of both exploitation and augmentation. In short, it offers a useful head-start in progressing sustainable development and in taking the concept beyond the state into society. Such is the importance accorded to NGOs in Agenda 21, that states are exhorted to foster their activities and their participation at all levels in the sustainable development process from policy-making, through decision-making, to implementation and review.[44]

Realizing these ambitious goals will require substantial and substantive change in the way in which states and the international community relate to civil society. Therefore it was somewhat surprising that the Commission on Sustainable Development (CSD), which is charged with official responsibility for fostering sustainable development, expressed the view as early as 1998 that sufficient progress had been made for it to:

> Welcome the trend . . . towards greater public participation and decentralization, including broader civil society consultation, citizen empowerment and increasing public/private partnerships and networks, resulting in more demand-driven efforts at capacity building,

[37] R. Sharp, 'Organizing for Change: People Power and the Role of Institutions' in J. Kirkby, P. O'Keefe, and L. Timberlake (eds.), *The Earthscan Reader in Sustainable Development* (London: Earthscan, 1995), 310 ff.

[38] The World Commission on Environment and Development (WCED), *Our Common Future* (Oxford: Oxford University Press, 1987).

[39] ibid. 23.

[40] ibid. 326–30.

[41] ibid. 27.3.

[42] ibid. 27.2.

[43] ibid. 327 and Agenda 21, n. 34 above, 27.3.

[44] Agenda 21, n. 34 above, 27.5, 6 and 8.

education and public awareness, science [*sic*] development and transfer of environmentally sound technology.[45]

While such developments would be laudable, the CSD's observation is premature, representing aspiration rather than reality, since no serious attempt has as yet been made to evaluate the impact of major group participation. The CSD at present seems to deem the opportunity for major groups (usually represented by NGOs) to participate in the debate on sustainable development sufficient in and of itself. The civil society groups themselves are however more likely to assess the usefulness of such participation on the basis of the impact which it has on the political endgame—and mere participation does not, of course, guarantee real influence in outcomes either in the political arena or the real world.

It is becoming increasingly important to address the barriers to effective public participation because the Agenda 21 approach to public participation seems to have set the scene for mainstreaming NGO involvement in international decision-making generally[46] and in particular in the realm of environmental law and policy.[47] The EU, for example, has increasingly drawn NGOs into the sphere of environmental law and policy not only in the context of Agenda 21[48] but also in more concrete areas.

However, even where NGO participation does occur in its optimum form, with real potential to influence decision-making procedures, it merely informs the process rather than necessarily exercising a decisive role and thus its legitimizing influence is curtailed. A cynical interpretation of the use made of public participation in this context might view it as providing a veneer of democracy that leaves the basic process unchanged. This chapter seeks to examine the effectiveness of the attempted transplantation of one element of democratic practice, public participation, to the international sphere in one concrete and reasonably well-developed area, environmental assessment in its varied forms.

IV. EA, SEA, and NGOs as Agents of Public Participation

Environmental assessment has arguably evolved beyond being a mere tool for assessing and addressing the environmental impacts of a wide variety of human activities to become a discipline in its own right encompassing a whole range of

[45] CSD Report on the Sixth Session, Economic and Social Council Official Records 1998, Supplement No. 9, 35, published on the Internet at: http://ods-dds-ny.un.org/doc/UNDOC/GEN/N98/166/67/PDF/N9816667.pdf.

[46] Commission on Global Governance, *Our Global Neighbourhood* (Oxford: Oxford University Press, 1995).

[47] Yamin, n. 17 above, 151.

[48] See, for example, the Commission's 1997 report, *Agenda 21—the First Five Years—Implementation of Agenda 21*, published on the Internet at: http://europa.eu.int/comm/environment/agenda21/implem.htm.

specific instruments. While geared initially to evaluating projects (project EA[49]) it is increasing and extending its reach back through the decision-making matrix to encompass programmes, plans, and even, most controversially, policies[50] (SEA). Latterly the development of EA has been aided in no small part by the fact that the versatility of the basic concepts that underpin it enabled it to be brought under the mantle of sustainable development. While sustainable development may be supposed to function as the rationale for the development of environmental law and policy and more in the twenty-first century, it suffers from a general weakness in its inherent vagueness. EA thus proved useful in providing a rare concrete focus for actualizing a sustainability-based approach to decision-making[51] and provided advantages in having at least a degree of established credibility in legal, policy, and especially practical terms. Sustainable development rhetoric provided a spur for further development of the EA process and the resulting symbiosis appears to be proving effective in progressing both agendas.

EA has a number of key strengths as a tool for progressing sustainable development[52] acting as a multi-output process by aiming ultimately to generate a more environmentally sustainable substantive decision. The fact that EA arrives at this point by encouraging wide participation (including public participation) in the decision-making process is highly significant as this course serves important governance goals in its own right. Ideally an EA serves a primarily deliberative purpose but at the same time it plays an educative role for all concerned.[53] At its best it can perform a number of educative tasks, serving to: 'advance understanding of the nature of social or environmental impacts and the acceptability of proposed mitigatory measures, as well as improve decision making, reduce conflicts or delays, and increase local co-operation between proponents and stakeholders in the implementation of the project'.[54]

The mutually educative view of EA, while interesting, needs to be approached with a degree of caution as its Habermas-inspired approach[55] assumes an equality of status among participants that is very arguable indeed in the EA context. If viewed instead from the point of view of equality of opportunity to participate, it

[49] The term Environmental Assessment is employed throughout in preference to the more cumbersome Environmental Impact Assessment (EIA).

[50] Policies pose the greatest challenge to SEA because they involve the broadest range of possible alternatives for examination and because they are ultimately political. Exposing them to scrutiny without unduly impinging upon the policy-makers' remit may prove problematic.

[51] C. George, 'Incorporating Sustainable Development into EIA' in *Sustainability and EIA/SEA* (1999), 18 EIA Newsletter, EIA Centre University of Manchester, published on the Internet at: http://www.art.man.ac.uk/EIA/nl18.geor.htm.

[52] See H. Wilkins, 'The Need for Subjectivity in EIA—Discourse as a Tool for Sustainable Development' (2003) 23 *Environmental Impact Assessment Review*, 401–14.

[53] ibid. 408.

[54] P. Francis, 'Stakeholder Involvement in EIA and SEA—World Bank Experience' (1999) 18 *EIA Newsletter*, EIA Centre University of Manchester, published on the Internet at: http://www.art.man.ac.uk/EIA/nl18wbk.htm.

[55] Discussed by Fischer, n. 9 above, 158.

may however provide a viable lens through which to view and evaluate the process.

Regardless of inequalities of participation, it is important to acknowledge that EA is necessarily as much a political as a legal or administrative process, a fact that is particularly clear where very controversial or environmentally sensitive matters are at stake, as is very often the case.[56] It is in this context that the democratic function of the EA process is most pronounced, as it employs public participation to import public values and preferences into the decision-making process. This in turn serves both to encourage citizen engagement with the issues and to promote increased public confidence in the procedure. Public participation plays a further role in EA in that it also influences the functioning and longevity of projects once executed as a result of its multi-faceted character.

Probably the ultimate benefit of public participation in the EA process though lies in the public profile and pressure that it generates which serve to ensure that environmental issues are highly visible in the ultimately political decision-making process. At the very least it can serve to open the political process up to a wider range of interests than just those of the proponents of an activity and the decision-maker dealing with it. In so doing, it locates the decision firmly in the public law sphere, preventing the unwelcome transmutation of a public law-based permitting process into something more akin to a private transaction that can result from closed or even just opaque decision-making processes. Such an approach serves to heighten the profile of environmental considerations and ensure that they are examined from a public interest perspective.

Nonetheless, it must be kept in mind that even where it operates at its optimum level, and employs public participation to full advantage, there are limits on what EA can deliver. Indeed, it could be said that ultimately EA serves to promote better decision-making, rather than to secure a better environment. In practice, though, EA can be hamstrung as a tool for both decision-making and public participation by legalistic demands for totally exhaustive information, demands which do not sit well with the needs of the real world, including decision-makers and the public. In real terms an overly legalistic approach to EA arguably converts it from a highly focused decision-making tool into a rather blunt instrument that cannot be employed to best effect. This tends to mean that the process tends to concentrate on minutiae rather than on matters of principle. The end result is often that the real issues are buried in such a mass of technical material that they can be very inaccessible in practice.[57]

More fundamentally EA is ultimately geared not to producing consensus or agreement among the public but rather to generating understanding of the issues.[58]

[56] Wilkins, n. 52 above, 404.

[57] C.C. Alton and P.B. Underwood, 'Let us make Impact Assessment more Accessible' (2003) 23 *Environmental Impact Assessment Review*, 141–53.

[58] ibid. 146.

For all of its obvious aspirational importance[59] and ubiquity, public participation provision is not a guarantee of successful engagement. Giving the public the opportunity to participate does not ensure that it will actually be taken up, as the public does not always realize the significance of involvement in time to take full advantage of the occasion.[60]

The identification of the relevant 'public' in the context of EA or SEA purpose will have a significant influence on the conduct and outcomes of the participation process.[61] As part of the function of EA is to legitimize processes and outcomes, it is important that identification of the public for the purposes of participation is objectively justifiable. This is required in order to prevent accusations by those who will inevitably be aggrieved whatever outcome is generated that the process has been 'massaged' in order to support a pre-determined course of action. This type of outcome cannot however be avoided simply by the provision of formal opportunities to participate in the decision-making process. That participation must be seen to be given due weight and not simply discounted in favour of scientific or technical submissions.[62] If the products of public participation are ignored and the process is merely employed by decision-makers in a formal fashion, the public will quickly (and rightly) become disillusioned and unwilling to engage in future EA exercises.

It rapidly became clear in both North American and European practice that project-based assessment often occurred too late in the decision-making process to do more than add a green gloss to the outcome and that a more pre-emptive approach was required. SEA is in many ways the logical corollary of project-based EA, though it is less than clear thus far, the concept being in its infancy, to what extent it can be extrapolated from EA. It has been defined in numerous ways,[63] a useful and fairly comprehensive definition being:

> ...an integrated, structured decision aid process, aiming to assess the environmental effects of strategic proposals (e.g., policies, plans and programmes) and their options, and to recommend possible measures to reduce negative effects or enhance positive ones. This process should include a written report and public involvement. Relevant and accountable authorities should use the conclusions of this process in their decision-making process.[64]

While there is broad agreement in principle that environmental impacts must be addressed on a strategic basis and not just project level, how this is actually to be achieved is a rather more contentious issue. SEA does however share the environ-

[59] S. Marks, *The Riddle of All Constitutions—International Law, Democracy and the Critique of Ideology* (Oxford: Oxford University Press, 2000), discussed in H. Cullen and K. Morrow, n. 23 above.

[60] Stookes and Razzaque, n. 14 above, 791.

[61] Wolfe *et al.*, n. 12 above, 441.

[62] ibid. 443.

[63] See N. Risse, M. Crowley, P. Vincke, and J. Waaub, 'Implementing the European SEA Directive—the Member States' Margin of Discretion' (2003) 23 *Environmental Impact Assessment Review*, 454–5.

[64] ibid.

mental focus of project-based EA and thus espouses similar core values and this arguably should provide us with a starting point (though only a starting point) from which to pursue its development. SEA is more versatile than EA, being, by its flexible nature,[65] an approach that lends itself to application across a wide variety of disciplines. In its inherent flexibility however lies one of its problems—it is considerably more difficult to pin down and actualize[66] than its project-based counterpart, which is by its very nature tied to very specific application. Thus while SEA is popularly regarded as a good idea in principle, rendering it workable in practice is fraught with difficulty. There is at least general consensus on the goal to be pursued: 'A precondition for the success of . . . SEA appears to be a capability to structure decision processes and to force decision makers to take environmental issues into account in a publicly accountable fashion'.[67]

When this is successfully achieved the SEA of plans and programmes should mesh together in such a way as to allow them to become progressively more streamlined as they descend the decision-making hierarchy, ultimately rendering project-based EA more straightforward that heretofore. Effective SEA must therefore above all be systematic[68] and has procedural advantages in addition to its projected substantive outcome of ensuring proactive consideration of resulting in sustainable decisions.

It is clear that public participation has an important role to play in SEA, in much the same fashion as in EA, since here too the issues are not merely concerned with scientific or technical considerations but also societal ethics and values. It is also highly significant that SEA is, by its very nature, more open ended than project EA and thus a flexible and iterative approach will be required in order to get maximum returns from the ongoing assessment process.[69] This very flexibility can have disadvantages for public participation in making already complex procedures still more difficult to tailor to a given context.

Public participation is however particularly problematic where SEA is concerned because the issues raised may appear to be too abstract to motivate substantial public engagement.[70] The need for involvement may only become fully apparent to affected communities at the project EA stage, by which stage the decision-making context will already have been set. This is one area where NGO involvement may prove decisive, as NGOs are better equipped to function at the relative level of abstraction required to engage with the issues at SEA level.[71]

[65] See M.R. Partidario, 'Elements of an [*sic*] SEA Framework—Improving the Added-value of SEA' (2000) *Environmental Impact Assessment Review*, 647–63.

[66] Fischer, n. 9 above, 159 ff.

[67] ibid. 161.

[68] ibid. 163.

[69] Wolfe *et al.*, n. 12 above, 439.

[70] Sharp, n. 37 above, emphasizes the central importance of personal interest in a decision as the motivation for the public to engage in decision-making processes, 311.

[71] B. Sheate, 'NGO Participation in EIA' (1996) 12 *EIA Newsletter*, EIA Centre University of Manchester, published on the Internet at: http://www.art.man.ac.uk/EIA/nl12ngo.htm.

Problems also arise because of the scale of the decision-making processes in question: 'The more intractable problem is that of scaling up. Above small group or community level, systems of representative democracy have to reconcile many complex and conflicting pressures'.[72]

It is here that NGOs can potentially provide not a manifestation of participative democracy, which becomes an artificial construct when it is extracted from its local setting, but instead an additional facet to representative democracy, specifically in promoting interests that are under-represented in its traditional form. In common with EA, however, SEA, even at its most successful, cannot always achieve a consensus that is acceptable to all. While the process may potentially encourage debate and provide the opportunity for a broader range of inputs into the decision-making process than has previously been available, it will not serve to insulate decision-makers from having to make hard (and of course unpopular) decisions.

V. Transboundary EA and SEA

The idea that states are prohibited from causing harm to the environmental interests of other states through the pursuit of their own ends has a long (if somewhat dubious[73]) pedigree in international environmental law, both in customary and more concrete form in Principle 21 of the Stockholm Declaration (reiterated in Principle 2 of the Rio Declaration[74]). On the other hand, and more in tune with state practice, transnational environmental assessment can be viewed as having its roots in the alternative interpretation of Principle 21 as imposing an obligation to employ due diligence to prevent significant transboundary harm to other states.[75] In any event, it has long been clear that activities that generate potential transboundary impacts are obvious candidates for environmental assessment procedures, a point emphasized by the endorsement of EA in Principle 17 of the Rio Declaration.[76] This was recognized, in outline at least, early in the development of the law in the European context in Directive 85/337/EEC on the Assessment of the Effects of certain Public and Private Projects on the

[72] See Sharp, n. 37 above, 326.

[73] J.H. Knox, 'The Myth and Reality of Transboundary Environmental Impact Assessment' (2002) 96 *American Journal of International Law*, 291–319.

[74] 'States have, in accordance with the Charter of the United Nations and the principles of international law, the sovereign right to exploit their own resources pursuant to their own environmental and developmental policies, and the responsibility to ensure that activities within their jurisdiction or control do not cause damage to the environment of other states or of areas beyond the limits of national jurisdiction.'

[75] ibid. 294.

[76] 'Environmental impact assessment, as a national instrument, shall be undertaken for proposed activities that are likely to have a significant adverse impact on the environment and are subject to a decision of a competent national authority.'

Environment (EIA Directive).[77] Article 7 of that Directive, which concerned itself primarily with domestic EA, created a rudimentary concept, transboundary environmental impact assessment (TEA), applicable at project level within the Community. Article 8 envisaged 'consultations' between states with regard to transboundary impacts producing information that would have to be considered in the decision-making process, though no indication was given as to the weight to be accorded to such information. The provisions relating to TEA in the EIA Directive were vague in themselves and were effectively nullified by the failure of the Directive to impose a transboundary element on EAs. These rather tentative provisions were soon superseded by the more comprehensive approach to transboundary EA in the Espoo Convention. The EU returned to the TEA issue in Directive 97/11/EC amending Directive 85/337/EEC on the Assessment of the Effects of certain Public and Private Projects on the Environment (EIA Directive)[78] and the SEA Directive,[79] discussed below.

Although imperfect in many ways, early domestic initiatives on TEA arguably provided a template for the development of concrete international environmental assessment regimes, such as those under the Espoo Convention, arguably proving more influential in this regard than abstract principles of law.[80] The most convincing explanation of both the ubiquity of EA and its spread to the transnational sphere is found in viewing it as the product of a complex intermixing of domestic and international social mores, political values and science, combining to provide the basis for legal initiatives. Ultimately, regardless of its source, the import of TEA is that it is no longer morally acceptable to cause environmental damage to other states in an unthinking and unjustified manner and that law can serve to ensure that environmental consequences are properly evaluated as part of decision-making processes at this level.

While international law has historically been regarded as the province of states and statecraft, the changing global order increasingly sees international law impacting not only on states but also on a range of non-state actors including NGOs and even individuals. As international environmental law increasingly imposes obligations on non-state actors,[81] the logical corollary has been the burgeoning developments of rights and other broader entitlements in this context. One area that has seen swift and radical development is that of public participation in TEA. Transboundary environmental assessments present special challenges for public participation arrangements, not least in coordinating pro-

[77] [1985] OJ L175/40.

[78] [1997] OJ 73/5.

[79] Dir. 2001/42/EC on the Assessment of the Effects of certain Plans and Programmes on the Environment [2001] OJ L197/30.

[80] Knox, n. 73 above, 296–301.

[81] J. Ebbesson, 'Innovative Elements and Expected Effectiveness of the 1991 EIA Convention' (1999) 19 *Environmental Impact Assessment Review*, 47–55.

cedures between often significantly different national systems.[82] Where two or more states are involved this can raise real practical difficulties and there is a danger that, in situations such as those under the Espoo Convention where the law provides for shared responsibility between parties for public participation, 'it may cause an attitude where "everybody has, and nobody takes" responsibility'.[83] Such problems are not necessarily insurmountable with careful forethought, for example by creating administrative 'maps' laying out basic institutional arrangements and procedures in a transparent and accessible way.[84]

Even where procedures do mesh well, this does not guarantee that TEA will successfully engage the public as this is not simply determined by procedural arrangements but also by cultural factors. States affected by transboundary problems can exhibit quite profound differences in their ethos of public participation; the public in former Soviet states for example often lack both the capacity and experience to engage with decision-making processes exhibited by their Scandinavian neighbours.[85]

Although it has become increasingly apparent in recent times that the activities of one state can impact on the interests of others and that environmental assessment can contribute to the prevention (or at least the reduction) of transboundary problems arising in this regard, the issue remains a highly charged one and tackling it is extremely problematic. This is particularly the case in respect of TSEA, which must inevitably address what are at root sovereignty conflicts if it is to have any practical impact. While TEA can itself raises such issues in respect of controversial projects, TSEA does so in an even more acute form, directing its attention at the freedom of states to develop plans and programmes applicable in their own jurisdictions. It may prove in the end that the notion of state sovereignty in its purest form cannot be reconciled with the realities of environmental constraints imposed by finite resources and pollution problems and that the doctrine may ultimately become attenuated because of this. For the present, however, sovereignty remains the dominant (if not the only) fact of the international legal system and TSEA, like other strategies for addressing environmental problems, must develop and function as best it can in the current legal and political milieu.

[82] Even systems that, given fairly similar legal cultures, would appear to present the prospect of fairly smooth cooperation mechanisms, such as the Scandinavian countries, can experience problems in practice where transboundary impacts are concerned. See A. Tesli and S.R. Husby, 'EIA in a Transboundary Context: Principles and Challenges for a Co-ordinated Nordic Application of the Espoo Convention' (1999) 19 *Environmental Impact Assessment Review*, 57–84.

[83] ibid. 81.

[84] T. Bunge, 'Transboundary Impacts and EIA—A German-Polish Research Project' (1997) 14 *EIA Newsletter*, EIA Centre University of Manchester, published on the Internet at: http://www.art.man.ac.uk/EIA/nl14gerp.htm.

[85] M. Hilden, 'Transboundary Impacts and EIA—Assessing Transboundary Impacts between Finland and Russia' (1997) 14 *EIA Newsletter*, EIA Centre University of Manchester, published on the Internet at: http://www.art.man.ac.uk/EIA/nl14inr.htm.

It is under the auspices of the UN/ECE Human Environment and Settlements Division through its Environment for Europe (EfE) process[86] that TSEA has been most seriously addressed to date. TSEA has been embraced in this context, not only for its own sake, but also as a tool to promote regional cohesion in the wake of the Cold War and as a precursor to the enlargement of the EU.[87] The first Ministerial Conference held as part of the Environment for Europe (EfE) process took place in Dobris in 1991. Its objective was to examine methods of cooperation to protect and improve the environment, culminating in developing an environmental programme for Europe in the longer term. To this end the conference agreed a number of outcomes including a set of basic (if rather general) guidelines for cooperation in the environmental sphere and initiated, as a cooperative endeavour between the UN/ECE and the European Commission, the first pan-European state of the Environment Report, *Europe's Environment—The Dobris Assessment*, which was eventually published in 1995.[88] This report, in providing a base-line survey of the state of Europe's environment, provided the necessary foundation for future action.

The Dobris meeting therefore represented the start of a continuing process but it was only at the second EfE Conference that the themes underpinning the topic of this chapter began to emerge as central concerns. Among the outcomes of the Second Ministerial Conference at Lucerne in 1993 was agreement on the ECE report on Elements for a Long-term Environmental Programme for Europe. This identified seven key elements as policy tools for achieving high shared environmental standards: these included environmental information and public participation. The meeting also endorsed the ECE Report on International Legal Instruments,[89] which demanded more effective implementation, monitoring, and compliance with international environmental law.

The process continued apace and the Third Ministerial Conference at Sofia in 1995 resulted in a Ministerial Declaration[90] based on the Lucerne principles, which included a reaffirmation of the importance of public participation. The meeting also endorsed the Environment for Europe Programme[91] containing recommendations for more concrete activities, including the development of a regional Convention on Public Participation. Interestingly, this process was to be moved forward with 'appropriate involvement of NGOs'.

[86] This section draws on the UN/ECE document Environment for Europe, published on the Internet at: http://www.unece.org/env/wgso/fromdobtokyiv.htm.

[87] Declaration by the Ministers of Environment of the Region of the United Nations Economic Commission for Europe, Fifth Ministerial Conference, Environment for Europe, Kiev, 21–3 May 2003, published on the Internet at: http://www.unece.org/env/documents/2003/ece/cep/ece.cep.94.rev.1.e.pdf para. 3–4.

[88] Published on the Internet at: http://reports.eea.eu.int/92-826-5409-5/en/.

[89] 2 Apr. 1993.

[90] 25 Oct. 1995.

[91] Published on the Internet at: http://www.unece.org/env/europe/epe.htm.

This was partly brought to fruition at the Fourth EfE Ministerial Conference, held in Aarhus in 1998, by the agreement of the UN/ECE Convention on Access to Information, Public Participation in Decision-making and Access to Justice in Environmental Matters[92] (Aarhus Convention). The Convention was adopted in part pursuant to pressure from NGOs and was partially shaped by their perspective and demands.[93] The fact that the Aarhus model did not simply pay lip service to broadening the base of environmental action in Europe is demonstrated by the fact that the Conference featured a parallel but independent NGO session entitled 'Strengthening Participatory Democracy for Sustainable Development'. The potentially profound significance of the Aarhus Convention should not be underplayed. It has, for example, been described by Kofi Annan, the Secretary-General of the UN, as: 'the most ambitious example of "environmental democracy" so far undertaken under the auspices of the United Nations'.[94]

The Fifth EfE Ministerial Conference in Kiev was originally to be held in 2002 but was held back until 2003 because of regional preparations for the World Summit on Sustainable Development. When it was eventually held it resulted in the Protocol to the Espoo Convention on Strategic Environmental Assessment.[95]

VI. The Aarhus Convention and EA

The Aarhus Convention came into force on 30 October 2001 and provides the second plank in the raft of mutually reinforcing measures pertaining to public participation in environmental decision-making heralded by the EfE process. Although chronologically subsequent to the Espoo Convention, the Aarhus Convention, by providing for the three basic pillars of access to information, public participation, and access to justice in the sphere of the environment, can logically be viewed as the necessary procedural foundation or at least as an enabling provision for subsequent concrete developments. The UN/ECE describes the Aarhus Convention as 'a new kind of environmental agreement'[96] and it certainly strives towards a number of ends that chime with modern environmental thought, linking the environment and human rights; acknowledging the interests of future generations; giving effect to a stakeholder-based approach to sustainable development; considering the nature of interactions between the public and public authorities in a democratic context; and last, but by no

92 24 June 1998.

93 Bodansky, n. 2 above, 618.

94 UN/ECE, 'Introducing the Aarhus Convention', published on the Internet at: http://www.unece.org/env/pp/welcome.html.

95 Published on the Internet at: http://www.unece.org/env/eia/sea_protocol.htm.

96 UN/ECE, 'Introducing the Aarhus Convention', published on the Internet at: http://www.unece.org/env/pp/welcome.html.

means least putting public participation to use in linking the public to international agreements. These themes and values have set the scene for the legal development of EA and SEA, in both domestic and transboundary contexts in the UN/ECE area.

As far as SEA is concerned, the most important provision of this Convention is Article 7, which provides for public participation in plans, programmes, and policies relating to the environment. Article 7 requires: 'appropriate practical... provisions for the public to participate during the preparation of plans and programmes relating to the environment, within a transparent and fair framework, having provided the necessary information to the public'.

While public participation is required in respect of plans and programmes, in the Aarhus Convention policies are not subjected to the same degree of control and signatories are merely exhorted by Article 7 to 'endeavour' to provide opportunities for public participation 'to the extent appropriate'. Where public participation does take place signatories are required to take 'due account' of the input that it produces.

If the public is denied its right to participate in the making of environmental plans and policies, in contradistinction to the situation applicable to projects under Article 6, there is no right under the Aarhus Convention to pursue the matter in the courts—under Article 9(2) the State party has discretion in this matter. This would seem to indicate a lower level of importance being accorded to public participation in strategic contexts than in project-based decision-making processes. The approach may be based on the idea that the public has less at stake in the former context than the latter. It is of course the case that, should the plan or programme eventually manifest itself in project form and the public is still denied an opportunity to participate effectively, it can take legal action at this point as of right. This state of affairs however potentially allows the public to be effectively denied the many advantages of early effective participation in the decision-making process.

While the Aarhus Convention more generally is a significant development both in principle and in practice, it is not without its flaws, and given its important role in supporting other developments in public participation in international environmental law, these may prove to be very significant indeed. While the Convention adopts generous definitions of the terms 'environment' and 'information', it is unfortunately rather less-well drafted when it comes to defining the term 'public' in Article 2, a highly significant matter given its central importance to the Convention. It appears not to be used in the sense that, given its context, might be expected (that is, of the 'public sphere') but rather it is taken to refer to the 'sum total of all society's potential actors'.[97] The term is broken

[97] V. Rodenhoff, 'The Aarhus Convention and its Implications for the "Institutions" of the European Community' (2002) 11 *Review of European Community and International Environmental Law*, 343–57, 344.

down into 'the public', defined in Article 2(4) as: 'one or more natural or legal persons, and in accordance with national legislation or practice, their associations, organizations or groups', and the 'public concerned', defined in Article 2(5) as: 'the public affected or likely to be affected by, or having an interest in, the environmental decision-making; for the purposes of this definition non-governmental organizations promoting environmental protection under national law shall be deemed to have an interest'.

It is significant that both aspects of the definition of 'public' attach importance to explicitly including environmental NGOs firmly within their scope. The central role envisaged for them is further enhanced by the provision in Article 3 encouraging state support for such groups. Taken together with the non-discrimination principle contained in Article 3(9), this seems to ensure a basically workable definition of the term 'public' as it applies to the UN/ECE region. One important caveat lies in the general cast of the Convention which, while it is on the one hand about empowering the public, on the other it keeps it firmly in its place by allowing states to act as 'gatekeepers' controlling access to Convention rights. Having said this, the right to public participation contained in the Aarhus Convention, although flawed in some respects, remains one of the best developed in international environmental law.

VII. The Espoo Convention and TEA

The Espoo Convention was signed on 26 February 1991 at Espoo and entered into force on 10 September 1997. While binding on its signatories as to outcome, the Convention does not require explicit incorporation into the law of signatory states. The Convention does however require the environmental assessment of proposed listed projects[98] that are likely to cause 'significant transboundary impacts'. Although the Espoo Convention has been enthusiastically embraced in principle, it has thus far been little applied in practice,[99] a matter often raised by NGOs.[100] Nonetheless it recognizes the importance of ensuring that the whole spatial impact of projects is addressed and puts in place a regime that addresses this issue in the potentially problematic situations that arise where such impacts cross national borders.[101]

In essence, the Convention creates a formal vertical model of information exchange, with obligations imposed on signatories, though it uses this model to

[98] Appendix I.

[99] M. Hilden and E. R. Furman, 'Assessment Across Borders—Stumbling Blocks and Options in the Practical Implementation of the Espoo Convention' (2001) 21 *Environmental Impact Assessment Review*, 537–51. This chapter is based on UN/ECE research into the application of the Espoo Convention in the two years after it entered into force.

[100] ibid. 542.

[101] UN/ECE, *Guidance on the Practical Application of the Espoo Convention*, published on the Internet at: http://www.unece.org/env/eia/guidance.html, Introduction, 3 ff.

introduce pronounced supplemental elements of a horizontal model, engaging the public in the TEA process.[102] It owes much of its approach and even elements of its wording to the EIA Directive,[103] expanding EA as practised under the Directive more convincingly and broadly in a transboundary context.[104] Having said this, the Espoo Convention also draws on other elements of international law, policy, and ideology, in particular relating to sustainable development, to give it shape.

One of the most significant achievements of the Espoo Convention is to provide a practical application of Principle 10 of the Rio Declaration by making public participation in TEA one of its key concerns. The term 'public' was originally defined by Article 1(x) of the Convention as meaning 'one or more natural or legal persons'. This definition was subsequently amended to include the clause 'and, in accordance with national legislation or practice, their associations, organizations or groups' in order to comply with the Aarhus Convention approach. The increasing infiltration of an NGO-friendly approach into international environmental law generally is indicated by this amendment. The practical reasons for invoking public participation in TEA was articulated in Decision II/3 of the Second Meeting of Parties to the EIA Convention as helping to:

(a) Improve relations between peoples and countries, and prevent transboundary environmental conflicts;
(b) Develop civil society and democracy in the countries of the ECE region;
(c) Promote the timely disclosure of relevant information to participants in the environmental decision-making process;
(d) Making people understand and respect the final decisions on projects; and
(e) Give an insight into environmental protection and long-term environmental problems.[105]

In this respect, the Espoo Convention outstrips earlier instruments by not only permitting public participation in this context but by actually requiring it as an integral part of the assessment process. In Article 2(6), the Convention espouses a number of key values, including the equality or non-discrimination principle, that serve to ensure that all affected publics, regardless of their state location, will be provided with equal opportunities to participate in the assessment process. In practical terms, this requires states to adopt a consistent, coherent, and coordinated approach to identifying issues to which the Convention applies, routes for information exchange, and public participation mechanisms. Article 3(8) provides:

[102] Tesli and Husby, n. 82 above, 75–6.

[103] See R.G. Connelly, 'The UN Convention on EIA in a Transboundary Context—A Historical Perspective' (1999) 19 *Environmental Impact Assessment Review*, 37–46, for a brief account of the development of TEA.

[104] Ebbesson, n. 81 above, 50.

[105] Published on the Internet at: http://www.unece.org/env/eia/publicpart.html.

The concerned Parties shall ensure that the public of the affected Party in the areas likely to be affected be informed of, and provided with possibilities for making comments or objections on, the proposed activity, and for transmittal of these comments or objections to the competent authority of the Party of origin, either directly to this authority or, where appropriate, through the Party of origin.

Under Article 6(1) the comments generated by the consultation exercise must be taken into account in arriving at a decision on a given project, but as with any other environmental assessment process, the information generated by an EA is only part of the material upon which a determination is arrived at and it is not necessarily decisive.

The teething troubles that have emerged under the Espoo regime include several that are centred on public participation; not least the significant differentials that are becoming apparent between signatory state practices and even more fundamentally in their 'philosophies' of environmental assessment.[106] The core of the problem lies in the fact that: 'public participation is not a universal concept that would be understood in the same way among all Parties'.[107]

Thus far the term 'public' in the Convention has been interpreted by signatories in a range of ways, varying from the literal, to the positively obtuse (whereby it is deemed to encapsulate only public authorities and specialist groups).[108] Perhaps if public participation is the coming concept in international environmental law, experience under the Espoo Convention will help to render its meaning less opaque. Even when the public has been defined for TEA purposes, engaging with the assessment process is fraught with difficulties generated not only by dissimilar legal provisions applying among signatory states but also by widely differing administrative arrangements, which can cause confusion in their own right. Further problems are encountered in the translation[109] of information that is generally necessary in a TEA context, though this problem could be remedied by introducing an obligation similar to that under the Convention on the Control of Transboundary Movement of Hazardous Wastes and their Disposal,[110] requiring responsible states to ensure that documentation is transmitted to affected states in a language appropriate to their needs.

Evidence suggests that the reasons behind the lack of application of the Espoo Convention in practice have a great deal to do with its content, which while undeniably detailed for international environmental law, is still rather inchoate by the standards of domestic law. The use of more concrete bilateral[111] or multilateral agreements, building upon the Convention but fleshing it out, is one way

[106] Hilden and Furman, n. 99 above, 544.

[107] ibid. 545.

[108] ibid.

[109] ibid. 546.

[110] Basel, 22 Mar. 1989 (1989) 28 *International Legal Materials*, 649.

[111] As advised by the 1999 Helsinki Workshop on the Practical Application of the Espoo Convention, quoted in Hilden and Furman, n. 99 above, 542.

to remedy this. While measures such as the SEA Directive (discussed below) will go some way to breathing life into the Espoo regime, there is still ample space for such instruments to progress TEA. It is certainly true that experience under the Espoo Convention has done a great deal to bring the considerable complexities of TEA to light; addressing them however will surely prove challenging to say the least.

VIII. The Kiev Protocol on TSEA

The Protocol to the Espoo Convention on Strategic Environmental Assessment (hereafter the Kiev Protocol) was signed at Kiev on 21 May 2003. Article 2(7) of the Espoo Convention had introduced a rather weak requirement that parties 'endeavour' to apply its provisions to policies, plans, and programmes, but, as might have been expected with a provision of this nature, little progress was achieved.[112] Article 2(7) did however provide the impetus for establishing an ad hoc working group on SEA that ultimately drafted the Kiev Protocol in January 2003. The drive behind the process lay in the identification by the UN/ECE of the importance of early positioning of strategic environmental assessment in the decision-making hierarchy in making it a 'key tool for sustainable development'.[113]

The Protocol was negotiated through the combined efforts of the Espoo and Aarhus governing bodies, the health sector, and NGOs and bears many of the hallmarks that would be expected as a result.[114] The preamble to the Protocol shows that it is, in many ways, an organic development of the Espoo Convention, drawing on the thinking that informed provisions for public participation in the EA process and applying it to SEA. The UN/ECE takes the view that, in respect of public participation at least, the objectives of SEA are the same as those of EA, namely promoting legitimacy and efficiency. The Preamble also firmly places the Protocol in the milieu of broader environmental law, referring specifically to the Rio Declaration on Environment and Development, 1992[115] and Agenda 21, 1992. Other international law developments resulting from the Third Ministerial Conference on Environment and Health, 1999 and the Johannesburg Declaration on Sustainable Development[116] and the Plan of Implementation adopted at the World Summit on Sustainable Development,[117] 2002 are also

[112] UN/ECE, *Guidance on the Practical Application of the Espoo Convention*, published on the Internet at: http://www.unece.org/env/eia/guidance.html in 'Specific Issues' at 4–6.

[113] UN/ECE, 'The Protocol on Strategic Environmental Assessment', published on the Internet at: http://www.unece.org/env/eia/introprotocol.htm.

[114] Kiev Ministerial Declaration, n. 87 above, para. 34.

[115] Specifically Principles 4 and 10.

[116] Published on the Internet at: http://www.un.org.esa/sustdev/documents/Johannesburg%20-Declaration.doc.

[117] Published on the Internet at: http://www.johannesburgsummit.org/html/documents/summit _docs/ 2309_planfinal.htm.

cited as underpinning the Protocol. The SEA Protocol is designed to be more 'cross-sectoral'[118] than its EA counterpart, and makes repeated reference to human health goals.[119] However, it is also arguable that, by so doing, the Protocol becomes more overtly anthropocentric in its outlook than the Espoo Convention. This may prove a retrograde step for the 'environmental' nature of assessment in principle, though on the other hand it may be a pragmatic move in strengthening the weight given to EA in practice.

The substantive elements of the Kiev Protocol fall under a number of heads.[120] First, there are a number of general provisions, including those on: assisting and guiding the public[121] and providing recognition and assistance to relevant associations.[122] Article 2(8) of the Protocol adopts the by now familiar definition of public as: 'one or more natural or legal persons and, in accordance with national legislation or practice, their associations, organizations or groups'. Thus, by the time the Kiev Protocol was drafted, NGO participation was being mandated as a matter of course in the context of public participation as the values and approach enshrined in the Aarhus Convention now routinely made their impact felt.

Secondly, under Article 4 of the Protocol, SEA is put in place for plans and programmes that are 'likely to have significant environmental, including health, effects' (Article 4(1)). Mandatory SEA applies under Article 4(2) in respect of plans and programmes for:

> . . . agriculture, forestry, fisheries, energy, industry including mining, transport, regional development, waste management, water management, telecommunications, tourism, town and country planning or landuse and which set the framework for future development consent projects listed in annex I (17 substantive areas are covered) and any other project listed in annex II (90 substantive areas are covered) that requires an environmental impact assessment under national legislation.

Article 4(3) of the Protocol makes provision for further SEA at the discretion of the Parties, dependent on whether the Parties consider that there are likely to be significant environmental effects, under Article 5(1) and Annex III. The Protocol also provides detailed provisions on the different stages of SEA. Plans and programmes relating to national defence, civil emergencies, financial and budgetary issues are excluded from the remit of the Protocol by Article 4(5).

Article 5(2) makes it clear that state-designated environmental and health authorities[123] are to be consulted during the screening process to determine if

[118] Kiev Ministerial Declaration, n. 87 above, para. 34.

[119] See e.g. Preamble, Art. 1, and Art. 4.

[120] Drawing on the analysis in the Commission's proposal for a Council Decision on the signature, on behalf of the European Community, of the Protocol on Strategic Environmental Assessment to the 1991 UN/ECE Convention on Environmental Impact Assessment in a Transboundary Context COM(2003)221.

[121] Art. 3(2).

[122] Art. 3(3).

[123] Art. 9.

significant effects are likely. Parties' obligations in respect of public involvement at this stage (under Article 5(3)) are however limited to endeavouring to provide opportunities to participate to the 'extent appropriate'. The same situation prevails with respect to the scoping stage under Article 6. Thus it appears that, at the earliest stages of the SEA process, the role of public participation is elastic, to say the least, and will be determined primarily by the wishes of states.

It is only when a draft plan or programme and an environmental report (under Article 7 and annex IV) have been produced that international law provides concrete rights for the public to participate. Article 8 lays out the measures mandated by the public participation requirements of the Protocol. These include an obligation on each Party to identify the relevant public (expressly including relevant NGOs under Article 8(3), once again giving effect to the Aarhus approach) for the purposes of informing them and allowing them to express their opinions about the draft plan or programme (Article 8(4)). Once identified, the relevant public must be given 'early, timely and effective opportunities' to participate, that is, when all of the options are still open (Article 8(1)), by making draft plans and programmes and their environmental reports publicly available[124] (Article 8(2)). To this end the provisions of Article 8(5) and Annex V identify the necessary information to be made available, covering not only the plan or programme but also the authority responsible for it, the procedures to be followed, the time limits to be applied, sources and scope of relevant information, and who to direct comments to. Annex V paragraph 4 also specifically requires that the public be informed if a transboundary strategic environmental assessment is to take place. Article 11 of the Protocol requires that due account is to be taken of comments submitted under Article 8 as part of the decision-making information and the public is to be informed both of the outcome and of how their comments have been considered.

Where TSEA is concerned, Article 10(1) of the Protocol places the primary obligation on the Party of origin to notify the affected Party as soon as possible. Under the same provision, affected Parties also enjoy a right to request such notification. The affected Party may then choose to take part in the consultation process prior to the adoption of the plan or programme in question, though it is not obliged to do so.[125] This matter is entirely in the hands of the state and not subject to review under the Protocol, thus it is possible to envisage a situation where an affected public, unable to generate sufficient political momentum to motivate its own government to engage with the TSEA process, could lose the opportunity to participate.

Where the affected Party does wish a TSEA to take place, the parties are required to agree on detailed arrangements to ensure that the public concerned in the former is informed and given the opportunity to participate within a reasonable time (Article 10 (4)). It is likely that plans and programmes deemed

[124] This may be done by electronic or other 'appropriate means'.

[125] Art. 10(3).

ripe for TSEA will be major in scale and/or particularly complex and these factors, compounded by the difficulties in conducting a transboundary consultation, point to the need to build in generous time-frames.

The Kiev Protocol also makes limited provision for the SEA of policies and legislation—though here the obligation is limited to endeavouring to 'ensure that environmental, including health, concerns are considered and integrated to the extent appropriate' (Article 13). This obligation is rather weak but may be sufficient to put the issue on the legal map in the same way that initial coverage in the Espoo Convention sowed the seed for further development of SEA in the Kiev Protocol itself.

Despite their flaws, the Espoo Convention and the Kiev Protocol do contain some of the most detailed procedures on transboundary environmental harm yet to be developed in international environmental law,[126] at least in part due to their close relationship with domestic legal provisions. The comparatively well-developed role for public (and particularly NGO) participation that they create is based on a long-standing commitment to fostering the role of civil society in the evolution of environmental policy and its implementation[127] that is beginning to crystallize into a workable system of legal entitlements. Revolutionary though developments to date have been, there is still however a long way to go to ensure that public participation plays a part in the substance as well as the form of lawful and environmentally sound decision-making.

IX. European Community Law and Policy, Public Participation, and TSEA

Community environmental assessment law now enjoys a well-established pedigree beginning with Directive 85/337/EEC on the Assessment of the Effects of Certain Public and Private Projects on the Environment (the EIA Directive).[128] The latest legal development in this area is Directive 2001/42/EC on the Assessment of the Effects of Certain Plans and Programmes on the Environment (the SEA Directive).[129]

The Community has long acknowledged the value of public participation, in particular through the NGOs' contributions, in delivering substantive outcomes and in fostering dialogue, partnership, and shared responsibility. NGOs are also viewed as having democratic value in bringing workable public participation into shaping policy and law.[130] Community policy development has done much to

[126] Ebbesson, n. 81 above, 50.

[127] Kiev Ministerial Declaration, n. 87 above, para. 12.

[128] [1985] OJ L175/40. [129] [2001] OJ L197/30.

[130] See the European Commission's 1997 report, *Agenda 21—the First Five Years—Implementation of Agenda 21*, published on the Internet at: http://europa.eu.int/comm/environment/agenda21/implem.htm, 15 ff.

propel the development of the law in regard to public participation, for example by the inclusion of SEA as a recognized strategic approach to meeting environmental objectives in the Decision No. 1600/2002/EC Laying Down the Sixth Community Environment Action Plan.[131] In addition, a second strand of support is found in the Community Environment Action Programme 2001–2010[132] (hereafter 6EAP), which builds firmly on the foundations of previous initiatives, and in particular 5EAP 'Towards Sustainability', in its commitment to building public participation in environmental decision-making.[133] Thus included in the objectives of the 6EAP is a commitment to: 'extensive dialogue with stakeholders, raising environmental awareness and public participation'[134] in environmental policy-making. To this end a number of priority actions have been identified, including the development of good practices of governance promoting wide and frequent consultation, strengthening and supporting[135] the role of environmental NGOs, and informing the general public.[136] This commitment to widening participation also extends to commitments to encouraging collaboration and partnership with NGOs, through supplying information pursuant to the Aarhus Convention, ensuring that environmental information is accessible to citizens, raising environmental awareness, and 'developing general rules and principles of good governance in dialogue processes'.[137]

X. The SEA Directive

The SEA Directive forms part of a raft of law and policy, including Directive 97/11/EC amending Directive 85/337/EEC,[138] through to Directive 2003/35/EC Providing for Public Participation in Respect of the Drawing Up of Certain Plans and Programmes relating to the Environment and Amending with regard to Public Participation and Access to Justice Directives 85/337/EEC and 96/62/EC,[139] providing for public participation in respect of the drawing up of plans and programmes relating to the environment. The latter Directive amends the EIA Directive[140] and Directive 96/61 concerning Integrated Pollution Preven-

[131] [2002] OJ L242/1, Art. 3(3).

[132] COM(2001)11, in particular 61–2.

[133] See also Dec. 1600/2002/EC, n. 130 above.

[134] ibid., Art. 2(3) and 6EAP, 62.

[135] This explicitly includes financial support and has been put into effect in Dec. 466/2002/EC Laying Down a Community Action Programme Promoting Non-Governmental Organizations Primarily Active in the Field of Environmental Protection [2002] OJ L75/1.

[136] ibid., Art. 10.

[137] ibid., Art. 3(9).

[138] [1997] OJ L73/5, which included enhanced provision for transboundary consultation in environmental assessment pursuant to the Espoo Convention.

[139] [2003] OJ L156/17.

[140] [1985] OJ L175/40.

tion and Control (IPPC Directive)[141] in order to give effect to the EU's obligations with respect to public participation in SEA of plans and programmes under the Aarhus[142] and Espoo Conventions. The Preamble to the SEA Directive clearly indicates both its international law[143] and theoretical roots.[144]

The SEA Directive is admittedly procedural in nature[145] but it is geared towards achieving multiple goals not only in improving the scope (both in the decision-making hierarchy[146] and in geographical terms[147]) and consistency of environmental assessment but also in increasing its democratic credibility. Paragraph 15 of the Preamble to the Directive articulates the latter purpose thus:

> In order to contribute to more transparent decision making and with the aim of ensuring that the information supplied for the assessment is comprehensive and reliable, it is necessary to provide that authorities with relevant environmental responsibilities and the public are to be consulted during the assessment of plans and programmes, and that appropriate time frames are set, allowing sufficient time for consultations, including the expression of opinion.

Under the SEA Directive, SEA is mandatory only in respect of a comparatively narrow class of plans and programmes and their modification, as outlined in Article 3(2). These are prepared and/or adopted by national, regional, or local authorities or by authorities operating under legislative procedures and are required by legislative, regulatory, or administrative provisions.[148] Only plans and programmes in categories listed in Article 3 are covered and then only where they are 'likely to have significant effects'.[149] Member States are empowered by Article 3(5) to determine on a case-by-case basis what amounts to a 'significant effect' subject to the guidance provided by Annex II to the Directive. The criteria contained in Annex II relate to the characteristics of the plans and programmes in question, their potential effects, and the area that may be affected and explicitly include transboundary effects. Thus SEA involves an explicit screening process based on matters of scale and seriousness of potential impacts. The areas covered comprise: agriculture, forestry, fisheries, energy, industry, transport, waste management, water management, telecommunications, town and country planning or land use (where they set the framework for project consents under the EIA Directive or are likely to affect Natura 2000 sites under Directive 92/43/EEC on the Conservation of Natural Habitats and of Wild Fauna and Flora (Habitats Directive)).[150] Beyond this core area, SEA lies at the discretion of Member States

141 [1996] OJ L257/26.
142 In particular Art. 7.
143 At paras. 3 and 7.
144 At paras. 4, and 5 in particular.
145 Preamble, para. 9.
146 Preamble, para. 5.
147 Preamble, para. 16.
148 Art. 2.
149 Art. 3(1). Art. 3(3) specifically provides that for small-scale or local plans and programmes EA is required only where they will generate significant effects.
150 [1992] OJ L206/7.

who may employ it more broadly under Article 3(4). Even where SEA does take place it is, of course, not, as with other EA processes, decisive in the decision-making process, but rather only one element of many for consideration.

Somewhat confusingly, the SEA Directive was not used to introduce a single universally applicable SEA system throughout the EU; other procedures exist and there are significant exceptions in place. Other SEA-type obligations continue to apply in Community law under Directive 79/409 on the Conservation of Wild Birds (Birds Directive),[151] the Habitats Directive, and Directive 2000/60/EC Establishing a Framework for Community Action in the Field of Water Policy (Water Framework Directive),[152] and coordination is therefore required between these regimes[153] and the SEA Directive. Arguably, consistency and public participation goals would have been better served by simply employing SEA in the form prescribed by the SEA Directive wherever appropriate. On the other hand, it is debatable, given the nature of SEA, whether a single 'one size fits all' model is workable or if an approach tailored to specific needs would be more viable. In the context of the SEA Directive, however, it would appear that there is an insufficient degree of difference between mainstream SEA and SEA-type assessments under the wild birds and water regimes to justify such differentiation.

Other exceptions to the SEA regime are also highly significant, covering plans and programmes relating to national defence or civil emergencies, budgets (which mirror the approach adopted in international law), and the controversial last minute addition[154] of the current tranche of structural funds[155] and the European Agricultural Guidance and Guarantee Fund.[156] While the exclusion of national defence and emergency issues from SEA coverage reflects the approach taken in other areas of environmental law, the broad exception for Community funding mechanisms is more questionable. Arguably, the Community's failure to apply SEA in the latter areas reflects poorly on the EU's acceptance of the obligations imposed by the Espoo Convention and the Kiev Protocol when its own activities rather than those of its Member States are concerned.

The exceptions adopted indicate a fairly minimalist approach to SEA in many respects, ostensibly prompted by fears of 'over-administration'.[157] This general reluctance to wholeheartedly embrace SEA is evident in respect of public partici-

[151] [1979] OJ L103/1.

[152] [2000] OJ L327/1.

[153] Preamble, para. 19.

[154] These exceptions were added to the Directive late in the negotiating process, against the will of the Commission, which cogently argued that they were harmful to the whole rationale of an integrated approach to SEA.

[155] Reg. (EC) No. 1260/1999 Laying Down General Provisions on the Structural Funds [1999] OJ L161/1.

[156] Reg. (EC) No. 1257/1999 on Support for Rural Development from the EAGGF and Amending and Repealing Certain Regulations [1999] OJ L160/80.

[157] L. Feldmann, M. Vanderhaegen, and C. Pirotte, 'The EU's SEA Directive—Status and Links to Integration and Sustainable Development' (2001) 21 *Environmental Impact Assessment Review*, 207.

pation, where the wording of the SEA Directive shadows the text of the Aarhus Convention, even where the latter is vague, and bears the hallmarks inevitably forged by compromise in international law instruments. During the law-making process following on the Aarhus Convention, the European Parliament attempted to flex its fledgling muscles under Article 251 of the EC Treaty to draw out and strengthen the impact of public participation in EA, but with little success.[158] Nonetheless, given the unusually (in an international law context) prescriptive requirements of the Aarhus and Espoo Conventions in relation to public participation, the SEA Directive still has a great deal to offer in this regard. Public participation forms a recurring theme, featuring prominently in Articles 6, 7, and 9 and also playing a significant role in Articles 3 and 8. The Directive, while setting out the basic parameters for participation, leaves the practicalities in the hands of Member States and therefore whether SEA is embraced on a deep or shallow level also remains in their control. 'Early and often' appear to be the watchwords for effective public participation in SEA embraced by the Directive. It needs to take place early enough in the decision-making process to be an effective consideration in deciding upon a course of action[159] and to be repeated throughout the process.

Where appropriate, transboundary SEA is covered by Article 7 of the Directive and the process is usually to be initiated through consultation with potentially affected Member States undertaken by the Member State developing the plan or programme in question. Thus the state-based obligations in respect of TSEA can, once again, be viewed as fitting into primary obligations placed on the initiating state and secondary entitlements resting on potentially affected states. In addition there is a default position whereby potentially affected Member States can request a TSEA if the initiating state fails to act.[160] There is however, once again, no obligation on potentially affected Member States to agree to a TSEA if they are not so inclined[161] and this creates the danger that affected publics may be left without an avenue to participate in the TSEA if their own government is not of the opinion that the potential environmental impacts generated will be sufficiently significant to take action. The central concern must be that local concerns may be forced to take a back seat in the context of broader interstate relations, ultimately frustrating the purpose of TSEA.

Where a TSEA is to be undertaken, the consultation arrangements put in place by Article 6 come into play and the Member States are required to identify the affected publics and arrange participation mechanisms, making special allowances for timetabling to accommodate the inevitably more complex processes of a

[158] See, for example, the Commission's Amended Proposal for a Directive Providing for Public Participation in Respect of the Drawing Up of Certain Plans and Programmes Relating to the Environment and Amending Directives 85/337 and 96/61 COM(2001)779.

[159] Art. 6(2).

[160] Art. 7(1).

[161] Art. 7(2).

TSEA. Where a TSEA is carried out, the information generated by the process is to be taken into account in the decision-making process in the same way as other elements of the assessment information[162] such as the environmental report under Article 5 and the fruits of domestic consultation under Article 6. Under Article 8 of the Directive, potentially affected Member States consulted under Article 7 are to be informed, in the same way as other participants in the TSEA, of the plan or programme adopted and supplied with a statement that accounts for how the EA information has been used, how environmental considerations have been integrated into it, and the reasons for choosing the plan or programme in question over alternatives considered. Further monitoring arrangements pursuant to Article 10 should be communicated to potentially affected Member States in the same way as to other participants in the assessment process. These measures are designed to ensure that, where it does occur, SEA is a weighty process that plays a significant role in the decision-making process and that its iterative nature is fully capitalized upon. Nevertheless, questions remain as to how the relevant 'public' is to be identified for a given SEA process, how its participative role is to be constituted, and how an appropriate form is to be determined. These issues raise matters of concern in any SEA, but even more so in the context of transboundary proceedings, and these issues must be resolved in order for the TSEA process to succeed in achieving the transparency, quality, and completeness required to give it legitimacy. The problem is that the TSEA provisions in fact provide only a very small role for the public and most of the participation entitlements in this area are mediated through the state. Arguably this approach represents, in substantive if not formal terms, a return to orthodoxy in international environmental law. It certainly falls short in spirit of the public participation ethos of the Aarhus and Espoo Conventions and the Kiev Protocol. These defects could in part be remedied by putting in place default mechanisms, allowing affected Member States' decisions not to engage with TSEA under Article 7 to be challenged by the public in their own states if they are dissatisfied. This approach would actually represent a shift in the locus of power in favour of the public and could reasonably have been expected in the context of a Community law regime that is not subject to the same limitations as general international law in terms of controlling state action.

The EU has not deemed it necessary to include SEA of policies and legislation under the SEA Directive. Given the weak nature of the obligation to endeavour to ensure that environmental implications are 'considered and integrated to the extent appropriate' applicable to this element of SEA in Article 13 of the Kiev Protocol, this inaction is unsurprising. The Commission has instead opted to address these issues at a policy level, through its Communication on Sustainable

[162] Art. 8.

Development[163] and its Communication on Impact Assessment,[164] which deal generally with the need to address the economic, social, and environmental aspects of sustainable development in a balanced fashion. In addition, the Commission has explicitly committed itself to harmonizing EU and UN/ECE provisions for SEA.[165]

XI. The Future?

The teething troubles experienced with EA and SEA may eventually be viewed simply as growing pains encountered as our approach to evaluating the impacts of our behaviour grows to maturity. If EA and SEA are viewed as introducing more sophisticated approaches to considering the environmental impacts of our actions, the next logical step is the introduction of still more demanding Sustainable Development Assessment (SDA).[166] While EA and, to a greater extent SEA, provide elements of consideration necessary to sustainable development and in particular environmental issues and serve to import process elements, notably public participation and equity issues, they deal with only part of the picture. Their role could arguably be enhanced by the introduction of integrated policy and project appraisal,[167] which would certainly serve to rationalize and probably augment the impact of current practice. It should be remembered that, while EA and its concomitant developments have passed comparatively quickly into legal and political orthodoxy, it is in fact a relatively recent development to give environmental factors anything like the same degree of consideration that is normally given to social and economic factors in decision-making processes. It is to be hoped that, in developing SDA, environmental considerations do not once again become subservient to more pressing human concerns. What is certain is that SDA will require the development of a much more complex,[168] fully integrated, and holistic approach than has hitherto been

[163] A Sustainable Europe for a Better World: A European Union Strategy for Sustainable Development COM (2001)264.

[164] COM(2002)276.

[165] Commission's proposal for a Council Decision on the signature, on behalf of the European Community, of the Protocol on Strategic Environmental Assessment to the 1991 UN/ECE Convention on Environmental Impact Assessment in a Transboundary Context COM(2003)221.

[166] B. Sadler, 'EIA and Sustainability' (1999) 18 *EIA Newsletter*, EIA Centre University of Manchester, published on the Internet at: http://www.art.man.ac.uk/EIA/nl18sadl.htm.

[167] ibid.

[168] George, n. 51 above, uses the Rio Declaration as a starting point for concretizing sustainable development in the context of EA, arriving at a checklist of eighteen points to test the process. Significantly, six of the key issues raised relate to public participation. See also, D. Devuyst, 'From EIA to Sustainability' in 'Sustainability and EIA/SEA' (1999) 18 *EIA Newsletter*, EIA Centre University of Manchester, published on the Internet at: http://www.art.man.ac.uk/EIA/nl18-devu.htm.

adopted to evaluating not only the environmental but also the social and economic impacts of human activities. This will surely prove to be at the very least a challenging proposition, but hopefully not an impossible one for the future development of our decision-making processes.

In any event, for reasons of sustainability alone it would seem that public participation in international environmental law and policy on an official level, though still quite a new phenomenon, is likely to play a central role in shaping our future decision-making processes. Thus far, significant development has occurred in allowing the public (often through NGOs) to have its say on matters directly affecting it in a more direct form, rather than being fully mediated and necessarily attenuated by the vagaries of representative democracy. While the implications of attempting to meld the competing approaches of representative and participatory democracy may not have been addressed, it is to be hoped that sufficient impetus has been created to prompt a constructive dialogue between the two. The potentially fundamental mismatch between representative and participatory democracy in international environmental law has yet to be meaningfully explored. While it may eventually be possible to reach some sort of accommodation between traditional top-down and newly favoured bottom-up means of governance, the fundamental differences between them will need to be explicitly addressed. For now, an attempt to apply a veneer of participative democracy to a system that remains substantively representative is likely only to throw the flaws of each into sharper relief.

A more optimistic view would be that the emerging symbiosis between international environmental law and NGOs, while it may not cure the defects of either, at the very least, by introducing broader participation in international environmental law and policy, may prove to be the beginning of an exciting experiment in governance for the current generation and those yet to come.

EU Chemicals Policy—A Foundation for Environmental Protection or a Missed Opportunity?

SHARRON MCELDOWNEY*

I. Introduction

Manufactured chemicals pervade every aspect of modern society and contribute to almost every activity we undertake. As an inevitable consequence humans and the environment are in contact with a diversity of solid, liquid, and even gaseous synthetic chemicals consisting of single chemical substances or complex mixtures and formulations. Environmental exposure occurs through a variety of pathways arising from the manufacturing process itself, the intended commercial use of a chemical, final disposal, and periodically through accident.

The variety of synthetic chemicals is vast, a point amply illustrated by the number of chemicals listed in the Chemicals Abstract Service's Registry which totals over nine million different synthetic chemicals.[1] Most of these will never be produced in large volumes, and will not be manufactured for the market. Nevertheless, a total of 400 million tonnes of approximately 100,000 different chemicals are produced annually throughout the world. In reality, 3,000 compounds represent 90 per cent of the total weight of manufactured chemicals commercially available across the globe.[2] Within the European Union (EU) 10,000 chemicals are marketed annually in quantities of more than ten tonnes and 20,000 in quantities between one and ten tonnes. In fact the total numbers of chemicals marketed,[3] and the number of chemicals with an annual market of ten tonnes[4] remain largely unaltered from values in the 1970s. Between 1981 and 1988, approximately 200 new synthetic chemicals came into commercial

* School of Biosciences, University of Westminster, England.

[1] See Chemical Abstracts Services Registry, CHEMCATS – Online Chemical Catalogs File, published on the Internet at: http://www.cas.org/CASFILES/chemcats.html.

[2] International Register of Potentially Toxic Chemicals (IRPTC), *About Chemicals and Chemophobia* (1983) IRPTC Bulletin 6.2.

[3] European Inventory of Existing Commercial Chemical Substances (EINECS) (London: HMSO, 1987).

[4] N. Haigh (ed.), *Legislation for the Control of Chemicals* (London: Institute for European Environmental Policy, 1995).

use,[5] balanced by other chemicals becoming obsolete or being no longer marketed. This cycle of addition and removal of chemicals from markets is driven by a variety of commercial factors, including profit margins, new technologies, the development of improved products, and regulatory forces.

The chemical industry is of major economic significance. It is the EU's third largest industry supporting three million jobs directly or indirectly in an estimated 36,000 Small and Medium Sized Enterprises (SMEs) as well as large multinational corporations. The value of the annual global production of chemicals in 1998 was approximately €1,244 billion. Of this 414 billion was produced within the EU.[6]

The regulation of chemicals has been relatively slow to develop within the EU. Historically, concentration was on controlling the disposal of solid waste and the discharge of effluent to the environment. These were tangible, identifiable, and often highly visible sources of environmental or human harm. The 1950s and 1960s, however, saw the first evidence that manufactured chemicals available on the market, and used commercially, could have adverse effects on the environment. The story of DDT is well known and documented, and similar concerns continue today for other pesticides. Major chemical accidents involving highly toxic and often long-lived chemicals served to further raise public awareness of chemical hazards in the late 1970s and 1980s. At Seveso in Italy (1976) 2,000 people suffered from dioxin toxicity and in Bhopal, India (1984) 2,500 people were killed and countless others disabled by the accidental release of a gaseous cyanide compound. Major chemical pollution incidents such as that at Basel, Switzerland, in 1986, which caused major pollution of the Rhine, served to underline the risks associated with chemicals and compounded the public's concern. There followed a number of initiatives within the EU to regulate the chemical industry with regard to major accidents and the commercial sale and use of chemicals. A prime concern was the establishment of the internal market in chemical substances by way of harmonization.

Strategies to regulate the manufacture, marketing, and use of chemicals to ensure environmental and human protection continue to evolve. At present, a variety of directives establish a regulatory framework for the chemical industry, manufactured chemicals, and their commercial use.[7] There are certain limitations in the existing framework, and in recognition of this the Commission published a White Paper entitled *Strategy for a Future Chemicals Policy*,[8] and have now published a draft Regulation taking the White Paper proposals forward.[9]

[5] OECD, *Report of the OECD Workshop on Ecological Effects Assessment* (Paris: OECD, 1989).

[6] See House of Lords (HoL) European Union Select Committee, *Thirteenth Report, Reducing the Risk—Regulating Industrial Chemicals* (London: HMSO, 2002).

[7] See L. Krämer, *EC Environmental Law* (London: Sweet & Maxwell, 2000).

[8] COM(2001)88 fin.

[9] Commission of the Eurpean Communities, Consultation Document concerning the Registration, Evaluation, Authorization and Restrictions of Chemicals (REACH), Vols. 1 to 7 (2003).

The regulation of the chemical industry raises difficulties that are not easy to resolve, and is highly controversial. The knowledge base about the impact and effects of many chemicals is severely limited.[10] The scientific estimation of the hazard and risk posed by individual chemicals is complex, expensive, and time-consuming. The prediction of risk is an essential component in setting environmental standards,[11] and it is noteworthy that chemical risk assessment contributes not only to product and process standards, but also to setting other environmental standards such as emission and quality standards. The techniques involved in the identification of chemical hazards may themselves be controversial and considered unacceptable, for example, the use of animal testing, and on occasion methods for establishing hazard may not have been fully developed.[12] The chemical industry is diverse, both in the chemicals produced and in the size of the companies. Many SMEs do not manufacture chemicals *de novo* but are engaged in mixing chemicals from suppliers into specific product formulations. Some of the resulting products use industrial chemicals in ways not originally envisaged, setting an additional challenge for the prediction of hazard and risk and for effective regulation.

The conflict between establishing adequate and robust protective and precautionary measures and maintaining the competitive strength of companies is particularly stark in the chemical industry. The cost and duration of risk assessments may reduce innovation, research, and product ranges, and may place further regulatory burdens on an already heavily regulated industry. The success of European chemical companies in a global market may be adversely affected. SMEs may be poorly equipped to cope with technical requirements arising from risk assessments. There are, also, underlying conflicts between a transparent regulatory process, and commercial sensitivity about information.

The EU White Paper and draft regulation[13] offers the opportunity to consider some of the problems raised by the environmental regulation of a complex and diverse industry. It is also timely to reflect on the challenges raised by hazard and risk assessment of chemicals, and the implications for regulation. The current

[10] See OECD, *Environmental Outlook for the Chemicals Industry* (Paris: OECD, 2001); Environment Agency, *Managing Chemicals for a Better Environment—The Environment Agency's Strategy* (Bristol: Environment Agency, 2002) and also the Royal Commission on Environmental Pollution, *Twenty-fourth Report, Chemicals in Products—Safeguarding the Environment and Human Health* (London: HMSO, 2003), Cm 5827.

[11] See Royal Commission on Environmental Pollution, *21st Report, Setting Environmental Standards* (London: HMSO, 1998), Cm 4053; J.F. McEldowney and S. McEldowney, *Environmental Law and Regulation* (Oxford: Oxford University Press, 2001), particularly 3–16 for a brief introduction to environmental standards.

[12] See Commission Communication on Community Strategy for Endocrine Disrupters COM(1999)706 fin., and OECD, *Detailed Review Paper Appraisal of Test Methods for Sex Hormone Disrupting Chemicals* (Paris: OECD, 2002), ENV/JM/MONO(2002)8.

[13] See Proposal for a Regulation concerning the Registration, Evaluation, Authorization and Restriction of Chemicals (Reach), Establishing a European Chemicals Agency and amending Directive 199/45/EC and Regulation (EC)... (on Persistent Organic pollutants) COM(2003)644.

framework for EU chemical regulation will be briefly reviewed, and the reasons why change is needed discussed. The regulatory proposals in the draft regulation and the conflicts and concerns surrounding them will be examined in detail.

II. Existing EU Regulation for Chemical Substances

A. Regulation and the Life-Cycle of Chemical Substances

It is helpful to consider the regulatory framework for the chemical industry in terms of the life-cycle of chemicals. This includes their development, manufacture, and formulation into products; storage, transport; marketing and use, and ultimate disposal. The manufacture of a chemical involves the formation of intermediates, and chemical substances are frequently modified or mixed with other chemicals downstream of the original production process. All chemicals and formulations pose different hazards and risks linked to uses, and may require risk management and risk reduction measures to ensure their safe use.

Existing EU chemical regulation encompasses a number of different elements. There are provisions for restriction on the marketing and use of chemicals pursuant to Directive 76/769/EEC on Restrictions on the Marketing and Use of Certain Dangerous Substances and Preparations (Marketing and Use Restrictions Directive).[14] Marketed chemicals must be classified, packed, and labelled depending on the hazards they present, with specific requirements for labelling and packaging based on 15 danger categories.[15] Labels contain diagrammatic symbols together with written phrases relating to specific risks (the R-phrases) and detailing the safe use of the product (the S-phrases). Professional users must receive safety sheets before delivery of dangerous chemicals. Similar requirements are placed on products, such as paints and solvents, that comprise mixtures of chemicals.[16] The transport of dangerous goods by road, rail, and sea falls under a number of directives that implement various international agreements.[17] Controls on the export of dangerous substances apply 'prior informed consent' (PIC)

[14] [1976] OJ L262/20. The Directive restricts or bans the use of a variety of chemicals and preparations as laid down in an annex to the Directive. This frequently amended Directive covers 42 chemical types incorporating 900 individual substances. Most chemicals are incorporated on the basis of their health impacts rather than environmental risks; for an explanation of restrictions on marketing and use, see Krämer, n. 7 above, 164–6.

[15] Dir. 76/769/EEC [1976] OJ L262/201.

[16] Dir. 99/45/EC relating to the Classification, Packaging and Labelling of Dangerous Preparations [1999] OJ L200/1, which replaced Dir. 88/379/EEC relating to the Classification, Packaging and Labelling of Dangerous Preparations [1988] OJ L187/14.

[17] Dir. 93/75/EC concerning Minimum Requirements for Vessels Bound for or Leaving Community Ports and Carrying Dangerous or Polluting Goods [1993] OJ L247/19; Annexes A and B to 94/55/EC of 21 November 1994 with Regard to the Transport of Dangerous Goods by Road [1994] OJ L275/1; Dir. 96/49/EC with Regard to the Transport of Dangerous Goods by Rail [1996] OJ L294/1.

procedures set out by the United Nations Environment programme (UNEP) and the United Nations Food and Agriculture Organization (FAO). Key in this regard is Regulation (EEC) No. 2455/92 concerning the Export and Import of Certain Dangerous Chemicals (Import and Export of Dangerous Chemicals Regulation),[18] which implements PIC arrangements, and requires notification of dangerous chemicals that have been 'banned or severely restricted on account of their effects on human health and the environment'. Such chemicals are largely listed in Annex 1 of The Marketing and Use Restrictions Directive, and also in Annex 1 to Directive 79/117/EEC Prohibiting the Placing on the Market and Use of Plant Protection Products Containing Certain Active Substances (Plant Protection Products Directive).[19] Workers are vulnerable to exposure to chemical substances and formulations at all stages in the life-cycle of chemicals, and their protection falls particularly under the framework Directive 80/1107/EEC on the Protection of Workers from the Risks related to Exposure to Chemical, Physical and Biological Agents at Work (Protection of Workers from Risks Directive).[20] This Directive, together with Directive 89/391/EEC on the Introduction of Measures to Encourage Improvements in the Safety and Health of Workers at Workplaces (Protection of Workers from Risks Directive), places restrictions on some specific chemicals in the workplace.[21] Exposure of people and the environment may also be caused by accidental chemical spillage or emission. Again, accident is possible throughout the life of a chemical, from production and formulation, to transport and use, and to final disposal. Directive 96/82/EC on the Control of Major Accident Hazards Involving Dangerous Substances (the Seveso Directive) deals with accident prevention during both the storage and use of chemicals by industry.[22]

The central theme of regulating chemicals must naturally fall on the chemicals themselves. It is the identification of hazards and the resolution of risks[23] associated with individual chemicals that provide the basis on which regulation relevant to the life-cycle of chemicals rests. The focus of the proposed EU legislation relates specifically to manufactured chemical substances, and has been developed largely to address perceived inadequacies in the existing regulation for chemical substances. It is worthwhile, therefore, briefly to consider current EU legislation for chemical substances.

[18] [1992] OJ L251/13.
[19] [1979] OJ L33/36.
[20] [1980] OJ L327/8.
[21] [1990] OJ L275/42.
[22] [1998] OJ L73/51.
[23] For an excellent summary of risk assessment and its limitations, see R. Nordbeck and M. Faust, 'European Chemicals Regulation and its Effect on Innovation: An Assessment of the EU's White Paper on the Strategy for a Future Chemicals Policy' (2003) 13 *European Environment*, 79–99.

B. Existing Regulation and Chemical Substances

There is a notable dichotomy in the way that the EU currently deals with chemical substances and preparations. Manufactured chemicals are divided between two categories, existing chemical substances and new chemical substances. Existing chemical substances are those marketed within the Community on 18 September 1981.[24] These chemicals are listed in the European Inventory of Existing Commercial Chemical Substances (the EINECS inventory),[25] which includes over 100,000 substances. Any chemical not on the EINECS inventory is considered a new chemical.

The regime for new chemicals includes the notification of regulatory authorities in the Member State where the chemical is produced at least 60 days prior to marketing. A technical (notification) dossier is an important part of notification and includes results from tests set down under Directive 67/548/EEC on the Classification, Packaging and Labelling of Dangerous Substances (Dangerous Substances Packaging Directive).[26] The testing scheme has three tiers depending on the amount of the substance to be marketed. Level 0 (or base level) and level 1 tests are for chemicals produced in quantities of equal to or more than 10 tonnes per year for each manufacturer or that have a total market of more than 50 tonnes per manufacturer. Level 2 tests are the most costly and detailed. They are for chemicals produced in quantities of 1,000 tonnes or over or that have a market of over 5,000 tonnes. Level 0 tests involve the establishment of a base level of physico-chemical data, ecotoxicity tests, and human toxicity tests. Greater detail and complexity is found in the level 1 tests. A proportion of all the level 1 tests may be required for chemicals (≥ ten tonnes annually) depending on the outcome of the base level tests, but for chemicals produced in quantities of ≥ 100 tonnes annually all the level 1 tests are required. Level 2 tests extend the range of tests. A degree of expertise is needed at this level of testing, since there is flexibility in selecting appropriate tests. The choice of tests is made after substantial discussions with the regulatory authority.[27]

Once the chemical notification has been received by a regulatory authority, it is checked for compliance requirements. The regulator then carries out a risk assessment on the chemical in the context of the likely levels of environmental and human exposure to the chemical, based on the proposed market. Thus, the manufacturer carries out the hazard assessment for the chemical and the regula-

[24] Dir. 79/831/EEC amending for the sixth time Directive 67/548/EEC relating to the Classification, Packaging and Labelling of Dangerous Substances [1979] OJ L259/10.

[25] See [1990] OJ C146/1 for the EINECS inventory; see also the European Chemical Bureau website, published on the Internet at: http://ecb.ei.jrc.it.

[26] [1967] OJ L196/1.

[27] See P. Calow (ed.), *Handbook of Environmental Risk Assessment and Management* (Oxford: Blackwell Science, 1998), in particular S.P. Felter *et al.*, 'Assessing Risks to Human Health from Chemicals in the Environment', 9–23 and J.C. Smrchek and M.G. Zeeman, 'Assessing Risks to Ecological Systems from Chemicals', 24–90.

tory authority the risk assessment.[28] A summary of the notification information and risk assessment is then sent to the Commission together with a proposal for classification and labelling of the chemical and for inclusion of the chemical on the European List of Notified Chemical Substances (the ELINCS list). All Member States receive copies of the information from the Commission, and can request more information or suggest further tests on the chemical. Decisions on the chemical then fall under committee procedure set out in the Dangerous Substances Packaging Directive. The Committee may either decide not to classify the chemical as dangerous or will require classification, packaging, and labelling of the substance based on the notification and other information. The chemical is then registered in ELINCS and incorporated in Annex I of the Dangerous Substances Packaging Directive. The name of the chemical, the category of danger associated with the chemical, the R-phrases and S-phrases, and the concentration limits of the chemical in a preparation that would qualify the preparation as dangerous under Directive 88/379/EEC relating to the Classification, Packaging and Labelling of Dangerous Preparations (Dangerous Preparations Directive) are included in the Annex.[29]

Risk assessment of a chemical substance or preparation may ultimately support a risk reduction strategy that involves restriction or even a ban on the marketing or use of the chemical, albeit the chemical complies with requirements under the Dangerous Substances Packaging Directive or the Dangerous Preparations Directive outlined above. Individual Member States may impose such restrictions, and the Commission must be notified. A safeguard procedure is then initiated, and a Community-wide decision on the substance restriction or ban is taken on the basis of majority voting.[30] The Commission may also instigate action on risk reduction measures for chemicals. Restrictions or bans on substances fall under Directive 76/769/EEC relating to Restrictions on the Marketing and Use of Certain Dangerous Substances and Preparations (the Marketing and Use Restrictions Directive), and are listed in Annex I of that Directive.[31] Inclusion of chemicals in the Annex involves detailed Community discussions that go to balancing risks and economic considerations. The majority of chemicals and preparations included in Annex I of the Directive present risks to human health; lower priority appears to be given to adverse environmental impacts.

[28] Hazard assessment is an identification of the intrinsic properties of a chemical that may result in adverse effects on the environment and humans. The hazard assessment together with an exposure assessment forms the basis of risk assessment.

[29] [1993] OJ L317/83.

[30] See Krämer, n. 7 above, 106 for an explanation of the basis for safeguard procedures.

[31] n. 15 above, with subsequent amendments, Annex I. Since 1979, a variety of chemicals have been restricted, e.g. asbestos, anti-fouling and leaded paints, cadmium, creosote, pentachlorophenol, chlorinated solvents, fire retardants, and PCB. Some other classes of chemicals have been restricted under separate Directives, e.g. mercury under Dir. 91/157/EEC on Batteries and Accumulators Containing Certain Dangerous Substances [1991] OJ L78/38 amended by Dir. 98/101/EC Adapting to Technical Progress Directive 91/157/EEC on Batteries and Accumulators Containing Certain Dangerous Substance [1999] OJ L1/1.

A further and intimidating problem surrounds the regulation of the more than 100,000 existing chemicals listed on the EINECS inventory (i.e., those on the market prior to 1981), of which some 30,000 are marketed in quantities of more than 1 tonne per annum.[32] The existing EU chemical regime is generally agreed to be operating poorly and exceptionally slowly. No risk management and risk reduction needs have been identified for the majority of these chemicals. Under the Dangerous Substances Packaging Directive manufacturers or importers use hazard data to classify, pack, and label an existing chemical prior to marketing within the Community. Classification of existing chemicals is to be progressively applied under a Committee procedure detailed in the Dangerous Substances Packaging Directive. This provides the risk assessment of the chemical and if a risk to humans or the environment is identified then the chemical is listed in Annex 1 to the Directive. Given the number of existing chemicals, it is not surprising that this is a gradual process. Indeed, it has taken 30 years to classify approximately 4,500 substances, 3,000 of which were considered hazardous and included in Annex I.[33] In response to the apparent slowness of the procedure for existing chemical substances, Regulation (EC) No. 793/93 on the Evaluation and Control of the Risks of Existing Substances (Existing Substances Regulation),[34] was introduced in the hope of hastening the process.

Under the Existing Substances Regulation, manufacturers or importers of chemicals marketed in quantities exceeding 1,000 tonnes must supply existing data on the chemical relevant for risk evaluation. This data, which includes existing information on effects and exposure to the chemical, is submitted to the European Chemicals Bureau, and included in the International Uniform Chemical Information Database,[35] which is administered by the Bureau. The first data sets were submitted in 1994 and 1995, and there is a triennial process of reporting. Priority setting follows the data collection stage and is based on the data supplied by manufacturers (or importers), a consideration of any gaps in existing knowledge on effects, and any information available from sources outside the EU. Priority lists of chemicals that appear to be in need of urgent risk assessment are then drawn up by the Commission. Reasons for selection include risks to the environment, indirect exposure, of humans via the environment, consumer exposure, and worker exposure. By 2000, four lists had been put in place containing 140 chemicals,[36] which include carcinogens or chemicals with chronic effects that relate to toxicity and ecotoxicity in particular. The identified

[32] See HoL European Union Select Committee, n. 6 above.

[33] See Krämer, n. 7 above, 160–2.

[34] [1993] OJ L224/34.

[35] European Chemical Bureau, published on the Internet at http://ecb.jrc.it, and International Uniform Chemical Information Database, published on the Internet at: http://ecb.jrc.it/existing-chemicals/.

[36] Reg. (EC) No. 1179/94 concerning the First List of Priority Substances as Foreseen under Council Regulation (EEC) No. 793/93 [1994] OJ L131/3, containing 42 chemicals; Reg. (EC)

priority chemicals are then allocated to Member States to take a full risk assessment forward.[37]

Member States nominate a suitable rapporteur for the assessment process. Manufacturers of listed chemicals must provide all data relevant to a risk assessment to the rapporteur within six months of the chemical being listed. If level 0 data is not available, a manufacturer must perform these tests and supply the data to the rapporteur within twelve months.[38] It is possible for the exemptions from these requirements to be granted by the rapporteur. In this case the Member State must be informed. Contested exemptions become subject to a committee procedure. Based on an evaluation of the available data, the rapporteur may consider that additional information or tests are needed. The final decision on whether a manufacturer is required to provide further data on a chemical and the time limits for submission is determined by the Committee. The rapporteur carries out the risk assessment. Regulation (EC) No. 1488/94 Laying Down the Principles for the Assessment of Risks to Man and the Environment of Existing Substances in Accordance with Council Regulation (EEC) No. 793/93[39] sets out the principles for the evaluation in terms of the physico-chemistry and toxicity of the chemical relevant to human health and the environment.[40]

The rapporteur informs the Commission of conclusions from the evaluation. As part of the report on the chemical the rapporteur may advise that:

1. Existing risk reduction measures for the chemical are adequate.
2. New risk reduction measures[41] should be taken, either through a ban or restriction on marketing and use of the chemical. In this case the rapporteur must provide a risk and cost benefit analysis outlining the advantages and disadvantages of the risk reduction measures and availability of substitute chemicals.
3. Further testing and/or other information on the chemical is needed.

No. 2268/95 concerning the Second List of Priority Substances as Foreseen under Council Regulation (EEC) No. 793/93 [1995] OJ L231/18, containing 36 chemicals; Reg. (EC) No. 143/97 concerning the Third List of Priority Substances as Foreseen under Council Regulation (EEC) No. 793/93 [1997] OJ L25/13, containing 32 chemicals; and Reg. (EC) No. 2364/2000 concerning the Fourth List of Priority Substances as Foreseen under Council Regulation (EEC) No. 793/93 OJ L273/5, containing 30 chemicals.

[37] To date, the UK has been allocated a total of 25 chemicals. Of these five are shared with other Member States. For a full breakdown of allocated chemicals under each Priority List, see HoL European Union Select Committee, n. 6 above.

[38] As set out in Dir. 67/548/EEC, n. 24 above, amended by Dir. 79/831/EEC amending for the Sixth Time Directive 67/548/EEC relating to the Classification, Packaging and Labelling of Dangerous Substances [1981] OJ 265/28, which is analysed in relation to new chemicals.

[39] [1994] OJ L61/3.

[40] Technical Guidance on Risk Assessment (Edition 2) is detailed by the European Chemical Bureau, and published on the Internet at: http://ecb.jrc.it/existing-chemicals/. A draft revision of the guidance (2003) is also available at this site.

[41] Technical Guidance of Risk Reduction is published on the Internet at: http://ecb.jrc.it.

It is possible for restrictions or a ban placed on a chemical to be recommended while at the same time requiring further information and testing. The decision on whether to adopt any risk reduction strategies is made under committee procedure. The Commission can propose any restrictions under the Marketing and Use Restrictions Directive.[42]

Since 1994, a total of 41 out of the 140 chemicals on the priority lists have had an EU risk assessment report completed,[43] and only a few of these substances[44] have so far been recommended for risk reduction strategies. Directives restricting the use of two of these substances have also been proposed by the Commission. These relate to C_{10-13} chloro-alkanes (short chain chlorinated paraffins) for use in the leather and metalworking industries[45] and diphenylether/pentabromo derivatives (pentabromodiphenyl ether) for all uses.[46] As yet none of the recommendations has been adopted.

C. Limitations in the Current Legislation for New and Existing Chemical Substances and Preparations

It is useful to identify some specific deficiencies in the existing legislation before considering the proposed regulation for chemicals. It is generally acknowledged that the process of notifying new chemicals has worked well and provides a 'sound basis for chemicals management'.[47] Undoubtedly, the Dangerous Substances Packaging Directive has resulted in substantial improvement in our knowledge on some 2,700 new chemicals that have been marketed since 1981. There are, inevitably, considerable economic costs linked to notification requirements for new chemicals. The industry itself carries a considerable burden in the testing of new chemicals and has frequently argued that the competitiveness of the EU chemical industry has been affected. One outcome of this 'regulatory burden' claimed by the industry is the diminution of product innovation with

[42] n. 14 above.

[43] See C.W.M. Bodar, F. Berthault, J.H.M. de Bruijin, C.J. van Leeuwen, M.E.J. Pronk, and T.G. Vermeire, *Evaluation of EU Risk Assessments Existing Chemicals* (*EC Regulation 793/93*) (The Hague: RIVM, 2002), 13 for a list of chemical substances that have finalized risk assessment reports.

[44] Rec. (EC) 1999/721 on the Results of the Risk Evaluation and on the Risk Reduction Strategies for the Substances: 2-(2-butoxyethoxy)Ethanol; 2-(2-methoxyethoxy)Ethanol; Alkanes, C_{10-13}, Chloro; Benzene, C_{10-13}-alkyl derivs. OJ [1999] L292/42; Rec. (EC) 2001/194 [2001] OJ L319/30 on the Results of the Risk Evaluation and the Risk Reduction Strategies for the Substances: Acrylaldehyde; Dimethyl Sulphate; Nonylphenol phenol, 4-nonyl-, Branched; Tert-butyl methyl ether; Rec. (EC) 2002/755 on the Results of the Risk Evaluation for the Substances: Ethyl Acetoacetate, 4-Chloro-o-cresol, Dimethyldioctadecylammonium Chloride OJ [2002] L181/35.

[45] COM(2000)260, OJ [2000] C337E/138.

[46] COM(2001)12, OJ [2001] C154E/112.

[47] European Commission, *Final Report of the SLIM Phase IV Team on Dangerous Substances (Directive 67/548/EEC, 1999)*, published on the Internet at: europa.eu.int/comm./environment/dansub/slim_report.pdf.

consequences for future competitiveness and global market share. There appears to be no conclusive evidence for a curb on innovation, however.[48]

New chemicals represent only 1 per cent by volume of chemical substances available on the EU market. Existing chemicals dominate the market, making an effective regulatory regime for these chemicals essential. The serious nature of the problem was recognized in the Fourth Community Action Programme on the Environment (1987–92),[49] which highlighted the urgent need for a regulatory structure to evaluate health and environmental risks arising from the myriad existing chemicals marketed within the EU. This concern led to the Commission proposal for the Existing Substances Regulation. Regrettably, it is difficult to feel sanguine about the effectiveness of the regime that was established for existing chemicals. Indeed the House of Lords' European Union Select Committee considered there to be 'a fundamental flaw in the Regulation'.[50] It is worth reiterating that priority setting in the Existing Substances Regulation is based on an evaluation of available data, and that chemicals on the priority lists are those where evidence exists to suggest serious adverse effects from exposure to the substance. Yet, less than 10 per cent of the 140 chemicals so far listed have reached the point where recommendations on risk reduction are being actively considered. Put in the perspective of the over 100,000 substances on the EINECS inventory, it is indeed difficult to have confidence in the working of the Existing Substances Regulation.

A number of fundamental problems in the Existing Substances Regulation have contributed to this slow progress. The process of chemical risk evaluation requires contributions from both the private and public sector. Industry provides data on a chemical that goes to identify the hazardous characteristics of a substance, while the designated rapporteur undertakes risk evaluation and management. This has a number of implications that affect the speed of the process. Assessment of risk by the rapporteur requires considerable resources and relies on Member States to respond adequately to the demands in terms of costs, staffing, and time. A lack of sufficient resources inevitably acts to slow the process of assessment and development of risk reduction measures. Most noteworthy perhaps with regard to an influence on the rate of assessments is the general framework of the Regulation. The EU White Paper points out that under the Regulation incentives for industry to provide data do not exist; in fact rather the reverse.[51] Any risk management or reduction measures are based on detailed risk assessments and on good evidence; delays in the provision of data, therefore, inevitably hinder the development and application of risk reduction measures. Thus, delays in the process lead to the chemical continuing to be marketed without new regulatory constraints. In addition, the Department for Environ-

48 See for discussion, Nordbeck and Faust, n. 23 above.

49 OJ [1987] C328/1.

50 HoL European Union Select Committee, n. 6 above.

51 See Commission White Paper, *Strategy for a Future Chemicals Policy*, n. 8 above, 19.

ment, Food and Rural Affairs (DEFRA) pointed out to the Select Committee[52] that chemical data sets on the International Uniform Chemical Information Database (IUCLID) are incomplete, further contributing to delays. This problem arises because under the Existing Substances Regulation manufacturers are only required to provide readily available information on a substance and not to remedy any mismatch between the needs of a common data set and the data that is actually available.

A key component of any chemical risk assessment is the end-use or uses of the chemical. This delineates the likely extent and routes of human and environmental exposure to substances through a large part of the chemical life-cycle. During the risk assessments of the priority list compounds so far examined under the Existing Substances Regulation, it has become clear that the chemical manufacturer may not foresee all the possible uses of the chemical.[53] In fact some 34 of the 41 substances so far evaluated had unforeseen uses by consumers.[54] Such unintended uses must be investigated in the risk assessment, slowing the process, particularly if the use is only identified towards the end of the assessment. Under the Existing Substances Regulation there is no requirement for downstream users to contribute to the risk assessment process and little information flow between producer and user. This leaves a lacuna in identifying all uses of a chemical, reducing the adequacy of risk evaluation and the appropriateness of any risk reduction measures.

An interesting point was raised by DEFRA in evidence to the Select Committee,[55] which was said to have contributed to delay in risk assessments on the priority chemicals under the Existing Substances Regulation. There is a tension between scientists and policy-makers 'with scientists wanting risk assessments to be as thorough as possible, while policy makers have only wanted enough information for risk reduction measures'. Such friction reflects the different dilemmas faced by scientists and policy-makers and also the different roles they perform in the process. Reducing scientific uncertainties and identifying effects of chemicals manifestly involves expanding the risk assessment process. Scientific confidence in outcomes becomes more robust when uncertainty is minimized, driving their desire to extend the assessment process. Policy-makers face pressures of other types. The criticisms and discontent that has arisen from the slow progress of the Existing Substances Regulation amply illustrate one pressure. Another is working within budgetary constraints, and recognition that any additional chemical assessment will further strain already tight budgets. There may also be a conflict between risk assessment and policy developments in other areas. One example of this is the use of animal testing. Some effects may at present only be testable using

52 n. 6 above.

53 ibid., para 68.

54 See Bodar *et al.*, n. 43, 13 for a list of chemical substances that have finalized risk assessment reports.

55 See HoL European Union Select Committee, n. 6 at para. 68.

animals. Yet there are substantial driving forces to reduce animal testing.[56] Policy-makers must strike a difficult balance between appropriate risk assessment and adequate precaution on one hand and the reduction of animal testing. That there is tension between the scientists and policy-makers is hardly surprising. It is possible, of course, that such tension may have beneficial effects. A workable balance between disproportionate assessment and too light an evaluation of risk may grow from these tensions through negotiation and discussion. A further complicating factor comes from the lack of consensus about the amount of information required before well-founded and justifiable risk reduction measures can be taken. In fact, Member States do not agree on how much information is needed.[57]

Other limitations exist within the overall regulatory framework for chemical substances within the EU. There is currently an important lacuna in chemical notification. The Dangerous Preparations Directive was replaced by Directive 99/45/EC bearing the same name, and which does not require their notification prior to marketing.[58] At present, inclusion of preparations under the old Dangerous Preparations Directive is based on the preparation containing more than the guide concentrations of individual chemicals set out in Annex 1 of the Dangerous Substances Packaging Directive. It is interesting to note that this Directive largely relates to health hazards, and not environmental impacts.[59] There is no requirement for risk evaluation linked to chemical formulations often produced by downstream users. The behaviour and impacts of chemicals can change when they are constituents of mixtures. Risk assessment of chemical formulations may be highly desirable on occasions, depending on the product, and this, together with notification, may have considerable benefits.

There has been no attempt within EU chemical legislation to restrict marketing and use of harmful chemicals if alternatives are available.[60] A policy to replace harmful chemicals with less hazardous and lower risk chemicals would clearly have advantages, but the problem of unforeseen effects can never be entirely discounted. Chlorofluorocarbons (CFCs) were originally used as refrigerants and propellants not because they are cheap to produce but because they are non-toxic and, it was originally thought, inert. The transport of CFCs to the stratosphere, their breakdown by sunlight releasing chlorine that reacted with stratospheric ozone was not foreseen. The potentially unpredictable effects of chemicals offer major challenges to any risk evaluation process. Even so, encouraging the substitution of chemicals that have known characteristics that pose

[56] See for a detailed discussion of this issue, Select Committee on Animals in Scientific Procedures, *Animals in Scientific Procedures*, Session 2001–2, Report. HL 150-I of 24 July 2002.

[57] See HoL European Union Select Committee, n. 6 at para. 68.

[58] Dir. 99/45/EC, n. 16 above, which replaced Dir. 88/379/EEC relating to the Classification, Packaging and Labelling of Dangerous Preparations [1988] OJ L187/27.

[59] See Krämer, n. 7 above, 161 and 163.

[60] ibid. 151–2.

particular risks, for example, they persist in the environment, are toxic or bioaccumulate, based on the best available science has obvious advantages. Any such measures would clearly involve the application of precautionary and preventative principles set out in Article 174 EC.

Existing EU legislation on chemicals has clear limitations and could be significantly improved to increase protection of humans and the environment. The draft Regulation sets out, in particular, to address problems related to the Existing Substances Regulation.

III. Legislative Proposals for the Future of EU Chemical Regulation

In 2001, the Commission published a White Paper on the Strategy for a future chemicals policy that proved controversial. A draft Regulation based on the White Paper, and responding to some concerns raised over proposals in the White Paper was published in May 2003 for an eight-week consultation.[61] The draft Regulation contains some 117 clauses, 16 annexes, and runs to 1,200 pages. It has proved as controversial as the White Paper and the Commission, after the consultation period, has conceded major changes to the draft Regulation. The changes are largely in recognition of concerns about its impact on the competitiveness of the chemical industry.[62] The target of the proposed Regulation is significantly to improve the speed at which chemicals are evaluated for risk and subsequently managed. It is the legislation for existing chemicals that has proved particularly wanting. Chemicals are ubiquitous in modern society, and their diversity together with our poor knowledge base on their potential to cause significant and perhaps irreversible harm makes efficient and effective regulation of chemicals imperative. The importance of the regulatory proposals cannot be understated and are certainly worthy of wide discussion.

A key element in the draft Regulation is the formation of a single entirely new regime for chemicals, bringing together regulation on new and existing chemical substances. The proposed single system consists of three main elements, registration, evaluation, and authorization, and is called REACH (Registration, Evaluation, and Authorization of Chemicals). The proposals appear to be based on three pieces of existing legislation:[63] notifying new chemicals, evaluating existing chemicals, and restricting marketing and use of chemicals.[64] Under each of the

[61] Commission Consultation Document concerning the Registration, Evaluation, Authorization and Restrictions of Chemicals (REACH), Vols. 1 to 7 available at the Internet at: http://europa.eu.int/comm./enterprise/chempd/whitepaper/reach.htm.

[62] See 'REACH caught up in EU's competitiveness agenda' (2003) 346 *The ENDS Report*, 51–3.

[63] See HoL European Union Select Committee, n. 6 above at para. 49.

[64] Dir. 67/548/EEC, n. 24 above. Dir 92/32/EC, n. 29 above. Dir. 76/769/EEC, n. 15 above. Reg. (EC) No. 793/93 on the Evaluation and Control of the Risks of Existing Substances [1993] OJ L84/1.

three elements of REACH there are significant proposals for change from existing legislation. The Commission has also proposed as part of the wide-ranging changes to establish a European Chemical Agency (ECA), which will have a key role in overseeing the REACH regime.

A. Registration

Registration under the Dangerous Substances Packaging Directive requires that new chemicals are notified 60 days prior to marketing within the EU and a technical (notification) dossier has to be submitted to the regulatory authorities (see above). This is to continue for new chemicals, and it is proposed that such a regime should be extended to existing chemicals. In contrast to the existing process, however, notification will be required before the chemical is produced or imported rather than as currently prior to marketing. Registration is intended in the draft Regulation to be mandatory for all chemicals manufactured or imported in amounts over one tonne annually—nearly 30,000 chemicals. A manufacturer or importer of an existing chemical will have to provide a 'registration dossier' on the chemical, broadly similar to a 'notification dossier' on new chemicals. The information required will vary with volume marketed, over ten, 100, and 1,000 tonnes, and with the properties of the compound and its uses. In general, the dossier will include information such as the chemical's intrinsic properties; all uses (including downstream uses) and accounting for all, but a maximum of 10 per cent, of the volume of the chemical imported or manufactured); routes and levels of human and environmental exposures; the projected production volumes; suggested hazard classification and safety data sheets; summaries of existing tests and preliminary risk assessments for the predicted uses; proposals for further testing; and a proposal for risk reduction and management measures. National authorities will decide what additional information is required to complete a registration dossier. As a result of the consultation on the draft Regulation, the Commission has reduced testing requirements for low tonnage chemicals. Any chemical produced or imported in quantities of one to ten tonnes per year per company will normally only require *in vitro* tests. In terms of any requirement for additional information, if this involves further testing, then lack of the information cannot be a basis for rejecting registration of the chemical. Thus submission of full data sets for registration may not be essential. There appears to be no incentive for manufacturers to complete full data packages before registration, potentially making the next stage in the process, evaluation, more onerous since decisions on data will be essential at this stage.

Thus it was intended under the May proposals for the Regulation that the manufacturer or importer would under Registration be required to provide chemical safety assessments (CSAs), documented in a chemical safety report (CRA), and ultimately undertake tests if appropriate data does not exist.

Moreover, a manufacturer must carry out the preliminary risk assessments linked to uses. This has subsequently been modified in the light of concerns about the costs of such a requirement. It is now intended that the duty will only apply to substances produced or imported in quantities of over ten tonnes per year per company, and only for 'identified uses'. The variety of end-uses must be established in conjunction with downstream users. CSAs must cover all the intended uses and entire life-cycle of a substance. Risk reduction measures will be based on the findings of the CSAs and must be applied throughout the supply chain of the chemical, including downstream uses. CSRs and safety data sheets will be passed down the supply chain and are required to be available to employees. Under the draft Regulation, a three-phase timetable for registration of chemicals exceeding production volumes of 1,000, 100, and one tonne was set of 2009, 2012, and 2017, respectively, if the legislation enters into force in 2006. Elements of this timetable have subsequently been softened in response to the consultation. There is the implication that if registration is not completed, there will be a ban on the marketing and use of the substance. The draft Regulation does not stipulate on what grounds registration can be rejected and a chemical banned from use.

There are a number of proposed exemptions from registration. A substance that is undergoing 'process-orientated research and development' has an up to ten-year exemption from registration. At present such exemption extends for only two years. Chemicals used only for research are currently exempted from notification if marketed in quantities of less than 100 kilograms; this is to be raised to one tonne. There has been considerable debate about registration requirements for intermediates, chemicals used for synthesis of other chemicals, some of which are marketed, as well as polymers. It is estimated that there are some 70–120,000 intermediates and some 70,000 polymers in use. There was considerable concern that a requirement to register these chemicals would not only incur excessive costs for industry but, because of the numbers of chemicals involved, would overwhelm REACH, and adversely affect any prioritization of the most hazardous chemicals.[65] These concerns raised on the White Paper were addressed by the Commission in the draft Regulation. It was intended that the majority of polymers would be exempted from REACH. This included all non-dangerous polymers and 'large' polymers. The remaining approximately 30,000 polymers were proposed to require only limited registration dossiers twelve years after the legislation came into force. 'Small polymers' classified as dangerous would require more extensive registration dossiers with shorter deadlines. The Commission has now reviewed requirements for polymers after consultation on the draft Regulation and it is intended that polymers should be excluded from registration and evaluation on the basis of costs involved. This will be reviewed in the future, and some polymers will still require authorization and restriction

[65] See 'Reforming EU Chemicals Policy: A Triumph of Hope over Experience?' (2003) 340 *The ENDS Report*, 30–3.

where risk management measures are required. Intermediates will similarly have a light touch. The intermediates that are solely a part of the process of synthesizing a marketable product and are not separated out from the process, that is the 'non-isolated' intermediates, will be entirely exempted from REACH. Other intermediates that are removed from the process and used on site or supplied to a maximum of two others will have limited registration requirements and the majority will have no additional tests required. The Commission has now removed the two-site restriction in view of its adverse impact on small producers involved in the preparation of formulations. Those intermediates supplied or marketed more widely will have the normal registration requirements.

Under the registration proposals, manufacturers will be required to submit far more information than is currently the case. The White Paper suggested that since more information is required in the registration dossier, delays arising from difficulties in obtaining information from manufacturers should be reduced. The onus has been placed firmly on industry. Since the lack of a complete dossier within the time constraints is likely to result in the chemical substance being banned from marketing, there is a substantial pressure on industry to comply fully with registration. This pressure is clearly absent from the current Existing Substances Regulation. However, it is clear in the draft Regulation that completeness is not gauged in terms of a full data set on a chemical, but rather in terms of all the required elements in the registration dossier being present. Registration will not be refused on the basis of incomplete data sets.

It is considered in the White Paper that the requirement for downstream users to contribute to the assessment process, providing information on uses, should substantially address the problem of unforeseen use of chemicals. It was originally intended in the draft Regulation that downstream users would have to undertake risk assessments under certain circumstances. If a chemical was used for a purpose not originally identified at the registration stage, then the user would have to undertake the risk assessment for that use and the part of the life-cycle of the chemical to which they contributed directly, including 'disposal and waste management'. This undoubtedly would have provided an incentive for downstream users to contribute fully to the registration process. There was a potential problem of the producer of a chemical minimizing the risk assessment they had to undertake by visualizing only a limited number of uses for a product, thereby pushing the burden and cost of assessment onto downstream users. This was addressed by proposing that companies must pay to use any assessment data produced by another company. After the consultation, however, the Commission agreed that downstream users should be exempted from preparing CSAs and CSRs, unless they specifically want to in order to maintain confidentiality of a particular use. The Commission believes that this will remove a considerable cost burden from downstream users, commonly SMEs. It may, however, have removed one of the drivers ensuring that downstream users contribute information on chemical uses under REACH. The draft Regulation sets out a number of rules to promote data sharing between companies as a technique to reduce testing costs. This falls into the following three categories:

1. Substances currently on the market—companies must notify existing studies for inclusion in the European Chemical Agency database during a pre-registration period eighteen months before registration deadlines.
2. Substances that are pre-registered by more than one company—companies must form a 'substance information exchange forum' and agree to sharing existing data, undertaking any new test that may be required and sharing costs. The requirement to share data is not binding, however.
3. New substances—there is an absolute ban on the repetition of more recent studies involving vertebrates. Any vertebrate studies can be passed on by authorities and there are mechanisms for companies that funded the studies to recover their costs.

B. Evaluation

The EU White Paper had proposed that evaluation should be a separate stage in the process of authorization. However this appears not to be the case in the draft Regulation. Even so, there are a number of proposals that relate to evaluation for certain chemicals under the REACH regime. Currently the Existing Substances Regulation requires a prioritization of chemical substances that are of particular concern. There is to be an extension of this prioritization process, as well as building on the evaluation of the technical dossier submitted for new chemicals. Under the proposals, a lead national regulatory authority, designated by the ECA, will qualitatively evaluate the registration dossier for a chemical and prepare a draft decision on the evaluation. The draft decision will include a judgement on whether and what further testing is required on a chemical substance based on the strategy for further testing, submitted by the manufacturer, for all chemicals that raise 'very high' concern as laid out in the Regulation, for example, toxic, mutagenic, or which have chemical structures that suggest reasons for concern, or exceed production values of over 100 tonnes annually. The evaluation by the lead Member State will, thus, determine the 'substance-tailored' assessment programme, focusing particularly on long-term effects. The investigation of chronic hazards, carcinogenicity and reproductive toxicity will continue as under the regime for new chemicals at the existing thresholds of 100 and 1,000 tonnes. As previously, once cumulative sales exceed trigger values, further testing on chemicals will be required. If there are a number of registrants, which is likely to be common, the draft decision will identify who is to be responsible for different tests. Downstream users may be exempted from contributing in this way after the consultation on the draft Regulation. There will, also, be a proposal for allocation of a coordinating role for the testing to one of the companies in order to ensure that replicate testing is minimized. Significantly, there will no longer be a full evaluation of every dossier on a case-by-case basis and the draft decision will not include an evaluation of the risk assessment in the registration dossier.

Draft decisions are to be passed to the registrants and downstream users for comment before circulation to all fourteen national regulatory authorities. Any disagreement by other national authorities on the draft decision will be referred to a committee of Member States' experts under the auspices of the ECA. Unanimous decisions by this committee will be binding. If there is not unanimity, then the draft decision will be referred to the Commission and will be referred to a committee of national representatives. There is a maximum time-limit of 195 days for the process, starting from the time when companies see the draft decision. The circulation of the draft decision between Member States and its consideration by committee is intended to harmonize the evaluation and requirements for further testing between national authorities, something which was lacking in the Existing Substances Regulation.

Evaluations undertaken by national authorities will be divided between:

1. 'Standard' evaluations—draft decisions are required two years after the registration deadline for chemical substances marketed in volumes of between 100 and 1,000 tonnes, and over 1,000 tonnes: 2014 and 2011 respectively.
2. 'Priority' evaluations—national authorities may assess a company's registration dossier and request further information. The authority then has twelve months to prepare the draft decision.

The Commission has predicted that of the order of 80 per cent of registered chemicals will require no further action after screening. The remaining 20 per cent (approximately 6,000 substances) will require full evaluation and may require further testing. No evaluation deadlines have been proposed for chemicals marketed in volumes of one to 100 tonnes.

Thus, the preliminary risk assessment by industry is central to the regulatory process. There is also the suggestion that risk assessments should be focused or 'targeted' rather than comprehensive as at present, and linked to waivers depending on exposure data. The Commission believes that this will be a more flexible system. This will help to contain the cost of assessments. One of the main causes for delays under the Existing Substances Regulation is the comprehensive nature of risk assessments, and it is suggested that targeted assessments should overcome this problem.

C. Authorization

There will be an authorization procedure for chemicals that are of 'very high concern' as laid down in the Regulation and identified under the evaluation process. Category 1 and 2 carcinogens, mutagens, or reproductive toxicants (CMRs), that is, substances that cause cancer, genetic mutation, or harm to reproduction, and persistent organic pollutants (POPs) were proposed to fall into this category in the White Paper. In fact, initial drafts of the White Paper suggested a requirement for authorization or restrictions on marketing, even amounting to a ban, on persistent, bioaccumulative, and toxic chemicals (PBTs) and very persistent and very bioaccumulative (vPvBs) chemicals. This was removed because of concerns raised by the Enterprise Directorate over the effect on competitiveness of the industry. Tensions between precautionary action to protect the environment and maintaining the competitiveness of industry are undoubtedly well illustrated in the evolution of EU chemical policy. There was, however, considerable unease expressed by a variety of stakeholders and Environment Ministers over the omission of PBTs and vPvBs from the final version of the White Paper. In response to these concerns, the draft Regulation includes these as chemicals of 'very high concern' if they meet specified criteria. A Member State can also make representations that a PBT or vPvBs gives rise to 'an equivalent level of concern'. Further, in recognition of the growing disquiet voiced internationally and within the EU, Member States can propose chemicals that have endocrine-disrupting capacities as giving rise to 'an equivalent level of concern'. Chemicals of 'very high concern' will be authorized for specified uses only if the use presents negligible risk, and will be banned from all applications not specifically authorized. Thus, if a high-risk chemical does not have authorization, it will not be marketable. This is a substantial change from existing requirements where a chemical can be marketed and used in the EU unless there is a specific restriction.

The first stage in the authorization process will involve the identification of chemical substances that should be authorized; setting time-limits on the period before prohibition of unauthorized uses; and determining the scope of exemptions. A committee of Member States' representatives will make the decision on whether a substance should enter the authorization process, based on proposals from the ECA or Member States. When a proposal is through a Member State, the procedure will take a total of 105 days and involves a number of steps. First, the dossier on the chemical produced by the initiating State will be circulated to other Member States. Any unresolved disagreements between States will go to the Commission, which will prepare a proposal for committee decision. Substances and uses needing authorization will, then, be determined at Community level.

The second stage in the authorization process is the actual authorization of the chemical for specified uses. Under current arrangements, restrictions on substances require a Council and Parliament Directive. In marked contrast, the draft Regulation assumes that authorization will predominantly be through a Committee procedure at Community level. Thus the Commission will make decisions on authorizations for substances marketed within the EU. In addition the Commission will authorize uses in products. The steps in the authorization procedure are:

1. The chemical substance will be included in an Annex to the Regulation.
2. This will be followed by a period within which manufacturers, importers, and downstream users will apply for authorization to the ECA. They will submit as part of the application for authorization a risk assessment on the chemical for specified uses, a socio-economic case on authorization for these uses, and a review of alternative technologies available for these uses. No universal deadlines for this stage of the authorization process are proposed; rather it is likely they will be set on a case-by-case basis.
3. The ECA will ask for comments from third parties on the alternative technologies or alternative substances. The Agency will then produce a draft opinion, containing a risk assessment of the chemical related to the uses for which application was made and a socio-economic analysis carried out by the ECA. This must be prepared within ten months of the application for authorization.
4. The draft opinion will be circulated to applicants who will have two months to comment on the findings.
5. There follows a three-month period during which the Commission must submit to committee a draft authorization decision.

Decision to authorize will be based on two grounds. A substance will be authorized for specified uses if the risks for those uses are 'adequately controlled'. Alternatively, there is the possibility of 'conditioned' authorization based on the socio-economic analysis furnished by industry, provided that the benefits outweigh the risks. In this case, decisions would be in the light of alternative chemicals or technologies being available. This availability, however, was 'insufficient grounds to refuse an authorization'. Objections by environmentalists on this aspect of the draft Regulation have resulted in the removal of the 'insufficient grounds to refuse authorization' rider. It is now explicit, however, that the risks associated with any alternatives must be considered. Authorization holders are under a duty to reduce exposure levels 'as low as technically' feasible without any qualification in terms of costs.

Authorization of chemicals may also be through a 'restrictions process'. This appears to be based on the existing Dangerous Substances Packaging Directive,[66] but importantly extends restrictions to the manufacture of chemicals.

Effectively, there will be an accelerated risk management process for chemicals that pose unacceptable risks to humans or the environment and require urgent risk reduction measures. Risk reduction measures will be established on the basis of targeted risk assessments. The process is initiated by the preparation of a dossier setting out the case for action. The dossier can be prepared by the ECA in response to a request by the Commission. Alternatively, the Agency may receive a dossier from a Member State, in which case the ECA will appoint rapporteurs to

[66] Dir. 76/769/EEC, n. 15 above.

confirm that the dossier meets the requirements set out in an Annex to the Regulation on chemical risk assessment and socio-economic analysis. Any shortfall from the Annex specification in the dossier is to be relayed to the Member State within 45 days. The Member State then has 30 days to bring the dossier up to the standard specified in the Annex. Failure to do so will end the procedure. There then follows a three-month period for comment on completed dossiers, which are published on the ECA's website. After the period for comment, the dossier goes to a risk assessment committee and a socio-economic analysis committee within the ECA. Both committees prepare an opinion on the restrictions proposed in the dossier within a six-month period. If there is a significant difference between the opinions of the two committees then the socio-economic analysis committee reviews its opinion within a 90-day period. The Commission then receives the opinions and submits a proposal on the chemical to a committee of Member States within three months.

It is clear that authorization and on occasion restrictions can be proposed at any time throughout the process and will not necessarily need to wait until risk assessments are completed. Authorizations will be time limited, with the possibility of an application being made for continued use. An authorization might incorporate a review period for particular uses of the authorized chemical, again linked to the possibility of application for continued use. Subsequent to the publication of the draft Regulation, the Commission has included a prioritization clause in the authorization process—substances with the 'highest expected regulatory outcomes' will be given priority. Enforcement of REACH will be by Member States, who are expected to monitor compliance and apply sanctions. This will be particularly difficult in the case of imported products (see below). It was originally proposed that substantial fines, up to 10 per cent of an offender's global turnover, might be applied for breach of the Regulation. The Commission, after the consultation period, has removed the figure of 10 per cent. The draft Regulation required that the ECA's website would provide the public with information on authorized chemicals, including risk assessments. Companies could claim some information as confidential but not test results for a chemical. The Commission has since amended and there are restrictions on disclosure of some information. The use and tonnages of chemicals, the 'full' composition of preparations, and links between manufacturers and downstream users will all be confidential except in cases of health or environmental emergencies. The name of the registrant may, also, be kept confidential.

Chemicals that are exclusively limited to being components in products do not require notification under the Dangerous Preparations Directive unless containing specified chemicals above guide concentrations set out in Annex 1 of the Dangerous Substances Packaging Directive, i.e. classified as 'dangerous'.[67] It is

[67] See Krämer, n. 7 above, 161 and 163.

proposed in the draft Regulation that any 'dangerous' substance contained in a product in quantities of more than one tonne per year per company must be registered. The requirement for registration is, however, based on a further criterion that there are reasonably foreseeable conditions that the chemical may be released to the environment in sufficient quantities to cause human health or environmental harm. If imported products contain 'dangerous' substances in quantities of more than 1 tonne but are not intended for release as part of their commercial use but release may cause harm, then they must be notified. The ECA is to decide whether registration will be needed in these cases. There is a general 'duty of care' on manufacturers and importers of products proposed in the draft Regulation. This has subsequently been replaced by a general principle that it is 'up to' companies to ensure this. There is, however, no requirement to disclose the chemicals that are in a product.

Under the authorization process there is a key and substantive change in the burden of proof. The existing regime puts the onus on the regulatory authorities to show chemicals pose unacceptable risks, not only through risk assessment but linked to cost-benefit analysis. The proposed Regulation reverses this and requires industry to justify a specified use of a chemical that might otherwise be banned. Essentially the burden of proof has been shifted to the manufacturer to demonstrate that the product is safe for specified uses. The draft Regulation proposed a duty of care on a manufacturer, importer, or downstream user to ensure that a chemical can be used safely, with no adverse effects on the environment or human health, under conditions that can be reasonably foreseen. The Commission has replaced the 'duty of care' by the phrase 'up to' companies to do, diluting the requirements in the face of strenuous objections from industry during the consultation.

D. The European Chemicals Bureau

The final major proposal discussed in the White Paper was the creation of a 'central entity', probably through the expansion of the European Chemicals Bureau. The Commission has now proposed the formation of the European Chemicals Bureau (ECA) with a key role in the expansion of chemical regulation as described above. At present the regime for new chemicals is largely decentralized with the manufacturer choosing the Member State in which to submit the notification dossier, and with that country carrying out the evaluation. There are provisions for the exchange of information between Member States, and the Commission resolves any disputes over individual chemicals. The Existing Substances Regulation provides a more centralized regime with the allocation, by the Commission, of lead Member States to undertake the risk assessment on priority list chemicals.

Under the proposed new Regulation the process will become much more centralized and the ECA will administer REACH undertaking the following functions:

1. Receive, and check for completeness, registration dossiers from manufacturers and importers, reports from downstream users.
2. Maintain a central database for the pre-registration phase of REACH and for registered chemicals.
3. Allocate substances to Member States for evaluation, support and coordinate this work and the decision-making process at this level.
4. Provision of the operational framework for authorization, coordinating and ensuring the smooth transfer of information on registration, authorization, and decisions between the parties involved in the process.
5. Maintain a classification and labelling inventory.
6. A range of technical functions including spot-checks and computerized screening of registered chemicals for characteristics of particular concern, preparation of guidance and software tools, drafting enforcement criteria and coordinating enforcement projects.

Thus, the ECA is intended not simply as a facilitator to administer the smooth operation of the REACH system and to maintain a chemical database, but rather to be proactive, overseeing and contributing to the process. The ECA of necessity, therefore, will be much larger than the European Chemical Bureau in order effectively to deliver its extensive role to manage chemical safety under the Regulation. National authorities will also have increased demands placed on them under REACH. The costs of the process will be predominantly borne by industry. Registration, evaluation, and authorization fees will be raised from manufacturers, importers, and downstream users and divided between the ECA and national authorities. The actual level of the fees is as yet unclear, and will undoubtedly prove to be highly controversial.

IV. Conclusion—Implications of REACH

It has been acknowledged that the Existing Substances Regulation has not worked effectively,[68] and it is largely to remedy this that the Commission has brought forward the far-reaching proposals in the draft Regulation. A broad sweep of changes proposed in the draft will have a major impact on the regulation not only of existing chemicals, but also of new chemicals. It has been

[68] See for example HoL European Union Select Committee, n. 6 above, and Royal Commission on Environmental Pollution, *Response to the Department of Environment, Transport and the Regions' Consultation on the European Commission's White Paper on Chemicals*, News Release, 26 April 2001.

generally accepted that the Dangerous Substances Packaging Directive has been an effective tool for regulating new chemicals, and in part this is reflected in the draft Regulation. Some of the principles and procedures for new chemicals are incorporated in the proposed new regime. The draft Regulation undoubtedly represents a bold attempt by the Commission to produce a unified system of regulation for chemicals, and address the problems identified in the Existing Substances Regulation. A unified system undoubtedly has attractions, but should not put in jeopardy the success story that was found in regulating new chemicals.

There are a number of fundamental changes proposed in the role of industry and downstream users in the regulatory process, and in the cost of regulation to businesses. In addition, there is a crucial change from current legislation in that industry must show a chemical is safe for specified uses rather than the regulator proving that use of a chemical poses unacceptable risks. The draft Regulation is highly complex, revolutionary rather than evolutionary, and likely to have major implications when implemented. A variety of issues may influence the effectiveness of the draft Regulation, and are worthy of some consideration.

The allocation of the Member State to undertake the evaluation of a chemical substance has a number of implications. It is a departure from the regime for new chemicals, since manufacturers will no longer be able to select the country in which to submit the technical (notification) dossier. Moreover, the intention is that the allocation between Member States should be proportionate and equal. This is to address the current situation where a number of Member States receive more notifications than others, in part as a reflection of the resources made available within a country to fulfil this role efficiently. A central entity, such as the one envisaged, should have the effect of harmonizing decisions, avoiding the problem of some Member States requiring risk reduction measures more frequently than others.

The slow working of the Existing Substances Regulation has been due in no small part to a lack of incentive, indeed considerable disincentive, for industry to supply data on a chemical to regulators. This effectively means that risk assessment and action on any necessary risk reduction measures, up to and including a ban, on use of the chemical is substantially delayed and the chemical can continue to be marketed. The draft Regulation introduces time limits on manufacturers and regulators throughout the REACH process, although these have subsequently been somewhat relaxed in the face of fierce criticism from industry. Even so, time limits will undoubtedly provide the impetus for a faster regime than currently exists. It does not appear, however, that many chemicals will be refused registration, and effectively banned from the EU market, on the basis of incomplete data sets. It will be at the evaluation stage that full and specified data sets will ultimately be required. The change in the approval (authorization) system may be a key mechanism to encourage manufacturers to be more proactive in generating full data sets. Positive approval of chemicals for specified uses and the onus on industry to demonstrate the safety of their product in order to obtain authorization or face a lack of approval for marketing, effectively a ban, should persuade industry to become more proactive in supplying data on existing chemicals.

As with the Existing Substances Regulation, the REACH process is set a formidable task. 'Full registration documents will be required for some 30,000 substances and perhaps 30,000 intermediates which are placed on the market, together with limited dossiers for some 40,000 other intermediates and 30,000 polymers—around 130,000 in total'.[69]

Approximately 5,000 of the substances are marketed in quantities of over 1,000 tonnes per year, and require the greatest testing. The workload for national regulators and the ECA is likely to be daunting, requiring substantial investment and resources. The expansion will be broadly funded by industry through fees for registration and evaluation, and for authorization. This funding will be divided between national regulators and the ECA. Clearly, for REACH to work effectively, funding must be at appropriate levels with considerable implications in terms of costs for industry. These costs remain opaque, and will be affected by the number of chemical substances going through the REACH process and the speed of their authorization, which will vary with testing requirements. Estimates for direct costs vary from €1.3 billion to €7 million, but the most likely scenario is for costs of €2.3–4 billion.[70] Manufacturers and downstream users have long held that such costs would stifle the competitiveness of the EU chemical industry in the global marketplace and the ability of industry to be innovative, and place an excessive burden particularly on SMEs.[71] This has now been addressed by the Commission reducing requirements set on downstream users, the majority of which are SMEs. Concerns have also been raised about the amount of product rationalization that might occur under REACH. This could potentially lead to a loss of lower volume and lower value chemicals from the marketplace, affecting downstream users in particular. The Commission counters this by pointing to the lengthy exemption from registration for chemical substances undergoing research and development (R&D), the raising of the registration threshold to 1 tonne annually rather than the present 10 kilograms for new substances, and the ending of the bias against new substances in the current legislation. The Commission also suggests that 'the requirements for authorization should encourage companies to increase their search for finding safer products',[72] in other words stimulating innovation. There is no requirement in the proposed legisla-

[69] n. 65 above.

[70] Risk & Policy Analysts Ltd., *Assessment of the Impact of New Regulations in the Chemical Sector* (prepared for the European Commission Enterprise Directorate-General), June 2002. An updated study by RPA was published in November 2003. E. Liikanen Press Conference on Chemicals, *The EU Chemical Strategy Working towards a Sustainable Approach.* Brussels, 7 May 2003.

[71] See for example R. Butler, 'EU rules alarm industry' (2003) 10 *Chemistry & Industry* 9; and *CEFIC* European Chemical Industry Council Press on the chemicals policy, Brussels, 6 May 2003.

[72] See e.g. *Questions and Answers on the New Chemicals Policy REACH.* Commission Press Release Memo/03/99, Brussels, 7 May 2003.

tion to encourage the use of safer alternatives, although recent changes to the draft Regulation no longer exclude the existence of alternative chemicals or technologies as a reason for not authorizing a chemical. It will be interesting for the future to assess the actual impact of the Regulation on innovation. A company must, of course, innovate to survive in a competitive market place, and it seems unlikely that this will change under the new Regulation. Much more likely is product rationalization to avoid the costs of REACH for low value and volume products. The implications of this are difficult to predict; it is unlikely that alternatives to low value chemicals will be either developed or easily provided to users. The lighter touch in regulation for low volume chemicals may, however, address some of this problem. It may be that inclusion of consideration of alternative chemicals and technologies in authorization may go some way to stimulate innovation in the direction of 'safer' products. Nordbeck and Faust doubt this and suggest that this would require further support than found in the draft Regulation.[73] There can be no doubt that encouraging industry in the development of chemical products and formulations less harmful to health and the environment is actually crucial for the future of environmental protection. It can be argued that this stands as a foundation stone of precaution for the future. Any regulatory structure that does not encourage the development of less harmful chemicals and their introduction into the marketplace will ultimately fail to ensure protection and sustainability for future generations.

In general, impacts of the Regulation on SMEs may be reduced through low volume substances requiring less registration information, the now much lighter touch for polymers, and the removal of the requirement for downstream users to undertake CSAs. SMEs characteristically manufacture in smaller volumes than large companies, and are frequently involved in product formulations including the production of polymers. The fact that the costs and resources needed for pre-registration and registration can be shared between companies may also go some way to reducing the burden on SMEs. It is essential in chemical risk assessment to consider all the uses of individual chemical substances, and the involvement of downstream users, often SMEs, in REACH is essential. Undoubtedly, SMEs will require substantial support, advice, and guidance to fulfil their role in the regulatory process, particularly if they choose to undertake CSAs. Downstream users must be proactive in identifying all uses for a chemical substance entering the Registration process; failure to do so will mean that risk assessments may be significantly flawed.

The costs of chemical risk assessment go beyond purely monetary and resource issues. Considerable concern has been voiced about the likely amount of animal testing under REACH, estimates by animal-rights groups suggest that up to twelve million animals might be used.[74] Animal testing is, of course, a conten-

[73] n. 23 above.

[74] n. 6 above. See also G. Murphy, 'Time runs Short for Opponents of Chemical-Testing Rules' (2003) 424 *Nature*, 241.

tious issue under existing legislation. There has been considerable pressure for change and for research into toxicological methods that offer an alternative to using animals in tests.[75] Such methods are difficult to develop and validate, but there is considerable international research collaboration to make alternatives available. The application of non-animal tests to toxicological assessments of industrial chemicals is, however, in its early stages. Undoubtedly, ethical concerns over animal tests have acted as a catalyst driving the development of techniques to avoid animal testing, but at present the science may not be adequate to meet the pressure. Other driving forces exist behind developing alternatives to animal tests, including cost and the fact that tests are often highly time-consuming, elements of considerable concern when developing a testing programme. The EU White Paper has a stated aim to promote non-animal testing and the Commission claims that proposed legislation for the REACH process will minimize animal testing through substantial use of existing data on chemical substances, through largely avoiding animal tests for chemicals produced at volumes of one to ten tonnes per year, through rigorous validation of end-points in tests to ensure they are relevant to the assessment; and avoidance of duplicate testing through data sharing.[76] Nonetheless, a great deal of animal testing will be required and a tension will remain until other testing methods become available.

A significant plank in the Commission's claim to minimize animal testing under REACH is that 'information requirements have been trimmed to enable smart and targeted testing, which takes into account the likely exposure by the use (s) of the substance to enable an adequate risk management'. A recent study, however, has raised considerable questions over the adequacy of targeted testing. The ECA and the Dutch Institute of Public Health (RIVM) undertook a study on the first 41 priority list compounds to complete the assessment process under the Existing Substances Regulation.[77] A number of noteworthy findings were made that have implications both for the current legislation and also for the proposed new Regulation. The findings of the report were:

1. The end point of risk evaluation for the rapporteur under the Existing Substances Regulation is to put forward one of three conclusions on the substance to the Commission. These are that existing risk reduction measures for the chemical are adequate; that new risk reduction measures are necessary; or that further data and testing on the substance is needed (see above). Only seven chemicals fell into the category that existing risk management was adequate.

[75] See e.g. Commons Select Committee on Animals in Scientific Procedures Report on *Animals in Scientific Procedures*, n. 56 above; and OECD, *Appraisal of Test Methods for Sex Hormone Disrupting Chemicals*, OECD Environment Health and Safety Publications Series on Testing and Assessment (2001) No. 21.

[76] *Questions and Answers on the New Chemicals Policy REACH.* Commission Press Release Memo/03/99, Brussels, 7 May 2003.

[77] Bodar *et al.*, n. 43 above.

2. The additional data or risk reduction measures for the remaining 34 substances were needed to resolve or limit risks to workers (80 per cent), to the environment (65 per cent), to consumers (35 per cent) and because of risks arising from indirect exposure of humans via the environment (35 per cent).
3. The reasons that the chemical substance was initially selected to be included in the priority lists, that is, the prediction of the group at risk, were often not substantiated, but rather emerged from the risk evaluation. It was notable that all three types of health risks were commonly underestimated, whereas risks to the environment tended to be overestimated. There were as many underestimates as overestimates of risk to consumers. The predictability of the risks associated with chemical substances appears poor.

It is evident from these findings that our knowledge of risks associated with specific chemicals is low, and appears to be a broadly inadequate basis to select priority chemicals. The fact that the majority of chemicals targeted in the initial priority lists under the Existing Substances Regulation required risk reduction action of some kind might not be reassuring, since it was often for different reasons than originally envisaged. Targeted testing on the basis of likely exposure and risks may then lack a firm foundation. The question must arise as to whether chemicals that are not prioritized may, in reality, pose significant risks. Unpredictability of chemical impacts has significant implications for the proposals for target testing under the draft Regulation. The Royal Commission on Environmental Pollution (RCEP) has criticized the REACH process as 'cumbersome and time-consuming' and

> The infeasibility of carrying on with traditional approaches for hazard and risk assessment and not exploiting fully new technologies and advances in computational assessment techniques are serious failings.... Where REACH fails is that it has been insufficiently radical in its approach to the actual process of assessing hazards and risks from chemicals.[78]

It may be that a more radical approach would answer not only the difficulties of targeted testing but also reduce animal testing.

Consideration of the RIVM study gives rise to another substantial and linked limitation in the REACH proposals. Chemical impacts may be unforeseeable, and it is this that, in the end, finally limits the effectiveness of any testing and assessment programme. Effects that were unforeseen or that had a different magnitude than predicted in risk assessments have often been identified through monitoring programmes. A recent example of this are a variety of chemicals that have endocrine-disrupting effects, with serious health and fertility implications

[78] The Royal Commission on Environmental Pollution, n. 10 above, 164.

for animals; the ecological stability of animal populations; and for humans.[79] Such effects were identified through environmental monitoring, not through hazard and risk assessments on chemicals. In fact, definitive tests for the endocrine disrupting capacity of chemicals are not yet established. The REACH process has not incorporated any mechanisms to link environmental monitoring with risk assessment, or feed into environmental monitoring programmes. In the Twenty-Fourth Report, the RCEP has strongly recommended that such a link should be made: 'Those responsible for overseeing the regulatory control of chemicals must have clearly defined routes through which they can influence environmental and monitoring programmes to deliver the required information, and that information must be integrated into the assessment process at all stages'.

The advantages of such a mechanism cannot be overstated. It would undoubtedly increase our ability to identify unforeseen impacts, and offer a method of continually reducing scientific uncertainty linked to a chemical substance or product. Failure to incorporate such a feedback loop into each stage of REACH is a highly significant omission. Inclusion of environmental and monitoring programmes would improve the efficacy of REACH immeasurably, and act as an important safeguard for the sustainable use of chemicals. In addition, REACH should incorporate some mechanism for continual review of data on a chemical, including monitoring and environmental programmes and also basic data sets on a chemical as knowledge on chemical substances improves. Periodic review, updating data, and incorporating monitoring data could be usefully performed by the ECA. If new material suggests a previously unknown hazard that should be incorporated in the risk assessment, the ECA should be able to revisit a CSA and require additional testing on a chemical.

The exceptionally limited registration requirement for intermediates, polymers, and products now proposed after the consultation on the Regulation also raises a number of questions that go to the robustness of the legislation in ensuring chemical safety. Intermediates that are not themselves marketed may exist in substantial quantities on manufacturing sites, and may be accidentally released to the environment. There may, however, be little a priori knowledge about the human and environmental health risks from any such release. Given the number of intermediates currently in existence, the Commission's decision to

[79] A well-known example of an endocrine disrupting chemical is tributyl tin (TBT) used in antifouling paints on the hulls of ships and yachts. The impact of TBT was first noted in the masculization of female dog whelks living in harbours and marinas and in the early 1980s this was linked to pollution from TBT. Since then, other examples of EDC action have been documented for other marine animals. It is, however, far from established that EDCs adversely affect humans although there is some suggestion that this may be the case. See the Royal Society, *Endocrine Disrupting Chemicals* (*EDCs*), published on the Internet at: http://www.royalsoc.ac.uk, for a useful summary of our current knowledge on EDCs. Concern is such, however, that the EU is developing strategies to deal with the EDCs, see Community Strategy for Endocrine Disrupters COM(99)706 and also *Implementation of the Community Strategy for Endocrine Disrupters*—A Range of Substances Suspected of Interfering with the Hormone Systems of Humans and Wildlife COM(2001)262.

give a light touch to intermediates is unsurprising both in terms of costs and avoiding overwhelming the new regulatory system. Yet, Seveso and Bhopal were both the result of chemical accidents and releases relating to intermediates at manufacturing plants. Similarly, polymers and mixtures of chemicals in products may behave very differently than the parent chemical substance(s) and knowledge of interactions and effects are frequently very limited.[80] It is in products that the majority of chemicals will come into contact with the environment and humans. The willingness of the Commission to embrace the estimation of risks associated with intermediates and mixtures of chemicals appears limited, particularly under pressure from industry and governments concerned about the competitive impact of the Regulation. This marks a failure in the evolving Regulation. REACH will not exert appropriate precautionary influence throughout the life-cycle of chemicals. RCEP's recommendation for incorporating information from monitoring programmes in the regulation of chemicals remains as valid for polymers and products as for individual chemicals. Here again, collection and review of information from monitoring and environmental programmes and other scientific data as they become available may go some way to balance the light regulatory regime proposed for intermediates, products, and polymers. This would not require industry to be involved in *de novo* testing, but could involve the ECA in an information collection and review role.

A further serious failing of the draft Regulation is the lack of positive incentives to use alternative substances or technologies that are less hazardous even if available. The Commission has removed from the draft Regulation the phrase that 'existence of alternative substances or technologies does not constitute sufficient reason to refuse an authorization'. They have stipulated that any alternatives must have a risk assessment, but have not made the existence of alternatives that pose lower risks sufficient reason to refuse authorization. For some time a key issue in chemicals policy has been the development of a process by which chemicals that are hazardous and high risk are replaced by safer, low risk substances.[81] Although it is recognized in the Commission White Paper as a laudable aim, the Commission appears to be relying on consumer pressure for safer products to act as the catalyst for this change. It is suggested that the availability of improved chemical safety data on the ECA website will raise awareness and facilitate pressure for change. This premise may prove to be unfounded. Public influence in catalysing change by industry is likely to be relatively unaffected unless producing companies and users are known. It is undoubtedly possible that certain chemicals become highly publicized *bêtes noires* if linked to substantial and adverse effects or if there is concerted speculation about such effects. However, given the sheer number of chemicals, and the fact

80 See McEldowney and McEldowney, n. 11 above, 50–77.

81 See HoL European Union Select Committee, n. 6 above, and The Royal Commission on Environmental Pollution, n. 10 above.

that they are commonly marketed in a diversity of products, it is difficult to visualize how consumer pressure might be effective in moving manufacturers towards the use of safer chemicals, particularly since there has been an extension of information that is confidential under the draft Regulation introduced after the consultation period. The lack of positive measures within the draft Regulation to encourage substitution of hazardous chemicals by safer alternatives by manufacturers is problematic. A more precautionary stance by the incorporation of mechanisms to promote the use and development of safe alternative chemicals by industry, as recommended by the RCEP throughout its Twenty-Fourth Report, would undoubtedly have substantially strengthened the Regulation. The EU White Paper and proposed Regulation are set within the overall framework of sustainable development. It seems an anathema to this concept that the proposed legislation is unlikely to achieve any real movement towards the substitution of safer chemicals.

The draft Regulation is inevitably controversial, and there are many detractors, not least the chemical industry. The proposed timetable for the introduction of REACH does not encourage the belief that there will be any rapid change in the status quo in terms of the vast numbers of chemicals that have not entered a regulatory process. Nor is there much to encourage the belief that our poor knowledge base on the impacts of most industrial chemicals will improve radically in the near future. Nor will REACH encourage substitution of chemicals by less harmful alternatives. The lack of incorporation of environmental and monitoring programmes within the REACH process is another major flaw in the Regulation, and targeted risk assessments, although laudable in reducing animal testing, may be based on false premises and in themselves cause unreliability in risks assessments. The ubiquity of industrial chemicals makes it essential that scientific uncertainties on their impacts are resolved and risk management measures are applied throughout the life-cycle of chemicals. This is a key foundation stone in setting product, process, emission, and quality standards to protect the environment and human health, and dilution of the process to assess risk within REACH challenges the setting of a wide range of environmental and health standards. One far-reaching change under the draft Regulation, however, will be a major achievement in the regulation of industrial chemicals within the EU. Use of industrial chemicals will be banned unless specifically approved. The onus is on industry to prove the safety of chemicals, not on regulators to prove unacceptable hazards and risks. It is the first step towards adopting greater precaution in our use of chemicals, and eschewing unsustainable practices in the chemical industry. Unfortunately, an opportunity has been missed. Positive measures to enhance the adoption of safer chemicals as part of REACH would have moved the chemical industry more forcibly towards sustainability.

Environmental Liability and Private Enforcement—Lessons from International Law, the European Court of Justice, and European Mining Laws

*Gerrit Betlem**

I. Introduction

This chapter examines legal developments at European Community (EC) level relevant to environmental liability provisions as contained in Directive 2004/35/EC on Environmental Liability with Regard to the Prevention and Remedying of Environmental Damage (Environmental Liability Directive).[1] It hence builds upon our earlier contribution in the second volume of this Yearbook, and covers legislative and judicial contributions during the period 2000–3. Those developments are critically reviewed in light of obligations imposed on the EC by an international Convention, empirical research into the deterrent effects of tort law, seminal case law of the European Court of Justice (ECJ), as well as comparative law research into the specialized field of mining law. The ECJ case law on private enforcement and the comparative analysis of mining law are covered to deal with those aspects of environmental liability which have, erroneously in my view, been left out of the Environmental Liability Directive.

First, a chronological account of events is provided (section II), followed by a discussion of the Council Common Position of September 2003 on the Environmental Liability Directive. As will be seen, from a private law perspective, the Common Position is perhaps most noteworthy for what it does not contain, that is, tort as an enforcement tool for public law standards. Having said that, the Environmental Liability Directive nonetheless will have an impact on private law

* Reader, University of Exeter (UK) This contribution has benefited from the EU-funded Research Project ERMITE (Environmental Regulation of Mine Waters in the European Union), contract no. EVK1-CT-2000–0078, and further develops my contribution to A.S. Hartkamp *et al.* (eds.), *Towards a European Civil Code* (The Hague/London/Boston: Kluwer, forthcoming). I am grateful to my colleagues Dr C. MacMaoláin and Professor A. Tettenborn for their comments on earlier drafts.

[1] Adopted after completion of this chapter. [2004] OJ L143/56. See G. Betlem and E. Brans, 'The Future Role of Civil Liability for Environmental Damage in the EU' in (2002) 2 *Yearbook of European Environmental Law*, 183–222.

in at least one respect: it may give rise to claims before civil courts with a view to recognition and enforcement abroad (section III). Next, a framework of empirical research into the deterrent effect of liability is provided (section IV). Section V of this chapter reviews an international Convention requiring effective access to justice to combat violations of environmental law by both private persons and public authorities (the Aarhus Convention). The next section (section VI) focuses on judicial developments in the Europeanization of (environmental) liability law within the above-mentioned framework of empirical research. Before drawing conclusions (section VIII), the *avant garde* of certain legislative techniques for removing barriers to effective access to justice under a number of European mining liability regimes is examined (section VII).

II. Chronology

A short reminder of the recent history of environmental liability law at the Community level may be useful. The legislative progress leading up to the adoption of the final text of the Environmental Liability Directive has been very slow. Indeed, many commentators were not sure whether the proposal would become law at all. However, the political climate in the first years of the 2000s differed from that in the 1990s in that there was a growing public concern over the environmental consequences of various pollution incidents that had occurred over the years, and the possible effects of releases of genetically modified organisms (GMOs) on public health and the environment.[2] This increased public environmental awareness provided an incentive for regulators to establish rules on environmental liability.

The first time that harmonization of environmental liability law was mentioned in an EC legislative instrument was in 1984, in Article 11(3) of Directive 84/631/EEC on the Supervision and Control within the European Community of the Transfrontier Shipment of Hazardous Waste (Hazardous Waste Directive),[3] pursuant to which the Council was under a duty to regulate the liability for damage caused by waste. Although this obligation has applied since 6 December 1984, legislative progress has so far resulted only in an Amended Proposal for a Council Directive on civil liability for damage caused by waste.[4] In any event, this duty to legislate no longer applies, since the Hazardous Waste Directive has been replaced by Regulation (EEC) No. 259/93 on the Supervision and Control of Shipments of Waste within, into and out of the European Community (Waste

[2] See generally C.P. Rogers, 'Liability for the Release of GMOs into the Environment—Exploring the Boundaries of Nuisance' (2003) 62 *Cambridge Law Journal*, 371–402.

[3] [1984] OJ L326/31 (no longer in force).

[4] [1991] OJ C192/6; see for an extensive commentary P. von Wilmowsky and G. Roller, *Civil Liability for Waste* (Frankfurt am Main: Peter Lang, 1992), Studies of the Environmental Law Network International, Vol. 2.

Shipment Regulation).[5] The Regulation, however, does not contain any reference to a regime for the liability of producers of waste, and liability is thus governed by the legal systems of the Member States. The Commission is proposing a complete overhaul of the Regulation in light of the Convention on the Control of Transboundary Movements of Hazardous Wastes and their Disposal (Basel Convention).[6] But even in that context, no harmonization of liability rules is being considered; the 2003 Proposal for a Waste Shipments Regulation is explicitly without prejudice to national or Community law on liability.[7] Nonetheless, it presumes that adequate liability rules are in place, as it does require operators to furnish evidence of insurance against liability for damage to third parties.[8]

In 1994, the European Parliament (EP) called for legislation in this area in a resolution calling on the Commission to submit a proposal for a directive on civil liability for environmental damage.[9] It took until 9 February 2000 for the Commission to publish the final version of the White Paper on Environmental Liability.[10] As will be seen, the Commission opted for a so-called horizontal regime, covering damage to the environment resulting from harmful activities generally, instead of sector-specific liability rules concerning, for example, liability for damage caused by GMOs or waste. The document sets out the structure of the likely future EC environmental liability regime. It contains the core elements and principles of a horizontal Environmental Liability Directive. The proposed regime is set up as a framework regime with minimum requirements and standards, and is to be completed over time and on the basis of experience with its initial application. The regime outlined in the White Paper has a closed character, and is linked with relevant EC environmental legislation. It covers two areas: damage caused by activities that bear an inherent risk of causing damage to the environment and that are subject to EC law, and damage to natural resources insofar as these are protected by Community law. A strict liability applies for damage caused by inherently dangerous activities, and a fault-based liability for damage to (what was called) biodiversity caused by activities not listed as dangerous. The regime will not be applied retroactively. Environmental damage that was caused in the past is considered to be a matter that should be dealt with by Member States.

[5] [1993] OJ L30/1 (as amended); in force since 1 May 1994.

[6] Basel (Switzerland), 22 Mar. 1989, Basel (entered into force 5 May 1992) (1989) 28 *International Legal Materials*, 3, 857.

[7] Proposal for a Regulation on Shipments of Waste COM(2003)379.

[8] ibid., Arts. 25(3), 26(8), and Annex II, No. 16. Unchanged in the Amended Proposal of 8/3/04, COM(2004)172.

[9] EP Res. on Preventing and Remedying Environmental Damage [1994] OJ C128/165. See also Opinion of the Economic and Social Committee on the Green Paper [1994] OJ C133/8, para. 2.2.1.

[10] COM(2000)66, published on the Internet at: http://europa.eu.int/comm/environment/liability/.

In January 2002, the European Commission adopted a Proposal for an Environmental Liability Directive, which marked the first formal step in the legislative process after the Commission issued its White Paper.[11] The White Paper outlined some of the key elements of an effective and practicable EU-wide environmental liability regime, including damage to persons, goods, and soil pollution, and also damage to nature. However, what is interesting (and perhaps regrettable) is that the civil liability regime of the White Paper is not reflected in the 2002 Proposal. The proposal underlines that the Directive does not give private parties a right of compensation relating to (threatened) environmental damage at all, even though it leaves intact any rights of recourse by operators against other polluters in situations of multiple party causation under national law. The proposal is confined to actions by public authorities against operators. This generally means proceedings under a public law regime, although this varies from jurisdiction to jurisdiction.[12] Any role whatever for civil liability as a tool of private enforcement by private actors against polluters and as a mechanism to overcome barriers to access to justice therefore has been categorically excluded. In my view, this is incompatible with the Aarhus Convention, of which the EC is a signatory. This is particularly curious, for a number of reasons.

First, the draft Directive was produced at a time when the EC had already signed the Aarhus Convention, and which it is suggested does require a private action to be available to non-public bodies to ensure compliance with environmental law by other non-public bodies (to be further discussed in section V below).

Secondly, the complete exclusion of civil claims by private parties negates a commitment undertaken by the Commission with the EP that a general liability regime would cover damage caused by GMOs. The EP therefore agreed not to press for liability provisions in the revised GMO Directive.[13]

To be sure, one of the reasons for this shift from private to public law is the fact that tort law nowadays operates in a regulatory context.[14] Crudely summarized, the historical development of environmental protection law is that it started with private law alone. In the common law world this was in the form of the torts of

[11] COM(2002)17, [2002] OJ C151E/132.

[12] See also R.G. Lee, 'EU Proposals on Environmental Liability—From a Private to a Public Law Framework' (2003) 34 *Journal of Business Law*, 180; Rogers, n. 2 above, 397.

[13] Betlem and Brans, n. 1 above. Dir. 2001/18/EC on the Deliberate Release into the Environment of Genetically Modified Organisms and Repealing Directive 90/220/EEC [2001] OJ L106/1, recital 16 of the preamble which reads: 'The provisions of this Directive should be without prejudice to national legislation in the field of environmental liability, while Community legislation in this field needs to be complemented by rules covering liability for different types of environmental damage in all areas of the European Union. To this end the Commission has undertaken to bring forward a legislative proposal on environmental liability before the end of 2001, which will also cover damage from GMOs.'

[14] See generally P. Cane, 'Tort as Regulation' (2002) 31 *Common Law World Review*, 305.

nuisance and trespass, in civilian jurisdictions by virtue of general provisions of the law of delict,[15] coupled with the doctrine of abuse of rights and maxims such as *sic utere tuo ut alienum non laedas*. But the emphasis shifted substantially from private to public law enforcement from the 1960s onwards,[16] mainly because tort law was not regarded adequate for environmental protection purposes. Some authors currently advocate a return to an all-or-nothing situation in the sense that public regulation should completely take the place of tort law.[17] Others prefer a complementary role for tort alongside and in conjunction with public law regulatory regimes.[18] It is nevertheless true that environmental law is, and is likely to remain, clearly dominated by regulatory command and control regimes with at most a subsidiary role for tort or delict.

However, that does not mean that there is no longer a meaningful role for old-style tort law. An illustrative example at EU level is product safety. There is a framework dealing with standards and procedures involving controls by public authorities at both EC and national level. In addition to Directive 2001/95/EC on General Product Safety,[19] an autonomous, harmonized, civil liability regime for damage caused by defective products in the form of Directive 85/374/EEC concerning Liability for Defective Products plays an autonomous role.[20] Indeed, an analogous approach was adopted for waste policy with the Commission's 1991 Amended Proposal for a Council Directive on Civil Liability for Damage Caused by Waste.[21] It includes a free-standing liability regime with strict liability of waste producers for damage resulting from their waste. This is a remarkably extensive liability, since not only does it encompass impairment of the environment as a whole, but it is no defence that the defendant complied with a permit

[15] e.g. *Code Civil*, § 1382 and its progeny.

[16] With origins in the nineteenth century, public bodies have long had extensive powers of interference: see, for example, the 'statutory nuisance' regime in England under the Public Health Act 1875, s. 91 ff.

[17] L. Bergkamp, *De vervuiler betaalt dubbel* [*The Polluter Pays Twice*] (Antwerpen/Gronigen: Intersentia, 1998); cf. P. Cane, 'Using Tort Law to Enforce Environmental Regulations?' (2002) 41 *Washburn Law Journal*, 427.

[18] M. Stallworthy, 'Environmental Liability and the Impact of Statutory Authority' (2003) 15 *Journal of Environmental Law*, 3; A. Arcuri, 'Controlling Environmental Risk in Europe—The Complementary Role of an EC Environmental Liability Regime' (2001) 15 *Tijdschrift voor Milieuschade en Aansprakelijkheidsrecht/Environmental Liability Law Review*, 37; see also K.S. Abraham, 'The Relation between Civil Liability and Environmental Regulation—An Analytical Overview' (2002) 41 *Washburn Law Review*, 379; M. Anderson, 'Transnational Corporations and Environmental Damage—Is Tort Law the Answer?' (2002) 41 *Washburn Law Review*, 399; K.N. Hylton, 'When Should We Prefer Tort Law to Environmental Regulation?' (2002) 41 *Washburn Law Review*, 515, and A. Kanner, 'Toxic Tort Litigation in a Regulatory World' (2002) 41 *Washburn Law Review*, 535.

[19] [2002] OJ L11/4.

[20] [1985] OJ L210/29, as amended by Dir. 1999/34/EC amending Dir. 85/374/EEC concerning Liability for Defective Products [1999] OJ L141 /20; a consolidated version is published on the Internet at: europa.eu.int/eur-lex/en/consleg/index1.html.

[21] [1991] OJ C192/6.

or regulatory requirements.[22] This mixed approach, it is submitted, is well suited to deal with risks that slip through the regulatory net.[23]

Neither has the Commission had any hesitation in promoting private enforcement in areas other than environmental law. Noteworthy in particular, apart from the case of product liability already mentioned, are competition law (including unfair commercial practices) and intellectual property (IP).[24] As for IP, a recently adopted directive focuses precisely on this issue.[25] It solely concerns the harmonization of sanctions and in particular private enforcement. A need for equal effectiveness of IP rights throughout the Community is identified; 'disparities between the systems of the Member States for enforcing intellectual property rights are prejudicial to the proper functioning of the Internal Market and make it impossible to ensure that intellectual property rights enjoy an equivalent level of protection throughout the Community';[26] 'current disparities also lead to a weakening of the substantive law on intellectual property and to a fragmentation of the Internal Market in this field'.[27] Therefore, effective enforcement of the substantive IP *acquis communautaire* 'must be ensured by specific action at Community level'.[28] Cannot the same argument be made for environmental protection? Before the case for private enforcement is further analysed from an empirical, international, and judicial perspective, the next section surveys the state of the legislative art until the end of 2003.

III. Council Common Position on Draft Environmental Liability Directive

As mentioned, the draft Environmental Liability Directive has shifted from a primarily private law to a predominantly public law regime. The basic features of the Proposal are retained in the Common Position of the Council.[29] This is not the place for a comprehensive analysis of the Common Position. Suffice it to

[22] On the issue of permit defence, see extensively P. Wennerås, 'Permit Defences in Environmental Liability Regimes—Subsidizing Environmental Damage in the EC?', published elsewhere in this volume.

[23] See Abraham, n. 18 above, 397.

[24] See Commission White Paper on Modernization of the Rules Implementing Arts. 85 and 86 of the EC Treaty [1999] OJ C132/1, Reg. (EC) No. 1/2003 on the Implementation of the Rules on Competition Laid Down in Arts. 81 and 82 of the Treaty [2003] OJ L1/1; Proposal for a Directive Concerning Unfair Business-to-Consumer Commercial Practices in the Internal Market and Amending Directives 84/450/EC, 97/7/EC and 98/27/EC (the Unfair Commercial Practices Directive), COM(2003)356; and Proposal for a Directive on Measures and Procedures to Ensure the Enforcement of Intellectual Property Rights COM(2003)46.

[25] Published on the Internet at: http://europa.eu.int/comm/internal_market/en/indprop/piracy/index.htm.

[26] Preamble, recital 8, COM(2003)46 at p. 29.

[27] Preamble, recital 9, ibid.

[28] ibid.

[29] Common Position (EC) No. 58/2003 of 18 September 2003 [2003] OJ C277E/10.

outline the main features and to represent some of these in Figure 1 and Table 1. For ease of future citation, this chapter hereafter refers to 'the Directive' rather than the 'Common Position'.[30]

Potentially liable persons covered by the Directive are 'operators', as defined in the Proposal. The scope of the Directive in terms of recoverable heads of damages is restricted to 'environmental damage', as defined (see Figure 1);[31] property damage as such, personal injury, and pure economic loss suffered by private parties are not included. Operators are obliged to take either preventive or remedial actions in case of (threatened) environmental damage. The determination of what action should be taken is dealt with in detail in Annex II. The central liability provision stipulates that operators 'shall bear the costs for the preventive and remedial actions taken'[32] (if they have not already executed them themselves). The Directive contains two forms of operator liability: strict liability, where environmental damage was caused by dangerous occupational activities,[33] and fault liability for any other non-dangerous activities but only insofar as damage to protected species and natural habitats are concerned.

The Community legislature leaves it up to the Member States whether operators, who must prove that they have not been negligent, may invoke compliance with an authorization as a defence; this is an important change to the original Commission Proposal which simply included the regulatory compliance defence as such. Likewise the so-called state-of-the-art defence: the Directive provides that Member States *may* allow operators not to bear the remediation costs regarding 'an emission or activity or any manner of using a product in the course of an activity which the operator demonstrates was not considered likely to cause environmental damage according to the state of scientific and technical knowledge at the time when the emission was released or the activity took place'.[34] The approach taken in respect of state of the art echoes that of the Product Liability Directive which likewise left this up to the Member States.[35] However, unlike the latter, the Environmental Liability Directive also allows for the regulatory compliance defence. The inclusion of this option is important in terms of the scope of the Directive.[36] Although there is limited overlap—the Directive explicitly considers

[30] On 30 Mar. 2004 the Council, at its 2,574th meeting on Justice and Home Affairs, adopted the Directive based on the text agreed in the Conciliation Committee, see PRES/04/76. The Directive has been adopted as Dir. 2004/35/EC on Environmental Liability with Regard to Preventing and Remedying Environmental Damage [2004] OJ L143/56.

[31] Art. 2(1)2 also defines 'damage'. It is not clear to me why this is done because 'damage' is restricted to detrimental impacts on natural resources, which in turn are circumscribed in exactly the same terms as the defined notion of 'environmental damage'.

[32] Art. 8.

[33] i.e. activities covered by existing EC environmental law and listed in Annex III of the Dir.

[34] Art. 8(4)b.

[35] See Art. 15(1)b of Dir. 85/374/EEC concerning Liability for Defective Products [1985] OJ L210/29.

[36] See in particular, on the Product Liability Directive, Case C-52/00, *Commission* v. *France* [2002] ECR I-3827; Case C-154/00, *Commission* v. *Greece* [2002] ECR I-3879; Case C-183/00, *María Victoria González Sánchez* v. *Medicina Asturiana SA* [2002] ECR I-3901.

the issue only in the context of multiple causation and where an operator had used a product in the course of its activities—it is interesting to consider the delineation between these two instruments to illustrate the different legislative techniques.[37] Member States are not allowed, even if they so wish, to introduce the regulatory compliance defence in their domestic strict product liability regimes (i.e. within the occupied field of the Directive); something which they are allowed to do under the Environmental Liability Directive. It is submitted that, although the practical effect of the Directive will be more profound than the original proposal, now that there is no longer a mandatory regulatory compliance defence, the added value of this text nonetheless remains unsatisfactory. This is particularly so with regard to damage caused by GMOs, in that the 'level EU-liability field' is limited to environmental damage within the meaning of the Directive, despite a harmonized system of licensing. The continued exclusion of traditional damage means that victims do not benefit from the strict liability.[38] The regime as outlined above may be summarized as shown in Figure 1.

'Habitat damage' is listed separately—despite its already being included in one of the three categories of 'environmental damage'—because the fault liability is only relevant to that type of loss (see Table 1).

Although the above confirms the primarily public law nature of the proposed Directive (notwithstanding its name), two aspects do have an impact on private (international) law: as mentioned, the contrast with liability of producers under

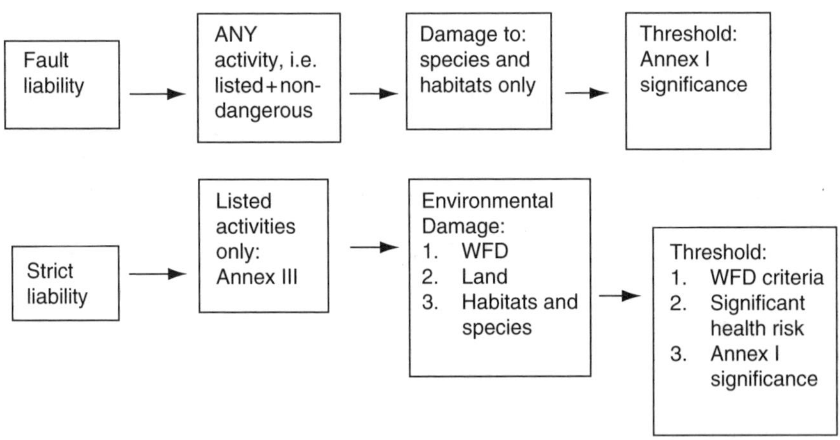

Figure 1. Scope and activities covered from types of liability of the perspective

[37] Cf. for a similar exercise within the Dutch Civil Code: J.H. Nieuwenhuis, *De Ramp op het Pikmeer—Bezwaren Tegen de Geest van het Post-moderne Aansprakelijkheidsrecht* [Disaster on the Pik-lake—Objections Against the Spirit of Post-modern Liability Law] (Deventer: Kluwer, 1997).

[38] Cf. Rogers, n. 2 above, 400–1, noting that the practical impact of the Draft as proposed by the Commission will be minimal.

Table 1. Scope from the perspective of types of loss

Type of damage	Nature of liability	Activities	Damage location	Threshold
Traditional damage[1]				
Habitat/species damage	Strict and fault	All activities	Annex I species and habitats	Annex I significance
Water damage[2]	Strict	Annex III activities	WFD waters	WFD criteria
Land damage	Strict	Annex III activities	Everywhere	Significant risk to human health

Notes:

[1] i.e property damage, personal injury, pure economic loss.

[2] i.e. 'any damage that significantly adversely affects the ecological, chemical and/or quantitative status and/or ecological potential, as defined in Directive 2000/60/EC'. Art. 1(1)(b) of Dir. 2000/60 Establishing a Framework for Community Action in the Field of Water Policy (Water Framework Directive (WFD)) [2000] OJ L327/1.

the Product Liability Directive, and the explicit recognition of potential claims by public authorities against operators based outside their territory.[39] In the absence of a comprehensive system of recognition and enforcement of foreign public law acts, it would seem to follow that such claims will have to brought under Member States' private laws and, if they also constitute a civil and commercial matter, will then benefit from the regime of Regulation (EC) No. 44/2001 on Jurisdiction and the Recognition and Enforcement of Judgments in Civil and Commercial Matters (Brussels I Regulation)[40] to obtain effect throughout the EU.[41]

Other important features of the Directive are the provisions on access to justice, financial security, and non-retroactivity. Natural and legal persons, including recognized NGOs, will have the right to request a public authority to take action; the latter's decision (not) to act must be subject to review by a court or other independent and impartial body. Access to justice therefore remains restricted to public law remedies (judicial review); no direct actions against operators are included. As will be further developed below, this approach only partly satisfies the requirements of the Aarhus Convention (in my view, access to civil remedies should be included). As for financial security, Member States are obliged to encourage its development, but it is not compulsory. By contrast, financial security is obligatory under the draft Mining Waste Directive, which is envisaged to function alongside the Environmental Liability Directive.[42] In

[39] Art.15(3).

[40] [2001] OJ L12/1; the so-called Brussels I Convention remains relevant for Denmark, see generally A. Briggs, *The Conflict of Laws* (Oxford: Oxford University Press, 2002), 52 ff.

[41] See for more details C. Bernasconi and G. Betlem, 'Licences, Liability and Cross-Border Pollution' (2003) 11 *Environmental Liability*, 83.

[42] See Art. 14 Financial guarantee and environmental liability of Proposal for a Directive of the European Parliament and of the Council on the Management of Waste from the Extractive Industries COM(2003)319.

addition, the Commission must within six years after the entry into force of the Directive report back to the EP and the Council on the availability of insurance and other kinds of financial security, which could include a proposal for a mandatory financial security system (Art. 14).

Finally, what will the temporal application of the new regime be like? In particular, will long latency damage be covered where loss emerges after the entry into force of the regime but resulting from events that took place before that moment in time? As is well known, the temporal application of any liability regime must be linked to the time when damage appears, when it was caused, or to a combination of both. The Directive focuses exclusively on events giving rise to damage—not on when any ensuing damage may surface. The watershed date envisaged under the Directive is the transposition date which is set at three years after entry into force (Spring 2007). Any damage (to natural resources only) which appears after that date but which was caused by 'an emission, event or incident that took place before' Spring 2007 is not covered by the Directive (Art. 17). The non-applicability is extended to emissions, events, or incidents occurring after that date when they derive from a specific activity that took place and finished before that date. In the absence of Explanatory Notes at the time of writing, it is difficult to gauge what is intended with respect to ongoing emissions resulting from past operations. Say for example that a mine is no longer functioning in Spring 2007 but mine waters flowing from it cause environmental damage after that date, will the regime apply or not? The text of the Directive would seem to be capable of being so construed that this situation is not covered, despite its not having wholly occurred in the past.

As will be seen, this approach is in marked contrast with at least one Member State's recent law on liability for environmental damage: the 2002 Dutch Mining Act (section VII below) and the general approach under traditional tort law for dealing with ongoing damaging situations (so-called continuing nuisances). It is submitted that if this is the correct approach to non-retroactivity as envisaged by the Community legislature, the effectiveness of liability is unduly restricted. In more general terms, the next section will report on empirical research on the capacity of liability rules to influence the conduct of operators.

IV. Deterrent Effect of Tort Law

There is anecdotal evidence in a recent Dutch article highlighting the ineffectiveness of public enforcement regimes, in particular judicial review; the authors advocate the use of civil remedies as a more effective enforcement tool.[43] Is there any further, more systematic, empirical proof for this belief in tort law as a tool of

[43] W.G.A. Hazewindus and C.J. van der Wilt, 'Rechtsbescherming Tegen Milieuoverlast—Een Pleidooi voor de Civiele Rechtsgang' [Legal Protection against Pollution—A Plea for Private Law Remedies] (2003) 78 *Nederlands Juristenblad*, 322.

enforcement? Schwartz has carried out extensive empirical research on the deterrent effect of tort.[44] He investigated industrial injury,[45] motorist liability, medical malpractice, product liability, non-profit and governmental agencies, occupiers' liability, and made a special study of the unique accident compensation scheme operating in New Zealand. The main aim of his work was to examine the view defended by many Law and Economics scholars that tort law was such a strong deterrent that no regulation at all was needed. He concluded that tort makes a significant contribution to risk prevention/minimization as a supplement to (or alongside) command-and-control systems of regulation. For example, worker compensation claims compared to an alternative of no employers' liability had reduced workplace deaths by 33 per cent;[46] a before-and-after study on the abolition of tort for car accidents in Quebec indicated an increase in fatalities, with similar results from New Zealand's complete exclusion of civil liability for all accidents; '[t]he general threat of liability clearly affects the behaviour of doctors';[47] and finally, the abolition of immunity from suit of certain non-profit organizations in the USA had spurred the introduction of risk management systems. More generally speaking, the latter point is important: it was only because of the threat of liability that risk managers were able to persuade managers of their companies to invest in risk prevention measures. It follows that empirical proof exists of the useful role tort plays as a deterrent of harmful conduct, either independent of or in conjunction with regulation.

V. The Aarhus Convention

Together with all the Member States, the European Community signed the Aarhus Convention in 1998.[48] To date, however, it has not ratified, approved, or adopted the Convention.[49] Of the three main components of the Convention—access to information, public participation in decision-making, and access to justice—only the first two have been covered fully by Community legisla-

[44] G.T. Schwartz, 'Reality in the Economic Analysis of Tort Law—Does Tort Law Really Deter?' (1994) 42 *University College of Los Angeles Law Review*, 377.

[45] See also, for an English case study, B. Pontin, 'Tort Law and Victorian Government Growth: The Historiographical Significance of Tort in the Shadow of Chemical Pollution and Factory Safety Regulation' (1998) 18 *Oxford Journal of Legal Studies*, 661.

[46] Schwartz, n. 44 above, 393.

[47] ibid. 401.

[48] Convention on Access to Information, Public Participation in Decision-Making and Access to Justice in Environmental Matters, Aarhus, 25 June 1998 (1999) 38 *International Legal Materials*, 517. In force since 30/10/01, published on the Internet at: http://unece.org/env/pp/.

[49] Website Aarhus Convention | Status of ratification, published on the Internet at: http://www.unece.org/env/pp/ (visited 1/4/04). Of the Member States after enlargement, the Convention is binding upon Belgium, Cyprus, Denmark, France, Hungary, Italy, Latvia, Lithuania, Malta, Poland, and Portugal. On 21 May 2003, in Kiev, the EC and the fifteen Member States signed an additional Protocol on Pollutant Release and Transfer Registers.

tion.[50] The Aarhus access to justice pillar, to date, has been given effect in Community law only as amendments to the IPPC and EIA Directives.[51] Notably this means that, as a matter of Community law, the Convention's provision on access to civil law remedies forms no part of the EC legal order. However, within the foreseeable future this should change as the Commission adopted an Aarhus 'package' in October 2003 to deal with this third pillar, including a draft Council Decision to approve the Convention[52] and a Proposal for a Directive on access to justice.[53] Community law needs to cover both the EC level as such and the level of domestic law in order to be able to undertake the obligations of the Convention under public international law.

Importantly, the third pillar of Aarhus—access to justice—is not limited to public law. On the contrary, according to Article 9(3), in addition to ensuring access of the public to legal mechanisms—mainly in the form of judicial review—in the event of non-compliance with the Convention's first and second pillars, that is, the provisions on access to information and public participation, access to courts must be made available to combat breaches of domestic environmental law by both private persons and public authorities.[54] Moreover, Article 9(4) requires parties to make effective remedies available, including injunctive relief, which are fair, equitable, timely, and not prohibitively expensive. Finally, the Article requires states to 'consider the establishment of appropriate assistance mechanisms to remove or reduce financial and other barriers to access to justice'.

The Commission Proposal for a Directive on Access to Justice restricts itself to explicit implementation of Article 9(3) in its Article 3 'Acts and omissions by private parties', which reads as follows: 'Member States shall ensure that members of the public, where they meet the criteria laid down in national law, have access to environmental proceedings in order to challenge acts and omissions by private persons which are in breach of environmental law'.

No mention is made of injunctive relief and civil proceedings are not included. The notion of 'environmental proceedings' is defined as 'administrative or

[50] Dir. 2003/4/EC on Public Access to Environmental Information and Repealing Dir. 90/313/EEC [2003] OJ L41/26.

[51] Dir. 2003/35/EC Providing for Public Participation in Respect of the Drawing Up of Certain Plans and Programmes Relating to the Environment and Amending with Regard to Public Participation and Access to Justice Directives 85/337/EEC and 96/61/EC [2003] OJ L156/17.

[52] Proposal for a Council Decision on the Conclusion, on behalf of the European Community, of the Convention on Access to Information, Public Participation in Decision-Making and Access to Justice in Environmental Matters, COM(2003)625.

[53] Proposal for a Directive on Access to Justice in Environmental Matters COM(2003)624, published on the Internet at: http://europa.eu.int/comm/environment/aarhus/.

[54] Art. 9(3) provides: 'In addition and without prejudice to the review procedures referred to in paragraphs 1 and 2 above, each Party shall ensure that, where they meet the criteria, if any, laid down in its national law, members of the public have access to administrative or judicial procedures to challenge acts and omissions by private persons and public authorities which contravene provisions of its national law relating to the environment'.

judicial review proceedings in environmental matters, other than... criminal matters'. However, it is difficult to see how the above-mentioned Aarhus requirements relating to effective remedies by members of the public against violations of the law by private actors can be satisfied without access to the civil courts. An indirect approach of asking the authorities to take steps, combined with judicial review in case of inaction, does not sound like an *effective* remedy to me.[55] In any event, under the proposal remedies against private persons are to be decided upon by national law.[56]

It follows, in my view, that Aarhus, at least as regards those states that have ratified it, includes obligations as regards states to ensure that their legal system includes effective civil remedies for the public (as defined in the Convention) against any person or entity breaching environmental protection law.[57] Although Article 9(3) Aarhus is explicitly referring only to violations of states' '*national* law relating to the environment' (emphasis added), in the context of EC law 'national' must be construed as including Community law, in particular directives and regulations within the meaning of Article 249 EC containing substantive environmental law.[58] This issue will arise even without ratification of Aarhus by the EU, because some Member States are already bound by the Convention and, of course, most of their *national* environmental law is nothing else than transposed *Community* law. Accordingly, private enforcement of EC environmental law is already legally required in some EU Member States.

Although highly significant in terms of harmonization, as a matter of international law, and of domestic tort law for the purpose of the enforcement of national environmental law, the Aarhus Convention does no more than concretize, in the context of environmental law, the more general obligation of states to provide effective remedies arising under provisions such as Articles 6 and 13 of the European Convention of Human Rights.[59] In the next section, it

[55] Admittedly, this as exactly what the Environmental Liability Directive does in its Art. 12. But that is no surprise as it explicitly restricts itself to claims by public authorities unlike the proposed Access to Justice Directive.

[56] Explanatory Memorandum, para. 3.3, COM(2003)624.

[57] See also S. Stec *et al.*, *The Aarhus Convention—An Implementation Guide*, UN Doc. ECE/CEP/72, New York and Geneva 2002, 123–5, published on the Internet at: http://unece.org/env/pp/, 130–6. It is true that the Convention requires access to a court of law *and/or* another body, but the latter must be an independent and impartial body established by law. Normally, only civil courts will be competent to deal with disputes between private actors. *Contra* V. Rodenhoff, 'The Aarhus Convention and its Implications for the "Institutions" of the European Community' (2002) 11 *Review of European Community and International Environmental Law*, 349. According to M. Lee and C. Abbot it is debatable whether a 'citizen suit' is required by this provision: M. Lee and C. Abbot, 'The Usual Suspects? Public Participation under the Aarhus Convention' (2003) 66 *Modern Law Review*, 105.

[58] See also Art. 2(1)g of the Proposed Access to Justice Directive which defines 'environmental law' in this way, COM(2003)624.

[59] Specifically in the environment sector, the same point has been made by the Global Judges Symposium meeting during the Johannesburg World Summit on Sustainable Development, which adopted the 'Johannesburg Principles on the Role of Law and Sustainable Development', 18–20 Aug. 2002, published on the Internet at: http://www.unep.org/documents/.

will be seen that a parallel obligation to make available private enforcement mechanisms arises under EC law as a result of a potentially seminal judgment of the ECJ.

VI. Private Enforcement and the ECJ's *Muñoz* Judgment

It is well known that lack of action by the Community legislature does not necessarily mean that Community law does not develop. Indeed, the ECJ, within the remit of its jurisdiction, can and has made significant contributions to the development of EC law.[60] Most notable in the present context is the consistent law on the role of private enforcement mechanisms in addition to the provisions of the Treaties (and secondary Community law) on a public law enforcement scheme. The latest step in this connection is the *Muñoz* case of 2002.[61] At issue was not environmental law as such but an analogous point: the right of a trader to seek enforcement of food quality standards against a competitor in civil proceedings. The ECJ ruled that the relevant regulations 'are to be interpreted as meaning that compliance with [the quality standards] must be capable of enforcement by means of civil proceedings instituted by a trader against a competitor'. This judgment has implications transcending the field of EC food law. Indeed, in my view, the *ratio decidendi* of this landmark ruling covers all usage of tort law as a tool of enforcing EC public law standards before national civil courts. The tort law of Member States must, as a matter of EC law, be made available as an effective private enforcement instrument. If necessary, restrictive requirements that act as obstacles to effective private enforcement must be modified or disapplied. We will therefore examine the case in more detail.

A. *Muñoz*—Facts and Legal Framework

EC law lays down quality standards for varieties of table grapes in two Regulations: Regulation (EEC) No. 1035/72 on the Common Organization of the Market in Fruit and Vegetables (Regulation on Fruit and Vegetables I),[62] and Regulation (EC) No. 2200/96 on the Common Organization of the Market in Fruit and Vegetables (Regulation on Fruit and Vegetables II).[63] Briefly summarized, they provide that these products may not be marketed in any other manner

[60] See e.g. S. van Erp, 'European Union Case Law as a Source of European Private Law—A Comparison with American Federal Common Law' (2001) 5.4 *Electronic Journal of Comparative Law*, published on the Internet at: http://www.ejcl.org/ejcl/54/art54-1.html.

[61] Case C-253/00, *Antonio Muñoz y Cia SA and Superior Fruiticola SA* v. *Frumar Ltd and Redbridge Produce Marketing Ltd* [2002] ECR I-7289. See also the case note by M. Biondi in (2003) 40 *Common Market Law Review*, 1241.

[62] [1972] OJ L118/1.

[63] [1996] OJ L297/1.

within the EC than in compliance with these standards. Checks must be made by the competent authorities of Member States to ensure that goods do indeed comply with those standards. Regarding table grapes, the regime prescribes an exhaustive system of marking and labelling. That is to say that a variety such as 'Superior Seedless' may not be named anything else but 'Superior Seedless'. In the United Kingdom (UK), the body entrusted with enforcement of these rules is the Horticultural Marketing Inspectorate (HMI). Applicable UK legislation imposes penalties for breach of the Community standards. The Spanish company Muñoz holds exclusive rights to grow these grapes. Competitors marketed their grapes in breach of these exclusive rights. The HMI took no action in response to complaints about mislabelling. Muñoz then sued them before the High Court, seeking an injunction as well as damages.[64] The English court held that the Regulations at issue here did not give the claimants a right of action in civil proceedings; the action therefore failed. On appeal, the Court of Appeal acknowledged that the question of a civil remedy for breach of the regulations was one of general importance in Community law; it accordingly made a referral for a preliminary ruling to the ECJ.[65]

B. Muñoz—the Judgment of the ECJ

The sole issue before the ECJ was whether the relevant food quality standards regulations gave rise to an obligation for traders in fruit and vegetables to comply with those standards, enforceable by means of civil proceedings instituted by competitors. In other words: do product standards laid down by EC (public) law entail, as a matter of EC law, a right of action under national tort law? On a few considerations, the ECJ answered in the affirmative. It started its reasoning by referring to the normative force of EC regulations under Article 249 EC, and their place in the hierarchy of sources of Community law. Regulations are of general application, directly applicable, and 'owing to their very nature . . . operate to confer rights on individuals which the national courts have a duty to protect'.[66] Secondly, the ECJ reaffirmed that those courts must ensure the full effectiveness of those Community rules; the classic *effet utile* requirement.[67]

Thirdly, the ECJ focused on the regulations at issue. It deduced from their preamble and scheme that the purpose of the common quality standards for fruit and vegetables is threefold:

(i) to exclude unsatisfactory products from the market;
(ii) to guide traders as to consumer requirements; and,
(iii) to facilitate fair competition between traders.

[64] See English High Court 26 Mar. 1999 *Muñoz* v. *Frumar* [1999] 3 CMLR 684 (Laddie J.).
[65] Judgment of 10 May 2000, unreported.
[66] ibid., para. 27.
[67] ibid., para. 28.

Accordingly, the ECJ held that the noted *effet utile*, and more specifically the practical effect of the traders' duty to comply with the standards:[68] 'imply that it must be possible to enforce that obligation by means of civil proceedings instituted by a trader against a competitor'.[69]

Finally, the ECJ underlines that the availability of tort claims strengthens the *effet utile* of the quality standards; it supplements enforcement by public authorities with a view to discouraging 'practices, often difficult to detect, which distort competition'.[70] Indeed, the ECJ considers civil actions by competitors 'particularly suited to contributing substantially to ensuring fair trading and transparency of markets in the Community'.[71] It follows that the ECJ's reply to the question referred is that the relevant Regulations, properly construed, include obligations imposed upon traders enforceable by civil action at the behest of other traders.

Three aspects of the judgment merit more detailed consideration in the context of this contribution: (i) the enforcement of regulations; (ii) the enforcement of directives and other EC law instruments; and (iii) the impact on the tort of breach of statutory duty.

C. Private Enforcement of Regulations

Under exactly what conditions should a tort claim be made available to enforce norms laid down in a Regulation? The answer is not clearly given in *Muñoz*, because there are some differences between the ECJ's judgment and the Advocate General's Opinion. In a word, the ECJ applied a wider, broad-brush, approach to the interaction between the violated norm and the civil action that should be available than the more precise and circumscribed approach of Advocate General Geelhoed. As pointed out, the ECJ requires that national law makes available a civil enforcement action to competitors as a matter of interpretation of both Fruit and Vegetables Regulations.[72] It does not say explicitly that only the directly effective provisions of the Regulations give rise to a civil action.

However, if read in conjunction with paragraph 27 of the judgment, this does seem to be the case because in that consideration it is essentially said that all Regulations automatically have direct effect.[73] Without partaking in the long-standing debate as to the equivalence or otherwise of 'directly applicable' and

[68] i.e. Art. 3(1) of both Reg. (EEC) 1035/72 and Reg. (EC) 2200/96, which reads, as far as relevant here: 'The holder of products covered by the quality standards adopted may not display such products or offer them for sale, or deliver or market them in any other manner within the Community than in conformity with those standards. The holder shall be responsible for observing such conformity'.

[69] Para. 30.

[70] Para. 31.

[71] ibid.

[72] Operative part and para. 32.

[73] Citing an earlier authority on this point: Case 34/73, *Fratelli Variola S.p.A.* v. *Amministrazione italiana delle Finanze* [1973] ECR 981.

'directly effective', it is submitted that it is somewhat misleading to regard each and every provision of a Regulation as directly effective by virtue of its nature. Most provisions will be, but some are not; for instance the duty to adopt sanctions or to designate competent authorities requires further action by Member States.[74] Accordingly, one would need to establish first and foremost whether a particular provision of a Regulation has direct effect and then to enquire whether it entails civil enforcement opportunities.

Hence, according to the Advocate General, the fundamental issue before the court is the availability of civil enforcement to a person where the designated public law enforcement body declined to take action (this important aspect of public–private interaction is returned to below). The Advocate General divided the preliminary question into three components:

— does a Regulation give a person a right to compliance by another person?; and, if so,
— does EC law require that that right can be enforced?;
— to what extent does EC law require national legal orders to provide for a civil action?[75]

After the Advocate General had established that the Fruit and Vegetable Regulations at issue intended to promote fair trading so that their protective scopes included competitors, he examined their direct effect in horizontal situations (trader versus trader). Applying well-established case law, there was no doubt that the crucial obligation in question had horizontal direct effect; that is, the addressee's duty not to market products in any other manner within the Community than in conformity with the standards. Under the Fruit and Vegetable Regulations, holders are responsible for observing such conformity.

Does this directly effective provision also confer rights on individuals? The fundamental criterion proposed by the Advocate General is a linkage between the protective scope of the violated norms, and the interests at stake.[76] In essence, this test is nothing other than the well-known *Schutznorm*—does the scope of protection of the norm infringed include the harmed interests of the claimant?—in the context of both EC liability law under Article 288 EC and domestic tort law.[77] In light of the scope of protection of the Fruit and Vegetable Regulations,

[74] T.C. Hartley, *The Foundations of European Community Law* (Oxford: Clarendon, 2003), 204. And see e.g. Art. 36 of Reg. (EEC) No. 259/93 on the Supervision and Control of Shipments of Waste Within, Into and Out of the European Community [1993] OJ L30/1 (as amended).

[75] Opinion, para. 22.

[76] ibid., paras. 46–9.

[77] See for EC law: Hartley, n. 74 at 468, P. Craig and G. de Búrca, *EU Law—Text, Cases and Materials* (Oxford: Oxford University Press, 2003), 549; the leading cases are: Joined Cases 5, 7 and 13–24/66, *Kampffmeyer and Others* v. *Commission* [1967] ECR 245 and Case C-282/90, *Industrie- en Handelsonderneming Vreugdenhil BV* v. *Commission* [1992] ECR I-1937. See for Dutch, English, and German law: *C. Asser's Handleiding tot de beoefening van het Nederlands burgerlijk recht, Verbintenissenrecht, Deel III, De verbintenis uit de wet*, by A.S. Hartkamp, 11th edn. (Zwolle: Tjeenk Willink, 2002), No. 197.

it was said that breaches by Frumar could result in an unlawful act with an adverse impact on Muñoz. The latter then has a right to compliance by the former under Community law. The ECJ presumably has implicitly agreed with the Advocate General on this *Schutznorm* point, in that it too underlined the aims and objectives of the Regulation, although the operative part of its judgment can be read more widely.

Secondly, does EC law require Member States to enable private enforcement? The most important aspect of *Muñoz* (both the judgment and the Opinion) is the obligation for national law to make available civil enforcement for competitors, as a supplement to the public enforcement regime. The Advocate General pointed out that the Fruit and Vegetable Regulations require a public law enforcement system. Crucially, this does not mean that it therefore excludes a private enforcement regime. Put differently, 'the Regulation grants no monopoly in regard to enforcement'.[78] Like the ECJ, the Advocate General considers civil actions by competitors a useful and necessary adjunct to public enforcement by supervisory authorities. A parallel is drawn with competition law, where EC policy is actively to encourage private enforcement. In this field, civil courts' powers exist alongside the enforcement functions of both the Commission and national competition authorities.[79]

The complementary role of public and private enforcement mechanisms as reaffirmed by the ECJ in *Muñoz* is certainly not a novel, freak, strand in its case law. On the contrary, it goes back to one of its earliest, and most important cases, *Van Gend & Loos*.[80] Of course this case is best remembered for the introduction of the concepts of direct effect and the new, autonomous, legal order of Community law. However, it also laid down the dual system of enforcement of EC law obligations by explicitly rejecting the argument by various Member States that the centralized, public, enforcement mechanism of Articles 226–8 EC is exclusive. Thus, it held that:

> A restriction of the guarantees against an infringement of Article 12 [now Art. 25 EC] by Member States to the procedures under Articles 169 and 170 [now 226 and 227 EC] would remove all direct legal protection of the individual rights of their nationals. There is the risk that recourse to the procedure under these Articles would be ineffective if it were to occur after the implementation of a national decision taken contrary to the provisions of the Treaty. The vigilance of individuals concerned to protect their rights amounts to an effective supervision *in addition to* the supervision entrusted by Articles [226] and [227] to the diligence of the Commission and of the Member States.[81]

[78] Opinion, n. 75 above, para. 55.

[79] ibid., paras. 58–62. See the Commission White Paper on modernization of the rules implementing Articles 85 and 86 of the EC Treaty [1999] OJ C132/1; Reg. (EC) No. 1/2003 on the Implementation of the Rules on Competition Laid Down in Articles 81 and 82 of the Treaty [2003] OJ L1/1; Case C-453/99, *Courage* v. *Crehan* [2001] ECR I-6297, and A.P. Kominos, 'New Prospects for Private Enforcement of EC Competition law: *Courage v. Crehan* and the Community Right to Damages' (2002) 39 *Common Market Law Review*, 447.

[80] Case 26/62, *NV Algemene Transport-en Expeditie Onderneming van Gend & Loos v. Netherlands Inland Revenue Administration* [1963] ECR 1.

[81] ibid., para. 13 (emphasis added).

It follows that right from the beginnings of EC law as a shared legal order within the Member States, the ECJ acknowledged the relevance of private enforcement in Community law and, more particularly, its complementary role to the public enforcement mechanism explicitly contained in the Treaty.[82] The three 'pillars' of the argument have since then been consistently confirmed and applied: (i) legal protection of individuals; (ii) dual enforcement mechanism, and; (iii) *effet utile*—perhaps most notably in the ECJ's landmark *Francovich* judgment on state liability for infringements of Community law.[83]

D. Private Enforcement of Directives

The analysis above dealt with the situation that specifically arose in *Muñoz*—civil enforcement of obligations addressed to individuals laid down in an EC regulation. The second question of assessing the *ratio decidendi* of *Muñoz* is: does the same apply when the relevant EC norm is contained not in a directly applicable regulation but in a directive? Strictly speaking, there is also a question about Treaty rules (as they were not in issue in *Muñoz*). However, it is obvious that Treaty provisions can qualify for civil enforcement in the wake of *Muñoz* as the very horizontal effect of Regulations was equated to the horizontal direct effect of relevant Treaty provisions in the Advocate General's Opinion.[84]

Most EC environmental law consists of directives, so the question concerning the implications of the judgment for the private enforcement of directives is particularly pertinent in the context of environmental liability.[85] Also, private enforcement can operate to reduce the implementation gap between the EC and national levels.[86] Of course, directives lack this *horizontal* direct effect.[87] However, they can nevertheless be decisive in disputes between private parties either under the doctrine of consistent interpretation of national law, or by way of so-called incidental effect following *CIA Security* and *Unilever Italia*.[88]

This being as it may, it can be argued that since the ECJ underlined the directly effective nature of regulations, *a contrario* they must be distinguished from

[82] Craig and de Búrca, n. 77 above, 404.

[83] Joined Cases C-6 and 9/90, *Andrea Francovich and Danila Bonifaci and others* v. *Italian Republic* [1991] ECR I-5357 at paras. 32, 33.

[84] See Nos. 43–5 referring to Case C-281/98, *Roman Angonese* v. *Cassa di Risparmio di Bolzano SpA* [2000] ECR I-4139.

[85] J.H. Jans, *European Environmental Law* (Groningen: Europa Publishing, 2000), Ch. 8.

[86] Commission Staff Working Paper, Fourth Annual Survey on the Implementation and Enforcement of Community Environmental Law 2002 SEC(2003) 804, 2.

[87] Case C-91/92, *Paola Faccini Dori* v. *Recreb Srl* [1994] ECR I-3325.

[88] C-194/94, *CIA Security International SA* v. *Signalson SA and Securitel SPRL* [1996] ECR I-2201; Case C-443/98, *Unilever Italia SpA* v. *Central Food SpA* [2000] ECR I-7535; see also C-77/97, *Österreichische Unilever GmbH* v. *Smithkline Beecham Markenartikel GmbH* [1999] ECR I-431 and Case C-159/00, *Sapod Audic* v. *Eco-Emballages SA* [2002] ECR I-5031. See generally Craig and de Búrca, n. 77 above, 211–27 and G. Betlem, 'The Doctrine of Consistent Interpretation—Managing Legal Uncertainty' (2002) 22 *Oxford Journal of Legal Studies*, 397.

directives which therefore do not qualify for '*Muñoz*-enforcement'.[89] However, in my view, this is not the correct approach. The better view is to focus on the analogy between state liability and liability of private persons for breach of Community law. After all, we are not talking about the use of EC law before national courts—either as a shield or as a sword—to displace or modify the application of some rule of Member State law deemed to be incompatible with Community law. At issue is only one point, which is precisely the question for preliminary ruling as formulated by the English Court of Appeal: the civil liability, under domestic tort law, of a private person vis-à-vis another private person for non-compliance with obligations under EC law.

What guidance does the analogy with State liability under *Francovich* principles give? There exists no previous ECJ case on Community liability of individuals for breach of EC law; the only direct precedent is the Opinion of Advocate General Van Gerven in *Banks*.[90] He contended that individuals are liable—just like Member States—as a matter of Community law, for breaches of directly effective provisions of EC law, such as Articles 81 and 82 EC on competition law (as the rule in issue of the ECSC Treaty was held not to produce any direct effect by the ECJ, the latter did not rule on the matter). In line with this conclusion, based on the scope of the *Francovich* liability and its place in the system of EC law, it is submitted that even in the absence of horizontal direct effect of directives, civil enforcement à la *Muñoz* must be made available for non-compliance with obligations laid down in a directive (after, of course, expiry of the transposition date), because it is no requirement of the *Francovich* liability that the infringed norm produces a direct effect.[91] Crucially, this was the case in *Francovich* itself.[92] Indeed, as has been well-established in post-*Francovich* case law, the decisive criterion is the conferral of rights on individuals.[93] It follows that at least for directives that create rights and obligations for individuals, '*Muñoz*-enforcement' must be made available.[94] There is also support for this view in the

[89] Para. 27 of *Muñoz*, n. 61 above. Opinion of Advocate General Geelhoed, Nos. 33–45. see also the head notes in [2003] 3 CMLR 26.

[90] Case C-128/92, *J. Banks & Co. Ltd v. British Coal Corporation* [1994] ECR I-1209. See also (briefly) Opinion Advocate General Jacobs in Joined Cases C-264/01, C-306/01, C-354/01 and C-355/01 of, *AOK Bundesverband and Others* of 22 May 2003 (published on the Internet at: http://www.curia.eu.int), No. 104; the ECJ did not deal with the matter, see its judgment of 16 March 2004. The issue is currently pending before the ECJ in Cases C-438 and 439/03, *Cannito* [2004] OJ C47/13.

[91] See also W. van Gerven *et al.*, *Tort Law* (Oxford: Hart Publishing, 2000), 895; S. Prechal, *Directives in European Community Law* (Oxford: Oxford Uuniversity Press, 1995), 329 and 331.

[92] Para. 26 of the judgment, n. 83 above.

[93] See most recently C-224/01, *Gerhard Köbler* v. *Republik Österreich* [2003] ECR nyr. (judgment of 30 September 2003), which, incidentally, itself concerns an application of the *Francovich* liability to a new situation, i.e. state liability for breach of Community law by a supreme court.

[94] See for an in-depth analysis of this distinction Opinion of Advocate General Jacobs in Case C-316/93, *Nicole Vaneetveld* v. *Le Foyer SA and Le Foyer SA* v. *Fédération des Mutualités Socialistes et Syndicales de la Province de Liège* [1994] ECR I763 and Opinion of Advocate Geeral Lenz in Case C-91/92, n. 87 above.

Muñoz judgment itself, where the ECJ refers to 'confer[ing] rights on individuals which the national courts have a duty to protect'.[95] So, even if the provision has no direct effect, but creates rights for individuals, they can enforce these rights via civil remedies before national courts against other individuals.

It could be argued that most environmental law provisions concern the public at large, imposing obligations on (primarily or even exclusively) public authorities. It is true that this may be so, but that still does not prevent public environmental law from conferring private rights on individuals.[96] This matter has already been addressed in previous case law both in the context of environmental law and in that of state liability. Directives on air pollution, drinking water, shellfish water, and on groundwater protection have been held to be capable of creating individual rights.[97] *Dillenkofer* leaves no doubt that Directive 90/314/EEC on Package Travel, Package Holidays and Package Tours (Package Travel Directive)[98] does not explicitly have to impose individual rights as such; they can be inferred from obligations imposed on the addressee of the norm.[99] The Package Travel Directive provided only that operators must provide sufficient evidence of security for the refund of money paid and for the repatriation of the consumer in the event of insolvency. According to the ECJ, this amounts to conferral of rights on consumers, mainly because of the aims and objectives of the Directive, which is consumer protection.[100] Thus, the requirement of the granting of rights by a provision of EC law, even if laid down in a directive which leaves considerable discretion to Member States, will generally be satisfied in EC (environmental) law. Finally, according to the English Court of Appeal, the notion of 'granting rights' for the purpose of a civil action also plays a significant part in ensuring compliance with the standards of Community public (environmental) law.[101]

E. Towards a European Breach of Statutory Duty

Thirdly and finally, what impact does *Muñoz* have on domestic tort law and in particular on 'breach of statutory duty'? Put differently, has it achieved any harmonization of national tort law? In modern societies, tort law functions in a regulatory context. All EU Member States recognize non-contractual liability for

[95] Para. 27, n. 61 above.

[96] This reasoning echoes Case 26/62, n. 80 above, 12; see also para. 31 of Joined Cases C-6 and C-9/90, n. 83 above.

[97] See Jans, n. 85 above, 213; Prechal, n. 91 above, 137; the cases are all *Commission* v. *Germany*: C-131/88 [1991] ECR I-825 (groundwater), Case C-58/89 [1991] ECR I-4983 (drinking water), Case C-59/89 [1991] ECR I-2607 (air); Opinion Advocate General Jacobs in Case C-237/90 [1992] ECR I-5973, No. 15 (drinking water); Case C-298/95 [1996] ECR I-6747 (shellfish water).

[98] [1990] OJ L158/59.

[99] Joined Cases C-178/94, C-179/94, C-188/94, C-189/94, and C-190/94, *Erich Dillenkofer, Christian Erdmann, Hans-Jürgen Schulte, Anke Heuer, Werner, Ursula and Trosten Knor* v. *Bundesrepublik Deutschland* [1996] ECR I-4845.

[100] Paras. 30–42 of the judgment; see also van Gerven, n. 91 above, 929.

[101] *Bowden* v. *Southwest Services Ltd.* [1999] 3 CMLR 180, para. 14 (C.A.).

violations of written public and private law obligations in some form or other, either literally as a 'breach of statutory duty' (England, Germany) or as part of a more general tort formula (France, the Netherlands).[102] One of the major elements of this tort is the matter of the protective scope. As noted above, generally speaking, liability for a violation of a written norm is circumscribed by a *Schutznorm* approach. Thus, only those who belong to a class of protected persons included in the protective scope of the violated norm are entitled to a civil remedy: in shorthand entitled the *Schutznorm* doctrine.[103] This norm applies both to domestic tort law and to Community liability.[104]

Even though the protective scope question features across all these legal systems, subtle differences in application by different courts do occur. For example, regarding the type of norms that may be relevant in order to constitute unlawfulness—in other words the meaning of 'statute' for this purpose—systems vary. Dutch law includes not only 'real' statutes, i.e. Acts of Parliament, secondary legislation etc., but also the conditions of a licence or permit issued under a statute, international conventions and even, in transnational situations, foreign laws.[105] German law, on the other hand, seems to be limited to domestic primary and secondary legislation. But, like Dutch law, provided the norm is a *Schutznorm*, a breach of a statute will always entail tortious liability.[106] By contrast, the starting point under English law is more or less the opposite: whenever the statute in question provides for a criminal sanction, a civil sanction would be excluded but for two exceptions:

(i) the statute intends to protect a particular class of persons;
(ii) the statute created a public right and a particular member of the public suffers specific, special loss, i.e. different from the rest of the public.[107]

A French equivalent of the Dutch, German, and English 'breach of statutory duty' does not as such exist, but the component of violation of a norm is subsumed under the notion of fault.[108] Having said that, any breach of the

[102] B.S. Markesinis and S.F. Deakin, *Tort Law* (Oxford: Oxford University Press, 1999), 336; B.S. Markesinis and H. Unberath, *The German Law of Torts—A Comparative Treatise* (Oxford: Hart Publishing, 2002), 885; Asser 4-III (2002), n. 77 above, No. 34; van Gerven, n. 91 above, 305.

[103] The term is presumably a kind of 'euro-German' as the 'real' legal German seems to be: *Schutzgesetzverletzung* (Markesinis and Unberath, n. 102 above, 885) or *Normzwecklehre* (Asser 4-III (2002) n. 77 above, No. 97).

[104] Van Gerven, n. 91 above, 894.

[105] Asser 4-III (2002), n. 77 above No. 34; Hoge Raad, 24 Nov. 1989 (1992) *Nederlandse Jurisprudentie* 404 (the *Interlas* case); see for discussions in English: G. Betlem, *Civil Liability for Transfrontier Pollution—Dutch Environmental Tort Law in International Cases in the Light of Community Law* (London: Graham & Trotman, 1993), 122 ff, and G. Betlem, 'Transboundary Enforcement: Free Movement of Injunctions' in S. Deimann and B. Dyssli (eds.), *Environmental Rights—Law, Litigation and Access to Justice* (London: Cameron/May, 1995), 184–229, published on the Internet at: http://www.ex.ac.uk/law/staff/betlem/index.html.

[106] Markesinis and Unberath, n. 102 above, 885–6.

[107] ibid. 343; Opinion Advocate General Geelhoed in *Muñoz*, n. 61 above, No. 55.

[108] J. Bell *et al.*, *Principles of French Law* (Oxford: Oxford University Press, 1998), 355–9. K. Zweigert and H. Kötz, *Introduction to Comparative Law* (Oxford: Oxford University Press,

criminal law in general automatically constitutes a civil fault, giving rise to non-contractual liability. In addition, breach of any other statute or statutory instrument (in French: a *lois* or *règlement*) likewise constitutes a tort within the meaning of the *Code Civil* provisions. Finally on French law, and most pertinently in the *Muñoz* context, an offence relating to anti-competitive practices entitles a victim suffering loss caused by it to recover damages.[109]

In the light of this brief *tour d'horizon*, it would seem to follow that the clearest impact of *Muñoz*'s civil enforcement requirements is on English law. In particular the complementary nature of private and public (including criminal) enforcement means a fundamental re-assessment of the approach of the English courts to 'breach of statutory duty'. A less restrictive approach to granting civil remedies is necessary. No great upheaval to the English law of torts will ensue, though, as legal doctrine in England already thought this was needed. In the specific context of liability—under English law—for directly effective Treaty provisions on competition law, the House of Lords had already acknowledged liability in damages for breach of Articles 81 and 82 EC. It held that those provisions not only promoted general economic prosperity in the common market, but also purported to protect private individuals suffering loss as a result of a violation of them; the relevant tort under English law being 'breach of statutory duty'.[110]

As for German law, in the post-*Muñoz* era, breach of a regulation will have to be included in the notion of 'statute/*Gesetz*' within the meaning of § 823-III Bürgerliches Gesetzbuch (BGB). The same can be said for Dutch law but that had already been held to be the case in any event; by the same token, it would seem that the ECJ's approach in *Muñoz* reflects established French tort law. Accordingly, like *Brasserie du Pêcheur* and *Factortame III* on state liability,[111] *Muñoz* constitutes yet another example of harmonizing effects on Member States' law of non-contractual liability by ECJ case law. The judgment is an important contribution to enhancing the effectiveness of food quality standards as well as other regulatory standards of Community law, including environmental law.

The next step is to ensure that the now mandatory availability of tort remedies are themselves effective. The next section will explore some solutions to overcome some of the barriers faced by claimants in tort actions adopted by various national legislators in the specialized field of mining law. It would appear that regular (environmental) tort law can learn lessons from mining law.

1998), 619; R. Youngs, *English, French and German Comparative Law* (London/Sydney: Cavendish, 1998), 219.

109 Bell *et al.*, n. 108 above, 359–60, 361–4; van Gerven, n. 91 above, 305.

110 Markesinis and Deakin, n. 102 above, 353: citing *Garden Cottage Foods v. Milk Marketing Board* [1984] AC 130.

111 Joined Cases C-46 & 48/93, *Brasserie du Pêcheur SA* v. *Bundesrepublik Deutschland and The Queen* v. *Secretary of State for Transport, ex. p. Factortame Ltd and others* [1996] ECR I-1029; van Gerven, n. 91 above, 951.

VII. European Mining Law

As said above, in the White Paper on Environmental Liability, the Commission acknowledged well-known obstacles for claimants in pollution cases, notably problems of proof of causation between polluters' action and ensuing harm. Two aspects in particular merit attention: the burden of proof of the causal link as well as the costs of the technical assessment/role of experts. The same type of problem arises in other contexts where evidence needed by claimants is in the possession of (potential) defendants. EC legislation has been adopted (or is proposed) to remedy the claimants' evidentiary plight in the fields of non-discrimination, consumer protection, and intellectual property.[112] So far, no action is being contemplated in the environmental sphere. However, this may change, and the Community legislature may then draw inspiration from Member States legislation dealing with damage caused by mining activities. The analogy with environmental harm is quite close, as mining activities have caused significant damage to the environment in recent years as well as the more classic form of mining-related damage: subsidence.[113]

This section provides a comparative overview of specific provisions on easing the claimant's litigation burden under mining laws of England, France, Germany, and the Netherlands.[114] Space does not permit a discussion of the broader context beyond brief introductions; the rules on burden of proof and the furnishing of technical evidence only are covered.

A. England

For the most part, liability rules under English mining law have been drawn up to deal with subsidence damage. There exists a common law right, which is an

[112] See Dir. 2000/78/EC Establishing a General Framework for Equal Treatment in Employment and Occupation [2000] OJ L303/16; Dir. 2000/43/EC Implementing the Principle of Equal Treatment Between Persons Irrespective of Racial or Ethnic Origin [2000] OJ L180/22; Dir. 97/80/EC on the Burden of Proof in Cases of Discrimination Based on Sex [1998] OJ L14/6 (amended by Directive 98/52/EC), consolidated version is available on the EUR-LEX website, published on the Internet at: http://europa.eu.int/eur-lex/en/consleg/index1.html. Consumer law: Dir.2002/65/EC concerning the Distance Marketing of Consumer Financial Services and Amending Dir. 90/619/EEC and Dirs. 97/7/EC and 98/27/EC [2002] OJ L271/16. Intellectual Property: Proposal for a Directive on Measures and Procedures to Ensure the Enforcement of Intellectual Property Rights COM(2003)46; the Directive has recently been adopted.

[113] Information regarding environmental damage and future EC law and policy is published on the Internet at: http://www.europa.eu.int/comm/environment/waste/mining/index.htm. In respect of mining activites, see e.g. J.M. van Dunné, 'Mijn en dijn in de ontwerp-Mijnbouwet' ['Yours and Mine' in the Dutch Mining Bill] (2002) 77 *Nederlands Juristenblad*, 560.

[114] This section reproduces parts of G. Betlem, E. Brans, K. Getliffe, and F. Groen, *Environmental Liability and Mining Law in Europe*, Report for Shared-Cost Action RTD Project ERMITE (Environmental Regulation of Mine Waters in the European Union), Contract No. EVK1-CT-2000-0078, European Commission Fifth Framework Programme, ENERGY, ENVIRONMENT

extension of a person's property rights. In addition, The Coal Mining Subsidence Act 1991 (CMSA) establishes statutory grounds for a party to claim damages, including in the form of remediation costs and depreciation in value, caused by subsidence, without the need to prove negligence.[115] Section 2 of the CMSA places a duty upon operators to take remedial action for any damage caused in the context of lawful coal-mining operations. Accordingly, this constitutes a form of strict liability with no defence of compliance with licence conditions and/or other statutory requirements. The CMSA is now being applied in conjunction with the 1994 Coal Industry Act.[116] Licence holders are liable for damage caused in their area of responsibility, as well as other potentially affected areas in the view of the licensing authority; the Coal Authority is responsible in any other case.[117] Where subsidence takes place in more than one area of responsibility, there is joint and several liability of the responsible parties.[118] Where the responsibility for subsidence damage has become the responsibility of a successor, the successor is liable regardless of whether the damage was caused or occurred before or after that time.[119]

Under English subsidence law, the plaintiff benefits greatly from the reversal of the burden of proof. This operates on the grounds that, for damage which is most likely to be subsidence damage, the onus is on the responsible person to show that the damage is not subsidence damage.[120] Of additional help to the plaintiff is the role of the Coal Authority (CA) as an information exchange. The CA is of extreme importance in the establishment of causation in that it serves as a source of information.[121] The CA may also reimburse reasonable costs incurred by the plaintiff in the pursuit of his/her claim where a successful case has been settled. These costs are anticipated where professional advice or assistance has been sought, for example, from a surveyor.[122] Once a claim has been made, the CA

AND SUSTAINABLE DEVELOPMENT, Key action 1: Sustainable Management and Quality of Water, copies are available from the Exeter CELS website, published on the Internet at: http://www.ex.ac.uk/law/cels/publications.html.

[115] Full texts are published on the Internet at: http://www.hmso.gov.uk.

[116] ibid.

[117] Sects. 37 and 43.

[118] Sect. 44.

[119] Sect. 43.

[120] CMSA 1991, s. 40(2), states: 'where in any proceedings under this Act the question arises whether any damage to property is subsidence damage and the circumstances are such to indicate that the damage may be subsidence damage, the onus shall be on the Corporation to show that the damage is not subsidence damage'.

[121] Coal Industry Act 1994, Part I, section 1(1)(d) states the duties of the Coal Authority to be, inter alia: 'facilitating the establishment and maintenance of arrangements for the information to which persons are to be entitled under this Act to be made available to them'. Part IV of the same Act sets out the rules relating to public access to information held by the Authority. The latter provision is strongly in favour of helping the plaintiff to access substantive independent information and is in keeping with the objectives of transparency.

[122] Sect. 38 of the Coal Mining Subsidence Act 1991. An explanation of claimant's surveyor's fees is published at the Internet at: http://www.coal.gov.uk/Services/subsidence/surveyorsfees.html.

appoints a Managing Consultant to supervise term contractors in the repair of the damage. Under the code of practice, measures are set out as to the means by which the Managing Consultants, Subsidence Assessors and term contractors carry out the remedial works.[123] Furthermore, under the 1994 Act, an Office of the Subsidence Adviser has been set up.[124] This is an independent person who advises and assists claimants; it is the duty of the Authority to give information. In addition, responsible parties must furnish factual information about subsidence.[125] The Subsidence Adviser will not conduct any research into questions of causation; his or her role is limited to the investigation of complaints and making recommendations.[126]

A. French Law—*Code Minier*

Liability of damage to owned natural resources caused by mining activities or mining waters is regulated by the French Mining Code. The Code puts on the person executing the mining works a presumption of strict liability for damage to the surface.[127] This means that he is obliged to pay for the restoration costs, even when it is not his fault. The justification for strict liability is the idea that the mining operator creates a risk, while he pursues a justifiable goal.[128] The French Mining Code also provides that in cases of the dissolution or insolvency of the operator, the rights and obligations of the *concessionaire* pass to the state after his concession expires.[129] Indeed, in general terms, the State functions as a second tier back-up guarantor where the operator is insolvent or cannot be traced. It is then liable for all the damage caused by the mining activities, while being subrogated in the rights the victim had against the operator.[130]

[123] Sect. F 'Remedial Action to Address Subsidence Damage' of the Code of Practice (Sept. 1996), Appendix II of the Coal Authority Environmental Policy, Mar. 2001.

[124] Sect. 46.

[125] The Coal Mining Subsidence (Provision of Information) Regulations 1994, SI 1994/2565.

[126] 'A Guide to Claimants' Rights', Department of Trade and Industry, Jan. 2002, available from the OSA website, published at the Internet at: http://www.cix.co.uk/~osanotts/index.html.

[127] Art. 75-1 French Mining Code (amended by Law No. 99-245 du 30 mars 1999 Art. 1 Journal Officiel No. 76 du 31 mars 1999, 4767); 'L'explorateur ou l'exploitant, ou à défaut le titulaire du titre minier, est responsable des dommages causés par son activité. Il peut toutefois s'exonérer de sa responsabilité en apportant la preuve d'une cause étrangère.' 'Cette responsabilité n'est pas limitée au périmètre du titre minier ni à la durée de validité du titre. En cas de disparition ou de défaillance du responsable, l'Etat est garant de la réparation des dommages mentionnés au premier alinéa; il est subrogé dans les droits de la victime à l'encontre du responsable.'
The term 'surface' is developed through case law.

[128] French jurisprudence accepts this '*risque à prendre*' liability in several cases, see A.J. Goedmakers, 'De aansprakelijkheid van de mijnbouwexploitant voor door mijnbouw toegebrachte schade an de oppervlakte' [Operator Liability for Damage Caused by Mining] (1999) 13 *Tijdschrift voor Milieuschade en Aansprakelijkheidsrecht/Environmental Liability Law Review*, 159, 167.

[129] Art. 29 III French Mining Code.

[130] Second part of Art. 75–1 French Mining Code, n. 127 above.

The person carrying out mining activities or the holder of an exclusive research permit is liable for damage caused by his activity, but he can be exonerated if he proves the existence of a foreign cause (*cause étrangère*). Causation, therefore, is decisive for this liability. To avoid placing the burden of proof on the property owner whose property is damaged, the French Mining Code applies the principle of 'presumption of causation', and places the onus of proving that the damage was *not* caused by mining on the person carrying out mining activities or the holder of an exclusive research permit.[131] The French Mining Code provides a second form of protection for the property owner by requiring operators to create a contingency fund for the payment of damage claims.[132]

Since Law 1999-245 amending the Mining Code, a Mining Risk Agency has been established. One of its tasks is to collect information about risks posed by mining activities (more particularly after closure), and to disclose this to any person or a collective of persons having an interest in the prevention or the reparation of damage.[133]

C. German Law—*Bundesberggesetz*

The 1980 German Federal Mining Act (*Bundesberggesetz*) includes rules on the prevention of damage, ownership rights, encroachments, duties to tolerate for landowners, and rights to compensation for landowners and others who are affected by mining activities. The rules on liability and compensation for mining damage (*Bergschäden*) can be found in sections 110–23, 170, and 170a (temporal aspects).

The Mining Act establishes a right to compensation for those who suffer personal injury damage (including death) and damage to things, including subsidence damage. This is a strict liability (*Gefährdungshaftung*) for the damage included in the definition of section 114; the latter contains a number of explicit exclusions, accordingly not subject to the strict liability, such as loss suffered by the miners and damage to third parties, which cannot be prevented by injunctive relief granted under the Civil Code.[134]

Damage due to subsidence is assessed on the basis of the loss of market value of the land, and under certain conditions an amount is added for the loss of (economic) use of the land.[135] Where the land cannot be used any longer for

[131] Civ. Ass. Plén. 13 février 1930 D 1930, 1, 57, *jand'heur.*

[132] Art. 74(1) French Mining Code: 'L'explorateur et l'exploitant de mines doivent, le cas échéant de travaux à faire sous des maisons ou lieux d'habitation, sous d'autres exploitations ou dans leur voisinage, donner caution de payer toute indemnité en cas de dommage.'

[133] In French: 'Agence de prévention et de surveillance des risques miniers', Art. 4 of Loi No. 99–245 du 30 mars 1999 relative à la responsabilité en matière de dommages consécutifs à l'exploitation minière et à la prévention des risques miniers après la fin de l'exploitation, J.O. Numéro 76 du 31 mars 1999, 4767.

[134] Section 906.

[135] Section 109.

economic purposes, and the damage is of certain significance, the owner may call on the mining company to buy the land. The German Mining Act also contains provisions on the burden of proof and information gathering. Section 120 notes that if subsidence damage occurs, or if there is compression or stretching of the surface in an area in which mining activities are taking place, it is presumed that the damage is caused by the mining company which is undertaking these activities (*Bergschadensvermutung*).[136] The existence of this provision is exceptional under German law, and acknowledges the difficulties victims face in proving causation.[137] This presumption of causation does not apply, *inter alia*, if it is has been established that the damage is the result of geological changes which cannot be attributed to mining activities (i.e. natural causes); the onus to prove this is on the operator.

The person who has suffered subsidence damage and who suspects that the damage is the result of mining activities taking place in the area (*Einwirkungsbereich*), has the right to get information from the company. Also interesting in that respect is section 125. According to this provision, the authorities may require the owner of a mining facility to monitor and measure the effects of his activities on the surface. Such activities are undertaken to reduce the burden of proving that the mining activities concerned resulted in subsidence damage. The measures are funded by the owner of the mining company (*Unternehmer*). The authorities can require monitoring activities for areas in which subsidence is expected and for which it is likely that it may cause apparent damage to things.

Finally, the Act empowers the Minister of Economy and Technology to adopt a Statutory Instrument establishing a Mining Damage Compensation Fund.[138]

[136] Full text in German: *Bundesberggesetz* § 120 Bergschadensvermutung:

(1) Entsteht im Einwirkungsbereich der untertägigen Aufsuchung oder Gewinnung eines Bergbaubetriebes durch Senkungen, Pressungen oder Zerrungen der Oberfläche oder durch Erdrisse ein Schaden, der seiner Art nach ein Bergschaden sein kann, so wird vermutet, daa der Schaden durch diesen Bergbaubetrieb verursacht worden ist. Dies gilt nicht, wenn feststeht, daß
   1. der Schaden durch einen offensichtlichen Baumangel oder eine baurechtswidrige Nutzung verursacht sein kann oder
   2. die Senkungen, Pressungen, Zerrungen oder Erdrisse
      (a) durch natürlich bedingte geologische oder hydrologische Gegebenheiten oder Veränderungen des Baugrundes oder
      (b) von einem Dritten verursacht sein können, der, ohne Bodenschätze untertägig aufzusuchen oder zu gewinnen, im Einwirkungsbereich des Bergbaubetriebes auf die Oberfläche eingewirkt hat.

(2) Wer sich wegen eines Schadens an einer baulichen Anlage auf eine Bergschadensvermutung beruft, hat dem Ersatzpflichtigen auf Verlangen Einsicht in die Baugenehmigung und die dazugehörigen Unterlagen für diese bauliche Anlage sowie bei Anlagen, für die wiederkehrende Prüfungen vorgeschrieben sind, auch Einsicht in die Prüfunterlagen zu gewähren oder zu ermöglichen.

[137] W. Frenz (Reinisch-Westfälische Hochschule Aachen), 'Berg-und Umweltrecht I, Vorlesung, WS 1998/1999, 1. Teil: Bergrecht', published on the Internet at: http://www.rwth-aachen.de/bur/Ww/VSkript0499.pdf, Nos. 83 and 88.

[138] Section 122 (*Bergschadensausfallkasse*).

It is envisaged to function as a second tier liability back-up fund in certain situations where exceptionally the operator and/or licence holder will not be able to compensate victims due to insolvency or the fact that the company no longer exists. The Fund is then liable in their place, and subrogates in the rights of victims against the companies. No Fund has been created so far.

D. The Netherlands—Mining Act 2002

Under the Mining Act 2002,[139] all mining operations are subject to a strict liability, analogous to the more general provision in the Dutch Civil Code (CC) dealing with damage caused by dangerous substances. A new version of Article 6:177 CC states that the mining operator shall be liable for damage caused by any emissions of substances (blow out) and earth movements linked to the mining activities, in particular subsidence damage. Compliance with a licence is no defence; the competent Dutch Minister affirmed this, arguing that most damage caused by mining can be expected to result from lawful activities.[140] No changes are made to the law of damages nor are there any specific restrictions on the categories of recoverable loss. Accordingly, all the 'normal' heads of damages listed in the Civil Code are available: property damage, personal injury, pure economic loss.[141]

For subsidence damage, liability is channelled to the operator who is/was in control at the time the damage became apparent. This liability 'sticks' in that the original operator remains liable even where a subsequent operator took over control of the mine. Likewise, if damage becomes known after closure, the last operator is liable. The provision on damage due to earth movements is restricted to loss becoming apparent after entry into force of the new Act (non-retroactivity).[142] There is a crucial difference between two types of event, emission of substances and earth movements, namely that the former is linked to the time of the event, whereas the latter is linked to the time of the occurrence of the loss. This constitutes a limited form of retrospectivity in that the new rules apply to events which occurred before the entry into force of the new Mining Act, insofar as the damage becomes known after that moment in time. The legislature took into account that a linkage to the event causing the damage would mean that the new rules would only apply in the distant future, given the frequent occurrence of

139 In Dutch: 'Wet van 31 oktober 2002, houdende regels met betrekking tot het onderzoek naar en het winnen van delfstoffen en met betrekking tot met de mijnbouw verwante activiteiten (Mijnbouwwet)' (2002) *Staatsblad*, 542. In force since 1 January 2003, see (2002) *Staatsblad*, 603.

140 See (2002) 16 *Tijdschrift voor Milieuschade en Aansprakelijkheidsrecht/Environmental Damage and Liability Law Review*, 89.

141 Betlem, n. 105 above, 498.

142 Mining Act 2002, Arts. 176–8 amending the Civil Code; Explanatory Memorandum to the Mining Bill (Mijnbouwwet), TK 1998–9, 26219, No. 3, 24 and 103.

long latency in this context; also because there is no fundamental change in the liability regime's harshness, this was considered unduly restrictive.[143]

As for rules on financial security and other mechanisms to relieve the victim's litigation burden, the Act stipulates that the Minister *may* rule that financial security must be arranged by the operator to cover liability for possible damage which, reasonably estimated, occurs by earth movements due to mining.[144] Under the 2002 regime, the Minister requests a Report from the operator on possible future damage, and decides the amount and the form of the financial security to the Minister's satisfaction. In addition, the Minister may require financial security for costs of enforcement measures, *inter alia* regarding abandoned mines.

It follows that there is no statutory duty to furnish financial security. However, the statute does establish a Mining Damage Guarantee Fund pursuant to Article 134 ff.[145] Its role is to function as a second tier liability back-up fund for compensating victims in the event of insolvency of the operator. Payments by the Fund include advance payments in certain circumstances, for example due to a need to limit ongoing damage.[146] The Fund is fed by yearly contributions from mining operators. In an international perspective, the chosen format reflects the International Oil Pollution Compensation Funds (IOPC) rather than a second tier back-up liability of the state with a right of recourse against those responsible for the damage, such as under French law.

In the context of assisting victims in their claims against operators, two mechanisms have been put in place. First, operators are required to measure and monitor earth movements up to 30 years after closure of the mine.[147] One of the functions of this duty is to facilitate damage assessment; knowledge will thus be available within the realm of the operator who shall grant access to this information to claimants.[148]

Secondly, the Dutch legislature did not opt for a system of a reversal of the burden of proof of causation, via a statutory presumption or otherwise. However, it did establish a Technical Commission Soil Movements (TechComm) which does not only have a general, abstract, advisory role, but is also involved in

[143] Explanatory Memorandum to the Mining Bill (*Mijnbouwwet*), TK 1998–9, 26219, No. 3, 104.

[144] Arts. 46–8. According to statements by the Minister during the Parliamentary proceedings, the Ministry does not think it is necessary to lay down a general financial security requirement, see EK 2001–2, 26219, No. 313a, 5.

[145] See also the Statutory Instrument of 6 Dec. 2002, (2002) *Staatsblad*, 604, ch. 8. In Dutch: *Mijnbouwbesluit*.

[146] Art. 140.

[147] Art. 41.

[148] 'Statement by Minister Jorritsma during Parliamentary proceedings of 27 Mar. 2002' (2002) 16 *Tijdschrift voor Milieuschade en Aansprakelijkheidsrecht/Environmental Damage and Liability Law Review*, 78.

advising victims on questions of causation and quantum of damages.[149] The statute requires a victim to address the allegedly liable operator within three months after knowledge of damage, or where he could reasonably have known about it. If no agreement is reached within another three months, the victim is then entitled to address the TechComm. For a modest fee, it will research, if necessary by appointing experts, whether there is a causal link between the victim's property loss and the mining activity, as well as the quantum of damages. The TechComm has the power to demand information from operators and can pass this on to the victim, unless an exception of the Freedom of Information Act applies.

It may be queried whether the 'limitation period' of three months is not too short. In addition, doubts have been expressed about the lack of independence of the TechComm—or the appointed experts:[150] should not parties appoint their own experts or simply leave this to the general civil procedure rules? Nonetheless, the advantages of this scheme for the victim are the small costs involved: €90 for natural persons—reimbursed where there may be a causal link. Also, if the appointment process is transparent and victims can genuinely trust the independence of the experts, this technique can be an effective form of mitigating the claimant's litigation burden.

E. Comparative Analysis

We can extract a number of salient features from the comparative overview, either in terms of common rules or country-specific provisions modifying general tort law in the light of enhancing the effectiveness of the legal protection against damage caused by mining. The jurisdictions studied share rules of strict liability for damage caused by mining; the strict liability is non-exclusive in that actions based on general tort law remain possible. The liable person is the operator and/or licence holder, either to the exclusion of any other potential defendants or not.

All systems provide for a form of mitigating the claimant's litigation burden. Techniques include statutory presumptions of causation, a technical advisory body providing assistance or research into the causal link between loss and event, duties to measure and monitor and disclose results to claimants—again in order to relieve the burden of proof of causation. Furthermore, guarantor systems are created, for example, by the obligation on individual mining operators to set up financial security, by compulsory contributions of the operators to a Compensation Fund, or by back-up liability of the State, with a right of recourse against operators.

149 Arts. 113–22.

150 G. van der Spek, 'Causalitieitsonzekerheid bij mijnschadeverhaal: de zaak Grouw' [Causal Uncertainty in the Grouw Case of Recovery of Mining Damages] (2002) 16 *Tijdschrift voor Milieuschade en Aansprakelijkheidsrecht/Environmental Liability Law Review*, 101–2.

VIII. Conclusions

The period 2000–3 has produced two developments in the communitarization of environmental liability law, a legislative one more notable for what it does not include rather than for what it does, and a judicial one: a landmark ECJ judgment on the mandatory availability of civil actions for the purposes of enforcement of Community law. The March 2004 Environmental Liability Directive does not include private rights of action against polluters. It will therefore fail to secure effective enforcement of substantive EC environmental law; particularly ineffective is the protection against harm caused by GMOs. In my view, this is out of step with the EU's international obligations (Aarhus) and with developments in ECJ case law as well as (future) national (case) law. It is also out of step with developments in other policy areas, notably intellectual property, where the Commission seeks to minimize disparities between Member State laws on remedies to ensure effective and uniform enforcement of the *acquis communautaire* in those fields. However, after the ECJ's *Muñoz* judgment, EU-wide availability of private enforcement mechanisms is required. This case contains the beginnings of a new genuinely European tort: breach of 'EC-statutory' duty. If and when private enforcement is being further developed in the environmental context, lessons can be learned from the Member States' laws on remedying damage caused by mining operations, in terms of increasing the effectiveness of tort liability. Barriers to access to justice have been removed there, or have been reduced by the establishment of appropriate assistance mechanisms, such as modifications to the burden of proof. The way forward is to do the same in the more general context of liability for environmental damage. In a word: by taking 'Aarhus' seriously.

Permit Defences in Environmental Liability Regimes—Subsidizing Environmental Damage in the EC?

*Pål Wennerås**

I. Introduction

On 23 January 2002, after nearly a decade of preparatory work,[1] the Commission proposed a Directive on Environmental Liability with regard to the Prevention and Remedying of Environmental Damage (Environmental Liability Directive).[2] The proposal is based on strict liability for a closed category of hazardous activities, but provides at the same time for a so-called 'permit defence', which precludes liability if the operator has complied with the administrative regulations governing his activity. As has become evident in the aftermath of the proposal, permit defence is considered a crucial element in a future environmental liability regime. Environmentalists argue that permit defence would jeopardize the success of the liability regime, whereas business claims that permit defence is necessary to ensure competitiveness of European industry. Meanwhile, an internally divided European Parliament (EP), on its first reading,[3] supported a compromise in which regulatory compliance may in some cases exempt operators from responsibility, and in other cases function as a 'mitigating factor' for the determination of responsibility and/or the costs which the operator may be held liable for. The Council, ending the first reading of the proposal, agreed to keep the permit defence, albeit in a modified form compared to the Commission proposal.[4]

* Researcher, Centre for Environmental Law, University of Amsterdam.

[1] The Commission issued a Green Paper as early as 1993, COM (93)47. However, one might say that the proposed Directive is a continuation of the Commission's first initiative in 1976 to include a provision on liability in the proposal for a Directive on Hazardous Waste. In the end, this clause was left out when the Directive was adopted in 1978; see L. Krämer, 'Liability For Damage to the Environment and the European Union' in conference paper presented at 'Approximation—The Never Ending Story', Tenth Anniversary of the Institute of Environmental Policy (Prague, 30–31 October 2002).

[2] [2002] OJ C151E/132.

[3] Position of the EP adopted at first reading on 14 May 2003 with a view to the adoption of a Directive of the European Parliament and of the Council on Environmental Liability with Respect to the Prevention and Remedying of Environmental Damage [2003] OJ C67 E/167.

[4] Common Position of the Council on the adoption of a Directive of the European Parliament and of the Council on Environmental Liability with Respect to the Prevention and Remedying of Environmental Damage [2003] OJ C277 E/10.

As demonstrated by a debate split along partisan lines, it obviously boils down to political choice whether a permit defence should temper the future environmental liability regime. However, in order to take an informed decision in this matter, it is necessary to have an understanding of the many complex issues that lie behind the seemingly straightforward notion of permit defence. This article will attempt to identify, analyse, and comment on the relevant questions which a permit defence raises in regard to the working of an environmental liability regime in the EC. More general questions, such as whether liability is an effective legal instrument or whether other mechanisms may be preferable, will not be discussed. Furthermore, an analysis of permit defence should arguably deal with individual sectors, taking into account the differences in risk potential and regulation. However, this is not possible within the confines of this contribution.

Section II will offer a general analysis of permit defence in a strict liability regime. The fundamental questions, that is, what the objectives of a strict liability regime are, and how a permit defence may affect them, will be dealt with. The remaining part will mostly consist of an analysis of the deterrent effect of strict liability. The first question is whether there is a need to supplement regulation with liability, followed by a discussion of the benefits of deterrence, and finally an examination of the costs of deterrence. Next, possible adverse spillovers from permit defence on command and control regulation and enforcement by private parties are explored. A general conclusion whether a strict liability regime should contain a permit defence is then formulated. In subsection G, I analyse the construction of permit compliance as a 'mitigating factor', and whether this may be a preferable alternative to a permit defence, or not having a permit defence at all.

Section III will apply the general analysis conducted in section II to analyse the Commission's proposal, taking into consideration the EP's and Council's amendments. The permit defence will be considered specifically in the light of the permitting requirements stipulated in Directive 96/61/EC on Integrated Pollution Prevention and Control (IPPC Directive).[5] The article concludes with an opinion as to whether the future EC environmental liability regime should contain a permit defence.[6]

II. Permit Defence and Mitigating Factors in Theory

A. Objectives of a Strict Liability Regime

In common with most strict liability regimes, the proposed Directive finds justification in the 'polluter pays principle'.[7] However, as is the case with principles,

[5] [1996] OJ L257/26.

[6] At the time of writing, Oct. 2003, the first reading by the EP and the Council had just been concluded.

[7] P. Cane, 'Using Tort Law to Enforce Environmental Regulations?' (2002) 41 *Washburn Law Journal*, 444: 'The polluter pays principle . . . is usually assumed to dictate strict liability'.

the polluter pays principle[8] is often afforded different meanings and economic, legal, and moral rationales.[9] In the following, I shall briefly touch upon three of the most important rationales: deterrence, reparation and corrective justice.

For the past two decades, most tort scholars have placed emphasis on the deterrent effect of liability—the creation of incentives for the prevention of future damages.[10] The preamble of the proposed Environmental Liability Directive reveals that the Commission also focuses on deterrence when it refers to the polluter pays principle.[11] The deterrence theory has been developed by economists such as Calabresi,[12] from the paradigm of wealth-maximization through an 'optimal level' of pollution. This theory assumes that the threat of liability will serve as an incentive for operators to limit the risk of damage, which may be realized by investing in preventive measures such as development of new technology and/or reducing levels of hazardous activities. In short, strict liability is believed to provide incentives for operators to do more than merely complying with existing regulation.

Another important objective of strict liability is the facilitation of compensation or reparation. Judging from the preamble of the proposed Environmental Liability Directive, this goal appears to be ancillary to prevention, albeit still important.[13] In relation to an environmental liability regime, which includes damages to unowned property, focus is on reparation rather than on compensation. Indeed, the proposed Environmental Liability Directive explicitly excludes responsibility for traditional damage, that is, compensation for damage to property or pure economic loss. In contrast to fault liability, where it is the conduct of the operator that triggers liability, damage is sufficient cause for responsibility in a strict liability regime. Strict liability should therefore, in theory, ensure reparation in all instances of damage but, due to, *inter alia,* the difficulty of proving causation, that promise has far from materialized.

Economic theories of law, such as the Calabresian wealth-maximization aim of deterrence, ignore the guilt of the operator, and do not link liability with moral responsibility. The libertarian viewpoint, as principally represented by Epstein,[14] posits that the focus should not be on efficiency or wealth-maximization which, he argued, represented invasions of individual autonomy in the name of the public good. The objective should instead be to ensure that the person

[8] The polluter pays principle is recognized in Art. 174(2) EC.

[9] H.C. Bugge, 'The Principles of "Polluter-Pays" in Economics and Law' in E. Eide and R. van den Bergh (eds.), *Law and Economics of the Environment* (Oslo: Juridisk Forlag, 1996), 57.

[10] The American Law Institute (1991) 1 *Reporter's Study on Enterprise Responsibility for Personal Injury* (ALI Study 1) in (1993) 30 *San Diego Law Review*, 390.

[11] Commission proposal, n. 2 above, Rec. 2.

[12] See G. Calabresi, 'Some Thoughts on Risk Distribution and the Law of Torts' (1961) 70 *Yale Law Journal*, 499; and G. Calabresi, *The Costs of Accidents—A Legal and Economic Analysis* (New Haven: Yale University Press, 1980).

[13] Commission proposal, n. 2 above, Rec. 14.

[14] R. Epstein, 'A Theory of Strict Liability' (1973) 2 *Journal of Legal Studies*, 151.

responsible for intruding on persons and property should make good the damage, regardless of fault. As much as no one should have a right to harm persons or property, nobody has a general, a priori, right to pollute.[15] Some have criticized the ethics of this manifestation of the polluter pays principle, on the basis that it disregards the benefits of certain harmful activities, and fails to provide any positive arguments for preferring the plaintiff to the defendant.[16] However, as Honoré points out,[17] the responsibility should lie with the person choosing to engage in certain conduct or activities. If a polluter decides to engage in an activity, usually because of commercial interests, the risk should lie with him, rather than the victim who was not consulted in the matter.[18]

A permit defence undermines all these objectives. The deterrent effect of strict liability, by many—including the Commission—considered the most significant objective, is seriously compromised by a permit defence, presuming that an activity is subject to regulation. In a heavily regulated field as environmental law, this means that the deterrent effect of strict liability is all but removed. The focus of this chapter will hence be on deterrence, and whether it is justifiable to remove this effect from a strict liability regime by allowing a permit defence. Before exploring deterrence and permit defence in some detail, we should be aware of the fundamental issues at stake. Should a liability regime function merely as an instrument of enforcing command and control regulation or should it, albeit indirectly, also play a regulatory role? Some pose the question as whether 'regulation . . . better achieves the goal of prevention [than liability]'[19] or determine when regulation is 'preferable',[20] or a 'superior, more precise instrument',[21] or conversely ask '[w]hen should we prefer tort law to environmental regulation?'.[22] However, to consider the relative advantages of regulation and liability in this context appears to be fundamentally flawed, as the question of permit defence revolves around whether these two instruments can function *together*, that is, if liability can and should supplement regulation. Thus, the question is whether the benefits of a regulatory dual-track regime outweigh its disadvantages.[23]

[15] Bugge, n. 9 above, 65.

[16] L. Bergkamp, 'The Proposed Environmental Liability Directive' (2002) 11 *European Environmental Law Review*, 329.

[17] T. Honoré, 'Responsibility and Luck—The Moral Basis of Strict Liability' (1988) 104 *Law Quarterly Review*, 530.

[18] Similarly, Cane, n. 7 above, 445.

[19] A. Arcuri, ' Controlling Environmental Risk in Europe—The Complementary Role of an EC Environmental Liability Regime' (2001) 15 *Tijdsschrift voor milieu aansprakelijkheid*, 37.

[20] L. Bergkamp, *Liability and Environment—Private and Public Law Aspects of Civil Liability for Environmental Harms in an International Context* (The Hague: Kluwer Law International, 2001), 233.

[21] L. Bergkamp, 'The Commission's White Paper on Environmental Liability—A Weak Case for an EC Strict Liability Regime' (2000) 9 *European Environmental Law Review*, 147.

[22] K.N. Hylton, 'When Should We Prefer Tort Law to Environmental Regulation' (2002) 41 *Washburn Law Journal*, 515.

[23] There are of course other relevant questions, e.g. whether other instruments may better supplement regulation, or perhaps other systems may be more efficient than a dual-track regime consisting of regulation and liability, but such general questions will not be considered here.

B. The Meaning of 'Permit Defence'

Put simply, permit defence allows an operator, who otherwise fulfils the conditions for liability, to be exempted from responsibility because of compliance with administrative regulations governing his activity. However, the term permit defence is often used indiscriminately for at least three different situations. The common meaning, which hereafter will be referred to as *permit defence*, means that the operator must defend himself in an administrative or judicial proceeding by providing evidence that he complied with the relevant regulation. Permit compliance may also *pre-empt* liability altogether, meaning that a liability suit cannot be initiated.[24] Finally, permit compliance can function as a *mitigating factor* in the determination of responsibility and/or the amount of costs which the operator may be held liable for.

The term 'permit defence' is often used as shorthand for the more accurate notion of 'regulatory compliance defence'. In this context 'regulation' is normally understood as any administrative requirements governing an activity, regardless of whether it is in the form of law, regulation, authorization, or permit.[25] Thus, it may not be necessary that the activity was specifically regulated in a permit, compliance with general requirements flowing from laws or regulations may also be sufficient to escape liability. However, additional conditions before a permit defence is applicable are usually required. These may imply that only specific regulations, such as permits, are relevant, or that the risk that caused the damage must have been specifically regulated in the permit. Such conditions therefore substantially narrow the scope of a permit defence. These issues will be dealt with further in the context of the design of the permit defence in the Commission's proposed Environmental Liability Directive.

Although this chapter concerns permit defence, it is important to note the close relationship with another exonerating factor: 'state of the art' defence. According to this defence, an operator is not held liable if his activities were not considered harmful according to the state of the scientific and technical knowledge pertaining at the time of the activity.[26] The strict division between these defences as applied by most academics can be misleading, since the permit defence not only consumes the 'state of the art defence', but goes further: thus, even though it was likely, according to the knowledge at the time, that the activity was going to cause environmental damage, the operator is still exempted from liability if he has complied with the relevant regulation. The justification for this far-reaching defence is founded on the belief that command and control regulation of industrial activities *is* based on existing scientific and technical knowledge.

[24] For example, Art. 9.1(b) in the Commission proposal, n. 2 above, stipulates that damage caused by an operator who complied with regulatory demands falls outside the scope of the Directive, i.e. permit compliance pre-empts the application of the proposed Directive on Environmental Liability.

[25] Commission proposal, n. 2 above, Art. 9(c).

[26] ibid., Art 9.1(d).

A polluter acting in compliance with a permit is thereby presumed to run his operation according to the best scientific and technical standards. However, as will be discussed below, regulation is not always based on the most advanced scientific and technical knowledge at the time of its drafting, and it will in any event seldom reflect modern scientific evidence throughout the often prolonged period between its drafting and updating.

C. The Problem—Exclusive Reliance on Regulation

Acknowledging a permit defence suggests that we are fully confident that command and control regulation on its own is capable of managing all environmental risks stemming from our diverse society. More specifically, permit defence assumes two basic conditions: first, that regulation represents stringent standards—as opposed to minimum requirements—and secondly, that our regulators are capable of determining such standards. However, many, if not most, environmental standards are in fact minimum requirements[27] which may provide insufficient grounds to exonerate operators of liability by virtue of their compliance with such minimum standards.[28] It seems moreover inevitable that command and control regulation, as any other type of regulatory instrument, will invariably contain gaps, and imperfections.[29] In order to set adequate and correct standards, regulators must have access to near perfect information. This presupposes both sufficient manpower and economic resources to gather (and subsequently process) the necessary information.[30] To the extent that authorities manage to collect sufficient information, it will often be of a general

[27] Art. 18(2) of 96/61/EC concerning Integrated Pollution Prevention and Control, n. 5 above, states that emissions values contained in other applicable directives shall be considered as 'minimum emission limit values'. See e.g. the US Restatement (Third) of Torts: Products Liability 4b (1997) [hereinafter Restatement] Comment: '[R]eflects the traditional view that the standards set by most product safety statutes or regulations generally are only minimum standards . . . they leave open the question whether a higher standard . . . should be applied. This is the general rule, applicable in most cases'.

[28] The American Law Institute (1991) 2 *Reporters Study on Enterprise Responsibility For Personal Injury* (ALI Study 2), 108; R.L. Rabin, 'Reassessing Regulatory Compliance' (2000) 88 *Georgetown Law Journal*, 2051: '[I]f the regulation sets nothing more than a minimum standard of safety, or floor, there is no correlative reason to treat compliance with it as a "safe harbour"', and at 2074; 'No serious commentator would argue for a regulatory compliance defence in circumstances where the agency regulations are considered as minimum standards rather than optimal standards'; R.B. Stewart, 'Regulatory Compliance Preclusion of Tort Liability: Limiting the Dual-Track System' (2000) 88 *Georgetown Law Journal*, 2173: 'In the case of regulatory programs designed to set a minimum standard, there is in principle no difficulty in allowing tort liability to play a supplemental role in addressing those risks that remain after the minimum standard has been satisfied'.

[29] ALI Study 2, n. 28 above, at 85–6.

[30] See e.g. T.O. McGarity, 'Beyond Buckman—Wrongful Manipulation of the Regulatory Process in the Law of Torts' (2002) 41 *Washburn Law Journal*, 567–70.

nature.[31] Collecting local information is costly, time-consuming, and difficult to gather.[32]

Regulators are also dependent on information from the regulated sector.[33] Hylton puts the importance of this deficit across strongly: 'Public enforcement agents cannot obtain enough information to design an intelligent scheme without access to private parties'.[34] Such information may, for obvious reasons, prove difficult to retrieve from industry. Another obstacle is that information about risks is a 'public good'.[35] Industry will therefore lack incentives to produce such data.

Regulators are moreover under constant pressure and lobbying from different interest groups during the decision-making process, bringing about risk of 'agency capture'.[36] The regulatory procedure consequently generally favours pressure groups over dispersed interests.[37] Furthermore, resourceful interest groups can be presumed to have larger influence than others.[38] Hence, industry will often have a considerable impact on the design of the regulation. There is also risk of bribery and corruption inside regulatory agencies.[39]

Another fundamental problem with regulation is that it is static. It is based on the knowledge available at the time of drafting. Changed factual circumstances, new scientific evidence concerning risks and harms, technological innovation, new manufacturing processes and so forth, often soon overtake regulation.[40]

[31] S. Shavell, 'Liability for Harm Versus Regulation of Safety' (1984) 13 *Journal of Legal Studies*, 365, where he comments that uniform regulatory standards, on the one hand, ignore that some individual polluters present an above average risk and, on the other hand, fail to acknowledge that some operators can take extra precautions more easily and cost-efficiently.

[32] Hylton, n. 22 above, 525 claims that 'almost all reliable information is probably local'.

[33] Shavell, n. 31 above, 360.

[34] Hylton, n. 22 above, 524.

[35] Shavell, n. 31 above, 360 (1984); Bergkamp, n. 20 above, 251.

[36] G. Becker, 'A Theory of Competition Among Pressure Groups for Political Influence' (1984) 98 *Quarterly Journal of Economics*, 371.

[37] Hylton, n. 22 above, 524. Others have questioned the validity of the 'agency capture' argument; see e.g. A. Ogus, *Regulation—Legal Form and Economic Theory* (Oxford: Clarendon Press, 1994) 57–8, 94–5, 106–7.

[38] Restatement (Third) of Torts, Section 4b stipulates that permit defence should not be recognized by the court unless it is confident that the regulatory process was full, fair, and thorough and reflected substantial expertise.

[39] Hylton, n. 22 above, 523–4: 'The firms who are likely to be regulated . . . have every incentive to bribe the legislators in order to shape rules to their liking. The legislators are motivated . . . to meet the demands of their constituents. But constituents cannot see the fine print in legislation, which concentrated interests groups, specifically regulated firms, can. This system is likely to produce regulatory legislation that seems on its face to impose harsh controls while under the surface providing significant protective shields to the regulated industry.'

[40] M. Stallworthy, 'Environmental Liability and the Impact of Statutory Authority' (2003) 15 *Journal of Environmental Law*, 21: 'Standards can fall out of line with developing understandings of technology and attendant risks. In an environmental arena beset with technical and political uncertainties, the sufficiency of ruling regulatory standards may be overtaken.'

Regulators do, of course, update regulation at regular intervals, but it is a difficult and costly task to do so sufficiently frequently.[41]

These examples strongly suggest that command and control regulation on its own cannot in all and every case manage to regulate all relevant risks, set proper standards, and take account of individual differences within industry and local environments.

D. The Case for Strict Liability

A strict liability regime without a permit defence provides operators with incentives to reduce risks until the cost of further abatement measures equals the cost of liability. 'Law and economics' scholars have therefore argued that operators will choose the optimal level of care, as this will reduce the expected costs, and they will choose the optimal level of activity because they will want to engage in the activity only when the additional gains exceed the associated costs of care and additional expected responsibility.[42] A permit defence thwarts these incentives altogether. However, economic theory underpinning strict liability has come under criticism lately. The promise of optimal levels of pollution relies on several uncertain assumptions, most notably 'perfect competition' and transparency for operators concerning costs and risks. In real life, strict liability will result in companies spending too many or too few resources on precautionary measures.[43] However, the claim that strict liability may not fulfil the promise of an optimal level of pollution is not a serious objection when strict liability is seen as an instrument of environmental protection rather than a mechanism for ensuring social welfare. The fact remains that strict liability will induce operators to take precautionary measures beyond what is required by virtue of regulation when the costs of such measures are less than the cost of damage.[44] Thus, companies may choose to invest in safer and cleaner production methods research, develop new technologies, gather information about risks, adopt risk-management plans, and so forth.[45] For operators of so-called 'ultra-hazardous' activities, strict liability

[41] See also ALI Study 2, n. 28 above, 85–6. In the Restatement (Third) of Torts, Section 4b, regulatory compliance defence should only be recognized when the regulation has been promulgated recently; see Rabin, n. 28 above, 2051.

[42] S. Shavell, [1987] *Economic Analysis of Accident Law* (Cambridge, Mass.: Harvard University Press, 1987) 23.

[43] For a thorough analysis, see P. Cane, *Atiyah's Accidents, Compensation and the Law* (London: Butterworths, 1999).

[44] Communication from the Commission, 'On the Road to a Sustainable Development' COM(2003)354, 30: [T]he company often has more information and know-how than the authority and is therefore in a better position to identify cost-effective measures to reduce emissions, provided the incentive is there'.

[45] Department for Environment, Food & Rural Affairs (UK) (DEFRA), 'Extended Partial Regulatory Impact Assessment On Proposals for a Directive on Environmental Liability' at 16 (2002): 'Removal [of permit defence] would place an additional incentive to treat permit conditions as minimum requirements'; K. Abrahams argues that liability will create incentives for discovery of new information that would not exist in the absence of such a threat, 'The Relation between Civil Liability and Environmental Regulation—An Analytical Overview' (2002) 41 *Washburn Law Journal*, 397; see also Rabin, n. 28 above, 2069.

may result in lower levels of activity when the risks outweigh the benefits.[46] This tendency is likely to be reinforced as 'green investors' shun businesses that may face liability. Increased lender liability may eventually reduce the number of environmentally unsound businesses, and force particularly damaging firms out of the market.[47] Likewise, the threat of liability has moved many insurers to impose stricter conditions upon their clients.[48] This may in turn push industry to undertake environmental audits or volunteer for environmental management schemes.[49]

The incentives caused by strict liability may not only serve environmental purposes; increased development of technology may create new business opportunities, and stimulate increased competition.[50] As strict liability forces operators to internalize the costs of environmental damage, running a 'green' and low risk facility becomes a business advantage.[51] Conversely, a permit defence regime may present environmentally counter-active incentives since moving beyond regulatory standards would place the operator at a competitive disadvantage.[52]

i. Lack of Deterrence?

Critics have questioned whether strict liability actually has the deterrent effect with which it has been credited.[53] Some have argued that insurance removes the incentives of strict liability, and creates risk of a 'moral hazard'.[54] However, as the

[46] Shavell, n. 42 above, 23.

[47] N. Gunningham, P. Grabosky and D. Sinclair, *Smart Regulation—Designing Environmental Policy* (Oxford: Clarendon Press, 1999), 114 and 116–17.

[48] ibid. 126, see also 78.

[49] ibid.

[50] Abrahams, n. 45 above, 398: 'The great strength of... [a] mixed system is that it leaves room for the economically venturesome'. This argument is disputed by Cane, n. 7 above, 464 because 'successful suits... in relation to compliant conduct would result in the driving up of regulatory standards'. It would appear, however, that Cane overestimates the regulatory eagerness of authorities and, in any event, it does not seem apt criticism that we should disregard the benefits in terms of increased flexibility provided by liability, simply because this flexibility may be removed by regulatory codification at a later stage.

[51] DEFRA, n. 45 above, 39, evaluating the effects of the proposed liability directive on competition, notes that 'environmental industries is an area in which UK has a competitive advantage and many of the operators are small and growing'.

[52] Cane, n. 43 above, 375.

[53] M. Faure, 'A Selection of Empirical Socio-Economic Research with Respect to the Functioning of Legal Rules and Institutions in Belgium and the Netherlands' (2001) 11 *European Journal of Law and Economics*, 207, argues that there is little evidence of preventive effect; see also T. Brennan 'Environmental Torts' (1993) 46 *Vanderbilt Law Review*, 6. P. Cane, 'Are Environmental Harms Special' (2001) 13 *Journal of Environmental Law*, 207–48, claims that, according to empirical evidence, liability has 'modest, if any, preventive effect', but, interestingly, in the article 'Using Tort Law to Enforce Environmental Regulations?' (2002) 41 *Washburn Law Journal*, 434, the same author comments that 'we don't really know how effective tort law is as a deterrent... the evidence we have about the deterrent impact of tort law is inconclusive and studies of the relative impacts of tort law and other deterrent mechanisms... are all but non-existent'.

[54] S. Rose-Ackerman, 'Public Law versus Private Law in Environmental Regulation—European Union Proposals in the Light of United States and German Experiences' in E. Eide and R. van den Bergh (eds.), *Law and Economics of the Environment* (Oslo: Juridisk Forlag, 1996), 17; Cane, n. 43 above, 368 and 384–6.

responsibility for damages is transferred from the operator to the insurer, the latter will have similar incentives to reduce the risk of damage. The insurance industry will therefore by different means, such as premiums according to risk differentiation or imposing specific conditions, for example, risk-management programmes or environmental auditing, seek to ensure that operators minimize risks.[55] Furthermore, large multinational enterprises are often self-insured. These firms often take 'deliberate, consciously planned judgements about whether to build a safeguard into a product or activity, precisely the type of enterprise decision that can and will take into account legal financial incentives'.[56]

It has also been claimed that small and medium-sized enterprises (SMEs) may have insufficient assets for the threat of liability to serve as an effective deterrent.[57] It should be noted, though, that deterrence is closely linked to the risk potential of the enterprise. If the risk potential is small, financially strapped firms will also have incentives to avoid damage. For activities that may cause significant damage, for example, chemical or biotechnological industry, risks of moral hazard can be avoided by compulsory insurance, or by requiring that the companies set aside money for restoration.[58]

Finally, it is often pointed out that there exists limited empirical evidence about the deterrent impact of tort law.[59] But there is even less evidence suggesting that liability *does not* have such deterrent effect.[60] In fact, the existing empirical evidence suggests that liability indeed has a deterrent effect, albeit perhaps not as strong as law and economics scholars have claimed.[61]

[55] Gunningham *et al.*, n. 47 above, 126, see also 78. For a different view, see Cane, n. 43 above, 368 and 388–90, who comments that there is 'no real evidence that fear of the loss of a no-claim bonus or of having to pay excess under a policy has any significant effect on the incidence of accidents'. This claim is, however, presented without any references to studies positively demonstrating that such an effect is absent. In addition, Cane questions the Calabresian theory that the market will induce insurers to set premiums based on risk differentiation (see G. Calabresi, 'The Decision for Accidents—An Approach to Non-Fault Allocation' (1965) 78 *Harvard Law Review*, 733–4) because the statistical methodology required is inaccurate and may add disproportionately high administrative costs.

[56] ALI Study 1, n. 10 above, at 391. See also H.A. Latin, 'Problem-Solving Behaviour and Theories of Tort Liability', (1985) 73 *California Law Review*, 677.

[57] Rose-Ackerman, n. 54 above, 17.

[58] This was recently introduced in France in response to an accident in Toulouse where the responsible operator lacked funds for restoration.

[59] See n. 53 above.

[60] The study by A. Alberini and D.H. Austin, 'Strict Liability as a Deterrent in Toxic Waste Management—Empirical Evidence from Accident and Spill Data' (1999) 38 *Journal of Environmental Economics and Management*, 20 reported that strict liability may have a less effective deterrent impact than fault liability, but—leaving aside the question whether this conclusion may have general value—it does not follow that liability, as an instrument, is not effective as an deterrent.

[61] G.T. Schwartz, 'Reality in the Economic Analysis of Tort Law—Does Tort Law Really Deter?' (1994) 42 *University College Los Angeles Law Review*, 377 (1994); D.H. Austin and A. Alberini, 'An Analysis of the Preventive Effect of Environmental Liability (2001), published on the Internet at: http://europa.eu.int/comm/environment/liability/followup.html. Studies on motor vehicle accidents and medical malpractice have shown that there is some deterrent value in liability exposure;

In sum, neither the theoretical nor the empirical challenge as to the deterrent effect of strict liability appears convincing.

ii. Over-Deterrence?

Ironically, it is also claimed that strict liability leads to over-deterrence.[62] Yet again, limited empirical evidence exists supporting this claim.[63] Admittedly, the United States (US) has experienced some cases where liability may have contributed to over-deterrence. This has predominantly been a problem in the pharmaceutical industry, where the threat of liability supposedly led manufacturers to exit the vaccine products market.[64] Being a heavily regulated area, the pharmaceutical sector bears much resemblance to the environmental sector. One of the implications of a dual-track regime in such an intensively regulated area is that the expenditure needed to fulfil the requirements of command and control regulation, in addition to possible subsequent liability, may place too heavy a burden on companies, especially on SMEs. Some refer to this scenario as the 'polluter pays twice'.[65]

There are several problems with these arguments, however. First, one should be careful with transposing experiences with the US tort system to the functioning of a public liability system in Europe. The problems connected with the US tort regime are largely due to its jury system[66]—with lay people not only ruling on the question of responsibility, but also determining the amount of damages—and the fact that punitive damages are awarded.[67] This has led to instances of exorbitant damages, which may have deterred companies from certain 'upper-tier' risk activities.[68] In Europe, it is generally judges that determine damages, whereas punitive damages are in principle not available in civil law systems.[69] Hence, the risk of over-deterrence is much smaller in Europe compared to the US.

see D. Dewees and M. Trebilcock, 'The Efficacy of the Tort System—A Review of the Empirical Evidence' (ALI Background Paper, 1991); Harvard Medical Practice Study Group, Patients, Doctors, and Lawyers: Medical Injury, Malpractice Litigation, and Patient Compensation in New York (1990) Harvard Study.

62 Rose-Ackerman, n. 54 above, 23 and 38–9; Stewart, n. 28 above, 2189 comments that 'the [ALI] study noted "indications" of over-deterrence in the case of certainly intensively regulated products'; Bergkamp, n. 20 above, 246.

63 Cane, n. 43 above, 367; Rabin, n. 28 above, 2075.

64 W.K. Viscusi, 'The Social Costs of Punitive Damages Against Corporations in Environmental and Safety Torts' (1998) 87 *Georgetown Law Journal*, 285. There are even claims that the fear of liability has prevented efforts to develop a vaccine for AIDS; see K.F. Clooney, 'AIDS Vaccine Manufacturers v. Tort Regime—The Need for Alternatives' (1992) 49 *Washington and Lee Law Review*, 559.

65 Bergkamp, n. 20 above, 236.

66 Cane, n. 7 above, 463.

67 ALI Study 1, n. 10 above, 391–2, referring to Huber, 'Safety and the Second Best—The Hazards of Public Risk Management in the Courts' (1985) 85 *Columbia Law Review*, 677.

68 Stewart, n. 28 above, 2169.

69 English and Irish tort law include punitive damages, albeit more limited than in the US.

Secondly, the very notion of over-deterrence is, in my opinion, questionable. In a dual-track regime, deterrence is precisely the objective of liability: By exposing companies to liability regardless of compliance, they are given incentives to go beyond compliance, use the newest technology, invest in risk management education for employees, seek safer production methods, take precautions and so on. These consequences are generally considered positive, so what then is over-deterrence?[70] Critics of liability seem to associate over-deterrence with any decrease of industrial activity as 'we lose the external benefits of the discontinued activity'.[71] However, activity levels decrease because the external costs of the activity have not been internalized. The demand has therefore been artificially high, causing suboptimal activity levels.[72] Hence, society does not in fact lose any external benefits, but gains a more efficient use of natural resources.[73]

iii. Distortion of Regulation?

Some academics have argued that permit defence is necessary to avoid adverse spillovers from liability arising out of command and control regulation.[74] First, it is claimed that regulatory standards reflect an optimal cost-benefit trade-off in terms of the beneficial effects of more stringent regulation measured against costs,[75] which additional costs imposed by a strict liability regime would distort.[76] The second claim is that liability without permit defence would reduce incentives to comply with command and control regulation. According to this theory, the regulation is set at an optimal cost-efficiency level, where the cost of compliance is equal to the costs of non-compliance. If the operator risked incurring additional costs in the form of liability, it would remove the incentives to comply with permits, as the accumulated costs would exceed the costs of non-compliance.[77] It should be noted that the corollary of the last argument is that liability actually offers incentives for operators, i.e. that liability serves as a deterrent. Hence, the economic distortion argument, proffered by, for instance,

[70] Cane, n. 43 above, 367 points out that the concept is problematic as the amount of care it is appropriate to take is itself a value-judgement.

[71] Bergkamp, n. 16 above, 329; and n. 20 above, 246.

[72] Shavell, n. 42 above, 23–4.

[73] Cane, n. 43 above, 375.

[74] See Rose-Ackerman, n. 54 above, DEFRA, n. 45 above, 34, raises the question whether an absence of permit defence may increase costs and make it harder to obtain financing for operators as they will encounter difficulties in persuading shareholders and insurers that compliance with permit conditions renders the risk of environmental liability acceptably small.

[75] The optimal level of regulation according to a cost-benefit analysis is when the marginal social costs of regulation equals the costs. Thus, the 'optimal' level of pollution is when marginal costs of further pollution control equal the marginal benefits of further abatement.

[76] Stewart, n. 28 above, 2173–5.

[77] Rose-Ackerman, n. 54 above, 23 and 38–9. In contrast, P. Burrows 'Commentary' in E. Eide and R. van den Bergh (eds.), *Law and Economics of the Environment* (Oslo: Juridisk Forlag, 1996), 47, argues that even if the costs of regulatory compliance and liability costs exceeds the value of the harm, it does not necessarily mean that the *expected* level of costs exceed the harm considering less than perfect enforcement. Hence, a dual-track regime would not lead to over-deterrence.

Rose-Ackerman and Bergkamp, offers at the same time support against claims that liability does not serve as a deterrent.[78] These claims of optimal regulation appear moreover to be mutually conflicting: in the case of cost-benefit trade-offs, optimal standards are understood as properly calibrated 'public choices',[79] whereas the compliance theory interprets optimal standards according to a purely economic theory of wealth maximization. Leaving these potential regulatory conflicts aside, the Achilles' heel of both theories is that they assume that regulators are capable of, and willing to enact, such optimal standards. However, as argued above, particularly because of the problem of imperfect information, it is unlikely that command and control regulation can be calibrated in such detail. In order to stipulate a regulatory standard where the costs of compliance equal the costs of non-compliance, regulators are dependent on information about costs from industry itself. However, for obvious reasons, industry is not likely always to be very forthcoming about such information. Even if it were, for example because of an obligation to submit such information, it is unlikely that industry is in a position to produce sufficient information about costs concerning a 'public good'. The problem of imperfect information is even more apparent in the case of societal cost-benefit trade-offs. Here access to a vast amount of information is required in order to take 'all' costs and benefits in to consideration. Regulators would also be required to balance incommensurable values, which itself calls into question whether there exists one 'optimal standard'.[80] Even if one presupposes that regulators are able to calibrate regulations and permits in such detail, these standards would be particularly vulnerable to scientific and technical development—and in the case of cost-benefits trade-offs, societal changes at large. Hence, 'optimal standards' are rapidly outdated, and would need constant amendment, something which is simply not realistic or even desirable.

It is, moreover, questionable whether today's regulatory standards in reality aim at enacting such optimal standards as described here.[81] Although cost-benefit analysis is frequently mentioned in regard to environmental policy-making and, moreover, is mentioned in the EC Treaty,[82] environmental regulation is still rarely based on cost-benefit analysis.[83] Furthermore, most existing standards in

[78] Similarly, Burrows, ibid., 43.

[79] R.L. Revez, 'Federalism and Environmental Regulation—A Public Choice Analysis' (2001) 115 *Harvard Law Review*, 553.

[80] Stallworthy, n. 40 above, 21: '[T]here is a crucial question as to whether regulation can in all circumstances achieve a proper balance between the various public interest factors involved in deciding upon acceptable levels of risk'.

[81] C.H. Schroeder, 'Lost in the Translation: What Environmental Regulation Does That Tort Cannot Duplicate' (2002) 41 *Washburn Law Journal*, 96, claims that 'environmental legislation [in the US, presumably] regularly establishes standards different from those chosen by cost-benefit consideration, standards that aim at protecting public health as much as possible within the limits of technical and economic feasibility'.

[82] Art. 174(3) EC.

[83] Bergkamp, n. 20 above, 459.

the EC not only often turn out to be minimum standards, by virtue of Articles 95 EC and 176 EC, they are so by definition.

Still, the most fundamental objection to be made against these theories lies in their failure to demonstrate that a supplementary liability regime necessarily distorts regulatory standards. It is difficult to understand why the expected costs of liability, as any other cost, could not be taken into account and internalized in the cost-benefit analysis undertaken by regulators.[84] This would counter the problem of distortion of 'optimal balance', as the standards would be set at a lower level in order to compensate for the costs of liability. Admittedly, it may be a difficult task to predict and calculate expected average costs of liability, but so is finding an 'optimal standard' in the first place. It should be reiterated that these distortion theories mainly stem from scholars who base their hypothesis on US tort law, which—due to its jury system and punitive damages—has failed to ensure uniform and consistent verdicts. In contrast, a civil law type of strict liability system ensures a higher level of uniformity and predictability, which should make it less difficult to calculate expected costs.

E. Adverse Spillover Effects From Permit Defence

i. Enforcement

If permit defence is available to polluters, liability will only function as an instrument for sanctioning non-compliance with environmental regulation. This is likely to deter individuals and NGOs from filing suits as they, in addition to the ordinary conditions for liability, will have to demonstrate that the operator breached his permit, and that the damage would not have occurred otherwise. Even if the operator ultimately bears the burden of proving that he acted in compliance with the permit, private parties will probably not risk going to court and incurring substantial legal fees without any evidence proving the opposite. But the sheer amount and complexity of today's regulation makes it very difficult fully to grasp the requirements placed on individual operators, and even more difficult to provide factual evidence that the operator has breached such conditions.[85] Perhaps most troubling of all, is that environmental regulation currently favoured in the Community often contains open-ended standards. This makes it very difficult to assess or prove that the operator was in breach. Prime examples are the water quality values in Directive 2000/60/EC establishing a Framework for Community Action in the Field of Water Policy (Water Frame-

[84] Liability could be seen as a sort of tax, along the lines of the Pigouvian tax which is construed in order to compensate for the market-failure concerning externalities. Similarly, in order to find optimal cost-benefit trade-offs, liability could be seen as part of the costs of regulation.

[85] In the EC, this situation is improving though, as permits are now publicly available; see Art. 15 of Dir. 96/61/EC, n. 5 above, and because of the implementation of a European Pollutant Emission Register (EPER) starting in June 2003 [2000] OJ L 192/36.

work Directive)[86] or such vague standards as 'Best Available Technology' (BAT).[87] Hence, it would seem that individuals will rarely have the necessary expertise or resources to pursue a liability case which hinges on the question whether the operator was in breach of his permit. Some of the largest NGOs may possess such knowledge, but they are not likely to have the financial capacity to bring more than a few such cases. In sum, a permit defence is likely to undermine private enforcement of the liability regime, leaving the effectiveness of the instrument dependent on the willingness of public authorities to bring claims.[88] However, public enforcement agents do not always have proper incentives: there is no direct connection between their interest and those of the potential victims they are supposed to protect, making them vulnerable to capture.[89]

ii. Regulation

If, by means of permit defence, industry is all but insulated from the responsibility of restoring environmental damage, regulators will be under political pressure to reduce risk of damage by adopting more comprehensive and stringent regulation, and tightening the terms of future permits.[90] Authorities will also have financial incentives to minimize risk through regulation, as private parties and NGOs are likely to turn their attention to the public purse, invoking state liability, for example on the basis of flawed risk regulation or insufficient permit requirements. Permit defence may affect future EC environmental regulation as well. At present, the EC environmental permitting process allows authorities to adjust the terms of permits to local circumstances.[91] Such local discretion may lead to disparities between liability exposures to operators in different parts of the EU, a result which would probably be corrected by increasing the stringency of EC legislation, causing inefficient increases in operating costs.[92] This situation is likely to favour neither business nor the environment. Environmentalists will note that the problems inherent in regulation remain, even though regulators will seek to create more complete and stringent regulation. As a consequence, one can expect increased regulatory gaps, posing a risk that the sector is insufficiently regulated in the meantime. Business will experience a more stringent and less flexible regulatory system, with permits containing terms which attempt to

[86] [2000] OJ L327/1.

[87] See H. Somsen, 'The Private Enforcement of Member State Compliance with EC Environmental Law—An Unfulfilled Promise?' (2000) 1 *Yearbook of European Environmental Law*, 337.

[88] It is interesting to note in this respect that empirical studies in the UK and elsewhere indicate that the regulator's discretion to prosecute environmental offences is rarely exercised in cases where the polluter was not at fault, despite being subject to strict liability; see Cane, n. 7 above, 444.

[89] Hylton, n. 22 above, 520; and McGarity, n. 30 above, 564–7.

[90] C. Clarke, *Update Comparative Legal Study*, 21–22, published on the Internet at: http://europa.eu.int/comm/environment/liability/followup.htm; DEFRA, n. 45 above, 16; Rabin, n. 28 above, 2076.

[91] See e.g. Art. 9(4) of Dir. 96/61/EC, n. 5 above.

[92] DEFRA, n. 45 above, 16.

make unforeseen damage virtually impossible, and drastically reduced emission allowances. The economic costs of such tightening are likely to be considerable.[93]

In fact, if one accepts the notion of over-deterrence, there is a more plausible risk of this occuring as a result of excessive regulation—stimulated by the application of permit defence—compared to the claim discussed previously concerning over-deterrence stemming from strict liability. As non-compliance with regulation or permits may result in withdrawal of permits as well as criminal sanctions, serious operators will have little choice but to comply with the regulation, or exit the market. Conversely, under strict liability, operators have freedom to choose whether they will make additional abatement measures according to their own cost-benefit calculations.

F. Relation to Fault Liability

Strict liability is evidently more onerous than fault liability, which is reflected in slightly different objectives. As seen above, there are environmental, economic, and moral grounds justifying strict liability over fault liability. Proponents of fault liability may similarly claim other viewpoints, justifying fault liability over strict liability. Leaving aside the discussion concerning the relative merits of the different policy aims, more important is that the choice of liability standard remains coherent with the policy aims it is supposed to further, that is, if deterrence is the main objective, the legislature should enact a strict liability regime capable of providing effective deterrence. However, if strict liability is accompanied by a permit defence, it will in reality come close to a fault regime.[94] Non-compliance with administrative statutes is normally considered sufficient proof of negligence, and the fault standard therefore becomes similar to strict liability. In most cases of environmental damage, the operator has acted in compliance with administrative permits,[95] and would thus be exempted from responsibility under a strict liability regime with permit defence. What remains covered by strict liability is therefore mainly damage that occurs because of accidents. Assuming that accidents for the most part are caused by fault, strict liability would result in responsibility in about the same number of cases as fault liability.

Strict liability with a permit defence may in fact prove to be less strict than fault liability.[96] Most fault liability regimes do not acknowledge permit compli-

[93] ibid.

[94] E. Rehbinder, 'Comments on Commission Working Document', published on the Internet at: http://europa.eu.int/comm/environment/liability/wrkdoc.htm; Stallworthy, n. 40 above, 18.

[95] In E. Eide and R. van den Bergh (eds.), *Law and Economics of the Environment* (Oslo: Juridisk Forlag, 1996), 51, it is claimed that 90% of all environmental damage stems from permitted pollution.

[96] Clarke, n. 90 above, 9.

ance as a sufficient reason to exempt the operator from responsibility:[97] 'Compliance with a legislative enactment or an administrative regulation does not prevent a finding of negligence where a reasonable man would take additional measures'.[98]

Since regulations and permits usually set minimum standards and/or may be seriously outdated, many operators will be held negligent even though they have complied with their permits. Thus, seeing that a permit defence can water down a strict liability regime to the point where it may even be less stringent than fault liability, one could question whether permit defence is logically compatible with strict liability—permit defence representing a compromise which removes the justification for strict liability, and ultimately threatens to undermine the policy aims that the regime is supposed to further.

G. Mitigating Factor in Theory

A more flexible and less far-reaching alternative to permit defence is to afford permit compliance relevance as a mitigating factor in the determination of responsibility and costs (hereinafter 'mitigating factor' or 'relative permit defence'). Still, a mitigating factor system carries most of the deficiencies discussed above in relation to permit defence, albeit to a lesser extent. The deterrent effect of strict liability is lessened as companies may be partially or wholly exempted from responsibility, but companies will still have some incentives to take precautionary measures as permit compliance does not insulate against liability. But a relative permit defence has other adverse effects which a regular permit defence does not have. Above, it was noted that a permit defence makes strict liability comparable with fault liability in terms of stringency, but the application of the two regimes are fundamentally different: the administration of the former hardly allows for any discretion, whereas the latter does. However, if strict liability is coupled with a relative permit defence, similar discretion is introduced as is the case in a fault system. As a consequence, many of the problems connected with fault liability will apply to strict liability, for example, lack of uniformity, risk of arbitrariness, and legal uncertainty.[99] This, in turn, especially in larger cases involving substantial economic costs, may make companies seek judicial review of the process, which will stimulate litigation and increased transaction costs.[100]

97 [US] Restatement (Third) of Torts: Product Liability, Section 4b, see Rabin, n. 28 above, 2050; F. Trinidade and P. Cane, *The Law of Torts in Australia* (Melbourne: Oxford University Press, 1999), 456–8.

98 Restatement (Second) of Torts 288C (1963–4).

99 H. Latin, 'Ideal versus real Regulatory Efficiency—Implementation of Uniform Standards and Fine Tuning Reforms' (1985) 38 *Stanford Law Review*, 1267 argues that, although flexibility may be efficient at a theoretical level, uniform standards significantly reduce decision-making and implementation cost and increase consistency and predictability. See also ALI Study 2, n. 28 above, 87–9.

100 Administrative costs will be higher than in a regular strict liability system as some risks will be processed and evaluated first through the regulatory system and then through the liability system,

Such a development would, moreover, raise concerns about whether courts should be allowed, albeit indirectly, to set standards, something which regulatory agencies arguably are better suited for. In the domain of fault liability, some commentators have voiced concerns about courts functioning as 'a form of appeal against standards set by regulators'.[101] This criticism appears misleading in relation to the functioning of a fault regime, as courts are traditionally careful not to intrude on the executive or legislature's competence, and can therefore be expected to act with some deference with regard to standards set by regulatory expert agencies. Hence, the application of fault liability is normally reserved for supplementing regulatory gaps, rather than securing the proficiency of standards. However, in a strict liability regime with a relative permit defence, it seems that courts in their judicial review would have to weigh the relevance and stringency of the regulatory standard, and on this basis decide whether to reduce the liability of the operator. The criticism of courts acting as appeal boards against regulation therefore seems fitting here.

Another crucial question is what standard should determine whether, and to what extent, compliance with permits should reduce the responsibility of the operator. As it obviously cannot be a strict standard, it would seem that one should apply a regular negligence norm: would a reasonable person take additional measures to those prescribed by the permit? If answered in the negative, the operator could in principle be entirely exempted from liability. Conversely, if a reasonable person would have taken measures that could have prevented the damage, permit compliance would not be a mitigating factor. Between these extremes are grey areas where perhaps a person should do a 'little more' than simply adhere to the permit, when the responsibility would supposedly be reduced. It seems evident that this level of flexibility and discretion may seriously complicate the administration of the liability regime and, in turn, undermine effective judicial review. In the context of the future EC environmental liability regime, should courts for instance have to assess the stringency of permits in the light of Best Available Technology Reference (BREF) documents, and on this basis consider to what extent permit compliance should reduce the responsibility of the operator?[102] Such a hybrid tort system would seem to carry the adverse effects of a fault liability system without the benefits stemming from strict liability.

often through repeated litigation of individual cases. See ALI Study 2, n. 28 above, 89; J. Coleman, *Risk and Wrongs* (Oxford: Oxford University Press, 1992), 226; H.C. Bugge, *Forurensningsansvaret* (Oslo: Universitetsforlaget, 1999), 102. In the USA, transaction costs in product liability and environmental liability cases have consumed up to two thirds of total outlays, leaving only the remaining third for compensation; see ALI Study 1, n. 10 above, 389.

[101] Cane, n. 7 above, 464.

[102] The Commission is in fact considering to what extent BREF documents, n. 85 above, can be used for purposes other than implementing the IPPC Directive; see Communication from the

Nonetheless, in the light of the polluter pays principle, it would still appear that a relative permit defence that reduces the responsibility of the operator is preferable to a permit defence which entirely exonerates the operator of liability. However, just as strict liability may be less onerous than fault liability—depending on the available defences—a relative permit defence may ultimately reduce responsibility in more cases than a narrowly defined permit defence. Thus, a 1991 Reporters Study by the American Law Institute (ALI) contained a proposal for a permit defence which, because of the stringency of its conditions,[103] would only be applicable in a limited number of cases, primarily in closely regulated areas.[104] In contrast, in a mitigating factor system, there is in principle no threshold for invoking permit compliance, but the nature of the permit will merely determine the extent to which the operator's responsibility shall be reduced. Furthermore, there is nothing hindering the authorities from affording permit compliance so much weight as a mitigating factor that little or no liability is conferred on the operator. As for judicial review, courts are likely to treat a regulatory standard set by expert agencies with some respect, the corollary of which is that permit compliance will probably be given considerable importance. In sum, it is conceivable that a relative permit defence may present a more serious exception to strict liability than a regular permit defence.

Due to the seemingly non-discretionary and automatic application of permit defence, it would appear to have advantages over a mitigating factor system in terms of uniformity, legal certainty, and transaction costs. However, this simplification can be misleading. As illustrated by the ALI permit defence draft, several conditions may need to be satisfied for reliance on a permit defence, some of which may involve difficult and discretionary assessments. Authorities—and in the case of judicial review, courts—may, for example, have to determine whether a regulatory standard is a minimum norm, or whether permits specifically regulate risks at issue. Some cases may also involve difficult evidentiary assessments as to whether the operator has fully complied with all relevant regulatory requirements. A permit defence may therefore merely change the nature of litigation, instead of reducing its actual amount.[105]

Commission 'On the Road to Sustainable Development' at 19 (COM (2003)354). However, BREF documents are not legally binding, but simply provide reference information.

[103] ALI Study 1, n. 10 above, 415–16: '[1] The regulation must have been produced by a specialized administrative agency with the statutory responsibility to monitor risk-creating activities in the area in question and to establish and regularly revise specific standards governing enterprise behaviour; [2] the agency must have addressed the specific risk in question in the case at hand and have made an explicit judgement about what type of legal controls are appropriate; [3] the enterprise in question must have complied with all the relevant standards prescribed by the Agency; [4] and the enterprise must also have disclosed to the regulatory agency any information in its possession (or which it had good reason to be aware) concerning both the hazards posed by the risk in question and the available means of controlling the risk'.

[104] ALI Study 2, n. 28 above, 101.

[105] For a similar view, see Rabin, n. 28 above, 2076–7.

Thus, although a comparison of the benefits and drawbacks of a regular permit defence and a mitigating factor system is complex, it would appear that the latter is not necessarily an attractive compromise. Simultaneously, application of a permit defence is more troublesome and likely to cause more litigation and legal uncertainty than is often claimed.

H. Interim Conclusion

It has been argued above that we should not rely exclusively on command and control instruments to manage all environmental harm stemming from our risk-oriented society. In addition to inevitable gaps in legislation and suboptimal standard-setting because of imperfect information, regulation may favour certain interests. It has been demonstrated that strict liability can play an important supplementary role in tandem with command and control instruments by providing an economic incentive for the regulatees to go beyond existing standards. Apart from beneficial environmental effects stemming from risk minimization, precautionary measures should normally be cost-efficient, since operators will take abatement measures to the extent that these cost less than a possible liability suit. Strict liability may also stimulate development of new technology and increase competition. By comparison, arguments in favour of a permit defence suffer from logical flaws or carry little weight. In addition, it has been seen that a permit defence may have adverse spillovers affecting regulation—not only from an environmental perspective, but also for business—and enforcement by private parties. Finally, it has been noted that a permit defence substantially changes the character of strict liability to the point where it becomes similar, if not inferior, to fault liability. This in turn raised the question whether a permit defence is in fact logically incompatible with a strict liability regime; permit defence represents a compromise that removes the justification for strict liability, and ultimately threatens to undermine the policy aims that the regime is purported to further. The alternative, a relative permit defence, mediates some of these deficiencies, but at the same time raises new problems by allowing authorities a discretionary role normally associated with fault liability regimes. This may in turn stimulate demand for judicial review, which would make the process more litigation-centric, add transaction costs, and undermine uniformity and legal certainty. Another fundamental question is whether courts are suited for—albeit indirectly—conducting judicial review of standards set by expert agencies.

For all these reasons, it appears that the adverse effects stemming from both a permit defence and a relative permit defence are so profound that neither should feature in a strict liability regime.

III. A Future European Environmental Liability Regime

A. Law in the Member States

A recent survey commissioned by the Commission revealed that the environmental liability regimes in most Member States are based on public/administrative law, virtually all of which prescribe strict liability.[106] No country has in recent years proposed new legislation based on fault liability.[107] 'State of the art' and permit defences are rarely available, although some Member States exonerate the operator for damages caused by licensed discharges of specific quantities or concentrations of pollutants.[108] An operator may similarly escape liability where development consents specify certain permitted instances of damage. However, the operator is normally not exempted from responsibility for indirect or unforeseen damage, although authorization of the activity may be treated as a mitigating factor when deciding the amount of liability to be imposed on the party responsible.[109]

Interestingly, in US torts law (products), an additional requirement before an operator can invoke permit defence is that the regulation or permit had been promulgated recently, and that the regulatory process was full, fair, and thorough as well as reflecting substantial expertise.[110]

Thus, permit defence is rarely accepted in European liability regimes. Where it is recognized as a ground for exemption of liability, the permit defence is restricted to cases in which the authorities have specifically authorized not only the emission, but also the damage. More often, the operator may only invoke permit compliance as a mitigating factor, the relevance of which depends on the nature of the permit.

B. The Proposed EC Environmental Liability Directive[111]

i. Strict Liability, Fault Liability, and Permit Defence

Before studying specifically the different models of permit defence favoured by the Commission, EP, and Council, respectively, we should briefly consider the basic features of the future EC liability regime. It is common ground that the liability regime should be based on strict liability for a closed group of activities

106 Clarke, n. 90 above, 9.

107 ibid.

108 Stallworthy, n. 40 above, 17; Clarke, n. 90 above, 21; DEFRA, n. 45 above, 15.

109 DEFRA, ibid.

110 Restatement (Third) of Torts, Section 4b 'Comment'.

111 This section is based on the legislative developments having taken place by Oct. 2003, i.e. shortly after the EP and the Council had concluded the first reading of the Commission's proposal.

that are considered hazardous, as listed in Annex 1 to the proposed liability directive. For biodiversity damage, the draft Environmental Liability Directive encompasses also other activities than those specified in Annex 1, but these activities are subject to fault liability. For the Annex 1 activities that are subjected to strict liability, a form of permit defence will most likely be provided for, the details of which will be considered further below. Nonetheless, according to the Commission's proposal and the Council Common Position, permit defence is not available if damage was caused by negligence or fault.[112] Put differently, an operator may in principle be held liable on the basis of fault liability even though acting in full compliance with the requirements governing his activity. Thus, although commentators have presented the future regime as strict liability with a permit defence, it might well be described as a fault liability scheme without a permit defence. The relationship between permit defence and subsidiary fault responsibility is not entirely clear though: it could be that the caveat of subsidiary fault liability is (superfluously) added to make clear that where damage is caused by an activity or risk which is not specifically regulated in the permit, the operator may still be held responsible. However, permit defence is normally not considered available in such a case, the consequence of which should be that the operator remains subject to strict liability, not fault liability. A different interpretation is that, even if the permit specifically regulated the risk causing the damage, authorities or courts shall apply a regular negligence test, posing the question, *inter alia*, whether a reasonable person would have taken measures additional to those stipulated in the permit. In this case, permit compliance will in reality not function as a defence, but merely as a mitigating factor in the determination of whether the operator acted negligently or not. Furthermore, it is noteworthy that, in the Council Common Position, the burden of proof has been reversed—the onus is on the operator to demonstrate that he was not at fault or negligent.[113]

As seen, there appears to be some tension between, on the one hand, the wish to have an uncomplicated system of strict liability and a permit defence, and, on the other hand, the wish to accommodate discretion for the authorities through the flexibility of a subsidiary fault liability mechanism.

ii. The Different Models of Permit Defence Contemplated by the Community

It is useful to consider different versions of permit defence systems promulgated by the Community's institutions in the framework of the decision-making

[112] See Art. 9(2) of the Commission proposal, n. 2 above; and Art. 8.4(a) of the Council Common Position, n. 4 above. The EP has not proposed a similar subsidiary fault responsibility, probably due to the fact that it favours a more flexible type of permit defence; see below.

[113] Council Common Position, ibid: 'The Member States may allow the operator not to bear the costs of remedial action where *he demonstrates* that he was not at fault or negligent' (emphasis added).

procedure which should eventually culminate in the Environmental Liability Directive. Article 9(1)(c) of the Commission's Proposal provides as follows:[114]

[T]his Directive shall not cover environmental damage or an imminent threat of such damage caused by:
(c) an emission or event allowed in applicable laws and regulations, or in the permit or authorisation issued to the operator.

Article 11.3 of the EP Position prescribes:[115]

[W]hen deciding the level of responsibility and the amount of financial compensation in respect of liability to be recovered from an operator, the competent authority and a reviewing court or tribunal shall take into account the following mitigating factors:
(a) an emission or activity specifically and explicitly allowed in applicable laws and regulations, or in the permit or authorisation issued to the operator. An emission or activity and its foreseeable effects, specifically and explicitly allowed in the permit or authorisation issued to the operator, can be considered as an exemption, so far as the usual risks within the framework of the authorisation are concerned. In the case of damage, the responsibility shall lie with the issuing authority.

Art 8.4 of the Council Common Position is articulated as follows:[116]

The Member States may allow the operator not to bear the costs of remedial actions taken pursuant to this Directive where he demonstrates that he was not at fault or negligent and that the environmental damage was caused by:
(a) an emission or event expressly authorised by, and fully in accordance with the conditions of, an authorisation conferred by or given under applicable national laws and regulations which implement those measures adopted by the Community specified in Annex III, as applied at the date of the emission or event.

First, the nature of the different permit defences should be examined. The Commission's proposal excludes from the scope of the Directive damage caused by activities that were carried out in compliance with a permit.[117] Hence, permit compliance would preclude any liability suit from being brought altogether. The EP, on the other hand, favours a compromise where regulatory compliance may in certain cases function as a mitigating factor, and in others as a defence. The Council's position is less clear: the text can be understood as referring to a regular permit defence, but may also be read as a relative permit defence. Considering that the paragraph does not contain any references to a mitigating factor scheme, and that it stipulates that the operator may not be required to bear 'the costs', instead of, for example, 'the full costs', it seems that the Council seeks to make available a regular permit defence. On the other hand, it is noteworthy that the Council, on the basis of the Greek Presidency Compromise Proposal, has removed the permit defence provision from the group of 'Exceptions' to the general heading of 'Prevention and Remediation Costs'. Linking permit compli-

[114] See n. 2 above. [115] See n. 3 above. [116] See n. 4 above.
[117] Stallworthy, n. 40 above, 18.

ance to costs, instead of the conditions for responsibility, suggests that permit compliance is not a defence, but a mitigating factor relevant for the determination of costs. But it could also simply mean that the Council, in contrast to the Commission's proposal, did not want permit compliance to *pre-empt* liability, but to apply as a defence. All things considered, the most likely interpretation is that the Council allows for a regular permit defence. Thus, the Community bodies have presented three distinctly different applications of permit compliance: 'permit pre-emption', 'permit defence', and permit as a 'mitigating factor'.

Secondly, there are also differences concerning the scope of the three proposed regimes. The Commission's proposal, supported by the Council, refers to an 'emission or event' allowed in applicable laws and regulations, or in the permit or authorization. However, the EP has substituted for 'event' 'activity'. The former arguably has a broader scope, as it connotes an ongoing situation, whereas the latter refers to individual situations. Indeed, Margot Walström has emphasized the importance of this distinction when claiming that the Commission's proposed permit defence is of limited application: 'It is worth stressing . . . that this provision [Art 9.1 (c)] does not refer to the activity as such but to "emission or event", that is a specific element of the activity considered as a whole'.[118]

If only permits that authorize an emission or event—as opposed to those that regulate an activity as such—are relevant, it would appear that permit defence is restricted to permits containing 'result requirements', as opposed to permits stipulating 'means requirements'.[119] Put simply, 'result permits' stipulate specifically the pollution which is permitted to result from the activity, either by setting emission limits or (imission) quality standards. 'Means permits', on the other hand, do not regulate the effects of the production, but the production methods, for example, by requiring BAT. Although permits have traditionally contained both result and means requirements, it is noteworthy that Directive 96/61/EC on Integrated Pollution Prevention and Control (IPPC Directive)[120] now allows national authorities to prescribe 'equivalent parameters or technical measures' instead of emission limits. Considering the trend of flexibility in today's regulation,[121] it is thus likely that future permits will increasingly consist of means requirements instead of result requirements. If so, it would appear that a significant part of future permits may not be invoked as permit defence.

Closely related is the question whether only the emissions and events must be authorized, or also their effects, that is, the damage occurring from the activity. As seen above, in national liability regimes where permit defence is recognized, it is only relevant for direct and foreseeable damage specifically authorized.

[118] Answer given by Mrs Walström on behalf of the Commission (31 July 2002) to written question P-2156/02 by Kathleen Van Brempt (PSE) to the Commission (11 July 2002).

[119] For a general analysis, see Bergkamp, n. 20 above, 242–3.

[120] See n. 5 above.

[121] See L. Krämer, 'Differentiation in EU Environmental Policy' (2000) 9 *European Environmental Law Review*, 133.

However, neither the Commission's proposal nor the Council's Common Position prescribes that the effects must be 'allowed', but only the 'emission or event' as such. It therefore seems that the damage must not be specifically authorized in the permit, but it leaves open the question whether the permit only exempts direct and foreseeable damage, or also indirect and unforeseen effects. The EP position, on the other hand, explicitly requires that not only the activity, but also that 'its foreseeable effects [have been] specifically and explicitly allowed in the permit . . . so far as the usual risks are concerned'. Conversely, if the permit merely allows the emission or activity, but not 'its foreseeable effects', the permit may not be used as a defence, but merely as a 'mitigating factor'. However, close reading of the EP position reveals seemingly illogical drafting: if the damage (effect) must have been 'specifically and explicitly' allowed in the permit, why is it necessary to add that the effect must be 'foreseeable' and concern 'usual risks'? Furthermore, it is not self-evident why foreseeability should be relevant in determining whether the operator should be held liable or not. In fact, the justification for the 'state of the art defence' is precisely that the operator should not be held liable for damages that could not be foreseen. An explanation may be derived from the fact that permits usually do not specifically and explicitly allow *damages*, but merely *emissions* or *events*. Thus, what the EP apparently seeks to achieve is to clarify in what situations a permit may be *interpreted as an implicit acceptance* of certain damage, that is, 'foreseeable effects' and 'usual risks'. This appears scarcely realistic: first, it should be noted that permits are not likely to be issued when it is clear beforehand that the activity will cause damage;[122] authorizations are normally restricted to activities which merely carry a *risk* of damage. Thus, permits are not about accepting damage, but regulating risk, and the issuing of a permit merely represents an effort by authorities to minimize this risk through the drawing up of certain requirements. Hence, it cannot be inferred from the mere fact that a permit has been issued that the authorities thereby have exempted the operator from responsibility if the risk should materialize and cause damage. Much as a driving licence does not exonerate motorists from responsibility for accidents, a permit issued to an industrial facility should not relieve the operator from carrying the risks of that activity.

A more far-reaching interpretation is that the EP actually requires that damage must have been specifically allowed in the permit, and that the notion of 'foreseeable effects' sets the outer limit for what the authorities may allow with regard to the liability of the operator.

Another question is to what extent an authorization in general instruments such as laws and regulations, as opposed to individually issued permits, may 'specifically' and 'explicitly' regulate a certain event. The EP has apparently been conscious of this problem, and has therefore differentiated between operations

122 Commission Q & A, published on the Internet at: http://europa.eu.int/comm/environment/liability/.

that are allowed in laws and regulations and situations where a permit or authorization has been issued. In the former case, compliance may serve as a mitigating factor only, whereas the operator may be entirely exempted from responsibility in the latter situation. However, neither the Commission nor the Council supports such a distinction.

It is noteworthy that the Commission and the EP, on the one hand, and the Council, on the other hand, differ on the scope of permit defence in respect of preventive and remedial responsibility. In the Commission proposal and the EP position, permit defence or mitigating factors apply to both situations, whereas the Council mentions permit defence in relation to costs of remediation only. Hence, according to the Council Common Position, it would seem that the operator would still be responsible for taking, or paying for, preventive measures.[123]

Before turning to the question whether a permit defence can properly function in the framework of EC environmental regulation, we should briefly pass comment on the merits of the different models of permit defence discussed above. The Commission has clearly proposed the most far-reaching model, whereby permit compliance precludes application of the liability directive altogether. Consequently, for reasons presented above, the only models worthy of consideration, in my opinion, are those of the Council and the EP respectively. However, a comparison is complicated by the fact that it is not entirely clear whether the Council has proposed a regular permit defence or a mitigating factor system. The following will assume that the former construction is the intended model. As noted above, a mitigating factor regime may not necessarily be more compatible with the 'polluter pays' principle than a narrowly defined permit defence. It is striking in this respect that, by virtue of use of the term of 'activity' instead of 'event', the EP's relative permit defence has a broader scope than the Council's permit defence. On the other hand, the EP's proposed defence is probably more narrowly construed than the Council's, due to the fact that it specifically requires that effects must be foreseeable and usual. In sum, it appears that the EP's compromise proposal, featuring both permit defence and a mitigating factor mechanism, is the alternative which departs the least from the polluter pays principle. It is of course noteworthy that the Council Common Position, unlike the EP position, leaves it to the Member States' discretion whether to acknowledge permit defence or not.[124] However, considering the great efforts made by a majority of the Member States in the Council to make permit defence available, it seems reasonable to assume that at least those countries will make use of this option.

[123] The costs of preventive measures could be considerable, e.g. if the operator is required to halt his activity while waiting for a risk assessment.

[124] Art. 8.4 of the Council Common Position: 'The Member States *may* allow the operator not to bear the remedial costs' (emphasis added).

iii. Subsidiary State Liability?

The ramifications of permit defence must be judged within the context of the question of subsidiary public responsibility. In view of the objective of effective reparation, it is vital that public authorities should be responsible for ensuring reparation in cases where permit defence exempts operators from the rigour of the 'polluter pays' principle. Public responsibility might also induce authorities to promulgate more comprehensive regulation, issue stricter permits, and more generally to apply the precautionary principle to a larger degree. As observed, these generally positive spillover effects on standard-setting are not sufficient to justify a permit defence—in some cases they may even have adverse environmental effects—but they should at least compensate for some of the loss of deterrence caused by permit defence. Considering that authorities indirectly contribute to damage by authorizing risky activities, the state bears a moral responsibility to ensure restoration. Moreover, in cases where damage occurs despite the operator complying fully with the permit, the authorities may have failed to regulate the activity satisfactorily altogether.

It is therefore of grave concern that the Commission and the Council reject state responsibility in cases where operators cannot be held responsible because of permit defence.[125] The EP, however, insisted on state liability in its first reading of the proposal.[126] Some may argue that it is not crucial whether or not the Environmental Liability Directive includes state liability as authorities may still be held liable under national law, or the *Francovich* doctrine if the errors stems from breach of EC law.[127] Yet, in most Member States it is very difficult—and in some cases impossible—to hold states responsible for insufficient regulation.[128] *Francovich* liability is unlikely often to apply to cases involving damage to natural resources, since such liability requires the breach of 'rights' of individuals, as well as economic loss.[129] In addition, since the requirements of EC law concerning the issuing of permits are few and general in nature,[130] it may in any event prove difficult to demonstrate a 'sufficiently serious breach'.[131]

C. Permit Requirements in the EC—the IPPC Directive

One cannot evaluate the virtues and disadvantages of permit defence without taking into account the legislative framework within which it operates; the

125 See Arts. 6.1 and 9.1of the Commission proposal, n. 2 above; as well as Arts. 5.3–5.4 and 6.3–6.4 of the Council Common Position, n. 4 above.

126 See Art. 11.3 (a) *in fine* of the EP position, n. 3 above.

127 Joined Cases C-6/90 and C-9/90, *Andrea Francovich and Danila Bonifaci and others* v. *Italian Republic* [1991] ECR I-5357.

128 Clarke, n. 90 above, 21; Stallworthy, n. 40 above, 21.

129 For a similar view, see W. van Gerven *et al.*, *Cases, Materials and Text on National, Supranational and International Tort Law—Scope of Protection* (Oxford: Hart Publishing, 1998), 445.

130 See L. Krämer, *EC Environmental Law* (London: Sweet and Maxwell, 2000), 48.

131 See e.g. Joined Cases C-174, 178–9 & 188–90/94 *Dillenkofer and Others* [1996] ECR I-4845, para. 25.

permitting process, and the nature and stringency of the permit requirements. Most activities mentioned in Annex 1 of the proposed Environmental Liability Directive are subject to a permit regime. However, many of the directives in Annex 1 lack specific substantive requirements for the issuing of permits. To the extent that directives contain emission limit values, they represent minimum standards.[132] Furthermore, the IPPC Directive,[133] which regulates most of the activities that fall within the scope of Annex 1 represents a major shift of environmental policy in the EC. Essentially, it moves away from Community-wide emission standards, and leaves principal responsibility for setting emission limits with national authorities.[134] This development in favour of decentralization stems from the belief that an integrated approach and cost-efficient regulation is most effectively realized locally.[135] To this end, authorities on a national, regional, or local level must enact emission limit values based on the ambiguous and cost-efficiency-oriented notion of Best Available Technology.[136] In the process, they must take into account technical characteristics of the installation, its geographical location, and local environmental conditions.[137] It is also noteworthy that emission limits are only required in respect of 'significant pollution'[138] and even so, national authorities are free to substitute emission limit

[132] See Art 18(2) of Dir. 96/61/EC, n. 5 above.

[133] ibid.

[134] Krämer, n. 121 above, 137: 'Of paramount importance for environmental policy is the permit system for industrial installations, which was set up by Directive 96/61 . . . The decision not to fix emission limit values for installations of the same type at Community level is a major shift of EC environmental policy in favour of more differentiation . . . Directive 96/61 will provide for EC-wide emission limit values only in exceptional circumstances; normally, such standards will be fixed at a local, regional or national level'.

[135] Communication from the Commission, 'On the Road to a Sustainable Development' COM(2003)354, 23.

[136] As seen from the definitions in Art. 2(11), the term 'best available technique' is clearly misleading, as it is based on a regular cost-benefit analysis, taking into account whether the technology may be implemented under economically viable conditions, whether they are produced inside the Member State in question (which, by the way, appears to conflict with Art. 28 EC), and whether they are 'reasonably accessible' to the operator. Indeed, the Commission Communication, ibid. 14–15, acknowledges that the notion of BAT is 'by nature dynamic and sufficiently flexible to allow the operator and authorities to take into account constraints from basic choices in the production process or plant layout and to respect cost-efficiency considerations. . . . This means that BAT can actually vary from one plant to another because costs and benefits can obviously vary. The fact that costs and benefits are elements in the definition of BAT also means that BAT inevitably is a balance between different environmental impacts and associated costs. Therefore, techniques may very well be better than BAT in terms of overall environmental performance or for one particular environmental aspect'.

[137] See Art. 9(4). See M. Doppelhammer, 'More Difficult than Finding the Way Round Chinatown? The IPPC Directive and its Implementation' (2000) 9 *European Environmental Law Review*, 203: 'This provision [Article 9.4] has a crucial impact. It enables national authorities to derogate from the BATs, which are already economically qualified, and to impose less stringent permit conditions whenever they consider this justified by the local environmental conditions'.

[138] It is not clear how 'significant pollution' compares to the definition of 'environmental damage' in the proposed environmental liability directive. The terms should ideally be aligned so that any pollution that potentially could result in environmental damage in the context of the liability directive should be considered 'significant' in relation to the IPPC Directive.

with 'equivalent parameters or technical measures'. In sum, it appears that the IPPC Directive does not seek to harmonize the substantive conditions for operating large installations in the EC, but rather provides for uniform procedural rules, leaving national authorities considerable discretion to determine the substance of permits.[139] The IPPC Directive therefore represents a fundamental move away from uniform standards, in favour of an emphasis on differentiation.[140]

This approach may have some virtues when the IPPC Directive is seen in isolation, but it clearly raises serious concerns when it is realized that it will also determine the effectiveness of the proposed Directive on Environmental Liability. After all, even though the latter is a proposal for a framework directive, it seeks to introduce a core of uniformity concerning environmental liability in the EC. It should be recalled that the Commission had to fend off allegations that the proposal was in breach of the subsidiarity principle by claiming that there was a need to have a uniform Community-wide liability regime in order, *inter alia*, to prevent 'forum-shopping' and ensure a level playing field.[141] This aim has been substantially undermined, since the lack of uniform permits will mean that the stringency of the liability regime will vary similarly throughout the Community.[142] In fact, one could argue that, if the liability regime recognizes a permit defence, and thereby fails to provide anything close to a uniform liability regime in the EC, the Directive will have lost its justification, and may indeed conflict with the subsidiarity principle.

In order to remedy this problem, there are two options. Either application of the permit defence must be reconsidered, or the IPPC Directive amended, so that more emission limits are fixed at Community level, thereby ensuring some degree of uniformity.[143] In the first option, this could take the form of either deleting the permit defence or applying permit compliance as a mitigating factor. Although a

139 In the (2001) 'First Report of Representative Limit Values', the Commission sought to verify the expected convergence of IPPC limit values within the Union on the basis of collected data from the Member States. Ironically, the Commission had to confess that it was impossible to meet this aim: 'The reason is not that Member States have not made a real effort, but rather that they all use very different ways of expressing limits, which they are perfectly allowed to do, since the [IPPC] Directive does not require harmonisation of these diverse practices', see Communication, n. 135 above, 10.

140 For a thorough analysis of the discretion inherent in the IPPC Directive, see J. Scott, 'Flexibility in the Implementation of EC Environmental Law' (2000) 1 *Yearbook of European Environmental Law*, 37.

141 See the explanatory memorandum in the Commission proposal, n. 2 above, 5.

142 Doppelhammer, n. 137 above, 206: 'Looking at the differences between northern and southern European countries in both standards of industrial development and attitudes to environmental protection, it seems likely that the emission limit values (ELVs) set at national level will vary considerably, thus bringing about distortions of competition'.

143 The Commission Communication, n. 135 above, 23, notes problems with the implementation of the IPPC Directive and warns that, 'if it becomes clear that in one or more Member States the authorities systematically set emission limit values that are too lenient and not based on BAT, it may be necessary to introduce additional Community emissions limit values'.

mitigating factor system itself raises problems of uniformity, the advantage would be that authorities or courts could take into account the stringency of the different permits, thereby ensuring, at least in theory, a level playing field even though permit requirements vary. It appears clearly advantageous to amend the proposed Directive on Environmental Liability instead of the IPPC Directive, as the exclusion of permit defence would strengthen the objective of the liability regime—ensuring application of the polluter pays principle—whereas re-orienting the IPPC Directive to centralized and uniform standard setting runs counter to the very idea of an integrated approach.[144]

Another problem with the IPPC Directive is that it only regulates large installations, SMEs falling outside its scope. SMEs may still be subjected to permits pursuant to some of the other directives in Annex 1 to the proposed Directive on Environmental Liability, but not all of them contain permit requirements, and some SMEs are in any event likely to fall below permit thresholds.[145] Thus, it would appear that many SMEs may operate without a permit that is relevant for the purposes of the proposed Directive on Environmental Liability, i.e. 'an authorization . . . which implements those measures adopted by the Community specified in Annex 3 [Annex 1 of the proposal]'.[146] This would in turn remove the possibility of invoking a permit defence. If so, one would have the paradoxical situation that SMEs are subject to a much stricter liability regime than large installations, which, because of their size, carry a higher risk potential than small and medium-sized enterprises.[147]

IV. Conclusions

Section II two of this article concluded that the adverse effects stemming from both a permit defence and a relative permit defence—or mitigating factor system as it is also called—are so profound that neither should feature in a strict liability regime. In Section III, it was noted that few of the EC Member States recognize permit defence, and the ones that do apply strict conditions before it may be invoked. Nonetheless, after having just completed the first reading of the proposed Environmental Liability Directive, it appears that some form of permit defence will be made available in a future EC regime. The Council seems to

[144] ibid.: 'Community-wide limit values undermine both the decentralised and integrated approach of the [IPPC] Directive, since they restrict the possibility for the competent authority to make pragmatic and environmentally- and economically-justified trade-off decisions'.

[145] DEFRA, n. 45 above, 21, notes however that SMEs may be covered in relation to discharge of dangerous substances, waste management, or water abstraction and impoundment.

[146] Art. 8.4a of the Council common position, n. 4 above.

[147] This would seem particularly ironic given that SMEs were excluded from the scope of the IPPC Directive due to fear of adverse effects on competitiveness; see Doppelhammer, n. 137 above, 201.

support a regular permit defence, the functioning of which is, however, muddled by the fact that it shall not be available if the operator was negligent. The EP, on the other hand, has sought to find a middle way where regulatory compliance may in some cases function as a mitigating factor and in others as a complete defence.

Perhaps as important as its stance on permit defence is the fact that the Council rejects any subsidiary responsibility for Member States to ensure restoration in cases where the operator cannot be held liable, for example, because of permit defence. The EP, however, insists that authorities must ensure restoration in these cases.

Finally, it was noted that a permit defence may undermine the prospect of a uniform environmental liability regime in the EC as permits issued under the umbrella of the IPPC Directive will vary substantially. Although a proposal for a framework directive, there may be concerns about its justification in light of the subsidiarity principle if it fails to establish even a core of uniformity. Since amending the IPPC Directive is not a viable option, consideration should be given to leaving out the permit defence, or at least settling for a mitigating factor system.

Against the background that there is no tradition of permit defence in Europe, and considering the abundance of general and EC specific arguments rejecting permit defence—underpinned by the well-established polluter pays principle—one may wonder why it nonetheless appears inevitable that such a defence will be made available in the future EC environmental liability regime. There are two major reasons for this misfortune. First, the Commission proposal, according to which permit compliance pre-empted the application of the proposed Directive on Environmental Liability altogether, was very weak. Thus, the Council was not given much to work with, and even the environmentally backwards permit defence eventually made available in the Common Position was an improvement by comparison. But perhaps most important is that the EP has been practically paralysed internally ever since the Legal Affairs and Internal Market Committee was given the lead role, instead of the Environmental Committee, and an 'enhanced Hughes procedure' was initiated. Apparently this choice was due to the fact that the EP's internal rules held that any matter concerning civil liability belonged to the Legal Affairs Committee. However, due to much criticism of the White Paper, the Commission changed policy and the proposed Directive on Environmental Liability is no longer based on civil liability, but public liability. Nonetheless, the struggle between the Legal Affairs Committee and the Environmental Committee delayed the EP's first reading so much that it was hardly in a position to influence the drafting of the Council Common Position, on which political agreement was reached within a month after the EP's first reading. The EP Resolution, on the other hand, bore inevitable signs of compromise. This is perhaps most evident from its dual-track model of both a permit defence and mitigating factor system. One can only hope that the added impetus provided by elections for an enlarged EP—which may be considered a 'make or break' deadline for the proposed Directive—can provide additional incentives for cooperation, and result in the EP taking a strong stand on, *inter alia*, the issue of permit defence.

Postscript

The EP surrendered on the issue of permit defence in the second reading and the subsequent conciliation procedure, and accepted the model favoured by the Council without proposing any amendments. EC Directive 2004/35 on environmental liability with regard to prevention and remedying of environmental damage was formally adopted on 21 April 2004.[148] The Member States have until 30 April 2007 to implement the Directive.

[148] [2004] OJ L143/56.

Between Enforcement and Toleration of Breaches of Environmental Law—Dutch Policy Explained

*ALLETA BLOMBERG AND LEX MICHIELS**

I. Introduction

This chapter focuses on tensions between the duty to enforce EC environmental law emanating from EC law, and practical and legal constraints faced by public authorities in the exercise of that obligation. The starting point is that many environmental directives contain obligations of result, and that Member States cannot rely on any justifications if they fail to comply with these obligations, which follow from Article 10 EC. Nonetheless, in individual cases where citizens or undertakings fail to comply with national implementing legislation, public authorities can, but may not always (immediately), initiate enforcement action. This follows from both legal obligations and practical realities. It will be argued that such (temporary) acquiescence, or toleration, does not necessarily amount to a breach of EC law if the result required by a directive is nonetheless realized.

In what follows we will explore the limits imposed by EC law on such acquiescence, as well as those following from the European Convention on Human Rights (ECHR). Next, it will be argued that, within those boundaries, (temporary) acquiescence is permitted, and may for important reasons also be necessary for the protection of all relevant interests. This policy may be pursued in a responsible way, such as is the case in the Netherlands, and has been accepted by Dutch courts. Dutch policy entails administrative decisions containing the conditions under which, for a specified period, the law will not be enforced. Such decisions may be judicially reviewed. On balance, this leads to better results compared to unregulated tolerance or, when it is denied that controlled acquiescence is a meaningful administrative tool, a situation in turn giving rise to belated, partial, or even non-enforcement.

Our focus is on activities requiring prior authorization (permits), because it is here that lawful acquiescence without an explicit prior decision in Dutch law is

* Respectively Senior Researcher and Professor at Utrecht University, Centre for Environmental Law and Policy.

normally not possible. We will commence with an overview of the Dutch enforcement system as it relates to environmental law, which will also involve a summary comparison with approaches in some other Member States.

II. Enforcement of Environmental Law in the Netherlands

The improvement of the enforcement of environmental law has received a great deal of attention during the last two decades. The Dutch legal system therefore provides a rather extensive set of enforcement tools. Several authorities enjoy competence to enforce environmental law, although there is a fairly sharp distinction between criminal and administrative enforcement. While criminal enforcement is the exclusive preserve of the Public Prosecutions Department—in conjunction with criminal investigators—in practice most enforcement is pursued by administrative authorities, which have primary responsibility for the enforcement of most environmental legislation. For this purpose, administrative authorities have three different sanctions at their disposal, which will be examined hereafter. Their ultimate objective is to put an end to breaches of environmental law, to prevent any recurrence of such breaches, and to undo the consequences of such violations.

To be sure, in many European countries, reparative instruments are called 'measures', and the word 'sanction' is used for punitive instruments. In the Netherlands, we use the word 'sanction' in a rather neutral sense to refer to each formal reaction of the public authorities to violations that impose an obligation on those responsible (for example, payment of a penalty or the obligation to carry out a clean-up order).

Before describing various sanctions, we need to specify which authorities play a role in public enforcement. In respect of breaches emanating from installations, and activities which (may) also occur outside installations requiring a permit, such as discharges, there will always be a public authority with competences to enforce. For large installations, this is the province, for smaller installations the municipality, which is also the competent authority in respect of undertakings whose activities have detrimental environmental effects, but which are not subject to a permit. On the basis of the *Wet Milieubeheer* (Environmental Management Act) and the associated *Inrichtingen en Vergunningenbesluit* (Decision on Installations and Permits), it can be precisely ascertained which authority has competences for each installation. These authorities, it should be noted, serve environmental imperatives as well as the public interest at large. For discharges in the aquatic environment, it is the board of a *Waterschap* (Water Authority) that is usually the competent authority. These are responsible for the maintenance of the quality of surface water. All authorities mentioned employ supervisors who investigate breaches. For many activities outside installations, the Minister is the competent authority, but in practice this power is exercised on his behalf by a national inspection authority. Actually, for such activities, criminal law plays a more prominent role than administrative law. As indicated, we will concentrate on activities giving rise to breaches that emanate from installations, and the practice of administrative acquiescence in such activities.

First, we shall discuss the three most important administrative sanctions. The first such sanction, called *bestuursdwang* (administrative coercion), gives the state the power actually to put an end to a breach. In the event of a breach, the relevant authority takes a decision announcing coercive action. In general, the administrative authority must specify a term within which the addressee can comply without attracting public interference. Once that term has expired and the addressee of the decision has not complied, the authority can take proactive measures. Moreover, the authority is entitled to execute the decision at the culprit's expense. According to the law, the decision announcing administrative coercion should not only be sent to the wrongdoer, but also—if applicable—to the persons entitled to the use of the object in respect of which enforcement action will be taken. These persons, however, do not have to bear the expenses if they are not also wrongdoers.

The second and most common sanction is the so-called *last onder dwangsom* (an administrative *astreinte* or, in other words, an order for periodic penalty payments). This is a corrective order backed up with a penalty: the wrongdoer who does not comply with the order has to pay a monetary sum for each violation (in case of repeated violations), or for the period of non-compliance (in case of continuous violations). Unlike *bestuursdwang*, the *last onder dwangsom* can only be imposed on wrongdoers who—according to the case law—also have to be able to bring an end to the illegal situation. The reason for this requirement is that the order would in effect be a fine if wrongdoers cannot end an illegal situation, because in that case they cannot prevent forfeiture. In practice, most wrongdoers are sensitive to this financial incentive, and discontinue breaches. This partly explains the relative popularity of the *last onder dwangsom* in the Netherlands.[1] Another reason for its attractiveness is that it implies fewer financial risks for the state than administrative coercion, as the wrongdoer must take all the measures to rectify the situation.

The third and most radical administrative sanction is revocation of a permit or exemption. After revocation, the wrongdoer in question is no longer entitled to perform the activity that was previously permitted. For this reason, this sanction is hardly used.

It is striking that Dutch administrative authorities do not have the power to impose punitive sanctions, such as fines or penalties. Punishing environmental misbehaviour is therefore reserved to the Department of Justice. Thus, to date, all Dutch administrative sanctions are reparative by nature. Yet, over the past few

[1] In comparison with *bestuursdwang*, the number of imposed administrative sanctions remains small.

years, in light of the aim to complement the set of instruments for sanctioning, there has been a call for the introduction of an administrative penalty in environmental law. There exist objections, however, which concern, *inter alia*, the fact that the introduction of a penalty that satisfies requirements of legal protection enshrined in national and especially international law will not add much to the current situation in terms of effective enforcement. Thus, administrative authorities fear multiple and lengthy procedures. Another objection is that punishment does not belong to the responsibilities of the administration. However, during these past few years an experiment has been carried out with the competence to impose an administrative transaction (akin to an out-of-court settlement). This created the possibility for administrative authorities to offer a transaction to those who are responsible for less serious environmental violations to avoid prosecution. If the transaction is paid then that is the end of the matter. However, in the event of refusals to pay, the administrative authority will forward the report of the breach to the Public Prosecutions Department. The prosecutor will then either offer a higher transaction, or will commence criminal proceedings. The advantage of this instrument, for the purpose of which the administration and the prosecutor clearly have to work together, is that the administration can also respond to isolated violations, and violations whose consequences cannot be rectified, in other words those cases where reparatory sanctions fail, without the perils of legal protection that are associated with administrative penalties. Refusal to pay means that the case will end up in the criminal system with its accompanying provisions of legal protection. It seems likely that the administrative transaction will soon be generally introduced.

Finally, we should briefly explain how parties may oppose a decision to acquiesce. *Anyone* may request a sanction,[2] and the authority must decide upon such a request within four weeks.[3] Administrative appeal against a negative or a belated decision is possible with the authority to which the request was addressed. Judicial review against that decision (or a belated one) is possible with the *Afdeling Bestuursrechtspraak van de Raad van State* (Council of State). Interim relief may be requested from the president of this court during the appeal and review procedures. It is likely that the right of appeal will be restricted to those directly and individually affected as of the end of 2004. This includes environmental Non-Governmental Organizations (NGOs) that specifically protect the environmental interest adversely affected by the decision to acquiesce, both in fact and formally in their articles of association.[4] The court can nullify a decision to acquiesce, as well as a request to enforce, in which case an authority will still have to take a decision to enforce.

[2] Art. 18.14 *Wet Milieubeheer*.

[3] ibid., Art. 18.16.

[4] Art. 2(3) *Algemene wet bestuursrecht* (General Administrative Law Act; hereafter referred to as GALA).

The Dutch range of instruments for criminal sanctioning is significantly more comprehensive than the set of administrative instruments. Virtually all environmental offences fall within the scope of the *Wet op de economische delicten* (Economic Offences Act). Apart from classical criminal sanctions, such as a pecuniary penalty and imprisonment, this law also contains reparatory instruments, including the imposition of obligations to restore what has been damaged, or the obligation to pay damages, and the possibility to close down businesses. This means that, compared to the administrative instruments, criminal instruments can attain a greater variety of enforcement targets. Punitive as well as reparatory goals can be pursued. Reparatory sanctions can serve to deal with offences that have already been committed (undoing the consequences) and also to prevent repetition (prevention). This means that neither the Proposed Directive on the Protection of the Environment through Criminal Law,[5] nor the Council Framework Decision on the protection of the environment through criminal law[6] will add to the current Dutch system. This is because almost all breaches of environmental law are already subject to criminal sanctions. Mandatory punitive sanctions (as opposed to the imposition of reparatory sanctions) could well turn out to produce disastrous environmental effects, that is, if this were to cause a shift from administrative to criminal enforcement. Our interpretation of the Proposed Directive, however, is that mere criminalization is required, and that the decision actually to impose criminal sanctions remains the preserve of Member States.[7]

Despite the lack of punitive administrative sanctions (for now), the Netherlands nevertheless has an extensive and effective set of instruments for the enforcement of environmental law. Nonetheless, application of these instruments can be considerably improved. In legal literature, a great deal of attention has been given in the past few years to the necessary professionalization of enforcement.[8] This has led to several initiatives to improve enforcement practice, including cooperation between the different bodies and persons that are involved in enforcement, enforcement on the basis of protocols, step-by-step procedures, and knowledge management. The Steering Committee entitled *Handhaven op Niveau* (Elevating Enforcement), which was set up in 2000 by the Dutch government, plays a stimulating and supporting role in this respect. This Committee was named after a 1998 report that contained many recommendations for the improvement of enforcement made by the Administrative and Civil Enforcement Committee. At the present time, considerable efforts are being made to realize effective enforcement, not just in theory, but also in practice.

[5] COM(02)544.

[6] Council Framework Dec. 2003/80/JHA of 27 Jan. 2003.

[7] Art. 4 of the Proposed Dir., n. 5 above.

[8] A.B. Blomberg, *Integrale handhaving van milieurecht* (s-Gravenhage: BJU, 2000), Commissie Bestuursrechtelijke en Privaatrechtelijke Handhaving, *Handhaven op niveau* (Deventer: Kluwer, 1998).

III. Lawful and Unlawful Acquiescence

Since the mid-1970s, the 'environmental court' in the Netherlands, the Council of State, has ruled that public authorities enjoy a degree of discretion in the enforcement of environmental law, but that only in special circumstances may enforcement be dispensed with.[9] In particular, it will have to be ascertained whether there exists 'real prospects' for compliance or termination of the activity. In other words, it is highly likely that the unlawful situation will cease to exist in the short term. The principles of legitimate expectation (explicit promise that there will be no enforcement) and non-discrimination (no enforcement has taken place in similar cases) can play a role in assessing the acceptability of temporary acquiescence.

For various reasons, action is not always taken against breaches of environmental law, even if the conditions specified above have not been fulfilled. There exists no reliable picture of the extent to which such tacit acquiescence occurs, but it may be feared that this is substantial. This kind of acquiescence, which undoubtedly also exists in other Member States, is illegitimate and unacceptable. A different matter is that not all breaches can be acted upon simultaneously. Resource shortage may result in a situation where no action is temporarily taken in respect of certain breaches. However, in this chapter we will focus on acquiescence on acceptable substantive grounds. We will posit that even in the case of a set of instruments that is optimal and properly applied, there remain cases in which enforcement is not necessarily the best solution. A classic example derived from practice concerns a regional rubbish tip operating with an expired permit. Dumping in that case was tolerated because the new dump could not yet be used.[10] Enforcement would have led to a situation in which inflammable waste would have accumulated in the region with detrimental consequences for the environment. Another example concerns a firm that decides to carry out an experiment to achieve 'greener' production processes, but in doing so violates conditions in a permit. If at the time of the experiment it is unclear what environmental requirements should be met, it is not possible to adjust the conditions of the permit before the experiment.[11] Recent research shows that

[9] *B en W van Gendt* v. *Gedeputeerde Staten van Gelderland*, Administrative Law Division of the Council of State (1996) 23 *Milieu en Recht*, 92.

[10] Voorzitter Afdeling Geschillen van Bestuur Raad van State (President of the Administrative Disputes Division of the Council of State) 12 January 1990, comment by G.T.J.M. Jurgens published in (1990) 320 *Administratiefrechtelijke Beslissingen* 952 (*Ehlers and others* v. *Gedeputeerde Staten van Gelderland*).

[11] This was at stake in *Hofstede* v. *Gedupteerde Staten van Zuid-Holland*, President of the Administrative Law Division of the Council of State (1994) 634 *Administratiefrechtelijke Beslissingen*, 1698.

such situations occur regularly in practice.[12] Preventing these types of experiments by rigidly enforcing the permit conditions would hamper favourable environmental technological development. That is why, in such cases, temporary deviations from the conditions of permits have been tolerated. In practice, it may be that an environmental permit is granted and takes effect but is later set aside after an appeal. If, in such a case, it is possible to grant a new environmental permit, it is not always reasonable to suspend the activity until the party concerned obtains a new permit. It may be clear from these examples that there can be imperative interests that go against enforcement in specific cases, especially when enforcement would lead to a situation where certain activities must cease or when enforcement has a reparatory nature.

In this connection, it could be suggested that a temporary permit should be granted, or a temporary change of a permit authorized. However, Dutch law does not as yet provide for this possibility. To be sure, a statutory power to grant temporary permits has disadvantages too. It would undermine the general rule, and the existence of such a possibility would stimulate its frequent use. Moreover, situations may arise where deviations from temporary permits will be tolerated. In addition, it will be hard to formulate clear statutory criteria for the exercise of power to issue temporary permits.

In all the examples that were mentioned above, important, legitimate interests of wrongdoers justified decisions not to enforce. In the Netherlands, this phenomenon is sometimes called 'administrative toleration'. This should be distinguished from the so-called judicial or criminal toleration by judicial authorities (the Public Prosecutions Department). In a sense, judicial toleration is a phenomenon that occurs much more often than administrative toleration, especially in environmental law. Given the primacy of administrative enforcement and the limited capacity to prosecute, most perpetrators of environmental offences are not prosecuted. The right to exercise prosecutorial discretion plays a part in the decision whether to prosecute or not. The Public Prosecutions Department only considers the prosecution of environmental offences to be expedient when these concern breaches of key provisions,[13] but even in such cases the Department will not always proceed to prosecute. This is not as serious as it seems. In practice, criminal enforcement consists mainly of punitive settlements (transactions, pecuniary penalties, and, incidentally, imprisonment), despite the existence of reparatory criminal sanctions in the Economic Offences Act. If (punitive) settlement does not occur, it has no direct consequence for the environment. This,

[12] C.W. Backes and A.B. Blomberg, 'Gedogen: Europese Grenzen en Nationale Oorzaken' in *Gedogen in het milieurecht*, Evaluatie Commissie Wet Milieubeheer 2002/6 (s-Gravenhage: Evaluatiecommissie Wet milieubeheer, 2002), 78.

[13] See its policy on the enforcement of environmental law (Openbaar Ministerie, *Strategie milieu—Strategiedocument voor de strafrechtelijke handhaving van milieurecht* (s-Gravenhage: Openbaar Ministerie, 1999).

significantly, is not the case when administrative toleration is concerned, because then a promise is made by the competent authority that the wrongdoer will—temporarily—not be forced by an administrative sanction to end his violation; nor will the state itself end the violation by coercive action (*bestuursdwang*). Administrative toleration is often a reason not to prosecute, among other things because of the notion that the state should present a common front. But, under certain circumstances administrative toleration can be a reason actually to take action, for example when the offender can be seriously blamed for the fact that the tolerated situation has come to exist.

The *Westpoint* case concerned this circumstance. An operator set up a transshipment company in the port of Amsterdam, and relied on obtaining the necessary permit and expected the competent administrative authority not to halt the operation of his company until the permit had been granted. Indeed, the authority did not enforce. As a result of the scheming on the part of this entrepreneur, however, the public prosecutor for the environment in Amsterdam felt that there was sufficient reason to start criminal proceedings, and Westpoint was convicted in a criminal court.[14] Therefore, in principle, administrative toleration does not stand in the way of criminal enforcement.

Actually, when tolerated situations come to exist, this cannot always be attributed to offenders because often the state is also to blame. For instance, research has shown that lack of clarity of environmental legislation, which is often very detailed and technically complicated, can lead to non-enforcement. It has also been shown that some regulations have been insufficiently attuned to actual practice. An example of this is Regulation (EEC) No. 259/93 on the Supervision and Control of Shipments of Waste within, into and out of the European Community (Waste Shipment Regulation).[15] This Regulation contains no lower limit, and therefore every small movement of waste has to fulfil its requirements. Operators and enforcement agencies have encountered difficulties with this aspect of the Regulation, but no support exists for the enforcement of such minor offences.[16] A specific problem in the Netherlands is the absence in environmental legislation of a suitable instrument for the regulation of temporary activities that require a permit. The regular procedure to grant a permit is considered too lengthy—it generally takes at least six months, while there exists no expedited procedure for adapting permits, and the power to waive the requirement for a permit is absent, with the result that many authorities tend

[14] It was fined 1 million guilders (€425,000), which is a large sum by Dutch standards, especially for an environmental violation; District Court of Amsterdam, *State* v. *Westpoint v.o.f*, with comment by F.C.M.A. Michiels (1996) 232 *Administratiefrechtelijke Beslissingen*, 769; comment by F. De Lange published in (1996) 23 *Milieu en Recht*, 127. The Court of Appeal reduced this amount to 100,000 guilders (€45,000); see Court of Appeal Amsterdam 22 Mar. 1997, (1997) 24 *Milieu en Recht*, 294.

[15] [1993] OJ L30/1.

[16] n. 12 above, 73.

to tolerate activities that are temporary.[17] More generally, decision-making procedures can lead to toleration when slow action on the side of the administration—which is not uncommon—unnecessarily hinders operational management by operators. In the eyes of the administration, too, strict enforcement would then be unreasonable.

The law therefore requires consideration of requirements other than enforcement for the decision whether or not to proceed with (administrative) enforcement. In Dutch enforcement law this is operationalized as follows. In principle, administrative enforcement is a discretionary power, which means that administrative authorities are 'free' to decide whether or not they will impose a sanction in the event of breaches of environmental law. Nevertheless, this discretion is circumscribed by the law since, like all administrative action, administrative enforcement has to meet certain legal requirements. These are set out in the *Algemene wet bestuursrecht* (General Adminstrative Law Act, hereinafter GALA), and have further evolved in case law. The most important rule in considering whether to impose an administrative order is that all interests directly involved, including the interest of the wrongdoer in continuing or repeating the violation, should be weighed.[18] Further, the adverse consequences of an order on affected parties should not be disproportionate compared to the purposes to be served by the order.[19] As a consequence, administrative authorities cannot impose an administrative sanction if enforcement is disproportionate. As part of a careful weighing of interests, authorities have to examine whether the unlawful situation can be legalized. *If* an unlawful situation can be legalized, and there are no policy reasons for not doing so, enforcement may be disproportionate. This principle sometimes results in situations of lawful non-enforcement; 'lawful' because the discretion not to enforce is used subject to certain accepted conditions. These conditions are laid down in the case law, and will be discussed in section VII.

IV. European Limits to Non-Enforcement

To a large extent, national environmental law emanates from European Community (EC) legislation, and consequently European law also conditions its implementation and enforcement. The most relevant rule of primary EC law is found in Article 10 EC, which lays down the principle of Community loyalty. Pursuant to this provision, Member States must take all measures necessary to guarantee fulfilment of obligations arising out of Community law, and must abstain from any measure which could jeopardize the attainment of the object-

[17] Cf. also F.C.M.A. Michiels, G.T.J.M. Jurgens, J.J. Vermeulen, M.A.M. Dieperink, and H. Grafhorst, *Gedogen met beschikkingen* ('s-Gravenhage: Ministerie van VROM, 2002), 99–100.

[18] Art. 3:4(1), GALA.

[19] ibid.

ives of the Treaty. Particularly from the first 'positive' obligation, the European Court of Justice (ECJ) has derived an obligation adequately to enforce directly effective EC law, as well as national implementing provisions. In addition, the ECJ has formulated some general requirements relating to enforcement: the sanctioning of violations of EC law should take place in the same manner as similar and equally serious breaches of national law. In addition, sanctions should be effective, proportional, and dissuasive.[20] In the Netherlands, it is generally assumed that the principle of Community loyalty as interpreted by the ECJ limits the scope for tolerance. However, complete clarity does not exist in this respect, partly because the cases brought before the ECJ usually concerns rather extreme cases: situations that are very serious from the point of view of environmental protection and/or situations in which insufficient measures have been taken during prolonged periods. Nonetheless, below we will attempt to indicate the limits imposed by EC law that affect the discretion enjoyed by national enforcement authorities, including those in the Netherlands.

First of all, it should be noted that administrative acquiescence will only be affected by EC law when an *EC* obligation is at stake. This is the case, for example, when EC law requires a permit for a certain activity and the competent authority of the Member State tolerates the exercise of this activity without a permit. This is different when EC law does not contain a permit obligation, but a Member State has chosen to use a permit system to comply with EC standards. Non-enforcement only amounts to an infringement of EC law if environmental quality standards are not met. If Member States can comply with European environmental standards in other ways, then administrative non-enforcement is not in breach of EC law. The substantive EC standard therefore answers the question whether toleration constitutes a possible violation of EC law.

Furthermore, it is important to note that only a few environmental directives contain provisions that, in case of violation, require Member States to respond immediately with a sanction. Most directives only require Member States to take 'appropriate measures' to ensure compliance with the aims of a directive. Enforcement action can be an appropriate measure but, as pointed out above, the result required by the relevant EC provision can sometimes—depending on the kind of obligation—also be achieved in other ways. Moreover, Member States may possess considerable freedom in the enforcement of EC law,[21] provided they meet the requirements formulated by the ECJ. In summary, national diversity of forms and methods of enforcement is ultimately limited by the objectives and results pursued by EC environmental law.[22] Section III explained that, in the

[20] Case C-68/88, *Commission* v. *Greece* [1989] ECR 2965.

[21] Case 50/76, *Amsterdam Bulb BV* v. *Produktschap voor Siergewassen* [1977] ECR 137. See also B.M. Veltkamp, *Implementatie van EG-milieurichtlijnen in Nederland* (Deventer: Kluwer, 1998), 268.

[22] C. Harding, 'Member State Enforcement of European Community Measures—The Chimera of "Effective" Enforcement' (1997) 4 *Maastricht Journal of European and Comparative Law*, 7.

Netherlands, toleration is seen as a consequence of the discretionary character of the competence to enforce. The question that needs to be answered is to what extent EC law allows for (temporary) non-enforcement, when the violation in question violates an obligation of EC law.

The ECJ has never explicitly ruled on the question of the extent to which acquiescence is permissible. It usually takes a strict stance, however, when it concerns compliance with EC obligations. If EC law contains an obligation of result, the mere observation that the required result has not been achieved generally suffices to assume a breach of the Treaty. The many arguments that Member States advance to justify non-compliance are routinely dismissed.[23] From the ECJ's case law it can be deduced that there are two possible grounds that may justify non-compliance with an obligation under EC law: the absolute impossibility of complying with EC law, and exceptional disproportional enforcement. Absolute impossibility of complying was argued in *Tafelwein* and *Blackpool*.[24] In neither of these cases did the ECJ accept this contention.

Tafelwein concerned breach of a duty to distil table wine. Germany argued that 'a decision ordering the immediate enforcement of the compulsory distillation notices would have served no purpose because when those notices were sent the quantities of table wine available from German producers were limited and it was difficult to envisage the purchasing of wine from producers established in other Member States'. Practical implementation problems, whatever their magnitude, are no justification: 'Although the German Government has contended that the implementation of measures of compulsory distillation according to that procedure would have given rise to practical difficulties, it has totally failed to demonstrate that such implementation was absolutely impossible'.

The ECJ added that it would have been more appropriate for the German government to notify those difficulties to the Commission, so that a solution could have been jointly pursued.

Blackpool concerned breach of Directive 76/160/EEC concerning the Quality of Bathing Waters (Bathing Water Directive).[25] The justifications advanced by the United Kingdom (UK) government were each summarily dismissed by the ECJ. In response to the UK exasperation that, 'if the latter interpretation were to prevail, any deviation from the limit values laid down in the annex to the directive would constitute an infringement of Article 4(1) of the Directive, even if the Member State concerned had taken all practicable steps to avoid

[23] J.H. Jans, H.G. Sevenster, and H.H.B. Vedder (eds.), *Europees milieurecht in Nederland* ('s-Gravenhage: Boom juridische uitgevers, 2000), 226; J.H. Jans, *European Environmental Law* (Groningen: European Law Publishing, 2000), 161–3 and J.H. Jans, R.de Lange, S. Prechal, and R.J.G.M. Widdershoven, *Inleiding tot het Europees bestuursrecht* (Nijmegen: Ars Aequi Libri, 2002), 279; H. Somsen, 'Discretion in European Community Environmental Law—An Analysis of ECJ Case Law' 40 (2003) *Common Market Law Review*, 1413–53.

[24] Case C-217/88, *Commission* v. *Germany* [1990] ECR I-2879 and Case C-56/90, *Commission* v. *United Kingdom* [1993] ECR I-4109.

[25] [1976] OJ L31/1.

such deviations', the ECJ did acknowledge that 'absolute physical impossibility' could provide a justification. The UK, however, had not succeeded in establishing the existence of such impossibility. Furthermore, it can be deduced from *Tafelwein* that the ECJ strictly applies this criterion: neither practical difficulties in implementation nor conflicting requirements in national case law emanating from independent national courts amount to 'absolute impossibility'. The same applies to lack of (financial) resources,[26] and fear of social conflict or disorderliness.[27] In *Spanish Strawberries*, for example, the free movement of agricultural products was hindered by large-scale protests by French farmers on the border between Spain and France.[28] Out of fear of even more serious disturbances, the French government did not wish to act too harshly, so that the hindrances continued. Before the ECJ, however, it could not be shown that there existed an actual threat to public order which could not be dealt with in other ways.

The second possible ground to justify non-compliance, exceptional disproportional enforcement, derives from the principle of proportionality, a generally acknowledged legal principle that is also regularly cited by the ECJ, especially in its case law on enforcement. Sanctions should not only be effective and dissuasive, but also proportionate. These requirements should be honoured by Member States, even when enforcement is the only way to comply with an obligation under EC law. In exceptional cases, this could justify acquiescence, even if an EC legal norm is at stake, that is, when non-enforcement is based on the principle of proportionality. In a recent preliminary ruling, the ECJ accepted a breach of Community law on that ground. Austria had not taken action against an environmental demonstration as a result of which the traffic on the Brenner Pass was blocked for hours. This obstruction to the free movement of goods—one of the fundamental freedoms laid down in the EC Treaty—was weighed against the interest of protecting basic rights, in this case the freedom of speech and the freedom of assembly (Articles 10 and 11 ECHR). Protection of those rights forms a legitimate interest that can in principle justify a violation of obligations of EC law.[29] However, we find it difficult to imagine cases in which violations of environmental law must be tolerated in the interest of the protection of fundamental rights. Rather, in section V, it will be shown that human rights impose limits on toleration. Enforcement of environmental law may however clash with the right to property (Article 1(1) first Protocol ECHR), but this fundamental right explicitly allows statutory exceptions in the general interest.

We are not familiar with other cases in which the ECJ has accepted a contention on the ground of proportionality, so it should be assumed that here too stringent requirements have to be met. Jans *et al.* therefore argue that acquies-

[26] Case C-52/95, *Commission* v. *France* [1995] ECRI-4443.

[27] Case C-265/95, *Commission* v. *France* [1997] ECR I-6959.

[28] ibid.

[29] Case C-112/00, *Eugen Schmidberger, Internationale Transporte und Planzüge* v. *Republik Österreich* [2003] ECR I-5659.

cence on the basis of the principle of proportionality can be justified only on the basis of effective and factual compliance with the EC standard within the short term.[30] The discretion of Member States only concerns the modality of enforcement; under certain circumstances temporary non-enforcement could be the most appropriate enforcement measure.[31] It should also be noted that disproportional enforcement can be avoided for the most part by means other than acquiescence, for example by offering compensation. Neither this justification nor the first justification referred to therefore offers any ground for (administrative) toleration.

According to Jans *et al.*, some room for acquiescence can be found in the case law of the ECJ that concerns setting less stringent standards than required by EC directives.[32] In principle, there is only room for a more liberal national regime when directives, whether or not subject to conditions, explicitly allow this. Many directives, for example, contain provisions on the basis of which temporary deviation from their requirements is allowed. However, from *Leybucht* it follows that there exists a kind of inherent competence to deviate even when there is no such provision, namely in cases in which higher interests are at stake than those which the directive aims to protect, or if it is a manifestation of 'ecological compensation'.[33] Those cases must concern extraordinary situations ('justifiable only on exceptional grounds').[34] In most Dutch cases involving toleration, these requirements will not be met.[35] Perhaps toleration can be justified on this ground in emergency situations, for example when the safety of people living in a certain area is at stake, but that kind of situation occurs only sporadically in practice.

Against the background of the restrictive case law set out above, the general consideration that the ECJ devoted to compliance with requirements in directives in a judgment of 9 November 1999 is remarkable.[36] In the San Rocco Valley, biological and chemical waste was systematically dumped illegally—without a permit—during a prolonged period, which resulted in health risks for the inhabitants of that valley, and harmful consequences for the local environment. The Italian authorities had taken several enforcement measures, such as placing a waste site under compulsory management, and imposing criminal sanctions on the operator of the site. The ECJ determined that the actual situation violated the requirements of the directive concerned, and condemned Italy. However, it also devoted some notable general considerations to the question whether the mere fact that a situation is not in conformity with objectives laid down in directives leads to the conclusion that a Member State has failed to fulfil its obligation under the provision in question:

From the fact that a situation is not in conformity with the objectives laid down in the first paragraph of Article 4 of the amended Directive, then, the direct inference may not in

[30] n. 23 above. [31] ibid. 281. [32] ibid. 180–3.

[33] Case C-57/89, *Commission* v. *Germany* [1991] ECR I-883. [34] ibid., consideration 21.

[35] Similarly Jans *et al.*, n. 23 above, 227–5.

[36] Case C-365/97, *Commission* v. *Italy* [1999] ECR I-7773.

principle be drawn that the Member State concerned has necessarily failed to fulfil its obligation under that provision to take the requisite measures to ensure that waste is disposed of without endangering human health and without harming the environment. However, if that situation persists and leads in particular to a significant deterioration in the environment over a protracted period without any action being taken by the competent authorities, it may be an indication that the Member States have exceeded the discretion conferred on them by that provision.[37]

Some authority for acquiescence could be inferred from these considerations. After all, the ECJ does not rule out temporary non-compliance, as long as the situation does not persist, and does not lead to a significant deterioration in the environment, especially when the Directive offers Member States some room for discretion when choosing the way in which they fulfil their obligations. On the other hand, this discretionary power may explain why the ECJ came to this particular consideration. Hence, the ECJ observed earlier:

Whilst that provision does not specify the actual content of the measures which must be taken in order to ensure that waste is disposed of without endangering human health and without harming the environment, it is none the less true that it is binding on the Member States as to the objective to be achieved, whilst leaving to the Member States a margin of discretion in assessing the need for such measures.[38]

The fact that the provision breached was of a framework character may explain the ECJ's more lenient stance. Nonetheless, this provision too has formed the basis for obligations for Member States.[39] Krämer explains the ECJ's judgment (in particular its acknowledgement of a degree of national discretion) by observing that any economic activity will result in some adverse environmental impact, and that it would be absurd if the exploitation of a waste dump in conformity with the relevant rules nonetheless amounted to a breach of Article 4 of the Directive.[40] However, the present case concerned an unlawful situation, which in our view means that Italy enjoyed no discretionary power. Although Italy was eventually condemned because it was clear that the requirements of the Directive had not been complied with for prolonged periods, and that great risks existed for public health and for the environment, the general observations in consideration 68 demonstrate more flexibility than the previous case law of the ECJ. According to Jans *et al.*, in *San Rocco* the ECJ did not look at the factual violation of the environmental provisions, but rather at the failure of the competent authorities to respond adequately.[41] However, under certain circumstances ac-

[37] ibid., consideration 68.

[38] ibid., consideration 67.

[39] Cf. J.R.C. Tieman, *Naar een nuttige toepassing van het begrip afvalstof* (Ph.D thesis, Utrecht University) (Deventer: Kluwer 2003), 131.

[40] L. Krämer, *Casebook on EU Environmental Law* (Oxford/Portland, Oregon: Hart Publishing, 2002), 347.

[41] Jans *et al.*, n. 23 above, 164.

quiescence can, in our opinion, be considered to be an adequate response to a specific problem, that is, under the circumstances discussed in section III. However, despite this islolated judgment,[42] it remains to be seen whether the ECJ wanted to introduce a new criterion relating to enforcement and, if that is the case, in what way the ECJ will develop its future cases. If the ECJ remains as strict as it is with regard to the two possible grounds that justify non-compliance, then EC law will leave little room for (administrative) non-enforcement, which would be regrettable in the light of what has been argued in section III. To put this in perspective, however, it can be argued that the cases that are brought before the ECJ usually concern extreme situations, in which there has already been a violation of the obligations of the directives for a long period of time, and usually also with obvious damage to the environment. Besides, it should be noted that the infringement procedure of Article 226 EC usually spans numerous years, during which Member States are granted plenty of opportunity to avoid condemnation by the ECJ, in the context of the pre-judicial phase. If no use is made of this opportunity, then non-compliance will have persisted over a considerable period of time (up to five years is no exception). This is, by Dutch standards too, unacceptable. The infringement procedure is hence not effective in combating acquiescence, other than perhaps in providing an incentive to comply which may be provided by the compliance letter. Evidently, Member States have an autonomous responsibility for securing compliance with EC law. We therefore do not argue that Member States should continue to tolerate breaches, merely because the infringement procedure does not pose much of a threat.

V. Limits to Non-Enforcement Posed by Human Rights Law

During the last decade, the authorities of several states have been confronted with the limits which the European Court of Human Rights (ECtHR) imposes on not taking action against environmental violations. As early as 1994, the ECtHR determined in *López Ostra* that Article 8 (on the protection of family life) can impose limits on activities that burden the environment.[43] Even though those activities were committed without a necessary permit, in that case the emphasis was not so much on the limits of toleration, but on the limits of the activities that could be allowed when these are a serious infringement of one of the rights contained in the ECHR. *Öneryildiz*[44] expressly concerned the limits of adminis-

[42] We are not familiar with later judgments that contain similar considerations.

[43] ECtHR 9 Dec. 1994, Series A 303, C *López Ostra* v. *Spain*.

[44] ECtHR 18 June 2002, appl. no. 48939/99, *Öneryildiz* v. *Turkey*. Meanwhile, the request by Turkey for a hearing by the Grand Chamber of the ECtHR has been granted.

trative toleration.[45] This limit is in any case exceeded when the right to life is affected (Article 2 ECHR). Because of the importance of this case we will briefly outline the facts.

Öneryildiz lived with twelve family members in a slum area on a waste dump that did not comply with the applicable technical requirements for such dumps. The occupation was illegal, but had been tolerated for a long time. A critical expert report from 1991, which mentioned the danger of an explosion by the accumulation of methane gas, did lead to discussion within the municipal authorities, but not to closure of the dump, or termination of its occupation. Nor did it lead to informing the occupants adequately. On 28 April 1993, an enormous explosion occurred, as a result of which nine of Öneryildiz's family members perished. Several legal procedures by Öneryildiz against the local authorities resulted in a few more or less symbolic convictions (the mayor of Istanbul and the mayor of one of the city quarters were both fined €9.70) and a similarly symbolic amount of damages of €2,285. At the ECtHR, Öneryildiz was more successful. The ECtHR was of the opinion that the right to life had been violated because the waste dump had not been closed, action had not been taken to stop illegal occupation, and the occupants had not been adequately informed. First, the ECtHR determined that the authorities simply should have been aware of the seriousness of the case:

> . . . the Court has been able to satisfy itself that, in respect of a field as technical as that of the operation of rubbish tips, it was impossible for the administrative and municipal departments responsible for monitoring the relevant installations not to have known of the risks inherent in methanogenesis or of the necessary preventive measures, particularly as there were specific regulations in the area which, moreover, were not in any way complied with.[46]

Subsequently, the ECtHR ruled that there was unmistakably a causal connection between the negligence on the part of the authorities, and the explosion: 'It observes that the factors referred to in the various expert reports attached to the file . . . suffice to establish a causal link between, on the one hand, those negligent omissions and, on the other, the occurrence of the accident on 28 April 1993 and the ensuing loss of lives'.[47]

This judgment implies that national authorities, in life-threatening situations, must ensure a level of supervision that allows them to be aware of any such threat, and act immediately. We will have to wait and see whether the Grand Chamber of the ECtHR will adhere to that judgment.

[45] On this case also M. Kuijer, 'Positieve verplichtingen voor een gedogende overheid' 28 (2003) *Nederlands Juristen Comité voor de Mensenrechten-bulletin*, 54–73, and T. Barkhuysen and M.L. van Emmerik, 'EHRM-uitspraak Öneryildiz tegen Turkije—Europese grenzen aan het gedogen van gevaarlijke situaties en aan beperkingen van overheidsaansprakelijkheid bij ongelukken en rampen' 4 (2003) *Overheid en Aansprakelijkheid*, 109–21.

[46] n. 44 above, consideration 79.

[47] ibid., consideration 81.

VI. Approaches in other Member States

The Netherlands has acquired a reputation for toleration, but how do other countries deal with non-compliance with environmental regulations? Hereafter, it will become clear that, in other Member States, environmental laws are similarly not always enforced. The causes of this are diverse. In general it reflects both a lack of sufficient attention to the enforcement of environmental law, and a consciously pursued policy in which strict enforcement is not seen as the most effective means to encourage compliance. Hereafter, we will briefly examine approaches adopted in France and Germany and the UK with regard to environmental offences, with the emphasis on administrative enforcement.

A. France

Inspection is mainly the duty of the *Inspection des installations classées*. There are three possible ways in which environmental law can be enforced: criminally, through punishment imposed by administrative courts, and through administrative enforcement.[48] The first avenue is that of traditional criminal law. After prosecution by the Public Prosecutions Department (or by the *ingénieurs des directions départementales de l'agriculture* for fisheries and by the *ingénieurs des services régionaux d'aménagement forestier* for hunting and the protection of forests), criminal courts can impose sanctions for the violation of environmental regulations. A possible punishment is a pecuniary penalty, or an injunction imposed on the wrongdoer prohibiting him from exercising his profession for a certain period of time, and publication of the conviction. In practice, there are hardly any criminal prosecutions. The police and the Public Prosecutions Department lack the necessary time and expert knowledge for the enforcement of environmental law. The social importance of the enforcement of environmental law is also not sufficiently recognized. Criminal enforcement of environmental law is exclusively repressive in nature and, in that respect, does not answer the need to repair environmental damage.

The second possibility is the imposition of sanctions by administrative courts (*le tribunal administratif*) by the *préfet*, who bases this claim on an official report, drawn up by the police or the inspector. Besides penalties, this court can also impose reparatory sanctions, *inter alia*, orders to close down a business. This possibility is the correct method when public property (*domaine public*) is at issue. Prosecution by the *préfet* by filing this claim is generally (as in criminal law) a discretionary matter, although in the case of damage to coastal areas prosecution is compulsory. Third parties, like environmental protection agencies, can enforce this duty in court.

[48] Cf. more elaborately M. Prieur, *Droit de l'environnement* (Paris: Dalloz, 2001), 850–63.

Finally, there is administrative enforcement. The mayor can impose sanctions in cases of less serious violations with the character of a nuisance (noise, odour). Administrative enforcement in respect of (bigger) industrial installations lies with the *préfet*. After a prior warning, he is competent to take measures at the wrongdoer's expense, and to close the installation down. In short, he is competent to take coercive action, and to revoke permits. He has a discretionary competence, and can therefore (and indeed will have to) decide in each specific case whether he will use this competence.[49] According to Auby, the *préfet* has a duty to take measures, but this may be limited to a warning (*a notice simple*).[50] In that sense, a discretionary competence does exist where it concerns 'real' sanctions. When it is unlawfully not used, third parties can hold the state liable for wrongfully neglecting to take action.[51] The practical value of this possibility depends on how wide-ranging the judicial review of the decision not to act is.

In French literature and case law, little is found regarding administrative acquiescence. Clearly, there is no consistent action against every violation in France, but French law is apparently available to act against this inconsistency, apart from the fact that the state may be guilty of wrongful neglect.

B. Germany

The complex and extensive German environmental law (partly federal, partly enacted by the *Länder)* is, as far as administrative enforcement is concerned, for the most part enforced by the *Länder*. Supervision lies in the hands of the authorities, and is supplemented by internal monitoring by companies. In addition, there is federal criminal enforcement. In practice, nothing will come from criminal enforcement.

In Germany, toleration is part of the broader term *informelles Verwaltungshandeln*. The term that is most commonly used for (administrative) toleration is *behördliche Duldung*. Decisions to tolerate are generally considered to be factual acts (*Realakte*) that are not binding (therefore, they are not decisions in the formal sense). They can, like other facts, of course be of influence on the lawfulness of sanction decisions that are taken after a period of toleration. According to part of the literature, under certain circumstances decisions to tolerate can have the character of a binding decision.[52] Other authors oppose

[49] ibid. 863.

[50] J.B. Auby, 'Public Environmental Law in France' in R.J.G.H. Seerden *et al.* (eds.), *Public Environmental Law in the European Union and the United States—A Comparative Analysis* (The Hague/London/New York: Kluwer Law International, 2002), 194.

[51] Conseil d'Etat 22 Mar. 1978 (Brélivet), (1981) 16 *Revue Juridique de l'Environnement*, 45.

[52] M. Malitz, *Zur behördlichen Duldung im Strafrecht—Grenzen informellen Verwaltungshandelns* (Berlin: Duncker & Humblot, 1995), 37.

this, because a declaration to tolerate would be in contravention of the law if it had the character of a decision.[53]

Informal action by administrative authorities is seen as less laborious and time-consuming, and more effective. The reasons to tolerate are, *inter alia*, the vagueness of some norms, material compliance with the intent of the author of the norms, and the fact that taking action after a long period of toleration would be unreasonable.[54] In environmental law, these reasons are more specifically: transitional situations, industrial accidents and disturbances, and the general interest that is served by continuation of the activity (for example in the case of waste disposal).

It is important to note that the German authorities have a discretionary competence to decide whether or not to enforce environmental law. Acquiescence in breaches of environmental law in principle is considered to be acceptable when there is no violation of any statutory regulation, the interests of third parties have been considered, and toleration occurs for a limited period of time.[55] In the administration of justice, there are different views on the question whether a decision to tolerate can be a criminal justification ground. In the early 1990s, the highest German criminal court occasionally accepted a declaration to tolerate as a justification ground and, in that sense, considered it to be equivalent to a permit.[56] The highest Dutch court has not gone this far.[57] German literature is also divided on the question whether a written declaration to tolerate can have a justifying effect in criminal law, even though, for example, action taken in breach of a declaration to tolerate can never be liable to punishment. In that sense, a declaration to tolerate cannot be deemed to be equivalent to a permit.[58] The possibility of criminal action is in any case accepted if there is only tacit toleration.[59]

C. United Kingdom

The public enforcement of environmental law in the UK is for the most part the responsibility of the Environment Agency. In the UK, toleration is not spoken or

[53] See G. Wenner, 'Die behördliche Duldung im Deutschen Recht—Ein neues Instrument informellen Verwaltungshandelns?' in R. Breuer (ed.), *Jahrbuch des Umwelt- und Technikrechts 1993* (Heidelberg: v. Decker, 1994), 313–14.

[54] W. Huisman, *Gedogen—een verschijnsel van alle tijden en alle plaatsen* ('s-Gravenhage/Amsterdam: Ministerie van Justitie, 1996), 39.

[55] Malitz, n. 52 above.

[56] Bundesgerichtshof 26 Apr. 1990, (1990) 37 *Entscheidungen des Bundesgerichtshof in Strafrecht*, 21–8. In contrast is Bundesgerichtshof, (1991) 11 *Neue Zeitschrift für Strafrecht*, 240 mentioned by M. Kloepfer, *Umweltrecht* (Munich: Beck, 1998), 477. Kloepfer himself is of the opinion that a declaration of toleration cannot be a ground for justification.

[57] See Supreme Court, *State* v. *X* (2002) 178 *Administratiefrechtelijke Beslissingen*, 764.

[58] M. Kloepfer and H. P. Viehaus, *Umweltstrafrecht* (Munich: Beck, 1995), 36 ff. and Kloepfer, *Umweltrecht*, n. 56 above, 477.

[59] See M. Rodi, 'Public Environmental Law in Germany' in Seerden *et al.*, n. 50 above, 243.

written about to any great extent. This is misleading, however. The enforcement style, when it concerns achieving compliance by wrongdoers of environmental law, is one that is unmistakably informed by policies of negotiation and persuasion. Toleration of a violation is regarded as a policy that can lead to compliance with another norm by virtue of a sort of moral appeal that extends from the attitude of the enforcer to the wrongdoer. The authorities that enforce, especially the Environment Agency, are convinced that this approach is the most effective, or at least more effective than a coercive and punitive approach. Furthermore, financial realities dictate that there are insufficient financial resources to pursue a formal legal approach in all cases in which violations occur. Added to this is the considerable self-discipline on the part of businesses. The Government relies, to an extreme extent, on this attitude, partly out of necessity, given the lack of sufficient formal coercive powers. There is no doubt that there are many cases in which rules are not complied with whilst public authorities are not aware of this, even if they could and arguably should be.

The UK policy could be acceptable as long as environmental norms are of a general character leaving considerable room for fixing emission limits and the like.[60] However, with the growth of binding EC rules, the UK can hardly comply with its EC obligations in this way, given the limits of toleration imposed by EC law. In part, toleration is avoided simply because the rules laid down are not precise, and if something is not prohibited or prescribed there can be no question of a violation and therefore no question of toleration. Environmental laws in the UK seem to be much more flexible than those in the Netherlands, and when there is a violation negotiation, rather than repressive enforcement, is the instinctive response. Finally, it should be noted that third parties seeking strict compliance may try to pursue this by way of civil law. In general, in the UK this will have more effect than urging the Environment Agency to take action.

D. Comparative Conclusions

It is striking that, although without a doubt toleration occurs everywhere, there exists little literature on the subject. It seems silence about this phenomenon is preferred in the UK and in France. In the Federal Republic of Germany this is clearly different. In all countries there exists a discretionary competence to enforce, with exceptions in this respect in France. From French administration of justice and literature, it is difficult to deduce how toleration is handled. It seems to remain simply elusive. In the UK, the Environment Agency deals with toleration much more openly. There are regulations on the way in which the discretionary competence to enforce should be used, and this implies the possibility of toleration. In Germany, there is an explicit recognition of toleration as a

[60] W. Huisman and C.M. Joubert, *Gedogen—een verschijnsel van alle tijden en alle plaatsen* ('s-Gravenhage/Amsterdam: Ministerie van Justitie, 1996), 62–5.

phenomenon. There is also a certain legal context, because decisions to tolerate can be binding under certain circumstances, at least according to some of the literature. In Germany, there is disagreement on the question whether and, if so, to what extent decisions to tolerate can be a ground for justifying criminal behaviour.

VII. The Dutch Approach: Quasi-Lawful Non-Enforcement

Not a single democratic constitutional state can ensure that all its laws are strictly complied with. The question therefore is how enforcement can best be realized. Apart from information and positive *stimuli* such as subsidies, enforcement is of great importance, both as *ex ante* incentive and *ex post* control. An effective enforcement policy would ideally consist of the following stages: proper supervision, and when a breach is found, negotiated attempts to end the breach in the short term and, if necessary, subsequently to impose a sanction. That is a perfectly sensible ambition, but because of structural lack of resources this will never be possible in all cases. However, more importantly, and at least more interestingly, it is not proper from a legal perspective to enforce in all cases where (strict) enforcement is possible. There are reasons why, under certain circumstances, it is more appropriate to tolerate than to enforce. Those reasons have been referred to in section III. But even then, this only applies in as far as toleration takes place in ways that ensure that all interests concerned are optimally protected. Before we indicate how toleration has found its place in Dutch law, and what requirements have been laid down in the case law, we will first deal with the term (administrative) toleration.

By toleration (or acquiescence) we mean a situation when a breach of legal rules has occurred, whilst an authority, in principle legally competent to act and actually capable of acting against the violation, has decided not to take any such action. Toleration thereby presupposes choice. He who cannot enforce, also cannot tolerate. Hence, authorities should first have knowledge of a violation, and a reasonable degree of supervision and investigation therefore is assumed. Toleration does not occur when no action is taken against a breach about which authorities had no knowledge, or could not reasonably have had any knowledge. In such cases what is at issue is an enforcement-obstructing factor. Insufficient resources, for example, can also be such a factor, at least temporarily. Finally, it is of importance that toleration can appear at several stages; after a violation has been discovered, but also when the enforcement process has begun but at a later stage is interrupted or no longer energetically pursued. Revoking the decision to punish, or not collecting forfeited coercive sums in certain circumstances, can be regarded as toleration.[61]

[61] Here we follow Michiels *et al.*, n. 17 above, 1.

We will now turn our attention to toleration of infringements by operators of installations requiring prior authorization (permits). This involves relatively few infringements compared to the total number of breaches of environmental law, but such instances have potentially serious impacts. Also, such activities as a rule are of a long-term nature, so that a long-standing relationship exists between the regulatee and the regulator. The latter is important for the attitude of both actors; a certain willingness to cooperate on both sides is vital for proper compliance.

A. Bringing Toleration *Sub Iudice* in the Netherlands

As early as in 1977, a written declaration to tolerate, implying that the competent authority would not use its competence to enforce in a certain case, was considered an (appealable) decision by the Dutch Council of State.[62] Since, then this has become established case law. In this respect, toleration has been legally recognized as the flip side of enforcement. This has had two significant consequences.

First, all legal requirements for decisions also govern decisions to tolerate. Since 1994, those requirements can be found in the GALA. In addition, specific requirements have been articulated concerning lawful toleration (with decisions) in case law and policy. In part, these are substantive in nature (such as the tolerability of the situation, and the period during which the violation in question can be tolerated), in part procedural. These requirements will be elaborated further below.

Secondly, it is possible in cases involving toleration to follow a procedure before the administrative courts. This can in any case occur when a decision to tolerate has been taken: a third party can appeal against this decision (after a preceding procedure for lodging an objection). It is more complicated if someone wishes to challenge the fact that, erroneously in his opinion, no declaration to tolerate has been granted. Only under certain conditions, which are not very clear, will the administrative court be prepared to consider this as a decision which can be challenged.

In principle refusal to grant a declaration to tolerate is therefore not seen as a decision,[63] but there are exceptions. The existence of a policy of tolerance, the favourable application of which is denied in a specific case, is seen as such an exception.[64] It has also been assumed that among the exceptions are cases in which violations have not yet commenced, and at the same time very important,

[62] President Legal Division of the Council of State, *X* v. *B en W van 's-Gravenhage* 1 (1980) Bouwrecht, 272.

[63] Administrative Law Division of the Council of State, *Meijer* v. *B en W van Ermelo* with comment by P.J.J. Van Buuren (1997) 343 *Administratiefrechtelijke Beslissingen.*

[64] Administrative Law Division of the Council of State, *Stevens* v. *B en W van Dalfsen*, with comment by F.C.M.A. Michiels (1999) 340 *Administratiefrechtelijke Beslissingen.*

concrete grounds exist to assume a legal obligation to tolerate.[65] However, this issue has not yet been full settled. Moreover, it should be noted that the text of Article 1:3(2) GALA explicitly provides that the rejection of a request for a decision amounts to a decision, which courts hence ignore. The court follows a comparable approach with regard to the revocation of a declaration to tolerate, which is also not regarded as a decision, except in special circumstances.[66]

All this does not alter the fact that it is possible to seek judicial review of declarations to tolerate before administrative courts, and to request that such declarations be overturned and compensation granted. The court nonetheless apparently has difficulty accepting all the consequences that result from the fact that the declaration to tolerate is an appealable decision.

B. Requirements for Non-Enforcement in Legislation: Case Law and Policy

Obviously, the law does not contain any specific provisions concerning toleration. Yet, the GALA contains numerous requirements for lawful action by administrative authorities, in particular decision-making. In addition, a number of important policy documents have been issued that indicate the circumstances in which violations may be tolerated, and which in addition lay down several complementary requirements. Finally, case law has also given rise to certain conditions and requirements, although these correspond to a large extent to those of the policy documents.

According to this case law and policy, it is possible to refrain from enforcing in those cases in which the interests that plead against enforcement outweigh the interests in favour of enforcement. In the case law a few more detailed situations are distinguished in which courts consider this condition to be satisfied. These are:

i. Situations in which Legalization can be Expected in the Short Term

One can think of situations in which a permit is requested, and there is no reason for not granting the permit, but more time is needed to formulate the specific permit conditions. In *Stichting Pantera*, for example, a permit had been granted to a sanctuary for predators. This was subsequently nullified by the court due to errors in the acoustical research that had formed the basis of the conditions regarding noise. During the period when new acoustical research was carried out and new conditions were drafted, operation of the sanctuary was tolerated, on

65 President of the Administrative Law Division of the Council of State, *Electrabel Nederland N.V.* v. *Gedeputeerde Staten van Gelderland*, with comment by F.C.M.A. Michiels (2002) 355 *Administratiefrechtelijke Beslissingen.*

66 Administrative Law Division of the Council of State, *ECO-composteerbedrijf BV* v. *Gedeputeerde Staten van Utrecht*, with comment by F.C.M.A. Michiels (2002) 219 *Administratiefrechtelijke Beslissingen.*

condition that the operator complied with the conditions in the draft permit (contained in a decision to tolerate).[67] It is also possible that an activity that is not permitted will no longer need a permit pursuant to a forthcoming amendment of the law.[68]

ii. Situations in which an Illegal Activity will Terminate in the Near Future, and the Activity Concerned has Occurred for a Prolonged Period

Relevant in this context also are situations that are a result of historical factors, such as businesses that have been situated in a particular location that is unfavourable to the environment, and that are to be relocated.[69] In anticipation of the relocation of the business, the illegal activity may then be tolerated, in which case there must exist concrete plans for a short-term relocation; vague plans are insufficient. Such cases are becoming increasingly rare, since public authorities have begun to take enforcement of environmental law seriously.

iii. Experimental Situations

This category concerns situations in which a specific experiment requires temporary violation of conditions. Importance is attached to the fact that the experiment may lead to knowledge concerning certain activities that may contribute to environmental protection. For example, an undertaking operating a thermic soil purification system by way of experiment was for some time allowed to clean soil polluted with dioxine and HCH. The new technical insights thus acquired could subsequently be used to determine whether an environmental permit could be granted for such activities.[70]

iv. Force Majeure

Force majeure involves situations in which certain activities have become inevitable because of special circumstances. A conflict then occurs between the duty to comply with a legal standard, and other interests requiring protection. *Scheepswerf Dodewaard* provides an example.[71] Five ships that had been brought to the dock of Scheepswerf Dodewaard for repair were left there when the customer

[67] Administrative Law Division of the Council of State, *Stichting Pantera* v. *B en W van Ooststellingwerf*, with comment by G.T.J.M. Jurgens (2000) 312 *Adminstratiefrechtelijke Beslissingen.*

[68] President of the Administrative Disputes Division of the Council of State, *Maessen and Geraedts* v. *B en W van Haelen*, with comment by G.T.J.M. Jurgens (1993) 209 *Adminstratiefrechtelijke Beslissingen.*

[69] President of the Administrative Law Division of the Council of State, *P. Daalders Aannemersbedrijf BV and G. Schot & Zn. BV* v. *B en W van Alkmaar*, with comment by F.C.M.A. Michiels (1995) 446 *Administratiefrechtelijke Beslissingen.*

[70] President of the Administrative Law Division of the Council of State, *Hofstede v. GS van Zuid-Holland* (1994) 634 *Administratiefrechtelijke Beslissingen*, 634.

[71] Administrative Law Division of the Council of State, *Ravestein Container Pontoon B.V.* v. *Gedeputeerde Staten van Gelderland en de minister van Verkeer van Waterstaat*, with comment by Schuiling (1997) 1 *Jurisprudentie Milieurecht*, 69.

went into bankruptcy. The state of the ships, which had already been bad, had deteriorated to a point where towing the ships for scrapping would have risked environmental damage. The risks associated with a towing operation exceeded those of an on-the-spot operation. The grant of a permit for on-the-spot demolition could not be awaited in view of the length of the permit procedure and quickly rising water levels. It was therefore decided to tolerate that the ships should be scrapped on the spot.

If a situation occurs in which refraining from enforcement is acceptable, and the administration plans to tolerate the activity in question, the administration has to take a decision to tolerate. In such circumatances, it must take into account, in chronological order, the following procedural and substantive requirements[72] (the legal basis for the requirement in question is placed in parentheses):

— as soon as the occasion arises, an admissible request for a permit needs to be submitted (case law and policy; in the case law, however, this requirement is not applied in all cases);
— the administration should inform itself of all the relevant information; in any case it must have knowledge of the nature and the consequences of the violation (Article 3:2 GALA);
— interested third parties should be given the opportunity to state their views (see Article 4:8 GALA; an exception to this rule is possible under Article 4:11(b) GALA);
— prior to taking a decision, the Inspectorate of the Environment should be given an opportunity to provide recommendations on the draft decision (policy);
— the Public Prosecutions Department should be informed of non-enforcement. On request (upon the initiative of the Public Prosecutions Department), consultation on the draft decision should take place (policy);
— the administration should weigh all the interests directly involved, and may not take a decision as to which the adverse consequences are disproportionate compared to the purposes to be served by the decision for one or more interested parties (Article 3:4 GALA);
— if it is inevitable that the decision has disproportionate adverse consequences for one or more interested parties, then in its decision the administration should award damages to those parties concerned. To date, in the case law, such a duty to award damages has only been accepted if and insofar as the damage-causing activity is tolerated in order to protect the public interest (Article 3:4, para. 2 GALA and case law);
— the decision to tolerate must set a specific time-limit, that should not exceed what is reasonably possible, and after which the illegal situation must be terminated (case law);

[72] n. 17 above, chs. 3 and 5.

— if possible, the decision to tolerate should include conditions (so-called 'tolerance conditions') that do justice to the interests that would be served by enforcement (Article 3:4(2) GALA and case law);
— the decision to tolerate should be based on proper and transparent reasons, and state the provisions that have been breached; the grounds for such toleration should reveal the reasons for tolerating the activity in question, as well as the way in which the administration has weighed the interests involved (Articles 3:46, 3:47, and 3:48 GALA);
— in the decision, it should be stated that the tolerated activity takes place at the wrongdoer's risk. Also, the decision should mention that it leaves the enforcement powers of other authorities intact (policy);
— the decision to tolerate should be notified to the wrongdoer; the decision should be notified to interested third parties that have stated their views, or to interested third parties that have not had opportunity to do so, and whose objections with respect to the tolerated activity are already known to the administration (Articles 3:41 and 3:43 GALA as well as case law);
— if there is a violation of the conditions under which the administration will refrain from enforcement, the wrongdoer should be urged to comply. If this has no effect, enforcement action should be taken against the original violation, but not until the decision to tolerate has been revoked (policy).

These thirteen requirements serve to prevent imprudent and careless toleration of illegal activities. They form a *quasi*-legal framework regulating non-enforcement. If the conditions for non-enforcement (the existence of an illegal situation that is worth tolerating) and these requirements for non-enforcement are actually met, one can speak of an extensive protection of the interests involved. Under certain circumstances, these interests can be better protected than by stringent enforcement. Still, a problem arises. We have seen that the Administrative Law Division of the Council of State requires that a decision to tolerate must include protecting conditions (the 'tolerance conditions'). At the same time, however, the Administrative Law Division is of the opinion that these conditions cannot themselves be enforced. After all, they are (extra-legal) conditions, and not legal standards the wrongdoer has to comply with.[73] To this day, constructions to enforce these conditions, even indirectly, have been rejected by the Administrative Law Division.[74] The problem therefore arises that if the conditions for granting a decision to tolerate are not complied with, it seems that there is only one way to proceed: withdrawal of the decision to tolerate and subsequent enforcement. However, under certain circumstances that could be disproportionate, namely if the infringement is minor in proportion to the interest that has

[73] Administrative Disputes Division of the Council of State, *Van Bentum Recyclingcentrale BV* v. *Gedeputeerde Staten van Zuid-Holland* (1994) 21 *Milieu en Recht*, 120.

[74] Administrative Law Division of the Council of State, *Veenis and Steenaart* v. *B en W van Woerden*, with comment by G.T.J.M. Jurgens (1996) 288 *Administratiefrechtelijke Beslissingen*.

been violated. If so, it would probably be necessary to tolerate the fact that the wrongdoer is not complying with one or more conditions, insofar as these are not of vital importance. After all, even in such situations, Article 3:4 GALA requires proper assessment of the interests directly involved, as well as proportionality between the purpose and the consequences.

v. Administrative Tolerance in Practice

The above-mentioned research by Michiels *et al.* shows that in 80 per cent of the cases in which a decision to tolerate is taken, these decisions include 'tolerance conditions' that ensure the same level of protection as permit conditions would. Hence, in those cases there is no added threat to the environment. The disadvantage of this informal method of regulation, however, is that in case of breach of the 'tolerance conditions', these conditions cannot be enforced separately, as we have already mentioned. For the remainder, we are under the impression that toleration often does not involve an explicit decision to tolerate, and rather takes place implicitly. This manifestation of toleration is not the method which we defend. All the reasons why legitimate non-enforcement in certain circumstances can be acceptable and even proper, do not apply to the implicit toleration of violations.

VIII. Conclusion

Enforcement of environmental law is a well-developed policy tool in the Netherlands, but many improvements can still be made. Those improvements concern both the desired broadening of the administrative enforcement toolbox, as well as better use of existing enforcement powers. This pleads for a more professional enforcement practice, and better cooperation among administrative authorities, and between administrative authorities and their judicial counterparts.

The possibility of lawful or unlawful toleration is subject to EC law and international human rights law. EC law sets strict limits on decisions to tolerate violations of environmental law, even though these limits are not very clear and the ECJ seems to leave some room for toleration. Nevertheless, within these limits there will always be situations in which stringent enforcement is inappropriate. The reasons for this reside notably in legislation that is insufficiently tailored to individual cases, the long duration of administrative procedures, as well as promises made to citizens that are based on incorrect assessments of the law by administrative authorities. As the administration has not only the right, but also the duty, to weigh all interests directly involved, which is generally the case in the countries we have examined, a decision to tolerate can, also in view of other written and unwritten rules, be the best outcome of that process.

Comparison of the Netherlands with some other Member States leads to the observation that the Netherlands and Germany, in contrast to France and the

UK, pay considerable dogmatic attention to the doctrine of lawful non-enforcement. In the Netherlands, case law has explicitly recognized that decisions to tolerate are decisions that can be challenged before administrative courts. The advantage of bringing toleration *sub iudice* (the Dutch way) is that lawful toleration can take place more openly, and therefore becomes reviewable. Several authorities and interested third parties are involved in the process, whereas the latter may take the matter to court. Administrative courts can then consider decisions to tolerate in the light of an extensive checklist of requirements with which lawful toleration has to comply. On balance, this leads to better results compared to a situation where toleration remains unregulated. Neither is it useful to deny that toleration may be a meaningful method of administration.

European Environmental Criminal Law—Recent Developments

*FRANÇOISE COMTE**

I. Introduction

The third paragraph of Article 1 of the Treaty on European Union (TEU)[1] provides that '[t]he Union shall be founded on the European Communities, supplemented by the policies and forms of co-operation established by this Treaty'. This has divided the TEU into the three well-known 'pillars': the original European Community (EC, the first pillar), and two new pillars: Common Foreign and Security Policy (CFSP, Title V, the second pillar) and Police and Judicial Cooperation in Criminal Matters (Title VI, the third pillar).

The two new pillars establish intergovernmental cooperation between Member States. There should be no conflict between the respective competencies defined under each of the three pillars, and the TEU contains a number of provisions to prevent this. Nonetheless, this is precisely what has occurred. A serious conflict has arisen between the European Commission (the Commission) and the Council of the European Union (the Council) over the issue of protection of the environment through criminal law. On 27 January 2003, the Council adopted Framework Decision 2003/90/JHA on Protection of the Environment Through Criminal Law (Framework Decision) under Articles 29, 31, and Article 34(2)(b) TEU (third pillar).[2] Earlier, on 13 March 2001, the Commission had also adopted a proposal for a Directive concerning Protection of the Environment Through Criminal Law[3] under Article 174 EC (first pillar).

* Official at DG Environment, Brussels. Opinions expressed are personal to the author. This article was written in July 2003 but updated on specific points in December 2003.

[1] The TEU was signed in Maastricht on 7 Feb. 1992, and entered into force on 1 Nov. 1993. The TEU was amended by the Treaty of Amsterdam, which was signed on 2 Oct. 1997 and entered into force on 1 May 1999, and by the Treaty of Nice, which was signed on 26 Feb. 2001, and entered into force on 1 Feb. 2003.

[2] [2003] OJ L29/55.

[3] COM(2001)139, [2001] OJ C180/238.

The two texts, bearing the same title and pursuing the same objective, have given rise to a serious inter-institutional conflict. The core question is on which pillar a requirement to provide for criminal penalties for breaches of EC environmental law should be based. The Council takes the view that this competence derives from the provisions of Title VI of the TEU (third pillar). The Commission considers that it derives from the provisions of EC law (first pillar).

Following adoption of the Framework Decision by the Council, the Commission decided, on 24 March 2003, to bring the matter before the European Court of Justice (ECJ). A judgment is sought that the Council has breached the rules governing the respective competencies of the Commission and Council under the EU and EC Treaties. The European Parliament (EP) and the European Economic and Social Committee (ECOSOC) have decided to intervene before the ECJ to support the Commission in its case against the Council.

On 19 November 2002, the tanker *Prestige* broke in two pieces about 130 miles off the Spanish coast, and sank to a depth of more than 3,000 metres. It was carrying 77,000 tonnes of heavy fuel oil, and the accident caused a major oil slick. Very soon after this accident, the Commission announced that it would introduce EC legislation requiring criminal sanctions in such cases. The instruments adopted by the Commission provide interesting insights into the criminal policy pursued by the Community legislator in environmental matters, and on the demarcation between the first and third pillars of the TEU.

The treaties are to be revised through a process that commenced with an Intergovernmental Conference in October 2003. Although it is too early to predict the way in which criminal matters will be treated in the new Treaties, it is interesting to observe how the Convention on the Future of Europe and the draft Constitution have addressed the issue.

This chapter has the following structure. First, it will be illustrated that there is a need to improve the implementation of EC environmental law (section II). Section III explores several initiatives to tackle environmental crime through criminal law. In this context, the proposal for a Directive on the Protection of the Environment Through Criminal Law (Criminal Environmental Law Directive) (section IV) and the Framework Decision (section V) will also be discussed. The inter-institutional conflict which has arisen will be explored (section VI) as well as the application of the Commission before the ECJ (sections VII and VIII). The *Prestige* incident will serve to illustrate the kind of measures the Commission decided to take in order to complement the criminal instruments already proposed in environmental matters (section IX). This chapter will conclude with some observations regarding the future for criminal environmental matters in the EU with particular reference to the European Convention's work and proposals (section X).

II. Implementation Deficits of EC Environmental Law

A. Why the Implementation of EC Environmental Law must be Improved

Whilst the first EC environmental directives were adopted in the 1970s,[4] today some 200 directives and regulations are in force. However, there remain numerous cases where Member States fail properly to comply with EC environmental law. Every year, the Commission's Directorate-General for the Environment receives a staggering number of complaints. In 2001, 600 complaints were received, and at the end of 2001, 301 infringement cases were pending against Member States. In 2001, the Commission referred 71 cases to the ECJ, and issued 197 reasoned opinions under Articles 226 and 228 EC. These represent over a third of the total number of complaints, and infringement cases that the Commission handles each year. They concern every piece of environmental legislation and all Member States.[5]

These trends are confirmed in the most recent annual survey on the implementation and enforcement of EC environmental law.[6] During 2002, 555 new complaints were registered by the Commission. These complaints, again, accounted for over one third of all infringements cases investigated. The Commission brought 65 cases against Member States before the ECJ, and issued 137 reasoned opinions (on the basis of Article 226 of the EC). The survey also provides statistical information about the different types of cases and gives a scoreboard per Member State and sector, showing the incidence of 'non-communication' (97 as of 31/12/2002), 'non-conformity' (89 as of 31/12/2002), 'bad application' and 'horizontal cases' (77 as of 31/12/2002).

Moreover, at the end of July 2003, the Commission announced numerous new legal actions against Member States.[7] The Commission has decided to take legal action under Articles 226 and 228 EC for breaches of EC environmental law. In particular, proceedings are being brought against ten Member States concerning water directives,[8] eight Member States concerning Directive 79/

[4] For example Dir. 75/439/EEC on the Disposal of Waste Oils [1975] OJ L194/23; Dir. 75/442/EEC on Waste [1975] OJ L194/39.

[5] See *Third Annual Survey on the Implementation and Enforcement of Community Environmental Law* (Jan. 2000 to Dec. 2001), Commission staff working paper SEC(2002)1041, 1 Oct. 2002.

[6] See *Fourth Annual Survey on the Implementation and Enforcement of Community Environmental Law* (2002), Commission staff working paper SEC(2003)804, 7 July 2002.

[7] Current statistics on infringements are published on the Internet at: http://europa.eu.int/comm/secretariat_general/sgb/droit_com/index_en.htm#infractions.

[8] See Commission's Press Release IP/03/1107, published on the Internet at: http://www.europa.eu.int (RAPID database). The Commission's action is aimed at the following instruments: Dir. 75/442/EEC on Waste [1975] OJ L194/39; Dir. 75/440/EEC concerning the Quality Required of Surface Water Intended for the Abstraction of Drinking Water in the Member States [1975] OJ L194/26; Dir. 80/778/EEC relating to the Quality of Water Intended for Human Consumption [1980] OJ L229/11; Dir. 91/271/EEC concerning Urban Waste-Water Treatment [1991] OJ L135/

409/EEC on the Conservation of Wild Birds (Birds Directive) and Directive 92/43/EEC on the Conservation of Natural Habitats and of Wild Fauna and Flora (Habitats Directive),[9] fifteen Member States concerning air pollution law,[10] and eight Member States concerning Directive 85/337/EEC on the Assessment of the Effects of certain Public and Private Projects on the Environment (EIA Directive).[11] These statistics underline the need to close the implementation deficit plaguing EC environmental law.

B. The Scale of Environmental Crime: Some Examples

It is very difficult to obtain reliable figures that can serve as a basis for evaluating the scale of environmental crime. This is simply because it is troublesome to gain insights into activities which are, by definition, clandestine. However, a few important examples of environmental crime such as the trade in endangered wildlife species, illegal waste disposal, including radioactive waste and materials, may illustrate the problem.

In terms of profits, trade in endangered wildlife species is thought to be second in importance only to drug trafficking. It is estimated to be worth between €2.1 and 3.7 billion.[12] One study confirms this, stating that: 'What is clear, however,

40; Dir. 76/160/EEC concerning the Quality of Bathing Water [1976] OJ L31/1; Dir. 80/68/EEC on the Protection of Groundwater Against Pollution Caused by Certain Dangerous Substances [1980] OJ L20/43; Dir. 91/676/EEC concerning the Protection of Waters Against Pollution Caused by Nitrates from Agricultural Sources [1991] OJ L375/1; Dir. 79/923/EEC on the Quality Required of Shellfish Waters [1979] OJ L281/47.

[9] See Commission's Press Release IP/03/1109, published on the Internet at: http://www.europa.eu.int (RAPID database). [1979] OJ L103/1; [1992] OJ L206/7.

[10] See Commission's Press Release IP/03/1069, published on the Internet at: http://www.europa.eu.int (RAPID database). The Commission's action is aimed at the following instruments: Dir. 2000/76/EC on the Incineration of Waste [2000] OJ L 332/91; Dir. 2000/69/EC relating to Limit Values for Benzene and Carbon Monoxide in Ambient Air [2000] OJ L313/12; Dir. 96/62/EC on Ambient Air Quality Assessment and Management [1996] OJ L296/55; Dir. 1999/30/EC relating to Limit Values for Sulphur Dioxide, Nitrogen Dioxide and Oxides of Nitrogen, Particulate Matter and Lead in Ambient Air [1999] OJ L163/41; Dir. 2001/81/EC on National Emission Ceilings for Certain Atmospheric Pollutants [2001] OJ L309/22; Dir. 2001/80/EC on the Limitation of Emissions of Certain Pollutants Into the Air from Large Combustion Plants [2001] OJ L309/1; Dir. 89/369/EEC on the Prevention of Air Pollution from New Municipal Waste Incineration Plants [1989] OJ L163/32; Dir. 1999/32/EC relating to a Reduction in the Sulphur Content of Certain Liquid Fuels and Amending Dir. 93/12/EEC [1999] OJ L121/13; Reg. (EC) No. 2037/2000 on Substances that Deplete the Ozone Layer [2000] OJ L244/1.

[11] See Commission's Press Release IP/03/1070, published on the Internet at: http://www.europa.eu.int (RAPID database), [1985] OJ L175/40.

[12] National Wildlife Crime Intelligence Unit (UK), information quoted in *Final Report: Organized Crime in the EU Member States*, study of 15 May 2003 for the Commission by Betreuungsgesellschaft für Umweltfragen, Dr Poppe MbH Umweltgutachtorganisation in cooperation with Max-Planck Institute for Foreign and International Criminal Law Freiburg (Germany). Although the study does not specify to which period these figures apply, it may be deduced from the context that this is a per year evaluation.

is that the financial cost of global illegal wildlife trade runs into billions of dollars and the environmental costs are immeasurable'.[13]

Wildlife trade covers many different types of animals and plants, including, for example, live or dead animals as collectors' items, products used for Traditional East Asian Medicine (TEAMs), skins and furs, food (including caviar), and timber. Wildlife trade flows are directed from South to North, going mainly from the less developed to more developed countries. Western Europe is important as a market for trade in endangered species, and as an intermediate destination.[14] It is also estimated that most of the live animals traded illegally are transported in very bad conditions.[15] For example, in the late 1980s, some 80 per cent of wild birds destined for the illegal trade died on the way to their destination during transport from Africa to Europe.[16]

Illegal trade in and disposal of waste and hazardous waste are even more difficult to evaluate than illegal trade in endangered species. The third environmental assessment report of the European Environment Agency (EEA) in 2003 stressed the 'lack of sound, reliable, comparable and available data'.[17] However, it is clear that environmental crime involving waste generates very high profits. There exist enormous cost differences between southern and northern countries concerning the treatment and disposal of hazardous waste. For instance, it is estimated that, in the late 1980s, 'the average cost of disposal of one tonne of hazardous waste in an OECD country was between US$ 100 and US$ 2000, while in Africa it was between US$ 2.50 and US$ 50'.[18] Illegal waste trafficking in Italy may give some idea of the extent of illegal activities involving waste in the whole of Europe. The Italian Parliamentary Commission, created in order to study illegal activities involving waste in Italy, estimated that 35 per cent of the 108 million tons of waste produced each year in that country are disposed of incorrectly or illegally, and that this generates an estimated turnover of about €7 billion, and a tax loss of at least €1 billion.[19]

The collapse of the former Soviet Union at the beginning of the 1990s led to a new and worrying form of smuggling in nuclear and radioactive material, an

[13] D. Cook, M. Roberts, and J. Lowther, *International Wildlife Trade and Organized Crime—A Review of the Evidence and the Role of the UK*, University of Wolverhampton, Regional Research Institute, June 2002.

[14] Switching Channels—Wildlife Trade Routes into Europe and the UK, a WWF/TRAFFIC Report, Dec. 2002.

[15] This is not true for legally traded animals, for which there exist strict controls.

[16] G. Hayman and D. Brack, *International Environmental Crime—The Nature and Control of Environmental Black Markets* (London: Royal Institute of International Affairs, 2002). Published on the Internet at: http://www.riia.org/pdf/research/sdp/RIIA%20Environmental%20Crime%20-Workshop%20Report.pdf.

[17] *Europe's Environment—The Third Assessment* (Copenhagen: EEA, 2003), 159.

[18] n. 16, above.

[19] Commissione Parlamentare d'inchiesta sul ciclo dei rifiuti e sulle attività illecite, as quoted in *Final Report: Organised Crime in the EU Member States*, n. 12 above.

activity which could have very serious environmental consequences. After the terrorist attack of 11 September 2001 in the United States (US), possession by terrorists of these materials became a source of grave concern in western countries in particular. Dispersal of these materials above large cities, in food chains, or drinking water could have disastrous consequences. In 1994, two spectacular seizures raised public concern. In Germany, luggage containing a very dangerous mix of plutonium oxides and uranium was seized by police on a commercial flight destined for Munich. In Tengen, in 1994, on the border between Germany and Switzerland, the police discovered in a garage a small lead cylinder, which contained extremely dangerous plutonium of military quality.

Against this background, it is not surprising that in recent years several initiatives at the international and EU levels have focused on tackling such environmental crime through criminal law.

III. Background of European Initiatives to Protect the Environment through Criminal Law

A. Convention of the Council of Europe on the Protection of the Environment through Criminal Law

In 1998, the Council of Europe adopted the Convention on the Protection of the Environment through Criminal Law.[20] This Convention is aimed at improving the protection of the environment at European level by using criminal law to deter and prevent conduct that is harmful to the environment. The Convention only addresses those activities which are most harmful to the environment, because criminal law is viewed as a solution of last resort. This Convention is the first international treaty to criminalize acts causing or likely to cause environmental damage, and as such constitutes a significant step towards effective protection of the environment.

Article 2 requires signatories to criminalize a number of serious environmental offences, defined by the Convention. Offences must have been committed intentionally or negligently, and must cause or be likely to cause lasting damage to the quality of the air, soil, water, animals, or plants, or result in the death of or serious injury to any person.

The Convention envisages both custodial and pecuniary sanctions, which may include reinstatement of the environment affected. The Convention addresses the issue of liability of legal persons. However, in view of the fact that some states embrace the basic principle that corporations cannot commit criminal offences,

[20] Strasbourg (France), 4 Nov. 1998 (not yet in force) (1999) 38 *International Legal Materials*, 2, 259, published on the Internet at: http://conventions.coe.int/Treaty/fr/CadreListeTraites.htm.

the Convention takes into account the different legal national traditions, and leaves open the possibility of imposing administrative sanctions and administrative measures on legal persons.

The Convention was signed on 16 November 1998, and will enter into force following the deposit of its third ratification. This number of ratifications has not yet been reached.[21]

B. The 'Danish Initiative'

In February 2000, Denmark presented to the Council an 'initiative with a view to adopting a Council Framework Decision on combating serious environmental crime', commonly referred to as the 'Danish initiative'.[22] It included some elements of the Council of Europe Convention, and was based on Articles 31 and 34(2)(b) TEU (third pillar).

IV. The Commission Proposal for the Criminal Environmental Law Directive

On 13 March 2001, the Commission adopted a proposal for the Criminal Environmental Law Directive.[23] Conceptually, this proposal is entirely novel, whereas the other two instruments share common foundations. The Commission's proposal is based on Article 174 EC (first pillar), and hence reflects what has become popularly known as the 'Community method'.

The Commission's position regarding EC competence in criminal matters is set out in a Commission staff working paper entitled 'Establishment of an *acquis* on criminal sanctions against environmental offences'.[24] EC competence is defended as follows:

> As concerns criminal sanctions the Community cannot purport to act in the criminal area in isolation—as there is no substantive Community competence in relation to criminal matters *per se*. However, to the extent that this is necessary for the achievement of Community objectives, the Community can oblige Member States to provide for criminal sanctions.

Article 175 EC defines general EC competence in environmental matters. Insofar as there is a failure properly to comply with EC environmental law, the Commu-

[21] For comments on the Convention, see for example C. Selin, 'Your Money or Your Life: A Look at the Convention on the Protection of the Environment through Criminal Law' (2001) 10 *Review of European Community and International Environmental Law*, 106–14.

[22] The 'Danish initiative': Initiative of the Kingdom of Denmark with a view to adopting a Council Framework Decision on combating serious environmental crime [2000] OJ C39/4.

[23] COM(2001)139, [2001] OJ C180/238.

[24] SEC(2001)227, 7 Feb. 2001.

nity legislator must require Member States to adopt effective, proportionate, and dissuasive penalties, including, where necessary, criminal penalties. This is the purpose of and hence justification for the proposed Criminal Environmental Law Directive. This reasoning is of general application, and therefore affects all branches of EC law. The sector of the environment serves as a legal laboratory,[25] but the outcome of this case is of importance to any matter in which the EC enjoys a general competence under the EC Treaty.[26]

i. General Outline of the Proposal

The proposed Criminal Environmental Law Directive establishes a number of basic principles that will allow Member States to adapt their criminal law whilst taking account of national traditions.[27] The central provision of the proposal for a Directive is Article 3, which requires Member States to ensure that certain activities are criminal offences: 'when committed intentionally or with serious negligence, as far as they breach the rules of Community law protecting the environment set out in the Annex and/or rules adopted by the Member States in order to comply with such Community law'. The Annex contains a selective list of 51 directives and regulations covering most types of environmental damage. It includes obligations the breach of which could cause substantial damage.

In accordance with the subsidiarity principle, the proposed Criminal Environmental Law Directive limits itself to obliging Member States to impose criminal penalties for breaches of EC environmental law. It leaves them considerable freedom to decide what type of criminal penalties they wish to impose, provided they are effective, proportionate, and dissuasive, in accordance with the case law of the ECJ on sanctions.[28] Member States are also free to adopt or maintain

[25] As often is the case in environmental matters. See for example the developments concerning the UN/ECE Convention on Access to Information, Public Participation in Decision-Making and Access to Justice in Environmental Matters (Aarhus Convention), Aarhus (Denmark), 25 June 1998 (entered into force 30 Oct. 2001) (1999) *38 International Legal Materials*, 3, 517. According to United Nations Secretary-General Kofi Annan this is 'the most ambitious venture in environmental democracy undertaken under the auspices of the United Nations'.

[26] The Commission made other proposals employing the same line of reasoning. See for example the Proposal for a Directive Council on the Criminal Law Protection of the Community's Financial Interests, COM(2001)272, [2001] OJ C240E/125, or the Proposal for a Directive on the Coordination of Procedures for the Award of Public Supply Contracts, Public Service Contracts and Public Works Contracts, COM(2000)275, [2001] OJ C29E/11. More recently, see also Proposal for a Regulation of Official Feed and Food Controls, COM(2003)52.

[27] The Commission mentioned the proposal for a Directive in its replies to several written and oral EP questions. For example, WQ E-0835/01 by C. Muscardini, [2001] OJ C318E/130; WQ E-1574/01 by L. Sbarbati, [2001] OJ C364E; WQ E-0382/01 by J. Titford, [2001] OJ C261E/101, OQ H-288/02 by M. Flemming, not yet published; WQ E-1514/02 by C. Muscardini, not yet published; WQ E-0087/03, van Brempt, not yet published; OQ 08/03 by Guido Sacconi, not yet published.

[28] Examples of ECJ rulings on Art. 10 EC are discussed below.

measures which are more stringent than those provided for in the proposal for a Directive.

In accordance with the proportionality and subsidiarity principles, the proposal does not regulate questions of criminal investigations, prosecutions, or procedure, which remain matters for the judicial authorities in Member States. These remain free to decide whether all offences must be prosecuted, and whether criminal penalties are to be imposed in minor cases, or where the impact on the environment is insignificant. The proposal also takes account of the fact that in some Member States the concept of criminal liability for legal persons does not exist. Article 4(b) allows those Member States to provide for penalties other than criminal penalties, as long as these are effective, proportionate, and dissuasive.

In short, the proposed Criminal Environmental Law Directive does not impose an obligation upon Member States to change their existing criminal law systems.[29] Rather, where necessary, they must supplement these.[30]

V. The Council's Framework Decision

As has been seen, Denmark made a proposal under the third pillar to adopt a Framework Decision on the Protection of the Environment through Criminal Law. This draft Framework Decision had evolved in the wake of the Commission's proposal for the Criminal Environmental Law Directive. The Commission had applied pressure on the Council to examine this proposal, and had firmly opposed the third pillar Framework Decision. It had argued that the right legal basis for legislation providing for criminal sanctions for breaches of EC environmental law is to be found in the first pillar. The Framework Decision adopted by the Council on 27 January 2003 had been amended to correspond more closely to the proposed Criminal Environmental Law Directive.[31] Its 'third pillar' legal basis was Articles 29, 31(e), and 34(2)(b) of the TEU. The definitions of serious environmental offences have been removed, and Article 2 closely resembles Article 3 of the proposed Criminal Environmental Law Directive, establishing the basic principle that Member States must ensure that national law provides for criminal penalties for breaches of environmental law.

[29] For example, Member States that have an administrative criminal law system will not be required to adopt another scheme for criminal justice but only, where necessary, to supplement it.

[30] For other views on the proposal for a Directive, see Y. Buruma and J. Somsen, 'Een strafwetgever te Brussel inzake milieubescherming?' (2001) 76 *Nederlands Juristenblad*, 795–7. See also C. Schrader, 'Europa bald mit Umweltstrafrecht?' (2001) 5 *Umweltmagazin*, 16–17.

[31] n. 2 above.

VI. Institutional Discord between the Commission and the Council

A. Support for the Community Legislator's Competence in Criminal Matters

It is worth noting that there is considerable support (examined below) for the Community legislator's competence in criminal matters.[32]

i. Relevant ECJ Case Law

The ECJ has never ruled directly on EC competence in criminal matters. It has, however, provided some guidance in its rulings in the context of Article 10 EC. Pursuant to this provision, the ECJ has ruled that Member States must adopt, where necessary, effective, proportionate, and dissuasive penalties, including criminal penalties, to ensure that EC law is observed, in accordance with Article 10 of the EC.

In *Commission* v. *Greece* the ECJ ruled that: 'where Community legislation does not specifically provide any penalty for an infringement or refers for that purpose to national laws, regulations and administrative provisions, Article 5 [now Article 10] of the Treaty requires the Member States to take all measures necessary to guarantee the application and effectiveness of Community law'.[33]

In *Hansen* the ECJ reiterated this principle in the same terms.[34] It provided further clarification in *Zwartveld* (1990). The ECJ ruled that: 'The principle of sincere co-operation not only requires the Member States to take all the measures necessary to guarantee the application and effectiveness of Community law, if necessary by instituting criminal proceedings but also imposes on Member States and the Community institutions mutual duties of sincere co-operation'.[35]

The ECJ reiterated this principle in *Nuñes*:

> Article 5 [now Article 10] of the Treaty requires the Member States to take all effective measures to penalize conduct harmful to the financial interests of the Community. Such measures may include criminal penalties even where the Community legislation only provides for civil ones. The penalty provided for must be analogous to those applicable to

[32] For academic comment on EC competence in criminal matters see, for example, G.Tesauro, 'La sanction des infractions du droit communautaire' *Congrès FIDE*, Lisbon, 23–6 Sept. 1992; J. Biancarell, 'L'ordre juridique communautaire a-t-il compétence pour instituer des sanctions?' in M. Delmas-Marty and H. Labayle, 'L'application du titre VI du Traité sur l'Union Européenne et la matière pénale' (1995) 1 *Revue Sciences Criminelles*, 35–64; C. Haghenau, 'Sanctions pénales destinées à assurer le respect du droit communautaire' (1993) 367 *Revue du Marché Commun et de l'Union Européenne*, 551.

[33] Case C-68/88, *Commission* v. *Greece* [1989] ECR 2965.

[34] Case C-326/88, *Anklagemyndigheden* v. *Hansen & Soen I/S* [1989] ECR I–2911.

[35] Case C-2/88, *J.J. Zwartveld and others* [1990] ECR I–3365.

infringements of national law of similar nature and importance, and must be effective, proportionate and dissuasive.[36]

Finally, in *Commission* v. *France*, the ECJ clearly stated that where a Member State does not provide for penalties for breaches of EC law, including criminal penalties, it infringes EC law: 'by failing, as regards the 1988 and 1990 fishing years, to take penal or administrative action against any master or other person responsible for fishing after imposition of a fishing ban, the French Republic has failed to fulfil its obligations under Article 5(2) of Regulation No. 170/83, in conjunction with Article 1(2) of Regulation No. 2241/87'.[37]

ii. The Council's Legal Service's Position

The Council's Legal Service has also spoken out in favour of EC competence in criminal matters. When preparing for the adoption of the Framework Decision, and in light of the Commission's proposal for a directive, the Council asked its Legal Service whether the draft Framework Decision contravened the provisions concerning competencies within the EU. The Legal Service notably replied that if the Community legislator considers that the only way of ensuring compliance with EC rules is to impose criminal penalties, it has legal capacity to require the Member States to impose such penalties. It added that, equally, if an area falls within the sphere of EC competence, it is not legally possible for the Union to adopt rules under the third pillar which would encroach on EC powers.

iii. The EP's position

The EP has supported the Community legislator's competence in this conflict. In its Recommendation on criminal sanctions and criminal law it stated that:

> the Community law system relies on general principles of law common to the national legal systems and on Article 10 of the EC Treaty, which enshrines the principle of loyal co-operation, for competence to require Member States to provide appropriate sanctions, including criminal law sanctions, to ensure fulfilment of obligations arising from the EC Treaty or its implementing measures, as recognized by the Court of Justice.[38]

The EP also unreservedly supported the Commission at its plenary session on 9 April 2002. Under the co-decision procedure, it adopted an Opinion on the proposal for a Directive, fully endorsing the Commission's stance.[39] At the same time it adopted an Opinion on the draft Framework Decision, which the Council had transmitted to it for consultation.[40]

[36] Case C-186/98, *Maria Amélia Nuñes and Evangelina de Matos* [1999] ECR I–4883.
[37] Case C-333/99, *Commission* v. *France* [2001] ECR I–1025.
[38] EP Doc. No. B5-0707/2001, 15 Nov. 2001, recital J.
[39] EP Doc. No. T5-0147/2002, Bull. 2002/4, point 1.4.53.
[40] EP Doc. No. T5-0151/2002.

B. The Procedural Confusion Resulting from the Inter-Institutional Conflict

The inter-institutional conflict gave rise to an unprecedented procedural phenomenon: two parallel legislative procedures were set in motion at the same time, one by the Council (to adopt the Framework Decision) and the other by the Commission and EP (to adopt the proposed Criminal Environmental Law Directive).

i. The Council's Refusal to Participate in the Co-Decision Procedure

The Council never wished to participate in the co-decision procedure within the framework of the first pillar. The Commission repeatedly invited it to do so, but it consistently refused to examine the proposal for a Directive. It only agreed to take account of the text as regards its most important provision, Article 3, which requires Member States to impose criminal penalties for breaches of EC environmental law by incorporating it into Article 2 of the Framework Decision. The Council effectively stole the substance of the proposal for a Directive, and transplanted it into its own Framework Decision.

ii. The EP's Acceptance of the Co-Decision Procedure and Support for the Commission

The Council, having finalized the draft Framework Decision in December 2001, consulted the EP again on the text, as provided under Article 39 of the TEU (third pillar). The EP had already delivered a favourable Opinion on the first draft (the Danish initiative).[41] As the text was substantially amended following adoption of the proposal for a Directive by the Commission, the Council consulted the EP again on the new draft.

The EP then adopted a courageous position, supporting the Commission in the conflict with the Council. It considered that the proposal for the Criminal Environmental Law Directive had been transmitted to it by the Commission in accordance with the usual co-decision rules (Article 251 EC), and that the co-decision procedure could begin. It decided to deliver an Opinion on the proposal for the Criminal Environmental Law Directive, although the Council had not asked it to do so. It also delivered a new Opinion on the draft Framework Decision (Article 39(1) TEU). The EP adopted the two Opinions simultaneously within the very short time-limit of three months provided for in Article 39(1) TEU.

The two Opinions are entirely complementary. The Opinion on the proposal for the Directive accepts its substance, and suggests several political and technical amendments. The Directive is the main legal instrument proposing the principle of criminalization under the first pillar. For aspects strictly falling within the

[41] EP Opinion, 7 July 2000 [2001] OJ C121/494.

scope of the 'third pillar' it must be supplemented by a Framework Decision. This division between a first pillar text (establishing the principle of criminal penalties) and a third pillar text (strictly limited to third pillar inter-governmental aspects) was anticipated by the Commission in the explanatory note to the proposal for the Criminal Environmental Law Directive. The Opinion on the Framework Decision substantially recasts the draft Framework Decision, removing the provisions requiring Member States to impose criminal penalties for breaches of environmental law—leaving the Directive to do this—and supplementing the Directive with provisions on the criminal liability of legal persons, jurisdiction, and extradition.

iii. The Commission's Strategy Fully to Utilize the Co-Decision Procedure

Following the EP's Opinion, the Commission adopted an amended proposal for the Criminal Environmental Law Directive in accordance with Article 250(2) EC, which stipulates that: 'as long as the Council has not acted, the Commission may alter its proposal at any time during the procedures leading to the adoption of a Community act. The European Economic and Social Committee becomes caught in the inter-institutional conflict'.[42]

The European Social and Economic Committee (ECOSOC) soon also found itself caught in the inter-institutional conflict. Having begun the co-decision procedure, despite opposition from the Council, the EP was now blocked by the Council's refusal to examine the EP's Opinion on the text—thereby preventing it from proceeding to a second reading. ECOSOC could not deliver an Opinion, as the EP had done under the co-decision procedure. It first had to be consulted by the Council under Article 262 EC. The Council never consulted ECOSOC, however, implicitly confirming its refusal to accept the co-decision procedure under the first pillar.

VII. The Case before the ECJ

A. The Commission's Application

Very early on, the Commission had announced its intention to challenge the legality of the Framework Decision before the ECJ if the Council went ahead and adopted it.[43] In a letter to the Belgian Minister for Environment,[44] Commissioners Wallström and Vitorino announced that, in the event that the Council intended to adopt the draft Framework Decision, they would propose to the Commission that proceedings be commenced before the ECJ in order to annul

[42] COM(2002)544, [2003] OJ C20E/284.

[43] Letter from Members of the Commission M. Wallström and A. Vitorino to the Council Presidency, 24 July 2001.

[44] At that time, the rotating Presidency of the Council was held by Belgium.

that act. A judgment would be sought that the Council had breached the rules governing the respective competencies of the Commission and Council under the EU and EC Treaties.

When the Council adopted the Framework Decision during the General Affairs Council of 27 January 2003, the Commission made, on the same day, a declaration to be annexed to the Framework Decision in which it reiterated its opposition to the legal basis of the adopted Framework Decision. The Commission also announced in this declaration that, since the Council had adopted the Framework Decision in spite of the EC competence, it reserved all the rights conferred on it by the Treaty.

This declaration has not been published in the Official Journal of the European Union (the Official Journal) as an annex to the Framework Decision, but appears in the monthly statement of the acts adopted by the Council. Within the context of its transparency policy, every month the Council publishes a 'statement of the acts adopted by the Council', which is accessible to the public. The monthly statement of January 2003 refers to the Commission's declaration.[45]

The action by the Commission was filed with the ECJ on 15 April 2003.[46] The Commission claims that the ECJ should declare that the Framework Decision is unlawful and annul it. The action is based on Article 35(6) TEU. This is the first time that such an action has been brought before the ECJ on this legal basis.[47] It provides the jurisdiction for the ECJ to review the legality of, *inter alia*, framework decisions;[48] hence, it is the equivalent of Article 230 EC. Article 35(6) of the TEU is, however, more limited in scope than Article 230 EC: the action is open only to Member States and the Commission.

The summary of the pleas in law, as published in the Official Journal, indicates that the Commission unreservedly supports the objectives of the Framework Decision but disputes the legal basis used, that is, Articles 29, 31(e), and 34(2)(b) TEU. The same reasoning is found in the press release of the Commission. The

[45] Document 6866/03 of the Council of the European Union, dated 28/02/2003. Annex II, declaration 17/03. The texts referred to in this can be obtained by sending an e-mail to: transparency@consilium.eu.int.

[46] Case C-176/03, *Commission* v. *Council* [2003] OJ C135/21. See also Commission's Press Release IP/03/461, published on the Internet at: http://www.europa.eu.int (RAPID database).

[47] The Commission brought an action before the ECJ under Art. 173 EC (now Art. 230 EC) for annulment of a Joint Action on Airport Transit Arrangements adopted by the Council on the basis of Article K.3 of the TEU. At the time, no specific legal basis existed in the TEU for such an action. See case C-170/96, *Commission* v. *Council* [1996] ECR I–2763.

[48] The Treaty of Amsterdam modified the provisions in Title VI of the TEU concerning Police and Judicial Cooperation in Criminal Matters, and extended the competence of ECJ within this title. Article 35(6) TEU reads as follows: 'The ECJ shall have jurisdiction to review the legality of framework decisions and decisions in actions brought by a Member State or the Commission on grounds of lack of competence, infringement of an essential procedural requirement, infringement of this Treaty or of any rule of law relating to its application, or misuse of powers. The proceedings provided for in this paragraph shall be instituted within two months of the publication of the measure'.

Commission considers that its proposed Criminal Environmental Law Directive, if adopted, would secure a better protection of the environment through criminal law than the Framework Decision. Because the Commission's action before the ECJ focuses on an essentially legal dispute about the correct basis, it will be difficult for European citizens to understand the significance of this case.

The main arguments first of all focus on the rule that the choice of the legal basis for a measure must, according to settled case law, rest on objective factors which are amenable to judicial review. Those factors in particular include the aim and the content of the measure.[49] In the present case, both the aim and the content of the Framework Decision belong to EC competence as defined for environmental policy in Articles 174 to 176 EC. To the extent that this is necessary for the achievement of EC objectives, the Community legislator can oblige Member States to provide for criminal sanctions in their national legal order. Article 47 TEU provides for the primacy of the EC Treaty.[50] It is therefore legally impossible to adopt an act on the basis of the TEU if a concurrent EC competence exists. In addition, in its pleas in law the Commission refers to the examples from the case law of the ECJ concerning Article 10 EC (obligation of cooperation between Member States and EC institutions) and to certain EC instruments which themselves define the type of sanctions to be adopted by the Member States.[51]

B. Intervention by the EP

The EP has supported the Commission in its action by intervening in the case.[52] This intervention is based on Article 40 of the Protocol on the Statute of the ECJ, which confers this right of intervention on Member States and institutions of the Communities.

According to this provision, 'an application to intervene shall be limited to supporting the form of order sought by one of the parties'. The EP will therefore not be able to submit additional arguments to those already raised by the Commission.

[49] See e.g. case C-271/94, *European Parliament* v. *Council* [1996] ECR I–1689, para. 14 and Case C-42/97, *European Parliament* v. *Council* [1999] ECR I–869, para. 36.

[50] Art. 47 of the TEU reads as follows: 'Subject to the provisions amending the Treaty establishing the European Economic Community with a view to establishing the European Community, the Treaty establishing the European Coal and Steel Community and the Treaty establishing the European Atomic Energy Community, and to these final provisions, nothing in this Treaty shall affect the Treaties establishing the European Communities or the subsequent Treaties and Acts modifying or supplementing them'.

[51] See e.g. Reg. (EEC) No. 2847/93 establishing a Control System Applicable to the Common Fisheries Policy [1993] OJ L 261/1.

[52] See Press Release of the Press Service of the Greens/EFA Group, EP, 3 Mar. 2003, published on the Internet at: http://www.greens-efa.org/.

The intervention illustrates the scope of the inter-institutional conflict. The EP, since the beginning of the conflict, has supported the Commission. As explained above, under the co-decision procedure, it simultaneously adopted Opinions on the proposed Criminal Environmental Law Directive and the draft Framework Decision, substantially recasting the latter, and supplementing the Directive with provisions strictly limited to third pillar intergovernmental aspects. The EP had already adopted a motion for a resolution on the Protection of the Environment through Criminal Law.[53] This resolution already called upon the Council to: 'refrain from taking any prior action regarding environmental law until after completion of the co-decision procedure for adoption of the proposed Directive of the EP and the Council on the Protection of the Environment through Criminal Law'.[54] and asked the Commission: 'to take the appropriate actions in the event the Council purported to adopt the draft Framework-decision Council on the Protection of the Environment through Criminal Law prior to the adoption of the proposed Directive'.[55]

The question can be asked whether the EP could have brought a direct action before the ECJ in this case. Article 35(6) TEU provides that the ECJ 'shall have jurisdiction to review the legality of framework decisions and decisions in actions brought by a Member State or the Commission'. The EP is therefore excluded from direct action under Article 35(6) TEU.

In the conflict between the Community legislator and the Council, the EP has been excluded from the legislative process by recourse to an incorrect legal basis in the third pillar. At an institutional level, the conflict between the Commission and the Council raises the question whether the EP can challenge a third pillar act, where that act has been adopted in breach of the rules governing EC competence. A similar question has already arisen regarding the EP's right to act under the former Article 173 EC (now Article 230 EC). On that occasion, the ECJ (in anticipation of future Treaty amendments) ruled that:

> an action for annulment brought by the EP against an act of the Council or the Commission is admissible provided that the action seeks only to safeguard its prerogatives and that it is founded only on submissions alleging their infringement. Provided that condition is met, the EP's action for annulment is subject to the rules laid down in the Treaties for actions for annulment brought by the other institutions.[56]

That case raises very similar questions to those of the present inter-institutional conflict over the right legal basis to be chosen for the protection of the environment through criminal law. The EP could have seized this opportunity to assert and strengthen its legislative prerogatives under the EC, by bringing a direct

[53] EP Doc. No. B85-0707/2001 EP Res. [2002] OJ C140E/524; See also EP doc. PE 319.680 'Working document on legal bases and compliance with Community law' (Committee on Legal Affairs and the Internal Market).

[54] See para. 6 of the Res.

[55] See para. 7 of the Res.

[56] Case C-70/88, *European Parliament* v. *Council* [1990] ECR I–2041.

action based on Article 230 EC. This would also have strengthened the Commission's position before the ECJ.

C. Intervention of the European Economic and Social Committee

ECOSOC could never deliver a final Opinion on the proposal for a Directive. According to Article 262 EC, 'the Committee must be consulted by the Council or by the Commission where this Treaty so provides'. In normal circumstances, the Council officially requests ECOSOC to deliver an Opinion. The Council in this instance never did so. From a procedural point of view, ECOSOC was deprived of the act which should have allowed it to render its final Opinion in plenary session.

ECOSOC, for legal reasons, did not wish to issue an Opinion on its own initiative.[57] It considered that it should follow the co-decision procedure, a first pillar procedure under which consultation of ECOSOC on legislative proposals is compulsory. A draft Opinion[58] supporting the Commission was adopted by ECOSOC's Agriculture, Rural Development and Environment Section on 11 July 2001, but no Opinion was adopted at a plenary session. The Committee's prerogatives as an advisory body under the first pillar legislative process, as provided for in Articles 257 to 262 EC, were therefore seriously undermined.

ECOSOC decided to support the Commission by intervening in the case before the ECJ. The basis for an intervention before the ECJ is again Article 40 of the Protocol on the Statute of the ECJ, which gives Member States and the institutions of the Communities the right to intervene in cases before the ECJ. This raises the question whether the intervention of ECOSOC will be accepted by the ECJ. According to Article 7 EC, ECOSOC does not belong to the 'institutions' of the EC. Article 7(2) EC only refers to ECOSOC 'acting in an advisory capacity'.[59]

This is the first time since the European Communities were founded that ECOSOC has seized the ECJ to support the Commission on a substantive issue

[57] This is possible under Art. 262(1) EC, last sentence, which reads as follows: 'It (ECOSOC) may issue an opinion on its own initiative in cases in which it considers such action appropriate'.

[58] Draft Opinion of the 'Agriculture, Rural Development and the Environment' section on the proposal for a Directive on the Protection of the Environment Through Criminal Law of 11 July 2001—DOC. NAT/114.

[59] Art. 7 EC (Nice version) reads as follows:

1. The tasks entrusted to the Community shall be carried out by the following institutions:
   — a EP,
   — a COUNCIL,
   — a COMMISSION,
   — a ECJ OF JUSTICE,
   — a ECJ OF AUDITORS.

   Each institution shall act within the limits of the powers conferred upon it by this Treaty.
2. The Council and the Commission shall be assisted by an Economic and Social Committee and a Committee of the Regions acting in an advisory capacity.

of EC law. ECOSOC considers that its legislative prerogatives have been clearly violated in the present case.

It might be argued that ECOSOC now finds itself in a similar position to that in which the EP established its legislative prerogatives in *EP* v. *Council*.[60] By making this intervention, ECOSOC is essentially asking for its role in the legislative process to be recognized. This is all the more important because the role of ECOSOC is currently being discussed within the framework of the future Treaties on European Union.[61]

D. Possible Interventions by Member States

It is possible that certain Member States opposed to any EC competence in criminal matters will intervene in support of the Council. In certain Member States, this may give rise to internal conflicts between ministries with responsibilities for the environment and justice affairs. Discussions in the Council leading up to the adoption of the Framework Decision were led only by national representatives of the ministries of justice. However, in some Member States, certain voices in national ministries for the environment expressed support for the proposed Criminal Environmental Law Directive.

E. Implications of the Commission's Case before the ECJ

The application of the Commission before the ECJ has no suspensive effect. Member States therefore have to transpose the Framework Decision in their national legal orders within two years from the date of adoption.[62] Under the third pillar, such transposition is not subject to the Commission's control,[63] in contrast with the position under the first pillar. A third pillar measure is also not subject to the same intensity of judicial review by the ECJ.[64]

It is difficult to predict the time-frame within which the ECJ will rule in this case, which will perpetuate institutional uncertainty over the division of competencies between the first and third pillars.[65] Even if the ECJ confirms the position

[60] See n. 49 above.

[61] ECOSOC in the draft Constitution is still proposed by the Convention to serve as an advisory body (see draft Constitution, part III. The Policies and Functioning of the Union, Title VI The functioning of the Union, Chapter one Institutional Provisions, Section 2 The Union's advisory bodies). The former Art. 262 EC is kept (New Article III–294).

[62] See Art. 10(1) of the Framework Decision.

[63] Art. 226 EC.

[64] Art. 234 EC.

[65] See L. Krämer, 'Die Rechtsprechung der EG-Gerichte zum Umweltrecht 2000 und 2001' (2002) 29 *Europäische Grundrechte Zeitschrift*, 483. For the period 2000–1, the average duration of procedures in environmental matters before the ECJ on the basis of Art. 226 EC amounted to 21 months. For procedures under Art. 234 EC, the average duration was 24 months. The data for procedures according to Art. 230 EC (23 months) are not reliable because the ECJ had to decide in only one case. However, on average, in environmental cases the duration of the procedure can normally be expected to come to an end within two years.

advanced by the Commission and the EP, it should be noted that no legal rule appears to oblige the Council to proceed with a first pillar proposal under the co-decision procedure. The only apparent legal route to force such action by the Council would be an action for failure to act under Article 232 EC for a violation of Article 175 EC, this being the correct legal basis for the adoption of the act.[66]

VIII. Arguments of the Commission before the ECJ

A. Legal Basis of the Action before the ECJ

The Commission has based its case exclusively on Article 35(6) TEU, probably because this application is the first of its kind. Article 35(6) TEU is the natural third pillar basis for an action challenging the legality of a framework decision adopted under third pillar provisions.

It is submitted, however, that the application could also have been based on Article 230 EC. Considering that the main purpose of the application is for the ECJ to determine the boundaries between EC competence (first pillar) and intergovernmental competence (third pillar), it could also have been based on the legal basis for instituting proceedings under the EC Treaty, that is, Article 230 EC.

The Commission's application seeks to challenge the legality of a third pillar act on the grounds that it encroaches upon EC competence. As stated above, the Council transplanted a substantial part of the proposal for the Criminal Environmental Law Directive into the Framework Decision and, most importantly, cut out its main provision (Article 3 requiring Member States to impose criminal penalties for breaches of EC environmental law). The very substance of the first pillar competence has been transferred to the third pillar. The ECJ will have to rule on the relationship between these two areas of competence. Insofar as the third pillar legislator may have encroached upon EC competence, the provisions of the third and first pillars have been infringed. The action of the Commission could then have been based on both Article 35(6) TEU and Article 230 EC.

B. The Substantive Arguments

The arguments raised by the Commission in support of its action before the ECJ do not appear very clearly from the summary as published in the Official Journal. The arguments may be subdivided into four categories:

66 Member States' arguments are indeed limited to disputing the EC's competence to adopt a proposal concerning criminal measures in case of serious violation of the environmental law. On the substance, the proposal is not really disputed. The Council Legal Service had issued an opinion to the effect that criminal competence must be recognized on the basis of Art. 175 EC. The fact that

(a) infringement of primary third pillar law;
(b) infringement of primary first pillar law;
(c) breach of the provisions of secondary first pillar legislation; and,
(d) procedural considerations.

i. Infringement of Primary Third Pillar Law

The requirement that Member States must provide for criminal penalties to ensure that environmental law is fully respected is central to EC competence in this area. The Council, as third pillar legislator, cannot adopt such a provision. Articles 29 and 47 TEU govern the structure of the treaties, establishing links between the pillars. They organize the division of powers between pillars, subordinating third pillar rules to those of the first pillar. In particular, Article 29 TEU clearly establishes that the provisions of the third pillar apply 'without prejudice to the powers of the EC'. Article 47 TEU stipulates that 'nothing in this Treaty shall affect the Treaties establishing the European Communities'. The Council, as third pillar legislator, hence is a supplementary legislator with limited competence. It cannot legislate on matters that are within the competence of the Community legislator.

Articles 29, 31(e), and 34(2)(b) TEU form the legal basis of the Framework Decision. The Council's powers as defined in these provisions must be interpreted restrictively. The Council is infringing the Treaty by extending the scope of Articles 29, 31(e), and 34(2)(b) TEU by encroaching upon an area of EC competence. In particular, Article 31(e) of the TEU, which defines the scope of the Union's competence under the third pillar, is limited to the areas of organized crime, terrorism, and drug trafficking.[67]

In adopting under the third pillar a Framework Decision requiring Member States to ensure that national environmental law provides for criminal penalties, the Council has challenged the architecture, organization, and equilibrium of the TEU. This is a precedent with serious implications for the development and scope of the Community method.

ii. Infringement of Primary First Pillar Law

EC competence in environmental matters is defined in Articles 174 and 175 EC. Having cut out and then transplanted the central provision of the proposal for a

the Council refused to adopt a common position in accordance with Art. 251(2) EC possibly does constitute a breach of Art. 175 EC. Case law relating to failure to act is limited to one case relating to the common transport policy (Case 13/83, *European Parliament* v. *Council* [1985] ECR 1513). In this case, the ECJ stated that a failure to act occurs only if the legislator's discretionary power is strongly reduced, and if the Treaty itself clearly fixes the result to be reached by the legislation.

[67] Article 31(e) reads as follows: 'Common action on judicial cooperation in criminal matters shall include:... (e) progressively adopting measures establishing minimum rules relating to the constituent elements of criminal acts and to penalties in the fields of organised crime, terrorism and illicit drug trafficking'.

Directive into the Framework Decision the Council stripped the Community legislator of its power to act. Reducing EC competence in this way infringes the EC Treaty. Adoption of the Framework Decision makes it impossible for the EC to utilize its competence for any other future instruments.

iii. Breach of Provisions of Secondary First Pillar Legislation—New Conditions for the Implementation of Community Law

Member States' environmental legislation is essentially of EC origin. The Framework Decision fundamentally amends EC environmental law, by introducing new conditions in respect of its implementation, namely that the act in question is 'unlawful', causes 'serious injury to any person' and/or 'substantial damage'. However, EC environmental law contains absolute prohibitions. There is no requirement that conduct be qualified as unlawful in order to be prohibited, or that serious injury to any person or substantial damage must occur.

Adoption of the Framework Decision therefore leads to an important amendment of a substantial part of EC environmental law by a third pillar text: the application of all the Directives and Regulations listed in the Annex to the proposal for a Directive on Criminal Environmental Law will henceforth be subject to new conditions. This breaches the principle that the instrument which amends an act must be of the same nature as the act itself.

A few examples, below, illustrate the consequences of the new conditions established by the Framework Decision. It will be seen that these conditions will impede effective implementation of EC environmental law.

Restrictive Conditions on the Application of Directive 75/439/EEC on the Disposal of Waste Oils (Waste Oils Directive)[68]

The Waste Oils Directive serves as a first example of the effects of the impact of the Framework Decision on the application of EC environmental law. Article 4 of the Waste Oils Directive provides: 'Member States shall take the necessary measures to ensure the prohibition of 1. any discharge of waste oils into internal surface waters, ground water, coastal waters and drainage systems . . . ; 2. any deposit and/or discharge of waste oils harmful to the soil . . . ; 3. any processing of waste oils causing air pollution'.

EC law already prohibits conduct which is harmful to the environment; in the instant case, the discharge of waste oil. All that needs be done to implement this obligation is to provide for penalties (a criminal one if necessary) for breaches. This should not be subject to any additional conditions, since the Directive does not provide for them. The fact that the penalty to be provided for in national law is a criminal one does not in any way alter Member States' obligations under Article 10 EC.

[68] [1975] OJ L194/23.

By contrast, the Framework Decision requires that conduct be *unlawful*.[69] It provides for such a condition in Article 2(b)–(g), thus covering a major proportion of environmental law, including waste law in Article 2(c), as follows:

Article 2
Intentional offences

Each Member State shall take the necessary measures to establish as criminal offences under its domestic law:

(a) . . .
(b) the unlawful discharge, emission or introduction of a quantity of substances or ionising radiation into air, soil or water which causes or is likely to cause their lasting or substantial deterioration or death or serious injury to any person or substantial damage to protected monuments, other protected objects, property, animals or plants;
(c) the unlawful disposal, treatment, storage, transport, export or import of waste, including hazardous waste, which causes or is likely to cause death or serious injury to any person or substantial damage to the quality of air, soil, water, animals or plants;
(d) the unlawful operation of a plant in which a dangerous activity is carried out and which, outside the plant, causes or is likely to cause death or serious injury to any person or substantial damage to the quality of air, soil, water, animals or plants;
(e) the unlawful manufacture, treatment, storage, use, transport, export or import of nuclear materials or other hazardous radioactive substances which cause or is likely to cause death or serious injury to any person or substantial damage to the quality of air, soil, water, animals or plants;
(f) the unlawful possession, taking, damaging, killing or trading of or in protected wild fauna and flora species or parts thereof, at least where they are threatened with extinction as defined under national law;
(g) the unlawful trade in ozone-depleting substances; when committed intentionally.

Requiring the conduct to be qualified as unlawful introduces a new condition for the implementation of EC environmental law. First, this is unnecessary: EC environmental law, adopted by the Council and the EP, does not provide for it. Secondly, it is difficult to apply, and will affect the consistency of the implementation of EC environmental law in Member States. The concept of unlawfulness will be interpreted differently from one Member State to another, and as a result EC environmental law will be applied unevenly. This could have serious environmental consequences, in particular as regards the environmental standards to be met by industry. The most polluting industries, for example, may well locate their operations in those countries with the most lenient penalties. This is even more likely to occur after the recent enlargement, which is unprecedented in scale.

[69] Art. 1 provides as follows: For the purposes of this Framework Decision (a) "unlawful" means infringing a law, an administrative regulation or a decision taken by a competent authority, including those giving effect to binding provisions of Community law aiming at the protection of the environment.

The Framework Decision also requires that conduct causes 'substantial damage' and 'serious injury to any person'. Article 2(b) of the Framework Decision reads:

> Each Member State shall take the necessary measures to establish as criminal offences under its domestic law: ...
>
> (b) the unlawful discharge, emission or introduction of a quantity of substances or ionising radiation into air, soil or water which causes or is likely to cause their lasting or substantial deterioration or death or serious injury to any person or substantial damage to protected monuments, other protected objects, property, animals or plants.

As explained above, the Waste Oils Directive provides for an absolute prohibition on the discharge of waste. The Framework Decision therefore requires proof of substantial damage to the environment for a criminal penalty to be imposed. This means that before a national court can impose criminal penalties, substantial damage to plants or animals must *de facto* be shown to have occurred. This is not required by EC environmental law. The imposition of penalties (civil or criminal) for failing to observe the requirements of these directives is not conditional upon fulfilment of such conditions. Merely failing to observe the obligations, by discharging used oils in contravention of the provisions, whatever the circumstances or consequences, is a punishable offence. To introduce as an additional precondition that substantial damage to the environment must have occurred is a regressive step both for the Directives and their transposing national measures. This is all the more evident, given that some Member States already provide for criminal penalties for breaches of EC environmental law.

Restrictive Conditions on the Application of Directive 91/689/EEC on Hazardous Waste (Hazardous Waste Directive)[70]

The Hazardous Waste Directive is a second example of the effects of the new conditions raised by the Framework Decision on the application of EC environmental law.

Article 2 of this Directive reads as follows:

> 1. Member States shall take the necessary measures to require that on every site where tipping (discharge) of hazardous waste takes place the waste is recorded and identified.
> 2. Member States shall take the necessary measures to require that establishments and undertakings which dispose of, recover, collect or transport hazardous waste do not mix different categories of hazardous waste or mix hazardous waste with non-hazardous waste ...

The Hazardous Waste Directive does not lay down any conditions for the recording, identification, disposal, recovery, collection, or transport of hazardous

[70] [1991] OJ L337/20.

waste, and notably does not stipulate that an accident must have occurred. By contrast, Article 2(c) of the Framework Decision reads:

> Each Member State shall take the necessary measures to establish as criminal offences under its domestic law: . . .
>
> (c) the unlawful disposal, treatment, storage, transport, export or import of waste, including hazardous waste, which causes or is likely to cause death or serious injury to any person or substantial damage to the quality of air, soil, water, animals or plants.

This means that for a criminal penalty to be imposed in a national court, an accident must have occurred. Proof must be shown, for example, of death or serious illness and a causal link must be established between this and the treatment or transport of hazardous waste.

Restrictive Condition on Application of Directive 96/82/EC on the Control of Major-Accident Hazards Involving Dangerous Substances (Seveso II Directive)[71]

The Seveso II Directive is a third example of the effects of the new conditions raised by the Framework Decision on the application of EC environmental law. The scope of the Seveso II Directive is very broad. In particular, Article 3(5) defines 'major accident' as:

> an occurrence such as a major emission, fire, or explosion resulting from uncontrolled developments in the course of the operation of any establishment covered by this Directive, and leading to serious danger to human health and/or the environment, immediate or delayed, *inside or outside* the establishment, and involving one or more dangerous substances (emphasis added).

Article 2(d) of the Framework Decision reads:

> Each Member State shall take the necessary measures to establish as criminal offences under its domestic law: . . .
>
> (d) the unlawful operation of a plant in which a dangerous activity is carried out and which, *outside the plant*, causes or is likely to cause death or serious injury to any person or substantial damage to the quality of air, soil, water, animals or plants. (emphasis added)

Damage within the plant is therefore excluded from the scope of the Framework Decision. National courts will not be able to impose any criminal penalties for this type of damage. Yet, the Directive applies to establishments which may employ large numbers of people who are exposed to the risk of very serious accidents that could cause death or serious health problems. Seveso (1976) and Toulouse (2001) are examples of the types of accident covered by the Seveso II Directive.[72]

[71] [1997] OJ L10/13.

[72] Seveso, Italy (10 July 1976): accident in a petrochemical plant (pesticides and herbicides)—more than 200 people injured and 730 people displaced; Toulouse, France (21 Sept. 2001): explosion in a petrochemical plant, 29 dead and 2,242 people injured. Details are published on the Internet at: http://www.uneptie.org/pc/apell/disasters/lists/disastersloc.html.

Restrictive Application of Regulation (EC) No. 338/97 on the Protection of Species of Wild Fauna and Flora by Regulating Trade therein (CITES Regulation)[73]

The CITES Regulation is a further example of the effects of the new conditions introduced by the Framework Decision on the application of EC environmental law. The obligations deriving from the 1973 Convention on International Trade in Endangered Species of Wild Fauna and Flora (CITES) are currently incorporated into EC law by the CITES Regulation.[74] The Convention mainly uses trade policy instruments to protect endangered species, imposing restrictions and controls on the trade in endangered species of fauna and flora. The CITES Regulation goes further than the CITES Convention, and divides endangered species of fauna and flora into four categories. The first covers endangered species (those listed in the CITES Convention and some other species). The CITES Regulation's criteria for defining endangered species are more stringent than those of the Convention. Trade in these species is prohibited (with some very limited exceptions, for example, if they are needed for scientific research). The second covers species which could be threatened with extinction. Trade in these species is subject to stringent conditions to prevent them from becoming an endangered species (import licence system). The third covers species protected in at least one country which is a contracting party to the Convention and has asked the other contracting Parties to CITES for assistance in controlling trade in that species (import notification system). The fourth covers species imported into the EC in large quantities (and therefore subject to an import notification system).

Article 2(f) of the Framework Decision provides:

> Each Member State shall take the necessary measures to establish as criminal offences under its domestic law: . . .
>
> (e) the unlawful possession, taking, damaging, killing or trading of or in protected wild fauna and flora species or parts thereof, at least where they are threatened with extinction as defined under national law.

The Framework Decision therefore covers only the (more limited) requirements established in national law under the CITES Convention. This leaves Member States free to choose whether or not to take into consideration the requirements of the CITES Regulation, a directly applicable instrument.

iv. The Council's Failure to Follow the Correct Procedure

In accordance with the principles established in Articles 29 and 47 TEU, the Council must refrain from acting under the third pillar before first pillar provisions are adopted. The Commission repeatedly requested that the Council

[73] [1997] OJ L61/1.

[74] Washington, DC (United States, 3 Mar. 1973) (1973) 12 *International Legal Materials*, 5, 1085; [1982] OJ L 384/8.

adhere to this principle when it was preparing to adopt the Framework Decision. Throughout, the Council refused to examine the proposal for the Criminal Environmental Law Directive in its capacity as *EC* legislator. This was a breach of its institutional obligation to examine the text under the co-decision procedure under Article 251 EC. The Council examined the proposal for the Directive only to expand and strengthen the text of the Framework Decision, thereby cutting out its substance.

The Council, by refusing to participate in the co-decision procedure, trapped the EC institutions in a blind alley. The Commission, the EP, and ECOSOC took the co-decision procedure as far as they could, but the adoption of the Framework Decision denies the EC legislator every opportunity to complete the legislative procedure for adopting the proposal for the Criminal Environmental Law Directive.

IX. The *Prestige* Disaster: The Consequences for Criminal Environmental Law

A. The *Prestige* Tanker Accident

On 13 November 2002, the *Prestige* tanker suffered serious damage off the Spanish coast. The *Prestige* was a 26-year-old single hull oil tanker flying the flag of the Bahamas. The weather was particularly bad, and the rescue operation was extremely difficult. The tanker requested an emergency evacuation of its crew. Ultimately, the ship broke into two, and sank on 19 November 2002. This accident caused the third major oil slick off the Galicia coast, which had already been struck by similar disasters in 1976 (Urquiola) and again in 1992 (Aegean Sea). It was also the third major oil slick in less than four years which heavily polluted the European coastline, following accidents with the *Erika* (1999) and *Baltic Carrier* (2001).[75]

B. The Commission's Reaction—Communication on Improving Safety at Sea in Response to the *Prestige* Accident

On 3 December 2002, two weeks after the sinking of the *Prestige*, and by way of response, the Commission issued a Communication to the EP and the Council on improving safety at sea.[76] It recalled that the Commission had already reacted

[75] Further factual information is published on the Internet at http://www.le-cedre.fr. Le Centre de Documentation, de Recherche et d'Expérimentations sur les Pollutions Accidentelles des Eaux (CEDRE) was created in 1978 as a result of the oil slick of the tanker *Amoco Cadiz*.

[76] COM(2002)681.

swiftly after the *Erika* accident in 1999, proposing a first set of measures in a Communication on Safety of the Seaborne Oil Trade (the Erika I package).[77] This had been supplemented by a Proposal for a Regulation establishing a European Maritime Safety Agency (the 'Erika II' package).[78]

The Communication of December 2002 mainly proposed an earlier application of the measures as intended in the Erika I and Erika II packages. In particular it proposed: the early establishment of the European Maritime Safety Agency,[79] closer monitoring of the performance of classification societies,[80] publication of an indicative list of substandard vessels under Directive 95/21/EC concerning the Enforcement, in Respect of Shipping using Community Ports and Sailing in the Waters under the Jurisdiction of the Member States, of International Standards for Ship Safety, Pollution Prevention and Shipboard Living and Working Conditions (Port State Control),[81] establishment of a trans-European data exchange network for vessel traffic monitoring,[82] and speeding up the preparation of plans to accommodate vessels in places of refuge.[83] The Commission also requested Member States to take the following measures: recruit a sufficient number of port control inspectors, take the measures necessary to achieve a sufficient inspection rate at all ports and anchorage areas in the Union, ratify without delay the Protocol Establishing a Supplementary Fund for Compensation for Oil Pollution Incidents (COPE fund),[84] and ensure that the fund covers damage up to €1 billion, and is fully operational before the end of 2003.

The Communication also proposed so-called 'additional measures', including revision of certain aspects of the international regime for liability and compensation for oil pollution. The Commission considers that there should be a better balance between the responsibility of the players involved in the transport of oil by sea, and their exposure to liability and a stricter application of the polluter pays principle. These measures to be taken by Member States at the international level should be *complemented at EC level by criminal sanctions*, which should be taken against any person who, intentionally or through gross negligence, causes marine pollution, whether deliberate or accidental. The Commission announced

[77] COM(2000)142. This 'Erika I' maritime safety legislation should have been transposed into national law by 22 July 2003. The European Commission has announced legal action against ten Member States for failure to implement this legislation. All Member States except Denmark, Spain, France, Germany, and the UK failed to notify implementing legislation by 22 July. See Commission's Press Release IP/03/1116, published on the Internet at: http://europa.eu.int (RAPID database).

[78] COM(2000)802.

[79] Reg. (EC) No. 1406/2002 establishing a European Maritime Safety Agency [2002] OJ L208/1.

[80] Dir. 94/57/EC on Common Rules and Standards for Ship Inspection and Survey Organizations and for the Relevant Activities of Maritime Administrations [1994] OJ L319/20.

[81] [1995] OJ L157/1.

[82] Dir. 2002/59/EC establishing a Community Vessel Traffic Monitoring and Information System and Repealing Directive 93/75/EEC [2002] OJ L208/10.

[83] ibid.

[84] COM(2000)802.

that it would, as an immediate step, envisage EC legislation introducing criminal sanctions and, in particular, would introduce a proposal for a directive on illegal discharges from ships.

In addition, at the European Council Summit of Copenhagen on 13 December 2002, the heads of State and Government of the EU Member States specifically referred to the need for specific measures related to liability and corresponding sanctions. The Justice and Home Affairs Council of 19 December 2002 agreed that complementary measures should be taken in order to 'strengthen the protection of the environment, in particular the seas, through criminal law'. It did not specify the legal basis for such complementary measures.[85]

On 5 March 2003, three months after the issuing of the Communication and three-and-a-half months after the *Prestige* accident, the Commission made a proposal for a Directive on Ship-Source Pollution and on the Introduction of Sanctions, Including Criminal Sanctions, for Pollution Offences (Ship-Source Pollution Directive).[86]

C. The Proposal for a Ship-Source Pollution Directive

i. Content of the Proposal

The content of the proposal is twofold. First, it incorporates existing international discharge rules for ship-source pollution into EC law. This regime is known as the MARPOL 73/78 standards.[87] The proposal for a Ship-Source Pollution Directive provides for detailed rules related to the enforcement of these standards. Secondly, the proposal for a Directive provides that violations of these discharge rules shall be deemed to be criminal offences.[88]

[85] Statement by the Justice and Home Affairs Council of 19 Dec. 2002.

[86] COM(2003)92. See also Commission's Press Release IP/03/316, published on the Internet at: http://www.europa.eu.int (RAPID database).

[87] The International Convention for the Prevention of Pollution from Ships, MARPOL 73/78 was adopted on 2 Nov. 1973 as a consequence of the *Torrey Canyon* accident in the English Channel; 2 Nov. 1973 (entered into force with the 1978 London Protocol on 2 Oct. 1983) (1973) 12 *International Legal Materials*, 6, 1439. The *Torrey Canyon* tanker spilled her entire cargo of 120,000 tons of crude oil into the sea. This was the biggest oil pollution accident ever seen up to that time. The Convention never entered into force, the number of ratifications being too low. A 1978 protocol introduced modifications to the original 1973 treaty text. The combined instrument—The International Convention for the Prevention of Marine Pollution from Ships, 1973, as modified by the Protocol of 1978 relating thereto (MARPOL 73/78)—entered into force on 2 Oct. 1983 for Annexes I (Oil) and II (Chemicals), the Annexes III to V covering harmful goods in packaged form, sewage, and garbage, being optional.

[88] See answers of the Commission to Parliament's questions: WQ by C. Bautista Ojeda, E-3405/02, not yet published; WQ by C. Tannock, P-3484/02, not yet published; WQ by D. Varela Suanzes-Carpegna E-3439/02, not yet published; WQ by E. Bakopoulos P-3642/02, not yet published; WQ by D. Sterckx, P-3796/02, not yet published; OQ by J. Cushnahan, H-0872/02, not yet published; OQ by Sir R. Atkins, H-799/02, not yet published; OQ by J. Hernandéz Mollar, H-815/02, not yet published; OQ by Camilo N. Román, J. Mendilice Pereiro, and D. Cohn-

The proposal for the Ship-Source Pollution Directive, as regards criminal sanctions, is built on the same legal foundations as the proposal for the Criminal Environmental Law Directive. It has been based on Article 80(2) EC, the legal basis for EC maritime policy.[89] The explanatory memorandum of the proposal for the Ship-Source Pollution Directive employs the same reasoning as the proposed Criminal Environmental Law Directive. Thus, although there is no explicit EC competence in relation to criminal matters *per se*, to the extent that this is necessary for the achievement of EC objectives, the EC can oblige Member States to provide for criminal sanctions (see above).[90]

There are fundamental differences between the proposal for the Ship-Source Pollution Directive, and the proposal for the Criminal Environmental Law Directive as regards criminal sanctions, and the way the two proposals are structured. The EC obligation—transposition of MARPOL rules and standards into EC law—is created by the proposal for a Ship-Source Pollution Directive. In contrast, the proposal for the Criminal Environmental Law Directive referred to existing EC environmental law (the Directives and Regulations set out in the Annex).

The proposal for a Ship-Source Pollution Directive presents a few elements that are innovative. The proposal covers both accidental and operational (deliberate) discharges. Article 2(3) of the proposal reads as follows: '"Illegal discharges" shall mean discharges in violation of Marpol 73/78 and shall include discharges resulting from damage to the ship or its equipment, which are exempted under Marpol 73/78 Annex I, regulation 11(b) and Annex II, regulation 6(b)'.

Deliberate discharges into the sea are a very common, though unacceptable practice. These discharges are covered as so-called 'operational' discharges, including tank cleaning operations and waste oil disposal. The explanatory memorandum to the proposal for a Directive quotes the following figures. In 2001, aerial surveillance detected 390 oil slicks in the Baltic Sea, and 596 in the North Sea. A Commission study for the Mediterranean Sea reports 1,638 illicit discharges in 1999.

Bendit, E-3404/02, not yet published; OQ by C. Nogueira Román, E-3362/02, not yet published; OQ by I. Rojo, H-863/02, not yet published; OQ by C. Nogueira Román, E-3597/02, not yet published; OQ by C. Nogueira Román, E-3590/02, not yet published; OQ by C. Nogueira Román, E-3601/02, not yet published; OQ by P. Casaca, E-3602/02, not yet published; OQ by P. Casaca, E-3603/02, not yet published; OQ by P. Casaca, E-3604/02, not yet published; WQ by R. Miguélez Ramos, E-716/03, not yet published; WQ by L. González Álvarez, E-1430/03, not yet published; WQ by J. Dhaene and C. Bautista Ojeda, E-1589/03, not yet published; WQ by D. Vlasto, E-1769/03, not yet published; WQ by J.P. Bebéar, P-1771/03, not yet published; WQ by B. Staes and J. Dhaene, E-2006/03, not yet published.

[89] Art. 80(2) EC (Nice version) reads: 'The Council may, acting by a qualified majority, decide whether, to what extent and by what procedure appropriate provisions may be laid down for sea and air transport'.

[90] See explanatory memorandum of the proposal for a Directive on Ship-Source Pollution, in particular para. 2.2. COM(2003)92.

The scope of the proposal is very wide as regards the notion 'ship'. Sea-going vessels, irrespective of their flag, and of any type whatsoever, operating in the marine environment, including hydrofoil boats, air-cushion vehicles, submersibles, and floating craft are covered.[91] The geographical scope of the proposal is also wide, as it covers all coastal waters of the EC and the high seas. The exclusive economic zone is covered to the extent that such a zone has been established, in accordance with international law, by a Member State.[92] The persons subject to sanctions cover the whole range of potential offenders, including natural and legal persons. The sanctions will be applicable to any person concerned with a ship, including the master, the owner, the operator, the charterer, and the classification society, who has been found to have caused or contributed to illegal pollution intentionally or by means of gross negligence. The penalties may, in the most serious cases, include custodial sentences.

Fines are referred to in Article 6, dealing with sanctions, and may not be insured against.[93] This point is very important, as owners of tankers may currently limit their financial liability if the accident is their fault. The proposal recognizes that it is important to cover the liability of legal persons. However, in certain Member States, a system of criminal sanctions against legal persons does not exist, and it would create difficulties to introduce a fundamental change in the underlying principles of national legal systems. For this reason, as in the proposed Criminal Environmental Law Directive, Member States are entitled to provide for measures other than criminal ones, as long as they are effective, proportionate, and dissuasive. The proposal for a Directive refers *inter alia* to fines (non-criminal ones), confiscation of proceeds, exclusion from entitlement to public benefits or aid, placed under judicial supervision and judicial winding-up orders.[94]

ii. The Link Between the Proposal for the Ship-Source Pollution Directive and the Proposal for the Criminal Environmental Law Directive

The proposal for the Ship-Source Pollution Directive refers several times to the proposal for the Criminal Environmental Law Directive, placing it within the general framework established by the latter.[95] The Ship-Source Pollution Directive is therefore to be considered specific or 'vertical', as opposed to the general or 'horizontal' proposal for a Ship-Source Pollution Directive.[96] Several problems

[91] See definitions in Art. 2(4).

[92] See Art. 3(1) of the proposal.

[93] See Art. 6(6) of the proposal.

[94] See Art. 6(5) of the proposal.

[95] See in particular in the introduction: 'In line with the Commission's proposal for a Directive on the protection of the environment through criminal law. . . .'

[96] The Commission underlined this point in answer to questions from MEPs. See for example: OQ of J. Hernandez Mollar, H-815/02, not yet published; WQ of R. Miguélez Ramos, E-716/03, not yet published; WQ of L. González Álvarez, E-1430/03.

arise, however, as regards the coherence between the two future EC Directives should both be adopted.

Article 3(a) of the proposed Criminal Environmental Law Directive specifically covers 'the discharge of hydrocarbons, waste oils or sewage sludge into water'. The *Prestige* was towed out into the open ocean where she sank. The 'discharge of hydrocarbons, waste oils or sewage sludge into water' therefore clearly occurred. This proposal may therefore be considered as covering the *Prestige* case. It refers in an Annex to the main EC legal instruments covering the most important types of pollution, which can be attributed to individuals or legal persons. At the time this proposal was adopted by the Commission, the only legislation referred to in the Annex arguably covering the 'discharge of hydrocarbons' is EC waste legislation, in particular the Directive 75/442/EEC on Waste.[97]

It is not the aim of this chapter further to elaborate on this point. It should simply be noted that the proposed Ship-Source Pollution Directive should, if adopted, be added to the list of instruments referred to in the Annex of the proposed Criminal Environmental Law Directive.

However, the compatibility of the future Ship-Source Pollution Directive with existing EC legislation will need to be carefully examined in order to avoid inconsistencies. *Prima facie*, the scope of EC waste legislation appears wider than the Ship-Source Pollution Directive. The proposed Ship-Source Pollution Directive refers to MARPOL rules, and incorporates them into EC law. It is therefore limited to the substances covered by Annexes I (Oil) and II (Chemicals) of MARPOL standards, the definitions of which do not correspond to those in EC waste legislation.[98] Moreover, the MARPOL rules, as incorporated in EC law, contain many exceptions and specific rules, which will make their implementation in EC law difficult, as is the case in international law.

D. The Second Commission Communication on the *Prestige*

On 5 March 2003, the Commission submitted a report to the European Council on action to deal with the effects of the *Prestige* disaster.[99] It insisted on mechanisms for cooperation between national authorities involving the Commission's monitoring and information centre. This would make it possible to respond immediately, for example, to Spanish authorities' requests for assistance with specialized resources.[100]

[97] [1975] OJ L194/39.

[98] On these matters see M. Hedemann-Robinson, 'Waste Management Law and the Marine Environment' (2003) 11 *Environmental Liability*, 89.

[99] COM(2003)105.

[100] Council Dec. 2001/792/Euratom establishing a Community Mechanism to Facilitate Reinforced Cooperation in Civil Protection Assistance Interventions [2001] OJ L297/7.

As far as criminal sanctions are concerned, the Commission indicated that it was on the verge of adopting a 'proposal for a Directive on Ship-Source Pollution, and the introduction of sanctions, including criminal sanctions'. It added that the proposal was to be adopted 'without excluding the possibility of undertaking other legislative initiatives'. Indeed, the Commission decided to complement the proposal for the Ship-Source Pollution Directive with a framework decision based on the third pillar, in order to enunciate the level of sanctions and other aspects where, in the Commission's view, a third pillar instrument complementing the Directive was required. The Commission therefore adopted a 'proposal for a Council Framework-Decision to strengthen the criminal-law framework for the enforcement of the law against ship-source pollution'.[101]

E. The Proposal for a Council Framework Decision to Strengthen the Criminal-Law Framework for the Enforcement of the Law against Ship-Source Pollution

i. The Proposal for a Framework Decision as a Complementary Instrument to the Directive

The Commission already envisaged the possibility of a first pillar instrument (the Directive) which would impose the obligation to provide for criminal sanctions in case of breach of EC environmental law on Member States, complemented by a third pillar instrument (a framework decision) strictly limited to third pillar aspects.

The explanatory memorandum of the proposal for a Criminal Environmental Law already provided that: 'beyond the rules of this Directive, further steps might have to be taken under the EU-Treaty, with regards to improved judicial co-operation... It may be envisaged to set up a framework-decision according to Article 34(2)(b) TEU. It could concern criminal jurisdiction, measures guaranteeing mutual extradition and/or coordination of prosecutions and investigations'.[102]

This is the same approach that the Commission adopted when deciding to adopt a proposal for a framework decision complementing the proposed Ship-Source Pollution Directive. The complementary character of the Framework Decision is clearly shown in its title, which uses the same terms as the proposal for a Directive: 'Framework Decision to strengthen the criminal-law framework for the enforcement of the law against ship-source pollution'. Articles 1 'Subject Matter' and 2 'Definitions' of the Framework Decision expressly refer to the Ship-Source Pollution Directive.

[101] COM(2003)227.

[102] See para. 5 of the explanatory memorandum.

ii. Main Points of the Proposal for a Framework Decision

The main and most important provisions are set out in Article 3 of the proposed Framework Decision. Article 3(1) of the Framework Decision relates to prison sentences, as provided for by the proposed Ship-Source Pollution Directive, for the 'most serious cases', listed in Article 6(4) of the proposal. It provides for a harmonization threshold, which is set between five and ten years' imprisonment. For cases that would not belong to the 'most serious cases', Member States remain free to provide for lower thresholds. The appraisal of the seriousness of cases as regards custodial sentences is left to each Member State. The proposed Framework Decision leaves it to Member States to interpret which case can be qualified as serious under its own legal system, but provides guidance for interpretation. It specifies four types of specific circumstances in which a case can be qualified as belonging to the 'most serious' ones.

The first specific circumstance is where the offence is committed in the context of a criminal organization. Curiously enough, the three other specific circumstances refer to offences causing death or serious injury of persons, substantial damage to water quality, animal or vegetable species, or to parts of them. These formulations appear to derive from the Framework Decision. As explained, they will lead to implementation difficulties by national courts.

Article 3(2) refers to the harmonization of penalties, and in particular the level of fines that Member States may impose in addition to, or in place of, a prison sentence as required by the proposed Directive. High-level penalties are envisaged, by reference to percentages of turnover or assets—from 1 per cent to 10 per cent of turnover for less serious cases and from 10 per cent to 20 per cent of turnover for the most serious cases. It is left to national legislation how these rules will be applied.

iii. Links between First and Third Pillar Competencies as Established under the Proposed Framework Decision

The proposal for a Framework Decision is based on Articles 29, 31, and 34(2)(b) TEU. The fifth recital refers to the (future) Ship-Source Pollution Directive, the aim of which is 'to undertake approximation (of legislation) with regard to the definition of the relevant offences and commission, participation and incitement, on the one hand, and the nature, possibly criminal, of the penalties that can be imposed'. The recital that follows provides: 'To supplement these provisions, there should be an approximation of, among other things, the level of penalties corresponding to the seriousness of offences in relation to the natural and legal persons who commit them or are liable for them'

In other words, the first pillar instrument (the Directive) provides for a partial approximation of legislation, limited to first pillar aspects. The third pillar instrument (the Framework Decision) complements the Directive, and remains limited to third pillar aspects. It is to be noted that in the Commission's proposal for a Framework Decision, the level of sanctions is addressed under the third pillar.

The delimitation of competencies under the first and third pillars is therefore now fixed by the Commission in the two proposals; the proposed Ship-Source Pollution Directive, and the complementing proposal for a Framework-Decision. The Commission's interpretation of the delimitation between the first and third pillars is now known. This could be an argument before the ECJ by the Commission in the action against the Council in order to show how it conceives the division of competencies between pillars. It could even be considered an argument in favour of the Commission, that the Commission already respects the jurisdiction established by these pillars.

However, it is submitted that it is not for the Commission to set in stone the distribution of competencies between first and third pillars. Its application to the ECJ precisely calls for the ECJ to reach a conclusion on the limits of these respective pillars.

Moreover, in the context of the revision of the treaties by the Convention and the intergovernmental conference, this exercise may be considered as a premature engagement by the Commission in difficult and subtle issues concerning the balance of power between institutions.

F. The Future of the Proposals of the Commission on Ship-Source Pollution

It is too early to be sure what will be the destiny of the proposed Ship-Source Pollution Directive and its complementing Framework Decision.[103] However, it appears that it is highly probable that the Council will manage the question as it did for the proposed Criminal Environmental Law Directive. It will hence probably wish to transfer the first pillar criminal part of the proposal for a directive to a new framework decision.

This would raise a problem for the Commission, which should oppose this manoeuvre as it did for the Council Framework Decision. However, even more than for the protection of the environment through criminal law, it will be difficult for the citizen to understand why the Commission, on pure legal matters, opposes measures which appear necessary in order to avoid further terrible oil slicks which may devastate whole coastal regions in Europe.

[103] A document published on the public register of the Council (Document 13584/03 dated 20 Oct. 2003) articulates the position of the different delegations during the debates within the working groups of the Council as follows: 'It appeared from the discussion in the TTE Council of 9 October 2003, in particular, that Member States were divided as regards the possibility to go beyond the existing international instruments, and that all Member States favoured a solution where the criminal sanctions would be dealt with under a parallel Framework-Decision, contrary to the opinion of the Commission'. Published on the Internet at: http://register.consilium.eu.int/.

Should the Council adopt such a framework decision, in order to be consistent with the present action before the ECJ, however, the immediate reaction of the Commission ought to be to take action against it on the same basis as the Framework Decision.

IX. The Future of Criminal Matters in the European Union

A. The Difficulty of the Distribution of Competencies is Connected with the Pillar Structure

The inter-institutional conflict over the protection of the environment through criminal law has arisen as a result of the TEU's pillar structure, which could remain a potential source of a great many conflicts. The blocking of EC action and the EC decision-making process, and the complexity of the procedures and legal instruments under the different pillars (even though the matters dealt with are substantively the same), do not make it easy for Europeans to understand the EU's institutional mechanisms, nor do they strengthen their legitimacy.

A solution is already anticipated by the treaties. Article 42 TEU, the so-called 'footbridge provision', provides for the transfer of areas falling within the ambit of inter-governmental cooperation to that of the EC. It expressly allows transfer of criminal matters referred to in Article 29 TEU (third pillar) to the first EC pillar. This transfer of powers would considerably simplify the work of the Community legislator. Under the Amsterdam Treaty, some matters have already been moved from the third pillar to the first: visas, asylum, immigration, the free movement of persons, and judicial cooperation in civil matters. Criminal policy may, likewise, ultimately be transferred to the EC.

B. The Convention's Solution

Judicial cooperation in criminal matters is treated in the draft Constitution under section 4 of Chapter IV, 'Area of Freedom, Security and Justice', which belongs to Title III, 'Internal Policies and Action'. Title III itself belongs to Part III of the draft Constitution, 'The Policies and Functioning of the Union'. The draft Constitution, therefore, suppresses the third pillar—integrating criminal matters into the policies of the Union and bringing matters within the Community method.

The draft Constitution exercises a certain self-restraint as regards approximation of laws, and provides that the criminal matters will be subject to minimum legislative approximation. The instrument for such a policy will be a European framework law. The framework law is the equivalent of the present directive. The main provision in this regard is Article III.167, which reads as follows:

> 1. A European framework law may establish minimum rules concerning the definition of criminal offences and sanctions in the areas of particularly serious crime with cross-border dimension resulting from the nature or impact of such offences or from a special need to combat them on a common basis.

The substantive areas of crime are defined in Article III.167(1), second paragraph as follows: 'terrorism, trafficking in human beings and sexual exploitation of women and children, illicit drug trafficking, illicit arms trafficking, money laundering, corruption, counterfeiting of means of payment, computer crime and organized crime'.

It may be regretted that environmental crime is not included in this list. However, it will be possible for the Council of Ministers to complete this list without making a revision of the Constitution by way of Article III.167(1), third paragraph: 'On the basis of development in crime, the Council of Ministers may adopt a European decision identifying other areas of crime that meet the criteria specified in this paragraph. It shall act unanimously after obtaining the consent of the European Parliament'.

As regards approximation of criminal law, Article III.167(2) finally provides specific rules, stating that the Council will be able to adopt minimum rules limited to the definition of criminal offences and sanctions. These minimum rules can be adopted by the Council when two cumulative conditions are fulfilled if:

1. the approximation of criminal legislation proves essential to ensure the effective implementation of a Union policy; and
2. the area of action must have been the subject of harmonization measures.

According to the commonly accepted interpretation, this allows it to cover, *inter alia*, environmental crime. Article III.167(2) reads as follows:

> 2. If the approximation of criminal legislation proves essential to ensure the effective implementation of a Union policy in an area which has been subject to harmonisation measures, a European framework law may establish minimum rules with regards to the definition of criminal offences and sanctions in the area concerned.

X. Conclusion

The need for action in criminal matters in the environmental field is obvious. The implications of environmental crime often are more serious than other types of crime, and incidents such as oil slicks appear to be more and more frequent. Some Member States already provide for criminal sanctions for breaches of environmental law. The level of criminal penalties in the EU, however, differs widely among Member States. For the same offence, after transposition of EC environmental law, sanctions can range from a few hundred to several thousand euro, and for imprisonment (natural persons) anything from a few days to several years. These discrepancies will become all the more pronounced in an EU of 25 Member States. Obvious distortions are created by the widely divergent financial consequences of environmental crime in different parts of the EU. This situation creates inconsistencies in the treatment of and even injustice between European citizens. It may even be argued that environmental crime is encouraged by these legislative distortions between Member States. These distortions, despite efforts by the new Member States to adopt the *acquis communautaire*, are likely to increase as a result of enlargement.

However, pollution knows and respects no borders. The *Prestige* disaster is there to remind us of that reality. Serious pollution of water, soil, and air, and the food and health scandals require coordinated action at the European level.

Integration of Environmental Protection into the EC Energy Policy

*Nele Dhondt**

I. Introduction

Over the past few decades, the European Union (EU) has developed an autonomous environmental policy. In the context of this policy, the EU adopted measures that were designed, for example, to control environmental pollution caused by power generation from fossil fuels. In the context of its policy relating to the energy sector, the EU has at the same time instigated the liberalization of the gas and electricity markets, designed, *inter alia*, to lower energy prices. It could be argued that such EU action is inconsistent with its environmental policy because low energy prices could result in increased energy consumption, and associated environmental problems.

A title specifically devoted to the environment was first included in the EC Treaty in 1987. Besides the 'objectives', 'principles', and 'criteria' of Community action relating to this field, this title provided a legal basis for such action. In addition, one of the provisions in the new title stipulated that 'Environmental protection requirements shall be a component of the Community's other policies'. After amendments to this Treaty provision by the Maastricht and the Amsterdam Treaties, the version currently in force reads: 'Environmental protection requirements must be integrated into the definition and implementation of the Community policies and activities referred to in Article 3, in particular with a view to promoting sustainable development'.

It could be argued that integration, as required by Article 6 EC, implies that measures relating to sectors such as energy and transport, or policies such as development cooperation, should be more 'in line with' or even 'supportive' of action relating to the protection of the environment. However, matters are not that straightforward. It is unclear whether this Treaty provision stands in the way of the adoption of any measure that is (actually or potentially) environmentally damaging, or whether it allows for environmentally damaging action to be taken. Does Article 6 EC require the addressees to give 'priority' to environmental concerns over other concerns? What if the measure in question is essential for the achievement of the non-environmental objectives of the Community? In other

* Solicitor, De Brauw Blackstone Westbroek, Amsterdam (the Netherlands).

words, the extent to which other policy areas must 'accommodate' environmental concerns, if at all, on the basis of this Treaty provision, is not entirely clear.

In this chapter, we will seek to identify the most plausible interpretation of the so-called integration principle of Article 6 EC. This interpretation will then be applied to the energy policy of the EU, with a view to examining the extent to which environmental protection requirements have been integrated into the Community's energy policy, as required by Article 6 EC. We will focus on the integration of environmental protection requirements into secondary energy law, rather than primary law. Neither will we deal with the question of the justiciability of the integration principle. It is sufficient to observe here that case law of the European Court of Justice (ECJ) does imply that the principle:

— could be used for reviewing the validity of secondary Community law (even if the review would be marginal); and

— is being used to interpret both primary and secondary Community law.[1] Even without tackling the issue of justiciability, however, it will appear from the overview below that the integration principle has had and is having a significant impact on the activities of the EC in relation to the energy field.

II. What do we Mean by 'Integration of Environmental Protection Requirements'?

On the basis of a comparison with other so-called 'horizontal' clauses in the EC Treaty,[2] and an examination of the aim of the principle (i.e. sustainable development), as well as relevant case law of the ECJ,[3] a most plausible interpretation may be identified. It could be argued that the integration requirement is a requirement to satisfy or apply the environmental protection requirements when developing and implementing other EC policies and activities. If it is accepted that the expression 'environmental protection requirements' relates to the objectives, principles, and criteria of Article 174 EC (the so-called environmental objectives, principles, and criteria),[4] it follows that these objectives, principles, and criteria can only apply in the context of other policy areas in the same way as they apply in the context of the environmental policy.

According to this interpretation, the integration principle means that the institutions must (not may) pursue environmental objectives, not only when

[1] See e.g. Case C-248/95, *Safety Hi-Tech* [1998] ECR I-4301, Case C-341/95, *Bettati* [1998] ECR I-4355, Case C-513/99, *Concordia Bus Finland* [2002] ECR I-7213.

[2] Art. 3(2) EC (equality between men and women); Art. 127(2) EC (employment); Art. 151(4) EC (culture); Art. 152(1) EC (public health); Art. 153(2) EC (consumer protection); Art. 157(3) EC (industry); Art. 159 EC (regional policy); Art. 178 EC (development cooperation). See N. Dhondt, *Integration of Environmental Protection into other EC Policies* (Groningen: Europa Law Publishing, 2003), 27–30 and 100–3.

[3] Case C-62/88, *Greece* v. *Council* [1990] ECR I-1527, para. 20.

[4] Dhondt, n. 2 above, 72–80.

acting on the basis of their powers to develop and implement an environmental policy but also when acting on the basis of their powers to determine and execute other policies (such as the agricultural, energy, and transport policies). Moreover, action must be based on the environmental principles and take account of the environmental criteria. In other words, besides the specific objectives of a policy area, action taken in the context of such a policy must also (systematically) contribute to the achievement of environmental objectives, be based on the environmental principles, and take account of environmental criteria. Consequently, the integration principle requires that every possible action is taken in the context of any policy area to help achieve environmental objectives.

The integration obligation is therefore more than a simple procedural requirement to take environmental requirements into account. Such a weak interpretation would grant overly wide discretionary powers to the Community institutions. At the same time this falls short of affording priority to environmental protection requirements. Priority would entail that environmental objectives, principles, and criteria should be applied *at all times*, even in case of a conflict or clash with specific and essential objectives of other policy areas. This result would be untenable, given the generally accepted view that there exists no hierarchy amongst Community objectives (cf. *Gleichrang* theory) (see also immediately below).

In sum, it may be argued that the strength of the integration concept varies along a continuum. On this continuum or spectrum, integration as required by Article 6 EC is situated in the middle, as is illustrated in Figure 1.

Article 6 EC requires that environmental objectives are pursued in the context of other policies to such a degree that a balance is reached, not between the various policy-specific objectives of the Community but between the various main objectives, as listed in Article 2 EC (economic, social, and ecological). This is also evidenced by the reference to sustainable development in Article 6 EC. This means that environmental concerns will prevail sometimes, with detrimental implications for various policies. However, on other occasions, it will be necessary to give temporary priority to economic considerations.

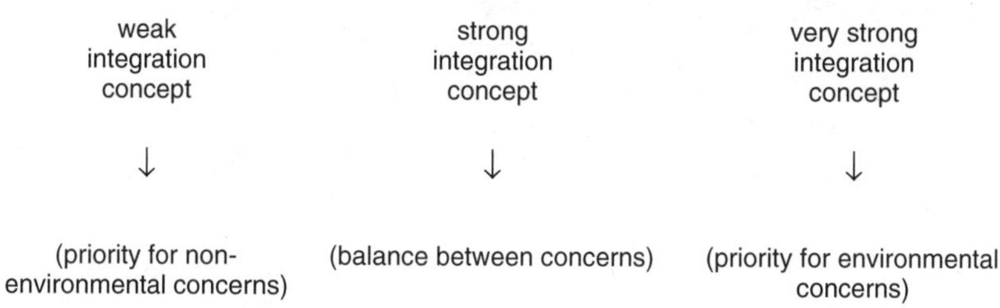

Figure 1. The force of the integration principle

Application of what has been suggested as the most plausible interpretation should result in achieving specific policy objectives in environmentally friendly ways, where possible (i.e. where there is no conflict). If policy objectives cannot be pursued or attained adequately in environmentally friendly ways (i.e. where there is conflict), the integration principle requires institutions to opt for the least environmentally damaging way or, in certain circumstances, radically to change or even to abandon the policy-specific objectives. The extent to which a policy-specific objective should be redefined or abandoned is determined by the requirement to find a balance between various policy-specific objectives so as to realize all principal goals of the Community (specified in Article 2 EC). If a policy-specific objective that is 'incompatible' (or in conflict) with environmental objectives is not or is no longer essential for realizing one or more general Community objectives, then it should be abandoned.

In connection with policy areas relating to sectors such as transport, energy, and agriculture, it would seem that integration requires specific objectives of such policy areas to be pursued in such a way that the environmentally optimal behaviour and practices (systems, methods, products, etc.) are stimulated or preferred over any alternative. Instances in which this occurs can be regarded as examples of '*integration efforts*'. At the same time, the instances in which the various policy areas (i.e. policy-specific legislation) have the opposite effect (in other words, fail to reflect environmentally optimal options) could be referred to as '*integration failures*'.

In the remainder of this chapter, both integration efforts and integration failures in EC energy policy will be examined. Essentially, the environmental impact of EC law relating to the energy sector will be analysed.[5] Before briefly describing legislation that makes up EC energy policy, some attention must be paid to the particularities of the energy sector, the context in which the EC energy policy has been developed, as well as a summary of the environmental effects of energy activities. The latter will allow an identification of (any) environmentally friendly, least environmentally damaging, and/or most environmentally damaging energy sources and methods. Next, this article will provide a brief description of the legislative measures that make up the EC energy policy. We will then examine, and evaluate more closely both integration efforts and integration failures. Finally, various types of integration will be distinguished on the basis of their intensity.

[5] I am aware of the fact that this could be regarded, at least partly, as a law and economics approach to the issue at hand, instead of a purely legal one. For similar research in relation to the environmental effects of agricultural policy, see M.A. Mekouar, *The Environmental Impact of Economic Incentives for Agricultural Production—A Comparative Law Study* (Rome: FAO, 1990), 1–67. This author observed that: 'relatively little attention has so far been paid to the environmental impact of the legal measures for the economic promotion of agricultural production. To what extent can the financial or fiscal incentives that are directed towards increased agricultural production harm or enhance the environment?...The issue has not yet received sufficient attention within this precise context, at least not on the part of the jurists'.

III. The European Community Energy Policy

A. Development of an Energy Policy

There is not one single but three relevant treaties for the energy sector. Besides the general energy policy in the context of the EC Treaty, a specific regime existed for coal under the ECSC (European Coal and Steel Community) Treaty and a specific regime still exists for nuclear energy under the Euratom (European Atomic Energy Community) Treaty. The ECSC Treaty expired on 23 July 2002, because it had been concluded for a fixed period of 50 years. The Euratom Treaty is still in force. In what follows, the main focus will be on energy-related legislation adopted under the EC Treaty. In this respect, it must be recalled that the scope of the integration clause seems to be limited to the EC Treaty. Occasionally, however, reference will be made in this chapter to relevant action under the ECSC and the Euratom Treaties, especially where this action seems to offset environmental benefits accrued under EC measures.

Like a common transport policy, it has proved difficult to develop and implement a common policy in relation to the equally sensitive energy sector. Although some EC legislation relating to the energy sector has been adopted over the years, it is not clear whether this really amounts to a common policy, hence the phrase 'EC Energy Policy' instead of 'Common Energy Policy'.

Contrary to the environmental, agricultural, and transport policies, for example, no separate title, and therefore no explicit legal basis, can be found in the EC Treaty in order to develop and implement a Common Energy Policy. Secondary law in relation to the energy sector has been based on many different provisions, including Article 308 (formerly Article 235) EC, a combination of Articles 47(2), 55, and 95 (formerly Articles 57(2), 66, and 100a) EC and Article 99 (formerly Article 103) EC. Since the entry into force of the Maastricht Treaty, Article 3 EC (the provision that lists the Community's activities) does include a reference to 'measures in the spheres of energy' (cf. Article 3(t), now Article 3(u) EC). In the Declaration on Civil Protection, Energy and Tourism, annexed to the Final Act of the Maastricht Treaty, the Intergovernmental Conference had even envisaged a discussion on the possible inclusion of a specific energy title. However, ultimately no specific title for energy policy was introduced into the EC Treaty by the Treaty of Amsterdam or by the subsequent Treaty of Nice. This would have required consensus among Member States as to the desired type of regulatory regime. Such consensus has not yet arisen because of the sensitivity of the sector.[6] Member States do not wish to cede powers pertaining to the regulation of the exploitation and utilization of their energy sources. Because

[6] See on the debate whether to include a specific title on energy or not: E.D. Cross, L. Hancher, and P.J. Slot in M.M. Roggenkamp *et al.*, *Energy Law in Europe—National, EU and International Law and Institutions* (Oxford: Oxford University Press, 2001), 219.

of lack of an explicit legal basis and specific energy objectives, the only option available to the Community was to work towards the creation of a liberalized energy market on the basis of the general provisions of the EC Treaty.[7] Over the years, a couple of other objectives have been added to this initial objective, as will appear from the overview of secondary legislation below.

That the Member States are reluctant to delegate powers to the Community in relation to such a sensitive sector as energy is also illustrated by a Treaty provision in the environmental title. In derogation from the normal decision-making procedure for the adoption of environmental legislation, Article 175(2) EC requires unanimity for measures 'significantly affecting a Member State's choice between different energy sources and the general structure of its energy supply'. In other words, measures that favour certain energy sources over others for environmental purposes require unanimity.[8]

A final reference to the energy sector in the EC Treaty can be found in the title on Trans-European Networks (TENs) (Articles 154–6 EC). The Treaty of Maastricht introduced a title on the development of TENs. Besides transport and telecommunications infrastructures, energy infrastructure was, and still is, a priority area for this type of Community action. The guidelines for Trans-European energy networks (TEN-E) will be discussed below in the paragraphs on 'Energy Infrastructure' (section III.D.*vii*).

Because the EC Treaty does not contain a specific title on energy policy, there also is no clear list of what the Community has to achieve in this area. However, some clues may be found in various policy documents produced by the Commission and the Council over the years.[9] In addition, the Council adopted resolutions concerning the 'energy policy objectives', usually for a period of ten years.[10] From these (early) policy documents and resolutions it appeared that the objectives of Community action relating to the energy sector are mainly:

[7] P.J.G. Kapteyn and P. Verloren van Themaat, *Introduction to the Law of the European Communities from Maastricht to Amsterdam* (London/The Hague/Boston: Kluwer Law International, 1998), 1231.

[8] See also J.H. Matláry, *Energy Policy in the European Union* (London: Macmillan, 1997), 67. In this context, reference should also be made to the Declaration on Article 130r EC (now Art. 174 EC), annexed to the Final Act of the SEA. In this Declaration, the Intergovernmental Conference observed that the Community's activities in the sphere of the environment may not interfere with national policies regarding the *exploitation* of energy resources. With this Declaration, Member States confirmed their sovereignty over mineral resources; Kapteyn and Verloren van Themaat, n. 7 above, 1231. See also L. Hancher, 'Energy and the Environment: Striking a Balance?' (1989) 26 *Common Market Law Review*, 486.

[9] For a discussion of the earliest policy documents see P.J.G. Kapteyn and P. Verloren van Themaat, *Introduction to the Law of the European Communities—After the Coming into Force of the Single European Act* (Deventer: Kluwer, 1990), 756–7, who mention the 1964 Protocol of Agreement between the Member States; the 1967 Council Decision on the policy for oil and natural gas; the 1968 Commission Communication 'First orientation for a common energy policy' and a 1973 Commission Communication.

[10] The 1974 Res. concerning Community Energy Policy Objectives for 1985 [1975] OJ C153/2; the 1980 Res. concerning Energy Policy Objectives for 1990 and Convergence of the Policies of the Member States [1980] OJ C149/1, and the 1986 Res. (EEC) concerning Energy Policy Objectives for 1995 and Convergence of the Policies of the Member States [1986] OJ C241/1.

(1) to integrate the sector within the common market, and
(2) to secure cheap energy supplies.

In addition, the need to tackle environmental problems was sometimes mentioned.[11] The Council adopted a resolution specifically on energy and the environment as early as 1975. The first Communication on energy and the environment only followed in 1990, however. Below, I will examine the extent to which the policy intentions in relation to energy and the environment were translated into concrete legal action (with or without reference to the integration clause).

B. The Energy Sector

It has already been observed that the energy sector is an essential and therefore very sensitive sector. The conditions under which energy products are produced, transported, distributed, and consumed determine the economic, social, and political environment of both industry and individuals.[12] The energy sector may be regarded as incorporating three types of activities:

(1) the production of primary energy, which is defined as: 'Energy embodied in natural resources (e.g. coal, crude oil, sunlight, uranium) that has not undergone any anthropogenic conversion or transformation';[13]
(2) the conversion of primary energy to derived energy (e.g. electricity and heat production);
(3) and the end use or the sector in which fuels are finally consumed.

C. Effects on the Environment[14]

Energy may be derived from various sources. The main sources are the 'fossil sources', which can be divided into 'solid fuels' (such as coal, lignite, and peat) and 'hydrocarbons' (oil and natural gas). Energy may also be derived from

[11] The 1974 Res. concerning Community Energy Policy Objectives for 1985 [1975] OJ C153/2.

[12] Commission, White Paper, 'An Energy Policy for the European Union' COM(95)682, 2.

[13] European Environment Agency (EEA), *Europe's Environment—The Dobris Assessment, Chapter 19—Energy* (Copenhagen: EEA, 2001), 1; The EEA, *Environmental Signals 2001—European Environment Agency Regular Indicator Report* (Copenhagen: EEA, 2001), 41, defines the 'energy supply sector' as the sector which includes coal, oil, and gas exploration and extraction, public electricity and heat production, refineries, and other industries engaged in transforming primary energy into other energy products.

[14] The data used for this section on the environmental effects of the energy sector is derived from the following publications: EEA, *Environmental Signals 2000—European Environment Agency Regular Indicator Report* (Copenhagen: EEA, 2000), 21–4; EEA, *Environmental Signals 2001—European Environment Agency Regular Indicator Report* (Copenhagen: EEA, 2001), 40–8; EEA, *Europe's Environment—The Dobris Assessment, Chapter 19—Energy* (Copenhagen: EEA, 2001); OECD, *Environmental Effects of Electricity Generation* (Paris: OECD, 1985), 9–154; OECD and International Energy Agency, *Benign Energy? The Environmental Implications of Renewables* (Paris: OECD/IEA, 1998), 13–113, and European Commission, *2000—Annual Energy Review* (Luxembourg: EC, 2001).

nuclear processes, or from so-called 'renewables' (such as energy from wind and sunlight). None of these energy sources is entirely environmentally neutral. To a greater or lesser extent, they all have negative environmental effects during their entire life-cycle; in other words, from their extraction through their processing to their end use. The effects of the various energy sources on the environment throughout their life-cycle will be analysed briefly next.

i. Fossil Fuels—Coal, Oil, and Gas

In Europe, almost half of the electricity is produced in thermal power plants using fossil fuels, in particular coal, oil, and gas. The use of these fossil fuels for power generation seriously damages the environment. First of all, generated this way, energy is a major user of natural resources. Besides fossil fuels themselves, other natural resources, especially water and land, are used. Electricity generation from coal, oil, and gas is also responsible for emissions, most notably, of CO_2, SO_2, and NO_x (carbon dioxide, sulphur dioxide, and nitrogen oxide) (contributing significantly to climate change, acidification, and the tropospheric ozone problem), as well as waste creation and noise pollution. In addition, the production and treatment, as well as the transportation and storage of these fuels, cause environmental problems.[15] Of course, further damaging effects are caused by their end use, when these fuels are consumed, for example, by transport or industry.[16] It is important to point out that of the three main fossil fuels, gas is considered to be the least environmentally damaging.[17]

ii. Renewable Energy Sources

The environmental impact of 'renewable energy sources' is considered to be less detrimental than the above-discussed, 'conventional' or 'non-renewable', energy sources. The main environmental benefit of introducing renewables such as hydropower, solar, photovoltaics (PV), wind, geothermal, and biomass (energy crops),[18] is that they cause significantly fewer emissions of atmospheric pollu-

[15] For example, these activities may lead to more air emissions (e.g. treatment of oil), spills and leaks (e.g. transport of oil by tankers), and the creation of waste (production and treatment of coal).

[16] Reportedly, around 80% of total worldwide anthropogenic CO_2 emissions find their origin in the combustion of fossil fuels, including that for transport and industry. Emissions in Europe are approximately 30% of this total. In 1990, around 95% of SO_2 emissions and 97% of NO_x come from the combustion of fossil fuels in Europe. Electricity generation and industry are responsible for the highest emissions, because they use most energy, as well as the highest sulphur-content fuels.

[17] The amount of CO_2 produced per unit of energy from coal is approximately 25% more than the amount from oil and half the amount from natural gas. Hence, natural gas is to be preferred over coal and oil from an environmental point of view.

[18] For example, biofuels are made out of biomass (plant oils, e.g. colza, soybean, sunflower; certain crops, such as sugar beets and cereals; organic waste material). Possible biofuels are bioethanol, biodiesel, ETBE (ethyl-tertio-butyl-ether), biogas, biomethanol, biodimethylether, and bio-oil. The list of biofuels usually also includes new fuels such as hydrogen. See Commission Communication on alternative fuels for road transportation and on a set of measures to promote the use of biofuels, COM(2001)547, 5.

tants than fossil fuels. Consequently, renewables offer a substantial means of reducing CO_2, but also SO_2 and NO_x emissions associated with, for example, electricity generation.[19]

Nonetheless, renewable energy sources are not completely environmentally neutral. While having major benefits in terms of emissions of air pollutants, for example, certain renewable energy sources raise other environmental problems. The negative side-effects of wind energy have received attention, for example. The concerns relate mainly to noise pollution, visual intrusion, land use, and bird strike.[20] Still, improved technology and careful site selection can significantly reduce the negative impact of wind farms. As for hydropower, a distinction must be made between small and large-scale hydropower. Significant environmental problems are associated, in particular, with the latter.[21] It is not surprising therefore that some discussion exists as to whether large-scale hydro can truly be regarded as a renewable energy source. Even more controversial is the question whether the category 'biomass', generally also regarded as a renewable, includes (in addition to energy crops and agricultural and forestry wastes) energy derived from landfill gas and waste incineration. Most controversial, however, is the suggestion to include nuclear energy under the term 'renewable energy sources'.

iii. Nuclear Energy

Although nuclear energy is an interesting energy source in terms of emissions of air pollutants and, in addition, the probability of accidents in EU plants is very low, it does give rise to a serious and very real waste problem. Long-term storage of radioactive waste remains problematic, as long as no proper solution has been found.[22]

iv. Combined Heat and Power (CHP)

CHP uses the 45 per cent to 70 per cent of energy that is lost as heat in conventional thermal power plants. Not only does it avoid the negative environmental impact of additional heat generation but, apparently, the total efficiency of CHP systems is higher than that of separately generated heat and electricity.[23]

[19] Whereas solid fuels, oil, and gas are 'carbon-intensive' in terms of their impact on climate change, renewables are 'low- or zero-carbon' energy sources. In particular, it has been estimated that, by 2020, up to 40% of current energy-related CO_2 emissions could be avoided that way.

[20] OECD and International Energy Agency, n. 14 above, 61–6. See also Cross *et al.*, n. 6 above, 1032.

[21] In particular, the impact on ecosystems (loss or change of habitat, change in water quality, change in flow characteristics, disruption of spawning migration, etc.) of the large plants is troublesome. OECD and International Energy Agency, n. 14 above, 73–9. See also EEA, *Environmental Signals 2000—European Environment Agency Regular Indicator Report* (Copenhagen: EEA, 2000), 23 and EEA, *Environmental Signals 2001—European Environment Agency Regular Indicator Report* (Copenhagen: EEA, 2001), 47.

[22] EEA, *Europe's Environment—The Dobris Assessment, Chapter 19—Energy* (Copenhagen: EEA, 2001), 3.

[23] EEA, *Environmental Signals 2001—European Environment Agency Regular Indicator Report* (Copenhagen: EEA, 2001), 46.

v. Energy Efficiency and Energy Conservation

The above clearly indicates that the environmental effects of activities relating to energy use vary substantially, depending on source. Environment impacts also differ depending on the efficiency of the technologies employed to generate and supply energy (operating efficiency of power-generating installations, and efficiency of energy distribution networks). Apart from efficiency *on the supply side*, negative effects can be controlled by encouraging efficient use of energy *on the demand side* (energy for transport, households, and industry). In this context, it is useful to employ the terms and definitions that the European Environmental Agency (EEA) proposed.[24] It defines '*energy efficiency*' as 'a measure of the overall efficiency of providing energy services, i.e. the efficiency with which energy is produced from primary resources, transformed into useful forms, delivered to end users and consumers'. The term '*energy conservation*' is usually reserved for 'energy saving on the demand side'. In what follows, the expressions 'energy saving' and 'rational use of energy' will be used as synonyms for the term 'energy conservation'.

Finally, it should be observed that negative effects on the environment originating from the generation of energy might also be controlled by way of pollution control technologies.

D. Main Features of Secondary Energy Law

i. Introduction

In this section, all legislation that is primarily aimed at furthering energy objectives will be described and analysed. This includes legislation that is exclusively aimed at achieving the energy objectives; legislation that predominantly pursues, along with energy objectives, environmental or other non-energy objectives as ancillary objectives, and legislation that simultaneously pursues one or more energy-related objectives, and one or more other (e.g. environmental) objectives.

ii. Economic Policy Measures—Oil Crisis Measures

Following the 1973 oil crisis, various efforts were made at the Community level to reduce its dependence on external energy sources. Part of these efforts consisted of the establishment of a crisis mechanism by way of a set of directives based on Article 103(4) EEC (Economic Policy).[25] Some of the action in this context preceded the oil crisis of 1973, which mainly concerned the obligation for Member States to maintain minimum stocks of certain energy products. There were measures such as restrictions on the use of natural gas and petroleum products, the monitoring of intra-Community trade in crude

[24] EEA, *Europe's Environment—The Dobris Assessment, Chapter 19—Energy* (Copenhagen: EEA, 2001), Box 19A.

[25] See also Kapteyn and Verloren van Themaat, n. 9 above, 758–9 and Kapteyn and Verloren van Themaat, n. 7 above, 1231.

oil and petroleum products, a common target for reducing consumption of petroleum products, and use of substitute fuel components in petrol.[26] Very few of these legislative acts contained an environmental element, although some had certain indirect environmental benefits, such as Decision 77/706/EEC on the Setting of a Community Target for a Reduction in the Consumption of Primary Sources of Energy in the Event of Difficulties in the Supply of Crude Oil and Petroleum Products,[27] which set a common target for reducing the consumption of primary energy sources in order to lessen the effects of energy supply difficulties. The directives laying down restrictions on the use of natural gas and petroleum products in power stations provide for an exception to the restrictions for 'special reasons relating to the protection of the environment' (Article 1(3) fourth indent and Article 1(2) fifth indent respectively). Although the environmental impact of these early Community acts will be discussed in greater detail below (Section IV.B.*i*), it may already be observed here that, in order to prevent or lessen the impact of energy supply difficulties, and thus improve security of energy supplies, the Community also adopted more structural measures. These are specifically aimed at encouraging the rational use of energy over the years. Directive 78/170/EEC on the Performance of Heat Generators for Space Heating and the Production of Hot Water in New or Existing Non-Industrial Buildings and on the Insulation of Heat and Domestic Hot-Water Distribution in New Non-industrial Buildings was such a measure.[28] Together with the other harmonizing legislation designed to promote rational use of energy, this measure will be discussed further below in Section III.D.*vi*. In addition, reference should be made to the support programmes for technological development in the hydrocarbons sector, discussed below in Section III.D.*viii*. Specific programmes designed to promote the rational use of energy—the SAVE programmes—are considered to be part of environmental policy. They are not examples of integration therefore. Consequently, they will not be discussed in this chapter further.

[26] Dir. 68/414/EEC Imposing an Obligation on Member States of the EEC to Maintain Minimum Stocks of Crude Oil and/or Petroleum Products [1968] OJ L308/14; Dec. 68/416/EEC on the Conclusion and Implementation of Individual Agreements Between Governments Relating to the Obligation of Member States to Maintain Minimum Stocks of Crude Oil and/or Petroleum Products [1968] OJ L308/19; Dir. 75/339/EEC Obliging the Member States to Maintain Minimum Stocks of Fossil Fuel at Thermal Power Stations [1975] OJ L153/35; Dir. 73/238/EEC on Measures to Mitigate the Effects of Difficulties in the Supply of Crude Oil and Petroleum Products [1973] OJ L228/1; Dir. 75/404/EEC on the Restriction of the Use of Natural Gas in Power Stations [1975] OJ L178/24; Dir. 75/405/EEC Concerning the Restriction of the Use of Petroleum Products in Power Stations [1975] OJ L178/26; Dec. 77/186/EEC on the Exporting of Crude Oil and Petroleum Products from One Member State to Another in the Event of Supply Difficulties [1977] OJ L61/23; Dec. 77/706/EEC on the Setting of a Community Target for a Reduction in the Consumption of Primary Sources of Energy in the Event of Difficulties in the Supply of Crude Oil and Petroleum Products [1977] OJ L292/9; Dir. 85/536/EEC on Crude-Oil Savings Through the Use of Substitute Fuel Components in Petrol [1985] OJ L334/20.

[27] [1977] OJ L292/9.

[28] [1978] OJ L52/32.

Now, an overview follows of the legislation adopted in order to further another one of the main objectives of the EC energy policy, the establishment of the internal energy markets.

iii. Market Operation

The White Paper, 'An Energy Policy for the European Union', called market integration 'the central, determining factor in the Community's energy policy'.[29] The underlying force of the market liberalization process is, reportedly, the need for economic efficiency in the energy sector, which should increase competitiveness of the European economy as a whole, and thus eventually growth of living standards.[30] For these purposes, the Community successively adopted Directive 94/22/EC on the Conditions for Granting and Using Authorizations for the Prospection, Exploration and Production of Hydrocarbons (Hydrocarbons Licensing Directive),[31] Directive 96/92/EC Concerning Common Rules for the Internal Market in Electricity (Internal Electricity Market Directive),[32] and Directive 98/30/EC Concerning Common Rules for the Internal Market in Natural Gas (Internal Gas Market Directive).[33] However, before turning to the content of these directives, some words must be devoted to the directives that started the process towards the establishment of internal energy markets, the so-called transit directives.

The Transit Directives

In 1990 and in 1991 respectively, Directive 90/547/EEC on the Transit of Electricity Through Transmission Grids (Electricity Transit Directive)[34] and Directive 91/296/EEC on the Transit of Natural Gas Through Grids (Gas Transit Directive)[35] were adopted. These Directives are both aimed at facilitating the electricity and gas transfers between grids,[36] where transport is situated within the EC, and involves the crossing of intra-Community frontiers. To this end, both directives set out certain conditions to be fulfilled in relation to the transfers. However, the Directives do not require Member States to establish

[29] COM(95)682, 3.

[30] Commission Communication on Single Market and Environment COM(99)263, 14 and Commission Communication on Completing the Internal Energy Market COM(2001)125, 2. As Hancher observes, with the establishment of the internal energy market, the Commission hoped to promote both intra-fuel and inter-fuel competition. This entails, for example, that French electricity should be able to compete with electricity produced in Germany, but also that gas for the generation of electricity should be able to compete more freely with other fuels (Hancher, n. 8 above, 477).

[31] [1994] OJ L164/3.

[32] [1997] OJ L27/20.

[33] [1998] OJ L204/1.

[34] [1990] OJ L313/30.

[35] [1991] OJ L147/37.

[36] Respectively high-voltage transmission grids, exclusive electricity distribution grids, and high-pressure transmission pipelines.

mandatory open access to grids.[37] In fact, it has been indicated that the Electricity Transit Directive did little more than formalize existing arrangements to manage exchanges between existing utilities.[38] As for references to the Community's environmental objectives, the preambles of both directives simply recall that, in completing the internal energy market, attention should be given to the objective of security of supply but also to objectives of environmental protection, in particular, in the form of environmentally compatible energy production methods.

Upstream Hydrocarbons (Oil and Gas) Sector

The first attempts to tackle the problematic conditions for access to the exploration and production of hydrocarbons (upstream oil and gas sector) were made in the context of the so-called Directive 90/531/EEC on the Procurement Procedures of Entities Operating in the Water, Energy, Transport and Telecommunications Sectors (Utilities Directive) of 1990.[39] However, the limited provisions in this legislation could not remove all barriers to entry created by national licensing systems.[40] Thus, in 1994, the Hydrocarbons Licensing Directive was adopted. The Preamble indicates that it is aimed at 'the greater integration, free from barriers to trade, of the internal energy market with a view to improving security of supply, reducing costs and improving economic competitiveness' (Preamble (2)). Indeed, this framework directive lays down certain general principles in order to ensure that the procedures for granting authorizations (licences) for the prospection, exploration, and production of hydrocarbons are open to all interested entities, possessing the necessary capabilities (Preamble (7) and Article 3) and, that the authorizations are granted on the basis of objective, published criteria (Articles 4 and 5). When granting an authorization, one of the procedures mentioned in Article 3(2) must be followed. On the one hand, authorizations relating to geographical areas that have been opened for prospection, exploration, and production (so-called 'open areas') can only be refused on the basis of the criteria in Article 5. No reference is made to environmental criteria in this provision. On the other hand, detailed obligations and conditions for the use of a specific authorization must be based on the need to ensure the proper performance of the activities in the relevant area (Article 6(1)), or, may be imposed if justified by a limited number of concerns, including, interestingly, environmental protection, protection of 'biological resources', and 'planned

[37] See on this issue, F. von Burchard and L. Eckert, *Natural Gas and EU Energy Law* (Baden-Baden: Nomos, 1995), 58 and D.S. MacDougall and T.W. Wälde (eds.), *European Community Energy Law—selected topics* (London/Dordrecht/Boston: Graham & Trotman/Martinus Nijhoff, 1994), 100.

[38] Cross *et al.*, n. 6 above, 284.

[39] [1990] OJ L297/1. In 1993, codified as Directive 93/38/EC Co-ordinating the Procurement Procedures of Entities Operating in the Water, Energy, Transport and Telecommunications Sectors [1993] OJ L199/84.

[40] Cross *et al.*, n. 6 above, 295–6.

management of hydrocarbon resources (for example the rate at which hydrocarbons are depleted or the optimization of their recovery)' (Article 6(2)).

In other words, Member States are not allowed completely to refuse licences relating to 'open areas' on the basis of environmental concerns. However, they can subject the exercise of the activities of prospecting, exploring for and producing of hydrocarbons to 'environmental conditions'. It is important to remember also that Member States retain the right to determine the areas within their territory to be made available for the exercise of the activities covered (i.e. retention of sovereign rights of Member States over the hydrocarbons resources on their territories) (Article 2(1)). In other words, Member States keep the discretion to determine which areas are opened up, and thus, subject to the rules of the Directive, which remain closed. The reasons why certain areas should remain closed are unlimited, and may therefore relate to environmental concerns. If a Member State wishes to refuse granting licences in relation to a certain area, it should keep that area closed for exploitation.[41]

Internal Electricity Market

The Preamble of the Internal Electricity Market Directive indicates that this Directive is aimed at gradually establishing the internal electricity market 'in order to increase efficiency in the production, transmission and distribution of this product, while reinforcing security of supply and the competitiveness of the European economy and respecting environmental protection' (Preamble (4)). It is also stressed that proposals for improving the operation of the internal electricity market will be necessary in the future, but no specific dates for further market liberalization are specified. The Directive sets out common rules for the organization of the sector, including rules on public service obligations (Article 3), generation or production (the construction of new generating capacity is opened up to competition) (Articles 4–6), transmission (Articles 7–9), and distribution (Articles 10–12) of electricity. An independent transmission system operator and an independent distribution operator must be appointed. Further rules concern unbundling and transparency of accounts (Articles 13–15) and access to the system (Articles 16–22). Article 19 provides that Member States must open up their national markets, be it gradually.[42]

As for environmental provisions, the following should be observed. First, it is provided that Member States may impose public service obligations relating to,

[41] On the basis of this provision, the Netherlands, for example, decided to exclude from licensing an area in the Waddenzee. Its decision was motivated by environmental concerns. See Article 2a Wet opsporing delfstoffen (1967), *Staatsblad* 258, as amended by Wet van 18 Mar. 1996 (1996) *Staatsblad* 199 and Explanatory Memorandum Wet 18 Mar. 1996, *Kamerstukken* II, 1994/95, 24078, NO. 3, 20. See also the *Biesbosch* case: Rechtbank Breda, 6 Nov. 2000 (2001) *Tijdschrift voor Milieu & Recht*, 64.

[42] The Directive sets minimum targets for market opening that correspond to 30% of domestic consumption in 2000 and 35% in 2003. Initial data on the implementation of this requirement showed that the majority of Member States had gone further than legally required in 2000. See Commission Communication on Completing the Internal Energy Market COM(2001)125, 4.

inter alia, environmental protection (Article 3(2)).[43] Secondly, for the construction of new generating capacity, Member States can choose between a licensing or a tendering procedure (Article 4). Pursuant to Article 5(1)(b), the criteria which Member States must fix when they opt for the licensing procedure may relate to 'protection of the environment'. Thirdly, Article 8(3) and Article 11(3) provide that Member States may require the transmission system operator and the distribution system operator, when dispatching generating installations, to give priority to generating installations using renewable energy sources or waste or producing combined heat and power. In addition, the distribution system operator is required to maintain a secure, reliable and efficient electricity distribution system in its area, 'with due regard for the environment' (Article 11(1)).

Internal Gas Market

The Internal Gas Market Directive is aimed at establishing the internal market in natural gas (Preamble (1), (3), and (5)). It seeks to do so by laying down common rules for the organization of the natural gas sector, including liquefied natural gas (LNG) (Articles 3–5) and the criteria and procedures applicable to the granting of authorizations for transmission, distribution, supply, and storage of natural gas (Articles 6–11). Further provisions relate to the unbundling and transparency of accounts (which are less far-reaching than the corresponding provisions in the Electricity Directive) (Articles 12–13) and network access (procedure of negotiated access or regulated access; equally less far-reaching) (Articles 15–16). The minimum targets for market opening are set at 20 per cent of the total annual gas consumption in 2000, 28 per cent in 2003, and 33 per cent in 2018 (Article 18).[44]

Just like the Internal Electricity Market Directive, the Internal Gas Market Directive allows Member States to introduce public service obligations which may relate to, *inter alia*, environmental protection (Article 3(2)).[45] Other environmental provisions relate to the following. Each transmission, storage, and/or LNG undertaking must operate, maintain, and develop secure, reliable, and efficient facilities, 'with due regard to the environment' (Article 7(1)). Each distribution undertaking has the same obligation: that is, to operate, maintain, and develop a secure, reliable and efficient system, with due regard to the environment (Article 10(1)). Finally, Article 23(2) requires that Member States apply certain objectives (fair and open access, achieving a competitive market,

[43] See also Preamble (13): 'Whereas for some Member States the imposition of public service obligations may be necessary to ensure security of supply and consumer and *environmental protection*, which ... free competition ... [alone], cannot necessarily guarantee' (emphasis added).

[44] Initial data on the implementation of this requirement showed that the majority of Member States had gone further than legally required in 2000. See Commission Communication on Completing the Internal Energy Market COM(2001)125, 4.

[45] See also Preamble (12): 'Whereas for some Member States the imposition of public service obligations may be necessary to ensure security of supply and consumer and environmental protection, which ... free competition ... [alone], cannot necessarily guarantee'.

avoiding abuse of dominant position), while taking account of such concerns as 'environmental protection', when they provide for access to upstream pipeline networks by eligible natural gas undertakings and customers.

Further Steps Towards Liberalization

Even though the above-discussed internal market directives require Member States to restructure their energy markets significantly, these are framework directives, which leave Member States substantial discretion as to the manner in which they do so.[46] For certain matters, such as how to bring about network access, several options are available. As a result, however, the state of liberalization varies significantly in the Member States.[47] Moreover, sometimes the vague wording of the legislation has led to interpretation problems.[48] In order to clarify some issues and remedy shortcomings in the current regime, as well as complete the liberalization process, the Commission presented a package of new proposals. This concerns, in particular, a proposal for a directive amending the Internal Electricity Market Directive and the Internal Gas Market Directive, supplemented by a proposal for a regulation on conditions for access to the network for cross-border exchanges in electricity.[49] In these proposals, fundamental issues, such as effective unbundling, third-party access, the importance of a regulator, and the content of the public service objectives are re-examined. Besides the possibility of environmental service obligations, the amendment would introduce an extra environmental provision in both the Internal Electricity Market Directive and the Internal Gas Market Directive. It would, in particular, require Member States to implement 'appropriate' environmental measures (proposed Article 3(3)).

It should be noted that, at its November 2002 meeting, the Transport Council reached an agreement on a final date for complete liberalization. Business users as well as domestic users should be free to choose energy suppliers, respectively, by 2004 and 2007.[50]

In summary, besides strengthening the Community's competitive position, most measures discussed above indicate that the opening of the respective energy market should reinforce security of energy supply. In addition, it is sometimes

[46] See also Cross *et al.*, n. 6 above, 220.

[47] See data on market opening in Annex 1 of Commission Communication on Recent Progress with Building the Internal Electricity Market COM(2000)297 and Commission Communication on Completing the Internal Energy Market COM(2001)125, 4–5.

[48] For the internal electricity market legislation see: Cross *et al.*, n. 6 above, 301–8.

[49] Proposal for a Directive Amending Directives 96/92/EC and 98/30/EC Concerning Common Rules for the Internal Market in Electricity and Natural Gas COM(2001)125, and Proposal for a Regulation on Conditions for Access to the Network for Cross-Border Exchanges in Electricity COM(2001)125.

[50] Transport Council Meeting, 25 November 2002, press release number 14337/02. In the meantime, the proposals have been through Parliament for a second reading and the Parliament amendments have been approved by the Council and the Commission (*Bulletin Quotidien Europe*, 2003/6, 1.4.65 and COM(2003)429).

provided that the process should occur while 'respecting the environment'. This intention is translated by means of the incorporation of environmental provisions, allowing, for example, public service obligations for environmental reasons.

iv. Price Transparency Regulation

Directive 90/377/EEC Concerning a Community Procedure to Improve the Transparency of Gas and Electricity Prices requires Member States to ensure that undertakings which supply electricity or gas to industrial end-users regularly communicate certain price-related information to the Statistical Office of the EC (SOEC).[51] The information relates to the prices and terms of sale, the price systems in use, and the breakdown of consumers and corresponding volumes of consumption. With this legislation, the Commission hoped to increase energy price transparency and thus ensure effective competition.[52] However, some authors have questioned the link between price transparency and effective competition. They observe that, on the contrary, uncertainty about the future behaviour of competitors can be a precondition for effective competition.[53] In addition, it is pointed out that price transparency can have a negative effect on the competitive situation of gas and electricity in relation to substitutive/alternative energies that are not subject to any transparency provisions. It seems that Directive 90/377/EEC presupposes the existence of such corresponding transparency regimes, since its preamble indicates that the information given pursuant to it will also enable comparisons with other energy sources, in particular oil, coal, fossil, and renewable energy sources.

In fact, a separate price transparency regime has existed for the oil sector since 1976. Directive 76/491/EEC Concerning Information and Consultation on the Prices of Crude Oil and Petroleum Products in the Community[54] was repealed and replaced, in 1999, by Council Decision 1999/280/EC Regarding a Community Procedure for Information and Consultation on Crude Oil Supply Costs and the Consumer Prices of Petroleum Products,[55] which sets out the current regime. Due to this transparency regime, it does not seem that competition between natural gas and oil, for example, is distorted.[56] However, no corresponding regimes exist for energy sources such as renewables.

[51] [1990] OJ L185/16.

[52] Apparently, the Commission pointed out that 'when energy prices are not transparent, they are capable of containing elements of State Aid unauthorized by the Commission or covering up anti-competitive practices by undertakings in breach of Community rules on competition'. See Cross, *et al.*, n. 6 above, 281.

[53] Von Burchard and Eckert, n. 37 above, 32.

[54] [1976] OJ L140/4.

[55] [1999] OJ L110/8. Also relevant in this context is Regulation 2964/95 introducing registration for crude oil imports and deliveries in the Community [1995] OJ L310/5.

[56] See also von Burchard and Eckert, n. 37 above, 37.

v. *Fiscal Harmonization*

Fiscal harmonization of the energy sector has remained very limited up to now. Energy products are heavily taxed in the EU, but the tax varies from product to product and from Member State to Member State.[57] To date, only excise duties on mineral oils have been harmonized to a certain extent. Efforts to introduce more harmonization, currently in the form of a proposal for restructuring the Community framework for the taxation of energy products, have been blocked in the Council. Below, the limited existing harmonization will be discussed as well as the proposals for further harmonization. The effects of both the current and the proposed tax regime on the realization of the Community's environmental objectives will be discussed more elaborately in the section on integration failures and efforts. It should be recalled in this context that, for areas where no secondary legislation applies, national legislation is reviewed against the background of relevant primary law, in particular Articles 23–4 and Article 90 EC.

Excise Duties on Mineral Oils

Excise duties on mineral oils have been harmonized to a limited extent.[58] In particular, Directive 92/82/EEC on the Approximation of the Rates of Excise Duties on Mineral Oils[59] introduces minimum rates of excise duty on mineral oils as a function of the use of each oil (fuel, industrial and commercial use, heating), while Directive 92/81/EEC on the Harmonization of the Structures of Excise Duties on Mineral Oils[60] defines the taxable products, and provides for required or possible exemptions and reductions. Despite the fact that, at first sight, this legislation seems to have a broad scope (in view of the definition of 'mineral oils' in Directive 92/81/EEC), certain important categories of hydrocarbons are not covered by the Community excise duty. Thus, pursuant to Article 2(3) of Directive 92/81/EEC, coal, lignite, peat, or other similar solid hydrocarbons and natural gas are not covered. The Directive allows Member States to apply to the products covered whichever rates they want as long as they exceed the minima. In this respect, it is interesting to point out that the Directive provides for the application of different rates of duty for different uses of the products, but it does not provide for different rates for different grades or types of the same product. For this purpose, a Member State must request an exemption

[57] Green Paper, 'Towards a European Strategy for the Security of Energy Supply' COM(2000) 769, 50.

[58] Dir. 92/82/EEC on the Approximation of the Rates of Excise Duties on Mineral Oils [1992] OJ L316/19 and Dir. 92/81/EEC on the Harmonization of the Structures of Excise Duties on Mineral Oils [1992] OJ L316/12. See also Dir. 92/12/EEC on the General Arrangements for Products Subject to Excise Duty and on the Holding, Movement and Monitoring of Such Products [1992] OJ L76/1. For comments on this legislation see: W. de Wit, *Nationale milieubelastingen en het EG-Verdrag* (Deventer: Kluwer, 1997), 90.

[59] [1992] OJ L316/19.

[60] [1992] OJ L316/12.

under Article 8(4) of the Directive. The legislation provides for several other types of exemptions and reductions.

Some exemptions are compulsory while others are optional for Member States. First, on the basis of Article 8(1) Directive 92/81/EEC, Member States are required to exempt completely, for example, mineral oils used as fuels for commercial air services and commercial navigation in Community waters. This exemption is, in other words, compulsory. Secondly, Article 8(2) provides for total or partial optional exemptions or reductions, *inter alia*, for mineral oils used for the production of electricity, and in CHP plants, for navigation on inland waterways, in the field of passenger and goods transport by rail, and in the field of pilot projects for the technological development of more environmentally friendly products (in particular in relation to fuels from renewable resources). Thirdly and finally, Article 8(4) provides for the possibility that the Council, acting unanimously on a proposal from the Commission, authorizes Member States to introduce further exemptions or reductions 'for specific policy considerations'. Article 8(5) provides that the Commission must re-evaluate the exemptions or reductions granted in terms of their compatibility with the Community's objectives of fair competition, good operation of the internal market, and environmental protection. In any event, the whole situation with regard to the exemptions and reductions had to be reviewed by the Council on the basis of a Commission report before 31 December 1996 (Article 8(6) EC).

The Commission did in fact produce a report in November 1996.[61] It gives a good overview of the exemptions and reductions granted to Member States on the basis of Article 8(4), and thus also of the 'specific policy considerations' which they have tried to achieve in this way.[62] In its report, the Commission neatly divides the exemptions and reductions granted into categories according to the concerns they relate to. A first grouping relates to transport issues, in particular, in relation to the air transport sector and the inland water navigation sector. A second category of exemptions/reductions was granted for industrial and commercial purposes and covers, for example, exemptions on fuel used in alumina production. Third and fourth areas relate to environmental concerns (e.g. differentiated rates to encourage use of cleaner fuels, e.g. low-sulphur diesel)

[61] Commission Report under Art. 8(6) of Dir. 92/81/EEC on the situation with regard to the exemptions or reductions for specific policy considerations as set out in Art. 8(4) of Dir. 92/81/EEC and concerning the obligatory exemption of mineral oils used as fuel for the purpose of air navigation other than private pleasure flying and the exemptions or reductions possible for navigation on inland waterways other than for private pleasure craft as set out in Art. 8(1) b and 8(2) b of the same Directive COM(96)549.

[62] Dec. 92/510/EEC (i.e. the Council's first decision in this matter, granting all Member States individual and specific derogations), Dec. 93/697/EC (relating to Belgium and Luxembourg, Greece, Italy, and Portugal), Dec. 95/585/EC (Belgium, Luxembourg, Finland, Austria, and Denmark), 96/273/EC (Italy, Austria, Sweden, and the UK), 96/418/EC (Ireland), Dec. 97/91/ EC (France), Dec. 97/92/EC (Sweden), Dec. 97/93/EC (France, Portugal, Greece, and Spain), and Dec. 97/136/EC (Belgium, Denmark, France, Italy, Ireland, Luxembourg, Austria, Portugal, Finland, Sweden, and the UK and Northern Ireland).

and regional policy aims (e.g. derogations for fuel consumed in particular regions). There is also a fifth and final category, entitled 'Other policy', e.g. derogations for fuel used by the armed forces, in vehicles used by disabled persons, in lighthouses, or in pumps used for drainage of flooded land and in desalination plants. As a result of its evaluation of these exemptions and reductions, the Commission proposed and the Council later adopted a new decision in which the previous authorizations to apply certain exemptions or reductions were extended, while certain others were abolished as of January 1998.[63] In addition, the Commission suggested certain interesting changes to the provisions of Directive 92/81/EEC, such as the suggestion to make the optional exemption in Article 8(2)(b) to the rate for fuel used for navigation on inland waterways compulsory. The various exemptions and reductions granted in this way over the years as well as the various review processes of the Commission and their consequences will be analysed in greater detail below, specifically with regard to their environmental relevance (sections IV.B.*ii* and IV.C.*iii*).

Biofuels

Despite the fact that they are not explicitly listed as fuels that are covered by the tax regime for mineral oils, biofuels or alternative fuels (such as bioethanol, biomethanol, etc.) nevertheless fall under the scope of this regime. The reason why is as follows. Article 2(3) of Directive 92/81/EEC provides that, in addition to the taxable products explicitly enumerated in the first paragraph, any product used as a motor fuel shall be taxed as such. The rate to be charged is that of the equivalent motor fuel (Article 2(2) of Directive 92/81/EEC). Several proposals aimed at changing this situation have been put forward.[64] The latest fits into a comprehensive strategy of the Commission aimed at promoting the use of these kind of fuels. The Commission envisages using both regulatory and fiscal instruments in this context.[65] The fiscal instrument consists of an amendment of Directive 92/81/EEC.[66] If adopted, this amendment would make it possible for Member States to reduce excise duties on biofuels (pure or blended) when used for heating or as motor fuels.

[63] Dec. 97/425/EC (general decision), repealed and replaced the previous Decisions in this field. It was in its turn repealed and replaced by Dec. 1999/880/EC (general decision), which was repealed and replaced by Dec. 2001/224/EC (general decision). The latter also replaces Dec. 1999/804/EC (France), Dec. 2000/266/EC (the Netherlands), Dec. 2000/433/EC (Germany), Dec. 2000/434/EC (UK and Northern Ireland), Dec. 2000/446/EC (Italy), and Dec. 2000/719/EC (France). Besides the general Dec. 2001/224/EC, there are also several decisions authorizing specific Member States, *inter alia*: Italy (Dec. 2001/226/EC), France (Dec. 2001/227/EC), the Netherlands (Dec. 2001/229/EC and Dec. 2002/263/EC), Denmark (Dec. 2002/264), etc. See also below sect. IV.C.*iii*.

[64] COM(92)36, amended Proposals COM(94)147 and COM(2001)547.

[65] The proposal using a regulatory instrument has been adopted as Dir. 2003/30/EC on the Promotion of the Use of Biofuels or other Renewable Fuels for Transport [2003] OJ L123/42. Its legal basis is Art. 175 EC.

[66] Dir. amending Dir. 92/81/EEC with Regard to the Possibility of Applying a Reduced Rate of Excise Duty on Certain Mineral Oils Containing Biofuels and on Biofuels COM(2001)547.

Carbon Dioxide Tax Turned Tax on Energy Products

The legislation described above resulted in little actual harmonization. As the Commission itself reported, excise duties on mineral oils vary significantly between Member States.[67] Two factors lie at the basis of this. First, reference may be made to the limited scope of existing harmonizing legislation, which is limited to certain mineral oils. No comparable harmonization has been introduced for competing energy products. Apparently, some Member States have established taxation for competing products, such as natural gas and coal, on their own initiative.[68] Secondly, the minimum rates laid down in Directive 92/82/EEC have not kept pace with the rates actually set by the Member States. In particular, the actual national rates of duty on motor fuels are a lot higher than the minimum Community rates.[69] These two issues have been addressed in the Commission's 1997 proposal for a common system for the taxation of energy products.[70] First of all, this proposal extends the current harmonization system for mineral oils to other competing energy products, including electricity, natural gas, and coal. Except for electricity, only the use of these products as motor fuel and heating fuel is taxed, not their use as raw materials or in chemical reductions or for electrolysis. Secondly, the proposal provides for the gradual increase of the minimum rates of excise duty.[71] The proposal is controversial, however, especially because of fears that a Community-wide high tax on energy will put the Community industry at a competitive disadvantage vis-à-vis third countries.[72] That is why the proposal provides for measures to reduce the tax burden on energy-intensive firms.

It is such concerns that 'killed' the previous Commission proposal in this field. Indeed, the 1997 proposal on a common system for energy taxation was not the first attempt of the Commission to introduce more fiscal harmonization. In 1991, the Commission proposed to introduce a common so-called carbon dioxide/energy tax.[73] The proposal had a dual purpose: on the one hand, fiscal harmonization, on the other hand, attainment of the 'CO_2-stabilization target' (i.e. stabilizing the CO_2 emissions in the Community at 1990 levels by the year 2000).[74] The

67 White Paper, An Energy Policy for the European Union COM(95)682, 18.

68 ibid

69 Commission report COM(95)285 final, 31; White Paper COM(95)682, 18 and Green Paper, 'Towards a European Strategy for the Security of Energy Supply' COM(2000)769, 51.

70 Proposal for a Council Directive Restructuring the Community Framework for the Taxation of Energy Products COM(97)30.

71 In fact, in its 1995 report on the rates of excise duties, the Commission had already proposed increasing the minimum rates for heating fuels while at the same time pointing out that this would require the scope of the duty to be extended to products not yet covered (COM(95)285, 30).

72 Kapteyn and Verloren van Themaat, n. 7 above, 1234. See A. Gonzalez-Calatayud, 'Substantive European Community Environmental Law: Atmospheric Pollution' (2002) *Yearbook of European Environmental Law*, 302–3.

73 Proposal for a Directive Introducing a Tax on Carbon Dioxide Emissions and Energy COM(92)226 (amended proposal COM(95)172).

74 See also Cross *et al.*, n. 6 above, 268 and de Wit, n. 58 above, 44.

tax base consisted of two components: it would be based on CO_2 emissions and on energy use (the calorific value of energy sources). The scope of the (proposed) tax was confined to motor and heating fuels. Raw materials were excluded, as were renewable energy sources (i.e. wind power, solar energy, biomass, biofuels, and small hydroelectric installations (less than 10 MW)). Special treatment (graduated tax reductions and conditional exemptions) was envisaged for energy-intensive firms in order to safeguard their international competitiveness.[75] The proposal also provided for tax incentives for investments in energy saving and CO_2 abatement. The tax was to be additional to existing harmonized excise duties, and it was to be levied at the stage of consumption in its final form (thus, imported products would have been liable for the tax). However, political agreement on this proposal turned out to be too difficult.[76]

In summary, it may be observed that fiscal harmonization relating to the energy sector has been limited to legislation on excise duties for mineral oils. Plans to extend this fiscal regime to other energy products, and to progressively increase the tax rates, have not been realized yet.

vi. Technical Harmonization

In this section, legislation setting out fuel quality specifications will be discussed, as it is considered energy law than rather environmental law: it is not solely or mainly aimed at furthering environmental objectives. In particular, it is equally designed to ensure that fuels, which comply with relevant requirements, can move freely in the internal market. Divergent national (technical) standards for fuels constitute trade barriers, which hamper the establishment and functioning of the internal market. It is national measures, which are aimed at furthering environmental objectives, that make these Community measures necessary. These EC measures are therefore different from 'environmental measures', such as Directive 88/609/EEC on the Limitation of Emissions of Certain Pollutants into the Air from Large Combustion Plants (Large Combustion Plants Directive),[77] that have 'implications for intra-Community trade' but that are not 'directly related' to both trade and environmental objectives.[78] The latter are discussed under the heading 'secondary energy-specific environmental legislation'.

Similar observations apply to legislation setting out energy efficiency requirements and energy labelling standards. Whereas early legislation was mainly aimed at eliminating technical barriers, the environmental aspect quickly became equally important. In particular, since the 1990s, the various directives usually

[75] At first, the introduction of this Community tax was conditional on other major industrial countries introducing a similar tax. This so-called conditionality clause disappeared in the amended proposal, however.

[76] See for the political process behind the proposal: Matláry, n. 8 above, 70.

[77] [1988] OJ L336/1, as amended by Dir. 2001/80/EC [2001] OJ L309/1.

[78] Hancher, n. 8 above, 501.

refer to the objective, in Article 175(1) EC, to ensure a prudent and rational use of natural resources as well as the Community's commitments in relation to climate change. The difference between this legislation and the legislation on fuel quality standards is that this legislation has been designed also, especially initially, to contribute to the objective of security of energy supply. In other words, the measures have three main objectives: eliminating trade barriers, environmental protection, and security of energy supply.

Harmonization of Fuel Quality Standards

A series of directives have progressively restricted the sulphur and lead contents of certain liquid fuels. The sulphur content of fuels was initially governed by Directive 75/716/EEC on the Approximation of the Laws of the Member States Relating to the Sulphur Content of Certain Liquid Fuels[79] until Directive 93/12/EEC Relating to the Sulphur Content of Certain Liquid Fuels replaced it.[80] The latter was in its turn amended by Directive 98/70/EC relating to the Quality of Petrol and Diesel Fuels and Amending Council Directive 93/12/EEC (Fuel Quality Directive)[81] (which was based on Article 95 EC (formerly Article 100a EC)) and by Directive 99/32/EC relating to a Reduction in the Sulphur Content of Certain Liquid Fuels and Amending Directive 93/12/EEC (Sulphur Directive)[82] (which, surprisingly, was based on Article 175(1) EC (formerly Article 130s(1) EC)). The Fuel Quality Directive contains environmental specifications, including the permitted sulphur content, for petrol and diesel fuels, that is, motor fuels, marketed within the EU territory.[83] This Directive followed the adoption of the so-called Auto-Oil I Programme, a programme specifically designed to control atmospheric emissions from road transport.[84] In this context, the Fuel Quality Directive complemented the directives setting out vehicle emission standards. A proposed directive is designed to confirm the fuel specifications for 2005, laid down in the Fuel Quality Directive.[85] But in the context of the proposal, the Commission also analysed the need to reduce sulphur levels in petrol and diesel even more.[86] In addition to fuel specifications relating to sulphur content in petrol and diesel, there is the Sulphur Directive, which sets out the maximum sulphur content of heavy fuel oil and gas oil.

[79] [1975] OJ L307/22.

[80] [1993] OJ L074/81.

[81] [1998] OJ L350/58.

[82] [1999] OJ L121/13.

[83] As of 1 Jan. 2000, this Dir. sets the maximum allowed sulphur content for petrol at 150 mg/kg (parts per million) and for diesel at 350 mg/kg. Both of these limits are to be reduced to 50 mg/kg by Jan. 2005.

[84] COM(96)248.

[85] COM(2001)241.

[86] Ultimately, the Commission decided to propose the mandatory *introduction* of sulphur-free petrol and diesel (i.e. petrol and diesel with a maximum sulphur content of 10 mg/kg) in every

Initially, the lead content of petrol was regulated in Directive 78/611/EEC on the Approximation of the Laws of Member States Concerning the Lead Content of Petrol.[87] Directive 85/210/EEC on the Approximation of the Laws of the Member States Concerning the Lead Content of Petrol repealed Directive 78/611/EEC, however, as of 31 December 1985.[88] It further lowered the maximum permitted lead content in (leaded) petrol. And finally, besides the maximum permitted sulphur contents of diesel and petrol, the Fuel Quality Directive also provided for the gradual elimination of leaded petrol by the year 2000 (while repealing Directive 85/210/EEC).[89]

Harmonization of Energy-Efficiency Standards (Including Labelling)

Despite the fact that the requirements discussed here are referred to as 'energy efficiency' standards, they in fact belong to the category of 'energy conservation' measures, as they are designed to save energy on the demand side. They lead to a more rational use of energy or, in other words, they amount to 'demand management of energy'. Directive 78/170/EEC, which sets minimum performance requirements for new heat generators for space heating and/or the production of hot water in non-industrial buildings, was the first (binding) Community act in this field, although various Council recommendations had preceded it.[90] Its Preamble clearly indicates that the standards were adopted so as to promote rational use of energy which, in its turn, was aimed at lessening 'the impact of the supply difficulties referred to in Article 103(4) of the Treaty'. At the same time, it obliquely observed that 'any improvement in the rational use of energy is generally beneficial to the environment'. This Directive is still in force. Over the years, more common energy efficiency standards have been set out in Community legislation. Some of them were adopted under the auspices of the so-called SAVE programmes, designed to promote rational use of energy by (financially) supporting certain Member State action in this field. They are considered to be part of environmental policy, and will therefore not be discussed further. Efficiency standards have been adopted for hot-water boilers, household electric refrigerators, freezers and combinations thereof, and ballasts of fluores-

Member State by Jan. 2005. As of Jan. 2011 (proposed by the Commission)/Jan. 2009 (political agreement by the Environment Council), *the use* of these kinds of fuels is to become mandatory in the Member States. This is, in other words, the end date for full market availability of the fuels in question. The proposal was in fact adopted as Dir. 2003/17/EC Amending Dir. 98/70/EC Relating to the Quality of Petrol and Diesel Fuels [2003] OJ L76/10.

87 [1978] OJ L197/19. It fixed the maximum value for the lead content of petrol between 0.40 and 0.15 g/l (Art. 2).

88 [1985] OJ L96/25.

89 [1998] OJ L350/58.

90 Dir. 78/170/EEC on the Performance of Heat Generators for Space Heating and the Production of Hot Water in New or Existing Non-Industrial Buildings and on the Insulation of Heat and Domestic Hot-Water Distribution in New Non-Industrial Buildings [1978] OJ L52/32, as amended by Dir. 82/885/EEC [1982] OJ L378/19. For some of the early Council recommendations: see Cross *et al.*, n. 6 above, 284.

cent lighting.[91] In addition, agreements have been negotiated with appliance manufacturers containing commitments similar to those in the legislation. In this context, the Commission negotiated an agreement on the reduction of stand-by losses of televisions and video recorders for example.[92] In contrast with the 1978 Directive, which referred to environmental protection only indirectly, the majority of the subsequent directives setting out mandatory energy-efficiency standards explicitly mention the objective to ensure a prudent and rational use of natural resources in Article 175(1) EC, as well as the Community's commitments in relation to climate change, beside the objective to eliminate technical barriers and promote the progressive establishment of the internal market.

Besides common energy-efficiency standards, the Community has adopted common rules on energy-efficiency labelling in order to increase consumers' awareness of the energy-efficiency of products. Such rules exist for a series of household appliances. Directive 92/75/EEC was adopted as a framework directive,[93] and various implementing directives followed.[94] Directive 92/75/EEC requires compulsory labelling of household electrical appliances. Before, Directive 79/530/EEC, and subsequent implementing directives, had tried to harmonize national rules on the labelling of the energy consumption of certain types of household appliances.[95] Based on Article 100 (now Article 94) EC, this Directive was said to be aimed at preventing non-tariff barriers to intra-Community trade, as well as promoting the rational use of energy, which would reduce supply difficulties of oil. As for the environment, the Preamble of Directive 79/530/EEC points to the beneficial environmental side-effects of the measure: 'any improvement in the rational use of the energy is generally beneficial to the environment

[91] Dir. 92/42/EEC on Efficiency Requirements for New Hot-Water Boilers Fired with Liquid or Gaseous Fuels [1992] OJ L167/17; Dir. 96/57/EC on Energy Efficiency Requirements for Household Electric Refrigerators, Freezers and Combinations thereof [1996] OJ L236/36; Dir. 2000/55/EC on Energy Efficiency Requirements for Ballasts for Fluorescent Lighting [2000] OJ L279/33.

[92] See Communication from the Commission, Action Plan to Improve Energy Efficiency in the European Community COM(2000)247, 9.

[93] Dir. 92/75/EEC on the Indication by Labelling and Standard Product Information of the Consumption of Energy and other Resources by Household Appliances [1992] OJ L297/16.

[94] Commission Dir. 94/2/EC implementing Dir. 92/75/EEC with regard to Energy Labelling of Household Electric Refrigerators, Freezers and their Combinations [1994] OJ L45/1; Commission Dir. 95/12/EC implementing Dir. 92/75/EEC with regard to Energy Labelling of Household Washing Machines [1995] OJ L136/1; Commission Dir. 95/13/EC implementing Dir. 92/75/EEC with regard to Energy Labelling of Household Electric Tumble Driers [1995] OJ L136/28; Commission Dir. 96/60/EC implementing Dir. 92/75/EEC with regard to Energy Labelling of Household Combined Washer-Driers [1996] OJ L266/1; Commission Dir. 97/17/EC implementing Dir. 92/75/EEC with regard to Energy Labelling of Household Dishwashers [1997] OJ L118/1; Commission Dir. 98/11/EC implementing Dir. 92/75/EEC with regard to Energy Labelling of Household Lamps [1998] OJ L71/1.

[95] Dir. 79/530/EEC on the Indication by Labelling of the Energy Consumption of Household Appliances [1979] OJ L145/1; Dir. 79/531/EEC Applying to Electric Ovens Dir. 79/530/EEC on the Indication by Labelling of the Energy Consumption of Household Appliances [1979] OJ L145/7.

(Recital (5))'. In contrast with this brief reference, the 1990s legislation refers explicitly to the environmental objectives of Article 175 EC.

vii. Energy Infrastructure

As for the development of trans-European networks (TENs) in the other areas, most notably transport and telecommunications, Community guidelines were adopted for the development of trans-European *energy* networks (TEN-E). Decision 1254/96/EC Laying Down a Series of Guidelines for Trans-European Energy Networks states, in Article 3, that the objectives of the development of TEN-E are:

(1) to allow the effective operation of the internal market (both in general and of the internal energy market, in particular);
(2) to help strengthen economic and social cohesion, and;
(3) to reinforce the security of energy supplies.[96]

To the first objective is added that the rational production, distribution, and utilization of energy resources and the development of renewable energy resources should simultaneously be encouraged. The Decision does not contain further instructions as to how exactly this should be done, except for the provision in Article 6, which contains criteria for determining whether an energy network project may be of 'common interest'. One of the criteria is whether the project displays 'potential economic viability'. Evaluation of economic viability must be based on a cost-benefit analysis, which must take account of all costs and benefits, including those 'in connection with environmental aspects'. Furthermore, a footnote to the indicative list of projects of common interest in the Annex recalls that the Decision is without prejudice to the Environmental Impact Assessment (EIA) of the projects.

In addition to Decision 1254/96/EEC setting out the TEN-E guidelines, Council Decision 96/391/EEC Laying Down a Series of Measures Aimed at Creating a More Favourable Context for the Development of Trans-European Networks in The Energy Sector was adopted.[97] It contains specific rules on cooperation between responsible entities in this area and Member States, as well as provisions on Community financial support for projects. It does not contain any explicit environmental provisions. As for financial support, the Decision provides that it should be granted in accordance with the relevant general regime, as laid down in Regulation (EC) No. 2236/95.[98] This Regulation defines the

[96] [1996] OJ L161/147.
[97] [1996] OJ L161/154.
[98] Reg. (EC) No. 2236/95 Laying Down General Rules for the Granting of Community Financial Aid in the Field of Trans-European Networks [1995] OJ L228/1. While the total TEN budget for the period 1995–9 was set at ECU 2, 345 million, the budget for the period 2000–6 is €4,600 million.

conditions and procedures for granting Community financial support to projects of common interest in the field of TENs (Article 1). Reference is made to the environment in a number of instances, which will be discussed in greater detail below (section IV.C.*ii*).

viii. Energy R&D and Demonstration Programmes

Over the years, more and more emphasis has been put on environmental benefits of certain technologies in the EC's energy research programmes. It concerns, most notably, technologies relating to renewable energy sources and technologies for a more rational and clean use of available energy sources (fossil fuels). These technologies had already been promoted in the past (1970s and 1980s). However, this was solely for security of energy supply reasons.[99] Since the 1990s, environmental objectives have been explicitly included as objectives of EC research support in the energy field.[100] One of the programmes even quotes

[99] Support programmes for technological development in the hydrocarbons sector, in particular, for the technological development connected with hydrocarbons prospection, production, storage, and transportation: Reg. (EC) No. 3056/73 on the Support of Community Projects in the Hydrocarbons Sector [1973] OJ L312/1, repealed by Reg. (EC) No. 3639/85 on a Programme of Support for Technological Development in the Hydrocarbons Sector [1985] OJ L350/25. Support for projects relating to energy-saving and alternative energy sources: (1) R&D projects: Dec. 73/176/EEC adopting a Programme of Research in New Technologies for the EEC (use of solar energy and recycling of raw materials) [1973] OJ L189/34; Dec. 75/510/EEC Adopting an Energy Research and Development Programme (1975–1979) [1975] OJ L231/1; Dec. 79/785/EEC Adopting an Energy Research and Development Programme (1979–1983) [1979] OJ L231/30; Dec. 85/198/EEC Adopting a Research and Development Programme in the Field of Non-Nuclear Energy (1985–1988) [1985] OJ L83/16; and (2) demonstration projects: Reg. (EEC) No. 1302/78 on the Granting of Financial Support for Projects to Exploit Alternative Energy Sources (1978–1983) [1978] OJ L158/3; Reg. (EEC) No. 1303/78 on the Granting of Financial Support for Demonstration Projects in the Field of Energy-Saving (1978–1982) [1978] OJ L158/6; Reg. (EEC) No. 1971/83 on the Granting of Financial Support for Pilot Industrial Projects and Demonstration Projects Relating to the Liquefaction and Gasification of Solid Fuels (applied until December 1983) [1983] OJ L195/1; Reg. (EEC) No. 1972/83 on the Granting of Financial Support for Demonstration Projects Relating to the Exploitation of Alternative Energy Sources and to Energy Saving and the Substitution of Hydrocarbons (applied until Dec. 1983) [1983] OJ L195/6 and Reg. (EEC) No. 3640/85 on the Promotion, by Financial Support, of Demonstration Projects and Industrial Pilot Projects in the Energy Field (applied until Dec. 1989) [1985] OJ L350/29. Whereas environment was not mentioned at all in the early measures and programmes of the 1970s, slowly but steadily, limited environmental references were introduced in the relevant legislation of the 1980s (see Art. 5(1) third indent Reg. (EEC) No. 1971/83; Art. 5(1) third indent Reg. (EEC) No. 1972/83; Art. 5(1) twelfth indent Reg. (EEC) No. 3639/85 and Art. 3(2) and Annexes I, II, III, and IV Reg. (EEC) No. 3640/85).

[100] In 1989 and in 1990 respectively, Dec. 89/236/EEC on a Specific Research and Technological Development Programme in the Field of Energy—Non-Nuclear Energies and Rational Use of Energy—1989 to 1992 (JOULE) [1989] OJ L98/13, and Reg. (EEC) No. 2008/90 Concerning the Promotion of Energy Technology in Europe (THERMIE) (1990–1994) [1990] OJ L185/1, were adopted as the new programmes for granting financial support to R&D (JOULE) and demonstration (THERMIE) projects in the energy field. The JOULE programme was supplemented by a specific R&D programme (Dec. 91/484/EEC [1991] OJ L257/37), which was implemented under the Third RTD Framework Programme, for the period 1990 to 1994 (Dec. 90/221/EEC [1990] OJ L117/28). In 1994, the demonstration part of THERMIE was merged with JOULE, and together they formed a new non-nuclear energy programme: the JOULE-THERMIE

the integration principle.[101] Under the current research programme, the environmental component continues to be strong, with particular attention for so-called sustainable energy systems.[102] In the short term, this entails that the Community's RTD efforts will focus on clean energy sources, savings and efficiency, and alternative motor fuels. In the medium to long term, efforts will concentrate on fuel cells, carriers/transport storage, renewable energy technologies, and capture and sequestration of CO_2.

In addition, it should be mentioned in this context that an environmental component was also incorporated in programmes relating to the two last stages of technology maturity, namely commercialization and market success. Decision 99/24/EC Adopting a Multiannual Programme of Technological Actions Promoting the Clean and Efficient Use of Solid Fuels (1998 to 2002) (CARNOT),[103] for example, was aimed at contributing to the improvement of security of energy supply, competitiveness, employment, but also the protection of the environment (Preamble) by promoting the use and development of clean solid fuel technologies (Article 1(2)).[104]

IV. Integration of Environmental Protection into the EC Energy Policy

A. Introduction

The purpose of this section is to evaluate the environmental effects of the above-discussed secondary legislation. In other words, we will examine whether, and if so, how Community action relating to the energy sector has stimulated

programme (Dec. 94/806/EEC [1994] OJ L334/87). The sub-programme relating to the energy sector implemented under the Fifth RTD Framework Programme (1999–2002) Dec. 182/1999/EC [1999] OJ L26/1 was called Dec. 1999/170/EC Adopting a Specific Programme for Research, Technological Development and Demonstration on Energy, Environment and Sustainable Development (1998 to 2002) (ENERGIE) [1999] OJ L64/58.

101 The Preamble of THERMIE does not just refer to the objective of prudent and rational utilization of natural resources in what was at the time Art. 130r EC (now Art. 176 EC), but also to the integration principle, be it in its initial form (i.e. environmental protection requirements are to be a component of the Community's other policies). This makes this regulation one of the few pieces of EC legislation that explicitly refers to the integration clause.

102 Sixth RTD Framework Programme (2002–2006), Dec. 1513/2002/EC [2002] OJ L232/1.

103 [1999] OJ L7/28. See also website DG Energy and Transport.

104 As for the last aim, in particular, it is designed to contribute to the reduction of polluting emissions arising from the use of fossil fuels in the Community. Under the programme, two instruments were used. So as to foster cooperation between the various actors in this field, it finances (a) the exchange of information and (b) the promotion of training and studies on clean solid fuel technologies. The total amount available for implementing the programme is €3 million (Art. 2). The CARNOT programme supplemented the (nuclear and non-nuclear) multi-annual framework programme for actions in the energy sector (1998–2002) (Dec. 99/21/EC [1999] OJ L7/16). In the context of the latter a total budget of €170 million was available in order to support (a) shared analyses and market monitoring; (b) international energy cooperation; (c) the promotion of

environmentally damaging practices and behaviour (integration failures). It will also be examined whether, and if so, how, Community action relating to this sector has stimulated environmentally friendly and/or the least environmentally damaging practices and behaviour (integration efforts). At the same time, this section analyses the instruments used for these purposes. A comparison of both failures and efforts to promote environmental objectives in the context of the energy policy should ultimately give an idea of what the overall environmental impact of that policy area is.

B. To What Extent does Energy Policy Prejudice Environmental Interests in the EU?

i. Direct Regulation

Effects of Early Oil Crisis Measures

Although some of the oil crisis measures had certain environmental benefits (e.g. Decision 77/706/EEC),[105] others were clearly problematic from an environmental point of view. Doubts existed especially in relation to Directive 75/404/EEC on the Restriction of the Use of Natural Gas in Power Stations,[106] which restricted use of natural gas in power plants. As mentioned above, compared to other conventional fuels, most notably coal and oil, natural gas is less polluting, especially in relation to air emissions. To discourage the use of this fuel in electricity generation may be regarded as an undesirable strategy from the environmental perspective. The fact that Directive 75/404/EEC allowed for an exception to the said restrictions for environmental reasons did not really change much because the exception was probably to be interpreted in a limited way. It took quite a long time, however, before the Directive was repealed. Certain Member States opposed abolition of the act so as to protect other energy sectors, in particular, the nuclear and the coal sectors.[107] The Preamble of Directive 91/148/EEC Revoking Directive 75/404/EEC on the Restriction of the Use of Natural Gas in Power Stations indicates that it does so partly for environmental and partly for political/economic reasons.[108] Although it has been noted that the

renewable energy sources; (d) rational and efficient use of energy resources; (e) the use of environmentally compatible solid fuels technologies; and (f) safe transport of radioactive materials and industrial cooperation promoting nuclear safety in Technical Assistence to the Common Wealth of Independent States (TACIS) countries. Art. 1(2) of the Decision setting out this programme; clearly stated that it shall primarily contribute to the balanced pursuit of the priority objectives of energy policy; in particular, security of supply, competitiveness, and environmental protection.

105 n. 27 above.

106 [1975] OJ L178/24.

107 Hancher, n. 8 above, 488. Hancher reports that the UK wanted to secure the future of its uneconomic nuclear sector, while West Germany wanted to safeguard its domestic coal industry.

108 [1991] OJ L75/52. The first relate to the fact that natural gas has specific advantages in terms of limiting air emissions. The latter consist of, on the one hand, certain operational advantages in terms of costs and efficiency of using natural gas and, on the other hand, the fact that the supply problems in relation to natural gas had ceased to exist.

Directive contributed towards the decline in the use of natural gas in power stations after 1975, it is argued at the same time that its purely quantitative impact was probably fairly small.[109] Directive 75/404/EEC was one of the few instances where a measure designed to further the security of energy supply objective was contrary to the attainment of the environmental objectives.

Effects of Liberalization Process

The question that will be dealt with here is whether the Community's efforts to liberalize energy markets may or will have negative effects for the environment. In this context, it is important to observe that the main objective of the liberalization project is to increase competition. Full or increased competition is expected to cause a drop in energy prices.[110] However, a decrease in energy prices is very likely to have negative environmental effects. The negative environmental impact could be twofold.[111] First, lower energy prices may reduce incentives to conserve energy. In other words, energy consumption may increase, which eventually leads to an increase in polluting emissions. At the same time, and this is the second negative effect, full competition and lower prices for electricity and gas may have a negative effect on the development of environmentally friendly energy sources and technologies such as renewables and CHP (which already require substantial investment as it is). As a result, the increase in energy consumption is likely to be based on fossil fuels, which are far more polluting, especially in terms of air emissions. The second negative effect, the trend towards increasing emissions resulting from higher consumption, reinforces the first.

Indeed, in its 2000 progress report, the Commission reported that the gradual introduction of competition in the electricity sector has caused electricity to drop in almost all Member States and for all kinds of consumers.[112] At the same time, the EEA confirmed that energy use in the EU grew relatively slowly in the early 1990s but that it is increasing more rapidly now.[113] Specifically in relation to the consequences for the development of CHP, the EEA reports that liberalization of energy markets in Finland and the United Kingdom has stimulated investment in CHP, but lower electricity prices may act against more investment in CHP

[109] Von Burchard and Eckert, n. 37 above, 49.

[110] *The Economist* reports that the two main (likely) consequences of energy liberalization, cheaper prices and a wave of corporate mergers, have already been felt in Britain since competition was introduced to the energy business (*The Economist*, 30 Nov. 2002, 58). See also, however, M. van der Woude, *EC Competition Handbook* (London: Sweet & Maxwell, 2002), 253. He has doubts about whether prices have really decreased as a result of the liberalization process.

[111] For these effects see: EEA, *Environmental Signals 2000—European Environment Agency Regular Indicator Report* (Copenhagen: EEA, 2000), 21 and European Environment Agency, *Environmental Signals 2001—European Environment Agency Regular Indicator Report* (Copenhagen: EEA, 2001), 40.

[112] Commission Communication on Recent Progress with Building the Internal Electricity Market COM(2000)297, 2–3. See also Commission Staff Working Paper, 'Integrating Environment and Sustainable Development into Energy and Transport Policies: Review Report 2001 and Implementation of the Strategies' SEC(2001)502, 12.

[113] EEA, *Environmental Signals 2001—European Environment Agency Regular Indicator Report* (Copenhagen: EEA, 2001), 40.

plants, which are capital intensive.[114] This is what happened in Germany where CHP generation has decreased.[115] Initially, the Commission was very careful in its statements on the negative effects of the liberalization process, but it eventually clearly acknowledged the areas of tension.[116]

The next questions are whether, first, besides the likely negative effects, the process also has positive effects for the environment and its protection and, secondly, efforts have been made to moderate the liberalization or mitigate the negative environmental effects in a certain way. These questions will be discussed below under the subsection on environmentally friendly (or less damaging) energy legislation.

ii. Economic/Market-Based Instruments

Fiscal Instruments—Environmentally Unfriendly Tax Exemptions and Reductions

As already observed, taxes and duties on energy differ significantly in the Community, both from product to product, and from Member State to Member State. The excise duties on mineral oils have been harmonized to a limited extent, but this legislation has not led to much harmonization in practice. The existence of this 'fiscal disorder' is regrettable, not merely because the fiscal disparities distort competition in the Community, but also because the potential of tax incentives as an effective tool to achieve aims such as the internalization of external costs is not exploited.[117] Up to now, attempts of the Commission to readjust this situation have failed, however.[118]

114 EEA, *Environmental Signals 2001—European Environment Agency Regular Indicator Report* (Copenhagen: EEA, 2001), 46.

115 On this issue, Krieglstein reports (F.B. Krieglstein, 'Renewable Energy Schemes and EC State Aids Provisions' (2001) 10 *European Environmental Law Review*, 52) that a CHP protection law was adopted in March 2000 'to protect the production of electricity in CHP plants from the effects of the liberalization of the German electricity market, in particular in terms of reducing market prices for electricity. The new law requires grid operators to purchase electricity produced from CHP plants at fixed prices, an approach similar to that followed for electricity from renewable energy sources. The protection under the new law will be limited in time however'.

116 Cf. White Paper, 'Energy for the Future: Renewable Sources of Energy' COM(97)599, 6–7 and 14–15; Commission Communication on the Single Market and the Environment COM(99)263, 14–15; Commission Green Paper, 'Towards a European Strategy for the Security of Energy Supply', COM(2000)769, 3 and 44; Commission Communication on 'Completing the Internal Energy Market' COM(2001)125, 22.

117 See also Commission Green Paper, 'Towards a European Strategy for the Security of Energy Supply' COM(2000)769, 50–5 and Cross *et al.*, n. 6 above, 267–9. In the Green Paper, the following is observed in relation to the tax regimes in the Member States: 'The principle of fiscal neutrality avoids distortion in the choice of factors of production and in consumer choice... Taxes on energy products in the Member States often follow the same hierarchy between products. Coal and natural gas are the least taxed and oil the most heavily taxed. Taxes are spent on renewable sources and coal benefits from State aid in the coal-producing countries. Coal is relatively lightly taxed, except in the northern EU States... Although it is perfectly logical to relieve coal of any tax burden while it is receiving substantial State aid, the result is to promote imported coal to the detriment of alternative but more heavily taxed energy sources such as natural gas and oil.'

118 See the Commission's unsuccessful attempts to introduce a CO_2 tax (COM(92)226, amended proposal: COM(95)172) and the difficulties surrounding the adoption of the subsequent proposal on taxation of energy products (COM(97)30). See further below section IV.C.*iii*.

Besides the mere fact that certain important energy sources (such as coal, lignite, peat, or other similar solid hydrocarbons used for heating purposes) fall outside the scope of the harmonized excise duty, the Community regime has been criticized for setting out minimum rates that are far too low. As already observed above (section III.D.*v*), one of the reasons why the Community legislation has resulted in little actual harmonization is exactly because common minimum rates have not kept pace with real national rates.[119] If the proposal for taxation of energy products were adopted, these minimum rates would increase progressively. However, the environmental benefits of such Community action would remain limited, because most Member States already apply tax rates above the proposed minima.[120]

The legislation contains other so-called 'environmental flaws'. First, it sets out a mandatory and total exemption for fuel used for commercial air services (Article 8(1)). This provision makes it impossible for a Member State to introduce a national tax on the use of aviation fuel, even if collected for environmental purposes, and only levied on domestic aviation. Thus, in *Braathens*[121] it was argued that the tax at issue was intended to protect the environment, and was charged not directly on fuel consumption, but on certain polluting emissions from aircraft used in national commercial aviation, making Directive 92/81/EEC completely irrelevant.[122] The European Court of Justice (ECJ) did not accept this argument, however. It held that there is a direct and inseverable link between fuel consumption and the polluting substances in question, so that the tax, both as regards the part calculated by reference to the emissions of hydrocarbons and nitric oxide and the part determined by reference to fuel consumption, which relates to carbon dioxide emissions, must be considered as levied on fuel consumption.[123] The ECJ concludes therefore that the collection of such a tax is

[119] In the 1995 White Paper (COM(95)682), the Commission noted: 'The difference between minimum rates and real rates set by governments is now so big, notably in respect of motor fuels, that any adjustment of the minimum rates in order to influence the market and improve convergence of excise duties will have to be of a substantial nature. Seen from an energy viewpoint, the removal of distortions resulting from a lack of approximation of Member States' effective rates, particularly on motor fuels, will have to be taken into account when considering a future fiscal structure on energy products'. See also Commission report on the rates of duty laid down in Dir. 92/79/EEC on the Approximation of Taxes on Cigarettes, Dir. 92/80/EEC on the Approximation of Taxes on Manufactured Tobacco Other than Cigarettes, Dir. 92/84/EEC on the Approximation of the Rates of Excise Duty on Alcohol and Alcoholic Beverages and Dir. 92/82/EEC on the Approximation of the Rates of Excise Duties on Mineral Oils COM(95)285, 10 and 25–6 and 28, where the Commission admits that 'environmental policy would favour a substantial increase in the level of excise duties on mineral oils and extension of the duty to products currently not covered'.

[120] J. Wiers, 'Transport and the Environment—The Ugly Face of the Internal Market' (1999) 18 *European Environmental Law Review*, 338. See also D. Grimeaud, 'Road Transport and Climate Change Concerns—The EC Approach' (1999) 7 *Environmental Liability*, 104. The Commission itself admitted to this in its 1998 Communication on Transport and CO_2—Developing a Community Approach COM(1998)204, 15.

[121] Case C-346/97 *Braathens* [1999] ECR I-3419.

[122] ibid., para. 16.

[123] ibid., para. 23.

incompatible with the provision in Article 8(1) of Directive 92/81/EEC.[124] Article 8(7) of Directive 92/81/EEC stipulates that the Council must review the exemptions for the commercial air transport sector before 31 December 1997 on the basis of a report of the Commission. In addition, it is explicitly indicated that the review should be based on the need to take account of the external costs entailed in this transport mode, and the implications for the environment. Thus, this could be regarded as a first step towards integration of environmental concerns into this field. The reason why this issue is discussed here, and not under the paragraphs on the instruments used to stimulate environmentally friendly practices, however, is because the review and its aftermath did not result in the abolition of the environmentally undesirable compulsory exemption.[125] Despite the fact that the Commission proposes to keep the preferential treatment for aviation fuel at Community level in place for now (in other words, no introduction of a Community tax on aviation fuel), it does recommend that:

[124] ibid., para. 26.

[125] In its 1996 review report, after briefly discussing the relevant international legal regime, the competitive position of the European air transport industry, but also the environmental consequences of the current situation and the necessity to internalize external costs, the Commission concluded that the excise duties on mineral oils should be extended to aviation kerosene as soon as the international legal situation allows the Community to levy such a tax on all carriers, including those from third countries (COM(96)549, 8–11). The Chicago Convention on International Civil Aviation of 1944 as well as many bilateral air service agreements provide for the obligatory exemption of aviation fuel from fuel taxes. The Council adopted the Commission report in June 1997, and subsequently requested the Commission to provide further information on the effects of such a tax (Res. of 9 June 1997). For these purposes, the Commission commissioned a study, which was finalized in 1998 (Analysis of the Taxation of Aircraft Fuel, Resource Analysis, Delft 1998). The Commission briefly commented on the results of this study in its Communication on Air Transport and the Environment (COM(1999)640, 11), but later devoted a separate (if rather short) Communication to the issue (Communication on Taxation of Aircraft Fuel COM(2000)110). For the reaction of the European Parliament (EP) to this Communication: see Res. A5-0334/2000 [2001] OJ C232/343). In this specific Communication, the Commission indicates that the results of the study confirm its own conclusions, as set out in the 1996 report. Taxation at Community level targeting exclusively intra-Community flights by Community air carriers would, at present, neither be practicable nor desirable, mainly for 'economic' reasons, but also in view of the fact that the positive environmental effects of such unilateral action would be comparatively minor. Quite logically, the study further confirmed that the introduction of kerosene taxation targeting all operations from Community airports would have significantly higher environmental benefits. This would require re-negotiation of bilateral air service agreements and of the relevant rules of the Chicago Convention, however.

The problems with imposing an aviation fuel tax have been discussed in the literature. Winter observes in this regard that imposing a tax for aviation fuel, similar to the petroleum taxes for road transport, is difficult for two main reasons. First, the costs are different (the airways have no construction costs, airports construction is partly financed through take-off and landing fees), and secondly, aeroplanes could be refuelled more easily than road vehicles in cheaper foreign countries. The kerosene tax would therefore only have a real impact if it was introduced internationally. In this respect, an aeroplane charge on the routes flown worldwide by domestic aeroplanes or a charge placed on the routes flown in domestic space may be more effective (G. Winter, 'On Integration of Environmental Protection into Air Transport Law—A German and EC Perspective' (1996) *Air & Space Law,* 140). See also G. Topmann in K. Button (ed.), *Transport Policy—Ways into Europe's Future* (Gütersloh: Bertelsmann, 1994), 196.

(a) efforts to change the relevant international regime in the context of the International Civil Aviation Organization (ICAO) are intensified;[126]
(b) each Member State is allowed to levy a tax on aviation fuel, either for domestic flights alone, or via bilateral agreements, on intra-Community flights.

Accordingly, the proposal for a Directive Restructuring the Community Framework for the Taxation of Energy Products provides in the proposed Article 13(1)(c) that Member States shall exempt from taxation, fuels used for the purpose of commercial air navigation, 'for as long as such products are obliged to be exempted under international obligations'.[127] Proposed Article 13(2) allows Member States to tax fuel used for domestic flights as well as for intra-Community movements, following bilateral negotiations. Allowing Member States to tax domestic flights would nevertheless constitute progress, since it would mean, for example, that Sweden could reintroduce the tax that the ECJ found in breach of the excise duties legislation (see *Braathens* case).

In addition to the mandatory exemptions of Article 8(1) of Directive 92/81/EEC, Article 8(2) and Article 8(3) of that same Directive allow Member States to apply exemptions or reductions in relation to taxation of heating fuels and motor fuels used for certain industrial and commercial purposes (e.g. in the field of the manufacture, development, testing, and maintenance of aircraft and ship; fuels used in agriculture, forestry, and inland fisheries, for stationary motors; fuels used for machinery used in construction, civil engineering, and public works). These exemptions or reductions might also be considered detrimental from an environmental point of view. The proposal for restructuring the Community framework on the taxation of energy products retains (possible) preferential treatment of some of these sectors.[128]

Finally, it should be observed here that more environmentally detrimental exemptions have been granted pursuant to Article 8(4) of Directive 92/81/EEC. As explained above, this provision allows for the Council to authorize individual Member States to apply certain exemptions or reductions from the harmonized excise duty on mineral oils 'for specific policy considerations'. On the basis of this provision, Member States have been allowed, for example, to exempt aviation fuel used in private pleasure flying (i.e. air navigation other than that covered by

[126] As for the latest developments on the international scene concerning this issue, it may be reported that it appears that the ICAO is still a long way from accepting the abolition of the mandatory exemption for aviation fuel. The attitude of the ICAO Council towards 'emission-related charges' seems less hostile, provided that charges are based on the costs of mitigating the environmental impact of aircraft engine emissions and to the extent that such costs can be properly identified and directly attributed to air transport. See Assembly Res. A33-7: Consolidated Statement of Continuing ICAO Policies and Practices Related to Environmental Protection—Appendix I—Oct. 2001 (see website ICAO—on file with the author).

[127] COM(97)30.

[128] ibid.

Article 8(1)),[129] or to allow the application of a reduced rate for diesel fuel for commercial vehicles.[130] A reduced rate was accepted also, for example, for enterprises with a very high consumption of energy (the so-called 'energy-intensive' enterprises).[131] The proposal for a Community framework on the taxation of energy products provides for tax refunds for energy-intensive firms in order to safeguard the competitiveness of European firms vis-à-vis third countries. At the same time, it should be observed here that some environmentally friendly exemptions and reductions have been allowed on the basis of Article 8(4) as well (see further below on how fiscal instruments are used to stimulate environmentally friendly or the least damaging practices, section IV.C.*iv*).

iii. Promoting R&D, Information Exchange, and/or Training

EC Programmes on R&D and Demonstration Projects

Community action in relation to non-nuclear energy research has been quite environmentally sensitive (see further below, section IV.C.*iv*). However, assistance has been granted to coal and nuclear research, respectively under the ECSC Treaty and the Euratom Treaty, as well. Coal is one of the most environmentally damaging energy sources. If nuclear energy is also regarded as such, R&D support should be considered as unwelcome from the environmental perspective. Despite the fact that this chapter concerns EC Energy Policy, and not the regulation of energy-related matters under the ECSC Treaty and the Euratom Treaty, it should nevertheless be observed that aid for research in both the coal and nuclear sectors has been substantial over the years. For research relating to nuclear energy, for example, a total budget of €979 million was available for the implementation of the Fifth Framework Programme of Euratom for research and training activities (1998–2002),[132] while a budget of €1,042 million was allocated to the energy sub-programme under the Fifth (EC) RTD Framework Programme (1998–2002).[133] These amounts are striking, especially in view of the fact that the first programme only concerns one type of energy source,

[129] Dec. 92/510/EEC, Dec. 96/273/EC Dec. 97/425/EC, and Dec. 1999/880/EC; authorizations now in Dec. 2001/224/EC which expires on 31 Dec. 2006.

[130] Dec. 97/425/EC, Dec. 99/880/EC, and Dec. 2000/446/EC—the latter applied until 31 Dec. 2000, both replaced by Dec. 2001/224/EC: in particular, Art. 2 and Annex II providing that the reduced rates apply for two years, in contradiction to other exemptions and reductions expiring in 2006.

[131] Dec. 97/92/EC, Dec. 97/425/EC, Dec. 99/880/EC, and Dec. 2001/224/EC (only to expire in 2006 it would seem).

[132] Dec. 1999/64/EC Concerning the Fifth Framework Programme of the European Atomic Energy Community (Euratom) for Research and Training Activities (1998–2002) [1999] OJ L26/34 and Dec. 1999/175/EC Adopting a Research and Training Programme (Euratom) in the Field of Nuclear Energy (1998–2002) [1999] OJ L64/142.

[133] Dec. 1999/170/EC Adopting a Specific Programme for Research, Technological Development and Demonstration on Energy, Environment and Sustainable Development (1998–2002) [1999] OJ L64/58 and website 'RTD info' DG Research (on file with the author).

while the latter concerns various energy sources.[134] It should be added, however, that the R&D programmes in relation to coal and nuclear energy do give some attention to relevant environmental issues, such as preference to R&D projects that help reduce greenhouse gas emissions derived from the coal industry.[135]

C. Does Energy Policy Support Environmental Interests in the EU?

i. Direct Regulation

Liberalization of the Electricity and Gas Markets

Besides negative environmental effects, identified and discussed above, certain more positive developments have been associated with the liberalization of the internal electricity and gas markets. The Commission has pointed, in particular, to improvements in generating plants, increased operational efficiency, and a switch to cleaner fuels in power production.[136] It expects the trend towards cleaner power generation plants to accelerate as market liberalization progresses. The EEA has confirmed these developments.[137]

It should be observed that these environmental benefits could be offset by the fact that increased competition pushes energy prices down, which leads to or could lead to increased energy demand—and thus increased emissions—as well as impeding the development of more environmentally friendly energy sources, as was explained above.[138] As for these negative side-effects of the creation of internal electricity and gas markets, certain mitigating action has been taken both

[134] See also Hancher, n. 8 above, 483–4. Hancher observes the following in this respect: 'Funding for this type of research has always been considerably lower than the Commission's support for nuclear power ([in footnote] Funding for non-nuclear R&D between 1987–91 has been reduced to 122 mecu, compared with 175 mecu granted in the previous four-year period). The Economic and Social Committee, as well as the EP has criticized the Commission's approach to the evaluation of projects for funding purposes as giving insufficient recognition to environmental considerations'.

[135] Appendix B of Dec. 2002/234/EC on the financial consequences of the expiry of the ECSC Treaty and on the research fund for coal and steel [2002] OJ L79/42, which provides for the legal basis of the new ECSC RTD programme.

[136] Commission Communication on Completing the Internal Energy Market COM(2001) 125, 22.

[137] Indeed, the EEA has confirmed that the liberalization process is partly responsible for the shift from coal to gas for electricity production, which, in turn, contributed to the reduction in CO_2 and acid gas emissions (EEA, *Environmental Signals 2000—European Environment Agency Regular Indicator Report* (Copenhagen: EEA, 2000), 22). The liberalization of the natural gas and electricity markets has stimulated electricity generators to choose 'the cheapest, most efficient and most flexible generating capacity' (EEA, *Environmental Signals 2001—European Environment Agency Regular Indicator Report* (Copenhagen: EEA, 2001), 44). The Agency adds that nuclear generation is currently regarded as an expensive option in the context of a liberalized market.

[138] EEA, *Environmental Signals 2000—European Environment Agency Regular Indicator Report* (Copenhagen: EEA, 2000), 21.

within the context of internal market legislation and outside of this legislation. Because it was realized that liberalized markets could halt or hinder the development of renewable energies and a less carbon-intensive system, internal electricity market legislation allows (but does not require) Member States to impose environmental service obligations, and give electricity from renewables and from CHP priority in dispatching.[139] In addition, Member States may set environmental criteria for the granting of authorizations for the construction of generating capacity. An example of a possible public service obligation in this context is the obligation for a distribution company to purchase electricity produced from renewable energy sources.[140]

It is interesting to examine the extent to which these provisions in the Internal Electricity Market Directive[141] can justify national regulatory schemes aimed at promoting renewable energy sources, such as the German scheme. Such a scheme was the subject of the *PreussenElektra* case.[142] Under German law, private electricity supply companies are required to purchase electricity produced from renewables in their area of supply at minimum prices (which are higher than real prices). The financial burden resulting from that obligation is shared between those electricity supply companies and upstream private electricity network operators. Especially interesting are the remarks of Advocate General Jacobs on the legality of this scheme. He does not believe that the mechanism established by German law is covered by any of the 'environmental provisions' of the Internal Electricity Market Directive. The reason for this lies in the fact that Article 3(2) of this Directive requires the public obligations to be non-discriminatory. The German purchase obligation imposed on network operators, however, applies only to electricity produced in Germany. Articles 8(3) and 11(3) of that same Directive concerning priority in dispatching cannot be used either, because they only allow a distinction between different modes of production of electricity. In its judgment, the ECJ is very brief. It does not really examine this question, but simply points to the priority clause in Articles 8(3) and 11(3) as an additional argument for its conclusion that the relevant German legislation is 'not incompatible' with Article 28 EC. Other arguments that the ECJ uses in this context are the aim and content of Community environmental measures which were

[139] Dir. 98/30/EC contains similar provisions in relation to the internal gas market.

[140] Cross *et al.*, n. 6 above, 303. Another example is given in the Commission's Communication on Completing the Internal Energy Market. It refers to the possible adoption of tariff structures to encourage energy-efficiency: 'These could be implemented through cuts to fixed charges leaving price signals on the variable use of electricity unchanged. Appropriate regulatory incentives would need to be in place in order to encourage such innovative tariff structures to emerge'. See COM(2001)125, 22.

[141] n. 32 above

[142] Case C-379/98, *PreussenElektra* [2001] ECR I-2099. On this case, see: J. Jans, case note (2001) 28 *Tijdschrift voor Milieu & Recht*, 258; H.H.B. Vedder, 'Het Europese recht en de stimulering van duurzame energie—Duitse windhandel' (2001) 7 *Nederlands Tijdschrift voor Europees Recht*, 147–55; S. de Vries, 'European Court of Justice: Case Report' (2001) 10 *European Environmental Law Review*, 193–205.

adopted in light of the Climate Change Convention, and the integration principle of Article 6 EC.

On the basis of all these considerations, the ECJ finds the German measure to be justified. It remains unclear, however, whether this justification occurs on the basis of a more liberal interpretation of Article 30 EC (i.e. by incorporating an 'environmental protection' ground), or a wider interpretation of the 'rule of reason' (by allowing the justification of discriminatory measures). It is also remarkable that the ECJ does not refer to the proportionality principle. This principle is usually at the centre of the ECJ's assessment of national trade barriers.[143] The vagueness of its reasoning is unfortunate, particularly in relation to the integration principle. Nevertheless, it may be concluded on the basis of this judgment that the integration principle plays some kind of role in the ECJ's review of national discriminatory measures. This, in itself, is an interesting conclusion.[144]

The first part of the judgment is entirely dedicated to the evaluation of the scheme in the light of the EC rules on State aid. On this matter, the ECJ concludes that the German scheme does not constitute State aid in the meaning of Article 87(1) EC.

The Commission has called for a strengthening of the existing provisions on public service obligations. In addition, it has expressed an intention to monitor the environmental consequences of market liberalization continuously. For this purpose, it has launched a study with the aim of assessing the environmental implications of market liberalization up to 2010.[145]

Fuel Quality Standards

As of 1975 (sulphur content) and 1978 (lead content), fuel quality standards have been set at the Community level. Continuous updating, amending, and replacing of the directives in question has resulted in cleaner conventional fuels.

[143] J. Jans, case note (2001) 28 *Tijdschrift voor Milieu & Recht*, 258.

[144] Advocate General Jacobs is more explicit about the role of the integration principle in this context. Jacobs suggests, while explicitly referring to the integration principle of Art. 6 EC, that the ECJ drops the condition that national measures must be non-discriminatory in order to be justifiable under the 'rule of reason'. In such a way, the Court could clarify its ambiguous case law in this area. Interestingly, Jacobs motivates this view on the basis of Art. 6 EC, indicating that this provision is 'not merely programmatic' but 'imposes legal obligations'. This means that special account must be taken of environmental concerns in interpreting the Treaty provisions on the free movement of goods (Opinion of Advocate General Jacobs in Case C-379/98, *PreussenElektra* [2001] ECR I-2099, paras. 231–2). De Vries believes that the Advocate General's opinion is in keeping with the presumption, based on Art. 6 EC, that the protection of the environment and the free movement of goods (particularly the principle of non-discrimination on the basis of nationality) are at least equally important. Whether a national measure is eventually justified depends on the proportionality of the measure; de Vries, n. 142 above, 203–5.

[145] Commission Communication on Completing the Internal Energy Market COM(2001)125, 8 and 24–5.

Energy Efficiency Standards and Labelling Rules

The above overview shows that, over the years, various harmonizing directives have been adopted aimed at promoting rational use of energy. They did so, in particular, by way of introducing common energy efficiency standards as well as efficiency labelling rules for respectively, heat generators (performance requirements in Directive 78/170/EEC)[146] and certain household appliances (labelling rules in Directive 79/530/EEC).[147] This early/initial action was adopted against the background of the oil crises and, thus, besides the objective to prevent the creation of trade barriers, was designed to help prevent energy supply difficulties and thus improve security of energy supply. The environmental benefits of the legislation were regarded as an accidental corollary.[148] From the beginning of the 1990s, however, the promotion of the rational use of energy or the 'demand management of energy' by way of energy efficiency requirements and complementary labelling rules was regarded as an important tool for contributing to environmental objectives. These objectives were, in particular, to ensure prudent and rational utilization of natural resources (in Article 175(1) EC) and, more importantly, the objective to reduce CO_2 emissions in the context of the climate change. Like the SAVE and ALTENER[149] programmes themselves, this harmonizing legislation evolved towards becoming strongly, if not predominantly, 'environmental'.

What the energy-efficiency standards and the labelling schemes hope to achieve is one thing. What they actually achieve is quite another, however. In 1998, a SAVE-financed study evaluated the energy-labelling scheme, and found that compliance with this scheme was relatively low.[150] Still, when applied, the scheme did seem to influence consumer choice.

ii. Cross-Compliance

The use of the mechanism of cross-compliance in order to integrate environmental requirements into energy policy is not very common. The overview of energy legislation below shows that certain forms of cross-compliance only appear in legislation on the TEN-E and on hydrocarbons licensing.

TEN-E

Environmental integration is pursued at two levels in the TEN legislation: first, at the level of the selection of projects of common interest, and, secondly, at the level of determining whether Community support can be granted for a particular

[146] n. 90 above.

[147] n. 95 above.

[148] Both Preambles simply pointed to the fact that 'any improvement in the rational use of energy is generally beneficial to the environment'.

[149] Dec. 646/2000/EC to adopt a Multi-Annual Programme for the Promotion of Renewable Energy Sources in the Community (1998–2002) [2000] OJ L79/1.

[150] See Commission Communication on Action Plan to Improve Energy Efficiency in the European Community COM(2000)247, 9.

project. The first level relates to the fact that the evaluation of the 'potential economic viability', one of the criteria for determining whether a project is of 'common interest', must be based on a cost-benefit analysis which must take account of all costs and benefits, including those relating to the environment (Article 6 of Decision 1254/96/EC).[151] As to the second level, it may be recalled that the general TEN Regulation (Regulation (EC) No. 2236/95)[152] makes the assessment of the environmental consequences of a project, according to Directive 85/337/EEC on the Assessment of the Effect of Certain Public and Private Projects on the Environment (EIA Directive),[153] a condition for granting financial support. This concerns a weak form of cross-compliance. It is weak, because it seems to concern a procedural obligation, which does not mean that a project is automatically ineligible for support if it has certain negative environmental consequences. Regulation (EC) No. 2236/95 also provides, however, that projects financed by the Community must comply, more generally, with Community law and policy, *inter alia*, in relation to environmental protection. This seems a somewhat stronger expression of cross-compliance. In addition, in the monitoring requirements, it is stipulated that the evaluation of the projects realized shall include an evaluation of their environmental impact (Article 15(4)).

Despite the incorporation of these environmental guarantees in TEN and TEN-E legislation, the Commission has expressed the view that the construction of new infrastructure should be encouraged as much as possible because of its importance for the internal energy market. The Commission even believes that the construction of new infrastructure is not a financial but a political problem. By this, it points especially to local opposition to the construction of new lines at strategic points, for example, around the Pyrenees or Alps. According to the Commission, the Community has to play a key role in ensuring that the operation of the market is not hampered by these 'physical constraints'.[154]

Hydrocarbons Licensing

Another piece of legislation that might be regarded as applying the cross-compliance instrument is represented by the legislation on hydrocarbons. It was discussed above how the Hydrocarbons Licensing Directive[155] allowed Member States to subject the exercise of these activities to environmental conditions. However, Member States cannot completely refuse to grant authorizations in so-called open areas on the basis of environmental concerns. If a Member State wishes to safeguard an area on the basis of its environmental value, it should keep it closed. The text of the Directive does not prohibit this, because it recognizes the sovereign rights of Member States over the hydrocarbons resources on their

[151] n. 96 above.

[152] n. 98 above.

[153] [1985] OJ L175/40.

[154] Commission Communication on Completing the Internal Energy Market COM(2001)125, 15–16.

[155] n. 31 above.

territories. Should the Community consider limiting these rights in the future, it would be advisable to leave Member States the possibility of excluding areas from exploitation for environmental reasons.

iii. Economic/Market-Based Instruments

Environmental Aspects of the Excise Duty on Mineral Oils

Above, more particularly in the paragraph on how fiscal instruments are used to encourage environmentally unfriendly practices, the elements in the legislation on mineral oils excise duties that are undesirable from an environmental point of view have been discussed. Here, the aspects of the same fiscal legislation that were designed to help promote environmental goals will be analysed. A first aspect consists of the fact that, in this legislation, the minimum rate set for unleaded petrol is lower than that set for leaded petrol. Article 4 of Directive 92/82/EEC[156] stipulates, in other words, that Member States must always differentiate the rates so that the rate charged for unleaded petrol is lower than that for leaded petrol. It is common knowledge that unleaded petrol is less environmentally damaging than leaded petrol. It is clear therefore that this provision was designed to contribute to the protection of the environment. Besides these differentiated minimum rates of excise duties on leaded and unleaded petrol, the legislation contains other 'environmental provisions'.

A second such 'environmental aspect' concerns some of the optional exemptions or reductions in the rate of duty, listed in Article 8(2) Directive 92/81/EEC.[157] The possible exemptions or reductions in relation to products (a) used in CHP plants; (b) for navigation on inland waterways (other than for private pleasure craft); (c) for rail transport (both of passengers and goods); and, (d) in the field of pilot projects for the technological development of more environmentally friendly products (in particular fuels from renewables) are interesting in this regard.

A third aspect of the legislation with environmental benefits is the result of certain exemptions or reductions of excise duties that are authorized for 'special policy considerations', on the basis of Article 8(4) of Directive 92/81/EEC. Apparently, the term 'special policy considerations' covers environmental concerns.[158]

[156] n. 59 above.

[157] n. 60 above.

[158] The reason for this lies in the fact that the authorized exemptions and reductions range from reduced or differentiated rates of excise duty for more environmentally friendly fuels, such as low sulphur diesel (in many decisions, for example, in Dec. 2001/229/EC), heavy fuel oil also complying with certain requirements relating to sulphur content (e.g. in Dec. 93/697/EC, Dec. 97/93/EC, Dec. 97/136/EC, and now in Dec. 2001/224/EC), or LPG used by waste-collection, drain-suction, and street-cleaning vehicles (Dec. 2000/266/EC) to exemptions or reductions for fuels used for more environmentally friendly practices, e.g. local public transport (in many decisions, e.g. Dec. 2000/433/EC), but also the application of a differentiated rate for petrol distributed from petrol stations equipped with a return system for petrol fumes (Dec. 95/585/EC). Interesting

A final aspect of the fiscal legislation with environmental relevance can be found in Article 8(5) of Directive 92/81/EEC. On the basis of this provision, the Commission shall propose and the Council subsequently adopt a measure that cancels any of the exemptions or reductions granted under Article 8(4) if it considers that these are no longer sustainable, *inter alia*, in light of the Community's environmental policy. This is especially important for the authorized exemptions that do not relate to environmental protection. It could be regarded as some form of cross-compliance: an authorization in relation to a non-environmental exemption can be repealed if contrary to environmental policy.[159]

Use of Fiscal Instruments to Promote Biofuels

As was explained above in the overview of energy legislation, biofuels (or alternative fuels) fall within the scope of the common fiscal regime for mineral oils, and therefore they must be subjected to the excise duty. This excise duty is applied to a selling price that is a lot higher than the cost of 'traditional' fuels, however, which means that the development of biofuels is seriously impeded, and market penetration is nearly impossible.[160] In view of their environmental benefits over traditional fuels, this situation is unattainable from an environmental perspective. A change could be near, however. The Commission presented a proposal for a directive to amend Directive 92/81/EC in order to allow Member States to apply a reduced rate of excise duty on biofuels.[161] It is interesting to observe that the proposed directive uses the same definition of 'biomass' as Directive 2001/77/EC on the Promotion of Electricity Produced

in relation to the differentiated rates for more environmentally friendly fuels is the occasional link of the authorizations with the fuel quality legislation, e.g. in Dec. 2001/229/EC: the low-sulphur diesel fuel for which the Netherlands wanted to apply a differentiated rate of excise duty complied with the environmental criterion laid down in Annex IV of Dir. 98/70/EC Relating to the Quality of Petrol and Diesel Fuels—the use of this fuel will be compulsory as of 2005 anyway. The fuel tax directives do not really refer explicitly to the possibility to differentiate on the basis of *the quality* of a product, so a lot of Member States have requested these individual authorizations in accordance with Art. 8(4) of Dir. 92/81/EEC in order to apply differentiated rates in relation to products with environmentally friendly characteristics.

If the proposal for an EC framework for the taxation of energy products is adopted in its current form, it will not be necessary anymore for Member States to request such authorizations. The proposal allows Member States to apply differentiated rates of taxation in relation to the same product, provided that these rates are higher than the minimum levels, and internal market and competition rules are respected.

[159] The proposal for restructuring the Community framework on the taxation of energy products retains this provision. COM(97)30.

[160] Commission Green Paper, 'Towards a European Strategy for the Security of Energy Supply' COM(2000)769, 53. See also Commission Communication on Alternative Fuels for Road Transportation and on a Set of Measures to Promote the Use of Biofuels COM(2001)547, 5, which mentions a €300/1,000 litre additional cost for biofuels compared to conventional fuels.

[161] Proposal for a Dir. Amending Dir. 92/81/EEC With Regard to the Possibility of Applying a Reduced Rate of Excise Duty on Certain Mineral Oils Containing Biofuels and on Biofuels COM(2001)547.

from Renewable Energy Sources in the Internal Electricity Market.[162] Until the proposed amendment is adopted, Member States may request an authorization to apply a differentiated rate of excise duty to biofuels in accordance with the procedure of Article 8(4) of Directive 92/81/EC.[163] Such an authorization is necessary if it does not concern pilot projects, because these are covered by Article 8(2)(d) (i.e. optional exemptions or reductions). It should be added that the proposed Directive on Restructuring the Community Framework for the Taxation of Energy Products also provides for the possibility of an exemption or reduction for biofuels, outside the context of a pilot project (proposed Article 14(1)(b) and (c)).[164]

Fiscal Instruments—The Energy Tax

After the failed attempts to introduce a common CO_2/energy tax, the Commission presented a different proposal aimed at establishing an overall tax system for energy products.[165] The Commission proposes that all energy products, not just the mineral oils (or hydrocarbons) are taxed. As appears from the preamble, the proposed Directive has a dual aim. It is designed, first, to reduce the distortions of competition in the internal energy market resulting from the current fiscal disorder and, secondly, to contribute to the attainment of certain environmental objectives, most notably, the objective to stabilize CO_2 emissions in the atmosphere. Interestingly, the proposed preamble includes an explicit reference to the integration principle. Indeed, this initiative may be regarded as a first step in the direction of the internalization of external costs, including those of an environmental nature, into energy prices.

However, two remarks should be made concerning this proposal. First, it makes no sense introducing such a common tax, for environmental purposes, if the current environmentally unfriendly fiscal exemptions and reductions are going to be upheld.[166] If adopted, the Directive would indeed repeal and replace

[162] [2001] OJ L283/33. Biomass shall mean the biodegradable fraction of products, waste and residues from agriculture (including vegetal and animal substances), forestry, and related industries, as well as the biodegradable fraction of industrial and municipal waste (Art. 2(b)).

[163] Such was the conclusion of the Court of First Instance (CFI) in *BP Chemicals* (Case T-184/97, *BP Chemicals* v. *Commission* [2000] ECR II-3145). In this judgment, the CFI annulled the Commission Decision in which it had decided that the domestic tax reductions on the biofuels in question constituted state aid compatible with the common market and that the scheme qualified as a pilot project within the meaning of Art. 8(2)(d) of Dir. 92/81/EEC. The CFI held that Art. 8(2)(d) could not be used but that there was no reason why a decision could not be adopted in accordance with Art. 8(4) of that same Dir. France was subsequently granted the necessary authorization on the basis of Art. 8(4) in Dec. 2002/266/EC [2002] OJ L92/22. See also Dec. 2002/265/EC authorizing Italy to apply a differentiated rate of excise duty to fuels containing biodiesel in accordance with Art. 8(4) of Dir. 92/81/EC [2002] OJ L92/19.

[164] COM(97)30.

[165] Proposal for a Dir. Restructuring the Community Framework for the Taxation of Energy Products COM(97)30.

[166] See in the same sense: K. Deketelaere, 'European Environmental Tax Policy—Proposal for a Policy Vision and a Legal Framework' (1996) *European Environmental Law Review*, 13: 'it should be

the current legislation on excise duties for mineral oils. In doing so, it would correct some of this legislation's environmental flaws as appeared from the analysis of the legislation above (i.e. minimum rates would increase; allowing tax on aviation fuel for domestic flights). Other shortcomings however, would remain in the same or other form, as also appeared above (e.g. flexible regime for certain energy-intensive firms; optional exemptions for certain industrial and commercial purposes changed into lower rates). An interesting element, not mentioned above, is the fact that tax refunds will be possible in order to encourage firms to invest in efficient use of energy.

The second remark relates to the envisaged effect of the proposed taxation. Some doubts exist as to whether the proposed minimum tax rates would reflect environmental costs fully, and thus have true environmental benefits.[167] It is interesting to know in this regard that, for a long time, the proposal was blocked in the Council. Political agreement was only reached in March 2003.[168] Naturally, the controversial nature of the proposal resulted in many compromises and weakened provisions. In fact, the proposal seems to provide for too many exemptions and transitional periods, both general and for specific Member States.

Fiscal Instruments—Proposal for Special Tax Arrangements for Diesel Fuel

For reasons of completeness, it should be added to the above that the Commission recently proposed to increase the minimum rate of excise duty on diesel by 2006 (for diesel used by commercial vehicles by 2010). Interestingly, Recital 1 of the proposed Preamble quotes Article 6 EC.[169] The proposal is said to be designed to contribute to a smooth operation of the internal transport market, reduce distortion of competition between operators, and also provide better environmental protection by applying the polluter pays principle.

clear that it is no use introducing a European environmental tax policy without abolishing the present environment-unfriendly (fiscal) regulations (e.g. tax concessions in respect of professional transportation costs). Hence, organizing a European coordinated and/or led "ecological clean-up" of such regulations should be the first task of the Community'.

[167] See the results of the so-called TREMOVE simulations, which suggested that the effect on the final fuel price of this proposal would have been less than the effects of non-fiscal components of the fuel price variation in the period 1999–2000 (European Commission, *Economic Papers—The Effects of Fuel Price Changes on the Transport Sector and its Emissions—Simulations with TREMOVE* (EC, 2002)). See also D. Grimeaud, 'Road Transport and Climate Change Concerns—The EC Approach' (1999) 7 *Environmental Liability*, 105 and J. Wiers, 'Transport and the Environment—The Ugly Face of the Internal Market' (1999) *European Environmental Law Review*, 338. Even the Commission has doubts: see COM(1998)204. In addition, it is necessary to be aware of unexpected negative side-effects for the environment. One of the dangers of the (old) CO_2/energy tax proposal was, for example, that it would probably have favoured nuclear energy. See further: E. Rehbinder, 'Environmental Regulation Through Fiscal and Economic Incentives in a Federalist System' (1993) 20 *Ecology Law Quarterly*, 69.

[168] MEMO/03/64 of 21 Mar. 2003.

[169] Proposal for a Dir. Amending Dir. 92/81/EEC and Dir. 92/82/EEC to Introduce Special Tax Arrangements for Diesel Fuel Used for Commercial Purposes and Align the Excise Duties on Petrol and Diesel Fuel COM(2002)410. See also IP/2002/1134 and *Bulletin Quotidien Europe*, 7/8-2002, No. 1.3.37.

In Sum

The use of fiscal instruments as tools for furthering environmental goals is limited to some fiscal incentives incorporated in the common tax regime for mineral oils. These incentives consist of some environmentally friendly exemptions or reductions, and are supplemented by the requirement for all exemptions and reductions granted on the basis of Article 8(4) not to be contrary to environmental policy. Progress in the integration of environmental requirements into this field would be made by the adoption of the proposed directive for a total tax system for energy products, and of the proposal on biofuel taxation. Unfortunately, the adoption of the first has been extremely difficult.

iv. Promoting R&D, Information Exchange, and/or Training

Research, Development, and Demonstration Projects

Whereas early 1970s legislation providing for Community financial support to energy research, development, and demonstration projects did not include any reference to the environment, some of the legislation of the 1980s contained an environmental component in the form of a requirement that the results of an EIA should be incorporated in the funding application.[170] Strictly speaking, this can be regarded as some (weak) form of cross-compliance: no financial support for research is granted unless there is an EIA. Energy-related research, development, and demonstration projects, which were supported by the Community, were aimed at stimulating technological development relating to the prospection for extraction, storage, or transportation of hydrocarbons; energy-efficiency, and the rational use of energy, and the development/exploitation of so-called alternative energy sources (the means). All of this was for the benefit of reducing the Community's dependence on imported energy sources, and thus to secure energy supply, in other words to reduce the risk of tensions on the energy market (the goal). It was only in the 1990s that legislation explicitly began to point to the environmental benefits of (promoting) some of this research. In other words, besides the security of energy supply, the environmental objectives became explicit aims of this type of Community action. The means in this field remained pretty much the same: the support was still aimed at promoting energy efficiency/the rational use of energy and alternative energy sources (more and more referred to as 'renewable energy sources'). One field that was added, however, was the support to research on clean solid fuel technologies.[171]

[170] This environmental component could be found in legislation on support programmes for technological development in the hydrocarbons sector (promoting technology relating to prospecting for, extracting, storing, or transportation of hydrocarbons) and on demonstration projects in the field of energy saving and alternative energy sources. The decisions on research and development projects relating to energy saving and alternative energy sources did not refer to environmental concerns at all.

[171] Starting under the THERMIE programme (see Annex III) and the specific programme which supplemented the JOULE programme (see Area 2).

Despite the fact that these research programmes seemed very promising from an environmental perspective, their implementation did not always proceed smoothly. For example, in 1998, the Court of Auditors presented Special Report No. 17/98 on Support for Renewable Energy Sources (RES) in the Shared-Cost actions of the JOULE-THERMIE Programme[172] and the Pilot Actions of the ALTENER Programme.[173] In this report, the Court concluded, *inter alia*, that the merger between JOULE and THERMIE had not been completed, that many of the THERMIE demonstration projects lacked major innovative elements, that proper scientific and financial management, monitoring, and control of all projects under these programmes were not guaranteed, and that coordination between the Commission services involved in the funding of the RES projects was insufficient. A general conclusion as to the success or failure of ALTENER[174] and the RES component of JOULE-THERMIE was impossible, however, because the overall objectives were not sufficiently precise.[175]

Information Exchange and Training

The instruments of information exchange and training have been introduced in the context of various energy programmes, such as the SAVE and ALTENER programmes (which seem predominantly environmental programmes), but also in the CARNOT programme.[176]

D. Comments

i. *Energy Objectives and the Environment*

As appeared from the overview of secondary legislation above, right from the start and until today, one of the main objectives of Community action relating to the energy sector has been of a political-economic nature. The objective to ensure security of energy supply mainly consists of trying to reduce the Community's dependence on imported energy sources. Besides the oil crisis measures in the 1970s and the beginning of the 1980s, this objective has been pursued, over the years, primarily in two ways by promoting energy efficiency and energy conservation (the latter is also referred to as 'demand management'), and by diversifying energy supply.[177] Diversification of energy supply has been attempted mostly by stimulating introduction and use of so-called 'alternative energy sources', later referred to as 'renewable energy sources'. Besides their positive impact on the

[172] n. 100 above.

[173] [1998] OJ C356/39.

[174] n. 149 above.

[175] [1998] OJ C356/52.

[176] n. 103 above.

[177] The Green Paper on security of energy supply also points to the possible negotiating of strategic partnerships with supplier countries as a means of reducing external energy dependence (COM(2000)769, 45). This topic belongs to the external dimension of the energy policy, which is not discussed in this chapter.

Community's security of energy supply situation, both strategies seem to have environmental benefits, and are therefore compatible with the Community's environmental objectives. However, initially, this synergy was not stimulated or even acknowledged (evidenced by early energy-efficiency standards and early programmes relating to R&D and demonstration projects encouraging energy conservation).[178] It was only at the beginning of the 1990s that the environmental benefits of this policy were explicitly recognized. As attention to the environmental problems caused by the energy sector grew, for example as a result of the climate change issue, the positive environmental aspects of this Community action were increasingly emphasized. By the time the 1995 White Paper was drafted, it was obvious that the promotion of energy efficient technologies and energy conservation efforts could achieve both security of energy supply and environmental goals (such as the reduction of CO_2 emissions).[179] The same is true for the promotion of renewable energy sources.[180] Thus, it is in this area that most efforts to integrate environmental concerns into energy policy have been made. It should be observed, however, that diversification of energy supply also seems to have been promoted for the purpose of keeping the option of nuclear energy open, for example, by way of supporting specific R&D in that area. If one regards this energy source as environmentally damaging, such support is undesirable from an environmental point of view.

From the beginning of the 1990s onwards (see transit directives at the beginning of this period), Community policy started focusing on the realization of another aim besides security of energy supply. It began to adopt concrete action for the *establishment of a common market in energy*. This objective appears less compatible with environmental objectives. Market integration was, and still is, in the first place regarded as a means to improve economic efficiency in the energy sector so as to increase the competitiveness of the European economy and thus economic growth. In other words, it is designed to contribute to the achievement of the economic objectives in Article 2 EC. Although it has been associated with certain positive environmental developments, it is feared that lower energy prices resulting from liberalization will undermine the positive effects of energy conservation measures as well as impede development of renewables.

Below, I will summarize the main integration failures and efforts, including the instruments used. Integration failures relate to, in particular, the (potential)

178 As noted above, early energy efficiency standards obliquely pointed to the fact that the action was generally beneficial to the environment. The research programmes aimed at encouraging energy conservation and alternative energy sources did not mention the environment in the 1970s while their successors in the 1980s included the requirement for an EIA to be attached to the funding application.

179 White Paper, 'An Energy Policy for the European Union' COM(95)682, 33. See also Cross *et al.*, n. 6 above, 1032.

180 See in this connection: Commission Green Paper, 'Towards a European strategy for the Security of Energy Supply' COM(2000)769, 42: 'The target of doubling the share of renewables forms part of a strategy of security of supply and sustainable development'.

adverse effects of the liberalization process, and the lack of internalization of environmental costs. On the one hand, integration efforts consist of certain (non-structural) measures, such as the promotion of cleaner conventional fuels and technologies, and the switch to less environmentally damaging energy sources. Simultaneously, integration efforts concern more 'structural' action in the form of promotion of energy conservation, in other words, demand management.

ii. Integration Failures

Despite certain benefits for the environment, for example its contribution to a switch to cleaner fuels in power generation, it is feared that the liberalization process, which causes energy prices to drop, will discourage rational use of energy, and thus make demand management more difficult, and hinder development of alternative energy sources. This would be logical, since the energy intensity of an economy is linked to energy prices. In other words, increases in real energy prices encourage energy conservation, while price decreases discourage energy conservation. That is why it is important that the full costs of the energy cycle are included in energy prices.[181] In this respect, a study estimated that the external costs of producing electricity, including damage to the environment and to health, amount to up to 1–2 per cent of the EU's GDP, not including the cost of global warming. The same research indicated that the cost of producing electricity from coal or oil would double, and the cost of electricity production from gas would increase by 30 per cent if external costs were internalized.[182] In order to internalize the external costs, the study suggests taxing damaging fuels and technologies, which would result in a substantial increase of energy prices. Although, to a limited extent, tax incentives in the energy field are used for environmental purposes, current EC fiscal legislation falls short of truly internalizing environmental costs. The scope of this legislation is limited and it allows for many environmentally undesirable exemptions or reductions. Consequently, existing legislation on excise duties on mineral oils has not led to any serious harmonization. The proposed CO_2/energy tax of 1992 might have been, and the proposed energy tax of 1997 may be a better attempt to start applying the polluter pays principle in this sector. The lack of a comprehensive internalization of environmental costs means that governments are effectively subsidizing those fuels that are most polluting.[183]

181 EEA, *Europe's Environment—The Dobris Assessment, Chapter 19—Energy* (Copenhagen: EEA, 2001), 13.

182 Report based on the results of the EXTERNE project: see Commission press release, IP/01/1047.

183 EEA, *Europe's Environment—The Dobris Assessment, Chapter 19—Energy* (Copenhagen: EEA, 2001), 113: 'energy extraction, production and consumption are inherently subsidised because market prices for various forms of fossil fuel energy do not take account of the cost of environmental damage resulting from atmospheric emissions. The increasing interest in incorporating these costs is likely to become a key influence on the demand for energy and in underlining the need for further improvements in energy efficiency in future' and G. Topmann in K. Button (ed.), *Transport Policy—*

In sum, the serious environmental damage caused by the energy sector may be regarded as being due to a combination of a market failure, that is, the market does not reflect environmental costs, and a government failure, which operates to reinforce the first. It may be argued that this amounts to a failure to integrate environmental concerns in energy policy. Under current legislation, the negative environmental effects of the internal market policy are only moderated by a limited number of other measures.

iii. Integration Efforts

Cleaner Conventional Fuels and Cleaner, Efficient Technologies on the Supply Side

The Community's efforts to promote cleaner conventional fuels through fuel quality standards (instrument of direct regulation) and fuel tax differentiation (fiscal instrument) may be regarded as integration efforts. Data show that the latter has been used successfully to phase out leaded petrol in the EU.[184] Clean (solid) fuel technologies were promoted by way of support of R&D, the promotion of training and information exchange, as well as regulation, in particular in the form of the Large Combustion Plants Directive. This Directive promoted use of pollution control technology, which led to a reduction in emissions of certain pollutants.[185] In addition, together with the liberalization process, which encouraged electricity generators to choose the cheapest, most efficient, and most flexible generating capacity, the Large Combustion Plants Directive in fact resulted in a switch from coal and oil to natural gas for electricity generation.[186] This switch contributed significantly to a fall in emissions of all major pollutants (including SO_2 and CO_2) between 1990 and 1998.

As for the promotion of CHP, no binding regulatory framework has been developed. There are only provisions in internal market directives and a non-binding Community strategy laid down in a 1997 Commission Communication.[187] This policy document sets out an EU indicative target of 18 per cent (of total gross electricity generation of the Community produced by CHP) by 2010, which means a doubling of the share of EU generation from CHP.[188]

Ways into Europe's Future (Gütersloh: Bertelsmann, 1994), 186: 'Since motor vehicle and mineral oil taxes do not cover the social costs actually incurred, the government in effect subsidizes that mode of transport which pollutes the environment most'.

184 EEA, *Environmental Signals 2000—European Environment Agency Regular Indicator Report* (Copenhagen: EEA, 2000), 27.

185 ibid. 22.

186 EEA, *Environmental Signals 2001—European Environment Agency Regular Indicator Report* (Copenhagen: EEA, 2001), 41–4.

187 Commission Communication on A Community Strategy to Promote Combined Heat and Power (CHP) and to Dismantle Barriers to its Development COM(97)514.

188 COM(97)514, 10. See also Cross *et al.*, n. 6 above, 315. The importance of financial support to promote CHP is illustrated by the fact that market penetration is especially high as a result of state aid in Denmark and the Netherlands, according to EEA (EEA, *Environmental Signals 2001—European Environment Agency Regular Indicator Report* (Copenhagen: EEA, 2001), 46).

Promotion of Less Environmentally Damaging Sources:Renewables

In internal market legislation, certain provisions have been incorporated that are aimed at mitigating negative environmental effects of the liberalization process. They might be used to help renewables and CHP overcome certain barriers. Besides the few provisions in internal energy market legislation, use of renewable energy sources is promoted mainly by way of R&D support in the context of the EC's energy-specific research programmes, and by way of information exchange, training, and related action in the context of the (predominantly environmental) ALTENER programme. Attention is given to the promotion of renewables in the Community guidelines on state aid for environmental protection. In addition, an environmental directive on renewables, setting out indicative targets for the share of energy derived from them, was adopted, but it proved impossible to agree on a common aid system for renewables. This is unfortunate in light of the results of a recent study which evaluated the effectiveness of various instruments used in different Member States designed to promote the development of renewables.[189] The study concluded that no single instrument could be identified as the ultimate key to success. Rather, it is a combination of different instruments, including support schemes, such as the fixed price scheme (entailing an obligation to purchase at a guaranteed price) that led to successful exploitation of renewable technology in certain Member States.

Promotion of Less Environmentally Damaging Energy Sources: Biofuels

The Commission has proposed to encourage the use of biofuels by way of fiscal regulation. Fuel tax differentiation to promote these fuels is possible under current legislation, but requires Member States to apply for individual authorizations. The proposed fiscal system, however, would provide for a general possibility to reduce excise duties on biofuels when used as heating or motor fuels. In addition, the Community has promoted these so-called alternative fuels in the form of financial support to relevant R&D projects in the context of various Community research programmes.

Limited Environmental Guarantees in TEN-E

Limited environmental guarantees are incorporated in the legislation on TEN-E. Use is made of the cross-compliance instrument in this respect.

Energy Conservation or Energy Demand Management

More fundamental than the above measures (including those aimed at promoting less environmentally damaging energy sources) is the strategy aimed at encouraging energy conservation, also referred to as a strategy of energy demand management. As observed, together with the measures aimed at encouraging the introduction and use of renewables (including biofuels), this strategy finds its

[189] EEA, Environmental issue report: 'Renewable Energies—Success Stories', 2001 (on file with the author).

origin in an attempt to reduce the Community's dependence on external energy sources and thus, to ensure energy supplies. Energy conservation has been encouraged at the Community level by way of various instruments, most notably, traditional command-and-control regulation (energy-efficiency standards and labelling rules), support to energy-specific R&D, and action relating to information exchange as well as training. The latter occurred or occurs in the context of the SAVE programmes, which are environmental programmes rather than energy programmes.

Chronology of Integration Efforts

It should be noted that the first explicit integration efforts were made in the context of fuel quality standards and implicitly in the context of energy-efficiency standards and R&D programmes. Both types of action were first adopted in the 1970s, before the integration principle was incorporated into the Treaty. The other integration efforts followed the adoption of energy-related legislation in new fields in the 1990s (i.e. environmental components of internal market legislation, TEN-E, and fiscal harmonization). Additional efforts are made in the context of proposed legislation (especially, in proposed fiscal regulation).

Assessment

In sum, most existing legislation does have an environmental component. However, it seems that this component is not always sufficient to lead to real environmental benefits. This is illustrated, for example, by the fact that, despite attempts to promote development of alternative energy sources, the use of fossil fuels remains predominant and,[190] despite energy conservation efforts, total energy consumption is increasing.[191]

[190] Despite efforts to promote use of alternative energy sources, data shows that energy use continues to be dominated by fossil fuel (see EEA, *Environmental Signals 2001—European Environment Agency Regular Indicator Report* (Copenhagen: EEA, 2001), 44. See also European Commission, *2000—Annual Energy Review* (Luxembourg: EC, 2001), 2). Oil is still the main energy source in the EU. Consumption of coal, lignite, and derivatives fell due to a switch to relatively cleaner fuels such as natural gas. Thus, the consumption of natural gas increased, but so did consumption of nuclear fuels. Finally, consumption of renewable energy rose. In 1998, its contribution in the EU amounted to 5.9%. The Commission itself has warned that oil dependence could reach 90% by 2020 if no specific measures are taken, especially in the transport sector (Commission Green Paper, 'Towards a European Strategy for the Security of Energy Supply' COM(2000)769, 39).

[191] Total energy consumption increased and remains linked to GDP. The energy intensity (or energy consumption per unit of GDP) fell, but less than the Commission had hoped for. See EEA, *Environmental Signals 2001—European Environment Agency Regular Indicator Report* (Copenhagen: EEA, 2001), 42–3. In addition, it is important to know that the decrease in energy intensity is not the result of energy efficiency measures, but rather of structural changes in the economy, such as the shift towards services (EEA, *Environmental Signals 2001—European Environment Agency Regular Indicator Report* (Copenhagen: EEA, 2001), 43). It should be recalled that once there was a time when energy consumption was de-coupled from GDP growth (as a result of the 1973 oil crisis) (OECD, *Environmental Effects of Electricity Generation* (Paris: OECD, 1985), 9).

Next Step

After having identified the specific integration efforts and failures in EC energy policy, various types of integration will now be distinguished depending on how strong and deliberate the integration is.

V. Various Types of Integration—Strength of the Integration

A. Integration Types

i. Introduction

Two different types of policy-specific objectives may be distinguished in relation to the environment and its protection: (potentially) 'compatible' objectives that may be adequately achieved in an environmentally friendly way, and 'incompatible' objectives that may not be achieved in such a way. In the first case, I shall refer to a 'no conflict situation', in the latter case to a 'conflict situation'. It seems that both 'no conflict' and 'conflict' situations are present in EC energy policy.

ii. No Conflict Situation

Compatible Objectives

It has been argued that this refers to a situation in which (non-environmental) policy-specific objectives are pursued in an environmentally friendly way. The question is whether EC energy policy contains (potentially) compatible objectives, and whether these have indeed been pursued in environmentally friendly fashion. It should be recalled in this respect that, initially, the objective of securing energy supply was not always promoted in an environmentally friendly way (see some of the early oil crisis measures). However, the means to achieve this objective have become more environmentally friendly. They consist of the promotion of energy-efficiency and conservation (which helps reduce demand), as well as of development of alternative energy sources. Both strategies have environmental benefits. Increasingly, they have been mentioned as components of the EC's strategy on climate change. On the other hand, the means to achieve security of supply by way of diversifying energy supply may not be entirely environmentally friendly to the extent that the option of nuclear energy is kept open.

Implicit Integration

The more compatible objectives are with environmental objectives, the easier it is to pursue the latter in the context of this policy. In such cases integration is almost automatic: by promoting one aim the other is promoted automatically. This will be referred to as 'implicit' integration.

The true test of integration lies in the extent to which a policy area and its incompatible objectives are adjusted or redesigned to help pursue environmental objectives, adhere to the environmental principles, and take account of environmental criteria. In other words, the true test lies in the extent to which 'explicit' efforts have been made to control or reduce negative environmental effects of another policy area.

iii. Conflict Situation

Mitigating/Non-Structural Versus Structural Integration

Often it will not be possible to achieve the objectives of a particular policy area adequately in an environmentally friendly way.[192] The most plausible interpretation of the integration principle requires that incompatible objectives are adjusted, so as to pursue them in the least environmentally damaging way possible or, even, that these objectives are redefined or abandoned, depending on the extent to which they are essential for the achievement of principal Community objectives.

It would seem that the more these policy-specific objectives are adjusted or dropped for environmental reasons, the stronger integration is in that specific policy area. Thus, various degrees of integration may be distinguished. A weak degree of integration occurs when the pursuit of an incompatible objective is made less damaging. A stronger degree occurs when a shift is promoted to less environmentally damaging action. Finally, the strongest degree of integration is when the cause of environmental damage is neutralized because the incompatible objective itself is completely dropped. A good example of the latter can be given in relation to the transport sector. Suppose that the Commission proposes measures that are designed to decouple transport growth from economic growth. Abandoning the objective to provide people and business with their ever-increasing need for mobility so as to fuel the economy would constitute a strong form of environmental integration.

Because such measures seem to tackle the 'root causes' of environmental degradation and appear to affect the policy area, its objectives, and the means to achieve these more fundamentally, I will refer to them as 'structural' measures.[193] Promotion of technological innovations and improvements resulting in less environmentally damaging methods, products, and systems, and/or a shift towards the least environmentally damaging practices, will mitigate or alleviate sector-specific environmental problems, but such action will not bring about

[192] Note the word 'adequately': the conflict situation includes the situation where there is an environmentally friendly way of pursuing the objectives but it is insufficient. A good example is the promotion of extensive farming systems in the context of the CAP. The CAP objectives should be pursued by stimulating these systems as much as possible (see special relationship between agricultural activity and environment).

[193] In the dictionary 'structural' is defined as 'relating to or affecting the structure of something' (*Collins Cobuild English Dictionary*).

'structural changes'. These measures will be referred to as 'non-structural' or 'mitigating' action. The question whether structural measures actually lead to less environmental damage or increased protection of the environment is a different matter, one which falls outside the scope of this chapter.[194]

Incidental versus Deliberate Integration

For an assessment of these integration efforts, it is necessary to examine whether they occurred specifically for environmental reasons, or whether policy-specific or other reasons or interests were playing a predominant role. In other words, it is important to establish whether a policy area, its objectives, and/or the means to achieve those objectives have been adjusted or redefined in order to help pursue environmental objectives, or whether other factors have pushed the policy area in a direction that (simply) happened to have positive consequences for the environment. The first type of integration may be termed 'deliberate' integration, the second 'incidental' integration. This distinction is based on the motives behind the measures. Again, just like integration in a no conflict situation, integration is 'easier' when other factors have pushed the policy area in question in the right direction. In the literature, this has been called 'a permissive structure for reforms' that allows for environmental protection requirements to be integrated.[195] One could also regard this as a conflict situation that has turned into a no-conflict situation. A good example of such incidental integration can be found in the Common Agricultural Policy (CAP). This policy area has known a couple of reform rounds that were designed to combat overproduction in various agricultural sectors. Some of these measures have had beneficial environmental side-effects. The integration has not always been succesful however, because the measures in question have not always been sufficiently specific.[196]

B. Integration in the EC Energy Policy

Integration in EC Energy Policy mainly results from the existence of the compatible objective to ensure security of energy supply (see also above, under no-conflict situation: *implicit integration*). In this context, a shift towards less environmentally damaging energy sources (renewables), as well as energy efficiency and conservation has been promoted. It appears that the environmental benefits of pursuing the compatible objective have been increasingly emphasized, instead of introducing new or further efforts to integrate environmental concerns. The failure to introduce a common energy tax is significant in this regard.

[194] For example, stimulating people to work from home might reduce transport but it might at the same time result in an increase of energy use or it might simply mean that people use their car more often at weekends.

[195] A. Lenschow, 'The World Trade Dimension of "Greening" the EU's Common Agricultural Policy' in J. Golub (ed.), *Global Competition and EU Environmental Policy* (London/New York: Routledge, 1998), 166.

[196] Dhondt, n. 2 above, 199–290.

Other integration efforts are of a deliberate but non-structural nature (e.g. fuel quality standards).

C. Is the Integration Sufficient in EC Energy Policy?

In sum, EC action towards integration in relation to the energy sector does not yet amount to a common policy. It seems that this observation also concerns the CHP. The liberalization process is not accompanied by measures resulting in true internalization of environmental costs. The integration principle in Article 6 EC probably does not require the market integration goal to be abandoned. After all, it is an important means to achieve some of the principal objectives of the Community. Nonetheless, it seems that the liberalization process and its potentially negative effects on the environment do require additional integration efforts. That is why I believe that current integration efforts are inadequate in light of what the integration principle requires. Although it includes demand-management measures, these appear insufficient to realize a true balance between various conflicting objectives. Finding this balance is exactly what integration is all about, the integration principle requires the Community to balance its main objectives, including those of an economic and environmental nature. It seems, however, that the energy policy has been and is being designed mainly to serve the economic objectives of the Community. It has been driven mainly by economic considerations. Integration in the context of the energy policy is therefore weak. It is, in other words, situated at the left end of the spectrum instead of in the middle.

What measures should be taken to improve this situation? It may be argued that serious, well-designed fiscal measures could have a more fundamental impact on the market, and a more consistent application of the polluter pays principle in EC energy policy seems to be needed. It should be observed in this regard that, at first sight, the energy taxation proposal, for which political agreement was reached in March 2003, appears to be insufficient. It allows for too many exemptions and transitional periods.

VI. Conclusion

The objectives to secure energy supply and to protect the environment are mutually supportive in action that is directed towards promoting renewables as well as towards demand management. However, because of the sensitive nature of the sector, it has been difficult to adopt a Community policy that truly influences the fuel choice of Member States. Initially, due to concerns relating to security of energy supply, and later also for environmental reasons, Community action has avoided radical measures of a fiscal nature determining the fuel mix in Member States. Rather, it has concentrated on a 'softer' form of coordination, aimed at promoting energy conservation and efficiency as well as, to a limited extent, cleaner energy sources. This policy has been pursued by way of technical harmonization, financial support of certain research, development, demonstration projects, and training, as well as information exchange programmes.[197] It is difficult to integrate environmental concerns into legislation harmonizing fiscal standards, as such harmonization has yet to occur. However, for integration to be realized, this seems to be the best way forward.

[197] See also R.H. Lauwaars and C.W.A. Timmermans, *Europees recht in kort bestek* (Deventer: W.E.J. Tjeenk Willink, 1999), 302.

Community Development Cooperation Law, Sustainable Development, and the Convention on Europe—From Dislocation to Consistency?

*Rhiannon Williams**

I. Introduction

The European Community (EC) Treaty sets out various provisions with regard to development law and sustainable development.[1] In this chapter it will be argued that they have been systematically ignored by the European Council and Commission, to the detriment of the least developed countries and the cause of sustainable development. Further, certain provisions of the draft Treaty establishing a Constitution for Europe, had they been adopted in December 2003, would have legitimized this approach, and would have allowed the further marginalization of development and environmental sustainability issues in developing countries. If the provisions in question were in future to be adopted without amendment, they could contribute to the existing downwards spiral of real and comparative poverty of the world's poorest peoples, which would continue to contribute to global insecurity. The other side of the coin is that, following the failure of the Brussels Intergovernmental Conference in December 2003, the Community could now seize the opportunity it ostensibly covets to demonstrate moral authority at international level, and to increase its effectiveness as a leading player on the international stage whose legacy in matters developmental, environmental—and economic—will endure.

The chapter is divided into five parts: current European Community (EC) and European Union (EU) Treaty provisions; a brief summary of the relevant provisions of the Cotonou Agreement; Community Policy; consideration of whether current EC policy could be challenged; and the potential impact of the Convention on Europe.

* Doctoral Research Fellow, Institute for European Studies, Vrije Universiteit Brussel.

[1] The chapter will follow the practice of the European Court of Justice (ECJ) with regard to the citation of Arts. of the Treaties. Thus, where a Treaty Art. is referred to as it stands after 1 May 1999, the number of the Art. is followed by two letters indicating the Treaty concerned: EU for the Treaty on European Union, and EC for the EC Treaty. But where a Treaty Art. is referred to as it stood before 1 May 1999, the number of the Art. is followed by the words 'of the Treaty on European Union' or 'of the EC Treaty'.

II. Current Treaty Provisions

A. On Development Cooperation

From its inception in 1957, the European Economic Community's (EEC) Member States were agreeing financially to support the economic and social development of their dependent territories. As those territories became independent, and as new Member States joined the EC, bringing with them concern for their own former territories, the first Lomé Convention was entered into in 1975 by the EC and a broader band of African, Caribbean, and Pacific (ACP) developing countries. The year 1985 saw the first explicit mention of an objective for EC development policy—poverty reduction, in Lomé III—followed by gender objectives, human rights, good governance, and the rule of law under Lomé IV and Lomé IV bis.[2] However, the first European constitutional provision for development aid did not appear until 1992, in the Treaty on European Union (the Maastricht Treaty). Under Title XVII on Development Cooperation were set out Articles 130u–130y of the EC Treaty. These were reproduced, almost entirely word for word, in the amended EC Treaty following the 1997 Amsterdam Treaty. Title XX EC is entitled 'Development Cooperation'. It comprises Articles 177 to 181, inclusive.

Article 177 EC (Article 130u of the EC Treaty) provides that:

1. Community policy in the sphere of development cooperation, which shall be complementary to the policies pursued by the Member States, shall foster:
   — the sustainable economic and social development of the developing countries, and more particularly the most disadvantaged[3] among them,
   — the smooth and gradual integration of the developing countries into the world economy,
   — the campaign against poverty in the developing countries.
2. Community policy in this area shall contribute to the general objective of developing and consolidating democracy and the rule of law, and to that of respecting human rights and fundamental freedoms.
3. The Community and the Member States shall comply with the commitments and take account of the objectives they have approved in the context of the United Nations and other competent international organisations.

There are no cases decided by or pending before the European Court of Justice (ECJ) on the interpretation of this Article. Indeed, the area generally is

[2] S.J.H. Dearden. 'Does the European Union's Development Policy Have Any Future?' Development Studies Association, European Development Policy Study Group (2001) Discussion Paper No. 24.

[3] This is not a defined term, but the UN designates as 'least-developed countries' those with a per capita income of less than US$1 per day, of which there are currently 49 (46 of which are ACP countries).

so little litigated that there is no 'development cooperation' field in the search form for ECJ case law on the Curia website. (An interesting exception to the general absence of case law is discussed below in relation to Article 181 EC.)[4]

'Developing countries' in Article 177 EC means all developing countries except those categorized by the Community as countries in transition (central and eastern European states). Community action with regard to these countries is based, somewhat unsatisfactorily, on the catch-all Article 308 EC.

Under Article 178 EC (Article 130v of the EC Treaty), 'The Community shall take account of the objectives referred to in Article 177 in the policies that it implements which are likely to affect developing countries'.

Article 179 EC (Article 130w of the EC Treaty) provides that:

> 1. Without prejudice to the other provisions of this Treaty, the Council, acting in accordance with the procedure referred to in Article 251, shall adopt the measures necessary to further the objectives referred to in Article 177. Such measures may take the form of multiannual programmes.
> 2. The European Investment Bank shall contribute, under the terms laid down in its Statute, to the implementation of the measures referred to in paragraph 1.
> 3. The provisions of this Article shall not affect cooperation with the African, Caribbean and Pacific countries in the framework of the ACP-EC Convention.

This was the only Article of the Development Title which was amended by the Amsterdam Treaty. The change lay in its paragraph 1, where mention to the procedure referred to in Article 251 EC was introduced. Article 251 EC sets out the *co-decision* procedure. Previously, any measures necessary to the furthering of the Article 177 EC objectives which were taken by the Council would have fallen under the *co-operation* procedure of Article 189c of the EC Treaty.

This change marked the only effective democratization of the implementation of the EC's development policy at that time.

In particular, it should be noted that, under this Article, the Council 'shall' adopt the measures necessary to further the objectives referred to in Article 177 EC. This is important when it comes to considering (see below) whether the nature of Article 177 EC is exhortatory or prescriptive.

Article 180 EC (Article 130x of the EC Treaty) provides that:

> 1. The Community and the Member States shall coordinate their policies on development cooperation and shall consult each other on their aid programmes, including in international organizations and during international conferences. They may undertake joint action. Member States shall contribute if necessary to the implementation of Community aid programmes.
> 2. The Commission may take any useful initiative to promote the coordination referred to in paragraph 1.

[4] Case C-268/94, *Portugal* v. *Council* [1996] ECR I-6177.

The coordination of Community and Member State development cooperation and aid is worthy of at least a full-length article in its own right, and will not be considered here. The tensions which may arise from the Community and the Member States' 'joint and several' responsibility for development cooperation are shown, however, in one of the few ECJ cases which touch on the development provisions of the EC Treaty:

Under Article 181 EC (Article 130y of the EC Treaty):

> Within their respective spheres of competence, the Community and the Member States shall cooperate with third countries and with the competent international organizations. The arrangements for Community cooperation may be the subject of arrangements between the Community and the third parties concerned, which shall be negotiated and concluded in accordance with Article 300.
>
> The previous paragraph shall be without prejudice to Members States' competence to negotiate in international bodies and to conclude international agreements.[5]

The case of *Portugal* v. *Council*[6] concerned an application by Portugal to annul a Council decision concerning the conclusion of a Cooperation Agreement between the EC and India. The decision was based on, *inter alia*, Article 130y of the EC Treaty (Article 181 EC). This case has been described as, 'the Court's first opportunity to define what development policy *was*,'[7] (as opposed to previous litigation, which had centred on what development policy was *not*, in comparison with commercial policy). Portugal put forward two main arguments:

(a) That recourse should have been had instead to Article 235 of the EC Treaty (Article 308 EC),[8] and to the participation of all the Member States in the conclusion of the Agreement, because the legal basis relied on conferred insufficient powers on the Community with regard to human rights and to various provisions concerning specific fields of cooperation. Portugal's application in this respect was dismissed, with the ECJ finding that:

> by declaring that 'Community policy... shall contribute to the general objective of developing and consolidating democracy and the rule of law, and to that of respecting human rights and fundamental freedoms', Article 130u(2) [of the EC Treaty] requires the Community to take account of the objective of respect for human rights when it adopts measures in the field of development cooperation.
>
> The mere fact that Article 1(1) of the Agreement provides that respect for human rights and democratic principles 'constitutes an essential element' of the Agreement does not justify the conclusion that that provision goes beyond the objective stated in Article

[5] This is identically worded to Art. 174(4) EC.

[6] See n. 4 above.

[7] S. Peers, 'Case note on Case C-268/94, *Portugal* v. *Council*' (1998) 35 *Common Market Law Review*, 539–55. See also the case note by N. Burrows, 'Development Cooperation Defined' (1997) 22 *European Law Review*, 594–8.

[8] The provision that if action by the Community should prove necessary to attain one of the Community objectives, and the Treaty has not provided the necessary powers, the Council shall, acting unanimously on a proposal from the Commission and after consulting the European Parliament, take the appropriate measures.

130u(2) of the Treaty. The very wording of the latter provision demonstrated the importance to be attached to respect for human rights and democratic principles, so that, amongst other things, development cooperation policy must be adapted to the requirement of respect for those rights and principles.[9]

The ECJ therefore found that, so far as Article 1(1) of the Agreement was concerned, the contested decision could be validly based on Article 130y of the EC Treaty (Article 181 EC) and,

(b) That as the Community's competence to conclude such an agreement was not exclusive, but was complementary to that of the Member States, the scope of some of the provisions of the Agreement, relating to specific matters falling within the sphere of cooperation, (e.g. energy, tourism and culture, drug-abuse control, and intellectual property), was such that the legal basis of the contested decision was inadequate. The ECJ held that:

> to require a development cooperation agreement concluded between the Community and a non-member country to be based on another provision as well as on Article 130y and, possibly, also to be concluded by the Member States whenever it touches on a specific matter would in practice amount to rendering devoid of substance the competence and procedure described in Article 130y.
>
> It must therefore be held that the fact that a development cooperation agreement contains clauses concerning various specific matters cannot alter the characterization of the agreement, which must be determined having regard to its essential object and not in terms of individual clauses, provided that those clauses do not impose such extensive obligations concerning the specific matters referred to that those obligations in fact constitute objectives distinct from those of development cooperation.[10]

In the light of those considerations, the ECJ considered the specific provisions of the Agreement, and then dismissed Portugal's application.

The ECJ found, as cited above, that Article 130u(2) of the EC Treaty (Article 177(2) EC) requires the Community to take account of the objective of respect for human rights when it adopts measures in the field of development cooperation because of the declaration that Community development cooperation policy 'shall contribute to' the general objective of respecting human rights and fundamental freedoms. It would seem logical to infer from the similar wording, therefore, that the Community is 'required' to take account of all three objectives cited in Article 177(1) EC (the sustainable economic and social development of the developing countries, and more particularly the most disadvantaged among them; the smooth and gradual integration of the developing countries into the world economy; and the campaign against poverty in the developing countries) when it adopts measures in the field of development cooperation because of the Treaty declaration that Community development policy 'shall foster' those objectives. 'Fostering' (in the presumably applicable sense of promoting the growth or development of) is at least as strong a concept, if not stronger, than

[9] See n. 4, at paras. 23 and 24. [10] ibid., at paras. 38 and 39.

'contributing to'. In addition, there is the provision of Article 178 EC, that the Community 'shall' take account of the Article 177 EC objectives in those of its policies likely to affect developing countries.

In further support of this argument is the finding of the ECJ at paragraph 37 of the judgment that, 'In order to qualify as a development cooperation agreement for the purposes of Article 130y of the Treaty, [Article 181 EC], an agreement must pursue the objectives referred to in Article 130u [Article 177 EC].'

It has, however, been posited that:

> . . . the [EC] Treaty expressly obliges that the Community development policy contribute to the *objective* of furthering human rights; it does not establish human rights protection as a superior rule governing the development policy. There is a gradual elision in the Court's reasoning as it finds, firstly, that Article 130U(2) requires the Community to 'take account' of this objective when adopting measures; secondly, that development policy 'must be adapted' to this request; and, thirdly, that such adaptation means that development policy is thus 'necessarily. . . subordinate' to the human rights objective.[11] In four paragraphs of legal alchemy, an objective to which Community policy was contributing has become a rule which that policy must obey. The grounds for this are simply that the Community institutions and the Member States believed this necessary.[12]

It is submitted that this is not a sound argument. The ECJ does not appear to be requiring of development policy any more than the Treaty does: the ECJ does not state that development policy must only be adapted to the human rights objective, or that this must be the overarching goal of that policy. The 'necessarily. . . subordinate' comment was made in the following context:

> With regard, more particularly, to the argument of the Portuguese Government that the characterization of respect for human rights as an essential element in cooperation presupposes specific means of action, it must first be stated that to adapt cooperation policy to respect for human rights necessarily entails establishing a certain connection between those matters whereby one of them is made subordinate to the other. In that regard, it should be borne in mind that a provision such as Article 1(1) of the Agreement[13] may be, amongst other things, an important factor for the exercise of the right to have a development cooperation agreement suspended or terminated where the non-member country has violated human rights.[14]

The Treaty does not provide that Community development policy 'may' contribute to the objective of furthering human rights, but that it 'shall' do so. Employing a suspension or termination clause for breach of human rights in a development cooperation agreement would appear to be an efficient and reasonable way to pursue fulfilment of that Treaty requirement.

[11] ibid., paras. 23, 24, and 26 of the judgment.

[12] Peers, n. 7 above.

[13] This provided that respect for human rights and democratic principles constituted 'an essential element' of the Agreement.

[14] n. 4 above, paras. 26 and 27 of the judgment.

As explained above, Community development policy must, under the EC Treaty, 'contribute to' the objective of furthering human rights, and 'foster' the objectives of: the sustainable economic and social development of the developing countries, and more particularly the most disadvantaged among them; the smooth and gradual integration of the developing countries into the world economy; and the campaign against poverty in the developing countries. Given that the duty to 'foster' appears to be at least as strong as—if not stronger than—that to 'contribute to', the same reasoning could be applied, *mutatis mutandis*, to those objectives, with the effect that development policy should be 'necessarily subordinate' to those objectives. But even if Peers is correct in his assessment that, 'The Court has delivered another judgment confusing what the Treaty *does* say with what it *should* say', it is submitted that the Treaty is sufficiently clearly worded for the Community to be 'required' to take account of all three objectives cited in Article 177(1) EC when adopting development cooperation measures.

The above argumentation may seem to be labouring the obvious, but in considering current Community development cooperation policy, questions which arise are: if one can argue that Community development cooperation generally, as set out in Communications from the Commission and Council, or that a development cooperation agreement for the purposes of Article 181 EC in particular, does not pursue the objectives referred to in Article 177 EC, then is that policy or agreement properly classified or founded in law? (In his Opinion in *Portugal* v. *Council*,[15] Advocate General La Pergola argued that 'It would be the failure to adopt a clause of that type [a democracy clause] that would compromise the legality of Community action, because compliance with the specific wording of Article 130u EC would no longer be guaranteed'.)[16] To what extent must those objectives be pursued? May one of the objectives be pursued to the exclusion of the others? How great is the scope for the Commission's or the Council's discretion in interpreting and implementing Article 177 EC? And to what extent should the Community be accountable with regard to showing the extent to which the objectives are being pursued in its general policy, or in each agreement, or with regard to each country?

Further questions arise with regard to compliance with Article 178 EC: to what extent *does* the Community take account of the Article 177 EC objectives in the policies that it implements which are likely to affect developing countries? Which policies might be included here? This provision could arguably include, *inter alia*, the Common Agricultural Policy, international trade policy, the Common Fisheries Policy, enlargement and international environmental policy. To what extent is the Community bound under Article 178 EC to record or

[15] n. 4 above.

[16] Para. 29 of Advocate General La Pergola's Opinion in Case C-268/94, *Portugal* v. *Council*, n. 4 above.

report how it has assessed and taken account of the Article 177 EC objectives in drawing up those of its policies likely to affect developing countries?

The development cooperation title of the EC Treaty seems to be no less prescriptive than the environment or consumer protection titles, yet in practice, its provisions appear to have been taken less seriously by the Community institutions. It is possible that this is because development policy is seen as being purely 'external'. However, one effect of globalization is that the boundaries between internal and external matters are becoming more blurred. In environmental and trade matters, for example, it is impossible in some areas to draw a line between internal and external policies and interests. The same is arguably true, if for different reasons, for development policy.[17] More importantly, the law is the law and should be applied as such. The EC has been allowed to maintain different levels of implementation of the two similarly worded policies. Those countries with an interest in the enforcement of the current EC Treaty provisions on development may not have considered whether it would be possible for them to be fully implemented, and few would be likely even to have the necessary resources to devote to analysing the Byzantine EC law and policy on the matter.

B. On the Relationship between Community Development and Common Foreign and Security Policy

Article 1 of the Treaty on European Union (TEU) provides in its third paragraph that, 'The Union shall be founded on the European Communities, supplemented by the policies and forms of cooperation established by this Treaty'. The Union's objectives are set out in Article 2 TEU, and include the achievement of 'balanced and sustainable development' (this is not stated to be limited to the Community), and the assertion of the identity of the Union on the international scene, in particular through the implementation of a common foreign and security policy. Article 3 TEU provides that the Union must respect and build upon the Community's *acquis communautaire*, and that the Union:

> shall in particular ensure the consistency of its external activities as a whole in the context of its external relations, security, economic and development policies. The Council and the Commission shall be responsible for ensuring such consistency and shall cooperate to

[17] Extract from the Executive summary of the *DAC Guidelines—Poverty Reduction*. See http://www.oecd.org/document/1/0,2340,en_2649_34621_1885953_19699_1_1_1, 00.html: 'in a rapidly globalizing world the social ills associated with poverty—disease, illicit migration, environmental degradation, crime, political instability, armed conflict and terrorism—can spread with greater ease across borders and continents. Compounding this are the pressures of population growth. Of the estimated increase of 2 billion people over the next 20 years, 97% will live in the developing world. Eradicating poverty is thus more than a moral and humanitarian imperative. It is also essential for global security and prosperity and for reducing environmental stresses. It is an international public good of the first order, serving the interests of all'.

this end. They shall ensure the implementation of these policies, each in accordance with its respective powers.

It is arguable that the *acquis communautaire* includes established development cooperation policies.[18] As pointed out by de Feyter, had a common foreign policy been included in the EC Treaty, it would have implied loss of sovereignty for the Member States. So it was included in the intergovernmental framework of the Treaty on European Union, where decision-making is unanimous. However, in the light of Article 3 TEU, that *acquis communautaire* will be built upon, and Union competencies will increase, so, '[i]nevitably, foreign policy and security considerations will impact upon the development cooperation policy, even with the safeguards provided on the acquis communautaire. The impact will grow as the Common Foreign and Security Policy (CFSP) policy gains in strength.'[19]

De Feyter goes on to consider Article 11 TEU, which sets out the objectives of the Union's CFSP. These are:

— to safeguard the common values, fundamental interests, independence and integrity of the Union in conformity with the principles of the United Nations Charter;
— to strengthen the security of the Union in all ways;
— to preserve peace and strengthen international security, in accordance with the principles of the United Nations Charter, as well as the principles of the Helsinki Final Act and the objectives of the Paris Charter, including those on external borders;
— to promote international cooperation;
— to develop and consolidate democracy and the rule of law, and respect for human rights and fundamental freedoms.

The factors which the Council has set out to be taken into account during the consideration of joint actions are: the geographical proximity of a region or country; whether there are important political interests in the political and economic stability of a region or country; and whether there are threats to the security interests of the Union. De Feyter asks whether, 'If one accepts that the objective of promotion of international co-operation includes development co-operation, this raises the interesting issue of whether these factors also have implications for the activities under the development co-operation chapter in the EC Treaty. In other words, should EC development co-operation in the future serve the goals of EU CFSP policy?' (with the concern that whilst CFSP goals may be relatively short term, those of development cooperation are usually medium to long term).[20]

[18] A. Koulaïmah-Gabriel, 'The EU and the Developing World—Coherence between the Common Foreign and Security Policy and Development Co-operation' in J. Forster and O. Stokke (eds.), *Policy Coherence in Development Co-operation* (London: Frank Cass, 1999), 353.

[19] K. de Feyter, *World Development Law Sharing Responsibility for Development* (Antwerpen: Intersentia, 2001), 111–12.

[20] ibid., 112.

It could be added here, that not only can a case be made for the classification of development cooperation as promoting international cooperation, but one could also argue that the first-cited[21] purpose of the UN 'to maintain international peace and security, and to that end: to take effective collective measures for the prevention and removal of threats to the peace' also includes development cooperation. Even though most wars are now civil rather than international, even civil wars may have a tendency to threaten international peace, and various studies indicate that high levels of poverty, and heavy dependence on resource-based primary exports, contribute significantly to the prevalence of civil war.[22] These are factors which development cooperation usually aims to alleviate. Further, Article 55, Chapter IX of the Charter of the United Nations provides that 'With a view to the creation of conditions of stability and well-being which are necessary for peaceful and friendly relations among nations based on respect for the principle of equal rights and self-determination of peoples, the United Nations shall promote: [*inter alia*] higher standards of living, full employment, and conditions of economic and social progress and development'. It is not just the organization which is bound by this provision. Article 56 states that, 'All Members pledge themselves to take joint and separate action in co-operation with the Organization for the achievement of the purposes set forth in Article 55'.

It is perhaps worth noting that the progress and development cited are described as being 'economic and social'. The current focus on economic development above all else is a more recent development.

C. On Development Cooperation and Sustainable Development

The relationship between Community development policy, sustainable development, and environmental protection is important in the light of the provisions of Article 177 EC, which sets out the three objectives to be fostered by Community development cooperation policy. However, the exact nature of their relationship is less clear in the context of the current policy of promoting poverty reduction as the principal aim of development cooperation policy.

Article 6 EC provides that, 'Environmental protection requirements must be integrated into the definition and implementation of the Community policies and activities referred to in Article 3 [these include 'a policy in the sphere of development cooperation'], in particular with a view to promoting sustainable development'.

[21] In Art. 1, Chapter 1 of the Charter of the United Nations.

[22] e.g. P. Collier and A. Hoeffler, 'Greed and Grievance in Civil War' World Bank Research—Working Paper, Mar. 2002; and P. Collier, I. Elbadawi, and N. Sambanis, 'Why are there so many Civil Wars in Africa? Prevention of Future Conflicts and Promotion of Inter-Group Cooperation' World Bank Research—Working Paper, Dec. 2000.

Providing some back-up to Article 6 EC there is Regulation (EC) No. 2493/2000 on Measures to Promote the Full Integration of the Environmental Dimension in the Development Process of Developing Countries.[23] The preamble includes, *inter alia*, the following justifications for the measure:

— the depletion of natural resources and environmental degradation have direct effects on economic development, and especially on the livelihoods of local communities, including indigenous peoples, and thus counteract the alleviation of poverty through sustainable development;

— the internal and external aspects of the EC's environment policy need to be coherent in order to effectively respond to the challenges identified in the United Nations Conference on Environment and Development (UNCED) and its follow-up processes;

— the European Parliament (EP) and the Council adopted Decision No. 2179/98, 'Towards Sustainability', which calls for a strengthened role for the Community in international cooperation in environment and sustainable development. The basic strategy of the Programme is to achieve full integration of environmental policy in other policies, including development policy; and

— sustainable development relies on the integration of the environmental dimension into the development process.

As Hain put it, in a paper submitted to the European Convention's Working Group on External Relations,[24] 'There is now an internationally agreed set of objectives—the Millennium Development Goals—and wider recognition of the links between development policy, security and sustainable development.'

Article 1 of Regulation (EC) No. 2493/2000 states that:

1. The Community shall support developing countries in their efforts to integrate the environmental dimension into their development process.

   To this end, the Community shall provide financial assistance and appropriate expertise aimed at drawing up and promoting the implementation of policies, strategies, tools and technologies for the pursuit of sustainable development.

2. Community support shall be provided directly to developing country stakeholders as well as indirectly through the strengthening of the environmental dimension of Community economic and development cooperation in order to ensure that full account is taken of environmental considerations in Community programmes.

3. The assistance and expertise provided under this Regulation shall complement and reinforce that provided through other instruments of development cooperation.

Article 1.1 talks of 'supporting' developing countries in 'their' efforts to integrate the environmental dimension into their development process. This is fine if the

[23] [2000] OJ L288/1. [24] WG VII—WD 27.

government of the developing country is making serious efforts in that regard, but would not enable the achievement of much, should the developing country not be concerned about such integration (which, as discussed below, the Commission has found is sometimes the case).

Article 1.2 goes rather further, talking of the 'indirect provision' of Community support through the strengthening of the environmental dimension of Community cooperation 'in order to ensure that full account is taken of environmental considerations in Community programmes'. This raises the question of what takes precedence if a Community programme does take full account of environmental considerations, but a developing country is not interested in taking account of those considerations. Should the developing state's 'ownership' of its sustainable development strategy take precedence, or should the Community be taking more of a view that it is standing in something akin to a fiduciary position, and that it should therefore use its financial advantage to insist on a fuller integration of the environmental dimension, in the long-term interests of the developing country? It could be argued that if someone chooses to shoot himself in the foot, that is his choice, but if you are aware of his intentions, and about to supply the gun, then your moral responsibility changes. (In addition, the Commission is under the Article 6 EC duty—mentioned above—to ensure that environmental protection requirements are integrated into the definition and implementation of Community policies and activities, including development cooperation policy. This is to be done 'with a view to promoting sustainable development'. The extent to which they must be integrated, however, or sustainable development promoted, is not specified.)

Article 2 provides a definition of 'sustainable development' for the purposes of the Regulation: 'the improvement of the standard of living and welfare of the relevant populations within the limits of the capacity of the ecosystems by maintaining natural assets and their biological diversity for the benefit of present and future generations'.

Article 3(1) sets out matters that should be addressed in particular by the activities to be carried out under the Regulation. The list of matters starts off with global and transboundary environmental issues, and then mentions three areas specifically relating to developing countries: environmental impacts related to their integration into the world economy; the inclusion in development cooperation projects of environmental considerations enabling the sustainable dimension of these projects to be distinguished, identified, and assessed; and the environmental impacts of macroeconomic and sectoral policies in developing countries. More general environmental matters are then listed, such as sustainable management and use of resources, the conservation of biological diversity, the management of freshwater resources, and environmental problems related to industrial activities, among others.

Article 3(2) sets out some of the activities eligible for funding. These include the raising of the awareness of local people in the development process with regard to the implications of sustainable development, in particular through information campaigns and training.

Article 3(3) provides that:

> In the selection, preparation, implementation and evaluation of activities, particular attention shall be paid to:
> — the contribution to the overall objective of eradicating poverty;
> — . . .
> — the potential for integration into the wider context of Community development cooperation policies and programmes . . .

These provisions are interesting because first, they refer to 'the overall objective of eradicating poverty', which is not what the Treaty provides with regard to the objectives of development policy (Article 177 EC sets out the three apparently equal objectives listed above), and secondly because of the reference to the 'potential' for integration (of what exactly—the specific activities selected?) into the wider context of Community development policy. This Regulation, which has its own financial framework (€93 million for the period from 2000 to 2006) does not automatically apply with regard to the integration of the environmental dimension in the wider context of Community development policy. So how is the environmental dimension integrated in that wider context? There is a plethora of possible sources to examine. In this chapter, two will be considered: at one level, there is the Cotonou Agreement between the Community and the ACP countries; and, at a slightly more detailed level, the country strategy papers (which set out the aid strategies for developing countries—ACP and non-ACP).

III. The Cotonou Agreement

The Cotonou Agreement was signed on 23 June 2000, and came into force on 1 April 2003, following its ratification by two-thirds of the ACP states (52 of the 78), the Community and its fifteen Member States. It is the latest in the series of agreements between the Community and the ACP states, following on from the Yaoundé and Lomé Conventions. It is a twenty-year agreement, whose objectives are set out in its Article 1. This explains that the Agreement was concluded 'with a view to contributing to world peace and security and to promoting a stable and democratic political environment'. However:

> The partnership shall be centred on the objective of reducing and eventually eradicating poverty *consistent with the objectives of sustainable development* and the gradual integration of the ACP countries into the world economy. *These* objectives and the Parties' international commitments *shall inform all development strategies* and shall be tackled through an integrated approach *taking account* at the same time of the political, economic, social, cultural *and environmental aspects* of development . . . *The principles of sustainable*

management of natural resources and the environment shall be applied and integrated at every level of the partnership. (emphasis added)

The central objectives appear to echo strongly the provisions of Article 177 EC, and the importance of environmental protection and sustainable development running hand in hand with poverty reduction seems to be clearly and strongly spelt out.

Article 3 provides that the Parties shall take all appropriate measures, whether general or particular, to facilitate the attainment of the objectives of the Agreement. Not only must they facilitate the attainment of those objectives, they 'shall refrain from any measures liable to jeopardize these objectives'. This provision is potentially extremely far-reaching. For example, would the implementation of a policy in a Communication or in a Treaty which effectively diminished or denied, or simply confused, the importance of the objective of sustainable development, count as a measure liable to jeopardize those objectives? It is arguable that certain Community measures and proposals could have such effects (see below). Further, if the Community fails to take the necessary action effectively to reform its CAP, could it be argued that this would be liable to jeopardize any of the objectives mentioned in the second paragraph of Article 1? Or if it fails to meet its emission limits under the Kyoto Protocol? Or if Community fisheries policy continues to damage the interests of coastal developing states?

'Sustainable development' is not specifically defined, but Article 9(1) makes an interesting comment on it (in relation to the 'political dimension'):

> Cooperation shall be directed towards sustainable development centred on the human person, who is the main protagonist and beneficiary of development; this entails respect for and promotion of all human rights.
>
> Respect for all human rights and fundamental freedoms, including respect for fundamental social rights, democracy based on the rule of law and transparent and accountable governance are an integral part of sustainable development.

First, this description is, on a personal, human level, broad. But does it fail to cover the environmental side of sustainable development? It is not necessarily an exhaustive definition. The respect for human rights is described as an integral *part* of sustainable development. Is that other part environmental? And *all* human rights are referred to. Would that include the right to a clean environment?

If the definition of sustainable development were to be taken to be limited to a narrow definition of human rights, then it would be far from the general understanding of what that phrase means, and would be very meanly defined. (Compare, for example, Article 2 of Regulation (EC) No. 2493/2000, as discussed above, whose definition of 'sustainable development' for the purposes of the Regulation is: 'the improvement of the standard of living and welfare of the relevant populations within the limits of the capacity of the ecosystems by maintaining natural assets and their biological diversity for the benefit of present and future generations'. Or the classic 1987 Brundtland Commission Report's, 'development that meets the needs of the present without compromising the ability of future generations to meet their own needs'.) It would also be odd, in that the objectives listed in Article 1 (and again in Article 19) are clearly based on the provisions of Article 177 EC. Although 'sustainable economic and social development' is also not defined in the EC Treaty, the sustainable development envisaged there is apparently not limited in the way a narrow interpretation of Article 9(1) of the Cotonou Agreement would be limited. Further, in the Preamble to the Cotonou Agreement, it refers to the pledges made at the Rio (Earth) Summit on environment and sustainability, in which sustainability was understood in the classic, Brundtland sense.

Happily, following on from Article 19(1) of the Cotonou Agreement, which restates that, 'The central objective of ACP-EC cooperation is poverty reduction and ultimately its eradication; sustainable development; and progressive integration of the ACP countries into the world economy', Article 20(1) (in the general framework chapter of the development strategies title) then provides that, 'The objectives of ACP-EC development cooperation shall be pursued through integrated strategies that incorporate economic, social, cultural, environmental and institutional elements that must be locally owned'. Those strategies must aim at five goals, of which one is, 'promoting environmental sustainability, regeneration and best practices, and the preservation of natural resource base'. That is much more what is usually understood by 'sustainability'. In addition, in accordance with Article 20(2), 'Systematic account shall be taken in mainstreaming into all areas of cooperation the following thematic or crosscutting themes: gender issues, environmental issues and institutional development and capacity building. These areas shall also be eligible for Community support.'

Referring back, also, the Article 1 Cotonou Agreement's objectives must be tackled through an 'integrated approach' which *takes account* of, *inter alia*, the environmental aspects of development. 'Taking account' is a somewhat loose concept, which would not necessarily lead to serious environmental protection. However, that Article also provides that the principle of the sustainable management of natural resources and the environment must be applied and integrated at every level of the partnership. That is much stronger, and potentially far-reaching.

Furthermore, Article 32 is devoted to the environment and natural resources. It provides that:

1. Cooperation on environmental protection and sustainable utilization and management of natural resources shall aim at:
    a. mainstreaming environmental sustainability into all aspects of development cooperation and support programmes and projects implemented by the various actors;
    b. building and/or strengthening the scientific and technical human and institutional capacity for environmental management for all environmental stakeholders;

c. supporting specific measures and schemes aimed at addressing critical sustainable management issues and also relating to current and future regional and international commitments concerning mineral and natural resources such as:
   i. tropical forests, water resources, coastal, marine and fisheries resources, wildlife, soils, biodiversity;
   ii. protection of fragile eco-systems (e.g. coral reef);
   iii. renewable energy sources notably solar energy and energy efficiency;
   iv. sustainable urban and rural development;
   v. desertification, drought and deforestation;
   vi. developing innovative solutions to urban environmental problems; and
   vii. promotion of sustainable tourism.

d. Taking into account issues relating to the transport and disposal of hazardous waste.

2. Cooperation shall also take account of:
   a. the vulnerability of small island ACP countries, especially to the threat posed by climate change;
   b. the worsening drought and desertification problems especially of least developed and land-locked countries; and
   c. institutional development and capacity building.

On the question of trade and the environment, Article 49 states that:

1. The parties reaffirm their commitment to promoting the development of international trade in such a way as to ensure sustainable and sound management of the environment, in accordance with the international conventions and undertakings in this area and with due regard to their respective level of development. They agree that the special needs and requirements of ACP states should be taken into account in the design and implementation of environment measures.
2. Bearing in mind the Rio principles and with a view to reinforcing the mutual supportiveness of trade and environment, the Parties agree to enhance their cooperation in this field. Cooperation shall in particular aim at the establishment of coherent national, regional and international policies, reinforcement of quality controls of goods and services related to the environment, [and] the improvement of environment-friendly production methods in relevant sectors.

This is an important area, but one which will not be considered in this chapter.

So under Articles 19, 20, and 32 of the Cotonou Agreement, when there is cooperation on environmental protection and sustainable utilization and management of natural resources, the above comprehensive list is what it must aim at. And the promotion of environmental sustainability must be aimed at in the ACP-EC cooperation strategies, which are to be used to pursue the objectives of ACP-EC development cooperation. So one would expect comprehensive coverage of environmental matters in all ACP-EC cooperation strategies.

Although these are vital enabling provisions, Commission officials in DG Development are concerned that no more than lip service is necessarily paid to them. The provision made in practice for environmental protection tends to be weak. Environmental matters are apparently almost always pushed by the European negotiators, but the ACP countries are not so interested in them. There is some examination of the country strategy papers in this regard below, following the consideration of Community policy (as opposed to law) on development cooperation.

IV. Community Policy

In understanding Community development cooperation policy, there are, in addition to the Treaty and Cotonou Agreement provisions, and amidst a plethora of policy documents, two Commission Communications whose contents are particularly illuminating. The first is the European Community's Development Policy.[25] The second is Towards a Global Partnership for Sustainable Development.[26]

A. 2000—A Fresh Strategy

In June 1995, the EU Development Council requested a full evaluation of EC development instruments and programmes. Three highly critical reports followed.[27] In May 1999, the Development Council concluded that various improvements were needed to enhance the relevance, efficiency, effectiveness, and visibility of Community development assistance. The Council therefore invited the Commission to elaborate a proposal for an overall policy statement.

In its Communication of April 2000, The European Community's Development Policy,[28] (Development Policy Communication), the Commission acknowledged that, 'A number of criticisms have been made by the DAC [the Development Assistance Committee of the OECD] or other stakeholders, especially the lack of an overall Community strategy [on development] and the fact that the objectives of Community development policy are too numerous, too vague and not ranked in any way'. The Communication goes on to state that the necessary strategy must be based on 'the Community's comparative advantages and specific characteristics'. These are then listed, and include: the Community's 'critical mass in financial terms but also in terms of economic and political weight

[25] COM(2000)212.

[26] COM(2002)82, discussed below.

[27] Evaluation of European Union Aid Managed by the Commission to ACP countries, 951338; Evaluation of EU Development Aid to ALA (Asia and Latin America) Countries, 951401; and Evaluation of Aspects of EU Development Aid to the Mediterranean Region, 951405.

[28] Communication from the Commission to the Council and the European Parliament, 'The European Community's Development Policy' (Development Policy Communication), COM (2000)212, 5.

and influence at an international level'; and the 'global dimension' of the Community's development policy. The environment is notable for its absence. On the next page, the Commission states, somewhat opaquely, 'Other activities of important interest to developing countries such as in the area of research, technology and environment, which are prolongations of internal policies, will play an important role supporting the main objective, [earlier identified as being poverty reduction]'.[29] The 'other' appears to refer back to the earlier mention of the 'more limited [though unspecified] number of core areas' on which Community development support 'has to be concentrated'. Why research, technology, and environment should be specifically designated 'prolongations of internal policies' is not clear, nor is the meaning of that phrase itself immediately comprehensible in this context.

Having apparently made it clear that the environment is to play a supporting role, the Communication then states that the 'Commission presented a Communication on the integration of environmental concerns into development to the Helsinki Council,[30] which will improve our strategy of how to consider environment in the elaboration and implementation of development policy'.

Immediately after this, the Communication goes on to explain that, 'The Helsinki Council asked the Commission to prepare a comprehensive development strategy dovetailing economic, social and environmental policies, to be presented in Gothenburg in June 2001. *Development policy will be an integral part of this overall sustainable development strategy*' (emphasis added). (The Council minutes actually state[31] that the Commission was 'invited to prepare a proposal for a long-term strategy dovetailing policies for economically, socially and ecologically sustainable development to be presented to the European Council in June 2001'. A strategy for development that is sustainable economically, socially, and ecologically is arguably different to a development policy which simply dovetails economic, social and environmental policies.)

So, in a tautologous few paragraphs, we learn that the environment will play an important role in supporting poverty reduction, the main objective of development policy. Meanwhile, development policy will be an integral part of the Community's overall sustainable development strategy, which strategy is to dovetail environmental, economic, and social policies. Environmental concerns are intricately interwoven here, but their precise status is far from clear. This Communication appears to be perpetuating exactly the same kind of presentational faults which it earlier admitted it had been widely criticized for.

Furthermore, the waters become yet muddier when the Commission's definition of 'poverty' is taken into account. It is explained[32] that poverty is now widely viewed as involving not just the absence of sufficient financial resources, but as being a 'multi-faceted concept'. The non-monetary factors included in this new

[29] ibid. [30] COM(1999)499.

[31] Presidency Conclusions, Helsinki European Council, 10 and 11 Dec. 1999.

[32] The Development Policy Communication, n. 28 above, 16.

definition include the 'lack of access to education, health, natural resources, employment, land and credit, political participation, services and infrastructure'.[33] The Commission concludes that, 'Reducing poverty therefore implies addressing these economic, political, social, environmental and institutional dimensions'. The threads of the material blur together as one strives to make out the main pattern: poverty reduction is the main aim of Community development policy, and environmental concerns constitute a supportive, or possibly dovetailing role, yet they are simultaneously in themselves part of the definition of poverty, and so must be addressed as part of that prioritized problem.[34]

Later on,[35] it is asserted that, 'The general objective of development cooperation is to encourage sustainable development that leads to a reduction in poverty in developing countries'. One begins to wonder how many people wrote the Communication, and whether there was any awareness of this pervading tautology. We all recognize a chair, whether it is the right way up, upside down, or lying on its side. Young children will draw mirror image or upside down letters because to them, letters are like the chair—the same, no matter which angle you view them from. Does it matter if the Commission takes a similar approach with regard to the prioritization of policy regarding development cooperation, the environment, and sustainable development? Could it be argued that these policy strands are all so entwined in a ball that the ball can be equally validly grasped or bounced, no matter which factor is on the top? Indeed, could it ever be a realistic possibility to identify a generally applicable, accurate hierarchy of these policies and objectives?

In addition, the Communication states that the Commission planned to present in the first half of 2000 a number of policy papers on the Community's external assistance. One of them was to cover, 'the coherence between development and other EU policies'.[36] The Commission has confirmed that a specific policy paper on this area was never presented. However, there is a Communication from Development Commissioner Nielson to the Commission which has not until now been publicly available. The Commission agreed, following a request by the author under Regulation (EC) No. 1049/2001 on public access to documents, to release to the author a copy of Towards Improved Consistency between the Community Development Policy and other Community Policies. It is available in an original[37] and an amended[38] form.

[33] ibid.

[34] One striking point here is the absence of any mention of the provisions of Art. 177 EC, following the Communication's identification of poverty reduction as the main objective of development cooperation. The Treaty provides for apparently equal weight to be given to the objectives of the sustainable economic and social development of the developing countries, their integration into the world economy, and the campaign against poverty. It is not explained in the Communication how this Treaty provision can suddenly be overridden by the provisions of a Communication.

[35] n. 28, at 17.

[36] ibid., 6.

[37] SEC(2000)728 of 22 Apr. 2000.

[38] SEC(2000)728/2 of 25 Apr. 2000.

The original referred to 'coherence' rather than 'consistency' in its title and contents, 'coherency' comprising, according to the Concise Oxford Dictionary, the qualities of logic and consistency, whilst 'consistency' is the state of being consistent and in conformity with other attitudes or practices—the logic is jettisoned in apparent deference to the Article 3 consistency provision of the EU Treaty.[39] The two papers are otherwise almost identical, with an introduction, and then sections on: the coherence/consistency of new Commission proposals; coherence/consistency in the implementation of policies; reporting; and monitoring. The only section which is amended other than with regard to coherence/consistency is that on coherence/consistency in the implementation of policies, and even that difference is largely a matter of presentation.

The section on the consistency of new Commission proposals explains that the Commission already takes its decisions in a collegial way, which 'means its procedures are to a large extent influenced by the pursuit of consistency'. In addition, internal Commission procedures are to play an important role: for all new proposals, 'it falls on' the leading ('*chef de file*') department to ensure that an assessment of the impact that the proposal may have on the objectives of development policy is reflected in the proposal. During inter-service consultations, DG Development (DG DEV) may then 'call consultations' to consider different methods of solving problems[40] if it considers that the proposal 'is significantly at odds with the objectives of the EC development policies or is likely to have a negative effect on development [*sic*] countries'. These consultations may be followed by a formal ad hoc meeting called by the Secretariat General. Ultimately, there may still be (as after any impact assessment) 'situations where the Commission may have to decide, after careful consideration of the Community's relative priorities, to present a policy proposal that may still create difficulties for the objectives of the development policy'.

With regard to consistency in the implementation of policies, a 'consistency focal point' 'will be established within DG Development'. In addition to screening new proposals, it will carry out a series of 'activities' under the first draft, and 'possible activities' under the amended document. It is odd that 'possible' is inserted here, as the later sentences are all couched in prescriptive ('will') rather than exhortatory ('may') terms. They are that the DG DEV focal point *will*:

— establish a database of selected Community legislation with a demonstrated or expected negative impact on the objectives of development policy, in order to allow for an efficient monitoring of the follow-up and implementation of these;

[39] That the Union shall, *inter alia*, ensure the consistency of its external activities as a whole in the context of external relations, security, economic, and development policies.

[40] Ranging from abandoning the proposal, to revising it, to adopting compensatory measures.

— promote analysis of relevant cases of inconsistent Community and/or national EU policies, for example, through the application of the OECD Development Aid Committee *Checklist on Policy Coherence*;
— facilitate independent evaluation studies to review the consistency aspects of specific areas of Community policy;
— prepare the background for discussion in the Council and Parliament when existing Community policies contradict each other or are contradicted by national policies.

The focal point 'will' also serve as a contact point and discussion partner for other Commission services and for representatives of developing countries and civil society organizations concerned with specific cases where inconsistency seems to occur.

The section on reporting explains that the Commission will report regularly on consistency to the Development Council (no longer meeting as such—see below), and will endeavour to keep the EP and the Council informed of decisions they are taking which may contradict development policy.

The monitoring section concerns the use of joint monitoring procedures with developing countries for the prompt identification of possible inconsistency between Community policies and the objectives of its development policy.

The Development Policy Communication then explains that, '[a] fresh strategy for the Community's development policy has to be established which builds on the positive achievements of the past, responds to the weaknesses of the EC performance, and which reflects the evolving international debate on development issues'.[41]

There are six areas addressed by the Communication before its conclusions are drawn: new challenges for development; the role of Europe; a comprehensive approach to development and poverty reduction; strategic activities; partnerships; and implementation. This chapter will consider new challenges for development, the role of Europe, and strategic activities,

i. New Challenges for Development

Under this title, the Commission explains how changing North–South relations over the last ten years have called development cooperation policies into question. At the international level, the new framework for development is centred on 'social and human aspects and on the sustainable management and use of natural resources and the environment'.[42] The impact of globalization is then considered: it has provided fresh opportunities for development in trade, investment, and access to know-how, as well as highlighting the importance of trade for the development process: 'Trade is the most efficient means to generate resources necessary for self-sustained development'.[43] However, 'Beyond its positive aspects, globalization involves increased risks of marginalization, if the country

[41] n. 28 above, 6. [42] ibid. 7. [43] ibid.

is not prepared to cope with these new opportunities. This will be the case in particular for the poorest countries... Moreover, the emergence of global environmental problems has brought a new level of interdependence between industrialized and developing countries.'[44]

The resulting 'need for co-operative efforts to solve problems means that there are an increasing number of Multilateral Environmental Agreements of which both the Community and its Member States are parties. Obligations deriving from those agreements should also be considered as part of the international development agenda. The strong focus on the integration of environmental concerns into all Commission development activities has to be seen as a sign of our commitment to the implementation of those obligations.'[45] In addition, notes the Commission, there needs to be more effective coordination between aid donors. To this end, frameworks are being drawn up at international level and, at the European level, 'strategy papers' are being prepared so as to foster 'better complementarity' between the Member States and the Community.[46]

ii. The Role of Europe

The Development Policy Communication states, 'The global projection of European values of democracy, social justice and sustainable development calls for an EU policy of solidarity. A trade and agricultural policy that takes greater account of the interests of developing countries should support this policy.'[47] The Commission explains that the Community has 'three principal means of action to pursue its objectives in the field of development—political dialogue, development cooperation and trade... The Community also acts through the external dimension of other Community policies, in particular in the areas of environment, research and technology and the information society. For instance, Community research activities in sustainable development (crop improvements, animal health, etc) clearly complement development policy goals.'[48] This again raises the question of whether the environment is just a matter complementary to Community development policy, whether development policy is an integral part of overall sustainable development strategy, and where exactly the environment falls in this mélange of policies and priorities.

Trade policy is highlighted in this section of the Communication. It is described as 'a key lever for development: at the multilateral level, by contributing to a fair and equitable multilateral trading system and thereby facilitating the integration of developing countries into the world trading system; at bilateral level by facilitating access to the markets of the developed countries. This involves taking into account the interests of developing countries... in international bodies regulating the framework of trade and investment, in particular the WTO.'[49] These assertions beg several questions, not least: who defines what

[44] ibid. [45] ibid. 9–10. [46] ibid. 10.
[47] ibid. [48] ibid. [49] ibid. 11.

constitutes a fair and equitable trading system; who is doing the 'taking into account'; and whether the WTO is capable of managing even-handedly to balance the interests of world trade and sustainable development or environmental protection when these clash. None of these questions is acknowledged, let alone tackled, at this point in the Communication.

The implementation problems in its aid system are recognized by the Commission, but it believes that these are 'mainly signs of a growth crisis'. The evaluations which had been made identified various problems, including the following: that the Community's aid system was too complex and fragmented in every way; tellingly, that policies were guided by the instruments rather than by policy objectives and clearly defined priorities; and that the EU's large disbursement did not entail proportional influence (for example, the EU financed 64 per cent of the cost of the African structural adjustment programmes, but had cumulative voting rights in the IMF of 27 per cent).

The Commission had committed itself to reform of these points 'through administrative reforms'. It has to be questioned whether such an approach could be sufficient to cope with such major problems. In addition, the Commission cites, without giving any example, the 'many innovative means and reforms' in the [Cotonou] Agreement. It calls for the support of the EP and the Member States in relation to the reform of complementarity, the instruments of financial control, and the procedures for Council oversight.

'Grossly under-exploited' is how the Commission describes the potential of the Community and the Member States for impact and action in development. It believes that the key to the release of this potential lies in better coordination, and in focusing on where Community action can offer added value. With regard to the Member States, for example, this could be in: the formulation of sectoral policies benefiting from the accumulated experience of the Member States, with their different experiences and approaches; the conveying of the culture and values of cooperation and collective action to developing countries; and the perception of the EU's 'distinct' profile with regard to the quality of sustainable development, following the importance attached to environmental considerations (*quod erat demonstrandum*?), European social values, and the diversity of European social systems.

iii. Strategic Activities—A New Framework for Activity

The Commission concludes that what is needed is a new, integrated framework for Community activities, drawn up with the central objective of poverty reduction. Under Article 177 EC, Community policy in the sphere of development cooperation is required to foster the three aims cited above, of which the campaign against poverty in the developing countries is the last mentioned. The sustainable economic and social development of the developing countries (and more particularly the most disadvantaged among them) is the first mentioned, and is therefore arguably at least as important an aim as any general campaign against poverty. It could be questioned whether the Commission/Community has the power unilaterally to decide to prioritize one of three apparently equal aims set out in the Treaty at the expense of the other two.

Beneath the statement of poverty reduction as the central objective, the Development Policy Communication sets out, '*Strategic areas* deriving from the Treaty' (emphasis added). These are, broadly, the three aims of Community development policy as set out in Article 177(1) EC and Article 177(2) EC. There are subtle differences, however.

The aims of Article 177(1) EC are required to be 'fostered', while that of Article 177(2) EC is to be 'contributed to' via Community development policy. In the Development Policy Communication, no distinction is made: the rough contents of both Articles are lumped together as 'Strategic areas deriving from the Treaty':

a. Sustainable development, in particular through promoting equitable growth, investment, employment, social and human development and environmental protection;
b. Integration into the world economy, including through support to regional cooperation and integration;
c. Fight against poverty;
d. Democracy, human rights, rule of law and when necessary peace-making and conflict prevention.

The Treaty requires the fostering of the sustainable development of the developing countries, 'and more particularly the most disadvantaged among them'. The Development Policy Communication fails to mention those words in italics. This is particularly significant when viewed alongside earlier words in the Development Policy Communication: '*In relative terms the emphasis of Community aid on the poorest nations has diminished. This is due to a globalization of Community policy and to new external priorities.*' The drop is startling: in 1986/7, the share of Community Official Development Assistance (ODA) to least developed countries was 51.3 per cent. By 1996/7, it had, according to the Communication, dropped to 33.6 per cent. The author asked the Commission for statistics on how much of the Community's budget has gone on development aid in each of the last ten years and, of that, what proportion had gone to the least developed countries. She also asked what proportion of European Development Fund (EDF) monies had gone to the least developed countries.

It might be assumed that this request was one for access to documents, but there are apparently no Commission documents printed specifically with a view to publicizing this information. The specific information requested was not provided, as it is apparently not collated in the format requested. The Commission did, however, forward statistics collated by the OECD.[50] (The 33.6 per cent cited in the Development Policy Communication was not exactly replicated in

[50] *Geographical Distribution of Financial Flows to Aid Recipients 1997–2001*, 2003 edition. OECD/DAC published on the Internet at the OECD web page: Net disbursements of ODA/OA by the EC to individual recipients (bilateral aid). Advance figures for the year 2002.

the figures provided by the Commission, but they provide a reasonably comparative indication of year-on-year provision of aid.)

The results, for net disbursements of Official Development Assistance/Official Aid (ODA/OA) by the EC, are shown in Table 1. The first row shows total annual disbursements of ODA/OA by the EC in millions of dollars; the second row shows the share which went to Least Developed Countries (LDCs), and the third row shows the second line as a percentage of the first.

The data for aid going to Central and East European Countries (CEEC) are shown in Table 2 (from the same source).

To take another OECD table: the percentage of total gross disbursements of ODA by the EC to sub-Saharan Africa was as shown in Table 3. The equivalent percentages for disbursements to Europe were as shown in Table 4. In addition, Figure 1 presents the data from a slightly different angle.

Table 1. ODA/OA by EC to LDCs (million dollars)

ODA/OA	1995	1996	1997	1998	1999	2000	2001	2002
Total	4722.8	5261.4	5156.3	5123.7	4910.9	4414	5517.1	5037.36
To LDCs	1565.1	1441.9	1332.8	1447.5	1273.2	996.3	1472.3	
LDCs (%)	33.1	27.4	25.8	28.2	25.9	22.6	26.7	

Note: Calculated by the author.

Table 2. ODA/OA by EC to Central and East European countries (million dollars)

ODA/OA	1995	1996	1997	1998	1999	2000	2001
Total	4722.8	5261.4	5156.3	5123.7	4910.9	4414.0	2187.9
To CEECs	610.9	946.9	959.2	1819.4	2213.7	2274.8	1472.3
CEECs (%)	12.9	17.9	18.6	35.5	45.1	51.5	67.3

Table 3. Percentage of total gross disbursements of ODA by the EC to Sub-Saharan Africa

1991–2	1996–7	2001–2
59.1	42.8	35.9

Note: Of the 51 countries in Sub-Saharan Africa, 33 are Least Developed Countries.

Source: Regional Distribution of ODA by Individual DAC Donors and Multilateral Agencies. Table 27, *The DAC Journal, Development Cooperation 2003 Report* Statistical Annex, 2004 edition.

Table 4. Percentage of total gross disbursements of ODA by the EC to Central and Eastern Europe

1991–2	1996–7	2001–2
8.4	11.2	25

EC

Gross Bilateral ODA, 2001-02 average, unless otherwise shown

Net ODA	2001	2002	Change 2001/2
Current (US$ m)	5,961	6,561	10.1%
Constant (2001 US$ m)	5,961	6,085	2.1%
In € (million)	6,656	6,962	4.6%
Net Official Aid (OA)			
Current (US$ m)	2,689	3,104	15.4%

	Top Ten Recipients of gross ODA/OA (US$ million)	
1	Poland (OA)	662
2	Romania (OA)	511
3	Hungary (OA)	416
4	Czech Republic (OA)	355
5	Ex-Yugoslavia Unsp.	311
6	Serbia and Montenegro	307
7	Turkey	291
8	Tunisia	261
9	Morocco	226
10	South Africa	187

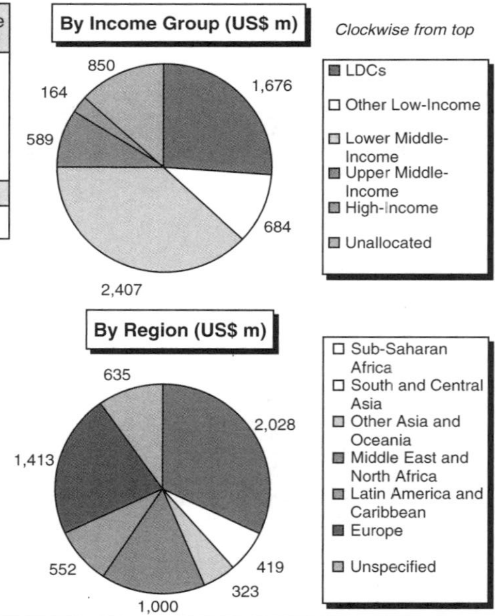

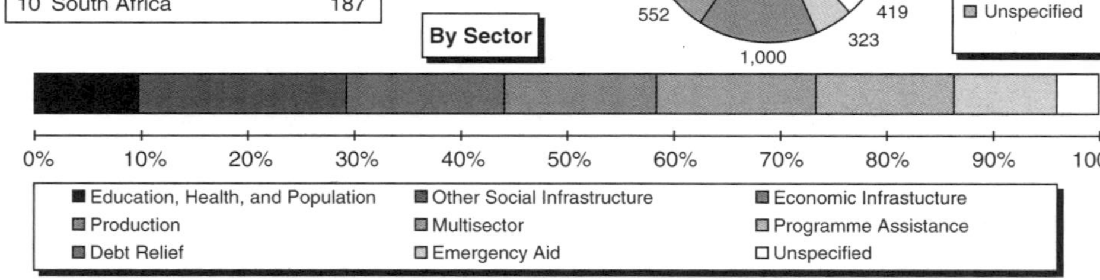

Figure 1. ODA/OA by the EC

Source: OECD.

So whilst the amount of Community ODA going to the least developed countries has seen a steady fall, which is just starting to pick up, the amount of Community OA to the CEEC has seen steady and steep year-on-year increases over the same period. Indeed, not one of the top ten recipients of gross EC ODA/OA in 2001–2 is a least developed country, with the top four being Poland, Romania, Hungary, and the Czech Republic. Meanwhile, 'Ethiopia has received more relief aid in the past 20 years than any other country on earth. But it has had less development aid than any other needy nation.'[51] (A further concern here is the possible impact of the new Member States on the EU's development policy later this year. As has been pointed out, 'Currently, these countries appear more interested in the ex-Soviet states and central Asia and tend to focus more on humanitarian aid than development cooperation. This raises the issue of whether the EU might, as a result of Enlargement, become less interested in Africa and the plight of the Least Developed Countries.')[52]

The author asked the OECD Development Assistance Committee (DAC) to what extent funding from the EDF is included in assessments of 'EU members' and 'EC' ODA, and what other sources of money are taken into account in each case. The reply explained that, to OECD's knowledge, 'EDF ODA disbursements are part of EC ODA, along with funds from the development budget (an assessed contribution) and, a third source from the EU's own revenues (for example, taxes levied on imports into the EU). The European Commission reports to the DAC its total combined flows so we are not able to identify separately these different sources in their data.'[53] The author is now asking the Commission for further clarification, in particular as to what proportion of EDF monies has gone to the least developed countries over the last ten years.

Reducing the development aid finance going to the most disadvantaged of the developing countries, whilst increasing the aid going to better-off countries, would appear only to be legally justifiable if in compliance with the EC Treaty. If it could be shown that the sustainable economic and social development of those most disadvantaged countries was not going to be fostered any the less by the loss of that money (for example, because other initiatives of Community development cooperation policy, such as the 'Everything But Arms' initiative or aid untying, would ensure equal or better fostering of their economic and social development), then a reduction in development aid would pose no problematic legal questions. Similarly, if the reason for reduction in development aid to the most disadvantaged developing countries had been given as its total inefficacy in any possible context (backed up by research), then it would be churlish to argue that the Community should continue to throw money into a black hole. But no such argumentation was made in the Development Policy Communication.

51 From an article by M. Buerk, *Sunday Times News Review*, 4 Jan. 2004, 2.

52 J. Mackie, 'Challenges for 2003—The Changing Framework of EU External Relations and its Implications for the ACP' (2003) 6 (*ECDPM InfoBrief*) (Maastricht: ECDPM, 2003).

53 E-mail to the author from dac.contact@oecd.org of 30 Jan. 2004.

Nor does the argument appear to be being made at a political level. In January 2004, Michael Lake, the Head of the EU Delegation in South Africa, explained at a conference[54] that the EU's first concern after enlargement would be the Union's 'ring of immediate neighbours'. He then asked where that left Africa, explaining that if the New Partnership for Africa's Development (NEPAD) 'bears fruit and good governance and the African countries really try, then there is an obligation on the EU to do more'. Bur first it needs 'results in terms of growth and improved governance. Otherwise we'll shut up shop and go home. We have other priorities.' He explained that the Union was asking, 'To maintain growth, where should we invest? China? Eastern Europe? Africa? Africa has to give the right answers.' Although he did not specify whether he meant here investment in trade or development, he had earlier stated that there are three pillars to EU/Africa international relations: development cooperation, preferential trade, and political dialogue. The emphasis here on the need for growth maintenance as a *sine qua non* for investment is interesting if it relates to development aid, as Article 177 EC works on the basis of development aid fostering economic development rather than vice versa. Public monies should not be thrown into a black hole, but is such an approach by the Community one which maximizes the likelihood of really helping the least developed countries? (It would ignore the possibility that development aid to those countries might be helping them maintain their status quo rather than deteriorating further.) A certain astringency of conditionality in the allocation of development aid may sometimes be no bad thing—in conjunction with other factors—but in the meantime, those other factors are more likely to be identified and implemented if Articles 177 and 178 EC are observed. If the EU adopts the approach that the countries with better growth and governance are those in which it will invest its development aid, it does not bode well for the least developed countries, which could find themselves in a Catch 22 situation.

Meanwhile, as the OECD notes in the Executive Summary of the Guidelines on Poverty Reduction, 'Sub-Saharan Africa has struggled with slow growth and *rising* poverty [emphasis added], partly linked to conflict and governance problems and it now faces the scourge of HIV/AIDS'.[55] The Community has not attempted to show that the reduction of its aid to the Least Developed Countries (LDCs) has had no effect on these figures.

Whilst the diminution of the emphasis of Community aid on the poorest nations identified in the Development Policy Communication has not been reversed, and although the 2001 figures have pulled up slightly to 26.7 per cent EC ODA to the least developed countries, they rest on the back of 2000's all time low of 22.6 per cent.

[54] Conference on the Relationship between Africa and the European Union, University of the Western Cape, South Africa, 22–3 Jan. The quotations are from the author's contemporaneous notes.

[55] Published on the Internet at: http://www.oecd.org/document/1/0,2340,en_2649_34621_1885953_119820_1_1_1,00.html.

Given the apparent prioritization in Community development policy of the alleviation of poverty, it is difficult to see how these figures can be justified by '*a globalization of Community policy*', though '*new external priorities*' (for example, in the form of accession and candidate countries) appear to be continuing to exert a growing influence.

There appears to be a lack of awareness at this point in the Development Policy Communication that it is arguably contrary to the Treaty for the Commission (or any Community institution) to choose simply to ignore a Treaty provision such as the reference in Article 177 EC to the fostering of, more particularly, the sustainable economic and social development of the most disadvantaged[56] developing countries in formulating a new priority for development cooperation because of a 'globalization' of policy (whatever that may mean) and the adoption of new—unspecified—external priorities. Of course, the Community can choose to prioritize one policy over another, but there are two matters which it should bear in mind if it does so: in reprioritizing the allocation of development cooperation monies within its development cooperation policy it must act in compliance with Article 177 EC, and in prioritizing other policies over development cooperation (and reallocating money between policies as a result), it must act in compliance with Article 178 EC.

An important question here is how direct the correlation is between the reduced amounts going to the developing countries, and the increased amounts of aid to eastern European countries. The view of interviewed Commission officials in DGs DEV and Environment (DG ENV) is that the two flows are directly linked, but it is difficult to follow any linkages directly because of the differing sources of the aid concerned. Most of the Community's development aid to LDCs is provided via the EDF. This does not come under the Community budget, is funded directly by the Member States, and is managed by a specific committee, with the Commission playing an important management role. The EDF budget is set by the Member States meeting in Council, with the agreements reached needing to be ratified by each Member State parliament. Further work needs to be done on tracing the flow of monies, but it is clear from the Development Cooperation Communication that the reason why the emphasis of Community aid on the poorest nations has diminished is because of the 'globalization of Community policy' and those 'new external priorities'. If the diverted money is not going to the CEEC, it is still apparently going to other Community policies, and these should therefore, under the development cooperation provisions of the EC Treaty, in particular Articles 177 and 178 EC, be identified and assessed for compliance with those provisions.

The trend of reduced funding going to the developing countries with greater investment in the eastern European accession countries shows no sign of abating.

[56] The most disadvantaged developing countries is an undefined term, but it is not unreasonable to suppose that there will be considerable overlap between such countries and those termed 'least developed countries'.

Following the collapse of the December 2003 summit on the draft constitution, Enlargement Commissioner Günter Verheugen warned that, 'The view in Berlin is that it will be hard to agree on the next financial perspectives if the decision-making system is not clear'.[57] The financial perspectives in question are those for the period 2007–13. Immediately prior to this (two days after the collapse of the summit), the Prime Ministers of the United Kingdom (UK), France, Germany, Sweden, the Netherlands, and Austria (proportionately large contributors to the Community budget) had sent Romano Prodi, the Commission President, the 'letter of the six' suggesting that the Union's budget be capped at 1 per cent of gross national income. If this were to happen, Poland and Spain would suffer significant financial disadvantage. Whether or not this suggestion was an attempt to punish those countries for failing to 'play ball', Verheugen insisted that, 'the core issue is not the distribution or redistribution of money. What is missing in the EU is not money, but political will, to have a more effective common foreign and security policy, and a stronger common policy on the budget and coordination of economic policies. These two elements are crucial.' In particular, he contended, if there were to be a cut in the EU's budget, it should not affect the ten accession countries, nine of which won referendums 'based on people's assumption that Europe would help improve their lives'. Crucially, he believes, 'morally, the promises must be maintained. If we must prioritize, then money should go first to the new Member States.'[58]

The use of 'morally' is interesting. There are indeed important moral questions at stake here. For example, what moral value should be placed on the previous pledge to help the world's least developed countries made in the EC Treaty, which pre-dated and, in legal terms, is more binding than an 'assumption' made by richer people in the accession countries? It could also be asked what moral value the greater need, and increasing relative poverty (in global terms), of those living in the least developed countries merits.

The acknowledgment in the Development Policy Communication of the diminution in Community aid to the poorest nations is followed by the disclaimer that, 'there is however a clear limitation in an analysis of poverty-focus on the sole basis of the categorisation of the recipient country by level of income'. It is quite true that many countries in the middle-income bracket have large percentages of their population below the poverty level, but this in itself does not justify the Community increasing its aid to other countries at the expense of the poorest countries (a) in apparent infringement of the EC Treaty, and (b) unless it can show that those monies have indeed gone to support those members of the population below the poverty line. Indeed, the wording of the suggestion on the next page as to how the Community could improve its secondary poverty focus suggests that cooperation programmes in middle-income countries had not been, and continued not to be, sufficiently poverty-focused.

[57] (2004) 9 *European Voice*, 18 Dec. 2003–14 Jan. 2004, 1. [58] ibid.

The Development Policy Communication goes on to state that three ways of enhancing and measuring the poverty focus of Community aid can be identified:

- Improving the *primary poverty focus*: meaning more concentration of efforts on LDCs and other Low Income Countries (LIC) category countries;
- Improving the *secondary poverty focus*: meaning more poverty-focused cooperation programmes in middle-income countries (MIC) where more than 20 per cent of the population lives under the poverty lines of $1/per day per capita;
- Improving the *tertiary poverty focus*: meaning greater focus on poverty reduction in cooperation programmes in all other developing countries.

With regard to improving the primary poverty focus, it is just not clear whether the Commission is saying, '*mea culpa*' with regard to the diminished emphasis on Community aid to the poorest nations since 1986, and intends to reverse the situation, or whether it is stating the situation as fact, and intending to allow the drop in aid to continue or to remain at the then current levels. What it calls for is *more concentration of efforts* on LDCs and other LIC category countries—does this mean more financial input, or a different approach to the deployment of monies already being disbursed in these countries? The waters are further muddied by the following paragraph: 'Improving the primary poverty focus is clearly limited by the setting of the political priorities and the consequences for the distribution of the financial resources to the regions.'[59] Can we assume that it refers back to the 'globalization of Community policy and to new [unspecified] external priorities' referred to on the previous page?

What the Commission means by improving the secondary poverty focus is also not as clear as it might be. Does 'more poverty-focused cooperation programmes' mean that there should be more such programmes, or that the current level of programmes should be more focused on poverty? And will monies continue to be disbursed for such programmes at the expense of primary poverty focus programmes?

When compared to DG DEV's Mission Statement, as available on the Commission's website in July 2003,[60] there are interesting differences. The Mission Statement provides that:

> the objective of Community development co-operation policy is to foster *sustainable development* designed to eradicate *poverty* in developing countries and to integrate them into the *world economy*. This can only be achieved by pursuing policies that promote the consolidation of democracy, the rule of law, good governance and the respect for human rights. Putting *equity* at the centre of its policies, the Directorate General

[59] n. 28 above, 20.

[60] Published on the Internet at: http://europa.eu.int/comm/dgs/development/mission_en.htm.

for Development gives priority to defending the interests of the most disadvantaged developing countries and the poorest sections of the population in economically more advanced developing countries. (Emphasis added)

This is much more a summary of Article 177 EC than in the Development Policy Communication. It also makes it less clear what the Commission's policy and priorities are.

For those working within DG DEV, the prioritization of poverty relief is seen as a helpful clarification, and they take the Development Policy Communication, not the Treaty or the Mission Statement, as their guiding rule. Whether it is legally acceptable, or even more efficient at achieving the aim of poverty reduction, remains to be seen. (It is convincingly argued in *Linking Poverty Reduction and Environmental Management*[61] that environmental improvement is not a luxury preoccupation that can wait until growth has alleviated income poverty, nor can it be assumed that growth itself will take care of environmental problems over the longer term as incomes rise and more resources are available for environmental protection. To improve the environmental soundness of growth, economic policies and decision-making need to better reflect the 'public goods' nature of many environmental goods and services by addressing the persistent policy and market failures that lead to their undervaluation and misuse.[62] Furthermore, it is frequently argued that the poor are the worst affected by environmental degradation. Or, as Martin Holland puts it, 'it seems foolish for the EU to establish development policy goals—such as poverty eradication—that are effectively unachievable. Less grandiose, but more attainable objectives are needed to enhance the reality of the EU's presence in a global context.').[63]

The Development Policy Communication refers to sustainable development 'in particular through promoting equitable growth, investment, employment, social and human development and environmental protection' as being a 'strategic area deriving from the Treaty'. The Treaty does not refer to any of those areas at all in this context, let alone as being relevant 'in particular'. It might be more helpful if the Commission clearly identified the Community's (and its own) obligations under the Treaty, and then separately listed through which means (in particular) it envisaged these as being most effectively achieved.

The Communication goes on to explain that:

Refocusing priorities in Community development aid is a necessity [because of the implementation problems which had been discussed earlier in the Communication]. Community development cooperation must do fewer things and do them better in order to ensure greater impact. In particular the Community has to decide in which areas of development cooperation it needs to concentrate its human resources in headquarters and

[61] Joint publication by the UK Department for International Development, DG DEV, UNDP, and the World Bank, July 2002.

[62] ibid. 23.

[63] M. Holland, *The European Union and the Third World* (Basingstoke: Palgrave, 2002), 244.

delegations. Such refocusing must be based on a combination of two main criteria: first, the areas chosen must contribute to the objective of poverty eradication and sustainable development; second, in the areas chosen Community action must have added value.[64]

Again, the Commission seems to be unaware of any need to refer to its obligations under the EC Treaty as a starting point for any identification of, or reference point for the refocusing of, priorities.

As it happens, poverty eradication and sustainable development do fall squarely within the priorities listed in Article 177(1) EC. However, there is again no reference to the Treaty obligation in the same Article for Community development policy to foster the sustainable economic and social development of, *in particular*, the most disadvantaged of the developing countries.

Following the presentation of this Communication, the Council and Commission made a Joint Statement on 10 November 2000[65] approving the proposed new strategy. In this statement, it was explained that, 'the main objective of Community development policy must be to reduce and, eventually, to eradicate poverty. This objective entails support for sustainable economic and social and environmental development, promotion of the gradual integration of the developing countries into the world economy and a determination to combat inequality.'

B. 2001—Commission Staff Working Paper, 'Integrating the Environment into EC Economic and Development Co-operation'

This excellent Working Paper[66] aims to explain how, given the major objective of poverty reduction, EC development aid can best help the developing countries to respond to their environmental challenges. It acknowledges that, 'A healthy environment is fundamental to the quality of life of current and future generations. Poor environmental quality undermines the developing countries' efforts to alleviate poverty and it will further jeopardize future prospects for sustainable economic and social development.' The impact of non-development policies on developing countries is clearly identified: 'the Community can have a major impact on the efforts of developing countries to integrate the environmental dimension in their development through improved policy coherence with fields such as trade, agriculture, fisheries and transport and energy'. The question of the extent to which such policy coherence has been, or needs to be, achieved cries out for examination, but would be too lengthy to include here.

[64] n. 28 above, 24.

[65] Council Press Release 12929/00. Published on the Internet at: http://europa.eu.int/comm/development/oct/polgui_en.htm. The use of a Statement in these circumstances is unusual. Such Statements are usually minuted in the Council conclusions or included as a footnote to those minutes.

[66] SEC(2001)609.

The Working Paper covers many areas, but if its suggestions were acted upon by all departments within the Commission, it would have a significant effect on the integration of the environment into the Community's development cooperation policies and practice.

On coherence with other policies, the Working Paper explains how DG DEV set up a coherence focal point in July 2000[67] whose task is to screen new policy proposals so as to ensure that the Community's policies vis-à-vis developing countries are consistent.

On programming issues, the Working Paper acknowledges that 'developing countries tend to invest too little into their national environment and demand for donor assistance in this area is limited. Therefore, the search for location-specific opportunities has to be systematically and actively promoted.' It lists various points at which such promotion could take place. These are timely—from an initial examination of the country strategy papers (see below), that promotion is sorely needed.

In conclusion, the Paper judges that achieving the environmental development target 'is extremely challenging and will require a fundamental shift in the approach of environmental integration'. To what extent has that shift been achieved? The next major Commission publication in the area gave some more cause for hope.

C. 2002—Commission Communication, 'Towards a Global Partnership for Sustainable Development'

In February 2002, the Commission published a Communication entitled, Towards a Global Partnership for Sustainable Development,[68] ('the Sustainable Development Communication'). It was drawn up jointly by DG DEV and DG Environment (DG ENV), who (in theory together with the rest of the Commission) share a sustainable development remit. And it appears to have been drawn up in disassociation from the Development Policy Communication.

In the Sustainable Development Communication, a quite different style and tone predominate. There are four main sections: the case for a global partnership; the challenge of integrating markets, governance, and internal policies through a global partnership; the EU's contribution: meeting priority objectives (the greater part of the paper); and implementing and reviewing the strategy.

[67] Referred to above in the discussion of SEC(2000)728/2, 'Towards Improved Consistency between the Community Development Policy and Other Community Policies'.

[68] Communication from the Commission to the European Parliament, the Council, the Economic and Social Committee and the Committee of the Regions, Towards a Global Partnership for Sustainable Development (Sustainable Development Communication) COM(2002)82.

i. The Case for a Global Partnership

This is in-your-face principles and need for reform at the international level. The first sentence sets out the ethos of the whole paper: 'To be sustainable, development must strike a balance between the economic, social and environmental objectives of society, in order to maximise well-being in the present, without compromising the ability of future generations to meet their needs'. The difference in tone and style compared to the Development Policy Communication is neatly demonstrated simply by comparing the two first sentences. The Development Policy Communication begins, 'Development policy is today one of the three principal components of the EU's external action, alongside trade policy and the political dimension'. It is more concerned with setting out or rearranging the status quo than with really grasping the nettle of what fundamentally needs to change. The Sustainable Development Communication makes a direct plea for stronger global governance and political institutions in order to create an effective counterweight to global market forces.

ii. The Challenge of Integrating Markets, Governance, and Internal Policies through a Global Partnership

Under this title, the Commission points out that globalization involves costs as well as benefits, and that intensive energy use, unsustainable exploitation of natural resources, and unwillingness to add environmental costs to the costs of production and transport 'are now threatening the resources base on which economic and social development depend... At the source of these unsustainable trends is the complex relationship between markets, global governance and national policy... What is needed is a global partnership which embraces all stakeholders.' The Commission suggests that the United Nations (UN) system (because of its role in the environmental, social, and economic spheres, and its universal membership) should take a lead in developing, together with the Bretton Woods institutions, the World Trade Organization (WTO), and the International Labour Organization (ILO), a global governance structure for sustainable development.

This section finishes with the Commission pointing out that the EU is 'well placed to assume a leading role in the pursuit of global sustainable development'. The reason given is that the EU, through its own evolution and its current enlargement policy, has pursued 'mutually supportive' strategies for stable economic growth, social development, and environmental protection. This, it is argued in the Communication, will provide valuable experience for tackling the same challenges at a global level. That experience will, inevitably, be based on its failures as well as its successes: although the EU has pursued those strategies, environmental degradation throughout the Community continues, in general, to increase, and it is possible to argue that stable economic growth has yet to be achieved. (Quite apart from the question of the extent to which economic growth is desirable from the point of view of sustainable development.)

This mooting of a leading role in the pursuit of global sustainable development follows on from the Presidency conclusions reached at the 2001 Göteborg European Council. The Council took the view then that:

Sustainable development requires global solutions. The Union will seek to make sustainable development an objective in bilateral development cooperation and in all international organisations and specialised agencies. In particular, the EU should promote issues of global environmental governance and ensure that trade and environment policies are mutually supportive.[69]

(The Council also seized that opportunity to put its own house in better environmental order, its official conclusions including the note that it had 'added an environmental dimension to the Lisbon process for employment, economic reform and social cohesion'. It is a little sobering to realize that the March 2000 Lisbon Council, which initiated the ten-year 'Lisbon Process' for employment, economic reform, and social cohesion, managed to do so without initially including any reference to environmental matters.)[70]

iii. The EU's Contribution—Meeting Priority Objectives

This section is broken down into six 'actions', each of which aims to complement the strategy endorsed by the Göteborg European Council. (At Göteborg, the Council agreed on its 'Strategy for Sustainable Development'. This strategy involved: a new approach to policy-making (based on the principle that the economic, environmental, and social effects of all policies should be subject to a sustainability impact assessment and that this should be taken into account in decision-making); the requirement for global solutions; the targeting of environmental priorities for sustainability—climate change, transport, public health, and natural resources; and integrating the environment into Community policies.)

The first three 'actions' are described as the 'components' of sustainable development, the last as 'necessary pre-conditions for success':

Economic (or 'Trade for Sustainable Development')

The priority objective here is 'to ensure that globalization contributes to sustainable development'. This is to be achieved via: the integration of the developing countries into the world economy; the provision of incentives for environmentally and socially sustainable production and trade; and better global financial market regulation to reduce volatility and abuse.

The upbeat tenor of the paper suddenly becomes suspiciously sanguine with the statement that:

The Doha Development Agenda (DDA) epitomises the integrated approach to managed globalization which the European Union is promoting, and creates the basis for further

[69] Presidency Conclusions, Göteborg European Council, SN 200/1/01 REV 1.

[70] See Presidency Conclusions, Lisbon European Summit, Press Release Lisbon (24 Mar. 2000) No. 100/1/00.

changes in the global system. The inclusion of talks on a wide range of issues such as the environment, competition, investment and trade facilitation will *ensure* [emphasis added] that market liberalization takes place within a broader regulatory framework.

Social

The priority objective here is to attain 'the International Development Targets and the Millennium Development Goals, in particular the target of halving extreme poverty in the world by 2015'.[71] The Millennium Development Goals are explained in the Sustainable Development Communication as the eight resulting from the UN General Assembly's Millennium Declaration of 2000: the eradication of extreme poverty and hunger; universal primary education; gender equality; reduction of child mortality; improved maternal health; the combating of diseases such as HIV/AIDS and malaria; environmental sustainability; and the development of a Global Partnership for Development—all 191 UN Member States have pledged to meet these goals by 2015. The International Development Targets are not defined or explained in the Sustainable Development Communication, but are presumably the goals set out by the OECD's DAC in 1996 when it adopted a new strategy called Shaping the 21 Century—the Contribution of Development Cooperation. The goals which the DAC set out to 'help to define' its 'vision of progress' (and which were heavily relied upon by the UN in drawing up its Millennium Declaration), were:

(1) Economic well-being: The proportion of people living in extreme poverty in developing countries should be reduced by at least one-half by 2015;

(2) Social development:

 (a) There should be universal primary education in all countries by 2015;

 (b) Progress toward gender equality should be demonstrated by eliminating gender disparity in primary and secondary education by 2005;

 (c) The death rate for infants and children under the age of 5 should be reduced in each developing country by two-thirds of the 1990 level by 2015. The rate of maternal mortality should be reduced by three-fourths during the same period;

 (d) Access for all of appropriate ages should be available to reproductive health services no later than 2015;

(3) Environmental sustainability and regeneration: There should be a current national strategy for sustainable development, in the process of implementation, in every country by 2005, so as to ensure that current trends in the loss of environmental resources—forests, fisheries, fresh water, climate, soils, biodiversity, stratospheric ozone, the accumulation of

[71] n. 68 above, 9, and with the definition of extreme poverty being taken as living on US$1 or less a day.

hazardous substances, and other major indicators—are effectively reversed at both global and national levels by 2015.

The Millennium Development Goals include, in addition, the combating of disease and the development of a Global Partnership for Development.

The EU action proposed by the Commission in this area includes furthering, 'the process of focusing European Union development policy on the central objective of poverty reduction, to be reflected in the tighter concentration of resources on LDCs and on the poorest groups in other developing countries'.[72]

This is interesting when compared to the equivalent part of the Development Policy Communication. Both refer to the central objective of poverty reduction (arguably contrary to Article 177 EC). But the provision that that objective should be reflected in the tighter concentration of resources on LDCs is in apparent conflict with the Development Policy Communication, which stated, as discussed above, that the emphasis on Community aid to the poorest nations had diminished because of the globalization of Community policy and new external priorities, and which did not appear to make any commitment to redressing the balance.

Sustainable Management of Natural and Environmental Resources

The priority objectives here are:

1. To ensure that current trends in the loss of environmental resources are effectively reversed at national and global levels by 2015; and
2. To develop sectoral and intermediate objectives in some key sectors—water, land and soil, energy and biodiversity.

The mention of 'national' in the first priority objective presumably refers to developing as well as to developed countries. Despite certain successes at the European level (such as in relation to emissions to air),[73] overall trends still vastly tend towards increasing loss.

The Commission confidently asserts that 'Some of the action included in the European Union's internal strategy will be instrumental in diminishing the ecological impact the European Union has on the rest of the world'. The action it has in mind is managing natural resources in a more sustainable manner and decoupling resource consumption and pollution from economic growth.

The global environmental problems identified in the paper are climate change (the most severe); lack of water resources; desertification and soil degradation; the increasing incidence of natural disasters; the depletion of fishing stocks and increasing damage to reefs; and exposure to hazardous chemicals.

The Commission's view is that there are three components of sustainable development: economic, social, and environmental. The overall division within

[72] ibid. 11. [73] (2002) 3 *Global Environmental Outlook*, UNEP.

the Commission with regard to the developing countries is that DG ENV deals with the environmental matters and DG DEV the rest.

Improving the Coherence of EU Policies

The priority objective here is to ensure that the objectives of sustainable development are progressively integrated into all EU policies, whilst respecting their internal and external dimensions. To enable this, they propose that the EU:

1. Ensures that an impact assessment is carried out for all major policy proposals analysing their economic, social, and environmental consequences, in accordance with the conclusions of the Göteborg European Council;
2. Continues to adapt key policies, including the Common Agricultural Policy ('CAP'), the Common Fisheries Policy, and EC policies on energy, transport, and industry to the internal and external objectives of sustainable development;
3. Tackles actual or potential problems of coherence whenever EU policies are formulated, reviewed, or reformed.

These three proposals can be more shortly referred to as impact assessment, adaptation to sustainable development, and coherence. Impact assessment and tackling coherence will be considered here. (Much remains to be done with regard to adapting key policies to the objectives of sustainable development.)

Impact Assessment

The Göteborg (Gothenburg) European Council met in June 2001, under the then Swedish Presidency of the Community. It noted that the Commission would include in its action plan for better regulation mechanisms to ensure that all major policy proposals include a sustainability impact assessment covering their potential economic, social, and environmental consequences.

The action proposed in the Sustainable Development Communication in this respect was the strengthening by all EU institutions of internal cooperation and coordination procedures so as to improve policy coherence, with the Commission to establish, by the end of 2002, a coherent methodology for impact analysis to assess the economic, social, and environmental consequences of all major policy proposals.

The Commission has indeed overseen the introduction of such an internal system. The Policy Coordination Unit of the Secretariat-General is responsible for the Commission's 'new Impact Assessment tool'. The year 2002 saw the adoption of two new communications setting out the new approach to policy development and the regulatory environment: the Better Regulation Action Plan[74] and the Communication on Impact Assessment.[75]

[74] Communication from the Commission, Action Plan on Simplifying and Improving the Regulatory Environment COM(2002)278.

[75] COM(2002)276.

The Better Regulation Action Plan

The purpose of this Communication was to present to the European Council an Action Plan introducing 'a strategy for further coordinated action to simplify the regulatory environment' so as to ensure a high level of legal certainty across the EU. It did not aim to deregulate the Community. Alongside this Communication, the Commission was launching 'two key measures': the establishment of minimum standards of consultation, and the definition of a consolidated impact assessment method for its key initiatives concerning policy and legislation.

The Communication on Impact Assessment

In the Communication on impact assessment (the IA Communication), the Commission explains that such assessment is being launched as a tool to improve the quality and coherence of the policy development process, and as a means of contributing to a more coherent implementation of the European Strategy for Sustainable Development.

'Sustainable Development' here should be taken to apply at a global level for several reasons. The first is that it explains in the IA Communication that the Commission is 'delivering on its Göteborg commitments to implement sustainable development and to establish a tool for sustainable impact assessment. *With respect to* [*these commitments*], *the Commission has added the external dimension of sustainable development* through its February 2001 Communication "Towards a Global Partnership for Sustainable Development"' (emphasis added). The second is that, as quoted in the Guidelines on Impact Assessment in the Commission (see below), 'Sustainable development should become the central objective of all sectors and policies. This means that policy-makers must identify likely spillovers—good and bad—onto other policy areas and take them into account. Careful assessment of the full effects of a policy proposal must include estimates of its economic, environmental and social impacts inside *and outside* the EU' (emphasis added). This quote comes from the Commission's Communication, A Sustainable Europe for a Better World: A European Union Strategy for Sustainable Development.[76] This was the Commission's proposal to the Göteborg European Council of June 2001. The Council's reaction was to welcome the Communication, and to confirm that 'sustainable development requires global solutions'. It concluded that, 'The Union will seek to make sustainable development an objective in bilateral development cooperation'.[77]

From 2003 onwards, the IA Communication foresees that impact assessment will be implemented in the Commission for all 'major initiatives'. These are defined as 'those which are presented in the Annual Policy Strategy or later in the Work Programme of the Commission'. Section 2 of the Communication further explains this definition:

[76] COM(2001)264. [77] SN 200/1/01 REV 1, 4 ff.

The principle is that all Commission legislative and all other policy proposals proposed for inclusion in the Annual Policy Strategy for the Commission and Work Programme... will be subject to the impact assessment procedure, provided that they have a potential economic, social and/or environmental impact and/or require some regulatory measure for their implementation. The basic criterion is therefore the submission of a proposal for inclusion on the Commission Annual Policy Strategy and/or Work Programme.

(The provision could be wide-ranging in effect—it is difficult to think of proposals which would not have a potential economic, social, and/or environmental impact.)

One conclusion which can be drawn from the above is that an impact assessment should, therefore, be made of each major law and policy proposal impacting on developing countries with regard to, *inter alia*, its environmental impact, where there is potential for such impact. This should be as true for proposals for law and policy relating to agriculture, fisheries, and competition as for measures traditionally seen as 'development' measures.

Section 1.2 of the IA Communication provides that, 'When carrying out an impact assessment, the Commission will seek a broad range of views and will be open and transparent in the process as set out in its Communication on general principles and minimum standards for consultation'[78] (The Standards for Consultation Communication). The potential involvement of developing countries in consultation processes relating to environmental matters is in fact specifically foreseen in that Communication, with the provision in the Minimum Standards section, paragraph B, 'Consultation Target Groups', that, for consultation to be equitable, the Commission should ensure adequate coverage of parties affected by the policy in a consultation process, and that in determining the relevant parties for consultation, the Commission should take into account, *inter alia*:

— the wider impact of the policy on other policy areas, e.g. environmental interests;
— the need to involve non-organized interests, where appropriate; and
— the need for a proper balance, where relevant, between the representatives of organizations in the EU and those in non-member countries, for example, developing countries.

The approach to impact assessment set out in the IA Communication is intended to 'integrate, reinforce, streamline and replace all the existing separate impact assessment mechanisms for Commission proposals'. It should be policy-driven, focusing on examining whether the impact of major policy proposals is sustainable and conforms to the principles of Better Regulation.

[78] Communication from the Commission, Towards a Reinforced Culture of Consultation and Dialogue—General Principles and Minimum Standards for Consultation of Interested Parties by the Commission COM(2002)704.

These impact assessment procedures are to be gradually phased in. The IA Communication provides at section 1.4 that, starting with the adoption of its work programme for 2003, the Commission will identify certain proposals which will be subject to an extended impact assessment (under section 3.2), and that the section 3.1 preliminary assessment will be required for all proposals submitted in the context of the Annual Policy Strategy[79] for 2004 that was supposed to be adopted in February 2003 and was actually adopted in March that year. On the basis of those preliminary assessments, the Commission, at the same time as adopting the Annual Policy Strategy, selected the proposals needing extended assessments from that Strategy and the Work Programme 2004. The IA Communication states that the system 'will be fully operational in 2004/5'. Because of the gradual introduction of the process, the IA statements for 2003 are expected to be 'less complete'. But 'the full level of detail' is expected from 2004.

Technical guidelines, explains the IA Communication, would be available by September 2002. These have indeed now been published as an internal Commission document.[80] Impact on developing countries is not specifically mentioned anywhere in the Guidelines, but there can be little doubt, given the points made above, that such impact must be taken into account where appropriate. In addition, the Guidelines exhort Commission officials to 'think outside the box', and not to limit assessment to familiar areas.

Section 3 covers the two stages in the Commission's IA process. The preliminary assessment should serve as a filter to help the Commission identify the proposals that should be subject to an extended IA. The preliminary IA 'must be established early in the policy formulation process as a condition for inclusion of a legislative or policy proposal in the Annual Policy Strategy prepared in February for the following year and, at the very latest, be finalised in November before inclusion [*sic*] into the Work Programme'.

In the filtering process (to decide which proposals should be subject to an IA), the Commission must take into account, *inter alia*:

— whether the proposal will result in substantial economic, environmental, and/or social impacts on a specific sector or several sectors, and whether the proposal will have a significant impact on major interested parties; and
— whether the proposal represents a major policy reform in one or several sectors.

'Sector' is undefined in the Communication, and no examples are given. Again, for the reasons given above, it is arguable that Community development law and/or the developing countries themselves are a sector. It is still puzzling. A sector is

[79] The Commission's Annual Policy Strategies set policy priorities and budgetary orientations.

[80] Although an internal document, anyone wishing to obtain a copy of 'Impact Assessment in the Commission Guidelines' need only apply to the Secretariat-General of the European Commission, which immediately released one to the author, when asked.

not a policy. A sector could mean part of society or part of a policy or part of an economic system. It could mean part of almost anything. The Merriam-Webster online default definition is 'a sociological, economic or political subdivision of society'. Later in the Communication, reference is made to 'horizontal multi-sectoral aspects'[81] and 'economic sector',[82] and there is one prior reference to 'sectoral assessments',[83] but these throw no light on the earlier intended meaning.

The structure of the Communication at this point is also puzzling. There are two sub-clauses beginning 'whether'. The first includes 'whether the proposal will result in substantial economic, environmental and/or social impacts on a specific sector or several sectors', '*and* whether the proposal will have a significant impact on major interested parties' (emphasis added). So do both those requirements together have to be satisfied before the decision can be made that a proposal should be subject to extended IA? On balance, such an approach would seem unlikely, given that they are all factors 'to be taken into account', not factors which automatically *per se* must lead to a determination one way or the other. The factors which might make an interested party a 'major' one are also not specified. Developing countries tend not to exercise great power or influence at the diplomatic level for obvious reasons. There is a risk here that although they might be significantly affected by a particular proposal, they might not be perceived as a 'major interested party'.

In parallel with the limitations on the Community's impact assessment Directives, the impact assessment of proposals under this Communication will not constitute a universal panacea. IA is just an assessment—it will not determine the resulting political action. As the Commission puts it in the Communication, it is foreseen as 'an aid to decision-making, not a substitute for political judgment'. Also, existing policies, or minor reforms to those policies, and their effects on the environment of developing countries cannot be assessed under the IA Communication.

If the Commission decides that extended impact assessment is necessary, then the responsible services must follow the technical guidelines for impact assessment issued by the Secretary-General (mentioned above), and the general method set out in Annex 2 of the IA Communication. The resulting report must form part of the inter-service consultation on the proposal, and a summary of the main findings should be included in the memorandum. In most cases, the extended impact assessment will begin after the Annual Policy Strategy decision of the spring and then reported on in order to enable the inclusion of the proposal in the autumn's Work Programme. It must have been completed by the time the proposal enters inter-service consultation.

The Commission states in the IA Communication that it will 'ensure full transparency on the results of impact assessment both for the preliminary and extended assessment'.[84] A Commission official has confirmed that 'full

[81] In sect. 3.2 (d). [82] In Annex 3, sect. 4. [83] In sect. 1.1. [84] In sect. 5.

transparency' does mean with regard to the public. That transparency will only take effect, however, once a proposal has been adopted by the Commission.

There are three annexes to the Communication, on: the format of the preliminary assessment statement; the components of impact assessment; and the indicative reporting format for the extended impact assessment. Annex 2 refers, in point 4.1, to how the distributive effects of environmental impacts will, when relevant, be analysed, and internal (to the EU) and external effects will be shown separately. At point 4.2 of the same annex, the Commission sets out the principles which it will follow in assessing impacts. These include:

— 'The economic, social and environmental impacts identified for the proposed option should be analysed and presented in a format that facilitates a better understanding of the trade-offs between competing economic, social and environmental objectives'; and
— 'When assessing impacts, strict cost-benefit analysis may not always supply the most relevant information; for example, the degree of irreversibility should also be considered. The precautionary principle[85] should also be applied when appropriate.[86] The impact on established policy objectives where available, should be assessed.'

One of the questions raised in Annex 3 is whether there will be impacts outside the EU (on the Candidate Countries 'and/or other countries'—the 'external impacts' referred to in Annex 2).

In 2003, the Commission aimed to carry out extended impact assessment (which officials refer to as 'Ex IA') for 43 (out of 244) of its initiatives. These 43[87] all fall within the Commission's three main priorities for 2003: enlargement; stability and security; and sustainable and inclusive economy. However, some have been cancelled, and some postponed—the Commission's list of which proposals fall into which category is not yet official, but it may be that the planned Ex IA for the proposal for a Regulation establishing a Joint Community Inspection Structure for Fisheries falls into one of these two groups.

It has been argued[88] that Community agricultural policy has a number of undesirable impacts on the economy and environment of developing countries. Bearing this in mind, it would have been interesting if, under the new Commission approach, the June 2003 CAP reform proposals had been subject to Ex IA. (A very brief assessment was carried out in the 2002 mid-term review of the CAP (COM(2002)394, summarized at p. 28 with regard to external effects), but this

[85] As set out in the Commission Guidelines on the Application of the Precautionary Principle COM(2000)1.

[86] And therein lies the rub.

[87] Communication on the Commission's Legislative and Work Programme for 2003 COM(2002)590, 25.

[88] e.g. in 'EU Hypocrisy Unmasked—Why EU Trade Policy Hurts Development' (2003) Oxfam Briefing Note, 5 May 2003.

could not be applied to what was actually agreed because of, for example, the exclusion from the reform proposals of areas such as sugar, cotton, and tobacco, and the deferral of the reform of milk subsidies.) However, the June 2003 CAP reform proposals had not been subject to Ex IA because their preparation had begun before the IA process became applicable. (It will not become compulsory for all proposals covered in the Communication until 2004.)

Tackling Coherence

The Development Policy Communication had explained that 'Art. 178 of the Treaty and common sense oblige the EU to check that the objectives of its development policy are taken into account when the implementation of other policies are [*sic*] likely to affect developing countries'. The many areas of Community policy for which such a check is relevant are acknowledged to include trade, agriculture, the environment, energy, and fisheries.

But there are two problems here: first, that such checks are not yet systematically carried out, even for important policies, and secondly, that even if such checks are made, and serious problems identified, the implementation of those other policies can still go ahead unimpeded.

DGs other than DG DEV are not yet at the stage of seriously studying and acknowledging the adverse impacts of other policies on the developing countries—certainly not systematically, and sometimes not at all. Development policy is still very much at the margin of Community policies generally, and always risks being sidelined.

Furthermore, much as environmental impact assessment under Directive 85/337 can in many cases enable development to go ahead once it has been established just how much damage will be caused, the Commission admits that, 'It is still possible that the EU makes the political choice to go ahead with a policy despite its potentially negative, indirect and unintended impact on developing countries'. Such a decision must be made 'in full knowledge of its indirect consequences. When various options are available, such policies *will have to be* implemented in the least damaging way to developing countries. *If necessary and possible*, measures and programmes *may* be devised to put developing countries in a position to offset or resist the negative, unavoidable effects of EU other [*sic*] policies' (emphasis added). This pursuit of improved coherence is 'the responsibility of all institutions . . . conflicting requests should be avoided or resisted, or, when equally legitimate, the conflict should be brought to the fore and solved'. It is noteworthy that the possibility does not appear to be allowed for that development policy might have any negative effects on other EU policies.

In the Sustainable Development Communication, the approach taken is that domestic EU policies may have negative 'spill-over' effects on other countries, particularly in the developing world. The Communication lists some areas where the Community has taken positive action, including the General System of Preferences and the 'Everything but Arms' Initiative. It notes that more systematic reviews of policies are needed, and mentions in particular the CAP and the Common Fisheries Policy. As the OECD DAC commented, with regard to those two Policies, 'These cases show how the pursuit of the legitimate interests of the EC may have potentially adverse consequences for the legitimate development interests of partner countries, despite Treaty obligations to pursue coherence with development policy'.[89]

Better Governance at all Levels

The priority objectives here are to ensure good governance within all countries, and to strengthen the legitimacy, participatory basis, coherence, and effectiveness of global economic, social, and environmental governance. Again the difference, when compared to the Development Policy Communication, which largely accepted the global governance status quo, is striking. The Sustainable Development Communication argues that, 'in the context of increasing interdependence, the imbalance between market forces on the one hand and governance institutions on the other has resulted in a "global governance gap." There is a growing consensus that the global governance system must urgently gain in legitimacy, coherence and effectiveness.'[90]

The Commission suggests that a stronger civil voice is needed in international fora, and that local communities must be allowed to play an important role. With regard to the UN, the Commission is strident: 'co-ordination among its various bodies, and between the UN Organisation and other international institutions *must* be strengthened and targeted towards global governance for sustainable development'[91] (emphasis added).

Financing Sustainable Development

The priority objective here is to ensure that there is adequate funding to attain the International Development Targets and the Millennium Development Goals. To achieve this, the Commission aims include: making 'decisive progress' towards reaching the UN target of 0.7 per cent of GNI in ODA; and identifying effective means of delivering and safeguarding 'global public goods'.[92] More funding will be needed to achieve the safeguarding of global public goods. This may mean just increased national contributions, or it may mean the introduction of new taxes, suggests the Commission, for example on currency transactions (a Tobin-type tax), on carbon, or on arms exports.

The Sustainable Development Communication then finishes with a few comments about the implementation and review of the strategy. What marks this Communication out is its acknowledgement that change and concerted

[89] Main Findings and Recommendations of the 2002 OECD DAC Peer Review of the European Community.

[90] n. 68 above, 15.

[91] ibid. 16.

[92] Defined by UNDP as public goods whose benefits reach across borders, generations, and population groups.

efforts are necessary in order to achieve a global partnership for sustainable development.

Both the Development Policy and the Sustainable Development Communications have fine aspirations, but the first suffers from internal inconsistencies and there is a lack of common coherence between the two. This is ironic, given the aspiration of both to improve coherency. The Sustainable Development Communication stemmed much more from an appreciation of a real need for change.

The response of the Development Council to the Sustainable Development Communication was positive, and it adopted a detailed set of conclusions as a result.[93] These supported the further emphasis on the fight against poverty, making globalization work for sustainable development, achieving sustainable patterns of consumption and production (in particular by decoupling economic growth from unsustainable natural resources use and environmental degradation), *reversing* environmental degradation, improving the coherence of EU policies, ensuring better governance at all levels, and increasing the financing of sustainable development.

Despite the serious points and quibbles raised about these Communications, the Commission is clearly, on paper, serious about doing something effective to protect the environment and to foster sustainable development in the developing countries. But how successful is it being in practice?

D. Country Support Strategies and the Restructured Commission

There used to be three Directorates General with responsibility for developing countries: DG 1, which dealt with the ACP countries and the Lomé Conventions, and DGs 1A and 1B, which were concerned with the eastern European and the Asian, Latin American, and Mediterranean countries. Each dealt with its own project cycles, identifying, programming, and evaluating its own projects. Each had its own system of contracts. DG DEV worked with the Lomé and Yaoundé Conventions, and with financial envelopes of five to ten years. The other two also worked in five to ten-year periods, but with a yearly budget cycle. This budgetary difference was a significant factor in the development of their different contracting and tendering procedures.

It was decided to move towards a uniform contracting system, and the fundamental restructuring of the Commission at the end of 1999 saw the creation of a new Directorate General for External Relations (often referred to as 'DG Relex', from the French 'Relations Extérieures'). DG DEV was also created, with the task of preparing the country support strategies. The 'Common Service[94] Relex' (SCR from the French 'Service Commun Relex') was created,

[93] Minutes of the 2429th Council meeting, 8958/02 Presse 147.

[94] 'Common services' are not a usual form of Commission service. A brief search of the Commission's database revealed no others. It was presumably termed 'common' because it was common to DGs Relex and DEV.

and took over the contracts and evaluation part of all project cycles. The fourth new creation was the EuropeAid Co-Operation Office, usually abbreviated to 'EuropeAid', which formally came into being on 1 January 2001, and which took over the responsibilities of the SCR. It describes itself on its website as 'a single department handling the Commission's external aid'. What this means is that it is responsible for all phases of the project cycles—their implementation—having taken over this responsibility from DGs DEV and Relex and the SCR. 'All phases' means: the identification and appraisal of projects and programmes; the preparation of financing decisions; implementation and monitoring; and the evaluation of projects and programmes.

The situation now, therefore, is that DG DEV, DG Relex, and EuropeAid are, between them, responsible for development policy and implementation.

i. DG Development and DG Relex

In its Mission Statement,[95] DG DEV explains that, *inter alia*, it 'contributes to the formulation, by the Commissioner for Development and Humanitarian Aid, of the Community's development co-operation policy for all developing countries and Overseas Countries and Territories (OCTs). In addition, DG DEV directly manages and coordinates Community relations with the 78 African, Caribbean and Pacific states (ACP) and the 20 OCTs.'

There are other jobs which the DG DEV officials perform, so the DG is, overall, responsible for:

(a) programming for the ACP countries, working within the framework of the Cotonou Agreement;
(b) drawing up development policy for all developing countries;
(c) preparing initiatives to promote the coordination of policies between the Community and Member States;
(d) lobbying internally (within the Commission) in an attempt to influence Community policy in other areas (for example, in agriculture and fisheries) further to Article 178 EC;
(e) involvement in the negotiation of multilateral environmental agreements.

With regard to (b), although in theory the policy guidelines drawn up by DG DEV should be followed by DG Relex, this is not always the case. DG Relex frequently follows its own policies and priorities. For example, the main document setting out DG DEV's development policy is the Development Policy Communication (see above). This sets out six priority areas, and includes the environment as a 'cross-cutting sector'. In its dealings with Indonesia and China, however, DG Relex has made the environment and natural resources a key factor. With regard to EC–China cooperation, its 'second focus' (after increased sustainability in China's economic and social reform process) will be the promotion

[95] Published on the Internet at: http://europa.eu.int/comm/dgs/development/mission_en.htm.

of sustainable development and assisting China to pursue a better balance between environmental protection, social development, and economic growth[96] (reflecting China's own priorities). With regard to EC–Indonesia cooperation, EC cooperation assistance concentrates on two sectors: good governance, and the preservation and sustainable management of natural resources (forests, water, communities, and environmental) in rural areas[97] (reflecting Indonesia's priorities). Where its countries do not wish to highlight environmental concerns in this way, DG Relex draws up standard country strategy papers (CSPs), where environmental matters are included as cross-cutting issues, for example, in the CSPs for Afghanistan.

The CSPs for the ACP countries administered by DG DEV show another pattern altogether. It has been commented on above that developing countries do not always desire there to be an environmental component to their aid agreements. Sometimes this indifference is so great that it will be reflected in the total, or almost total, absence of environmental provision in the CSP. This is unfortunately the case with, for example, Barbados, Benin, Central African Republic, Eritrea, the Gambia, and Ghana.

Another policy difference between DGs DEV and Relex lies in their strategy for incorporating environmental concerns. The environment and rural development unit of DG DEV has a strategy for incorporating environmental concerns which was approved by a Development Council conclusion of May 2001. Meanwhile, the General Affairs Council approved a separate strategy for integrating the environment into development cooperation for the DG Relex countries. In this, there is more focus on conflict prevention. (Such a situation may be less likely to arise again as there will be no more separate meetings of the Development Council. The Seville European Council in 2002 decided to reduce 'sectoral formations' of the Council from 20 to 9. Development matters are now discussed at the General Affairs and External Relations Councils (GAERCs) in May and November.)

There is, within the Commission, some disquiet at the ad hoc nature of these developments, but, as one official put it, 'it's not necessarily worse [than all following the same policy strategy]'. The situation appears to have arisen not out of internal attempts to create pockets of power, but from a better motive: in negotiations with China and Indonesia, there were more opportunities to prioritize environmental objectives because those countries expressed more interest in environmental matters in the context of EC development cooperation. Such an approach gives the Commission a greater margin of manoeuvre with regard to the inclusion of environmental provisions. With the ACP countries, much of the initiative to include environmental matters apparently comes from the EC side,

[96] The China Country Strategy Paper, 2002–2006, published on the Internet at: europa.eu.int/comm/external_relations/china/csp.

[97] The Indonesia Country Strategy Paper, 2002–2006, published on the Internet at: http://www.europa.eu.int/comm/external_relations/indonesia/csp/02_06_en.pdf.

because, for most ACP countries, the environment is not a priority issue. (This may be understandable when one compares poverty figures. But it raises the question as to what the responsibility of the Community is towards grindingly poor countries with regard to insisting on the inclusion of environmental concerns in development negotiations and agreements.) There is also the question of designation to bear in mind: when, in Mauritius, 80 per cent of aid was spent on water and sanitation, it was an environmental matter, but it was not categorized as that.

With regard to (c), the officials lobby with the intention of defending the interests of the developing countries. Sometimes that lobbying is at DG level, for example with regard to policies emanating from DG ENV, sometimes by an individual unit, for example, the environment and rural development unit of DG DEV when fisheries are being discussed. DG ENV has been working on many initiatives, following up on the sixth Environment Action Programme and Johannesburg. It has therefore been developing many strategies, for example that on soil. These can be viewed within DG DEV as being very Europe-oriented, and as seeing Europe 'as an island'. DG DEV sees part of its job as being to persuade all other DGs that many of their proposed policies would have effects extending beyond Europe, and affecting developing countries. A self-assessment is that they are 'sometimes successful', one example of recent perceived success being input to DG ENV's pre-strategy on natural resource use. DG DEV felt that this had overlooked the interests of the developing countries, but that it has now been amended to take these interests into account. However, as one official explained, it has not yet been agreed on as formal strategy.[98]

Another area where DG DEV has been lobbying is fisheries agreements. These are very European-interest oriented (with countries like Spain exercising great lobbying influence), often at the expense of the interests of the developing countries, because the fisheries agreements to date are simply not in the interests of small fishermen. This is an area where DG DEV's lobbying is largely unsuccessful. Although DG Fisheries has come up with token plans with regard to training and plants, these consistently fail to address the real problem: that small fishermen are deprived of their catch.

With regard to involvement in the negotiation of multilateral environmental agreements ((d) above), DG DEV has a representational function. In almost all cases DG ENV is the '*chef de file*' during such negotiations, for example with regard to climate change and biodiversity. That means that DG DEV will make its contribution to the negotiations through the DG ENV filter. In one area only is DG DEV *chef de file*: desertification (since the countries most concerned and affected by desertification are the developing ones).

[98] For further information, see the DG ENV website, which includes the text of the Commission Communication, Towards a Thematic Strategy on the Sustainable Use of Natural Resources COM(2003)572.

A constant problem for DG DEV is that its committed and stretched staff are constantly asking unsuccessfully for more resources in terms of money and personnel. Lobbying for these is part of the run-up to the Strategic Planning Process. But DG DEV has very little influence on the negotiations because the whole process is very centralized, and it is a weak, peripheral DG. (Even the building which houses the DG is kilometres away from most of the Commission's buildings, which tend to cluster around the main Commission building where the College of Commissioners meets in the centre of the 'European quarter'.)

ii. EuropeAid

It took some time for EuropeAid to get to grips with all its responsibilities, but relations between it and DG DEV are apparently now working smoothly. For example, every two years, the Commission sets guidelines for the budget lines for the developing countries. Agreement on these between DG DEV and EuropeAid took six-to-nine months in 2002, but was far speedier and less fraught in 2003.

EuropeAid aspires to be accountable, but the perception in DG DEV is that its accountability—to DG DEV—is very weak. DG DEV would like the Commission to make available the results of all environmental evaluations of the projects for which EuropeAid is responsible. It keeps a register of these, but this is not yet accessible to DG DEV, let alone the public. For 200 on-going projects, DG DEV would like to see 200 published environmental impact assessments (EIAs). At the moment, the lack of information is so dire that the DG does not even know *which* projects have been evaluated, let alone the results of those assessments. The whole project information database is very weak, and it is hard to find information, even down to learning which projects involve environmental issues. EuropeAid has, apparently, just started to apply the OECD DAC sector codes to the projects. This should provide a little more information than at present on each project.

In theory, the environment is being integrated into the Country Support Strategies. However, DG DEV is not told whether the environmental measures have been implemented, and they cannot follow each strategy up, on top of their normal work. There are around 130 strategies, 70 for the ACP. Sometimes if DG DEV tries to achieve follow-up, it is successful, at other times not. There is no policy or coherency on the matter.

In addition to all the concerns raised above, it is relatively easy to insert into a programming document for Surinam, for example, that the environment will be dealt with as a cross-cutting issue, but being able to confirm that it has been so dealt with is quite another matter. A DG DEV official commented that the DG's main successes are its communications and policies—the implementation of these is a different story.

V. Could the EC be Challenged with regard to its Reduction of ODA to LDCs?

It is argued above that the Community institutions are acting contrary to the EC Treaty in failing to foster 'more particularly' the sustainable economic and social development of the most disadvantaged among the developing countries. If this is correct, can anything be done about it?

There are provisions in the EC Treaty allowing for legal challenges to the European institutions. The European ECJ and the Court of First Instance (CFI) are bound to ensure that in the interpretation and application of the EC Treaty the law is observed.[99] In the circumstances in question, one could argue that the Commission or Council, or both, are *acting*, in taking decisions which effectively mean that they are neglecting their obligation under the EC Treaty to foster 'more particularly' the sustainable economic and social development of the most disadvantaged among the developing countries. One could also argue that they are *failing to act* to foster that development.

Acting: any relevant 'acts' could be challenged as infringements of the Treaty under Article 230 EC, but only by a Member State, the EP, the Council or the Commission. It would be astonishing were a Member State to choose to take such action—their Foreign Ministers sit on the External Relations Council, and they have chosen to change the focus of Community aid over the past decade away from the least developed countries to other 'new external priorities'. The Council and Commission would not challenge for similar reasons, and the EP, whilst it has shown consistent support and concern for the cause of the developing countries, would have to overcome considerable internal support for maintaining the current situation from the point of view of facilitating accession, for example.

Such 'acts' can also be challenged by any natural or legal person, who may institute proceedings against a decision addressed to that person or against a decision which, although in the form of a regulation or a decision addressed to another person, is of direct and individual concern to the former. Could this provision be used by a developing country to challenge the Community's development aid policy? Showing direct and individual concern is fraught with difficulty. Potentially more interesting is the next possibility.

Failure to act: any relevant 'failure to act' could be challenged under Article 232 EC by the Member States and other Community institutions. Such a challenge would again, for the reasons given in the previous paragraph, be extremely unlikely.

[99] Art. 220 EC.

In addition, any natural or legal person may call upon the institution(s) concerned to act. If, within two months of being so called upon, the institution concerned has not defined its position, within a further two months a complaint may be made to the ECJ that the institution(s) in question have failed to address to that person any act (other than a recommendation or opinion). It would not be by any means a clear-cut case,[100] but there would appear to be grounds for considering whether one or more of the least developed countries could mount such a challenge. The first step in such an action, (calling on the institution to define its position) would not involve immediate action before the ECJ, and all the costs that that would entail. It could, however, lead to an interesting response, and maybe further action, even if no court case was actually brought, as in *The Liberal Democrats* v. *European Parliament*.[101] In that case, the Liberal Democrats, a UK political party, applied for a declaration that, by failing to draw up proposals for direct elections to the EP in accordance with a uniform procedure in all Member States, the EP had infringed various treaty provisions and an Act annexed to a Council Decision. The publicity involved led to the rectification of the failure after the action had been brought and the Advocate General had published his Opinion, but before a decision had been given. There was therefore no need for the ECJ to give a decision. The parties each bore their own costs.

Should a call to act be made by one or more of the LDCs soon, it might help focus the minds of those negotiating the next EU Financial Perspectives (a six-to-seven-year overall budget framework which will 'set the levels of the nine major chapters of the EU budget for 2007–13 and the degree of annual variations. . . . The availability of funds for development cooperation in the EU budget is thus constrained for these seven years by the overall size of the External Relations Chapter allocation and the competing needs of other external action requirements. These negotiations are therefore also a crucial moment to redefine the relative priority the EU attaches to its major policy areas: if the budget allocated to EU agriculture (the CAP) is to be reduced and increased funds allocated to external policy this is the moment to ensure that it happens.').[102] It might also be relevant to the negotiation of the 10th EDF in 2006.

[100] Obvious issues which arise include: the difficulty of proving that money spent elsewhere and via different funds would otherwise have gone to the least developed countries, and whether the ECJ would consider it had jurisdiction over the EDF, as its budget is set in the Council, and the agreements must be ratified by the Member States' parliaments. (It does not fall under the general Community budget, even though a heading has been reserved for the Fund in that budget since 1993.) These issues might pose less of a problem should the EDF be budgetized, as proposed by the Commission in its Communication Towards the Full Integration of Co-operation with ACP Countries in the EU Budget COM(2003)590. However, as the Commission has stated that funding to the least developed countries has fallen because of new external priorities, it could be asked to state what those new priorities are, and the increased funding to policies concerned with those new priorities could then be assessed.

[101] Case C-41/92, *The Liberal Democrats* v. *European Parliament* [1993] I-3153.

[102] Mackie, n. 52 above.

Even if no legal challenge were to be feasible, the argument that the EC Treaty provisions should not be ignored could be made in relevant debates, discussions, and assessments of Community development cooperation theory and practice.

In addition, two other avenues of action might be explored: the submission of a petition to the EP's Committee on Petitions, and the making of a complaint to the European Ombudsman.

Petitions can be submitted to the EP by EU citizens, non-Community residents in the EU, and the members of any natural or legal person with its headquarters in an EU Member State. Such petitions may relate to matters of general concern, individual complaints, or a request for the Parliament to take a stance on a matter of public interest. The subject of the petition has to fall within the sphere of EU activities. These include development cooperation policy. As the EP's website[103] explains, depending on the circumstances, the Committee on Petitions may:

- Ask the European Commission to provide information regarding compliance with the relevant Community legislation,
- Refer the petition to other EP committees for further action,
- Submit a report to the EP to be voted on in plenary,
- Draw up an opinion and ask the President of the EP to forward it to the Council and/or European Commission for action.

The European Ombudsman 'investigates complaints about maladministration by the institutions and bodies of the European Community'.[104] Any EU Member State citizen, anyone living in an EU Member State, and all natural and legal persons with a registered office in the EU may complain to the Ombudsman. There is no need to show direct or individual concern with regard to the alleged maladministration. As explained in the citizen's guide,[105] if 'an institution fails to do something it should have done, if it does it in the wrong way or if it does something it should not have done, there may be reason to complain to the Ombudsman'. There is a time limit: complaints must be made within two years 'of the date when you got to know the facts on which your complaint is based and you must already have contacted the institution or body concerned, for example by a letter'.[106] If maladministration is found, and the issue not resolved during the inquiry, the Ombudsman will attempt to find a 'friendly solution'. If that does not work, he can make a draft recommendation, calling on the institution to put the maladministration right. If that recommendation is not accepted, the Ombudsman may make a special report to the EP.

[103] Published on the Internet at: http://www.europarl.eu.int/petition/help_en.htm.

[104] *What can the European Ombudsman Do for You? A Guide for Citizens.* Published on the Internet at: http://www.euro-ombudsman.eu.int.

[105] ibid.

[106] ibid.

(And where the maladministration cannot be put right, the Ombudsman can address a 'critical remark' to the institution.) If a complaint is made, the Ombudsman will not investigate it at the same time as any legal case is under way. But as making a complaint to the Ombudsman is free, that might be a more appropriate first step to take in any event.

VI. The Convention on Europe

In December 2003, the Brussels summit of European Heads of Government, which was held with the aim of agreeing on the terms of a new European constitution, was abandoned after Spain and Poland were unable to agree some of the proposed terms, and were not prepared to compromise in respect of those provisions. Their concerns related to voting rights: they did not wish to surrender the voting rights granted to them under the Nice Treaty. Under that Treaty, each would have 27 votes, with Germany, Britain, France, and Italy possessed of 29 votes each. That weighting is of concern to Germany in particular, which has a population of 80 million—double that of either Poland or Spain—and which contributes roughly 25 per cent of the total EU budget. Poland will, initially at least, be contributing proportionately little to that budget. The Germans and the French, alarmed by such a prospect, had argued at the summit for the introduction instead of a double-majority voting system, requiring new laws to be approved by at least 13 of the 25 countries, representing at least 60 per cent of the population. This would have increased their power, and reduced that of Poland and Spain. There is now a pressing need to agree on how cooperation and collaboration can fairly be achieved.

But those were not the only differences proposed in the draft constitution. Most of those interested in European affairs will be aware of other pressing issues which now remain in need of urgent resolution, for example: the need for the election of a president, in place of rotating the presidency every six months; and the question of European defence policy, and its relationship with the North Atlantic Treaty Organization (NATO).

In addition to the well-known issues, however, much of what the EC Treaty currently sets out with regard to development cooperation would have been changed, or neutered, had the recommendations of the Convention on Europe been adopted. There has already been a great deal written about the place of development policy in the evolution of the EU's external action policy (for example, with regard to what will happen to the position of High Representative for the Common Foreign and Security Policy, or the taking of external relations decisions within the Council and Commission, together with the integration of development matters into those decisions), so this chapter will not be examining those aspects of the draft constitution. Nor will this chapter be considering the draft constitution from the point of view of the conservation of the environmental *acquis*, as the battle to retain that *acquis* has already been documented.[107]

In its last section, this chapter will focus on the proposals made in the draft constitution with regard to the amendment of the existing Treaty provisions on development cooperation which were considered in detail above.

A. Background

At the European Council meeting in Laeken in December 2001, the EU Heads of State issued a Declaration on the Future of the European Union.[108] This was divided into three parts: Europe at a crossroads; challenges and reforms in a renewed union; and convening of a convention on the future of Europe.

The Declaration asked, in the context of whether there could be a better division and definition of competence in the European Union, 'What amendments should be made to the Treaty on the various policies? How, for example, should a more coherent common foreign policy and defence be developed?' And later on in the same part, in a paragraph on the need for more democracy, transparency, and efficiency in the European Union, the Council asks, 'How should the coherence of European foreign policy be enhanced? How is synergy between the High Representative and the competent Commissioner to be reinforced? Should the external representation of the Union in international fora be extended further?' Development policy is not mentioned. The coherence of European foreign policy is apparently of particular concern to the Ministers.

Interestingly, in the preface to the draft constitution, it is stated that, 'The Convention was asked to draw up proposals on three subjects: how to bring citizens closer to the European design and European Institutions; how to organise politics and the European political area in an enlarged Union; and how to develop the Union into a stabilising factor and a model in the new world order'. Whether the provisions of the draft constitution would have achieved the last aim is disputable.

Part III, on the convening of a convention on the future of Europe, explained that such a convention would be convened 'in order to pave the way for the next Intergovernmental Conference'.[109] It was to be composed of the 'main parties involved in the debate on the future of the Union', and it was to 'consider the key issues arising for the Union's future development, and try to identify the various possible responses'. The Declaration then stated that:

> It [the Convention] will draw up a final document which may comprise either different options, indicating the degree of support which they received, or recommendations if consensus is achieved.

[107] I. Christopoulou and T. Long, 'Conserving the Environmental Acquis—An Assessment of the European Convention' (2004) 10 *Environmental Law Network International*, 1.

[108] SN 300/1/01 REV 1, Annex I.

[109] i.e. the Dec. 2003 Brussels summit.

Together with the outcome of national debates on the future of the Union, the final document will provide a starting point for discussions in the Intergovernmental Conference, which will take the ultimate decisions.

The 'final document' (of options or recommendations to act as a starting point) was presented to the Italian Presidency of the European Council by the Chairman of the Convention, Valéry Giscard d'Estaing, on 18 July 2003, in the form of a 'full draft Treaty establishing a Constitution for Europe'. In the accompanying 'Rome Declaration', the draft was described as 'a success because it is a finished product, with no loose ends to be tied up, no options left open. It is in the general interest.' A call was made to 'have the text left as it stands. Reopening it, even in part, would cause it to unravel.'

This was a startling claim to make in respect of a document that was supposed to consist of options or recommendations to act as a 'starting point' for discussions in the Intergovernmental Conference.

Further, eight of the Convention members put their names to an 'Alternative Report', *The Europe of Democracies*,[110] in which they question the legitimacy of the draft European Constitution, arguing, in particular, that the 'draft EU constitution was never drafted through normal democratic methods' because:

— the applicant countries were treated as observers in the Praesidium and had no real say;
— only three political families were represented in the powerful Praesidium which drafted the 'tunnel vision text';
— the members were refused the right to have their amendments translated, distributed, discussed, and voted upon;
— the Convention had no Members for those halves of the respective populations which rejected the Maastricht Treaty in France or the Nice Treaty in Ireland;
— not one Eurosceptic or Eurorealist was allowed to observe or to participate in the work in the Praesidium, or in any of its assisting secretariats.

The final claim of those eight dissenting Convention members was that 'Giscard did not allow democracy and normal voting in the Convention. The draft Constitution runs counter to all democratic principles.'

These are serious points,[111] and criticism came from other quarters too. Quite apart from the reservations of various Member States, which created such stumbling blocks at the Brussels summit in December 2003, European Commission President, Romano Prodi, referred to the draft as a 'step backwards' as it failed to wrest away from Member States their vetoes in taxation and foreign

[110] CONV 851/03 (2003) 'Report from the Presidency of the Convention to the President of the European Council', Annex III, 21.

[111] For further commentary see A. Arnull, 'Editorial' (2003) 28 *European Law Review*, 573–4.

policy, and he had sympathy with the arguments of the smaller states that the proposed changes could lead to the larger countries dominating the EU, whilst a weakened Commission looked on. (Because, for example, of the proposals to replace the rotating presidency with a permanent presidency, and to reduce the number of Commissioners so that not every Member State will always have one). In addition, Gisela Stuart, a German-born British Labour Party MP, who was the only female member of the thirteen members of the Praesidium of the Convention on the future of Europe, published her grave reservations about the procedures of the Praesidium and the resulting draft constitution in a Fabian Society pamphlet.[112] Amongst her criticisms were the following:

— 'Laeken had posed a number of specific questions but rather than answering them, after six months of general debates the Praesidium presented the Convention members with a skeleton structure of a constitution. Without debate, it was simply accepted that this was the most appropriate way of fulfilling the Laeken mandate.'[113]

— The monthly plenary debates were confined to short inspirational speeches with detailed specific discussions reserved for written contributions and the working groups. The Convention had decided early on that it would not take votes, for resaons explained by Valéry Giscard d'Estaing: 'They tried this in the previous Convention on the Charter of Fundamental Rights and found it to have been a very bad idea. Literally thousands of amendments flooded in, and commentators often remarked how difficult it was to see from the outside how decisions were reached on what was deemed to have support and what was discarded. All I can say is that it was equally difficult from the inside.'[114]

— 'It was at [a dinner] that the skeleton of the draft constitution was given to members of the Praesidium in sealed brown envelopes the weekend before the public presentation. We were not allowed to take the documents away with us. Just precisely who drafted the skeleton, and when, is still unclear to me, but I gather much of the work was done by Valéry Giscard d'Estaing [a French politician and former President of the Republic 1974–81] and Sir John Kerr [a British career diplomat and the Secretary-General of the European Convention] over the summer. There was little time for informed discussion, and even less scope for changes to be made.'[115]

— 'It was only in the final months of the Convention that simultaneous translation was provided for Praesidium meetings and we could be accompanied by an assistant to give legal advice.... It was not unusual for texts to arrive late and only in French.'[116]

[112] G. Stuart, *The Making of Europe's Constitution* (London: The Fabian Society, 2003).
[113] ibid. 19. [114] ibid. 19–20. [115] ibid. 20–1. [116] ibid. 21–2.

— 'In the final stages of the Convention, a number of delegates, myself included, made it clear that we could not endorse the text as it stood and that it should be regarded as no more than a basis for future discussions . . . Yet, hardly was the ink dry on the Draft than this was turned into an endorsement by all those present and governments were warned not to open up the carefully achieved compromises.'

When it comes to matters of policy, Ms Stuart does not mention Community development policy, despite listing the following as examples of substantive Union external action policies which are defined in the draft constitution: common and foreign security policy; common commercial policy; cooperation with other countries; and humanitarian aid.

Similarly, there appears to have been little reaction, if any, at Member State level to the proposed changes to treaty provisions on development cooperation, which give a nod towards, but arguably take backward steps with regard to, the statement in the Preamble to the draft Constitution that the reunited Europe wishes to 'strive for peace, justice and solidarity throughout the world'.

B. The Provisions of the Draft European Constitution

i. General—In Relation to the Sustainable Development and Development Cooperation

The draft Treaty establishing a Constitution for Europe[117] is divided into parts. Part I has no overall title, but its individual titles comprise, in order: the definition and objectives of the Union; fundamental rights and citizenship of the Union; Union competences; the Union's institutions; the exercise of Union competence; the democratic life of the Union; the Union's finances; the Union and its immediate environment; and Union membership. The draft treaty provides in its Article 3(4) (in Title I) that:

In its relations with the wider world, the Union shall uphold and promote its values *and interests*. It shall contribute to peace, security, the *sustainable development of the earth*, solidarity and mutual respect among peoples, free and fair trade, *eradication of poverty* and protection of human rights and in particular children's rights, as well as to strict observance and development of international law, including respect for the principles of the United Nations Charter. (emphasis added)

Article 13 sets out 'Areas of shared competence'. (It follows on from Article 12's listing of those areas where the Union would have exclusive competence: in establishing the competition rules necessary for the functioning of the internal market; monetary policy for the Member States in the euro-zone; the common

[117] CONV 850/03, 'Draft Treaty Establishing a Constitution for Europe, submitted to the President of the European Council in Rome', 18 July 2003.

commercial policy; the customs union; and the conservation of marine biological resources under the common fisheries policy.) The environment is listed as one of the areas of shared competence in Article 13(2). Article 13(4) provides that, in the area of development cooperation, 'the Union shall have competence to take action and conduct a common policy; however, the exercise of that competence may not result in Member States being prevented from exercising theirs'. This serves neatly to underline the meaninglessness of the word 'common' when applied to a Community policy. The original idea had been that such a policy should be exclusively and completely common to the Community, as the first common policy, the Common Agricultural Policy, was. The word has come to be applied over time to policies such as the Common Transport Policy or the Common Foreign and Security Policy, where the Member States continue to develop and exercise their own policies in tandem with Community policy, without challenge by the European Commission as guardian of the Treaty. To provide for the Union exercise of a 'common' development cooperation policy alongside the exercise by individual Member States of their own, different, development cooperation policies simply illustrates the point.[118]

ii. Provisions relating to Development Cooperation

Article 13(4) (in Title III) states that, 'In the areas of development cooperation and humanitarian aid, the Union shall have competence to take action and conduct a common[119] policy; however, the exercise of that competence may not result in Member States being prevented from exercising theirs'.

Title V of Part II of the draft Treaty is entitled, 'The Union's External Action'. Its chapter IV (following on from 'Provisions Having General Application', 'Common Foreign and Security Policy', and 'Common Commercial Policy') is 'Cooperation with Third Countries and Humanitarian Aid'. It proposes a radical re-writing of the Treaty provisions on development cooperation, in three articles.

Article III-218 provides that:

1. Union policy in the sphere of development cooperation shall be conducted within the framework of the principles and objectives of the Union's external action. The Union's development cooperation policy and that of the Member States complement and reinforce each other.
   Union development cooperation policy shall have as its primary objective the reduction and, in the long term, the eradication of poverty. The Union shall take account of the objectives of development cooperation in the policies that it implements which are likely to affect developing countries.

[118] See also for mention of the variable meaning and lack of control over the use of 'common' when applied to Community policies, F. Dehousse and C. Maczkovics, 'Les arrêts open skies de la Cour de justice: l'abandon de la competence externe implicite de la Communauté?' (2003) 11 *Journal des Tribunaux Droit Européen*, 225–36.

[119] Whether a policy is 'common' or not now has no legal impact. It is a matter of political aspiration. European Member States remain far from being able to agree on a truly common development cooperation policy.

2. The Union and the Member States shall comply with the commitments and take account of the objectives they have approved in the context of the United Nations and other competent international organisations.

Article III-219 states that:

1. European laws or framework laws shall establish the measures necessary for the implementation of development cooperation policy, which may relate to multi-annual cooperation programmes with developing countries or programmes with a thematic approach.
2. The Union may conclude with third countries and competent international organisations any agreement helping to achieve the objectives referred to in Article III-193 [which would include the fostering of 'the sustainable economic, social and environmental development of developing countries, with the primary aim of eradicating poverty']. Such agreements shall be negotiated and concluded in accordance with Article III-227 [the procedure for negotiating and concluding international agreements].

   The first subparagraph shall be without prejudice to Member States' competence to negotiate in international bodies and to conclude international agreements....
3. The European Investment Bank shall contribute, under the terms laid down in its Statute, to the implementation of the measures referred to in paragraph 1.

The role of the EP throughout these provisions remains sadly minimal.

Article III-218 would squarely set the EU's development cooperation policy 'within the framework' of the EU's external action. Obviously, coherency is good, but one danger here lies in the possible subsummation of the longer-term goals of development policy in the shorter-term and potentially more economically influenced general external action policies of the EU.

A sweeping change in terms of Treaty provision (though not practice) would be the proposed introduction of just one primary objective for EU development cooperation policy: the reduction and, in the long term, the eradication of poverty. Of particular significance here is that the most disadvantaged developing countries could no longer claim any priority over the other developing countries, which they can do currently (in theory, at least) in relation to the Community's duty to foster their sustainable economic and social development. The EU could, in compliance with its duties under the draft Treaty, if approved, focus most of its development aid on the poor in the more developed developing countries, thus benefiting from the extra economic benefits and global influence this would bring, whilst 'legitimately' leaving the most disadvantaged developing countries for later consideration and increase in aid.

It should also be mentioned here that the Convention's Working Group on External Action had recommended with a 'very large consensus'[120] on the following text defining the 'Principles and Objectives' of EU external action:

[120] 'The Final Report of Working Group VII on External Action to the Members of the Convention', CONV 459/02, WG VII 17, of 16 Dec. 2002, para. 2.

1. The Union's action on the international stage will be guided by, and designed to advance in the wider world, the values which have inspired its own creation, development and enlargement: democracy, the rule of law, the universality and indivisibility of human rights and fundamental freedoms, the principles of human dignity, equality and solidarity, and respect for international law in accordance with the principles of the Charter of the United Nations. The Union will seek to develop relations and build partnerships with countries, and regional or global organisations, who share these values. It will promote multilateral solutions to common problems, in particular in the framework of the United Nations.
2. The European Union will define and pursue common policies and Union actions, and will work for a maximum degree of cooperation in all fields of international relations, in order:
    (a) to safeguard the common values, fundamental interests, independence and integrity of the Union;
    (b) to consolidate and support democracy, the rule of law, human rights and international law;
    (c) to preserve peace, prevent conflicts and strengthen international security, in conformity with the principles of the United Nations Charter;
    (d) *to foster the durable [sic—this appears to be a translation error which should have read 'sustainable']*[121] *economic and social development of developing countries, with the primary aim to eradicate poverty, in particular in low income countries*; [emphasis added]
    (e) to encourage the integration of all countries into the world economy, including through the progressive abolition of restrictions on international trade;
    (f) to develop international measures to preserve the environment and global natural resources, and ensure sustainable development;
    (g) to assist populations, countries and regions confronting man-made or natural disasters;
    (h) to promote an international system based on stronger multilateral cooperation and good global governance.

The Convention decided to set up working groups on 'specific subjects which are difficult to go into in depth at plenary sessions' in order to 'look at issues more closely'.[122] The guiding criterion for the composition of the Working Groups was 'specific expertise',[123] the composition being determined by the Praesidium[124] on that basis. The External Action Working Group, like all

[121] Despite Bobby McDonagh, representative of the Irish Government and alternate member of the Convention, having pointed out the need for the word to be changed in his comments on the revised draft final report of the Working Group on External Action, WG VII—WD 64.

[122] Published on the Internet at: http://european-convention.eu.int/grptrav.asp?lang=EN&Content/WGI.

[123] Note from the Secretariat to the Convention on 'Working Groups: Second Wave', CONV 206/02, para. 4.

[124] The Praesidium consisted of: the Convention Chairman (Valéry Giscard d'Estaing); its two vice-chairmen; and nine members of the Convention (representatives of the three governments holding the Presidency of the Union during the Convention (Spain, Denmark, and Greece); two national parliament representatives, two representatives of the European Parliament, and two representatives of the Commission.

the working groups, was set a mandate. The original mandate[125] posed five questions:

1. How should the interests of the EU be defined and formulated?
2. How should the consistency of the EU's activities be ensured, coordinating all the instruments available to it (including development aid, humanitarian action, financial assistance, trade policy, etc.)?
3. What can be done to ensure that the decision-making process allows the EU to act rapidly and effectively on the international stage? How far could the Community method be extended to other fields of action and how could it be made more effective? What easing of the rule of unanimity might be considered?
4. What lessons may be drawn from the experience gained from the creation of the post of High Representative for the Common Foreign and Security Policy (CFSP)? What scope for initiative may be assigned to him? How can it be ensured that he has the necessary resources, including financial resources, at his disposal?
5. What amendments to arrangements for the external representation of the EU would increase the EU's influence at international level? How could better synergy be achieved between the diplomatic activity of the EU and of the Member States?

The second question rather begs several questions relating to development aid. It classifies development aid as an 'instrument' available to the EU in its external action. It is not. It is currently a Treaty obligation *per se*. Further, under neither that mandate, nor the annotated version,[126] is there to be any consideration of the efficacy of Community development policy, or consideration as to how it could best be rationalized or its aims achieved. The amended mandate recalls that, 'the challenges of globalization require the EU to fulfil its international role by using effectively and coherently all the resources at its disposal'. Rather more subtly, a little later on the amended mandate notes that, 'The different policies and their instruments are interlinked; for example a decision related to development co-operation or humanitarian aid can have an important impact on foreign policy and *vice versa*'. This may be true, but there is no explicit recognition that often development policy and external relations may be pursuing aims which do not easily fuse in the short term. Development policy (unlike humanitarian aid) tends to work in a long-term perspective, and foreign policy tends to operate more, though far from exclusively, in the short to medium term. (As acknowledged in the amended mandate: 'All agree that it is important for the EU to have a dynamic foreign policy that is capable of responding promptly to international developments'.)[127]

[125] CONV 206/02, 19 July 2002.
[126] CNV 252/02 of 10 Sept. 2002.
[127] Para. 7.

Under the TEU, the EU 'shall in particular ensure the consistency of its external activities as a whole in the context of its external relations, economic and development policies'.[128] This sits slightly uneasily with the Praesidium's Discussion Paper on EU External Action,[129] which explains that 'The main policies in the area of external relations in which the Community was given a role from its inception (and which remain to this day) come under two distinct headings: trade and development co-operation'.[130] However, the EU Treaty appears to provide that the Community's 'external activities' include each of 'external relations policy', 'security policy', 'economic policy', and 'development policy'. In other words, development policy would appear to be presented here as a self-contained policy (and external relations policy as another), not, as claimed in the Praesidium's 'Reflection Paper'[131] one of the two 'distinct headings' in the area of external relations (the other being trade). Was this an attempt by the Convention to deprive development cooperation of its status as a policy in its own right?

The issue had been considered by the Working Group on External Action, which, 'while recognising that development policy has its specific purposes, which are reflected among the principles and objectives of EU external action, underlines the need for ensuring coherence between development cooperation and other aspects of EU external action as well as external aspects of internal policies, since development assistance should be considered as an element of the global strategy of the EU vis-à-vis third countries'. This view, upholding the current Treaty provisions, was turned on its head by the Praesidium in the (general) conditions outlined above by Gisela Stuart.

The External Action Working Group also found within its ranks 'a high degree of support in favour of the integration of the European Development Fund (EDF) into the overall EU budget and thus making it subject to the same procedures applicable to other areas of financial assistance'. It stressed, however, that such integration 'must be accompanied by improvements to the effectiveness and poverty focus of EU development programmes in general, and *should not reduce the volume of aid directed towards ACP countries*'[132] (emphasis added). In part B of the Working Group on External Action's Final Report ('the Detailed Report of Discussions'), it was explained that there had been 'a high degree of support in favour of the integration of the EDF into the Community budget' and that 'some' had pointed out that such integration should in no case lead to a reduction in the volume of aid directed towards ACP countries.

Should the EDF be integrated into the Community budget? Poul Nielsen, the Development Commissioner, certainly thinks so. He said in his address[133] to the Working Group on External Relations that, 'The European Development Fund represents an essential part of [the] EU's development co-operation. Under the

[128] TEU, Art. 3. [129] CONV 161/02, 3 July 2002. [130] Para. 3.
[131] CONV 161/02, as described in CONV 459/02, p. 11, and CNV 2002/02, p. 2.
[132] CONV 459/02, sect. 9, second para. 8. [133] 15 Oct. 2002, WG VII—WD 9.

9th EDF, 13.5 billion Euros are available for development co-operation with the ACP countries until 2007. Nevertheless, the EDF is not an integral part of the EU. It is therefore not subject to parliamentary control by the European Parliament.

'This is an anomaly. The EDF is an important policy domain of the EU and should as such be [as] subject to normal parliamentary control as other policy domains. The integration of the EDF in the General Budget would achieve this objective. Moreover, it would bring distinct benefits in terms of simplification, as it would allow for a single legal framework for the management of development funds.'[134]

The Convention totally ignored—on paper[135]—the recommendation that the EDF should be integrated into the EU budget. It also excised one recommendation made in the report by the External Action Working Group, the effect of which would, if incorporated in a new European constitution, be of particular significance for the least developed countries. The Convention maintained the provision that would have required the Community to foster sustainable development in the developing countries, with the primary aim of eradicating poverty, but deleted the specification that the primary aim of poverty eradication should apply in particular in low income countries. During the plenary session of the European Convention of 20 December 2002, there was a debate on the final report of the Working Party on External Action. Jean-Luc Dehaene (a Belgian politician, Prime Minister of Belgium 1992–9, and Vice Chairman of the Convention) presented the report. In the Summary Report of that Plenary Session,[136] it is explained that 'The central question in the debate was what arrangements, both in terms of Treaty change and reform of working methods, would help the Union to become a stronger global player, capable of defending its interests and promoting its values.... Some welcomed the fact that the principles and objectives indicated that development policy should have as its primary aim the eradication of poverty, *in particular in low income countries* [emphasis added] while others were concerned that such a reference could limit the range of action of EU development policy.' There was no voting in the arena, and the provision 'in particular in low income countries' disappeared. Although it seems slightly odd that some members were worried about the provision limiting

[134] For a detailed discussion of the issue of budgetization, see: F. Faria and A. Koulaïmah-Gabriel, *Budgetisation of the European Development Fund—Issues, Implications, Opportunities*, published on the Internet at: http://www.ecdpm.org/Web_ECDPM/Web/Content/Download.nsf/0/09FF2ABEB09AE04BC1256D25004EB564/$FILE/98-63-E-Budgetisation.pdf.; and the Communication from the Commission, Towards the Full Integration of Co-operation with ACP Countries in the EU budget COM(2003)590.

[135] A statement to the opposite effect was made orally, during debate of the terms to be included in the draft constitution. (It is this to which the Commission refers in towards the Full Integration of Co-operation with ACP Countries in the EU Budget—ibid.—when it states that the Convention recommended the budgetization of EU/ACP co-operation.)

[136] CONV 473/02.

the range of EU action when the comparative part of Article 177 EC has as yet to have any such effect, this concern adds weight to the argument that the least developed countries may be able to rely on Article 177 EC morally, if not legally, to argue for a greater share of Community aid funds.

Article III-218(1) contains the interesting statement that 'The Union shall take account of the objectives of development cooperation in the policies that it implements which are likely to affect developing countries'. The 'objectives of development cooperation' as such are not defined in the draft treaty. What we do have is Articles III-193 and III-194. These are long, but worth transcribing.

Article III-193 provides that:

1. The Union's action on the international scene shall be guided by, and designed to advance in the wider world, the principles which have inspired its own creation, development and enlargement: democracy, the rule of law, the universality and indivisibility of human rights and fundamental freedoms, respect for human dignity, equality and solidarity, and for international law in accordance with the principles of the United Nations Charter. [Principles]

   The Union shall seek to develop relations and build partnerships with third countries, and international, regional or global organisations, which share these values. It shall promote multilateral solutions to common problems, in particular in the framework of the United Nations. [Objectives]

2. [More objectives] The Union shall define and pursue common policies and actions, and shall work for a high degree of cooperation in all fields of international relations, in order to:
   (a) safeguard the common values, fundamental interests, security, independence and integrity of the Union;
   (b) consolidate and support democracy, the rule of law, human rights and international law;
   (c) preserve peace, prevent conflicts and strengthen international security, in conformity with the principles of the United Nations Charter;
   (d) foster the sustainable economic, social and environmental development of developing countries, with the primary aim of eradicating poverty;
   (e) encourage the integration of all countries into the world economy, including through the progressive abolition of restrictions on international trade;
   (f) help develop international measures to preserve and improve the quality of the environment and the sustainable management of global natural resources; in order to ensure sustainable development;
   (g) assist populations, countries and regions confronting natural or man-made disasters;
   (h) promote an international system based on stronger multilateral cooperation and good global governance.

3. The Union shall respect the principles and objectives listed in paragraphs 1 and 2 in the development and implementation of the different areas of the Union's external action covered by this Title and the external aspects of its other policies.

   The Union shall ensure consistency between the different areas of its external action and between these and its other policies. The Council of Ministers and the Commission, assisted by the Union Minister for Foreign Affairs, shall ensure that consistency and shall cooperate to that effect.

The list of objectives includes several relating directly to development cooperation, and the whole list is an apparently prescriptive provision with regard to the objectives cited. However, that admirable list may come to be seen as a worthy shopping list or wish-list rather than hard law in itself, because of the provisions of Article III-194:

1. On the basis of the principles and objectives referred to in Article III-193, the European Council shall identify the strategic interests and objectives of the Union. European decisions[137] of the European Council on the strategic interests and objectives of the Union shall relate to the common foreign and security policy and to other areas of the external action of the Union. Such decisions may concern the relations of the Union with a specific country or region or may be thematic in approach. They shall define their duration, and the means to be made available by the Union and the Member States.

   The European Council shall act unanimously on a recommendation from the Council of Ministers, adopted by the latter under the arrangements laid down for each area. European decisions of the European Council shall be implemented in accordance with the procedures provided for by the Constitution.
2. The Union Minister for Foreign Affairs, for the field of common foreign and security policy, and the Commission, for other fields of external action, may submit joint proposals to the Council of Ministers.

So the 'objectives of development cooperation' referred to in Article III-218 are arguably those which remain to be decided on by the Council, in accordance with Article III-194. This appears to provide for the ad hoc identification, in an unlimited number of different European decisions, of the relevant objectives for development cooperation in relation to an area of external action, relations with a specific country or region, or a particular theme. Although such an approach could lend itself to the EU being able to tailor its policies as appropriate, it also holds the potential for uncertainty, incoherency, short-term approaches to long-term problems, and the politicization of development policy.

One criticism which can be levelled at current development cooperation policy is how it has been laid out almost exclusively in Communications and conclusions. Article III-219(1) would require 'European laws or framework laws' (the equivalent of regulations and directives—see Article 33 of the draft Treaty), to establish the measures necessary for the implementation of development cooperation policy. This increased legal certainty would be welcome.

137 'European decisions' is the proposed new name for decisions under Arts. 34 and 36 of the draft Treaty.

In short, if the proposed draft Treaty provisions in question were to come into force as currently worded, the poorest countries would be likely to lose out in theory, and probably in continuing reality, and whilst some extra certainty would be gained from the provision that the implementation measures for development cooperation policy would have to take a more legally binding form, there could be a corresponding lack of certainty arising from the potential diversification of objectives applied to individual countries and policies.

It is interesting to refer back here to the Presidency conclusions to the European Council meeting in Laeken, December 2001: under the title, 'Europe's new role in a globalized world'. The conclusions included the following, somewhat purple, yet comfortingly aspirational prose:

> Beyond its borders . . . the European Union is confronted with a fast-changing, globalized world . . . religious fanaticism, ethnic nationalism, racism and terrorism are on the increase, and regional conflicts, poverty and underdevelopment still provide a constant seedbed for them . . . The European Union's one boundary is democracy and human rights. The Union is open only to countries which uphold basic values such as free elections, respect for minorities and respect for the rule of law. Now that the Cold War is over and we are living in a globalized, yet also highly fragmented world, Europe needs to shoulder its responsibilities in the governance of globalisation. The role it has to play is that of a power resolutely doing battle against all violence, all terror and all fanaticism, but which also does not turn a blind eye to the world's heartrending injustices. In short, a power wanting to change the course of world affairs in such a way as to benefit not just the rich countries but also the poorest. A power seeking to set globalisation within a moral framework, in other words to anchor it in solidarity and sustainable development.

It is not clear that the provisions of the draft Treaty would achieve this aim.

VI. Conclusion

In 1980, China and India accounted for the majority of the world's poor. Both have seen strong, if not spectacular, economic growth since then, which has led to significant poverty reduction in those countries.[138]

However, more than one billion people, one in six of the world's population, still survive (or fail to) on €1 or less per day, many of them in sub-Saharan Africa. Meanwhile, the environment continues to degrade at a staggeringly fast rate: see the conclusions of the *Global Environment Outlook* 3.[139] UNEP concludes[140] that despite the environmental achievements of the past thirty years, such

[138] David Dollar of the World Bank, in a live Internet discussion of Feb. 2004. http://discuss.worldbank.org/chat/ddollar-globalization.php.

[139] n. 73 above.

[140] ibid. 298.

as action relating to stratospheric ozone, air pollution, land management, and fresh water, the measures taken have been insufficient to counteract the pressures imposed by 'increasing poverty and uncontrolled consumption'. There is 'indisputable evidence of continuing and widespread environmental degradation'.

Current approaches are not working well enough. In 1960, the world's richest 20 per cent had an income 30 times higher than the 20 per cent poorest. By 1995, this was 82 times higher.[141]

One small point of good news is that 2002 saw an increase in total ODA by the 22 DAC member countries[142] of 4.9 per cent in real terms. This amounted to 0.23 per cent of combined GNI [gross national income], up from the all-time lows of 0.22 per cent GNI in 2000 and 2001. But this should be placed in the context of consistent falls since the 0.33 per cent GNI which had been consistently achieved until 1992 (and the 0.5 per cent of the 1960s, cited by World Bank President, James D. Wolfensohn).[143] The rise follows the 2002 International Conference on Financing for Development, which was held in Monterrey, Mexico. However, if DAC member countries fulfil the commitments they made at the Monterrey Conference, their ODA would still only rise to 0.26 per cent GNI by 2006 (with the exception of the EU Member States, who, before the Monterrey Conference, had already committed themselves to increasing their collective ODA to 0.39 per cent GNI by 2006).[144]

Denmark, Luxembourg, the Netherlands, Norway, and Sweden were the only countries to meet the UN ODA target of 0.7 per cent GNI in 2002. Belgium has committed itself to achieving that figure by 2010, Ireland by 2007, and France by 2012. The United States (US) increased its ODA to 0.12 per cent GNI.[145] Despite the urgent need for such aid, the US had managed just 0.20 per cent GNI in 1991, which was down to a staggeringly low 0.11 in 2001. Although the US remains the world's largest donor in volume terms, this should be set in the context of its having given, every year since 1994, the lowest percentage of GNI as ODA of any of the OECD-DAC countries.[146]

What is astonishing, and shaming, in the 'developed' world's approach to aiding developing countries, is the frequent avoidance of the awkward fact that it is still far from managing to achieve sustainable development itself. In the

[141] Report on Human Development (UNDP, 1998).

[142] The DAC member countries account for 95% of worldwide ODA disbursements. They are: Australia, Austria, Belgium, Canada, Denmark, Finland, France, Germany, Greece, Ireland, Italy, Japan, Luxembourg, Netherlands, New Zealand, Norway, Portugal, Spain, Sweden, Switzerland, the United Kingdom, and the United States.

[143] World Bank Press Release of 29 Dec. 2003, 'Fighting Poverty for Peace'.

[144] Taken from OECD news release (2003).

[145] Source for all these statistics: OECD DAC. Published on the Internet at: http://www.oecd.org/document/42/0,2340,en_2649_34447_ 2507754_1_1_1_1,00.html.

[146] OECD-DAC figures.

foreword to the *Global Environment Outlook 3*,[147] it is stated that, 'Despite the wealth of technologies, human resources, policy options, and technical and scientific information at our disposal, humankind has yet to break decisively with unsustainable and environmentally unsound policies and practices. What emerges from the data, analysis and forecasts contained in this report is the compelling need to go beyond taking stock to taking action.' The continuing deterioration of the state of the global environment is put down to the twin evils of poverty and excessive consumption. We are failing to do enough to address world poverty, and we continue to do practically nothing to address increasingly excessive consumption in the (over-)developed world.

It is an unpalatable conclusion, and one which politicians prefer to steer clear of. Nielson, the European Commission's Development Commissioner, said in a speech in 2002,[148] 'The challenge is massive. We need a fundamental change in the way we think and work. The development model championed by the rich is economically and socially unsustainable. It simply leaves too many people out.' He identifies three main aspects of our current 'global sustainability crisis': deep and widespread poverty, with the gap between rich and poor continuing to grow;[149] increasing pressure on the environment and natural resources; and non-inclusive globalization which has led to increasing economic, financial, and political instability in the world. His conclusion is that, 'In order to make globalisation sustainable we need a much better balance between the global market forces on the one hand and global governance and political institutions on the other'. This is true, but it can be seen why such pronouncements fail to engage ordinary people—the responsibility for global poverty, environmental pressures and world instability is not perceived as 'personal'. What is all too often missing is any mention of the need for people in developed countries to reduce their consumption, modify their expectations, and take responsibility for the need to give more.

With regard to the dislocation between the EC Treaty provisions on development cooperation and Community development cooperation policy and practice, either the law should be amended, or the policy and practice changed.

Should the law be changed? Stuart[150] was quoted as saying on the failure of the summit, 'I think this is really wise—we can now go back to the drawing board'.[151] This may be particularly true in the case of the Community's development cooperation policy.

[147] UNEP (London: Earthscan Publications Ltd, 2002), p. xiv.

[148] Speech of 8 Feb. 2002, published on the Internet at: http://europa.eu.int/comm/commissioners/nielson/speeches/20020208_en.htm.

[149] He comments that since 1960 the polarization of income between the richest and poorest 20% of the world's population has tripled, to 90:1.

[150] n. 112, above.

[151] *The Observer*, 14 Dec. 2003.

If the draft provision that poverty reduction is always to be the prime objective of EU development policy were to become law, without the specific mention of any particular responsibilities towards the least developed countries, such an approach could lead to problems with regard to the environmental integrity of the developing countries, particularly the least developed, and even more so if their aid income diminishes further. Although it is too early to be able to predict what is likely to happen, it would not be in the best interests of the developing countries, of the world's environment, or of long-term peace, for an over-simplistic, poverty-focused strategy to be applied, particularly if disproportionately large amounts of aid were to continue to make their way to the richer developing countries without the global consequences of that policy having been fully considered.

Should policy be changed? If the arguments made above are correct, the Community must justify its reduction of aid to the least developed countries. If it could argue convincingly that aid reduction has no effect on the least developed countries, it would be difficult to fault the reduction in funding. But could that really be the case? More financial resources could be diverted to the least developed countries, but would such direct aid help? It has conspicuously failed in the past, arguably because of poor governance and inadequate economic policies. Debt relief could be considered. The International Monetary Fund (IMF) has stated that the current multilateral debt relief programme is not enough to bring Africa's debts down to 'sustainable' levels. It has therefore suggested that more grants should be made by the developed countries. Could more financial resources be fruitfully put towards AIDS/HIV, for example in areas like education or anti-retroviral drugs, now that their prices are plummeting? Failing any useful potential for increased funding on the ground, could those resources be put towards research on how to most efficiently help improve governance, or education and skills, or establishing sound property rights?

Even if it could be established that no greater financial input in aid to, or research about, the least developed countries would have any beneficial effect, the Community should then ask itself whether there is anything else it could do. Under the EC Treaty, the three Article 177 EC aims do not have to be fostered by purely financial means—indeed, Article 178 EC makes it very clear that other policies may be of significance for the achievement of the Article 177 EC objectives. What effect would the lifting of various agricultural and trade barriers have? Or wholesale reform of the CAP? Or compliance with the Kyoto Protocol?

Has the Community actively explored the above and other possible avenues for the disbursement of aid to, or the fostering of the Article 177 EC objectives in, the least developed countries? It would appear not, as the Commission has stated that the reduction in its aid to the least developed countries was due to other policy priorities.

Or are both law and policy reform necessary? It could be argued that not only should any future proposed Treaty changes be more carefully thought through, more Community development aid should also be allocated to the least developed countries (and less aid given, if necessary, to more developed countries), whilst greater emphasis should be placed on ensuring that sustainable development considerations are taken into account in, for example, the Country Support Strategies. The OAC recommends that the European Community should:

> Bring ODA allocations into better alignment with the principal aim of poverty reduction [and review] the balance between pursuing long-term development objectives and the flexibility needed for external relations policies. There are discussions within the EU to improve sustainability and poverty reduction including: budgetization of the European Development Fund; increased allocation of ODA to social sectors; and the classification of allocations along DAC lines. The DAC believes these suggestions, while potentially useful, are insufficient to address the fundamental requirements. In order to translate the primary aim of poverty reduction into more effective ODA allocations, there is a need to work towards resource allocation criteria and to reform the budgetary process in a way that meets several different strategic requirements—to reduce the number of budget lines, to promote flexibility, and to enhance accountability further to the European Parliament and the Council of Ministers.[152]

The OECD DAC also recommends, *inter alia*, reviewing and improving the coherence of internal Community policies with development objectives and developing the institutional framework for coherence.

In the short term, recognition and observance of duties laid down under the EC Treaty, particularly those towards the 'most disadvantaged developing countries', would, it is submitted, contribute to the achievement of those recommendations.

However, even if the policies and laws espoused under the new Treaty were to achieve the necessary fine balance between poverty reduction and the sustainable development of developing countries, if European policies are truly to be able to foster effective sustainable development, the developed countries would themselves have to at least be on course to achieve sustainable development, and reverse their unsustainable patterns of production and consumption. We would have to change our behaviour and expectations. These are heavily ingrained,[153] despite repeated research results apparently showing that, once enough is being earned to cover life's basic needs (around £14,000 per annum to cover food, shelter, and healthcare), happiness is not proportionately related to further income rises. Indeed, the constant drive towards affluence appears to be rendering people in developed countries significantly unhappier than previous generations.[154] Nevertheless, given politics and human nature, it

[152] Main Findings and Recommendations of the OECD DAC 2002 Peer Review of the European Community.

[153] Recent research shows that, in the UK, 60% of people believe that they do not have enough to buy all they need, whilst among those earning more than €50,000 a year, 40% say they are unable to buy enough of life's luxuries: *The Sunday Times* News Review, 7 Sept. 2003.

[154] *The Times*, 3 July 2003 and 26 June 2003.

appears temptingly easier to stick our heads into the reassuring sands of fine words, and leave our children to cope with the results of our inaction. The world's stability and environment is our family silver. We in the developed countries are on the verge of going down in history as a disgracefully selfish and profligate generation.

CURRENT SURVEY

Substantive European Community Environmental Law

I. Atmospheric Pollution

Alexandra González-Calatayud *

A. Introduction

The survey year 2002 was one of high expectations for progress in important areas of atmospheric pollution law, particularly regarding climate change. Implementation of obligations stemming from the Kyoto Protocol[1] to the United Nations (UN) Framework Convention on Climate Change (UNFCCC)[2] had gained importance and urgency, since parties reached an agreement for the operating mechanisms the previous year. However, other areas also demanded attention, such as the daughter directives to the 1998 Air Framework Directive, and pollution sources such as shipping fuels.

B. Legislation Adopted

i. Energy Efficiency of Buildings

The Commission Proposal for a Directive on the Energy Performance of Buildings was one of the main legal dossiers on energy efficiency in 2002.[3] The draft aimed at setting a Community-wide framework to coordinate Member States' efforts, but leaving practical implementation to the Member States. The beginning of the legislative procedure in 2001, with the reading in the European

* Trade Policy Officer with the Royal Society for the Protection of Birds (RSPB), London (United Kingdom).

[1] Kyoto (Japan), 10 Dec. 1997 (not yet in force) (1998) 37 *International Legal Materials* 1, 22.

[2] New York, NY (United States), 9 May 1992 (entered into force on 21 Mar. 1994) (1992) 31 *International Legal Materials* 4, 849.

[3] COM(2001)226, [2001] OJ C213E/266.

Parliament (EP) energy committee, had announced disagreements between the Council and the EP, in particular on the date of entry into force of the proposed Directive. However, these differences disappeared once the EP in full had to vote on the draft. The first reading even made Members of the European Parliament (MEPs) look less radical than Ministers, as they voted to allow Member States until 2005 to transpose the Directive, and until 2010 to apply energy certification to all buildings.[4] The Commission had originally proposed 2003 both as the date of entry into force and as the deadline for full certification, whereas the Council had suggested 2004 and 2008, respectively. The significance of delaying widespread implementation until 2008 or 2010 was that this would substantially diminish the Directive's ability to help reduce carbon dioxide (CO_2) emissions for buildings by the time of the first commitment period under the Kyoto Protocol, commencing in 2008. The EP also amended the scope of the draft by extending its application to office buildings on industrial sites. Moreover, it introduced several changes addressing the need for better cooling systems that would reduce the need for air-conditioning in southern Member States. Both the EP and the Council wanted approval of the proposed Directive as swiftly as possible, in order to avoid a second reading, and worked closely together towards this goal. In late August 2002, a compromise was struck based on a six-year implementation deadline (i.e. one year less than preferred by the Council),[5] which was backed by the EP's plenary in October. Finally, Directive 2002/91/EC on the Energy Performance of Buildings (Building Energy Efficiency Directive)[6] was adopted on 16 December 2002. By January 2006, Member States must have set up energy certification schemes for the energy performance of all buildings, and must carry out regular inspections of boilers and air-conditioning systems. States lacking an infrastructure to do so have up to three additional years to create one. The Directive does not establish EU-wide minimum efficiency standards and requires Member States to lay down their own national minimum standards. The methodology to set national standards will have to take into account differences in climate and include factors relating to insulation, heating, ventilation, lighting, building orientation, heat recovery, and use of renewable energy sources.

ii. Auto/Oil Programme

Within the framework of the Auto/Oil Programme, two amendments to Directives were adopted in 2002. The first concerned Directive 98/70/EC relating to the Quality of Petrol and Diesel Fuels and Amending Council Directive 93/12/EEC (Fuel Quality Directive),[7] and the second amendment was to Directive 97/24/EC on Certain Components and Characteristics of Two- or Three-Wheel Motor Vehicles (Motorcycles Directive).[8] The latter was

[4] *ENDS Environment Daily*, 7 Feb. 2002. [5] *ENDS Environment Daily*, 3 Oct. 2002.
[6] [2003] OJ L1/65. [7] [1998] OJ L 350/58. [8] [1997] OJ L 226/1.

the most advanced of the two dossiers.[9] Conciliation talks started in early 2002 and were concluded in March, when the most contentious of the issues, the dates for compulsory emission standards, was agreed.[10] Technical negotiations completed in January, on a draft worldwide test cycle for motorcycle emissions under the auspices of the UN Economic Commission for Europe (UN/ ECE), paved the way for the political agreement between the Council and the EP. On 19 July, Directive 2002/51/EC on the Reduction of the Level of Pollutant Emissions from Two- and Three-Wheel Motor Vehicles and Amending Directive 97/24/EC (Motorcycles Directive)[11] was adopted. The revised Motorcycles Directive prescribed limit values for motorcycle emissions of carbon monoxide, hydrocarbons, and nitrogen oxides to apply from 1 April 2003, while tougher limits will take effect on 1 January 2006. Compliance with EU limits for 2003 will be based on an existing test cycle designed for cars, while compliance with 2006 limits will be allowed using either the car test cycle or the new motorcycle test cycle. Both testing systems will be valid for motorcycles for several years, giving industry flexibility for the phasing in of new specific emission tests. The Commission will be undertaking additional work that could result in a further tightening of emission limits, including new limits for particulates and the introduction of a specific motorcycles test cycle for measuring emissions.

In the case of the amendment of the Fuel Quality Directive it was the Council that got its way in the final stages of the co-decision procedure.[12] The key stumbling block was the extension of the scope of the Directive to non-road vehicles, such as agricultural tractors or construction equipment. The Parliament's environment committee had insisted that non-road vehicles should be covered by the draft's requirements to introduce mandatory sulphur-free fuels by 2009.[13] However, during conciliation talks in December, the EP failed in its bid to include them and the issue will now be decided after a review by the Commission in 2005. Following the conciliation talks, in 2005, the Commission will have to propose initial fuel quality standards for off-road fuels alongside a revision of emission standards for off-road vehicle engines. According to the conciliation text, petrol and diesel with a sulphur content of no more than 10 ppm will be mandatory throughout the EU from January 2009. As of 2005, Member States will also have to supply low-sulphur fuel at sufficient locations to allow the circulation of new low-emission engines requiring the cleaner fuel.

[9] Commission Proposal for a Directive amending Directive 97/24/EC on Certain Components and Characteristics of Two or Three Wheel Motor Vehicles COM(2000)314, [2000] OJ C337E/140.

[10] Conciliation text of 30 Apr. 2002.

[11] [2002] OJ L252/20.

[12] Commission Proposal for a Directive on the Quality of Petrol and Diesel Fuels and Amending Directive 98/70/EC COM(2001)241, [2001] OJ C213E/255.

[13] EP document A5-0293/2002, 10 Sept. 2002, *rapporteur* H. Hautala.

iii. Air Quality Daughter Directives

Only two so-called 'daughter directives' to Directive 96/62/EC on Ambient Air Quality Assessment and Management (Air Quality Framework Directive)[14] were pending for adoption in 2002, one regulating emissions of ozone, the other emissions of polyaromatic hydrocarbons (PAHs) and three heavy metals (cadmium, arsenic, and nickel).

The proposed Directive on Ozone was the most advanced of the two dossiers. A draft text had been hammered out in conciliation during 2001, and only the approval of the EP plenary and the Council was still required. Hence, early in 2002, on 12 February, Directive 2002/3/EC relating to Ozone in Ambient Air (Ozone Directive)[15] was adopted. Member States must have transposed it by 9 September 2003. The Directive sets long-term objectives equivalent to the World Health Organization's (WHO) new guideline values and target values for ozone in ambient air, to be attained where possible by 2010. These targets follow Directive 2001/81/EC on National Emission Ceilings for Certain Atmospheric Pollutants (NEC Directive).[16] Transparency requirements include public notification where ozone levels exceed or are predicted to exceed 180 ug/m3 as a one-hour average, and a public alert where levels are above 240 ug/m3. Member States' authorities must take short-term action if thresholds are exceeded, following examples given in a Commission guidance report that has yet to be drafted.

iv. Non-Road Mobile Petrol Machinery

Directive 2002/88/EC amending Directive 97/68/EC on Measures against the Emission of Gaseous and Particulate Pollutants from Internal Combustion Engines to be Installed in Non-road Mobile Machinery[17] was adopted without major problems in October 2002. It expands the scope of Directive 97/68/EC from diesel engines to petrol-engine equipment ranging from lawnmowers and chain saws to trimmers, cutters, and generating sets. In the EU they represent 10 to 15 per cent of all Volatile Organic Compounds (VOCs), thus contributing significantly to ozone pollution. An initial set of emission limits will take effect eighteen months after entry into force, in August 2004. A second round of tighter limits will be introduced between 2004 and 2010, depending on engine type.

C. Legislation in Progress

i. Greenhouse Gas Emissions Trading Directive

Another item that figured high on the agenda in 2002 was the Commission Proposal for a Directive establishing a Framework for Greenhouse Gas Emissions

[14] [1996] OJ L296/55. [15] [2002] OJ L67/14. [16] [2001] OJ L309/22.
[17] [2002] OJ L35/28.

Trading within the European Community and Amending Directive 96/61/EC.[18] The EP's legal affairs committee, one of several to adopt opinions on the dossier, started the debate in late March, calling for major alterations to the draft Directive. Focusing on what was going to become one of the major sticking points of the proposal, the committee's *rapporteur* rejected the recommendation that all initial allowances should be allocated to firms free of charge. Instead, a certain percentage of emission allowances should be auctioned and revenues recycled to industry and Member States to ensure overall revenue neutrality. The Commission had proposed complete free allocation in the first instance, but the committee argued that this would end up allocating emissions simply according to past levels, without rewarding early action or reflecting the polluter-pays principle (through lower impacts on consumers and taxpayers that would be guaranteed by auctioning). The *rapporteur* further recommended extending the trading scheme's scope from just CO_2 to the three fluorinated gases (F-gases) included among the six greenhouse gases under the Kyoto Protocol. Regarding the Directive's addressees, it was urged that chemical plants and aluminium producers be added to the list of sectors required to take on a cap on emissions, if their annual releases exceeded 50,000 of CO_2 equivalent. The reading in the EP's environment committee, later in the year, confirmed the recommended extension in scope to cover more industrial sectors and gases. However, much of the debate in this committee centred around the mandatory or voluntary nature of company participation in the cap-and-trade arrangement during the trial period. The Commission was adamant it should be mandatory and the environment committee backed that view, anticipating problems at the reading in the Council, where three Member States (Germany, the United Kingdom (UK), and Finland) were strongly arguing for the voluntary line. This forecast became slightly more certain when the EP plenary supported this amendment and voted for the climate emission trading scheme to be mandatory. However, responding to the potential concerns in the Council, it introduced a clause fleshed out in the environment committee, giving firms limited rights to opt out of the scheme in the first three years. This opt-out clause would allow firms to abstain from trading for the first three years, subject to a commitment to make equivalent emission cuts and, crucially, approval from the Commission. Another major addition was the introduction of allowances-auctioning for 15 per cent of available allowances. According to the amendment, all resulting revenues would have to be recycled back to industry for environmental purposes. It further demanded a cap on the amount of emission allowances available for distribution by governments. The plenary also endorsed the amendments of its committees and extended the scope of the Directive to include all six Kyoto greenhouse gases, rather than just CO_2, as well as the emissions from chemical and aluminium plants.

[18] COM(2001)581, [2001] OJ C75E/33.

After several delays, a deal between Germany's governing parties to abandon opposition to Commission proposals for mandatory rather than voluntary participation allowed the dossier to be debated in the Council in December.[19] The resulting first reading agreement was based on a compromise proposal drafted by the Danish presidency. It retained the opt-out possibility devised by Parliament for individual installations or industry sectors during the first three years of the scheme, with the conditions of equivalent emission cuts and approval from the Commission. The deal also foresaw that exempted companies would be subject to the same reporting and verification requirements, carrying equivalent penalties for non-compliance, as plants within the trading scheme. After the beginning of the first commitment period in 2008, no further opt-outs would be allowed. The arrangement satisfied the three Member States that had been most resistant to a fully mandatory scheme and, with the aforementioned conditions, even seemed acceptable to the Commission. Also agreed was the possibility for Member States to allow installations within an industrial sector to form voluntary trading pools for the whole duration of the scheme. This mechanism was put forward by Germany, as a way of safeguarding existing domestic carbon reduction commitments by relieving firms of the possibility to take on individual emission caps.[20] With regard to the allocation method, the Council recommended that all emission allowances be free of charge in the first phase, with a possibility to auction up to 10 per cent of available allowances in the second phase starting in 2008. However, the Commission would retain the right of veto over national emission allowance allocation plans. Also from 2008, Member States would be able to apply for the inclusion of greenhouse gases other than CO_2 in national emission trading, again subject to approval by the Commission based on EU competition and internal market rules, as well as availability of reliable monitoring methods.

Finally, the Council considered it desirable to link the emissions trading scheme and the Kyoto Protocol's flexible mechanisms (the joint implementation scheme and clean development mechanism), allowing firms to buy credits from these projects to make up allowance shortfalls. The Commission announced plans to develop a separate draft directive to this effect.

ii. Renewable Energy

The legislative procedure for the two draft Directives on biofuels, proposed in 2001, lingered on during all of 2002.[21]

The first, Commission Proposal for a Directive on the Promotion of the Use of Biofuels for Transport,[22] planned the setting of a mandatory minimum level of

[19] *ENDS Environment Daily*, 15 Oct. 2002 and 9 Dec. 2002.

[20] *ENDS Environment Daily*, 27 Nov. 2002.

[21] See also A. Catalayud, 'Atmospheric Pollution' (2003) 3 *Yearbook of European Environmental Law*, 363–4.

[22] COM(2001)547, [2001] OJ C103E/205.

biofuels as a proportion of fuels sold from 2005, starting with 2 percent and rising in annual steps to 5.75 percent by 2010. The mandatory nature of the target became the cause of major dissent between the Council and the EP. When energy ministers, meeting in June 2002, first debated the draft, they preferred to maintain the numerical targets as proposed by the Commission, but only as indicative and optional, rather than compulsory. However, the EP rejected the Council's agreement to make targets for increased biofuels penetration voluntary.[23] MEPs also voted to support biofuel development, although only for use as a 'pure' fuel and not for blending with fossil-derived counterparts. However, the Council practically won the battle over the nature of the biofuel targets when, in November 2002, it rubber-stamped a common position that established non-binding targets and, in order to avoid a potential battle with the EP, governments said they would refuse to adopt the second proposed Directive dealing with the fiscal side of biofuel promotion, unless they got their way with the targets.[24] Since the latter Directive required unanimity among Member States and gave the EP only a consultative role, this meant that, in practice, MEPs would have to give in if they wanted both Directives to be adopted. More in tune with Parliament, the Council also decided to reject the possibility proposed by the Commission to include subsidiary minimum targets for blending biofuels with conventional fuels.

The second proposed Directive in the biofuels package, Commission Proposal for a Directive amending Directive 92/81/EEC with regard to the Possibility of Applying a Reduced Rate of Excise Duty on Certain Mineral Oils Containing Biofuels and on Biofuels,[25] also suffered from delays, due to political battles. In the draft, the Commission had proposed to allow Member States to reduce excise duties on biofuels by up to 50 per cent, or the relevant fraction in blended fuels. The draft did seem to have the backing of the Council, but then in early June, when Ministers were due to approve the Directive apparently without discussion, the UK blocked the approval at the last minute, to punish France for opposing the energy tax package.[26] Ultimately, unanimous approval from the Council was reached later that month. Ministers also voted that the tax dispensation should be more generous than originally proposed by the Commission, with a 100 per cent duty relief instead of only 50 per cent. According to the agreement, the exemption would be available until 2012, but would not run for more than six consecutive years. Voting by the EP on both sets of Directives was delayed until 2003.

iii. Energy Efficiency

In a surprise move in November 2002, the Commission merged its proposals for minimum energy efficiency standards for consumer appliances (or end-use

[23] EP document T5-0361/2002, 4 July 2002.

[24] *ENDS Environment Daily*, 19 Nov. 2002.

[25] COM(2001)547, [2001] OJ C103E/217.

[26] *ENDS Environment Daily*, 5 June 2002. France is the strongest supporter of fiscal aids for biofuels.

equipment), with the setting of eco-design requirements, in a Draft Commission Proposal for a Directive on Establishing a Framework for Eco-Design of End-Use Equipment.[27] Originally, the intention had been to create a separate directive for appliance energy efficiency. The motives behind this move have been indicated as being opposition from a wide section of industry, particularly on the draft eco-design Directive, that had emerged in April 2002.[28] The new draft proposed to cover all end-use equipment regardless of their energy source. More significantly, however, it was suggested as a framework directive, meaning that products would only be subject to eco-design or energy efficiency requirements following the adoption of implementing measures. This was not the case under the eco-design draft circulated in April that would have covered all product categories from the outset. Reactions to the working paper text from industry and environmental groups were mixed. Industry called for maximizing self-regulatory undertakings in achieving the future Directive's aims, while some non-governmental organizations (NGOs) pressed to have the two proposals separated again. The Commission stated that a formal proposal might emerge in early 2003.[29]

In July 2002, the Commission released a much-awaited proposal for a Directive supporting combined heat and power (CHP) generation. The Proposal for a Directive on the Promotion of Co-generation based on a Useful Heat Demand in the Internal Energy Market[30] was generally received as disappointing. Its overriding objective was to create a framework to support and facilitate the installation and proper functioning of electrical co-generation plants where a useful heat demand exists or is foreseen. No mandatory targets for co-generation market shares were suggested, despite demands from the CHP industry. Rather, the draft encouraged the Commission to consider the introduction of 'indicative objectives'. It further proposed that only plants above a 50-megawatt threshold should be eligible for financial support. MEPs also disagreed over the draft during discussions in the first stage of the co-decision procedure. In December 2002, the industry committee's *rapporteur* drafted a report proposing more than 50 amendments, including the setting of binding targets and dropping of the 50-megawatt threshold to qualify for financial support.[31] The text also attempted to define co-generation through a complicated formula that was received with little enthusiasm by fellow MEPs. At the closing of the survey period, the first EP reading was foreseen for early 2003.

iv. Energy Taxation

During 2002, it was first Spain's and then Denmark's turn to try to reach adoption of the difficult energy taxation dossier, but like all their predecessors

[27] Distributed among stakeholders on 31 Oct. 2002.

[28] *ENDS Environment Daily*, 7 Nov. 2002.

[29] *ENDS Environment Daily*, 3 Dec. 2002.

[30] COM(2002)415, [2002] OJ C291E/182.

[31] *ENDS Environment Daily*, 4 Dec. 2002.

in this capacity, they failed, despite valiant attempts by officials and diplomats. Efforts to bring the dossier forward were certainly not something that was expected from Spain, which used to be the main opponent to the energy taxation. However, following an agreement by EU leaders in March 2002 to adopt an energy tax package by the end of the year, the Spanish Finance Ministry drafted a proposal that was presented to the Council in May.[32] It included recommendations for minimum national excise duty rates on various fossil energy products plus electricity, to be introduced within four years. A long series of exemptions, comprising electricity, gas, and coal used by households and charities, as well as all coal used for electricity generation as a chemical reductant in electrolysis and lime, cement, glass, and ceramics production, was also foreseen. It was, in particular, the long list of exemptions that attracted most criticisms from the Commission, and prompted the Taxation Commissioner to characterize the proposal as 'a Gruyere cheese with too many holes'.[33] Eventually, like all preceding proposals for an EU-wide energy tax, this proposal also floundered when it was put on the negotiating table of EU Finance Ministers in June 2002, after France rejected the compromise proposal. Under the Danish presidency of the Council, the dossier was on the agenda twice, in November and December 2002, but both times Ministers failed to reach a final agreement. This was primarily due to three major unresolved issues: first, the possibility of setting national tax levels below the EU minimum; secondly, tax breaks for certain sectors; and thirdly, the taxation of diesel road fuel. The main stumbling block was Germany, which apparently objected to reduced tax rates on diesel for road hauliers, zero tax rating for energy-intensive industries, and reduced taxes for firms with good environmental track records.[34] Agreement on the dossier was finally deferred to 2003.

v. Acidification

This survey year was not one of much activity in the field of acidification legislation. Two important directives entered into force this year: Directive 2001/81/EC on National Emission Ceilings for Certain Atmospheric Pollutants (NEC Directive),[35] and Directive 2001/80/EC on the Limitation of Emissions of Certain Pollutants into the Air from Large Combustion Plants (Large Combustion Plants Directive).[36] Several Member States started the procedures to transpose this new legislation into national law.

The Commission contemplated proposing a Directive imposing limits on volatile organic compounds (VOCs) in decorative paints and varnishes. It had been pressured to do so by the Member States, which under the NEC Directive were to take on individual caps on total VOC emissions, but feared they would

32 *ENDS Environment Daily*, 7 May 2002.

33 Ibid.

34 *ENDS Environment Daily*, 5 Dec. 2002.

35 [2001] OJ L309/22.

36 [2001] OJ L309/1.

be unable to meet the strict ceilings.[37] Subsequently, in May 2002, the Commission released a first working document containing a draft proposal for a Directive and a cost-benefit analysis of the plans. The draft proposal imposed limits on VOCs in decorative paints and varnishes to be met in 2007, with a second phase of tighter controls to be introduced in 2010. Separate limits would be applied to vehicle coatings from 2007. The new legislation was estimated to lead to a reduction in VOC emissions of 280,000 tonnes by 2010, presenting estimated health benefits from reduced air pollution of over €580 million, annually. Conversely, the Commission estimated the cost of reducing solvent content at between €108 million and €157 million per year by 2010. The draft proposal received mixed responses, with criticism coming, in particular, from the solvents sector that contested the cost-benefit analysis made by the Commission.

After a period of consultation, on 23 December 2002, the Commission finally put forward its Proposal for a Directive on the Limitation of Volatile Organic Compounds Due to the Use of Organic Solvents in Decorative Paints and Varnishes and Vehicle Refinishing Products and Amending Directive 1999/13/EC.[38] The proposal differed little from the plans outlined in May. Limits for solvents to be met by 2007 would range from 50 grams of VOC per litre of product (g/l) to 750 g/l, depending on product type. From 2010, the lowest limit would be 30 g/l. For vehicle coatings only one phase was suggested, starting 1 January 2007, and imposing limits from 200 to 850 g/l. The proposed Directive was based on Article 95 EC, thus requiring Member States wanting to apply tougher limits to provide justification based on paragraphs 4 and 5 of Article 95 EC.

vi. Ozone

In November 2002, the Commission announced a Proposal for a Regulation amending Regulation (EC) No. 2037/2000 as regards the Critical Use and Export of Halons, the Export of Products and Equipment Containing Chlorofluorocarbons and Controls on Bromochlormethane.[39] The proposal was motivated by problems of export and control of ozone-depleting substances that emerged in the application of the present legislation. The proposed Regulation contained four amendments: (i) introduction of time-frames for reducing (where justified) the use of halons for critical uses, when reviewing Annex VII, to ensure that progress is made in reducing the scope of the use of halons for critical uses; (ii) establishment of Export Authorization Numbers to enable the Commission to track exports of halons and control whether they were being used for critical uses in the importing country; (iii) clarification of Article 11 of Regulation (EC) No. 2037/2000 on Substances that Deplete the Ozone Layer (Ozone Regulation),[40] to restrict only the export of used refrigeration and air-conditioning

[37] *ENDS Environment Daily*, 12 Apr. 2002.
[38] COM(2002)750.
[39] COM(2002)642, [2002] OJ C45E/297.
[40] [2000] OJ L244/1.

equipment containing chlorofluorocarbons (CFCs) and not other products and equipment containing foam blown with CFCs; and (iv) strengthening of the controls for the new substance listed in Annex II (bromochloromethane), by including them in the scope of the provisions applying to controlled substances, to enable the EU to meet all its obligations under the Montreal Protocol on Substances that Deplete the Ozone Layer (Montreal Protocol).[41] The co-decision procedure for the proposed Regulation was planned to commence in early 2003.

vii. Air Quality—Daughter Directives

A proposal for a fourth so-called 'daughter directive' to Directive 96/62/EC on Ambient Air Quality Assessment and Management (Air Quality Framework Directive)[42] had been delayed in 2001, while more research was carried out into the health benefits of planned strict air quality standards on four carcinogenic pollutants. Following the results of this study and strong protests by industry against mandatory targets, the Commission issued a draft proposal in October 2002 containing non-binding targets, set at the same level as originally planned in 2001. These targets included 6 nanograms per cubic metre (ng/m^3) for arsenic, 5 ng/m^3 for cadmium, 20 ng/m^3 for nickel and 1 ng/m^3 for benzo-a-pyrene (BaP), used as a marker for polyaromatic hydrocarbons (PAHs). The targets would be accompanied by tough monitoring and reporting provisions requiring Member States to explain local exceedances. Should these occur, governments would have to show that all cost-effective anti-pollution measures had been taken. Sources of pollution would have to be disclosed, as well as the number of people exposed above target levels. At the end of the survey period, the Commission was planning to issue a proposal for a directive in early 2003.

D. Policy Documents

i. CO_2 Monitoring

In December 2002, the Commission launched its third annual report under Council Decision 93/389/EEC, as amended by Decision 99/296/EC for a Monitoring Mechanism of Community Greenhouse Gas Emissions.[43] The report assessed the actual and projected progress of the Community and the Member States towards fulfilling their reduction commitments under the Kyoto Protocol. It concluded that with its present policies the EU will emit 4.7 per cent less greenhouse gases in 2010 than in 1990, compared with its Kyoto Protocol target of reducing emissions by 8 per cent. However, it also suggested that this reduction could be boosted to over 12 per cent if further efforts were made. The

41 Montreal (Canada), 16 Sept. 1987 (entered into force on 1 Jan. 1989) (1987) 26 *International Legal Materials* 6, 1541.

42 [1996] OJ L296/55.

43 COM(2002)702.

emission reductions achieved so far were mainly due to lower emissions in a few Member States (notably Germany and the UK), while nine Member States, headed by Spain, Ireland, and Portugal, were far off track in meeting their targets under the EU burden-sharing. The report also included, for the first time, information on emissions in the EU candidate countries, which were all on track to meet their reduction targets under the Kyoto Protocol. Emission trends in the transport sector remained of particular concern. With the exception of Finland, all Member States showed large increases in their transport emissions. The sector has seen the biggest increase of actual greenhouse gas emissions between 1990 and 2000, in particular of CO_2 and N_2O, while emissions in industry and households have decreased.

ii. CO_2 Emissions from Passenger Cars

One of the most important environmental policy documents presented by the Commission during 2002 was the Communication to the Council and the European Parliament on the Taxation of Passenger Cars in the EU.[44] It represented the fourth element of the strategy to meet a long-term EU target of reducing average new car emissions to 120 grams per kilometre (g/km) by 2010.[45] The Communication examined ways to restructure existing vehicle taxes so as to put more emphasis on environmental objectives. In particular, it recommended that the taxation of new passenger cars be more directly related to their CO_2 emissions. In 2002, the UK was the only Member State to apply a CO_2-based road tax. The Communication also recommended that taxation of the use of company cars (e.g. when people pay income tax on the use of a company car given in lieu of remuneration) should also include a clear and strong incentive to use more CO_2-efficient cars. According to the conclusions of a recent study undertaken for the Commission, a differential CO_2 tax on car use would be essential to produce significant emission reductions, while raising existing taxes would reap only small emissions savings. Moreover, meeting the 120 g/km target would unavoidably lead to either a higher proportion of diesel cars or the 'downsizing' of vehicle sales. Analysis was also made of current passenger-car taxation systems and ways of improving their coordination so as to remove tax obstacles and distortions to free movement of passenger cars within the Internal Market. Registration taxes were identified as the biggest problem and the Commission recommended their gradual reduction and even abolition. They should be replaced by annual road taxes and fuel taxes, so that the tax burden would remain the same but would be related to the use of a car rather than to its acquisition. The Communication also recommended a certain degree of approximation of annual road taxes to prevent car market fragmentation. The Commis-

[44] COM(2002)431.

[45] The other three elements of the strategy are a voluntary agreement with the car industry under which emissions are supposed to fall to 140 g/km by 2008, and two directives on monitoring and labelling of car CO_2 emissions.

sion indicated that it may present proposals for Community legislation on the basis of the Communication and in the light of the results of consultations with interested parties.

The Commission also presented its annual report on the 1998 voluntary agreement between the EU and the car industry to reduce CO_2 emissions from new passenger cars.[46] Under the agreement, car manufacturers committed to reducing CO_2 emissions on average by 140 g/km, to be achieved by 2009 by the Japanese and Korean car associations JAMA and KAMA, respectively, and by 2008 by the European ACEA. ACEA and JAMA were closest to achieving their target, while KAMA had only achieved a reduction of 0.9 per cent. Failure by any of the associations to meet their commitments would force the Commission to put forward legislation. The report also contained the first account of the operation of the monitoring scheme set up by Decision 1753/2000/EC establishing a Scheme to Monitor the Average Specific Emissions of CO_2 from New Passenger Cars,[47] to measure the broader goal of achieving average CO_2 emissions from new cars of 120 g/km by 2005, or by 2010 at the latest. It concludes that the first will not be met, but the second can be reached.

iii. Auto/Oil Programme

In June 2002, the Enterprise Directorate General of the Commission launched a call for evidence[48] to determine whether the EU should further toughen limits on heavy goods vehicles foreseen in Directive 1999/96/EC.[49] Under the Directive, limits on emissions of NO_x by lorries are due to be tightened in October 2006, but the Commission is asking for views on the possibility of strengthening limits in October 2008 for new-type approvals and in October 2009 for new engines.

iv. CO_2 from Air Transport

Not much progress was made in 2002 in terms of reduction of CO_2 emissions from the aviation industry. In December, the Commission-sponsored Advisory Council for Aeronautics Research in Europe (ACARE) presented the findings of its first year of work in a comprehensive Strategic Research Agenda (SRA). The report addressed the challenges that aviation faces in its third generation, including environmental challenges, and proposed the reduction of noise, fuel consumption, and CO_2 emissions by 50 per cent, and nitrogen oxide (NO_x) levels by 80 per cent. The reductions in CO_2 emissions will be pursued by undertaking

[46] Published on the Internet at: http://europa.eu.int/eur-lex/en/com/pdf/2002/com2002_0693en01.pdf.

[47] [2000] OJ L202/1.

[48] *ENDS Environment Daily*, 11 June 2002.

[49] Dir. 1999/96/EC relating to Measures to be Taken against the Emission of Gaseous and Particulate Pollutants from Compression Ignition Engines for Use in Vehicles, and the Emission of Gaseous Pollutants from Positive Ignition Engines Fuelled with Natural Gas or Liquefied Petroleum Gas for Use in Vehicles and Amending Council Directive 88/77/EEC [1999] OJ L44/1.

research in aerodynamics, weight reduction, and by improving the technology configuration. Research will also concentrate on alternative aircraft fuel such as hydrogen.

v. Shipping Fuel

Another air emission source tackled by the Commission in 2002 was shipping fuel. A first comprehensive survey of the contribution of shipping to emissions of several major pollutants in the EU was published in August. Following that, the Commission released a new strategy to reduce the impact of ships' atmospheric emissions on the environment and human health in November. The strategy, comprising a Communication[50] and an accompanying Proposal for a Directive,[51] was aimed at imposing limits on the sulphur content of fuel used in shipping. It set a 1.5 sulphur limit on all seagoing vessels in the North and Baltic Seas and the English Channel. In addition to the sulphur proposal, the strategy set out a number of other important actions, including a push for tougher global emissions standards at the International Maritime Organization (IMO), the development of new market-based measures to reduce ship emissions beyond regulatory standards, and the creation of a new Clean Marine Award scheme to promote low-emission shipping in the EU.

E. International Cooperation

i. Kyoto Protocol

From a symbolic point of view, the European Union's (EU) most important regulatory achievement in 2002 was the ratification of the Kyoto Protocol. The first step in this process was the adoption of Council Decision 2002/358/EC concerning the Approval, on Behalf of the European Community, of the Kyoto Protocol to the United Nations Framework Convention on Climate Change and the Joint Fulfilment of Commitments Thereunder.[52] The final text was agreed on 4 March 2002, allowing time for national Parliaments to approve their respective ratification instruments before the end of May, the deadline the EU had set itself for ratification to allow an eventual entry into force of the Protocol during the UN World Summit on Sustainable Development (Johannesburg Summit) in September.[53] Ultimately, only an eleventh-hour adoption of the necessary legal instruments by the Greek and Italian Parliaments would allow the EU to meet this deadline. On 31 May, representatives of all EU governments and the

[50] Communication from the Commission to the European Parliament and the Council—A European Union Strategy to Reduce Atmospheric Emissions from Seagoing Ships COM(2002)595.

[51] Proposal for a Directive Amending Directive 1999/32/EC as regards the Sulphur Content of Marine Fuels, COM(2002)595, [2002] OJ C45E/277.

[52] [2002] OJ L130/1.

[53] Johannesburg (South Africa), 26 Aug.–4 Sept. 2002.

European Commission formally ratified the Kyoto Protocol.[54] However, in the meantime, it had become clear that the hoped-for entry into force of the Protocol during the Johannesburg Summit would be impossible, as too few industrialized countries had ratified in time. Nonetheless, the EU's ratification was a crucial political gesture, and the fact that all its Member States also simultaneously ratified gave legally binding force to the bloc's collective target to cut greenhouse gas emissions by 8 per cent between 1990 and 2008–12.[55]

The EU was not so successful at international level, where only limited progress was achieved at the Eighth Conference of the Parties (COP-8) to the United Nations (UN) Framework Convention on Climate Change (UNFCCC)[56] in New Delhi (India). For COP-8, the EU Environment Ministers adopted a detailed resolution beforehand, setting out their goals for the negotiations. They called for greater cooperation with the UN conventions on desertification and biodiversity, and hoped the talks would set the scene for negotiations to decide further emission cuts after the end of the Kyoto Protocol's first commitment period in 2012. None of these goals was, unfortunately, achieved in what was to be a very low-key conference. With regard to the most important objective for the EU, the agreement on tougher emission targets for rich countries and movements towards targets for developing countries, the United States of America (US) and developing countries sidelined the issue and blocked its inclusion in the final declaration.[57] Reluctantly, EU negotiators were forced to accept this, since otherwise the meeting would have ended without a declaration and, according to the Danish head of the EU delegation, Steen Gade, this would have been 'a feather in the cap' of the US, who opposed the Kyoto Protocol.[58] Limited progress was achieved on the Protocol's clean development mechanism, agreed to become fully operational from the first quarter of 2003. Negotiators also agreed a system of harmonized emissions data presentation.[59]

ii. Renewable Energy

Renewable energy also figured high on the agenda at the Johannesburg Summit, in September 2002.[60] The EU fought hard to get targets for renewable energy into the resulting Johannesburg Plan of Action, but missed this objective due to resistance by, in particular, the US. In response to this failure, however, the EU

[54] *ENDS Environment Daily*, 23 May 2002.

[55] *ENDS Environment Daily*, 30 May 2002.

[56] New York, NY (United States), 9 May 1992 (entered into force on 21 Mar. 1994) (1992) 31 *International Legal Materials* 4, 849.

[57] The New Delhi Declaration was published on the Internet at: http://unfccc.int/resource/docs/cop8/07.pdf.

[58] *ENDS Environment Daily*, 4 Nov. 2002.

[59] *Earth Negotiations Bulletin* (12/209), Nov. 2002, published on the Internet at: http://www.iisd.ca/.

[60] n. 53 above.

launched a 'coalition of like-minded states' for States willing to increase their use of renewable energy through specific targets. The Johannesburg Plan of Action also refers to the Kyoto Protocol, with States that have ratified the Protocol 'strongly urging others to follow suit'.

iii. Ozone

The Fourteenth Meeting of the Parties (MOP-14) to the Montreal Protocol on Substances that Deplete the Ozone Layer (Montreal Protocol)[61] took place in Rome (Italy) from 25 to 29 November 2002. The main item on the agenda was the Multilateral Fund replenishment, but also of concern were the phasing out of methyl bromide, illegal trade in ozone-depleting substances (ODS), compliance procedures, destruction of ODS, and synergies between ozone depletion and climate change.[62] During the two-week long negotiation, delegates had to reach agreement on the appropriate level of replenishment for the Multilateral Fund for the next triennium. The funding for 2003–5 was considered by many to be particularly crucial, since the so-called Article 5 Parties (i.e. developing countries) must now comply with their commitments to cut their use of CFCs, halons, and CTC by 50 per cent, by the end of the triennium, with smaller cuts required in methyl bromide and methyl chloroform. After several days of negotiation, delegates agreed the figure of US$573 million using an ingenious solution of including interest to be accrued over the triennium as a bridge between the 'bottom lines' of donor and developing countries. Although this figure came close to the recommended level, some delegates pointed out that it was only a fraction more than the previous replenishment, and that the US$23 million contribution accruing from interest could hardly be relied upon. Also, developing countries expressed concern that the reclassification of some economies in transition as Article 5 Parties might lead to greater demands on the Multilateral Fund.

iv. Convention on Long-Range Transboundary Air Pollution

At the UN Economic Commission for Europe (UN/ECE) annual working group meeting in Geneva (Switzerland), new models allowing more accurate predictions of pollutant hot spots emerged. It was hoped that this could lead to a shift away from a blanket precautionary approach towards the setting of heavy metal emission limits, and allow efforts to be targeted according to geographic necessity so as to maximize benefits. The protocols signed under the UN/ECE Convention on Long-Range Transboundary Air Pollution (LRTAP)[63] are due to be revised in 2004 and 2005.

[61] Montreal (Canada), 16 Sept. 1987 (entered into force on 1 Jan. 1989) (1987) 26 *International Legal Materials* 6, 1541.

[62] *Earth Negotiations Bulletin* (19/24), Dec. 2002, published on the Internet at: http://www.iisd.ca/.

[63] Geneva (Switzerland), 13 Nov. 1979 (entered into force on 16 Mar. 1983) (1979) 18 *International Legal Materials* 6, 1442.

v. Persistent Organic Pollutants

There was much optimism among delegates at the Sixth Meeting of the Intergovernmental Negotiating Committee (INC-6) to the United Nations Environment Programme (UNEP) Stockholm Convention on Persistent Organic Pollutants (Stockholm POPs Convention).[64] Having completed the negotiation process in 2001, they enthusiastically embraced the next task of ensuring that the Convention is both ratified and fully implemented in a timely manner. Many observers speculated that the Convention would enter into force within two years—at least one year ahead of schedule. Four key dimensions of the Convention were discussed during INC-6 through which to gauge progress towards ratification and implementation: national implementation plans (NIPs), technical assistance, Convention financing, and the POPs Review Committee (POPRC). Discussions on the latter two issues were the most contentious. A technical assistance contact group was created to formalize arrangements relating to guidance on technical assistance, the capacity assistance network (CAN), the feasibility study on regional and subregional centres, and the case studies on regional and subregional centres. Furthermore, the INC-6 established an Expert Group on best available techniques and best environmental practices (BAT/BEP), whose task will be to guide the delivery of BAT/BEP as they pertain to measures to reduce or eliminate releases from unintentional production. Results concerning the POPRC were not as encouraging. This committee will have the task of reviewing proposed additions to the scope of the Convention. The extent to which it will be able to add new chemicals, particularly those with high commercial value, will be the true test of the Convention's mettle. In that vein, several delegates suggested that postponing POPRC issues and focusing on the relatively non-controversial twelve POPs already covered, may promote early ratification. However, it is suspected that many countries that have not yet ratified the Convention may try to use the POPRC process to ensure that they are not unnecessarily burdened by amendments to the POPs' Annexes.

F. Conclusions

The survey year was certainly not as active as could have been anticipated in January. Few new proposals were made and progress consisted almost exclusively of the adoption of dossiers that had been started in previous years. Especially disappointing in this regard was the fact that a proposal for the fourth daughter directive regulating polyaromatic hydrocarbons was not issued, and that there was no progress at all in tackling CO_2 emissions from aviation.

However, there was notable progress in the proposal for an EU-wide emissions trading scheme and the timely ratification of the Kyoto Protocol by the EU could

[64] Stockholm (Sweden), 22 May 2001 (not yet in force) (2001) 40 *International Legal Materials* 3, 531.

also be hailed as a success. Furthermore, it is to be welcomed that the Commission is trying to tackle important emissions coming from the shipping sector, where little movement has been made at international level. With the adoption of the Sixth Environmental Action Programme and the positive feedback to the thematic strategy deriving from it in the form of the Clean Air for Europe (CAFE) strategy, it is to be expected that the coming years will bring further important advances in atmospheric pollution legislation.[65]

[65] Dec. 1600/2002/EC of the European Parliament and of the Council laying down the Sixth Community Environment Action Programme [2002] OJ L242.

II. Biotechnology

*THIJS ETTY**

A. Introduction

For the policy area of biotechnology, the survey year 2002 was something of a transitory period. Many developments in law and policy built on the major progress of the foregoing two years, which included the adoption of a revised directive on deliberate environmental release of genetically modified organisms (GMOs),[1] and the conclusion of an international protocol on biosafety.[2] Other developments prepared for important advances in the coming year(s), including proposed regulations on genetically modified (GM) food and feed,[3] and on their traceability and labelling,[4] on transboundary movement of GMOs,[5] and a proposed directive on environmental liability.[6] However, since the journey is often as important as the ultimate destination, the year was by no means stagnant.

One vital objective for the Commission, during 2002, was to set the stage for a lifting of the *de facto* moratorium on GM foods and crops in the European Union (EU). In place since 1998, the moratorium has caused the Commission increasing headaches, in particular with a view to the looming and intensifying threat of an international trade dispute. The United States of America (US) continued to step up pressure on the EU to lift the allegedly illegal trade ban, threatening to initiate a dispute-settlement proceeding in the World Trade Organization (WTO). Given estimates that US farmers have lost hundreds of millions of dollars each year in exports to the EU, since 1998, the prospect of litigation was cause for serious concern for the Commission. In addition to international trade law, the moratorium might also be contested under Community law, at the European Court of Justice (ECJ), notably by agro-alimentary biotechnology corporations. Although the newly revised Deliberate Release Directive[7] was intended to pave the way towards a lifting of the ban, the Environment Ministers failed to reach agreement on a Commission proposal to this end, at the 2378th Council Meeting on 29 October 2001. In particular, Austria, Denmark, France, Greece, Italy, and Luxembourg were adamant that the moratorium stay in place until sufficient rules for traceability and labelling were in place. The Commission's final attempt to end this impasse, by proposing that

* Researcher at the Centre for Environmental Law, University of Amsterdam (Member of the Ius Commune Centre for Environmental Law, ICCEL), Amsterdam (the Netherlands).

[1] Dir. 2001/18/EC, n. 9 below.

[2] Cartagena Biosafety Protocol, n. 19 below. See also discussion at sect. F.*i*. below.

[3] n. 27 below. [4] n. 28 below. [5] n. 23 below.

[6] n. 35 below. [7] n. 9 below.

those rules, as laid down in its July 2001 legislative proposals, could voluntarily be implemented by industry prior to their adoption, was also rejected by the Ministers.[8] Despite Commissioners' predictions that the approval process for GMOs in the EU would recommence on 17 October, with the entry into force of the revised Deliberate Release Directive, by the end of 2002, the *de facto* moratorium was still firmly in place.

B. Legislation Adopted

i. Deliberate Release of GMOs

On 12 March 2001, the European Parliament (EP) and Council adopted Directive 2001/18/EC on the Deliberate Release of Genetically Modified Organisms into the Environment Repealing Directive 90/220/EEC (Deliberate Release Directive).[9] The revised Directive generally maintained the basic framework and structure of its 1990 predecessor,[10] while introducing important improvements to, *inter alia*, the efficiency, effectiveness, and notably, the transparency of authorization procedures for the marketing or (field) testing of GMOs. As noted in the introduction above, the revised Directive did not have the hoped-for effect of ending the *de facto* GMO moratorium in the EU.

The deadline for transposition of the provisions of the Directive into the national laws of the Member States was 17 October 2002. This date passed with only a single Member State, namely Denmark, having fulfilled this obligation.[11] Consequently, the Commission opened infringement proceedings against the other fourteen Member States, for non-communication of transposition measures.[12]

In 2002, the Commission and the Council adopted four Decisions to supplement the revised Deliberate Release Directive. Following these amendments, the new authorization process could become fully operational.

First, on 24 July, the Commission adopted Decision 2002/623/EC establishing Guidance Notes Supplementing Annex II to Directive 2001/18/EC on the Deliberate Release into the Environment of Genetically Modified Organisms and

[8] See Council Minutes Pres. 273, No. 12994/01. See also 'Early EU Gene Crop Approvals on the Cards' *ENDS Environmental Daily*, 8 Oct. 2001,

[9] [2001] OJ L106/1. See e.g. B. Sheridan, *EU Biotechnology Law and Practice—Regulating Genetically Modified & Novel Food Products* (Bembridge: Palladian Law Publishing, 2001), 29–96; S. Franceson, 'The New Directive 2001/18/EC on the Deliberate Release of Genetically Modified Organisms into the Environment—Changes and Perspectives' (2001) 10 *Review of European Community & International Environmental Law* 3, 309–20; D. Lawrence, J. Kennedy, and E. Hattan, 'New Controls on the Deliberate Release of GMOs' (2002) 11 *European Environmental Law Review* 2, 51–6.

[10] Dir. 1990/220/EEC on the Deliberate Release of Genetically Modified Organisms into the Environment [1990] OJ L117/15.

[11] Commission, Twentieth Annual Report on Monitoring the Application of Community Law (2002) COM(2003)669, 44.

[12] ibid., Annex IV, 34–5. See also sect. D.*i.* below.

Repealing Directive 90/220/EEC.[13] According to Article 4(3) of the Deliberate Release Directive, Member States (or where appropriate the Commission) must ensure for each authorization request, on a case-by-case basis, an accurate assessment of the potential risk associated with the intended GMO release. These environmental risk assessments, outlined in Annex II to the Directive, provide the basis for authorization decisions and appropriate risk management strategies. The Guidance Notes established by Decision 2002/623/EC supplement this Annex by outlining the objectives and principles, as well as the methodology, for such environmental risk assessment. The objective was to assist both notifiers and competent authorities, and to further enhance the transparency (to the general public) of the assessments and authorization procedures. The Decision laid down six steps for the analysis in the environmental risk assessments: (i) identification of characteristics which may cause adverse effects; (ii) evaluation of potential consequences of each adverse effect, if it occurs; (iii) evaluation of the likelihood of the occurrence of each identified potential adverse effect; (iv) estimation of the risk posed by each identified characteristic; (v) application of management strategies for risks from the deliberate release or marketing; and (vi) determination of overall risk.

Secondly, on 3 October, the Council adopted Decision 2002/811/EC establishing Guidance Notes Supplementing Annex VII to Directive 2001/18/EC on Deliberate Release into the Environment of Genetically Modified Organisms and Repealing Directive 90/220/EEC.[14] Notifications under Part C of the Deliberate Release Directive, for (commercial) market placements of GMOs, must contain proposed plans for post-marketing monitoring, according to Articles 13(2), 19(3), and 20 of the Directive. Such monitoring plans are intended to enable tracing and identification of any direct or indirect, immediate, delayed, or unforeseen effects on human health or the environment of GMOs as or in products. Monitoring plans should be drawn up in accordance with Annex VII, and Decision 2002/811/EC supplemented this Annex with detailed guidance on the objectives, general principles, and design of such plans.

Thirdly, also on 3 October, Council adopted Decision 2000/812/EC establishing Pursuant to Directive 2001/18/EC the Summary Information Format Relating to the Placing on the Market of Genetically Modified Organisms as or in Products.[15] This Decision provided the Summary Information Format which notifiers must use to draw up the summary of the dossier for their submission to a competent authority for a Part C (market placement) release authorization, under Article 13(2)(h) of the Deliberate Release Directive. The Summary Information Format reflects the need to enable the fullest possible exchange of relevant information between notifiers, the competent authorities of the Member States, the Commission, and the public. To this end, the Format ensures that relevant information is presented in a standardized and accessible way. It is made explicit

[13] [2002] OJ L200/22. [14] [2002] OJ L280/27. [15] [2002] OJ L280/37.

that this information cannot form the (sole) basis of an environmental risk assessment.

Fourthly and finally, again on 3 October, the Council adopted Decision 2002/813/EC establishing, Pursuant to Directive 2001/18/EC, the Summary Notification Information Format for Notifications Concerning the Deliberate Release into the Environment of Genetically Modified Organisms for Purposes other than for Placing on the Market.[16] This Decision serves, essentially, the same purpose as the aforementioned Decision 2002/812/EC,[17] but now in respect of so-called Part B notifications, for purposes other than market placement (most notably, field experimentation with GM crops).

ii. Cartagena Biosafety Protocol

On 25 June 2002, the Council adopted Decision 2002/628/EC concerning the conclusion, on behalf of the European Community, of the Cartagena Protocol on Biosafety.[18] This formal approval of the Cartagena Protocol on Biosafety (Cartagena Biosafety Protocol)[19] to the Convention on Biological Diversity (CBD)[20] followed its signature on 24 May 2000. The EU was the twentieth Contracting Party to ratify the Protocol.[21]

C. Legislation in Progress

i. Transboundary Movements of GMOs

By signing the Cartagena Biosafety Protocol, on 24 May 2000, the EC committed itself to the Protocol's provisions on, *inter alia*, the transboundary movements of GMOs.[22] Although Community legislation contains provisions on imports of GMOs and GM crops that are largely consistent with the Protocol's provisions, rules for exporting GMOs to third countries were lacking. Hence, the Commission drafted a Proposal for a Regulation on the Transboundary Movement of Genetically Modified Organisms,[23] which was presented on 18 February 2002. Article 32 of the Deliberate Release Directive had invited the Commission to draft a legislative proposal to bring the Community GMO regime in conformity with the Protocol, in particular concerning exporting requirements. The latter include, notably, an Advance Informed Agreement Procedure, under Articles 7 to

[16] [2002] OJ L280/62.

[17] ibid.

[18] [2002] OJ L201/48.

[19] Montreal (Canada), 29 Jan. 2000 (entered into force 11 Sept. 2003) (2000) 39 *International Legal Materials* 5, 1027.

[20] Rio de Janeiro (Brazil), 5 June 1992 (entered into force 29 Dec. 1993) (1992) 31 *International Legal Materials*, 818.

[21] See Commission Press Release, IP/02/927, 25 June 2002.

[22] Referred to as 'living modified organisms' or 'LMOs' in the context of the Biosafety Protocol.

[23] COM(2002)85, [2002] OJ C151E/121.

10, 12, and 14 of the Cartagena Biosafety Protocol. Essentially, the proposed rules prescribe that exports of GMOs should be notified to the country of import, allowing it to make an informed decision, based on scientifically sound risk assessment. To this end, in accordance with the precautionary principle, a common system of notification and information is set up for exports and unintentional transboundary movements of GMOs to third countries, 'in order to contribute to ensuring an adequate level of protection in the field of the safe transfer, handling and use of GMOs that may have adverse effects on the conservation and the sustainable use of biological diversity, taking also into account risks to human health'.[24] To ensure efficient and appropriate responses to unintentional transboundary movements of GMOs that are likely to harm the conservation and sustainable use of biological diversity, or human health. States from which such movements originate must immediately inform the potentially affected States, as well as the Biosafety Clearing House (BCH),[25] established under the Protocol, and any other relevant international organizations.

On 24 September, the EP endorsed the Proposal subject to several amendments, which related, in particular, to: (i) clarifying the definition of 'exporter' and, hence, the legal competence and responsibility of the natural or legal person who arranges transboundary movements of GMOs; (ii) ensuring that no first intentional transboundary movement of a GMO intended directly or indirectly for deliberate release into the environment takes place without the prior consent of the importing party; (iii) avoiding duplication of notifications in the event of movement of the same GMO to another country; (iv) ensuring that a GMO which may be subject to transboundary movements for direct use as food or feed or for processing may not be exported unless it is authorized for the same use within the EC; and (v) to improve transparency and traceability.[26] At the 2457th Council Meeting, on 17 October 2002, the EU Environment Ministers reached political agreement on a Common Position, which will be formally adopted at the next session, early in 2003. The second reading in the EP was planned for the first half of 2003, and it is likely that adoption of the Regulation will be possible soon thereafter.

ii. GM Food and Feed, Traceability and Labelling

In July 2001, the Commission had presented two important legislative proposals concerning GM food and feed, and its traceability and labelling: a Proposal for a Regulation on Genetically Modified Food and Feed,[27] and a Proposal for a Regulation concerning Traceability and Labelling of Genetically Modified Organisms and Traceability of Food and Feed Products Produced from Genetically Modified Organisms and Amending Directive 2001/18/EC.[28]

[24] ibid., Art. 1. [25] See sect. F.*i.* below for more details.
[26] EP Doc. No. A5/2002/289 [2002] OJ C273E/104.
[27] COM(2001)425, [2001] OJ C304E/221.
[28] COM(2001)182, [2001] OJ C304E/237.

The EP had its first reading for both Proposals in July 2002, which resulted in a significant amount of (substantive) amendments.[29] Although the EP broadly supported the proposals, there were many points of disagreement between the Institutions. Essentially, the EP demanded more stringent provisions for traceability and labelling, and importantly, a more restrictive threshold than proposed by the Commission for adventitious presence of transgenic material in food and feed products. The proposed new regulations are intended to 'complete the EU's regulatory framework for GM foodstuffs', to further facilitate a trustworthy, transparent, and environmentally sound approach to GMOs, GM food, and GM feed, and to ensure consumer choice through strict and comprehensible labelling. In particular, the GM Food and Feed Regulation was designed to incorporate all rules, procedures, and measures governing not only GM food but also feed, into a single, comprehensive legal act, which would replace the Deliberate Release Directive. In turn, the specific objective for the Traceability and Labelling Regulation would be to establish a comprehensive framework of extensive traceability and labelling requirements for both GM foods and animal feeds, facilitating environmental monitoring, the consumer's 'right to know', and possible withdrawals of products where necessary. In the context of the latter regulation, it is envisaged that a system be established to develop and assign unique identifier codes to individual GMOs, to facilitate the traceability throughout the production and consumption chain. Further proposals to this end will be made by the Commission in the near future.

The proposed Food and Feed Regulation would replace the current authorization rules for GMOs and GMO-containing products, creating a single authorization procedure for all applications of the GMOs, and doing away with simplified, or shortened, procedures as existed, for example, under Regulation (EC) No. 258/97 concerning Novel Foods and Novel Food Ingredients (Novel Foods Regulation),[30] and the Deliberate Release Directive. The proposed Traceability and Labelling Regulation is intended to extend and tighten the existing labelling rules for GMOs and GM foods, while introducing for the first time such requirements for animal feeds. Major bones of contention were, in particular, the scope of the regulations (e.g. as to the type of products and organisms they should cover), and the thresholds for adventitious presence of GM material, below which, under restricted circumstances, neither labelling nor authorization would be necessary.

Following the many EP amendments in the first reading, the Commission amended its proposals in September[31] and October 2002.[32] On 28 November 2002, at the 2456th Council Meeting, the EU Environment Ministers reached

[29] EP Doc. No. A5/2002/229 [2002] OJ C271E/275 (Traceability and Labelling), EP Doc. No. A5/2002/225 [2002] OJ C271E/283 (Food & Feed).

[30] [1997] OJ L 43/1.

[31] COM(2002)515, [2002] OJ C331E/308 (Traceability and Labelling).

[32] COM(2002)559 (Food & Feed).

political agreement on a Common Position[33] for the GM Food and Feed Regulation. Subsequently, on 9 December 2002, at the 2473rd Council Meeting, the Ministers also reached political agreement on a Common Position[34] on the proposed Traceability and Labelling Regulation.

Both Common Positions will be formalized at the next meeting of the Ministers, early in 2003, and will then be sent to the EP for the second reading. Adoption of the (contentious) regulations may be expected for the second half of 2003.

iii. Environmental Liability

Finally, in January 2002, following almost a decade of contentious preparations, the Commission adopted a long-awaited Proposal for a Directive on Environmental Liability with regard to the Prevention and Remedying of Environmental Damage.[35] The Commission proposed a framework to prevent damage to the environment, and if necessary, remediate such damages, based on the polluter-pays principle. The liability rules would not have retrospective effect. One of the most vital differences between the original draft proposals and this final Proposal is that the Directive would create a liability regime under public administrative law, rather than civil law. Hence, competent public authorities would be responsible for preventing and remedying environmental damage, or rather, for having liable operators undertake these tasks. In accordance with the subsidiarity and proportionality principles, the Member States would be to decide when measures should be taken by the liable operator or by the competent authorities, or a third party acting on their behalf. Individuals or qualified public interest groups would have to address these authorities in respect of their (potential) damage, or the authority's action or inaction. The authorities (or third parties having acted on their behalf) must, in turn, recover their prevention or remediation costs from the liable operators.

Under the proposed Directive, environmental damage would include: (i) damage to wildlife and biodiversity in sites designated under national or Community nature conservation laws, (ii) damage to waters covered by Community legislation, and (iii) land contamination (soil and subsoil) that could create serious public health hazards.

This compromised scope of the Directive, as compared to earlier drafts, excludes specific environmental damage by GMOs. Many commentators, in particular environmental organizations, have argued that the Directive's scope should be widened so as also to include less severe damage and damage to biodiversity outside designated nature conservation areas. Moreover, some have

[33] See Commission Press Release IP/02/1770, 29 Nov. 2002.

[34] See Commission Press Release IP/02/1836, 10 Dec. 2002.

[35] COM(2002)17, [2002] OJ C151E/132. See also the 1993 Green Paper COM(1993)47, and the 2000 White Paper COM(2000)66.

urged incorporation of the definition of 'biodiversity' under the CBD,[36] in order to include more comprehensive damage caused by GMOs. However, the Commission has ruled this extension out, arguing that this would raise delicate questions as to the quantification of such damage, and the appropriate threshold of damage-entailing liability. Criticism has also been voiced in relation to the proposals to include a 'permit defence' and 'state-of-the-art' defence under the Directive, which might considerably diminish the liability for the biotechnology industry, in particular, in view of the authorization processes and the extremely rapid development of 'state-of-the-art' in this sector, and the current lack of scientific certainty as to the effects and impacts of GMOs.

The issue of scope is, and likely will be, a matter of fierce debate between the Institutions and the Member States. The first reading in the EP was delayed until the first quarter of 2003, and significant EP amendments may be expected from that reading. Sceptical of the outcome of the legislative process, some have voiced suggestions to establish a separate liability regime, specifically for GMO-related damage.

D. Case Law and Enforcement Activity

i. Deliberate Release Directive

According to Article 34 of the Deliberate Release Directive,[37] the Member States were to 'bring into force the laws, regulations and administrative provisions necessary to comply with this Directive by 17 October 2002'. However, only Denmark communicated national transposition measures to the Commission before this date. Hence, on 21 November 2001, the Commission sent letters of formal notice to all Member States, except Denmark, for not having transposed the Directive in due time.[38] It is noteworthy that even in 2002, there were still Member States that had not transposed the former Deliberate Release Directive 90/220/EEC.[39]

ii. Contained Use Directive

Directive 98/81/EC amending Directive 90/219/EEC on the Contained Use of Genetically Modified Micro-Organisms (Contained Use Directive)[40] should have been transposed by the Member States by 5 June 2000. However, by the end of 2002, several Member States still had not adopted and communicated to the Commission the appropriate measures to bring their national legal systems into conformity with the provisions of the Directive. Actions against Germany and Greece were withdrawn in the second half of 2002,[41] but by the end of 2002,

[36] n. 20 above. [37] n. 9 above.

[38] Commission Report, n. 11 above, Annex IV, 34–5. [39] ibid.

[40] [1998] OJ L330/13.

[41] Case C-2001/346, *Commission* v. *Germany*, action withdrawn on 16 Oct. 2002; Case C-2001/371, *Commission* v. *Greece*, action withdrawn on 18 Sept. 2002.

the Commission was still pursuing non-transposition (or infringement) proceedings against Belgium, Spain, France, Luxembourg, and Austria.[42]

iii. Access to Environmental Information

There was one case in 2002 involving biotechnology law which deserves some attention, although its merits were rather more relevant for the horizontal instrument of access to information on the environment. On 5 December 2002, Advocate General (AG) Tizzano presented his Opinion in Case C-316/01, *Eva Glawischnig*.[43] The case involved a preliminary ruling by an Austrian administrative court, on three questions relating to Directive 90/313/EEC on the Freedom of Access to Information on the Environment (Access to Information Directive).[44] In particular, the ECJ was asked whether 'information relating to the environment' within the meaning of the Directive, should be interpreted to include details of examinations carried out by Austrian administrative authorities to monitor compliance with labelling requirements for GM foodstuffs, under Regulation (EC) No. 1139/98 concerning the Compulsory Indication of the Labelling of Certain Foodstuffs Produced from Genetically Modified Organisms of Particulars other than those Provided for in Directive 79/112/EEC.[45] Dr Eva Glawischnig, Austrian parliamentarian for the Green Party, considered that the term 'environment' in the context of the Access to Information Directive also covered human beings and human health, and that, hence, access should also be granted to information related to the latter categories. In her opinion, compliance-monitoring data related to failures to comply with specific authorization conditions or labelling requirements for dangerous products (*in casu* foodstuffs containing GMOs) constituted information related to the protection of human health and the environment that should be publicly accessible, since the effects on the human body of consuming GM foods are unknown.

Referring to the ECJ's ruling in *Mecklenburg*,[46] Advocate General Tizzano noted that it was necessary to determine the purpose of Regulation (EC) No. 1139/98, as the public authorities' activities must be 'act[s] capable of... protecting the state of one of the sectors of the environment covered by the directive', in order for their data to constitute 'information relating to the environment'.[47] He agreed with the Commission and the Austrian Government that the purpose of the Regulation was not to protect human health or the environment, but rather informing consumers.

[42] See Commission Report, n. 8 above, 48.

[43] Case C-316/01, *Eva Glawischnig v. Bundesminister für Soziale Sicherheit und Generationen* [2002] ECR I-5995 (not yet reported), Opinion of Advocate General Tizzano of 5 Dec. 2002.

[44] [1990] OJ L158/56.

[45] [1998] OJ L159/4.

[46] Case C-321/96, *Mecklenburg* [1998] ECR I-3809.

[47] Case C-316/01, n. 43 above, paras. 25 and 26, referring to Case C-321/96, ibid., para. 21.

Hence, in the Advocate General's opinion, the information requested by Glawischnig did not relate to activities or measures designed to protect the environment within the meaning of the Access to Information Directive.[48]

This interpretation of the term 'environment' under the Access to Information Directive is, arguably, very literal and restrictive. The ECJ, which will give its ruling in this case in 2003, is not likely to reach a different conclusion, but it may be questioned whether this effective curtailing of the public's right to environmental information is in conformity with the United Nations Economic Commission for Europe (UN/ECE) Convention on Access to Information, Public Participation in Decision-Making and Access to Justice in Environmental Matters (Aarhus Convention).[49]

It is submitted that rulings like these, although not surprising under current EC legislation, will do nothing to improve the public's confidence in the transparency of the regulation of GM technologies, in particular in relation to food. It is difficult to see an upward trend of transparency in the regulation of biotechnology, in view of cases like the above, and legislative developments such as in the United Kingdom (UK), which in 2002 adopted secrecy rules barring the public's right to access to information relating to industrial plants and applications involving GMOs.[50]

E. Policy Documents

i. Life Sciences and Biotechnology—A Strategy for Europe

In January 2002, the Commission presented the Communication Life Sciences and Biotechnology—A Strategy for Europe.[51]

The Commission had announced in March 2001 at the Stockholm European Council, in the context of the Lisbon European Council's Strategy, that it would present a Communication setting out a strategic vision for life sciences and biotechnology up to 2010, including proposals for how best to address ethical issues. In preparation of the final Communication, a working document had been distributed among stakeholders in September 2001, as a basis for a broad public consultation. Some 320 responses were received, *inter alia* from Member State governments and public authorities, the European Group on Ethics, industry, professional associations, academics, and private individuals.

[48] ibid., para. 36.

[49] Aarhus (Denmark), 25 June 1998 (entered into force 30 Oct. 2001) (1999) 38 *International Legal Materials* 3, 517.

[50] See Genetically Modified Organisms (Contained Use) (Amendment) Regulations 2002, SI 2002/163; see also e.g. 'Post-September 11 secrecy over COMAH, GMO sites' (2001) 28 *Environmental Data Services Report* 323, 40–1. 'Secrecy Rules for Dangerous GMOs' (2002) 29 *Environmental Data Services Report*, 49, and 'DEFRA Dallies over Disclosure of GM Crop Locations' (2002) 29 *Environmental Data Services*, 44–5, and 'Government Paves Way to Secrecy over GM Crop Locations' (2003) 30 *Environmental Data Services* 336, 48–9.

[51] COM(2002)27, [2002] OJ C55/3.

In the Communication of January 2002, the Commission proposed a strategy for the EU to develop sustainable and responsible policies to address three basic questions: (i) How can the EU best attract the human, industrial, and financial resources to develop and apply life sciences and biotechnology to meet society's needs and concerns (including health, ageing, food, the environment, and sustainable development) and increase its competitiveness?; (ii) How can the EU deliver effective, credible, and responsible policies that enjoy the confidence and support of its citizens?; and (iii) How can the EU best respond to global challenges, develop its domestic policies with a clear international perspective, and act internationally to pursue its interests?[52] The Commission stressed the need for responsible, science-based, and people-centred policies on an ethical basis, to respond to what it calls a 'technology revolution'.[53] To implement this strategy, the Commission proposed an open, collaborative, and sustained process to develop coherent and credible policies.

The strategy also included a 30-point Action Plan, which could be grouped into two broad categories, respectively aimed at strengthening the 'value creation chain', and at improving effective governance. The actions propose concrete measures by the Commission and the Community (Member States), as well as recommendations for other public and private actors, such as local authorities, industry, and all other interested parties, in order to 'harvest the potential' of the various applications of biotechnology. An important proposed action is the setting up of a Stakeholders' Forum for life sciences and biotechnology.

Although the strategy notes many potential and current (environmental) benefits of biotechnology, such as bioremediation, and bio-catalysis (creating 'clean industry' through the use of enzymes in industrial processes), it also noted the potential risks. Particular attention was also given to the sustainable and equitable use of technological advances, *inter alia* in relation to developing nations. Generally, the importance of a 'European agenda for international collaboration' was underlined.

The Commission stressed the significance of governance, which it defined as 'attention to the way public authorities prepare, decide, implement and explain policies and actions'.[54]

It proposed five main 'action lines' along which to apply the 'highest standards of governance' in life sciences and biotechnology: (i) societal dialogue and scrutiny should accompany and guide the development of life sciences and biotechnology; (ii) life sciences and biotechnology should be developed in a responsible way in harmony with ethical values and societal goals; (iii) informed choice should facilitate demand-driven applications; (iv) science-based regulatory oversight should enhance public confidence; and (v) basic regulatory principles and legal obligations should be respected to safeguard the Community single market and international obligations.[55]

[52] ibid. 5. [53] ibid. 3. [54] ibid. 11. [55] ibid. 11–17.

F. International Cooperation

i. Cartagena Biosafety Protocol

The Cartagena Protocol on Biosafety (Cartagena Biosafety Protocol)[56] to the Convention on Biological Diversity (CBD)[57] was adopted on 29 January 2000, following over half a decade of preparatory work and negotiations. The objective of the Protocol is to protect biodiversity and human health from potential adverse effects of living modified organisms (LMOs), resulting from biotechnology.

To this end, the Protocol aims to establish an Advanced Informed Agreement (AIA) procedure which would allow countries to make informed decisions on whether to import genetically modified organisms (GMOs), as well as a Biosafety Clearing House (BCH) to facilitate the exchange of information and especially assist developing countries through an Action Plan for Building Capacities for Effective Implementation. It distinguishes between two categories of LMOs: first, LMOs for deliberate release into the environment of the country of import (e.g. seeds or crops to be planted), and secondly, LMOs 'in transit, for contained use, or intended for direct use as food or feed, or for processing' (e.g. harvested crops, such as soybeans for use in food). The first category is subject to the AIA procedure, involving detailed written information and consent from the importers and exporters. For the second category of LMOs, instead, information must be sent on any new LMO to the BCH, where the information will be available to potential importers. Shipments containing the latter category of LMOs must be labelled as 'may contain LMOs', and should indicate that they are not intended for introduction into the environment.

The Biosafety Protocol was signed by the EU on May 2000, and ratified on 25 June 2002.[58] There had been a strong push to ratify before the United Nations (UN) World Summit on Sustainable Development (WSSD)[59] in August and September 2002. In fact, originally, there had even been hopes of having the Biosafety Protocol enter into force prior to the Summit. However, these hopes were quashed at the third meeting of the CBD's Intergovernmental Committee on the Cartagena Protocol (ICCP) in The Hague (the Netherlands) from 22 to 26 April 2002. Although 110 States had signed the Protocol at that time, only 17 of these had ratified, making entry into force (after 90 days following the fiftieth ratification) before the WSSD highly unlikely, if not impossible.

The third meeting of the ICCP, directly after the Sixth Conference of the Parties (COP-6) of the CBD, established two Working Groups for the following subjects: (i) information sharing, handling, transport, packaging and identifica-

[56] Montreal (Canada), 29 Jan. 2000 (entered into force 11 Sept. 2003) (2000) 39 *International Legal Materials* 5, 1027.

[57] Rio de Janeiro (Brazil), 5 June 1992 (entered into force 29 Dec. 1993), (1992) 31 *International Legal Materials*, 818.

[58] n. 21 above.

[59] Johannesburg (South Africa), 26 Aug.–4 Sept. 2002.

tion, monitoring and reporting, and other issues for effective implementation, and (ii) liability and redress, compliance, and capacity building.[60] Unsurprisingly, perhaps, the most contentious issues debated involved liability, compliance, and transport, packaging, and identification. Under Article 18 of the Biosafety Protocol, Parties are required to consider the need for and modalities of developing standards for the handling, transport, packaging, and identification practices for LMOs. In this context, Parties are divided between those supporting the general identification system for shipments that 'may contain' LMO (as currently stated in the Protocol), and those favouring a more specialized system with 'unique identification codes' for genetic material.

G. Miscellaneous

i. Co-Existence of GM, Conventional, and Organic Crops

With new rules for authorizing, tracing, and labelling GMOs and GM food and feed in the pipeline, the next major hurdle for the EC to take in the area of agrobiotechnology is the controversial issue of 'co-existence'. The imminent new GMO regime is likely, in the short- or mid-term future, to result in a significant increase of commercial planting and harvesting of GM crops throughout the EC. To be sure, this will also lead to an increase in adventitious presence of GM or transgenic material in non-GM conventional or organic crops. Hence, the thus far (in the EC context) somewhat theoretical problem of co-existence of GM and non-GM conventional and organic crops has now become highly realistic and urgent. In order for farmers in all three agricultural production systems to be able to generate their respective produce freely and without hindrance, the seeds, crops, and harvests should be separated, to avoid 'cross-contamination' or 'admixture' (i.e. the adventitious mixing of GM and non-GM corps as a result of, *inter alia*, seed impurities, cross-pollination, and harvesting, storage, and shipment practices).

On the issue of co-existence, early in 2002, the Commission was embroiled in a controversy over whether or not it had concealed a report by the Joint Research Centre (JRC), completed in January 2002.[61] The environmental NGO Greenpeace, who leaked the report in May, claimed to possess an accompanying letter to the report by JRC Director General Barry McSweeney, in which he allegedly suggested that 'given the sensitivity of the issue, I would suggest that the report be kept for internal use within the Commission only'.[62]

[60] See Report of the Intergovernmental Committee for the Cartagena Protocol on Biosafety on the Work of its Third Meeting, Document UNEP/CBD/ICCP/3/10, Published on the Internet at: http://www.biodiv.org/doc/meetings/bs/iccp-03/official/iccp-03-10-en.pdf.

[61] See e.g. (2002) 29 *Environmental Data Services Report* 329, 11–2; and 'GMO Co-existence with Conventional Crops, JRC' (2002) 4 *Environmental Law Review*, 270.

[62] See Greenpeace Press Release, 'EU Suppresses Study Showing Genetically Engineered Crops Add High Costs for All Farmers and Threaten Organic', of 16 May 2002, published on the Internet at: http://archive.greenpeace.org/pressreleases/geneng/2002may16.html.

Ultimately, following these allegations, on 22 May 2002, the Commission published the report Scenarios for Co-Existence of Genetically Modified, Conventional and Organic Crops in European Agriculture.[63] The report was a synthesis of the results of a study which the JRC had undertaken at the request, in May 2000, of the Commission's Directorate General (DG) Agriculture. It was based on six individual studies performed under the auspices of the JRC: (i) analysis of potential risks of contamination; (ii) analysis of necessary adjustments of farming practices; (iii) overview of existing segregation methods; (iv) analysis of financial losses in case of contamination; (v) farm-level monitoring of GMO content in non-GM crops; and (vi) review of GMO detection and quantification techniques.

Drafting policy and rules for co-existence were among the proposed actions under the Communication on Life Sciences and Biotechnology—A Strategy for Europe.[64] Under Action 17, the Commission committed itself to take 'initiative[s] to develop, in partnership with Member States, farmers and other private operators, research and pilot projects to clarify the need, and possible options, for agronomic and other measures to ensure the viability of conventional and organic farming and their sustainable coexistence with genetically modified crops'.[65]

The JRC study was a first step towards addressing these issues, and trying to assess the consequences of the introduction and possible increase of GM crops, and to identify appropriate measures for the minimization of adventitious presence of GMOs below the proposed thresholds under the upcoming new GM food and feed legislation. Moreover, it also served to devise appropriate monitoring systems for verification, and estimated the implementation costs of effective co-existence measures, monitoring systems, and potential liability or insurance systems to cover possible financial damage as a result of admixtures.

The study used as case studies three arable crops, which were selected not only for representing different biological features, but also as these might be the most likely candidates for large(r) scale commercial growing in the EU: oilseed rape for seed production, grain maize used for feed production, and potato for direct consumption and food processing. The researchers used two key assumptions for their estimations: first, that GM crops would have a market share of 10 per cent and 50 per cent in the study regions, and secondly, that GM contamination thresholds of 0.1 per cent, 0.3 per cent, and 1.0 per cent would apply.

The JRC study indicated that while estimated levels of adventitious presence of GM crops did not change dramatically between the two market share scenarios (10 per cent or 50 per cent) of GM crop, under current farming practices, estimated levels of adventitious presence of GM crops in non-GM crops significantly varied depending on the crop and farm type (e.g. as much as 2.2 per cent

[63] Published on the Internet at: http://www.jrc.cec.eu.int/download/GMCrops_coexistence.pdf.
[64] See n. 42 above. [65] ibid. 42.

for a conventional intensive maize farm or as low as 0.1 per cent for an organic potato farm).

Under a 0.1 per cent threshold, in both market share scenarios, co-existence with non-GM crops was deemed virtually impossible, while at 0.3 per cent and 1.0 per cent, co-existence 'might technically be possible but economically difficult because of the costs and complexities' of the necessary changes in farming practices.[66] The general conclusion was that compliance with the 1 per cent threshold for adventitious presence would probably be possible, but would require changes to farming practices (e.g. effective monitoring systems, in particular for conventional and organic crops). However, in the particular case of organic crops, it would be very difficult to maintain sufficient separation between GM and organic crop varieties in order to comply with the 0.1 per cent standard for organic certification.

As a result, also with a view to the need for insurance for damages, farmers in these sectors would probably face significant additional production costs, at an average of approximately 15 per cent. However, it was noted that the probability of admixtures, and hence the extent of requisite preventive measures, was highly crop-specific. For example, the prudent co-existence of GM and non-GM oilseed rape might involve additional production costs of up to 50 per cent. Unsurprisingly, organic farmers would be the hardest hit in this regard.

The Commission is likely to follow this report with a large-scale policy debate on co-existence, in 2003, as a basis for future policy or legislation. This debate will, logically, also include the question of whether Community liability rules should be enacted to allow compensation for economic loss in the event of admixtures or contamination.

ii. Eurobarometer

A Eurobarometer survey of public opinion towards biotechnology in the EU, published in December 2001, presented broad evidence of public scepticism towards GM technologies.[67] The survey results were based on questioning of approximately 1,000 people in each Member State during the summer of 2001. It indicated that 71 per cent of EU citizens reject GM foods outright, although the proportion was slightly less among 15- to 24-year-olds, at 64 per cent. Furthermore, 86 per cent of Europeans were risk averse, and 86 per cent wanted to be better informed about GM foods before eating them, while a staggering 95 per cent insisted on having a right to know and choose what to eat. Another interesting result was that people's perceptions that GMOs may hold environmental risks grow parallel to their general level of scientific literacy. Hence, of

[66] JRC Report, n. 54 above, 6.

[67] Eurobarometer 55.2, *European, Science and Technology*, Dec. 2001, published on the Internet at: http://europa.eu.int/comm/public_opinion/archives/ebs/ebs_154_en.pdf.

people with the lowest level of scientific understanding in the survey, 43 per cent thought that GMOs could be detrimental to the environment, while approximately the same percentage were unsure. In contrast, of the people with high levels of scientific understanding, 66 per cent acknowledged potential environmental risks, while only 22 per cent were undecided. Generally, approximately 60 per cent of those surveyed saw potential for adverse environmental effects. Thirty-three per cent of people felt that media attention had exaggerated the dangers of GM technologies.

H. Conclusion

While many developments did occur during 2002, these were mostly follow-ups to progress in 2000 and 2001, or build-up to likely developments during 2003. It is clearly noticeable, though, that Community environmental consumer health and environment legislation and policy on biotechnology are now rapidly advancing. Of course, inevitably in regulating such an exceptionally rapidly evolving technology, regulation will always be lagging behind somewhat. However, the Commission has expressed its intention to move from such a response-based approach to a more proactive stance in the regulation of biotechnology. The Communication on Life Sciences and Biotechnology—A Strategy for Europe serves as a good example of this aspiration.

Many important developments are to be expected for the year to come. Not only is it likely that crucial legislation will be adopted, including the regulations on GM food and feed, traceability of GM food and feed, and transboundary movements of GMOs, and perhaps even the proposed environmental liability directive (although this appears less likely), policy discussions will touch upon vital issues in the regulation of modern biotechnology, such as the debate on co-existence of GM and non-GM crops. The coming year(s) will also witness the practical application of the updated authorization regime for GMOs and GM food products, under the revised Deliberate Release Directive. Member States will have to continue their efforts to implement the new rules.

Noteworthy events will also be likely to take place at the international level, with continuing negotiations and discussions within the context of the Cartagena Biosafety Protocol, and notably, with the increasingly unavoidable WTO complaint by the US (and possibly other major GM-crops exporters, such as Canada) against the EU's *de facto* moratorium on (imports of) GMOs. In this respect, the EU is faced with a difficult dilemma. On the one hand, it may be hoped that the proposed new legislation for GMOs and GM foods, once adopted, will serve to diffuse this looming 'trade war'. However, on the other hand, it is submitted that those very rules, given their strictness and continued precautionary approach, may just as well ignite an additional international trade dispute.

III. Nature Conservation

Agustín Garcia-Ureta *

A. Legislation Adopted

i. Birds and Habitats Directives

Directive 79/409/EEC on the Conservation of Wild Birds (Birds Directive),[1] and Directive 92/43/EEC on the Conservation of Natural Habitats and of Wild Fauna and Flora (Habitats Directive),[2] remained unaltered. No amendments were made to Regulation (EC) No. 338/97 on the Protection of Species of Wild Fauna and Flora by Regulating Trade Therein (CITES Regulation).[3]

ii. Biosafety

Following the Commission's proposal,[4] the Council adopted Decision 2002/628/EC concerning the Conclusion, on Behalf of the European Community, of the Cartagena Protocol on Biosafety.[5] The Cartagena Protocol on Biosafety (Cartagena Biosafety Protocol)[6] to the Convention on Biological Diversity (CBD),[7] had been signed on behalf of the EC on 24 May 2000, in Nairobi (Kenya). The Protocol provides a framework for the safe transfer, handling, and use of living modified organisms (LMOs) resulting from modern biotechnology that may have adverse effects on the conservation and sustainable use of biological diversity.

iii. Forests

The European Parliament (EP) and the Council adopted Regulation (EC) No. 804/2002 amending Regulation (EEC) No. 3528/86 on the Protection of the Community's Forests against Atmospheric Pollution,[8] and Regulation (EC) No. 805/2002 amending Regulation (EEC) No. 2158/92 on Protection of the Community's Forests against Fire.[9] The old Regulations were to expire on 31 December 2002.

* Lecturer in Law, University of the Basque Country, Bilbao (Spain).

1 [1979] OJ L103/1.
2 [1992] OJ L206/7.
3 [1997] OJ L61/1.
4 Proposal for a Council Decision Concerning the Conclusion, on Behalf of the Community, of the Cartagena Protocol on Biosafety, 13 Mar. 2002, COM(2002)127, [2002] OJ C181E/258.
5 [2002] OJ L201/48.
6 Montreal (Canada), 29 Jan. 2000 (entered into force 11 Sept. 2003) (2000) 39 *International Legal Materials* 5, 1027.
7 Rio de Janeiro (Brazil), 5 June 1992 (entered into force 29 Dec. 1993) (1992) 31 *International Legal Materials*, 818.
8 [2002] OJ L132/1.
9 [2002] OJ L132/3.

iv. Sixth Environmental Action Programme

The EP and the Council adopted Decision No. 1600/2002/EC laying down the Sixth Community Environment Action Programme.[10] Article 6 of the Decision enumerates the objectives and priority areas for action on nature and biodiversity. The objectives are as follows: (i) halting biodiversity decline with the aim to reach this objective by 2010 (including prevention and mitigation of impacts of invasive alien species and genotypes); (ii) protection and appropriate restoration of nature and biodiversity from damaging pollution; (iii) conservation, appropriate restoration, and sustainable use of marine environment, coasts, and wetlands; (iv) conservation and appropriate restoration of areas of significant landscape values, including both cultivated and sensitive areas; (v) conservation of species and habitats, with special concern for preventing habitat fragmentation; and (vi) promotion of a sustainable use of the soil, with particular attention to preventing erosion, deterioration, contamination, and desertification.

The above-mentioned objectives are to be pursued by means of several priority actions. Article 6 specifies nine actions. Among them, the following may be highlighted:

(a) On biodiversity: ensuring the implementation and promoting the monitoring and assessment of the Community's biodiversity strategy and the relevant action plans; promoting research on biodiversity, genetic resources, ecosystems, and interactions with human activities; developing measures to enhance sustainable use, sustainable production, and sustainable investments in relation to biodiversity; encouraging coherent assessment, further research, and cooperation on threatened species; promoting at the global level a fair and equitable sharing of benefits arising from the use of genetic resources to implement Article 15 of the CBD on access to genetic resources originating from third countries; developing measures aimed at the prevention and control of invasive alien species including alien genotypes; establishing the Natura 2000 Network and implementing the necessary instruments and measures required for its full implementation and for the protection, outside the Natura 2000 areas, of species protected under the Habitats and Birds Directives; promoting the extension of the Natura 2000 Network to the Candidate Countries;

(e) Promoting the integration of conservation and restoration of the landscape values into other policies including tourism, taking account of relevant international instruments;

(f) Promoting the integration of biodiversity considerations in agricultural policies;

(g) Promoting sustainable use of the seas and conservation of marine ecosystems, including sea beds, estuarine and coastal areas. Special attention for

[10] [2002] OJ L242/1.

sites holding a high biodiversity value through, *inter alia*, further promoting the protection of marine areas, in particular with the Natura 2000 Network, as well as by other feasible Community means; and

(h) Implementing and further developing strategies and measures on forests incorporating the following, *inter alia*, elements: improving existing Community measures which protect forests and implementing sustainable forest management, *inter alia*, through national forest programmes, in connection with rural development plans, with increased emphasis on the monitoring of the multiple roles of forests in line with recommendations adopted by the Ministerial Conference on the Protection of Forests in Europe and the United Nations Forum on Forests and the Convention on Biodiversity, and other fora.

B. Legislation in Progress

In July 2002, the Commission submitted a Proposal for a Regulation concerning Monitoring of Forests and Environmental Interactions in the Community (Forest Focus).[11] The scheme is to be built on the achievements of Regulation (EEC) No. 3528/86 on the Protection of the Community's Forests against Atmospheric Pollution,[12] and Regulation (EEC) No. 2158/92 on the Protection of the Community's Forests against Fire.[13] The proposal provides a multi-annual framework to cover (initially) a six-year period from 2003 to 2008. The main objective of the Proposal is to contribute towards the protection of forest ecosystems in the Community by monitoring their conditions. According to the Commission, this objective cannot be sufficiently achieved by the Member States acting individually. Rather, Community action should be taken in order to ensure harmonized data collection and the provision of policy-relevant information at Community level, to assist the evaluation of ongoing Community measures to promote the conservation and sustainable management of forest ecosystems. Several aspects are considered in the Proposal: (a) nearly 44 per cent of the total land area of the EU is covered with forests and other wooded areas. Forest ecosystems fulfil various functions with economic, social, and ecological significance. Furthermore, forest ecosystems are also habitat for various species of plants and animals; (b) forest ecosystems are exposed to serious threats from air pollution, fires, climatic change, and attacks from parasites and diseases. Most of these threats can have cross-border effects and can seriously upset and even destroy forest ecosystems; (c) forest ecosystem conditions, changes in these

[11] COM(2002)404, 15 July 2002 [2002] OJ C20E/67.

[12] [1986] OJ L326/2. It was amended by Reg. (EC) No. 307/97 [1997] OJ L51/9, which was annulled by the ECJ, since the Council should have taken the former Art. 130 EC (now Art. 175 EC) as sole legal basis (see Joined Cases C-164/97 and C-165/97, *EP* v. *Council* [1999] ECR I-1139). It was subsequently replaced by Reg. (EC) No. 1484/2001 [2001] OJ L196/1.

[13] [1992] OJ L217/3.

conditions, forests ecosystems, reaction to environmental stress, and the effects of policies can only be traced by means of monitoring; and (d) changes in forest ecosystem conditions as well as the reasons for these changes may be recognized at an early stage, thereby allowing the adoption of timely and appropriate measures in due time.

The scheme is to be based on the following activities: (i) establishment of a monitoring programme on air pollution effects on forests; (ii) setting up forest fire monitoring; (iii) continuous evaluation of the efficiency of monitoring activities in the assessment of forest ecosystem conditions and the further development of monitoring activity; and (iv) establishment of new monitoring activities on forest biodiversity, soils, climate change, and carbon sequestration after the development of appropriate monitoring methods, provided that the necessary additional financial resources are made available by the budgetary authority. In order to make full use of the results derived from these actions, the Member States are expected to carry out monitoring activities. The collection of data as well as studies, experiments, and demonstration projects shall be implemented under multi-annual national programmes (three-year periods). The proposed Framework Regulation will provide co-financing of up to 50 per cent of the eligible costs for monitoring activities and database platforms, as well as for studies, experiments, and demonstration projects to be carried out by Member States in the context of their national programmes. In order to conduct monitoring of air pollution effects on forests and on forest fires, to develop new monitoring activities, and to improve the scheme, €52 million shall be provided for the period 2003–6. For 2007 and 2008, the annual amount of €13 million may be increased in order to fund new activities, provided the budgetary authority approves such an increase.

In September 2002, the Commission presented a Proposal for a Council Decision on the Community Position to be Adopted on Certain Proposals Submitted to the Twelfth Meeting of the Conference of the Parties to the Convention on International Trade in Endangered Species of Wild Fauna and Flora (CITES), Santiago, Chile, 3–15 November 2002.[14] In view of the effects of decisions taken by the Conference of the Parties on the implementation of the CITES Regulation,[15] it was necessary to adopt a Community position on proposals submitted to the Conference. According to the Proposal, draft resolutions on interpretation and implementation of CITES and proposals to amend the appendices prepared by Member States or by the Commission were discussed by the Committee of Member States constituted under the CITES Regulation at a meeting on 17 May 2002. All proposals and working documents that were approved were subsequently submitted to the CITES Secretariat, including a document seeking to repeal two earlier Conference Resolutions on implementation of CITES by the Community. The Commission indicated in the Proposal

[14] COM(2002)516, 17 Sept. 2002 [2002] OJ C331E/319.

[15] n. 3 above.

that in the light of the enactment of the CITES Regulation, and the fact that all fifteen Member States were already Parties in their own right (following ratification by Ireland in the early months of 2002), those Resolutions were out of date and should be repealed. The Presidency also submitted a draft Decision calling upon all Parties who had not yet done so to ratify the Gaborone amendment, allowing Regional Economic Integration Organizations such as the EC to become a Party.

C. Case Law

i. Birds Directive

In Case C-202/01, *Commission* v. *France*,[16] the Commission made three basic claims: (i) that France had not classified territories as Special Protection Areas (SPAs) in sufficient measure, in terms of either number or size; (ii) that the classified areas were not sufficiently varied and representative to offer protection to all the species of wild bird listed in Annex I to the Birds Directive and to migratory species not listed in that Annex; and (iii) that protection of the SPAs was, in many cases, not sufficiently ensured. It also alleged, specifically, that France had failed to designate the site Plaine des Maures as an SPA.

Since France had not challenged the allegations regarding the need to classify as SPAs areas of land sufficient in both quantitative and qualitative terms in the light of the scientifically determined characteristics of sites, the European Court of Justice (ECJ) found no difficulties in upholding these. The Commission had referred to the 1994 French inventory of sites of importance for the conservation of birds (ZICO). In its opinion, that inventory, compatible with the March 2000 edition of the 'Important Bird Areas' inventory drawn up at Community level by the Commission (IBA), identified 285 ZICOs in the metropolitan area of France, and constituted the best scientific evidence available for the comprehensive assessment of the classifications throughout the French territory. In the absence of inventories contradicting the conclusions of the inventory of ZICOs, France should have classified as SPAs all the zones regarded as ZICOs.

The French government stated that, as at 17 July 2001, there were 117 SPAs, totalling almost 900,000 hectares, or 41 per cent of the number of ZICOs, and 19 per cent of their surface area. However, it acknowledged that additional classifications were needed for compliance with Article 4 of the Directive. In addition, it argued that the Directive did not require classification as SPAs of all of the territories referred to in the 1994 ZICO or the 2000 IBA inventories. In its opinion, those territories were inappropriate for identification as 'the most suitable territories' to be classified as SPAs. In addition, the approach taken in the 1994 ZICO and the 2000 IBA inventories was more comprehensive than that which guided the drawing up of the IBA inventory in 1989. Therefore, the

[16] [2002] ECR I-11019.

latter was the only one to concentrate on 'the most suitable territories', while the other inventories were much broader. However, having said that, France also acknowledged that six of the 116 species of wild birds listed in Annex I found on French territory were not protected in at least one SPA. In the light of the foregoing, the ECJ held that France had not, in sufficient measure, classified as SPAs the most suitable territories for the conservation of the species of wild bird listed in Annex I and of migratory species.[17] In addition, several Annex I species were not 'in any event' protected by any SPA designation on French territory at the end of the period laid down in the reasoned opinion.[18] This combination of factors allowed the ECJ to declare that, without considering whether all the territories listed as ZICOs should have been classified as SPAs, France had failed to classify the territories most suitable for the conservation of the aforementioned species.[19]

The Court also considered whether the designation of the Plaine des Maures was adequate in the light of the Directive. The Commission had not only challenged the incorrect application of Articles 3 and 4 of the Directive, but claimed that Plaine des Maures did not fully comply with those provisions. Three arguments were to sustain this allegation: first, that by classifying only 879 hectares of the site as an SPA (while for that site the ZICO covered 7,500 hectares), France had also failed to fulfil its obligation under Article 4(1) and (2). Secondly, by undertaking to extend the SPA of the site from 879 to 4,700 hectares, France at the same time had acknowledged the inadequacy of the land area then classified as an SPA on that site. Thirdly, that since 7,500 hectares of the site were listed in the ZICO inventory, it had to be classified in its entirety as an SPA, unless it could be demonstrated that the Directive did not require this. In contrast, France held that the Commission had not put forward any legal arguments specifically relating to an insufficiently large area on the Plaine des Maures being classified as an SPA. Moreover, the Commission had not even briefly set out the points of law necessary to conclude that there had been an infringement specifically relating to this site. In respect of the surface classified as an SPA, France found many difficulties to provide sound grounds. It acknowledged that the classification of 879 hectares, in force at the end of the period laid down in the reasoned opinion, was not sufficient, but noted that this infringement had ended with the enlargement of the SPA to 4,537 hectares, notified to the Commission on 17 May 2001. The ECJ held that the Commission had stated to the requisite legal standard the legal basis for the claim that the site had not been classified as an SPA in sufficient measure.[20] The French government itself had acknowledged, in its rejoinder, that the points of law on which that claim was based could be inferred from the Commission's arguments relating to the first claim. Concerning the territorial surface of the SPA, the ECJ held that France had acknowledged 'unreservedly' that it had not, at the end of the period

[17] ibid., para. 19. [18] ibid., para. 20. [19] ibid., para. 21. [20] ibid., para. 26.

laid down in the reasoned opinion, classified as an SPA a sufficient part of the territory of the Plaine des Maures. However, following one of the allegations brought forward by the Commission concerning the need to preserve the variety of species included in the Directive, the Court observed that it was not in dispute that this site sheltered 23 species of wild birds listed in Annex I, as well as several migratory species not listed in that Annex, some of which made that zone one of great ornithological interest.[21] Consequently, without answering the question whether all the territory listed as ZICO should have been classified as an SPA, the Court upheld the Commission's allegations and declared a corresponding breach of Article 4(1) and (2) in respect of that particular site.

In Case C-117/00, *Commission* v. *Ireland*,[22] the Commission brought an action under Article 226 EC claiming that Ireland had failed to take all the measures necessary to comply with Article 3 of the Birds Directive, in respect of the red grouse, and with the first sentence of Article 4(4) of that Directive, and Article 6(2) of the Habitats Directive in respect of the Owenduff-Nephin Beg Complex SPA. As regards Article 3 of the Birds Directive, the Commission indicated that the habitat of the red grouse was hill land and bog and that its diet consisted of common heather. However, this plant species was under serious threat from overgrazing in Ireland. The Commission cited various studies which showed that there had been a very marked decline in red grouse populations and a significant reduction in areas where the species was found, including its mating grounds.

The ECJ first recalled the wording of Article 3 of the Birds Directive, requiring Member States to take requisite measures to preserve, maintain, or re-establish a sufficient diversity and area of habitats for all the species of birds covered by the Directive. Pointing to its standing case law, the Court noted that this obligation existed before any reduction was observed in the number of birds or any risk of a protected species becoming extinct had materialized.[23] It also noted that a 1993 report of the Irish Wildbird Conservancy had identified the red grouse as one of the country's twelve most endangered breeding birds. It also indicated that the numbers of red grouse had diminished by more than 50 per cent over the last twenty years. In addition, a comparison of two scientific works, *The Atlas of Breeding Birds in Britain and Ireland—1968–1972* and *The New Atlas of Breeding Birds in Britain and Ireland—1988–1991*, revealed a significant contraction in the range in which the species was present and in which the species bred. The ECJ concluded that it was not in dispute that the breeding range of the red grouse, which was given a full entry in Annex II/1 to the Birds Directive, coincided, to a large extent, with the areas designated by the Irish Heritage Council as having been degraded by overgrazing. It noted that Ireland had acknowledged that, in general terms, it was reasonable to conclude that red grouse populations had been affected by the consequences of overgrazing on

[21] ibid., para. 29. [22] [2002] ECR I-5335. [23] ibid., para. 15.

their habitats. Ireland had also stated that the red grouse was dependent on common heather (being the predominant plant species on many Irish heaths, raised bogs, and uplands) and that it would be designating a very large area of those types of habitat (probably in excess of 250,000 hectares) as Special Areas of Conservation (SACs) within the meaning of the Habitats Directive. This should provide mechanisms to control the overgrazing. The ECJ also cited an Action Plan for Ireland's twelve most threatened breeding bird species prepared in 1995 by the Irish Wildbird Conservancy, according to which it was essential to properly manage pasturelands as part of priority actions. These consisted, initially, in halting the decline in red grouse populations and in their areas of distribution and, subsequently, in repopulating the areas of distribution previously abandoned. In the light of the foregoing, the ECJ held that Ireland had not taken all the measures necessary to safeguard a sufficient diversity and area of habitats for the red grouse for the purposes of Article 3 of the Birds Directive.[24]

The Commission's second claim concerned the infringement of the first sentence of Article 4(4) of the Birds Directive and Article 6(2) of the Habitats Directive. Both provisions require the Member States to take appropriate steps to avoid, *inter alia*, deterioration of habitats in SPAs classified pursuant to Article 4(1) of the Birds Directive. The Commission maintained that Ireland had failed to take the necessary measures to prevent the blanket bog of the Owenduff-Nephin Beg Complex SPA from being damaged by overgrazing. The Commission argued that the general reduction of 30 per cent in the mountain sheep quota decided upon during the winter of 1998–99 was inadequate, if consideration was given to all areas affected by overgrazing. Recalling settled case law, the ECJ held that the question whether a Member State failed to fulfil its obligations was to be determined by reference to the situation prevailing in that State at the end of the period laid down in the reasoned opinion. Hence, measures adopted after 8 June 1998 could not be taken into account.[25] Secondly, it noted that it was 'undisputed' that the Owenduff-Nephin Beg Complex had been classified as an SPA since October 1996. As regards land classified as an SPA, Article 7 of the Habitats Directive provided that the obligations arising under the first sentence of Article 4(4) of the Birds Directive were replaced, *inter alia*, by the obligations arising under Article 6(2) of the Habitats Directive as from the date of implementation of this Directive (10 June 1994), or the date of classification under the Birds Directive, where the latter date was later. Therefore, it followed that Article 6(2) of the Habitats Directive, rather than the first sentence of Article 4(4) of the Birds Directive, had applied to the Owenduff-Nephin Beg Complex SPA since October 1996.[26] Accordingly, the Commission's plea was dismissed insofar as it was based on infringement of Article 4(4). By contrast, the ECJ had to confine itself to considering whether there had been an infringement of Article 6(2) of the Habitats Directive.

[24] ibid., paras. 16–20. [25] ibid., para. 24. [26] ibid., para. 25.

The Court noted that whilst the Commission pursued no claim of infringement against Ireland in relation to the 10,000 hectares in State ownership and upon which grazing was very light, it was clear from the documents before it that other parts of the Owenduff-Nephin Beg Complex SPA had been seriously damaged. The ECJ expressly cited a conservation plan for the SPA, completed on 22 August 2000, by the heritage service of the Department of Arts, Heritage, Gaeltacht and the Islands. According to this plan some blanket bog and heath areas within the site were heavily eroded due to the excessive numbers of sheep. The ECJ also observed that in their correspondence with the Commission preceding the reasoned opinion, the Irish authorities had already recognized that this SPA was heavily stocked with sheep, which were penetrating into the uninhabited valleys and mountain slopes. Ireland had also acknowledged that damage caused by overgrazing was particularly severe on the slopes west of Lough Feeagh and that this had contributed to the decline in the numbers of Greenland white-fronted geese. Furthermore, it had recognized that it was necessary not only to take measures to stabilize the problem of overgrazing, but also to ensure recovery of damaged habitats.[27] Accordingly, the ECJ came to the conclusion that Ireland had failed to fulfil its obligations under Article 6(2) of the Habitats Directive.

ii. Habitats Directive

In Case C-324/01, *Commission* v. *Belgium*,[28] the Commission claimed that Belgium had failed to take all the measures necessary to ensure the full and proper transposition of Articles 1, 4(5), 5(4), 6, 7, 12, 13, 14, 15, 16(1), and 22(b) and (c) of the Habitats Directive. Belgium did not dispute the Commission's complaints regarding the Flemish Region. The ECJ held that since the parties had agreed that the measures in force at the end of the period laid down in the reasoned opinion did not ensure the full transposition of the provisions of the Directive, the Commission's application was well founded.[29] As regards the Brussels Capital Region, the Court considered three different claims. First, the failure to transpose the second sentence in the first subparagraph of Article 6(4) of the Directive. Article 6 defines the system for SACs and sites of Community importance. It reads:

1. For special areas of conservation, Member States shall establish the necessary conservation measures . . .
2. Member States shall take appropriate steps to avoid, in the special areas of conservation, the deterioration of natural habitats and the habitats of species . . .
3. Any plan or project not directly connected with or necessary to the management of the site but likely to have a significant effect thereon . . . shall be subject to appropriate assessment of its implications . . .

[27] ibid., paras. 28–31. [28] [ECR] 2002 I-11197. [29] ibid., para. 14.

4. If, in spite of a negative assessment of the implications for the site and in the absence of alternative solutions, a plan or project must nevertheless be carried out for imperative reasons of overriding public interest, including those of a social or economic nature, the Member State shall take all compensatory measures necessary to ensure that the overall coherence of Natura 2000 is protected. It shall inform the Commission of the compensatory measures adopted . . .

Belgium did not deny the Commission's claim that no provision had been adopted requiring the competent authorities to inform the Commission of the compensatory measures adopted for the Brussels Capital Region. However, it argued that the transposition of this provision could not be achieved by legislation. In its opinion, the provision had 'no normative scope' since it creates neither rights nor obligations for a general category of individuals. The ECJ rejected that claim by holding that each of the Member States to which a directive was addressed is obliged to adopt, within the framework of its national legal system, all the measures necessary to ensure that the directive was fully effective, in accordance with the objective it pursued. The purpose of the second sentence of the first subparagraph of Article 6(4) was to enable the Commission to consider whether the compensatory measures adopted were such as to ensure that the overall coherence of the Natura 2000 Network was protected and, depending on the circumstances, to draw the appropriate conclusions.[30] Therefore, in the absence of a provision in national law laying down adequate detailed rules concerning information on the compensatory measures adopted by this region, it was not possible to ensure that this provision had full effect and attained its objective. The ECJ concluded that 'uncertainty at the domestic level concerning the procedure to be followed in order to comply with the obligation to inform is likely to hinder compliance with that obligation and, consequently, the attainment of its objective'.[31]

The second claim concerned the failure to transpose Article 7 of the Directive, which reads:

Obligations arising under Article 6(2), (3) and (4) of this directive shall replace any obligations arising under the first sentence of Article 4(4) of Directive 79/409/EEC in respect of areas classified pursuant to Article 4(1) or similarly recognised under Article 4(2) thereof, as from the date of implementation of this Directive or the date of classification or recognition by a Member State under Directive 79/409/EEC, where the latter date is later.

Rather than deny the allegation, Belgium contended that there was no need to transpose this provision, as the Brussels Capital Region had not considered it necessary to implement Article 6 in national law. The ECJ dismissed this reasoning. It first recalled that Article 7 provided that the system for protecting SACs defined in Article 6(2), (3), and (4) of the Habitats Directive was to replace

[30] ibid., para. 20. [31] ibid., para. 21.

the system of protection of SPAs under Article 4(4) of the Birds Directive. However, in the absence of any national measure requiring the application to SPAs of the system of protection for SACs, the attainment of the objective of Article 7 could not be satisfactorily ensured. In order to ensure the full application of that provision in law and not only in fact, and to satisfy the requirement of legal certainty, the Member States had to provide a precise legal framework for the field in question.[32] Hence, the Commission's claim was well founded.

Finally, the Commission had alleged failure to comply with Article 22(c) of the Habitats Directive, which requires Member States to promote education and general information on the need to protect species of wild fauna and flora and to conserve their habitats and natural habitats. It claimed that the Brussels Capital Region had not notified to it any laws, regulations, or administrative provisions forming the basis for the implementation of this provision. In contrast, the Belgium stated that the Region had complied with this provision through various agreements financing nature education programmes. However, the ECJ observed that no measure likely to ensure the implementation of Article 22(c) had been notified to the Commission and, hence, upheld the claim.[33]

Case C-103/00, *Commission* v. *Greece*[34] concerned an Article 226 EC action against Greece, on 17 March 2000. The Commission alleged that Greece had failed to adopt measures to establish and implement an effective system of strict protection for the sea turtle (*Caretta caretta*) on the Greek island of Zakinthos, as required by Article 12(1)(b) and (d) of the Habitats Directive. Article 12(1) provides that Member States must take requisite measures to establish a system of strict protection for the animal species listed in Annex IV(a) in their natural range, including the sea turtle. Accordingly, they must prohibit: (i) all forms of deliberate capture or killing of specimens of those species in the wild; (ii) deliberate disturbance of these species, particularly during the periods of breeding, rearing, hibernation, and migration; (iii) deliberate destruction or taking of eggs from the wild; and (iv) deterioration or destruction of breeding sites or resting places. Those measures were in force as from 10 June 1994, the deadline for implementation of the Directive, and they are directly enforceable.

The situation of deterioration in the conservation conditions for the sea turtle on the island of Zakinthos had been criticized by some NGOs. The island had been proposed as a site of Community importance within the framework of the Habitats Directive for being a vital breeding region for the sea turtle.

In July 1998, the Commission requested information from Greece on protective measures for that species on the island, and sent officials to verify whether any such measures had been implemented. Several activities contrary to the Directive's aims were identified, including lack of supervision or notices on the beaches, illegal presence of pedalos and boats in the protected sea area, a

[32] ibid., paras. 26–7. [33] ibid., para. 33. [34] [2002] ECR I-1147.

significant number of beach umbrellas, deckchairs, and illegal buildings and works on various beaches. In the pre-litigation procedure, the Greek authorities had held that several measures had been implemented, such as port regulations, programmes for monitoring sea turtles, and public information and awareness campaigns. Nevertheless, the Commission concluded that by not having taken the measures to introduce an effective system of protection, Greece had failed to fulfil its obligations under Article 12(1)(b) and (d) of the Directive. The Greek authorities replied that a draft presidential decree on the creation of a marine park of Zakinthos had been submitted to the Council of State for finalization. Also, a committee had been established to draft a special presidential decree, of a general nature, containing financial provisions applicable to all the protected natural regions in Greece. Moreover, Greece notified the Commission of its intention to draft a third presidential decree on compensatory measures for the marine park of the island. Finally, it announced a series of measures including demolition of all illegal buildings on beaches, the establishment of a national land register, the prohibition of vehicle access to the beaches, the replacement of the lighting which disturbed the sea turtles, and the removal of deck-chairs and beach umbrellas. Nevertheless, the Commission concluded that Greece had still not adopted the necessary measures to introduce an effective system of protection for the sea turtle.

In June 1999, the Commission sent a reasoned opinion to Greece demanding compliance within two months from the date of its notification. Greece then informed the Commission that a budget for a public information programme and for the supervision, cleaning, and protection of the sand beaches had been approved for the summer of 1999, and that beach umbrellas had been removed or reduced. However, the Commission remained unconvinced and brought its action before the ECJ.

The key question under consideration in this case was whether the Greek measures were compatible with the protection requirements set out in the Directive, particularly in Article 12(1)(b) and (d). A Decree of 22 December 1999 had classified as a national marine and regional parks the islands and sea areas where the habitats of the sea turtles were located.[35] In addition, it indicated that nesting figures available for the sea turtle over the last fifteen years did not show that the number of nests had decreased. However, the ECJ found that the 1999 Decree had been approved after the expiry of the two-month time limit laid down in the Commission's reasoned opinion. Therefore, according to standing case law, the Court was not entitled to take it into account.

This conclusion made it unnecessary to examine whether the system of protection for the sea turtle provided for by the 1999 Decree met the Directive's

[35] Namely, the land and sea regions of the bay of Laganas and the Strofada islands, and the coastal areas of the communes of Zakinthos and Laganas.

requirements.[36] The ECJ held that it was undisputed that one of the bays located in the island was a vital breeding region for the turtle. It also recalled a report prepared by the Greek Council of State recommending the prohibition of the opening of new access routes to the beaches, and the creation of infrastructures such as kiosks, tents, or parking facilities.[37] The ECJ observed that Greece had not been able to show that the measures allegedly adopted before the expiry of the reasoned opinion's deadline constituted a system of strict protection for the sea turtle pursuant to Article 12(1)(b) and (d) of the Directive.[38] Therefore, it was apparent that Greece had failed to adopt a consistent legal framework within the prescribed time-limit that was capable of ensuring strict protection for the sea turtle against any deliberate disturbance during the breeding period and against any deterioration or destruction of its breeding sites. The fact that it did not appear that the number of nests of that species had decreased over the last fifteen years did not, of itself, call these findings into question.[39] This final remark must be considered in the light of Article 1(i) of the Habitats Directive, which reads:

> The conservation status will be taken as 'favourable' when:
> — population dynamics data on the species concerned indicate that it is maintaining itself on a long-term basis as a viable component of its natural habitats, and
> — the natural range of the species *is neither being reduced* nor is likely to be reduced for the foreseeable future, and
> — there is, and will probably continue to be, a sufficiently large habitat to maintain its populations on a long-term basis.[40]

It seems that Greece relied on this definition to contend that there was no infringement of Article 12, but the ECJ contested this, holding that no coherent legal framework had been adopted. Apart from the failure to adopt a consistent legal framework, the Commission also claimed that Greece had not adopted specific measures for the protection of the sea turtle, and in fact it had found the aforementioned list of activities carried out contrary to Article 12(1)(b). Although Greece had not disputed these allegations, nonetheless, the ECJ found it necessary to highlight the different dangers faced by sea turtles and the reasons that those activities were incompatible with Article 12(1)(b), and that they were not isolated occurrences.[41] The judgment in this case reflects the Court's strict position regarding the scope of the measures that must be adopted and the interpretation of the Directive's general prohibitions. This represents an important constraint for the Member States, since the degree of protection required by the Directive is rather high in the case of the species listed in Annex IV. The argument brought forward by Greece that the number of turtles had not decreased was also rejected since the Habitats Directive does not simply aim to maintain the status quo concerning species protection in Europe.

[36] Case C-103/00, n. 34 above, paras. 23–5.
[37] ibid., para. 28.
[38] ibid., para. 29.
[39] ibid., para. 31.
[40] Emphasis added.
[41] Case C-103/00, n. 34 above, para. 37.

iii. Animals Used for Experimental Purposes

Case C-152/00, *Commission* v. *France*[42] concerned the French transposition of Directive 86/609/EEC on the Protection of Animals Used for Experimental and other Scientific Purposes.[43] The Commission questioned the validity of the French provisions transposing Articles 4, 7, 11, 12, 18, and 22 of the Directive. France had notified three measures: (i) Decree No. 2001–464 of 29 May 2001, amending Decree No. 87–848, (ii) an Order of 20 June 2001 regarding good laboratory practices for veterinary medicines, and (iii) an Order of 14 March 2000 on good laboratory practices. However, the ECJ recalled settled case law and declared that whether a Member State had failed to fulfil its obligations is to be determined by reference to the situation in the Member State at the end of the period laid down in the Commission's reasoned opinion. Therefore, none of the national provisions could be taken into account by the Court in its consideration of the Commission's action.[44]

The first Commission complaint concerned the failure to transpose Article 4 of the Directive. This provision obliges Member States to ensure that experiments using animals considered as endangered under Appendix I of the Convention on International Trade in Endangered Species of Wild Fauna and Flora (CITES)[45] and Annex C.I. of its implementing Regulation (EEC) No. 3626/82,[46] are prohibited unless they are in conformity with the Regulation and the objects of the experiment are either research aimed at preservation of the species in question, or essential biomedical purposes where the species in question exceptionally proves to be the only one suitable for those purposes. France argued that it followed from the combined effect of several provisions of Decree No. 87–848 that, for experiments using endangered species covered by Article 4 of the Directive, as a condition for its granting, the licence application must identify an essential medical purpose for the experiment and verify the exclusive suitability of the particular endangered species. However, the ECJ took a different view in holding that it was sufficient to observe that such consequences did not follow 'at all' from the wording of the French provisions, and that mere administrative practices (which by their nature could be changed as and when the authorities pleased and which were not published widely enough) could not be regarded as a proper fulfilment of the obligation imposed on Member States.[47]

The Court also dismissed the French argument that protected species were only rarely bred in captivity in France, whereas the conditions relating to their

42 [2002] ECR I-6973.

43 [1986] OJ L358/1.

44 Case C-152/00, n. 42 above, para. 15.

45 Washington, DC (United States), 3 Mar. 1973; (1973) 12 *International Legal Materials* 5, 1085.

46 [1982] OJ L384/1. It was subsequently repealed and replaced by Reg. (EC) No. 338/97 (CITES Reg.), n. 3 above.

47 Case C-152/00, n. 42 above, para. 19.

importation from third countries, laid down by Articles 4 and 8 of the CITES Regulation[48] were sufficient to guarantee the result required by that provision. The ECJ first held that it was unnecessary to rule on the scope of Articles 4 and 8 of the CITES Regulation, as it sufficed to observe that those provisions concerned the import of, and trade in, but not experiments on, protected species. With regard to the fact that the protected species were only rarely bred in captivity in France, it indicated that, since failure to comply with an obligation imposed by a rule of Community law was in itself sufficient to constitute a breach, the fact that such a failure had had no adverse effects was irrelevant.[49] Therefore, the Commission's complaint was fully upheld.

As regards the incorrect transposition of Article 7(3) of the Directive, the Commission claimed that the French legislation contained no provisions prescribing the taking into account of the criteria which were to govern the choice of experiments, species, and animals, listed in Article 7(3) of the Directive. In contrast, France argued that consideration of a licence application for experiments under Article 5 of Decree No. 87–848 allowed for verification of the compliance with the conditions of Article 7(3) of the Directive. However, the ECJ held that, assuming that this was the case, such a verification rested on a mere administrative practice, and was insufficient to constitute proper transposition.[50] As regards the general prohibition to carry out experiments on animals taken from the wild, unless experiments on other animals were not sufficient, the ECJ observed that the French rules were not such as to ensure the proper transposition of the second subparagraph of Article 7(3) of the Directive. Those rules concerned only certain animal species living in the wild and did not relate to their capture or transport unless experiments on such species were envisaged. Furthermore, the possible taking into consideration of the requirements prescribed in Article 7(3), if that was in fact what happened, was not prescribed by a binding provision but came about as a result 'of a mere administrative practice'.[51]

In its third complaint the Commission claimed that, in violation of Article 11 of the Directive, French legislation did not require prior verification of the conditions for the setting free of animals used for experiments. France relied upon Article 2 of Decree No. 87–848, stating that 'the observation of animals under conditions that do not cause them any suffering' should not be regarded as experiments. The ECJ first defined the scope of Article 11. By specifying that the setting free of an animal could be allowed where necessary for the legitimate purposes of the experiment, that provision showed that the setting free of an animal used for an experiment within the meaning of the Directive could only be allowed insofar as it formed an integral part of the experiment, that is, when further observations were still to be made. Therefore, contrary to the

[48] n. 3 above.
[49] Case C-152/00, n. 42 above, para. 21.
[50] ibid., para. 25.
[51] ibid., paras. 26–7.

Commission's submission, Article 11 was in no way intended to authorize an animal to be set free after the conclusion of the experiment.[52] However, contrary to the French submission, the ECJ held that there was nothing to suggest that this provision contemplated the setting free of animals for the purposes of experiments in progress only insofar as animals taken from their natural environment were concerned.[53] The Commission was also held to be wrong in maintaining that Article 11 obliged Member States to adopt provisions enabling a designated authority, at the request of researchers, to authorize animals used for an experiment to be set free when necessary for the legitimate purposes of the experiment and upon satisfaction of the other conditions.[54] Article 11 showed that, where its strict conditions were satisfied, the authority had discretion (but no obligation) to grant a licence to set animals free. In the light of Article 24 of the Directive, Member States were free to apply or adopt stricter measures to ensure the protection of animals used for experimental purposes or to control or restrict the use of animals for certain experiments. It followed from the latter provision that Member States were, in particular, entitled to prohibit any setting free of animals used in an experiment, or even to allow this, under the conditions laid down by Article 11, only insofar as it concerned animals taken from the wild.[55] Therefore, the ECJ held that France had not fulfilled its obligations. The national provisions did not ensure that the setting free, in the sense contemplated in Article 11 of the Directive, was possible only under the conditions specified by that provision. Article 2(b) of Decree No. 87–848, a provision relating to the observation of animals put in conditions which involved no suffering, was completely irrelevant to the decision, since Article 11 of the Directive only covered the setting free of animals used for an experiment, that is, use for scientific purposes capable of causing pain, suffering, distress, or lasting harm to the animal. Secondly, France had not substantiated its assertion that the scientific purposes for which experiments on animals were allowed by the Decree were such as to exclude experiments necessitating animals to be set free. The fact that the capture and transport of certain protected species as well as game taken from the wild were subject to a regime of prior authorization was no more likely to ensure the correct implementation of Article 11 of the Directive.[56]

The ECJ upheld the Commission's allegation regarding the failure to transpose Article 12(2) of the Directive, since France had not disputed that this provision had not been transposed into national law.[57]

As regards the incomplete transposition of Article 18(1) and (3) of the Directive, concerning the marking of cats, dogs, and non-human primates in breeding, supplying, or user establishments within the meaning of the Directive, France relied on several provisions to argue that the obligations set out in the Directive were correctly transposed. However, the ECJ held that those various

[52] ibid., para. 38. [53] ibid., para. 39. [54] ibid., para. 40.
[55] ibid., para. 41. [56] ibid., paras. 43–6. [57] ibid., para. 48.

measures did not provide that the individual marking had to take place before weaning and in the least painful manner possible, as required by Article 18(1) of the Directive.[58]

The final complaint concerned Article 22(1) of the Directive regarding the recognition by the Member States of the validity of data generated by animal experiments carried out in the territory of another Member State for one of the purposes listed in Article 3 of the Directive. France argued, *inter alia*, that this provision imposed on Member States merely an obligation to use their best endeavours, evidenced by the words 'as far as possible' in its paragraph 1. The ECJ indicated that it was clear from settled case law that Article 22 required the adoption of appropriate transposition measures. However, on the expiry of the period laid down in the reasoned opinion, France had not adopted any measure aimed at giving effect to Article 22(1) of the Directive.[59] Hence, the Commission's complaint was also upheld.

D. Policy Documents

i. Resolutions, Reports, and Policy Documents on Nature Conservation

In March 2002, the Commission issued a Report on the Application of Directive 79/409/EEC on the Conservation of Wild Birds—Update for 1996–1998, Based on Information Supplied by the Member States on the Application of National Measures Adopted Pursuant to the Directive.[60] According to the report, almost 25 per cent of species regularly observed in Europe underwent 'a substantial decline in numbers over the last 20 years'. The decline in the case of most diminishing bird populations was the result of changes in land use and management techniques. The intensification of agriculture was the main (or at least one) contributing factor for 42 per cent of declining species. Another important factor was habitats destruction and damaging, especially in wetlands. Hunting, capture, killing, and sale sometimes had an adverse effect on those threatened species, but this was usually of a secondary nature.

The establishment of the network of Special Protection Areas (SPAs) by Member States during the three-year period of the report was as follows:

- *Austria*: 58 SPAs were designated, totalling 11,333 kilometres.
- *Belgium*: No new areas were designated, the protected surface area was not extended.
- *Denmark*: No new areas were designated, the protected surface area was not extended. However, numerous measures were taken to avoid the deterioration of habitats and to prevent significant disturbance. At national level, nature restoration projects were initiated and partially

[58] ibid., para. 53. [59] ibid., para. 59.
[60] COM(2002)146, 25 Mar. 2002.

completed in SPAs at an estimated cost of DKR 90 million, some of which came from LIFE funds. A new order of November 1998 specified for the competent authorities that impact studies concerning projects liable to affect an SPA had to contain an assessment of their impact on protected bird species.

— *Finland*: 439 SPAs were designated. Those areas comprised 2 national parks and 311 protection areas on private land. By the end of 1998, the protected network covered more than 29,311 kilometres, or 8 per cent of the national territory.

— *France*: 10 new SPAs were designated, totalling 807 kilometres. By the end of 1998, 109 SPAs had been designated with a total surface area of 7,877 kilometres. In addition, 9 nature reserves covering a total surface area of 13,000 hectares were created in order to conserve bird habitats.

— *Germany*: 65 new SPAs were designated, totalling 5,584 kilometres. By the end of 1998, 551 SPAs had been designated, with a total surface area of over 14,000 kilometres. Any planned project resulting in major changes within SPAs required prior approval by the competent authorities.

— *Greece*: 26 new SPAs were designated, totalling 3,049 kilometres. By the end of 1998, 52 SPAs had been designated, with a total surface area of 4,965 kilometres.

— *Ireland*: 25 new SPAs were designated, totalling 587 kilometres. By the end of 1998, 100 SPAs had been designated with a total surface area of 2,165 kilometres.

— *Italy*: 121 new SPAs were designated, totalling 6,397 kilometres. By the end of 1998, 201 SPAs had had been designated with a total surface area of 9,561 kilometres.

— *Luxembourg*: 7 new SPAs were designated, totalling 34 kilometres. By the end of 1998, 13 SPAs had been designated with a total surface area of 160 kilometres.

— *The Netherlands*: 7 new SPAs were designated, totalling 233 kilometres. By the end of 1998, 30 SPAs had been designated with a total surface area of 3,509 kilometres.

— *Portugal*: No new areas were designated, the protected surface area was not extended.

— *Spain*: 21 new SPAs were designated, totalling 7,853 kilometres. By the end of 1998, 170 SPAs had been designated with a total surface area of 33,191 kilometres.

— *Sweden*: 302 SPAs were designated. By the end of 1998, the protected network covered more than 21,360 kilometres, or 5 per cent of the national territory.

— *United Kingdom*: 74 new SPAs were designated. By the end of 1998, 187 SPAs had been designated with a total surface area of over 7,660 kilometres, forming an extension of 4,000 kilometres compared to the end of the previous reporting period (1993–5).

In sum, during this reporting period (1996–8), a total of 1,155 new SPAs were designated, extending the protected surface area by nearly 90,548 kilometres (including 62,004 kilometres for the three new Member States). Hence, the protected surface area doubled as compared to the previous reporting period. By 31 December 1998, there were 2,403 SPAs, with a combined surface area of 162,450 kilometres, or approximately 7 per cent of the entire EU territory.

During the reporting period, a major study of Important Bird Areas (IBAs) in Europe was carried out by BirdLife International. The study identified IBAs on the basis of ornithological criteria, and covered the entire continent of Europe. Results were published in 2000. A total of 3,619 IBAs were identified (1,997 sites of global importance, 1,176 sites of continental importance, and 446 sites of importance for the EU), of which 2,342 were situated in the EU. An evaluation of the degree of designation achieved in the EU (situation of September 1999) indicated that while 54 per cent of the IBAs identified as being important (1,260 sites) were included, in whole or in part, in no less than 1,375 SPAs designated by the fifteen Member States, there were 1,082 SPAs (46 per cent) which had still not been designated as SPAs, and only four Member States had designated over 75 per cent of their IBAs.

The Report acknowledged that while progress had been made since the end of the reporting period, by December 2001, when the report was completed, there were still 'major shortcomings in several Member States'.

Most Member States did not make major changes to the general system of protection for all species of birds covered under Article 5 of the Birds Directive. The exceptions were Belgium, Finland, the Netherlands, and Sweden. The Commission Report indicated that the required conditions of Article 6 regarding the authorization of marketing activities in respect of the species mentioned in Annex III, Part 2 to the Birds Directive, were met in all of the Member States and that there had been no major amendment of the law during the reporting period. As regards Article 7, concerning exploitation, hunting, and capture, no major changes were introduced in Austria, Belgium, Finland, Germany, Luxembourg, Sweden, and the United Kingdom (UK). Changes were made in Denmark, France, Greece, Ireland, Italy, Portugal, and Spain. As regards Article 8, which concerns forbidden hunting methods, the Commission indicated that the Member States had adopted the necessary measures 'often ahead of the Directive's entry into force'. Major derogations from the system of protection of Article 9 of the Directive were compiled in the Report.

It also referred to the research programmes adopted and to projects focusing on actions identified as the most urgent for protected species. Moreover, it contained information on the introduction of bird species not naturally occurring in the territory of the Member States.

On 9 May 2002, the Environment Ministers adopted the so-called El Teide Declaration 'Natura 2000: A partnership for Nature'. In this Declaration they recognized the commitment of the European Heads of State in the Gothenburg Summit conclusions to take positive action to halt the decline of European biodiversity, and the priority given to this in the Sixth Environmental Action Programme. They also recognized the outstanding importance of Natura 2000 as a network of natural and semi-natural areas dedicated to ensure the conservation of Europe's most valuable habitats and wildlife. It was also noted that the success of Natura 2000 was to require the support of European citizens, especially of local people and landowners, and their participation in the decisions on the implementation of the conservation and management of the areas involved. In the Declaration, the Member States committed themselves to:

(i) finalize in the shortest delays the full implementation of the Natura 2000 Network;
(ii) promote awareness and understanding of Natura 2000;
(iii) promote the development of partnerships involving the broad range of stakeholders in the conservation and management of Natura 2000 sites;
(iv) support the sharing of experience and good practice in managing the Natura 2000 Network;
(v) support the sustainable use and management of Natura 2000 areas such as educational and recreation purposes; and
(vi) ensure that the needs of Natura 2000 were effectively implemented in other Community policies.

Finally, the Member States recognized that those objectives required targeted resources. During an Informal Ministerial Meeting in Brussels on 12 July 2002, all thirteen EU candidate countries (Bulgaria, Cyprus, Czech Republic, Estonia, Hungary, Latvia, Lithuania, Malta, Poland, Romania, Slovakia, Slovenia, and Turkey) signed the El Teide Declaration, committing themselves to tackling the problem of biodiversity loss in their respective countries.

In October 2002, the Commission issued the Communication Towards a Strategy to Protect and Conserve the Marine Environment.[61] The sixth Environment Action Programme required the development of a strategy for the protection and conservation of the marine environment with the overall aim to promote sustainable use of the seas and conserve marine ecosystems, since the marine environment is subject to a variety of threats. These threats include loss or degradation of biodiversity and changes in its structure, loss of habitats, contamination by dangerous substances and nutrients, and possible future effects of climate change. As regards the loss of biodiversity and the destruction of habitats,

[61] COM(2002)539, 2 Oct. 2002.

the Communication set out three objectives: (i) to halt biodiversity decline by 2010; (ii) to ensure a sustainable use of biodiversity through the protection and conservation of natural habitats and of wild fauna and flora in the first instance in the European seas, *inter alia*, by restoring marine ecosystems and re-establishing certain trophic levels affected by human activities, and by preventing the human-induced introduction of new non-indigenous species, genetically modified organisms (GMOs), and disease organisms; and (iii) in relation to the reform of the Common Fisheries Policy, a change in fisheries management to reverse the decline in stocks and ensure sustainable fisheries and a healthy ecosystem, both in the EU and globally.

Since the Communication acknowledged that these objectives are often of a political and aspirational nature rather than specific, measurable, or time-related, their realization could involve a range of different measures. As regards biodiversity and habitats conservation, the communication included four actions:

(1) the development of an ecosystem-based approach, including ecosystem benchmarks and targets to ensure conservation and sustainable use of biodiversity;

(2) the implementation of the Habitats and Birds Directives in the marine environment including Exclusive Economic Zones (EEZs). For the attainment of this action the Commission is to develop, by 2005, together with the regional marine conventions, a programme aimed at enhancing the protection of species and habitats in European waters;

(3) the adjustment of the fishing effort and capacity in line with long-term management plans to secure sustainable harvest of fish resources and propose measures to reduce discards, incidental by-catches, and impact on habitats;

(4) the preparation, in the International Maritime Organization (IMO) framework, of an international convention for the control and management of ships' ballast water and sediments. In 2005–6, regional ballast-water management plans should be developed, and in 2004–5 it should be reviewed whether (and if so, to what extent) a complementary initiative for controlling the introduction of new non-indigenous species by ships ballast water would be necessary.

E. International Cooperation

In March 2002, the Council drew up its conclusions in preparation for the Sixth Conference of the Parties to the Convention on Biological Diversity, held in The Hague (the Netherlands) from 7 to 19 April 2002.[62] The Council stressed the importance of a strategic plan both to support implementation of the

[62] *Bulletin Quotidien Europe*, 3–2002, point 1.4.22.

Convention on Biological Diversity and to provide input from the convention to the World Summit on Sustainable Development in Johannesburg (South Africa) in September 2002. It emphasized the need for adoption of a multi-year programme of work for the convention to guide and monitor implementation of the strategic plan. On access and benefit-sharing as related to genetic resources, the Council believed that transactions involving genetic resources had to be based on material transfer agreements and that harmonization of these agreements was desirable. On invasive alien species, the Council recognized that the introduction of such species was one of the main recorded causes of biodiversity loss and therefore required monitoring at national and international level. In cases of intentional introduction of such species, the burden of proof for the safety of ecosystems, habitats, or species had to be with the person or institution responsible for introducing them. In cases of unintentional introduction, appropriate mechanisms had to be established securing their safety. On forest biological diversity, the Council considered that the sixth conference of the parties should adopt a revised, expanded work programme. It also reaffirmed the importance of forest biological diversity, given the crucial role which forests play in conserving the world's biological diversity.

In June 2002, the Council approved certain conclusions regarding the Sixth Conference of the Parties to the Convention on Biological Diversity. The Council took stock of ten years of the 'Natura 2000' project covering the internal dimension of biodiversity and stressed the common European responsibility for protecting the common natural heritage and biodiversity. It emphasized the need for designation of SPAs for birds, the participation of all stakeholders, particularly of the rural community, raising public awareness, and effective administrative instruments to protect the designated sites and to allow the adoption of appropriate management measures and monitoring processes. It also welcomed the outcome of the Sixth Conference of the Parties, including the commitment to reverse the alarming rate of biodiversity loss at all levels by 2010, the work programme on forest biological diversity, the guidelines on access to genetic resources, and the guiding principles for invasive alien species.[63]

The Community participated in the Twelfth Meeting of the Conference of the Parties to the Convention on International Trade in Endangered Species of Wild Fauna and Flora (CITES),[64] held in Santiago (Chile) from 3 to 15 November 2002.[65] The Conference achieved progress on several matters. It first made a call for the Parties which had not yet done so to ratify the Gabarone amendment so that the EC could become a Party in its own right. Also, a 6 per cent increase in contributions to the Convention's budget was agreed. A decision was adopted on big-leaf mahogany (*Swietenia macrophylla*) in order to allow greater cooperation

[63] *Bulletin Quotidien Europe*, 6–2002, point 1.4.37.

[64] Washington, DC (United States), 3 Mar. 1973; (1973) 12 *International Legal Materials* 5, 1085.

[65] *Bulletin Quotidien Europe*, 11–2002, point 1.4.43.

between exporting and importing countries to ensure that only legally and sustainably harvested timber was traded. Similarly, a decision was taken regarding the monkey puzzle (*Araucaria araucana*) and tree of life *(Guaiacum sanctum)* timber. Other decisions concerned the basking shark (*Cetorhinus maximus*), whale shark (*Rhincodon typus*), and seahorses (*Hippocampus*) to remedy the underprotection of those species at international level. The Conference rejected a proposal submitted by Japan to downlist protection of the Minke whales (*Balaenoptera acutorostrata*) and Bryde's whales (*Balaenoptera edeni*). As regards elephants, the Conference decided to postpone, until May 2004, the imposition of strict conditions on a one-off sale of ivory from existing legal stocks in South Africa, Botswana, and Namibia. It also adopted a decision to improve enforcement of anti-poaching measures and control of illegal trade in ivory.

F. Miscellaneous

i. Written Questions by Members of the European Parliament

In 2002, Members of the European Parliament (MEPs) submitted several questions regarding the interpretation, application, and enforcement of the Birds and Habitats Directives. In its answer to Written Question E-2055/01,[66] the Commission indicated that hunting was a legitimate activity and, in many cases, if properly managed under strict conditions, not incompatible with maintaining species of birds in a good state of conservation. It identified site management plans involving the parties concerned as the most appropriate framework for defining such conditions on a case-by-case basis. In addition, in the same answer the Commission provided certain guidelines regarding the concept of significant disturbance. It indicated that as far as sites protected under the Habitats Directive were concerned, game hunting was 'highly unlikely to cause a problem', except for a small number of species. Conditions governing the concepts of disturbances were to be assessed in the light of the general state of conservation of the species or habitats concerned and in the light of local conditions. At a particular site, disturbances were generally appraised on a case-by-case analysis. The Commission considered that a species was disturbed when the data relating to the population dynamic of that site showed that, compared with the initial situation, the species in question could no longer constitute a viable element of the site concerned. That appraisal was to be carried out in accordance with the site's contribution to the coherence of the Natura 2000 Network.

In its answer to Written Question E-1278/02,[67] the Commission indicated that it was for the Member States to decide on the most appropriate measures for

[66] Jean-Louis Bernié, 'Natura 2000 Network-Application of Article 6(2) of Habitats Directive—Concept of Significant Disturbance' [2002] OJ C40E/172.

[67] Toine Manders, 'Evaluation of Implementation of Directives on Wild Birds and Habitats' [2002] OJ C277E/177.

the management of conservation areas, while ensuring their nature conservation values. It noted that 'any presumption of a complete ban on tourism in designated areas cannot be justified on the basis of Community Directives'. The Commission did not believe, with respect to the principle of subsidiarity, that it was appropriate to call for an evaluation of the implementation of the Birds and Habitats Directives in the Netherlands to identify undesirable side-effects, since it had no competence to limit the power of Member States to decide on management measures for Natura 2000.

In its answer to Written Question P-2680/01,[68] the Commission acknowledged that, to date, none of the Member States had met all its obligations under the Habitats Directive, whilst they had made significant progress in proposing sites pursuant to Article 4 thereof. In response to Written Question P-2722/01,[69] the Commission declared that any substantial withdrawal of sites proposed by Member States for the Natura 2000 Network had to be justified in terms both of the eligibility of those sites according to the scientific criteria of Annex III to the Habitats Directive, and of an analysis of the representation of the habitat types and habitats of species of Community interest found in the sites. It noted that 'should such withdrawal result in any habitat types or habitats of a species of Community interest being insufficiently represented, the Member State will have to propose new sites to make good the shortfalls revealed at the biogeographical seminars'.

The accession of new Member States and the application of the Habitats Directive were also considered by MEPS. In its answer to Written Question E-1299/01,[70] the Commission pointed out that, prior to accession, candidate countries were under no obligation to identify protected areas under Community legislation. However, it strongly recommended the candidates to respect the requirements of Community (nature protection) law. In response to Written Question E-1032/02,[71] the Commission indicated that as long as candidate countries had not yet prepared their lists of sites of Community importance for the Natura 2000 Network, the following types of sites were to be regarded as environmentally sensitive areas in the field of nature protection: (i) sites listed in the latest inventory on Important Bird Areas (IBA) for candidate countries and, if available, equivalent more detailed scientific inventories endorsed by national authorities; (ii) wetlands of international importance designated under the Convention on Wetlands of International Importance especially as Waterfowl Habitat (Ramsar Convention),[72] or qualifying for such protection; (iii) areas to

[68] Hans-Gert Poettering, 'Implementation of the Habitats Directive' [2002] OJ C81E/201.

[69] Yves Butel, 'Natura 2000—Habitats Directive—France—Rescission by Court Decision of the Forwarding of Lists of Areas in France—Impact on Biogegraphical Seminars' [2002] OJ C81E/204.

[70] Erik Meijer, 'Nature Conservation and Environmental Protection in Poland during the Run-Up to its Accession to the European Union' [2002] OJ C40E/31.

[71] Elizabeth Lynne, 'Destruction of Valuable Wildlife Habitats across Eastern and Central Europe as a Result of the Development of Transport Infrastructure' [2002] OJ C309E/75.

[72] Ramsar (Iran), 2 Feb. 1971 (entered into force 21 Dec. 1975) (1972) 11 *International Legal Materials* 5, 963.

which the Convention on the Conservation of European Wildlife and Natural Habitats (Bern Convention)[73] applied, in particular sites meeting the criteria of the Emerald Network; and (iv) areas protected under national nature conservation legislation. In cases where Community pre-accession funding for large infrastructure developments was concerned, similar standards to those set by Community environmental legislation had to be applied before any Community funding could be granted to the candidate countries.

ii. Monitoring of the Application of Community Law

In February 2002, the Commission sent a reasoned opinion to Spain for non-compliance with Directive 86/609/EEC.[74] In March 2002, the Commission adopted several decisions against eight Member States. A reasoned opinion was sent to France concerning inadequate protection of the important bird site Basses Corbières, since remedial measures taken, following a judgment of the ECJ in Case C-374/98,[75] were still inadequate.[76] In addition, the Commission sent a further reasoned opinion concerning grassland habitats in the Vosges Mountains due to the development of new vineyards threatening the habitats. Portugal also received a reasoned opinion following an investigation into a complaint about the damage done to a bird site at the Ria de Aveiro, an SPA under the Birds Directive, by a 4-kilometre-long dyke.[77] A letter of formal notice was addressed to Italy for its failure to amend its legislation concerning wild birds following the judgment in Case C-159/99.[78] The ECJ had ruled that Italy had permitted the capture and keeping in captivity of three species of wild birds, *Passer italiae, Passer montanus*, and *Sturnus vulgaris*, contrary to the provisions of the Birds Directive.[79] A futher letter of formal notice was sent to Ireland for its failure to comply with the judgment in Case C-67/99 concerning the designation of protected sites.[80] The ECJ had ruled that Ireland had failed to send the Commission the complete list of proposed protected sites required under the Habitats Directive by the June 1995 deadline. Ireland had considerably increased its list of sites compared to the date on which the ECJ based its judgment (February 1998). However, according to the Commission, there were still significant omissions from the list in the area of raised bogs, salmon rivers, and offshore cold-water coral reefs.[81] A reasoned opinion was sent to Spain because of an irrigation project threatening 12 per cent of the surface area of an SPA in the province of Zamora in Castilla y Leon.[82] Luxembourg also received a reasoned opinion due,

73 Bern (Switzerland), 19 Sept. 1979 (entered into force 1 June 1982).
74 n. 43 above. Commission Press Release IP/02/294.
75 Case C-374/98, *Commission* v. *France* [2000] ECR I-10799.
76 Commission Press Release IP/02/413. 77 ibid.
78 Case C-159/1999, *Commission* v. *Italy* [2001] ECR I-4007.
79 Commission Press Release IP/02/413.
80 Case C-67/99, *Commission* v. *Ireland* [2001] ECR I-5757.
81 Commission Press Release IP/02/413. 82 ibid.

first, to its failure to designate a number of bird sites as SPAs as required under the Birds Directive and, secondly, to ensure that designated SPAs benefited from a legal regime providing adequate protection.[83]

The Commission decided to refer Germany to the ECJ because aspects of German federal and state hunting legislation contravened the Birds Directive. Both federal and state regulations allowed the hunting of certain species during periods of migration and reproduction, contrary to the Directive.[84] An action was also brought against Austria because a golf course extension had caused damage to habitats of the globally endangered corncrake, *Crex crex*, in the Enns Valley. In the Commission's view, the government of the state of Styria had not, when approving the extension, taken sufficient account of the nature impact assessment which it had carried out in accordance with the Habitats Directive.[85]

In April 2002, the Commission sent a letter of formal notice to Ireland demanding compliance with the 2001 judgment in Case C-354/1999,[86] concerning Directive 86/609/EEC.[87] As no response was received following this letter, the Commission decided to initiate Article 228 EC infringement proceedings.

In July 2002, the Commission adopted several decisions against ten Member States for non-implementation of the Birds and Habitats Directives.[88] The Commission decided to send a reasoned opinion to France, under Article 228 of the Treaty, for non-compliance with an ECJ ruling in Case C-96/98,[89] regarding the failure to fully designate and protect the Marais Poitevin wetland as an SPA. Although it acknowledged that France had made some progress towards meeting the ruling, shortcomings still remained since not all the habitats that were important for birds had been designated, and there was a lack of information on certain measures, including those required to reverse previous cases of serious habitat damage. The Commission decided to bring an action before the ECJ against Finland concerning official approval of spring hunting of waterfowl, contravening the prohibition in the Birds Directive on hunting during the breeding and rearing seasons. It also sent a reasoned opinion to Finland on hunting, stating that the Finnish practice of granting licences for the hunting of wolf, brown bear, and lynx did not respect the conditions set out in the Habitats Directive. Licences were regularly granted without a link to individuals causing serious damage and in spite of alternative solutions being available. A further reasoned opinion was sent for failing to properly apply safeguards required by the Habitats Directive to a power-line project affecting important natural sites.

[83] ibid. [84] ibid. [85] ibid.

[86] Case C-354/1999, *Commission* v. *Ireland* [2001] ECR I-7657.

[87] Commission Press Release IP/02/294.

[88] Commission Press Release IP/02/1060.

[89] Case 96/98, *Commission* v. *France* [1999] ECR I-8531.

An action was brought before the ECJ against Luxembourg concerning gaps in its network of SPAs and weaknesses in its legislation for protecting such areas. A (limited) number of SPAs still needed to be designated, and Luxembourg should develop an adequate legal protection regime for all designated areas. A reasoned opinion was sent to Italy concerning the approval of a development plan for tourism and sport centres, holiday villages, and hotel complexes in the municipality of L'Aquila. The Commission considered that this plan could affect the designated SPA in the Parco Nazionale Gran Sasso Monti della Laga, as well as 22 sites nominated for protection under the Habitats Directive within the area. No proper environmental impact assessment (EIA) had been carried out or considered before the plan was approved. The UK received a reasoned opinion for allowing environmentally damaging dredge-fishing operations to take place in Carmarthen Bay without having carried out a prior EIA. According to the Commission, that site was also inadequately designated under the Birds Directive, as no SPA had been declared for the common scoter. Portugal received a reasoned opinion due to its failure to fully designate Moura/Mourão/Barrancos as an SPA, and because it had approved the siting of a paper production plant in the area in spite of the negative effects on wild birds and their habitats. Sweden received a reasoned opinion because the list of sites it had nominated as part of the Natura 2000 Network under the Habitats Directive was inadequate. Finally, the Commission decided to forward a letter of formal notice to France, Italy, Luxembourg, the Netherlands, and Spain, for failing to send their first general report on the implementation of the Habitats Directive (1994–2000), which was due by September 2001.

In October 2002, the Commission decided to refer Austria to the ECJ for allowing the killing of birds of prey in the State of Lower Austria, breaching the hunting provisions of the Birds Directive.[90] Lower Austria granted exemptions for the killing of birds of prey alleging that such killing was needed to protect smaller wild birds and animals such as the pheasant and the grey partridge. However, the Commission questioned the use of that justification to allow the killing of natural predators in high numbers.

In December 2002, the Commission sent a reasoned opinion to France for failing to designate and protect an important bird site in the Department of Loire-Atlantique under the Birds Directive.[91] The Commission also announced its intention to refer the Netherlands to the ECJ due to shortcomings in Dutch legislation for implementing the Habitats Directive. It considered that the legislation, first, did not provide adequate safeguards for sites under the Natura 2000 Network, secondly, failed to adequately provide for the monitoring of habitats and species, and finally, omitted measures for certain plant species protected under the Directive. Two reasoned opinions were addressed to Germany. The first concerned a project to construct a wind farm in Lower Saxony at

[90] Commission Press Release IP/02/1564.

[91] Commission Press Release IP/02/1923.

a site identified as being important for the conservation of wild birds. The second reasoned opinion was issued due to failure to nominate two important areas in Bavaria as proposed Natura 2000 sites. This case also concerned Germany's failure to apply adequate safeguards to protect those sites in relation to a motorway.

The Commission began proceedings under Article 228 EC against Greece for failure to comply with the judgment in Case C-103/00.[92] Greece had been condemned for failing to adopt and apply adequate measures to protect the breeding and resting places of the rare Mediterranean sea turtle, *Caretta caretta*, on the island of Zakynthos. In the Commission's view, the situation remained unsatisfactory. A reasoned opinion was also sent to Greece for designating an insufficient number of SPAs, and for failing to properly protect the lagoon of Messolonghi-Aitolikon, a wetland internationally recognized as an important habitat for wild birds.

The Commission decided to send a reasoned opinion to Ireland for failing to properly safeguard an SPA in the Boyne Estuary. The area had suffered from illegal waste disposal operations. Furthermore, adequate compensatory measures had not been taken to make up for a temporary loss of mudflats, which were being used as a site for waste storage. Finally, Italy received a reasoned opinion for approving a ski-run and ski-lift at two sites in the Abruzzo region protected under the Habitats Directive. In the Commission's opinion the project would destroy certain priority habitats and interfere with breeding and resting places of wolf, bear, and chamois. It also considered that the project was inconsistent with the objectives of EC nature conservation funding in the area.

[92] Case C-103/00, *Commission* v. *Greece* [2002] ECR I-1147.

IV. Waste

*Geert van Calster**

A. Legislation Adopted

i. Waste Electrical and Electronic Equipment and Restrictions of the Use of Hazardous Substances in Electrical and Electronic Equipment

According to expectations,[1] conciliation proceedings between the European Parliament (EP) and Council were required for the adoption of Directive 2002/96/EC on Waste Electrical and Electronic Equipment (WEEE Directive)[2] and Directive 2002/95/EC on the Restriction of the Use of Certain Hazardous Substances in Electrical and Electronic Equipment (RoHS Directive).[3] The Directives oblige Member States to set up collection points and collection systems for discarded material, prior to 2005. Consumers will be able to deposit their Waste Electrical and Electronic Equipment (WEEE) at these points, free of charge. The EP had wanted to include a provision which would have obliged Member States to ensure that per inhabitant, at least 6 kilograms of discarded material would have to be collected, annually. However, the Council opposed this, and eventually a compromise was struck at a target of 4 kilograms by the end of 2006.

With respect to the waste collected from households, the producers themselves will be responsible for financing collection and disposal. Consequently, any fee which currently is raised from the consumer to finance the regime will have to be phased out. This includes, for instance, the current fee in the Flemish Region, known as 'Recupel'. Another sticking point was the question as to whether producers should be individually responsible for financing the collection and disposal of their own products, or whether this would be organized as a collective responsibility.[4] Industry split between supporting both options, with a strong argument made in favour of the former, in that allegedly only individual responsibility is likely to encourage innovative, environmentally friendly design. Ultimately, the WEEE Directive withheld individual responsibility, which the EP most certainly can count as a victory. For goods marketed prior to 2005, producers often cannot ascertain which goods should be counted as 'theirs', usually simply because the brand name is not clearly indicated. A pro rata system will operate for such products, with manufacturers active at the time having to bear the costs. So as to ensure that recycling is encouraged, the WEEE Directive

* Associate Professor, Institute of Energy and Environmental Law (IMER), Collegium Falconis, K.U. Leuven; Member of the Brussels Bar, DLA Caestecker, Brussels (Belgium).

[1] See e.g. G. van Calster, 'Waste' (2003) 3 *Yearbook of European Environmental Law*, 441–2.

[2] [2002] OJ L37/24.

[3] [2002] OJ L37/19.

[4] See van Calster, n. 1 above.

includes a provision to discourage the use of technical means which hamper recycling, such as ink cartridges that cannot be refilled. With respect to the RoHS Directive, the bone of contention was the time at which the prohibition on the use of the substances concerned ought to kick in. The compromise reached effectively blocks the use of substances such as lead, cadmium, mercury, and hexavalent chromium in electrical appliances, as of 1 July 2006.

ii. Waste Statistics

The new Regulation (EC) No. 2150/2002 on Waste Statistics (Waste Statistics Regulation)[5] establishes a very extensive regime for waste statistics, building on the Commission insistence that proper statistical information is paramount to achieve the most effective waste regulation. It is noteworthy that the regime may be extensive, but nevertheless was reduced by almost half, compared with the original proposal.[6] The Regulation, which entered into force at the end of December 2002, obliges Member States to collect elaborate data as of 2004. A pan-European report, which the Commission will compile on the basis of the national data submitted to it, will be compiled for the first time early in 2008. As noted, the Regulation, its direct applicability, and the sheer size of the reporting duties, illustrate the importance which the Commission attaches to reporting duties in the waste sector.

iii. End-of-Life Vehicles

By Decision 2002/525/EC amending Annex II of Directive 2000/53/EC on End-of-Life Vehicles,[7] the Commission has amended Directive 2000/53/EC on End-of-Life Vehicles (ELV Directive).[8] Under the Directive, the Commission is required to evaluate certain hazardous substances prohibited pursuant to Article 4(2)(a). The Commission concluded that certain materials and components containing lead, mercury, cadmium, or hexavalent chromium, should be exempt or continue to be exempt from the prohibition, since the use of these hazardous substances in those specific materials and components is still unavoidable. Furthermore, the Commission argued that some exemptions from the prohibition for certain specific materials or components should be limited in their scope and temporal validity, in order to achieve a gradual phase-out of hazardous substances in vehicles, given that the use of those substances in such applications will become avoidable.

[5] [2002] OJ L332/1.

[6] Draft Council Regulation (EC) on Waste Management Statistics COM(1999)31, [1999] OJ C87/22.

[7] [2002] OJ L170/81.

[8] [2000] OJ L269/34.

iv. Sixth Environmental Action Programme

Although not typically thought of as being legislation in the strict sense of the word, the Sixth Environmental Action Programme (EAP-6)[9] does formally fall within that category. Article 8 includes a long list of proposed actions with respect to waste law and policy. Arguably the most remarkable proposal may be found in Article 8(2)(ii)(a): 'developing a set of quantitative and qualitative reduction targets covering all relevant waste, to be achieved at Community level by 2010. The Commission is invited to prepare a proposal for such targets by 2002.'

Waste prevention may occupy the highest spot of the waste management hierarchy, precious little specific action has, however, so far been taken to translate that priority into specific action. That is not to say, of course, that waste prevention may not have been a side-effect of all the measures taken to deal with waste in an environmentally sound manner, once the waste has been produced. However, looking at attempts to target waste prevention specifically, these have been cumbersome, to say the least. One specific example is the development of packaging standards, as a technical translation of the 'essential requirements' of Directive 94/62/EEC on Packaging and Packaging Waste (Packaging and Packaging Waste Directive).[10] These are aimed precisely at reducing the very production of packaging. However the European Standardization Organization (CEN) has so far failed in its task to develop the standards to the Commission's satisfaction.[11] Previous difficulties notwithstanding, the Commission's environment officials do seem to have opted for an ambitious drive to kick-start more specific preventive action. In particular, the Commission is considering drafting specific targets for waste prevention. No doubt, some time will lapse between this initial expression of ambition and the eventual proposal for specific legislation. In particular, it would seem paramount for the Commission to wait for reliable data to be submitted by the Member States, in line with the recently adopted new Waste Statistics Regulation.[12]

v. Animal By-Products

The new Regulation (EC) No. 1774/2002 laying down Health Rules concerning Animal By-Products not Intended for Human Consumption[13] is relevant for the waste sector, in particular in view of its provisions aiming to ensure better coordination with existing waste legislation. There was particular uncertainty

[9] Dec. 1600/2002/EC laying down the Sixth Community Environment Action Programme [2002] OJ L242/1.

[10] [1994] OJ L365/10.

[11] See also van Calster, n. 1 above, 437–41.

[12] n. 5 above.

[13] [2002] OJ L273/1.

with respect to the relation between Directive 91/156/EEC amending Directive 75/442/EEC on Waste (Waste Framework Directive)[14] and Directive 90/667/EEC laying down the Veterinary Rules for the Disposal and Processing of Animal Waste, for its Placing on the Market and for the Prevention of Pathogens in Feedstuffs of Animal or Fish Origin and Amending Directive 90/425/EEC (Animal Waste Directive).[15] It was one of the basic objectives of the new Regulation to clarify this link with EC environmental law. The other core provisions of the Regulation concern: (i) the banning from the food chain of material originating from corpses or disapproved material; (ii) a new legal framework for the sector of animal by-products; and (iii) imports from third countries. In order to do so, three potential destinations are put forward for both unprocessed and processed animal by-products: waste disposal;[16] recovery;[17] or marketing.[18]

However, Commission sources reveal that the coordination with respect to the exact relationship between the two aforementioned Directives, between DG Environment and DG Agriculture, has been far from optimal. Reportedly, it should not be excluded that the legal service of the Commission may still enter the fray, in order to fine-tune the mechanism of the Directive and the Regulation.

vi. Italian Exemption from Permit Duty for Hazardous Waste

In accordance with Article 11 of the Waste Framework Directive and Article 3 of Directive 91/689/EEC on Hazardous Waste (Hazardous Waste Directive),[19] a Member State may grant exemption from the permit duty provided for in Article 10 of the Waste Framework Directive for establishments and undertakings which recover hazardous waste (i.e. not those which dispose of it). This is only possible, however, under the following circumstances: (i) if the Member State adopts general rules listing the type and quantity of waste and laying down specific conditions (limit values for the content of hazardous substances in the waste, emission limit values, type of activity), and other necessary requirements for carrying out different forms of recovery; (ii) if the types or quantities of waste and methods of recovery are such that the conditions imposed in Article 4 of the Waste Framework Directive are complied with (i.e. the protection of the environment has to be guaranteed); (iii) if the establishments or undertakings thus exempt are registered with the competent authorities; and (iv) if the Commission, after having verified the conditions above, concludes that *in casu* they have been fulfilled.

[14] [1991] OJ L78/32.

[15] [1990] OJ L363/51, repealed by Reg. (EC) No. 1774/2002, n. 13 above.

[16] e.g. landfill, burial, or incineration.

[17] e.g. co-incineration.

[18] e.g. processing in destruction companies, entailing production of animal and saturated fats for use in animal feed, and manure.

[19] [1991] OJ L337/20.

By Decision 2002/909/EC on Italian Rules Waiving Permitting Requirements for Undertakings and Establishments Recovering Hazardous Waste under Article 3 of Directive 91/689/EEC on Hazardous Waste,[20] the Commission approved the relevant Italian application, after considerably lengthy analysis, as well as consultation of the other Member States.

vii. Waste Acceptance Criteria for Landfills

With some delay, the Commission has proposed, and the Council has adopted, the criteria which (per type of waste) determine the leakage limits for a variety of pollutants.[21] These limits had to be proposed by the Commission in accordance with Article 16 of Directive 1999/31/EC on Landfill of Waste (Waste Landfill Directive).[22] In particular, for those Member States where landfill remains an important part of waste management techniques (in particular the United Kingdom (UK)), these criteria are crucial for the implementation of the Directive.

B. Legislation in Progress

i. Packaging and Packaging Waste

All hopes that updating the quantitative targets of the Packaging and Packaging Waste Directive[23] could be done swiftly have surely been frustrated.[24] First, the Commission dithered as to whether the update should merely focus on the targets themselves, or should include other elements of the Directive as well. Subsequently, the Commission decided that, for the moment at least, it would limit itself to 'merely' proposing updating the targets. Now, however, the proposed targets are themselves subject to intense scrutiny by industry and Member States alike (just as the Directive itself remains one of the most heavily lobbied pieces of EC legislation). The Commission proposes a general target for recovery of minimum 60 per cent and maximum 75 per cent (in the current text: 50 and 65 per cent, respectively) weight of packaging waste. Moreover, the Commission proposes for recycling minimum 55 per cent and maximum 70 per cent. The Council advocates minimum 60 per cent for recovery, and minimum 55 per cent for recycling (i.e. minima identical to the Commission proposal), with however maximum 80 per cent for recycling, and no maximum at all for recovery generally. The Council proposes for this to be realized by the end of 2008. The

[20] [2002] OJ L315/16.

[21] Dec. 2003/33/EC establishing Criteria and Procedures for the Acceptance of Waste at Landfills Pursuant to Art. 16 of and Annex II to Dir. 1999/31/EC [2003] OJ L11/27.

[22] [1999] OJ L182/1, instructing the Commission to specify specific criteria and/or limit values for each class of landfill.

[23] n. 10 above.

[24] See also van Calster, n. 1 above, 437–41.

EP, for its part, seeks a minimum of 65 per cent for recycling, and a minimum of 60 per cent for recovery, to be realized by 2006.

In light of the likely continuing disagreement, conciliation proceedings would seem almost inevitable.

ii. Transfrontier Shipments of Waste

In order to bring the Community regime on transfrontier shipments of waste into line with both the Convention on the Control of Transboundary Movements of Hazardous Wastes and their Disposal (Basel Convention),[25] and the Organization for Economic Cooperation and Development (OECD) regime under OECD Council Decision C(92)39/final on the Control of Transboundary Movements of Wastes Destined for Recovery Operations,[26] the Commission is currently preparing a proposal to replace the Community's current three list system, under Regulation (EEC) No. 259/93 on the Supervision and Control of Shipments of Waste within, into, and out of the European Community (Waste Shipment Regulation),[27] with a dual list system.

The 'red list' of wastes is to disappear, leaving just two lists: the amber list for hazardous wastes, and the green list for non-hazardous wastes (which can, in principle, be freely traded). Hiccups are to be expected, however, given that the initial plans of the Commission would seem to include stricter requirements than the OECD regime, at least in a number of respects.

C. Case Law

i. Abfall Service

Following hard on the heels of *DaimlerChrysler*,[28] of December 2001, *Abfall Service*[29] illustrates some of the difficulties that still arise from the attempts of the Waste Shipments Regulation to resolve the tension between free movement and the environmental regulation of waste transfers. The Regulation governs, *inter alia*, the monitoring and control of shipments of waste between Member States. Different rules apply to waste destined for recovery or disposal. Whilst 'recovery' and 'disposal' are not defined terms, reference is made to the lists of disposal or recovery operations in Annexes IIA and IIB to the Waste Framework Directive.

Abfall notified the Austrian Bundesminister für Umwelt (BMU), as the competent authority of dispatch, of its intention to ship hazardous waste to

[25] Basel (Switzerland), 22 Mar 1989, Basel (entered into force 5 May 1992) (1989) 28 *International Legal Materials* 3, 857.

[26] 30 Mar. 1992, as amended by OECD Dec. C(2001)107, 14 June 14 2001, published on the Internet at: http://www.olis.oecd.org/olis/2001doc.nsf/linkto/c(2001)107-final.

[27] [1993] OJ L30/1.

[28] Case C-324/99, *DaimlerChrysler AG* v. *Land Baden-Württemberg* [2001] ECR I-9897.

[29] Case C-6/00, *Abfall Service AG (ASA)* v. *Bundesminister für Umwelt, Jugend und Familie* [2002] ECR I-1961.

Germany. According to that notification, the waste in question was slag and ashes produced as a by-product in the operation of waste incinerators, subsequently treated. The waste was to be deposited in a former salt-mine, to secure hollow spaces (mine-sealing). In the notification documents, Abfall classified the treatment of the waste to be shipped as a recovery operation coming within the scope of the operation listed in R5 of Annex IIB to the Waste Framework Directive ('recycling/reclamation of other inorganic materials'). The German competent authority informed Abfall that there appeared to be no reason for it not to approve the notification classifying the shipment as a recovery operation. The BMU raised an objection to the shipment under the Regulation. They claimed that the planned shipment in fact constituted the disposal operation referred to in D12 of Annex IIA ('permanent storage (e.g. emplacement of containers in a mine, etc.)'). Abfall challenged the BMU's decision before the Verwaltungsgerichtshof. In particular, it claimed that the ground stated for the objection, namely that the planned operation was not a recovery operation but a disposal operation, was not in accordance with those laid down in the Regulation.

A number of questions on the shipment of waste were referred to the European Court of Justice (ECJ), first as to whether the competent authority of dispatch is entitled to verify the accuracy of the classification of the shipment, and if so whether that is grounds for objecting to a shipment.

The ECJ confirmed its ruling in *DaimlerChrysler*, that the question of shipments of waste is regulated by the Regulation in order to ensure the protection of the environment. It also confirmed that the cases in which Member States may object to a shipment of waste between Member States are exhaustively listed in the Regulation.[30] However, it added that the provisions defining the objections to shipments of waste presuppose that the purpose of the shipment has first been correctly classified.

The ECJ held that the need for correct classification of the shipment of waste follows, first, from the provisions in the Regulation specifying different grounds for objecting to a shipment depending on whether it is destined for disposal or recovery. It stems also, more generally, from the Regulation as a whole, which applies different procedures depending on the destination of the waste. One of the Regulation's aims is to render shipments of waste for recovery easier than shipments of waste for disposal, by laying down less restrictive rules for the former. This aim would be jeopardized if the classification of the purpose of those shipments were not scrutinized. Further, Article 26 requires Member States to prohibit and punish any illegal traffic, in particular resulting from a knowingly false classification of the purpose of the shipment by the notifier, and Article 30(1) expressly imposes a general duty on Member States to take the requisite measures to ensure that waste is shipped in accordance with the provisions of the Regulation. In addition, the ECJ held that it follows from the system established

[30] Art. 4(3) for shipments destined for disposal and Art. 7(4) for shipments destined for recovery.

by the Regulation that all the competent authorities to which that notification is addressed must check that the classification by the notifier is consistent with the provisions of the Regulation, and object to a shipment which is incorrectly classified. The Court rejected Abfall's contention that the competent authorities of destination and the competent authorities of dispatch should not both be required to verify the accuracy of the notifier's classification of the shipment because this could lead to different classifications of the same shipment. It held that the risk of such different classifications is inherent in the system established by the Regulation, which simultaneously confers on all the competent authorities the responsibility of ensuring that the shipments are carried out in accordance with the Regulation. The ECJ also rejected Abfall's arguments that the principle of freedom of movement of goods and the principle of primacy of recovery of waste together imply that the competent authority of dispatch is not entitled to raise an objection on the ground of incorrect classification. First, objection on that ground can be made only if that classification is inconsistent with the Regulation, not in order to restrict trade between the Member States. Secondly, the principle of primacy of recovery of waste, which is intended to encourage recovery, by definition, only applies to waste which is, in fact, intended for recovery. The ground for the objection must, according to the ECJ, be the classification error itself, rather than one of the grounds set out in the Regulation. The time periods laid down in the Regulation apply to such an objection.

The other main element of the reference by the national court was a question as to whether deposit of waste in a disused mine necessarily constituted a disposal operation, or whether such deposits should be assessed on a case-by-case basis, and if so, on what criteria. The ECJ stated that the intention of Annexes IIA and IIB to the Waste Framework Directive is to list the most common disposal and recovery operations, and not precisely and exhaustively to specify all the disposal and recovery operations covered. Some methods of disposal or recovery of waste may not expressly be mentioned in the Annexes, notably because they did not come into use until after the most recent adaptation of those Annexes. Some operations are capable of falling within the wording of Annex IIA or IIB. However, any treatment of waste falling within the scope of the Directive must be classifiable either as disposal or recovery of waste, in order that the separate rules established by the Directive for those two categories of operations can be applied, and similarly for the application of the Regulations. The deposit in this case could, on its face, be brought within either of the Annexes (D12 of IIA, R5 of IIB).

The ECJ held that the deposit of waste in a disused mine did not necessarily constitute a disposal operation for the purposes of D12 of Annex IIA. The deposit must be assessed on a case-by-case basis to determine whether the operation is a disposal or a recovery operation within the meaning of the Directive. The term 'recovery operation' may generally imply a prior treatment of the waste, but it does not follow from Article 3(1)(b), or from any other provision of the Directive, that the fact that waste has been subject to such a treatment is a necessary condition for classifying an operation as recovery. Neither is the hazardous or non-hazardous nature of the waste, of itself, a relevant criterion for assessing whether a waste treatment operation must be classified as recovery.

According to the ECJ, the essential characteristic of a waste recovery operation is that its principal objective is that the waste serve a useful purpose in replacing other materials which would have had to be used for that purpose, thereby conserving natural resources. It is for the national judge to apply that criterion in the present case, in order to classify the deposit of the waste at issue in a disused mine as either a disposal operation or a recovery operation.

Following the decision in *DaimlerChrysler*, limiting the opportunities for the State of dispatch to restrict waste export on environmental grounds, in this decision the ECJ confirmed that the State of origin of waste does maintain significant responsibility in waste transfers. Moreover, its approach to the term 'recovery', whilst falling far short of a free-standing definition, may prove useful given the problems to which that term has given rise.

ii. Palin Granit

The meaning of 'waste' in EC law has caused serious difficulties of interpretation in the Member States, and has been the subject of many references to the ECJ. The decision in *Palin Granit*[31] is interesting for its consideration of residues from industrial (or here: mining) operations, and the distinction in that context between 'waste' and a useful industrial by-product.

Waste is defined under the Waste Framework Directive as any substance or object in the categories set out in Annex I which the holder discards or intends or is required to discard. Annex I to the Directive, headed 'Categories of waste', includes under head Q11 'Residues from raw materials extraction and processing (e.g. mining residues, oil field slops, etc.)'. The final head, Q16, is a catch-all category, covering 'any materials, substances or products which are not contained in the above categories'. The reference in this case was made in the course of an appeal against the grant of an environmental licence to Palin Granit to operate a granite quarry. Palin Granit's application included a plan for management of the leftover stone and mentioned the possibility of recovering that stone by using it as gravel or filling material. It also stated that the leftover stone from the quarrying would be stored on an adjacent site.

The licence granted by the municipal authority was subsequently set aside, on the ground that the leftover stone was waste and its storage landfill. Under Finnish law, municipal authorities are not competent to grant an environmental licence for a landfill. Palin Granit brought an appeal challenging the classification

[31] Case C-9/00, *Palin Granit Oy and Vehmassalon Kansanterveystyön Kuntayhtymän Hallitus* [2002] ECR I-3533.

of the leftover stone as waste. Since some of the submissions of the parties were made before the important decision in *ARCO Chemie*,[32] the ECJ revisited some of the basic issues in that decision. It confirmed that the scope of the term 'waste' turns on the meaning of the term 'discard'. It also followed its standing case law in holding that the term 'discard' must be interpreted in light of the aim of the Waste Framework Directive, that is the protection of human health and the environment against harmful effects of waste, and the aim of Article 174(2) EC, which provides that Community policy on the environment is to aim at a high level of protection and is to be based, in particular, on the precautionary principle and the principle that preventive action should be taken. The concept of waste, accordingly, cannot be interpreted restrictively. The ECJ confirmed that the fact that a substance undergoes a recovery or disposal operation listed in the Directive does not, in itself, mean that a substance has been discarded. Neither, however, does the fact that the leftover stone is capable of being reused (for embankment work or for building harbours and breakwaters) preclude the leftover stone from being considered as waste. The Court referred to the importance of determining whether a substance is a production residue, that is to say, a product not in itself sought for a subsequent use. *In casu*, the production of leftover stone was not Palin Granit's primary objective. The leftover stone was only a secondary product and the undertaking sought to limit the quantity produced. According to its ordinary meaning, waste is what falls away when one processes a material or an object and is not the end-product which the manufacturing process directly seeks to produce.

However, the ECJ also considered a counter-argument, that materials resulting from a manufacturing or extraction process, the primary aim of which is not the production of that item, may be regarded not as a residue. They may, instead, be regarded as a by-product which the undertaking does not wish to discard, but intends to exploit or market on terms which are advantageous to it, in a subsequent process, without any further processing prior to reuse.

The ECJ held that this interpretation would not be incompatible with the aims of the Waste Framework Directive. It found no reason to hold that the provisions of this Directive apply to goods, materials, or raw materials which have an economic value as products, regardless of any form of processing, and which, as such, are subject to the legislation applicable to those products. However, the ECJ had regard to the obligation to interpret the concept of waste widely in order to limit its inherent risks and pollution. It held that the reasoning applicable to by-products should be confined to situations in which the reuse of the goods, materials, or raw materials is not a mere possibility but a

[32] Joined Cases C-418/97 and C-419/97, *ARCO Chemie Nederland Ltd* v. *Minister van Volkshuisvesting, Ruimtelijke Ordening en Milieubeheer (C-418/97) and Vereniging Dorpsbelang Hees, Stichting Werkgroep Weurt and Vereniging Stedelijk Leefmilieu Nijmegen* v. *Directeur van de Dienst Milieu en Water van de Provincie Gelderland (C-419/97)* [2000] ECR I-4475.

certainty, without any further processing prior to reuse, and as an integral part of the production process. In addition to determining whether a substance constitutes a production residue, the degree of likelihood that that substance will be reused, without any further processing prior to its reuse, is relevant to determining whether something is discarded. If, in addition to the mere possibility of reusing the substance, there is also a financial advantage to the holder in so doing, the likelihood of reuse is high. In such circumstances, the substance in question must no longer be regarded as a burden that its holder seeks to discard, but as a genuine product.

In this case, the ECJ held that the reuse was not certain and was only foreseeable in the longer term. The answer to the main question asked by the national court therefore was that the holder of leftover stone resulting from stone quarrying, which is stored for an indefinite length of time to await possible use, discards or intends to discard that leftover stone. Hence, it should be regarded as 'waste' within the meaning of the Waste Framework Directive.

The ECJ referred to its holding in *ARCO Chemie* to the effect that the circumstance that a residue is unsuitable for its use, or requires special precautions due to its environmentally hazardous nature, may provide evidence that the holder has discarded it, or intends or is required to discard it. It is clear, however, that the fact that leftover stone has the same composition as other stone, poses no risk to health or the environment, and is capable of immediate use, does not mean that it cannot be waste.

The decision on this reference is not really surprising, given the ECJ's consistently tough and purposive approach to the meaning of 'waste'. It is part of a long line of decisions on boundaries between waste and raw materials. Whilst we are still no closer to a tight and comprehensive definition of waste, this decision does take us somewhat closer to understanding the impact of reusability on the definition of waste.

iii. Commission *v.* Denmark

What a pity indeed. The Commission had taken a particularly long time to decide to press ahead with a procedure against Denmark, on the grounds that elements of the Danish packaging regulations are incompatible with the Packaging and Packaging Waste Directive, and/or with Articles 28–30 EC on the free movement of goods. Advocate General Colomer had already advised, by and large siding with the Commission. The incoming Danish Government has however substantially changed the regime (including the controversial prohibition of aluminium cans), which, in turn, led to the Commission striking the case off the register.[33] A judgment of the ECJ would have been very welcome, in particular with a view to clarifying the general relationship between free trade and

[33] Order of the ECJ of 11 Sept. 2002—Removal from the Register, Case C-246/99, *Commission* v. *Denmark* [2002] ECR I-6943.

the environment, as well as, more specifically, the degree of harmonization brought about by the Packaging and Packaging Waste Directive. Another hot topic is the authority of the 'essential requirements' of the Directive—a recurrent topic of the so-called 'New Approach' in Community harmonization. It has to be said that the new Danish regime, which essentially amounts to a deposit and return scheme, in itself raises a number of questions vis-à-vis EC law.

iv. Eco-Emballages

In *Eco-Emballages*, the ECJ had been asked by a French court to review the legality of a number of provisions in the French implementing legislation of the Packaging and Packaging Waste Directive.[34] The Court, however, rebounded the questions, in line with long-standing case law on the respective duties of national courts and the ECJ.

C. International Cooperation

i. International Standards for the Dismantling of Shipwrecks

The cumbersome negotiation of international standards for the dismantling and recycling of shipwrecks, within the framework of the Basel Convention,[35] have finally delivered at the end of December 2002. The standards are, however, not binding. Similar standards were agreed for lead batteries, plastics waste, biomedical waste, and medical waste. At the Sixth Conference of the Parties (COP-6), 9–13 December 2002, in Geneva (Switzerland), an attempt was made to give the Convention a new lease of life, by taking a number of initiatives, the most important of which would seem to be the Strategic Plan for the Implementation of the Basel Convention (to 2010). The Plan sets out priorities for international action in the area of hazardous wastes and other wastes, up to the year 2010. It focuses, *inter alia*, on treating some 'priority waste streams' with more urgency, in particular waste pesticides, lead batteries, waste oils, polychlorobiphenyls (PCBs), and electronic wastes. Highlighting priority waste streams is an interesting development, in particular if one considers that a similar initiative of the European Commission in the 1990s, has not delivered.

ii. OECD Three-List Regime Abolished

In particular so as to bring its listing regime in line with the Basel Convention, the OECD has changed its three-list system for transfrontier shipments of waste (red, amber, green), to a two-list system (amber and green, for hazardous and non-hazardous wastes respectively).[36] Whilst the structure of the lists may now be identical, substantial differences remain, for example as to which waste figures

[34] Case C-159/00, *Sapod Audic* v. *Eco-Emballages SA* [2002] ECR I-5031.

[35] n. 25 above. See also van Calster, n. 1 above, 456.

[36] OECD Dec. C(2001)107, n. 26 above.

on which list. As noted in section B.*ii* of this survey, the new EU regime will be very similar (albeit not identical) to either the OECD or the Basel Convention regime.

D. Prominent National Developments

i. German Packaging Legislation Withstands Barrage of (National) Court Challenges—European Threat Remains

In early 2003, the German Government introduced a deposit-return scheme on one-way packaging, following industry's and retailers' failure to reach the refill quota of 72 per cent, which the Government had imposed. A variety of trade associations, as well as individual companies, have initiated a truly impressive series of court challenges to the regulations. Their arguments are based upon both German law (in particular German constitutional law) and EC law. The majority of these cases have hitherto failed, in particular on procedural grounds as well as on grounds of German law. The opponents of the regime can, however, keep on hoping. Indeed, first, one of the courts involved in the procedure (Stuttgart) has requested a preliminary ruling from the ECJ, with respect to the compatibility of the inherent discrimination vis-à-vis one-way packaging with the Packaging and Packaging Waste Directive. Moreover, the Commission is continuing its pursuit of Germany. Germany has, indeed, been taken to the ECJ on the basis that, in the Commission's view, the Packaging and Packaging Waste Directive does not offer room for absolute priority of refillable packaging over one-way packaging.

ii. Italian Decree Gives 'Authentic Interpretation' of 'Waste'—Tension with Courts and the Commission

Article 14 of the Italian Decree-Law 138/02 of 8 July 2002[37] gives an 'authentic interpretation' of the concept of 'waste' in Italian law. This is reminiscent of earlier attempts by the Italian legislator to interpret restrictively the concept of 'waste'.[38] It holds that there is no intention to 'discard' a substance, when it can be reused without prior treatment, and insofar as there is no threat of damage to the environment. The legislative intervention would seem to be aimed in particular at scrap metal, as well as wood chips, and would seem inspired by previous interventions of Advocate General Jacobs (since rejected). At least one

[37] *GURI* 158 of 8 July 2002; converted into Law 178 of 8 Aug. 2002, *GURI* 187 of 10 Aug. 2002. See also the 'Italy' survey by F. Francioni and M. Montini, in this volume, sections F and I.

[38] See its previous legislation, which led to Joined Cases C-304/94, C-330/94, C-342/94 and C-234/95, *Criminal Proceedings against Euro Tombesi and Adino Tombesi* (C-304/94), *Roberto Santella* (C-330/94), *Giovanni Muzi and Others* (C-342/94) *and Anselmo Savini* (C-224/95) (*Euro Tombesi*) [1997] ECR I-3561. See also the case report by G. van Calster in (1998) 4 *Columbia Journal of European Law* 1, 166–72.

Italian judge has already dismissed the definition outright, because of its apparent incompatibility with EC law, and the Commission has also initiated an enquiry.

E. Miscellaneous

i. Verol Recycling—*Distinction Recovery/Disposal*

It seems that no matter how many judgments the ECJ issues with respect to EC waste legislation, practice continues to supply further questions. In *Verol Recycling*,[39] the main proceedings arise out of two notifications by Verol Recycling Limburg BV of its intention to ship waste from the Netherlands to Belgium. The first notification concerned 2,000 tonnes of a compact mixture of waste glue, sealant, resin, and paint and waste containing silicon, with sawdust. The second notification concerned 1,000 tonnes of sediment with a low halogen content, with sawdust. In both cases the waste was to be used as fuel in cement kilns and as a raw material in the process for producing clinker in cement factories. In that process, the national court explained that the energy obtained from burning the waste is a substitute for energy obtained from burning primary raw materials, namely other fuel, and the ash residues from the incinerated waste are a substitute for primary raw materials, namely sand. More precisely, the organic component of the mixtures of waste at issue is incinerated and the residue of the inorganic component is used for the production of clinker. Thereafter, nothing remains of the waste. The Dutch Minister consented to the planned shipments, subject to the condition that for each planned movement of waste with a chlorine content of 1 per cent or less, the waste to be exported had to have a calorific value of over 11,500 kilo Joules per kilogram (kJ/kg), and that for each planned movement of waste with a chlorine content of over 1 per cent the waste to be exported had to have a calorific value of over 15,000 kJ/kg. The Minister based those conditions, *inter alia*, on relevant Dutch policy documents, which, as regards recovery with use principally as a fuel, take the calorific value linked to the chlorine content of the waste as the relevant criterion. For an operation to constitute recovery, hazardous waste with a chlorine content of 1 per cent or less must have a minimum calorific value of 11,500 kJ/kg. For an operation to constitute recovery, hazardous waste with a chlorine content of over 1 per cent must have a minimum calorific value of 15,000 kJ/kg.

Verol contended before the national court that the Minister was wrong to attach the abovementioned conditions to its consent. In its view, the use in question of the waste in the cement industry in Belgium should be regarded unconditionally as recovery within the meaning of Article 1(f) read in conjunction with Annex IIB to the Directive. It considers that the operation concerned is

[39] Case C-116/01, *SITA EcoService Nederland BV, formerly Verol Recycling Limburg BV* v. *Minister van Volkshuisvesting, Ruimtelijke Ordening en Milieubeheer* (not yet reported), Opinion by Advocate General Jacobs delivered on 14 Nov. 2002.

an operation R1 'Use principally as a fuel or other means to generate energy', R3 'Recycling/reclamation of organic substances which are not used as solvents', and R5 'Recycling/reclamation of other inorganic materials', within the meaning of the Annex. Verol argues that the processing of the waste in the combined procedure results in the complete use of the waste and that, in adopting his decision, the Minister wrongly failed to take account of the efficiency of the combined procedure as a whole and instead took as a basis the nature and composition of the waste.

Advocate General Jacobs opined, first of all, that the scheme of both the Directive and the Regulation suggest that whether waste is to be correctly classified as intended for disposal or recovery for the purposes of the Regulation is determined by the correct classification of the first operation to which the waste is to be subject. Furthermore, Jacobs revisited his opinion (and the ruling) in *Abfall Service*,[40] to opine that the operation at issue constituted 'use principally as a fuel or other source of energy' under head R1 of Annex IIB, provided that (i) the greater part of the waste is used as a fuel and (ii) the energy generated thereby is principally used in the sense that the greater part of the energy generated thereby is used. Hence, in Jacobs' view, it is clear that, in order for the requirements of head R1 to be satisfied, it is not necessary for all the waste to be used as a fuel. In passing, Jacobs rejected minimum calorific value determined on the basis of national criteria as a valid criterion for the operation to be regarded as recovery. The unacceptable consequences of Member States being permitted to apply their own criteria in such a way are evident from the diverse minimum calorific values which certain Member States require of waste in order for its incineration with recovery of heat generated to be classified as a recovery operation under head R1 in Annex IIB. That is not to say that a uniform criterion based on calorific value might not be a useful and workable means of distinguishing between recovery and disposal operations if set at Community level. However it appears that it has not been possible to agree such a criterion, to date. The ECJ is expected to issue its judgment in this case at the beginning of 2003.

ii. German Export of Waste Solidarity Fund—Illegal Customs Duty

In the view of Advocate General Tizzano, in Case C-389/00,[41] Germany levies a customs duty (evidently prohibited by the EC Treaty) by having established a solidarity fund, and levying obligatory contributions for it, in the waste sector. The fund is aimed at financing the return of shipments of waste, and/or their processing, as provided for by the Waste Shipments Regulation. It is noteworthy that the contributions come over and above the financial security which exporters already have to provide. Tizzano subscribed to the Commission's arguments, and

[40] n. 29 above.

[41] Case C-389/00, *Commission* v. *Germany* (not yet reported), Opinion of Advocate General Tizzano delivered on 14 Nov. 2002.

rejected Germany's arguments, such as that the levy actually constitutes a contribution for a service provided.

iii. Waste Incineration—Disposal or Recovery?

In two opinions which have already caused serious debate, Advocate General Jacobs discussed the implications and potential applications of the distinction between recovery and disposal, as made in *Abfall Services*.[42] The first Opinion, in Case C-458/00,[43] concerned the refusal of export of waste, by the Luxembourg authorities. The authorities make recourse to the proximity principle. The waste concerned is municipal waste which the holder seeks to incinerate in the waste incineration facilities of the municipality of Strasbourg. Jacobs revisited the judgment in *Abfall Services*, where the ECJ ruled that the principal objective of a recovery operation is that the waste serve a useful purpose in replacing other materials which would have had to be used for that purpose, thereby conserving natural resources. In the case of waste being incinerated in a plant developed for that purpose, the answer to that question is, in the view of Jacobs, clearly 'no'; in the absence of available waste, there would be no incineration. In those circumstances it would not be right, in his opinion, to describe the operation as recovery simply because, whenever waste is available and incinerated, the heat generated by the incineration is used, wholly or partly, as a means to generate energy. Jacobs referred, *inter alia*, to a number of policy documents of the Council of Ministers, which warn against systematic transports of large quantities of household waste between the Member States, on the grounds that this may lead to negative consequences for the environment. In the second Opinion, in Case C-228/00,[44] Advocate General Jacobs continued the same line of reasoning with respect to the principal objective. Incineration facilities in Belgian cement kilns have as their principal objective the creation of energy, for use in the production process. Incinerating wastes in such installations, therefore, needs to be viewed as a recovery operation, given that other, primary resources, would have been used, should waste not have been available. Consequently, according to Jacobs, Germany cannot make recourse to the proximity principle to object to such shipments, given that the proximity principle can only be used vis-à-vis waste intended for disposal.

The judgment of the Court in both cases, *inter alia* with respect to the relevance of the calorific value of the waste concerned, arguably will be paramount in deciding the future of the incineration of domestic waste in Europe. A ruling is expected for the beginning of 2003.

[42] n. 29 above.

[43] Case C-458/00, *Commission* v. *Luxembourg* (not yet reported), Opinion of Advocate General Jacobs delivered on 26 Sept. 2002.

[44] Case C-228/00, *Commission* v. *Germany* (not yet reported), Opinion of Advocate General Jacobs delivered on 26 Sept. 2002.

iv. Flanders Warned for Refusal to Export Garden Waste

At the end of 2002, the Commission announced that it had sent a 'reasoned opinion' to Belgium, with respect to the refusal by the Flemish Waste Agency for a waste processor to export garden and kitchen waste to The Netherlands. The Agency systematically refuses the export of such waste. The reason cited for such refusal is the priority which Flemish waste management plans grant to processing such waste in Flanders itself. This would seem at odds with the Waste Shipments Regulation. Should Belgium be taken to the Court of Justice about this issue (which seems very likely), the judgment will offer an opportunity to clarify the room which Member States have to refuse exports of waste purely on the basis of national waste management plans. In view of the legal hierarchy between the Regulation and the Treaty Articles on the free movement of goods, the answer would seem to be fairly obvious.[45]

v. The Concept of 'Recycling'

In an Opinion on the Packaging and Packaging Waste Directive, in *Mayer Parry Recycling*,[46] Advocate General Alber ventured into the controversial issue of defining the concept of 'recycling' (albeit within the sole context of that Directive). In a case with considerable economic interest because of the tradeability of the certificates at stake, Mayer Parry Recycling (MPR) argued that the scrap metal involved is fully recycled after the processing in its facilities, and hence, at that time, ceases to be waste. Alber had a different view, emphasizing, *inter alia*, that in his view the concept of 'recycling' involves a procedure, the result of which entails 'a higher degree of processing' than the original material that is being processed. Other than this view on the concept of recycling, the Opinion is important with respect to the relationship between the Packaging and Packaging Waste Directive and the Waste Framework Directive. Alber viewed the former as *lex specialis* vis-à-vis the latter, and consequently argued that identical concepts need not have exactly the same meaning in both Directives.

vi. CEN Mandate for Product Standards for Solid Recovered Fuels

The Commission has given the most prominent of European standardization bodies, CEN, a mandate in the framework of so-called Solid Recovered Fuels (SRFs).[47] These are fuels originating from non-hazardous waste, which are used as a means of recovering energy in waste incineration and co-incineration facilities covered by the scope of application of Directive 2000/76/EC on the

[45] See, however, the confusion caused by the ECJ's views on exhaustion in *DaimlerChrysler*.

[46] Case C-444/00, *The Queen, on the Application of Mayer Parry Recycling Ltd* v. *Environment Agency and Secretary of State for the Environment, Transport and the Regions, and Corus (UK) Ltd and Allied Steel and Wire Ltd (ASW)* (not yet reported), Opinion of Advocate General Alber delivered on 4 July 2002.

[47] Mandate M325 of 26 Aug. 2002.

Incineration of Waste (Waste Incineration Directive).[48] SRFs are classified in the European Waste List[49] under heading 19-12: wastes from the mechanical treatment of waste (e.g. sorting, crushing, compacting, pelletizing) not otherwise specified, sub-heading 19-12-10: combustible waste (refuse-derived fuel).[50] The Commission's initiative was triggered by the fact that, in practice, co-incineration of SRFs requires that incineration facilities enjoy a stable, homogeneous supply of pre-treated waste which can be traded between producers and buyers of SRFs. Product standards can facilitate that process. The Commission has created something of a stir with the mandate. Its text foresees that recyclable waste need not necessarily be excluded from the scope of the product standards. This has led to accusations that the Commission is implicitly changing the waste management hierarchy.

48 [2000] OJ L332/91.

49 Dec. 2000/532/EC replacing Dec. 94/3/EC establishing a List of Wastes Pursuant to Article 1(a) of Dir. 75/442/EEC on Waste and Council Dec. 94/904/EC establishing a List of Hazardous Waste Pursuant to Article 1(4) of Dir. 91/689/EEC on Hazardous Waste [2000] OJ L226/3 (as amended).

50 Note that this only includes non-hazardous waste: hazardous waste is included in heading 19-12-11.

V. Water

*MARK STALLWORTHY**

A. Introduction

i. The 'Implementation Gap'

There are well-known difficulties faced by those seeking to secure the implementation of environmental legislation across jurisdictions generally. These include problems in working at the limits of scientific understanding (including as to substances in common use and their interactions).[1] The sector is moreover particularly prone to problems caused by pollution from diffuse sources. But it also has to be said that the field of environmental regulation, particularly within the European Union (EU), continues to encounter other systemic problems. As for the mechanisms under Community legislative structures, even where there exists apparent clarity in the scope and content of schemes of control, there has been a high degree of difficulty in securing transposition by Member States. More importantly, once transposed, there have been severe deficiencies in performance. The now annual Commission reports on implementation and enforcement confirm that there are continuing difficulties in securing timely and proper implementation by Member States of European Community (EC) environmental laws.[2]

The most significant challenge therefore that continues to beset Community environmental law concerns the question of implementation. Commentators widely point to an implementation deficit. This is perhaps inevitable in the context of an EU legal structure with two built-in weaknesses. First, direct, hierarchical legal controls over those (in effect, Member States) with responsibilities for implementation are restricted; and, secondly, legislative outputs afford high levels of discretion.[3] Moreover, the political ramifications of policy-making and legal implementation are highly complex. Thus it is necessary for EU legislation to accommodate contrasting national approaches and regulatory styles.[4]

* Senior Lecturer, Norwich Law School, University of East Anglia (United Kingdom).

1 It is argued, e.g., that disputes as to nature of health risks and appropriate indicators and analytical methods were a main reason for the delay in producing reforms to bathing waters legislation (n. 18 below): see R.K.W. Wurzel, *Environmental Policy-Making in Britain, Germany and the European Union—the Europeanisation of Air and Water Pollution Control* (Manchester: Manchester University Press, 2002), 259.

2 See Commission Report—Third Annual Survey on the Implementation and Enforcement of Community Environmental Law SEC(2002)1041.

3 See M. Glachant, *Implementing European Environmental Policy* (Cheltenham: Edward Elgar, 2001), 26–7.

4 See, comparing UK and German stances, Wurzel, n. 1 above, 29–30; for an interesting transatlantic comparison, see D. Vogel, *National Styles of Regulation—Environmental Protection in Great Britain and the United States* (Ithaca, NY: Cornell University Press, 1986).

It is perhaps inevitable that a combination of ambiguous responsibilities, problematic power relationships, and differentiated concerns about resources have hindered levels of implementation.[5] That said, such consequences of the playing out of structural tensions can be defended on the basis that they reflect the functional realities of unity and diversity, national and supranational priorities, and heterodox distribution of powers; it is argued that implementation deficits accordingly help to maintain a delicate, 'post-decisional', balance between EU and Member State political forces.[6]

ii. Directions in Community Water Legislation

These deficiencies can be seen in connection with the programmatic arrangements demanded by the generation of water legislation that now in force should be having an increasing impact. An illustration of this problem is the legislation aimed at controlling non-point source nitrate pollution from agricultural sources. Here the legislative approach has been through risk area designations and action programmes, based upon non-mandatory codes of good agricultural practice, supplemented where necessary by mandatory codes and action programmes on the basis of the designation of nitrate-vulnerable zones.[7] The implications for investment, and the political sensitivities of imposing additional burdens upon the agricultural sector, are significant, and levels of non-compliance have been problematic. The Commission has noted recent improvements in most Member Sates in matters of transposition, setting up of monitoring networks, issuing codes of practice, and zone designations. However, it has also regretted what has amounted to 'a delay of 5 years or more by Member States to fulfil their commitments for implementation of the Directive and an effective reduction of nitrogen (N) losses from agriculture to water'.[8]

And yet, Community water legislation's legislative mix has seen considerable successes. There has, furthermore, in recent years been a marked increase in sophistication of legal mechanisms employed. Now, to supplement basic reliance upon the setting of quality standards and emission limits, as subsequently reinforced through sectoral strategies and integrated control systems, the EU has embarked upon a further, third phase. Directive 2000/60/EC establishing a Framework for Community Action in the Field of Water Policy (Water

[5] See H. Ingram and A. Schneider, 'Improving Implementation through Framing Smarter Statutes' (1990) 10 *Journal of Public Policy* 1, 67.

[6] See A. Jordan, *Environmental Policy in the European Union* (London: Earthscan, 2002), 320–2 (and, generally, ch. 17); citing D. Puchala, 'Domestic Politics and Regional Harmonization in the European Communities' (1975) 27 *World Politics*, 496.

[7] Dir. 91/676/EEC concerning the Protection of Waters against Pollution caused by Nitrates from Agricultural Sources [1991] OJ L375/1, especially Arts. 3, 4, and 5.

[8] Commission Report—Implementation of Council Directive 91/676/EEC concerning the Protection of Waters against Pollution Caused by Nitrates from Agricultural Sources—Synthesis from Year 2000 Member States Reports COM(2002)407, 43.

Framework Directive)[9] is to form the centrepiece of this new era in environmental policy. It is as yet too early to reach conclusions as to the likely success of this policy—not least because the due transposition date of end 2003 will constitute but the formal domestic commencement of a lengthy implementation process across a fifteen-year time-frame. And yet, the measure has both symbolic and strategic significance. Thus 'a fundamental rethink of Community policy [has led to] agreement on the need for a more political approach to water quality management, and the development of a framework water directive designed to offer a more strategic approach to water quality issues'.[10]

B. Legislation Adopted

i. A Framework for Community Water Protection

The Commission has committed itself to a high profile programme of information and supporting projects in connection with the gradual incorporation of the provisions of the Water Framework Directive into national laws.[11] It is from the first emphasizing participation on the part of stakeholders in order to ensure effective implementation.[12] The first major deadline is for transposition into the laws of Member States, and this must occur by the end of 2003. Thus by that date it will be necessary for national and regional water laws to have been adapted to the requirements of the Directive (and River Basin Cooperation Agreements to have come into operation). With the term date of 2015 in mind (and meeting the objective of good status, taking into account qualitative and quantitative aspects), deadlines will proceed to come thick and fast once the transposition is in place. For instance, detailed analyses of pressures and impacts on waters, in light of environmental objectives, should have been completed before the end of 2004. This is to include analyses of economic impacts, including as to issues of cost effectiveness.

Proposals as to both method and timing of deadline compliance are a matter of controversy in certain quarters. There is, for instance, criticism that the United Kingdom (UK) is continuing with its (seemingly traditional) policy of piecemeal implementation and compliance as near to deadlines as possible.[13] Experience

[9] [2000] OJ L327/1.

[10] J. McCormick, *Environmental Policy in the European Union* (Basingstoke: Palgrave, 2001), 196 (and, generally, ch. 7).

[11] See e.g. Commission, LIFE Focus: Water, an Essential Resource—Life and the New European Water Policy (Nov. 2002), published on the Internet at: http://europa.eu.int/comm/environment/life/infoproducts/water_en.pdf.

[12] Commission, The Water Framework Directive—Tap Into It! (2002), published on the Internet at: http://europa.eu.int/comm/environment/water/water-framework/pdf/brochure_en.pdf.

[13] See the UK Government's continuing consultation process: Department for Environment, Food and Rural Affairs, Second Consultation Paper on the EC Water Framework Directive (Nov. 2002), published on the Internet at: http://www.defra.gov.uk/environment/consult/waterframe2/pdf/waterframe2-1.pdf.

suggests that this has in the past tended to show up flaws in implementation in due course, and indeed to put pressure upon compliance deadlines further down the legislative 'pipeline'. At the same time, there is little doubt that, for all the variety of water legislation in place, it is widely recognized in bureaucratic circles that serious problems remain to be addressed. Once again, taking the UK by way of illustration, the government during 2002 produced its water policy strategy.[14] This has the stated aim of producing, in due course, an integrated water strategy, including as to policies for its uses across sectors. Thus, the paper proceeds along a theme of sustainable development, which echoes the sustainability objectives underlying the Water Framework Directive. It is clear from its wording that agriculture lies at the forefront of concerns (carefully balanced by reference to the requirement that EU legislation take better account of impacts upon farming), together with a variety of further issues of water management, including as to resources and development demands.

The kinds of structural problems faced, in places barely addressed by potential legal solutions, and touched upon in the strategy document, will be recognizable across Member State jurisdictions. Just three examples are offered here, from the lengthy list produced in the paper. First, there are serious challenges in terms of integration, including as to issues of water quality and flood controls, but also now increasingly in terms of sustainable development planning, as well as abstraction, use, and biodiversity issues.[15] Secondly, there is an endemic challenge posed by the external environmental costs of the diffuse pollution resulting from intensive forms of agricultural use which have arguably been demanded by both political and institutional structures within the EU, and perhaps also by consumers themselves.[16] A third challenge comes from a more surprising quarter, and concerns the growing problems in terms of energy use that enhanced water quality provisions place upon the water industry (and so to issues of global warming and climate change). In this latter respect, such can be linked to increasing treatment standards obligations placed upon water companies and deriving from the EU legislation, such as on bathing, shellfish, and urban wastewater.[17]

It will readily be seen that these challenges raise fundamental questions as to the principles that underlie EU environmental policy under the Treaty: especially as to remediation at source and the polluter pays principle. Thus more holistic approaches (assisted by new river basin management arrangements) entail

[14] Department for Environment, Food and Rural Affairs, Directing the Flow—Priorities for Future Water Policy (Nov. 2002), published on the Internet at: http://www.defra.gov.uk/environment/water/strategy/pdf/directing_the_flow.pdf.

[15] See e.g. S. Tromans, 'Too Much or Too Little—Water Management and the Land Use Planning System' (2001) 29 *Journal of Planning Law*, 64–78.

[16] See e.g. Department of Environment, Food and Rural Affairs, Agriculture and Water—A Diffuse Pollution Review (June 2002), published on the Internet at: http://www.defra.gov.uk/environment/water/dwpa/reports/dwpa01.htm.

[17] See 'Water Sector Awakes to Energy Test' (2002) 26 *Environmental Data Services Report*, 329.

extending beyond the clean up demands made upon those bodies (such as water and sewerage companies) that receive and treat emissions (whether point source or diffuse) of others. In order to achieve greater internalization of costs, it will become necessary increasingly to engage a broad range of stakeholders, especially including farming and manufacturing interests. Yet others (such as highway authorities and other developers on land) must likewise be part of this process, as well as end consumers (notwithstanding that they in any event arguably already bear the ultimate cost of water treatment facilities). Such issues will provide some of the more acute problems across Member States as each moves to meet the deadlines set by the Water Framework Directive.

C. Legislation in Progress

i. Bathing Water

During 2002, the Commission finally produced a Proposal for a Directive concerning the Quality of Bathing Water.[18] The intention has been to update the regulatory scheme, notwithstanding the fair degree of success under Directive 76/160/EEC Concerning the Quality of Bathing Water (Bathing Water Directive).[19] Indeed, around 85 per cent of EU coastal waters are believed to be compliant with current (guide value) standards. The proposal has long been awaited (since indeed the middle of the 1990s), and follows formal consultation involving much that has been included in the eventual draft in 2000.[20] Amongst the measures dropped from the original proposal was that to extend controls to leisure activity waters (water sports).[21] This will reduce costs, especially as regards the continued use of long waste-water sea outfalls. Moreover, monitoring requirements become more flexible, especially where consistent compliance is achieved, and sampling would be considerably reduced as compared with current levels.[22]

Stated objectives are the improvement of health standards, greater management effectiveness, and increased public participation in the processes of monitoring and control. The draft, in part, reflects consistent challenges in the environmental field, in terms of the development in scientific knowledge and particularly in epidemiological understanding. It likewise seeks to take account of technological advances subsequent to those ruling at the time of the original controls being laid down.[23] Parameters have been rationalized more heavily than had originally been anticipated, with a reduced focus on two bacteriological indicator parameters (by reference to Intestinal *Enterococci* and *Escherischia*

[18] COM(2002)581, [2002] OJ C45E/127.

[19] [1976] OJ L31/1.

[20] Commission Communication—Developing a New Bathing Water Policy COM(2000)860.

[21] See n. 18 above, Explanatory Memorandum, para. 4.3.

[22] ibid., paras. 4.7–4.8.

[23] See Wurzel, n. 1 above.

coli).[24] The aim is to impose microbiological quality standards that result in the achievement of tighter controls over faecal pollution. As before, there will be guide values (excellent water class) and mandatory values (good water class).[25]

Significantly, the proposal places reliance upon an improved, more proactive, managerial approach to water quality assessment and analysis and control methods.[26] Classification will be on a three-yearly trend basis, thereby avoiding over-reliance, as at present, on annual results. Sampling and monitoring requirements would be reduced for good waters and excellent waters on the basis of trends over a first and subsequent three-year periods.[27] Nevertheless, in contrast, a twice-monthly sampling requirement would be retained for waters categorized as poor. Management will involve the assessment of sites that are likely sources of contamination, and management plans are to be produced in consultation with the public, and tied to more advanced information systems,[28] including as to the plans themselves and monitoring data. Poor quality waters would be subject to annual management review, with a view to both protecting and informing the public; good waters would be reviewed, with a view to 'preventive' measures, every two years; and excellent waters would be reviewed on a three-year cycle.[29] Improved communication arrangements will include, as well as the media and beach postings, use of the Internet.[30] Remedial measures would be required where standards are not met, although it seems that the risks of enforcement action would be reduced. For instance, a failure to meet mandatory levels may be treated as compliant on a temporary basis provided that measures are taken both to prevent human exposure to pollution during that season and to produce improvement within three years.

As to cost impacts, the stricter faecal contamination limits will require considerable investment, particularly in agricultural areas with high levels of animal stock rearing. Whilst this issue must be addressed for the purposes of the Water Framework Directive, the deadlines there are to have controls in place and in force by 2009 and 2012, respectively. In terms of timing, therefore, should prior controls come into force in terms of the proposed new Bathing Waters Directive, then it is likely that significant, targeted investments (and higher levels of agricultural subsidy) will be required in order to ensure compliance.

Overall, it appears that higher levels of flexibility are to be accorded to Member States in respect of implementation. Although the proposal is for the Directive to come into force within two years of adoption, the full picture may not be clear for some while yet, given that transposition of the Water Framework Directive will be influential in developments here, as in other areas.[31] For instance, under that measure, in place of an approach based upon standards

[24] See n. 21 above, paras. 4.4–4.6.
[25] See n. 18 above, Arts. 4 and 9, and Annexes I (columns B, C) and II.
[26] See n. 21 above, paras. 4.9–4.10. [27] See n. 18 above, Annex IV.
[28] ibid., Arts. 15, 16. [29] ibid., Art. 10. [30] See n. 21 above, para. 4.13.
[31] ibid., para. 4.2.

and deadline setting, water quality objectives must be integrated for each river basin, and these are to extend to bathing waters (as well as drinking waters, valuable habitats, and aquatic ecology generally). Concerns at seemingly reduced levels of control may be alleviated at least in respect of the scope of requirements retained within the new draft proposal. Further, a more integrated approach to activities upstream should facilitate the improvement of waters within river basins.

ii. Groundwater

Part of the project under the Water Framework Directive for securing an integrated regulatory approach is to secure the repeal and replacement of first phase directives, such as Directive 80/68/EEC on the Protection of Groundwater against Pollution Caused by Certain Dangerous Substances (Groundwater Pollution Directive).[32] In order to produce further reductions in groundwater pollution a draft Directive is anticipated for 2003. The aim will be to provide for common indicators for the assessment of the chemical status of groundwaters together with harmonized criteria for monitoring programmes and obligations as to measures to be taken in response.

iii. Marine Conservation

The Commission has proposed that the spirit of integration be extended into marine policy at EU level.[33] Thus far, policy and law have developed in a sectoral way, and without concentrated attention being given to issues of integration. Indeed, developments of protections in this context, unsurprisingly, owe much to other, regional, geo-political structures, rather than to specifically EU mechanisms. These include, in particular, arrangements under the Convention for the Protection of the Marine Environment for the North East Atlantic (OSPAR Convention).[34] This Convention is a major element in the regional regulation of sources of marine pollution caused by releases of land-based hazardous substances.[35]

The draft EU strategy is one of the Commission's responses to commitments under the Sixth Environmental Action Programme (EAP-6).[36] It sets out a series of objectives which broadly purport to accord with a holistic approach to protection of the marine environment, as for instance in development of the

[32] [1980] OJ L20/43.

[33] Commission Communication—Towards a Strategy to Protect and Conserve the Marine Environment COM(2002)539.

[34] Paris (France), 22 Sept. 1999 (entered into force on 25 Mar. 1998) (1993) 32 *International Legal Materials* 3, 759–804. See also Cooperation Agreement for the Protection of the Coasts and Waters of the North-East Atlantic Against Pollution [1993] OJ L267/22.

[35] See e.g. Dec. 98/249/EC on the Conclusion of the Convention for the Protection of the Marine Environment of the North-East Atlantic [1998] OJ L104/2.

[36] Dec. 1600/2002/EC laying down the Sixth Community Environment Action Programme.

notion of good ecological quality of waters. Given that EU policies already impact in this area, there are inevitable echoes of approaches elsewhere, including as to limits on hazardous substances, and sustainable fishing. Likewise, attention will be focused upon the development of policies affecting the marine environment, including: protecting biodiversity, addressing eutrophication problems, reducing radioactive discharges, and strengthening oil pollution restrictions. Whilst the proposal is at an early stage, it appears that a key feature will be the issue of integration of policies which impact here, and attention to links between marine ecology and threats to human health.

iv. Pesticides

A further aspect of the process of integration, long-awaited, is the perceived need for controls upon pesticide use.[37] This is indeed another of the thematic strategies required under the terms of the new EAP-6. Whilst pesticides have been tackled in the limited enforcement arena of drinking water legislation,[38] there has been a considerable gestation period of around a decade before EU proposals for regulation of their use have appeared. The Commission has now produced a draft strategy document for this purpose.[39] The proposed time-frame is for implementation by 2006.

Implementation would take the form of the development of national plans to contain programmes for pesticide reduction. Standard features appear in the paper, such as the emphasis upon wider participation. However it appears that (perhaps in accordance with the spirit of the Water Framework Directive in its wider context) a high degree of discretion is to be left in the hands of Member States. At this stage, for instance, the Commission has stepped back from proposing quantitative reduction targets and deadlines. Doubtless in the hope of pre-empting extreme resistance from certain Member States, there is also no proposal made for the introduction of a pesticides tax.

D. Case Law and Enforcement Activity

i. Dangerous Substances

The sector of water law regulated by Directive 76/464/EEC on Pollution Caused by certain Dangerous Substances Discharged into the Aquatic Environment of the Community (Dangerous Substances Discharge Directive)[40] provides an illustration of the insistence of the ECJ upon programmatic implementation where this is required. There is accordingly a need for 'comprehensive and

[37] See e.g. Commission Communication—Directions Towards Sustainable Agriculture COM(99)22, [1999] OJ C173.

[38] Case C-340/96, *Commission* v. *United Kingdom* [1999] ECR I-2023.

[39] Commission Communication—Towards a Thematic Strategy on the Sustainable Use of Pesticides COM(2002)349.

[40] [1976] OJ L129/23.

coherent programmes for reducing pollution, based on studies of the waters affected and setting quality objectives'.[41] Schemes will not constitute programmes within the meaning of the Directive where they 'give no indication either as to the quality objectives pursued as regards the substances referred to . . . or as to the deadlines for implementing those plans'.[42] It seems that the main obstacle to compliance has related to the failure to establish programmes incorporating quality objectives with a view to the reduction of pollution by the listed substances into the aquatic environment, for the Court will approach anything less as amounting to a defective implementation.[43]

As can be seen from the large number of recent enforcement cases referenced in the previous paragraph, the Commission continues to regard the dangerous substances legislation as being beset with high levels of Member State non-compliance. Thus it has reported that 'proceedings have been started against most Member States over their implementation of [the Dangerous Substances Directive] and of the directives setting levels for individual substances'.[44] Thus, in numerous instances Member States have not yet notified sufficient measures to ensure compliance with Article 7 of the Directive, and numerous infringement procedures have been instigated.[45] Overall, the Commission's proactive enforcement policies seem set to continue. Its dangerous substances implementation report states that compliance with the Directive is improved considerably by the further use of infringement procedures.[46] Looking at the wider picture, dovetailing the Directive into the Water Framework Directive is assisted by its requirements for pollution reduction programmes, as these are regarded as 'building blocks' toward eventual implementation of the Water Framework Directive, according to its Article 11.

ii. Nitrates

The EU legislation on nitrates pollution continues to see a high degree of enforcement activity on the part of the Commission. This is not only in terms of Article 226 EC (for failure to fulfil Treaty obligations) but also widely under Article 228 EC (for non-compliance with ECJ judgments).[47] The UK, for instance, had been held in 2000 to be in breach of Directive 91/676/EEC on the Protection of Waters against Pollution Caused by Nitrates from Agricultural

[41] Case C-384/97, *Commission* v. *Greece* [2000] ECR I-3823, para. 42.

[42] Case C-261/98, *Commission* v. *Portugal* [2000] ECR I-5905, para. 29; see also Case C-184/97, *Commission* v. *Germany* [1999] ECR I-7837, para. 39.

[43] Case C-152/98, *Commission* v. *Netherlands* [2001] ECR I-3463; see also Case C-184/97, ibid.

[44] Commission Report, n. 2 above, 17.

[45] See e.g. Case C-384/97, n. 41 above; Case C-261/98, n. 42 above; Case C-207/97, *Commission* v. *Belgium* [1999] ECR I-275; and Case C-206/96, *Commission* v. *Luxembourg* [1998] ECR I-3401.

[46] Commission Report—Assessment of Programmes under Article 7 Of Directive 76/464/EEC (Nov. 2001), published on the Internet at: http://europa.eu.int/comm/environment/water/water-dangersub/article7ofdirective77464eec.pdf.

[47] See Commission Report, n. 2 above, 19–20.

Sources (Nitrates Directive),[48] both as to designation criteria and time limits.[49] The UK has faced considerable problems in producing a scheme to achieve compliance. Proposals were eventually produced which involved the designation of either 100 per cent or 80 per cent of England land area (from a base of just 8 per cent under the original, defaulting arrangements),[50] but following a critical response from the agricultural lobby the extent of designation has subsequently been reduced to 55 per cent.[51] There remains a threat of further enforcement proceedings under Article 228 EC, and it would in such circumstances be necessary to satisfy the Court that all measures necessary to comply with obligations to designate vulnerable zones, as well as drawing up action programmes, had been adopted in accordance with Articles 3(1)(2) and 5 of the Nitrates Directive.

An illustration of the insistence on the part of the ECJ upon requisite compliance with the objectives of the Directive can be seen in a 2002 judgment in Case C-258/00, *Commission* v. *France*.[52] The proceedings concerned domestic methodology which purported to limit (for the purposes of control) the identification of eutrophic waters on grounds that in some conditions (including as to flowing brackish waters and both stagnant and flowing hard freshwaters) phosphorous was a controlling factor. The Member State in part placed reliance upon scientific arguments, an illustration of which can be seen in an extract from a French Environment Ministry Circular concerned with designations under the Directive. Thus:

> at the stage where one can speak of eutrophication . . . excessive growth of aquatic plant life thus appears to be the result of the complex and subtle interplay between a number of diverse and variable factors. To establish a relationship of cause and effect from its appearance, its nature, its intensity and its frequency is an extremely difficult task, precisely because of that complexity and subtlety of interactions.[53]

In interpreting the obligations placed upon Member States under the terms of Articles 1, 3(1), and 3(2) of the Directive the ECJ sought to apply the tried and tested objectives-based approach. This was based upon the recognition that, as a matter of fact, nitrogen pollution from agricultural sources was a contributing factor. Thus, notwithstanding the wide discretion afforded to Member States for the purposes of identification of designable waters,[54] an essential obligation

[48] [1991] OJ L375/1.

[49] Case C-69/99, *Commission* v. *United Kingdom* [2000] ECR I-10979.

[50] Department of Environment, Food and Rural Affairs, How Should England Implement the 1991 Nitrates Directive? (Dec. 2001); published on the Internet at: http://www.defra.gov.uk/environment/consult/nitrate1201/index.htm.

[51] See 'Government Caves in on Nitrates' (2002) 26 *Environmental Data Services Report*, 330.

[52] [2002] ECR I-5959.

[53] ibid., para. 49, citing a Circular of 5 Nov. 1992 concerning the Directive and the Initial Designation of Vulnerable Zones.

[54] See e.g. Case C-293/97, *The Queen* v. *Secretary of State for the Environment and Ministry of Agriculture, Fisheries and Food, ex p. H.A. Standley and Others and D.G.D. Metson and Others* (*Standley*) [1999] ECR I-2603, paras. 37–9.

applied to the task of identification, 'to respect the objectives of the Directive, namely, the reduction of water pollution caused by nitrates from agricultural sources'.[55] Moreover, it was not acceptable that a Member State's exercise of discretion as to the identification of waters falling within the terms of the Nitrates Directive could result in 'a large portion of nitrogen-bearing waters falling outside the scope of the Directive'.[56]

It appears, therefore, that the ECJ was careful to distance itself from detailed engagement in scientific argument. The Court made this clear in pronouncing as follows: 'Without having to take account of the many scientific reports and studies cited . . . it should be noted that restricting the scope of the Directive to exclude certain categories of waters owing to the supposedly fundamental role of phosphorous in the pollution of those waters is incompatible with both the logic and the objective of the Directive'.[57]

Where disputes of a scientific or technical nature concerning a Directive subsequently arise, and fall to be decided as a matter of interpretation, it appears that a legalistic approach in favour of mandatory compliance is likely to prevail.[58] Altered understandings will accordingly be as far as possible confined to policy processes within the EU. This does little for flexibility, but it does partly insulate the integrity of current legislation from the kind of systemic conflictual processes referred to above.[59]

In an important enforcement action against Germany, the ECJ has held that the process of discounting (by 20 per cent) nitrate emission figures, to take account of evaporation upon the spreading of livestock manure,[60] was a substantive breach of the requirements of the Directive.[61] Germany argued that, as a result of evaporation, such nitrogen would not enter groundwater sources as a direct result of 'livestock manure applied to the land'.[62] The Commission argued that a large proportion of the same would eventually return to the land (presumably by such factors as precipitation). An arguably narrow, legalistic point of construction concerned what process(es) amounted to application of manure. Purporting to approach interpretation on the principled basis of context,[63] the ECJ found a range of indicators in the Directive which enabled the conclusion that the process extended beyond actual spreading. The Court relied upon sections of the Preamble: for instance the statement that the Directive had the aim of reducing direct or indirect pollution of waters by nitrates from

[55] Case C-258/00, n. 52 above, para. 53; see also Case C-293/97, ibid.

[56] Case C-258/00, n. 52 above, para. 54; cf. Case C-133/94, *Commission* v. *Belgium* [1996] ECR-I 2323.

[57] Case C-258/00, n. 52 above, para. 45.

[58] Cf. Case C-152/98, *Commission* v. *Netherlands* [2001] ECR I-3463; and Case C-71/97, *Commission* v. *Spain* [1998] ECR I-5991.

[59] See sect. A above.

[60] Art. 5(4) of the Nitrates Dir., and measures contained in Annex III.

[61] Case C-161/00, *Commission* v. *Germany* [2002] ECR I-2753.

[62] Para. 2.1 of Annex III to the Nitrates Dir.

[63] See, further, Case C-156/98, *Commission* v. *Germany* [2000] ECR I-6857, para. 50.

agricultural sources and to prevent further such pollution in order to protect human health, living resources, and aquatic ecosystems.[64] Moreover, there appeared to be 'no distinction (made) between the beginning and the end of the application process'.[65]

The Court found a failure to fulfil obligations arising under the Directive. Accordingly, in view of:

> both the context and objectives of the Directive, . . . the decisive criterion which the Directive lays down for limiting pollution by nitrates from agricultural sources is the amount of nitrogen applied to land by spreading on its surface, by injection into the land, by placing below the surface of the land or by mixing with the surface layers of the land, and not the amount of nitrogen actually penetrating into the land.[66]

In other words, in view of the determination that the process of application should not be restrictively interpreted, the grounds for such discounting by the Member State from calculations of maximum levels must necessarily be rejected. There is some irony in the potential implications of such a broad statement in the light of the first law of thermodynamics. Notwithstanding this, the result is, arguably, beneficial when viewed from the wider perspectives of those concerned at the cumulative extent of environmental threats faced by humankind.

iii. Urban Waste-Water

Alongside the Nitrates Directive, Directive 91/271/EEC on Urban Waste-Water Treatment (Urban Waste-Water Directive)[67] also targets pollution from phosphates and nitrates (and resulting problems such as eutrophication). Its implementation deadlines are gradually coming into force, as for instance a 1998 deadline for implementing advanced sewerage treatment in areas deemed sensitive to discharges. There is a looming 2005 end-date for full effectiveness. Following the Commission's 2001 report that proceedings in the event of implementation failures were to be taken against seven Member States, numerous infringement procedures were ongoing in 2002.[68] An updated, cumulative report has criticized what are described as 'major shortcomings in most Member States as regards compliance with the obligations of the Directive'.[69] The Commission cites implementation delays in most Member States, and defects in treatment standards affecting large centres of population, together with failures to recognize the sensitive nature of aquatic environments that receive waste-water from large cities and consequent problems of downstream marine

[64] Recitals 6 and 11.

[65] Case C-161/00, n. 61 above, para. 40, citing Art. 2(h) of the Nitrates Dir.

[66] ibid., para. 46.

[67] [1991] OJ L135/40.

[68] Commission Report—Implementation of Council Directive 91/676/EEC of 21 May 1991 concerning Urban Waste-Water Treatment, as amended by Commission Directive 98/15/EC of 27 February 1998—Situation at 31 December 1998 COM(2001)685, 43.

[69] ibid. 47.

eutrophication. Problems have also been encountered because of information and reporting deficits.[70]

The Commission continues to be concerned as to defaults in two major respects, namely, in meeting designation obligations in respect of sensitive areas; and, further, in compliance with urban waste-water treatment requirements under the terms of the Directive. Proceedings have, for instance, been commenced in connection with alleged insufficient and incorrect designation of vulnerable zones under Article 5.[71] Other pending actions include those laid against Belgium (late implementation in respect of the provision of sewers and waste-water treatment plants) and France (lack of identification of sensitive areas and insufficiencies in water treatment).[72] The Commission retained concerns as to whether adequate action had been taken in respect of certain waters in the UK, including shellfish waters and certain estuaries.[73] There was a possibility of potential proceedings in respect of failures correctly to designate and to review sensitive and less sensitive areas under the terms of the Directive.[74]

Italy has been condemned for failure to fulfil obligations under Article 5(1) in respect of urban waste-water treatment in the Milan area.[75] Here, discharge of untreated waste-water into a tributary of the river Po eventually drained into an area identified as a sensitive area (the Po Delta, along with a part of the coastal area of the north-west Adriatic). The Court ruled that it was of no consequence that the discharges to the relevant sensitive areas could be said to be indirect (given a distance in excess of 300 kilometres from the city). Any other interpretation of the obligation would undermine the objectives of the Directive.[76]

iv. Bathing Water

Reference has already been made above to new legislative proposals in the area of bathing water which have the dual aim of tightening up controls of contamination in targeted respects and otherwise upon introducing greater flexibility into the regulatory regime.[77] The proposed new Directive thus takes account of technological and scientific developments in the quarter of a century since the previous lead Directive. The whole tenor of encouragement of greater transparency and public and stakeholder participation chimes in with one of the essential objectives underlying the Water Framework Directive.

Control of bathing waters is one of the areas of regulation where the Commission feels that most progress has been made.[78] Likewise, it is one of the areas

70 ibid. 47–8.

71 Case C-419/01, *Commission* v. *Spain* [2003] ECR I-4947.

72 Commission Report, n. 2 above, 18–19.

73 'New "Sensitive Area" Designations May Not be Enough' (2002) 26 *Environmental Data Services Report*, 326.

74 Commission Report, n. 2 above, 19.

75 Case C-396/00, *Commission* v. *Italy* [2002] ECR I-3949.

76 See n. 17 above, Art. 5(2).

77 See sect. C.*i.* above; in particular COM(2002)581, n. 18 above.

78 See e.g. Explanatory Memorandum, n. 21 above, para. 1.

within the Commission's beat that is most amenable to enforcement in the event of defects in compliance, given demanding standards and high levels of monitoring in place. Thus, the Commission has stated that 'proceedings are still under way against most Member States since implementation still falls far short of the [Bathing Water] Directive's requirements'.[79] In 2002, the ECJ ruled against the Netherlands in respect of failure to conform to quality values and sampling frequencies.[80]

An illustration of the (attritionally) long time-frames of litigation can be seen in the saga of enforcement against the UK for non-compliance with the Bathing Waters Directive. In 1993, judgment had been given against the UK for non-compliance with mandatory quality values in respect of certain bathing waters in the north-west of England.[81] The ECJ had applied a purposive approach to the review of the exercise of discretion in the designation of bathing waters for the purposes of the Directive.[82] The UK had argued that all practicable steps had been taken, that compliance was not possible, that the duty was conditional, and, in effect, that due diligence (towards the achievement of the required standards) had been exercised. The ruling reasserted the state's responsibility to ensure conformity with objective characteristics.[83] This ruled out reliance on particular national circumstances as a reason for breach, outside the formal derogation process, and the notion of taking all practicable steps afforded no acceptable ground of defence.[84] Proceedings now, at last, appear to have come to an end, as the Commission has withdrawn Article 228 EC proceedings for non-compliance with the original judgment of the Court,[85] on the basis that bathing waters were compliant with the mandatory standards.[86]

Meanwhile, as in the above-mentioned case, there appears to be a catalogue of further Commission investigations into non-compliance with ECJ judgments under the terms of the Bathing Waters Directive. For instance, it was reported that infringement proceedings remained open against Germany.[87] This followed an earlier judgment for failure in due time to adopt steps to ensure conformity with limit values and to meet prescribed minimum sampling frequencies, it again being insufficient to take all reasonably practicable measures.[88] A further

[79] See Commission Report, n. 2 above, 16.

[80] Case C-268/00, *Commission* v. *Netherlands* [2002] ECR I-2995.

[81] Case C-56/90, *Commission* v. *United Kingdom* [1993] ECR I-4109.

[82] ibid., para. 43.

[83] ibid., para. 33.

[84] ibid., paras. 43–4, although physical impossibility (not there established) had been arguably left open.

[85] Case C-85/01, *Commission* v. *United Kingdom*, withdrawn.

[86] Cf. Case C-278/01, *Commission* v. *Spain* [2003] ECR-I 0000 (not yet reported), concerning alleged non-compliance with the judgment in Case C-92/96, *Commission* v. *Spain* [1998] ECR I-505.

[87] Commission Report, n. 2 above, 16.

[88] Case C-198/97, *Commission* v. *Germany* [1999] ECR I-3257; see Art. 6(1) of the Bathing Waters Dir.

illustration followed an earlier finding against Belgium of non-compliance with the Directive's objective requirements, brought about by non-conformity with limit values and the unjustified removal from designation of certain inland waters,[89] the Commission instigating formal Article 228 EC procedures.[90]

v. Drinking Water

Directive 98/83/EC on the Quality of Water Intended for Human Consumption (Drinking Water Directive)[91] repeals the original Directive 80/778/EEC relating to the Quality of Water for Human Consumption,[92] which should be fully replaced by 25 December 2003. The due date for transposition was 25 December 2000, and the Commission has already been concerned as to potential infringements of the new legislation on the part of a number of Member States in the adoption and communication to the Commission of fully transposed measures.[93] Notwithstanding its shortening shelf life, a small number of cases remain concerned with the 1980 Directive, in which the Commission appears concerned to instigate proceedings.[94] In an important judgment requiring interpretation of the Directive, the ECJ has emphasized once more its interpretation to the effect that legislative mandatory values are absolute requirements.[95] This case against Ireland concerned non-compliance with microbiological parameters for such water.[96] On the general question of compliance, it is established law that compliance failure cannot be justified by reference to reasonably practicable (usually investment-related) measures.[97] The Court was unimpressed with the *de minimis* arguments as to the slight nature of the risks, in effect substantial compliance: 'However strenuous the efforts . . . to improve the quality of drinking water on its territory may have been . . . in respect of water quality, Article 7(6) of Directive 80/778 does not establish a mere duty of diligence but an obligation to achieve a particular result'.[98]

The proceedings broke new ground in that enforcement also concerned non-compliance by a large proportion of so-called 'group water schemes'. These schemes cover around 145,000 rural households in Ireland in areas of thin population density. They are developed through community effort and grant-aided by the state. Of this number, the action concerned inadequacy of supply in

[89] Case C-307/98, *Commission* v. *Belgium* [2000] ECR I-3933.

[90] See further Case C-368/00, *Commission* v. *Sweden* [2001] ECR I-4605.

[91] [1998] OJ L330/32.

[92] [1980] OJ L229/11.

[93] During 2002, the Commission announced its intention to take proceedings against Belgium, Spain, and the UK.

[94] See Wurzel, n. 1 above, 18.

[95] Case C-316/00, *Commission* v. *Ireland* [2002] ECR I-10527.

[96] Art. 2 (and Annex I, setting out the relevant parameters) of Dir. 80/778, n. 92 above.

[97] See Case C-340/96, n. 38 above; see also Case C-337/89, *Commission* v. *United Kingdom* [1993] ECR I-4109.

[98] Case C-316/00, n. 95 above, para. 37.

respect of the 55,000 of these households which were in schemes that did not connect with public water supply networks, but were reliant upon private sources (such as springs, boreholes, rivers, or lakes). The Court ruled that such schemes fell within the scope of the Directive. Earlier authority indicated that a supply derived from private sources was excluded from the provisions.[99] However, this case was distinguished on the basis that it must be interpreted as restricted to waters 'directly drawn by the individual for his own use. By contrast, a situation where the water is supplied to several users by way of a supply network is clearly covered by the concept of supply to consumers'.[100] The schemes under dispute were accordingly held to fall within the terms of the Directive.

The distinction, whilst arguably justified, was based on the seemingly unnecessarily narrow view that such a network's extraction and distribution process 'prevent it from being individually monitored by each user'.[101] Yet, once the determination is made that a facility is a supply network, it clearly becomes irrelevant that only a small number of customers are served.[102] Moreover, domestic regulations in effect exempting such schemes from equivalent controls (by failing to place a direct duty of compliance upon providers, but rather warning as to unacceptable risks and recommendations for action) amounted to a failure to ensure the binding character of the quality parameters contained in the Directive.[103]

Meanwhile, the Commission has several further cases under way concerning infringements of Directive 75/440/EEC concerning the Quality Required of Surface Water intended for the Abstraction of Drinking Water in the Member States (Surface Waters Directive).[104] These relate to defaults in relation to the preparation of systematic action plans for the purposes of safeguarding water quality, including as to nitrates and pesticides; and disputes concerning criteria applicable to exemptions.[105] Moreover, following ECJ judgment against France in respect of nitrate content of waters used for abstraction of drinking waters in excess of limit values,[106] the Commission reported the possibility of further action under Article 228 EC procedures in the event of non-compliance. By contrast, in another proceeding, against Italy, action had been withdrawn in respect of an alleged breach of the requirement to produce a systematic action programme for the Lombardy Region.[107]

vi. Shellfish Waters

Directive 79/923/EEC on the Quality Required of Shellfish Waters (Shellfish Water Directive)[108] requires appropriate designation and preparation of improve-

[99] Case C-42/89, *Commission* v. *Belgium* [1990] ECR I-2821.
[100] Case C-316/00, n. 95 above, para. 44.
[101] ibid., para. 44.
[102] ibid., para. 45.
[103] ibid., para. 49.
[104] [1975] OJ L194/26.
[105] ibid., Art. 4(2)(3).
[106] Case C-266/99, *Commission* v. *France* [2001] ECR I-1981, paras. 29–30.
[107] Case C-375/00, *Commission* v. *Italy*, withdrawn.
[108] [1979] OJ L281/47.

ment programmes and adequate monitoring. Following receipt of information and assurances as to both designation and appropriate improvement programmes and monitoring arrangements, the Commission has dropped threatened enforcement proceedings for non-compliance against the UK.

D. Conclusions

Finally, whilst recognizing the continuing difficulties in securing improved environmental performance in this sector of EU policy-making, over a quarter century of water regulation at Community level has seen a pervasive, growing acceptance—albeit grudging in places, often on grounds of resource implications—by Member States. It has been said that, generally:

> the European institutions have together developed a policy that demands local coordination, complicated interactions with specific water institutions, and recently even massive financial transfers. As a policy it has survived direct legal conflict with member states such as Britain and the challenge from those wishing to roll back the EU's environmental competencies. Judged from this perspective, perhaps what is most surprising is the extent to which EU involvement has been so readily accepted.[109]

A gradual political climate change reflects the development of new traditions, and the impact of heightened public expectations (and public interest group involvement).[110] It is, for instance, notable that Commission documents now routinely commence by reference to 'growing public concerns'.[111] And greater public participation is being built into new regulatory structures, as under the Water Framework Directive and the new Bathing Water Directive.[112]

For all the concerns at implementation, the key innovative feature of the Water Framework Directive lies in its attempt to set up a truly integrative approach to water quality and water availability. This potentially groundbreaking contribution cannot be over-emphasized. Without such an approach, alongside 'more of the same' in terms of periodic set-piece EU struggles to modernize legislation and thereafter (with questionable efficiency) to ensure compliance, reliance upon other legal mechanisms would remain extremely problematic. An extreme illustration of this can be seen in the United States, where progress in the cause of environmental protection, including as to water pollution, often relies upon citizen suits. Their potential impact there has been welcomed by some

[109] A. Weale, G. Pridham, M. Cini, D. Konstadakopulos, M. Porter, and B. Flynn (eds.), *Environmental Governance in Europe—An Ever Closer Ecological Union?* (Oxford: Oxford University Press, 2000), 378.

[110] See Jordan, n. 6 above, 321.

[111] e.g. Commission Report, n. 8 above, 7.

[112] The pending incorporation of the Aarhus Convention into EC law will accelerate this process. See UN/ECE Convention on Access to Information, Public Participation in Decision-Making and Access to Justice in Environmental Matters (Aarhus Convention), Aarhus (Denmark), 25 June 1998 (entered into force 30 Oct. 2001) (1999) 38 *International Legal Materials* 3, 517.

commentators, even suggesting a potential 'to transform water pollution law by forcing federal and state governments to focus on ambient water quality in whole watersheds rather than the use of mandated technology controls by individual dischargers'.[113] Such developments are interesting, but from a European perspective the potential inefficiencies (as well as the vagaries attaching to structural restrictions across Member States, as for instance in respect of standing) are in part what led to the continuing acceptance of the need for regulatory structures. For all the encouragement of access to justice, there have thus far been few signs of a serious contribution on the part of individual or group actions under such doctrines as direct effect and *Francovich* in this field.[114]

Given continued reliance upon regulatory arrangements, it is however to be regretted that problems of implementation are not confronted head on at the earlier stages of policy deliberations (and attendant compromises being reached). This would be beneficial in two particular ways. First, better quality legislation would emerge. Secondly, Member States might find themselves able to 'buy in' to the implications of legislative outputs.[115] The crucial need for improvements in the quality of law making is now recognized.[116] As the third phase of EU legislative intervention unfolds, as under the Water Framework Directive, harmonization, as between instruments, will be a crucial factor towards progress. This will apply as between the Framework, Urban Waste-Water, and Nitrates Directives, for instance, as regards parameter setting, monitoring arrangements, and comparisons of impact and efficiency of measures.[117] Concerns persist as to how satisfactorily these approaches will achieve harmonization across Member States. And yet there is a degree of optimism that, overall, enhanced levels of implementation will result.[118] In particular, a successful and effective implementation of the Framework Directive will be crucial to future progress in the management of water resources and ecosystems within the European Union.

[113] See J.S. Harbison, 'Private Enforcement of Public Values in US Courts—Justiciability Barriers in Environmental Law' (2001) 3 *Environmental Law Review* 4, 264–81, citing, at 266, *Sierra Club et al.* v. *Hankinson*, 939 F. Supp. 865 (N.D. Ga. 1996).

[114] Joined Cases C-6/90 and C-9/90, *Andrea Francovich and Danila Bonifaci and Others* v. *Italy* [1991] ECR I-5357; see High Court, *Bowden* v. *South West Water* (1998) 6 Environmental Law Reports, 445; cf. Court of Appeals, *Bowden* v. *South West Water* (1999) 7 Environmental Law Reports, 438.

[115] See K. Collins and D. Earnshaw, *The Implementation and Enforcement of EC Environmental Policy* (1992) 1 *Environmental Politics* 4, 213–49.

[116] See e.g. Commission Communication—Implementing Community Environmental Law, COM(96)500.

[117] See Commission Report, n. 8 above, 43–4.

[118] See e.g. Glachant, n. 3 above, 27.

VI. Horizontal Instruments

*Benjamin J. Richardson**

A. Legislation Adopted

i. Environmental Impact Assessment

The European Community (EC) environmental impact assessment (EIA) legislation has been substantially modernized in recent years, and is arguably the most important of the 'horizontal' instruments of environmental governance in the Community. Environmental policy instruments that can work across sectors, often using incentive and informational mechanisms, can stimulate a more integrated and comprehensive system of governing environmental affairs. Assessing the environmental impacts of development proposals, as well as plans and programmes, helps generate information to enable more informed, precautionary decision-making and so prevent environmental harms from arising or, where they do, minimizing the extent of such harms.

The first Community EIA law was Directive 85/337/EEC on the Assessment of the Effects of certain Public and Private Projects on the Environment.[1] In 1997, this Directive was overhauled by Directive 97/11/EC Amending Directive 85/337/EEC on the Assessment of the Effects of certain Public and Private Projects on the Environment,[2] which entered into force on 14 March 1999. The new Directive introduced changes relating to the screening of projects, obligations to consider alternative development options, improved integration of EIA processes with other environmental regulation procedures, and a widening of impact assessment to include transboundary effects. Further ambitious reforms were engineered in June 2001, with the passage of the so-called 'strategic assessment Directive', Directive 2001/42/EC on the Assessment of the Effects of Certain Plans and Programmes on the Environment (SEA Directive).[3]

The SEA Directive provides a procedural framework for ensuring that the environmental consequences of certain plans and programmes are identified and assessed during their preparation. Article 3 of the SEA Directive requires an environmental assessment of all plans and programmes which: (i) are prepared for agriculture, forestry, fisheries, energy, industry, transport, waste management, water management, telecommunications, tourism, town and country planning, or land use, and which set the framework for future development consent of projects identified in the Annexes of Directive 85/337/EEC; or (ii) which have been determined to require an assessment pursuant to Directive 92/43/EEC on

* Associate Professor, Osgoode Hall Law School, York University, Toronto (Canada).

1 [1985] OJ L175/40. 2 [1997] OJ L73/5. 3 [2001] OJ L197/30.

the Conservation of Natural Habitats and of Wild Fauna and Flora (Habitats Directive).[4] The SEA Directive not only applies to internal national plans and programmes, but also those deriving from EC legislation. However, it does not apply to national or EC policies, although of course there may not always be a bright line distinction between a 'policy' and a 'plan' or 'programme'. Also excluded are plans and programmes for which the sole purpose is to serve national defence or civil emergency, and financial or budget plans and programmes. Despite these shortcomings, through the SEA Directive, the EC is able to take a more comprehensive and holistic approach to environmental assessment, in accordance with the 'integration' principle introduced in Article 6 EC by the Treaty of Amsterdam.[5]

Although the SEA Directive does not formally apply to policies, the EC has been looking at ways better to link environmental assessment with other forms of social and economic assessment in government planning and policy-making. On 6 May 2002, the Commission issued a Communication on Impact Assessment, wherein it spelt out a campaign 'to launch impact assessment as a tool to improve the quality and coherence of the policy development process, [and so contribute] to a more coherent implementation of the European strategy for Sustainable Development'.[6] To be phased in over 2003–4, the Commission's aim is to foster a more 'integrated' impact assessment system to replace the current, seemingly ad hoc approach to impact assessment regarding legislative and policy proposals. These comprise, apart from environmental assessment, requirements for business impact assessment, gender assessment, regulatory impact assessment, and so on. The aim, therefore, is to include environmental assessment in a broader, coherent web of policy and regulatory impact assessments that are to canvass a range of social, economic, and environmental factors simultaneously in the spirit of sustainable development. The Commission's Communication builds on earlier statements to this effect contained in its Better Regulation Action Plan,[7] and the White Paper on Governance.[8] This focus on integrated impact assessment methods, in turn, naturally builds on the SEA Directive. By seeking to integrate the environment into social and economic decision-making at the beginning of the policy cycle, the Commission's initiatives should help fulfil the integration principle of Article 6 EC. The primary shortcoming with traditional EIA methods is that they react to development proposals rather than foreseeing and steering them.[9] Strategic, holistic, forms of impact assessment can help mitigate this problem by offering a systematic and comprehensive process of assessment of

[4] [1992] OJ L206/7.

[5] Consolidated version of the Treaty of the European Community [1997] OJ C340/3.

[6] COM(2002)276, para. 1.

[7] Commission Communication—Action Plan on Simplifying and Improving the Regulatory Environment COM(2002)278.

[8] European Governance—A White Paper COM(2001)428, [2001] OJ C287/1.

[9] See C. Wood and N. Djeddour, 'Strategic Environmental Assessment—EA of Policies, Plans and Programmes' (1992) 10 *Impact Assessment Bulletin*, 3.

the environmental impacts of plans and policies which mould subsequent decision-making on specific developments and other activities.[10]

ii. Eco-Management and Audit Scheme

The Community's Eco-Management and Audit Scheme (EMAS) encourages companies, on a voluntary basis, to establish site- or company-wide environmental management and audit systems, and periodically to publish environmental performance reports that are independently verified by accredited auditors. The EMAS was established in 1993 by Regulation (EEC) No. 1836/93 allowing Voluntary Participation by Companies in the Industrial Sector in a Community Eco-Management and Audit Scheme,[11] and substantially revised in 2001 by Regulation (EC) No. 761/2001 allowing Voluntary Participation by Organisations in a Community Eco-Management and Audit Scheme.[12] Along with the Community eco-label scheme, EMAS was portrayed in the Sixth Community Environment Action Programme (EAP-6) published in 2002 as 'the backbone of the Community's environmental protection policy'.[13]

Targeting companies in the industrial sector, the 1993 EMAS Regulation aimed to promote ongoing environmental performance improvements of corporate activities by committing participating firms to evaluate and improve their own environmental performance. The Regulation obliged Member States to establish a review mechanism, by which independent verifiers who are approved by accreditation bodies can validate compliance to the scheme. Upon receipt of an appropriate recommendation from the verifier, a Member State's designated competent authority can then register the business in question as EMS-compliant. To be registered, an organization must adopt an environmental policy containing, in summary, commitments to: comply with all relevant environmental legislation; prevent pollution; and achieve continuous improvements in environmental performance.

To spur wider interest in EMAS, and to extend the practice into other areas of the market, in 2001, the EC extensively revamped EMAS in the 2001 Regulation, which entered into force in April 2001. The principal problem with the 1993 Regulation was its narrow focus on industrial sites rather than environmental policies and management practices at a company level. Its form also made it difficult to encompass the environmental practices of the influential financial services sector, such as bank lending.[14] The main elements of the 2001 EMAS

[10] See R. Therivel and M.R. Partidario (eds.), *The Practice of Strategic Environmental Assessment* (London: Earthscan, 1996).

[11] [1993] OJ L168/1.

[12] [2001] OJ L114/1.

[13] Dec. 1600/2002/EC laying down the Sixth Community Environment Action Programme [2002] OJ L242/13.

[14] See B.J. Richardson, 'Implications of Recent Changes to the EMAS and Eco-label Regulations for the Financial Services Sector' (2002) 14 *Environmental Law and Management* 2, 131.

Regulation were: (i) the extension of the scope of EMAS to all sectors of economic activity, including public authorities;[15] (ii) the integration of ISO 14001 as the required environmental management system (although EMAS continues to differ from the ISO standard with regard to legal compliance, communication, and environmental performance); (iii) the potential extension of EMAS to an entire organization rather than a specific site of that organization; (iv) a strengthening of the role of the corporate environmental statement to improve the transparency of the communication of environmental performance between companies and the wider community; and (v) more emphasis on consideration of indirect environmental effects including financial investments, administrative decisions, and procurement procedures.

In theory, the primary attraction for companies to participate in EMAS—a voluntary scheme—is the prospect of regulatory relief, improved market reputation, and cost savings through more frugal resource consumption.[16] By the close of 2002, there were a total of 3,797 EMAS registrations, slightly down from 3,912 at the beginning of 2002, but well up on numbers of a few years ago (e.g. 3,417 at the beginning of 2000, and 2,775 at the beginning of 1999).[17] Germany still massively dominates the registrations, with some 2,500 EMAS-registered industrial sites or companies, followed at a distance by Spain and Austria with about 300 registrations each, and, competing for the wooden spoon, a paltry 75 registrations in Britain and a mere 40 in France.[18] In some instances, EMAS registrations have been withdrawn or terminated following poor environmental practice. For example, the chemical producer AH Marks recently withdrew from EMAS following the United Kingdom (UK) Environment Agency's recommendation that it be suspended from the British EMAS register after unauthorized pollution emissions.[19] In EAP-6 it was acknowledged that 'whilst the uptake of EMAS by companies has been encouraging, additional measures need to be considered that will help significantly increase the proportion of companies that publish rigorous and audited environmental or broader sustainable development reports'.[20] In particular, the Programme recommended that specific attention be given to tailoring these tools to the needs of small and medium-

[15] 'To any organisation dedicated to improving its overall environmental performance', Art. 3 of Reg. (EC) No. 761/2001, n. 12 above.

[16] See F. Watzold, 'EMAS and Regulatory Relief in Europe—Lessons from National Experience' (2001) 11 *European Environment* 1, 37; R. Fairley, 'Environmental Policy and Audit—What's in It for Us?' (1995) 7 *Environmental Law and Management*, 31.

[17] Statistics on EMAS registration are published on the Internet at: http://europa.eu.int/comm/environment/emas.

[18] Per head of population, however, Austria has relatively the highest EMAS registrations, followed closely by Germany.

[19] See 'Agency Flexes its Muscles on EMAS' (2003) 26 *Environmental Data Services Reports*, 338, 3; 'Chemical Company's EMAS Registration Suspended Following IPC Breach' (2003) 128 *Environment Information Bulletin*, 1.

[20] n. 13 above, 16.

sized enterprises (SMEs), although it did not elaborate on how this should be done.[21]

Although there have been no legislative amendments to the EMAS regime since the 2001 revision, apart from a technical corrigendum,[22] the Commission has been active in strengthening the framework for implementation of the Scheme. Primarily, the Commission adopted seven 'guidance' documents aimed at ensuring that the EMAS Regulation is applied uniformly by all Member States, and at giving practical support to organizations in the implementation of the scheme. Three of these guidance documents have been adopted as annexes to a Commission Decision (guidance on the entity, on verification frequency, and on the EMAS logo),[23] and the remaining four guidelines have been adopted as annexes of a Commission Recommendation.[24]

One of the acclaimed advantages of corporate environmental management systems such as EMAS is that they should allow participating businesses to obtain preferential treatment from regulators given that certification of adoption of an environmental management system should be plausible evidence of a company's compliance with environmental law. Participation in voluntary agreements with environmental regulators can also provide an equivalent function. Recently, the Commission has proposed a new system for voluntary environmental agreements at Community level, which could be linked to the EMAS.[25] In its Opinion on the Commission's proposal, the Economic and Social Committee (ESC) recommended that 'participation in a voluntary environmental agreement [be] a criterion in the award of an eco-label or EMAS certification'.[26] Such a policy would surely strengthen the incentive to be EMAS-registered, for it would be a necessary precondition to enter into voluntary environmental agreements, as an alternative to further environmental regulation.

iii. Eco-Labelling

Eco-labelling is a market-based, voluntary instrument that works to promote consumer preference for products and services that have a lower environmental impact during their life-cycle. It also provides consumers with more information

[21] ibid., 16–17.

[22] Corrigendum to Reg. (EC) No. 761/2001, [2002] OJ L 327/10.

[23] Dec. 681/2001/EC on Guidance for the Implementation of Regulation (EC) No. 761/2001 allowing Voluntary Participation by Organisations in a Community Eco-Management and Audit Scheme, [2001] OJ L247/24.

[24] Rec. 680/2001/EC on Guidance for the Implementation of Regulation (EC) No. 761/2001 allowing Voluntary Participation by Organisations in a Community Eco-Management and Audit Scheme, [2001] OJ L247/1.

[25] Commission Communication—Environmental Agreements at Community Level Within the Framework of the Action Plan on the Simplification and Improvement of the Regulatory Environment, COM(2002)412.

[26] Opinion of the ESC on the Commission Communication—Environmental Agreements at Community Level Within the Framework of the Action Plan on the Simplification and Improvement of the Regulatory Environment, [2003] OJ C61/142, para. 2.7.

regarding the environmental quality and effects of products and services so as to enable them to make more informed purchasing decisions.[27] Because it potentially affects a plethora of environmental policy situations, eco-labelling is a classic horizontal policy instrument. However, as it is both a voluntary and a selective tool, eco-labelling lacks the compulsion and universality that some other environmental policy measures can impart.

The eco-labelling scheme was originally constituted by Regulation (EEC) No. 880/92 on a Community Eco-Label Award Scheme,[28] and was revised in July 2000 by Regulation (EC) No. 1980/2000 on a Revised Community Eco-Label Award Scheme.[29] Apart from the Eco-Label Regulations, environmental information labelling requirements also come from EC energy legislation providing for the classification of products according to their energy efficiency. An extensive legislative programme for energy efficiency labelling of household appliances was undertaken in the 1990s.[30]

Under the scheme, products that satisfy precise ecological performance criteria are awarded the 'Flower' logo, which can be marketed to demonstrate to consumers that a product has superior environmental credentials. The 2000 amendments streamlined the scheme, widened its scope to cover labelling of services, introduced decreased fee structures, and increased the scheme's transparency and opportunity for stakeholder involvement. The primary reason for the amendments was that the 1992 Regulation was considered not to have achieved a satisfactory level of market penetration, mostly because of the limited range of goods it covered. The European Union (EU) Eco-labelling Board (EUEB) is the central body of the scheme. The Board consists of the national competent bodies (the authorities responsible for implementing the eco-label award scheme at national level) and members of the Consultation Forum (comprising representatives of consumer and environment non-governmental organizations (NGOs), trade unions, industry, and business interest groups). The EUEB provides the core secretariat function, and contributes to the setting and reviewing of eco-label criteria.[31]

The Community eco-labelling scheme did not experience any major revisions during 2002, which was a period of administrative refinement and clarification.

The Commission intends to review the scheme again before September 2005, in accordance with the recommendation of EAP-6, 'to assess the progress and

[27] See generally J.A. Grodsky, 'Certified Green—The Law and Future of Environmental Labeling' (1993) 10 *Yale Journal on Regulation*, 147; Organization for Economic Co-operation and Development, *Eco-Labelling—Actual Effects of Selected Programmes* (Paris: OECD, 1997).

[28] [1992] OJ L99/1.

[29] [2000] OJ L237/1.

[30] See e.g. Dir. 96/60/EC implementing Dir. 92/75/EEC with regard to Energy Labelling of Household Combined Washer-Driers [1996] OJ L266/1; and Dir. 98/11/EC implementing Dir. 92/75/EEC with regard to Energy Labelling of Household Lamps [1998] OJ L71/1.

[31] See further A. Nadai, 'Consumer "Sovereignty" and Policy Issues in the Development of Product Ecolabels' [2001] 11 *European Environment* 1, 14.

effectiveness of the Community Eco-Label scheme'.[32] In particular, EAP-6 suggested that financial incentives be used to complement the scheme, to encourage consumer uptake of eco-labelled products.[33] Some commentators have criticized the scheme as being too narrow, focusing on ecological issues without reference to social labelling. For example, it has been suggested that the scheme be modernized to promote fair trade with developing countries, enabling products and services to be judged according to fair trade criteria.[34]

Since the 2000 revisions came into effect, the number of eco-labelled products sold increased by 300 per cent by the end of 2002.[35] Two new product groups were added to the scheme in 2002: vacuum cleaners and tourist accommodation. The latter marks a seminal milestone, as tourism accommodation is the first ever extension of the eco-label scheme to the 'services' sector, following the amendment to the Eco-Label Regulation. During 2000, the laundry detergents product group was revised, to strengthen its environmental criteria. The revision of the eco-label for detergents has coincided with EC plans to develop a new, comprehensive environmental regulation on detergents.[36] By the close of 2002, there were 125 product groups in the eco-label scheme (each group containing various products), of which 43 are textile products (the largest group), followed by 31 indoor paint and varnish product groups. Disappointingly, national implementation of the voluntary scheme remains highly uneven. France and Italy share the title for holding the most product groups labelled (27 each), compared to the UK, at the bottom, with only two product groups.[37]

B. Legislation in Progress

i. Access to Environmental Information and Public Participation

Community legislative proposals regarding public participation in environmental decisions and access to environmental information were further advanced during 2002. This paved the way for adoption of new directives scheduled for early 2003, in order to bring EC law into conformity with the United Nations Economic Commission for Europe (UN/ECE) Convention on Access to Information, Public Participation in Decision-Making and Access to Justice in Environmental Matters (Aarhus Convention).[38] The Convention seeks to promote

[32] n. 13 above, 18. [33] ibid., 18–19.

[34] See C. MacMaolain, 'Ethical Food Labelling—The Role of European Union Free Trade in Facilitating International Fair Trade' (2002) 39 *Common Market Law Review* 2, 295.

[35] Statistics cited in the Eco-Label scheme's newsletter, EU Eco-Labelling Board, *The Flower* (2002) 3.

[36] See ESC Opinion on the Commission Proposal for a Regulation on Detergents COM(2002)485, [2003] OJ C95/24.

[37] EU Eco-Labelling Board, *The Flower* (2002) 3; see also 'Patchy Progress for EU Eco-Label' (2002) 25 *Environmental Data Services Reports* 335, 36.

[38] Aarhus (Denmark), 25 June 1998 (entered into force 30 Oct. 2001) (1999) 38 *International Legal Materials* 3, 517.

government accountability, transparency, and responsiveness in environmental decision-making by providing high standards for public involvement in government decision processes. It posits standards for citizens' involvement in environmental matters and enforcement of environmental law, focusing on three areas: first, public rights of access to environmental information; secondly, public rights to participate in decision-making processes; and thirdly, access to justice for the public (e.g. to courts).[39] The Convention entered into force on 30 October 2001, but has yet to be ratified by all EC Member States and the EC itself.

Since 2000, the EC has been advancing two legislative proposals to give effect to the Aarhus Convention and thus pave the way for its ratification. These upcoming new directives on environmental information and public participation are intended to supersede the current Directive 90/313/EEC on the Freedom of Access to Information on the Environment (Access to Information Directive).[40] The purpose of the 1990 Directive is to require Member States to ensure the public has access to information on the environment held by public authorities, without needing to demonstrate an interest, within a reasonable time-frame, and at an affordable cost. Experience to date with the Access to Information Directive has revealed some shortcomings in its design and implementation that warrant legislative change.[41] The first amendment proposal, presented by the Commission in June 2000, was for a second-generation directive on public access to environmental information, to reflect the changes in the way information is created, collated, and transmitted.[42] The proposal aimed to: (i) establish public rights of access to environmental information and to ensure that information is made available and disseminated to society, in particular by harnessing new information technologies; (ii) provide a wider definition of 'environmental information' than stated in the 1990 Directive, as well as to clarify the definition of 'public authorities' subject to the information provision rights; (iii) impose a shorter time-frame within which public authorities must respond to valid requests for information; (iv) clarify the exceptions to the release of information; (v) clarify the charges which may be imposed on applicants for information; (vi) introduce two review procedures (administrative and judicial) to reconsider access-refusal decisions; and (vii) provide new arrangements for so-called 'active supply' of information by public authorities, not based on public request.

39 For an overview, see J. Jendroska, and S. Stec, 'The Aarhus Convention—Towards a New Era in Environmental Democracy' (2001) 9 *Environmental Liability* 3, 140.

40 [1990] OJ L158/56.

41 See findings in Report from the Commission to the Council and the European Parliament on the Experience Gained in the Application of Council Directive 1990/313/EEC of 7 June 1990, on Freedom of Access to Information on the Environment, COM(2000)400; see also R. Hallo (ed.), *Access to Environmental Information—The Implementation and Implications of Directive 90/313/EEC* (London/The Hague/New York: Kluwer Law International, 1996).

42 Commission Proposal for a Directive on Public Access to Environmental Information COM(2000)402, [2000] OJ C337/156, as amended by COM(2001)303, [2001] OJ C240E/289.

During 2002, the European Parliament (EP) and Council reached agreement on the joint text of the proposed new directive on environmental information. The agreement, reached in a conciliation committee on 6 November, introduced some amendments to the Commission's original proposal.[43] It was agreed that public authorities must respond to an information request within one month, albeit in exceptional cases this can be extended by another month. Further, public bodies may charge fees to recoup administrative costs of collecting information, and higher charges may be levied for companies seeking to obtain data that may have commercial applications. Another agreed amendment is a new provision on quality standards to ensure that data that is current, accurate, and comparable has been incorporated. Consequently, a public authority must explain why it cannot disclose information requested, such as due to confidentiality requirements. Also, the Directive's definition of 'environmental information' was amended to include contamination of the food chain.

On 10 December 2002, agreement was also reached between the EP and Council in conciliation on the second proposal to fulfil the Aarhus Convention: the proposed directive on public participation.[44] Rights of public participation in environmental decision-making have long been a feature of EC environmental legislation, but they have been confined to specific instruments and limited situations. Notably, for example, the 1985 EIA Directive allows the public to comment on key information with environmental relevance and to influence decision-making in relation to specific projects likely to have significant effects on the environment. The new proposal provides for public participation in a much wider policy context. The draft Directive, which was presented in January 2001 as a Commission Proposal, provides for public participation in decision-making in relation to environmental plans and programmes.[45] Among the changes, the directive would amend the existing EIA Directive and Directive 96/61/EC on Integrated Pollution Prevention and Control (IPPC Directive),[46] in accordance with Article 7 of the Aarhus Convention, requiring provision for public participation in the preparation and review of certain plans and programmes.

The recent conciliation agreement between the EP and Commission settled possible exemptions from the public participation requirement for plans and programmes serving national defence interests, provided for wider public participation in the updating of permits under the IPPC Directive, and provided for the opening up of directives on waste, nitrates, and air quality, to public participation.[47] The EP also succeeded in adding a clause requiring the

[43] European Commission, Parliament, Council Conciliation Committee Public Access to Environmental Information, C/02/346, 7 Nov. 2002.

[44] Commission Proposal for a Directive providing for Public Participation in Respect of the Drawing Up of Certain Plans and Programmes relating to the Environment and Amending Directives 85/337/EEC and 96/61/EC, COM(2000)839, [2000] OJ C154E/123.

[45] ibid.

[46] [1996] OJ L275/26.

[47] European Commission, 'Parliament—Council Conciliation Committee Agreement on Public Participation in Environmental Plans and Programmes', C/02/396, 16 Dec. 2002.

Commission to consider a future amendment to the Directive to widen its scope to include other environmental plans and programmes. However, the draft Directive's coverage is limited to participation concerning specific items of EC legislation rather than participation in the legislation-making process itself.

C. Case Law and Enforcement Activity

i. Environmental Impact Assessment

In 2002, the Commission continued to take various enforcement actions against Member States for infringements against the EIA Directive. Most notably, the Commission successfully applied to the European Court of Justice (ECJ) for a declaration that France had failed to comply with the EIA Directive by not setting the appropriate laws and related mechanisms in train. Article 3(1) of the Directive provides that the Member States are to bring into force the laws, regulations, and administrative provisions necessary to comply with that Directive by 14 March 1999, at the latest, and to inform the Commission thereof forthwith. The Commission took the view that the EIA Directive had not been transposed into French law within the prescribed period and hence, on 26 January 2000, issued a Reasoned Opinion requesting France to adopt the requisite measures within two months of its notification. In subsequent correspondence with the Commission during 2000 and 2001, the French Government explained that its existing environmental statutes covered most of the provisions of the EIA Directive, and that a new draft Decree was in train that would bring three categories of projects within the scope of the domestic legislation which did not yet come within that scope. The latter included wind farms, initial afforestation, and the use of uncultivated or semi-cultivated land for intensive agricultural purposes. The Commission considered France's measures as insufficient to transpose the provisions of the EIA Directive in their entirety and, having no other information in its possession concerning the adoption of the national measures announced, launched legal action against France by application to the ECJ on 17 September 2001.

The Commission's pleadings to the Court alleged that France had failed to transpose the requirements of Articles 1(7) and 1(11) of the EIA Directive, relating to the establishment of a framework procedure and mandatory public information, respectively. In upholding the Commission's application, the ECJ affirmed that mere administrative procedures and practices (such as France relied upon), which by their nature are alterable at will by the authorities and are not given the appropriate publicity, cannot be regarded as constituting the proper fulfilment of a Member State's obligations.[48] The ECJ stressed that it was not open to a Member State to plead a practice followed in its internal legal order,

[48] Case C-348/01, *Commission* v. *France* [2002] ECR I-10249.

and that additional legislative measures (as France later promised) were needed to fulfil the requirements of the Directive.

The Commission also cited Belgium before the ECJ over failures to implement the EIA Directive within the stipulated time-frame.[49] Although, during 1999 and 2000, the Commission had received communications from the Belgian authorities regarding proposed laws to implement the EIA Directive for the Walloon region, the Commission was not satisfied that these provisions transposed the Directive in full for the whole of Belgium, and thus instigated the action after having issued a Reasoned Opinion to Belgium. The ECJ upheld the action, finding that measures must also be undertaken by Belgian federal authorities to determine whether or not implementation of the EIA Directive was complete.

Incomplete transposition of the EIA Directive by the Spanish Government also resulted in the Commission applying to the ECJ for enforcement action.[50] There has been a long history of complaint from the Commission regarding Spain's efforts to implement the EIA Directive, dating back to the early 1990s. The Commission's application related principally to Spain's apparent failure to maintain in force legislation that enables an assessment of the environmental effects to be undertaken in the whole of the national territory in respect of certain classes of project listed in Annex II to the Directive and, in a large part of that territory, regarding many other classes of project enumerated in the same Annex. At national level, Legislative Royal Decree 1302/1986 on the assessment of environmental impact[51] constituted Spain's first measure transposing the 1985 EIA Directive. Later, the 1997 Directive was transposed into Spanish law by Royal Decree-Law 9/2000 amending Legislative Royal Decree 1302/86.[52] In addition, EIA measures for projects listed in Annex II of the Directive proposed in special areas of conservation (SACs) were required by Royal Decree 1997/1995 establishing measures to help guarantee biodiversity through conservation of natural habitats and wild flora and fauna.[53] Moreover, for many sectors of activity, Spain had specific national laws, containing provisions relating to the assessment of the impact of projects on the environment.

The Commission successfully argued before the ECJ that the Spanish legislation did not comply with the Directive, in particular Article 4(2), on the ground that it exempted most of the projects covered by Annex II from the impact assessment obligations. The ECJ stressed that Article 4(2) does not empower the Member States to exclude generally and definitively from the obligation of assessment one or more classes of projects mentioned in Annex II, although it acknowledged that Member States may establish the criteria and/or thresholds

49 Case C-319/01, *Commission* v. *Belgium* [2002] ECR I-10779.

50 Case C-474/99, *Commission* v. *Spain* [2002] ECR I-5239.

51 Official State Gazette (BOE) 155, 30 June 1986.

52 Official State Gazette (BOE) 241, 7 Oct. 2000.

53 Official State Gazette (BOE) 310, 28 Dec. 1995.

necessary to determine which of the projects covered by Annex II are to be subject to an assessment (taking into account not only the size of projects but also their nature and location). The ECJ found that Legislative Royal Decree 1302/1986 listed only four classes of projects among the 83 set out in Annex II to the Directive. It also found that Royal Decree 1997/1995, which, according to the Spanish Government, reproduced all the classes of projects listed in Annex II to the Directive, in fact concerned only projects affecting special areas of conservation established under the Habitats Directive.[54] The ECJ noted that the choice of such a criterion, within essentially a limited number of rural areas, significantly eviscerated the scope for environmental assessment of projects in Spain. It also found, contrary to Spanish assertions, that the EIA Directive was not subject to additional implementing measures at the level of the autonomous communities and cities.

The fourth environmental assessment case heard by the ECJ in 2002 concerned Luxembourg's failure to transpose the EIA Directive rules into national law.[55] The Commission took the view that Luxembourg's draft Decree of 1999 to give effect to the Directive only authorized the adoption of the provisions necessary for the transposition. The Commission sent Luxembourg a Reasoned Opinion in January 2000, restating its complaint and requesting compliance within two months. Before the ECJ, Luxembourg did not dispute the lack of transposition, but it claimed that all possible measures had been taken by its authorities to transpose the Directive at the earliest possible opportunity and that, accordingly, the Commission should withdraw its action. Reaffirming its previous statements, the ECJ held that Member States must strictly adhere to deadlines agreed in Community legislation and a Member State may not plead provisions, practices, or circumstances existing in its internal legal system in order to justify a failure, as in Luxembourg's case, to comply with the obligations and time-limits laid down in a directive.

At the close of 2002, the Commission was commencing further enforcement action against Luxembourg for failure to comply with the aforementioned ECJ ruling, and was pursuing another ten wayward Member States for various infringements of the EIA legislation.[56] Ireland received a Reasoned Opinion for failing to carry out a prior EIA on a peat extraction project in the environmentally sensitive Moud's Bog, of County Kildare. The Commission resolved to

[54] n. 4 above.

[55] Case C-366/00, *Commission* v. *Luxembourg* [2002] ECR I-1749; see also J. Lowther, 'Failure to Implement Environmental Assessment Directive' (2002) 14 *Environmental Law and Management* 2, 93.

[56] The following information on enforcement action is drawn from the following Commission press releases: 'Commission Pursues Infringement Proceedings Against Eight Member States for Non-Compliance with the Environmental Impact Assessment Directive', IP/03/117, 24 Jan. 2003; 'Commission Questions Environmental Impact Assessment Measures in Portugal, Greece and Spain', IP/02/1574, 29 Oct. 2002; 'Environmental Impact: Commission Acts Against Ireland, Italy, Portugal and France for Non-Compliance with EU Law', IP/02/411, 14 Mar. 2002.

refer the UK to the ECJ for failing to carry out an EIA on a large multiplex cinema and leisure complex in London. It also referred Austria to the Court following the failure of the *Länder* Burgenland, Carinthia, and Salzburg to adopt EIA rules for projects involving the restructuring of rural landholdings. Proceedings were initiated against Italy following the Italian authorities' decision that an EIA was unnecessary for a yacht marina project at Fossacesia, which threatened a nearby area nominated for special protection under the Habitats Directive. Spain also came to the Commission's attention again, in this instance for failing to apply the EIA Directive appropriately in the case of three linked urban development cases. Adding to its enforcement load, the Commission referred Portugal to the ECJ for not correctly carrying out a prior EIA on the final section of the Lisbon to Algarve motorway, near the habitat of the endangered Iberian Lynx. Greece also faced enforcement action over its blatant failure to conduct an EIA of a waste-water treatment plant at Gerani, Crete. The Commission also sent a Reasoned Opinion to the Greek Government to ensure adequate EIA measures for the Mamidakis petrochemical plant in Lesbos, which had been operating without a permit since 1997 on a site nominated for special protection under the Habitats Directive. Finland also faced the prospect of enforcement action because legislation notified to transpose the 1997 amendment to the EIA Directive in the Province of Åland did not ensure that all projects likely to have significant environmental impacts would be subject to a development consent procedure. A Reasoned Opinion was also issued to Sweden to ensure amendment of national legislation so as to require adequate EIAs prior to the decommissioning and dismantling of nuclear power plants and reactors. Finally, Germany received a Final Written Warning because *Länder* had apparently failed to (correctly) implement the EIA Directive in relation to road construction projects.

ii. Access to Environmental Information

The only significant case law, during 2002, on the Access to Information Directive was the Opinion given in relation to the Austrian Case C-316/01, *Eva Glawischnig*.[57] By order of 25 July 2001, the *Unabhängiger Verwaltungssenat Wien* (Independent Administrative Chamber of Vienna) referred three questions to the ECJ for a preliminary ruling on the interpretation of the Access to Information Directive. The Austrian court requested advice on whether details of examinations carried out by Austrian administrative authorities to monitor compliance with the rules on the labelling of certain foodstuffs produced from genetically modified organisms (GMOs), posited by Regulation (EC) No. 1139/98 concerning the Compulsory Indication of the Labelling of Certain Foodstuffs Produced from Genetically Modified Organisms of Particulars other than those

[57] Case C-316/01, *Eva Glawischnig* v. *Bundesminister für soziale Sicherheit und Generationen* [2002] ECR I-5995, Opinion of Advocate General Tizzano of 5 Dec. 2002.

Provided for in Directive 79/112/EEC,[58] could constitute 'information relating to the environment' within the meaning of the Access to Information Directive. In his Opinion, Advocate General Tizzano determined that the purpose of Regulation (EC) No. 1139/98 was not to protect human health or to protect the environment, and nor was the purpose of the examinations carried out by Austrian authorities to ensure compliance with the Regulation. Accordingly, the Opinion concluded that the information requested by Glawischnig did not relate to activities or measures designed to protect the environment within the meaning of the Access to Information Directive. It reasoned that:

> administrative documents relating to the monitoring of instances of incorrect labelling, pursuant to Council Regulation (EC) No. 1139/98 . . . revealing the name of the manufacturer of foodstuffs and the description of the product in respect of which a complaint has been made, the name of the manufacturer of foodstuffs and the description of the product in respect of which administrative penalties have been imposed, and the frequency with which such penalties have been imposed, cannot constitute 'information relating to the environment' within the meaning of [the Directive].[59]

D. International Cooperation

i. Eco-Labelling

An energy labelling agreement concluded in 2001 between the United States of America (US) and the EC, which was recently annulled by the ECJ, has highlighted the continuing tensions between EC environmental and commercial policies.[60] Efforts to promote international cooperation and standardization in energy product labelling unravelled when the ECJ ruled that the Council had negotiated the agreement on the wrong legal basis. The background to the voided agreement is the US Environmental Protection Agency's 'Energy Star Program', launched in 1992 as a voluntary labelling programme for office equipment.[61] The US programme aims to encourage manufacturers to introduce energy-saving features and to stimulate consumer awareness of the energy losses of office equipment in stand-by mode. The programme was subsequently extended to cover a range of consumer appliances and equipment. The Energy Star logo is offered to equipment that meets certain rules concerning energy consumption adopted under the programme. Following the success of the US programme (which was emerging as a universal international standard), the Commission

[58] [1998] OJ L159/4.

[59] n. 57 above, para. 36.

[60] Dec. 2001/469/EC concerning the Conclusion on Behalf of the European Community of the Agreement between the Government of the United States of America and the European Community on the Coordination of Energy-Efficient Labelling Programs for Office Equipment [2001] OJ L172/1. The detailed arrangements for implementing this Agreement at Community level have been put forward in: Reg. (EC) No. 2422/2001 on a Community Energy-Efficient Labelling Programme for Office Equipment [2001] OJ L332/1.

[61] Published on the Internet at: http://www.energystar.gov.

decided that, rather than develop a separate energy-labelling scheme for office equipment in the Community, the wiser course would be simply to adopt the US Energy Star Program. Accordingly, agreement was reached with the US in December 2000 for coordinating energy-efficient labelling programmes for office equipment, applying the US model. However, the Energy Star Agreement was not intended to restrict the ability of each party to maintain and develop other energy and environmental product labelling programmes in their respective jurisdictions. On 14 May 2001, following a favourable opinion from the EP, the Council approved the Energy Star Agreement on behalf of the Community on the basis of Article 175(1) EC, in conjunction with elements of Article 300 EC.[62] The legality of the agreement was challenged before the ECJ by the Commission in Case C-281/01, *Commission* v. *Council*.[63] On 12 December 2002, the ECJ annulled the agreement, concluding that the Council should have chosen Article 133 EC (common commercial policy, an exclusive Community competence) as the legal basis for the decision to conclude the agreement on behalf of the Community, instead of Article 175(1) EC (environmental policy, a competence shared with the Member States). According to the Court, the commercial policy objective pursued by the agreement was predominant. Although the ECJ accepted that the Energy Star Agreement had both commercial trade dimensions and an environmental policy component, it concluded that the agreement was *predominantly* a commercial policy measure. The Court reasoned:

> It is clear from the terms in which the Energy Star Agreement is couched . . . that the Energy Star labelling program is essentially intended to enable manufacturers to use, in accordance with a procedure for the mutual recognition of registrations, a common logo to identify for consumers certain products complying with a common set of energy-efficiency specifications which they intend to sell on the American and Community markets. An instrument having a direct impact on trade in office equipment is therefore involved. . . . It is true that in the long term, depending on how manufacturers and consumers in fact behave, the programme should have a positive environmental effect as a result of the reduction in energy consumption which it should achieve. However, that is merely an indirect and distant effect, in contrast to the effect on trade in office equipment, which is direct and immediate.[64]

The Court added that such an agreement, although dealing with non-binding labelling provisions, could constitute an obstacle to international trade and hence could cause problems in terms of obligations under the World Trade Organization (WTO) agreements. In any event, the ECJ's decision amounted to only a temporary setback to plans to establish the EC's Energy Star Programme, which was legally constituted in early 2003.[65]

[62] n. 60 above.
[63] [2002] ECR I-12049.
[64] ibid., paras. 40–1.
[65] Dec. 2003/168/EC establishing the European Community Energy Star Board [2003] OJ L67/22.

VII. Miscellaneous Instruments

Diane Ryland *

A. Legislation Adopted

i. Action Plans

Decision 1600/2002/EC lays down the Sixth Community Environment Action Programme.[1] The Programme (EAP-6) constitutes a framework for the Community's environmental policy for a ten-year period, starting from July 2002. Environmental objectives are set out in four priority areas: (i) climate change, (ii) nature and biodiversity, (iii) environment and health and quality of life, and (iv) natural resources and wastes. As well as promoting the adoption of policies and approaches that contribute to the achievement of sustainable development in the accession candidate countries, the Programme includes the objective of pursuing ambitious environmental policies internationally. Provision is made for the development of thematic strategies in order to pursue the four priority environmental aims of the Programme. First, objectives on tackling climate change include, *inter alia*, realization by 2005 of demonstrable progress in achieving the commitments under the Kyoto Protocol[2] to the United Nations (UN) Framework Convention on Climate Change (UNFCCC).[3] Towards this end, a framework of actions is identified, inclusive of the development of Community Carbon Dioxide (CO_2) emissions trading, in order to implement international climate commitments and to reduce greenhouse gas emissions, for example, in the energy and transport sectors and in industrial production. The use of fiscal measures is promoted, in particular a Community framework for energy taxation. Environmental agreements with industry sectors on greenhouse gas emissions will be encouraged. In the second instance, halting biodiversity decline, the protection and appropriate restoration of nature and biodiversity from damaging pollution, and the sustainable use of both the marine environment and soil are, *inter alia*, objectives pursued under the Programme. Actions to be undertaken comprise: (i) promotion of research, (ii) establishing the Natura 2000 network and its consequential technical and financial instruments and extending it to the candidate countries, (iii) promoting Community coordination concerning accidents and natural disasters, and (iv) developing thematic strategies on soil protection and the protection and conservation of the marine environment.

* Senior lecturer in law, European Policy Research Centre, University of Lincoln, Lincolnshire (United Kingdom).

1 [2002] OJ L242/1.

2 Kyoto (Japan), 10 Dec. 1997 (not yet in force) (1998) 37 *International Legal Materials* 1, 22.

3 New York, NY (United States), 9 May 1992 (entered into force on 21 Mar. 1994) (1992) 31 *International Legal Materials* 4, 849.

Thirdly, objectives concerning environment and health and quality of life comprise, *inter alia*: (i) contributing to a better quality of life through an integrated approach concentrating on urban areas, (ii) reducing the impacts of dangerous chemicals and pesticides on human health, (iii) achieving levels of water and air quality that do not give rise to significant impacts on and risks to human health and the environment, and (iv) substantially reducing the number of people regularly affected by long-term average levels of noise. Reinforced research programmes and scientific expertise feature among the priority actions in order to pursue these objectives, as does a framework of national and international actions concerning chemicals and pesticides, and also implementation of Directive 2000/60/EC establishing a Framework for Community Action in the Field of Water Policy (Water Framework Directive),[4] and revision of Directive 76/160/EEC concerning the Quality of Bathing Water (Bathing Water Directive).[5] Further measures and strategies are envisaged on air quality and the urban environment. Noise reduction and mitigation are prioritized actions. Fourthly, resource and energy efficiency, reducing waste generation and disposal, and encouraging reuse, recovery, and recycling are key objectives of EPA-6. Priority actions for achieving these objectives are: developing thematic strategies on the sustainable use and management of resources, and on waste recycling, developing and implementing measures on waste prevention and management, and revising legislation on waste. A series of strategic approaches to meeting the Programme's environmental objectives comprise: developing new Community legislation and amending existing legislation, encouraging more effective implementation and enforcement of Community environmental legislation, further efforts for integrating environmental protection requirements into the preparation, definition, and implementation of Community policies and activities, promotion of sustainable production and consumption patterns through the use of a blend of instruments including market-based and economic instruments, encouraging collaboration and partnership, ensuring the consumer receives environmental information, and supporting environmental integration in the financial sector. These approaches will be pursued under the Programme with actions that, *inter alia*, develop general principles of good governance within which stakeholders are consulted, and which strengthen participation in the dialogue process by non-governmental organizations (NGOs). Further actions under the Programme include ensuring the environment is a priority for Community research programmes and ensuring the provision of regular information.

The European Parliament and the Council adopted Decision 466/2002/EC laying down a Community Action Programme Promoting Non-Governmental Organisations Primarily Active in the Field of Environmental Protection.[6] Activities falling within the general objectives of this Programme should involve contributions to the development and implementation of Community environ-

[4] [2000] OJ L327/1. [5] [1976] OJ L31/1. [6] [2002] OJ L75/1.

mental policy and legislation in different regions of Europe. Also promoted is the systematic involvement of NGOs at all stages of the Community environmental policy-making process, by ensuring relevant representation in stakeholder consultation meetings and public hearings. In addition, the Programme will contribute to the strengthening of small regional or local associations working to apply the *acquis communautaire* in relation to the environment and sustainable development in their local area. In order to qualify for a grant an NGO must, *inter alia*, be active at a European level. Target areas for support are those given priority under EAP-6,[7] namely: limiting climate change; nature and biodiversity—protecting a unique resource; health and environment; ensuring the sustainable development of natural resources; and waste. The financial framework for the implementation of this Programme, for the period 1 January 2002 to 31 December 2006, is €32 million.

ii. Cohesion Fund

The Commission adopted Regulation (EC) No. 1386/2002 laying down Detailed Rules for the Implementation of Regulation (EC) No. 1164/94 as regards the Management and Control Systems for Assistance granted from the Cohesion Fund and the Procedure for making Financial Corrections.[8]

iii. Energy

Directive 2002/91/EC on the Energy Performance of Buildings (Building Energy Efficiency Directive)[9] promotes the improvement of the energy performance of buildings within the Community, taking into account outdoor climatic and local conditions, as well as indoor climate requirements and cost-effectiveness. It lays down requirements as regards: (i) the general framework for a methodology of calculation of the integrated energy performance of buildings; (ii) the application of minimum requirements on the energy performance of new buildings; (iii) the application of minimum requirements on the energy performance of existing large buildings that are subject to major renovation; (iv) energy certification of buildings; and (v) regular inspection of boilers and of air-conditioning systems in buildings and in addition an assessment of the heating installation in which the boilers are more than 15 years old.

iv. Financial Instruments

Regulation (EC) No. 2012/2002 establishing the European Union Solidarity Fund[10] was adopted, to enable the Community to respond in a rapid, efficient

[7] n. 1 above.

[8] [2002] OJ L201/5. It applies in respect of eligible measures that fall within Art. 3 of Reg. (EC) No. 1164/94, and was first approved after 1 Jan. 2000.

[9] [2003] OJ L1/65.

[10] [2002] OJ L311/3.

and flexible manner to emergency situations. Assistance from the Fund may mainly be mobilized when a major natural disaster with serious repercussions on living conditions, the natural environment, or the economy, in one or more regions or one or more countries, occurs in the territory of a Member State or a country involved in accession negotiations with the European Union (EU). The term 'major disaster' is defined under the Regulation. The aim of the Fund is to complement the efforts of the States concerned and to cover a share of their public expenditure in order to help the beneficiary State to carry out the following emergency operations, depending on the type of disaster: (i) immediate restoration to working order of infrastructure and plant in the fields of energy, water and waste water, telecommunications, transport, health and education; (ii) providing temporary accommodation and funding rescue services to meet the immediate needs of the population concerned; (iii) immediate securing of preventive infrastructures and measures of immediate protection of the cultural heritage; and (iv) immediate cleaning up of disaster-stricken areas, including natural zones.

v. Implementation

Regulation (EC) No. 1406/2002 establishing a European Maritime Safety Agency[11] was adopted for the purpose of ensuring a high, uniform, and effective level of maritime safety and prevention of pollution by ships within the Community. The Agency has been endowed with the task of providing the Member States and the Commission with the technical and scientific assistance needed, and with a high level of expertise, in order to help them to apply Community legislation in the field of maritime safety and prevention of pollution by ships, to monitor its implementation, and to evaluate the effectiveness of the measures in place.

On 27 June 2002, the EP and the Council adopted Directive 2002/59/EC establishing a Community Vessel Traffic Monitoring and Information System and repealing Directive 93/75/EEC.[12]

vi. Research and Development

The EP and the Council adopted Decision 1513/2002/EC concerning the Sixth Framework Programme of the European Community for Research, Technological Development and Demonstration Activities, Contributing to the Creation of the European Research Area and to Innovation (2002 to 2006).[13] The maximum overall amount for Community financial participation in the entire Sixth Framework Programme, which will be implemented by specific programmes, will be €16,270 million. Seven priority thematic areas are identified, including, *inter alia*, food quality and safety, sustainable development, global

[11] [2002] OJ L208/1. [12] [2002] OJ L208/10. [13] [2002] OJ L232/1.

change, and ecosystems, which will receive €685 million and €2,120 million, respectively.

The Council issued Decision 2002/834/EC adopting a Specific Programme for Research, Technological Development and Demonstration: 'Integrating and Strengthening the European Research Area' (2002–6).[14] The objectives and technological priorities for this specific programme include, *inter alia*: food quality and safety, sustainable development (sustainable energy systems and sustainable surface transport), global change, and ecosystems. An indicative amount of €685 million for food quality and safety is confirmed, as is €810 for sustainable energy systems, €610 for sustainable transport systems, and €700 for global change and ecosystems.

Further programmes were established by Decision 2002/835/EC adopting a Specific Programme of Research, Technological Development and Demonstration: 'Structuring the European Research Area' (2002–6),[15] and Decision 2002/836/EC adopting a Specific Programme of Research, Technological Development and Demonstration to be carried out by means of Direct Actions by the Joint Research Centre (2002–6).[16]

A further framework programme was adopted by Decision 2002/668/Euratom adopting the Sixth Framework Programme of the European Atomic Energy Community (Euratom) for Nuclear Research and Training Activities, also Contributing to the Creation of the European Research Area (2002–6).[17] The financial reference amount for the implementation of this programme will be €1,230 million allocated to priority thematic areas which include, *inter alia*, the management of nuclear waste, radiation protection, and other areas in the field of nuclear technologies and safety.

Decision 2002/837/Euratom adopting a Specific Programme (Euratom) for Research and Training on Nuclear Energy (2002–6),[18] created an allocation of €940 million for the execution of this new Programme.

Decision 2002/838/Euratom adopting a Specific Programme for Research and Training to be carried out by the Joint Research Centre by means of Direct Actions for the European Atomic Energy Community (2002–6)[19] was adopted.

vii. Statistics

Regulation (EC) No. 2150/2002 on Waste Statistics (Waste Statistics Regulation)[20] establishes a framework for the production of Community statistics on the generation, recovery, and disposal of waste. Member States and the Commission, within their respective fields of competence, and in accordance with the Regulation, are required to produce Community statistics on the generation, recovery, and disposal of waste, excluding radioactive waste, which is already covered by other legislation.

[14] [2002] OJ L294/1. [15] [2002] OJ L294/44. [16] [2002] OJ L294/60.
[17] [2002] OJ L232/34. [18] [2002] OJ L294/74. [19] [2002] OJ L294/86.
[20] [2002] OJ L332/1.

Decision 2367/2002/EC on the Community Statistical Programme 2003 to 2007.[21] Under the Environment Title, the main effort of the statistical programme will, *inter alia*, be to: improve core environmental statistics, mainly waste, water, and environmental expenditure statistics, with a focus on statistics needed for environmental indicators and to put in place the necessary legislation for such statistics; produce easily understandable environmental and sustainability indicators in cooperation with other Commission services and the European Environment Agency (EEA).

viii. Use of Instruments

The Commission adopted Directive 2002/31/EC implementing Directive 92/75/EEC with regard to Energy Labelling of Household Air-Conditioners,[22] and Directive 2002/40/EC implementing Directive 92/75/EEC with regard to Energy Labelling of Household Electric Ovens.[23]

A Decision of the Committee of Permanent Representatives sets up an ad hoc high-level group on energy taxation.[24] Its objective is to prepare the work of the Council with a view to reaching consensus on the guidelines for the taxation of energy products and an agreement on the adoption of an energy tax directive.

B. Policy Documents

i. Action Programmes

The Commission presented its Proposal for a Decision adopting a Multi-Annual Programme for Action in the Field of Energy: 'Intelligent Energy for Europe' Programme (2003–6), based on Article 175(1) EC.[25] Concerns for the medium- and long-term security of energy supply and for the integration of sustainable development and environmental protection in energy[26] and in the energy aspects of transport[27] underpin the programme. It covers four specific fields of action: (i) rational use of energy and demand management (SAVE); (ii) new and renewable energy sources (ALTENER); (iii) energy aspects of transport (STEER); and (iv) promotion at international level, particularly with the developing countries, of cooperation in the fields of renewable energy sources and energy efficiency (COOPENER). Six types of action are planned for each field of activity: (i) design and implementation of strategies, development of standards, studies, etc.; (ii) creation of structures and financial and market instruments, including local and regional planning; (iii) promotion of systems and equipment to ease the

[21] [2002] OJ L358/1. [22] [2002] OJ L86/26.

[23] [2002] OJ L128/45. [24] [2002] OJ C148/1.

[25] COM(2002)162, [2002] OJ C203E/47. See also Commission Press Release IP/02/524.

[26] Commission Green Paper, 'Towards a European Strategy for the Security of Energy Supply' COM(2001)769.

[27] Commission White Paper, 'European Transport Policy for 2010: Time to Decide' COM(2001)370.

transition from demonstration to marketing; (iv) development of information and education structures and utilization of the results; (v) monitoring; and (vi) assessment of the impact of the actions.

The programme will be implemented by targeted initiatives, or 'key actions', relating to one or more specific fields of action. These will be defined when the work programme is established and include, for example: sustainable energies for the islands; economic buildings; energy and urban safety; water and energy; striving for 100 per cent renewable energy sources; green transport; learning about sustainable energy; etc. A detailed work programme will specify, *inter alia*, funding arrangements and rules on participation; selection criteria and the arrangements for applying them, and the methods and instruments for monitoring and utilizing the results of the actions. It will include the definition of performance indicators; the indicative timetable for the implementation of the work programme; the procedures for coordinating and linking up with other Community policies; and the operational arrangements to encourage the participation of remote and outlying regions and of small and medium-sized enterprises (SMEs). Financial assistance under the programme will be allocated on the basis of benefit to the Community of the activity, expected impact, and origin of the initiative. As a general rule, aid may not exceed 50 per cent of the total cost. A budget of €215 million is proposed for the duration of the programme from 2003 to 2006, broken down into individual annual amounts in respect of each of the four specific fields of action. Provision is made for an additional budget from 2004, as a result of enlargement.

In its Communication towards a Thematic Strategy for Soil Protection,[28] in response to the EAP-6 Decision,[29] the Commission develops an approach to protect soils against erosion and pollution. A distinction is made between soil and land use, the latter of which will be the subject of a separate Communication, under preparation, provisionally entitled Planning and the Environment—the Territorial Dimension. In order to prevent soil contamination, the Commission intends to propose legislation on mining waste, sewage sludge, and compost, and to pursue the integration of soil protection concerns in other EC policies. Furthermore, working with Member States, candidate countries, and relevant stakeholders, the Commission will prepare a proposal for soil monitoring legislation and also a Communication on erosion, the decline in soil organic matter, and contamination with recommended actions.

In addition, and in accordance with EAP-6, the Commission adopted a Communication, Towards a Thematic Strategy on the Sustainable Use of Pesticides,[30] with the aim of reducing the impact of pesticides on human health and the environment. Objectives include improving controls on the use and distribution of pesticides, replacing the most dangerous active substances with safer

[28] COM(2002)179; Commission Press Release IP/02/592.
[29] n. 1 above. [30] COM(2002)349.

non-chemical alternatives, encouraging pesticide-free farming, and establishing a transparent monitoring and reporting system. The purpose of the Communication is to launch a consultation with farmers, growers, and all stakeholders, prior to the Commission developing the thematic strategy for approval in 2004.

EAP-6 also refers to the development of a thematic strategy for the protection of the marine environment with the objective of promoting sustainable use of the seas and conserving marine ecosystems. To this end, the Commission has presented a Communication towards a Strategy to Protect and Conserve the Marine Environment.[31] This document, *inter alia*, reviews current information on the environmental status of the seas and oceans, identifying the main threats. It reviews the development and implementation of policies to control these threats, also reviewing monitoring assessment and research. Gaps in knowledge are identified and conclusions drawn as to what needs to be done, identifying operational and institutional objectives for the EU. An action plan and a work programme are set out for the Commission, Member States, candidate countries, and stakeholders, to work together in order to define and develop a thematic strategy for the protection and sustainable use of the marine environment.

The Commission has presented a Proposal for a Regulation concerning Monitoring of Forests and Environmental Interactions in the Community.[32] The aim is to provide a framework for a Community scheme to contribute towards the protection of forest ecosystems in the Community by monitoring the conditions of these ecosystems. The framework regulation will be implemented by Commission regulations, which will, *inter alia*, prescribe general aspects of the monitoring activities and procedures to be followed for reporting and for the national programmes. It is intended that the scheme will run for six years, from 1 January 2003 to 31 December 2008, with the provision of €52 million for the period 2003 to 2006, and further consideration to be given to raising the annual amount of €13 million in order to fund new activities for 2007 and 2008.

The Commission presented a Communication setting out a Community Action Plan to Integrate Environmental Protection Requirements into the Common Fisheries Policy.[33]

On the Energy Framework Programme, the Commission issued a Communication: Comments of the Commission on the Conclusions of the Mid-term Assessment of the Energy Framework Programme (1998–2002).[34] The Panel of experts conducting the assessment concludes, *inter alia*, that there is a real need for a new energy programme to follow the current Energy Framework Programme. The Panel recommends, however, that it should evolve to a single programme retaining three current areas of activity, namely, energy efficiency, renewable energy, and international cooperation, and that a new area should be included on the energy aspects of transport. A lack of resources, both financial and human, is noted.

[31] COM(2002)539. [32] COM(2002)404. [33] COM(2002)186.
[34] COM(2002)448.

ii. Energy

The Commission presented a Proposal for a Directive on the Promotion of Co-generation based on a Useful Heat Demand in the Internal Energy Market.[35] Reinforced efforts are needed to promote high-efficiency combined heat and power in the internal energy market. Co-generation is not just an end in itself but contributes to the objectives of security of energy supply and the energy-efficiency targets of climate change policy. It is recognized, in the short term, that regulatory certainty and financial support may be needed where the internal energy market is not fully completed and where internalization of energy costs is not reflected in energy prices. The long-term objective is the establishment of an additional diverse and efficient energy supply system within the EU.

As explained in a Communication on the Internal Market in Energy: Coordinated Measures on the Security of Energy Supply,[36] the Commission has presented:

— A Proposal for a Directive concerning the alignment of measures with regard to security of supply for petroleum products;[37]

— A Proposal for a Directive concerning Measures to Safeguard Security of Natural Gas Supply;[38]

— A Proposal for a Directive repealing Directives 68/414/EEC and 98/93/EC imposing an obligation on Member States to maintain minimum stocks of crude oil and/or petroleum products, and Directive 73/238/EEC on Measures to Mitigate the Effects of Difficulties in the Supply of Crude Oil and Petroleum Products;[39] and

— A Proposal for a Decision repealing Decision 68/416/EEC on the Conclusion and Implementation of Individual Agreements between Governments relating to the Obligation of Member States to Maintain Minimum Stocks of Crude Oil and/or Petroleum Products and Decision 77/706/EEC on the Setting of a Community Target for a Reduction in the Consumption of Primary Sources of Energy in the Event of Difficulties in the Supply of Crude Oil and Petroleum Products.[40]

The Commission Communication Nuclear Safety in the European Union[41] is a step towards adopting a Community framework for nuclear safety and solutions for the management of nuclear waste. It is recognized that there is a need to add safety standards for nuclear installations during and at the end of their working life to the *acquis communautaire* on radiation protection; all the more so in an enlarged EU. A significant number of nuclear installations in the current Member States, however, are coming towards the end of their active lives.

[35] COM(2002)415, [2002] OJ C291E/182; Commission Press Release IP/02/1124.
[36] COM(2002)488. [37] [2002]OJ C331E/249. [38] [2002] OJ C331E/262.
[39] [2002] OJ C331E/279. [40] [2002] OJ C331E/280. [41] COM(2002)605.

There is uncertainty as to the availability of financial assistance to ensure safe decommissioning, and a lack of safe solutions for the management of nuclear waste. Also, the opening of negotiations on trade in nuclear materials with Russia should result in the development of Community legislation concerning the safety of first-generation power stations still in operation in Russia. This Communication includes two proposals for Directives: a Draft Proposal for a (Euratom) Directive Setting Out Basic Obligations and General Principles on the Safety of Nuclear Installations; and a Draft Proposal for a Directive (Euratom) on the Management of Spent Nuclear Fuel and Radioactive Waste, both of which are presented by the Commission to the group of experts from Member States designated by the Scientific and Technical Committee for opinion in conformity with Article 31 Euratom. The Commission is also proposing to the Council a Draft Decision authorizing the Commission to Negotiate an Agreement on Trade between Euratom and the Russian Federation on Trade in Nuclear Materials. This Decision is the subject of a separate Communication.[42]

iii. Implementation

Commission Communication, Better Monitoring of the Application of Community Law,[43] sets out various actions to improve the monitoring of the application of EC law. The Commission is of the opinion that in certain areas of the application of Community law where legal disputes are numerous, such as the environmental sphere, it should be possible to have more effective recourse to national courts. The Commission is, therefore, considering adopting a proposal for a directive implementing the third pillar of the United Nations Economic Commission for Europe (UN/ECE) Convention on Access to Information, Public Participation in Decision-Making and Access to Justice in Environmental Matters (Aarhus Convention),[44] and will consider the possibility of a supplementary initiative to establish non-judicial procedures for the handling of complaints. In its annual report on monitoring the application of Community law, the Commission will give an account of the implementation of the measures set out in this Communication.

iv. Use of Instruments

The Commission Report on Environmental Technology for Sustainable Development[45] assesses how environment technology can promote growth and employment and protect the environment. Market barriers and other obstacles are preventing realization of the full potential of environment technology. The

[42] See Commission Press Release IP/02/1616.

[43] COM(2002)725.

[44] Aarhus (Denmark), 25 June 1998 (entered into force 30 Oct. 2001) (1999) 38 *International Legal Materials* 3, 517.

[45] COM(2002)122; Commission Press Release IP/02/416.

Commission, therefore, aims to work with stakeholders from industry, researchers, non-governmental organizations, and governments both within the EU and the candidate countries to develop an action plan to promote clean technologies. Environmental technologies, according to the Report, include 'integrated' technologies that prevent pollutants being generated during the production process, as well as new materials, energy and resource-efficient production processes, environmental know-how, and new ways of working. The Commission recognizes the need to remove market obstacles and to internalize environmental costs in market prices, in order to exploit fully the potential of environmental technologies, and to provide incentives for further research and development in this field. The Report concludes that environmental technologies offer a natural bridge between the economic, social, and environmental goals of an enlarged EU.

Furthermore, the Commission has adopted a Proposal for a Directive on Environmental Liability with regard to the Prevention and Remedying of Environmental Damage.[46] Based on the Environment Title of the EC Treaty and the polluter pays principle, a framework is proposed under which environmental damage would be prevented or necessary restorative measures would be taken. Environmental damage would include damage having serious adverse effects on biodiversity (in areas protected under national or European law), damage to waters covered by the Water Framework Directive,[47] and land damage creating serious potential or actual harm to public health as a result of soil and subsoil contamination. The operators of the activities listed in Annex I, having caused the imminent threat of, or, the environmental damage, will be potentially liable under the draft Directive for preventive or remedial costs. Operators of activities outside Annex I may also be liable for preventive or remedial costs in respect of biodiversity damage, solely where they are at fault or are negligent. Within a framework allowing flexibility, and in accordance with the principle of subsidiarity, when environmental damage occurs Member States are required to ensure that the damage is remedied. Ultimately, restoration costs incurred by the competent authority or by a third party on its behalf must be recovered from the liable operators. Common rules on the restoration objectives to be achieved, and how to identify and choose appropriate restorative measures are laid down at Community level in the proposed Directive. Exemptions and limitation periods, *inter alia*, are drafted into this prospective liability regime.

The Commission has also presented a Communication on Environmental Agreements at Community Level within the Framework of the Action Plan on the Simplification and Improvement of the Regulatory Environment.[48] Environmental agreements at Community level are those by which stakeholders undertake to achieve pollution abatement, as defined in environmental law, or environmental objectives set out in Article 174 EC. The Commission is of the

[46] COM(2002)17, [2002] OJ C151E/132. [47] n. 4 above. [48] COM(2002)412.

opinion that these agreements have a potentially valuable role to play in complementing, but not replacing, other policy instruments, notably legislation. These agreements should be distinguished from the environmental agreements entered into by the Member States as a national implementation measure of Community directives. They are also different instruments to the multilateral environmental agreements (MEAs) concluded and implemented by the Community, to the extent of its competence. Environmental agreements may, first, be purely spontaneous decisions initiated by stakeholders, for example, industry and environmental NGOs, in a broad range of areas in which the Commission has not proposed legislation. The Commission encourages stakeholders to be proactive in developing such agreements. Secondly, they can be a response by stakeholders to an expressed intention of the Commission to legislate. Thirdly, the Commission can initiate them. Environmental agreements, however, are not negotiated with the Commission. They can be acknowledged by the Commission either by an exchange of letters, by a Recommendation by the Commission, by a Recommendation accompanied by an EP and Council Decision on monitoring, or under co-regulation decided by the Community legislators. Parties to environmental agreements must be considered to be representative, organized, and responsible by the Commission, Council, and the EP. In particular, the Commission encourages environmental agreements in the context of the PVC Strategy, Integrated Product Policy, waste management, and climate change.

In the Communication Taxation of Passenger Cars in the European Union—Options for Action at National and Community Levels,[49] the Commission proposes policies and options for future action in the field of passenger car taxation. Priority objectives concern the protection of both the environment and the Internal Market. The possibility of vehicle taxation systems for passenger cars being based partially or totally on CO_2 parameters is examined, as is better coordination, and later approximation, of passenger car taxation in order to remove tax obstacles and distortions to free circulation of passenger cars within the Internal Market.

C. International Cooperation

i. Climate Change

In April 2002, the Council adopted Decision 2002/358/EC concerning the Approval, on Behalf of the European Community, of the Kyoto Protocol to the United Nations Framework Convention on Climate Change and the Joint Fulfilment of Commitments Thereunder.[50]

[49] COM(2002)431. [50] [2002] OJ L130/1.

ii. Biosafety

The Cartagena Protocol on Biosafety (Cartagena Biosafety Protocol)[51] to the Convention on Biological Diversity (CBD)[52] was approved for the EC by Council Decision 2002/628/EC on the Approval, on Behalf of the European Community, of the Cartegena Protocol on Biosafety.[53] The Protocol establishes a framework for transboundary movement, based on the precautionary principle, for the safe transfer, handling, and use of living modified organisms resulting from modern biotechnology that may have adverse effects on the conservation and sustainable use of biological diversity, or pose risks to human health.

iii. Civil Liability for Bunker Oil Pollution Damage

Decision 2002/762/EC authorizing the Member States, in the interest of the Community, to sign, ratify, or accede to the International Convention on Civil Liability for Bunker Oil Pollution Damage 2001[54] was adopted to allow Member States to sign, ratify, or accede to the International Convention on Civil Liability for Bunker Oil Pollution Damage 2001 (Bunkers Convention),[55] subject to certain conditions laid down in the Decision.

iv. Integrated Coastal Zone Management

Recommendation 2002/413/EC concerning the Implementation of Integrated Coastal Zone Management in Europe[56] was issued in 2002. Therein, *inter alia*, the need for cooperative action is recognized. Member States are urged to encourage, enter into, or maintain dialogue and implement existing conventions with neighbouring countries, including non-Member States in the same regional sea, to establish mechanisms for better coordination of responses to cross-border issues.

v. Global Partnership for Sustainable Development

In the Commission Communication, Towards a Global Partnership for Sustainable Development,[57] the external dimension of the EU's approach to sustainable

[51] Montreal (Canada), 29 Jan. 2000 (entered into force 11 Sept. 2003) (2000) 39 *International Legal Materials* 5, 1027.

[52] Rio de Janeiro (Brazil), 5 June 1992 (entered into force 29 Dec. 1993) (1992) 31 *International Legal Materials*, 818.

[53] COM(2002)127, [2002] OJ L201/48. The Commission has presented a Proposal for a Regulation on the Transboundary Movement of Genetically Modified Organisms COM (2002)85, [2002] OJ C151E/121.

[54] [2002] OJ L256/7.

[55] London (United Kingdom), 23 Mar. 2001 (not yet in force).

[56] [2002] OJ L148/24.

[57] COM(2002)82. An internal strategy is established in Commission Communication A Sustainable Europe for a Better World—A European Union Strategy for Sustainable Development COM(2001)264.

development is outlined. The Commission is of the opinion that globalization, that is, expansion in the movement of goods, services, capital, technology, ideas, and people around the world, involves costs as well as economic benefits. Intensive energy use, unsustainable exploitation of natural resources, and unwillingness to add environmental costs to the costs of production and transport are, according to the Commission, threatening the resource base on which economic and social development depend. Therefore, the need is perceived for a framework in which market forces can be used to maintain and increase growth, to create jobs, to preserve the environment, and to strengthen social cohesion. This will require collective effort, globally, regionally, and nationally. Priority objectives include: harnessing trade for sustainable development; fighting poverty and promoting social development; sustainable management of natural and environmental resources; improving the coherence of EU policies; better governance at all levels; and financing sustainable development. The EU's contribution towards these ends is set out in a series of action plans.

vi. Water Management in Developing Countries

In the Communication, Water Management in Developing Countries—Policy and Priorities for EU Development Cooperation,[58] the Commission responds to the challenge of providing water and sanitation in developing countries. It is an attempt to deal with the growing scarcity and decreasing quality of global water resources. The challenge is identified as being to ensure sustainable and equitable access to safe water for all its uses, with special attention to the basic needs of the poor. Integrated water management and poverty reduction strategies would include, *inter alia*, regional integration and cooperation, and food security and sustainable rural development. Acting within an integrated water resources management framework, meeting basic needs for water supply and sanitation is identified as the essential priority. Towards this end, action is needed to provide sustainable water services, and to expand sanitation coverage and the provision of hygiene education, especially since urbanization is placing increasing strain on water supplies, drainage systems, and sewerage services. In addition, ensuring water-food security and protecting water ecosystems are vital components of poverty reduction. International trade and climate change impact on water security and are, therefore, necessary elements in an integrated water resource management strategy.

vi. Ships Oil Pollution

The Commission presented a Proposal for a Decision on the Signing of a New Protocol to the Barcelona Convention concerning Cooperation in Preventing Pollution from Ships and in Combating Pollution of the Mediterranean Sea by Oil and Hazardous and Noxious Substances in Cases of Emergency.[59]

[58] COM(2002)132. [59] COM(2002)11.

In addition, the Commission has presented an Amended Proposal for a Regulation on the Establishment of a Fund for the Compensation of Oil Pollution Damage in European Waters, and Related Measures.[60]

vii. Radioactive Waste

Furthermore, the Commission issued proposals for two Decisions: to approve on behalf of the European Atomic Energy Community (Euratom),[61] and to conclude for the EC,[62] respectively, the International Joint Convention on the Safety of Spent Fuel Management and the Safety of Radioactive Waste Management.

viii. Prior Informed Consent

The Commission has also submitted a Proposal for a Decision Approving, on Behalf of the European Community, the Rotterdam Convention on the Prior Informed Consent Procedure for Certain Hazardous Chemicals and Pesticides in International Trade.[63]

ix. Safety at Sea

The Commission has adopted a Communication on Improving Safety at Sea in Response to the Prestige Accident,[64] in which it places emphasis on the need for rapid, effective application of existing Community legislation. Additionally, the Commission proposes specific measures for the carriage of heavy fuel oil.[65] The Commission also considers that certain aspects of the international regime for liability and compensation for oil pollution need to be revised. Furthermore, the Commission proposes, *inter alia*, that penal sanctions should be taken against any person who, through gross negligence, causes marine pollution, whether deliberate or accidental. It recommends accession on the part of the Community to the International Maritime Organization (IMO), and calls upon the Member States to work with the Commission within the IMO, in order to establish a code of practice to be followed by flag States and to develop flag State audit procedures. In partnership with oil companies, the Commission aspires to conclude a voluntary agreement on a Community code of conduct on the carriage of oil products by sea. The Commission has published an indicative blacklist of a total number of 66 ships, representing thirteen flags.

[60] COM(2002)313, [2002] OJ C227E/487.

[61] [2002] OJ C51E/258.

[62] [2002] OJ C51E/260.

[63] COM(2001)802, [2002] OJ C126/E274. Convention was signed in Rotterdam (the Netherlands), 11 Sept. 1998 (not yet in force) (1999) 38 *International Legal Materials* 1, 1.

[64] COM(2002)681.

[65] Proposal for a Regulation amending Regulation (EC) No. 417/2002 on the Accelerated Phasing In of Double Hull or Equivalent Design Requirements for Single Hull Tankers and repealing Council Regulation (EC) No. 2978/94, COM(2002)780.

D. Miscellaneous

i. Cohesion Fund

The main points of Decisions Granting Financial Assistance under Regulation (EC) No. 1164/94 Establishing a Cohesion Fund, as amended by Regulations (EC) No. 1264/99 and (EC) No. 1265/99 have been published.[66]

The Commission has issued the Annual Report of the Cohesion Fund (2001).[67] In 2001, 48.5 per cent of the total Cohesion Fund commitments went to the transport sector, concentrating on railways. The environment accounted for 51.1 per cent of commitments under the Fund for 2001, the priorities remaining the supply of drinking water and the treatment of waste water and solid waste. Besides the direct financing of infrastructure to treat waste-water and waste, the Commission continued its efforts to implement environmental legislation by ensuring the correct application of certain directives, for example Directive 92/43/EEC on the Conservation of Natural Habitats and of Wild Fauna and Flora (Habitats Directive),[68] and Directive 91/271/EEC on Urban Waste-Water Treatment (Urban Waste-Water Directive),[69] as a prior condition for granting finance.

The final amount, after indexation, of the resources of the Cohesion Fund for 2001 was €2,715 million. Of this amount, Spain received 61.8 per cent, divided between the environment, 51.7 per cent and transport, 48.3 per cent. Greece was allocated 17.2 per cent of the appropriations, 54.2 per cent going to the environment and 45.8 per cent to transport. Ireland was awarded 4.3 per cent of the total appropriations in 2001, apportioned between the environment 34.6 per cent and transport 65.4 per cent. Portugal was granted 16.8 per cent of the Cohesion Fund resources in 2001, in the ratio of 52.2 per cent for the environment and 47.8 per cent for transport. On 25 July 2002, Portugal announced a public deficit of 4.1 per cent of GDP, above the reference level of 3 per cent. This prompted the Commission to follow the excessive deficit procedure laid down in the Council Resolution on the Stability and Growth Pact in preparing a report to the Economic and Financial Committee for its opinion.

ii. Energy

The Commission has presented a Proposal for a Directive on the Control of High Activity Sealed Radioactive Sources.[70]

In addition, the Commission has adopted a Proposal for a Council Decision Approving a Commission Regulation on the Application of Euratom safe-

[66] Spain-2001 [2002] OJ C126/3; Greece-2001 [2002] OJ C126/9; and Portugal-2001 [2002] OJ C126/12.

[67] COM(2002)557.

[68] [1992] OJ L206/7.

[69] [1991] OJ L135/40.

[70] COM(2002)130, [2002] OJ C151E/298.

guards,[71] in accordance with developments in the fields of nuclear and information technology.

iii. Financial Instruments

A Proposal for a Regulation on the Granting of Community Financial Assistance to Improve the Environmental Performance of the Freight Transport System, has also been presented by the Commission.[72]

iv. Implementation

In its Nineteenth Annual Report on Monitoring the Application of Community Law,[73] the Commission reports on the application of EC law in 2001. One-third of the complaints and infringement cases for non-compliance with Community law investigated by the Commission in 2001 concerned the environment. During 2001, the Commission brought 71 cases against Member States before the European Court of Justice (ECJ) and delivered 197 Reasoned Opinions on the basis of Articles 226 and 228 EC, which combined represents a 40 per cent increase compared with 2000. Several factors are reported to have contributed to the increasing number of cases concerning the environment. These include: (i) regular monitoring by the Commission of the conformity with directives of the implementing measures notified by Member States; (ii) increasing public concern over environmental issues; (iii) organizational difficulties experienced in Member States, as a result of constitutional and administrative structures under which responsibility lies for implementing environmental law; (iv) the wide scope of EC environmental legislation; and (v) the non-existence or inefficiency of complaint mechanisms in Member States.

The Commission adopted a Decision on 23 May 2001 to refer Spain for the second time, under Article 228 EC, with a request for a daily penalty payment of €45,600, for failing to comply with an ECJ judgment concerning the Bathing Water Directive.[74] The Article 228 EC referrals instigated in 2000 against the United Kingdom (UK) and Germany were dropped since, in each case, the necessary measures were taken to comply with the ECJ's earlier judgment. In 2001, the Commission considered that Greece had complied with the Court's judgment of 7 April 1992. In its second judgment of 4 July 2000, in Case C-387/97,[75] the ECJ imposed a financial penalty of €20,000 per day for failing to comply with its first judgment. The case concerned infringements of Directive 75/442/EEC on Waste (Waste Framework Directive)[76] and Directive 78/319/EEC on Toxic and Dangerous Waste.[77] In March 2001, the illegal solid waste

[71] COM(2002)99, [2002] OJ C227E/224. [72] COM(2002)54, [2002] OJ C126E/354.
[73] COM(2002)324. [74] n. 5 above.
[75] Case C-387/97, *Commission* v. *Greece* [2000] ECR I-5047.
[76] [1975] OJ L194/39, amended by Dir. 91/156 [1991] OJ L78/32.
[77] [1978] OJ L84/43.

dump in Kouroupitos in the region of Chania was closed and the waste was treated in an appropriate installation. Greece paid a total of €5,400,000 in penalty payments for the period from July 2000 to March 2001.

Several seminars were held in 2001, in which Commission representatives explained the correct implementation of complex environmental directives to Member States' competent authorities in order to prevent, in the first instance, their incorrect application. Five directives in the air sector were to be transposed by Member States during 2001. Infringement proceedings have been taken for failure to notify national measures implementing these directives. The Commission also started infringement proceedings against thirteen Member States, of which eleven are still open, in respect of Directive 2000/14/EC relating to the Noise Emission in the Environment by Equipment for Use Outdoors.[78] This Directive repeals, from 3 January 2002, nine directives concerning noise levels of different products.

v. Information

The European Environment Agency (EEA) issued its Thirty-First Environmental Issue Report—Energy and Environment in the European Union.[79]

The Commission has adopted a Proposal for a Regulation amending Regulation (EEC) No. 1210/90[80] as regards the Budgetary and Financial Rules applicable to the European Environment Agency and the European Environment Information and Observation Network and Access to the Agency's Documents.[81]

vi. State Aid

The Commission has announced its intention to continue to apply the current Community Framework for State Aid for Research and Development,[82] until 31 December 2005.[83]

vii. Statistics

The Commission's Proposal for a Decision on the Community Statistical Programme 2003–7,[84] has been published. The draft Decision sets out, *inter alia*, the main statistical efforts under the Environment Title for the next five years.

The EEA has published the EU's greenhouse gas emission figures for 2000. They were 3.5 per cent lower than in the base year 1990.[85]

[78] [2000] OJ L162/1.

[79] Luxembourg: Office for Official Publications of the European Communities, 2002, published on the Internet at: http://www.eea.eu.int.

[80] [1990] OJ L120/1. As amended by Reg. (EC) No. 933/1999, [1999] OJ L117/1.

[81] COM(2002)406, [2002] OJ C331E/59.

[82] [1996] OJ C45/5; as amended [1998] OJ C48/2; cf. [2001] OJ C78/24.

[83] [2002] OJ C111/3.

[84] [2002] OJ C75E/274.

[85] Published on the Internet at: http://org.eea.eu.int/documents/newsreleases/greenhouse_gas_emission; see also Commission Press Release IP/02/636.

viii. Trans-European Networks

An Amended Proposal for a Regulation amending Regulation (EC) No. 2236/95 laying down General Rules for the Granting of Community Financial Aid in the Field of Trans-European Networks[86] has been submitted by the Commission.

The Commission has adopted a Proposal for a Decision amending Decision 1254/96/EC laying down a Series of Guidelines for Trans-European Energy Networks.[87]

Also, the Commission has presented an Amended Proposal for a Decision amending Decision 1692/96/EC on Community Guidelines for the Development of the Trans-European Transport Network.[88]

The 2000 Annual Report on Trans-European Networks has been issued by the Commission.[89]

ix. Use of Instruments

The Commission Proposal for a Directive establishing a Scheme for Greenhouse Gas Emission Allowance Trading within the Community and amending Directive 96/61/EC[90] has been published.

The Commission Proposal for a Directive amending Directive 92/81/EEC with Regard to the Possibility of Applying a Reduced Rate of Excise Duty on Certain Mineral Oils Containing Biofuels and on Biofuels[91] has also been published.

Furthermore, the Commission has presented a Proposal for a Directive amending Directive 92/81/EEC and Directive 92/82/EEC to Introduce Special Tax Arrangements for Diesel Fuel used for Commercial Purposes and to Align the Excise Duties on Petrol and Diesel Fuel.[92]

In addition, the Commission has presented an Amended Proposal for a Directive on the Promotion of the Use of Biofuels for Transport.[93]

The Commission has also presented an Amended Proposal for a Directive on the Protection of the Environment through Criminal Law.[94]

A Report from the Commission on Environmental Technology for Sustainable Development forms the basis of the Commission's intention to develop an action plan for promoting environmental technologies in 2003.[95]

The Commission Communication Implementing the Community Strategy to Reduce CO_2 Emissions from Cars[96] is the third annual report on the effectiveness of the strategy. It covers the period 1995 to 2001 and reports, *inter alia*, on the operation of the monitoring scheme established under Decision 1753/2000/EC.[97]

[86] COM(2002)134, [2002] OJ C151E/291. [87] [2002] OJ C151 E/207.

[88] COM(2002)542. [89] COM(2002)344.

[90] [2002] OJ C75E/33. [91] COM(2001)547, [2002] OJ C103E/217.

[92] COM(2002)410, [2002] OJ C291E/221.

[93] COM(2002)508, [2002] OJ C103E/205.

[94] COM(2002)544. [95] COM(2002)122. [96] COM(2002)693.

[97] Dec. 1753/2000/EC establishing a Scheme to Monitor the Average Specific Emissions of CO_2 from New Passenger Cars [2000] OJ L202/1.

The Third Progress Report under Decision 93/389/EEC as amended by Decision 99/296/EC for a Monitoring Mechanism of Community Greenhouse Gas Emissions[98] has been issued by the Commission. It assesses the actual and projected progress of Member States and the Community towards fulfilling their greenhouse gas emission commitments under the UNFCCC[99] and the Kyoto Protocol thereto.[100] The EC, as a whole, met its greenhouse gas stabilization target in 2000 under the UNFCCC, and emissions for that year are in line with the Kyoto target path for 2008–12. Overall, greenhouse gas emissions in 2000 decreased by 3.5 per cent compared to 1990, slightly less than in 1999 (−4 per cent). CO_2 emissions were 0.5 per cent below 1990 levels while CH_4 and N_2O emissions decreased by 16 per cent and 20 per cent, respectively. In the EU, greenhouse gas emissions per capita decreased by 7 per cent, from 11.5 tonnes in 1990 to 10.8 tonnes in 2000. The 'business-as-usual' scenario (with existing measures) suggests that in 2010, EC emissions will have decreased by only 4.7 per cent leaving a gap of 3.3 per cent to the Kyoto target. All Member States except three have identified additional policies and measures to achieve their respective Burden Sharing target. Acceding Member States are not part of the burden sharing agreement. They are subject to individual 8 per cent targets, except Hungary and Poland, which each have a reduction commitment of 6 per cent.

[98] COM(2002)702; Commission Press Release IP/02/1835.

[99] n. 3 above. [100] n. 2 above.

VIII. Case Law of the European Court of Justice

*Jos Janssen**

A. Introduction

The survey year 2002 was not a very fruitful one in terms of environmental law judgments of the European Court of Justice (ECJ), in particular due to the low number of preliminary references. Whereas the ECJ handed down some 20 judgments on infringements of environmental directives under Article 226 EC, there were only two preliminary rulings under Article 234 EC concerning the interpretation of 'genuine' environmental legislation, both concerning waste issues. Thus, this survey provides support for the view that private enforcement of EC environmental law pursuant to Article 234 EC indeed seems to be 'an unfulfilled promise'.[1] Furthermore, it confirms the rather unsurprising observation of the Commission that the Member States still have difficulties in the timely and correct implementation, as well as the proper practical application, of European Community (EC) environmental law, given the number of judgments under Article 226 EC.[2] In fact, in 2002 alone, the Commission brought 65 new cases against Member States on the basis of Article 226 EC.[3] As a general observation, there seems to be a growing emphasis on practical implementation of environmental directives, meaning that the ECJ increasingly requires factual situations to be in accordance with obligations laid down in directives.[4] At a more substantive level, the most important news of 2002 was that the ECJ clarified the concept of 'waste for recovery' in *Abfall Service*.[5] Furthermore, as to the substance of the integration principle, laid down in Article 6 EC, the ECJ ruled in *Concordia Bus* that environmental concerns may be taken into account in awarding public service contracts under the EC public procurement rules.[6]

* Lecturer at the Centre for Environmental Law, University of Amsterdam (the Netherlands).

[1] See H. Somsen, 'Private Enforcement of EC Environmental Law: an Unfulfilled Promise?' (2000) 1 *Yearbook of European Environmental Law*, 311–60.

[2] See Commission Report—Fourth Annual Survey on the Implementation and Enforcement of Community Environmental Law SEC(2003)804, 6.

[3] In its Annual Survey, ibid., the Commission builds upon the following typology of infringement cases: (i) non-communication (failure to adopt the measures to transpose directives and to communicate them to the Commission within the prescribed time-limit); (ii) non-conformity (transposition measures are not in conformity with directives); and (iii) horizontal bad application (failure to implement certain derived or secondary obligations contained in the Community acts, e.g. setting out plans, classifying sites and designating areas, adopting programmes, submitting monitoring data, reporting, etc.).

[4] See also J.H. Jans, *European Environmental Law* (Groningen: Europa Law Publishing, 2000), referring to 'factual' infringements of Community standards, at 164.

[5] Case C-6/00, n. 28 below.

[6] Case C-513/99, n. 68 below.

B. Atmospheric Pollution

i. Commission v. France, *and* Commission v. Spain

Community legislation on atmospheric pollution includes two directives on the prevention of air pollution from new and existing municipal waste incineration plants, respectively: Directive 89/369/EEC on the Prevention of Air Pollution from New Municipal Waste Incineration Plants[7] and Directive 89/429 on the Reduction of Air Pollution from Existing Municipal Waste Incineration Plants[8] (Municipal Waste Incinerators Directives). In 2002, the Commission brought two cases before the ECJ concerning alleged infringements of these Directives by France and Spain. In both judgments, the ECJ held that the correct transposition in domestic law of the provisions of the Municipal Waste Incinerators Directives was not sufficient to comply with the obligations of these Directives (implementation in law), but that it was also required that the incineration plants had, in actual fact, been commissioned and operated in accordance with the requirements of the Directives (implementation in fact).

In the case against France, according to the Commission, the Member State had failed to adopt the necessary measures to ensure that all incinerators at that time operating in France were operated in accordance with the combustion conditions laid down in the Directives.[9] It is interesting to note that as a result of a complaint that one particular incinerator did not comply with the combustion conditions in the Municipal Waste Incinerators Directives, the Commission became aware of a survey and a press release from the French Ministry of Regional Planning and the Environment, which revealed that several incinerators did not comply with the operating conditions laid down in the Directives. On the basis of this information, made public by the French authorities themselves, the Commission decided to issue a letter of formal notice. The French Government argued, *inter alia*, that both Directives' provisions had been correctly transposed into national law and that there were measures to ensure their effective application. However, the Commission alleged that the measures were insufficient since, four years after expiry of the time-limit, they still had not enabled the result required by the Directives for all French incinerators. France's chief defence was that, pursuant to the Municipal Waste Incinerators Directives, Member States are required only to make incinerator operators subject to certain obligations, and that this obligation is binding on the Member States as to the objective to be achieved, but leaves a margin of discretion in assessing the need for the measures to be adopted. According to the French Government, the fact that a situation is not in conformity with the objectives of a directive does not, per se, mean that the Member State has failed to fulfil its obligation.

[7] [1989] OJ L163/32.
[8] [1989] OJ L 203/50.
[9] Case C-60/01, *Commission* v. *France* [2002] ECR I-5679.

However, the ECJ generally held that it follows from Article 249 EC that one of the principal characteristics of directives is precisely that they are intended to achieve a specified result, yet there may be great differences in the types of obligations which directives impose on Member States, and hence also in the results that must be achieved. It distinguished between three different types of obligations: (i) directives requiring legislative measures to be adopted at national level and compliance with those measures to be subject to judicial review;[10] (ii) directives laying down that Member States are to take the necessary measures to ensure that certain objectives formulated in general and unquantifiable terms are attained, whilst allowing some discretion as to the nature of the measures to be taken;[11] and (iii) directives requiring Member States to obtain very precise and specific results after a certain period.[12]

The finding that an infringement has occurred depends on the type of obligation imposed. According to the ECJ, the Directives *in casu* supplemented Directive 84/360/EEC on the Combating of Air Pollution from Industrial Plants,[13] by introducing detailed and precise requirements applicable to both new and existing municipal waste incineration plants. For example, Article 4(1) of Directive 89/369/EEC and Articles 2(a) and 4 of Directive 89/429/EEC state that gases resulting from combustion of waste must be raised to a temperature of at least 850°C, for at least two seconds, in the presence of at least 6 per cent oxygen. Furthermore, Article 5(1) of both Directives specifies that these standards for temperature and oxygen content are minimum values to be observed at all times during the operation of the incinerator. From this, the ECJ concluded that the Municipal Waste Incinerators Directives impose on Member States obligations, formulated in clear and unequivocal terms, to achieve a certain result, in order that their incineration plants meet detailed and precise requirements within the stated time-limits. *In casu*, the ECJ deemed it insufficient for a Member State (merely) to take all reasonably practicable measures to achieve the result imposed by the Directives.[14]

In the case against Spain, the Commission claimed that incineration plants at Mazo and Barlovento were not covered by an authorization to operate as required by Article 2 of Directive 89/369/EEC.[15] The Spanish Government claimed that Article 2 was implemented in Spanish law by Royal Decree 1088/1992 on limiting emissions into the atmosphere of certain polluting agents from municipal

[10] See e.g. Arts. 4 and 8 of Dir. 84/450/EEC concerning Misleading Advertising [1984] OJ L250/17.

[11] See e.g. Art. 4 of Dir. 75/442/EEC on Waste [1975] OJ L194/39, as amended by Dir. 91/156/EEC, [1991] OJ L78/32.

[12] See e.g. Art. 4(1) of Dir. 76/160/EEC concerning the Quality of Bathing Water [1976] OJ L31/1.

[13] [1984] OJ L188/20.

[14] See, to that effect, with regard to Dir. 76/160/EEC, n. 12 above, Case C-268/00, *Commission* v. *Netherlands* [2002] ECR I-2995, paras. 12–14.

[15] Case C-139/00, *Commission* v. *Spain* [2002] I-6407.

waste incineration plants,[16] and that Article 2 could only be infringed if no rule implementing it in the national legal order had been adopted. It was clear that the Commission did not allege that Spain had not (correctly) implemented Directive 89/369/EEC. Rather, the Commission's complaint related to two specific cases in which certain obligations under the Directive had not been complied with. In this regard the ECJ referred to the parallel case *Commission* v. *France*,[17] reiterating that Directive 89/369/EEC imposes obligations, formulated in clear and unequivocal terms, in order to achieve a certain result, to the effect that national incineration plants meet detailed and precise requirements within the stated time-limits. Accordingly, a Member State will comply with its obligations under this Directive (and hence achieve the result prescribed therein) only if, in addition to correct implementation of the provisions of that Directive into domestic law, the incineration plants located in its territory have, in actual fact, been commissioned and operate in accordance with the requirements of the provisions of the Directive.[18] Thus, the ECJ held that the correct transposition in domestic law of the provisions of Directive 89/369/EEC is not sufficient to comply with the obligations it imposes. Furthermore, the Court ruled that Spain had infringed Article 7 of the Directive by not having equipped two incineration plants with auxiliary burners. The Spanish Government tried to justify these infringements by relying on the absence of negative effects on the environment from the operation of the furnaces in question, but this was not accepted by the ECJ. That is, even if the impact of those plants on the environment had been environmentally acceptable, this would not relieve Member States from complying with Articles 6 and 7 of the Directive. The ECJ added that a Member State has complied with its obligations under the Directive, and thus achieved the requisite results, only if the incineration plants located in its territory have been commissioned and operate in accordance with the requirements of the Directive. In other words, the Directive requires implementation not only in law, but also in fact.

C. Chemicals

i. Netherlands *v.* Commission

Pursuant to Article 2a of Directive 76/769/EEC on Restrictions on the Marketing and Use of Certain Dangerous Substances and Preparations (Marketing and Use Restrictions Directive),[19] the Commission has the power to adapt the Directive to technical progress by way of a comitology procedure, instead of Article 95 EC. In *Netherlands* v. *Commission*,[20] the Netherlands argued that the Commission had exceeded its powers by adopting a provision on the

[16] Official State Gazette (BOE) 235 of 30 Sept. 1992. [17] n. 9 above.
[18] Case C-139/00, n. 15 above, para. 27. [19] [1976] OJ L262/201.
[20] Case C-314/99, *Netherlands* v. *Commission* [2002] ECR I-5521.

basis of Article 2a, allowing Austria and Sweden to continue to apply existing restrictions on cadmium. In contrast to Article 95 EC, this provision provides for the possibility of immediate amendments to Annex I to the Directive when new risks to human health and the environment are detected. If the Commission seeks to rely on this procedure it must have sufficiently reliable scientific data proving the necessity of introducing new restrictions on the use of the substance or preparation concerned. However, *in casu*, the provision amending Annex I did not include any new restriction on the use of cadmium at Community level, but merely permitted Austria and Sweden to maintain existing restrictions. Hence, the ECJ held that the contested provision could not be regarded as an adaptation to technical progress of Annex I, and granted the request of the Netherlands for annulment.

D. Nature Conservation

i. Commission *v.* Ireland

In Case C-117/00 against Ireland,[21] the Commission alleged that this Member State had infringed Article 3 of Directive 79/409/EEC on the Conservation of Wild Birds (Birds Directive),[22] by not having ensured sufficient diversity and area of habitats for the red grouse. The Commission also claimed that Ireland had failed to prevent the blanket bog of the Owenduff-Nephin Beg Complex special protection area (SPA) from being damaged by overgrazing, in breach of Article 4(4) of the Birds Directive and Article 6(2) of Directive 92/43/EEC on the Conservation of Natural Habitats and of Wild Fauna and Flora (Habitats Directive).[23] With regard to the infringement of Article 3 of the Birds Directive, the Commission argued that the habitat of the red grouse is hill land and bog, and that its diet consists principally in common heather, which it also uses for building its nests and for protection from predators. Consequently, areas of bog and hill land are the only suitable habitats for the red grouse. However, heather is particularly vulnerable to overgrazing and in Ireland it was under serious threat from overgrazing. In addition, various studies showed that there had been a very marked decline in red grouse populations. The Irish Government claimed that the Commission had failed to prove that the facts of the complaint had the effect of reducing the red grouse's habitats to such a degree that it is no longer sufficient for its conservation. Referred to its standing case law, the ECJ held that Member States' obligations under Article 3 of the Birds Directive exist before any reduction is observed in the number of birds, or any risk of a protected species becoming extinct has materialized.[24] Furthermore, the ECJ inferred from evidence presented that the numbers of red grouse had indeed diminished, and that

[21] Case C-117/00, *Commission* v. *Ireland* [2002] ECR I-5335.

[22] [1979] OJ L103/1. [23] [1992] OJ L206/7.

[24] See Case C-355/90, *Commission* v. *Spain* [1993] ECR I-4221, para. 15.

the breeding range of the red grouse coincided largely with areas having been degraded by overgrazing. The Commission's complaint was accordingly upheld.

The Commission further claimed that the adverse effects of overgrazing by sheep on Ireland's largest SPA, the Owenduff-Nephin Beg Complex, constituted an infringement of Article 6(2) of the Habitats Directive and of Article 4(4) of the Birds Directive. Pursuant to these provisions, Member States are to take appropriate steps to avoid deterioration of habitats in SPAs classified pursuant to Article 4(1) of the Birds Directive. Although there was no infringement in relation to 10,000 hectares in State ownership on which grazing had been diminished, other parts of the SPA had seriously been damaged by the excessive numbers of sheep grazing there. With regard to these other parts of the SPA, the ECJ held that Ireland had infringed Article 6(2) of the Habitats Directive.

ii. Commission *v.* Greece

Under Article 12(1)(b) and (d) of the Habitats Directive, Member States are required to take the requisite measures to establish a system of strict protection for animal species listed in Annex IV(a). At issue in Case C-103/00 was Greece's alleged failure to take such measures in order to protect the sea turtle *Caretta caretta* on the island Zakinthos.[25] In particular, Greece had failed to avoid disturbances during the turtle's breeding period and activities which might bring about deterioration or destruction of its breeding sites. Rather exceptionally, the Commission carried out on-the-spot investigations twice in July and August 1999. Commission officials found that the protective measures on the beaches used for breeding by the sea turtle *Caretta caretta* were inadequate. They found in particular that there was no supervision and no notices on the beaches, there were pedalos and boats in the sea area where their use was prohibited, there were a significant number of beach umbrellas and deckchairs on various beaches, and there were illegal buildings on the beach. The Greek Government did not dispute these findings. On the basis of the Commission's findings, the ECJ concluded that the use of mopeds on the beach and the presence of pedalos and small boats in the sea, which, in addition, were not isolated occurrences, constituted deliberate disturbance of the species during its breeding period. Furthermore, the presence of buildings on a breeding beach was held liable to lead to the deterioration or destruction of the breeding site. Accordingly, the ECJ ruled that Greece had failed to fulfil its obligations under Article 12(1)(b) and (d) of the Habitats Directive.

iii. Commission *v.* Belgium

The Commission also brought an action against Belgium for incomplete transposition (by several Belgian regions) of various provisions of the Habitats

[25] Case C-103/00, *Commission* v. *Greece* [2002] ECR I-1147.

Directive.[26] As regards the Flemish Region, the Commission claimed that it had failed to adopt the necessary measures to ensure the transposition of Articles 1, 4(5), 5(4), 6, 7, 12, 13, 14, 15, 16(1), 22(b), and 23(2) of the Habitats Directive. This was not disputed by the Belgian Government. Furthermore, the Brussels Capital Region had failed to implement certain provisions because it did not deem transposition necessary. It failed, for example, to adopt a provision requiring authorities to inform the Commission of compensatory measures adopted pursuant to Article 6(4) of the Directive. According to the Belgian government, transposition of Article 6(4) could not be achieved by legislation, because it has no normative scope and it does not create rights or obligations for a general category of individuals. The ECJ considered that in the absence of a provision in national law which lays down adequate detailed rules concerning information on the compensatory measures adopted, it would not be possible to ensure that the second sentence of the first subparagraph of Article 6(4) had full effect and attained its objective. Uncertainty at the domestic level concerning the procedure to be followed in order to comply with the obligation to inform, is likely to hinder compliance with that obligation and, consequently, the attainment of its objective. Similarly, the ECJ held that Article 7, providing that the system for protecting special areas of conservation defined in Article 6(2), (3), and (4) of the Habitats Directive is to replace the system of protection arising from the first sentence of Article 4(4) of the Birds Directive, requires transposition into national legislation. In order to ensure full application of that provision in law, and not only in fact, and to satisfy the requirement of legal certainty, Member States must provide a precise legal framework for the field in question.[27] It can, moreover, be deduced from this judgment that the duty for Member States to promote education and general information on the need to protect species of wild fauna and flora and to conserve their habitats, as laid down in Article 22(c) of the Directive, requires transposition into national law, rather than guaranteeing the financing of nature-related education programmes and concluding agreements thereto.

E. Waste

i. Abfall Service

In *Abfall Service*,[28] the Austrian company Abfall Service notified to the competent authorities its intention to ship 7,000 tonnes of hazardous waste to the German Salzwerke AG, where it was to be deposited in a former salt-mine in order to secure hollow spaces (mine-sealing). According to Abfall Service, the treatment

[26] Case C-324/01, *Commission* v. *Belgium* [2002] ECR I-11197.

[27] See to that effect Case C-360/87, *Commission* v. *Italy* [1991] ECR I-791, paras. 11 and 13.

[28] Case C-6/00, *Abfall Service AG (ASA)* v. *Bundesminister für Umwelt, Jugend und Familie* [2002] ECR I-1961.

of the waste to be shipped constituted a 'recovery' operation, which was approved by the competent authority of destination in Germany. The Austrian authorities, however, raised an objection to the shipment under Article 7(4)(a) of Regulation (EEC) No. 259/93 on the Supervision and Control of Shipments of Waste within, into and out of the European Community (Waste Shipment Regulation),[29] since the planned shipment, in fact, constituted a disposal operation. That decision was challenged by Abfall Service before an Austrian administrative court, which subsequently referred several preliminary questions to the ECJ.

First, the national court sought clarification as to whether the competent authority of dispatch within the meaning of Article 2(c) of the Waste Shipment Regulation is competent to verify whether a proposed shipment classified in the notification as a 'shipment of waste for recovery' does, in fact, correspond to that classification. According to Abfall Service, the authority of dispatch was not competent to verify the accuracy of the notifier's classification of the shipment, in particular since only the competent authority of destination would be able to acquire the information relating to the recovery installation and the costs of recovery and disposal in the country of destination, which would enable it to raise an objection in full knowledge of the facts. The ECJ, however, held that: 'it follows from the system established by the Regulation that all the competent authorities to which that notification is addressed must check that the classification by the notifier is consistent with the provisions of the Regulation and object to a shipment which is incorrectly classified'.[30]

In particular, this obligation derives from Article 26 of the Regulation, which requires Member States to prohibit and punish any illegal traffic, and from Article 30(1) of the Regulation, which expressly imposes a general duty on Member States to take the requisite measures to ensure that waste is shipped in accordance with the provisions of the Regulation. Another important question the ECJ had to deal with was whether the deposit of waste in a disused mine constitutes a disposal operation or a recovery operation. The ECJ observed that neither the Waste Shipment Regulation nor Directive 75/442/EEC on Waste (Waste Framework Directive)[31] contains a general definition of disposal or recovery of waste, but merely refer to Annexes IIA and IIB to the Waste Framework Directive, in which various operations falling within the scope of those concepts are listed. Furthermore, the intention of both Annexes is to list the most common disposal and recovery operations, and not precisely and exhaustively to specify all the disposal and recovery operations covered by the Directive. In case a waste operation cannot be brought within one of the operations or categories of operations referred to in Annexes IIA or IIB, it must be classified on a case-by-case basis in light of the Directive's objectives. As to the criterion to be

[29] [1993] OJ L30/1. [30] Case C-6/00, n. 5 above, para. 40.
[31] [1975] OJ L194/39, amended by Dir. 91/156, [1991] OJ L78/32.

used in order to classify the waste operation, the ECJ ruled that it follows from Article 3(1)(b) and the Fourth Recital of the Waste Framework Directive that the essential characteristic of a waste recovery operation is that its principal objective is that the waste serve a useful purpose in replacing other materials which would have had to be used for that purpose, thereby conserving natural resources. According to the ECJ, the national judge had to apply that criterion *in casu*, in order to classify the deposit of waste in a disused mine as either a disposal operation or a recovery operation. In view of its previous considerations, the ECJ held that the deposit of waste in a disused mine does not necessarily constitute a disposal operation and that it must be assessed on a case-by-case basis to determine whether the operation is a disposal or a recovery operation. Given the definition provided by the ECJ in this judgment, such a deposit constitutes a recovery operation if its principal objective is that the waste serve a useful purpose in replacing other materials which could have been used for that purpose.

ii. Palin Granit

Another episode in the never-ending story of the definition of 'waste' can be found in *Palin Granit*,[32] in which the ECJ had to rule on the issue whether leftover stone resulting from quarrying was to be regarded as waste. The judgment provides a useful overview of recent case law of the definition of waste under the Waste Framework Directive. Pursuant to Article 1(a) of the Directive, 'waste' means 'any substance or object in the categories set out in Annex I which the holder discards or intends or is required to discard'. The decisive element in this definition is the meaning of the term 'discard',[33] which must be interpreted in the light of the aim of the Waste Framework Directive and of Article 174(2) EC. Hence, the concept of waste cannot be interpreted restrictively.[34] In addition, the question whether a given substance is waste must be determined in the light of all the circumstances, regard being had to the aim of the Waste Framework Directive and the need to ensure that its effectiveness is not undermined.[35] In any event, neither the fact that the leftover stone had undergone a treatment operation referred to in the Waste Framework Directive, nor the fact that it could be reused, sufficed to decide whether that stone was waste for the purposes of the

[32] Case C-9/00, *Palin Granit Oy and Vehmassalon Kansanterveystyön Kuntayhtymän Hallitus* [2002] ECR I-3533.

[33] See Case C-129/96, *Inter-Environnement Wallonie ASBL* v. *Région Wallonne* [1997] ECR I-7411, para. 26.

[34] See Joined Cases C-418/97 and C-419/97, *ARCO Chemie Nederland Ltd* v. *Minister van Volkshuisvesting, Ruimtelijke Ordening en Milieubeheer* (*C-418/97*) *and Vereniging Dorpsbelang Hees, Stichting Werkgroep Weurt and Vereniging Stedelijk Leefmilieu Nijmegen* v. *Directeur van de Dienst Milieu en Water van de Provincie Gelderland* (*C-419/97*) (*ARCO Chemie*) [2000] ECR I-4475, paras. 36–40.

[35] ibid., paras. 73, 88, and 97.

Directive.[36] According to the ECJ, other considerations were more decisive, such as the fact that the holder stores the leftover stone for an indefinite period to await possible use, or discards or intends to discard it. Accordingly, the leftover stone is to be classified as waste within the meaning of the Directive. In addition, it is not relevant for this determination where the leftover stone is stored, what its composition is, or the fact that the stone does not pose any real risk to human health or the environment.

iii. Waste Management Plans

In 2002, there were three judgments concerning inadequate waste planning concerning France, the United Kingdom (UK), and Spain.[37] The ECJ condemned all three Member States for having breached Article 7(1) of the Waste Framework Directive, Article 6(1) of Directive 91/689/EEC on Hazardous Waste (Hazardous Waste Directive),[38] and Article 14 of Directive 94/62/EEC on Packaging and Packaging Waste (Packaging and Packaging Waste Directive),[39] which require the adoption of various waste management plans. In order to ensure compliance with these judgments, the Commission is following up these cases under Article 228 EC.[40] As regards the defences raised by the Member States for breaching the planning requirements in these Directives, it is noteworthy that France claimed that the delay of seven years in drawing up waste management plans 'as soon as possible', for the purpose of Article 7(1) of the Waste Framework Directive, was *inter alia* due to the fact that it had set itself more ambitious objectives than those pursued by the Directive. However, the ECJ held that this did not relieve France of its obligation to comply, at the very least, with the requirements of the Directive within the period allowed.

iv. Disposal of PCBs and PCTs

The disposal of Polychlorinated Byphenyls (PCBs) and Polychlorinated Terphenyls (PCTs) is regulated by Directive 96/59/EC on the Disposal of Polychlorinated Byphenyls and Polychlorinated Terphenyls (PCB/PCT Directive).[41] Article 11(1) requires that Member States draw up plans for the decontamination and/or disposal of inventoried equipment and PCBs contained therein, in accordance with Article 4 of the Directive. In 2002, the ECJ ruled against Luxembourg, Italy,

[36] See on these points, respectively, *ARCO Chemie*, n. 34 above, para. 82, and Joined Cases C-206/88 and C-207/88, *Criminal Proceedings against G. Vessoso and G. Zanetti* [1990] ECR I-1416, para. 9, and Joined Cases C-304/94, C-330/94, C-342/94, and C-234/95, *Criminal Proceedings against Euro Tombesi and Adino Tombesi (C-304/94), Roberto Santella (C-330/94), Giovanni Muzi and Others (C-342/94) and Anselmo Savini (C-224/95) (Tombesi)* [1997] ECR I-3561, para. 52.

[37] Case C-292/99, *Commission* v. *France* [2002] ECR I-4097; Case C-35/00, *Commission* v. *United Kingdom* [2002] ECR I-953; and Case C-466/99, *Commission* v. *Italy* [2002] ECR I-851.

[38] [1991] OJ L337/20.

[39] [1994] OJ L365/10.

[40] See Commission Report, n. 2 above, 16.

[41] [1996] OJ L243/31.

France, and Spain, for not having communicated the necessary measures to the Commission under the PCB/PCT Directive.[42] In the case against Luxembourg, the ECJ defined specific requirements as regards the content of the plan. Although Article 11(1) merely states that Member States must draw up plans, the ECJ held that the first indent of this provision, read in conjunction with the tenth and sixteenth Recitals of the Preamble to the Directive, indicates that in drawing up plans, Member States are obliged to compare the amount of inventoried equipment and quantities of PCBs contained therein which must be disposed of or decontaminated with the disposal or decontamination facilities available for that purpose. The plan must also enable the designation of appropriate types of treatment for the various categories of equipment and contained PCBs. In order fully to satisfy the obligations arising from this provision, the plan must be specific and in conformity with the general system for disposal of PCBs under the Directive.[43]

F. Water

i. Bathing Water in the Netherlands

According to the Commission, the monitoring of bathing waters is becoming increasingly common and water quality is improving,[44] as required by Directive 76/160/EEC concerning the Quality of Bathing Water (Bathing Water Directive).[45] Nevertheless, the application of the Directive is still problematic, as is illustrated by the fact that the Netherlands was condemned for the poor quality of its bathing waters, which did not conform with the Directive's limit values. Member States are obliged take all requisite measures to achieve these limit values by no later that ten years after notification of the Directive.[46]

ii. Drinking Water in Ireland

In Case C-316/00, *Commission* v. *Ireland*,[47] the Commission alleged that Ireland had failed to ensure compliance with certain microbiological parameters of Annex I to Directive 80/778/EEC relating to the Quality of Water for Human Consumption (Drinking Water Directive).[48] Moreover, it had failed to reflect, in national legislation, the binding character of the requirements of Annex I in relation to group water supplies. In essence, this case concerned 'group water

[42] Case C-174/01, *Commission* v. *Luxembourg* [2002] ECR I-1171, Case C-46/01, *Commission* v. *Italy* [2002] ECR I-2094, Case C-177/01, *Commission* v. *France* [2002] I-5137.

[43] See, to that effect, Joined Cases C-232/95 and C-233/95, *Commission* v. *Greece* [1998] ECR I-3343, paras. 34–6, and Case C-207/97, *Commission* v. *Belgium* [1999] ECR I-275, para. 39.

[44] See Commission Report, n. 2 above, 11.

[45] [1976] OJ L31/1.

[46] See Case C-56/90, *Commission* v. *United Kingdom* [1993] ECR I-4109, para. 43.

[47] [2002] ECR I-10527.

[48] [1980] OJ L229/11, last amended by Dir. 98/83/EC [1998] OJ L330/32.

schemes', which have been set up to secure drinking water supply to remote rural areas of Ireland. Each such group water scheme provides two or more households with drinking water, using a common or shared source and a distribution system which is owned, operated, and maintained by a cooperative group formed in a rural area. Ireland submitted that the Drinking Water Directive does not apply to group water schemes, relying on the ECJ ruling in Case 42/89, *Commission* v. *Belgium*.[49] In that case, the ECJ had held that the Directive applies only to water supplied for human consumption and not to water from private sources, which, the Irish Government argued, should be considered to include group water schemes. However, the ECJ held that the exclusion, in that ruling, of 'private sources' from the scope of the Directive, must be understood as limited to wells and other private water sources where the water is directly drawn by the individual for his own use. By contrast, a situation where the water is supplied to several users by way of a supply network clearly is covered by the concept of supply to consumers, and thus falls within the scope of the Directive. Unlike water drawn by an individual for his own use, water supplied to several users by way of a supply network undergoes extraction and distribution processes, which prevent it from being individually monitored by each user. According to the ECJ, the group water schemes are characterized by the fact that the water supplied to the users through the schemes cannot be monitored by those users individually. Thus, the ECJ ruled that the Irish group water schemes fall within the scope of the Drinking Water Directive. Consequently, Ireland was condemned for not having ensured compliance with certain microbiological parameters of Annex I to the Directive both with regard to public water supplies and group water schemes.

iii. Protecting Water against Nitrates

In 2002, the ECJ decided two cases on Directive 91/676/EEC on the Protection of Waters against Pollution Caused by Nitrates from Agricultural Sources (Nitrates Directive).[50] These cases concerned proceedings against France and Germany, for lacking or insufficient designation of vulnerable zones as required by Article 3 of the Nitrates Directive, and for the failure to establish proper action programmes to reduce water pollution caused by nitrogen compounds in those zones, as required by Article 5.

In the case against France,[51] the main issue was that France had limited the identification of eutrophic waters[52] to zones in which nitrogen is the controlling

[49] Case 42/89, *Commission* v. *Belgium* [1990] ECR I-2821, para. 17.

[50] [1991] OJ L375/1.

[51] Case C-258/00, *Commission* v. *France* [2002] ECR I-5959.

[52] Art. 2(i) of the Nitrates Dir. defines 'eutrophication' as 'the enrichment of water by nitrogen compounds, causing an accelerated growth of algae and higher forms of plant life to produce an undesirable disturbance to the balance of organisms present in the water and to the quality of the water concerned'. The waters referred to in Art. 3(1) affected by pollution or which could be so

factor, that is, to coastal zones and shallow stagnant, brackish waters. This implied that major classes of waters, such as flowing brackish waters and harsh freshwaters, could never be designated as eutrophic, even though there was, in fact, pollution by nitrates from agricultural sources, or a real risk of such pollution. According to the ECJ, this clearly would be incompatible with the Directive, which requires Member States to identify polluted waters or those which could be so affected in order to take certain measures to reduce water pollution caused or induced by nitrates from agricultural sources and to prevent further such pollution. Implicitly referring to the precautionary principle, the Court further held that understanding of the subject is still imprecise and incomplete, which would make it incompatible with the logic and objective of the Directive a priori to exclude from its scope major classes of waters. Furthermore, although Member States have been granted a wide discretion in the identification of waters referred to in Article 3(1) of the Directive, because of the assessments which they are called upon to carry out in that context,[53] it nevertheless remains the case that when they carry out that identification, they are obliged to respect the objectives of the Directive. In particular, this includes the reduction of water pollution caused by nitrates from agricultural sources. Thus, the Court ruled that the exercise of that discretion may not result in a large portion of nitrogen-bearing waters falling outside the scope of the Directive.

In *Commission* v. *Germany*,[54] the Commission contended that the German legislation implementing the action programmes for vulnerable zones was not in conformity with certain mandatory measures prescribed by Article 5(4)(a) of the Nitrates Directive. These include measures ensuring that for each farm or livestock unit, the amount of livestock manure applied to the land each year (including by the animals themselves) shall not exceed a specified amount per hectare.[55] This amount is 170 kilograms of nitrogen per hectare (kg N/ha), but Member States may allow an amount of manure containing up to 210 kg N/ha for the first four-year action programme. According to the German implementing legislation, in the application of farmyard livestock manure to the land, account could be taken of nitrogen loss resulting from inevitable losses during spreading, up to a maximum of 20 per cent of the total amount of nitrogen determined before spreading. The Commission argued that this may lead to the spreading of amounts of nitrogen greater than those allowed by the Directive and

affected are defined according to, *inter alia*, the criteria listed in Annex IA, one of which refers to eutrophication.

[53] See Case C-293/97, *The Queen* v. *Secretary of State for the Environment and Ministry of Agriculture, Fisheries and Food, ex p. H.A. Standley and Others and D.G.D. Metson and Others* (*Standley*) [1999] ECR I-2603, paras. 37 and 39.

[54] Case C-161/00, *Commission* v. *Germany* [2002] ECR I-2753.

[55] See Annex III, measures to be included in action programmes as referred to in Article 5(4)(a) of the Dir.

that, as a result, a large proportion of the amounts of nitrogen which escape into the air could eventually fall back onto the land and into watercourses. The ECJ considered that the ultimate purpose of the Directive is to reduce direct or indirect pollution of water by nitrates from agricultural sources and to prevent further such pollution in order to protect human health, living resources, and aquatic ecosystems. Accordingly, the ECJ decided that the decisive criterion for limiting pollution by nitrates from agricultural sources is the amount of nitrogen applied to the land by spreading on its surface, by injection into the land, by placing below the surface of the land, or by mixing with the surface layers of the land, and not the amount of nitrogen actually penetrating into the land. Thus, the ECJ concluded that the use of another criterion for calculating the maximum permissible amount of livestock manure to be applied was not in accordance with the Directive.

iv. Urban Waste-Water in Milan

Article 5(2) of Directive 91/271/EEC on Urban Waste-Water Treatment (Urban Waste-Water Directive)[56] requires that all urban waste-water originating from agglomerations having a population equivalent (p.e.) of more than 10,000, and which discharges into a sensitive area, is subjected to treatment more stringent than that mentioned in Article 4 of the Directive.[57] In Case C-396/00,[58] the Commission alleged infringement of the Urban Waste-Water Directive by Italy since the city of Milan (2.7 million inhabitants) had been discharging its urban waste-water without any prior treatment into a catchment area draining into areas of the delta of the Po river and the north-west coast of the Adriatic Sea. Both areas had been (partly) identified as sensitive areas by the Italian authorities. According to the Italian Government, it was not required to subject the waste in question to more stringent treatment insofar as it did not, at least not directly, discharge into an area identified as sensitive. The ECJ ruled that it is clear from Article 5(2) of the Directive that the urban waste-water of Milan, having a p.e. of more than 10,000, and being discharged into a sensitive area, had to be subjected to more stringent treatment than provided for by Article 4. In this regard, it makes no difference whether the waste-water is discharged directly or indirectly into a sensitive area, since the Directive does not make this distinction. Any other interpretation would undermine the objective of protecting the environment, under Article 1 of the Directive and Article 174(2) EC, which provides that Community environmental policy aims at a high level of protection.

[56] [1991] OJ L135/40.

[57] Art. 2 of the Urban Waste-Water Dir. defines 1 p.e. as 'the organic biodegradable load having a five-day biochemical oxygen demand (BOD5) of 60 g of oxygen per day'.

[58] Case C-396/00, *Commission* v. *Italy* [2002] ECR I-3949.

G. Horizontal Instruments

i. Environmental Impact Assessment

Directive 85/337/EEC on the Assessment of the Effects of certain Public and Private Projects on the Environment[59] was amended by Directive 97/11/EC amending Directive 85/337/EEC on the Assessment of the Effects of certain Public and Private Projects on the Environment (EIA Directive).[60] Three Member States, Luxembourg, Belgium, and France, were condemned for not having brought into force before the transposition deadline of 14 March 1999 the legislation necessary to comply with the revised EIA Directive.[61]

In a fourth case, against Spain,[62] the Commission alleged that Spanish legislation did not comply with Articles 2(1) and 4(2) in conjunction with Annex II to the 1985 EIA Directive. In particular, Spanish legislation exempted most of the projects covered by Annex II from the obligation to assess their environmental effects. According to the Spanish Government, Article 4(2) grants Member States considerable latitude to decide whether the classes of projects listed in Annex II must be made subject to an assessment. Referring to its standing case law, the ECJ made four general points on Member States' discretion under Article 4(2). First, Article 4(2) does not empower the Member States generally and definitively to exclude from the obligation of assessment one or more classes of projects mentioned in Annex II,[63] since the concept of 'classes' of projects must be understood to mean not the twelve categories in Annex II, but the subdivisions of those categories.[64] Secondly, Member States may establish criteria and/or thresholds necessary to determine which of the projects covered by Annex II are to be subject to an assessment.[65] Thirdly, when establishing those thresholds and/or criteria, Member States must take into account not only the size of projects, but also their nature and location.[66] Fourthly and finally, national provisions of a general or sectoral nature which require the assessment of the environmental impact of certain types of projects, must satisfy the requirements set out in Article 3 of the Directive, as well as the procedural rules in Articles 5 to 9 which concern, *inter alia*, public information.

[59] [1985] OJ L175/40.

[60] [1997] OJ L73/5.

[61] Case C-366/00, *Commission* v. *Luxembourg* [2002] ECRI-1749; Case C-319/01, *Commission* v. *Belgium* [2002] ECR 1-10779 Case C-348/01, *Commission* v. *France* [2002] ECR I-10249.

[62] Case C-474/99, *Commission* v. *Spain*

[63] Case C-133/96, *Commission* v. *Belgium* [1996] ECR I-2323, paras. 41–3.

[64] Case C-301/95, *Commission* v. *Germany* [1998] ECR I-6135, paras. 39–43.

[65] Case C-72/95, *Aannemersbedrijf P.K. Kraaijeveld BV and Other* v. *Gedeputeerde Staten van Zuid-Holland* (*Kraaijeveld*) [1996] ECR I-5403, paras. 49–53.

[66] Case C-392/96, *Commission* v. *Ireland* [1999] ECR I-5901, paras. 65–7.

H. Miscellaneous

i. Concordia Bus—*Greening Public Procurement?*

A particularly interesting judgment in 2002 concerns the integration of environmental protection into other EC policies as required by Article 6 EC.[67] In *Concordia Bus*,[68] the ECJ had to answer the question whether in awarding a public contract for the provision of urban bus transport services under EC public procurement rules to the most economically advantageous tender, the contracting authority may take into account environmental criteria. Article 36(1)(a) of Directive 92/50/EEC relating to the Coordination of Procedures for the Award of Public Service Contracts[69] states that the criteria on which the contracting authority may base the award of contracts may, where the award is made to the economically most advantageous tender, be various criteria relating to the contract. These include quality, technical merit, aesthetic and functional characteristics, technical assistance and after-sales service, delivery date, delivery period or period of completion, and price. Although the Directive does not refer to any criteria relating to environmental protection concerns, the Commission has argued that environmental elements can serve to identify the most economically advantageous tender, in cases where these elements imply an economic advantage for the purchasing entity, attributable to the product or service which is the object of the procurement.[70]

The ECJ held that the criteria which may be used for the award of public contracts to the economically most advantageous tender are not listed exhaustively[71] and that Article 36(1)(a) cannot be interpreted as meaning that each of the award criteria must necessarily be of a purely economic nature, since it cannot be excluded that not purely economic factors may influence the value of a tender from the point of view of the contracting authority. In addition, the ECJ referred to the purpose of coordinating at Community level the procedures for the award of public contracts being to eliminate barriers to free movement of goods and services.[72] In the light of that purpose and also of the integration principle of Article 6 EC, the ECJ concluded that Article 36(1)(a) does not exclude the possibility for the contracting authority of using criteria relating to the preserva-

67 See on the Art. 6 EC integration principle: N. Dhondt, *Integration of Environmental Protection into other EC Policies, Legal Theory and Practice* (Groningen: Europa Law Publishing, 2003); see also the chapter by Dhondt, 'Integration of Environmental Protection into the EC Energy Policy', in this volume.

68 Case C-513/99, *Concordia Bus Finland Oy Ab, formerly Stagecoach Finland Oy Ab* v. *Helsingin kaupunki and HKL-Bussiliikenne* (*Concordia Bus*) [2002] ECR I-7213.

69 [1992] OJ L209/1.

70 Commission Interpretative Communication on the Community Law Applicable to Public Procurement and the Possibilities for Integrating Environmental Considerations into Public Procurement COM(2001)274, [2001] OJ C333/13, 33.

71 See also to that effect Case C-19/00, *SIAC Construction Ltd* v. *County Council of the County of Mayo* [2001] ECR I-7725, para. 35.

72 ibid., para. 32.

tion of the environment when assessing the economically most advantageous tender. It has been argued that this judgment does not point towards an extremely strong interpretation of Article 6 EC, and that it would have been interesting to see what the ECJ would have decided if the question had been whether the authorities are *required*, where relevant, to include environmental criteria, as reward criteria.[73] Following this ruling, it is clear that the contracting authorities may take into account ecological criteria in awarding public service contracts under Directive 92/50/EEC, but Article 6 EC does not oblige them to do so.

ii. Legal Basis of CAP Regulation Promoting Environmentally Friendly Production

In a preliminary reference in Case C-336/00,[74] an Austrian court asked the ECJ to rule on the validity of Regulation (EEC) No. 2078/92 on Agricultural Production Methods Compatible with the Requirements of the Protection of the Environment and the Maintenance of the Countryside.[75] More precisely, the question was whether the Regulation was valid notwithstanding its legal basis of the former Articles 42 and 43 EC (now Articles 36 and 37 EC), rather than the former Article 130s EC (now, after amendment, Article 175 EC). The ruling provides a clear example of the application of the 'centre of gravity' theory in determining the correct legal basis for a Community measure. Referring to standing case law, the ECJ held that the choice of the legal basis for a Community measure must rest on objective factors which are amenable to judicial review, including, in particular, the aim and the content of the measure.[76] Furthermore, if examination of a Community act shows that it has a twofold purpose or twofold component and if one of these is identifiable as main or predominant, whereas the other is merely incidental, the act must be founded on a sole legal basis, that is, the one required by the main or predominant purpose or component. Exceptionally, if it is established that the act simultaneously pursues a number of objectives, indissociably linked, without one being secondary and indirect in relation to the other, such an act may be founded on the various corresponding legal bases.[77]

In casu, it was common ground that Regulation (EEC) No. 2078/92 simultaneously pursued objectives of agricultural policy and environmental protection. Furthermore, the ECJ held that the former Articles 130r and 130s EC (now, after amendment, Articles 174 and 175 EC) are intended to confer powers on the Community to undertake specific action on environmental matters, while leaving intact its powers under other provisions of the Treaty, even if the measures in

[73] Dhondt, n. 67 above, 164.

[74] Case C-336/00, *Austria* v. *Martin Huber* [2002] ECR I-7699.

[75] [1992] OJ L215/85.

[76] See Case C-300/89, *Commission* v. *Council* (*Titanium dioxide*) [1991] ECR I-2867, para. 10.

[77] See to that effect, ibid., paras. 13 and 17.

question pursue at the same time one of the objectives of environmental protection.[78] Next, the ECJ referred to the integration principle in the former Article 130r EC and the current Article 6 EC, which provides that environmental protection requirements are to be a component of the EC's other policies, so that a Community measure cannot be part of Community action on environmental matters merely because it takes account of those requirements.[79] As regards the former Article 43 EC (now Article 37 EC), the ECJ referred to its settled case law that this provision is the appropriate legal basis for any legislation concerning the production and marketing of the agricultural products listed in Annex II to the EC Treaty, which contributes to the attainment of one or more of the objectives of the common agricultural policy (CAP) set out in the former Article 39 EC (now Article 33 EC).[80]

The ECJ concluded on the basis of the Preamble and Article 1 of Regulation (EEC) No. 2078/92 that the main purpose of the Regulation's support measures was to regulate the production of agricultural products within the meaning of Annex II to the Treaty, in order to promote the transition from intensive cultivation, of better quality, with farmers being compensated for the financial consequences of this by the granting of aid. According to the ECJ, the fact that the Regulation was of a nature such as to promote more environmentally friendly forms of production—which is certainly a genuine objective, but an ancillary one, of the CAP—cannot, in itself, justify the legal basis being constituted not only by the former Articles 42 and 43 EC (now Articles 36 and 37 EC), but also by the former Article 130s EC (now Article 175 EC).

[78] Case C-405/92, *Etablissements Armand Mondiet SA* v. *Armement Islais SARL (Mondiet)*, [1993] ECR I-6133, para. 26.

[79] ibid. para. 27.

[80] Case C-180/96, *United Kingdom* v. *Commission* [1998] ECR I-2265, para. 133.

Environmental Law in the Member States

I. Austria

*Karl Weber**

A. Introduction

Not much progress was made in Austrian environmental law during 2002. As in previous survey years, European Community (EC) legislation was implemented, without requiring any fundamental legal reforms. Primarily, reforms were to be noticed at the level of the *Länder*, some of which improved their nature protection laws or reoriented their environmental organization. The judicature of the supreme courts, which is of great importance for the development of environmental law in Austria, showed a large degree of continuity, without any major developments in 2002. Although this survey year cannot be characterized as a milestone, the consolidation and careful reforms also did not cause any deterioration of Austrian environmental law. Finally, in the international cooperation realm, one major development did occur, with the coming into force of the implementing protocols of the Alpine Convention.[1]

B. Atmospheric Pollution

Since the 1988 constitutional amendment[2] legislative competence for air quality protection has been divided between *Bund* and *Länder*, pursuant to Article 10(1)(c)(12) of the *BundesVerwaltungsgesetz* (B-VG) (Austrian Federal Constitution). Provisions of the *Länder* that, following the revised allocation, were no longer within their competence, were to remain in force as part of the federal legislation. As a result, legislation in this field has become highly unsystematic, in particular relating to heating systems and incineration of industrial bio-gene material. In 2000, the federal government set out to simplify matters by replacing the scattered provisions with a uniform regime on the incineration of bio-gene material outside industrial plants. The *Bundesluftreinhaltegesetz* 2000[3] (Federal Clean Air Act) was adopted, requiring the preservation of clean air, and

* Professor of Public Law, University of Innsbruck (Austria).

[1] Discussed in sect. H.*iii.* below.

[2] BGBl 1988/685; see P. Bußjäger, 'Was bedeutet "Luftreinhaltung, unbeschadet der Zuständigkeit der Länder für Heizungsanlagen"?' (1996) 12 *Zeitschrift für Verwaltung*, 521–30.

[3] BGBl I 2002/137.

prohibiting disturbance and nuisance to third persons. Only officially permitted air pollutions and measures in connection with normal farming were exempted from this prohibition.

The *Kraftstoffverordnung* (General Order on Fuel), based on the *Kraftfahrgesetz* 1967[4] (Law on Motor Vehicles) regulates the mixture of fuel. An amendment to the *Kraftstoffverordnung*[5] implemented Commission Directive 2000/71/EC Adapting the Measuring Methods as laid down in Annexes I, II, III, and IV to Directive 98/70/EC to Technical Progress as Foreseen in Article 10 of that Directive.[6] Consequently, for several types of fuel, stricter rules will now apply for limiting values and testing procedures. An amendment was made to the *Kraftfahrgesetz*[7] to ban elements of fuel that can cause air pollution or excessive formation of greenhouse gas. It also added a prohibition on excessive noise or atmospheric pollution from motor vehicles.

Efforts are being undertaken in Austria to use natural vegetable oils, especially rape, for energy production. This was taken into account by a *Verordnung* (general order) of the *Land* Vorarlberg, which introduced emission limits for vegetable oils used in heating systems.[8]

C. Chemicals

Although several *Verordnungen* were adopted in the field of chemicals law, this only brought marginal changes to rules for packaging and labelling of hazardous substances and mixings.[9] Amendments were made to the classification of several chemicals as well as details concerning monitoring.[10]

D. Biotechnology

The *Gentechnikgesetz*[11] (law on genetic engineering) was amended,[12] to implement the revisions made by Directive 98/81/EC amending Directive 90/219/EEC on the Contained Use of Genetically Modified Micro-Organisms (Contained Use Directive).[13] The new law subjects scientific work done with genetically modified organisms (GMOs) and genetically modified micro-organisms (GMMs) to stricter security checks. The participation of the public in the hearing procedure was also improved. The rules on the deliberate release, and the putting into circulation, of GMOs remained unchanged.

E. Nature Conservation

The nature conservation laws of the Austrian *Länder* contain provisions for the protection of the landscape, of species of wild animals and plants, and their basis

[4] BGBl 1967/267 idF BGBl 2002/32. [5] BGBl II 2002/56. [6] [2000] OJ L87/46.
[7] BGBl I 2002/80. [8] LGBl 1994/92 idF LGBl 2002/9. [9] See BGBl II 2002/186.
[10] See BGBl II 2002/428. [11] BGBl 1994/510. [12] BGBl I 2002/94.
[13] [1998] OJ L330/13.

for life. Objects protected by those laws are the natural landscape as well as the cultivated land. The amendment of the Nature Conservation Law in Salzburg tightens the provisions on the weighing of the interests for permits.[14] Now public interests are given priority over other interests, albeit not always. Economic interests, which until recently had justified quite a number of intrusions upon the natural balance, were very much restrained. The amended law is obviously orientated towards Directive 92/43/EEC on the Conservation of Natural Habitats and of Wild Fauna and Flora (Habitats Directive),[15] which also provides strict criteria for the weighing of interests in cases of intrusions upon the natural balance.

The *Land* Kärnten also adopted a far-reaching amendment to its Nature Conservation law.[16] Henceforth, the extraction of stone, gravel, sand, and loam for commercial purposes is subject to permits, and intrusions upon natural or naturally conserved stretches of running water are handled more restrictively. More attention is also awarded to the protection of species and the protection of rare types of landscape.

F. Waste

Pursuant to Article 10(1)(c)(12) B-VG, the competences for waste management are divided between the *Bund* (legislation and execution of waste management concerning hazardous waste), and the *Länder* (waste management concerning non-hazardous waste). In addition, the so-called *Bedarfskompetenz* (competence in case of need) allows, in case of an 'objective necessity', the *Bund* to adopt uniform federal regulations in the field of non-hazardous waste.

One of the most controversial questions in Austrian waste law concerns the definition of 'waste'. It was repeatedly argued that the Austrian interpretation of 'waste' did not correspond with the Community definition. This criticism lost its foundation with the *Abfallwirtschaftsgesetz* 2002 (AWG)[17] (Waste Management Law). In this law account was taken of the point of view of the Commission, which in particular had criticized the fact that numerous types of waste accumulating within companies were exempted from the purview of the Waste Management Law. The Commission had also prosecuted this at the European Court of Justice (ECJ). The AWG 2002 now defines 'waste' along the general (Community) criteria of the term, and in accordance with the relevant ECJ and Austrian supreme courts' case law.

In correspondence with the EC law, the term '*Abfallbehandlung*' (treatment of waste) is introduced as the general term for all the activities concerning waste in the purview of waste management. The former complicated distinctions were replaced by a division into utilization procedure (*Verwertungsverfahren*) and disposal procedure (*Beseitigungsverfahren*), also taking into account EC law.

[14] LGBl 2002/1.
[15] [1992] OJ L206/7.
[16] LGBl 2002/12.
[17] BGBl 2002/102.

Moreover, the terms '*Abfallbesitzer*' (holder of waste) and '*Abfallerzeuger*' (producer of waste) were defined more precisely according to Community guidelines. The *Bedarfskompetenz* (competence in case of need) was also extended regarding non-hazardous waste. Henceforth also, the fundamental general provisions for non-hazardous waste shall be laid down by federal law. The *Länder* will only have competence to adopt independent regulations in the field of the collection of domestic rubbish and bulky refuse and the organization of collection systems within the local communes. Considering the very detailed EC guidelines in this field, this appears quite justified. The provisions on duties to report and record were reformed as well as the provisions on monitoring of businesses as regards matters of waste management, where special electronic data management is used. This also refers to the close-to-home systems of collection and utilization, where repeatedly deplorable state of affairs had been complained about. For the time being, the AWG 2002 concluded a discussion dating back many years about a modern waste management law that is conformable to EC law. In the years to come, the relevant *Verordnungen* for a detailed implementation of the law will have to be adapted to the new system of regulations. However, in the more immediate future, amendments to the AWG 2000 will be inevitable due to the highly dynamic nature of EC waste legislation. In Tyrol, the new definition of 'waste' of the federal AWG was implemented by the amendment to the AWG in 2002.[18] At the same time, numerous provisions were tightened, procedural improvements were introduced, and monitoring measures were regulated more precisely. At the level of the *Verordnungen* the AWG was implemented in the field of old vehicles. An *Altfahrzeuge-Verordnung*[19] (general ruling on old vehicles) laid down that vehicles should be recycled as much as possible.

G. Horizontal Instruments

i. Environmental Impact Assessment

The *Umweltverträglichkeitsprüfungsgesetz* 2000[20] (UVP-G) (law on the assessment of environmental effects), which remained unchanged in 2002, was subject to the attention of the supreme courts. The tendency of the court practice shows that the judiciary is rather restrictive in the interpretation of the UVP-G.[21] Several public-interest groups that prosecuted illegalities in various proceedings could not carry through their legal point of view.

Based on Article 3 UVP-G, a general order on strained (air) areas was adopted, implementing Directive 97/11/EC amending Directive 85/337/EEC on the Assessment of the Effects of certain Public and Private Projects on the Environment (EIA Directive).[22] Various territories of the communes in *Kärnten*

[18] LGBl 2002/3. [19] BGBl II 2002/407. [20] BGBl 1993/697 idF 2002/50.
[21] See VfGH 22 June 2002, V 53/01, and VfGH 26 June 2002, V 73/01.
[22] [1997] OJ 73/5.

(Carinthia), *Oberösterreich* (Upper Austria), *Steiermark* (Styria), *Tirol* (Tyrol), and *Wien* (Vienna) were enumerated and declared protected territories pursuant to category D of Annex 2 to the UVP-G.

ii. Access to Information

Directive 90/313/EEC on the Freedom of Access to Information on the Environment (Access to Information Directive)[23] was implemented in federal law by the *Umweltinformationsgesetz* 1993[24] (UIG) (Law on Environmental Information), and in consequence, with variable intensity, also by provisions of the *Länder*. In the past, the *Länder* often lagged behind in the implementation, leading to repeated criticism, but during this survey year many took further steps to improve this.

In 2002, the Styrian *Umweltschutzeinrichtungengesetz*[25] (Law on Environmental Institutions) was amended and extended. Applications for environmental information shall now be rewarded without any unnecessary delay, at the latest within eight weeks. Possible impediments to requested information must be appropriately communicated to the applicants. In such cases, the applicant can apply for a *Bescheid* (ruling) that has to be given by the authority. A survey amongst the official authorities of *Bund* and *Länder* showed that this right to environmental information is, in practice, only very sparsely exercised. In the first place, it is mostly the NGOs that use this right to environmental information. The limited application of the right owes much to the establishment of *Umweltanwaltschaften* (environmental advocacies) in the *Länder*, which are burdened with the legal task of informing citizens.[26] Consequently, much of the information is not passed on by the authorities themselves but rather by the *Umweltanwaltschaften*.

iii. Integrated Pollution Prevention and Control

The Austrian legislator has not yet achieved the adoption of a general and standardized law on industrial plants in order to implement Directive 96/61/EC on Integrated Pollution Prevention and Control (IPPC Directive)[27] with one single law. For the moment, three separate laws serve to implement IPPC requirements in Austria. The *Gewerbeordnung*[28] (Industrial Code), the *Abfallwirtschaftsgesetz*[29] (Waste Management Law), and the *Wasserrechtsgesetz*[30] (Water Law) implemented the provisions on industrial plants sector-specifically at the level of the *Bund*. The *Länder*, which do not play a central role, but nevertheless are not unimportant in the implementation of the IPPC Directive, also took various measures during the survey period.

[23] [1990] OJ L158/56. [24] BGBl 1993/495 idF BGBl I 2001/108.
[25] LGBl 1988/78 idF LGBl 2002/24. [26] See also sect. H.*ii*.
[27] [1996] OJ L275/26. [28] BGBl 1994/13 idF BGBl I 2003/23.
[29] BGBl I 2002/102. [30] BGBl 1959/215 idF BGBl I 2002/156.

At federal level, a *Verordnung* on the report of pollutant-emission-freight[31] was adopted. This serves the drawing up of a Community pollutant-emission register, as prescribed by the IPPC Directive. Regulated herein are the reports on emissions, control of plausibility by the competent authority, and the referrals to the *Bundesumweltamt* (Federal Environmental Authority) and to the European Commission.

At the level of the *Länder*, Kärnten adopted an IPPC law on industrial plants.[32] It applies to heating systems with a power of more than 50 megawatts for the generation of energy, for large plants for intensive livestock-keeping, and for large plants for slaughtering and disposal or utilization of animal bodies, insofar as this is not subject to the *Gewerbeordnung* (Industrial Code) or the *Abfallwirtschaftsgesetz* (Waste Management Law). The erection or substantial alteration of plants requires a permit. The amended permit procedure includes a public hearing. If a permit is granted, the authority has to work towards having the project carried out according to the latest developments in technology, and must ensure an optimal avoidance of risks to the environment.

The Environmental Protection Law[33] of Oberösterreich was also amended[34] with regard to the IPPC Directive. Here as well, compulsory permit requirements were introduced, pollutant-emission limits were tightened, the public was given a right to make statements, and the monitoring of plants was newly regulated.

H. Miscellaneous

i. Major-Accident Hazards—Seveso II

The amendment[35] to the environmental protection law of Oberösterreich also contains new provisions on the prevention of accidents with dangerous substances. These substances are exhaustively enumerated. Businesses with a large amount of such substances are subject to special measures for the prevention of accidents. Hence compulsory reports, the setting up of a security concept, a security report, and an emergency plan are required. Businesses are obliged to inform the public about dangers and the appropriate conduct in case of accidents.

ii. Environmental Advocacy

In Burgenland, the *Umweltanwalt* (environmental advocate) was fully regulated by a specific *Umweltanwaltschaftsgesetz*[36] (Law on Environmental Advocacy). Henceforth, environmental advocates shall be competent to participate in the administrative procedure, having to attend to the environmental interests. They

[31] BGBl II 2002/300. [32] LGBl 2002/52. [33] LGBl 1996/84 idF LGBl 2002/152.
[34] LBGl 2002/83. [35] LGBl 2002/83. [36] LGBl 2002/78.

also possess the right of initiative for the remedy of deplorable state of affairs, rights of information, the right to examine draft laws and general orders, the duty to report to the *Landtag* (legislative body of the land). Importantly, they must also provide professional advice and information to citizens. A constitutional provision provides the *Umweltanwaltschaft* in Oberösterreich with the quality not to be subject to directives of the *Landtag*.

A constitutional law of the *Land* Oberösterreich, the *Bürger(innen)rechtegesetz*[37] (Law on the Rights of Citizens) extends direct democracy at the level of the *Land*. In the field of environmental protection such citizens' rights are of particular importance because it is especially here that numerous public-interest groups exist, which, on the basis of this law, in the future will have an increased influence on the adoption, amendment, or abrogation of *Länder* legislation or administrative measures. If more than 3 per cent of the electorate supports a petition, this must be discussed by the competent organ. Where a petition supported by at least 8 per cent of the electorate is not pursued, a citizen referendum must be held.

iii. Convention on the Protection of the Alps

Of great (future) importance is the coming into force of the first eight implementing protocols and the Protocol on Dispute Settlement[38] to the Convention on the Protection of the Alps (Alpine Convention).[39] Austria not only ratified the Alpine Convention but also provided the protocols with direct binding nature (general transformation).[40] In Austria, the Convention constitutes a particularly important set of agreements, as the greater part of the country is situated within the Alps and is therefore to a great extent included in the protective provisions. Implementation of the Alpine Convention had not yet started in 2002, as this will require several legal adjustments by the *Bund* and *Länder*, in coming years.

[37] LGBl 2002/5.

[38] Austria ratified the implementing protocols on 10 July 2002. The protocols entered into force on 18 Dec. 2002, following ratification by the three necessary states: Liechtenstein, Austria, and Germany.

[39] Salzburg (Austria), 7 Nov. 1991 (entered into force 6 Mar. 1995).

[40] BGBl III 2002/230–238.

II. Belgium

Kurt Deketelaere and Bernard Vanheusden***

A. Atmospheric Pollution

i. Climate Change

A Flemish Decree of 22 February 2002,[1] a Walloon Decree of 21 March 2002,[2] and a federal Law of 26 September 2001,[3] confirmed the Kyoto Protocol[4] to the United Nations (UN) Framework Convention on Climate Change (UNFCCC),[5] and the Annexes A and B. The Belgian Government ratified the Kyoto Protocol on 31 May 2002. The Belgian target encompassed a reduction (by 2010) of greenhouse gases of 7.5 per cent of 1990 levels. This very ambitious target is also incorporated in the Federal Plan on Sustainable Development 2000–2004.[6]

A Royal Decree of 2 April 2003 amended the Royal Decree of 9 January 2000, which determined the general rules of the consultation of the public on the draft of the federal plan on sustainable development.[7]

A Cooperation Agreement of 14 November 2002 between the Federal State,[8] the Flemish Region,[9] the Walloon Region,[10] and the Brussels Capital Region,[11] concerning drawing up, executing, and following up the National Climate Plan (and reporting under the Kyoto Protocol), entered into force on 13 November 2003. Furthermore, in view of the Kyoto Protocol, on 2 June 2003, the Walloon Region entered into a sector agreement with Fedichem Wallonie Energie, representing the chemical sector, on the reduction of the specific emission of greenhouse gases and the improvement of energy efficiency.[12]

ii. Ambient Air Quality

The Walloon Government finally implemented Directive 96/62/EC on Ambient Air Quality Assessment and Management (Air Quality Framework Directive),[13]

* Professor of Law, University of Leuven (Belgium); Visiting Senior Fellow, Institute of Advanced Legal Studies, University of London (United Kingdom).

** Research Assistant, Limburg University Centre (Belgium).

1 *Moniteur Belge*, 23 Mar. 2002.

2 *Moniteur Belge*, 3 Apr. 2002.

3 *Moniteur Belge*, 26 Sept. 2002.

4 Kyoto (Japan), 10 Dec. 1997 (not yet in force) (1998) 37 *International Legal Materials* 1, 22.

5 New York, NY (United States), 9 May 1992 (entered into force on 21 Mar. 1994) (1992) 31 *International Legal Materials* 4, 849.

6 Published on the Internet at: http://www.icdo.fgov.be.

7 *Moniteur Belge*, 11 Apr. 2003.

8 Law of 11 Apr. 2003, *Moniteur Belge*, 15 July 2003.

9 Decree of 10 July 2003, *Moniteur Belge*, 19 Aug. 2003.

10 Decree of 13 Nov. 2003, *Moniteur Belge*, 5 Dec. 2003.

11 Ordinance of 22 May 2003, *Moniteur Belge*, 27 June 2003.

12 *Moniteur Belge*, 7 July 2003.

13 [1996] OJ L296/55.

by a Decision of 5 December 2002,[14] following a Commission Reasoned Opinion, of 8 February 2000.

A Royal Decree of 3 October 2002 replaced the Royal Decree of 7 March 2001 concerning the denomination, characteristics, and sulphur content of diesel oil for heating.[15] It transposed, well beyond the deadline of 1 July 2000, Directive 1999/32/EC on the Sulphur Content of Certain Liquid Fuels (Sulphur Directive).[16]

Two Decisions of the Flemish Government, of 18 January 2002 and 25 January 2002,[17] modified its Decision of 1 June 1995, containing general and sectoral provisions on environmental hygiene. This implemented, well beyond the deadline of 19 July 2001, Directive 1999/30/EC laying down Limit Values for Sulphur Dioxide, Nitrogen Dioxide and Oxides of Nitrogen, Particulates and Lead in the Ambient Air.[18]

A Decision of the Walloon Government of 13 November 2002,[19] and a Decision of the Brussels Capital Government of 3 June 2003 determined emission ceilings for certain atmospheric pollutants,[20] implementing Directive 2001/81/EC on National Emission Ceilings for Certain Atmospheric Pollutants (NEC Directive).[21] The Directive was to be transposed by 27 November 2002. The Walloon Government transposed Directive 2001/80/EC on the Limitation of Emissions of Certain Pollutants into the Air from Large Combustion Plants (Large Combustion Plants Directive)[22] by a Decision of 13 November 2002,[23] also before the 27 November 2002 deadline. The Directive was also transposed by the Brussels Capital Government, by Decision of 21 November 2002.[24] A Decision of the Brussels Capital Government of 18 April 2002 fixed long-term objectives, target values, and an alarm and information barrier for ozone concentrations in the air.[25]

A Royal Decree of 20 February 2003 amended the Royal Decree of 3 February 1999 on the protection of the air against the emission of gaseous and particulate pollutants from internal combustion engines to be installed in non-road mobile machinery.[26] This transposed Directive 2001/63/EC Adapting to Technical Progress Directive 97/68/EC relating to Measures against the Emission of Gaseous and Particulate Pollutants from Internal Combustion Engines to be Installed in Non-Road Mobile Machinery.[27] Transposition had been required by 30 June 2002, and Belgium received a formal notice letter of the Commission on 27 September 2002.

Two decisions of the Flemish Government of 14 March 2003 modified the Decision of the Flemish Government of 1 June 1995 containing general and

[14] *Moniteur Belge*, 10 Feb. 2003.
[15] *Moniteur Belge*, 23 Oct. 2002.
[16] [1999] OJ L121/13.
[17] *Moniteur Belge*, 14 Feb. 2002, and 19 Feb. 2002.
[18] [1999] OJ L163/41.
[19] *Moniteur Belge*, 14 Dec. 2002.
[20] *Moniteur Belge*, 19 June 2003.
[21] [2001] OJ L309/22.
[22] [2001] OJ L309/1.
[23] *Moniteur Belge*, 19 Dec. 2002.
[24] *Moniteur Belge*, 21 Dec. 2002.
[25] *Moniteur Belge*, 11 June 2002.
[26] *Moniteur Belge*, 11 Mar. 2003.
[27] [2001] OJ L227/41.

sectoral provisions on environmental hygiene.[28] The latter Decision was also amended by a Decision of the Flemish Government of 19 September 2003, which also amended the Decision of the Flemish Government of 6 February 1991 on environmental permits.[29] Together, these Decisions transposed the following directives:

— NEC Directive;[30]
— Directive 2000/69/EC relating to Limit Values for Benzene and Carbon Monoxide in Ambient Air;[31]
— Directive 2001/91/EC Adapting to Technical Progress for the Eighth Time Annex I to Directive 76/769/EEC on Restrictions on the Marketing and Use of Certain Dangerous Substances and Preparations (Hexachloroethane);[32] and
— Directive 2002/3/EC relating to Ozone in Ambient Air (Ozone Directive).[33]

The Decisions took into account Regulation (EC) No. 2037/2000 on Substances that Deplete the Ozone Layer (Ozone Regulation).[34] A Decision of the Brussels Capital Government of 20 November 2003 regarding cooling systems[35] also transposed the Ozone Regulation.

iii. Organic Solvents

Four Decisions of the Brussels Capital Government of 3 July 2003[36] limited the emissions of volatile organic compounds (VOCs) in certain activities and installations, transposing Directive 1999/13/EC on the Limitation of Emissions of Volatile Organic Compounds Due to the Use of Organic Solvents in Certain Activities and Installations (Solvent Emissions Directive),[37] well beyond the deadline of 1 April 2001. The Directive was also implemented in the Walloon Region, by Decision of 4 July 2002.[38]

B. Biotechnology

i. Biosafety

The Cartagena Protocol on Biosafety (Cartagena Biosafety Protocol)[39] to the Convention on Biological Diversity (CBD),[40] was approved, in 2002, for the

[28] *Moniteur Belge*, 14 Apr. 2003. [29] *Moniteur Belge*, 10 Oct. 2003.
[30] n. 21 above. [31] [2000] OJ L313/12. [32] [2001] OJ L286/27.
[33] [2002] OJ L67/14. [34] [2000] OJ L244/1. [35] *Moniteur Belge*, 9 Dec. 2003.
[36] *Moniteur Belge*, 6 Aug. 2003, 13 Aug. 2003, and 26 Sept. 2003.
[37] [1999] OJ L85/1. [38] *Moniteur Belge*, 21 Sept. 2002; Err., 4 Oct. 2002.
[39] Montreal (Canada), 29 Jan. 2000 (entered into force 11 Sept. 2003) (2000) 39 *International Legal Materials* 5, 1027.
[40] Rio de Janeiro (Brazil), 5 June 1992 (entered into force 29 Dec. 1993) (1992) 31 *International Legal Materials*, 818.

German-speaking Community by a Decree of 7 October 2002,[41] and for the Walloon Region by a Decree of 13 November 2002.[42] The Protocol was approved by the Brussels Capital Region by an Ordinance of 3 April 2003.[43]

ii. Contained Use

A Decision of the Walloon Government of 18 April 2002 amended the General Regulation on Protection at Work with regard to the contained use of genetically modified and/or pathogenic organisms.[44] This Decision implements, almost eleven years beyond the expiry of the deadline, Directive 90/219/EEC on the Contained Use of Genetically Modified Micro-Organisms (Contained Use Directive).[45] A Decision of the Walloon Government of 4 July 2002 laid down the sectoral conditions regarding the contained use of genetically modified or pathogen organisms, and further implemented the Contained Use Directive.[46]

C. Chemicals

i. Pesticides and Biocides

A Decree of 21 December 2001 regarded a decrease of the use of pesticides, herbicides, and fungicides by the public services in the Flemish Region.[47] A Ministerial Decision of 18 February 2002 amended the Royal Decree of 28 February 1994 on the keeping, placing on the market, and the use of pesticides and herbicides for agricultural use.[48] This implemented Directive 2001/36/EC amending Directive 91/414/EEC concerning the Placing of Plant Protection Products on the Market (Pesticides Directive).[49] A Ministerial Decision of 26 February 2002 executed Article 59(1), (1)(b), and (2)(1)(b) of the Royal Decree of 5 September 2001 regarding the placing on the market and the use of biocides.[50] These provisions stipulate the know-how requirements for 'registered salesmen' of Class A biocides, or 'recognized users' of biocides. A Ministerial Decision of 6 March 2002 determined the list of companies, as foreseen in Article 56(2) of the Decree.[51] A Royal Decree of 22 May 2003 concerned the placing on the market and the use of biocides.[52] It incorporates provisions of three directives: Directive 67/548/EEC on the Classification, Packaging and Labelling of Dangerous Substances (Dangerous Substances Packaging Directive);[53] Directive 1999/45/EC on the Classification, Packaging, and Labelling of Dangerous Preparations;[54] and Directive 98/8/EC concerning the Placing of Biocidal Products on the Market (Biocides Directive).[55]

[41] *Moniteur Belge*, 15 Nov. 2002. [42] *Moniteur Belge*, 4 Dec. 2002.
[43] *Moniteur Belge*, 28 Apr. 2003. [44] *Moniteur Belge*, 24 Apr. 2002.
[45] [1990] OJ L117/1, last amended by Dir. 98/81/EC, [1998] OJ L330/13.
[46] *Moniteur Belge*, 21 Sept. 2002. [47] *Moniteur Belge*, 31 Jan. 2002.
[48] *Moniteur Belge*, 13 Mar. 2002. [49] [2001] OJ L164/1.
[50] *Moniteur Belge*, 9 Mar. 2002. [51] ibid. [52] *Moniteur Belge*, 11 July 2003.
[53] [1967] OJ L196/1, as amended. [54] [1999] OJ L200/1, as amended.
[55] [1998] OJ L123/1.

ii. Marketing, Use, Packaging, and Labelling of Dangerous Substances and Preparations

Several measures were taken to transpose Community legislation concerning marketing and use, packaging, and labelling of dangerous substances and preparations. Two Royal Decrees of 9 January 2000[56] and 18 July 2002[57] modified the Royal Decree of 5 October 1998, restricting marketing and use. A Royal Decree of 17 July 2002 modified the Royal Decree of 24 May 1982,[58] transposing Directive 2001/59/EC Adapting to Technical Progress for the Twenty-Eighth Time Directive 67/548/EEC on Classification, Packaging and Labelling of Dangerous Substances,[59] which was due by 30 July 2002. A Royal Decree of 17 July 2002 modified the Royal Decree of 11 January 1993,[60] transposing Directive 1999/45/EC on the Classification, Packaging, and Labelling of Dangerous Preparations,[61] Directive 2001/58/EC Amending for the Second Time Directive 91/155/EEC Defining and Laying Down the Detailed Arrangements for the System of Specific Information Relating to Dangerous Preparations in Implementation of Article 14 of Directive 1999/45/EC and relating to Dangerous Substances in Implementation of Article 27 of Directive 67/548/EEC,[62] and Directive 2001/59/EC.[63] A Royal Decree of 25 October 2002 modified the Royal Decree of 25 February 1996,[64] transposing (in time) Directive 2002/62/EC Adapting to Technical Progress for the Ninth Time Annex I to Directive 76/769/EEC on Restrictions on the Marketing and Use of Certain Dangerous Substances and Preparations (Organostannic Compounds).[65]

A Royal Decree of 13 February 2003[66] forbade the bringing on the market of textile detergents containing phosphate and intended for domestic use, transposing Directive 98/34/EC laying down a Procedure for the Provision of Information in the Field of Technical Standards and Regulations.[67] A Royal Decree of 26 April 2003[68] transposed Directive 2003/2/EC of 6 January 2003 relating to Restrictions on the Marketing and Use of Arsenic (Tenth Adaptation to Technical Progress to Directive 76/769/EEC).[69] A Royal Decree of 18 June 2003[70] transposed into Belgian law Directive 2002/45/EC amending for the Twentieth Time Directive 76/769/EEC relating to Restrictions on the Marketing and Use of Certain Dangerous Substances and Preparations (Short-Chain Chlorinated Paraffins).[71] A Royal Decree of 30 October 2003[72] transposed Directive 2002/61/EC amending for the Nineteenth Time Directive 76/769/EEC relating to

[56] *Moniteur Belge*, Err., 31 Aug. 2002.
[57] *Moniteur Belge*, 9 Aug. 2002.
[58] *Moniteur Belge*, 29 Aug. 2002.
[59] [2001] OJ L225/1.
[60] *Moniteur Belge*, 29 Aug. 2002; Err., 19 Dec. 2002.
[61] [1999] OJ L200/1.
[62] [2001] OJ L212/24.
[63] n. 59 above.
[64] *Moniteur Belge*, 1 Nov. 2002.
[65] [2002] OJ L183/58.
[66] *Moniteur Belge*, 25 Feb. 2003.
[67] [1998] OJ L204/37.
[68] *Moniteur Belge*, 6 May 2003.
[69] [2003] OJ L4/9.
[70] *Moniteur Belge*, 8 July 2003.
[71] [2002] OJ L177/21.
[72] *Moniteur Belge*, 24 Dec. 2003.

Restrictions on the Marketing and Use of Certain Dangerous Substances and Preparations (Azocolourants).[73]

iii. PCBs and PCTs

With a Decision of 13 December 2001, the Walloon Government modified its Decision of 25 March 1999 on the disposal of polychlorinated biphenyls (PCBs) and polychlorinated terphenyls (PCTs),[74] thereby transposing Directive 96/59/EC on the Disposal of Polychlorinated Byphenyls and Polychlorinated Terphenyls (PCB/PCT Directive).[75]

iv. Prior Informed Consent

A Federal Law of 7 October 2002[76] approved the Convention on the Prior Informed Consent Procedure for Certain Hazardous Chemicals and Pesticides in International Trade (Rotterdam PIC Convention),[77] including its Annexes I to V.

v. Road Transport of Dangerous Goods

A Royal Decree of 6 February 2003 concerned training certificates for drivers of vehicles that transport radioactive substances by road,[78] implementing Directive 94/55/EC on Transport of Dangerous Goods by Road.[79] The Decree also took into account the United Nations Economic Commission for Europe (UN/ECE) European Agreement concerning the International Carriage of Dangerous Goods by Road (ADR).[80]

vi. Persistent Organic Pollutants

The United Nations Environment Programme (UNEP) Stockholm Convention on Persistent Organic Pollutants (Stockholm POPs Convention)[81] and its Annexes was approved in the Walloon Region by a Decree of 27 November 2003.[82]

[73] [2002] OJ L243/15.

[74] *Moniteur Belge*, 25 Jan. 2002.

[75] [1996] OJ L243/31.

[76] *Moniteur Belge*, 13 Jan. 2003.

[77] Rotterdam (the Netherlands), 11 Sept. 1998 (not yet in force) (1999) 38 *International Legal Materials* 1, 1.

[78] *Moniteur Belge*, 28 Feb. 2003.

[79] [1994] OJ L319/7.

[80] Geneva (Switzerland), 30 Sept. 1957 (entered into force on 29 Jan. 1968), published on the Internet at: http://www.unece.org/trans/danger/publi/adr/adr_e.html.

[81] Stockholm (Sweden), 22 May 2001 (not yet in force) (2001) 40 *International Legal Materials* 3, 531.

[82] *Moniteur Belge*, 8 Dec. 2003.

D. Nature Conservation

i. Habitats and Fauna and Flora

A Royal Decree of 21 December 2001[83] finally implemented Directive 92/43/EEC on the Conservation of Natural Habitats and of Wild Fauna and Flora (Habitats Directive).[84] The Commission had declared Belgium in default, several times, lastly on 23 July 1999. The Royal Decree regulates the protection of species in sea areas under Belgian jurisdiction. A Ministerial Decision of 9 April 2002 amended several Annexes to the Royal Decree of 3 May 1994 on the combating of organisms that are harmful to plants and plant products,[85] in order to fulfil the obligations under Directive 2002/28/EC of 19 March 2002 amending Certain Annexes to Council Directive 2000/29/EC on Protective Measures against the Introduction into the Community of Organisms Harmful to Plants or Plant Products and against their Spread within the Community.[86] The Directive should have been implemented by 31 March 2002. A Ministerial Decision of 11 April 2002 amended the Ministerial Decision of 30 May 2001 on the recognition of protected zones exposed to particular plant health risks in the Community,[87] transposing (within the deadline) Directive 2002/29/EC amending Directive 2001/32/EC as regards Certain Protected Zones Exposed to Particular Plant Health Risks in the Community.[88]

In the light of a comprehensive adaptation of the Flemish legislation with regard to nature conservation, a Decree of 19 July 2002[89] amended the following legal texts: (i) Decree of 21 October 1997 on nature conservation and natural environment; (ii) Decree of 13 June 1990 on woods; (iii) Decree of 16 April 1996 on landscape care; (iv) Decree of 21 December 1988 on the establishment of the Flemish Land Agency; (v) Law of 22 July 1970 on land consolidation; (vi) Decree of 23 January 1991 concerning protection of the environment against pollution by fertilizers; and (vii) Law on the control on road traffic, coordinated by Royal Decree of 16 March 1968.

A Decision of the Flemish Government of 24 May 2002 implemented Article 4(1) of the Habitats Directive, by determining the areas proposed to the Commission as special areas of conservation (SACs).[90] A Decision of the Brussels Capital Government of 28 November 2002 amended the Decision of the Brussels Capital Government of 26 October 2000 on the conservation of natural habitats and of wild fauna and flora.[91] This was necessary fully to transpose the Habitats Directive. The Commission had submitted, on 28 August 2001, a demand for a determination of a proof of default. The Advocate

[83] *Moniteur Belge*, 14 Feb. 2002.
[84] [1992] OJ L206/7.
[85] *Moniteur Belge*, 12 Apr. 2002.
[86] [2002] OJ L77/23.
[87] *Moniteur Belge*, 12 Apr. 2002.
[88] [2002] OJ L77/26.
[89] *Moniteur Belge*, 31 Aug. 2002.
[90] *Moniteur Belge*, 17 Aug. 2002.
[91] *Moniteur Belge*, 20 Dec. 2002.

General followed the Commission's motivations in his Opinion of 12 September 2002.

A Decision of the Flemish Government of 28 February 2003 concerned nature guiding plans.[92] A Decision of the Flemish Government of 27 June 2003 established conditions for the recognition of nature reserves and of environmental associations managing a terrain, and on the granting of subsidies.[93]

A decision of the Walloon Government of 23 January 2003[94] indicated the wetlands of international importance, according to the Convention on Wetlands of International Importance especially as Waterfowl Habitat (Ramsar Convention).[95]

ii. Birds

A Decree of 18 January 2002 modified the Federal Law of 12 July 1973 on nature conservation.[96] A Royal Decree of 9 September 1981 regarding the protection of birds in the Flemish Region was amended by two Decisions of the Flemish Government of 8 March 2002[97] and 7 June 2002,[98] taking into account Directive 79/409/EEC on the Conservation of Wild Birds (Birds Directive).[99]

iii. Fish

The Walloon Government, in a Decision of 28 February 2002, restricted the catching, keeping, and transporting of fish species caught in waterways and canals in the Walloon Region.[100] A Decision of the Walloon Government of 7 March 2002 amended the Decision of the Walloon Regional Executive of 11 March 1993 that executed the Federal Law of 1 July 1954 on river fishing.[101]

Annex V and Appendix 3 to the Convention for the Protection of the Marine Environment of the North-East Atlantic (OSPAR Convention)[102] was approved by a Walloon Decree of 16 October 2003.[103] The Annex concerned the protection and conservation of ecosystems and biological diversity of the maritime area.

iv. Wood and Forests

Three Decisions of the Flemish Government of 7 June 2002 concerned, first, the sale of wood and other products coming from public woods; secondly, the procedure and the conditions concerning the public sales of these products;

[92] *Moniteur Belge*, 27 Mar. 2003.
[93] *Moniteur Belge*, 12 Sept. 2003.
[94] *Moniteur Belge*, 31 Oct. 2003.
[95] Ramsar (Iran), 2 Feb. 1971 (entered into force 21 Dec. 1975) (1972) 11 *International Legal Materials* 5, 963.
[96] *Moniteur Belge*, 13 Feb. 2002.
[97] *Moniteur Belge*, 4 Apr. 2002.
[98] *Moniteur Belge*, 18 July 2002.
[99] [1979] OJ L103/1.
[100] *Moniteur Belge*, 8 Mar. 2002.
[101] *Moniteur Belge*, 16 Mar. 2002.
[102] Paris (France), 22 Sept. 1999 (entered into force on 25 Mar. 1998) (1993) 32 *International Legal Materials* 3, 759–804.
[103] *Moniteur Belge*, 24 Oct. 2003.

and thirdly, the determination of the form of the licence to cut down trees in public woods and the procedure of delivery.[104] A Decision of the Walloon Government of 5 September 2002 granted subsidies concerning woods policy to public persons,[105] executing Regulation (EC) No. 1257/1999 on Support for Rural Development from the European Agricultural Guidance and Guarantee Fund (EAGGF).[106]

The Flemish Government was very active, during 2003, with regard to woods and forests policy. A Flemish Decree of 9 May 2003 introduced an exemption from death duty for woods and an exemption from death duty and property tax for grounds situated in the Flemish Ecological Network.[107] On 27 June 2003, the Flemish Government issued four Decisions concerning forest conservation,[108] concerning: (i) determination of criteria for sustainable forest conservation in the Flemish Region; (ii) conservation plans for forests; (iii) subsidies for conservationists of public and private forests; and (iv) the recognition and the subsidizing of forest groups and the way members of the forest conservation can cooperate in recognized groups.

A Decision of the Flemish Government of 3 October 2003[109] implemented Directive 1999/105/EC on the Marketing of Forest Reproductive Material,[110] missing the deadline of 1 January 2003. An Ordinance of 27 November 2003 modified the Law of 19 December 1854 containing the Wood Code and regulating the transfer of public woods and forests.[111]

v. Conservation of Bats

The Agreement on the Conservation of Bats in Europe (EUROBATS),[112] approved by Decree of 23 March 2001, has been ratified by a Decision of the Flemish Government of 3 May 2002.[113] A representative of the Flemish Government deposited, on 14 May 2003, for the Flemish Government, the Walloon Government, and the Brussels Capital Government, the ratification instruments for EUROBATS.[114] It entered into force in Belgium, according to Article XII, on 13 June 2003.

vi. Soil and Landscapes

Two Decisions of the Flemish Government of 12 October 2001[115] and 14 June 2002[116] almost completely modified the Decision of the Flemish Government of 5 March 1996 establishing the Flemish regulation on soil decontamination,

[104] *Moniteur Belge*, 20 July 2002 and 30 July 2002. [105] *Moniteur Belge*, 22 Oct. 2002.
[106] [1999] OJ L160/80. [107] *Moniteur Belge*, 2 June 2003.
[108] *Moniteur Belge*, 10 Sept. 2003. [109] *Moniteur Belge*, 13 Nov. 2003.
[110] [2000] OJ L11/17. [111] *Moniteur Belge*, 11 Dec. 2003.
[112] London (UK), 4 Dec. 1991 (entered into force on 16 Jan. 1994), published on the Internet at: http://www.eurobats.org.
[113] *Moniteur Belge*, 24 July 2002. [114] *Moniteur Belge*, 2 June 2003.
[115] *Moniteur Belge*, 2 Feb. 2002; Err., 1 Mar. 2002.
[116] *Moniteur Belge*, 7 Aug. 2002.

executing the Flemish Decree of 22 February 1995 on soil decontamination. Two Decisions of the Flemish Government, of 22 February 2002[117] and of 13 December 2002,[118] listed the clean-up actions that the Flemish Waste Company *ex officio* will start and will continue in 2002 and 2003, respectively, for the Flemish Region, while a Decision of 24 October 2003 lists the clean-up actions foreseen for 2004.[119] The Cooperation agreement of 13 December 2002 on the execution and financing of the soil decontamination of filling stations was approved by an Ordinance of 20 December 2002,[120] by a Walloon Decree of 15 May 2003,[121] by a Flemish Decree of 18 July 2003,[122] and by a Federal Law of 26 August 2003.[123]

A decision of the Flemish Government of 17 January 2003 modified the decisions of the Flemish Government of 12 October 2001 and 14 June 2002,[124] amending the Decision of the Flemish Government of 5 March 1996 establishing the Flemish regulation on soil decontamination. Two Flemish Decrees, of 27 June 2003[125] and of 19 December 2003,[126] amended the soil decontamination Decree of 22 February 1995 and created a Soil Protection Fund.

Three decisions of the Flemish Government of 4 April 2003 concerned protected landscapes. They established, *inter alia*, a bounty system for protected landscapes and several supervisory committees.[127] The European Landscape Convention[128] was approved by a Flemish Decree of 18 July 2003,[129] and for the Brussels Capital Region by an Ordinance of 13 February 2003.[130]

vii. International Trade in Endangered Species—CITES

A Programme Law of 24 December 2002[131] amended the Federal Law of 28 July 1981 containing the approval of the Convention on International Trade in Endangered Species of Wild Fauna and Flora (CITES).[132]

E. Waste

i. Waste Management

The Walloon Region Decree of 27 June 1996 concerning waste by introducing a take back duty for certain goods or waste was modified by a Decree of 20

[117] *Moniteur Belge*, 27 Apr. 2002.
[118] *Moniteur Belge*, 24 Jan. 2003.
[119] *Moniteur Belge*, 3 Dec. 2003.
[120] *Moniteur Belge*, 26 Feb. 2003.
[121] *Moniteur Belge*, 10 July 2003.
[122] *Moniteur Belge*, 19 Aug. 2003.
[123] *Moniteur Belge*, 29 Sept. 2003.
[124] *Moniteur Belge*, 31 Jan. 2003.
[125] *Moniteur Belge*, 12 Sept. 2003.
[126] *Moniteur Belge*, 31 Dec. 2003.
[127] *Moniteur Belge*, 20 June 2003.
[128] Florence (Italy), 20 Oct. 2000 (not yet in force), published on the Internet at http://www.coe.int.
[129] *Moniteur Belge*, 5 Sept. 2003.
[130] *Moniteur Belge*, 5 May 2003.
[131] *Moniteur Belge*, 31 Dec. 2002.
[132] Washington, DC (United States), 3 Mar. 1973; (1973) 12 *International Legal Materials* 5, 1085.

December 2001.[133] A take back duty was introduced for certain wastes with a view to the valorization or the management of these wastes, by a Decision of 25 April 2002.[134] The Brussels Capital Government also introduced such a take back duty, by a Decision of 18 July 2002.[135]

A Walloon Decree of 19 September 2002 amended the Decree of 27 June 1996 on waste.[136] A Brussels Capital Region Ordinance of 21 March 2002 amended the Ordinance of 19 July 1990 that established the Regional Agency for Tidiness.[137] A Decision of the Brussels Capital Government of 28 February 2002 regarded the administrative fines concerning the levy on the drainage of waste-water.[138] The Brussels Capital Government determined with a Decision of 25 April 2002 the list of waste and dangerous waste.[139] A Regulation of 18 July 2002 amended the Regulation of 15 July 1993 on the disposal of waste by means of collections within the Brussels Capital Region.[140] A Decision of the Flemish Government of 22 February 2002 modified the Decision of the Flemish Government of 17 December 1997 on the establishment of the Flemish Regulation on Waste Prevention and Control.[141]

Five decisions of the Walloon Government of 27 February 2003[142] implemented Directive 2000/53/EC on End-of-Life Vehicles (ELV Directive),[143] Directive 2000/59/EC on Port Reception Facilities for Ship-Generated Waste and Cargo Residues (Port Waste Facilities Directive),[144] and Directive 2000/76/EC on the Incineration of Waste (Waste Incineration Directive).[145] The latter Directive was also implemented in the Brussels Capital Region, by a Decision of 21 November 2002.[146]

ii. Landfill of Waste

A Decision of the Brussels Capital Government of 18 April 2002 regarded the dumping of waste.[147] Annex II to this Decision was subsequently modified by a Decision of 13 November 2003 modified,[148] in order to implement Directive 1999/31/EC on Landfill of Waste (Waste Landfill Directive),[149] as well as Decision 2003/33/EC of 19 December 2002 establishing Criteria and Procedures for the Acceptance of Waste at Landfills Pursuant to Article 16 of and Annex II to Directive 1999/31/EC.[150]

133 *Moniteur Belge*, 6 Feb. 2002.
134 *Moniteur Belge*, 18 June 2002.
135 *Moniteur Belge*, 27 Sept. 2002.
136 *Moniteur Belge*, 27 Sept. 2002.
137 *Moniteur Belge*, 5 Apr. 2002.
138 *Moniteur Belge*, 18 Apr. 2002.
139 *Moniteur Belge*, 12 June 2002.
140 *Moniteur Belge*, 7 Aug. 2002.
141 *Moniteur Belge*, 26 Apr. 2002.
142 *Moniteur Belge*, 10 Mar. 2003, 13 Mar. 2003, 14 Mar. 2003,
143 [2000] OJ L269/34.
144 [2000] OJ L332/81.
145 [2000] OJ L332/91.
146 *Moniteur Belge*, 20 Feb. 2003.
147 *Moniteur Belge*, 17 May 2002.
148 *Moniteur Belge*, 18 Dec. 2003.
149 [1999] OJ L182/1.
150 [2003] OJ L11/27.

iii. Animal Waste

A Decision of the Flemish Government modified the Decision of the Flemish Government of 24 May 1995 on the collection and the processing of animal waste,[151] in order to comply with Decision 2001/25/EC Prohibiting the Use of Certain Animal By-Products in Animal Feed.[152] Two Decisions of the Flemish Government of 13 July 2001,[153] and a Decision of the Flemish Government of 19 July 2002,[154] amended the Decision of the Flemish Government of 24 May 1995 on the collection and the processing of animal waste. A Decision of the Brussels Capital Government of 28 November 2002 concerned the disposal of animal waste and the installations for the processing of animal waste.[155]

iv. Shipments of Waste

A Decision of the Walloon Government of 13 November 2002 modified the Decision of the Walloon Government of 9 June 1994 on the application of Regulation (EEC) No. 259/93 on the Supervision and Control of Shipments of Waste within, into and out of the European Community (Waste Shipment Regulation).[156]

The Amendment to the Convention on the Control of Transboundary Movements of Hazardous Wastes and their Disposal (Basel Convention)[157] were approved by a Flemish Government Decree of 6 December 2002,[158] a Walloon Decree of 10 April 2003,[159] and a Federal Law of 6 March 2003.[160]

v. Port Waste Reception Facilities

Finally, the Flemish Government implemented the Port Waste Facilities Directive,[161] by a Decision of 14 March 2003. The Directive had to be implemented before 28 December 2002, and the Commission had already sent a proof of default on 22 January 2003. The Decision amends the Decision of the Flemish Government of 17 December 1997 on the establishment of the Flemish Regulation on Waste Prevention and Control.[162]

vi. Packaging Waste—Product Norms

A Law of 28 March 2003 amended the Law of 21 December 1998 regarding product norms for the promotion of sustainable production and consumption patterns and for the protection of the environment and public health.[163] A Royal

[151] *Moniteur Belge*, 16 Jan. 2002. [152] [2001] OJ L6/16.
[153] *Moniteur Belge*, 14 Mar. 2002 and 9 Apr. 2002. [154] *Moniteur Belge*, 13 Aug. 2002.
[155] *Moniteur Belge*, 19 Dec. 2002. [156] [1993] OJ L30/1.
[157] Basel (Switzerland), 22 Mar 1989, Basel (entered into force 5 May 1992) (1989) 28 *International Legal Materials* 3, 857.
[158] *Moniteur Belge*, 24 and 31 Dec. 2002. [159] *Moniteur Belge*, 18 Apr. 2003.
[160] *Moniteur Belge*, 28 Oct. 2003. [161] n. 144 above.
[162] *Moniteur Belge*, 14 Apr. 2003. [163] *Moniteur Belge*, 29 Apr. 2003.

Decree of 15 May 2003 amended the Royal Decree of 25 March 1999 on the determination of product norms for packaging,[164] transposing Decision 1999/177/EC establishing the Conditions for a Derogation for Plastic Crates and Plastic Pallets in Relation to the Heavy Metal Concentration Levels established in Directive 94/62/EC on Packaging and Packaging Waste,[165] and Decision 2001/171/EC establishing the Conditions for a Derogation for Glass Packaging in Relation to the Heavy Metal Concentration Levels established in Directive 94/62/EC on Packaging and Packaging Waste.[166]

vii. Radioactive Waste

A Royal Decree of 18 November 2002 regulated the recognition of equipment for the storage, processing, and conditioning of radioactive waste.[167] A Federal Law of 2 August 2002[168] confirmed the Joint Convention on the Safety of Spent Fuel Management and on the Safety of Radioactive Waste Management.[169]

F. Water

i. Water Management and Water Framework Directive

A very important Flemish Decree of 18 July 2003 concerned the integrated water policy,[170] implementing Directive 2000/60/EC establishing a Framework for Community Action in the Field of Water Policy (Water Framework Directive),[171] prior to the deadline of 22 December 2003.

A Walloon Decree of 22 October 2003 amended the Decree of 15 April 1999 on the circulation of water and the establishment of a Public Agency for Water Management.[172] A Walloon Decree of 22 October 2003 amended the Decree of 7 March 2001 on the reform of the Walloon Agency for Water Distribution.[173]

ii. Nitrates

With regard to the Decree of 23 January 1991 concerning the protection of the environment against the pollution by fertilizers, a Decision of the Flemish Government of 5 October 2001 executed Article 33ter,[174] a Decision of the Flemish Government of 15 March 2002 executed Articles 14(6), and 17(8),[175] and a Decision of the Flemish Government of 14 June 2002 revised and

[164] *Moniteur Belge*, 18 June 2003.
[165] [1999] OJ L56/47.
[166] [2001] OJ L62/20.
[167] *Moniteur Belge*, 3 Dec. 2002.
[168] *Moniteur Belge*, 25 Dec. 2002.
[169] Vienna (Austria), 5 Sept. 1997 (entered into force 18 June 2001), published on the Internet at: http://www.iaea.or.at/worldatom/Documents/Legal/jointconv.shtml.
[170] *Moniteur Belge*, 14 Nov. 2003; Err., 5 Dec. 2003.
[171] [2000] OJ L327/1.
[172] *Moniteur Belge*, 27 Nov. 2003.
[173] *Moniteur Belge*, 27 Nov. 2003.
[174] *Moniteur Belge*, 9 Jan. 2002.
[175] *Moniteur Belge*, 26 Apr. 2002.

amended the vulnerable water zones as mentioned in Article 15(3), (4), and (5).[176] By this last amendment, the Flemish Government complied with Directive 91/676/EEC on the Protection of Waters against Pollution Caused by Nitrates from Agricultural Sources (Nitrates Directive).[177] A Decision of the Flemish Government of 24 May 2002 altered the Decision of the Flemish Government of 20 April 2001 regulating the voluntary, complete, and definitive closing-down of the production of all animal manure, coming from pigs.[178] A Decision of the Walloon Government of 10 October 2002 concerned the sustainable management of nitrogen in agriculture,[179] further transposing the Nitrates Directive. By a Decree of 7 February 2003,[180] and of 28 March 2003,[181] the Flemish Government twice amended the Decree of 23 January 1991 concerning the protection of the environment against pollution by fertilizers. The Walloon Government decided on 18 September 2003 to modify its Decision of 10 October 2002 regarding the sustainable management of nitrogen in agriculture.[182]

iii. Surface Waters

A Flemish Government Decree of 21 December 2001 modified the Federal Law of 26 March 1971 on the protection of surface waters against pollution.[183] The Flemish Government granted, with a Decision of 18 January 2002, a regional contribution to public authorities taking care of polders or of water maintenance outside the polders for the execution of certain water works.[184] It also established the procedure for subsidizing these works. A Flemish Government Decision of 28 June 2002 executed Chapter IIIbis of the Law of 26 March 1971 on the protection of surface waters against pollution.[185] Chapter IIIbis had already been executed by a Decision of the Flemish Government of 16 February 1993, which was amended by two Decisions of the Flemish Government of 1 February 2002[186] and 22 March 2002.[187]

Two Flemish Decrees, of 27 June 2003[188] and 19 December 2003,[189] amended the Law of 26 March 1971 on the protection of surface waters against pollution. A Walloon Decree of 22 October 2003 amended the Decree of 7 October 1985 on the protection of surface waters against pollution.[190]

iv. Groundwater and Drinking Water

A Flemish Government Decision of 28 June 2002 executed Chapter IVbis of the Decree of 24 January 1984 on measures with regard to the management of

[176] *Moniteur Belge*, 17 July 2002.
[177] [1991] OJ L375/1.
[178] *Moniteur Belge*, 31 May 2002.
[179] *Moniteur Belge*, 29 Nov. 2002.
[180] *Moniteur Belge*, 24 Feb. 2003.
[181] *Moniteur Belge*, 8 May 2003.
[182] *Moniteur Belge*, 29 Oct. 2003.
[183] *Moniteur Belge*, 29 Jan. 2002.
[184] *Moniteur Belge*, 25 Apr. 2002.
[185] *Moniteur Belge*, 1 Aug. 2002.
[186] *Moniteur Belge*, 19 Apr. 2002.
[187] *Moniteur Belge*, 17 May 2002.
[188] *Moniteur Belge*, 12 Sept. 2003.
[189] *Moniteur Belge*, 31 Dec. 2003.
[190] *Moniteur Belge*, 27 Nov. 2003.

groundwater.[191] A Walloon Region Decree of 12 December 2002 modified the Decree of 30 April 1990 on the protection and the exploitation of groundwater and of water that can be processed to drinking water.[192] A Flemish Government Decree of 24 May 2003 concerned drinking water.[193] A Decision of the Brussels Capital Government of 24 January 2002 regulated the quality of tap water in the Brussels Capital Region.[194] This measure was necessary to implement Directive 98/83/EC on the Quality of Water Intended for Human Consumption (Drinking Water Directive),[195] which had to be implemented by 23 November 2000. The Directive was also implemented in the Flemish Region, by a Decision of 13 December 2002,[196] and in the Walloon Region by a Decree of 12 December 2002.[197] Furthermore, the Walloon Government issued a Decision of 2 October 2003 regarding the procedure to be followed in the event of harm being done to drinking water.[198]

v. Urban Waste-Water

Two Walloon Decrees, of 12 December 2002[199] and of 22 October 2003,[200] modified the Decree of 30 April 1990 on the introduction of a tax on the drainage of industrial and household waste-water and amended the Decree of 30 April 1990 on the introduction of a tax on the drainage of industrial and household waste-water. A Decision of the Walloon Government of 22 May 2003 regarded the general regulation for the decontamination of urban waste-water,[201] implementing Directive 91/271/EEC on Urban Waste-Water Treatment (Urban Waste-Water Directive).[202]

vi. Dangerous Substances

A Walloon Ministerial Decision of 12 July 2002 established a programme for the reduction of water pollution caused by the dangerous substance polycyclic aromatic hydrocarbon.[203] The Walloon Government established by a Decision of 13 June 2002 the investment programme 2000–4 for the decontamination and the protection of water extractions.[204] A Decision of the Walloon Government of 12 September 2002 amended the list of relevant substances meant in the Decision of the Walloon Government of 29 June 2000 on the protection of surface water against pollution caused by certain dangerous substances.[205] A Brussels Capital Ministerial Decision of 11 April 2003 determined a programme to reduce the water pollution caused by certain dangerous substances,[206]

[191] *Moniteur Belge*, 1 Aug. 2002.
[192] *Moniteur Belge*, 14 Dec. 2002.
[193] *Moniteur Belge*, 23 July 2003.
[194] *Moniteur Belge*, 21 Feb. 2002.
[195] [1998] OJ L330/32.
[196] *Moniteur Belge*, 28 Jan. 2003.
[197] *Moniteur Belge*, 14 Jan. 2003; Err., 20 May 2003.
[198] *Moniteur Belge*, 27 Oct. 2003.
[199] *Moniteur Belge*, 14 Dec. 2002.
[200] *Moniteur Belge*, 27 Nov. 2003.
[201] *Moniteur Belge*, 10 July 2003.
[202] [1991] OJ L135/40.
[203] *Moniteur Belge*, 31 Aug. 2002.
[204] *Moniteur Belge*, 31 Aug. 2002.
[205] *Moniteur Belge*, 17 Oct. 2002.
[206] *Moniteur Belge*, 23 May 2003.

transposing Directive 76/464/EEC on Pollution Caused by certain Dangerous Substances Discharged into the Aquatic Environment of the Community (Dangerous Substances Discharge Directive).[207]

vii. Agreement between Belgium/Netherlands on the Maas

A Walloon Region Decree of 13 November 2002[208] approved the Agreement between the Kingdom of Belgium and the Kingdom of the Netherlands that regulates the shipping and the recreation on the Common Maas.[209] The Agreement was also approved by a Federal Law of 15 March 2002.[210]

The Walloon Region also approved by a Decree of 27 November 2003[211] the International Conventions on the Protection of the Schelde and the Maas, and their Annexes.[212]

G. Horizontal Instruments

i. Environmental Impact Assessment

Environmental impact assessment (EIA) in the Walloon Region was organized by a Decree of 4 July 2002.[213] A Decision of the same date listed the projects that were subjected to EIA and the classified installations and activities,[214] implementing Directive 97/11/EC amending Directive 85/337/EEC on the Assessment of the Effects of certain Public and Private Projects on the Environment (EIA Directive).[215] A Royal Decree of 7 September 2003 determined the procedure for permitting and authorization of certain activities in the sea areas under the competence of Belgium,[216] implementing into Belgian law Directive 85/337/EEC on the Assessment of the Effects of certain Public and Private Projects on the Environment.[217] Another Royal Decree of 9 September 2003 further implements the 1985 EIA Directive, concerning the rules with regard to EIA in execution of the law of 20 January 1999 on the protection of the marine environment in the sea areas under the competence of Belgium.[218]

ii. Integrated Pollution Prevention and Control

A Walloon Decision of 4 July 2002[219] implemented Directive 96/61/EC on Integrated Pollution Prevention and Control (IPPC Directive).[220] A Decision of the Brussels Capital Government of 18 April 2002 imposed an obligation to

207 [1976] OJ L129/23. 208 *Moniteur Belge*, 4 Dec. 2002.
209 Brussels (Belgium), 6 Jan. 1993. 210 *Moniteur Belge*, 6 Mar. 2003.
211 *Moniteur Belge*, 8 Dec. 2003.
212 Ghent (Belgium), 3 Dec. 2002, published on the Internet at: http://www.cipm-icbm.be.
213 *Moniteur Belge*, 21 Aug. 2002. 214 *Moniteur Belge*, 21 Sept. 2002; Err., 4 Oct. 2002.
215 [1997] OJ L73/5. 216 *Moniteur Belge*, 17 Sept. 2003; Err., 25 Sept. 2003.
217 [1985] OJ L175/40. 218 *Moniteur Belge*, 17 Sept. 2003.
219 *Moniteur Belge*, 21 Sept. 2002; Err., 4 Oct. 2002. 220 [1996] OJ L275/26.

report on operators of certain classified activities,[221] taking into account Decision 2000/479/EC on the Implementation of a European Pollutant Emission Register (EPER) according to Article 15 of Directive 96/61/EC concerning Integrated Pollution Prevention and Control.[222]

iii. Access to Information

The Belgian Government ratified the United Nations Economic Commission for Europe (UN/ECE) Convention on Access to Information, Public Participation in Decision-Making and Access to Justice in Environmental Matters (Aarhus Convention),[223] and its Annexes I and II, on 21 January 2003. The Convention was approved for the Walloon Region by a Decree of 13 June 2002,[224] for the Brussels Capital Region by an Ordinance of 7 November 2002,[225] for the Flemish Region by a Decree of 6 December 2002,[226] and finally, by a Federal Law of 17 December 2002.[227] The Aarhus Convention will enter into force for Belgium on 21 April 2003.

iv. Eco-Label

Two Royal Decrees of 11 June 2003 concerned the European Eco-Label scheme under Regulation (EC) No. 1980/2000 on a Revised Community Eco-Label Award Scheme (Eco-Label Regulation).[228] The first modified the Royal Decree of 29 August 1997 concerning the Committee for the granting of the European eco-label. The second modified the Royal Decree of 13 January 1999 on the determination of the amount and the method of payment of the costs and rights related to the European eco-label.[229]

H. Miscellaneous

i. Major-Accident Hazards—Seveso II

A Walloon Decision of 4 July 2002[230] implemented Directive 96/82/EC on the Control of Major-Accident Hazards Involving Dangerous Substances (Seveso II Directive).[231] A Federal Law of 26 May 2002 amended the Law of 21 January 1987 on the risks of heavy accidents with certain industrial activities.[232]

By two Decrees of 1 March 2002,[233] the Flemish Government approved the United Nations Economic Commission for Europe (UN/ECE) Convention on

[221] *Moniteur Belge*, 31 May 2002. [222] [2000] OJ L192/36.

[223] Aarhus (Denmark), 25 June 1998 (entered into force 30 Oct. 2001) (1999) 38 *International Legal Materials* 3, 517.

[224] *Moniteur Belge*, 3 July 2002. [225] *Moniteur Belge*, 22 Nov. 2002.

[226] *Moniteur Belge*, 7 Jan. 2003. [227] *Moniteur Belge*, 24 Apr. 2003.

[228] [2000] OJ L237/1. [229] *Moniteur Belge*, 4 July 2003.

[230] *Moniteur Belge*, 21 Sept. 2002; Err., 4 Oct. 2002. [231] [1997] OJ L10/13.

[232] *Moniteur Belge*, 27 June 2002. [233] *Moniteur Belge*, 12 Apr. 2002.

the Transboundary Effects of Industrial Accidents[234] (and its Annexes I to XIII), and the International Labour Organization (ILO) Convention No. 174 on the Prevention of Major Industrial Accidents.[235]

ii. Energy

A Decision of the Flemish Government of 29 March 2002 concerned the public service obligations to stimulate the rational energy use.[236] A Royal Decree of 16 July 2002 installed mechanisms to stimulate electricity generated from renewable energy sources.[237] A Decision of the Walloon Government of 30 May 2002 concerned the award of subsidies for the amelioration of energy efficiency and for the stimulation of a more rational energy use in the private sector (AMURE).[238] A Decision of the Walloon Government of 4 July 2002,[239] amended by a Decision of 28 November 2002,[240] was intended to stimulate environmentally friendly electricity.

In 2003, the Federal State as well as the three Regions introduced a substantial amount of energy legislation. With regard to the national policy, several laws dealt with nuclear energy. First, a Law of 31 January 2003 concerned the gradual abandonment of nuclear energy for industrial electricity production.[241] Secondly, a Law of 2 April 2003 modified the Law of 15 April 1994 on the protection of the public and the environment against the dangers resulting from ionizing radiation and on the Federal Agency for Nuclear Control.[242] Thirdly, a Law of 11 April 2003 concerned the provisions for the dismantling of nuclear power stations and for the management of nuclear fuel that was irradiated in these nuclear power stations.[243] Lastly, a Royal Decree of 17 October 2003 established the nuclear and radiological emergency plan for the Belgian territory.[244] Existing legislation in this area has been elaborated and completed as follows during 2003. A Decision of the Flemish Government of 4 April 2003 amended its Decision of 28 September 2001 concerning the promotion of the generation of electricity from renewable sources of energy.[245] A Flemish Decree of 4 July 2003, one of 10 July 2003, and one of 18 July 2003 amended the electricity Decree of 17 July 2000, on the one hand with regard to the public service obligations, on the other hand with regard to the introduction of a system of heat and power certificates and with regard to

[234] Helsinki (Finland), 17 Mar. 1992 (entered into force 19 Apr. 2000) (1992) 31 *International Legal Materials* 6, 1330.

[235] Geneva (Switzerland), 22 June 1993 (entered into force 3 Jan. 1997), published on the Internet at: http://www.ilo.org/public/english/protection/safework/accidis/index.htm.

[236] *Moniteur Belge*, 4 May 2002; Err., 23 May 2002.

[237] *Moniteur Belge*, 23 Aug. 2002.

[238] *Moniteur Belge*, 2 July 2002.

[239] *Moniteur Belge*, 17 Aug. 2002.

[240] *Moniteur Belge*, 28 Dec. 2002.

[241] *Moniteur Belge*, 31 Jan. 2003.

[242] *Moniteur Belge*, 2 May 2003.

[243] *Moniteur Belge*, 15 July 2003.

[244] *Moniteur Belge*, 20 Nov. 2003.

[245] *Moniteur Belge*, 30 Apr. 2003.

the public lighting.[246] A Decision of the Flemish Government of 26 September 2003 modified the decision of the Flemish Government of 29 March 2002 on the public service obligations to promote rational energy use.[247] A Decision of the Walloon Government of 15 May 2003,[248] and one of 26 June 2003,[249] amended the decision of the Walloon Government of 4 July 2002 on the stimulation of environmentally friendly electricity. A Decision of the Walloon Government of 10 April 2003 regarded the public service obligations on the electricity market.[250]

iii. Environmental Policy

The Financial Protocol of 4 October 2002 to the Cooperation Agreement of 5 April 1995 between the Federal State, the Flemish Region, the Walloon Region, and the Brussels Capital Region on international environmental policy, was approved by a Federal Law of 4 April 2003,[251] a Flemish Decree of 18 July 2003,[252] and a Walloon Decree of 2 October 2003.[253] A Decision of the Flemish Government of 14 June 2002 regarded the provincial and local environmental planning and the environmental council.[254] By doing so, the Decision executed Articles 2.1.16, 2.1.18, 2.1.22, and 2.1.24 of the Decree of 5 April 1995 on general provisions with a view to environmental policy.

A Walloon Decree of 20 December 2001 concerns environmental agreements.[255]

iv. Environmental Permits

The Decision of the Flemish Government of 6 February 1991 establishing the Flemish regulation on environmental permits has been amended by a Decision of the Flemish Government of 5 October 2001,[256] and a Decision of the Flemish Government of 31 May 2002.[257] With regard to the Brussels Capital Region, several modifications concerning the environmental permits can be found in an Ordinance of 6 December 2001.[258] Two Walloon Decrees of 4 July 2002 and one Decree of 19 September 2002 modified the Decree of 11 March 1999 regarding the environmental permit.[259] A Decision of the Walloon Government of 4 July 2002 stipulated the general conditions to exploit institutions that fall under the Decree of 11 March 1999, regarding the environmental permit.[260] Another Decision of the Walloon Government of 4 July 2002 concerned the

[246] *Moniteur Belge*, 8 Aug. 2003, 11 Aug. 2003, and 14 Aug. 2003.
[247] *Moniteur Belge*, 31 Dec. 2003.
[248] *Moniteur Belge*, 26 May 2003.
[249] *Moniteur Belge*, 15 July 2003.
[250] *Moniteur Belge*, 13 June 2003.
[251] *Moniteur Belge*, 2 July 2003.
[252] *Moniteur Belge*, 5 Sept. 2003.
[253] *Moniteur Belge*, 16 Oct. 2003.
[254] *Moniteur Belge*, 8 Aug. 2002.
[255] *Moniteur Belge*, 6 Feb. 2002.
[256] *Moniteur Belge*, 9 Jan. 2002.
[257] *Moniteur Belge*, 19 June 2002.
[258] *Moniteur Belge*, 2 Feb. 2002.
[259] *Moniteur Belge*, 18 July 2002, 9 Aug. 2002, and 27 Sept. 2002.
[260] *Moniteur Belge*, 21 Aug. 2002; Err., 1 Oct. 2002.

procedure and several measures for the execution of the Decree of 11 March 1999 regarding the environmental permit.[261]

v. Environmental Taxation and Subsidies

A Decision of the Flemish Government of 11 January 2002 regarded the aid for ecology investments by enterprises.[262] This Decision was necessary to bring the aid into line with the Community guidelines on State aid for environmental protection.[263] A Royal Decree of 2 December 2002 amended the Royal Decree of 14 February 2001 regarding the introduction of a bounty system to promote the installation of LPG in cars.[264]

A Law of 30 December 2002 contained several fiscal provisions with regard to environmental taxes.[265] A Decision of the Brussels Capital Government of 30 April 2003 determined the conditions for the award of a subsidy for works to preserve a protected estate.[266] A Decision of the Walloon Government of 10 April 2003 concerned the award of subsidies to public authorities and to non-commercial institutions, for the realization of studies and works that aim at a better energy performance for buildings.[267] A Decision of the Flemish Government of 13 June 2003 amended its Decision of 5 July 2002 on subsidies for urban renewal projects.[268] The Decision of the Flemish Government of 18 May 2001 on the granting of subsidies for the application of environmentally friendly agricultural production methods and for the preservation of genetic diversity, first was amended by a Decision of the Flemish Government of 13 June 2003,[269] and subsequently was replaced by a Decision of the Flemish Government of 3 October 2003.[270] The Brussels Capital Government in a Decision of 17 July 2003 regulated the granting of subsidies for the urban renewal task of the Regional Development Agency for the Brussels Capital Region.[271] Two decisions of the Flemish Government of 10 October 2003 determined the specific rules for the subsidizing of projects with regard to sustainable environmental policy, as well as for the recognition and the subsidizing of environmental associations.[272] A Walloon Decree of 22 October 2003 modified the Decree of 25 July 1991 with regard to the tax on waste in the Walloon Region.[273] A programme Law of 22 December 2003 contained certain provisions on the energy tax, and on environmental taxes.[274]

[261] *Moniteur Belge*, 21 Sept. 2002; Err., 4 Oct. 2002.
[262] *Moniteur Belge*, 9 Apr. 2002.
[263] [2001] OJ C37/3.
[264] *Moniteur Belge*, 6 Dec. 2002.
[265] *Moniteur Belge*, 17 Apr. 2003.
[266] *Moniteur Belge*, 26 May 2003; Err., 19 June 2003.
[267] *Moniteur Belge*, 28 May 2003.
[268] *Moniteur Belge*, 1 Aug. 2003.
[269] *Moniteur Belge*, 12 Aug. 2003.
[270] *Moniteur Belge*, 23 Oct. 2003.
[271] *Moniteur Belge*, 12 Sept. 2003.
[272] *Moniteur Belge*, 4 Nov. 2003 and 10 Dec. 2003.
[273] *Moniteur Belge*, 19 Nov. 2003.
[274] *Moniteur Belge*, 31 Dec. 2003.

III. Denmark

Peter Pagh *

A. Introduction

Following elections at the end of 2001 a new government came to power based on a right-wing majority in parliament. The new conservative/liberal alliance was expected to cause substantial changes to Danish environmental policy during 2002. However, environmental policy, from a European perspective, was hardly amended in the period under survey. No substantial developments occurred in the policy areas of climate change, nature conservation and preservation, restrictions on pollution, waste treatment, or chemicals law. The majority of environmental legislation adopted during 2002 concerned implementation of European Community (EC) legislation. However, regarding foreign environmental aid the new government did make substantial changes: funding was significantly cut and the administration was removed from the Ministry of the Environment to the Ministry of Foreign Affairs.

Regarding Danish national environmental law several developments are worth noting. First, whereas the former government had introduced a number of new green taxes and increased existing green taxes to a total revenue of approximately €9 billion, the new government introduced a tax-stop. Thus, green taxes as economic tools for environmental protection were stricken from the Danish political agenda. Secondly, the new government loosened the firm restrictions on land use outside the cities by amending the Physical Planning Act.[1] Thirdly, in February 2002, the government established a new Environmental Assessment Institute (EAI). The institute is an independent governmental body financed by the State and is headed by the internationally well-known Danish political scientist and statistician, Björn Lomborg.[2] The EAI does not deal with environmental assessment in the ordinary sense. Rather, it performs economic and environmental analyses based on the concept of environmental efficiency. To date, the institute's reports have not affected existing legislation, nor have they sparked new (draft) legislation.[3]

The first half of 2002 also saw the Danish Presidency of the European Union (EU). In this capacity, Denmark presented the EU position at the Earth Summit in Johannesburg (South Africa). Neither the Danish national goals nor the EU

* Professor of environmental law, University of Copenhagen (Denmark).

[1] Act No. 383 of 6 June 2002.

[2] See e.g. B. Lomborg, *The Sceptical Environmentalist—Measuring the Real State of the World* (Cambridge: Cambridge University Press, 2001). Lomborg and his book have stirred fierce discussions among environmental scientists and environmentalists.

[3] Reports from the Institute are published (in English) on the Internet at: http://www.imv.dk/en/index.htm.

position were overly ambitious, rather focusing on realistic goals; in particular the need for clean water and sanitary facilities, such as sewerage and water-purifying plants in developing nations.

B. Atmospheric Pollution

i. Ambient Air Quality

The Ministry of Environment decided to attempt to overcome past complications in the implementation of the EC Directives on ambient air quality,[4] by issuing Statutory Order No. 58 of 23 January 2003 on ambient air quality. The new order is intended to implement not only Directive 96/62/EC on Ambient Air Quality Assessment and Management (Air Quality Framework Directive),[5] but also its daughter directives: Directive 1999/30/EC laying down Limit Values for Sulphur Dioxide, Nitrogen Dioxide and Oxides of Nitrogen, Particulates and Lead in the Ambient Air,[6] and Directive 2000/69/EC relating to Limit Values for Benzene and Carbon Monoxide in Ambient Air.[7] However, this new implementation effort also appears to be insufficient. The Directives prescribe that 'Member States shall determine the penalties applicable to breaches of the national provisions adopted pursuant to this Directive. Those penalties shall be effective, proportionate and dissuasive'.[8] However, the Statutory Order does not contain any provisions on penalties. According to the Danish Environmental Protection Agency (EPA), this is because all obligations arising from the Statutory Order are addressed at governmental bodies, including the EPA itself. It claims that it is sufficient that the Commission can take infringement action against the Danish State. Although this argument seems rather unconvincing, at the time of writing, the Commission had not yet initiated any infringement procedure.

ii. National Emission Ceilings

Similar problems relating to penalty provisions exist in the Danish implementation of Directive 2001/81/EC on National Emission Ceilings for Certain Atmospheric Pollutants (NEC Directive).[9] The emission ceilings and the public participation provisions of the NEC Directive have been implemented by Statutory Order No. 21 of 8 January 2003 on national emission ceilings for sulphur dioxide, nitrogen oxides, volatile organic compounds and ammonia, leaving the obligation to set up action programs to the EPA. Although Article 14 of the NEC Directive contains a penalty provision similar to those of the ambient air quality Directives, the Statutory Order does not contain any penalty provisions.

[4] See P. Pagh, 'Denmark' (2003) 3 *Yearbook of European Environmental Law*, 579.
[5] [1996] OJ L296/55. [6] [1999] OJ L163/41. [7] [2000] OJ L313/12.
[8] Art. 11 of Dir. 1999/30/EC, and Art. 9 of Dir. 2000/69/EC.
[9] [2001] OJ L309/22.

iii. Volatile Organic Compounds

Directive 1999/13/EC on the Limitation of Emissions of Volatile Organic Compounds Due to the Use of Organic Solvents in Certain Activities and Installations (Solvents Emissions Directive)[10] should have been implemented in all Member States by April 2001. Over a year after this deadline, it was implemented in Denmark by Statutory Order No. 350 of 29 May 2002 on VOC. This delay, which was criticized by Parliament, was excused by the EPA with reference to the necessary consultations with the Commission on the interpretation of certain provisions. From an outsider's perspective, this excuse appears rather surprising since it implies that Denmark had voted in favour of the Directive without being fully aware of its legal implications.

Directive 97/68/EC relating to Measures against the Emission of Gaseous and Particulate Pollutants from Internal Combustion Engines to be Installed in Non-road Mobile Machinery[11] was implemented by Statutory Order No. 844 of 11 October 2002 on restrictions of air pollution from non-road mobile machinery.

C. Chemicals

It is well known that the EC has almost exhaustively legislated chemicals. Hence, the major national efforts in this field of environmental law involve implementation and interpretation of EC legislation. In some cases, Denmark has adopted supplementary legislation, such as Statutory Order No. 552 of 2 July 2002 on certain industrial greenhouse gases prohibited from import, sale and use of new products containing hydrofluorocarbons (HFCs), perfluorocarbons (PFCs), and sulphurhexafluoride (SF6).

The pre-emptive effect of EC legislation on chemicals has been cause for great political concerns as to appropriate national responses. One example is the restrictions on use of organotin compounds (TBT) as bottom paints on sea vessels. By Statutory Order No. 926 of 18 November 2002 amending Statutory Order No. 1042 of 17 December 1997 on restrictions on the use and marketing of certain dangerous chemicals, Denmark implemented Commission Directive 2002/62/EC Adapting to Technical Progress for the Ninth Time Annex I to Council Directive 76/769/EEC on Restrictions on the Marketing and Use of Certain Dangerous Substances and Preparations (Organostannic Compounds),[12] prohibiting the application or re-application to ships of organotin compounds which act as biocides in anti-fouling systems.

However, the Danish EPA did not find the restrictions under the Directive sufficient. As a result, these were supplemented by a special Danish system adopted by Statutory Order No. 761 of 25 September 1999 on restrictions on the import, sale, and use of biocidal bottom paint. Taking into account that the Directive entailed exhaustive legislation, it is doubtful that this Statutory Order is

[10] [1999] OJ L85/1. [11] [1997] OJ L59/1. [12] [2002] OJ L183/58.

in accordance with EC law. In fact, the Order has neither been notified nor approved under Article 95(6) EC. What is more, comparable German legislation was rejected by the Commission in Decision 2001/570/EC on Draft National Provisions Notified by the Federal Republic of Germany on Limitations on the Marketing and Use of Organostannic Compounds.[13]

A more general approach to avoid or escape the aforementioned pre-emptive effect has been issuing recommendations to consumers or business not to buy or sell certain chemical substances or chemical products which are considered dangerous. Such an approach has, in particular, been used with the marketing of cosmetics, which are subject to exhaustive EC legislation under Directive 76/768/EEC on Cosmetic Products.[14] However, it is to be doubted that this approach is in accordance with EC law. If certain cosmetic products are considered dangerous, the national authorities are obliged to take action and inform the Commission. The fact that the Danish EPA might be overruled by the Commission cannot serve as an excuse for not applying the procedure required under the Directive. To date, however, the Commission has not pursued this matter.

D. Nature Conservation

After many years, at the end of 2002, the Danish Ministry of Environment officially recognized the insufficiency of the Danish implementation of Directive 92/43/EEC on the Conservation of Natural Habitats and of Wild Fauna and Flora (Habitats Directive).[15] The implementation problems concern at least four aspects of the Directive.

First, the Danish implementation of the protection required under Article 6 of the Habitats Directive does not address or oblige citizens in any way. Only authorities are committed by it.

Secondly, the Danish protection of designated sites does not include protection against existing use of land. Until the European Court of Justice (ECJ) ruling in Case C-117/00, *Commission* v. *Ireland*,[16] the Danish authorities believed that protection under Article 6(2) of the Directive does not require restrictions on existing use. The ruling underlined the faultiness of this official Danish interpretation. However, this was problematic since under Section 73 of the Danish Constitution, such interference in the use of private land might require expropriation and compensation to affected landowners. Taking into account the number of landowners affected by the designated areas (which cover approximately 7 per cent of the national territory), it is not an easy task to bring the Danish nature protection legislation into compliance with EC obligations. To date it remains unclear how this will be undertaken. This misinterpretation

[13] [2001] OJ L202/37.
[14] [1976] OJ L262/169.
[15] [1992] OJ L206/7.
[16] [2000] ECR I-5335.

(and others) by the Danish authorities of the scope of protection under the Habitats Directive has been fiercely debated in Parliament.

Thirdly, the scope of the Danish implementation of Article 6(3) of the Habitats Directive does not cover all projects and plans.

Fourthly, the implicit distinction in Article 6(3) between *screening* to identify projects and plans which must be subject to an assessment and the assessment is not reflected in Danish implementation or practice.

E. Waste

As reported in previous volumes of this *Yearbook*,[17] Danish waste legislation has been challenged in a number of litigations for non-compliance with the EC law. Contrary to expectations, none of the pending cases was decided by the ECJ during 2002. Some cases have been settled, for example Case C-209/98, *Sydhavn Sten & Grus* v. *Københavns Kommune*,[18] in July 2002. A compromise was struck which gave the private company minor compensation and access to collect and receive construction waste in the future. However, the legally troublesome questions were never decided by a court of law, and the legality of the waste system in the City of Copenhagen remains disputed. The same uncertainty is seen regarding the opening letter from the Commission of 2001: it is unclear whether the Commission will follow up with a reasoned opinion or close the case.

Whatever the outcome may be on the pending cases and complaints, the Minister of Environment has set up a new committee to consider a general reform of Danish waste legislation. The outcome of this committee's efforts is expected in the course of 2004.

[17] See P. Pagh, 'Denmark' (2002) 2 *Yearbook of European Environmental Law*, 462; and P. Pagh, 'Denmark' (2003) 3 *Yearbook of European Environmental Law*, 581–3.

[18] [2000] ECR I-3743.

IV. Finland

*Pekka Vihervuori**

A. Atmospheric Pollution

i. Kyoto Protocol

The obligations under the Kyoto Protocol[1] to the United Nations (UN) Framework Convention on Climate Change (UNFCCC)[2] were approved by a special Act in May 2002.[3] The more concrete domestic arrangements were left to be completed in 2003.

ii. Solvents Emissions and Large Combustion Plants Emissions

Due to the problems connected to the legal consequences of administrative plans under Finnish law, the Environmental Protection Act of 2000[4] was complemented in 2002.[5] Introduced was the possibility to use either a specified Cabinet decision or a Decree, instead of a mere plan, for the implementation of Directive 1999/13/EC on the Limitation of Emissions of Volatile Organic Compounds Due to the Use of Organic Solvents in Certain Activities and Installations (Solvent Emissions Directive)[6] and Directive 2001/80/EC on the Limitation of Emissions of Certain Pollutants into the Air from Large Combustion Plants (Large Combustion Plants Directive).[7]

Following the adoption, in October 2001, of the Large Combustion Plants Directive, a new specific emission Decree on the reduction of sulphur and nitrogen oxide emissions and of particle emissions from power generation boilers and gas turbines with a rated thermal input of at least 50 MW, was issued under the Environmental Protection Act.[8] It is now required by the inserted Section 43(4) of the Environmental Protection Act that in issuing permit provisions for

* Professor at the Helsinki University of Technology; Justice at the Supreme Administrative Court, Helsinki (Finland).

1 Kyoto (Japan), 10 Dec. 1997 (not yet in force) (1998) 37 *International Legal Materials* 1, 22.

2 New York, NY (United States), 9 May 1992 (entered into force on 21 Mar. 1994) (1992) 31 *International Legal Materials* 4, 849.

3 *Suomen Säädöskokoelma* (SS) (Official Legislation Journal) 383/2002.

4 SS 86/2000. In Finnish: *Ympäristönsuojelulaki*; in Swedish: *Miljöskyddslagen*. See also P. Vihervuori, 'Public Environmental Law in Finland' in R.J.G.H. Seerden, M.A. Heldeweg, and K.R. Deketelaere (eds.), *Public Environmental Law in the European Union and the United States—A Comparative Analysis* (The Hague/London/New York: Kluwer Law International, 2002), 129–70.

5 SS 944/2002.

6 [1999] OJ L85/1.

7 [2001] OJ L309/1.

8 SS 1017/2002.

large combustion plants the possibility of joint production of electricity and heat shall be taken into account, where technically and economically feasible, and taking the situation in energy market and delivery as a starting point. Operators of power generation boilers and gas turbines with a fuel capacity of at least 50 MW are obliged to notify the environmental authorities on malfunction or breakdown of the abatement equipment.

The Large Combustion Plants Directive imposes on each Member State a duty to define and implement a national emission reduction plan for existing plants. As mentioned above, the legal consequences of administrative plans are traditionally problematic in the Finnish legal system. Despite the provisions in Sections 26 and 50 of the Environmental Protection Act, such problems again emerged with the implementation of the Directive. The difficulties resulted in taking into account two alternatives to implement the reduction plan provisions. Hence, two new provisions were added to the Environmental Protection Act. According to the inserted Section 110a of the Environmental Protection Act, in order to implement the Directive's environmental obligations, the Cabinet is empowered to decide on a common obligation for certain individual operators to reduce emissions, and on the detailed assignment of such obligations to each operator within a certain branch, and, where necessary, on the amendment of such obligations. However, lacking such a Cabinet decision, the obligations of the operators on the reducing of emissions shall be based on a Government Decree. Where the Cabinet decision differs from a valid Environmental Permit, the former shall be upheld. On the other hand, permit provisions may go beyond the requirements of the Cabinet decision, as far as is necessary to meet the requirements for granting the permit or in order to safeguard an environmental quality standard required by a Government Decree. Operators' organizations may suggest proposals for the Cabinet decision, making the decisions somewhat similar to voluntary agreements. Following the inserted Section 110b of the Environmental Protection Act, various authorities and interested parties must be heard during the preparation of a Cabinet decision.

The obligations based on the Solvent Emissions Directive were also implemented in 2002. Pursuant to the Directive, national plans may be used to reduce Volatile Organic Compound (VOC) emissions regarding existing activities and installations. The aforementioned new provisions in Sections 110a and 110b of the Environmental Protection Act also apply to the Solvent Emissions Directive. The existing Decree on the limitation of emissions of volatile organic compounds due to the use of organic solvents in certain activities and installations was amended to also contain the possibility of implementation through such a plan, finally approved by the Cabinet.[9]

[9] SS 435/2001, amended by SS 1267/2002.

B. Nature Conservation

i. Vuotos Reservoir *Case*

The prolonged procedure concerning the water reservoir project *Vuotos* in the Kemijoki river system in Lapland came to an end, at least from a legal point of view, as the Supreme Administrative Court *Korkein hallinto-oikeus* (KHO) finally settled this permit case. A permit for the project, including a reservoir of 242 square kilometres, a hydroelectric plant, and continuous regulation of the water level, had been given in February 2000 by the (then) Water Court. Appeals by various persons and organizations, based on several judicial grounds of both domestic and European Community (EC) law, were lodged in the Vaasa Regional Administrative Court. This appellate court of first instance, competent for the whole country in Water Act and Environmental Protection Act cases, settled the case on 14 June 2001. The permit was annulled by virtue of Section 5 of Chapter 2 of the Water Act, following the wording in Act 467/1987. According to this unconditional and absolute clause, no permit for a water-constructing project may be granted if the project would endanger public health, cause considerable and far-reaching detrimental impacts in the natural conditions of the environs or in water nature or its activities, or if the project would to a large extent deteriorate the preconditions for local settlement or business conditions. All the remaining grounds for appeals, including those regarding environmental impact assessment (EIA) or the provisions of Directive 79/409/EEC on the Conservation of Wild Birds (Birds Directive),[10] remained unanswered, since the permit was annulled. This case constituted the first time that a permit was denied by virtue of Section 5 of Chapter 2 of the Water Act. As a rule, denials have been based on a less striking provision in Section 6 of the same chapter (applied by the Water Court), where the economic, social, and environmental 'pros and cons' are measured against each other. Pursuant to Section 5, however, the economic arguments are irrelevant. The ruling received enormous publicity and strongly varying opinions of both a legal and non-legal nature were presented. The applicants, headed by the governmentally owned hydroelectric company *Kemijoki Oy*, appealed to the KHO. The judgment in appeal was rendered on 18 December 2002.[11] In the explanatory part of the judgment, the KHO noted, *inter alia*, the action brought by the Commission against Finland before the European Court of Justice ECJ, in Case C-240/00.[12] In this case, the Commission sought a declaration stating that Finland had failed to fulfil its obligations under Article 4(1) and (2) of the Birds Directive, by not fully and definitively having classified special protection areas (SPAs). As an example, the Commission had mentioned the topical wetlands of Kemihaara as sites that

[10] [1979] OJ L103/1. [11] Decision 3339, KHO 2002:86.

[12] Case C-240/00, *Commission* v. *Finland* [2003] ECR I-2187.

should have been classified as SPAs. At the time of the KHO ruling in the *Vuotos Reservoir* case, the infringement procedure had not yet been decided, and only the opinion of Advocate General (AG) Léger, of 25 April 2002, was available.[13] However, the judgment of the KHO, like that of Vaasa Regional Administrative Court, was based on domestic legislation, specifically Section 5 of Chapter 2 of the Water Act. Although, ultimately, the KHO also decided to annul the permit (by six votes to one), its reasoning was in many respects different from that of the Vaasa Regional Administrative Court. Like the ruling of the Vaasa Regional Administrative Court, the KHO's verdict left the questions regarding the alternative alleged grounds for disapproval of the permit unanswered, due to the fact that one obstacle to the permit was sufficient for its annulment.

ii. Vuosaari Harbour Project

Among the other rulings of the KHO, those regarding the *Vuosaari* harbour project in Helsinki have been significant, at least in the public debate and the media. On 26 June 2002, the appeals against the relevant land use plans for this project were finally settled.[14] A partly adjacent area had been proposed by the Government as a Natura 2000 Network site pursuant to Directive 92/43/EEC on the Conservation of Natural Habitats and of Wild Fauna and Flora (Habitats Directive),[15] and notified to the Commission as an SPA under the Birds Directive.[16]

Following environmental impact assessments, it had been concluded that the harbour project would deteriorate the natural values for which the site had been designated. These assessments were subsequently amended, and the Ministry of the Environment (having adopted the regional land use plan) had held that neither the harbour nor its traffic connections had a significant effect on the natural values for which the site had been designated. In contrast, the KHO reasoned that Section 66(1) of the Nature Conservation Act[17] required an overall assessment on the habitat. Due to the appeals, particular focus had been given to certain bird conditions at the edge of the site. According to the KHO, annual changes of bird populations did not, as such, result in infringement of the ban on deterioration under Section 66, unless the populations diminished or disappeared. Hence, the impacts on the woods, bushes, grass, and other characteristics of the habitats of the species for which the areas had been designated were to be taken into account. The planned bridge over a narrow bay decreased, to some extent, the amount of bushes and other vegetation within the site. Harbour activities were expected to cause noise that would impact the site. However,

[13] Ultimately, in its judgment of 6 Mar. 2003, the ECJ issued the declaration against Finland as sought by the Commission.

[14] Decision 1607, KHO 2002:48.

[15] [1992] OJ L206/7.

[16] EC site number FI0100065, *Mustavuoren lehto ja Östersundomin lintuvedet*. See P. Vihervuori, 'Finland' (2003) 3 *Yearbook of European Environmental Law*, 595.

[17] SS 1096/1996.

according to the KHO, the project would not result in the destruction of the immediate habitat of any bird species for which the site had been designated, or in the destruction of any area suitable as habitat of such bird species. Nevertheless, the KHO held that the natural values of the site would, according to the assessment procedure, be deteriorated by the project. The assessment did not prove that this deterioration would be focused on the natural values for which the site has been designated. Given the importance of such findings for the application of Section 66(1) of the Nature Conservation Act and of Article 6 of the Habitats Directive, the appeals were rejected.

On 24 October 2002, in a subsequent case under the Water Act, regarding the same project, the KHO rejected all the appeals regarding the respective water law permit.[18] The KHO, in a complicated procedural situation and among several judgments of an entirely domestic law nature, in respect of the impacts on the neighbouring Natura 2000 site referred to its aforementioned ruling of 26 June 2002. It held that, even when the cumulative impacts of various factors were taken into account, and given the lack of any new relevant information on this question, it could find no infringement of the Natura 2000 provisions.

iii. Flying Squirrel

According to Article 12(1) of the Habitats Directive, Member States shall take the requisite measures to establish a system of strict protection for the animal species listed in Annex IV in their natural range, prohibiting, *inter alia*, deterioration or destruction of breeding sites or resting places. The flying squirrel, *Pteromys volans*, is a protected species under Article 12 of the Habitats Directive, which, within the present geographical area of the EU, only lives in Finland. Its protection, with possibly significant impacts on land use, forestry, traffic connections, and so on, has been widely debated, in particular regarding its exact scope and content. At the domestic level, the protection is primarily based on Section 49(1) of the Nature Conservation Act,[19] but the wording of this provision in relation to Article 12(1) of the Habitats Directive has been contested. Several judicial proceedings on this issue were pending in 2002.

On 20 November 2002, the KHO ruled in a case concerning a land use plan that land areas where the flying squirrel has been observed may be assigned for residential construction only after examination of the connecting routes of the species and assessment of the protection of the breeding sites and resting places.[20] Because this had not taken place in the planning procedure *in casu*, the plan was annulled. Several other cases concerning the flying squirrel were still pending at the end of 2002. By the end of June 2003, several cases had been settled by the KHO, in particular the widely known forestry-related case of *Konikallio* in southern Finland.

[18] Decision 2638, KHO 2002:64.

[19] SS 1096/1996.

[20] Decision 2975, KHO 2002:78.

D. Waste

i. Palin Granit

In Case C-9/00, *Palin Granit*,[21] on 31 December 1999, the KHO had sought a preliminary ruling from the ECJ in the proceedings between *Palin Granit Oy* and *Vehmassalon Kansanterveystyön Kuntayhtymän Hallitus*. Its questions concerned the interpretation of the notion of waste under Article 1(a) of Directive 91/156/EEC amending Directive 75/442/EEC on Waste (Waste Framework Directive).[22] In its judgment of 18 April 2002, the ECJ held that: 'the holder of leftover stone resulting from stone quarrying which is stored for an indefinite length of time to await possible use discards or intends to discard that leftover stone, which is accordingly to be classified as waste within the meaning of Council Dir. 75/442/EEC'[23] and 'the place of storage of leftover stone, its composition and the fact, even if proven, that the stone does not pose any real risk to human health or the environment are not relevant criteria for determining whether the stone is to be regarded as waste'.[24]

Following the ECJ's preliminary ruling, on 5 November 2002, the KHO settled the domestic case.[25] According to this ruling, leftover stone resulting from stone quarrying by the applicant company which was to be stored in the vicinity of the quarrying but outside the quarrying area specified in the quarrying permit (for an indefinite length of time, to await possible use, discards or intends to discard that leftover stone) was to be classified as 'waste' within the meaning of the Waste Act.[26] The place of storage of leftover stone in the vicinity, its composition, and the assumption (even if proven) that the stone did not pose any real risk to human health or the environment, were not relevant criteria for determining whether the stone was to be regarded as waste.

ii. AvestaPolarit Chrome

The related Case C-114/01, *AvestaPolarit Chrome Oy*,[27] was still pending in 2002. In this case, the KHO had asked the ECJ for guidance as to the criteria for determining whether, in a series of defined circumstances, leftover rock resulting from the extraction of ore and/or ore-dressing sand resulting from the dressing of ore in mining operations was to be regarded as 'waste' within the meaning of the Framework Waste Directive.

[21] Case C-9/00, *Palin Granit Oy and Vehmassalon Kansanterveystyön Kuntayhtymän Hallitus* [2002] ECR I-3533.

[22] [1991] OJ L78/32.

[23] Case C-9/00, n. 21 above, para. 39.

[24] ibid., para. 51.

[25] Decision 3055, KHO 2002:82.

[26] SS 1072/1993.

[27] [2003] ECR I-0000 (not yet reported).

F. Horizontal Instruments

i. Integrated Pollution Prevention and Control

In order fully to bring it in line with Directive 96/61/EC on Integrated Pollution Prevention and Control (IPPC Directive),[28] several minor technical amendments were made to the Environmental Protection Act.[29] The practical effects of these mainly formal clarifications are allegedly very small.

Although the Act is, in many respects, based on the IPPC Directive, it covers a substantially larger number of activities and installations. Against this background, the development of domestic administrative and judicial practice is highly interesting.[30] However, only a few interesting cases were finally settled during 2002. A KHO judgment of 8 May 2002[31] concerned an environmental permit for a petrol station under the Environmental Permit Act. An existing station, located in an area designated as an important groundwater area, was to be renewed and enlarged. Double wall tanks with a leak detector systems were to be used and the ground was to be covered with a tight layer of plastic, as well as overfill prevention, and so on. Two additional provisions on further technical safeguard measures had been included in the permit decision by the Municipal Environmental Authority, but the Vaasa Regional Administrative Court removed these provisions at the request of the applicant. In turn, the KHO, in the appeal lodged by the Regional Environmental Centre, restored the provisions. The acceptability of the site as such was procedurally not at stake before the KHO. On 11 February 2003, a slightly different petrol station case was decided, also concerning a groundwater area.[32] The permit application, irrespective of meeting the level of best available techniques (BAT), was rejected because additional measures concerning the subsoil were deemed necessary.

At the closing of the survey period, several cases were pending concerning the notion of 'totality of activity' under Section 2 of the Environmental Protection Decree,[33] as compared to the notion of 'installation' under Article 2(3) of the IPPC Directive. These notions are crucial for the determination of the necessary minimum scope for a permit. On 6 February 2002, the KHO passed a verdict in one of these cases.[34] Although the case concerned a permit application that was clearly below the level of the IPPC Directive, the facts were nevertheless interesting. The animal shed at stake was intended for 30 milk cows, 12 young cows, 33 beef cows, and 23 young cows under eight months. An environmental permit was required under Section 1(1)(11a) of the Environmental Protection Decree, because the listed level of 30 milk cows was reached. The totality of activity, making up the scope of the permit, was created by the technical and production

[28] [1996] OJ L275/26. [29] SS 506/2002. [30] See Vihervuori, n. 16 above, 591–2.
[31] Decision 1037, KHO 2002:36. [32] Decision 294. [33] SS 169/2000.
[34] Decision 248.

totality consisting of, in addition to the milk cows, all the other animals mentioned, as well as the storing of manure sludge in two nearby tanks and the spreading of manure sludge in the fields located in the neighbourhood of the shed. The relationship of spreading of manure sludge to main activities was generally still an open question by the end of 2002, pending in several cases before the KHO. In this respect, on 30 June 2003, the KHO passed down two important rulings.[35]

G. Miscellaneous

i. Ecological Criteria in Public Contracts

In 2002, the ECJ gave its ruling in the important Case C-513/99,[36] concerning the acceptability of ecological criteria in public contracts. The KHO had referred questions to the ECJ under Article 234 EC on the interpretation of Articles 2(1)(a), (2)(c) and (4), and 34(1) of Directive 93/38/EEC Coordinating the Procurement Procedures of Entities Operating in the Water, Energy, Transport and Telecommunications Sectors,[37] and Article 36(1) of Directive 92/50/EEC relating to the Coordination of Procedures for the Award of Public Service Contracts.[38] On 17 September 2002, the ECJ ruled, *inter alia*, that Article 36(1)(a) of Directive 92/50/EEC must be interpreted as meaning that where, in the context of a public contract for the provision of urban bus transport services, the contracting authority decides to award a contract to the tenderer who submits the economically most advantageous tender, it may take into consideration ecological criteria such as the level of nitrogen oxide emissions or the noise level of the buses, provided that they are linked to the subject-matter of the contract, do not confer an unrestricted freedom of choice on the authority, are expressly mentioned in the contract documents or the tender notice, and comply with all the fundamental principles of Community law, in particular the principle of non-discrimination.[39] Furthermore, the ECJ held that the principle of equal treatment does not preclude the taking into consideration of criteria connected with protection of the environment, such as those at issue in the main proceedings, solely because the contracting entity's own transport undertaking is one of the few undertakings able to offer a bus fleet satisfying those criteria.[40]

[35] Decision 1568, KHO 2003:40; and Decision 1569.

[36] Case C-513/99, *Concordia Bus Finland Oy Ab, formerly Stagecoach Finland Oy Ab* v. *Helsingin Kaupunki and HKL-Bussiliikenne* [2002] ECR I-7213.

[37] [1993] OJ L199/84, as amended by [1994] OJ C241/21, and [1995] OJ L1/1.

[38] [1992] OJ L209/1.

[39] Case C-513/99, n. 36 above, para. 69.

[40] ibid., para. 86.

V. France

Nathalie Hervé-Fournereau *

A. Introduction

> We are the first generation aware of the risks threatening our planet. The first. And we are probably the last generation capable of stopping what is irreversible.[1]

The noteworthy speech made by French president Jacques Chirac at the United Nations (UN) World Summit on Sustainable Development (Johannesburg Summit),[2] in September 2002, emphasized the awareness of the acuteness of global environmental affairs. It underlined France's willingness to play a leading part in favour of a development that could 'satisfy the needs of current generations, without jeopardising the needs of future generations',[3] hence respecting ecological balance. Whereas the survey year 2002 highlighted France's strengthened intentions, paradoxically, it appears as a transitional year and one of continuous tensions fostered between French law and European Community (EC) environmental law. This transitional year can be explained by the change of government (and a political majority within the French National Assembly) following the presidential elections in May 2002. During 2002, the designation of the Ministry in charge of environmental matters was changed to 'Ministry of Ecology and Sustainable Development' ('which is not a play on words'),[4] and a Secretary of State was appointed for sustainable development. Furthermore, the (female) Ecology and Sustainable Development Minister promised to promote a pragmatic, transparent approach to get 'the ministry out of the ghetto where it had been confined'.[5] This shift in approach,[6] far from pleasing the majority of

* Researcher in Environmental Law at CNRS (National Centre for Scientific Research), member of IODE (Institut de l'Ouest Droit et Europe) and UMR (Mixed Research Unit) 6050 CNRS, department of CEDRE (Centre for European Research), University of Rennes I, 'Jean Monnet' European Pole, Rennes (France).

[1] J. Chirac, President of the French Republic, speech at Johannesburg Summit, 2 Sept. 2002. All speeches noted in this survey are published on the Internet at: www.environnement.gouv.fr.

[2] Johannesburg (South Africa), 26 Aug.–4 Sept. 2002.

[3] Definition given by the Brundland Report: World Commission on Environment and Development, *Our Common Future* (Oxford: Oxford University Press, 1987).

[4] Speech by Minister of Ecology and Sustainable Development R. Bachelot, delivered at the National Assembly on 25 Oct. 2002, to present the 2003 budget.

[5] ibid.

[6] The Ministry's website presents a Communiqué of 16 May 2002 on the sustainable commitment for ecology. Among the notable statements made by the Minister regarding the domains of nuclear power or hunting, a statement of 8 May 2002 (one day after her inauguration) reads: 'the least polluting industry is the nuclear industry', while she was quoted in the newspaper *Le Monde* on 8 May 2002 as having said: 'Any rejection of the nuclear energy, any moratorium, could be a terrible threat for the future and for the environment'.

the French environmental protection activists, is coupled with the defeat of the Bill concerning water in February 2002, and with the launch of a series of national debates on hunting, national heritage management, water, risks, and energy, which were intended to result in legislative action in 2003 or 2004. This research is carried out specifically with a Community perspective with regard to the commitments made by France. Among the many general actions launched by the new government following Community policy developments, are the preparation of an environmental charter, and of a national strategy for sustainable development.

The environmental charter was prepared, 'relying upon', in the words of President Chirac, the French Constitution. The presidential 'will' to see France 'become the crucible of a new art of living for the twenty-first century' nurtured the debates supervised by a commission in charge of drafting the charter. Since June 2002, this commission has been chaired by palaeontologist Yves Coppens. The environmental charter, which was being drafted in 2002, is meant to establish constitutionally recognition of the right to a healthy and well-balanced environment and of certain environmental principles. It was expected to be introduced to the Parliament by spring 2003.

The preparation of a national strategy for sustainable development was officially initiated in November 2002, at the governmental seminar on sustainable development. At this seminar, a selection of sixty actions was presented, falling into the following six themes: (i) economic activity; (ii) town and country planning and management; (iii) security, safety, and police; (iv) information and participation; (v) exemplary state; and (vi) international action. A national council on sustainable development and an interdepartmental comity were scheduled to be set up in 2003.

Once again, during this survey period France was laggard in transposing and implementing EC environmental secondary legislation, and hence was yet again confronted with a multitude of national and Community litigation. Even if, according to standing case law of the European Court of Justice (ECJ),[7] these failures to respect Community law were to be assessed 'by reference to the situation prevailing at the end of the period laid down in the reasoned opinion', and hence would not constitute 'a topical reality of the state of law respect', they still illustrate the complexities and the loopholes in the French legal system concerning environmental matters. Henceforth, the fear of incurring possible penalties by the ECJ for failing to comply with its judgments rendered since 2000 clearly appears in French debates and legislative proposals. Nevertheless, the policy towards sustainable hunting, of the Minister of Ecology and Sustainable Development, heralds the accentuation of judicial and political strife in the framework of the enforcement of Directive 79/409/EEC on the Conservation of Wild Birds (Birds Directive).[8]

[7] See e.g. recently Case C-60/01, *Commission* v. *France* [2002] ECR I-5679, para. 36.
[8] [1979] OJ L103/1.

B. Atmospheric Pollution

i. Climate Change

Following its ten-year programme aimed at fighting climatic change, adopted in 2000, France continued the dialogue started in 2001 with industry in order to conclude voluntary commitments to reduce greenhouse gases.[9] Industry is expected to submit a scheme of voluntary commitments to the government whose modes will have to be discussed with the Ministry of Ecology and Sustainable Development and the Ministry of Economy. Those forthcoming thoughts and actions come in the wake of the Community's proposals and debates in order to put in place a future European market of emission licences.

A national observatory to monitor the effects of global warming was set up within the framework of the ten-year national strategy. In addition, in December 2002, France adopted Decree 2002/1508 relating to the indication of fuel consumption and carbon dioxide (CO_2) emissions of new personal automobiles. This constituted a response to the late transposition of Directive 1999/94/EC relating to the Availability of Consumer Information on Fuel Economy and CO_2 Emissions in Respect of the Marketing of New Passenger Cars.[10] In this respect, in April 2002, the European Commission filed a petition with the ECJ to note France's failure to respect the deadline for transposition.

ii. Municipal Waste Incineration

Since 1996,[11] France has (belatedly) undertaken a large-scale programme to standardize all municipal waste incineration plants, in order (slowly) to comply with Directive 89/369/EEC on the Prevention of Air Pollution from New Municipal Waste Incineration Plants,[12] and Directive 89/429/EEC on the Reduction of Air Pollution from Existing Municipal Waste Incineration Plants.[13] Because of the French laxness, the Commission had started proceedings with the ECJ in February 2002. Rejecting France's arguments,[14] in June 2002, the ECJ noted that France had failed to fulfil its Community obligations by not taking all the required and appropriate measures to ensure that the total number of incinerators in France were exploited in conformity with the combustion

[9] See N. Hervé-Fournereau, 'France' (2003) 3 *Yearbook of European Environmental Law*, 602.

[10] [1999] OJ L12/16.

[11] In 1996, an inquiry by the Ministry of Environment indicated that 40 incinerators (with a capacity superior to 6 tons of waste per hour) did not comply with the combustion conditions imposed by EC law. In late 1999, 7 incinerators still were not in conformity.

[12] [1989] OJ L163/32.

[13] [1989] OJ L203/50.

[14] France argued that Member States keep a margin of discretion and that it is impossible directly to infer from a *de facto* situation of non-conformity with the objectives of Directives that a Member State has forcefully breached its duties. It was underlined in this case that the breach of a Community norm by a legal entity, which is in no way linked to the public authority, did not constitute a failure. Moreover, France argued that all reasonable and possible measures had been taken so as to reach the result imposed by Community texts.

conditions imposed by Directives 89/369/EEC and 89/429/EEC, or that their exploitations were stopped in due time, namely by 1 December 1990 for new facilities and by 1 December 1996 for existing facilities.[15] Parallel to this, the government pledged to enforce compliance with Community Directives by ordering the prefects to ensure that laws were being enforced.[16] According to an estimate by the Ministry of Ecology and Sustainable Development, in late 2002, two units out of a total of 36 incineration plants (high and low processing capacity), according to norms in May 2002, would have conformed to standards, while 31 would be stopped and three suspended for repairs.

C. Chemicals

In October 2001, shortly after the major industrial accident at the AZF (subsidiary of the Total/Fina/Elf trust) plant in Toulouse, an investigation commission was set up in order to assess the safety of industrial plants and research centres.[17] The Commission Report, presented in January 2002, highlighted the weaknesses of the programmes for prevention and handling of major industrial hazards. It stressed the importance of improving scientific knowledge concerning the dangerous chemical substances used at industrial plants. In this context, the French Environmental Health Security Agency, established in 2001 and inaugurated in November 2002, has included the appreciation of the health impact of (dangerous) chemicals in its research programme. Finally, the investigation commission's report encouraged, in particular, a proactive approach for France at the Community level in the field of chemicals policy. France should play a leading part in the implementation of the actions presented in the 2001 Commission White Paper—Strategy for a Future Policy in the Domain of Chemicals.[18]

D. Biotechnology

In the controversial domain of biotechnology, a public debate about genetically modified organisms (GMOs) and field experimentation with genetically modified (GM) crops took place in France between November 2001 and February 2002. The resulting report confirmed the acuteness of public concerns and the lack of transparency and dialogue regarding biotechnology.[19] It stressed the necessity of proper citizen consultation about GMOs and of a parliamentary debate about issues related to biotechnology.

In the meantime, in July 2001, the European Commission initiated proceedings before the ECJ[20] regarding France's failure sufficiently to transpose Directive

[15] Case C-60/01, n. 7 above. [16] Circular of 27 June 2002.

[17] See Hervé-Fournereau, n. 9 above, 608–9. [18] COM(2001)88.

[19] *Rapport a la Suite du Débat sur les OGM et les Essais au Champ*, 7 Mar. 2002, published on the Internet at: http://www1.environnement.gouv.fr/IMG/pdf/20020307-rapport-ogm.pdf.

[20] Case C-296/01, *Commission* v. *France* [2003] ECR I-0000 (not yet reported).

90/220/EEC on the Deliberate Release into the Environment of Genetically Modified Organisms (Deliberate Release Directive).[21] The case will likely be decided by the end of 2003.

D. Nature Conservation

i. Natura 2000

Once again, in 2001 and 2002,[22] France was condemned by the ECJ for not having designated a sufficient number of special protection areas (SPAs) under the Birds Directive,[23] and special areas of conservation (SACs) under Directive 92/43/EEC on the Conservation of Natural Habitats and of Wild Fauna and Flora (Habitats Directive).[24] In Case C-202/01,[25] the ECJ concluded that 'without it being necessary to consider whether all the territories listed as ZICOs should be classified as SPAs',[26] France had not, within the period laid down, in sufficient measure, classified as SPAs the territories most suitable for the conservation of species of wild bird listed in Annex I to the Birds Directive and of migratory species not listed therein. It also states that France had failed to meet its Community obligations by not having classified as an SPA (in due time) a sufficient area of land on the Plaine des Maures.[27] This allegation was not contested by the French government.

As a result of these new condemnations, once more, France has made itself vulnerable to financial penalties for non-compliance with the rulings, and perhaps even to suspensions in the granting of Community structural funds. Wary of these possible consequences, France renewed its efforts to fulfil its obligations under the Natura 2000 Network.[28] At the end of 2002, France had designated 119 SPAs (comprising 936,000 hectares, or 1.7 per cent of the French national territory) under the Birds Directive, and had proposed to the Commission 1,172 new SACs (comprising approximately four million hectares, or 7.4 per cent of the French national territory) under the Habitats Directive.[29] Taking advantage of these boosted intentions, the Minister of Ecology and Sustainable

[21] [1990] OJ L117/15.

[22] Case C-220/99, *Commission* v. *France* [2001] ECR I-5831; and Case C-202/01, *Commission* v. *France* [2002] ECR I-11039.

[23] n. 8 above.

[24] [1992] OJ L206/7.

[25] n. 22 above.

[26] ibid., para. 21. ZICOs are French sites of importance for bird conservation.

[27] ibid., para. 30.

[28] Circular of 3 May 2002 on the contractual management of Natura 2000 sites (Ministry Bulletin 2002/6); Circular of 26 July 2002 relating to the restart of the talks about Natura 2000 (Ministry Bulletin 2002/7); Circular of 25 July 2002 on Natura 2000. All circulars and bulletins are published on the Internet at: www.environnement.gouv.fr.

[29] In 2002, the Marais Poitevin, the site d'Arjuzanx, the Marseilles islands, the Hyères islands, the Basses Corbières, the estuary and the marshes of lower Seine were registered in the Natura 2000 Network (Ministry Bulletin 2003/1).

Development explicated the Ministry's ambition to 'shift the protection of the natural patrimony towards a concerted management of species and habitats based on solid scientific data'.[30] She stressed the necessity of improving knowledge and of the scientific basis for interventions, and the need to promote a partnership approach relying on transparency and proximity.[31]

ii. Hunting

The reactivation, in 2002, of the debate on hunting did not improve conciliation or support from all participants, including the environmental protection associations. While a new law on hunting is expected to be adopted in 2003, during 2002, the Government clashed with the Council of State concerning the dates of opening and closing of the hunting season.[32] In December 2002, advocating conditions for sustainable hunting, the new Government set up a think-tank for hunting issues. Under the previous government, in January 2002, the Council of State had already cancelled a part of the Decree of 1 August 2000 relating to the opening of the hunting season for some water game species.[33] It had also referred a question to the ECJ for a preliminary ruling on the conformity of French provisions permitting the capture or any rational exploitation of a small number of goose, wood pigeon, and thrush, until 20 February.[34] In particular, it wanted to know whether it was possible to depart from the dates of opening and closing of the hunting season under Article 7(4) based on Article 9(1)(c) of the Birds Directive. Finally, by a ruling of 20 December 2002,[35] the Council of State annulled the orders of 18 July 2002 on the opening of the hunting season for migratory birds (except the woodcock and the turtle dove) due to their non-compliance with Article 7(4) of the Birds Directive.

E. Waste

In response to its Community commitments and the orders issued by the ECJ in the field of waste law, the government adopted a series of texts, including Decree 2002/540 relating to the classification of waste, which was implemented by a Circular of 3 October 2002. As discussed above, efforts were made to standardize all municipal waste incinerators.[36]

[30] Circular of 3 May 2002 on the regional orientations of wild fauna and improvement of the quality of habitats (Ministry Bulletin 2002/6).

[31] Decree 2002/1000 of 17 July 2002 relating to the national observatory of wild fauna and its habitats, JORF of 18 July 2002.

[32] JORF of 23 July 2002.

[33] Council of State, 25 Jan. 2001, *Bird Protection League, Aspas and Roc*, No. 224850.

[34] Case C-180/02, pending.

[35] Council of State, 20 Dec. 2002, *League for the Protection of Wild Fauna and for the Defence of Non Hunters*, No. 250255-250256-250257.

[36] See sect. B.*ii*.

i. End-of-Life Vehicles

A Decree was adopted with the aim of organizing the collection and disposal of old tyres. Directive 2000/53/EC on End-of-Life Vehicles (ELV Directive)[37] had obliged the Member States to ensure that operators put in place systems to collect old vehicles and old parts. The appropriate facilities for storing old tyres were mentioned among the processing sites in Annex I.

ii. Landfill of Waste

The first of July 2002 represented a transition date in the domain of waste, in particular for landfill of waste. As from this date, according to Article L541–24 of the Environment Code, landfill of waste will only be allowed for ultimate waste. A Circular of 27 June 2002 was dedicated to this deadline set by the French authorities. With the adoption of the Order of 30 December 2002 on waste landfill, France is gradually improving its compliance with Directive 1999/31/EC on Landfill of Waste (Waste Landfill Directive),[38] and is beginning to ensure that waste-recycling procedures are put into place.

iii. Waste Management

In Case C-292/99,[39] the ECJ ruled that France had failed to establish waste management schemes for its national territory, and management schemes for certain regions or departments for waste containing polychlorobiphenyls (PCBs), for care waste, and for special domestic waste. Moreover, the waste management schemes that had been adopted did not include specific chapters relating to packaging waste. Thereby, France had failed to fulfil its obligations under Directive 91/156/EEC amending Directive 75/442/EEC on Waste (Waste Framework Directive),[40] Directive 91/689/EEC on Hazardous Waste (Hazardous Waste Directive),[41] and Directive 94/62/EEC on Packaging and Packaging Waste (Packaging and Packaging Waste Directive).[42] The French arguments relating to the technical nature of the subject, or to the litigation responsible for the delays in devising management schemes, were rejected by the Court. It also did not accept France's arguments relating to the interpretation of the phrase 'as soon as possible', concerning the allotted time to conceive the required management schemes. France had argued that the words 'as soon as possible' constituted an indication of a time-limit which replaced any general provision concerning time-limits in the Community instrument concerned, and is not limited in time.[43] The ECJ noted that 'as soon as possible' should be interpreted as stipulating, in principle, 'a reasonable period for compliance by the competent authorities of each Member State with that particular obligation, that period

[37] [2000] OJ L269/34. [38] [1999] OJ L182/1.

[39] Case C-292/99, *Commission* v. *France* [2002] ECR I-4097.

[40] [1991] OJ L78/32. [41] [1991] OJ L337/20. [42] [1994] OJ L365/10.

[43] Case C-292/99, n. 39 above, para. 34.

being unconnected with the period laid down for transposition of the Directive'.[44] The ECJ estimated that the time lost by France (the time-limit laid down in the Reasoned Opinion expired seven years after the publication of the provisions) did not constitute a reasonable delay.[45]

iv. PCBs

In case C-177/01,[46] the ECJ noted France's failure to communicate to the Commission a list of inventories of machines containing higher amount of PCBs than 5 dm^3, a scheme of decontamination and/or disposal of listed machines and of the PCBs they contain, as well as a project concerning the collection and the future elimination of the machines which had not been listed, according to Article 4(1) of Directive 96/59/EC on the Disposal of Polychlorinated Byphenyls and Polychlorinated Terphenyls (PCB/PCT Directive).[47] The time-limit for transposition had expired in March 1998. Again, the technical difficulties argued by France to justify its belatedness were not accepted by the Court. Following this ruling, France completed its national inventory of machines containing PCBs. The PCB national commission was to prepare the national elimination programme, which should be ratified in 2003.

F. Water

The change of government, in May 2002, sounded the death knell for the Bill relating to water up for vote in the first reading by the National Assembly in spring 2002. The Minister of Ecology and Sustainable Development indicated 'great weaknesses' in the text and noted that there was 'insufficient consultation'. This defeat, in favour of launching a national debate on water policy in 2003, granted more respite to farmers opposed to the introduction of a tax on nitrogen. The goal clearly to re-examine the entire French water policy in order to adopt an efficient water management scheme, should provide France with an opportunity to ensure compliance with EC water law and with the rulings of the ECJ.

i. Water Framework Directive

Referring to the current situation of the intentions and of the very mitigated assessment of the obtained achievements and of the existing litigation, a Bill was drafted in 2002 to transpose Directive 2000/60/EC establishing a Framework for Community Action in the Field of Water Policy (Water Framework Directive).[48] A Circular of 2 February 2002 was dedicated to the elaboration of the documents concerning the assessment in enforcement of Articles 5 and 6 of the Water Framework Directive. Given that this Community text was inspired by the

[44] ibid., para. 41. [45] ibid., para. 45.
[46] Case C-177/01, *Commission* v. *France* [2002] ECR I-5137.
[47] [1996] OJ L243/31. [48] [2000] OJ L327/1.

French water management approach by catchments basins, its implementation should not raise many institutional difficulties. However, in order to fulfil the obligations of result concerning the good ecological and chemical health of water by 2015, a change of methodology in the assessment of the quality of water must be achieved. Above all, this will also require adoption of a very stringent and effective enforcement strategy for the prescribed standards.

ii. Urban Waste-Water

In an attempt not to further increase France's already substantial delays in the implementation of Directive 91/271/EEC on Urban Waste-Water Treatment (Urban Waste-Water Directive),[49] in 2002, quite a large number of (in principle non-restricting) Circulars were adopted. For instance, a Circular of 20 December 2002 aimed at collecting data relating to towns' water-treatment plants was submitted in time for the deadline of the Waste-Water Directive. A Circular of 3 May 2002 concerned conformity to standards by the water-purifying systems of local authorities.

iii. Nitrates

Directive 91/676/EEC on the Protection of Waters against Pollution Caused by Nitrates from Agricultural Sources (Nitrates Directive)[50] also inspired legislative action during 2002. A Circular of 8 April 2002 concerned the review of the list of vulnerable zones, following litigation before the ECJ. The designation of vulnerable zones under the Nitrates Directive has become a bone of contention for the national and Community judiciary.[51] The Commission's petition with the ECJ, in 2000, to question France's failure to designate vulnerable zones, presented the ECJ with an opportunity to assess the French methodology for the identification and designation of vulnerable zones.[52] The Commission argued that the French designation was insufficient due to improper enforcement of Articles 3 and 6 and Annex I of the Nitrates Directive. In particular, it questioned the failure to designate the Baie de Seine as a vulnerable zone. Furthermore, the Commission argued that due to the improper methodology used by France for the identification of affected waters, 'flowing brackish waters and hard freshwaters, both stagnant and flowing, could never be designated as eutrophic within the meaning of the Directive, given that, according to the circular, it is phosphorus and not nitrogen which is the controlling factor in those cases'.[53] In turn, France claimed

[49] [1991] OJ L135/40.

[50] [1991] OJ L375/1.

[51] See e.g. Council of State, 21 Jan. 2001, *The Ile de France Farmers Trade-Unions Federation*, No. 220203–222980, in which the Council of State rejected the request to annul an Order of the Prefect of Ile de France concerning the first review of the delimitation of vulnerable zones according to the Nitrates Dir.

[52] Case C-258/00, *Commission* v. *France* [2002] ECR I-5959.

[53] ibid., para. 25.

that the Directive required 'identification as polluted waters only of eutrophic waters with respect to which the control of nitrates is possible by measures applying to agriculture and would make optional the designation of the whole of the territory as a vulnerable zone', and hence, the methodology proposed by the Commission would lead to the 'identification as polluted of all waters containing nitrates, even at a reasonable level—that is to say, in practice, all Community waters'.[54] The ECJ agreed with the Commission that the French methodology was flawed by preventing large water areas from ever being designated as eutrophic, irrespective of the (imminent) presence of agricultural nitrate pollution.[55] It concluded that it would be incompatible with the Directive's logic and objective to restrict its scope to exclude certain categories of waters owing to the supposedly fundamental role in their pollution of phosphorus,[56] and hence, that France disregarded the Directive by a priori excluding from its scope major classes of waters, such as those mentioned in the Circular.[57] While recognizing the margin of discretion in the designation of waters, the ECJ held that Member States are obliged to respect the objectives of the Directive, and thus, that the exercise of that discretion may not result, as *in casu*, in a large portion of nitrogen-bearing waters falling outside its scope.[58] Concerning the non-identification of the Baie de Seine waters, France explained that this area was not eutrophized in the meaning of the Directive, and that there had been no impact to this area as a result of it not being designated as a vulnerable zone. However, the ECJ noted that even if eutrophication was not evident in the Seine bay itself, it would, nonetheless, contribute to the eutrophication of the North Sea.[59] The Court concluded that the interpretation of 'eutrophication' and the methodology chosen by France were too restrictive and hence incompatible with the Directive, and that France had not taken 'the appropriate steps to identify waters affected by pollution and, consequently, to designate the corresponding vulnerable zones'.[60]

iv. Dangerous Substance Discharges

In Case C-130/01,[61] the Commission brought proceedings before the ECJ over France's alleged failure to adopt pollution reduction programmes, including quality objectives for the 99 hazardous substances listed under Directive 76/464/EEC on Pollution Caused by certain Dangerous Substances Discharged into the Aquatic Environment of the Community (Dangerous Substances Discharge Directive).[62] France had also failed to communicate summaries of the programmes and the results of their implementation in accordance with Article 7 of the Directive. Two categories of hazardous substances are distinguished under the Directive: List I concerns certain highly hazardous substances for which the

[54] ibid., para. 34. [55] ibid., para. 46. [56] ibid., para. 45. [57] ibid., para. 50.
[58] ibid., para. 54. [59] ibid., para. 67. [60] ibid., para. 70.
[61] Case C-130/01, *Commission* v. *France* [2003] ECR I-5829. [62] [1976] OJ L129/23.

Council will set limit values, while List II contains 99 substances with a noxious effect on water that could be restricted to a certain area, and the substances (families or groups) quoted in List I for which no limit values have been set by the Council. The Water Framework Directive has come to replace the Dangerous Substances Discharge Directive.

G. Horizontal Instruments

i. Environmental Impact Assessment

In Case C-348/01,[63] the Commission brought proceedings before the ECJ against France for its failure sufficiently to transpose Article 1(7) and (11) of Directive 97/11/EC amending Directive 85/337/EEC on the Assessment of the Effects of certain Public and Private Projects on the Environment (EIA Directive),[64] before the deadline of 14 March 1999. France argued that it had always properly enforced the framework procedure, introduced by Article 1(7), at the request of developers. However, a mere internal practice could not be sufficient, the Court recalled, correctly to transpose Community provisions. Under Article 1(11) it is compulsory to inform the public of the reasons for a decision. The Commission claimed that the French implementing provisions did not ensure transposition of the provisions regarding projects different from those relating to classified facilities. In November 2002, notwithstanding the fact that, in the meantime, France had drafted a Decree to transpose Article 1(7), and enacted a Law to transpose Article 1(11),[65] the ECJ agreed with the Commission that timely and sufficient transposition had not been achieved.[66]

ii. Major-Accident Hazards—Seveso II

In January 2002, the report of the investigation commission on the safety of industrial plants and research centres and the protection of individuals was published, in the aftermath of the September 2001 AZF plant disaster in Toulouse.[67] The report encouraged the creation of a hazard culture and a European approach for industrial security, especially within the context of the heterogeneous domain of chemistry. It lists some 90 improvement measures covering six themes: (i) hazard reduction at the roots, (ii) human factor problem, (iii) transparency and pluralism of expertise, (iv) control of town planning, (v) compensation for victims, and (vi) judicial proceedings. The Bill to ensure control of technological hazards, now entitled the Bill relating to the prevention of technological and natural hazards and to the compensation of damages, was inspired by some of the suggestions made in the report. Since the Toulouse

[63] Case C-348/01, *Commission* v. *France* [2002] ECR I-10253. [64] [1997] OJ L73/5.

[65] Law 2002/276 of 27 Feb. 2002 relating to the democracy of proximity, JORF of 28 Feb 2002, 3808.

[66] Case C-348/01, n. 63 above, para. 20. [67] See further sect. C above.

accident, the 670 facilities classified under Directive 96/82/EC on the Control of Major-Accident Hazards Involving Dangerous Substances (Seveso II Directive)[68] have had to update their studies on hazard and propose security improvement schemes. The objective to increase the number of inspectors for classified facilities (currently 750) was reinstated by the new government of May 2002. According to a Ministry Communiqué of 27 August 2002, some 150 positions for additional inspectors were to be created by the end of 2003.

H. Miscellaneous

i. Integration

Parallel to the Community process that aims to integrate environmental requirements into all other policies, France has stated its ambition to realize its commitment to the ecological consistency of its public policies. In this context, particular attention is awarded to the objective of sustainable development, for which a national strategy was prepared in 2002. However, the intentions of environmental integration are sometimes watered down by other political and socio-economic issues. The reform of the Common Fisheries Policy[69] and the pending reform of the Common Agricultural Policy illustrate in veritable terms the French ambiguities and the complexities of the integration of environmental concerns. The qualification of farmsteads according to the concept of integrated farming teaches us a lot about the political will needed to ensure a real reconciliation of agricultural and environmental interests. For example, referring to farmsteads which (apart from a few minor exceptions) simply comply with existing legislation as examples of 'integrated farming' is baffling.[70] Echoing the Commission Recommendation of 30 May 2001 on the Recognition, Measurement and Disclosure of Environmental Issues in the Annual Accounts and Annual Reports of Companies,[71] France decided to oblige companies quoted on the Paris stock exchange to provide their shareholders with an annual report comprising, in addition to the usual data, information 'on the way the company takes into account the social and environmental consequences of its activity'.[72] Two statutory texts were adopted in 2002 in order to enforce this new obligation

[68] [1997] OJ L10/13.

[69] See N. Hervé-Fournereau, 'La réforme de la politique Commune de la pêche et la protection de l'environnement: du conditionnel au présent imparfait' in C. Flaesch-Mougin, D. Charles le Bihan, and C. Lequesne (eds.), *La politique Européenne de la pêche—vers un développement durable?* (Rennes: Apogée, 2003), 107–36.

[70] Decree 2002/631 of 24 Apr. 2002 relating to the qualification of farmsteads in accordance with integrated farming, JORF of 28 Apr. 2002.

[71] [2001] OJ L156/33.

[72] Law 2001/420 of 15 May 2001 relating to new economic regulations, JORF of 16 May 2001, 7776.

of transparency and of information.[73] Hence, too slowly but carefully, the will to promote effective integration of environmental concerns in company management is beginning to takes shape.[74]

[73] Decree 2002/221 of 20 Feb. 2002, JORF 44 of 21 Feb. 2002, 3360; Order of 30 Apr. 2002, JORF of 5 May 2002.

[74] On this subject see also N. Hervé-Fournereau, *L'entreprise et le droit Communautaire de l'environnement* (Rennes: Apogée, 2000).

VI. Germany

*Michael Rodi**

A. Introduction

The survey year 2002 witnessed an unusually active German legislature, with new enactments in virtually every field of environmental law. To a large extent, this activity can be traced back to the compulsory implementation of European Community (EC) legislation. Among the events worth noting were the adoption of the Act on the Phase-out of Nuclear Power, the new Federal Nature Conservation Act, the new Water Resource Management Act, and the Act on the Further Development of the Ecological Tax Reform. Waste policy was characterized by a contentious debate on the mandatory deposit on beverage packages. Finally, once again, courts were forced to deal with difficulties arising from *de facto* protection areas under the Habitats and Birds Directives.

B. Atmospheric Pollution

In the area of atmospheric pollution, an amendment to the Emission Control Act[1] and the Twenty-Second Emission Control Ordinance on Emission Limit Values for Air Polluting Substances[2] entered into force on 18 September 2002, thereby implementing the new Community directives on air quality. Directive 96/62/EC on Ambient Air Quality Assessment and Management (Air Quality Framework Directive)[3] called for air quality assessments pursuant to uniform measuring methods and criteria. Against this background, emission limits (that may not be exceeded after specified deadlines) were laid down by the first two so-called daughter directives: Directive 1999/30/EC laying down Limit Values for Sulphur Dioxide, Nitrogen Dioxide and Oxides of Nitrogen, Particulates and Lead in the Ambient Air[4] and Directive 2000/69/EC relating to Limit Values for Benzene and Carbon Monoxide in Ambient Air.[5] In addition, a duty to inform the population sets in whenever certain alarm thresholds are breached. In cases where such a breach appears likely, the authorities are required to set out action

* Professor of Law, University of Greifswald (Germany).
The following abbreviations will be used throughout this chapter: *Bundesgesetzblatt*—Federal Law Gazette (BGB1.); *Gemeinsames Ministerialblatt*—Common Ministerial Gazette (GMBl.).

1 Siebtes Gesetz zur Änderung des Bundes-Immissionsschutzgesetzes, BGBl. I 2002, 3622.

2 Zweiundzwanzigste Verordnung zur Durchführung des Bundes-Immissionsschutzgesetzes (Verordnungüber Immissionswerte für Schadstoffe in der Luft—22. BImSchV), BGBl. I 2002, 3626.

3 [1996] OJ L296/55.

4 [1999] OJ L163/41.

5 [2000] OJ L313/12.

plans detailing measures to reduce emissions. The amended Emission Control Act will now facilitate this by broadening the powers of German authorities with regard to possible sources of pollution, in particular industrial plants and car traffic. The limit values required under the daughter directives have been included in the amended Twenty-Second Emission Control Ordinance, which considerably tightens the requirements on measurements and monitoring as well as on adequate and timely information of the general public.

It is the Technical Instructions on Clean Air, however, and not the Ordinance, which translate the permit requirements of the Emission Control Act into concrete terms as regards air pollution. On 30 July 2002, the Federal Government published a restatement[6] of the former Technical Instructions on Air Quality Control (*TA Luft*), which dated from 1986 and did not meet the new EC standards. Moreover, the differing standards contained in the Emission Control Ordinance and the *TA Luft* would have led to considerable legal uncertainty. It adapts existing standards to European standards and introduces a new standard for benzene as well as new methods to assess existing and additional pollution loads. Altogether, the amendment was designed to implement the concept of integrated environmental protection as introduced by Directive 96/61/EC on Integrated Pollution Prevention and Control (IPPC Directive).[7] For that purpose, Article 5(1)(3) of the *TA Luft* establishes basic requirements for the integrated prevention of environmental pollution.

The Third Emission Control Ordinance of 24 June 2002[8] aims at further reducing levels of sulphur dioxide in the air by implementing Directive 1999/32/EC on the Sulphur Content of Certain Liquid Fuels (Sulphur Directive).[9] From 1 January 2008, the limit on the sulphur content of light heating oil will be cut by 50 per cent to 0.1 per cent. For heavy heating oil, that limit is set at 1 per cent and has been in effect since 1 January 2003.

Further adaptation will be required in the near future to accommodate Community legislation, in particular Directive 2002/3/EC relating to Ozone in Ambient Air (Ozone Directive),[10] which has been adopted as the third daughter directive of the Air Quality Framework Directive; and Directive 2001/81/EC on National Emission Ceilings for Certain Atmospheric Pollutants (NEC Directive).[11] In this regard, the Federal Government has already submitted a draft Ordinance on the Reduction of Summer Smog, Acidification and

[6] Erste Allgemeine Verwaltungsvorschrift zum Bundes-Immissionsschutzgesetz (Technische Anleitung zur Reinhaltung der Luft—TA Luft), GMBl. 2002, 511.

[7] [1996] OJ L275/26.

[8] Dritte Verordnung zur Durchführung des Bundes-Immissionsschutzgesetzes (Verordnung über den Schwefelgehalt bestimmter flüssiger Kraft-oder Brennstoffe—3. BImSchV), BGBl. I 2002, 2244.

[9] [1999] OJ L121/13.

[10] [2002] OJ L67/14.

[11] [2001] OJ L309/22.

Eutrophication.[12] Another draft[13] sees to the adaptation of the Seventeenth Emission Control Ordinance[14] to the new Directive 2000/76/EC on the Incineration of Waste (Waste Incineration Directive).[15] Finally, a draft amendment of the Ordinance on Large Combustion Plants (the Thirteenth Emission Control Ordinance)[16] brings about some necessary changes pursuant to the new Directive 2001/80/EC on the Limitation of Emissions of Certain Pollutants into the Air from Large Combustion Plants (Large Combustion Plants Directive).[17]

It is also worth noting that an Ordinance on the Amendment of Emission Control Legislation of 6 May 2002[18] has altered the Twenty-First Emission Control Ordinance.[19] It requires the gradual establishment of an automatic surveillance system for vapour recovery systems at petrol pumps.

C. Biotechnology

The Second Act Amending the Act on Genetic Engineering[20] aims at implementing Directive 98/81/EC amending Directive 90/219/EEC on the Contained Use of Genetically Modified Micro-Organisms (Contained Use Directive).[21] It also alleviates permit and control procedures for (scientific) activities involving genetic engineering.

D. Chemicals

On 28 June 2002, the Act on Biocidal Products[22] entered into force, followed on 7 July 2002 by the Ordinance on Biocidal Products.[23] These instruments

[12] Published on the Internet at: http://www.bmu.de/de/1024/js/download/b_vo.

[13] Published on the Internet at: http://www.bmu.de/de/800/js/download/b_bimsch.

[14] Siebzehnte Verordnung zur Durchführung des Bundes-Immissionsschutzgesetzes (Verordnung über Verbrennungsanlagen für Abfälle und ähnliche brennbare Stoffe—17. BImSchV), BGBl. I 1990, 2545, 2832.

[15] [2000] OJ L332/91.

[16] Published on the Internet at: http://www.bmu.de/de/1024/js/download/b_immission_dreizehn.

[17] [2001] OJ L309/1.

[18] Verordnung zur Änderung immissionsschutzrechtlicher Vorschriften, BGBl. I 2002, 1566.

[19] Einundzwanzigste Verordnung zur Durchführung des Bundes-Immissionsschutzgesetzes (Verordnung zur Begrenzung der Kohlenwasserstoffemissionen bei der Betankung von Kraftfahrzeugen—21. BImSchV), BGBl. I 1992, 1730.

[20] Zweites Gesetz zur Änderung des Gentechnikgesetzes (2. GenTG-ÄndG), BGBl. I 2002, 3220.

[21] [1998] OJ L330/13.

[22] Gesetz zur Umsetzung der Richtlinie 98/8/EG des Europäischen Parlaments und des Rates vom 16. Februar 1998 über das Inverkehrbringen von Biozid-Produkten (Biozidgesetz), BGBl. I 2002, 2076.

[23] Verordnung zur Umsetzung der Richtlinie 98/8/EG des Europäischen Parlaments und des Rates vom 16. Februar 1998 über das Inverkehrbringenvon Biozid-Produkten und zur Änderung chemikalienrechtlicher Verordnungen, BGBl. I 2002, 2514.

implement the Directive 98/8/EC concerning the Placing of Biocidal Products on the Market (Biocides Directive).[24] As a result, the licensing, marketing, and use of biocidal products are regulated in a comprehensive way in Germany. These new provisions have resulted in an amendment of the Chemicals Act, which now contains a separate chapter on biocides. The Biocidal Act focuses on the conditions for licensing.

E. Nature Conservation

i. Nature Conservation Act

On 4 April 2002, a new Nature Conservation Act entered into force,[25] adapting the previous Act (dating from 1976) to current Community legislation and the principle of sustainable nature conservation. Given that the federal act is limited to establishing a legal framework, it will be up to the individual *Länder* to amend their respective nature conservation acts. One of the fundamental elements of the new law is the promotion of sustainable agriculture by defining clear requirements of good practice (e.g. limiting the use of fertilizers and imposing documentation duties). The participatory rights of citizens in the legislative process are strengthened and associations granted legal standing (for the first time on a nationwide basis). The *Länder* may extend this right to further procedures and issues. Besides updating the process of designating protection areas, the new act establishes a network of connected biotopes comprised of at least 10 per cent of the overall area assigned to the conservation of biological diversity. Furthermore, the amendment plays a role in restructuring the energy supply in Germany, establishing conditions for the use of offshore wind energy, in particular in the Exclusive Economic Zone (EEZ) within 12 and 200 sea miles off the coast. The Government will be able to designate conservation areas in the EEZ in accordance with Directive 79/409/EEC on the Conservation of Wild Birds (Birds Directive)[26] and Directive 92/43/EEC on the Conservation of Natural Habitats and of Wild Fauna and Flora (Habitats Directive).[27]

ii. Habitats and Birds Directives

The concepts of *de facto* protection areas developed by the European Court of Justice (ECJ) or potential special protection areas (SPAs) developed by the *Bundesverwaltungsgericht* (Federal Administrative Court), continued to keep the courts busy.[28] In a decision of 31 January 2002,[29] concerning the Baltic

[24] [1998] OJ L123/1.

[25] Gesetz zur Neuregelung des Rechts des Naturschutzes und der Landschaftspflege und zur Anpassung anderer Rechtsvorschriften (BNatSchNeuregG), BGBl. I 2002, 1193.

[26] [1979] OJ L103/1.

[27] [1992] OJ L206/7.

[28] See also M. Rodi, 'Germany' (2003) 3 *Yearbook of European Environmental Law*, 616–17.

[29] *Bundesverwaltungsgericht* Case 4 A 15/01, (2002) 21 *Neue Zeitschrift für Verwaltungsrecht*, 1103; (2002) 117 *Deutsches Verwaltungsblatt*, 990; (2002) 24 *Natur und Recht*, 539.

Sea Motorway (A20) crossing at Wakenitz, an ecologically sensitive area north of Hamburg, the Federal Administrative Court specified and modified its jurisprudence on the concepts of nature protection areas. In line with standing ECJ case law, *de facto* bird protection areas have to be protected in accordance with the strict criteria of Article 4(4) of the Birds Directive.[30] Member States have a certain degree of discretion based on scientific findings in deciding which areas are most suitable for the conservation of endangered species according to Article 4(1) and (2) of the Directive.[31] According to the Federal Administrative Court, quantitative and qualitative criteria determine the ornithological value of an area. Qualitative criteria refer to the sensitivity and the level of the threat to specific species and their specific requirements regarding habitats. Quantitative criteria refer to the overall quantity of species living in a specific area in relevant numbers. Moreover, the Court modified its jurisprudence regarding potential SPAs. In the past, the existence of such an area was assumed when it fulfilled the criteria of Article 4(1) of the Birds Directive and if its integration into a coherent ecological network seemed plausible, or the only reasonable choice.[32] According to a recent decision, however, this shall henceforth be the case when habitats and species in the sense of Annex I or II are present in the area and clearly fulfil the criteria of Annex III (phase 1). Thus, it is no longer sufficient that the nomination of an area may be justifiable under the preceding criteria on the basis of a scientific assessment. A potential protection area requires that no doubts remain in the scientific assessment as to whether the criteria of Annex III are met, so that notification becomes compulsory.

In a ruling of 17 May 2002,[33] the Federal Administrative Court elaborated on the assessment of alternative solutions under Article 6(4) of the Habitats Directive. Alternative solutions have to be assessed whenever a project is expected to have a significant negative effect on a site in a special area of conservation (SAC). In that case, the court treated a potential SAC as a site of Community importance listed in accordance with Article 4(2); it argued that the protection regime of Article 6 had to be directly applicable, as the Commission possessed no discretion in including the site on the list as an area of priority natural habitat types or priority species. In examining the existence of alternative solutions, it further specified and broadened its quite narrow understanding of project alternatives as

30 Case C-374/98, *Commission* v. *France* [2000] ECR I-10837.

31 See e.g. Case C-355/90, *Commission* v. *Spain* [1993] ECR I-4221; Case C-3/96, *Commission* v. *The Netherlands* [1998] ECR I-3031; also *Bundesverwaltungsgericht* Case 4 A 15/02, (2003) 22 *Neue Zeitschrift für Verwaltungsrecht*, 485; (2003) 118 *Deutsches Verwaltungsblatt*, 534.

32 *Bundesverwaltungsgericht* Case 4 A 9/97, (1998) 17 *Neue Zeitschrift für Verwaltungsrecht*, 96; (1999) 107 *Entscheidungen des Bundesverwaltungsgerichts*, 1; *Bundesverwaltungsgericht* Case 4 C 2/99, (2000) 19 *Neue Zeitschrift für Verwaltungsrecht*, 1171; (2001) 110 *Entscheidungen des Bundesverwaltungsgerichts*, 302; *Bundesverwaltungsgericht* Case 6 B 23/00, (2001) 20 *Neue Zeitschrift für Verwaltungsrecht*, 92; (2001) 116 *Deutsches Verwaltungsblatt*, 375.

33 *Bundesverwaltungsgericht*, Case 4 A 28/01, (2002) 21 *Neue Zeitschrift für Verwaltungsrecht*, 1243; (2002) 117 *Deutsches Verwaltungsblatt*, 1486; (2002) 24 *Natur und Recht*, 739; (2003) 116 *Entscheidungen des Bundesverwaltungsgerichts*, 254.

developed in its first decision concerning the Baltic Sea Motorway. In order to discern an alternative from a different project, the Court referred to the objectives and purposes of the original project. Under that test, a project would remain an alternative whenever the objective(s) could be reached, even if that occurred in a less than optimum manner; the duty of assessing alternatives would lose its purpose if the exact same degree of objective achievement were required. If a project is thereby found to be an alternative and not another project, a further step requires an assessment of its feasibility, which is assumed if there are no obstacles of a legal or practical nature. In this regard, the Federal Administrative Court clarified that the criteria used to assess alternatives on the basis of Article 6 of the Habitats Directive differed from those in national planning law. An alternative in the sense of the Directive constitutes a legal obstacle to the project, and cannot be overcome by way of the balancing of interests known in German planning law. In view of the character of Article 6(4) of the Directive, which is designed as an exception, that could only be done in line with the concept of the greatest possible protection of protected habitats and species.

F. Waste

i. Packaging Waste—Deposit Scheme

In the area of waste law, legal and political controversy centred on a compulsory deposit to be levied on the packaging of certain beverages from 1 January 2003 onward. A deposit is to be charged on the packaging of beer, mineral water, and carbonated soft drinks, irrespective of the type of packaging (i.e. cans, disposable glass, or disposable plastic bottles). This requirement already applied under the regulatory system of the 1991 Packaging Ordinance, which remained unchanged in this regard after the 1998 amendment.[34] According to that rule, producers and purchasers are obliged to take back product packaging at the place of sale or delivery. This burdensome obligation can be averted by installing a collective and functioning recycling system on a private basis. Against that legal background, the company Duales System Deutschland Ltd, known for its identifying label, the *Grüne Punkt* ('green dot'), collected, *inter alia*, disposable beverage packaging. A legal condition imposed on such activity under Articles 8(1) and 9(2) of the Packaging Ordinance is the achievement of a minimum collection and reusage quota of 72 per cent per year. Should the quota fall below that limit for two consecutive years, the privilege of collective recycling on a private basis ends, with a return to the obligations of taking back packaging and levying a deposit for the beverage packaging in question. According to a survey by the Federal Government, such a violation of the minimum quota had occurred in 2000 and 2001, and thus the obligation to charge deposits entered into force

[34] Verordnung über die Vermeidung und Verwertung von Verpackungsabfällen (Verpackungsverordnung—VerpackV), BGBl. I 1998, 2379.

automatically on 1 January 2003. All legal proceedings by the manufacturers and traders seeking temporary relief remained unsuccessful.[35] Regarding a pending constitutional complaint, the *Bundesverfassungsgericht* (Federal Constitutional Court)[36] made clear that this was not yet a final decision on the legality of the deposit system. Only the Administrative Court of Düsseldorf[37] has so far held the opinion that there was no sufficient legal basis in the Waste Law and Recycling Act.[38] However, this decision was overruled by the Federal Administrative Court on the basis of procedural issues.[39] Moreover, the compatibility of the packaging Ordinance with EC law is still unclear. The Administrative Court of Stuttgart[40] submitted a case to the ECJ, regarding the compatibility of Paragraphs 6, 8, and 9 of the Ordinance with Directive 94/62/EEC on Packaging and Packaging Waste (Packaging and Packaging Waste Directive),[41] and Article 28 EC.

ii. End-of-Life Vehicles

On 1 July 2002, the Act on the Disposal of End-of-Life Vehicles entered into force,[42] adopted to implement Directive 2000/53/EC on End-of-Life Vehicles (ELV Directive).[43] Its main objective is to ensure that end-of-life vehicles (ELVs) can be returned to the producer (or importer) free of charge from 2007 onwards (for vehicles bought after July 2002, that date is brought forward to July 2003). Manufacturers, importers of cars, and operators of disposal facilities have to reach specific quotas of exploitation and recycling.

iii. Waste Oil

In its judgment of 9 September 1999 in Case C-102/97,[44] the ECJ had sentenced Germany for not fully complying with Directive 87/101/EEC amending Directive 75/439/EEC on the Disposal of Waste Oils (Waste Oil Directive).[45]

[35] See e.g. *Oberverwaltungsgericht Berlin*, Case 2 S 6/01, (2002) 117 *Deutsches Verwaltungsblatt*, 630; (2002) 15 *NVwZ-Rechtsprechungs-Report*, 720; *Oberverwaltungsgericht Berlin*, Case 2 S 44/02, confirmed by *Bundesverfassungsgericht*, Case 1 BvR 2305/02; *Oberverwaltungsgericht Münster*, Case 7 VR 1/02, confirmed by *Bundesverfassungsgericht*, Case 1 BvR 2351/02.

[36] *Bundesverfassungsgericht*, Case 1 BvR 2351/02.

[37] *Verwaltungsgericht Düsseldorf*, Case 17 K 1907/02, (2002) 21 *Neue Zeitschrift für Verwaltungsrecht*, 1269; dissenting *Verwaltungsgericht Berlin*, Case 10 A 349/02.

[38] Gesetz zur Förderung der Kreislaufwirtschaft und der Sicherung der umweltverträglichen Beseitigung von Abfällen (Kreislaufwirtschafts- und Abfallgesetz-KrW-/AbfG), BGBl. I 1994, 2705.

[39] *Bundesverwaltungsgericht*, Case 7 C 31/02.

[40] *Verwaltungsgericht Stuttgart*, Case 19 K 2019/02, (2002) 21 *Neue Zeitschrift für Verwaltungsrecht*, 1274; (2002) 55 *Neue Juristische Wochenschrift*, 3656.

[41] [1994] OJ L365/10.

[42] Gesetz über die Entsorgung von Altfahrzeugen (Altfahrzeug-Gesetz—AltfahrzeugG), BGBl. I 2002, 2199.

[43] [2000] OJ L269/34.

[44] Case C-102/97, *Commission* v. *Germany* [1999] ECR I-5051.

[45] [1987] OJ L42/43.

Above all, Germany was condemned for not having established the primacy of processing waste oil to base oil in the Waste Oil Regulation of 1987.[46] On 16 April 2002, the requisite amendment was finally adopted by Germany, thereby introducing said primacy.[47]

iv. Landfill of Waste

A new Ordinance on Landfill of Waste[48] comprehensively regulates landfills and long-term storage facilities in accordance with the state of the art of technology. Together with the Ordinance on the Storage of Waste from Human Settlements,[49] it aims at fully implementing Directive 1999/31/EC on Landfill of Waste (Waste Landfill Directive).[50] The Ordinance on Landfill of Waste sets up detailed technical and organizational requirements as to the establishment, features, operation, shutdown, and post-shutdown maintenance of landfills and long-term storage facilities. In particular, it focuses on standards of reference requiring special advance treatment of a number of waste types. As a result, the quantity of waste and the amount of harmful substances will (supposedly) be reduced, making landfill sites safer, in combination with requirements regarding the choice of location, the underground foundation as well as sealing systems.

v. Commercial Wastes

The Commercial Wastes Ordinance of 19 June 2002,[51] which entered into force on 1 January 2003, aims at counteracting the practice of mixing different kinds of waste in order to circumvent the obligation of making waste available to parties responsible for waste disposal. According to Article 3 of the Ordinance, producers and those in possession of commercial waste are under an obligation to keep certain types of reusable waste (e.g. paper, cardboard, glass, plastic, and metal) separate from waste that cannot be recycled. Such waste must be made available to the competent parties responsible for waste management, according to Article 7. Pre-treatment facilities for mixed wastes are only allowed under the condition that a recovery quota of at least 85 per cent is reached on an average annual basis (Articles 5 and 7). This Ordinance reacts to a practice previously backed by the judiciary: producers and those in possession of commercial waste have traditionally tried to circumvent the obligation of making waste available

[46] Altölverordnung, BGBl. I 1987, 2335.

[47] Verordnung zur Änderung abfallrechtlicher Bestimmungen zur Altölentsorgung, BGBl. I 2002, 1360.

[48] Verordnung über Deponien und Langzeitlager (Deponieverordnung—DepV), Art. 1 der Verordnung über Deponien und Langzeitlager und zur Änderung der Abfallablagerungsverordnung, BGBl. I 2002, 2807.

[49] Verordnung über die umweltverträgliche Ablagerung von Siedlungsabfällen (Abfallablagerungsverordnung—AbfAblV), BGBl. I 2001, 305.

[50] [1999] OJ L182/1.

[51] Verordnung über die Entsorgung von gewerblichen Siedlungsabfällen und von bestimmten Bau- und Abbruchabfällen (Gewerbeabfallverordnung—GewAbfV), BGBl. I 2002, 1938.

for disposal to the responsible public entities, because the entities engaged in waste recycling are, as a rule, private entities offering services at lower prices. Thus, producers and those in possession of commercial waste have tended to 'escape' into recycling by declaring waste 'reusable'. This was made possible by the practice of mixing waste that had originally been separated. In accordance with case law of the Federal Administrative Court,[52] such combined waste has been treated as a homogeneous type of waste as long as the combination did not interfere with any applicable duties to keep waste separate. Since the Court could not identify any such obligations, the producers and other persons in possession of commercial waste could intentionally mix their waste in a specific manner to avoid the obligation of delivering waste for disposal.

G. Water

i. Federal Water Management Act

The Federal Water Management Act was amended on 25 June 2002,[53] mainly to implement Directive 2000/60/EC establishing a Framework for Community Action in the Field of Water Policy (Water Framework Directive).[54] The Directive aims at an integrated concept of water management. The amendment of the national act introduces some new definitions (e.g. river basin district) and integrates terrestrial ecosystems and wetlands into the scope of the legal framework, provided these depend directly on the ecological functions of water. Furthermore, it implements the management of water resources on the basis of river basin areas and the obligation to coordinate the transboundary management of water resources between different *Länder*.[55] This includes setting up an inventory, assessing the status quo, and determining far-reaching planning and measure programmes. It sets up new ecological management objectives for ground, coastal, and surface water. As the Water Management Act is a framework act, many detailed provisions will have to be set up by the *Länder*. The greatest challenge basis for the legislature and administration in this regard will be the implementation of transboundary coordination.

ii. Waste-Water

According to the Federal Water Act, the discharge of waste-water can only be authorized if the pollutant discharge is kept at a minimum through application of appropriate procedures by using the best available technology (BAT). The

[52] See *Bundesverwaltungsgericht*, Case 3 C 4/00, (2000) 19 *Neue Zeitschrift für Verwaltungsrecht*, 1178.

[53] Siebtes Gesetz zur Änderung des Wasserhaushaltsgesetzes, BGBl. I 2002, 1914.

[54] [2000] OJ L327/1.

[55] Ten in Germany: Danube, Rhine, Meuse, Ems, Weser, Elbe, Eider, Oder, Schlei/Trave, and Warnow/Peene.

Waste-Water Ordinance defines this standard more precisely. The Fifth amendment of the Waste-Water Ordinance, of 2 July 2002,[56] provides a common standard for waste-water from municipalities and from seven industrial and commercial sectors. It implements, *inter alia*, provisions of Directive 91/271/EEC on Urban Waste-Water Treatment (Urban Waste-Water Directive),[57] and Directive 2000/76/EC on the Incineration of Waste (Waste Incineration Directive).[58]

H. Energy

i. Heat and Power Co-Generation

On 1 April 2002, the new Heat and Power Co-Generation Act[59] entered into force, replacing its predecessor of 12 May 2000.[60] It aims at safeguarding, promoting, and modernizing energy production in combined heat and power plants, and also seeks to facilitate the market introduction of fuel cells. In line with the Renewable Energies Act, the electricity from combined heat and power plants is promoted through attractive fixed rates paid by the grid operators in addition to the current market price. These supplementary rates are calculated on a degressive basis and are differentiated in accordance with the type of production plant.

ii. Energy Efficiency

Another instrument of climate change policy, the Energy Saving Ordinance of 16 November 2001,[61] largely entered into force on 1 February 2002. Its objective is the reduction of energy consumption by establishing standards for the heating and insulation of buildings. It implements several Community directives and integrates the Insulation Ordinance and the Heating Plant Ordinance, which expired on 1 February 2002. Energy used for the heating of rooms and warm water production, in particular, will be reduced by its provisions. Energy consumption patterns within new buildings will henceforth be restricted to a standard based on the benchmark of 'low energy buildings'. Moreover, the ordinance introduces technology standards for certain facilities, new documentation procedures, and facilitated use of renewable energy sources. As for existing buildings, stricter energy standards are introduced whenever the building

[56] Fünfte Verordnung zur Änderung der Abwasserverordnung, BGBl. I 2002, 2497.

[57] [1991] OJ L135/40.

[58] [2000] OJ L332/91.

[59] Gesetz für die Erhaltung, die Modernisierung und den Ausbau der Kraft-Wärme-Kopplung (Kraft-Wärme-Kopplungsgesetz—KWKG), BGBl. I 2002, 1092.

[60] Gesetz zum Schutz der Stromerzeugung aus Kraft-Wärme-Kopplung (Kraft-Wärme-Kopplungsgesetz), BGBl. I 2000, 703.

[61] Verordnung über energiesparenden Wärmeschutz und energiesparende Anlagentechnik bei Gebäuden (Energieeinsparverordnung—EnEV), BGBl. I 2001, 3085.

undergoes significant alterations, and certain older boiler models will have to be shut down. There will also be new requirements regarding thermal insulation of upper floor ceilings and piping.

iii. Wind Power Generation

The generation of wind power typically results in a conflict with established principles of noise emission control and landscape conservation.[62] During 2002, again, these conflicts occupied the administrative courts. In a ruling of 17 December 2002,[63] the Federal Administrative Court had to decide on issues of planning law. In order to promote this source of renewable energy, wind power plants erected in areas outside of municipalities are privileged under building legislation. This privilege has been combined with a planning instrument for municipalities, enhancing the balanced development of rural areas in order to avoid a deterioration of the landscape. It authorizes municipalities to determine the location of wind power plants in their local development plans. The Court recently issued a decision on the conditions and extent of this competence. Municipalities are not allowed to withhold their entire terrain from the establishment of wind power plants. Moreover, they may not designate unsuitable areas, effectively preventing rather than coordinating the erection of windmills. On the other side, municipalities are not obliged to designate all suitable areas, either. In the event of planning conflicts arising between the promotion of wind energy and other public interests, the municipality may decide in favour of the latter whenever justified by important reasons of urban planning.

I. Horizontal Instruments

i. Eco-Management and Audit Scheme

The national provisions on the eco-management and audit scheme (EMAS) have been adapted to Regulation (EC) No. 761/2001 allowing Voluntary Participation by Organizations in a Community Eco-Management and Audit Scheme (EMAS).[64] The corresponding Implementation Act[65] entered into force on 21 August 2002.[66] The most relevant changes include (i) facilitated participation for enterprises with more than one site by allowing registration of an 'organization'

[62] Some conflicts of maritime windmill parks with nature conservation law have recently been regulated in the new Nature Conservation Act, n. 25 above.

[63] *Bundesverwaltungsgericht*, Case 4 C 15/01, (2003) 22 *Neue Zeitschrift für Verwaltungsrecht*, 733.

[64] [2001] OJ L114/1.

[65] Gesetz zur Ausführung der Verordnung (EG) No. 761/2001 des Europäischen Parlaments und des Rates vom 19. März 2001 über die freiwillige Beteiligung von Organisationen an einem Gemeinschaftssystem für das Umweltmanagement und die Umweltbetriebsprüfung (EMAS) (Umweltauditgesetz—UAG), BGBl. I 2002, 3187.

[66] Gesetz zur Änderung des Umweltauditgesetzes, BGBl. I 2002, 3167.

rather than individual sites, (ii) stricter supervision of environmental verifiers or verifying organizations by introduction of regular supervision, at least once every two years, and (iii) even greater commitment to the objective of having only such organizations registered under EMAS which fully comply with their environmental obligations. Participating organizations are dedicated to improving their environmental performance. As part of the auditing process, they are also required to forward a verified statement of their performance to the public. This voluntary commitment can then be rewarded on the basis of the so-called Ordinance on Privileges,[67] which, for instance, can provide for more lenient supervision in the ambit of command-and-control regulation. Moreover, authorities must take documents on EMAS participation into account during permit procedures.

ii. Eco-Taxation

The Act on the Further Development of the Ecological Tax Reform of 23 December 2002[68] is the third act within the ecological tax reform. In 1999, the first Act implemented the ecological tax reform,[69] while the second Act increased the tax rates for energy in several steps.[70] The new third Act seeks to eliminate some weaknesses and reform the system of tax abatements. Thus, the reduced tax rate for industry, agriculture, and forestry is raised from 20 per cent to 60 per cent. This will not, however, significantly improve the overall ecological outcome, as the *Spitzenausgleich* (tax cap) has been retained, albeit in an amended guise. This system limits the payable tax burden in accordance with the benefits gained by companies from revenue recycling (reduced social insurance contributions). Under previous legislation, the eco-tax was refunded to the extent that the burden arising from these increased tax rates was 1.2 times greater than the tax relief gained from reductions in social security contributions. This system has now been changed, as it places labour-intensive industries at a disadvantage. According to the new rules, 95 per cent of the taxes paid in excess of benefits will be refunded.

J. Miscellaneous

i. Noise

The new Ordinance on Technical Devices and Mechanical Noise[71] implements Directive 2000/14/EC relating to the Noise Emission in the Environment by

[67] Verordnung zum Erlass und zur Änderung immissionsschutzrechtlicher und abfallrechtlicher Verordnungen, BGBl. I 2002, 2247.

[68] Gesetz zur Fortentwicklung der ökologischen Steuerreform, BGBl. I 2002, 4602.

[69] Ersten Gesetz zum Einstieg in die ökologische Steuerreform, BGBl. I 1999, 378.

[70] Zweiten Gesetz zur Fortführung der ökologischen Steuerreform, BGBl. I 1999, 2432.

[71] Verordnung zur Einführung der Geräte- und Maschinenlärmschutzverordnung, BGBl. I 2002, 3478.

Equipment for Use Outdoors.[72] It replaces several specific ordinances on noise control and affects 57 different kinds of appliances and machines for outdoors operation. All these devices have to carry a label indicating noise emission limits guaranteed by the producer. Particularly loud appliances and machines have to respect emission standards that will be further tightened after four years. In addition to these provisions regulating market access and commerce, the Ordinance sets up new rules limiting the use of such appliances in specific areas, such as residential zones.

ii. Nuclear Law and Radiological Protection

On 27 April 2002, the Act on the Structured Phase-out of the Utilization of Nuclear Energy for the Commercial Generation of Electricity[73] entered into force. It is based on an agreement of 14 July 2000 between the Government and the four biggest energy supply companies.[74] It changes the purpose of the Act from promoting nuclear energy to a structured phase-out, according to Article 1. Key features are a ban on the construction of new commercial nuclear power plants and a limitation of the residual operating life of existing nuclear power plants to 32 years from the time of their first operation. This is calculated on the basis of a maximum permitted residual electricity volume for each individual power plant, which can be transferred to newer plants. Waste management is now restricted to direct final disposal. Operators will be obliged to erect and use interim storage facilities at the location of the respective plants.

The amendments of the Radiological Protection Ordinance[75] and the X-Ray Ordinance,[76] both of 18 June 2002, were primarily aimed at implementing Directive 96/29/Euratom, Laying Down Basic Safety Standards for the Protection of the Health of Workers and the General Public against the Dangers arising from Ionizing Radiation,[77] Directive 97/43/Euratom on Health Protection of Individuals against the Dangers of Ionizing Radiation in Relation to Medical Exposure and Repealing Directive 84/466/Euratom.[78] They reduce the limit values for the population to 1 millisievert (mSv) per year and for those exposed to radioactivity through their occupation to 20 mSv per year.

[72] [2000] OJ L162/1.

[73] Gesetz zur geordneten Beendigung der Kernenergienutzung zur gewerblichen Erzeugung von Elektrizität, BGBl. I 2002, 1351.

[74] See the Supplement to (2000) 19 *Neue Zeitschrift für Verwaltungsrecht*.

[75] Art. 2 Verordnung zur Änderung der Röntgenverordnung und anderer atomrechtlicher Verordnungen, BGBl. I 2002, 1869.

[76] Art. 1 Verordnung zur Änderung der Röntgenverordnung und anderer atomrechtlicher Verordnungen, BGBl. I 2002, 1869.

[77] [1996] OJ L159/1.

[78] [1997] OJ L180/22.

VII. Greece

*Christopher Petrou**

A. Introduction

The dominant influence of European Community (EC) legislation and funding on Greek environmental policy during 2002 seems to have pushed national objectives and priorities to the background, to some extent. Greece typically follows up closely and contributes regularly to the development of international and European environmental policy, as it participates in all relevant proceedings.[1] At the United Nations (UN) World Summit on Sustainable Development (Johannesburg Summit)[2] in September 2002, Greece presented two important policy proposals. First, the Type II Initiative on 'Water for the Poor', part of the European Union (EU) Water for Life Initiative, was focused on the reduction of the number of people in Mediterranean countries without access to safe and clean water and to sanitation.[3] Secondly, Greece officially announced the Type II Initiative for education and the creation of nuclei of trainers for the environment and sustainability, belonging to a single Mediterranean Network.

Also in 2002, Greece made fundamental amendments to Law 1650/1986 on the protection of the environment (Environmental Protection Framework Law),[4] with the adoption of a new Law 3010/2002,[5] in order fully to transpose Directive 97/11/EC amending Directive 85/337/EEC on the Assessment of the Effects of certain Public and Private Projects on the Environment (EIA Directive)[6] and Directive 96/61/EC on Integrated Pollution Prevention and Control (IPPC Directive).[7]

In addition, a comprehensive national legislative plan for the environment, based on a wide-ranging administrative and economic process and setting specific legal objectives and targets, was established in order to better achieve and substantiate Greece's ambition to build on its natural and cultural heritage. For this purpose, the development strategy of the Community Support Framework III (CSF) 2000–2006 established basic objectives in order to combat unemployment, to promote equal opportunities of education and training, to reinforce the

* Senior Researcher at the European Public Law Center, University of Athens; Legal Advisor at the Ministry of Foreign Affairs; Lawyer in the Athens Bar Association, Athens (Greece).

[1] Greece has ratified all relevant international Conventions, or is in the process of doing so.

[2] Johannesburg (South Africa), 26 Aug.–4 Sept. 2002.

[3] The proposal was supported by other Mediterranean countries, international institutions (OECD, UNEP, World Bank), NGO, and the private sector.

[4] Official Gazette, Vol. A, 160.

[5] Official Gazette, Vol. A, 117, 30 May 2002.

[6] [1997] OJ L73/5.

[7] [1996] OJ L275/26.

industrial foundation of the country, and to promote new technologies through the integration of the major infrastructure investments, that is, natural gas, electricity, oil, and so on.

The Council of State also played a positive role in defining the content of framework environmental legislation and providing a practical interpretation of the term 'sustainable development'.[8] In 2001, important modifications were made to Article 24 of the Greek Constitution, including the introduction of an explicit right to an environment protected by the State.[9] This new right is highly important in that it provides consolidation of citizens' legal resistance against activities that threaten the environment and intervention for the preventive guarantee of ecological balance. Concomitant with this right, the State now has a formal obligation to prevent or repress activities that harm the natural and cultural environment.[10] With this consolidated individual environmental right, citizens now have an explicitly recognized opportunity actively to pursue protection of the environment, either individually or represented by ecological non-governmental organizations (NGOs). The new right has already been subject to judicial review, during 2002. In its judgment No. 613/2002, the High Court of Greece held that the protection of the natural and cultural environment under the new Article 24(1) of the Constitution constitutes an obligation for the State.

B. Atmospheric Pollution

The Environmental Protection Framework Law[11] established the basic framework for the development of air management policy and made provisions for the monitoring, prevention, and control of air pollution. Within this framework, EC Directives also formed the legal basis for air management regulation in Greece. However, the Commission decided to take legal action against Greece for failing to transpose (adequately) Community secondary legislation on air quality and air emissions, and in June 2002 issued a Reasoned Opinion concerning Greece's failure to adopt the requisite legislation to transpose Directive 1999/13/EC on the Limitation of Emissions of Volatile Organic Compounds Due to the Use of Organic Solvents in Certain Activities and Installations (Solvent Emissions Directive).[12]

[8] Council of State No. 613/2002.

[9] See G. Sioutis and C. Petrou, 'Greece' (2003) 3 *Yearbook of European Environmental Law*, 627.

[10] See G. Sioutis, 'La protection de l'environnement depuis la revision constitutionnelle de 2001' (2002) 3 *Revue Européenne de Droit de l'Environnement*, 39–50; G. Sioutis, *Constitutional Guarantees of Environmental Protection* (Athens/Komotini: Ant. N. Sakkoulas Publishing, 1985), 119–24; G. Sioutis, *Environmental Law—Public Law and the Environment* (Athens/Komotini: Ant. N. Sakkoulas Publishing, 1993), 41–64; G. Sioutis, 'Public Environmental Law in Greece' in R. Seerden and M. Heldeweg (eds.), *Comparative Environmental Law in Europe—An Introduction to Public Environmental Law in the EU Member States* (Antwerp: MAKLU, Ius Commune Europaeum Publishing, 1996), 193–211; and A. Tachos, *Law of Environmental Protection* (Thessaloniki: Ant. N. Sakkoulas Publishing, 1995), 50–4.

[11] n. 4 above.

[12] [1999] OJ L85/1.

According to the National Strategy for Sustainable Development and to the needs for enforcement and monitoring of air quality management, the reduction of air pollutants remains a matter of priority in Greek environmental policy. The need for a significant limitation of carbon dioxide (CO_2) emissions compared to the increase in energy, transport, and pollution, constitutes a principal area of action and measures for the reduction of environmental pressures.[13] In this context, on 10 December 2002, Joint Common Decision 8407/395 was adopted to implement Directive 2001/100/EC amending Directive 70/220/EEC on Measures to be taken Against Air Pollution by Emissions from Motor Vehicles.[14]

Furthermore, by Law 3017/2002,[15] Greece ratified the Kyoto Protocol[16] to the United Nations (UN) Framework Convention on Climate Change (UNFCCC).[17] This fits within the strategy to promote sustainable development and to implement and further elaborate national policies and measures with this aim. Greece considers climate change as one of the major environmental hazards, in view of the rising pressures of desertification, water scarcity, increased global temperature. Hence, Greece is committed not to increase the releases of the six greenhouses gases covered by the Kyoto Protocol by more than 25 per cent, as compared to 1990 emissions.

C. Chemicals

i. Classification, Packaging, and Labelling of Dangerous Substances

The Commission sent a Reasoned Opinion to Greece for its failure to adopt and communicate the texts required to implement (before the deadline of 1 June 2001) Directive 2000/32/EC Adapting to Technical Progress for the Twenty-Sixth Time Directive 67/548/EEC on the Classification, Packaging and Labelling of Dangerous Substances.[18] The procedure was eventually terminated in June 2002, after Greece had completed this implementation. It did so by a Joint Ministerial Decision of Ministers of National Economy and Economics of 31 January 2002, also transposing Directive 2000/33/EC Adapting to Technical Progress for the Twenty-Seventh Time Directive 67/548/EEC on the Classification, Packaging and Labelling of Dangerous Substances.[19] The Decision also

[13] Greece's emissions of CO_2 per unit of GDP are among the highest in the EU. Since the mid-1990s, the Ministry of Environment has launched a major restructuring of the energy sector, including a range of measures aimed at improving the fuel mix for electricity generation, primarily through the use of natural gas and promoting energy conservation in the transport, industrial, and residential and commercial sectors.

[14] [2002] OJ L16/32.

[15] Official Gazette, Vol. A, 1117, 30 Feb. 2002.

[16] Kyoto (Japan), 10 Dec. 1997 (not yet in force) (1998) 37 *International Legal Materials* 1, 22.

[17] New York, NY (United States), 9 May 1992 (entered into force on 21 Mar. 1994) (1992) 31 *International Legal Materials* 4, 849.

[18] [2000] OJ L136/1.

[19] [2000] OJ L136/90.

ensured transposition of Directive 2000/21/EC concerning the List of Community Legislation Referred to in the Fifth Indent of Article 13(1) of Directive 67/548/EEC.[20] The principal effects of this national measure were the adaptation to technical progress of physio-chemical properties, toxicity, and eco-toxicity of substances and preparations. It also updated the requirements for the protection of animals used for experimental and other scientific purposes.

Furthermore, in September 2002, Ministerial Decision 265 of the Minister of National Economy and Economics[21] transposed into national law Directive 2001/60/EC Adapting to Technical Progress Directive 1999/45/EC on Classification, Packaging and Labelling of Dangerous Preparations.[22]

ii. Biocides and Pesticides

As a result of Community requirements in the field of plant protection products, efforts have been made in Greece to develop a comprehensive strategy in this field. In this context, Greece adopted Joint Ministerial Decision 89648 of 25 February 2002,[23] and modified Presidential Decree 115/1997,[24] in order to improve the implementation of Directive 2001/36/EC amending Directive 91/414/EEC concerning the Placing of Plant Protection Products on the Market (Pesticides Directive).[25] The purpose of the Greek legislator was to improve the data requirements based on experience gained during the evaluation of several new active substances consisting of micro-organisms, in particular in view of the major developments as regards occupational health, consumer exposure, and environmental risks. Concomitantly, the 2001 amendments to Annex I of the Pesticides Directive[26] were incorporated into the national framework by Joint Ministerial Decision of the Ministers of National Economy and Economics 89619 of 19 February 2002, Joint Decision 102692 of 24 July 2002, and Joint Ministerial Decision of the Ministers of National Economy, Economics and Agriculture 93586 of 2 May 2002 amending Annex I of Presidential Decree 115/2997.[27] Henceforth, the Greek administration shall review existing author-

[20] [2000] OJ L103/70.

[21] Official Gazette, Vol. B, 1214, 19 Sept. 2002.

[22] [2001] OJ L226/5.

[23] Official Gazette, Vol. B, 241, 28 Feb. 2002.

[24] Official Gazette, Vol. A, 104.

[25] [2001] OJ L164/1.

[26] Dir. 2001/87/EC amending Annex I to Dir. 91/414/EEC concerning the Placing of Plant Protection Products on the Market to Include Acibenzolar-S-Methyl, Cyclanilide, Ferric Phosphate, Pymetrozine and Pyraflufen-Ethyl as Active Substances [2001] OJ L276/17; and Dir. 2001/99/EC amending Annex I to Dir. 91/414/EEC concerning the Placing of Plant Protection Products on the Market to Include Glyphosate and Thifensulfuron-Methyl as Active Substances [2001] OJ L304/14; and Dir. 2000/80/EC amending Annex I to Dir. 91/414/EEC concerning the Placing of Plant Protection Products on the Market, so as to Consolidate that Annex and Include a Further Active Substance (Lambda-Cyhalothrin) [2000] OJ L309/14; and Dir. 2001/21/EC amending Annex I to Dir. 91/414/EEC concerning the Placing of Plant Protection Products on the Market to Include Amitrole, Diquat, Pyridate and Thiabendazole as Active Substances [2001] OJ L69/17.

[27] Official Gazette, Vol. B, 602, 16 May 2002.

izations and shall grant new authorizations in accordance with these amended provisions, also by providing a longer period of time for the submission and assessment of the complete dossier of each plant protection product.

iii. PCBs and PCTs

The Commission issued a final written warning concerning Greece's failure adequately to transpose Directive 96/59/EC on the Disposal of Polychlorinated Byphenyls and Polychlorinated Terphenyls (PCB/PCT Directive).[28]

iv. Chemical Weapons

Law 2991/2002[29] gave effect to the United Nations (UN) Convention on the Prohibition of the Development, Production, Stockpiling and Use of Chemical Weapons and on their Destruction.[30]

D. Biotechnology

In accordance with EC legislation in the field of biotechnology, national regulations were adopted for research and development with, and the placing on the market and labelling and the use of, genetically modified organisms (GMOs). In this context, Greece adopted Joint Ministerial Decision 11642/1943 of 26 June 2002 of the Ministers of National Economy and Economics, of Interior Public Administration and Decentralization of Development, of Environment, Urban Planning, and Public Works, of Agriculture and of Providence.[31]

In Case C-371/01, *Commission* v. *Greece*[32] Advocate General (AG) Jacobs delivered his opinion on 6 June 2002, stating that Greece had failed to fulfil its obligations under the Treaty by not adopting within the prescribed time-limit the requisite measures to fully comply with Directive 98/81/EC amending Directive 90/219/EEC on the Contained Use of Genetically Modified Micro-Organisms (Contained Use Directive).[33]

E. Nature Conservation

Greece is characterized by a rich biodiversity in a wide variety of species and ecosystems. In 2002, 4 per cent of flora and 22 per cent of fauna in Greece was considered endangered.[34] During the survey year, as in recent years, several

28 [1996] OJ L 243/31.

29 Official Gazette, Vol. A, 35, 27 Feb. 2002.

30 Paris (France), 13 Jan. 1993 (entered into force on 29 Apr. 1997) (1993) 32 *International Legal Materials* 3, 800–3.

31 Official Gazette, Vol. B, 831, 2 Aug. 2002.

32 Case C-371/01, *Commission* v. *Greece*, not yet reported.

33 [1998] OJ L330/13.

34 See N.S. Magaris, *Around Greece with a 'Skeptical Environmentalist'* (Athens: Ellenika Grammata, 2003).

measures were taken with the aim of conserving this biodiversity, also on an international level. For example, in June 2002 Greece ratified[35] the amendments to Article XXI of the Convention on International Trade in Endangered Species of Wild Fauna and Flora (CITES).[36] Also, with Law 3040/2002[37] Greece ratified the Agreement between the Hellenic and the Turkish Republics concerning the Cooperation on Plant Protection.[38] On the Community level, efforts were made towards the implementation of EC nature conservation laws, including the drafting of a national inventory of NATURA 2000 sites.[39] Noteworthy developments on the national level included the establishment of a Forest Cadastre, and of a new management body for National Marine Park of Zakynthos, and the publication of Law 2742/1999 on physical planning and sustainable development.[40]

i. Habitats Directive

On 30 January 2002, the European Court of Justice (ECJ) condemned Greece in Case C-103/00, *Commission* v. *Greece*[41] in an Article 226 EC procedure concerning Greece's failure to adopt measures to establish and implement an effective system of strict protection for the sea turtle *Caretta caretta* on the island of Zakinthos, as required by Article 12(1)(b) and (d) of Directive 92/43/EEC on the Conservation of Natural Habitats and of Wild Fauna and Flora (Habitats Directive).[42] On 4 and 5 September 2002, another official mission was conducted by representatives of the Commission. Although the representatives recognized that efforts had been made to comply with the judgment, they nonetheless concluded that gaps in the protection system remained. Most of the regulatory and implementing measures were still not in place, and illegal constructions and objects had not been removed from important turtle habitat beaches. Hence, in December 2002, the Commission again initiated proceedings against Greece, this time under Article 228 EC, and submitted a letter of formal notice.

ii. Birds Directive

A reasoned opinion was also sent to Greece for designating an insufficient number of special protection areas (SPAs) under Directive 79/409/EEC on the

[35] Law 3026/2002 of 28 June 2002.

[36] Washington, DC (US), 3 Mar. 1973; (1973) 12 *International Legal Materials* 5, 1085.

[37] Official Gazette Vol. A, 184, 9 Aug. 2002.

[38] Athens (Greece), 1 Nov. 2001 (entered into force 22 Feb. 2003).

[39] The Natura 2000 sites combined cover 18% of Greece's land surface (or approx. 2,360,000 hectares), excluding the entirely marine sites.

[40] See also C. Petrou, 'Les nouvelles tendances du droit de l'environnement en Grèce (du 1er janvier au 1er juin 2001)' (2001) 2 *Revue Européenne de Droit de l'Environnement*, 169–82.

[41] [2002] ECR I-1147.

[42] [1992] OJ L206/7.

Conservation of Wild Birds (Birds Directive).[43] The Greek list of SPAs as Natura 2000 sites was insufficient, according to the Commission. While some recent progress has been made and the number of designated SPAs now stands at 110, the Commission considers that a further 76 sites merit designation. The Commission also noted Greece's failure to properly protect the lagoon of Messolonghi-Aitolikon, a wetland internationally recognized as an important habitat for wild birds. The appropriate legal framework for ensuring the effective protection of the bird habitats in the lagoon is still not in place. In addition, the site is being adversely affected as a result of illegal construction projects and inadequate controls on waste disposal.

iii. Wild Fauna and Flora

The legislative framework for nature conservation dates from 1950, when Law 1469/1950 concerning the preservation of landscapes of outstanding beauty was adopted. Laws 996/1971 and 998/1979 developed the framework for a forestry code that also addressed the protection of flora, fauna, and habitats. Law 177/1975 established the legal framework for hunting control, elaborated by numerous ministerial decisions. In 1981, Greek Presidential Decree 1180/1981 on the protection of native flora and wildlife was adopted, listing 916 plants, 139 vertebrates, and 82 invertebrates. On 10 December 2002, Presidential Decree 365/2002[44] was adopted to transpose the new requirements set out by Directive 2000/29/EC on Protective Measures against the Introduction into the Community of Organisms Harmful to Plants or Plant Products and against their Spread within the Community.[45] However, following a complaint that the mortality rate of Eleonora's falcon, *Falco eleonorae*, a bird of prey on Crete was disturbingly high because of the over-use of pesticides, the Commission asked Greece for information on the specific measures it had taken to protect the species and to comply with EU nature conservation legislation.

F. Waste

The Commission issued a final written warning concerning Greece's failure adequately to transpose various EC waste laws regarding general waste management, shipments of waste, hazardous waste, landfill of waste, waste oils, packaging waste, and polychlorinated biphenyls (PCBs) and polychlorinated terphenyls (PCTs). These EU laws required that waste disposal operations be carried out safely, operated only if they have a permit and pose no risk to human health or the environment. They also set requirements for the safe movement of waste, stipulate strict conditions with regard to landfills, and seek to reduce waste

[43] [1979] OJ L103/1.
[44] Official Gazette, Vol. A, 307, 10 Dec. 2002.
[45] [2000] OJ L169/1.

from packaging. The Commission is concerned that by not implementing these laws correctly Greece will face problems such as illegal or poorly managed landfill sites.

i. Landfill of Waste

The production of solid wastes is an inevitable result of production processes and consumption. Greece has promoted several measures for the expansion and the organization of related infrastructure, conveying responsibility for planning and management of waste to the regions. The Greek authorities are implementing new regional plans to reduce the large number of landfill sites that are still operating illegally, and have stated that they have reduced the number of illegal sites from a total of 2,810 at the end of 2001 to 1,458 in May 2002.[46] However, despite such efforts, the problem still persists.[47] The lack of institutional, technical, and administrative measures for waste in Greece, and the large number of illegal or uncontrolled waste disposal sites, inspired action from the Commission. In 2002, it sent a Reasoned Opinion, and subsequently initiated infringement proceedings, against Greece for having failed to adopt and communicate to the Commission, by the deadline of 16 July 2001, national legislation to implement Directive 1999/31/EC on Landfill of Waste (Waste Landfill Directive).[48] Of particular concern was the fact that Greece had allowed numerous unauthorized landfill sites to operate illegally.

ii. Waste Oils

The Commission also issued a letter of formal notice to Greece for failure to comply with several provisions of Directive 87/101/EEC amending Directive 75/439/EEC on the Disposal of Waste Oils (Waste Oil Directive).[49] In particular, the Commission considered that the failure to implement technical measures in order to ensure the collection and safe disposal of waste oils and the failure to prioritize waste oil regeneration when there was no technical, economic, or organizational constraint to prevent this, to be a violation of the Waste Oil Directive.

iii. Hazardous Waste

Furthermore, Greece received a letter of formal notice to put in place an adequate plan for the management of hazardous waste in the region of Thriassio, near Athens, and to avoid the pollution of groundwater by hazardous waste, as required by Directive 91/156/EEC amending Directive 75/442/EEC on Waste (Waste Framework Directive).[50]

[46] See Petrou, n. 40 above.

[47] See C. Petrou, *Le régime de la protection de l'environnement dans le cadre de la Communauté Européenne* (Athens: Bruyant, 2000), 450–64.

[48] [1999] OJ L182/1.

[49] [1987] OJ L42/43.

[50] [1991] OJ L78/32.

iv. End-of-Life Vehicles

On 21 April 2002, the deadline for the implementation of Directive 2000/53/EC on End-of-Life Vehicles (ELV Directive)[51] passed, without Greece having adopted and communicated implementing measures. Hence, the Commission issued a Reasoned Opinion to ensure swift transposition. The adoption of Law 2992/2002[52] and Joint Ministerial Decision 1002901/67/2002[53] on procedures and conditions for the qualification of solid wastes as old vehicles does not appear to satisfy this requirement.

G. Water

i. Urban Waste-Water Treatment

The coastline of Greece stretches over 15,000 kilometres and there are approximately 3,000 Greek islands. Sixty per cent of the Greek population resides in the coastal areas. These areas are currently used mainly for tourism, fishing, and some urban development. For these areas, significant progress was made for waste-water management, as waste-water treatment plants now service approximately half of the national population. In addition, 98 per cent of the Greek coasts meet the standards set by Directive 76/160/EEC concerning the Quality of Bathing Water (Bathing Water Directive).[54] The national legislation on integrated coastal management aims at protecting water resources and establishes the measures and limits for solid waste management, keeping in mind the National Plan for the management of solid wastes. Notwithstanding this progress, the Commission brought an action against Greece for non-compliance with EU water quality legislation, in particular concerning surface water, bathing water, drinking water, shellfish water, urban waste-water, and nitrates. In addition, on two occasions the Commission referred Greece to the ECJ under Article 226 EC for non-implementation of Directive 91/271/EEC on Urban Waste-Water Treatment (Urban Waste-Water Directive).[55] The first complaint concerned Greece's failure to meet the 1998 deadline for installing tertiary treatment for the region of Elefsina. The second complaint related to the inadequate waste-water treatment in Athens. The city of Athens eventually benefited from a major new treatment plant at Psyttalia, capable of treating waste produced by five million people. However, the stricter waste-water treatment measures that were required to protect the receiving waters of the Gulf of Saronikos (which recent studies have shown to be eutrophic) were not operational at the end of 2002. Greece also received a Reasoned Opinion under Article 226 EC for failing to designate the Gulf of Thermaikos as sensitive. Finally, the Commission issued a letter of formal notice for Greece's failure to provide sufficient information on

[51] [2000] OJ L269/34. [52] Official Gazette, Vol. A, 54, 20 Mar. 2002.
[53] Official Gazette, Vol. B, 57, 24 Jan. 2002. [54] [1976] OJ L31/1.
[55] [1991] OJ L135/40.

how the Urban Waste-Water Treatment Directive was (to be) implemented. This related in particular to the lack of a general implementation report and of information on industrial sectors.

H. Horizontal Instruments

i. Environmental Impact Assessment

Directive 97/11/EC amending Directive 85/337/EEC on the Assessment of the Effects of certain Public and Private Projects on the Environment (EIA Directive)[56] was transposed into the Greek legal order by Law 3010/2002.[57] The Council of State has repeatedly dealt with the incorporation of Community environmental impact assessment (EIA) provisions.[58] The legislative gaps in the Greek transposition of the 1985 EIA Directive 85/337/EEC have been cause for much jurisprudence of the Council of State, as has its implementation, including the adoption of 'qualitative criteria' concerning the localization, description, and evaluation of direct and indirect environmental effects of certain projects. Since 1997, the Mamidakis petrochemical storage plant located in the Gulf of Geras, by the island of Lesbos, has been operating illegally. Not only had it been operational without a permit since 1997, there had also not been an adequate prior EIA, notwithstanding its location near a Natura 2000 site. This site hosted many rare habitats and species earmarked for conservation and protection under the Habitats Directive. Greek legislation implementing the EIA Directive did require that prior assessment should have been carried out for the plant, and the Council of State declared the EIA procedures carried out in 1996 and in 2000 null and void. The Commission considered that, by allowing this plant to function in such a sensitive location without adequate prior EIA having been done, Greece had breached its obligations under both the EIA Directive and the Habitats Directive. Hence, the Commission issued formal notices demanding compliance through adequate impact assessment measures.

ii. Integrated Pollution Prevention and Control

On 25 April 2002, Law 3010/2002[59] was adopted to transpose Directive 96/61/EC on Integrated Pollution Prevention and Control (IPPC Directive).[60]

iii. Access to Information

Guaranteeing the right of access to information and securing a change in the tradition of secrecy in public administration constitute vital tasks for the Greek

[56] [1997] OJ L73/5.

[57] Official Gazette, Vol. A, 91, 25 Apr. 2002.

[58] M. Assimakopoulou, *Environmental Impact Assessments and the Jurisprudence of Greek Council of State* (Athens: Nomos Kai Fysis, 1994).

[59] n. 57 above.

[60] [1996] OJ L275/26.

administration in order to create a culture of openness, transparency, and accountability. Despite various restrictions, recently certain progress has been made to this end.[61] This includes the increased application of electronic innovations to the dissemination of public administration information. Moreover, amendments were made to the 1995 Joint Ministerial Decision 77921/1440 concerning public access to environmental information, by the adoption, in February 2002, of Joint Ministerial Decision 49987 of the Ministers of National Economy and Economics, Interior, Public Administration and Decentralization.[62] Although current Greek legislation on the environment contains certain provisions for public participation and access to information on activities that may create environmental effects, their practical application has shown a number of deficiencies. An example is the case of the Eleonora's falcon, *falco eleonorae*, a bird of prey on Crete. Following several complaints about alleged breaches of EC public participation and information requirements related to information on the mortality rate of this particular falcon, the Commission decided to initiate infringement proceedings against Greece.

I. Miscellaneous

i. Noise

The Commission issued formal notices to Greece to adequately implement Directive 2000/14/EC relating to the Noise Emission in the Environment by Equipment for Use Outdoors.[63] The Directive stipulates that equipment can only be placed on the market if it satisfies certain requirements on noise emissions and providing that the correct information on guaranteed noise levels is clearly displayed. The implementation deadline was 3 July 2001, and Greece failed to inform the Commission that the rules had been implemented on a national level by this date.

J. Conclusion

Greece will assume the EU's rotating presidency during a difficult and important period. The accession of ten new Member States and their harmonization with Community rules and ethos will be accompanied by a deeply rooted conviction on the necessity to preserve the environment as the basis for well-being and quality of life. However, Greece's determination to cooperate with the other EU Member States and the Commission to put into action the Johannesburg Application Programme and Type B Initiatives, as well as the promotion of an

[61] C. Petrou, 'Les contingences de transparence et le souci européen pour la démocratisation du débat environnemental' (2002) 3 *Revue Européenne de Droit de l'Environnement*, 40–6.

[62] Official Gazette, Vol. B, 592, 16 May 2002.

[63] [2000] OJ L162/1.

EU Sustainable Development Strategy, both within and outside the EU may set out new goals and priorities. It may also suggest ways by which the Johannesburg Conclusions may be implemented. One of the priorities of the Greek Presidency will be the implementation of a ten-year programme on Sustainable Development and Consumption, emphasizing the role of clean technologies on ecological efficiency and suggesting ways to separate economic development from environmental devaluation, both conceptually and in practice.

Special attention will be also paid to the combination of environmental sustainability and the EU's international economic competitiveness. This may be realized through the increased efficiency in the use of resources, as well as through the added value from 'green' products and services. The Greek Presidency will, moreover, seek to strengthen the EU's initiatives as regards water and energy. In particular, according to the EU Statement on the Renewable Sources of Energy, the Greek Presidency will develop actions including an international chemicals strategy, countering poverty, preservation of natural resources, prevention of biodiversity depletion, financing of development, commerce, and governance. However, the Greek Presidency will also stress the implementation of the EU and the National Sustainable Development Strategies, based on the Gothenburg European Council guidelines. Among the priorities for the environment is also the EU's Sixth Environment Action Programme, which is directly linked with the Sustainable Development Strategy and its thematic sections.

VIII. Ireland

Yvonne Scannell *

A. Introduction

Ireland has a reputation for being quite conscientious in the implementation of European Community (EC) legislation, but less so with international law conventions. In order to keep the following report of interest to the European, and international reader, a comprehensive description of legislative developments or jurisprudence will not be given. Rather, a selection will be made of the most interesting topics in Irish environmental law as influenced by EC law. Primarily, in 2002, such topics concerned waste management, environmental impact assessment (EIA), integrated pollution prevention and control (IPPC), and access to justice. Important case law in these areas of law touched upon fundamental principles (including the precautionary principle, the polluter pays principle, and the proximity principle) and on approaches to risk, responsibility, and liability. Finally, the generous *locus standi* in environmental cases granted by Irish courts was considered again in several cases during 2002.

B. Waste

i. Waste Framework Directive

Irish authorities are finding it very difficult to implement the Waste Framework Directive (Directive 91/156/EEC amending Directive 75/442/EEC on Waste (Waste Framework Directive)).[1] Competent authorities (in practice local authorities) making waste management plans encounter enormous problems identifying sites for waste recovery and disposal activities. Moreover, the prospect of having an incinerator in an area generates a level of paranoia akin to that generated by a leaking nuclear facility. Elected members of local authorities continuously refuse to comply with the Directive when making (or refusing to make) waste management plans. The result has been that the power to make waste management plans is now vested in unelected county managers. To date, the Department of Agriculture has paid nearly €59 million for storing meat and bone meal as there are no facilities for its disposal in Ireland and an attempt to provide them was abandoned when wealthy objectors initiated a judicial review of the local planning authority's decision to grant planning permission.[2] So

* Professor of Law, Trinity College Law School; Consultant with Arthur Cox Solicitors, Dublin (Ireland).

[1] [1991] OJ L78/32.

[2] This was the background to *O'Brien* v. *Tipperary South Riding County Council*, High Court, 22 Oct. 2002. See discussion of the case in sect. C.*i.*, at n. 20 below.

controversial are waste management facilities that section 26 of the Protection of the Environment Act 2003[3] now provides that the review, variation, or replacement of a waste management plan is an executive function, that is, must be made by (unelected) county and city managers and not, as was formerly the case, by the elected members of local authorities. This curtailment of the democratic powers of elected members is regrettable and may even have constitutional implications. It was only made because the elected members of most local authorities had virtually abdicated their functions relating to the provision of waste management facilities under the Waste Management Acts 1996–2001.[4]

ii. Boyne Valley and Newgrange Environmental Protection League Ltd *v.* Environmental Protection Agency

Many decisions to grant licences for waste management facilities are challenged in the courts. In *Boyne Valley and Newgrange Environmental Protection League Ltd* v. *Environmental Protection Agency*,[5] the applicant sought leave to apply for judicial review to quash a decision granting a waste licence. To do this, he had to prove that he had 'substantial grounds' for bringing the action under section 43(5) of the Waste Management Act 1996. His main grounds were that the Environmental Protection Agency (EPA) had no jurisdiction to grant a waste licence for a landfill facility when a waste management plan required by the Waste Management Act 1996 and compliant with the Waste Framework Directive had not been adopted, when the actual site of the proposed landfill had not been identified as required, he alleged, by the Directive, and when the EIA had not addressed the environmental impacts of the proposed landfill. The planning authority which granted planning permission for the facility had carried out an EIA, but only into the planning aspects. O'Caoimh J. refused leave to apply. He held that a waste plan under earlier legislation was a valid plan for the purposes of granting a licence under the 1996 Act. Transitional provisions in the Waste Management Act 1996 ensured that this was the case. He also held that the Directive did not require competent authorities to identify *all* waste disposal facilities in advance. As to the EIA point, the court held that the applicant had not established this. The fact that the EPA file did not record in any particular form that an assessment had been carried out, did not mean that it had not been carried out. Section 26 of the Protection of the Environment Act 2003 coperfasted aspects of this decision by providing that an application for planning permission may not be refused solely on the ground that the proposed development is not specifically referred to in the relevant waste management plan if the development will facilitate the achievement of the objectives of that plan. This removes one potentially good ground for obtaining leave to apply for a judicial review.

[3] No. 27/2003, 14 July 2003.

[4] No. 36/2001, 17 July 2001.

[5] High Court, 17 Apr. 2002.

iii. Hogan *v.* Waterford County Manager

The proximity principle became the focus of arguments in *Hogan* v. *Waterford County Manager.*[6] In that case the relevant waste management plan drawn up under the Waste Management Act 1996 identified several potential waste disposal sites in east Waterford for waste disposal facilities because most of the population of the county lived there. When no suitable site was identified, the County Manager proceeded to investigate possibilities in west Waterford and eventually located a site that appeared to satisfy the criteria for environmentally acceptable landfills. He proceeded to commission an EIS for the site. Elected members of the council passed a resolution requiring the county manager not to proceed with the site identification process, alleging that locating a site in west Waterford would be a material contravention of the applicable waste management plan and a violation of the proximity principle enshrined therein. Leave to apply for judicial review was refused because the application, although made within the statutory time limits, had not been made 'promptly' as required under Order 84, Rule 21 of the Rules of the Supreme Court. Herbert J. did remark that the substantive merits of a case could be a factor in deciding whether or not to extend the time for applying. However, he considered that the applicants did not have a good case, remarking that the proximity principle (which he equated to the principle of rectification at source, citing Case C-2/90, *Commission* v. *Belgium*)[7] did not override all other environmental considerations such as the suitability of the most proximate sites. He held that the objective was to strike a best balance in the interest of protecting the environment and public health. In this case, the court held that there was no departure from the proximity principle and no variation of the waste management plan.

iv. De Burca *v.* Wicklow County Council

In *De Burca* v. *Wicklow County Council,*[8] the applicant applied for a mandatory injunction to compel the county council to adopt a waste management plan as required under the Waste Management Act 1996 and the Waste Framework Directive. The High Court exercised its discretion not to grant the injunction because it considered that the matter was being actively pursued at the time the applicant applied for the injunction.

v. Wicklow County Council *v.* Fenton

The most important case involving waste law during 2002 was *Wicklow County Council* v. *Fenton.*[9] This case resulted from the discovery of large amounts of wastes (some of them hazardous) illegally dumped on lands belonging to a Mr Fenton. The local authority concerned proceeded to sue not only Mr Fenton but

[6] High Court, 30 Apr. 2003. [7] [1992] ECR I–4431. [8] High Court, 22 Mar. 2002.
[9] High Court, 31 July 2002 [2002] *Irish High Court Directory*, 102.

also Swanliffe Ltd. (trading as Dublin Waste), the waste company which had sent waste to his landfill, and the directors of Swanliffe under sections 57 and 58 of the Waste Management Act 1996. These sections enable any person to take enforcement action against the person holding, recovering, or disposing of waste when it is being held, recovered, or disposed of in a manner that causes or is likely to cause environmental pollution (section 57) or against a person who has held, recovered, or disposed of waste in a manner which is causing or has caused environmental pollution (section 58). While both sections deal with situations where pollution is actually occurring, section 57 also deals with when it has not happened but is likely to occur and section 58 deals with where it has happened in the past.

Dublin Waste, in an effort to spread the liability, tried to join two private hospitals from which they had collected hospital wastes as notice parties, but this attempt was foiled by a judgment of O'Sullivan J. in *Wicklow County Council* v. *Fenton*,[10] who held that the third party procedure was not permissible in this kind of case under waste management legislation. This finding is entirely consistent with the decision of the Supreme Court in *Mahon* v. *Butler*,[11] to the effect that, as a result of the summary nature of proceedings of this type, it would be inappropriate to allow complex issues of law or fact to be determined in the same way. O'Sullivan J. also held that the nature of the remedy under the injunction proceedings was such that it could not properly be described as involving a 'wrong' within the meaning of the Civil Liability Act 1961, which sets time-limits for bringing proceedings.

On the main issues of the case, O'Sullivan J.'s judgment is notable for his interpretation of the concept of 'environmental pollution' as defined in waste law, and for a remarkably wide application of the polluter pays principle. O'Sullivan held that the mere presence of a risk constitutes 'environmental pollution' as defined in section 5 of the Waste Management Act 1996, and that 'environmental pollution is *caused* if a *risk* is created to waters, the atmosphere, land, soil, plants, or animals'.[12] It is submitted that the court went too far in this finding. Almost any human activity could cause a risk of environmental pollution: pollution is where the risk is significant. Section 5 requires that the endangerment to human health and the environment must be 'to a significant extent'. No guidance was given on what 'significant' means, although the court assumed that the risk was significant, saying that the precautionary principle applies when the court is making orders for the protection of the environment and the remediation of pollution.

On the polluter pays principle, O'Sullivan J. went further than any previous Irish court in expressly endorsing, interpreting, and applying the principle almost as if it were a rule of law rather than a politico-legal principle, the status of which

[10] High Court, 3 Nov. 2002 [2003] *Irish Law Reports Monthly*, 279.
[11] Supreme Court, 1 Aug. 1997 [1997] *Irish Reports*, 369; [1998] *Irish Law Reports Monthly*, 284.
[12] n. 7 above, para. 7.

is hotly debated. Having stated that the purpose of the Waste Management Act 1996 was to give effect to the Waste Framework Directive, and to the polluter pays principle in Council Recommendation 75/436/Euratom/ECSC/EEC regarding Cost Allocation and Action by Public Authorities on Environmental Matters,[13] which is specifically incorporated in section 5 of the 1996 Act, the learned judge stated that the principle applies to 'the interpretation of domestic law intended retrospectively to deal with situations where the polluter has caused environmental pollution in breach of the law, or, for example, the terms of a licence'.[14] It should be noticed that breach of the terms of a licence does not necessarily involve the creation of a risk of pollution. In considering the case against each defendant, O'Sullivan J. held, endorsing the English decision in *Empress Car Co. (Abertillery) Ltd* v. *National Rivers Authority*[15] that a person causes pollution when his act or omission brings about or contributes to bringing about pollution notwithstanding the absence of proof of intention, foreseeability, or recklessness and notwithstanding that the act of a third party or some natural event might have intervened as a contributing factor or subsequent link in the causal chain linking the person to the environmental pollution. Indeed, the learned judge considered that requiring proof of intention, recklessness, or foreseeability would be to violate the polluter pays principle, which requires that the polluter should pay rather than an innocent party or the community at large. In any event, the learned judge found that both Fenton and Dublin Waste were negligent. The chain of causation between Dublin Waste and a lorry driver (who was an independent contractor) was not broken by a truck driver who, it was alleged, had illegally dumped hazardous wastes on Fenton's land. This was because Dublin Waste and Fenton should have ensured that he acted properly. The hospitals who generated the wastes were also exonerated under sections 57 and 58 because the cause of the environmental pollution was Dublin Waste's failure to comply with their waste licence and the court considered that it would be a violation of the polluter pays principle to hold the hospitals liable. This finding somewhat contradicts the learned judge's earlier statement on the polluter pays principle although it must surely be correct.

Orders requiring comprehensive remediation of the landfill were made against Dublin Waste and/or Mr and Mrs Moriarty (the directors of Dublin Waste), if it proved unable or unwilling to remediate. The landowner, Mr Fenton, was required by order under section 57(1)(c) to facilitate the carrying out of the works and to pay half of the costs and expenses of remediation on an application by Dublin Waste for this contribution. Dublin Waste, Fenton, and Mr and Mrs Moriarty were made jointly and severally liable for the costs and expenses of the enforcing authority. Mr and Mrs Moriarty, the directors of Swanliffe Ltd., were held personally liable. This was an unexpected finding because, under planning legislation, which is phrased similarly to waste legislation on corporate liability,

[13] [1975] OJ L194/1. [14] n. 7 above, para. 24. [15] [1997] 2 AC 22.

the veil of incorporation is not easily lifted to make directors personally liable. However, O'Sullivan J. held that waste legislation, unlike planning legislation, was enacted to transpose European directives and that Mr and Mr Moriarty were polluters as defined in Recommendation 75/436/Euratom/ECSC/EEC, that is, 'someone who directly or indirectly damages the environment or who creates conditions leading to such damage'.[16] Consequently, O'Sullivan J. held that the polluter pays principle requires that 'domestic company law of limited liability should be suspended and the veil of incorporation lifted in order to ensure the full application of this principle and other objectives of the European Waste Directives'[17] when a company directed to comply with court orders is not able for financial or other reasons to comply with them.

C. Horizontal Instruments

i. Environmental Impact Assessment and Integrated Pollution Prevention and Control

Undoubtedly the most fertile source of litigation in environmental law is Directive 97/11/EC amending Directive 85/337/EEC on the Assessment of the Effects of certain Public and Private Projects on the Environment (EIA Directive).[18] This Directive has been implemented by a mammoth amount of legislation covering all kinds of activities for which EIA is required. Most of the projects listed in the Annexes to the Directive are authorized under planning legislation. Many of these projects are liable to cause polluting emissions. For this reason, an integrated pollution control (IPC) licence under the Environmental Protection Agency Act 1992 is required from the EPA for many of projects for which EIA is required. In implementing the EIA Directive, the Irish legislature chose to allocate the assessment of the land-use or planning elements of these projects to planning authorities and to allocate the assessment of the environmental pollution aspects to the EPA, which has a specialist expertise in environmental pollution matters. Accordingly, in dealing with applications for projects for which both EIA and an IPC licence were required, planning authorities were prohibiting by section 98 of the Environmental Protection Agency Act 1992[19] from considering the risk of environmental pollution from any IPC activity and from refusing permission or attaching pollution control conditions to any authorization granted for an IPC project. These matters were for the EPA. Environmentalists, and others opposing projects, objected to this policy alleging, *inter alia*, first, that the division of responsibility for assessing the environmental

[16] n. 11 above, Annex, para. 3.

[17] n. 7 above, para. 115.

[18] [1997] OJ L73/5.

[19] Since amended; planning authorities can now refuse permissions for environmental pollution reasons.

impacts of EIA/IPC projects would lead to a failure to consider the interactions referred to in Article 3 of the EIA Directive, and secondly, that the division of responsibility could, in practice, result in a failure to consider particular impacts because there are not always discrete boundary lines between planning and environmental pollution. The classic example given was the height of a chimney built to disperse pollutants. This could be both a planning (visual impact) and an environmental pollution matter (height relevant to dispersion of pollutants). This objection became a single transferable argument which has now been used at least ten times by environmentalists and others in judicial review proceedings challenging the validity of planning decisions or the planning process itself. Applicants for judicial review were encouraged by the fact that the European Commission had questioned the validity of the Irish implementation measures in a reasoned opinion.[20] Unfortunately, the courts have not yet definitively ruled on the matter.

Decisions in two cases in 2002 involved applicants for judicial reviews seeking interlocutory injunctions restraining the Planning Appeals Board from holding oral (public) hearings into appeals made against decisions granting permissions for projects which required both planning permissions and IPC licences.

In the first decision, *Martin* v. *An Bord Pleanála*,[21] the applicant sought to injunct a public hearing of an appeal against a decision to permit a municipal waste incinerator. O'Sullivan J. refused an interlocutory injunction because damages would not have been an adequate remedy to the notice party developer and on balance of convenience grounds, although he intimated that there was some merit in the applicant's arguments.

In the second decision, *O'Brien* v. *Tipperary South Riding County Council*,[22] an interlocutory injunction was granted. O'Caoimh J. considered, *inter alia*, that the legal issues raised as to whether the EIA Directive had been correctly implemented could not be determined by the Planning Appeals Board, being an administrative tribunal. *Martin* was distinguished because the applicant in *O'Brien* gave an undertaking as to substantial damages and because he had directly challenged the validity of the decision. The developer in *O'Brien* subsequently agreed to abandon the project so the case did not proceed to a full hearing on its merits. *Martin* subsequently sought leave to apply for judicial review of the Planning Appeal Board's decision to permit the incinerator. This had not been heard at the time of writing of this survey.

Another issue which arose because of section 98 of the EPA Act 1992 was whether it prevented a planning authority or the Planning Appeals Board from considering the environmental pollution implications of a development

[20] C(2001)2253, 25 July 2001.

[21] High Court, 24 July 2002 [2002] *Irish High Court Directory*, 82; [2003] *Irish Law Reports Monthly*, 257.

[22] High Court, 22 Oct. 2002.

when considering if an EIA was required for a project which did not meet the thresholds for mandatory EIA. In *O'Connell* v. *Environmental Protection Agency*,[23] Butler J. held that it did not, because the wording of the prohibition merely prohibited consideration of environmental pollution matters when a planning authority was deciding whether or not to permit a project, not when it was deciding whether or not an EIS was required. No statable case had been made out that the respondent failed to have regard to relevant considerations in deciding that an EIS was not required. The applicant has appealed this decision to the Supreme Court.

Several more judicial reviews on EIA matters are awaiting hearings.

ii. Access to Justice

The Irish courts continue to favour public interest litigation and are relatively generous in according *locus standi* (or standing) to environmentalists and to companies formed expressly to litigate environmental cases. The *locus standi* of a limited liability company to bring judicial review proceedings in a planning matter was again considered in *Ballintubber Heights Ltd.* v. *Cork Corporation*.[24] The applicant company sought to challenge a decision of a planning authority to grant planning permission. At the same time, a shareholder and director of the same company had made an administrative appeal to An Bord Pleanála. The only proprietary interest relevant to the proposed development which the company had was an option to purchase neighbouring lands granted by its shareholders immediately before the judicial review proceedings were issued. In refusing leave to appeal, O'Caoimh J held that the interest of the applicant company appeared to have been created to enable it to bring the proceedings, and this interest was best described as remote. Moreover, he held that the applicant company was not entitled to rely on an (alleged) representation made to the directors/shareholders of the company by the planning authority.

Until very recently, losing parties to environmental cases were very reluctant to ask for, or pursue, orders for costs made against unsuccessful objectors to developments or environmental authorizations. This reluctance is fast disappearing. In *O'Connor* v. *Nenagh Urban District Council*[25] O'Connor, a notice party, sought to recover his costs when the case brought against the administrative authority (the local planning authority) which granted him a planning permission failed. The High Court awarded him his costs. The unsuccessful applicant for judicial review then appealed to the Supreme Court. Denham J. held that, while there was an element of public interest in the case, the application as originally drafted sought specific remedies potentially detrimental to O'Connor,

[23] High Court, 25 Apr. 2002 [2002] *Irish High Court Directory*, 46.
[24] High Court, 21 June 2002.
[25] Supreme Court, 16 May 2002 [2002] *Irish Supreme Court Directory*, 40.

the notice party developer. The notice party, who was a necessary party, had fully participated in the trial, was an entirely innocent party, and had acted in good faith at all times. Accordingly, there was no compelling reason why O'Connor, having been successful in the proceedings, should not be awarded his costs. The normal rule is that costs are awarded only to the successful party in a case.

IX. Italy

*Francesco Francioni and Massimiliano Montini**

A. Introduction

During 2002, the Italian Parliament initiated deliberations on a new Draft Law,[1] aimed at obtaining a delegation of powers for the drafting of new decrees and consolidated texts in the environmental sector, which had been presented by the government in October 2001.[2] The act is intended to reorganize and coordinate all the existing laws and regulations around some well-defined subject areas, such as waste management and disposal and soil clean-up, water resource management and pollution prevention, soil protection and measures against desertification, protection of wild flora and fauna and management of natural protected areas, responsibility for environmental damage, and horizontal instruments including Environmental Impact Assessment (EIA) and Integrated Pollution Prevention and Control (IPPC) procedures. Although the legislative procedure for the Draft Law did not come to a conclusion during the period under survey, its ultimate adoption is one of the priorities of the present Government.

In the meantime, awaiting this formal delegation of powers, Parliament adopted Law 137/02 on 6 July 2002,[3] to empower the government to adopt a consolidated text to reorganize and improve the *existing* legislation on cultural and environmental heritage. This is a somewhat surprising development, in view of the fact that merely three years earlier Legislative Decree 490/99[4] of 29 October 1999 had been adopted for this very purpose, by the previous government.

In August 2002, shortly after the adoption of the European Community's (EC) Sixth Environmental Action Programme (EAP-6), the Italian Inter-Ministerial Committee for Economic Planning (CIPE) adopted the national environmental strategy for sustainable development.[5] The strategy is organized around four priority areas, drafted in accordance with EAP-6: (i) combating climate change and protection of the ozone layer; (ii) conservation of nature and biodiversity; (iii) preservation and improvement of the quality of the environment and the quality of life in the urban environment; and (iv) sustainable use of natural resources and waste production. The strategy aims for an integrated

* Respectively Professor and Lecturer at the Faculty of Law, University of Siena (Italy).

1 Draft Law 1798, presented to the Chamber of Deputies on 19 Oct. 2001.

2 See F. Francioni and M. Montini, 'Italy' (2003) 3 *Yearbook of European Environmental* Law, 657.

3 *GURI* 158 of 8 July 2002.

4 Ordinary Supplement to *GURI* 302 of 27 Dec. 1999.

5 Deliberation of CIPE of 2 Aug. 2002, Ordinary Supplement to *GURI* 205 of 30 Oct. 2002.

approach, cross-cutting all policy areas, in line with the EC's environmental Integration Principle, as laid down in Article 6 EC Treaty.

B. Atmospheric Pollution

i. Fuel Quality

In the field of air pollution prevention from motor vehicles, two Decrees deserve mention. First, Decree of the Ministry of Transport of 25 January 2002[6] implemented Commission Directive 2001/27/EC Adapting to Technical Progress Directive 88/77//EC relating to Measures to be Taken against the Emission of Gaseous and Particulate Pollutants from Compression-Ignition Engines for Use in Vehicles, and the Emission of Gaseous Pollutants from Positive-Ignition Engines Fuelled with Natural Gas or Liquefied Petroleum Gas for Use in Vehicles.[7] The act contains certain criteria to homologize vehicles for air pollution reduction and prevention. Secondly, Decree of the President of the Council of Ministers 29/02 of 29 January 2002[8] prohibits the marketing of conventional fuels which do not contain (a small quota of) organic fuels (so-called 'bio-fuels').

ii. Industrial Air Pollution

In the field of industrial air pollution, mention should be made of the Decree of the President of the Council of Ministers of 8 March 2002,[9] which establishes the merceological characteristics of the combustibles and the technological characteristics which industrial and domestic combustion plants must respect, in order to reduce air pollution.

iii. Ambient Air Quality

Progress was made during 2002 in the application process of Directive 96/62/EC on Ambient Air Quality Assessment and Management (Ambient Air Quality Framework Directive),[10] which was implemented in Italy by Legislative Decree 351/99 of 4 August 1999.[11] Two of its daughter directives were transposed by Decree of the Ministry of Environment 60/02 of 2 April 2002,[12] namely: Directive 1999/30/EC relating to Limit Values for Sulphur Dioxide, Nitrogen Dioxide and Oxides of Nitrogen, Particulate Matter, and Lead in Ambient Air,[13] and Directive 2000/69/EC relating to Limit Values for Benzene and Carbon Monoxide in Ambient Air.[14] In addition, the technical bodies and modalities for ensuring the quality of the monitoring systems used for ambient air quality evaluation and management were identified by Decree of the Ministry of Envir-

[6] *GURI* 38 of 14 Feb. 2002. [7] [2001] OJ L107/10. [8] *GURI* 60 of 12 Mar. 2002.
[9] *GURI* 60 of 12 Mar. 2002. [10] [1996] OJ L296/55. [11] *GURI* 241 of 13 Oct. 1999.
[12] Ordinary Supplement 77 to *GURI* 87 of 13 Apr. 2002. [13] [1999] OJ L163/41.
[14] [2000] OJ L313/12.

onment of 20 September 2002.[15] Finally, Decree 261/02 of the Ministry of Environment of 1 October 2002[16] laid down technical directives for the preliminary evaluation of ambient air quality, and criteria for the elaboration of the plans and programmes prescribed by Legislative Decree 351/99.[17]

iv. Climate Change

Italy's ratification of the Kyoto Protocol[18] to the United Nations (UN) Framework Convention on Climate Change (UNFCCC),[19] was formalized by Law 120/02 of 1 June 2002.[20] Subsequently, in December 2002, the Italian Inter-Ministerial Committee for Economic Planning (CIPE) adopted revised guidelines for the Italian policies and measures to combat climate change, supplementing and amending the original 1998 guidelines.[21]

v. Ozone Layer

With the aim of protecting the ozone layer, the Decree of the Ministry of Environment of 20 September 2002[22] determined the technical norms and modalities for the prevention of emissions into the atmosphere which can occur as a result of the recovery of equipment containing ozone-depleting substances, in accordance with Law 549/1993 of 28 December1993 on the protection of the ozone layer.[23]

D. Chemicals

Two directives concerning the management of dangerous substances were implemented during 2002. First, Decree of the Ministry of Environment of 14 June 2002[24] implemented Commission Directive 2001/59/EC Adapting to Technical Progress for the Twenty-Eighth Time Council Directive 67/548/EEC on Classification, Packaging and Labelling of Dangerous Substances.[25] Secondly, Decree of the Ministry of Environment of 7 September 2002[26] regulated the modalities for the (public) information required for the marketing of dangerous substances by implementing Commission Directive 2001/58/EC Amending for the Second

[15] *GURI* 231 of 2 Oct. 2002.

[16] *GURI* 272 of 20 Nov. 2002.

[17] n. 11 above.

[18] Kyoto (Japan), 10 Dec. 1997 (not yet in force) (1998) 37 *International Legal Materials* 1, 22.

[19] New York, NY (United States), 9 May 1992 (entered into force 21 Mar. 1994); (1992) 31 *International Legal Materials* 4, 849.

[20] Ordinary Supplement 129 to *GURI* 142 of 19 June 2002.

[21] Deliberation of CIPE 123 of 19 Dec. 2002, *GURI* 68 of 22 Mar. 2003.

[22] *GURI* 230 of 1 Oct. 2002.

[23] *GURI* 305 of 30 Dec. 1993.

[24] Ordinary Supplement 197 to *GURI* 244 of 17 Oct. 2002.

[25] [2001] OJ L225/1.

[26] *GURI* 252 of 26 Oct. 2002.

Time Directive 91/155/EEC Defining and Laying Down the Detailed Arrangements for the System of Specific Information Relating to Dangerous Preparations in Implementation of Article 14 of Directive 1999/45/EC and Relating to Dangerous Substances in Implementation of Article 27 of Directive 67/548/EEC (Safety Data Sheets).[27]

E. Nature Conservation

i. CITES

Decree 7 of the Ministry of Environment of 8 January 2002[28] instituted the National Register for the detention/possession of animal and plants species included in Annexes A and B of the Convention on International Trade in Endangered Species of Wild Fauna and Flora (CITES),[29] as implemented by Regulation (EC) 338/97 on the Protection of Species of Wild Fauna and Flora by Regulating Trade Therein.[30] The Decree was adopted pursuant to Article 5 of Law 150/92 of 7 February 1992.[31] Moreover, a new marine protection area was created around Isola Asinara, by means of Decree of the Ministry of Environment of 13 August 2002.[32]

F. Waste

In the field of application of the Italian framework law on waste management, Legislative Decree 22/97, it is worth recalling Decree 138/02 of 8 July 2002.[33] This contains the long-debated 'authentic interpretation' of the notion of 'waste', which updates and partially modifies the original notion of waste contained in Law 22/97. The problem with such an 'authentic interpretation' lies in the fact that the notion of waste in Italian law is derived directly from EC law and the present authentic interpretation is considered by the Commission not to be in conformity with the relevant provisions of EC law.[34]

Moreover, the Ministry of Environment issued Decree 161/02 of 12 June 2002,[35] implementing the provisions of Articles 31 to 33 of Legislative Decree 22/97, determining the recovery activities dealing with dangerous waste which can be carried out following the so-called 'simplified procedures'. In more concrete terms, such procedures substantially consist in a communication to the competent Province which may substitute in certain circumstances the usual request for an authorization for the recovery of dangerous waste which normally ought to be filed to the competent Region.

[27] [2001] OJ L212/24. [28] *GURI* 252 of 26 Oct. 2002.
[29] Washington, DC (US), 3 Mar. 1973; (1973) 12 *International Legal Materials* 5, 1085.
[30] [1997] OJ L61/1. [31] *GURI* 44 of 22 Feb. 1992. [32] *GURI* 298 of 20 Dec. 2002.
[33] *GURI* 158 of 8 July 2002; converted into Law 178 of 8 Aug. 2002, *GURI* 187 of 10 Aug. 2002.
[34] European Commission, Communication C(2002)3868. [35] *GURI* 177 of 30 July 2002.

G. Water

With reference to the application of the Italian framework law on the protection of water from pollution, on water quality management, and on the regulation of waste water discharges: Legislative Decree 152/99, Decree of the Ministry of Environment of 20 September 2002,[36] contains the modalities to be used by the Regions and the autonomous Provinces of Trento and Bolzano to report to the State on the relevant information regarding the quality of the waters.

As regards the implementation and application of Directive 76/160/EEC concerning the Quality of Bathing Water (Bathing Water Directive),[37] Decree 92 of 10 May 2002[38] contains a further shift to 31 December 2003 of the date of entry into force of the discipline provided by Decree 109/93 of 13 April 1993,[39] with specific reference to the parameter of the 'dissolved oxygen'.

H. Horizontal Instruments

i. Environmental Impact Assessment

Legislative Decree 190/02 of 20 August 2002[40] sets criteria for the planning, approval, and realization of the so-called strategic public infrastructures of a prominent national interest and on the approval of private industrial settlements and infrastructures of a prominent national interest, as singled out pursuant to the provisions of Law 443/01 of 21 December 2001.[41] To this effect, the Decree introduces a new 'fast-track' administrative procedure for the approval of such infrastructures and other projects of a prominent national interest, which is coordinated directly by the government through the Inter-Ministerial Committee for Economic Planning (CIPE). A specific environmental impact assessment (EIA) procedure is provided by this Decree for infrastructures and other projects that fall within its scope of application. Such a procedure derogates from the ordinary EIA procedure in many respects, *inter alia*: first, these procedures are conducted in an early phase of the approval of the projects and hence are based on a preliminary, rather than the definitive, version of the project. Secondly, the final approval of the project is left to a technical-political body, namely the CIPE, rather than to a purely technical body, for example, the Ministry of Environment.

ii. Integrated Pollution Prevention and Control

The provisions of Directive 96/61/EEC on Integrated Pollution Prevention and Control (IPPC Directive)[42] in Italy are currently in force only with regard to

[36] Ordinary Supplement 198 to *GURI* 245 of 18 Oct. 2002. [37] [1976] OJ L31/1.

[38] *GURI* 110 of 13 May 2002; converted into Law 140/02 of 11 July 2002, *GURI* 162 of 12 July 2002.

[39] *GURI* 87 of 15 April 1993; converted into Law 185/1993 of 12 June 1993, *GURI* 137 of 14 June 1993.

[40] Ordinary Supplement 174 to *GURI* 199 of 26 Aug. 2002.

[41] *GURI* 299 of 27 Dec. 2001. [42] [1996] OJ L275/26.

existing plants pursuant to Legislative Decree 372/99 of 4 August 1999.[43] While awaiting the full and complete implementation of this Directive, several Decrees have been enacted by the Ministry of Environment in order to guarantee the correct application of the IPPC provisions. For instance, by means of Decrees of 23 November 2001[44] and of 26 April 2002,[45] the Ministry of Environment established the format and the modalities for the filing of relevant data on emissions into air, water, and soil that IPPC plants must submit to the competent authorities for the inventory of all existing emissions. Moreover, by means of Decree of 24 July 2002,[46] the Ministry of Environment determined a new timetable for the filing of the request for the issuance of the IPPC authorization as far as energy production plants falling within the State competence are concerned.

I. Miscellaneous

i. Taxation and Subsidies

A new set of eco-incentives for the acquisition of new cars with lower levels of polluting emissions, following the first set which was in place in 1997–8, was put in place during 2002 and 2003 by Decree 138/02.[47] The new set of eco-incentives, which was conceded to those buyers of new cars with catalytic converters that give back to the seller an old car with no catalytic converter, include an exemption for three years from the annual State tax on cars, and a waiver for the provincial registration charges.

The market in 'green certificates', which are issued to the producers of energy from renewable sources, is now ready to become operational, following the Decree of the Ministry of Productive Activities of 18 March 2002,[48] which updated the provisions of Legislative Decree 79/99 of 16 March 1999[49] and partially modified Decree of the Ministry of Productive Activities of 11 November 1999.[50] According to the basic provisions of Law 79/99, each producer or importer of energy which operates in the Italian market must demonstrate that at least 2 per cent of its electricity is produced from renewable sources. Where producers or importers do not meet this threshold limit through their own production or imports, they are obliged to acquire an equivalent amount of 'green certificates' on the market, so as to promote the generation of energy from renewable sources.

ii. Planning Law

Legislative Decree 198/02 of 4 September 2002[51] contains principles and criteria on the installation of telecommunication infrastructures, which are deemed to be

[43] *GURI* 252 of 26 Oct. 1999.
[44] Ordinary Supplement 29 to *GURI* 37 of 13 Feb. 2002.
[45] *GURI* 126 of 31 May 2002.
[46] *GURI* 229 of 30 Sept. 2002.
[47] *GURI* 158 of 8 July 2002; converted into Law 178 of 8 Aug. 2002, *GURI* 187 of 10 Aug. 2002.
[48] *GURI* 71 of 25 Mar. 2002.
[49] *GURI* 75 of 31 Mar. 1999.
[50] *GURI* 292 of 14 Dec. 1999.
[51] *GURI* 215 of 13 Sept. 2002.

'strategic', pursuant to the provisions of Law 443/01 of 21 December 2001.[52] The main novelty introduced by this Decree is that the telecommunication infrastructures listed in Article 4 (essentially comprising all radio, TV, and mobile telephone antennae) are considered to be 'works of a national interest' and hence are deemed to be automatically compatible with any land-planning destination and any land-planning municipal regulation. Moreover, as to the authorization procedure for the installation of such infrastructures, the Decree prescribes that the so-called 'silent assent' procedure applies. Thus, if within 90 days from the filing date of an authorization request for the installation of a telecommunication infrastructure with the competent local authority (ordinarily, the local municipality) no administrative decision has been made, the request is considered to have been accepted by default.

[52] *GURI* 299 of 27 Dec. 2001.

X. The Netherlands

*Jonathan Verschuuren**

A. Introduction

The political climate in the Netherlands changed quite profoundly in 2002 and 2003, as evidenced by the two new government programmes following the two consecutive national elections during this period. Neither programme paid much attention to environmental policy, except for an intention to 'deregulate' this field of policy. Moreover, under both consecutive governments, the Cabinet Minister position for environmental policy was replaced by a Secretary of State. There was a general impression that environmental legislation was too detailed and too strict for businesses. During the first half of 2003, all environmental legislation in the Netherlands was reviewed in order to identify provisions that could be abolished. Although at the close of the survey period, the government had yet to introduce concrete proposals, it was clear that many pieces of legislation would be brought back to European (minimum) standards. Hence, national provisions that went beyond what is strictly necessary as a consequence of European Community (EC) law were 'in the danger zone'. The May 2003 government programme stated that 'no new policy measures will be introduced that are stricter than the measures imposed by European legislation'.[1]

Already, this conservative approach has had an effect on the position of the Dutch environmental performance within the European Union (EU). In its report *Environmental Balance 2003*, the National Institute of Public Health and the Environment (RIVM) concluded that the Netherlands was devolving from a front runner to an average environmental performer.[2] According to the report, not only had the Netherlands no longer used its opportunity to set standards that went beyond EC requirements, it was also confronted with an increasing number of infringement procedures.[3] It also showed that the Netherlands had the highest density of population, industry, cattle, and transportation of the EU. Also, the damage caused by acids, nitrates, and phosphates to the soil, surface, groundwater, and generally to nature, was worst in the Netherlands, compared to all other Member States.[4]

* Professor of European and International Environmental Law, Tilburg University (the Netherlands).

[1] The May 2003 Government Programme (*Regeerakkoord*), entitled 'Co-operate, More Jobs, Less Rules', was published on the Internet at: http://www.regering.nl (Dutch), or http://www.government.nl (English).

[2] *Milieubalans 2003 (Environmental Balance 2003)* (Bilthoven: RIVM, 2003), published on the Internet at: http://www.rivm.nl.

[3] ibid. 121–43.

[4] ibid. 15.

Finally, an important development occurred in the case law of the Administrative Law Division of the Council of State (Administrative Law Division), the highest administrative court in the Netherlands. In October 2002, the Administrative Law Division ruled in a case concerning Directive 76/464/EEC on Pollution Caused by certain Dangerous Substances Discharged into the Aquatic Environment of the Community (Dangerous Substances Discharge Directive).[5] It held that competent authorities were no longer allowed directly to apply provisions of directives having direct effect, insofar as this would be disadvantageous for individual citizens.[6] In such cases, the authority must apply national legislation. However, should someone (e.g. the applicant or a third party) explicitly invoke a provision having direct effect, the competent authority would be obliged to apply the Community provision instead of national legislation. To underpin this ruling, the Administrative Law Division referred to the European Court of Justice (ECJ) judgment in *Arcaro*.[7] The reasoning of this ruling received much criticism,[8] not only for appearing contrary to Article 10 EC and the *Kraaijeveld* judgment of the ECJ,[9] but also due to its many (im)practical implications. For instance, it obliged competent authorities to prepare two separate decisions: one based upon national law (should the Directive not be invoked), and one based upon EC law. In the event the Directive was not invoked during the decision-making process, but *was* brought up in a subsequent court procedure, the competent authority's decision could be quashed. In fact in later cases, the Administrative Law Division itself tested, on its own motion, administrative decisions against provisions of Directive 96/61/EC concerning Integrated Pollution Prevention and Control (IPPC Directive)[10] that had taken direct effect, even in cases where this was disadvantageous for the applicant of the environmental permit.[11]

B. Atmospheric Pollution

i. Greenhouse Gases

In the spring of 2003, although at that time Directive 2003/87/EC establishing a Scheme for Greenhouse Gas Emission Allowance Trading within the Commu-

[5] [1976] OJ L129/23.

[6] Administrative Law Division of the Council of State, *De Maatschap A* v. *Dijkgraaf en Hoogheemraden van het Hoogheemraadschap Amstel, Gooi en Vecht*, 23 Oct. 2002 (2002) 47 *Administratiefrechtelijke Beslissingen*, 418 (annotation by Backes).

[7] Case C-168/95, *Criminal Proceedings against Luciano Arcaro* [1996] ECR I-4705.

[8] See e.g. J. Verschuuren, 'Afdeling bestuursrechtspraak worstelt met rechtstreekse werking EG-richtlijnen' (2003) 9 *Nederlands Tijdschrift voor Europees Recht*, 75–7.

[9] Case C-72/95, *Aannemersbedrijf P.K. Kraaijeveld BV e.a.* v. *Gedeputeerde Staten van Zuid-Holland* [1996] ECR I-5403.

[10] [1996] OJ L257/26.

[11] See e.g. Administrative Law Division of the Council of State, *Vereniging Milieudefensie e.a.* v. *Het College van B & W van Hof van Twente*, 19 Feb. 2003 (2003) 16 *Administratiefrechtelijke Beslissingen* 129 (annotation by Verschuuren).

nity and Amending Council Directive 96/61/EC[12] had not yet been adopted, a proposal to add a chapter on emissions trading to the Dutch Environmental Management Act (EMA) was published. The extremely short implementation period that was included in the Directive (31 December 2003) was the reason for this unique situation of the national implementation legislation being drafted parallel to the drafting of the Directive.

ii. Air Quality Daughter Directives

The Commission started an infringement procedure against the Netherlands for not having implemented time on Directive 2000/69/EC relating to Limit Values for Benzene and Carbon Monoxide in Ambient Air.[13] The delay in the implementation of this second so-called 'daughter Directive' to Directive 96/62/EC on Ambient Air Quality Assessment and Management (Air Quality Framework Directive)[14] was caused by discussions between the Environment Secretary and Parliament on the way all daughter Directives should be implemented. The first daughter Directive, Directive 1999/30/EC laying down Limit Values for Sulphur Dioxide, Nitrogen Dioxide and Oxides of Nitrogen, Particulates and Lead in the Ambient Air,[15] was implemented with the adoption of the Decree on Air Quality, setting environmental quality standards on the basis of the EMA.[16] The Secretary had the intention to implement the second daughter Directive by amending the Decree on Air Quality. However, Parliament requested implementation of both daughter Directives by Act of Parliament. Parliament has the right to make such requests under Article 21(5) of the EMA. The Council of State had serious objections against repealing the Decree on Air Quality and starting a (lengthy) legislative procedure, risking more delays and more infringement procedures. Still, Parliament insisted on introducing a new Act of Parliament on air quality. In April 2003, the Secretary finally agreed to do so and announced a proposal for a new Act implementing all three daughter Directives.[17]

C. Chemicals

i. Biocides and Pesticides

The implementation of Directive 98/8/EC concerning the Placing of Biocidal Products on the Market (Biocides Directive)[18] caused much unrest in the Dutch Parliament. According to the (former) Minister, the Directive allowed Member

[12] [2003] OJ L275/32.
[13] [2000] OJ L313/12.
[14] [1996] OJ L296/55.
[15] [1999] OJ L163/41.
[16] *Bulletin of Acts and Decrees 2001*, No. 269. See J. Verschuuren, 'The Netherlands' (2003) 3 *Yearbook of European Environmental Law*, 682.
[17] Parliamentary Documents II, 2002–2003, No. 27 793, 9.
[18] [1998] OJ L123/1.

States to ban products from the market prior to, and awaiting, Community assessment. Industry argued that all existing products should remain on the market prior to Community assessment. Parliament forced the Minister to incorporate his suggestions into a revised proposal, not only for biocides, but also for pesticides that had not yet been assessed at Community level under Directive 91/414/EEC concerning the Placing of Plant Protection Products on the Market (Pesticides Directive).[19] The revised Pesticides Act,[20] in which both Directives were implemented, entered into force in December 2002.

ii. Integration of Regulations on Chemicals and Products into the EMA

Although the legislature reserved chapter 9 of the 1993 EMA for a future integrated regulation on substances and products, to date, this chapter contains no articles. It is unclear whether the new government programme will further delay the proposal of new legislation.[21] Since new EC measures are expected in the near future, concerning both products[22] and chemicals,[23] it may be decided to keep existing laws relating to substances and chemicals (most importantly the Chemical Substances Act) unchanged, awaiting EC initiatives.

D. Nature Conservation

In October 2000, the Commission notified the Dutch government that neither the current nor the proposed legislation on nature protection was fully in compliance with a number of provisions of Directive 79/409/EEC on the Conservation of Wild Birds (Birds Directive)[24] and Directive 92/43/EEC on the Conservation of Natural Habitats and of Wild Fauna and Flora (Habitats Directive),[25] in particular Article 6 of the latter.[26] In December 2001, a proposal to amend the Nature Protection Act 1998, implementing Article 6 of the Habitats Directive, was sent to Parliament.[27] The proposal received criticism for a number of reasons. For example, it stated that the provisions of Article 6 of the Directive were to be applied by *any* authority preparing *any* decision that might have a negative impact on a Special Protection Area (SPA) or a Special Area of Conservation (SAC). The proposal did not explicitly state *which* decision

[19] [1991] OJ L230/1.

[20] *Bulletin of Acts and Decrees* 2002, No. 461.

[21] In Feb. 2003, the Secretary still wanted to proceed with the integration of the Chemical Substances Act in the EMA, Parliamentary Documents II, 2002–2003, No. 27 646, 11.

[22] Future Integrated Product Policy is described by the Commission on the Internet at: http://europa.eu.int/comm/environment/ipp/futuredevelopments.htm.

[23] White Paper on the Strategy for the Future Chemicals Policy, COM(2001)88.

[24] [1979] OJ L103/1.

[25] [1992] OJ L206/7.

[26] See H.E. Woldendorp, 'Europese actiepunten inzake het Nederlandse natuurbeschermings-beleid' (2002) 29 *Milieu & Recht* 4, 94–9.

[27] Parliamentary Documents II, 2001–2002, 28 171, 1–3.

or *which* authority, or whether one competent authority had final responsibility for the application of the provisions of both Directives. Moreover, no changes were made to existing legislation relating to areas that were already protected under national law. Hence, two regimes existed for areas protected under the Nature Protection Act 1998: one regime for SPAs and SACs, and a different regime for nature protection areas not (yet) designated as SPAs or SACs.[28] Following this criticism, a whole series of amendments was proposed by Parliament. Also, the two national elections of 2002 and 2003 seriously slowed down the legislative process, so that it may take a while before the Habitats Directive is fully implemented in the Netherlands.

In March 2002, the Administrative Law Division referred five questions to the ECJ for a preliminary ruling on the interpretation of the Habitats Directive.[29] All five questions related to Article 6 of the Directive, *inter alia* to the relationship between its second and third paragraph, to the terms 'appropriate steps' in Article 6(2), and 'appropriate assessment' in Article 6(3), and to the role of the precautionary principle in applying Article 6. The case concerned a decision by the Secretary of State for Agriculture, Nature, and Fisheries to allow mechanical fishing for cockles in the Waddensea, which would probably lead to deterioration of the food supply of birds for which this area was designated as an SPA under the Birds Directive.

Dutch courts continue to render many decisions in cases on the Birds and Habitats Directives.[30] A much-publicized case on the construction of a new north–south motorway through the province of Limburg along the east bank of the River Meuse showed that areas that are expected to be proposed as future SACs to the Commission do not yet receive full protection under Article 6 of the Habitats Directive. The motorway was planned to cross two areas that had been proposed as future SACs to the Commission. However, the Council of State found that an alternative route would also be harmful to nature (although this alternative route, on the west bank of the river, did not cross any protected areas), and it hence considered that it would be up to the competent authorities to select the most convenient route.[31] In this way, in this author's view, the Council of State did not give proper weight to the legal consequences of the Habitats Directive. The fact that there were other important natural elements present on the west bank is, from a legal perspective, less important than the fact that two

[28] See J. Veltman, 'De Natuurbeschermingswet opnieuw op de helling' (2002) 29 *Milieu & Recht* 4, 100–7.

[29] Administrative Law Division of the Council of State, *Landelijke Vereniging tot Behoud van de Waddenzee* v. *Secretary of State of Agriculture, Nature and Fisheries*, 27 Mar. 2002 (2002) 29 *Milieu & Recht* 7/8, 222–8 (annotation by Verschuuren).

[30] For an overview, see J. Verschuuren, 'Nogmaals kokkels, hamsters en woelmuizen: recente ontwikkelingen rond de implementatie van de Vogel- en Habitatrichtlijn in Nederland' (2003) 9 *Nederlands Tijdschrift voor Europees Recht* 1/2, 34–8.

[31] Administrative Law Division of the Council of State, *Stichting Milieufederatie Limburg a.o.* v. *Gedeputeerde Staten van Limburg*, 13 Nov. 2002 (2003) 30 *Milieu & Recht* 2, 41–50.

areas on the east bank were proposed as future SACs. The good news is that, during the survey period, the designation of SPAs under the Birds Directive and the selection of SACs under the Habitats Directive were concluded in a satisfactory manner. The decision, published in March 2000, to designate 43 new SPAs has stood the test in court,[32] while further SPAs were designated as recently as May 2003. With these final decisions, designation of SPAs has now been concluded. In May 2003, the Minister sent the Commission the final version of the list of proposed future SACs.[33] A total of 141 areas were included in the list and, although a final judgment from the Commission has to be awaited, this list is believed to be quite satisfactory.

E. Waste

The ECJ judgments on the definition of waste in Joined Cases C-418/97 and C-419/97, *Arco Chemie/EPON*[34] finally caused Dutch waste policy and legislation to be brought fully into conformity with the terminology used in Directive 75/442/EEC on Waste (Waste Framework Directive).[35] Commission Decision 2000/532/EC replacing Decision 94/3/EC establishing a List of Wastes Pursuant to Article 1(a) of Council Directive 75/442/EEC on Waste and Council Decision 94/904/EC establishing a List of Hazardous Waste Pursuant to Article 1(4) of Council Directive 91/689/EEC on Hazardous Waste[36] also caused changes in the national waste legislation. Chapter 10 of the EMA on waste was completely revised and renumbered,[37] the Decree on Hazardous Wastes was replaced with the Ministerial Order European Waste List,[38] and the National Waste Management Plan was also revised.[39] This by no means indicates that all problems concerning the terms 'waste', 'disposal', and 'recovery' have been solved. There have been new preliminary rulings by the ECJ in Dutch cases on the question whether certain activities should be regarded as disposal or as recovery.[40] These

[32] Administrative Law Division of the Council of State, *Koninklijke Nederlandse Jagersvereniging a.o.* v. *Secretary of State of Agriculture, Nature and Fisheries*, 18 Mar. 2003 (2003) 30 *Milieu & Recht* 3, 65.

[33] All information on the selection, designation, and proposals of SACs and SPAs is published by the Ministry on the Internet at: http://www.minlnv.nl/natura2000.

[34] Joined Cases C-418/97 and C-419/97, *Arco Chemie Nederland Ltd.* v. *Minister van VROM*, and *Vereniging Dorpsbelang Hees and Others* v. *Directeur van de dienst Milieu en Water van de Provincie Gelderland and Others* [2000] ECR I-4475.

[35] [1975] OJ L194/39, amended by Dir. 91/156 [1991] OJ L78/32.

[36] [2000] OJ L226/3.

[37] *Bulletin of Acts and Decrees* 2001, No. 346.

[38] *Government Gazette* 2002, 62.

[39] *Government Gazette* 2003, 23.

[40] Joined Cases C-307/00 to C-311/00, *Oliehandel Koeweit BV and Others* v. *Minister van Volkshuisvesting, Ruimtelijke Ordening en Milieubeheer* [2003] ECR I-1821; and C-116/01, *SITA EcoService Nederland BV, formerly Verol Recycling Limburg BV* v. *Minister van Volkshuisvesting, Ruimtelijke Ordening en Milieubeheer* [2003] ECR I-2969.

decisions again showed that all questions regarding waste can only be answered on a case-by-case basis, and that it is difficult for the national authorities to come up with criteria to facilitate concrete decision-making.[41]

F. Water

i. Framework Water Directive

A proposal to implement Directive 2000/60/EC establishing a Framework for Community Action in the Field of Water Policy (Water Framework Directive)[42] in Dutch legislation was sent to Parliament in March 2003.[43] The Directive is to be mainly implemented in the Water Management Act. The legislature proposed to make as few adjustments to existing law as possible. For example, instead of a series of river basin management plans for each river basin, there will be only the existing National Water Policy Plan containing the programmes for each of the rivers basins in the Netherlands. Unless the Parliamentary debates bring major changes to this proposed 'limited implementation', the Netherlands may encounter problems for not having fully implemented this important Directive. The Directive itself has been criticized for not paying sufficient attention to issues relating to groundwater quantity.[44] In an integrated approach, groundwater quantity management is as important as groundwater quality, surface water quantity, and surface water quality management. In the Netherlands, measures to combat dehydration of the soil have led to high groundwater levels, in rural as well as urban areas. This has caused new problems, illustrating the need for an overall integrated water management.

ii. Dangerous Substances Discharge

In October 2002, the Administrative Law Division issued an important ruling on direct effect, in a case concerning Article 3(4) of Directive 76/464/EEC on Pollution Caused by certain Dangerous Substances Discharged into the Aquatic Environment of the Community (Dangerous Substances Discharge Directive).[45] According to Article 3(4), permits for discharging Annex I substances may be granted for a limited period only. However, Article 8.17 of the Dutch EMA only lists several specific situations in which a permit may be granted for a limited period, not including the circumstance that an Annex I substance is to be discharged. Hence, Article 3(4) of the Directive was not

[41] See further Verschuuren, n. 16 above, 685; and G. van Thyne, 'De draagwijdte van het begrip "afvalstof" na het Arco/EPON-arrest voor de Vlaamse en Nederlandse rechtspraktijk' (2001) 49 *Sociaal Economische Wetgeving* 9, 290–301.

[42] [2000] OJ L327/1.

[43] Parliamentary Documents II, 2002–2003, 28 808, 1–3.

[44] P. de Putter, 'Grondwaterpeilbeheer in de Europese Kaderrichtlijn Water' (2002) 29 *Milieu & Recht* 11, 291–5.

[45] [1976] OJ L129/23.

correctly implemented into Dutch legislation. According to the Administrative Law Division this provision takes direct effect, but only if invoked by an interested party.[46]

iii. Nitrates

The civil law case between environmental non-governmental organizations (NGOs) and the Minister of Agriculture, Nature Management and Fisheries, discussed in last year's survey,[47] was brought before the Dutch Supreme Court. The case concerned the implementation of Directive 91/676/EEC on the Protection of Waters against Pollution Caused by Nitrates from Agricultural Sources (Nitrates Directive).[48] In 1999, a District Court had declared Dutch policy regarding nitrates from agricultural sources unlawful because it did not follow the Directive, and ordered the Minister to adapt the policy accordingly.[49] However, according to the Higher Court, ordering the Minister to adopt (implementing) legislation is beyond the competence of the courts, as this would infringe on the principle of division of powers. Moreover, the Higher Court held that the case had been brought before the ECJ in an Article 226 EC procedure by the Commission, preventing Dutch courts to interfere in the same case.[50] In March 2003, the Supreme Court rendered its judgment in this case. It confirmed that national courts were barred from forcing the State to enact legislation implementing EC law, while noting that the ECJ does have such powers. Since the decision whether or not to implement EC secondary legislation is of a political nature, it holds no role for the (national) judiciary. The Court argued that this point of view did not limit citizens' rights, because individual citizens still can, in administrative procedures, invoke provisions that have direct effect, and since the opportunity to claim damages under the *Francovich*[51] doctrine remains intact. Meanwhile, the ECJ ruling in the infringement procedure against the Netherlands for not having implemented the Directive is anxiously awaited. In November 2002, Advocate General (AG) Léger concluded by condemning the Netherlands in this case.[52]

[46] See also sect. A, at n. 5 above. For further commentary, see H.F.M.W. van Rijswick and R.J.G.M. Widdershoven, 'Een gemiste kans—de tijdelijke vergunning voor de lozing van zwartelijststoffen' (2002) 2 *Tijdschrift voor omgevingsrecht* 6, 229–35.

[47] Verschuuren, n. 16 above, 687.

[48] [1991] OJ L375/1.

[49] District Court The Hague, *Stichting Waterpakt and Others v. Netherlands State*, 23 Nov. 1999 (2000) *Tijdschrift voor Milieu en Recht*, no. 24 (annotation by J. Jans and J. Verschuuren).

[50] Higher Court The Hague, *Netherlands State* v. *Stichting Waterpakt and Others*, 2 Aug. 2001 (2001) *Tijdschrift voor Milieu en Recht*, no. 95 (annotation by J. Jans and J. de Jong).

[51] Joined cases C-6/90 and C-9/90, *Andrea Francovich and Danila Bonifaci and Others* v. *Italy* [1991] ECR I-5357.

[52] Case C-322/00, *Commission* v. *The Netherlands*, Opinion of 7 Nov. 2002, not yet reported.

G. Horizontal Instruments

i. Integrated Pollution Prevention and Control

For some time, many commentators have claimed that the Dutch legislation concerning ammonia emissions from intensive bio-industry is contrary to Article 9(4) of Directive 96/61/EC concerning Integrated Pollution Prevention and Control (IPPC Directive).[53] Finally, in November 2002, the Administrative Law Division expressed the same opinion. It held that the Ammonia and Livestock Farming (Interim Measures) Act did not guarantee that emission limit values were based upon the best available techniques (BAT), taking into account the geographical location and the local environmental conditions. Instead of applying the relevant provisions of the Act, the competent authority should have granted a permit that was in line with the provisions of Article 9(4) of the IPPC Directive, which takes direct effect.[54] Although this particular problem was only temporary, as the Ammonia and Livestock Farming (Interim Measures) Act has since been replaced with a new Ammonia and Livestock Farming Act,[55] there were more problems concerning the implementation of the IPPC Directive. The Commission pointed out that the Dutch EMA does not guarantee that the goals of the Directive will be achieved. In her 2002 dissertation on environmental permits, Jongma extensively identified the differences between IPPC and the EMA, especially as concerns the obligation to base emission limit values on BAT.[56] These differences have now also been acknowledged at the Ministry for the Environment, resulting in the drafting of a proposal to more precisely adopt the formulations of the IPPC Directive in the provisions of the EMA concerning the granting of environmental permits. It is expected that this proposal will be sent to Parliament in 2003.

ii. Environmental Impact Assessment and Strategic Environmental Assessment

Work was undertaken during the survey period on the drafting of a proposal to implement Directive 2001/42/EC on the Assessment of the Effects of Certain Plans and Programmes on the Environment (SEA Directive).[57] The need to implement this Directive, together with the general wish to deregulate

[53] [1996] OJ L257/26.

[54] Administrative Law Division of the Council of State, *A. Bosscher* v. *B & W van Hof van Twente*, 13 Nov. 2002 (2003) 4 *Administratiefrechtelijke Beslissingen*, 27 (annotation by M.P. Jongma). See on this and similar subsequent decisions J.M. Verschuuren, 'Rechtstreekse werking IPPC-richtlijn en ambtshalve toetsing' (2003) 9 *Nederlands Tijdschrift voor Europees Recht* 5, 124–6.

[55] *Bulletin of Acts and Decrees* 2002, No. 93. See also Verschuuren, n. 16 above, 687–8.

[56] M.P. Jongma, *De milieuvergunning—een onderzoek naar het beschermingsniveau en de soorten voorschriften* (Deventer: Kluwer, 2002), with summary in English.

[57] [2001] OJ L197/30. See e.g. S. Pieters, 'Implementatie van de strategische m.e.r. (SMB)-richtlijn' (2002) 29 *Milieu & Recht* 12, 308–11.

environmental law,[58] resulted in proposals for more drastic revisions of the entire system of environmental impact assessment (EIA) in the Netherlands. Under the existing Dutch laws, several plans cannot be decided on after an EIA has been carried out. In future, these plans will be brought under the duty to carry out a strategic environmental assessment (SEA) under the SEA Directive, instead of an EIA, thereby considerably reducing the administrative burden for decision-makers.

H. Miscellaneous Developments

i. Environmental Liability

The Commission Proposal for a Directive on Environmental Liability with regard to the Prevention and Remedying of Environmental Damage[59] has been widely welcomed.[60] Although, according to some, the proposal does not go far enough (especially with regard to the exception in Article 4 of damage caused by actions that were allowed in laws, regulations, permits, or other authorizations), it does provide interesting and important new features. For example, the fact that the proposal defines damage as 'a measurable adverse change' to natural resources, and that 'interim losses' are covered by the Directive, are considered important additions to national liability law.

ii. Environmental Protection through Criminal Law

The Commission Proposal for a Directive on the Protection of the Environment through Criminal Law[61] raised some criticism as well, although a larger influence of the EU on environmental criminal law generally was considered to be inevitable.[62] The main criticism is that the proposal differs quite substantially from the Council of Europe (COE) Convention on the Protection of Environment through Criminal Law,[63] in particular concerning the role of administrative law. According to some, the Commission should recognize that the environment is worthy of protection through the criminal system per se, not only if, and insofaras, a rule set by the competent authority has been broken.[64]

[58] See sect. A above.

[59] COM(2002)17, [2002] OJ C151E/132.

[60] See e.g. E. Bauw, 'Het lange wachten beloond? Het voorstel voor een richtlijn milieuaansprakelijkheid' (2002) 8 *Nederlands Tijdschrift voor Europees Recht* 7/8, 186–90; and E.H.P. Brans, 'Voorstel van de Europese Commissie voor een richtlijn milieuaansprakelijkheid (COM(2002)17)' (2002) 29 *Milieu & Recht* 5, 137–45. See also on the White Paper E.H.P. Brans, *Liability for Damage to Public Natural Resources—Standing, Damage and Damage Assessment* (The Hague/London/New York: Kluwer Law International, 2001), 177–240.

[61] COM(2001)139, [2001] OJ C180E/238; amended proposal COM(2002)544, [2002] OJ C20E/284.

[62] See e.g. Ton de Lange, 'Naar een Europees milieustrafrecht?' (2002) 29 *Milieu & Recht* 1, 2–6.

[63] Strasbourg (France), 4 Nov. 1998 (not yet in force), (1999) 38 *International Legal Materials* 2, 259.

[64] See de Lange, n. 62 above, 3.

XI. Portugal

*Pedro Machado**

A. Introduction

There were relatively few legal developments in environmental law in Portugal during 2002. This was due to the resignation of the Prime Minister in mid-December 2001, and the consequent need for new elections. These elections took place on 17 March 2002, and led to a new coalition government, comprising the Social Democratic Party (PSD) and People's Party (PP), which took office on 6 April 2002 and whose programme was approved by parliament at the end of April 2002. Article 2 of the Organic Law of the new government, adopted by Decree-Law 120/2002 of 3 May 2002,[1] instituted an innovative Ministry for the Cities, Town and Country Planning and the Environment, replacing the former Ministry of the Environment and Town and Country Planning.

On the other hand, the controversy concerning the question of co-incineration of hazardous industrial waste, which has been a subject of dispute since 1999 between the local populations, non-governmental organizations (NGOs), and the government, on the one hand, and the government and parliament, on the other, practically came to an end. Although the tendency has yet to be confirmed in coming years, it appears that highly pressing global concerns over climate change and the preservation of the ozone layer are receiving increased attention from the government and are, therefore, becoming central to the government's environmental agenda. There has also been increased concern with reinforcing the representation of the municipalities on decision-making bodies with environmental responsibilities, as well as with delegating to them a range of licensing powers in relation to dangerous substances.

In terms of case law, there were no judicial decisions issued by the Community courts regarding Portugal in the field of environmental law. Only an opinion of Advocate General Stix-Hackl on the incomplete transposition of Directive 75/439/EEC on the Disposal of Waste Oils (Waste Oils Directive)[2] was delivered in the course of 2002. The Portuguese Constitutional Court also did not hand down any decisions on questions of environmental law during the period under survey.

B. Atmospheric Pollution

Decree-Law 119/2002 of 20 April 2002 was adopted to comply with the obligations arising from Regulation (EC) No. 2037/2000 on Substances that

* Ph.D. Researcher at the European University Institute, Florence (Italy).

[1] (2002) *Diário da República*, No. 102, I-A, 4188.

[2] [1975] OJ L194/23.

Deplete the Ozone Layer.[3] The law designates the *Instituto do Ambiente* (Institute of the Environment) as the authority charged with carrying out the obligations set out in the Regulation. It also institutes the procedures for granting permits for the production, import, and utilization of the substances regulated, and the recovery of the same substances already in use, as well as the bodies with sectoral competencies for issuing an opinion prior to decisions on these permits. Finally, the law designates the bodies with powers to monitor compliance, and establishes a list of penalties for offences against the new rules.

More recently, Decree 35/2002 of 5 November 2002 of the Ministry for Foreign Affairs[4] has approved the amendments to the Protocol on Substances that Deplete the Ozone Layer (Montreal Protocol)[5] to the United Nations Environment Programme (UNEP) Vienna Convention for the Protection of the Ozone Layer (Ozone Convention).[6] The amendments in question introduced (i) a ban on the import and export of methyl bromide (the controlled substance in Annex E) from any State not party to the Protocol; (ii) a ban on the export of used, recycled, and reclaimed quantities of a controlled substance, other than for the purpose of destruction, where (after the phase-out date applicable to it) a Party is unable, despite having taken all practicable steps to comply with its obligation under the Protocol, to cease production of the substance for domestic consumption, other than for uses agreed by the Parties to be essential; and (iii) a system for licensing the import and export of new, used, recycled, and reclaimed controlled substances that destroy the ozone layer (Annexes A, B, C, and E to the Protocol).

On the subject of climate change, the National Programme for Climate Change (PNAC) was opened to public discussion during January and February 2002, and the results of this process were accommodated, where deemed relevant.[7] This is the first programme with the specific objective of controlling and reducing emissions of greenhouse gases in compliance with the obligations deriving from the Kyoto Protocol[8] to the United Nations (UN) Framework Convention on Climate Change (UNFCCC),[9] and the sharing of responsibilities within the European Union (EU) as a result of this Protocol. Moreover, it is designed to anticipate the impacts of climate change and proposes a set of measures intended to reduce the negative effects associated with such impacts. The main objectives listed under the PNAC are, *inter alia*: (i) quantification of

[3] [2000] OJ L244/1.

[4] (2002) *Diário da República*, No. 255, I-A, 7059.

[5] Montreal (Canada), 16 Sept. 1987 (entered into force on 1 Jan. 1989) (1987) 26 *International Legal Materials* 6, 1541.

[6] Vienna (Austria), 22 Mar. 1985 (entered into force on 22 Sept. 1988) (1987) 26*International Legal Materials* 6, 1516.

[7] The PNAC was published on the Internet at: http://www.iambiente.pt/docs/5018/pnacvd.pdf.

[8] Kyoto (Japan), 10 Dec. 1997 (1998) 37 *International Legal Materials* 1, 22.

[9] New York (United States), 9 May 1992 (entered into force 21 Mar. 1994) (1992) 31 *International Legal Materials* 4, 849.

the reduction efforts for compliance with the obligations assumed; (ii) identification of sectoral responsibilities for emissions of greenhouse gases; (iii) definition of policy principles and conditions for implementation; (iv) identification of the Portuguese participation in the flexible mechanisms provided for under the Kyoto Protocol; and (v) definition of the monitoring and review system.

C. Chemicals

Another area that has been touched by the decentralization impetus that has characterized many of the amendments to Portuguese environmental legislation during 2002 was chemicals law. Decree-Law 267/2002 of 26 November 2002 adopted a new procedural framework for the licensing and monitoring of facilities where liquid and gas petroleum fuel is stored and supplied.[10] In this case, the relevant powers have been entrusted to the municipalities, with the exception of certain facilities in view of their size, the extremely hazardous nature of the fuels stored, the operations carried out, or their strategic interest for the country. In the latter case, powers are retained by the central authorities, in particular by the relevant departments of the Ministry of Economy. In addition to establishing a well-structured and sound procedural framework, this law institutes mandatory regular inspections of facilities, mandatory up-to-date insurance policies covering potential damages resulting from the activities carried out in the facilities, and the creation of a central database allowing for swift emergency planning in the event of a crisis in supply.

D. Nature Conservation

In terms of nature conservation policy, Decree-Law 203/2002 of 1 October 2002 amended the existing legal framework for National Ecological Reserves (REN),[11] originally approved by Decree-Law 93/90 of 19 March 1990.[12] Under the new legal framework, a National Commission for the REN has been established, comprising representatives of different ministries, a representative of the National Association of Municipalities, and two citizens of recognized standing appointed by the Ministry of the Environment. The National Commission is responsible for delimiting and managing the areas included (or to be included) in the REN. The dismantling of several ministries and departments in recent years has, however, made the composition of the National Commission obsolete. It was also felt that the municipalities were underrepresented. In view of this, Decree-Law 203/2002 not only updated the references to ministries and departments but also increased the representation of Portuguese municipalities on the

[10] (2002) *Diário da República*, No. 273, I-A, 7400.
[11] (2002) *Diário da República*, No. 227, I-A, 6644.
[12] (1990) *Diário da República*, No. 65, I-A, 1350.

National Commission. Its membership was extended, on an ad hoc basis, to one representative of the municipalities concerned when new REN boundaries are to be decided.

The legal framework for the National Network of Protected Areas (RNAP), adopted originally by Decree-Law No. 19/93 of 23 January 1993,[13] was amended by Decree-Law 221/2002 of 22 October 2002.[14] The changes were, once again, motivated by the need to increase representation of the municipalities in the management and decision-making process for the RNAP. In this regard, the advisory powers legally enjoyed by the municipalities have been strengthened, in the case of the appointment of the chairman of the RNAP executive board, by making these powers binding. In addition, the RNAP advisory board, composed of representatives of the municipalities, has been given added powers with regard to permits for acts or activities to be carried out in the protected areas. The outcome of the consultation in this field was made binding with Decree-Law 221/2002.

E. Waste

The most noteworthy developments in Portuguese waste law during 2002 revolved around this issue of co-incineration of (hazardous) industrial waste. Given the vital relevance of environmental impact assessment (EIA) in this discussion, the co-incineration saga will be analysed in the paragraph on Horizontal Instruments, in section F.*i* below.

F. Horizontal Instruments

i. Environmental Impact Assessment

The new government decided to put an end to the highly disputed controversy over the 1997 co-incineration programme for industrial waste in Portugal and the environmental impact assessment procedure associated therewith. This issue had dominated the domestic environmental agenda since 1999,[15] and an Independent Scientific Commission for the Environmental Control and Monitoring of Co-incineration had been established by Law 20/99 of 15 April 1999[16] and Decree-Laws 120/99[17] and 121/99 of 16 April 1999.[18] Its report on the treatment of hazardous industrial waste was issued in May 2000. The recommendation

[13] (1993) *Diário da República*, No. 19, I-A, 271.

[14] (2002) *Diário da República*, No. 244, I-A, 6848.

[15] See P. Machado, 'Environmental Law in the Member States—Portugal' (2002) 2 *Yearbook of European Environmental Law*, 529–30, and P. Machado, 'Environmental Law in the Member States—Portugal' (2003) 3 *Yearbook of European Environmental Law*, 695–7.

[16] (1999) *Diário da República*, No. 88, I-A, 2012.

[17] (1999) *Diário da República*, No. 89, I-A, 2026.

[18] (1999) *Diário da República*, No. 89, I-A, 2031.

contained in this report to use co-incineration in cement plants for treating hazardous industrial waste and, following the analysis subsequently conducted, the indication of two sites for the implementation of the co-incineration process, provoked fierce controversy, which evolved from confrontation between government and the local populations to an institutional conflict between government and parliament. The calling of new elections at the end of 2001 halted the decision-making process on the issue of co-incineration and thus also the controversy surrounding this issue.

On 19 April 2002, the new Minister of the Cities, Town and Country Planning and the Environment ordered the suspension of the experimental co-incineration trials that were being held in two cement plants. More important, however, has been the enactment of Decree-Law 175/2002 of 25 July 2002,[19] the adoption of which was motivated, according to the preamble, by the new government guidelines on waste management. Under these guidelines, the prevention of waste production and the promotion and development of integrated systems of collection, treatment, and improvement are central to waste management. In the particular case of hazardous industrial waste, the new law states that prevention, re-utilization, and recycling should be given priority over 'last line' solutions, such as co-incineration in cement plants. In addition to these guidelines, it was judged that a rigorous assessment of the current situation with regard to the production of hazardous industrial waste has not yet been made and that, until a sound and complete inventory on this issue is produced, a decision on the best solution for the treatment and management of this type of waste cannot be made. On the basis of these considerations, Decree-Law 175/2002 dismantled the Independent Scientific Commission for the Environmental Control and Monitoring of Co-incineration. Although more definitive conclusions on the issue of co-incineration are only to be expected in the course of 2003, the discontinuation of this commission appears to be an indication of the current government's reluctance towards co-incineration as a solution for the management of hazardous industrial waste.

G. Miscellaneous

i. Noise

In keeping with the same rationale of strengthening municipal powers in the legislation on nature conservation, Decree-Law 259/2002 of 23 November 2002[20] amended Decree-Law 292/2000 of 14 November 2000,[21] which in late 2000 introduced into the Portuguese legal system new regulations on noise pollution. In this regard, special permits for noisy activities are now administered

[19] (2002) *Diário da República*, No. 170, I-A, 5479.
[20] (2002) *Diário da República*, No. 271, I-A, 7368.
[21] (2000) *Diário da República*, No. 263, I-A, 6511.

by the municipalities, which have also taken on a more prominent role in enforcement activities, such as monitoring and application of penalties.

It is worth mentioning that noise pollution was probably the busiest field in terms of new legislation in 2002. Following the introduction of the new legal framework for noise pollution, Decree-Law 76/2002 of 26 March 2002[22] incorporated into Portuguese law Directive 2000/14/EC on Noise Emission in the Environment by Equipment for Use Outdoors.[23] Decree-Law 76/2002 was intended, further to the transposition of this Directive, to establish the requirements for the marketing of outdoor equipment. In addition, the law was aimed at ensuring that the public is adequately informed on the noise emission levels for outdoor equipment. In this regard, it establishes a set of obligations for manufacturers and producers in respect of indication of the level of noise emission on such equipment.

The other major legislative act in the domain of noise pollution was Decree-Law 129/2002 of 11 May 2002.[24] It introduced new regulations on the acoustic requirements for buildings, and represented a shift from the area of construction law to that of environmental law. Indeed, the acoustic protection of buildings, traditionally, has been subject to the regulations governing construction; in particular the General Regulations on Urban Buildings, which were adopted by Decree 38 382 of 7 August 1951.[25] Given the specific nature of the acoustic quality of buildings, the government saw fit to have it approved by an autonomous legislative act, namely Decree-Law 129/2002, instead of having such a specific matter governed by the regulations on noise pollution. At the same time, the acoustic requirements for buildings were considered to be an environmental issue and, as such, were approved as regulations pertaining to environmental, rather than construction, law.

H. Case Law

The only case involving Portugal, in the area of environmental law, to come before the Community courts during 2002 was Case C-392/99.[26] The action was lodged by the Commission against Portugal for failure to fulfil its obligations under Community law, namely: Articles 6(2), 8(2)(a), 13, and 17 of the Waste Oils Directive, as amended by Directive 87/101/EEC;[27] Article 10(1) EC; and Article 249(3) EC. The Commission's claims related to the permit procedure applicable to certain undertakings that dispose of waste oils, the conditions governing the disposal of residues from the combustion of waste oils, the inspection procedure for undertakings that dispose of waste oils, and the duty

[22] (2002) *Diário da República*, No. 72, I-A, 2879.
[23] [2000] OJ L162/1.
[24] (2002) *Diário da República*, No. 109, I-A, 4421.
[25] (1951) *Diário do Governo*, No. 166, 715.
[26] Case C-392/99, *Commission* v. *Portugal* [2003] ECR I-3373.
[27] [1987] OJ L42/43.

to convey information to the Commission. On 7 March 2002, Advocate General (AG) Stix-Hackl handed down his opinion in this case.[28]

The aim of the Waste Oils Directive was to protect the environment from the harmful effects of discharging, depositing, and treating waste oils. In order to achieve this aim Member States were obliged—under the original version of Articles 2 to 4 of the Directive—to take the necessary measures to ensure the safe collection and disposal of waste oils and to ensure that, as far as possible, they were disposed of by recycling. The principal aim of the revision of the Waste Oils Directive by Directive 87/101/EEC was to give priority to the processing of waste oils by regeneration in view of the energy savings this process can achieve. Articles 1 to 6 of the original text of the Waste Oils Directive were entirely replaced by new provisions.

In this legal context, the Commission claimed that Portugal was in breach of said provisions of the (amended) Directive by: (i) failing to adopt provisions whereby, before granting a permit to undertakings that regenerate waste oils or use them as fuel, the competent authority may satisfy itself that health is appropriately protected where waste oils are used as fuel, and that the best available technology not entailing excessive cost is used where waste oils are regenerated or used as fuel; (ii) failing to lay down that residues from the combustion of waste oils are to be disposed of in accordance with Article 9 of Directive 78/319/EEC on Toxic and Dangerous Waste (Toxic and Dangerous Waste Directive)[29] and, from 27 June 1995, in accordance with Article 9 of Directive 75/442/EEC on Waste,[30] which (as amended by Directive 91/156/ EEC and pursuant to Directive 91/689/EEC on Hazardous Waste[31]) replaced Article 9 of the Toxic and Dangerous Waste Directive; (iii) by failing to provide for periodical inspections of undertakings that regenerate waste oils or use them as fuel, or for examination of trends in the state of technical development and/or of the environment with a view to revising, where necessary, permits granted to those undertakings; and (iv) failing to convey to the Commission information concerning its technical expertise and the experience gained and results obtained through the application of measures taken pursuant to the amended Waste Oils Directive. Advocate General Stix-Hackl was of the opinion that the first, third, and fourth claims were well founded,[32] whilst he found the second to be partly inadmissible, to the extent that obligations did not exist under Article 9 of the Toxic and Dangerous Waste Directive.[33]

As regards the rulings of the Portuguese Constitutional Court issued in 2002 in the field of environmental law, no decisions were handed down dealing either with environmental protection alone or with a potential conflict between a constitutional objective or a fundamental right and environmental protection as a constitutionally protected guarantee.

[28] Opinion of AG Stix-Hackl issued on 7 Mar. 2002, in Case C-392/99, n. 26 above.
[29] [1978] OJ L84/43. [30] [1975] OJ L194/29. [31] [1991] OJ L377/20.
[32] n. 28 above, paras. 52, 111, 125, and 127. [33] ibid., para. 79.

XII. United Kingdom

*Ben Pontin**

A. Introduction

In a quiet year for Britain's legislatures,[1] the highlight of this survey is the House of Lords' ruling on causation in the negligence case of *Fairchild*.[2] Other highlights include EU-inspired amendments to secondary legislation in the fields of air, waste, and biotechnology; and influential domestic policy debates affecting the evolution of environmental law that were had in areas of taxation, genetically modified organisms (GMOs), and agriculture. Agriculture, inevitably, was a prominent issue. The foot and mouth epidemic of 2001 cast a long shadow throughout the year. In particular, it was the main catalyst behind the dissolution of the Ministry of Agriculture, Fisheries and Food (MAFF)[3] and the consequential resettlement of environmental affairs within a new department: the Department of the Environment, Food and Rural Affairs (DEFRA). This shifting in the executive frontiers of environmental policy attracted considerable criticism within Parliament.[4]

B. Atmospheric Pollution

i. Ozone Depleting Substances and Air Quality Objectives

The survey year began with difficulties surrounding the coming into force of European ozone controls contained in Regulation (EC) No. 2037/2000 on Substances that Deplete the Ozone Layer.[5] Transposed into domestic law by the Environmental Protection (Control of Ozone Depleting Substances) Regulations 2002,[6] this new and comprehensive regime controlling the production, marketing, trade in, and emissions of ozone-depleting substances (ODS)

* Burgess Salmon Environmental Law Research Unit, Faculty of Law, University of the West of England, Bristol (UK).

[1] The Scottish Parliament passed the Protection of Mammals (Scotland) Act 2002. This prohibited certain forms of hunting wild mammals, and thus represents an animal welfare measure more than one of nature conservation.

[2] *Fairchild* v. *Glenavon Funeral Services Ltd* [2002] 3 *Weekly Law Reports* 89, discussed in sect. H below.

[3] MAFF Dissolution Order (SI 2002/794).

[4] See the House of Commons Committee on Environment, Food and Rural Affairs, Tenth Report, Session 2001–2002, *The Role of DEFRA* (HC 991).

[5] [2000] OJ L244/1. These regulations had already come into force in respect of ozone-depleting substance (ODS) in the business sector. The outstanding measures were those concerning ODS contained in domestic goods.

[6] SI 2002/528. The EU legislation also necessitated amendment to Britain's waste regulations: Waste Management Licensing (Amendment) (England) Regulations 2002 (SI 2002/674).

required, *inter alia*, local authorities to remove ODS from domestic refrigerators prior to disposal. As the mountains of appliances awaiting safe disposal grew, it became apparent that local authorities lacked the technology necessary to comply with their obligations.[7] By the end of 2002, the technology had been disseminated and practical compliance problems eased.

Setting national air quality objectives for ozone has proved more challenging and long drawn out than for other pollutants.[8] Directive 2002/3/EC relating to Ozone in Ambient Air[9] (the third 'daughter directive' to Directive 96/62/EC on Ambient Air Quality Assessment and Management)[10] is thus something of a breakthrough, in requiring Member States to transpose target values for ozone into national law by 9 September 2003. The Government considered implementing this Directive early, in the course of implementing Directive 2000/69/EC relating to Limit Values for Benzene and Carbon Monoxide in Ambient Air[11] (the second 'daughter directive'), but, in the event, it was decided to implement each Directive in turn. Thus, the Air Quality (England) (Amendment) Regulations 2002[12] implement only the second daughter directive's provisions relating to objectives for benzene and carbon monoxide. These amend regulations of 2000.[13]

ii. Large Plant and Incinerators

Directive 2001/80/EC on the Limitation of Emissions of Certain Pollutants into the Air from Large Combustion Plants (Large Combustion Plants Directive)[14] reformed EC law relating to emissions from large combustion plants. Its central provisions were transposed into national law by the Pollution Prevention and Control (Combustion Plants) (England and Wales) Directions 2002.[15] These directions demonstrate, once again, Britain's scepticism towards emission limit values, preferring more flexible means of achieving the necessary environmental quality objectives. As an alternative to emission limit values applicable to each plant, the Large Combustion Plants Directive allowed Member States to implement a 'national plan' setting out practical measures for achieving the requisite environmental quality. The directions follow the national plan approach, as embodied in the 'UK Plan for the Reduction of Emissions into the Air of

[7] 'Report Blames Government for £40 m Fridge Mountain', *The Guardian*, 20 June 2002.

[8] The problem is the existence of major transboundary sources of ozone, beyond the control of individual Member States.

[9] [2002] OJ L67/14.

[10] [1996] OJ L296/55.

[11] [2000] OJ L313/12.

[12] SI 2002/3043.

[13] e.g. Air Quality (England) Regulations 2000 (SI 2000/928).

[14] [2001] OJ L309/1.

[15] These apply to plants requiring a permit under the Pollution Prevention and Control Act 1999. See also the Environment Protection (Combustion Plants) (England) Directions 2002, relating to plants requiring an authorization under Part I, Environmental Protection Act 1990.

Sulphur Dioxide and Oxides of Nitrogen from Existing Large Combustion Plants'.[16]

Directive 2000/76/EC on the Incineration of Waste (Waste Incineration Directive)[17] amends earlier EC waste incineration legislation with two aims in mind: first, to provide for greater stringency in the pollution control standards to be achieved by these plant; and secondly, greater resource efficiency so as to contribute to improvements in environmental quality more broadly. The Directive was transposed by the Waste Incinerator (England and Wales) Regulations 2002.[18] These regulations provide robust licensing conditions for preventing pollution from incinerators and important resource conservation measures, including the requirement that heat is recovered as far as practicable.[19]

C. Chemicals

Early in 2002, Parliament[20] addressed itself to the theme of UK and EU chemicals policy. The House of Lords expressed 'serious concern' at the 'lack of knowledge about the impact of many chemicals on the environment and human health'.[21] UK chemicals policy is largely in the hands of the Department for Environment, Food and Rural Affairs (DEFRA) and the Health and Safety Executive (HSE). The Health and Safety at Work etc. Act 1974 places a duty on any person who manufactures, imports, or supplies any substance for use at work to ensure that the substance is safe and without risks to health when properly used, and to carry out such tests and examinations as may be necessary. Risks to the environment are addressed within the framework of the Environmental Protection Act 1990. This contains powers to prohibit or restrict the importation, use, or storage of any substance in order to protect the environment (and indeed human health). The 1990 Act also established an Advisory Committee on Hazardous Substances.

Chemicals are deeply connected with issues of free movement of goods. Because of this, the EU has taken a particularly prescriptive line in legislating in this area.[22] With very little scope for developing a national regulatory approach, Britain has instead begun to experiment with precautionary risk assessment decision-making in cooperation with industry and other stakeholders. The cornerstone of this voluntary approach is the UK Chemical Stakeholders Forum,

[16] Available on the Internet at: http://www.defra.gov.uk.

[17] [2000] OJ L332/91.

[18] SI 2002/2980.

[19] Regulation 5. Another related provision is that incineration residues should be minimized and recycled where appropriate.

[20] House of Lords Select Committee on the European Union, Thirteenth Report 2001/2002, *Reducing the Risks–Regulating Industrial Chemicals* (HL Paper).

[21] ibid., para. 25.

[22] Beginning with Dir. 67/548/EEC on the Classification, Packaging and Labelling of Dangerous Substances [1967] OJ L196/1.

an advisory body with a truly diverse stakeholder membership.[23] Its key achievement of 2002 was to persuade the Government to seek an agreement with industry for the control of two chemicals of particular concern.[24]

D. Biotechnology

Directive 2001/18/EC on the Deliberate Release into the Environment of Genetically Modified Organisms and Repealing Council Directive 90/220/EEC (Deliberate Release Directive)[25] was transposed into domestic law by the Genetically Modified Organisms (Deliberate Release) Regulations 2002,[26] replacing earlier regulations of 1992. The main features of the reform are: phasing out of GMOs containing antibiotic resistance markers; more robust risk assessments covering long-term effects, backed by post-release monitoring requirements; and beefed-up public consultation procedures. Whilst the regulations bring Britain's laws into formal compliance with those of the EU, the main practical developments over the survey year were elsewhere. They surrounded the voluntary moratorium on commercial cultivation of GM crops agreed with industry in 1999. This agreement renders the legislation somewhat superfluous, at least for the time being.

In the previous UK survey, it was noted that momentum was gathering behind the idea of a national public debate, which would contribute to the decision whether to lift the moratorium.[27] This debate began to take clearer shape on 31 May 2002, when the Government asked the (independent) Agriculture and Environment Biotechnology Commission (AEBC) to advise on the terms of reference for the debate and on how a large-scale debate of the kind envisaged should be structured and executed.[28] In line with the AEBC's advice, the Public Debate Steering Board was set up, consisting predominantly of individuals connected with the AEBC, but with some representation by the Government too. It first met in September 2002, with a view to producing a final report by September 2003. An early assessment of the unfolding debate found that the Steering Group was in pursuit of a genuinely deliberative debate (rather than a mere poll of opinion or a referendum).[29] September 2003 is thus awaited with

[23] Alongside chemical industrialists, sit representatives from the environmental pressure group, Friends of the Earth, and the animal welfare group, British Union for the Abolition of Vivisection. Membership also includes representatives from the political party, the Green Alliance. See UK Chemical Stakeholders Forum, *Annual Report 2001/2002* (London: DEFRA, 2003), 6.

[24] ibid., 3. The chemicals were nonylphenol and octylpohenol (and their ethoxylates).

[25] [2001] OJ L106/1.

[26] SI 2002/2443.

[27] B. Pontin, 'United Kingdom' (2003) 3 *Yearbook of European Environmental Law*, 729.

[28] This section draws on S. Brown, 'The Agriculture and Environment Biotechnology Commission—Independent *and* Influential?' (2003) 15 *Environmental Law and Management* 2, 85–91.

[29] For a discussion of deliberative decision-making, see J. Steele, 'Participation and Deliberation in Environmental Law—Exploring a Problem Solving Approach' (2001) 21 *Oxford Journal of Legal Studies* 3, 415–42.

interest, although ultimately, of course, the key decisions are likely to be taken at an EU level, where an elaborate regulatory regime has been established that is unlikely to be held in perpetual abeyance.

E. Nature Conservation

During 2002, most of the outstanding provisions of the Countryside and Rights of Way Act 2000 were brought into force.[30] The new regime is thought to be working smoothly, with many further designations of Sites of Special Scientific Interest (SSSIs),[31] and no significant litigation before the courts.[32] The 'mapping process' (relating to access issues) got under way with secondary legislation on the point.[33] Policy-wise, England was given its own biodiversity strategy, under the auspices of the Countryside and Rights of Way Act 2000 (CROWA 2000).[34] In Scotland (to which CROWA 2000 does not apply), the Land Reform Bill continued its long passage through the Scottish Parliament.

Directive 1999/22/EC relating to the Keeping of Wild Animals in Zoos (Zoo Directive)[35] is concerned mainly with the welfare of animals, but its recital signals a wider objective: 'the need to ensure that zoos adequately fulfil their important role in the conservation of species'. National implementing measures were required to be in place by 9 April 2002, but the survey year passed without the necessary measures being taken.[36] This is somewhat of an embarrassment for Britain, as the Zoo Directive owes much to Britain's Presidency of the EU in 1998.[37] Farming practices are of course fundamental to nature conservation in many important ways. In 2001, the Government set up the Policy Commission on the Future of Farming and Food, to advise on how to create a sustainable, competitive, and diverse farming and food sector. Its report, entitled *Farming and Food—A Sustainable Future*, was published in January 2002.[38] Chapter 4 is of particular interest. Having outlined in graphic detail the legacy of environmental degradation which resulted from changes in farming practices introduced immediately after the Second World War, the Commission focuses on imaginative but practical ways in which farmers can achieve effective environmental stewardship.

[30] e.g. Countryside and Rights of Way Act 2000 (Commencement No. 3) (Wales) Order 2002 (SI 2002/2615) (W 253).

[31] As reported on the Internet at: http://www:english-nature.org.uk.

[32] Cf. the human rights case, *The Queen (Aggregate Industries Ltd)* v. *English Nature and the Secretary of State* [2002] *ENDS Report*, May 57, discussed in sect. 'I' below.

[33] e.g. Countryside Access (Provisional and Conclusive Maps) (Wales) Regulations 2002 (SI 2002/1796) (W 171).

[34] *England's Biodiversity Strategy—Working with the Grain of Nature* (London: DEFRA, 2002).

[35] [1999] OJ L94/24.

[36] Although the Zoo Licensing Act 1981 does partially implement the Directive.

[37] See N. Parpworth, 'The Licensing of Zoos—A Reformed Regime' (2003) 15 *Environmental Law and Management* 3, 175–218.

[38] Policy Commission on the Future of Farming and Food, *Farming and Food—A Sustainable Future* (London: Cabinet Office, 2002).

Carrots (metaphorically), more than sticks, are considered to be the way forward. This was endorsed in the Government's *Strategy for Sustainable Farming and Food*.[39] A specific example of the voluntary approach to agricultural environmental stewardship in this context is the Action Plan to Develop Organic Farming and Food in England.[40]

F. Waste

Directive 1999/31/EC on Landfill of Waste (Waste Landfill Directive)[41] provided Europe with its first landfill-specific legislation. It was implemented in the UK, a year late, by the Landfill (England and Wales) Regulations 2002.[42] The Regulations reform the Pollution Prevention and Control (England and Wales) Regulations 2000,[43] the Waste Management Licensing Regulations 1994,[44] and the Environmental Protection (Duty of Care) Regulations 1991.[45] Earlier, in 2000, the Directive's strategic requirements relating to reducing dependency on landfill were implemented in the *Waste Strategy for England and Wales*,[46] which continued to apply throughout the survey year.

As in the past, waste regulation occupied the courts on an almost daily basis throughout 2002. The relationship between criminal and civil sanctions for waste infractions under the Environmental Protection Act 1990 was highlighted in *The Queen* v. *Ivory Plant Hire*.[47] One of the defendant company's directors was imprisoned for twelve months for a series of fly tipping offences. For the first time since 1999, and possibly only the second time ever, the Environment Agency sought to invoke powers for the court to disqualify an individual from holding a company directorship under section 11(1) of the Company Directors Disqualification Act 1986.[48] A similar request was made of another of the company's directors, who had been convicted of these offences but not imprisoned. The individuals were disqualified for ten years and five years respectively.

In *Murray* v. *Derbyshire County Council*,[49] the Court of Appeal ruled on the legal status of the 'general objective' contained in Article 4 of Directive 91/156/EEC amending Directive 75/442/EEC on Waste (Waste Framework Directive).[50] The Council had given consent for an extension of a landfill site—a decision which was challenged on the basis that insufficient regard had been paid to the environmental objective in Article 4. Previously, the Court of Appeal had ruled that this provision was simply one material consideration among many.[51] Pill LJ in *Murray* took a different line: 'An objective in my judgment is something

[39] *Strategy for Sustainable Farming and Food* (London: DEFRA, 2002).
[40] Available on the Internet at: http://www.defra.gov.uk/farm/organic/actionplan/actionplan.htm.
[41] [1999] OJ L182/1. [42] SI 2002/1559. [43] SI 2000/1973.
[44] SI 1994/1056.
[45] SI 1991/2839. [46] Cm 4693, London, 2000. [47] [2002] *ENDS Report*, Oct. 60.
[48] SI 1986/2067. [49] [2002] *ENDS Report*, Mar. 55. [50] [1991] OJ L78/32.
[51] *The Queen* v. *Bolton MDC ex p. Kirkman* (1998) 25 *Journal of Planning and Environmental Law*, 687.

different from a material consideration . . . An objective which is obligatory must always be kept in mind when making a decision even while the decision maker has regard to other material considerations'.[52]

Thus, a decision which gave such weight to other (non-environmental) factors as to involve a plain and flagrant disregard for the objectives could be illegal. On the facts, however, the grant of planning consent was lawful.

G. Water

The survey year closed with considerable ground still to cover in order for Britain to comply with Directive 2000/60/EC establishing a Framework for Community Action in the Field of Water Policy (Water Framework Directive).[53] In October 2002, the Government entered a second phase in its public consultation on measures for implementing the Directive.[54] It is clear from this consultation paper that the issue of controlling diffuse pollution is the most challenging. What is unclear is the appropriate regulatory response. Chapter 11, in particular, revealed that issues as fundamental as the identity of the competent regulatory authority remained open to suggestion.[55] Indeed, the Environment Agency's effectiveness in its present role as policer of rivers pollution offences under the Water Resources Act 1991 was called into question in quite dramatic fashion in *Hart* v. *Anglian Water*.[56] When the Environment Agency did not prosecute after a sewage pollution incident involving the defendants, Mr Hart brought a private prosecution. The £200,000 (approximately €300,000) fine handed down by the Magistrates is thought to be the largest ever for an offence of that kind.

In October 2002, the law was at last brought into compliance with Directive 91/676/EEC on the Protection of Waters against Pollution Caused by Nitrates from Agricultural Sources (Nitrates Directive),[57] which Britain was held to have breached in Case C-69/99, *Commission* v. *UK*.[58] The Nitrate Vulnerable Zones (Additional Designations) (England) (No. 2) Regulations 2002[59] added 47 per cent to existing Nitrate Vulnerable Zones (NVZ) coverage. As a consequence, over 50 per cent of agricultural land now falls within the NVZ scheme of protection. The 'Action Programme' of which this protection consists remains unchanged.

[52] n. 49 above.

[53] [2000] OJ L327/1. See in particular the concerns expressed by Members of Parliament in the Environment, Food and Rural Affairs Committee, Fourth Report, Session 2002–2003, *Water Framework Directive* (HC 130).

[54] *Second Consultation Paper on the Implementation of the EC Water Framework Directive* (2000/60) (London: DEFRA, 2002).

[55] ibid., para. 11.69.

[56] [2002] *ENDS Report*, Mar. 54.

[57] [1991] OJ L375/1.

[58] [2000] ECR I-10979.

[59] SI 2002/2614.

H. Horizontal Instruments

During 2002 there were developments in the law relating to access to environmental information,[60] environmental impact assessment (EIA),[61] town and country planning,[62] and human rights.[63] Important debates concerning taxation took place,[64] and there has been progress with the execution of the UK's pilot emissions trading scheme.[65] However, two developments of interest and importance are particularly noteworthy. One is the environmental dimension to the draft Companies Bill, published in July 2002 as part of the White Paper, *Modernising Company Law*.[66] The other is the relaxation in the causation requirements of a negligence action, brought about by the House of Lords' judgment in *Fairchild*.[67]

i. The Emerging Environmental Dimension to Company Law Reform

Modernising Company Law is a bold (and generally warmly received) policy document in which the Government set out the case for the assimilation of the 'environment' within company law. For example, it is proposed that all directors be under a duty to take account of the company's impact on the environment, where material,[68] whilst directors of Britain's largest companies will be required to publish an annual operating and financial review (OFR), which could include information about the company's environmental performance. Part of the rationale for this is grounded in the concept of corporate responsibility. Of course, this rather nebulous concept touches on the environment, but only as one consideration alongside many others of a social, ethical, and indeed commercial nature. The Company Law Review Steering Group relied exclusively on this rationale.[69]

Another part of the rationale, as expressed in the White Paper, is grounded firmly in established environmental principles and objectives. In the context of the general environmental duty on all company directors, the environment

[60] Freedom of Information (Commencement No. 2) Order 2002, SI 2002/2812.

[61] e.g. Environment Impact Assessment (Scotland) Amendment Regulations, SI 2002/324.

[62] e.g. in the field of enforcement, *inter alia*: Town and Country Planning (Enforcement Notices and Appeals) (England) Regulations, SI 2002/2682; and Town and Country Planning (Enforcement) (Determination by Inspectors) (Inquiries) (England) Procedure Rules, SI 2002/2685.

[63] The human rights reasoning of the High Court in *Marcic* v. *Thames Water Utilities plc* (2001) 66 *All England Law Reports* 3, 698 was upheld by the Court of Appeal: [2002] EWCA Civ 65. See also the extension of *The Queen (Alconbury)* v. *Secretary of State* (2001) 66 *All England Law Reports* 1, 929 to SSSI designations in *Pioneer Aggregates*.

[64] Environmental Audit Committee, Second Report, Session 2001–2002, *Pre-Budget Report 2001–A New Agenda?* (HC 363).

[65] See the website of the UK Emissions Trading Group on the Internet at: http://www.uketg.com.

[66] Cm 5553, London, 2002.

[67] n. 2 above.

[68] The concept of materiality is to be fleshed out by Government guidance.

[69] Set up by the Government in 1998 to oversee an initial consultation process and make recommendations for reform.

(in relation to other social concerns) is stated by the Government to be 'first amongst equals'.[70] Of the reporting provisions, the Government states: 'The new requirement to report, for example, on material environmental issues would be a major contribution to both broad corporate social responsibility and sustainable development initiatives'.[71] Is this one of the clearest examples yet of what might be involved in 'fourth phase' environmental law?[72]

ii. Causation—the Fairchild *Case*

In the year that the European Commission published proposals for a public law system of environmental remedies, the House of Lords decision in *Fairchild*[73] signalled that common law, private law, is willing to respond to changing perceptions of responsibility for environmental risk and harm. The claim was based on employees who had contracted asbestos-related diseases, whose causes were attributed to exposure to asbestos in the workplace. Each of the defendants had, at the material time, acted carelessly, but it was impossible to prove that any one or more acts of carelessness caused the harm. The court was faced with a difficult choice. Application of the established test of causation (i.e. that a defendant must be proved to have materially contributed to the *cause* of the disease or injury) would have served the interests of legal certainty, but offended morality. It would have shielded from liability undeserving defendants whose carelessness had exposed individuals to risk. An alternative was to relax traditional doctrine, so that it extended to material contribution to the *risk* of disease, and so on. In a judgment deeply infused with moral reasoning, the House of Lords unanimously preferred the latter. Profoundly important in itself, this decision could also turn out to have implications beyond negligence, encompassing, in particular, private nuisance.

I. Miscellaneous

> There has been some concern that the level of fines and sentences given in environmental cases are not high enough. This has led to a situation where, for some unscrupulous companies and individuals, it is cheaper to commit an offence and continue to pay the fines rather than comply with the law and pay the real cost, including the environmental and social cost, of polluting.[74]

Costing the Earth—Information for Sentencer, published in 2002, provides magistrates (many of whom are unused to adjudicating on environmental crimes) with

[70] n. 66 above, para. 4.31.

[71] ibid., para. 4.32.

[72] G. Winter, 'Perspectives for Environmental Law—Entering the Fourth Phase' (1989) 1 *Journal of Environmental Law* 1, 38–47.

[73] n. 2 above.

[74] *Costing the Earth—Information for Sentencer* (London: Magistrates' Association/Environmental Law Foundation, 2002), para. 1.1.

a sentencing 'toolkit'. It is an important contribution to an area of environmental justice that has long been recognized as weak, but where—until this handbook—there had been little attempt at concerted action to improve matters.[75] Perhaps next year, as a result, robust sentences such as those handed down in *Hart*[76] will become more typical.

J. Conclusion

The year 2002 deserves to be remembered as the year when the courts recaptured their spirit of innovation in relation to the common law, seemingly lost in several high-profile cases previously.[77] *Fairchild* has been described as the most important tort case since *Donoghue* v. *Stevenson* (1932).[78] Whilst this should be treated with caution in that the House of Lords stressed that the case turned on its own particular facts (as ever), nonetheless, in attributing overriding importance to morality in defining legal wrongs, it may have far-reaching implications. In criminal cases too, the courts have shown remarkable responsiveness. *Hart* reveals that the courts are prepared to 'reward' private prosecutors who step in to protect the public interest where public regulators look on. More innovation and creativity of this kind in 2003 will invite advocates of a specialized environmental court to reconsider the strength of their case.

In administrative terms, a number of conclusions can be drawn. The task of transposing EC legislation by the date due continues to pose problems, as was the case in 2002 in the context of ozone, landfill, nitrates, and zoos. Not all law has its origins in the EU, however, and in 2002 there were imaginative unilateral developments in areas of public participation in decision-making (relating to GMOs), economic instruments (relating to tradeable emission permits), and perhaps most significant of all, company law reform. Interestingly, much of the impetus has come from Whitehall, with the environment having a comparatively low profile in terms of major achievements in the devolved regions.[79] With important Scottish legislation due to be enacted in the fields of water and nature conservation, this conclusion may need to be revisited in 2003.

[75] For a solution to a different aspects of the problem, see: the Proceeds of Crime Act 2002; and the creation of the National Wildlife Crime Intelligence Unit (Apr. 2002), (2002) 14 *Environmental Law and Management*, 105.

[76] n. 56 above.

[77] e.g. *Cambridge Water v. Eastern Counties Leathers* [1994] 2 AC 264; *Hunter* v. *Canary Wharf* [1996] 44 *Weekly Law Reports* 2, 348.

[78] Freshfields Bruckhaus Beringer, *Fairchild—A Donoghue v Stevenson for the 21 Century?* (London: FBP, 2002).

[79] See e.g. P. Hunter, 'Devolution—Evolution or Revolution? Environmental Law and Policy in Scotland and the Effects of Devolution' (2002) 14 *Environmental Law and Management* 2, 339.

XIII. EU Candidate Countries

Marie Soveroski *

A. Introduction

Preparations for membership of the European Union (EU) continued to dominate the legislative and political agendas of the candidate countries in 2002.[1] Transposition of legislation in the lead-up to accession[2] resulted in the adoption of a multitude of national legislation. The year was a particularly significant one with respect to enlargement and environmental policy, as accession negotiations with most of the candidate countries on this chapter of the *acquis communautaire* were concluded in December. Hence, the transition periods allowed to these countries in order to comply with European Community (EC) environmental law have now been settled.

An overview of the legislation adopted, as well as areas identified for priority attention, are reflected in the results of the accession negotiations, as well as in the European Commission's annual Regular Reports on the progress these countries made towards preparation for EU membership. A brief presentation on environmental measures adopted in the candidate countries is presented first, with an overview of the results of the negotiations following.

B. Country Reports

i. Bulgaria

Bulgaria slowly worked its way through transposition obligations, although the Commission noted that it has not always complied with the agreed schedule for transposition. Examples of the latter were in the areas of genetically modified organisms (GMOs) and industrial accident risk management. In April 2002, Bulgaria adopted regulations on maximum allowable levels of radioactive contamination in agricultural products and foodstuffs, and a law on Safe Use of Nuclear Energy, in June. In July, legislation was adopted controlling the import and export of dangerous substances and on risk assessment of new chemical substances. Bulgaria adopted a framework Environmental Protection Act in

* Director, European Centre for Judges and Lawyers, European Institute of Public Administration (EIPA), Antenna Luxembourg (Luxembourg).

[1] The countries addressed here are Bulgaria, Cyprus, Czech Republic, Estonia, Hungary, Latvia, Lithuania, Malta, Poland, Romania, Slovakia, and Slovenia. Although Turkey has also now been officially recognized as a candidate country, as accession negotiations have not yet commenced, analysis of its progress with respect to adoption of the *acquis communautaire* is not systematically pursued in this survey.

[2] All candidate countries except Bulgaria, Romania, and Turkey will join the EU on 1 May 2004.

September 2002, which provides the basis for further legislative measures such as on environmental impact assessment (EIA), access to environmental information, and integrated pollution prevention and control (IPPC). Waste legislation was also adopted with respect to end-of-life vehicles (ELVs).[3]

While progress in the area of water quality protection was slower than anticipated, some progress was made with respect to transposition of Directive 2000/60/EC establishing a Framework for Community Action in the Field of Water Policy (Water Framework Directive),[4] Directive 91/271/EEC on Urban Waste-Water Treatment (Urban Waste-Water Directive),[5] Directive 98/83/EC on the Quality of Water Intended for Human Consumption (Drinking Water Directive),[6] and Directive 76/160/EEC concerning the Quality of Bathing Water (Bathing Water Directive).[7]

In August 2002, Bulgaria adopted its Law on Biological Diversity, which included provisions as required by Directive 79/409/EEC on the Conservation of Wild Birds (Birds Directive),[8] and Directive 92/43/EEC on the Conservation of Natural Habitats and of Wild Fauna and Flora (Habitats Directive).[9] While welcoming the legislation, the Commission identified this as an area where the lack of administrative capacity, at both the national and sub-national level, was problematic. To remedy the situation, with respect to implementation and enforcement of environmental law in general, the Bulgarian Council of Ministers authorized the hiring of over 500 additional persons to staff the Ministry of Environment, the Executive Environmental Agency, regional inspectorates, and the River Basin Directorates. In addition, River Basin Directorates (management authorities) were established, as well as a department within the Environment Executive Agency to deal with IPPC.[10]

With respect to identifying priorities for future action, the Commission indicated that particular attention should be paid to the development of waste management plans, designation of sensitive areas and discharge permitting in the area of water quality control, industrial pollution and risk management, and chemicals policy, as well as improving capacity in the areas of GMOs and nature protection.[11]

ii. Cyprus

One of the major pieces of environmental legislation adopted in Cyprus was the Law for the Environmental Impact Assessment of Certain Projects, implemented

[3] Commission of the European Communities, '2002 Regular Report on Bulgaria's Progress Towards Accession' COM(2002)700 final, SEC(2002)1400, 9 Oct. 2002 (Bulgaria Report), 102–3.

[4] [2000] OJ L327/1.

[5] [1991] OJ L135/40, as amended by Dir. 98/15/EC [1998] OJ L67/29.

[6] [1998] OJ L330/32.

[7] [1976] OJ L31/1.

[8] [1979] OJ L103/1.

[9] [1992] OJ L206/7.

[10] Bulgaria Report, n. 3 above, 102–3.

[11] ibid. 104.

in February 2002.[12] Cyprus sought compliance with EC requirements on industrial pollution control and risk management through regulations adopted under its Health and Safety at Work Law, in December 2001, which addressed control of major accidents and hazards. In March 2002, the Type Approval of Motor Vehicles Law was amended, including expanding coverage for non-road mobile machinery. A month later, the Law on Packaging and Packaging Waste was adopted, along with related implementing regulations. Framework legislation was adopted as a basis for transposition of the 'new approach' directives on noise from vehicles and machinery. In May 2002, regulations on Polychlorinated Biphenyls is (PCBs) and Polychlorinated Terphenyls (PCTs), waste oils, and batteries and accumulators were adopted. The Water Pollution Control Bill, agreed upon in June, addressed the transposition requirements of a number of EC water quality protection measures, as well as some requirements of the IPPC Directive.[13]

The Radiation Protection Law was adopted in June, and a regulation on information to be provided to the public in the event of a radiological emergency was adopted in July. A bill on noise from household appliances was approved by the Council of Ministers in July, and regulations adopted under the Petroleum Law were amended, in pursuit of compliance with EC air quality control requirements.[14]

Legislative integration of environmental protection considerations took place in a few policy areas. With respect to agricultural policy, this included adoption of provisions on the use of fertilizers and pesticides and establishment of a legal framework for promotion of organic cultivation. In the transport sector this was done in the context of the adoption of a strategy on 'sustainable mobility' in new land-use plans adopted for urban areas.[15] In order to improve administrative capacity, additional staff were hired by the Environment Service, while implementing programmes were adopted in the areas of carbon dioxide (CO_2), ozone, and waste management strategies, chemicals and other pollutants, IPPC, and habitat protection.[16]

The Commission's Regular Report indicated that particular attention should be paid to adoption of air quality and hazardous waste management legislation, as well as measures dealing with industrial pollution and risk management, chemicals, GMOs, and noise.[17]

iii. Czech Republic

Czech implementing EIA legislation, the Act on Waste, and the Act on Packaging Waste, all came into force in January 2002. A multitude of implementing decrees

[12] Commission of the European Communities, '2002 Regular Report on Cyprus's Progress Towards Accession' COM(2002)700 final, SEC(2002)1401, 9 Oct. 2002 (Cyprus Report), 97.

[13] ibid. 97–8.

[14] ibid. 98–9.

[15] ibid. 97. [16] ibid. 99. [17] ibid.

was adopted addressing specific waste streams, such as hazardous waste and batteries, as well as for water quality protection. The Act on Air Protection, addressing control of air pollution, protection of the ozone layer, and actions against climate change, was adopted in February, and came into force in July. It required the development of action plans in areas where limit values for certain pollutants are exceeded, and established a new category of control with respect to large combustion facilities.[18]

The Act on Integrated Pollution Prevention and Control was also adopted in February 2002, and entered into force in January 2003. An IPPC Agency was established within the Czech Environment Institute in support of this. A Government Regulation concerning noise emissions from products came into force in April 2002, while the Act on Biocides and related implementing legislation, adopted in pursuit of EC requirements on chemicals, came into force in July. An amendment to the Atomic Act, adopted in December 2001, also came into effect in July 2002, along with related implementing legislation. With this, the Czech transposition in the area of radiation protection and emergency preparedness, as well as with respect to transport of radioactive materials, was completed.[19]

The Act on Municipalities, adopted in June 2002, elaborated environmental responsibilities to be taken over by municipalities commencing in January 2003. Czech penal law was also amended, with certain acts of non-compliance with nature protection legislation (by both natural and legal persons) being defined as criminal offences.[20]

Administrative coordination, if not capacity, was an issue identified by the Commission. The latter expressed the view that, despite the established system for permitting, inspections, and enforcement in the area of water quality control, the division of responsibility among a large number of authorities weakened enforcement efforts.[21] With respect to other priority areas, the Commission indicated that particular attention should be paid to adoption of legislation on EIA, titanium dioxide waste, and industrial pollution/risk management, water quality and nature protection, as well as implementation of existing legislation. Significantly, while waste management and river basin management plans, as well as action programmes for air quality, still need to be adopted, the Czech Republic lacks the data on compliance and non-compliance needed to be able to develop such strategies.[22]

iv. Estonia

Estonia's legislative efforts have not only been motivated by the requirements of the EC environmental *acquis* but also by the provisions of its own National Environmental Action Plan, and by the Baltic Sea Agenda 21. With respect to

[18] Commission of the European Communities, '2002 Regular Report on Czech Republic's Progress Towards Accession' COM(2002)700 final, SEC(2002)1402, 9 Oct. 2002 (Czech Report), 104–5.

[19] ibid. 105–6. [20] ibid. 106. [21] ibid. 107. [22] ibid. 106 and 108.

such cross-border efforts, Estonia signed an agreement with Finland, in February 2002, on Environmental Impact Assessment in a Transboundary Context.[23]

The Protected Natural Objects Act was amended in December 2001, in order to comply with requirements of the Habitats Directive. The Hunting Act, adopted in April 2002, brings Estonian legislation in line with the EC *acquis*, except with respect to the hunting of bears, which continues to be legal in Estonia. The IPPC Act entered into force in May 2002, establishing a standard format for public notification and applications for permits. Three implementing pieces of legislation, related to the Contained Use of GMMs Act, of November 2001, were adopted in January 2002. This brought Estonian legislation close to compliance with EC requirements in the area of GMOs and GMMs.[24]

A regulation on the protection of water from nitrate pollution from agricultural sources came into effect in February 2002, partially aligning Estonia legislation with EC rules. An amendment to the Water Act, which came into effect in April 2002, established requirements for discharges of dangerous substances and water permits. Two regulations adopted under the Water Act, in June 2002, completed alignment with EC law with respect to drinking water. Regulations were also approved on water quality protection related to the operation of oil products terminals, in December 2001; professional certification requirements for persons involved with water surveys, in January 2002; and water sampling methods, in May 2002. The Regulation on Environmental Noise and Measurement Methods, approved in April 2002, also moved compliance closer in this area.[25]

In pursuit of EC requirements in the area of air quality control, the Government approved, in June and July 2002, regulations establishing emission limits with respect to non-road mobile machinery, and related to the production and processing of cellulose, cement, and timber. Estonia adopted regulations under its Waste Act and Packaging Act, bringing its legislation into compliance with EC requirements with respect to asbestos waste, waste reporting, a national packaging information system, waste shipments, and a waste catalogue. In addition, a Government Regulation was adopted in August 2002, defining hazardous waste.[26]

Despite considerable progress in adopting environmental protection legislation, the Commission noted that important framework legislation on air quality and radiation protection is still missing. It further pointed out that Parliamentary acts are still needed with respect to waste, nature protection, biocides, and chemicals, and that implementing legislation is still lacking with respect to waste, noise, industrial pollution, chemicals, and GMOs.[27]

[23] Commission of the European Communities, '2002 Regular Report on Estonia's Progress Towards Accession' COM(2002)700 final, SEC(2002)1403, 9 Oct. 2002 (Estonia Report), 96.

[24] ibid.

[25] ibid.

[26] ibid. 95. [27] ibid. 96–7.

v. Hungary

Hungary had a busy legislative programme in 2002, particularly with respect to waste and water issues. Legislation on waste and on packaging and packaging waste was adopted in May 2002, while over the course of the year legislation was adopted in pursuit of EC requirements with respect to incineration of waste, titanium-dioxide waste, the compilation of lists of waste, and hazardous waste, and establishment of fines for incorrect waste management. Legislation was also adopted for drinking and bathing water quality, and discharges of dangerous substances into water. Moreover, legislation was passed concerning waste-water and sewage, including on the determination of waste-water agglomerations, on registration and reporting with respect to urban waste-water, and establishing fines for violations.[28]

In July 2002, air quality control legislation was adopted with respect to non-road mobile machinery, and on consumer information to be provided on fuel economy and CO_2 emissions of new passenger cars. Legislation was also adopted to comply with EC legislation on the marketing and use of certain dangerous substances and preparations.[29]

Laws controlling the emission of noise from equipment for use outdoors entered into force in January 2002, while rules on the permitting of transboundary shipments of radioactive waste entered into force in April 2002. Legislation to comply with Directive 96/82/EC on the Control of Major-Accident Hazards Involving Dangerous Substances (Seveso II Directive)[30] also came into effect in 2002. An IPPC Bureau was established within the Environment Ministry's Institute for Environmental Management, to support effective implementation of the IPPC Directive.[31] Hungary has pursued establishment of such institutional and administrative expert bodies in a number of areas. For example, a Permitting Authority for GMOs was established within the Ministry of Economic Affairs. Moreover, the Hungarian National Environmental Council was established, as an advisory body bringing together representatives of the scientific community, NGOs, and industry, as a means to support the integration of environmental considerations into all policy areas.[32]

In order to further improve its administrative capacity in the environmental protection area, responsibility for water management and air quality monitoring were given to the newly reformulated Ministry of Environment and Water Management from, respectively, the Ministry of Transport and the Ministry of Health. Further, an inter-ministerial working group meets on a regular basis to deal with issues of transposition and implementation of environmental legislation.[33]

[28] Commission of the European Communities, '2002 Regular Report on Hungary's Progress Towards Accession' COM(2002)700 final, SEC(2002)1404, 9 Oct. 2002 (Hungary Report), 104.

[29] ibid. 103.

[30] [1997] OJ L10/13.

[31] Hungary Report, n. 28 above, 104. [32] ibid. 103–4. [33] ibid. 104–5.

With respect to identifying priorities for future action, the Commission observed that legislation was still lacking on air quality (concerning sulphur content of fuels, ozone, and designation of zones and agglomerations), ELVs, nature protection, biocidal products, asbestos, and GMOs, with particular urgency being ascribed to adoption of a National Waste Management Plan and Regional Environmental Inspectorate Plans. Air quality monitoring and programmes, as well as implementation of Directive 1999/31/EC on Landfill of Waste (Waste Landfill Directive),[34] were also considered pressing.[35]

vi. Latvia

In its Regular Report, the Commission stated that Latvia had made particular progress in bringing its legislation into alignment with the *acquis* in the areas of water quality, waste management, nature protection, and noise.[36] During 2002, Latvia adopted legislation on urban waste-water treatment, discharges of dangerous substances into surface water, groundwater protection, nitrates, and on the protection of the quality of bathing water, drinking water, and fisheries water. In January 2002, legislation was adopted identifying all of Latvia as a sensitive area with respect to the urban waste-water Directive. With respect to waste, Latvia adopted rules dealing with the temporary storage of hazardous waste and the handling of packaging waste in July, and formulated a National Waste Management Plan in August. It also adopted legislation with respect to the landfill of waste, and disposal of waste oils, PCBs and PCTs, and batteries and accumulators.[37]

Several measures were adopted in May 2002, to enhance the strength of nature protection, including legislation elaborating the criteria for establishing protected areas. A State Environmental Monitoring Programme was established, containing provisions on protection of biological diversity, and a Nature Protection Board began operating. With respect to noise, legislation was adopted regulating both indoor and outdoor equipment and appliances.[38]

In pursuit of compliance with EC air quality requirements, Latvia amended its regulations on volatile organic compound (VOC) emissions from storage and distribution of petrol, in January 2002, and adopted new legislation on fuel quality and on air quality with respect to benzene and carbon monoxide, and a regulation on conformity assessment of petrol and diesel fuel, in June and July. Legislation on large combustion plants was adopted in August. In pursuit of industrial pollution control and risk management, an IPPC-modelled permitting system was put into place, and a new division on IPPC and major accident hazards control was established within the State Environmental Inspectorate.

[34] [1999] OJ L182/1.

[35] Hungary Report, n. 28 above, 105–6, and 108.

[36] Commission of the European Communities, '2002 Regular Report on Latvia's Progress Towards Accession' COM(2002)700 final, SEC(2002)1405, 9 Oct. 2002 (Latvia Report), 104.

[37] ibid. 105. [38] ibid. 105–6.

A government regulation on notification and risk assessment of new chemical substances was also adopted in August. Implementing regulations were agreed with respect to work-related and medical exposures to radiation, and the handling of radioactive waste.[39]

A Council for Sustainable Development was established in March 2002, chaired by the Prime Minister. Latvia's Strategy for Sustainable Development was adopted in August. Like Estonia, Latvia is also involved with the Baltic Sea Agenda 21.[40]

According to the Commission's Regular Report, compliance with the *acquis communautaire* is still lacking with respect to the sulphur content of certain fuels, ELVs, chemicals, GMOs, and nuclear safety and radiation protection (basic safety standards). Moreover, transposition still needs to be completed with respect to nature protection and water quality, in particular for water management law and drinking water. The Commission stated that close attention should be paid to the implementation of EC rules on waste management (in particular regarding permitting), air quality (ambient air quality programme), water quality (designation of vulnerable zones and preparation of action plans, review of permits), industrial pollution control (issuing of integrated permits), and chemicals (administrative capacity). The Commission also noted that the distinctions between permitting, compliance, verification, and enforcement activities should be clarified and strengthened, as should, generally, the role of the Regional Environmental Boards.[41]

vii. Lithuania

Lithuania made progress in complying with EC rules on ambient air quality and reduction of VOC emissions from storage and distribution of petrol. Studies were carried out to determine the most appropriate way to enhance compliance with Directive 1999/32/EC on the Sulphur Content of Certain Liquid Fuels (Sulphur Directive).[42] Ministerial orders were issued at the end of 2001 and the beginning of 2002, on protection of groundwater, rules for the establishment of an inventory on dangerous substances, nitrate pollution, and designation of institutions responsible for various water quality protection issues. A law on pollution-related charges, including packaging and other waste-related goods, was adopted in January 2002. Three ministerial orders on packing waste were adopted in June 2002. In April 2002, the National Waste Management Plan was adopted, with amendments being made to the law on waste management in July 2002. The biggest problem identified by the Commission in the area of waste management was with respect to hazardous waste, for which only temporary storage was currently available.[43]

[39] ibid. [40] ibid. 104–5.
[41] ibid. 107. [42] [1999] OJ L121/13.
[43] Commission of the European Communities, '2002 Regular Report on Lithuania's Progress Towards Accession' COM(2002)700 final, SEC(2002)1406, 9 Oct. 2002 (Lithuania Report), 106–7.

In December 2001, legislation on habitat and wildlife protection was amended, while implementing legislation with respect to species of Community importance was adopted. A list of proposed sites of Community importance was drafted in April 2002. A division was established between the Nature Protection Department of the Ministry of Environment, responsible for GMOs, and a consultative committee on GMOs. Provisions on issuing certificates for GMOs and related product use were adopted, while provisions on testing for eco-toxicity of chemical substances, and on data collection, processing and dissemination, were approved in January and February 2002, respectively. The national licensing system for ozone-depleting substances was updated in March.[44]

Rules on integrated industrial permitting were adopted in February, and on collection of emission data in March. In more horizontal areas, a special working group of the National Sustainable Development Commission was established to develop a sustainable development strategy. Legislation on access to environmental information was also adopted, by means of amendments to the framework Law on Environmental Protection, which entered into force in January 2002.[45]

The Commission's Regular Report noted that compliance with the *acquis* is still lacking with respect to biocides, risk assessment and other information on GMOs, waste incineration, VOC emissions, and permitting guidelines, packaging waste and waste oils, and nature protection. Regulation of noise is a particular problem, as no transposition has yet taken place in this sector.[46]

viii. Malta

Like a number of other candidate countries, Malta established a National Commission for Sustainable Development, in February 2002, chaired by its Prime Minister.[47]

The 2001 Maltese Waste Management Strategy provides for specified treatment of waste in three categories: demolition waste, municipal and hazardous waste, and actions with respect to three landfills. Regulations on the disposal of waste, including hazardous waste, and controlling shipments of radioactive waste, were adopted in December 2001, while regulations on sewage sludge came into effect in Spring 2002.[48]

Malta adopted a regulation on freedom of access to environmental information, and added several related amendments to the Development Planning Act. In June 2002, regulations were adopted on ambient air limits for benzene and carbon monoxide, sulphur content of liquid fuels, and consumer

[44] ibid. 107.

[45] ibid. 106.

[46] ibid. 108–9.

[47] Commission of the European Communities, '2002 Regular Report on Malta's Progress Towards Accession' COM(2002)700 final, SEC(2002)1407, 9 Oct. 2002 (Malta Report), 84.

[48] ibid. 85.

information on fuel economy and CO_2 emissions of new cars, as well as regulations on waste oils, batteries and accumulators, PCBs and PCTs, and landfill of waste. Regulations were also adopted in June on capture and hunting of wild animals, in order to complete the transposition of the Habitats Directive, and on IPPC and control of emissions from large combustion plants.[49]

Regulations were adopted on the contained use and deliberate release of GMOs. A Chemicals Control Board was established in January 2002 to coordinate activities in this area, particularly with respect to intra-Ministerial coordination. In March 2002, regulations were adopted under the Product Safety Act on household appliances and outdoor equipment noise. Regulations were also adopted on urban waste-water treatment, nitrate pollution of waters, water quality for fish life, and the quality of surface and groundwater.[50]

Malta made concerted efforts to improve its administrative capacity in the environmental policy area, with the establishment, in March 2002, of the Malta Environmental and Planning Authority, as provided for in its Environmental Protection Act of 2001. Related reorganization included the renaming of the Ministry of Environment and Resources as the Ministry for Resources and Infrastructure (MRI), and of the Ministry for Home Affairs as the Ministry for Home Affairs and Environment. The new Environmental and Planning Authority was established under the latter Ministry. The Maltese Resources Authority (MRA), responsible for carrying out permitting and management of environmental infrastructures, and the Waste Management Service Agency, responsible for the new waste management strategy, were established under the MRI. The Commission noted that, as both MEPA and MRA have permitting responsibilities, a coordinated permitting system needs to be created, particularly considering the requirements of the IPPC Directive.[51]

The Commission identified priority areas for requisite implementing legislation, including air quality (non-road mobile machinery), waste (packaging and ELVs), water quality (drinking water, bathing water, and the Water Framework Directive), nature (birds), industrial pollution (major accident hazards), chemicals (biocides, animal protection), nuclear safety and radiation protection (basic safety standards, emergency information to the public, and medical exposure), as well as on foodstuffs.[52]

ix. Poland

Poland struggled with its schedule for transposition of the environmental *acquis*, shifting its original target date from 2000 to 2001. While it was largely successful in meeting this target with respect to acts of Parliament, there were substantial delays in the adoption of implementing legislation. The Commission noted that this was particularly true in the areas of water quality, industrial pollution control, risk management, and chemicals. Ministerial regulations were con-

[49] ibid. [50] ibid. [51] ibid. 86–7. [52] ibid. 87.

sidered to be lacking in most areas, but particularly with respect to air quality, water, chemicals, IPPC, nature conservation, and packaging waste and waste landfills. The Commission also indicated that it noted no progress during 2002 with transposition in the areas of air and water quality protection, and nuclear safety and radiation protection.[53]

Provisions were adopted with respect to EIA and access to environmental information, although transposition is still not complete in these areas. Regulations were also adopted pursuing compliance with Directive 75/442/EEC on Waste (Waste Framework Directive),[54] Directive 75/439/EEC on the Disposal of Waste Oils (Waste Oil Directive),[55] and the Birds, Habitats, and Seveso II Directives. Regulations concerning ozone-depleting substances were also adopted.[56]

One of the particular challenges that faced Poland stemmed from its recent administrative reform. Implementation of environmental policy and law was significantly decentralized, in some cases with responsibility going to newly established regions and districts. National and regional EIA Commissions were planned, but not yet established.[57] Despite this (or because of it), Poland made efforts to provide institutional support for implementation. For example, the Centre for Best Available Techniques was established to provide support for implementation of the IPPC Directive,[58] as was a Commission on GMOs, and the Office of the Inspector for Chemical Substances and Preparations.[59]

The Commission seemed the most critical of the lack of a systematic approach in Poland. National programmes for protection of air quality and for waste management were still not completed, and most measures were pursued on a case-by-case basis.[60]

x. *Romania*

The Commission's observations on Romania's efforts in the environmental protection field were mixed. It noted that much legislation was adopted, but also that this appeared to have been done without taking into consideration the administrative and financial costs involved in implementation. For example, despite adoption of most of the requisite implementing legislation, the National Environmental Fund still had not become operational. In some cases, the Commission's criticism was based on the lack of foundation for measures

[53] Commission of the European Communities, '2002 Regular Report on Poland's Progress Towards Accession' COM(2002)700 final, SEC(2002)1408, 9 Oct. 2002 (Poland Report), 107–8 and 110.

[54] [1975] OJ L194/39, amended by Dir. 91/156 [1991] OJ L78/32.

[55] [1975] OJ L194/22.

[56] Poland Report, n. 53 above, 107–8.

[57] ibid. 108–9.

[58] Of the installations covered, 70% will be overseen at district level (ibid.).

[59] ibid. 107.

[60] ibid. 107–9.

adopted. For example, in the area of industrial pollution control and risk management, an Emergency Ordinance on industrial pollution prevention, reduction, and control was adopted. However, implementation requirements, such as drawing up a list of enterprises that will be covered, were still lacking. The Commission even went so far as to postulate that it 'is therefore likely that many of these laws will prove impossible to implement and will have to be amended'.[61]

Another area the Commission criticized as being of more form than substance was the integration of environmental protection into other policy areas. Although Romania has an Inter-Ministerial Committee responsible for such coordination, its meeting in 2002 was the first since 1999. The Commission did note that committees responsible for water basin management were active.[62]

With respect to legislative measures adopted in 2002, a Government Order on VOCs from storage and distribution of petrol, and a governmental decision on the emission of gaseous and particular pollutants from internal combustion engines, were adopted. Legislation was also adopted pursuing transposition of a mass of EC waste legislation, including Directive 94/62/EEC on Packaging and Packaging Waste (Packaging and Packaging Waste Directive),[63] Directive 2000/76/EC on the Incineration of Waste (Waste Incineration Directive),[64] Directive 91/689/EEC on Hazardous Waste (Hazardous Waste Directive),[65] and the Waste Framework, Packaging and Packaging Waste, Waste Landfill, and Hazardous Waste Directives.

Norms and standards were adopted for discharge of waste water, and the quality of water intended for human consumption, fish life, and bathing. The Commission noted significant progress with respect to transposition in the area of radiation safety, although it was particularly concerned about the lack of legislation on EIA, which it felt must become a priority.[66]

xi. Slovakia

Slovakia was considered to have made good progress with respect to both the adoption of environmental legislation and in the improvement of its administrative capacity to implement and enforce this legislation. A National Strategy for Sustainable Development was agreed by Parliament in April 2002. The Nature and Landscape Protection Act, which transposes the requirements of the Birds and Habitats Directives, will come into effect in 2003.[67]

[61] Commission of the European Communities, '2002 Regular Report on Romania's Progress Towards Accession' COM(2002)700 final, SEC(2002)1409, 9 Oct. 2002 (Romania Report), 104–5.

[62] ibid. 104.

[63] [1994] OJ L365/10.

[64] [2000] OJ L332/91.

[65] [1991] OJ L337/20.

[66] (Romania Report), n. 61 above, 104–5.

[67] Commission of the European Communities, '2002 Regular Report on Slovakia's Progress Towards Accession' COM(2002)700 final, SEC(2002)1410, 9 Oct. 2002 (Slovakia Report), 100–1.

In February 2002, the National Waste Management Programme was approved, while an Order of the Ministry of Environment established uniform methods for the analytical inspection of waste. In August 2002, Parliament adopted the Act on Packaging, transposing the Packaging and Packaging Waste Directive. With respect to water quality, the Act on the Protection of People's Health, which entered into force in January 2002, along with some of its implementing decrees, transposed the requirements of the Bathing Water and Drinking Water Directives. The Slovak Water Act, adopted in June 2002, transposed a number of requirements of individual water Directives, although it does not fully transpose the Water Framework Directive. The Act on Public Water Supply and Sewage, partially transposing the Urban Waste-Water Directive, entered into force in July 2002.[68]

Also in July 2002, the Slovak Air Protection Act was adopted. The Act set air quality targets and penalties for pollution violations, and identified competent local and central authorities in this area. It brings Slovak legislation into compliance with the EC obligations of Directive 96/62/EC on Ambient Air Quality Assessment and Management (Air Quality Framework Directive),[69] and the Waste Incineration Directives, as well as some requirements of Directive 2001/80/EC on the Limitation of Emissions of Certain Pollutants into the Air from Large Combustion Plants (Large Combustion Plants Directive).[70]

Many important pieces of legislation entered into force in 2002. Full transposition compliance with the *acquis* in the area of radiation protection was achieved with the entry into force, in January 2002, of an amendment to the Law on the Protection of Human Health. The Act on the Use of Genetic Technologies and GMOs, and its implementing provisions, entered into force in April and June 2002, respectively. The Act on the Prevention of Major Industrial Accidents, transposing the Seveso II Directive, entered into force in July. The Act on Environmental Labelling of Products, and the Act on an Environmentally Oriented Management and Audit System, both entered into force in January 2003.[71]

Although the Commission noted that Slovakia was quite advanced with respect to alignment with the environmental *acquis*, it noted that transposition was still lacking in the areas of industrial pollution,[72] particularly with respect to the IPPC Directive and Directive 1999/13/EC on the Limitation of Emissions of Volatile Organic Compounds Due to the Use of Organic Solvents in Certain Activities and Installations (Solvents Emissions Directive).[73]

Further the Commission noted challenges in environmental protection administration. Slovakia has a four-tiered system of administration, with responsibilities being shared among national, regional, district, and municipal

[68] ibid. 101. [69] [1996] OJ L296/55. [70] [2001] OJ L309/1.
[71] (Slovakia Report), n. 67 above, 101–2. [72] ibid. 102. [73] [1999] OJ L85/1.

authorities. A number of areas of responsibility for administrative capacity were transferred to the local and regional level of government, as a result of the decentralizing administrative reform of 2001. For example, responsibility for forestry devolved from the district, to the municipal, level. Further decentralization was envisaged, in particular in the areas of water and waste management, and nature and landscape protection.[74] In some respects, this contributed to further complicating an already complex permitting system.[75]

Priority was attached by the Commission to Slovakia's task of finalizing transposition of the IPPC Directive and strengthening implementation capacity, particularly in the areas of discharge of dangerous substances, IPPC and waste permitting, and water pollution reduction programmes.[76]

xii. Slovenia

Slovenia achieved basic harmonization with the environmental *acquis* in most areas, with the 'notable exception' of the IPPC Directive. It was also considered to have strong administrative capacity in this area. The Strategy for the Economic Development of Slovenia addressed the issues of integration of environmental protection measures into other policy areas, particularly with respect to transport, energy, and agricultural policies. The operational programme for recovery and recycling of packaging waste was adopted in March 2002. Slovenia's transposition of legislation on VOCs was completed with the adoption of two governmental decrees on the emissions of halogenated VOCs from installations, adopted in May 2002.[77]

Slovenia adopted its Water Act in July 2002. The Act addressed the requirements of a number of EC water law Directives, in respect of all waters (marine, surface, underground, and coastal areas). Implementing legislation was adopted fulfilling some requirements of the Water Framework Directive. Adoption, in May 2002, of a Decree regulating discharges from textile washing and dry-cleaning facilities brought Slovenian legislation into alignment with all EC standards for discharges of dangerous substances into waters. Slovenian law was also brought in line with Community requirements for waters for aquaculture.[78]

Strategies for the protection of the brown bear, and on biodiversity conservation, were adopted in January 2002. Together with implementation of measures to comply with the Birds Directive, as well as adoption of a measure to complete compliance with provisions of the Zoo Directive, these efforts reflect Slovenia's compliance with the environmental *acquis* in the area of nature protection. In January 2002, Decrees were adopted on the content and drawing

[74] (Slovakia Report), n. 67 above, 103.
[75] ibid. 102–3.
[76] ibid. 104.
[77] Commission of the European Communities, '2002 Regular Report on Slovenia's Progress Towards Accession' COM(2002)700 final, SEC(2002)1411, 9 Oct. 2002 (Slovenia Report), 94–5.
[78] ibid. 95.

up of protection and rescue plans in relation to industrial pollution control and risk management. Further decrees followed, in May 2002, on the reduction of risk to the environment caused by major accidents involving chemical substances, in pursuit of compliance with the Seveso II Directive. Provisions were also adopted on removal of materials containing asbestos, completing EC *acquis* compliance in this area. Legislation on GMOs was adopted in July 2002, to protect biodiversity, public health, and consumers, and to regulate imports and exports of GMO. The Ionizing Radiation Protection and Nuclear Safety Act was adopted in July 2002.[79]

Slovenia streamlined the structure of its Ministry of Environment and Spatial Planning and reduced the number of divergent actors responsible for the environment. An Environmental Agency was established, centralizing authority that had formerly been spread over several institutions. A Nature Conservation Institute was also established.[80]

The Commission indicated that Slovenia's priorities should be transposition related to the IPPC Directive, as well as completion of the transposition with respect to EIA, air quality and nature protection, and control of radiation and noise.[81]

C. Accession Negotiations

The accession negotiations on the environment chapter of the *acquis* were closed in December 2001 with Cyprus, the Czech Republic, Estonia, Hungary, Latvia, Lithuania, Malta, Poland, Slovakia, and Slovenia. In June 2003, negotiations were concluded with Bulgaria, leaving the environment chapter open only with Romania.[82]

All eleven countries have been granted transitional arrangements (derogations in time) with respect to the Urban Waste-Water Directive,[83] which must be implemented by Member States by 31 December 2005. Not surprisingly, considering its size, Malta is expected to come into compliance the quickest, having been granted a derogation until 31 March 2007.[84] Lithuania was granted a derogation until the end of 2009, the Czech Republic and Estonia until the end of 2010, and Cyprus until the end of 2012.[85] Bulgaria is to comply by the

[79] ibid.

[80] ibid. 96.

[81] ibid.

[82] The derogations granted are included in Part Four, on Temporary Provisions, of the Treaty of Accession, signed 16 Apr. 2003, in Athens (Greece).

[83] n. 5 above.

[84] AA2003/ACT/Annex XI/en 3304–3306.

[85] Lithuania has an intermediate target compliance date of 31 Dec. 2007 for agglomerations with a population equivalent of more than 10,000 (AA2003/ACT/Annex IX/en 2834); the *Czech Republic* shall comply by the date of accession for 18 agglomerates with population equivalents of 10,000 inhabitants, while for 36 additional agglomerates this has been extended until 31

end of 2014. The remaining countries, Hungary, Latvia, Poland, Slovakia, and Slovenia, were granted transition periods up to the end of 2015.[86]

All countries except Estonia were also granted derogations in time with respect to the Packaging and Packaging Waste Directive.[87] Cyprus, the Czech Republic, and Hungary are expected to comply with this Directive by the end of 2005.[88] Lithuania was granted until the end of 2006 to comply, while Latvia, Poland, Slovakia, and Slovenia have until the end of 2007.[89] Malta must comply by 2007 for beverage containers, and generally by the end of 2009.[90] Bulgaria is to comply by the end of 2011.

All countries except Latvia and Slovenia requested and received derogations in time with respect to the Large Combustion Plants Directive.[91] Hungary must comply by the end of 2004, Malta by the end of 2005, and the Czech Republic

Dec. 2006 (AA2003/ACT/Annex V/en 2562); *Estonia* has an intermediate target for all agglomerates with population equivalents of more than 10,000 of 31 Dec. 2009 (AA2003/ACT/Annex VI/en 2604); *Cyprus* received derogations until 31 Dec. 2008 for the cities of Limassol and Paralimni, 31 Dec. 2009 for Nicosia, and 31 Dec. 2011 for Paphos (AA2003/ACT/Annex VII/en 2623).

[86] *Hungary* must comply by 31 Dec. 2008 for agglomerations in sensitive areas with population equivalents of more than 10,000, and by 31 Dec. 2010 for agglomerations in normal areas with population equivalents of more than 15,000. For biodegradable industrial waste-water, it has until 31 Dec. 2008 for 10 specifically identified facilities (AA2003/ACT/Annex X/en 3240); *Latvia* has an intermediate target of 31 Dec. 2008 for agglomerations with a population equivalent of more than 100,000, and 31 Dec. 2011 for agglomerations with a population equivalent between 10,000 and 100,000 (AA2003/ACT/Annex VIII/en 2779); *Poland* has multiple intermediate targets based on percentages of total biodegradable load. Special provisions were also agreed for biodegradable industrial waste-water (AA2003/ACT/Annex XII/en 3821–3822); *Slovakia* also has intermediate targets based on biodegradable load. By 31 Dec. 2010 it should comply for all agglomerations with population equivalents of more than 10,000 (AA2003/ACT/Annex XIV/en 4688); *Slovenia* has the same intermediate targets as Hungary with respect to agglomerations (AA2003/ACT/Annex XIII/en 4492).

[87] n. 63 above.

[88] *Cyprus* and the *Czech Republic* have intermediate targets relating to the recycling of plastics, paper, and cardboard, and overall recycling and recovery rates (AA2003/ACT/Annex VII/en 2622), (AA2002/ACT/Annex V/en 2561); *Hungary's* intermediate targets relate to plastics and overall recovery rates. A further derogation was set for a recycling target of 46% from 2005 onwards (AA2003/ACT/Annex X/en 3239).

[89] *Lithuania* has intermediate targets for 2004 for recycling plastics and metals and overall recycling rate, and intermediate targets for overall recovery rates for 2004 and 2005 (AA2003/ACT/Annex IX/en 2833); *Latvia* and *Poland* have annual intermediate targets for recycling plastics and for overall recovery rates for 2004 through 2006 (AA2003/ACT/Annex VIII/en 2776–2777), (AA2003/ACT/Annex XII/en 3816); *Slovakia* has intermediate targets for recycling metal and overall recovery rate for 2004 through 2006 (AA2003/ACT/Annex XIV/en 4686); *Slovenia's* intermediate targets, for 2004–2006, are for plastics and overall recovery rates (AA2003/ACT/Annex XIII/en 4491).

[90] Malta has been given incremental intermediate targets for recycling plastics and overall recovery targets for 2005 to 2008. It may restrict marketing of packaging not complying with its legislative requirements that carbonated beverages with less than 2% alcohol content must be sold in refillable glass bottles or dispensed from metal kegs until 31 Dec. 2007 (AAA2003/ACT/Annex XI/en 3302).

[91] n. 70 above.

and Slovakia by the end of 2007.[92] Cyprus was granted special provisions with respect to acceptable emission limitations.[93] Bulgaria, Estonia, Lithuania, and Poland anticipated having particular problems complying with the requirements of this Directive and hence were granted considerably longer transition periods. Bulgaria must comply by the end of 2014, Estonia and Lithuania by the end of 2015, and Poland by the end of 2017.[94]

For Poland and Lithuania specific concerns were expressed in the Annex to the Treaty of Accession as to the distortion of competition these derogations may cause. Whether this was a result of particular concerns with respect to these countries, or the length of the transition periods involved, or whether it merely reflected the fact that negotiations were conducted by different teams for different countries, is not clear. The Annex states expressly that the Commission will intensely scrutinize these countries' compliance plans, that it will expect a shortened schedule for compliance should economic development allow for increased investments to achieve compliance, and that infringement proceedings might be brought if the Commission, 'in consultation with the Member States', does not consider measures taken to be sufficient.[95]

The next most frequently granted transition period was with respect to Directive 94/63/EEC on Emissions of Volatile Organic Compounds for the Storage of Petrol and its Distribution from Terminals to Service Stations (VOC Emissions Directive).[96] Malta was given until the end of 2004 to comply, Poland until the end of 2005, Estonia until the end of 2006, Lithuania and Slovakia until the end of 2007, and Latvia until the end of 2008.[97] Bulgaria is expected to come into compliance by the end of 2009. The Czech Republic, Cyprus, Hungary, and Slovenia are expected to be in compliance at the time of their accession.

[92] *Hungary*'s derogations refer to emission limit values for SO_2, NO_2, and dust at eight boiler facilities (AA2003/ACT/Annex X/en 3245); *Malta*'s derogation is limited to emission limit values for dust (AA2003/ACT/Annex XI/en 3308); the *Czech Republic*'s derogations involve two heating plants at Přerov and Nová Hut (AA2003/ACT/Annex V/en 2562); *Slovakia*'s transition period covers SO_2, NO_2, and dust emissions from three specific boilers (AA2003/ACT/Annex XIV/en 4691).

[93] Emission limits of 1700 mg N/m^3 apply to combustion plants at Dhekelia and Vasilikos until there is an upgrade or a significant change to these boilers, natural gas becomes available on the island, Cyrpus becomes an exporter of electricity, or the currently operating boilers are closed (AA2003/ACT/Annex VII/en 2624).

[94] Estonia's intermediate targets involve emission limits for SO_2 and dust at several combustion facilities, some of which must be closed by 1 Jan. 2008. It must also 'make all efforts' to see that by 2012 SO_2 emissions from oil shale fired plants do not exceed 25,000 tonnes (AA2003/ACT/Annex VI/en 2605–2606); *Lithuania*'s transition period is for three combined heat and power plants and is in respect to SO_2 and NO_2 emissions (AA2003/ACT/Annex XI/en 3299–3300); *Poland*'s derogation until 2017 was the longest under the environment chapter (AA2003/ACT/Annex XII/en 3835–3844).

[95] AA2003/ACT/Annex IX/en 2835–2836 (Lithuania). AA2003/ACT/Annex XII/en 3844 (Poland).

[96] [1994] OJ L365/24.

[97] AA2003/ACT/Annex XI/en 3299–3300 (Malta); AA2003/ACT/Annex XII/en 3811 (Poland); AA2003/ACT/Annex VI/en 2601–2602 (Estonia); AA2003/ACT/Annex IX/en 2832

With respect to the requirements of the IPPC Directive[98] which comes into effect for existing Member States in 2007, derogations in time have been allowed for existing installations in five countries; all new installations must be in compliance. Latvia and Poland have been granted until the end of 2010, while Bulgaria and Slovakia have until 31 December 2011,[99] and Slovenia until 30 October 2011.[100] Fully coordinated permits for all the temporarily exempted facilities must be issued by 30 October 2007, identifying binding timetables for achieving full compliance.

Malta, Estonia, and Latvia were granted transition periods for compliance with the Drinking Water Directive,[101] until the end of 2005, 2013, and 2015, respectively.[102] Hungary was allowed to grant derogations for arsenic until 25 December 2009 without being required to communicate this decision to the Commission, albeit not for drinking water intended for food processing.[103] In other water quality areas, Malta, Poland, and Slovakia were granted transition periods with respect to compliance on provisions limiting the Directive 76/464/EEC on Pollution Caused by certain Dangerous Substances Discharged into the Aquatic Environment of the Community (Dangerous Substances Discharge Directive).[104] Malta and Slovakia[105] were granted transition periods with respect to Council Directive 86/280/EEC on Limit Values and Quality Objectives for

(Lithuania); AA2003/ACT/Annex XIV/en 4683–4684 (Slovakia); AA2003/ACT/Annex VIII/en 2775–2776 (Latvia).

[98] n. 13 above.

[99] *Latvia* has transition periods for 15 facilities, two of which must come into compliance by 31 Dec. 2008 and another one year later (AA2003/ACT/Annex VIII/en 2781); *Poland* was given intermediate target compliance dates for installations that will not be expected to be in compliance immediately upon accession (AA2003/ACT/Annex XII/en 3823–3834); *Slovakia*'s derogations were aimed at ten facilities, with one needing to comply by the end of 2009 and three by the end of 2010 (AA2003/ACT/Annex XIV/en 4690).

[100] The country-specific nature of the accession negotiations is reflected in the fact that for the fifteen identified facilities the intermediate targets for Slovenia, which run from 2008 until 2011, all are for 30 Oct., as opposed to 31 Dec. for all other countries and most other derogations (AA2003/ACT/Annex XIII/en 4493).

[101] n. 6 above.

[102] For *Malta*, the fluoride and nitrate parameters will not apply until 31 Dec. 2005 (AA2003/ACT/Annex XI/en 3306); *Estonia* has a temporary derogation with respect to parameters for colour, hydrogen ion concentration, iron, manganese, odour, and turpidity, until 31 Dec. 2007 for distribution systems serving more than 2,000 persons and with respect to chloride, conductivity, and sulphates until 31 Dec. 2008 (AA2003/ACT/Annex VI/en 2605); *Latvia*'s derogation relates to the value limits for bromate, trihalomethanes, aluminium, iron, manganese, and oxidizability, with intermediate deadlines for compliance of 31 Dec. 2008 for municipalities with more than 100,000 inhabitants, and three years later for those with between 10,000 and 100,000 (AA2003/ACT/Annex VIII/en 2779).

[103] AA2003/ACT/Annex X/en 3241.

[104] [1976] OJ L129/23.

[105] *Malta* was granted derogations in time running from 30 Sept. 2004 until 31 Mar. 2007 for five identified facilities with respect to chloroform discharge, and from 31 Dec. 2004 until 31 Mar. 2007 with respect to trichloroethylene and percholoroethylene for three of these facilities (AA2003/ACT/Annex XI/en 3303–3304). *Slovakia*'s derogation, until 31 Dec. 2006, is for the facility at Šal'a (AA2003/ACT/Annex XIV/en 4687).

Discharge of certain Dangerous Substances included in List I of the Annex to Directive 76/464/EEC.[106]

Malta was granted transition periods with respect to Directive 83/513/EEC on Limit Values and Quality Objectives for Cadmium Discharges,[107] for three specific facilities, with total compliance being required by 31 March 2007.[108] Poland was also granted derogations with respect to mercury and cadmium discharges regulated by a number of Community measures until 31 December 2007.[109] Slovakia was granted a transition period until 31 December 2006 for Directive 84/156/EEC on Mercury Discharges from Sectors Other than the Chlor-Alkali Electrolysis Industry[110] for one specific chemical facility in Nová-ky.[111]

With respect to the Waste Landfill Directive,[112] permanent sites within Latvia used for temporary storage of hazardous waste produced within the country will not be considered landfills until 31 December 2004.[113] Poland also received transition periods for this Directive, extending until 1 July 2012, with various intermediate targets and dates identified.[114] A transition period until 2014 was agreed, with respect to Bulgaria, for the landfill of certain liquid wastes. Estonia's special reliance on oil shale for energy was taken into account here, with the Directive's provisions on liquid and corrosive waste not applying to oil shale deposited in existing landfills until 16 July 2009. Estonia will be required progressively to reduce the amount of non-complying ash according to a schedule agreed in the negotiations.[115]

Hungary and Slovakia were granted transition periods relating to Directive 94/67/EC on Incineration of Hazardous Waste (Hazardous Waste Incineration Directive).[116] This extends until 30 June 2005 for five incinerators for waste oils and other liquid waste, 14 incinerators of hospital waste, and 18 incinerators and co-incinerators of solid and liquid hazardous waste in Hungary, and until 31

[106] [1986] OJ L181/16, as last amended by Dir. 91/692/EEC [1991] OJ L377/48.

[107] [1986] OJ L291/1, as last amended by Dir. 91/692/EEC [1991] OJ L377/48.

[108] AA2003/ACT/Annex XI/en 3302–3303.

[109] The transition period refers to the requirements of Dir. 82/176/EEC on Limit Values and Quality Objectives for Mercury Discharges by the Chlor-Alkali Electrolysis Industry [1982] OJ L81/29; Dir. 83/513/EEC on Limit Values and Quality Objectives for Cadmium Discharges [1983] OJ L291/1; Dir. 84/156/EEC on Limit Values and Quality Objectives for Mercury Discharges by Sectors Other than the Chlor-Alkali Electrolysis Industry [1984] OJ L74/49; and Dir. 86/280/EEC on Limit Values and Quality Objectives for Discharges of certain Dangerous Substances included in List I of the Annex to Dir. 76/464/EEC [1986] OJ L181/16; all as last amended by Dir. 91/692/EEC [1991] OJ L377/48 (AA2003/ACT/Annex XII/en 3819–3822).

[110] [1984] OJ L74/49, as last amended by Dir. 91/692/EEC [1991] OJ L377/48.

[111] AA2003/ACT/Annex XIV/en 4686–4687.

[112] n. 34 above.

[113] AA2003/ACT/Annex VIII/en 2778.

[114] The Polish derogations address water control and leachate management, protection of soil and water, gas control and stability, AA2003/ACT/Annex XII/en 3817–3818.

[115] AA2003/ACT/Annex VI/en 2603.

[116] [1994] OJ L365/34.

December 2006 for 11 hospital incinerators and seven hazardous waste incinerators in Slovakia.[117]

Cyprus was granted a one-year transition period with respect to the Sulphur Directive,[118] with the expectation that it will seek a derogation under the Directive during that time.[119] Poland also received a derogation with respect to this Directive, with the sulphur restrictions on heavy fuel oils not applying until 31 December 2006.[120]

Bulgaria, Hungary, Latvia, Malta, Poland, and Slovakia were granted derogations in time for Regulation (EEC) No. 259/93 on the Supervision and Control of Shipments of Waste (Waste Shipment Regulation),[121] with respect to certain shipments of waste.[122] Hungary and Malta must comply by the end of 2005, Bulgaria by the end of 2009, Latvia by the end of 2010, and Poland by the end of 2012. For all these countries, however, there is also the requirement that competent authorities must object to certain shipments destined for recovery at facilities exempted from the IPPC, Waste Incineration, or Large Combustion Plant Directives, as relevant to each country.

Individual transition periods for various measures were also granted. Latvia received a derogation in time until 31 December 2004 with respect to Directive 87/217/EEC on the Prevention and Reduction of Environmental Pollution by Asbestos,[123] with respect to landfill of waste containing asbestos fibres and dust.[124] Malta was granted transitional arrangements until 31 December 2008 under the Birds Directive,[125] for the trapping of finches to establish a captive breeding system.[126] Estonia was given a derogation with respect to the Habitats Directive,[127] with respect to the hunting of lynx.[128] Latvia and Poland were granted transition periods with respect to Directive 97/43/Euratom on Health Protection of Individuals against the Dangers of Ionizing Radiation in Relation to Medical Exposures,[129] as regards certain radiological equipment and practices.

[117] AA2003/ACT/Annex X/en 3242–3244 (Hungary), AA2003/ACT/Annex XIV/en 4689–4690 (Slovakia).

[118] n. 42 above.

[119] AA2003/ACT/Annex VII/en 2621.

[120] AA2003/ACT/Annex XII/en 3811.

[121] [1993] OJ L30/1, last amended by Reg. (EC) No. 2557/2001 [2001] OJ L349/1.

[122] AA2003/ACT/Annex X/en 3238 (Hungary); AA2003/ACT/Annex VIII/en 2777 (Latvia); AA2003/ACT/Annex XI/en 3300–3301 (Malta); AA2003/ACT/Annex XI/en 3300–3301 (Poland); AA2003/ACT/Annex XII/en 3812–3816 (Slovakia).

[123] [1987] OJ L85/40.

[124] This waste must be handled specially, being packed in double bags and buried separately at marked sites (AA2003/ACT/Annex VIII/en 2780).

[125] n. 8 above.

[126] AA2003/ACT/Annex XI/en 3307.

[127] n. 9 above.

[128] The Commission will provide a report to the Council five years after accession on whether this exception should continue. AA2003/ACT/Annex VI/en 2608.

[129] [1997] OJ L180/22.

Latvia's derogation runs until 31 December 2005,[130] while Poland has one year longer to comply.[131]

D. Conclusions

If success in the area of environmental policy and law were to be measured by transposition compliance with the *acquis communautaire*, based on the information presented above the Czech Republic could be deemed to have earned the gold medal. Having agreed to transition periods only with respect to the Urban Waste-Water Directive, the Packaging and Packaging Waste Directive, and the Large Combustion Plant Directive, this would seem to indicate that it is the country most prepared for taking on the obligations of the environmental *acquis*. Lithuania would have earned silver, having agreed to only four derogations: for these same three measures plus the Volatile Organic Compounds Directive. Slovakia would take the bronze, with transition periods only deemed necessary with respect to these four Directives plus the IPPC Directive.

However, the relatively limited number of transition periods agreed (as compared to the requests at the opening of negotiations on this chapter) is probably as much a reflection of the resistance of the EU and its Member States to granting transition periods in this chapter of the *acquis*, as it is of extensive preparedness on the part of the candidate countries. It had been made clear, especially by the Commission, that transition periods would not be granted for horizontal, or in principle for nature protection measures, or where derogations could disrupt the functioning of the internal market. Hence, the initial negotiating position of the Czech Republic (and many other candidate countries) indicating a desire for derogations on the Habitats, Birds, or Nitrates Directives had to be abandoned. Other requests were significantly cut back in the final agreements. Even the negotiations on EC measures which would require significant financial investments were tough, with stringent limitations and tight timetables for compliance included.[132]

While the transposition efforts in the candidate countries are drawing to a close, the more challenging aspects of implementation and enforcement are only barely beginning.

130 AA2003/ACT/Annex VIII/en 2782.

131 AA2003/ACT/Annex XII/en 3844.

132 See M. Soveroski, 'Central and Eastern European Countries' (2002) 2 *Yearbook of European Environmental Law*, 562–6.

REVIEWS OF BOOKS

Cradle to Cradle: Remaking the Way We Make Things, William McDonough and Michael Braungart. New York: Northpoint Press; A Division of Farrar, Straus and Giroux, 2002, 208 pp., $25.00. ISBN 0865475873

An imaginative book aimed at designers and scientists makes for interesting reading for lawyers, and has relevance for a wide range of legal spheres including Impact Assessment and Standardization. *Cradle to Cradle: Remaking the Way We Make Things* attempts to unify values of technology, business, and environmental protection with a new set of 'design principles' for sustainability.

McDonough, an American architect, and Braungart, a German chemist, come together to argue that current industrial practices are so flawed that increased regulation and reforms aimed at reducing consumption will fail to alleviate environmental destruction and merely slow down its path. Against industrialists and environmentalists alike, the authors charge that the current poor design features of conventionally made products combined with misdirected reform efforts lead to inefficient recycling and large quantities of waste. Instead, the authors propose a new approach to the design of products and systems which embraces consumption and growth, but within a framework where every stage of a product's use and reuse is planned—a 'cradle to cradle' approach where even the disposal of a product is devised as an input into another cycle.

In imitating nature, the authors hope their design principles will create a system where 'waste equals food', much like the blossoms of a cherry tree. This system depends on a strict division between 'biological' and 'technical' nutrients and a notion of 'products as service' (such as television sets that are rented and upgraded rather than bought, consumed, and discarded). As an example, the book itself comes from and is destined to remain within the closed loop 'technosphere'; it is made from plastic, its durability and white aesthetic attempting to improve on recycled paper versions and the future uses of its constituent parts already planned. It is a nice symbol for setting out a vision where innovation and intelligence can produce things of no waste.

Why is this book being reviewed in a law journal and what is its use for law? First, texts such as Daniel Farber's *Eco-Pragmatism* remind us of the multidisciplinary nature of environmental law, and understanding new scientific conceptions and design principles can only advance the law's goals and effectiveness. Here, one can learn about a redesign of the current 'monstrous hybrids' that describe the technical and biological parts of products such as running shoes, read about architectural innovations such as the future construction of factories along naturally cleansing wetlands, and become aware of spurious effects of some 'eco-efficiency' principles such as increased heating insulation, which, without appropriate design, may increase unhealthy indoor pollutants.

More importantly for our purposes, however, is the manner in which law may serve to improve upon the innovative suggestions contained in *Cradle to Cradle*. The prime example is in the chapter titled 'Respect Diversity'. Here, McDonough and Braungart propose an analytical tool based on a design 'pyramid', which features 'Ecology' at the peak and 'Equity' and 'Economy' at the two edges of the base. Using this tool, designers and producers ask a series of questions from points in the pyramid, starting with economic considerations ('can I make a profit?') to social issues ('are employees earning a living wage?, are people treating one another with respect?') to environmental issues ('is it fair to pollute a river?, are we obeying nature's laws?, does waste equal food?').

The idea of this pyramid will already be familiar to environmental lawyers, who have worked for many years with the notion of Environmental Impact Assessment (EIA) and its broader incarnation, Sustainability Impact Assessment (SIA). Procedural guarantees for the former are required within a number of international and regional conventions, guidelines of multilateral funding institutions, domestic statutes, and the practice of national development agencies. A useful example of the latter is the European Commission's new impact assessment procedure, which imposes a wide-ranging series of questions for new policies within its work programme.[1] The preliminary assessment statement published as part of the Commission's Communication includes a mandatory description of the problem that the policy/proposal is expected to tackle and an indication of the economic, social, and/or environmental 'potentially unsustainable trends associated with the problem'. This holistic approach compares exactly with the design pyramid advocated in *Cradle to Cradle*. In fact, law plays a central role in this process: when policy-makers are required to answer various social and ecological questions as part of SIA, they will look to a jurisdiction's health and safety laws, environment and labour standards, and even safeguards for corporate responsibility. McDonough and Braungart's designers must do this also, as the book could have pointed out.

The other major legal counterpart to the design principles of *Cradle to Cradle* (which is also not included in the book but which will be obvious to environmental lawyers) is standardization. Standards bodies such as the International Organisation for Standardisation (ISO) and the European Committee for Standardisation (CEN) currently produce standards ranging from product design, energy efficiency, and technical processes. Readers may be aware, for example, of the preparation of a Communication by the European Commission examin-

[1] See Communication from the Commission on Impact Assessment COM(2002)276.

ing the Integration of Environmental Aspects into European Standardization.[2] The working group, which held public consultations in September 2003, acknowledged the importance of a systematic consideration of environmental principles along with economic and social aspects of standardization. Of benefit to this inquiry would be McDonough and Braungart's ideas for the environmentally conscious design of products, and the positioning of standard measurements and tests along the entire 'cradle to cradle' cycle.

Aside from a crude acceptance of systems theory, in which the authors generalize that regulation is a 'signal of design failure', and assert that commercial and guardianship (governmental) spheres of society must be kept separate, *Cradle to Cradle* makes little reference to legal norms or analysis. This is perhaps understandable given the scope of the work, but the effect denies the transformative potential of law. Readers of the book are therefore encouraged to consider the legal relevance and ramifications of the important design principles advocated by McDonough and Braungart, both in relation to SIA and standardization, but also in broader legal areas. For example, the effect of legal incentives within the current system, such as the WTO agreement on technical barriers to trade, must be borne in mind in the development and application of product and systems standards. In addition, any state involvement in the pricing of goods to reflect their true costs within the 'technosphere' will have to fit alongside obligations to respect tariff bindings and discipline the use of trade-distorting subsidies, or alternatively create exceptions within the multilateral trading regime. Legal techniques to enforce these 'good design principles', and the appropriate role of national, regional, and international trade and environmental institutions and standards bodies, give rise to crucial questions for lawyers and require a similar bent towards innovation as valuably contained in *Cradle to Cradle*.

MARGARET A. YOUNG
University of Cambridge

Environment and Statecraft: The Strategy of Environmental Treaty-Making, Scott Barrett. Oxford: Oxford University Press, 2003, 446 pp., £27.50 hb. ISBN 0199257337

Despite the flurry of international environmental treaty-making since the early 1970s—presently well over 300 multilateral and bilateral treaties—the global environment according to most criteria has hardly improved. The mass of environmental treaties may have slowed and moderated the worst excesses, but not halted the overall negative trajectory. In a global chessboard of competing

[2] See Communication from the Commission: Integration of Environmental Aspects into European Standardisation COM(2004)130. See also the report on Integration of Environmental Aspects into European Standardization—Public Consultation, published on the Internet at: http://europa.eu.int/comm/environment/standardisation/stan_public_cons.pdf.

state powers, coupled with the amorphous influence of transnational corporations and other non-state economic entities, international environmental agreements barely seem able to change behaviour. Those treaties that enjoy broad international participation tend to do so because they do not require much from states and lack enforcement machinery. Conversely, the more ambitious environmental treaties, which contain tough environmental standards and credible compliance sanctions, attract few states.

Most academic literature on the subject of reform is long on rhetoric and morality, but short on practicalities. In this context, Professor Scott Barrett's *Environment and Statecraft* is a hugely important book. He explains why international treaties are needed to protect the shared environment, and why some treaties succeed while others fail. Taking an instrumental and economic approach to the problem of international environmental cooperation, Barrett offers a hopeful thesis, revealing the structural weaknesses of those many treaties that have failed and unearthing the key ingredients of the few that work. Drawing from a variety of different cases, Barrett argues that the successful treaties strategically manipulate incentives, and make it in the interests of sovereign states to protect rather than harm the environment.

In doing so, *Environment and Statecraft* propounds a theory of how states can cooperate in protecting their shared environmental resources, whether it is southern blue fin tuna, the Aral Sea, or the global climate. The book's key assumption is that treaties must be self-enforcing—namely, individually rational, collectively rational, and fair. Such treaties, Barrett argues, work only if they are self-enforcing. Every nation wishes to avoid paying to protect the environment. But each also recognizes that, if every nation took this stance, the general outcome would be worse. Therefore, effective treaties are ones that can strategically manipulate the incentives states have to exploit the environment, combining both carrots (e.g. technology transfer and financial assistance) and sticks (e.g. reciprocity and trade restrictions). Barrett's theory integrates a number of disciplines, including economics, negotiation analysis, and game theory, but he goes beyond existing literature on these topics by looking at their application to specific environmental problems, notably his concluding chapter on the Kyoto Protocol.

There are many reasons why environmental agreements fail. One reason is that large economic and geographical asymmetries among countries complicate the negotiations to achieve an equitable share of the burden of environmental protection. Also, due to the public good nature of the global environment, which implies non-excludable environmental benefits for all countries, countries may prefer to free-ride, that is, to profit from the cleaner environment provided by countries participating in agreements, without paying the costs. The lack of a supra-national authority capable of enforcing international environmental laws is a further cause of failure.

Yet, despite these and other obstacles, Barrett finds examples of effective international environmental cooperation. Among the most successful environmental treaties cited are the 1911 North Pacific Fur Seal Treaty and the 1987 Montreal Protocol to protect the ozone layer. What is so special about these agreements? According to Barrett, they worked (i.e. saved seals or reduced ozone-depleting chemicals) because each contained mechanisms that were able to deter non-compliance and non-participation. Only a handful of countries have not ratified the Montreal Protocol (they include Afghanistan and Iraq, which have had other preoccupations). The Protocol offered a range of financial and technological benefits that helped attract record international participation, which was coupled with trade sanctions against products containing or made by using CFCs, and mechanisms for withdrawing financial assistance should states step out of line. In the case of the North Pacific Fur Seal Treaty, it reversed a precipitous decline in the population of fur seals caused by over-hunting. It achieved this by banning hunting at sea, where they were common property and therefore over-exploited: seals could then be taken only on the territory of individual governments, which acquired an interest in protecting them. That produced an overall gain (more seals), which could be distributed to make all nations better off, and thus give them an incentive to abide by their agreement.

However, Barrett cautions that there is no single blueprint for international environmental treaty-making. The conditions that allow one treaty to succeed may be wholly absent for another. Thus, Barrett points out that in the case of the Montreal Protocol, the costs of implementing the Protocol were relatively low and the benefits from complying—notably the avoidance of skin cancers and eye cataracts—were enormous. For the Kyoto Protocol, however, Barrett sees the balance between costs and benefits as much less promising. Whilst the small island states of the South Pacific have much to fear from rising sea levels, agriculture in Canada and Russia (two big producers of fossil fuels) may benefit from a predicted warmer and wetter climate.

Rejecting the Montreal Protocol as a model for the Kyoto Protocol, Barrett argues it should follow the environmental standards and technology approach taken in the MARPOL[3] oil pollution and shipping treaties. Barrett argues that the Kyoto Protocol offers weak incentives for participation and compliance, and he tries to solve this problem by suggesting an alternative climate regime based on common incentives for climate-friendly technology research and development (R&D). In particular, Barrett advances the idea of a cooperative funding of basic R&D with respect to energy-saving, climate-friendly technologies on the one hand, and the implementation of various standards directed towards the international adoption and diffusion of new technologies on the other. He concludes, therefore, that the Framework Convention on Climate Change of 1992 be

[3] International Maritime Organization (IMO) International Convention for the Prevention of Pollution from Ships (MARPOL), 2 Nov. 1973 (entered into force with the 1978 London Protocol on 2 Oct. 1983) (1973) 12 *International Legal Materials* 6, 1439.

extended through the negotiation of a new standards protocol and a cooperative R&D protocol.

Not all of Barrett's conclusions seem so plausible. For example, his suggestion that regional environmental problems are easier to remedy than global environmental problems unfortunately does not appear congruent with the evidence. Many of the most inept and hopeless environmental treaties are regional ones, such as the ASEAN Agreement on the Conservation of Nature and Natural Resources, 1985, and the Apia Convention on Conservation of Nature in the South Pacific, 1976. Possibly, the more global in character an environmental problem is, the more publicity and resources can be generated towards reaching agreements to solve such problems.

Overall, Barrett's lucidity and analysis of international environmental cooperation and treaty-making make this book one of the most significant in its field in recent years. It should be staple reading for all international environmental scholars and policy-makers.

BENJAMIN J. RICHARDSON
Osgoode Hall Law School

Civil Liability for Environmental Damage: A Comparative Analysis of Law and Policy in Europe and the United States, Mark Wilde. The Hague: Kluwer Law International, 2002, 341 pp., €110.00 hb. ISBN 9041118918

Environmental Damage in International and Comparative Law: Problems of Definition and Valuation, edited by Michael Bowman and Alan E. Boyle. Oxford: Oxford University Press, 2002, 360 pp., £65.00 hb. ISBN 0199255733

Notwithstanding the burgeoning of international environmental law, its penetrative limitations in terms of enforcement mechanisms are readily apparent in the field of securing redress for environmental harm. Indeed, problems are pervasive in the sense that, as Bowman and Boyle's title suggests, international law is beset by root difficulties of definition and valuation. The authors' edited collection seeks to fill a persisting gap, therefore, by focusing upon questions of compensation, especially for natural resource loss and damage to ecosystems. Their volume results from a project instigated by the Environmental Law Commission of the British Branch of the International Law Association. Its framework offers an international law analysis informed by overviews of approaches to the treatment of environmental harm in selected national jurisdictions. These form a somewhat eclectic mix, and contributions vary across a range of potential categories of heads of legal action. Whilst the comparative approach is more apparent than real, Bowman's introduction offers an incisive survey of priorities and contradictions addressed in these discrete chapters. To an extent,

Wilde's treatment, if less detailed (for instance, in the treatment of German approaches as compared with Wetterstein's chapter 12 in Bowman and Boyle) appears the more comparative, given that consideration across jurisdictions is woven into the fabric of the author's argument.

Wilde's project is explicitly directed at the law of tort, and specifically as to its potentiality as part of a liability system of environmental regulation. This eventually leads him into an extensive discussion of the implications of the European Commission's White Paper on Civil Liability (now a draft Directive, and, given its timing, referenced separately in an Appendix). It must be said that the proposal presently appears to be metamorphosing into a scheme more 'public regulatory' than 'civil liability' in flavour. For all that, a considerable strength of Wilde's book lies in a rigorous testing of civil liability analyses, combined with an avowedly theoretical approach. The author, much as might a brave motor mechanic, is willing to strip his subject down to its component functional parts, and, having sought to identify the conceptual underpinnings (no easy task), he goes on to test their utility in his chosen context.

A broad sketch of the reach of the book is that liability issues are addressed along the following lines: first, deliberating upon the foundations for, and obstacles to, establishing liability for environmental damage; next, investigating the capacities of tort in an environmental protection role; and finally, in light of experience elsewhere and particularly in view of the debate within Europe, offering a model for environmental protection through civil liability. The chapter (2) laying the foundations is not surprisingly an exercise in analysis of English common law (and might be commended to undergraduate and masters students of environmental law). Likewise, the discussion of obstacles to effective performance (in chapter 3) is domestic in content, although interesting common law analogies elsewhere are drawn. This may have been a selective exercise, but the approach is eminently justified on grounds of scale. In the section on remedies, discussion of economic loss (and, briefly, questions of contingent value: compare Hanley's specialist economic treatment in Bowman and Boyle, chapter 3) is informed by US experience, especially in the legal aftermath of the *Exxon Valdiz* 1989 oil spill. The theme is revisited in chapter 10, where the author points out that traditional valuation methods pay scant attention to resource values beyond those contemplated by (commercial) use valuation. Further, the doctrinally intractable problems associated with the withholding of injunctions is succinctly addressed, with good use made of the paradigm US authority of *Boomer* v. *Atlantic Cement Co.* (New York Court of Appeals, 1970). It is in Wilde's treatment of theoretical perspectives (chapter 4) that sustained consideration of experience elsewhere (again, mainly common law perspectives) is offered, both as to economic analysis and in a thought-provoking discussion of 'corrective versus distributive justice arguments'. Here, the author also considers the problem of historic pollution (briefly concluding that it may be effectively addressed but not through tort mechanisms) and the conundrum of insurance (non-)availability.

More problematic territory is encountered as regards private enforcement of a public (environmental) interest. Subject to there being some opportunity for regulatory standards to inform actions, in default of 'citizen action' provisions, opportunities are generally restricted. Reading the contrasting contributions of the reviewed volumes to the continuing debate as to the appropriate basis for securing remediation for environmental harm, this reviewer became more convinced than ever before as to the centrality of conceptions of property if genuine solutions are to be found. Hardin's warnings as to the consequences of the 'tragedy of the commons' in the face of problems of resource despoliation and scarcity were rooted in the need for property.[4] Yet as Cole has recently pointed out, many have failed to recognize that each of Hardin's solutions (essentially through private property and regulatory regimes) 'involves the imposition of property rights'.[5] Wilde is acutely aware of a need to put property at the centre of the debate, although this only becomes apparent some way into the argument (and came as a pleasant, and stimulating, surprise). In considering wider doctrinal implications—as did Stone in the ground-breaking 'Do Trees Have Standing?'—Wilde appears to accept Gray's idea of an extended concept of equitable property. This Wilde argues is more fertile territory than human rights-based arguments.[6] The lucid exposition here relies heavily on the US Supreme Court's 2000 ruling in *Friends of the Earth* v. *Laidlaw Environmental Services* (itself a considerable rowing back from the 1992 decision in *Lujan* v. *Defenders of Wildlife*). It has to be said, however, that the wording of the EC's draft Civil Liability Directive leaves possibilities for more extensive rights some way off, and more general access to justice provisions following transposition of commitments under the Aarhus Convention may in due course have greater impact. The treatment of access in Wilde's chapter 8 must now be read in light of current rethinking on the part of the Commission.

It moreover appears generally that treatment of the EC's civil liability proposals (chapters 5 and 6) has become somewhat dated (already) given the differences between the 2000 White Paper and 2002 draft Directive (as referred to above, a short Appendix was inserted). However the discussion is a valuable one, as Wilde addresses the utility of strict liability approaches towards achieving environmental objectives (by reference to extant and future environmental legislation). Indeed, the discussion of 'development risk' and 'regulatory compliance' defences assumes increased relevance in light of the (initial terms of the) proposed Directive. Choice of the fault and strict liability mix has remained almost exclusively a matter for Member States, and here (just as in the following chapter 7, concerned with causation), discussion is informed

[4] G. Hardin, 'The Tragedy of the Commons' (1968) 162 *Science*, 1243–8.

[5] D.H. Cole, *Pollution and Property—Comparing Ownership Institutions for Environmental Protection* (Cambridge: Cambridge University Press, 2002).

[6] Here he would presumably ally with the views of Miller. See e.g. C. Miller, *Environmental Rights—Critical Perspectives* (London: Routledge, 1998).

by the fruits of research into the legal approaches across a range of Member States.

The culmination of the argument (and focus hinted at throughout) appears in chapter 10. Here the limitations of tort as a means of environmental protection are exposed and cumulated. He points to palliative steps, such as use of strict liability approaches; relaxed causation tests; greater reliance upon injunctive relief; and extending standing to represent the public interest in natural resources, especially to NGOs. However, any more effective role for civil liability may depend upon the development of property conceptions that reject (well, more politely, reinvent) those of free market liberalism. Wilde subscribes to a similar view and calls for a reappraisal of the functions of property.[7] The way to such (environmental) heaven is strewn with systemic obstacles. Nevertheless, Wilde feels that this is more likely to prove effective than seemingly more incremental EC routes to individual enforcement of Member State obligations under ruling EC legislation.

If Wilde is thus concerned with the representational problem in securing environmental protection through civil liability, then a twin systemic limitation—the nature of environmental damage itself—is the main subject of the treatment in Bowman and Boyle. Whilst the intricate weave of Wilde's single-minded work is inevitably missing, much of this collection likewise offers stimulating perspectives. For instance, an understanding of the potentiality and limits of the EC's nascent (form of) civil liability regime would be enhanced by a reading of Edward Brans' comparison with the US Oil Pollution Act in terms of remedial consequences. The central concern of this book, and what appeared to be the major disciplinary binding agent between the contributors, is with questions of definition as to the elements of environmental harm and its measurement and valuation. Whilst such a task was perhaps of Herculean proportions, it was also of inestimable value given the pervasiveness of such questions at all jurisdictional levels. Within the text, discussion of environmental harm is invigorated by breadth of treatment. This is especially pronounced in roughly the first (or 'international') half of the book, exemplified by the juxtaposition of economic valuation methods (by Hanley, in chapter 3) and Bowman's own ethical investigation into intrinsic value (chapter 4). In this vein, if the general impression of Bowman and Boyle, especially as to national treatments, was that content erred on the side of selectivity and succinctness, there was also much illumination, partly on the latter account. Thus, responsible for offering an overview of common law approaches, Schoenbaum provided a thoughtful summation of deficiencies in the definition and measurement of damages for the purposes of private law.

Standing is not a substantial theme of the Bowman and Boyle collection. But the synergies between representational issues (as stated, crucial to the discussion in Wilde) and the focus in their volume upon harm raise crucial questions. Thus

[7] See K. Gray, 'Equitable Property' (1994) 47 *Current Legal Problems*, 157.

De la Fayette (discussing the definitional gap as to 'environmental damage' in international liability regimes) contrasts traditional tort approaches and recognizes—especially given the importance of restoration—the need for new duty regimes. This raises key questions as to the role of NGOs and citizens as alternative regulators. Questions of valuation should not be severed from those of property (in the sense of rights, obligations, and enforcement). Ultimately, questions of standing are central to finding effective solutions. Whilst this does not appear to have been consistently developed as a linking theme, wider references to (the lack of) *actio popularis* appear (as in Reid's discussion of liability in Scotland, chapter 14). Moreover, Reid is right to quote Himsworth's assertion that perhaps the most important question of all is 'who may be entitled to sue in respect of the damage and who should be the recipient of any compensation awarded'.[8] Some fuller explanation is offered by Nukhet Turgent (chapter 16) and Wetterstein (chapter 12), respectively concerning Turkish and German law, where restrictive approaches to standing will make familiar reading. It would have offered fruitful comparison had a contribution from the Netherlands (and in this respect also the United States) been included.

Overall, these volumes provide informative and stimulating fare in their mutual concerns with problems in securing protection for wider environmental interests. Wilde's discussion of civil liability takes him beyond the doctrinal restraints of English tort law, with the assistance of comparative perspectives alongside the potential of EC proposals, whilst the focus for Bowman and Boyle is upon environmental harm, where the arguments most nearly converge in the respective discussions of the nature of remedies and imperatives of environmental restoration. Here, notwithstanding that answers are not forthcoming in international law at present, Boyle (chapter 2), distils the environmental problematic in the valuation argument as follows: 'overcoming the objection that something which is not necessarily "property" and which may have no "market value" has no financial and economic worth'.

Whilst Boyle asserts that this task is not one for lawyers alone, he might have added that political complexities render the search for solutions precarious indeed. This is especially the case if resolution is to be found in reformed approaches to public interest representation. In the same volume, Hanley's discussion of 'WTP' (Willingness to Pay) and 'WTAC' (minimum Willingness to Accept Compensation) methods concludes by saying that 'if environmental damage litigation becomes more widespread in Europe . . . rulings on property right allocations will be a vital part of the process'. It is here that Wilde's exposition is at its most considerable. As modern politicians are wont to say, citizenship is as much about obligations as rights. Whether the increasingly limited aspirations of the Community for incursions into domestic civil liability

[8] C. Himsworth, 'Unsustainable Developments in Law-Making for Environmental Liability?' in J. Hayward and T. O'Neill, *Justice, Property and the Environment* (Avebury: Aldershot, 1997).

terrain might in due course engender fresh thinking as to equitable property and the public interest is much to be doubted. The reconfiguration of property in political mindsets in modern liberal market economies offers a tough challenge. Still, Wilde's compelling appraisal is an excellent contribution to the debate, just as the Bowman and Boyle volume emphasizes the crucial importance of developing workable, accepted notions of environmental harm, and of what should be required by way of enforceable alleviation.

MARK STALLWORTHY
Norwich Law School,
University of East Anglia, Norwich

Environmental Principles: From Political Slogans to Legal Rules, Nicolas de Sadeleer. Oxford: Oxford University Press, 2003, 400 pp., £60.00 hb. ISBN 0199254745

Environmental principles have become the hallmark of environmental law and in the last decade principles such as sustainable development, the polluter pays principle, the prevention principle, and the precautionary principle have found their way into policy, legislation, case law, and legal reasoning. Despite the ubiquitous nature of such principles, there has been no wholesale academic analysis of them. Commentary has tended to be ad hoc and has focused on particular developments or particular principles rather than the implications of such principles for environmental law *writ large*. De Sadeleer in this ambitious and wide-ranging book provides such an analysis. The book focuses on three different principles that he sees as profoundly interdependent—the polluter pays principle, the principle of prevention, and the precautionary principle. He argues that not only do these principles represent different approaches to risk but also that their deployment in legal reasoning is a significant feature of contemporary environmental law.

The first section of the book contains a substantive overview of the three principles in which each principle is subject to careful analytical scrutiny. De Sadeleer devotes most of his attention to the precautionary principle and considers the operation of the principle in a number of different jurisdictions and in distinct contexts such as standard setting and the imposition of liability. The author argues that each principle symbolizes a different approach to risk, progressing from a curative model (the polluter pays principle) through to a preventive model (the principle of prevention) and onwards to an anticipatory model (the precautionary principle). This depiction of these principles reflects much of the discussion in the sociological literature about risk in the last decade.[9]

[9] e.g. U. Beck, *Risk Society—Towards a New Modernity* (London: Sage Publications, 1992) and F. Ewald, 'Risk in Contemporary Society' (2000) 6 *Conneticut Insurance Law Journal*, 365.

Commentators have argued that there has been a fundamental shift in how risk is defined, perceived, and managed. De Sadeleer describes this shift as a 'reflex towards security' (p. 225). This link between the sociological literature and the legal utilization of the principle is an interesting one and makes these chapters a valuable resource for anyone who is thinking about these principles.

De Sadeleer's analysis does not stop there however. The second section of the book places these principles in the broader context of environmental law and legal reasoning. De Sadeleer argues that the three principles he is analysing lie at the interface between modern and post-modern law. Modern law, he argues, requires a legal system to be hierarchical, autonomous, and consisting of general and abstract rules. A post-modern legal system in contrast is individualized, open, and consisting of 'mingling yet competing' norms (p. 248). He argues that while environmental principles have arisen in a post-modern context, they bring a rationality to the legal system and are thus not a complete break with modern law. These directing principles are an 'antidote' (p. 264) against post-modernism because they (among other things) refine the purposes of environmental law, codify it, delimit discretionary power, and promote legal certainty. In considering their legal status, he shows that they can be used as a justification for judicial activism and can act to reconcile conflicting norms. The role that such principles play in 'balancing' is particularly stressed by de Sadeleer and the last chapter of section two looks at that role in the environment versus trade legal debate.

Environmental Principles is based on an impressive range of sources. A considerable body of secondary and primary material underpins discussion of the principles, and the theoretical aspects of the book have clearly been informed by extensive reading on the part of de Sadeleer. The end result is a book that is sweeping in its scope. On the one hand, the expansiveness of the book is its great strength. Here is a book that provides a theory of environmental principles and not just a description of them. On the other hand, however, the vastness of this book is also its greatest weakness in that its all-embracing coverage is sometimes at the expense of careful reasoning. There are a number of examples of this and while none of them is fatal to de Sadeleer's core argument, they do detract from it. Thus for example, de Sadeleer's argument that directing principles are closely connected to a human right to environmental protection (pp. 275–89) reads more as wishful thinking than a rigorously constructed argument. His emphasis on the uniqueness of environmental principles as a form of legal reasoning is not always convincing. This is particularly so when the relationship he describes between post-modern and modern law is clearly not restricted to environmental law. Moreover, in the first section there is a tendency for him to 'precaution spot'.[10] Some examples were taken out of context and some examples were cases where the principles were not explicitly being deployed (e.g. the precautionary

[10] See (2002) 9 *Maastricht Journal of European and Comparative Law*, 7.

approach in the United States, pp. 139–47) and thus their utility to his wider argument was unclear. De Sadeleer does take into account comparative analysis in other parts of his book and clearly his arguments about post-modern law also have a bearing on how one considers examples from other jurisdictions, but these arguments did not seem to be fully integrated into the first section of the book.

Overall, *Environmental Principles* is an exciting and passionate book. As can be seen from above, the argument that de Sadeleer puts forward is not inconsequential. This is not just a book about the growing popularity of these principles but is really a sustained argument about the nature of contemporary environmental law. As such, it is an important work and it will, without a doubt, become a touchstone for debate in this area.

LIZ FISHER
Corpus Christi College, Oxford

Competition Law, Environmental Policy and Producer Responsibility: Experiences in the Netherlands from a European Perspective, Hans Vedder. Groningen: Europa Law Publishing, 2002, 204 pp., £39.00 hb. ISBN 907681078

From an institutional as well as academic perspective, the relationship between EU competition and environmental policy remains at a fairly basic and underdeveloped stage. In practice, the 'integration' commitment in Article 6 of the EC Treaty continues to operate largely in the shadows, not least as far as the implementation of EU competition policy is concerned. Whilst, for instance, the EC Treaty contains a number of directly effective prohibitions on anti-competitive behaviour (e.g. Articles 81–2 and 86 EC), no such norms exist in primary EU law in order to outlaw anti-environmental behaviour. Articles 174–6 EC, post-Nice, remain confined to providing the legal framework for legitimizing political and legislative action in relation to environmental protection at a secondary level. This imbalance means that EU legislative initiatives designed to coordinate private actions within a particular commercial sector with the aim of enhancing environmental protection have to pass through the gateway of EU competition law scrutiny, with all that entails. Vedder's book provides some interesting insights into the problems and tensions, practical and legal, that have arisen between competition and environmental norms in the particular context of legislating for environmental safeguards on the management of waste electrical and electronic equipment (WEEE).

The author analyses how EU and Dutch competition law affect the application of environmental legislation on the management of WEEE. The foreword reveals that the book is the result of a study into the problems that may arise from the possible conflict between competition and environmental law in the field of

WEEE management, which was commissioned by the Amsterdam Centre for Environmental Law in 2000. The Netherlands have been one of the few EU countries that have had some experience in terms of legislating for and organizing the management of WEEE prior to the recent adoption of EU's own environmental instrument,[11] in order to improve on the state of reuse and recycling and also to apply the principle of producer responsibility in relation to such waste. Many of the problems that have arisen in the Netherlands in terms of reconciling competition and environmental priorities are set to reappear in variegated forms across the EU with the recent adoption of the EU's own WEEE Directive,[12] which has left considerable leeway for Member States to organize collection and eventual recovery or disposal of the various waste fractions.

The book commences with a systematic introductory overview of the various sources of environmental and competition law that have a bearing on WEEE management, Dutch and European, before outlining areas of conflict and synergy between the respective sectors of competition and environmental law. However, given that it was originally completed in 2001 in Dutch before being translated into English in 2002, the book only considers the key elements of the draft proposal of the WEEE Directive and not the final legal instrument itself. Vedder then goes on to consider the methods by which separate collection of WEEE is organized and the various competition law issues that may arise and have arisen in the Netherlands as a result. Consonant with the principles of polluter pays and extended producer responsibility, both Dutch (and now EU law) on WEEE contain requirements that producers are to shoulder most of the responsibility and cost of organizing separate collection as well as treatment of WEEE, with a view to minimizing disposal routes and maximizing recovery options. These are coupled with requirements to ensure that consumers have systems made available to them to return WEEE free of charge (e.g. to the municipal waste department or to distributors on an 'old for new' basis). The author reveals that in the Netherlands producers and importers have overwhelmingly favoured entering into collective arrangements on meeting their joint obligations as opposed to organizing collection on an individualistic basis. The preference for pooling resources in meeting these substantial as well as technically complex environmental obligations is not surprising, given the clear cost advantages to be gained by most EEE suppliers. The Dutch system of collection arrangements has been constructed on the basis of a fixed fee agreed between producers passed though to consumers, with the fee to be indicated separately from the price tag on EEE products at the point of sale. The tension with competition law arises from the fact that these collective arrangements may fall within the scope of the prohibitions contained in Dutch and EU prohibitions on anti-competitive agreements, principally Article 81 EC. Within the context of

[11] 1998 Dutch White and Brown Goods Order.

[12] Dir. 2002/96/EC on Waste Electronic and Electrical Equipment [2003] OJ L37/24.

Dutch competition law, the question has arisen as to whether such arrangements may possibly be exempted from the cartel prohibition or found to be outside its scope. The author outlines a number of decisions taken by the Dutch Competition Authority which have determined that attempts at passing on fixed fees to the end consumer and indicating such fees separately on the invoice are unduly restrictive of competition. The author rightly points out that this analysis ignores the weight and scope of the 'polluter pays' principle, which should play an overriding role in terms of analysing environmental agreements, according to which both consumers and producers are constituent members of the polluting community. From an environmental protection perspective, fixed fee systems with separate invoicing appear to have many advantages, not least in providing consumers with an incentive to participate in recovery and therefore ensuring a high level of separate collection.

The middle part of the book examines various possible solutions that may be found within and outside the existing Dutch and EU legal frameworks for reconciling the conflicting perspectives that competition and environmental norms may bring to bear on WEEE management. Vedder explores whether existing European Court of Justice jurisprudence might be used in support of excluding or exempting fixed fee arrangements from the prohibition contained in Article 81 EC: for example, with reference to the *Albany*[13] ruling on refining the scope of the definition of undertakings caught by the prohibition; jurisprudence on compulsory cartels; appreciability; rule of reason analysis; and Article 81(3) EC exemption criteria. The book also considers the compatibility of such collection systems with other EU fundamental rules of law, such as in relation to the free movement of goods as well as providing an illuminating if brief comparative survey of various European countries' positions in relation to competition scrutiny of environmental agreements of this kind.

What emerges overall from Vedder's analysis is that there is relatively little clarity as to where the legal boundaries are set in relation to collective agreements on environmental protection, especially as far as EU competition law is concerned. The European Commission has begun to set out some ground rules in relation to privatized management of waste,[14] such as in relation to the packaging sector, but these have not been detailed enough to provide a clear analysis of the relative benefits to be gained from the establishment of collective fixed fee arrangements. For instance, the existing guidelines on horizontal cooperation agreements in the environmental sector[15] are woefully inadequate, simply stating that in relation to assessing whether environmental agreements should receive an

[13] Case C-67/96, *Albany International BV* v. *Stichting Bedrijfspensioenfonds Textielindustrie* [1999] ECR I-5751.

[14] See e.g. summary in the *European Union Competition Policy, Thirtieth Report on Competition Policy 2001* (European Commission DG Competition) OOPEC (ISSN 16095111), 25.

[15] Commission Notice—Guidelines on the Applicability of Article 81 of the EC Treaty to Horizontal Cooperation Agreements [2001] OJ C3/2.

exemption under Article 81(3) EC 'it should be very clearly demonstrated that a uniform fee, charged irrespective of individual costs for waste collection, is indispensable for the functioning of an industry-wide collection system'. The problem is compounded by the fact, with the prospective entering into force of the new Regulation[16] on enforcement of EU competition rules in May 2004, that the European Commission is no longer devoting resources to issuing any guidance in the form of informal guidance or as Article 81(3) EC exemption decisions. National competition authorities and courts are now to have powers and responsibility for applying Article 81 EC in its entirety. However, in this particular case, such authorities and courts have little or no precedent to go on, a factor that threatens to fracture the application of enforcement of EU competition (and, in the context of WEEE management, also EU environmental legislation) within the Union. A way out may be for the European Commission, acting in the public interest on its own initiative, to make a finding of inapplicability in relation to particular existing or draft collective agreements in accordance with Article 10 of the new Regulation. Alternatively, it could draft some more detailed and comprehensive guidelines on the scope of Article 81 EC in relation to environmental agreements. Such initiatives would be particularly useful in the run up to the transposition deadline[17] in relation to the WEEE Directive. I understand that some informal work is in progress on this front within DG Competition, but I remain sceptical as to the level of political priority that this will receive.

In summary, the book provides a useful overview of the various competition law issues that arise and need to be tackled where Member States elect to use the mechanism of private environmental agreements in order to enforce EU environmental legislation. From Vedder's analysis, it is far from clear that the EU and Dutch legal frameworks are duly equipped to ensure that environmental considerations are fully taken into account in terms of current practice for competition scrutiny purposes. The WEEE Directive itself makes specific provision for Member States being able set up collective or individual schemes for collection and treatment of WEEE from private households.[18] In addition, for a transitional period, they are entitled to opt for a system which permits the costs of collection and treatment to be shown separately to consumers.[19] The question remains open though as to the reasons why the European Commission applied such a limitation and whether or not this decision serves to assist in the implementation of producer responsibility, let alone the 'polluter pays' principle, in WEEE management. Since the book was written, there have been a number of

[16] Reg. (EC) No. 1/2003 on the Implementation of the Rules of Competition Laid Down in Arts. 81 and 82 of the Treaty [2003] OJ L1/1.

[17] 13 Aug. 2004.

[18] See Art. 8(2).

[19] Art. 8(3).

important legal important developments that need now to be taken on board, such as the WEEE Directive itself and Regulation (EC) No. 1/2003. The book's chapter on the international context is now out of date as far as part of the references to United Kingdom competition law are concerned. Notwithstanding these limitations, this book is an excellent reference guide to examining core EU competition and environmental legal issues that underpin environmental agreements, one of the increasingly favoured mechanisms of enforcing environmental standards within the EU.

MARTIN HEDEMANN-ROBINSON
Brunel University, London

The European Convention and the Future of European Environmental Law, edited by Jan Jans. Groningen: Europa Law Publishing, 2003, 146 pp., £20.00 pb. ISBN 9076871132

This is the first volume in a projected series of publications by the Avosetta Group. This group is an informal association of lawyers whose 'main purpose is to further the development of environmental law in the European Union and its Member States'. Its participants are invited 'in recognition of their distinction in European environmental law'. The high reputation of the group's participants and of the contributors to this work would lead to high expectations of their series of publications. This first volume, with slight reservations, meets such expectations.

An initial difficulty comes, though, with the absence of any clear statement of the mission of the volume. Edited collections, such as this, normally start with an editor's introductory section highlighting the themes, linking the papers, and explaining the objectives of the collection. This is absent here. It would have been particularly valuable because the genesis of the work is not typical; in particular it preceded a major constitutional reform event and grew from a meeting to draw up a resolution on how environmental issues should be dealt with in that process. There is though no indication of the proposed relationship between the resolution and the papers in this volume, nor if either was sent as a position paper to the Convention itself, to institutions, to Member States, or NGOs.

Having said that, the authors in each chapter take a broadly consistent approach. They evaluate the law on a particular area, consider whether the existing EC constitutional framework and its interpretation by the European Court of Justice (ECJ) and by the national courts fulfils environmental objectives, and, in particular, whether there is scope for improvement by amendments to the Treaty itself.

In the first chapter, Winter examines the role of the environmental principles. His overall approach is typical in that it exhibits fine judgement in considering when existing treaty provisions are sufficient, whether a treaty amendment should take place, or whether any necessary changes would be better at the sub-Treaty policy and law level. He concludes that no major change to the constitutional status of the principles is required, as the courts have developed an effective role for the principles. His suggestions for reform are limited to a number of clarifications, for example, highlighting the sustainable use of resources in Article 174(1) EC. Some of the detailed steps in the elaboration of the argument, though, are a little under-developed. In his discussion of the conflict between free movement of goods and environmental protection, for example, his conclusion from *Rewe-Zentral*[20] that 'environmental protection has priority according to the case-law of the Community' over-simplifies. Similarly, he highlights *Danish Bottles*[21] as a case showing that environmental protection can act to limit the effect of the rules on free movement, but doesn't state that the reverse is also true, as is evident from the case itself.

A similar contrast between stimulating and well-judged overall conclusions and occasional lapses in detailed argumentation are evident in Ermacora's evaluation of the constitutional right to a clean environment. In discussing the European Court of Human Rights jurisprudence on Article 8 ECHR in cases like *Guerra*,[22] for example, he asserts that the right to a healthy environment 'is included in the concept of the right to respect for private and family life'. It may be a small point but this overplays the impact of the Article 8 ECHR cases. Environmental pollution might in some very limited circumstances be the cause of an Article 8 breach, but this falls far short of saying that the right to environment is 'included' in Article 8 ECHR.

This highlights a key feature of this volume. If you are interested in expert views on the need for reform of the constitutional aspects of EC environmental law then there are some fascinating ideas here. The work should not be viewed, however, as providing a comprehensive outline and in-depth analysis of the various areas addressed.

Epiney, in a very strong contribution, discusses the division of competence between the Member States and the EC. Whilst broadly supporting the current system, she is highly critical of the reservation, in Article 175(2) EC, of the unanimity voting procedure for certain subjects. Jans, in his chapter, 'EU Environmental Policy and the Civil Society', makes a similar strong argument for the European Convention to grasp the issue of standing to appear before the ECJ and Court of First Instance (CFI). In particular, he urges the legislative institutions to take up the invitation from the ECJ, in the *UPA* case,[23] to rethink the 'direct and

[20] Case 120/78, *Rewe Zentrale* v. *Bundesmonopolverwattung für Branntwein* [1979] ECR 649.

[21] Case 302/86, *Commission* v. *Denmark* [1988] ECR 4607.

[22] ECtHR 19 Feb. 1998, 116/1996/735/932, *Guerra and Others* v. *Italy*.

[23] Case C-50/00/P, *Unión de Pequeños Agricultores* v. *Council* [2002] ECR 1-6677.

individual concern' test. Jans suggests that the issue could be resolved satisfactorily simply by enacting the *Schoppenstadt* formula in the Treaty, but with the omission of the words, 'and individual'.

One distinctive and impressive feature of this volume is its reformatory character. Most texts will have a strong critique and evaluation of what has taken place, including sometimes forthright views on what the legislators or courts have done wrong. It is rarer to see, on the scale outlined here at any rate, proposals for ways of dealing better with a situation. Critiquing, or reviewing, the constructive attempts of others can be a deal easier than the construction itself.

Montini's chapter on the issue of external competence is a useful overview, particularly on WTO obligations. It doesn't, however, relate to the European Convention. There are no recommendations for Treaty amendments, and no explicit evaluation of the issue in terms of need for reform of the current Treaty.

Krämer's consideration of the future role of the ECJ in developing environmental law is very stimulating. In addressing the problem of delay, for example, he advocates empowering the Commission to make 'findings of law' that Member States could appeal up to the ECJ if they wished. He further suggests decentralized complaint receipt centres in each Member State to reinforce the role of citizen complaints in bringing to light breaches of Community law. These creative suggestions do prompt consideration by the reader, though it would have been useful to see their implications explored in more detail by the author.

In a well-balanced final chapter, Bándi points out the difficulty that enlargement states will have in complying with the EC environmental *acquis*. He goes on though to point out that the constitutional right to a clean environment in South Eastern European and Central Eastern European states is often better formulated (and in the case of Hungary, judicially applied) than in their Western neighbours. He stresses that this strength should not be watered down by EC membership.

The volume concludes with the resolution of the Avosetta Conference on the European Convention. This crystallizes some of the Treaty reform ideas suggested in the earlier chapters. There are some interesting aspects of the resolution that are not really taken up by any of the contributors, for example, paragraph 9 on the idea of a *Komptenz-Katalog* and the dangers of a strengthened subsidiarity principle.

Overall then this is a stimulating if flawed volume. Its strengths are in the expertise of its contributors and the constitutional reform ideas presented. Its principal flaws are a certain unevenness between the contributions and the lack of an explicit objective for the work. The group's website, www.avosetta.org is also worth a visit.

MICHAEL G. DOHERTY
Lancashire Law School, University of Central Lancashire

EC Agricultural Law, 2nd edition, J.A. Usher. Oxford: Oxford University Press, 2002, 254 pp., £60.00 hb. ISBN 019826823

EC Agricultural Law is the second edition of a book previously published, in 1988, by Clarendon Press, under the title *Legal Aspects of Agriculture in the European Community*. The first edition was warmly welcomed as a valuable examination of an area of European Community (EC) law that had otherwise been largely ignored by legal research. This is equally true of the second edition. The preface to the first edition drew attention to the frequency and bulk of EC legislation concerning the Common Agricultural Policy (CAP). In the period since the publication of the first edition, the CAP has undergone several major reforms, in particular with the introduction of the MacSharry reform measures in 1992, the Agenda 2000 reforms in 1999, and the introduction of the single currency. At one level, therefore, this second edition is significant in providing a more up to date discussion of the legal framework within which the CAP operates. However, as is the nature of the CAP, the present edition has been overtaken by a further set of reforms, the Mid Term Review of the CAP, agreed by the Council in 2003. Nevertheless, despite this, it will be apparent, from the comments that follow, that this book continues to provide an important examination of the legal framework of the CAP. Indeed, as will also be apparent, it is also likely to be a valuable edition to library collections on EC law for other reasons.

The author has divided the book into nine chapters. Seven of these chapters are based upon the chapter format of the first edition and two are new. Chapter one is deceptively entitled 'Agriculture in the EC Treaty'. It is not simply an examination of the agriculture title in the EC Treaty. Instead the author provides a very interesting account of the interaction between the CAP and other aspects of EC trade law. Additionally he provides an analysis of the manner in which terms such as 'agricultural goods' or 'agricultural produce' have been interpreted in EC law. Chapter two then examines the manner in which the objectives of the CAP, set out in Article 33 of the EC Treaty, have been interpreted and applied. Additionally in this chapter, the author also explains how litigation concerning the CAP has been the source of many of the EC's general principles of law. Chapter three is one of the new chapters within the book. This chapter examines the impact that international trade negotiations have had on the CAP and, perhaps more importantly, upon CAP reform. From here the author moves into a detailed analysis of individual aspects of the CAP. Chapter four examines EC legislation that has established common measures to govern the production and trade in particular agricultural produce. Chapter five then explains the financial mechanisms through which the CAP is financed. This must be one of the most complex areas of EC law. However, the author must be congratulated for his remarkably clear and concise account of this area. Chapter six is the second new chapter included within this edition. In one of the most novel aspects of the book, the author here includes a chapter on the Common Fisheries Policy. Chapter seven examines the extent to which national authorities retain powers to act unilaterally despite the fact that EC measures exist concerning agricultural production and trade. This tackles the thorny issue of the extent to which Member States are able to operate national agricultural policies within the structure of the CAP. The author's examination of the mechanisms of the CAP also acknowledges that the CAP is not merely about agricultural production and trade. In this regard, Chapter eight deals with the policies developed by the EC to deal with the structural problems that have long existed both within the agriculture sector and within rural areas in general. Finally the book concludes, in chapter nine, with a chapter that deals with administrative issues. This very interesting chapter deals with issues such as the processes through which EC legislation on the CAP is both adopted and enforced and also the methods through which it has been implemented and enforced within the United Kingdom.

Overall, the author has provided a very comprehensive, yet readily intelligible, explanation of a variety of legal issues associated with the CAP. This is particularly true of the legal structure of the CAP itself and of the laws that apply in relation to agricultural trade. Such explanations will undoubtedly be of value to both postgraduate students and professionals who have an interest in European agricultural law. It is true that the book was published before the Council reached its recent agreement on further reforms to the legal framework of the CAP. These reforms will enter into force in 2004 and 2005 and will principally affect CAP market policy as described in chapter four. Even so, the underlying legal structure described in that chapter will remain unchanged, though some individual aspects of the law will change. One example of this will be the introduction of a single farm payment to replace separate payments in respect of differing aspects of agricultural production. However, many other legal issues examined by the author in the book will be unaffected. Consequently, the book continues to provide a very valuable analysis of the legal framework of the CAP. Elsewhere the author's explanation of the role of agricultural cases, before the ECJ, in developing the EC's general principles of law will also be of interest to all students of EC law. This is equally true of the discussion of administrative issues that is contained in the final chapter. On a critical note, however, readers seeking an environmental perspective are likely to be disappointed. The book provides the author with little space to examine policy issues affecting the CAP. Consequently the author does not focus upon the development of environmental measures within the CAP and the book does not examine in any detail the measures adopted by the EC to encourage farmers to avoid environmental damage or those that have been adopted in order to foster agriculture's role in enhancing the environment.

BRIAN JACK
Queen's University of Belfast

Deterrence, Insurability and Compensation in Environmental Liability: Future Developments in the European Union, edited by Michael Faure. New York/ Vienna: Springer-Verlag, 2003, 408 pp., €92 pb. ISBN 3211838635

At first glance this publication, rooted as it is in the environmental liability regime proposed by the Commission in its White Paper of 2000, may appear to have been overtaken by subsequent developments. However, the issues it addresses, particularly its primary focus upon financial assurance arrangements, are of pertinence today. Indeed, this book can be viewed as timely given the publication in 2003 of the Council's Common Position on the proposed Environmental Liability Directive, which defers any commitment on compulsory insurance or guarantees.

The editor presents three studies undertaken for the European Commission by the Maastricht Institute for Transnational Legal Research (METRO) post publication of the White Paper on Environmental Liability in 2000. The Commission's brief together with a copy of the White Paper, are appended as annexes. The goals as expounded in the Editorial Foreword/Introduction are (taking the White Paper as a starting point): to explore the possibilities for a regime of environmental liability and insurance, which will provide for optimal compensation, and to investigate the efficacy of alternatives to traditional insurance. An interesting methodology is employed that combines traditional comparative legal analysis and legal economic analysis. This is justified by reference to the request by the Commission to formulate proposals in line with economic efficiency and the White Paper, which also draws on comparative legal research.

The first and by far the largest of the three studies is by Faure and Grimeaud and is entitled 'Financial Assurance Issues of Environmental Liability'. Chapter II of the study sets out a theoretical framework for principles of liability. In order to assess the efficiency of the White Paper regime, the authors proceed to undertake an economic analysis in line with the White Paper's commitment to provide a regime that goes beyond compensation and acts as an incentive for prevention to would-be polluters. The White Paper is measured against the theoretical model, and issues such as retroactivity and the nature of the strict liability rule are addressed. The authors conclude that the proposals are efficient because the strict liability rule is limited to specific (generally unilateral) dangerous activities and fault-based liability is adopted for bilateral accidents resulting from non-dangerous activities. If environmental liability is to have an impact upon incentives for polluters, then, it is also argued that no retroactivity is correct. Interestingly, these features of the White Paper are broadly reproduced in the latest EC environmental liability proposals.

Chapter III addresses possible defences, again based upon the framework of the second chapter and again analysed from an economic perspective. It is of note that the authors conclude that regulatory compliance should not exclude operators from liability other than in exceptional circumstances. This has been an area of considerable debate in the European Parliament and the Council and indications that the regulatory compliance defence contained in the first proposal for a Directive might be jettisoned have, so far, not borne fruit. Chapter IV applies the theoretical framework of Chapters II and III to the environmental liability regimes in the legal systems of some of the Member States, focusing upon Flanders and the Netherlands. It is conceded that this is a brief snapshot rather than in-depth comparative analysis. However, it would have been interesting to see this expanded, at least in so far as the same features of the theoretical framework are considered in each of the legal systems examined.

The central focus of the study surrounds the Commission's concern over insurability of the proposed White Paper regime and this forms the subject of the subsequent chapters. An outline of general principles of insurability identified in the literature is applied to environmental liability and the White Paper proposals in Chapters V and VI. It is of particular note that the authors stress that this section is merely a consideration of theoretical conditions that may enhance insurability and is not an empirical work. They (correctly, it is submitted) warn that ultimately it will be the insurance industry that will decide upon whether the risks involved are insurable. Three areas that impact upon insurability are highlighted for examination: predictability, defences, and capacity. Predictability is a particular hurdle when dealing with the notion of damage to biodiversity. However, the authors are encouraged by the White Paper's remediation costs approach (maintained in the draft Directive). An issue not explored in depth and of interest in the light of recent debate and development is the impact upon insurability of a regulatory compliance defence.

The so-called 'judgement proof' problem may arise in cases of insolvency or transfer of assets and compulsory insurance could provide a possible answer here. Both the benefits and potential dangers of mandatory coverage are assessed in Chapter VI and the conclusion arrived at that such dangers warrant caution with regard to introduction of compulsory insurance (advice which has evidently been heeded by the Commission). In Chapter VII, the authors scrutinize the arguments for and against financial limits to liability and suggest that such limits might encourage the development of an insurance market. It is, however, noted that limits would contravene the polluter pays principle on which both the White Paper and the subsequent draft Directive are explicitly stated to rest. Chapter VIII provides a brief glance at interdependencies between liability and insurance and, somewhat paradoxically given the purpose of the study, the authors conclude that the nature of the regime should be framed by reference to the theoretical model outlined in the preceding text and not 'according to vague notions concerning insurability' (p. 211). One of the aims of this study was to assess alternatives to traditional liability insurance and this forms the subject of Chapter IX. The financial security options under examination include self-insurance, bank guarantees, and funding pools. Another interesting alternative is put forward in the form of first party insurance as, seemingly successfully, employed in the Netherlands. The chapter concludes with a very brief look at compensation funds that might act as a back-up where insolvency is an issue or liability cannot be established. Arguably such a back-up regime is essential, particularly given the prevalence of pollution from non-point sources, and yet in the most recent proposals there is not even a mandatory requirement for remediation of orphaned sites.

Chapter XI is dedicated to the second study: 'A Market-based Analysis of Financial Insurance Issues Associated with US National Resource Damage Liability' by Boyd. Whereas study one was primarily desk-based, studies two and three are market-based. Boyd's study considers the US experience with mandatory financial assurance, focusing upon national resource damage liability under US Statutes (primarily OPA and CERCLA). Section B provides a conceptual justification of financial assurance requirements and section C details US national resource damage law in the guise of federal and state law as well as the common law. Finally section D considers approaches to damage assessment and valuation. The author advocates mandatory financial assurance and concludes that, although national resource damage coverage is perhaps problematic for underwriters/guarantors, such damage represents only a small fraction of the cost of environmental liabilities as a whole. In fact, he argues, markets have developed quite readily and the cost of premiums is absorbable (indeed costs are falling). Fears of bankruptcy and insurance market failure have been, according to Boyd, over-exaggerated.

The second market-based study, presented by Lahnstein, provides an analysis of financial assurance issues in Germany, Austria, Italy, and Spain. It sets out to be complementary to the Boyd study and considers how regimes differ in the chosen Member States by reference to (for example) ecological damage and *ex ante* versus *ex post* restoration. The author concludes that approaches to compensation for ecological damage differ widely. However, one common feature is that no broad coverage is evident for compulsory insurance and Lahnstein sees it as having 'only small practical importance' (p. 330). In the Member States examined, there is nonetheless fairly widespread coverage for existing traditional liabilities, although the perception is that the percentage of claims for expenditure for ecological damage is not of a high level.

The availability of insurance for an EC environmental liability regime (including coverage for ecological damage) has been a particular concern of the Commission and commentators. The results of the studies contained in this book are drawn upon in the Explanatory Memorandum to the draft Directive and they seem to have led the Commission to take a favourable view upon insurability. The Council's recently published common position requires Member States to 'take measures to encourage the development of financial security instruments and markets' and requires the Commission to report within a time period and possibly submit proposals for mandatory financial security. However, as the authors warn, insurability, in the end, will depend upon the willingness of underwriters to insure. Certainly the studies presented by Faure may yet provide some 'food for thought' for both legislator and industry alike.

JULIE ADSHEAD
University of Salford

Casebook on EU Environmental Law, edited by Ludwig Krämer. Oxford: Hart Publishing, 2002, 392 pp., £35.00 pb. ISBN 1841131725

As the 'father' of European environmental law, and an author of many books and publications in the field, Ludwig Krämer needs little introduction. He begins this latest work with just praise for the 'outstanding' work of the European Court of Justice (ECJ) in developing and interpreting environmental law. The book is a selective guide to the case law of the ECJ in environmental law, and is aimed at all, from practitioners to students, with the purpose of increasing 'understanding and comprehension of the reasoning of the Court'. The fifty cases chosen for inclusion are arranged thematically, with excerpts from each decision followed by the author's commentary.

The book presupposes a certain degree of knowledge and so there is neither introduction nor introductory chapter. An explanation of the structure and purpose of this work is to be found in the brief preface; in this sense it adheres to its role as a casebook.

There are six chapters, covering general principles, so-called 'horizontal problems', water and air, products and noise, nature protection, waste management, and finally 'procedural questions'. It is an impressive undertaking. The majority of the fifty cases included, and certainly all those that deserve it, are accompanied by comprehensive and thought-provoking discussion. A number of what might be considered the 'classic' decisions of the ECJ in environmental protection are to be found within this casebook, each thoroughly analysed.

The first chapter begins with an involved discussion of what would appear to be a rather unpromising case in environmental policy terms: a dispute between the Parliament and the Council, concerning the proper legislative basis for a Community measure on forestry and environmental protection. It is essentially a 'turf war' between two institutions, and one might think that it does not bode well for what is to follow. In fact it is a very appropriate starting point. The case highlights a number of issues and tensions in Community environmental policy and law-making: the paternalistic, institutional, and formalistic nature of the Community; the difficulties in finding a correct legal basis for legislative measures (Professor Krämer observes that in this case 'the principal aim of product-related environmental measures is doubtful'); the apparent conflict between differing policy objectives, in this case environmental protection and agricultural policy; and perhaps more generally the need for a sensible redrafting and restructuring of the Treaties. It also reminds us that Community policy on the environment, which has in many ways been very effective, has succeeded despite these apparent difficulties.

The first chapter includes a number of interesting cases on 'general principles', such as the right of a Member State to adopt more protective measures than exist at Community level, and to regulate economic activity outside the Community; the right of individuals to rely directly on environmental directives; the obligation on Member States to achieve the aims of Community legislation; and the proper interpretation of Community law. We are reminded of the fundamental tension present in law-making by a community of nations: Member States lose the right to regulate, as they see fit, much activity which could harm the environment, but at the same time each Member State gains the benefit of uniform standards (and, hopefully, high standards) of regulation in both trade and environmental protection across the Community.

Presumably for reasons of space, this chapter omits discussion of other issues, such as the interaction of Community law and international treaty obligations (in particular the WTO), and the application of principles of environmental law (in particular the precautionary principle and the proximity principle). Similarly, whilst the author notes (in relation to the *Peralta* case[24] on the regulation by Italy of oil-dumping by shipping in international waters) that protection of the marine environment is one particular weakness in Community environmental policy, it is a shame that he does not expand upon this comment, as no doubt Professor Krämer would have some interesting things to say on what is yet to be achieved by the Community in the field of environmental policy.

Many seminal decisions of the ECJ are to be found here,[25] such as *Kraaijeveld* (in relation to which the author observes that in a densely populated and highly developed area such as the EU 'a proper assessment of environmental impacts should be of much wider application than is required by the EIA directive and its subsequent amendment') and *Bozen*, on environmental impact assessment. In addition, less well-known but very interesting decisions, such as the *Mecklenburg* case on Directive 90/313/EEC on Access to Environmental Information, are also included. The author notes that the recent Aarhus Convention is based in large measure on Directive 90/313/EEC, and includes a short discussion of the Convention, although he does not venture any thoughts on the impact and future interpretation of Aarhus.

As both a survey of significant decisions, and an analysis of the jurisprudence contained in them, some parts of the book are very strong. The cases on water

[24] Case C-379/92, *Criminal Proceedings against Matteo Peralta* [1994] ECR 3453.

[25] Case C-72/95, *Aannemersbedrijf P.K. Kraaijeveld BV e.a.* v. *Gedeputeerde Staten van Zuid-Holland* [1996] ECR 1-5403; Case C-435/97, *World Wildlife Fund (WWF) and Others* v. *Autonome Provinz Bozen and Others* [1999] 1-5613; Case C-321/96, *Wiltaeln Mecklenburg* v. *Kreis Pinneberg—Der Landrat* [1998] 1-3809.

and air 'standards' are well explained, and those on nature conservation are thorough. Likewise, the author broadens the horizons of the environmental lawyer by including less well-known cases on products standards and consumer protection, as well as the classic cases. Where Community policy has succeeded, for example in the reduction of ozone-depleting gases, it is given due credit; where there is a long way to go, as is the case with biotechnology, the author does not hesitate to say so.

At times Professor Krämer is happy to introduce his personal viewpoint (he does not, for instance, see any overall benefit in genetically modified organisms) and the book is all the better for that. The cases chosen remind us that environmental policy, like any other area of life, has its trends and fashions: 'eco-labelling' was once a topic of some debate, but it has been largely forgotten; GMOs may go the same way (however unlikely that may seem at present).

The selection of cases for inclusion in a book such as this will depend, in large measure, on personal choice and (no doubt) differing opinions. However, there are some notable omissions: the chapter on waste management includes no recent decisions of the ECJ on the definition of 'waste' (although the central debate is set out in the discussion of *Tombesi*), which is perhaps one of the most intractable issues in environmental law at present. The otherwise broad chapter on nature conservation omits the important *Santona Marshes* case. There is some discussion of state aids for environmental purposes, but the important decision in *PreussenElektra* is not included. The *Danish Bees*, *Danish Bottles*, *Belgian Waste*, and *Veal Crates* cases do not merit a mention, perhaps because of their vintage.[26]

Considerable wisdom and insight will be found within this text, although the structure of the book makes it a little unwieldy at times. A chapter in which the author presents an overall analysis of the various cases, or the overarching principles in the ECJ's policy, and suggests future trends or developments would have made a valuable addition. It would be interesting to know Professor Krämer's views on whether the ECJ will adopt a courageous or cautious approach to interpreting the Treaties after the accession of a number of new Member States. Because the survey of cases (and indeed law) does not purport to be comprehensive, one requires a reasonable level of knowledge of this field in order to use the book; on the other hand, the inclusion of some basic cases, and exclusion of others, may give rise to debate.

[26] Joined Cases C-304/94, C-330/94, C-342/94, and C-234/95, *Criminal Proceedings against Euro Tombesi and Adino Tombesi (C-304/94), Robert Santella (C-330/94), Giovanni Muzi and others (C-342/94) and Anselono Savini (C-224/95)* [1997] ECR 1-3561; Case C-379/98, *Preussen Elektra AG* v. *Schleswig AG, in the presence of Windpark Reussenköge III GmbH and Land Schleswig Holstein* [2001] ECR 1-2099; Case C-355/90, *Commission* v. *Spain* [1993] ECR 1-4221; Case C-67/97, *Criminal Proceedings against Ditlev Bluhme* [1998] ECR 8033; Case 302/86, *Commission* v. *Denmark* [1988] ECR 4607; Case C-290, *Commission* v. *Belgium* [1992] ECR 1-4431; Case C-1/96, *The Queen* v. *Minister of Agriculture, Fisheries and Food ex p. Compassion in World Farming Ltd.*

Ultimately, this is a wide-ranging work, containing sharp analysis and no little insight (which, given the identity of the author, is not surprising). Students, academics, and practitioners should benefit from reading and re-reading this work.

JEREMY PIKE
Barrister
2 Harcourt Buildings

World Resources 2002–2004, Decisions for the Earth: Balance, Voice and Power. New York: World Resources Institute, 2003, 328 pp., $27.00 pb. ISBN 1569735328. Also available on the Internet at http://pubs.wri.org/pubs

Recent years have witnessed a remarkable growth of consensus that greater public participation is desirable in environmental decision-making. This report, the tenth in the *World Resources Series*, is firmly part of this consensus, arguing that public involvement is a crucial element of environmental governance.

Such widespread consensus should perhaps not be unexpected. After all, public participation is able to appeal to so many, from green political theorists trying to escape both green authoritarianism and the limitations of liberal representative democracy, to technocrats looking for 'free' information, to politicians and developers who want to see public and private projects introduced with the minimum of public opposition. Some want better decisions, some more democracy. The consensus goes alongside what are, on the whole, relatively poorly defined objectives, and a wide range of meanings for participation. Of the diverse rationales for public participation in environmental decision-making, this report places participation firmly in the camp of improving substantive outcomes. This is on the one hand a question of environmental quality: environmental degradation is linked to a flawed decision-making process. The faith in tools of openness, information, and involvement to bring about improvements in environmental quality is striking, and not fully explained. That is not the full extent of a good outcome, however, in this report. A good outcome in this report implies not only environmental quality, but also, and crucially, fairness. Fairness, usually linked in this debate with the quality of a process, is here also far more basically concerned with distribution, principally the distribution of natural resources.

It is hardly surprising that public participation fails to deliver on all its promises in practice. And it is practice that is the most significant feature of this report. *Decisions for the Earth* examines mechanisms of environmental decision-making and environmental governance around the world, identifying examples of good and bad practice. The report argues that better environmental governance is one of the most direct routes to fairer and more sustainable use of natural resources. And the 'access principles', that is access to information, access to decision-making, and access to justice, are a fundamental part of that improved environmental governance.

This report is not the place to look for sustained theoretical analysis, or indeed detailed discussion of legal provisions on access. The report's value lies in its detailed discussion of the *application* of the access principles, which it views as the building blocks of good environmental governance. Whilst information on legal rights and obligations can be obtained relatively easily, environmental lawyers know as well as anybody that progressive legislation is only the beginning. Changing cultures and expectations on the ground is the greater challenge. Notwithstanding the chorus of consensus that surrounds participation, it is well recognized that there is a certain lack of progress on the ground. It is not too surprising to learn from the report, for example, that access to information is characterized by 'strong laws, weak implementation' (p. 51).

So, we are provided in this report with a very wide range of illustrations of access to information, participation, and access to justice in a range of different national and sectoral contexts. The illustrations absorb cases of absence of access, flawed access initiatives, and genuine success stories. Chapter 3 discusses the 'access initiative', in which a coalition of 25 civil society groups measured access to information, access to decision-making, and access to justice in nine different (and diverse) countries. It is of course terribly difficult to get objective and comparable information on access in different systems and different sectors. Whilst the discussion here is not without its flaws (in particular, the methodology and measurement criteria are not entirely clear), it is an interesting and ambitious initiative. And notwithstanding the very clear agenda in this report, the discussion is generally balanced. The challenges of participation are not shirked; by way of example, the report discusses some of the potential difficulties of reliance on NGO involvement (p. 75). Whilst firmly in favour of enhanced access, the report is willing to criticize initiatives that do not come up to scratch.

The main focus of this report is on developing countries, and particularly natural resource development. The book is, however, truly international, and discusses a range of examples from different countries and sectors. In addition, Chapter 6 discusses corporate decision-making, and Chapter 7 access to international decision-making. The (perhaps misplaced) optimism felt at EU level that participatory mechanisms will cut a path through the democratic deficit, which is so resistant to change by representative mechanisms, resonates also in other regional and international bodies.

This report is published collaboratively by United Nations Development Programme, the United Nations Environment Programme, the World Bank, and the World Resources Institute. As one might expect from a publication of this nature, the prose style is rather dry, and the output not radical. The report ends with a series of recommendations for action. Five criteria are put forward by which to 'define our drive for better environmental governance' (p. 215). We are to: 'adopt environmental management approaches that respect ecosystems'; 'build the capacity for public participation'; 'recognize all affected stakeholders'; 'integrate environmental sustainability in economic decision-making'; 'strengthen global environmental cooperation' (p. 221). None of this is very groundbreaking, even if all are very challenging in practice. The strength of *Decisions for the Earth* lies not in this reinforcement of some well-established ideas, but in underlining the importance of an active rather than passive approach to public participation, and in the discussion of how it works in practice. Given that the practice and culture of administrations and businesses dictate the reality of public involvement in decision-making, and that the most sophisticated legal provisions can be empty in practice, that makes this a useful book for environmental lawyers.

MARIA LEE
King's College London

Eco-nomics: What Everyone Should Know about Economics and the Environment, Richard R. Stroup. Washington: Cato Institute, 2003, 91 pp., $9.95 pb. ISBN 1930865449

Conventional wisdom has it that environmental problems stem from unconstrained economic development, which justifies government regulation and, in some cases, public ownership of environmental goods. But this view of relations between the economy and the environment has always been too simple, as economists have pointed out since at least the 1960s. For one thing, environmental market failures cannot automatically justify government intervention because governments fail too, and sometimes the costs of government failure, including the environmental costs, exceed the costs of market failure. (This has obvious but underappreciated implications for the 'Polluter Pays Principle'.) Moreover, markets do not only cause environmental harm; they can be enlisted to help improve environmental protection, as Richard Stroup shows in his new book, *Eco-nomics*.

Stroup's concise and readable introduction to environmental economics argues that the chief problem with environmental protection is not too much but too little economics. It includes a good deal of anecdotal evidence of government failure, and explains how market-based solutions can help. This alone makes the book valuable reading, particularly for those inclined to believe that markets simply *cause* environmental problems and governments simply *resolve* them. But this should not be the only book one reads about environmental economics because it is not well balanced. Like other works in the 'free market environmentalist' literature, Stroup's book focuses almost exclusively on problems of government failure, while minimizing the very real problem of market failure.

The 'free-market environmentalist' argument runs generally as follows: The basic problem of environmental protection is the lack of well-defined and enforced private property rights in environmental goods. If all resources were privately owned, they would be adequately protected against over-use and degradation by (1) the incentives private resource owners naturally possess to maximize the long-run economic values of the resources they own, and (2) common-law remedies, such as nuisance and trespass, that protect privately owned resources from the depredations of others.

There are several problems with the basic 'free market environmentalist' thesis, not least of which is the fact that property rights are costly, sometimes prohibitively costly, to define and enforce. In addition, common-law remedies for environmental protection often fail because of high transaction costs and diseconomies of scale. Nuisance and trespass law do not cope well with large-scale problems affecting large numbers of people. For this reason, direct government regulation is sometimes both necessary and preferable.

To his credit, and in contrast to many of his fellow 'free-marketeers', Stroup expressly acknowledges these deficiencies in the standard 'free-market environmentalist' thesis. Nevertheless, his book's unwavering focus is on problems of government failure, as if those problems are far more responsible than market failures for environmental harms. Stroup's default principle seems to be that markets (which Stroup associates with 'cooperation') are good; politics (which he associates with 'conflict') are bad. He is, of course, entitled to that belief, which many no doubt share. His bias may even be a useful corrective to the typical environmentalist bias against any use of economic analysis in policy-making. The fact of the matter, however, is that government is not *always* the source of environmental problems, and markets are not always the solution. Indeed, there is no reason to believe that government is more responsible than markets for environmental problems.

Stroup's bias would be less troublesome if he did not try to mask it by pretending that his analysis is 'objective' and 'dispassionate'. His analysis is informed, just like everyone else's, by ideological predispositions. Much of *Eco-nomics* reads more like a lawyer's brief than a judicial clerk's memo.

Eco-nomics is filled with anecdotes that highlight problems of government failure in environmental protection. He refers to: forest management policies that exacerbate fire damage by preventing the removal of dead and dying trees, against the advice of forestry experts; national park management decisions to close campsites that are profitable, but not for the local land managers; federal endangered species protection policies that create perverse incentives for private landowners to eradicate species habitat; one-size-fits-all pollution-control standards that ignore regulated parties' differential costs of compliance; government irrigation projects that provide water for special interests, such as agriculture, at prices below the cost of provision; and so on. All of these problems are real. What is unrealistic is the implication that government is the primary source of environmental problems, many (or any) of which might be effectively resolved or avoided by a simple combination of private property rights and free markets.

How likely is it, for example, that private property, markets, and the common law would resolve the problem of endangered species? At several points in his book, Stroup mentions the Nature Conservancy—a private organization, which preserves land and other resources by engaging in market transactions. In fact, the Nature Conservancy is the largest *private* landowner in the United States. But the largest single tract of Nature Conservancy land is just 56,000 acres—a vast parcel for a private landowner but only a tiny fraction of the designated 'critical habitat' (845,000 acres) of just one endangered species: the peninsular big-horn sheep.[27] In the absence of government regulation, ownership, or subsidies, it is doubtful that big-horn sheep habitat, or the habitat of any *non-commodity* resource, would be protected through the coordinated efforts of private landowners. The transaction costs of such a private enterprise would likely be prohibitive.

One basis of Stroup's preference for private over public ownership is his sense that public resource managers are comparatively short-sighted. Only private landowners, Stroup suggests, have an incentive to maximize the long-run value of the resources they own. But this belief is not well supported by economic theory or available empirical information about how private resource owners actually behave. The most we can legitimately expect is that private owners will manage the resources they own so as to maximize their private values, whether based on economic, ideological, political, religious, ecological, or other principles. There is no reason to suppose (a) that their private values equal social values or (b) that they operate according to (inherently subjective) discount rates that are lower than those of public land managers.

Another of Stroup's more controversial assertions is that environmental goods are just like any other economic goods in society; consequently, he concludes, there is no reason to treat them differently. But many environmental goods *are* different because (1) not all of their values are priced, or are even capable of being priced, in markets, and (2) they are likely to be under-supplied by markets because private producers cannot capture enough of the benefits to cover the costs of providing them. In other words, many environmental amenities are *public goods*. There is no more reason to believe that a combination of private property, markets, and the common law will produce sufficient environmental protection than that they would produce sufficient amounts of national defence or criminal justice.

Again, this is not to say that Stroup is wrong to claim that private property and markets have substantial utility for environmental protection. He may even be right that these tools are presently 'underappreciated' and, as a consequence, underutilized in environmental policy. But their utility is far more limited than Stroup's book suggests.

DANIEL H. COLE
Indiana University School of Law at Indianapolis (USA)

[27] See D.H. Cole, *Pollution and Property—Comparing Ownership Institutions for Environmental Protection* (Cambridge: Cambridge University Press, 2002).

The Precautionary Principle in the 20th Century: Late Lessons from Early Warnings, edited by Poul Harremoës, David Gee, Malcolm MacGarvin, Andy Stirling, Jane Keys, Brian Wynne, and Sofia Guedes Vaz. London: Earthscan Publications, Ltd., 2002, 268 pp. £17.95 pb. ISBN 1853838934

All nations face risks to safety, health, and the environment. Many of these risks cannot easily be quantified. Suppose that genetic modification of food becomes common. Will human health be jeopardized? If global warming continues at its current pace, what, precisely, will happen in England and France? Do electromagnetic fields create a serious risk of cancer? For that matter, what are the risks of a serious terrorist attack in New York, London, or Paris? For public officials, the most general question is how to proceed in the absence of good evidence about how to quantify social risks.

In many nations, and the European Community in particular, the increasingly popular answer is: Follow the Precautionary Principle (PP). This PP is not always clearly defined. In fact it is easy to find a range of different definitions. But in all its incarnations, the PP counsels regulators to act even in the face of considerable uncertainty. For those who endorse the PP, it is better to be safe than sorry; hazards should be controlled whether or not we have clear proof of harm.

This book, a multi-authored volume from the European Environment Agency, can be seen as a kind of lawyer's brief in favour of the PP. It is extremely well done, and it makes for informative and powerful reading. The basic goal is to offer a wide range of cases in which regulators ignored early warning signs, demanded clear evidence, and ultimately waited until it was too late. Through the sheer accumulation of examples, the authors offer evidence that the PP makes a great deal of sense. But they have theoretical ambitions as well. They want both to sharpen and to deepen our understanding of what the PP means and requires.

What, exactly, is the PP? In answering this question, the authors draw on an analogy to medicine and public health, where, they urge, 'the benefit of doubt about a diagnosis is usually given to the patient ('better safe than sorry')'. They suggest that the PP requires that in many contexts, 'there is a need to act to reduce potential hazards *before* there is strong proof of harm, taking into account the likely costs and benefits'. And they urge that the PP, properly understood, requires much more. It calls for early research and monitoring, for a general reduction of environmental burdens, for promoting clean production and innovation, and for cooperation among stakeholders. The PP can therefore be seen as a way of giving the benefit of the doubt to safety, health, and the environment. A special goal is to forestall disasters or irreversible harm while also promoting wide public participation in risk regulation.

Supporting the argument for precautions, the authors' case studies deal with a wide range of environmental problems: overused fisheries, radiation, benzene, asbestos, PCBs, halocarbons, DES, antimicrobials, sulphur dioxide, MTBE in petrol, chemical contamination of the Great Lakes, TBT antifoulants (with the intriguing subtitle 'a tale of ships, snails and imposex'), hormones in the promotion of growth, and mad cow disease. Most of the chapters follow a simple structure. An activity, product, or process is introduced; early warnings suggest the existence of a possible hazard; the warnings are ignored; and serious harms ensue. Consider, for example, the case of MTBE, a fuel additive designed to replace lead. Use of MTBE was originally justified on many grounds. It is expensive, and it appeared to be environmentally desirable, a promising method for reducing ozone and carbon monoxide pollution. Unfortunately, MTBE also has adverse environmental and health effects. Worse of all, it leads to significant groundwater contamination. In addition, it might be carcinogenic. In retrospect, the use of MTBE was a big mistake. Could the adverse effects have been anticipated? The authors answer affirmatively: 'The persistency, mobility and high production volume of MBTE should have prompted systematic, comprehensive investigation' at an earlier stage. Regulators ignored quite serious risks.

The authors offer many similar examples. For many decades, it has been suspected that benzene causes serious health risks to workers; recommendations for reduced exposure went unheeded for decades. With respect to asbestos, there were early warnings at the start of the twentieth century, suggesting that exposure could cause cancer. Much tragic loss could have been avoided by attending to these warnings. Since the 1930s, PCBs have been suspected of causing serious harm to human health. But regulation was minimal, with governments requiring an indefensibly high level of proof. Bovine spongiform encephalopathy (BSE) is the authors' most recent illustration. Notwithstanding early indications of a real risk, the UK government's 'policy was not precautionary. Its primary objective was rather one of trying to diminish, as far as possible, the short-term adverse impact of BSE on the profitability of the food industry and the level of public expenditure.'

In two concluding chapters, the authors draw lessons from these case studies. The most serious problem is that while adequate information was frequently available at an early stage, no action was taken until too late. Sometimes short-term economic and political considerations were the source of the problem. For the future, the authors suggest that regulatory action should be taken 'when there are reasonable grounds for concern', and that regulators should avoid the pervasive temptation to wait for more information ('paralysis by analysis'). They insist that it is important to respond not just to uncertainty (where outcomes can be identified, but probabilities cannot be), but also to ignorance (where neither outcomes nor probabilities can be identified). In the environmental domain, surprises are pervasive. Consider, for example, the effects of halocarbons on the ozone layer; for long periods, 'the very possibility of an "ozone hole" was unappreciated'.

The authors also contend that in order to be precautionary, public officials should focus not only on the most direct impacts but also on a wide range of adverse effects, especially those that are irreversible. Continuing monitoring is important to catch early warning signs and to identify gaps in scientific knowledge. Hence early research is indispensable. The authors also make a plea for informing the PP with the standard tools of risk assessment, including a systematic assessment of both 'pros' and 'cons' and careful evaluation of alternatives. But the authors are democrats, not merely technocrats. They want to 'enfranchize' many interest groups at an early stage, ensuring that experts are made sensitive to local values and priorities. Thus they urge the importance of professional risk communication, replacing 'a sound-bite culture' with more sustained discussion of both ignorance and uncertainty. At the same time, they contend that regulators should pay attention not only to specialists, but also to ordinary people, who may have local knowledge grounded in real world conditions.

This is a valuable book, full of sensible discussions, useful insights, and helpful guidance for the future. But it would not be difficult to produce a mirror-image book, directly opposed to the PP, and basing the opposition on case studies in which government greatly overreacted to misleading 'early warnings' and took steps that turned out to be wasteful, hysterical, self-defeating. In fact Wildavsky, a distinguished political scientist, has produced exactly that book, a collection of studies of risk regulation, mostly in the environmental area, in which early warnings spurred steps that ranged from excessive to counterproductive.[28] Wildavsky does not much like the PP. In any case it would be too crude to suggest that nations should always take aggressive regulatory steps in the face of early warnings. We need to know a great deal about the nature of those warnings and those steps.

The authors are aware of this point. They suggest that officials should scrutinize claimed justifications and benefits alongside potential risks. In a sense, they argue for a marriage of two apparent adversaries: the PP (favoured in Europe) and cost-benefit analysis (increasingly favoured in the United States). I believe that the marriage has real promise. Properly applied, cost-benefit analysis is attuned to risks that have a low probability of occurring; it does not neglect low-probability, high-consequence hazards. If there is a 5 per cent chance of a loss of 10,000 lives, then there is serious reason for concern. What cost-benefit analysis cannot easily handle are situations of uncertainty and ignorance, in which the benefits of risk reduction cannot be quantified. In these circumstances, the PP calls for careful monitoring of the situation, especially to guard against serious and irreversible damage, and also for regulatory steps, at least when they do not themselves impose significant costs.

But I think that the authors' presentation suffers from two problems. First, they underplay some of the theoretical complexities raised by the PP. They write as if the question is: *Precautionary or not*? But this seems to me an incoherent question. The real question is this: *Precautionary with respect to what*? Our world is filled with multiple risks, and hazards might well arise from action, inaction,

[28] A. Wildavsky, *But is it True?* (Cambridge, Mass.: Harvard University Press, 1999).

and everything in between. We can certainly take precautions against particular risks. But we cannot be precautionary in general. Consider, for example, the risks associated with genetic engineering of food. The PP, properly understood, might seem to call for stringent regulation. But what if regulation itself causes risks, and what if we are, with respect to those risks, in a situation of either uncertainty or ignorance? To see the problem, simply notice that defenders of genetic engineering contend that they will be able to produce safe and low-cost food, with special promise for people in the poorest nations. Under the PP, the question is not whether they are right. It is whether regulation of their activities creates risks—and it does. Whenever risk regulation produces substitute risks, or eliminates 'opportunity benefits', it threatens to run afoul of the PP. Precautions need not be precautionary.

The problem is pervasive. Suppose, for example, that the PP is invoked to justify stringent controls on greenhouse gases. It would be easy to say that such controls would themselves violate the PP. The reason is that regulatory controls might well create a host of risks, including those that stem from substitute processes and technologies (which have hazards of their own) and those that come from the sheer fact of increased prices. If costs of energy go up, many people will have less money, producing more poverty and unemployment. To say the least, neither of these is good for people's health. My claim is not that greenhouse gases should be uncontrolled. It is that in answering whether and how much to control them, the PP is unhelpful. Because risks are generally on all sides of social situations, it is literally impossible to be 'precautionary' in general. If the point continues to be obscure, continue the much-discussed case of DDT. In some nations, DDT has been said to be the cheapest and most effective way of controlling the spread of malaria. Is it precautionary to ban DDT, or to allow it? The United States (US) do not embrace the PP, but in some of its anti-terrorist policies and even in the war with Iraq, the US were very much acting in a precautionary fashion. The problem is that those very actions have created risks—and hence seem to run afoul of the PP. Taken for all that it is worth, the PP forbids every course of action, including inaction. It is not possible to be universally precautionary. In deciding what to do, we need to make a more refined inquiry into the multiple variables at stake.

This problem is closely related to another one. For all their sensible observations, the authors do not provide much of a framework for regulators to follow. In place of a framework, they outline a number of 'late lessons', amounting to an unruly, heterogeneous, and sometimes platitudinous list. The criticism should not be overstated; the list points in useful directions. But I do wonder about the authors' endorsement of public participation in these highly technical areas, where people's fears can get the better of them. More generally, I wonder whether it might not be best to adopt not a PP but a hierarchy of precautionary responses. The better the evidence, the more intrusive the response. When the evidence of harm is weak, we might support continuing monitoring and research. As it increases, we might move to the somewhat more aggressive step of requiring public disclosure of risks, and from there to imposing regulatory restrictions of various sorts, with flat bans only when the evidence of harm is strong. And if the product or process does not carry much in the way of benefits, then the argument for stringent precautions is strengthened. Distributional issues are of course central here. If the risk would be borne by people who are already suffering from extreme disadvantage, there is all the more reason to do something about it. And if risk reduction would impose special hardship on the poor, then we should be cautious, even precautionary, about precautions.

The authors of this valuable book have hardly provided the last word about appropriate precautions. Both theory and practice need far more development. But the case studies here, and the sensible lessons that the authors draw from them, provide an excellent place to start.

CASS R. SUNSTEIN
University of Chicago

DOCUMENTS

Ludwig Krämer *

I. Summaries of Communications, Green Papers, and White Papers

A. Communication from the Commission: Towards a Thematic Strategy for Soil Protection[1]

When adopting the Sixth Environmental Action Programme,[2] the European Parliament (EP) and the Council had asked the Commission to present, before 2005, seven 'thematic strategies' on soil protection, marine protection, the sustainable use of pesticides, urban environment, air pollution, management of resources, and waste recycling. The present Communication has the objective to prepare the thematic strategy on soil protection.

The Communication is structured in ten chapters. After a short introduction (1) the functions and distinctive features of soil are described (2). Chapter (3) deals with the threats to soil and shortly discusses erosion, decline in organic matter, contamination, sealing, compaction, decline in biodiversity, and floods and landslides. The international dimension (4) and the problems of Member States and candidate countries are mentioned briefly (5). Chapter (6) mentions relevant EC policy, chapter (7) the existing soil data gathering systems. Chapter (8) suggests the way forward. The final chapters deal with a work plan and timetable for future EU policy (9) and the conclusions (10).

The Communication was adopted before the Sixth Environmental Action Programme, implying that its authors knew what they wanted, irrespective of the subsequent opinions of the Council, the EP, or the Member States. This suspicion is strengthened by the assertive tone of the Communication, and the fact that regulatory measures are not presented as options for future policy, but announced as matters of fact. This includes a Proposal for a Directive on the Management of Waste from the Extractive Industries,[3] a review of Directive 86/

* European Commission, DG Environment, Brussels (Belgium). Professor of Law, University of Bremen (Germany). The author expresses his personal views.

[1] COM(2002)179.

[2] Dec. 1600/2002/EC laying down the Sixth Environmental Action Programme [2002] OJ L242/1.

[3] COM(2003)319.

278/EEC on the Protection of the Environment, and in Particular of the Soil, when Sewage Sludge is Used in Agriculture,[4] a proposal for a directive on compost and biowaste, another proposal for soil monitoring legislation that is to be presented in 2004, and a communication on soil erosion, soil organic matter decline, and soil contamination, as well as examination of an amendment to Directive 92/43/EEC on the Conservation of Natural Habitats and of Wild Fauna and Flora (Habitats Directive).[5] Proposals regarding other policies such as agriculture, research, transport, and regional policy are much less concrete, which once more underlines the need to integrate environmental requirements into other policies.

The Communication is rather technical, and concentrates on past and future action, in the context of which questions of EC competence are not raised.

B. Commission Staff Working Paper: Environmental Integration in the External Policies of the General Affairs Council[6]

In the context of the so-called 'Cardiff Process', the Commission has elaborated a number of strategy documents in order to implement Article 6 EC, and integrate environmental requirements into other policies.[7] This Communication focuses on the integration of environmental requirements into foreign policy. The Commission notes that Article 6 EC does not apply to foreign policy pursued within the framework of the second pillar of the Treaty on European Union (TEU), and that Article 174 EC requires promotion of international action in the field of the environment. The overall EC strategy must be to provide a framework for a coherent and ambitious approach to environmental concerns by the European Union (EU) in its external relations: 'By maximizing the integration of environmental concerns into external policy, alongside economic and social aspects, the EU will further contribute to its goal of achieving sustainable development at the global level, as well as within its own territory'.

Chapter 2 deals with efforts to raise the profile of environmental issues in the context of the EU's relations with third countries. The Commission indicates its intention better to integrate environmental requirements into all forms of bilateral and multilateral dialogue. It states:

> The theory that growth must come first, and will later provide sufficient assets to put things right, is superficially attractive to some developing and transitional/industrialised countries. Such approaches must be changed, by pressing for better integration of the

[4] [1986] OJ L181/612.

[5] [1992] OJ L206/7.

[6] SEC(2002)271, 7 Mar. 2002.

[7] See summaries in (2002) 2 *Yearbook of European Environmental Law,* 622 (general questions), 628 (agriculture), 632 (economic and development cooperation); (2003) 3 *Yearbook of European Environmental Law,* 826 (fisheries policies).

often institutionally weak environment component into our partners' overall planning of their development, or transition to market economy.

As true as this is, everything will depend on tangible action yet to be taken.

Chapter 3 deals with a number of horizontal aspects relating to the integration of environmental requirements into post-conflict reconstruction, conflict prevention activities, and governance and human rights discussions. The Commission undertakes to promote the principles of the United Nations Economic Commission for Europe (UN/ECE) Convention on Access to Information, Public Participation in Decision-Making and Access to Justice in Environmental Matters (Aarhus Convention).[8]

In chapter 4, which deals with trade issues, the Commission recognizes that the relationship between trade and environment is a difficult one. It approvingly quotes the Ministerial Declaration of the Doha Conference 2002, which stated that 'no country should be prevented from taking measures for the protection of human, animal or plant life or health, or for the environment at the levels it considers appropriate, subject to the requirement that they are not applied in a manner which would constitute a means of arbitrary or unjustifiable discrimination' and declares this statement a 'very important political advance'.

Although a number of the Communication's statements were written prior to the World Summit in Johannesburg in 2002, the Communication remains useful as a manifestation of the EU's attitude to environment and foreign (trade) policy. Indeed, as the United States (US) are withdrawing their support for international environmental issues, whether it likes it or not, the EU is gradually becoming a global environmental player. Much would be gained for the environment, if the objectives and principles mentioned in the Communication were actually applied in day-to-day international practice.

C. Communication from the Commission: Towards a Strategy to Protect and Conserve the Marine Environment[9]

This Communication, which has no table of contents, is structured in nine chapters. After the introduction (chapter 1), in which it is soberly stated that 'at the EU level, there exists no overall, integrated policy for marine protection', the environmental quality status of, primarily, Europe's regional seas—Baltic Sea, North East Atlantic, Mediterranean Sea, Black Sea—is described in chapter 2 and annex 1. This description is very largely based on the different reports which have been elaborated under regional marine conventions. Marine ecosystems and biodiversity are under threat, and annex 1 summarily describes twelve particular causes. These include overfishing, introduction of non-indigenous species,

[8] Aarhus (Denmark), 25 June 1998 (entered into force 30 Oct. 2001) (1999) 38 *International Legal Materials* 3, 517.

[9] COM(2002)539.

increasing intensity of human activity along the coasts, pollution (by hazardous substances, oil, metals, radionucleides, microbiologicals, or litter), eutrophication, accidents, and climate change. Chapter 3 and annex 2 review policies and legislation that exist in the form of a wealth of EC legislation and international (regional) conventions, the impact of which is different from one regional sea to the other. Chapter 4 examines knowledge gaps regarding the quality status of the marine environment, and shortcomings of existing monitoring systems.

Chapters 5 and 6 draw overall conclusions, and acknowledge that after an analysis of existing EC legislation and regional conventions together it remains unclear 'whether the aggregate of these measures is sufficient to afford the desired level of protection and conservation'. It is suggested that future marine policy should set an ambitious, clear and coherent set of objectives with a view to promoting sustainable use of the seas, and conserving marine ecosystems. Chapter 7 articulates no less than fourteen environmental objectives, many of them to be realized by 2010 or 2020. The majority of these are rather general.[10] Chapter 9 proposes 23 concrete actions to realize the different objectives which are accompanied by a timetable (annex V).

The Communication intends to intensify cooperation with regional conventions and implementation of existing legislation. It is vague on the question what regulatory and implementing action should be taken by which body. However, as a first document on a thematic strategy regarding the marine environment, it provides a very useful political overview on the nature of the problems faced, and underlines the necessity of future action.

D. Communication from the Commission: Structural Indicators[11] Report from the Commission: Analysis of the 'Open List' of Environment-Related Headline Indicators[12]

At the Lisbon European Council of March 2000, the EU set itself the goal to become, by 2010, the most dynamic, competitive, sustainable knowledge-based economy, enjoying full employment and strengthened economic and social cohesion. The Gothenburg Summit of 2001 added an environmental dimension, so that there are now three objectives under the heading of sustainable development: economic growth, social cohesion, and environmental protection.

The problem of measuring environmental progress is addressed by these two papers, the first not being limited to environmental issues. The Lisbon European

[10] For example, in respect of objective 3: 'a change in fisheries management to reverse the decline in stocks and ensure sustainable fisheries and healthy ecosystems, both in EU and globally'; objective 4: 'reach concentrations of such (hazardous) substances in the marine environment near background values for naturally occurring substances and close to zero for man-made synthetic substances'; and objective 10: 'The objective is to reach a quality of the environment where levels of contaminants do not give rise to significant impacts on or risks to human health or well being'.

[11] COM(2002)551.

[12] COM(2002)524.

Council had asked for a list of structural indicators which would allow an objective assessment of progress made towards the Lisbon objectives. The Communication discusses this list of structural indicators, which consists of 42 structural indicators, grouped in six classes of seven indicators each (in brackets the number of sub-indicators): General economic background (11); employment (21); innovation and research (16); economic reform (23); social cohesion (21); and environment (16).

These are the environmental indicators adopted by the European Council of Copenhagen 2002.

(1) Greenhouse gases emissions.
(2) Energy intensity of the economy.
(3) Transport:
- — volume of transport (tonne- and passenger-km) relative to Gross Domestic Product (GDP);
- — volume of freight transport relative to GDP;
- — volume of passenger transport relative to GDP;
- — modal split of freight transport—per cent share of road;
- — modal split of passenger transport—per cent share of cars.

(4) Urban air quality:
- — population exposure to air pollution by ozone;
- — population exposure to air pollution by particulate matter.

(5) Municipal waste:
- — municipal waste collected;
- — municipal waste landfilled;
- — municipal waste incinerated.

(6) Share of renewable energy.
(7) Natural resources:
- — fish stocks in European water;
- — protected areas for biodiversity (Habitats Directive);[13]
- — protected areas for biodiversity (Birds Directive).[14]

In its 2003 report to the European Council, the Commission used these indicators to report on the implementation of the Lisbon strategy. It may be wondered whether these indicators really allow for an assessment of environmental trends. However, one should be aware that hardly any other indicators exist for which data are available. The fact that the development of such criteria has been blatantly neglected is undoubtedly a serious deficiency of environmental policy, given the fact that they are vital for policy and the financial consequences that flow from it.

13 Dir. 92/43/EEC on the Conservation of Natural Habitats and of Wild Fauna and Flora [1992] OJ L206/7.

14 Dir. 79/409/EEC on the Conservation of Wild Birds [1979] OJ L103/1.

The Commission's report seeks to address this deficiency. The report, mandated by the Council, analyses 34 environmental indicators; the intention is to create a pool of indicators from which seven environment-related indicators for the annual 'Lisbon Progress Report' can be distilled. The report classified the indicators into different groups, according to whether they are based on sound science and up-to-date data are available from reliable sources, and whether they are comparable.

Group I contains six indicators which can be produced more or less immediately.[15] For group II indicators, data are currently incomplete or not sufficiently up to date.[16] Group III indicators concern data that are inadequate, incomparable, or incomplete in coverage.[17] Group IV enumerates indicators which have yet to mature, and are therefore not viable for use in the near future.[18]

The report further discusses indicators for sustainable development related to public health, and concludes that the number of persons killed in road traffic accidents could be an appropriate indicator.

For lawyers, this work may appear rather futile. However, it is clear that future progress in environmental protection will be measured with reference to these indicators, and financial means will be made available according to the trends which they reveal. It is necessary, therefore, critically to discuss the advantages and disadvantages of different indicators, and if appropriate propose more suitable alternatives.

E. Communication from the Commission: A Framework for Target-Based Tripartite Contracts and Agreements between the Community, the States and Regional and Local Authorities[19]

This brief Communication is not limited to the sphere of the environment. It develops an instrument that might gain some importance in environmental policy, if there should exist political will to use it.

[15] The indicators of group I are: greenhouse gases emissions (six gases); distance-to-target and sectoral breakdowns; energy consumption by mode of transport; urban population exposure to air pollution (by ozone and particulate matter); emissions of air pollutants (ozone precursors, particulate matters, and SO_2); fish stocks in European marine waters; area devoted to organic farming.

[16] Group II: transport intensity of GDP; modal split of transport; municipal waste collected, landfilled and incinerated; recycling rate of selected materials (glass and paper/cardboard); nitrate and phosphorous concentration in rivers; protected areas (for biodiversity: nitrogen balance).

[17] Group III: investment in transport infrastructure by mode (passengers and freight); recycling rate of selected materials (extended to other materials); hazardous waste generated; discharges of pollutants (nutrients, organics, chemicals in water; quality of drinking water; resources productivity indicators or material intensity (GNP/total material requirement) (by type of resource); pesticides consumption; evolution of land use by main categories.

[18] Group V: exposure of the population to high levels of transport noise; average journey length and time per person, by mode and purpose; internalization of the external costs in the transport sector; exposure to and consumption of toxic chemicals; waste prevention; valorization rate of selected materials—intensity of material use (GNP/total material requirement); biodiversity index; contaminated and eroded soil.

[19] COM(2002)709.

The Communication differentiates between tripartite contracts—contracts between the EC represented by the Commission, a Member State, and regional and local authorities—'in direct application of binding secondary Community law (regulations, directives or decisions)', and tripartite agreements concluded between those same partners 'outside a binding Community framework'. According to the Commission, use of tripartite contracts presupposes that regulations, directives, or decisions contain enabling clauses authorizing the Commission to conclude such a contract. Furthermore, the contract itself must stipulate that the Member State in which the tripartite contract is performed alone is responsible for its due performance, in particular with regard to Article 226 EC.

The Communication sees room for tripartite contracts or agreements because of the need for diversity within the EC. This is particularly essential in policy areas with a strong territorial impact where it is essential to take local circumstances into account. Environmental policy is quoted as one example where regional diversity, and hence flexibility in shaping and implementing action, is desirable. Tripartite arrangements might involve regional and local authorities (cities) more closely in European policies.

Such tripartite contracts/agreements for the environment appear to be particularly promising in those areas which cannot be effectively regulated by binding environmental provisions. Examples include the urban environment, coastal zone management, as well as environmental protection measures in third countries. Tripartite environmental agreements with Gibraltar or Ceuta/Melilla, with Kaliningrad or the northern part of Cyprus might also be considered.

Until mid-2003, no environmental pilot project had been envisaged, even though the interest in regions and cities in EU matters is quite remarkable.

F. Communication from the Commission: Developing an Action Plan for Environmental Technology[20]

This Communication is a follow-up of an earlier communication of 2002.[21] The Commission's intention is to deliver an action plan on environmental technology by the end of 2003. The present Communication is a preliminary analysis concerning a limited number of areas, which is to form the basis for a dialogue with stakeholders. Chapter 1 introduces the subject, placing it in the context of the Lisbon strategy. Chapter 3 provides examples of current research areas. Chapters 4 to 7 specify these issues for four sectors: climate change, sustainable production and consumption, water, and soil protection. Chapter 8 details a possible way forward. For each of the four sectors, an 'issues group' is to be set up. For production and consumption, as well as water, some details are specified:

[20] COM(2003)131.

[21] Commission, Environmental Technology for Sustainable Development COM(2002)122.

25 to 30 persons participate, representing governments, experts, scientists, professional industrial and environmental organizations.

For each sector except soil, the different obstacles—regulatory, economic, social, and technical—are briefly explored. These barriers are to be discussed in the issues groups with the aim of finding ways to overcome them. The paper concludes by formulating a number of questions for stakeholders, who are invited to respond. Reactions from the public and the issues groups is to be used for the adoption of a Commission action plan by the end of 2003.

G. Communication from the Commission: Choosing to Grow: Knowledge, Innovation and Jobs in a Cohesive Society—Report to the Spring European Council, 21 March 2003 on the Lisbon Strategy of Economic, Social and Environmental Renewal[22]

This so-called Spring report informs on progress in the implementation of the Lisbon strategy. As observed above, in Lisbon (March 2000), the European Council launched a strategy to make the EU the most dynamic, competitive, sustainable knowledge-based economy, enjoying full employment and strengthened economic and social cohesion by 2010. The Gothenburg European Council added the environmental dimension to this. The Commission is requested to report once a year on progress with regard to the strategy.

While the first Spring report[23] contains almost no reference to the environment, this second report puts some effort into including environmental issues. The report's roadmap until 2010, however, merely specifies the economic and, marginally, social steps to be taken by 2010, but is silent on environmental measures. It continues by discussing employment questions, boosting investment and productivity, improving social cohesion, and, under the heading 'sustainable development', environmental trends. It is worthwhile reproducing this section in full as it is, with a reference to environmental indicators[24] and 'stimulating the take up of environmental technologies', the report's only reference to the environment:

> With less than two years since Gothenburg the pace and direction of progress in this area is difficult to assess. Certain industrial sectors have succeeded in cutting emissions while increasing output. There are positive signs in terms of policy development and implementation—particularly in terms of developing the global perspective of sustainability. On the basis of the data available for 2000, the worrying trends that were observed at the time of the launch of the Union's sustainable development strategy have continued. These trends highlight the need to accelerate efforts, reflected in recently adopted and pending proposals, to address unsustainable trends. Clean, environmental technologies may have a particular role.

22 COM(2003)5.

23 Commission, The Lisbon Strategy—Making Things Happen COM(2002)14.

24 See COM(2002)14, 8.

As regards activities over the next year, the report underlines 'the need of renewed effort to implement EC environmental legislation, complement it through the use of economic instruments to provide the right signals and incentives to change behaviour, as well as removing damaging subsidies, and using fewer resources or using and reusing them more efficiently'. This should support the decoupling needed to ensure that the economy can grow faster without increasing pressure on the environment. Concrete measures concern the continued reduction in greenhouse gas emissions, improved air quality, and compliance with the Kyoto commitments.

Overall, it is not quite clear how these different references, statements and conclusions will contribute towards the aim of sustainability by 2010.

H. Communication from the Commission: Forest Law Enforcement, Governance and Trade (Flegt): Proposal for an EU Action Plan[25]

The Communication is structured into an executive summary (1); an introduction (2); a description of the origins and scope of the action plan (3); the action plan itself taking up 15 of the 23 pages of the Communication (4); coordination and programming (5); and a short indication of the next steps (6). Annex I summarizes ongoing initiatives for improved forest law enforcement, Annex II international trade in timber, and Annex III the Bali Declaration of 2001 on forest law enforcement and governance.[26]

This Communication and the proposed action plan are necessary because of the 'substantial and growing' problem of illegal logging, which constitutes a significant share of trade in timber worth over €150 billion per year. The action plan suggests:

— support of timber-producing countries. This will consist of political, administrative, and technical cooperation and support, including financial support within the limits of the budget;

— trade in timber. The main EU timber imports—except from North America—originate from Central Africa, Russia, Tropical South America, and South-east Asia. The EU will try to find multilateral solutions to the problem of illegal logging, consider the elaboration of a regulation to promote voluntary export licensing systems in third countries, and examine an import ban for illegally harvested timber;

— public procurement. The plan provides that the EU will endeavour to use only certified timber in public procurement procedures;

[25] COM(2003)251.

[26] Ministerial Declaration, on Forest Law Enforcement and Governance, East Asia Ministerial Conference, Bali Indonesia, 11–12 Sept. 2001. Published on the Internet at: http://www.abc.net.au/4corners/content/2002/timber_mafia/resources/balideclaration.pdf.

— private initiatives in the context of corporate social responsibility, and the elaboration of private codes of conduct or standards will be encouraged;
— accompanying measures, which will include use of existing legislative instruments (concerning money laundering, trade in endangered species, and so on), and examination of conflict timber issues (i.e. timber money used to finance local conflicts).

The action plan is subject to endorsement by the Council and the EP.

I. Communication from the Commission: Towards a Thematic Strategy on the Prevention and Recycling of Waste[27]

In the same manner as the reports on soil and marine environment protection, this Communication prepares the ground for the thematic strategy which the Commission is to propose by 2004/5, pursuant to the Sixth Environmental Action Programme. It is divided into ten chapters. After a short introduction (1), the environmental challenge posed by waste is discussed (2). In that respect, the Communication notes the trend of increased waste generation. It observes that waste prevention and recycling can reduce the environmental impacts of resource use, the extraction of primary raw materials and its environmental consequences, as well as the impact of the transformation of raw materials in production processes. Chapter 3 assesses the Community's waste management policy, which needs to be further developed. Chapter 4 discusses the problem of setting targets for waste prevention and recycling. Chapter 5 concerns the building blocks for a future thematic strategy. As regards waste prevention, this concerns measures aimed at quantitative and qualitative waste prevention, and other measures such as waste prevention plans, best technology guidelines, and instruments to promote waste recycling. It also tables the idea of setting up an EC-wide level playing field for recycling, in the form of, *inter alia*, targets for waste materials, and the setting of EC-wide instead of national targets. Chapters 6 to 10 deal with health, enlargement, international cooperation, and the future development of the thematic strategy. Annexes articulate EC waste legislation (I) and trends in waste generation and management (II).

The link between waste prevention and waste recycling established by the Communication, goes beyond the orientation of the Sixth Environmental Action Programme, and is to be welcomed. As regards waste prevention, the core phrase is the following: 'As all materials used in an economy sooner or later become waste, major changes in waste generation require changes in production and consumption patterns. This requires policy approaches which go beyond waste policy in its strict sense and enter into fields such as resource management and Integrated Product Policy'.[28] The Communication is a discussion paper, and it

[27] COM(2003)301. [28] COM(2003)301, 28.

remains to be seen which of these instruments will come to form part of the thematic strategy.

J. Communication from the Commission: A European Environment and Health Strategy[29]

After a brief introduction (1), The Communication articulates the rationale and objectives of the strategy (2). Chapter 4 reviews past activities, chapter 5 the core elements of the strategy, and chapter 6 the strategy itself. Chapter 7 deals with implementation and chapter 8 draws conclusions. Annexes identify: (A) EU policies related to environment and health; (B) research in this area; (C) international actions on environment and health.

The objectives of the strategy are:

— to reduce disease caused by environmental factors in the EU;
— to identify and to prevent new health threats caused by environmental factors to strengthen EU capacity for policy-making in this area.

Core elements of the strategy are an *integrated* approach with regard to information, research, impact on other policies, cycle of pollutants, and intervention and participation of stakeholders. Furthermore, the strategy will be incremental and concentrate on children and accession countries. It intends to set up an Integrated European Environment and Health Monitoring and Response System which will focus on data sharing, improvement availability, accessibility and comparability of data, assessment of existing knowledge, and review of existing policies.

During the first cycle of the strategy, it will be attempted better to understand the link between environmental factors and (a) childhood respiratory diseases, asthma, and allergies, (b) neurodevelopment disorders, (c) childhood cancer, and (d) endocrine disrupting effects. The viability of a European Biomonitoring System, which appears to have considerable potential, will be examined. Three pilot projects on dioxins, heavy metals, and endocrine disrupters will be launched, and harmonized environment and health indicators will be developed. Research will be promoted and exposure to air pollutants reduced. Heavy metals, electromagnetic fields, and urban environment-related health problems will be tackled.

As regards implementation, a consultative group on environment and health will be set up in 2003, made up of Member States, private experts, academics, economic interests, and Non-Governmental Organizations (NGOs). The group will cooperate with technical working groups. Several conferences intend to elaborate details of the strategy and its implementation. The suggested acronym of the strategy is SCALE (Science, Children, Awareness, Legal instruments, Evaluation).

[29] COM(2003)338.

K. Communication from the Commission: Integrated Product Policy[30]

This Communication follows a Commission Green paper of 2001 on the same topic.[31] After a brief introduction, the paper explains why a product dimension to environmental policy is needed (2). Chapter 3 describes the Integrated Policy (IPP) approach which, as it is perceived by the Commission, contains five elements—life-cycle thinking, working with the market, stakeholder involvement, continuous improvement, and a variety of policy instruments. Chapter 4 attributes three key roles to IPP: contributing to addressing the environmental challenges, supplementing existing product-related policies by virtue of a more extensive 'life-cycle'; providing a conceptual framework; and strengthening co-ordination and coherence between existing and future environment-related product policy instruments.

Chapter 5 establishes the framework conditions for continuous environmental improvement. As tools for creating the right economic and legal framework for IPP, taxes and subsidies, voluntary agreements, standardization, public procurement and other legislation are suggested. The chapter also advocates promotion of life-cycle thinking and better informing consumers so as to facilitate informed choice. Chapter 6 invites suggestions for pilot products for which life-cycle approaches could be used. Concrete proposals are announced for the end of 2003. Annex I recapitulates the comments to the Green Paper of 2001, and annex II examines possible roles and responsibilities of stakeholders.

Overall, the Communication does not go significantly beyond the Communication of 2001. The detailed comments and suggestions by the Council,[32] the EP,[33] and the Committee of the Regions[34] have only very sporadically been taken up.

II. Summary of Reports

A. Report from the Commission on the Application of Directive 79/409/EEC on the Conservation of Wild Birds (1996–1998)[35]

The report is a follow-up to the report of March 2000.[36] It is once more based on Member States' information, and hardly contains any independent assessment by the Commission. The report is based on information available under the different provisions of Directive 79/409/EEC on the Conservation of Wild Birds (Birds Directive).[37]

30 COM(2003)302.
31 COM(2001)68; see (2003) 3 *Yearbook of European Environmental Law*, 824.
32 Council Res. of 7 June 2001, not published.
33 European Parliament, Res. of 17 Jan 2002 [2002] OJ C271E/394.
34 [2001] OJ C357/53.
35 COM(2002)146.
36 See summary in (2002) 2 *Yearbook of European Environmental Law*, 645.
37 [1979] OJ L103/1.

The latest status of European bird species was published by BirdLife International in 1994. The study identified 514 species, out of which 319 species (62 per cent) have a conservation status that is considered to be generally satisfactory, whilst 195 species (38 per cent) have an unsatisfactory status. Almost 25 per cent of species regularly observed in Europe have undergone a substantial decline in numbers over the last 20 years: 'Their decline mirrors what is happening to many animal or plant groups: a pronounced deterioration in biodiversity in Europe, both in the distribution and the abundance of species'.

A major cause for this decline is the intensification of agriculture (affecting 42 per cent of declining species) and destruction of or damage to habitats. Another study on Important Bird Areas (IBAs) by BirdLife International, identified 3,619 IBAs in Europe, of which, 2,342 were situated within the EU. Out of these, 1,082 sites (46 per cent) had still not been designated as Special Protection Areas (SPAs) under the Birds Directive. More than 20 years after adoption of the Birds Directive, only four Member States had designated over 75 per cent of their IBAs.

The report also specifies the number of derogations granted by Member States under Article 9 of the Birds Directive: 89 for France, 323 for Spain, 375 for Italy, 729 for the United Kingdom (UK), and 1,162 for Germany. My conclusion from these figures is that either not all Member States expressly request derogations or that these are not granted.

It is also noteworthy that in the UK a voluntary two-year ban on the use of lead shot was tried, but that did not lead to a general change in ammunition. As a result, the UK Government has announced that the best solution would be to prohibit by law the use of lead shot in wetlands.

Overall, the report is largely based on information provided by Member States. As it frequently refers to previous reports ('no change compared with the previous period'), it is not very transparent for lay-persons.

B. Commission: Nineteenth Annual Report on Monitoring the Application of Community Law (2001)[38]

This report relates to the monitoring of the application of environmental law in the year 2001. However, no comparison with earlier reports is possible, as the basis for statistics changed again. Also, information regarding letters of formal notice is normally not provided and in general no effort is made to allow the reader to make comparisons or draw conclusions. The report notes that:

- in cases of complaint on refusal to grant access to environmental information, the Commission normally advises to use the national channels of appeal;
- many complaints regarding environment impact assessment (EIA) require examination of the question whether Member States exceeded their discretion in deciding whether to subject a project to EIA, and whether the

[38] COM(2002)324.

EIA was of a proper quality and received sufficient weight in the decision-making process;

- infringement procedures were started against thirteen Member States for not having transposed Directive 2000/14/EC Relating to the Noise Emission in the Environment by Equipment for Use Outdoors;[39]
- The amount of the penalty paid by Greece under Article 228 EC in *Commission* v. *Greece* was €5,400,000;[40]
- the Commission started proceedings under Article 226 EC against all Member States except Austria in respect of waste management plans under different waste directives;
- the Commission started proceedings under Article 226 EC against eleven Member States for failing to afford priority to the regeneration of waste oil and instead burning it, contrary to the requirements of Directive 75/439/EEC on the Disposal of Waste Oils (Waste Oil Directive);[41]
- Directive 1999/31/EC on Landfill of Waste (Waste Landfill Directive)[42] had been transposed in time by four Member States (Denmark, France, Austria, and Sweden);
- by the end of 2001, there were 32 environmental judgments by the ECJ which had still not been implemented by Member States, in respect of which the Commission started or considered starting procedures under Article 228 EC.

Overall, lack of transparency considerably reduces the value of the report, which otherwise could have been a very effective instrument for improving application of EC environmental law. In this context, it should be noted that the Commission published a document regarding relations with complainants about infringements of EC law,[43] and issued two communications on improved monitoring of the application of EC law.[44]

C. Report from the Commission: Implementation of Ambient Air Quality Directives (80/779/EEC,[45] 82/884/EEC,[46] and 85/203/EEC)[47]

This report is extremely short (eight pages) and disappointing. It refers to earlier reports from 1995 and before, which are hardly available any more, and refers to annual reports published by the European Topic Centre on air quality. The latter

[39] [2000] OJ L311/51. [40] Case C-387/97, *Commission* v. *Greece* [2000] ECR I-5047.
[41] [1975] OJ L194/22. [42] [1999] OJ L182/1. [43] COM(2002)141.
[44] COM(2002)471 and COM(2002)725/4.
[45] Dir. 80/779/EEC on Air Quality Limit Values and Guide Values for Sulphur Dioxide and Suspended Particulates [1980] OJ L229/30.
[46] Dir. 82/884/EEC on a Limit Value for Lead in the Air [1982] OJ L378/15.
[47] COM(2002)609.

are said to provide detailed information on air pollution levels and trends without, however, specifying their contents. The report thus limits itself to summarizing instances that were reported by Member States where air quality limits were exceeded.

The report does not analyse the (widely varying) number of measuring stations in Member States, their location, measuring methods, and so on. These are all aspects which are most relevant for assessing the effectiveness of the Directives. The report acknowledges that there are substantial differences in the way Member States measure air quality and report results to the Commission, but fails to report on any efforts to reduce these differences. The reader therefore cannot acquire a picture of the present situation.

As regards Directive 80/779/EEC on Air Quality Limit Values and Guide Values for Sulphur Dioxide and Suspended Particulates, in total fourteen stations reported on breaches of one standard in 1997, and again in 1998, and thirteen stations in 1999. Most of the breaches concerned suspended particulate. For Directive 85/203/EEC on Air Quality Standards for Nitrogen Dioxide, five Member States reported breaches in 1997 (thirteen stations), three in 1998 (nine stations), and four in 1999 (ten stations). No breach of Directive 82/884/EEC on a Limit Value for Lead in the Air was reported.

No judgement is made as to whether this information was complete, or whether the measures adopted to avoid repetition had been sufficient, whether there were repeated breaches, and so on. On the basis of this report, the reader hence does not get an impression regarding compliance with the requirements of the Directives in Member States.

D. Report from the Commission: Implementation of Directive 91/676/EEC on the Protection of Waters against Pollution Caused by Nitrates from Agricultural Sources (Nitrates Directive)[48]

Directive 91/676/EEC on the Protection of Waters against Pollution Caused by Nitrates from Agricultural Sources (Nitrates Directive)[49] requires Member States to report on the implementation of the Directive every four years. This second report by the Commission[50] summarizes the reports received during 2000–1, when all EC Member States with the exception of the UK had submitted reports. However, the scope of the report goes far beyond a synthesis of national reports. It starts by describing (A) the problem of eutrophication in the EC, where at present some nine to ten million tons of nitrogen from mineral fertilizers are generated per year. Of these, some eight million tons originate from animal husbandry, and are subsequently spread on agricultural soil.

48 COM(2002)407. 49 [1991] OJ L375/1.

50 For the first report, see (2000) 1 *Yearbook of European Environmental Law*, 567.

Chapter B starts by summarizing the content of the national reports and of the second action programmes elaborated for the period 2001–5. The reports/programmes are rated well in Belgium, Denmark, Germany, France, Ireland, Luxembourg, Netherlands, and Austria, and relatively badly in Spain, Italy, Portugal, and the UK.

As for water, the report notes (B.2.2) that about 20 per cent of EU monitoring stations suffer nitrate concentrations over 50 mg NO^3/l, and 40 per cent over 25 mg NO^3/l. For surface waters, 60 per cent of monitoring stations show nitrate concentrations far below 10 mg NO^3/l. For coastal waters, insufficient data exists. Generally, Member States have difficulties in preparing a forecast of the impact of their action programmes on water quality.

Overall, about 38 per cent of the EU area is at present designated as a vulnerable zone, where Member States are obliged to take measures in order to reduce nitrate inputs into the soil or the water. Denmark, Germany, Luxembourg, Netherlands, Austria, and Finland designated their whole territory, France 48 and Greece 11 per cent. The remaining Member States designated less than 10 per cent. The Commission considered this designation insufficient in the case of the nine Member States that did not designate the whole of their territory. The discrepancy is particularly pronounced for Belgium, Spain, Italy, Portugal, and Sweden.

The present rate of compliance of existing action programmes with the Directive's requirements is insufficient overall in the Netherlands, Germany, Greece, Spain, Italy and Austria. Most Member States fail to comply with measures concerning restricted periods for fertilizer application.

The report goes on to describe a number of positive actions taken, the effects of some national measures, and actions taken by the Commission. At present, there are 23 cases pending under Article 226 EC, among them seven cases are pending before the ECJ. Overall, the report concludes that awareness of Member States with regard to nitrate problems has increased. Many achievements of the Directive will only become apparent after some years, but a number of success stories can already be noticed in some regions.

In general, the nature of the report is more technical than legal. It offers plenty of information and provides a general overview of the problem of nitrates in EC waters.

E. Report from the Commission: Monitoring Greenhouse Gases (Commission Report for a Monitoring Mechanism of Community Greenhouse Gas Emissions)[51]

The report is the third progress report regarding the monitoring of greenhouse gas emissions.[52] It does not indicate which period exactly it covers. As it was prepared on the basis of two reports from the European Environment Agency

[51] COM(2002)702.

[52] See also (2002) 2 *Yearbook of European Environmental Law*, 653.

(EEA) which cover the period up to 2000, it may be assumed that this report mainly limits itself to data up to 2000, although some data refers to the end of 2001, and legislative and political references often refer to 2002.

As regards the reporting requirements of Member States, it is stated that this is 'still poor for most Member States'. Nevertheless, all Member States reported data on their national greenhouse gas inventories for 2000. Generally, the data regarding CO_2, N_2O, and CH_4 is more complete than the other three greenhouse gases, HFCs, PFCs, and SF_6.

Between 1990 and 2000, total greenhouse gas (GHG) emissions decreased by 3.5 per cent.[53] This was largely the result of cuts in emissions in Germany due to increasing efficiency in German thermal electricity production, and economic restructuring in the five new *Länder* after German reunification. In the UK, cuts were mainly the result of switches in electricity production from oil and coal to gas, and implementation of N_2O abatement measures in the chemical industry. By 2000, Luxembourg, Sweden, and the UK had already complied with their requirements under the Kyoto Protocol and the EC burden sharing agreement (compliance date 2008–12). If the progressive alignment towards 2008 is taken into account,[54] France, Finland, and Germany are to be included in the group of 'complying States'.

The report once more draws attention to the transport sector, where between 1990 and 2000 emissions of CO_2 gases increased by 18 per cent, and emissions of N_2O by even more than 100 per cent. Increases were particularly high in Ireland, Spain, Portugal, and Greece.

The report also gives information on the ten accession countries, which are all below the targets fixed under the Kyoto Protocol, mainly because of the changes in the economic system in these countries after 1990.

The report concludes by drawing attention to the fact that 'a majority of Member States will have to take considerable efforts to achieve their respective burden-sharing target'. Overall, the report contains a considerable amount of mostly rather technical information on GHG emissions within the EC.

F. Report from the Commission: Application of Regulation (EC) No. 1049/2001[55] (Access to Documents Held by EC Institutions)[56]

This is the first annual report on the application of Regulation (EC) No. 1049/2001 regarding Public Access to European Parliament, Council and Commission Documents, which became operational by the end of 2001. However, since there existed earlier rules on access to documents, comparison with previous years is

[53] The figures for the different Member States were: Austria +2.7; Belgium +6.3; Denmark −1.7; Finland −4.1; France −1.7; Germany −19.1; Greece +21.2; Ireland +24; Italy + 3.9; Luxembourg −45.1; Netherlands +2.6; Portugal + 30.1; Spain +33.7; Sweden −1.9; UK −12.9.

[54] This is expressed by a distance-to-target indicator.

[55] [2001] OJ L145/43.

[56] COM(2003)216.

possible. The report only covers access to Commission documents. In the present context, information relating to the environment is of particular interest.

In 2002, there were 991 requests for access to documents (1991: 450). In 33.5 per cent of these cases, access was refused. The main reason for refusing access was the 'protection of the purposes of inspections, investigations and audits (35.9 per cent of all refusals)'. This figure relates mainly to the almost systematic refusal by the Commission to grant access to letters of formal notice or reasoned opinions under Article 226 EC. However, in my opinion, these documents form no part of inspections, investigations, or audits.

Where an applicant appeals against a refusal, the Commission issues a confirmative decision. In 2002, there were 96 applications for a confirmative decision. In 66.9 per cent the original refusal was upheld, in 9.2 per cent partial access was granted, and in 23.9 per cent full access was granted.

Only 6.2 per cent of all applications made in 2002 concerned environmental matters (2001: 16.3 per cent). In one instance, the important *Mühlenberger Loch* case of Hamburg, the matter has been submitted to the Court of First Instance (CFI) which is to give a judgment. The issue in this case is whether the Commission rightly refused access to a letter of Chancellor Schröder, in which he intervened in favour of the construction of an airport within a protected habitat.

Overall, the report is not very informative as it does not detail the different reasons for refusing access. The reader can thus not verify whether the Commission indeed ensures 'the widest possible access to documents'.[57]

G. Report from the Commission: Implementation of Five Waste Directives (1998–2000)[58]

This long report (145 pages) discusses, respectively, Directives 75/442/EEC on Waste (Waste Framework Directive),[59] 91/689/EEC on Hazardous Waste (Hazardous Waste Directive),[60] 75/439/EEC on the Disposal of Waste Oils (Waste Oil Directive),[61] 86/278 on the Protection of the Environment, and in Particular of the Soil, when Sewage Sludge is Used in Agriculture (Sewage Sludge Directive),[62] and 94/62/EEC on Packaging and Packaging Waste (Packaging and Packaging Waste Directive).[63] A chapter containing conclusions and articulating future prospects ends the report.

[57] Art. 1 of Reg. (EC) No. 1049/2001, n. 56 above.

[58] COM(2003)250.

[59] [1975] OJ L194/39, amended by Dir. 91/156 amending Dir. 75/442/EEC on Waste [1991] OJ L78/32.

[60] [1991] OJ L337/20.

[61] [1975] OJ L194/22.

[62] [1986] OJ L181/612.

[63] [1994] OJ L365/10.

For each of the five Directives, the incorporation into national law is examined, followed by a discussion of its application. This allows a detailed analysis of the different problems associated with the Directives, which cannot all be mentioned here. The main concerns are the definition of waste; the hierarchy of principles and the preference for landfilling or incineration compared to recycling; waste management planning; data availability and statistics; record keeping; and the administrative control of waste management. By the end of 2002, the Commission was running 45 procedures against Member States for not living up to their obligations under these five Directives.

The overall state of implementation of the waste directives is found to be unsatisfactory.[64]

H. Report from the Commission: The Operation of Directive 98/34/EC Laying Down a Procedure for the Provision of Information in the Field of Technical Standards and Regulations (1999 to 2001)[65]

Directive 98/34/EC Laying Down a Procedure for the Provision of Information in the Field of Technical Standards and Regulations is an internal market directive.[66] It requires Member States to notify draft national legislation, in order to prevent the creation of technical barriers to trade. As notification to the Commission is followed by a mandatory standstill and Member States cannot really adopt their legislation before having received clearance from all other Member States and the Commission, this Directive has developed into an effective instrument for the prevention and elimination of technical barriers in the internal market.

For the environment, the Directive is important mainly in two ways. First, national environmental legislation violates Article 28 EC ruling out its adoption. Secondly, environmental law, in particular EC environmental law, very frequently meets the objection that the trend is for deregulation, and that legislation is to be avoided. In this context, the statistics contained in the report are interesting.

Between 1999 and 2001, Member States notified 1,872 draft texts (1999: 591; 2000: 751; 2001: 530). The main sectors were agricultural products and foodstuffs (18.9 per cent); telecommunications (15.9 per cent); transport (15.2 per cent); building and construction (14.7 per cent); and mechanical engineering (6.7 per cent). The 114 environmental measures notified (including packaging) only represented 5.9 per cent of all notifications. This serves to demonstrate the limited role environmental law should play in the discussion on deregulation, and the political character of claims that the EC should adopt fewer environmental measures. This data may also explain the Council's statement in the

[64] n. 57 above, 145. [65] COM(2003)200. [66] [1998] OJ L204/37.

Sixth EC Environmental Action Programme that 'legislation remains central to meeting environmental challenges'.[67]

The report also contains data regarding activities of national, European, and international standardization organizations. In the three years covered by the report, 11,444 new standardization activities were initiated. The majority originated from the European Committee for Standardization (CEN) and the European Committee for Electrotechnical Standardization (CENELEC): 40 per cent and more in each of the three years. Once more, these figures show that claims supporting deregulation of environmental matters are of a political nature. If economic operators are of the opinion that there are too many rules, they might first consider reducing the number of new standards.

I. Report from the Commission on the Application and Effectiveness of Directive 85/337/EEC on the Assessment of the Effects of certain Public and Private Projects on the Environment (EIA Directive)[68]

This 130-page long report consists of two parts. Part 1 is a summary of findings and actions to be taken with regard to the EIA Directive.[69] This part is not significantly different from the last chapter of part 2 on the 'effectiveness of the EIA Directive as a whole'. Part 2 is a review carried out by the Impact Assessment Unit of the School of Planning, Oxford Brookes University, UK. Part 2 covers 90 pages and is followed by two annexes. Annex I reproduces the questionnaire which was answered by Member States; annex II provides a table with thresholds for projects that fall under annex 2 of the EIA Directive.

As the report's factual content is exclusively based on information derived from national administrations, conclusions regarding the practical application of the Directive need to be approached with caution. Indeed, while national legislation transposing the Directive might be in compliance with the requirements of the Directive, this might not reflect actual practice. The report thus expressly indicates that 'from the review of the information assessed here it is very difficult to draw any firm conclusions on the role Environmental Impact Assessment (EIA) plays in project decision-making';[70] 'the main problem lies with the application and implementation of the directive and not, for the most part, with the transposition of the legal requirements of the Directive'.[71] In particular, the report does not deal with the issue of sanctions for non-compliance, with what happens if an EIA is required but not carried out, or carried out without participation of the public concerned; with omission of administrations to make

[67] n. 2 above, recital 12.

[68] COM(2003)334.

[69] Dir. 85/337/EEC on the Assessment of the Effects of Certain Public and Private Projects on the Environment [1985] OJ L175/40.

[70] n. 68, above, 95.

[71] ibid. 98.

public its reasons for reaching any given decision; or with any other serious omissions in the procedure.

Nonetheless, the report provides much information on a number of details. Thus, numerous Member States included golf courses in the EIA requirement, although the Directive does not mention them. Other projects mentioned are genetically modified organism (GMO) installations, shooting ranges, intensive rearing of cattle and calves, and military practice grounds. The number of EIAs per year varies from ten to twenty (Austria) to 6,000–7,000 (France), with Germany detailing more than 1,000, Greece specifying 1,600, Ireland 178, Portugal 92, the UK 500, whilst no (precise) data was as available for Italy and Spain.

These differences also reflect the different thresholds used for Annex II projects. An afforestation project requires an EIA when it exceeds 20 hectares in Italy; this figure is 30 hectares for Denmark, 50 for Germany, 100 for Belgium (Wallonia), 200 for Finland, and 350 for Portugal. Indicative thresholds are sometimes lower. For cement manufacture the mandatory threshold is 300,000 tonnes annual production capacity in Austria, and 500,000 in Belgium (Flanders); France has a threshold of 5 tonnes per day, Italy and Belgium (Wallonia) of 500 tonnes per day, Germany of 1,000 tonnes per day. In the Netherlands there is no mandatory threshold, whilst Greece, Ireland, Denmark, Belgium (Brussels), and Finland always require an EIA.

Other aspects cover the examination of alternatives, the 'salami-slicing' (dividing a project into several smaller parts in order to avoid EIA) and public participation. The report contains no information regarding actual decisions concerning projects. Finally, the Commission's announcement on initiatives deals with further research, the publication of a guidance document, training of officials, continuation of monitoring compliance, and future amendments to the Directive.

Index